D1736526

"This is a superb collection, edited by two of the leading lights in the field. This volume provides a splendid view of the rich and varied terrain of contemporary metaethics, with contributions by an all-star roster of philosophers. Those looking to familiarize themselves with what is happening in metaethics today need look no further than this immensely helpful handbook."

Russ Shafer-Landau, *University of North Carolina at Chapel Hill*

"This is an extremely valuable, comprehensive volume of essays on metaethics. The contributors, whether veterans or new voices, provide knowledgeable and original perspectives on just about every aspect of contemporary metaethical theory."

Jamie Dreier, *Brown University*

THE ROUTLEDGE HANDBOOK OF METAETHICS

This *Handbook* surveys the contemporary state of the burgeoning field of metaethics. Forty-four chapters, all written exclusively for this volume, provide expert introductions to

- the central research programs that frame metaethical discussions
- the central explanatory challenges, resources, and strategies that inform contemporary work in those research programs
- debates over the status of metaethics, and the appropriate methods to use in metaethical inquiry

This is essential reading for anyone with a serious interest in metaethics, from those coming to it for the first time to those actively pursuing research in the field.

Tristram McPherson is Associate Professor of Philosophy at The Ohio State University.

David Plunkett is Assistant Professor of Philosophy at Dartmouth College.

ROUTLEDGE HANDBOOKS IN PHILOSOPHY

Routledge Handbooks in Philosophy are state-of-the-art surveys of emerging, newly refreshed, and important fields in philosophy, providing accessible yet thorough assessments of key problems, themes, thinkers, and recent developments in research.

All chapters for each volume are specially commissioned, and written by leading scholars in the field. Carefully edited and organized, Routledge Handbooks in Philosophy provide indispensable reference tools for students and researchers seeking a comprehensive overview of new and exciting topics in philosophy. They are also valuable teaching resources as accompaniments to textbooks, anthologies, and research-orientated publications.

Recently published:

The Routledge Handbook of Philosophy of Imagination
Edited by Amy Kind

The Routledge Handbook of the Stoic Tradition
Edited by John Sellars

The Routledge Handbook of Philosophy of Information
Edited by Luciano Floridi

The Routledge Handbook of the Philosophy of Biodiversity
Edited by Justin Garson, Anya Plutynski, and Sahotra Sarkar

The Routledge Handbook of Philosophy of the Social Mind
Edited by Julian Kiverstein

The Routledge Handbook of Philosophy of Empathy
Edited by Heidi Maibom

The Routledge Handbook of Epistemic Contextualism
Edited by Jonathan Jenkins Ichikawa

The Routledge Handbook of Epistemic Injustice
Edited by Ian James Kidd, José Medina and Gaile Pohlhaus

The Routledge Handbook of Philosophy of Pain
Edited by Jennifer Corns

The Routledge Handbook of Brentano and the Brentano School
Edited by Uriah Kriegel

The Routledge Handbook of Metaethics
Edited by Tristram McPherson and David Plunkett

The Routledge Handbook of Philosophy of Memory
Edited by Sven Bernecker and Kourken Michaelian

The Routledge Handbook of Evolution and Philosophy
Edited by Richard Joyce

The Routledge Handbook of Mechanisms and Mechanical Philosophy
Edited by Stuart Glennan and Phyllis Illari

The Routledge Handbook of Libertarianism
Edited by Jason Brennan, Bas van der Vossen, and David Schmidtz

For a full list of published *Routledge Handbooks in Philosophy*, please visit
https://www.routledge.com/Routledge-Handbooks-in-Philosophy/book-series/RHP

THE ROUTLEDGE HANDBOOK OF METAETHICS

Edited by
Tristram McPherson and David Plunkett

LONDON AND NEW YORK

First published 2018 by Routledge

2 Park Square, Milton Park, Abingdon, Oxfordshire OX14 4RN
52 Vanderbilt Avenue, New York, NY 10017

Routledge is an imprint of the Taylor & Francis Group, an informa business

First issued in paperback 2019

Library of Congress Cataloging in Publication Data
Names: McPherson, Tristram Colin, 1975- editor. | Plunkett, David, editor.
Title: The Routledge handbook of metaethics / edited by Tristram McPherson and David Plunkett.
Description: New York: Routledge, 2017. |
Series: Routledge handbooks in philosophy | Includes index.
Identifiers: LCCN 2016046199 | ISBN 9781138812208 (hardback)
Subjects: LCSH: Metaethics.
Classification: LCC BJ21 .R685 2017 | DDC 170/.42–dc23
LC record available at https://lccn.loc.gov/2016046199

ISBN: 978-1-138-81220-8 (hbk)
ISBN: 978-0-367-85607-6 (pbk)

Typeset in Minion Pro and Frutiger
by Deanta Global Publishing Services, Chennai, India

Contents

PART II: CENTRAL PROBLEMS AND STRATEGIES IN METAETHICS

PART III: THE STATUS AND METHODOLOGY OF METAETHICS

Contributors

Derek Baker is Associate Professor of Philosophy at Lingnan University in Hong Kong. He works on issues in metaethics and moral psychology, including expressivism, rational coherence, motivation, and self-knowledge.

Melissa Barry is Professor of Philosophy at Williams College. Her work focuses on normative objectivity and its connection to practical reasoning and motivation. Recent articles include "Constructivist Practical Reasoning and Objectivity" (*Reading Onora O'Neill*, 2013) and "Humean Theories of Motivation" (*Oxford Studies in Metaethics* 5, 2010).

Matthew S. Bedke is Associate Professor of Philosophy at the University of British Columbia. He specializes in metaethics. Some of his recent work explores the nature of normative authority and the nature and epistemology of intuitions.

Gunnar Björnsson is a Professor of Practical Philosophy at Stockholm University. He works on issues in metaethics, moral responsibility, shared moral agency, and philosophy of language, with recent work appearing in, among other places, *Mind*, *Noûs*, *Ethics*, and *Philosophy and Phenomenological Research*.

Elisabeth Camp is Associate Professor of Philosophy at Rutgers University, New Jersey.

Jennifer Carr is Assistant Professor of Philosophy at the University of California, San Diego.

Matthew Chrisman is Reader in Philosophy at the University of Edinburgh. His research is focused on ethical theory, the philosophy of language, epistemology, and political philosophy. He has published a monograph, *The Meaning of 'Ought'* (Oxford University Press, 2016), on metaethics and the semantics of normative modals, and a textbook, *What Is This Thing Called Metaethics?* (Routledge, 2016).

Terence Cuneo is the Marsh Professor of Intellectual and Moral Philosophy at the University of Vermont. He is the author of *The Normative Web* (Oxford University Press, 2007), *Speech and Morality* (Oxford University Press, 2014), and *Ritualized Faith* (Oxford, 2016).

Stephen Darwall teaches at Yale University. He has written widely on the foundations and history of ethics. His most important books include *Impartial Reason, The British Moralists and the Internal 'Ought', Welfare and Rational Care, Philosophical Ethics,* and *The Second-Person Standpoint.*

Tom Dougherty is a member of the philosophy faculty at the University of Cambridge and also of Trinity Hall. He researches and teaches moral and political philosophy.

Billy Dunaway received his PhD from the University of Michigan in 2013, was previously a postdoctoral research fellow at the University of Oxford, and is currently Assistant Professor of Philosophy at the University of Missouri—St. Louis.

David Enoch is the Rodney Blackman Professor in the Philosophy of Law at The Faculty of Law and the Philosophy Department at the Hebrew University in Jerusalem. He works primarily in metaethics, normative ethics, political philosophy, and the philosophy of law.

David Faraci completed his PhD in Philosophy at Bowling Green State University in 2012. He is currently a faculty fellow at the Georgetown Institute for the Study of Markets and Ethics at Georgetown University. His primary areas of research are the epistemology and metaphysics of ethics.

Stephen Finlay is Professor of Philosophy at the University of Southern California. He is the author of *Confusion of Tongues: A Theory of Normative Language* (2014).

Karen Jones is Senior Lecturer in Philosophy at the University of Melbourne. She has written extensively on trust, what it is, and when it is justified. She also writes on emotions and rationality. Much of her work is from a feminist perspective.

Richard Joyce is Professor of Philosophy at Victoria University of Wellington, New Zealand. He is author of *The Myth of Morality* (Cambridge University Press, 2001), *The Evolution of Morality* (MIT Press, 2006), *Essays in Moral Skepticism* (Oxford University Press, 2016), and numerous articles on metaethics and moral psychology.

Doug Kremm is a PhD student in Philosophy at Harvard University. He works primarily in ethics, metaethics, and their history, focusing on issues in moral psychology, philosophy of action, and philosophy of language.

Nicholas Laskowski is completing his PhD in Philosophy at the University of Southern California. His research primarily lies at the intersection of metaethics, normative ethics, and the philosophy of mind.

Dustin Locke is Associate Professor of Philosophy at Claremont McKenna College. He works primarily in epistemology, most recently authoring essays on moral epistemology and the relationship between rational belief and rational action.

Errol Lord is Assistant Professor of Philosophy at the University of Pennsylvania. He works in ethical theory, epistemology, philosophy of action, and aesthetics. He has published in *Mind, Oxford Studies in Metaethics, Philosophy and Phenomenological Research*, and *Philosophical Studies*, among other places.

Matt Lutz is Associate Professor of Philosophy at Wuhan University in Wuhan, China. He works on issues in metaethics and epistemology.

Tristram McPherson is Associate Professor of Philosophy at The Ohio State University. He works primarily in metaethics and in applied ethics, and his work is often inspired by interest in methodological and metaphilosophical questions.

Barry Maguire is Research Assistant Professor at the University of North Carolina, Chapel Hill. He was previously a Bersoff Fellow at New York University. He received his PhD in Philosophy from Princeton and BA in Politics, Philosophy, and Economics from Balliol College, Oxford.

Daniel Nolan is the McMahon-Hank Professor of Philosophy at the University of Notre Dame. He is the author of *Topics in the Philosophy of Possible Worlds* (Routledge) and *David Lewis* (Routledge), and articles in journals including *Noûs, Philosophy and Phenomenological Research, Philosophical Studies*, and the *Journal of Moral Philosophy*.

Howard Nye is Associate Professor of Philosophy at the University of Alberta. He works primarily in the areas of normative ethics, practical ethics, and metaethics. He is particularly interested in how conceptual issues can affect substantive ethical debates, especially in the context of the relationships among well-being, morality, and practical reasons.

Jonas Olson is Professor of Practical Philosophy at Stockholm University. He is the author of *Moral Error Theory: History, Critique, Defence* (2014) and co-editor of *The Oxford Handbook of Value Theory* (2015), both published by Oxford University Press.

Hille Paakkunainen is Assistant Professor of Philosophy at Syracuse University. She works in metaethics, philosophy of action, and epistemology. A native of Finland, she received her PhD from the University of Pittsburgh, and her undergraduate degree from the University of Glasgow, Scotland.

David Plunkett is Assistant Professor of Philosophy at Dartmouth College.

Peter Railton is the Gregory S. Kavka Distinguished University Professor at the University of Michigan.

Debbie Roberts is Lecturer in Philosophy at the University of Edinburgh. Her research is focused primarily on metaethics and metanormative theory.

Connie S. Rosati is Associate Professor of Philosophy at the University of Arizona. Her research interests are principally in metaethics and the philosophy of law. Her recent publications include "The Makropulos Case Revisited: Reflections on Immortality and Agency" and "The Moral Reading of Constitutions."

Gideon Rosen is Professor of Philosophy at Princeton University.

Jacob Ross is Associate Professor of Philosophy at the University of Southern California. He specializes in ethics and epistemology. His writings have appeared in such venues as the *Philosophical Review*, *Mind*, *Ethics*, and *Philosophy and Phenomenological Research*.

Karl Schafer is Professor of Philosophy at the University of California, Irvine. Previously, he was Associate Professor of Philosophy at the University of Pittsburgh. He has held a Lawrence S. Rockefeller Fellowship at Princeton University, a Humboldt Fellowship at Humboldt Universität zu Berlin, and an ACLS Ryskamp Fellowship. His primary philosophical interests lie in ethics, epistemology, Hume, and Kant.

Joshua Schechter is Associate Professor of Philosophy at Brown University. He works in epistemology, the philosophy of logic, and metaethics, among other areas. Much of his current research concerns the epistemology of a priori beliefs and basic rules of inference.

Mark Schroeder is Professor of Philosophy at the University of Southern California. He is the author of five books and over sixty research articles, mostly about metaethics, normative ethics, and related topics. *Explaining the Reasons We Share* (Oxford University Press, 2014) collects eleven essays about the relationship between normative ethics and metaethics.

François Schroeter is a Senior Lecturer in Philosophy at the University of Melbourne. His research focus is on ethics, metaethics, and moral psychology.

Laura Schroeter is a Senior Lecturer in Philosophy at the University of Melbourne. She has written extensively on concept individuation, metasemantics, two-dimensional semantics, and the meaning of normative terms.

Andrew Sepielli is Assistant Professor of Philosophy at the University of Toronto.

Alex Silk is Lecturer in Philosophy at the University of Birmingham. His research is primarily in philosophy of language and metaethics. He recently completed a book (*Discourse Contextualism: A Framework for Contextualist Semantics and Pragmatics*, Oxford University Press) defending contextualism about a range of expressions that have figured in recent contextualism/relativism debates.

Michael Smith, currently McCosh Professor of Philosophy at Princeton University and Distinguished Visiting Focus Professor in Monash University Philosophy Department's Focus Program on Belief, Value, and Mind, is the author of *The Moral Problem* (1994), and *Ethics and the A Priori* (2004), and the co-author with Frank Jackson and Philip Pettit of *Mind, Morality, and Explanation* (2005).

Amia Srinivasan is a Lecturer in Philosophy at University College London and a Prize Fellow at All Souls College, Oxford. She works on topics in epistemology, ethics, social and political philosophy, and feminism.

Chandra Sripada is Associate Professor of Philosophy and Psychiatry at the University of Michigan and works on issues in cognitive science and moral psychology from cross-disciplinary perspectives.

Isidora Stojanovic is a Research Director at Centre National de Recherche Scientifique and is affiliated with the Jean-Nicod Institute in Paris. She holds a PhD in Cognitive Science from École Polytechnique and a PhD in Philosophy from Stanford University. She works primarily in philosophy of language and semantics. She has published articles in *Erkenntnis, Inquiry, Linguistics and Philosophy, Southern Journal of Philosophy,* and *Synthese,* on topics such as context-dependence, assertion, value judgments, aesthetic adjectives, future contingents, and the semantics-pragmatics interface.

Teemu Toppinen is a postdoctoral fellow at the University of Helsinki. Most of his work focuses on all sorts of things metaethical. For example, he is developing a novel, relational version of expressivism and exploring applications of the expressivist/quasi-realist package both within and outside of ethics.

Elizabeth Tropman is Associate Professor of Philosophy at Colorado State University. She has published articles on moral knowledge, moral intuitionism, moral explanation, and moral realism.

Pekka Väyrynen is Professor of Moral Philosophy at the University of Leeds. He is the author of *The Lewd, the Rude and the Nasty: A Study of Thick Concepts in Ethics* (Oxford University Press) and has published articles on a wide range of topics in metaethics.

Kenneth Walden is Assistant Professor of Philosophy at Dartmouth College. His work focuses on ethics, epistemology, aesthetics, and Kant.

Jack Woods is a University Academic Fellow in Mathematical Philosophy at the University of Leeds. He works in the philosophy of logic, the philosophy of language, and metaethics, though not necessarily in that order.

Acknowledgments

Editing this volume has been a rewarding experience, and we are grateful to all of those who have helped to make it a success. First and foremost, we thank our authors for their extraordinary contributions to this volume. We would also like to offer enthusiastic praise for our research assistants, Lea Schroeder and Jamie Fritz, who together offered extremely helpful and timely comments on almost all of the chapters. We also owe both Jamie Fritz and Derek Haderlie for their help on the index. Our editor at Routledge, Andrew Beck, was unfailingly helpful from conception to completion of the project. Nick Craggs, Laura Briskman, and Elizabeth Vogt, also at Routledge, were a pleasure to work with through the whole process. We are grateful to the referees on our initial proposal, who helped us better shape the volume. Finally, we would like to thank our former teachers who helped develop our interests in metaethics over the years, and who encouraged us to pursue work in the field. We here owe particular thanks to Melissa Barry, David Braddon-Mitchell, Sarah Buss, Stephen Darwall, Andy Egan, Allan Gibbard, Gilbert Harman, Nadeem Hussain, Frank Jackson, Tom Kelly, Christine Korsgaard, Philip Pettit, Peter Railton, Gideon Rosen, Michael Smith, Sharon Street, Evan Tiffany, and David Velleman.

Thanks also go to David Braddon-Mitchell for the cover image (Dolerite Bluff near Mt. Anne, SW Tasmania. Image © 2012 David Braddon-Mitchell).

Preface

This *Handbook* aims to provide a survey of the contemporary state of the burgeoning field of metaethics. We hope this book will be a useful reference for anyone with a serious interest in metaethics, ranging from those coming to it for the first time to those actively pursuing research in the field.

As we explain in our introductory chapter, "The Nature and Explanatory Ambitions of Metaethics," we understand metaethics in terms of a broad explanatory project, rather than in terms of a static list of specific questions. This project, we claim, is to explain how actual ethical thought and talk—and what (if anything) that thought and talk is distinctively about—fits into reality. (For more on what we mean by this, see our introductory chapter.) A remarkable range of issues and controversies arise in the context of this explanatory project, and the chapters of this volume provide expert introductions to many of those that currently animate discussion in metaethics.

We have organized the volume into three sections. The first section, "Central Organizing Options in Metaethics," introduces seven influential research programs in metaethics. It is common to regiment metaethics into such broad research programs, and we think it can often be valuable to do so, for such research programs seek to execute illuminating broad strategies for systematically accomplishing the central explanatory project.

At the same time, we think it is important not to be overly focused on these research programs as such, and the unified systematic views they aspire to construct. As metaethics has matured, a great deal of the most important work in the field has focused instead on developing distinctive challenges, argumentative strategies, and resources that serve to potentially buttress or undermine various systematic options and broad research programs. These topics are the focus of the second section, "Central Problems and Strategies in Metaethics."

Almost all of the assumptions required to even frame a unified metaethical theory are controversial, and this controversy has attracted increasing interest as metaethics has matured. The third part of the *Handbook*, "The Status and Methodology of Metaethics," introduces some of these debates.

This volume can be used in different ways, depending on the aims of the reader. Readers with a strong background in metaethics need no guidance from us: they can simply locate what they are interested in and dive in. For those coming to the subject for the first time, we recommend starting with our introductory chapter and then perhaps a few chapters from the first section of the book, before turning to chapters from the second and third sections. At the same time, however, it might well be that a reader coming to the subject for the first time is particularly grabbed from the start by one of the topics in the second or third sections in the book, and thus might be better off starting there.

This volume complements—rather than replaces—important existing resources for learning about metaethics. For example, we think the metaethical beginner would do well to pair this book with an excellent textbook, such as Matthew Chrisman's *What Is This Thing Called Metaethics?*, Alex Miller's *Contemporary Metaethics: An Introduction*, or Mark van Roojen's *Metaethics: A Contemporary Introduction*. (Note that, of these three textbooks, the latter two assume more philosophical background than Chrisman's.) One valuable feature of all of these textbooks is that they provide illuminating overall frameworks to help the reader organize her thinking about metaethics. They thus help make the sometimes overwhelming complexity of the topic a little more manageable. This volume can also be usefully complemented by collections of influential work in the field, such as Stephen Darwall, Allan Gibbard, and Peter Railton's *Moral Discourse and Practice* or Terence Cuneo and Russ Shafer-Landau's *Foundations of Ethics*. We purposefully organized this volume ahistorically, in order to better represent the vibrant and complex nature of the current state of the field. However, much of the best work in metaethics has been deeply informed by awareness of the historical roots of contemporary questions and debates, as well as by direct engagement with issues, positions, and arguments developed by philosophers who previously worked on metaethics (or connected subfields). Given this, Stephen Darwall's *Philosophical Ethics* would serve as a wonderful historically focused complement to our volume.

This volume aims to capture some of the exciting ways that metaethics is currently developing. As we emphasize in our introduction, we expect that the field will continue to make progress in years to come. We hope that this volume is a useful resource for those who will transform the field.

Introduction

The Nature and Explanatory Ambitions of Metaethics

Tristram McPherson and David Plunkett

INTRODUCTION

This volume introduces a wide range of important views, questions, and controversies in and about contemporary metaethics. It is natural to ask: What, if anything, connects this extraordinary range of discussions? This introductory chapter aims to answer this question by giving an account of metaethics that shows it to be a unified theoretical activity. According to this account, metaethics is a theoretical activity characterized by an explanatory goal. This goal is to explain how actual ethical thought and talk—and what (if anything) that thought and talk is distinctively about—fits into reality.

We begin by introducing and developing this account, and illustrating it via discussion of a simple illustrative metaethical theory: Simple Subjectivism. We then explain important upshots of the characterization. Our account is novel and controversial, as is the status of metaethics as a theoretically fruitful project. We thus compare our account to competing characterizations of the field, and explain how our account permits us to address certain challenges to the theoretical significance of a distinctively metaethical project. In the conclusion, we explain why, given our account, one might think that metaethics *matters*, and explain how we understand the history and future of self-conscious metaethical theorizing. As we will emphasize, we should expect new ways of approaching the explanatory project at the heart of metaethics to emerge in the coming years, as the tools and resources we have for tackling that project expand. Our hope is that by emphasizing the centrality of the explanatory project itself, rather than just focusing narrowly on the views that have been developed so far by those engaged in that project, we can help encourage and facilitate the development of new questions, arguments, and views that help move the field forward.

THE PROPOSAL

In the Introduction, we promised to argue that metaethics is a *unified* theoretical activity. To get a feel for this claim, consider the following three groups of questions:

Group 1:   Is it good to be vegetarian?
When (if ever) is abortion ethically permissible?
How much should I give to charity?
Is assisted suicide ethically okay?

Group 2:   Is it always ethically permissible to promote the best outcome?
Do facts about virtuous agents explain facts about right action?
Do the actual outcomes of an action typically explain whether it is right or wrong, or are the expected outcomes the ones that matter?

Group 3:   What are we doing when we sincerely utter simple ethical sentences such as 'Killing innocents is wrong'? Are we expressing beliefs about some subject matter? Or are we doing something else?
Are ethical judgments necessarily motivating?
Are there ethical facts?
Can armchair reflection provide ethical knowledge?
How does ethics relate to the kinds of facts that we study in the natural and social sciences?

The questions in Group 1 are often regarded as core questions in *applied ethics* (or "practical ethics" or "case ethics"). Those in Group 2 are often regarded as core questions in *normative ethics* (or "systematic ethics" or "ethical theory"). And those in Group 3 are often regarded as core questions in *metaethics*. So we can sharpen our initial question about what unifies metaethical discussion by asking: Does it make sense to group the Group 3 questions (and others like them) together, in a way that excludes questions in Groups 1 and 2? And if so, *why* does that make sense?

One reason it might make sense to group these questions together is that the groupings are sociologically significant. Certain people (e.g., a certain subset of professional philosophers) tend to group them together, and it could be useful to track these tendencies. However, we think that the Group 3 questions—at least as they arise in many philosophical contexts—share a deeper theoretical unity. The first step toward seeing this unity is to notice that we can understand each of these questions as arising naturally in the context of very general attempts to explain central apparent features of ethical thought and talk. Consider three examples.

First, it appears to many of us that speakers who express systematically divergent ethical views are often thereby engaged in genuine disagreement, rather than merely "talking past" each other. One natural attempt to explain this appearance involves answering the first Group 3 question by claiming that simple ethical sentences express genuine beliefs about a shared factual subject matter. If correct, this would help vindicate the appearance of genuine ethical disagreement, because conflicting beliefs about a single matter of fact constitute a paradigmatic form of genuine disagreement.

Second, consider the range of distinctive roles that ethical thoughts appear to play in deliberation and action. For example, when someone sincerely judges that she ought to perform an action, we typically expect that she will perform it, if given the opportunity. One natural way to explain this would involve answering the second Group 3 question by claiming that ethical judgments necessarily motivate. Because motivation is central to the explanation of action, this view could help explain why we expect that people will act on their ethical judgments.

Third, consider the appearance that we have considerable ethical knowledge. Answering the third and fourth Group 3 questions by claiming that there are ethical facts, and that armchair reflection can provide knowledge of those facts, would be natural components of a theory that attempted to vindicate this third appearance.

The three apparent features of ethical thought and talk just mentioned are instances of the three sets of puzzles—about shared ethical subject matter, the practicality of ethics, and ethical knowledge—that Mark van Roojen (2015, chapters 2–4) plausibly claims are central to contemporary metaethics. As van Roojen points out, most systematic meta-ethical theories will aim to address each of these sets of puzzles. One way to do this is to offer explanations intended to *vindicate* the relevant appearances. (Our examples were the beginnings of such vindicating explanations.) However, it is also possible to respond to these puzzles by attempting to *explain away* the apparent feature in question, purporting to show it to be misleading. For example, someone who denied that armchair reflection could provide ethical knowledge might seek to offer a compelling explanation of why we are tempted to believe this method could provide it.

These examples suggest that answers to the paradigmatic Group 3 questions can be used to naturally address certain explanatory concerns. We claim further that what unifies these questions is a distinctive explanatory aim. Our account (which draws on views developed in McPherson 2012 and Plunkett and Shapiro forthcoming) proposes that we can understand what metaethics is in terms of this explanatory aim:

Metaethics: Metaethics is that theoretical activity which aims to explain how actual ethical thought and talk—and what (if anything) that thought and talk is distinctively about—fits into reality.

The next section will unpack the many moving parts of this account. However, even before clarifying the details, it should be plausible that this account provides a unifying explanation of the significance of the three appearances mentioned above. Genuine ethical disagreement is a central apparent feature of actual ethical thought and talk, as is the range of distinctive roles that ethical judgments appear to play in deliberation. And the appearance that we have considerable ethical knowledge is a central aspect of the apparent relationship between ethical thought and talk on the one hand, and what that thought and talk is distinctively about, on the other.

This account also suggests a clear way of explaining the contrast between metaethics, on the one hand, and normative and applied ethics, on the other. For these other projects can themselves be understood as each having a characteristic and distinct explanatory aim. Roughly, these projects aim to explain what we ought to do, either in specific salient clusters of contexts (applied ethics), or with maximal explanatory generality (systematic normative ethics).

Explaining the Account

We now explain each element of our account of metaethics. Before we proceed, however, it will be useful to flag a central element of our approach. Many of the terms we use in our account of metaethics are themselves the sites of intense metaethical controversy. To gloss these terms too precisely would thus be an attempt to *adjudicate* central metaethical debates. Because our aim here is to illuminate the nature of the metaethical project, we will aim as much as possible to avoid such adjudication. The result is that our account of the explanatory project that unifies metaethics is a *schematic* one. We take this to be a virtue of our account: we think that metaethics is a project that can be pursued in many different ways, depending especially on one's commitments in other areas of philosophy such as the philosophy of language, metaphysics, epistemology, etc.

In light of this, we will typically aim to orient the reader to our way of understanding metaethics by offering paradigm cases of the notions that we deploy. We begin in this spirit by considering our account's focus on *ethical* thought and talk. Paradigms of ethical thought and talk include the Group 1 and Group 2 questions mentioned in the Introduction (the questions in applied ethics and normative ethics), together with thought and talk that directly *answers* those questions. It also includes thinking or uttering prosaic claims like *embezzling is unethical* or *you ought to call your friend back tonight*. (We return to the issue of characterizing the ethical in the section "Ethics, Morality, and Robust Normativity," below.)

Next, consider the account's focus on ethical *thought and talk*. It is common for much of metaethics to focus narrowly here: for example, to provide an account of the meaning of the term 'ethically good', or of what it is to have the thought that an action is right. While such a narrow focus may be useful for some purposes, ethical thought and talk as we are understanding it includes much else, including a range of kinds of ethical expressions (beyond 'ethically good') and a range of ethical thoughts (beyond those about which actions are right). Moreover, it is worth underscoring here that we take it to include patterns of ethical discourse and reasoning, and (if there are such things) presentational and emotional states that have ethical content.

Our reference to *actual* ethical thought and talk identifies metaethics as a *hermeneutic* or *interpretative* project. Metaethics is about the sort of ethical thought and talk that people actually engage in—including those parts that we might come to think are mistaken, unfortunate, or misguided. This characterization reflects an important feature of much metaethical practice. Consider two examples: First, one core metaethical question is whether—and under what conditions—people are motivated by their ethical judgments (see David Faraci and Tristram McPherson's chapter "Ethical Judgment and Motivation"). This is a question about the connection between *actual* patterns of ethical thought and motivation, rather than those we might wish for. Second, an important research program in metaethics is *error theory*. Error theorists claim that our *actual* ethical thought and talk commit us to some sort of objectionable error, such as belief in things that do not exist (see Jonas Olson's chapter "Error Theory in Metaethics"). Our reference to actual thought and talk is intended to bring out the hermeneutic character of the project as illustrated by these examples, and not (for example) to stipulate that metaethicists ignore *counterfactual instances* of ordinary ethical thought and talk.

Because we understand metaethics as a hermeneutic project, we distinguish metaethics from certain projects that aim to reform or replace our use of expressions like 'ethically right' or 'ethical obligation'. For example, some error theorists think that while ethical talk commits one to false metaphysical views, it nonetheless plays certain important functions in our lives. Some of these philosophers propose replacing our existing ethical thought and talk to eliminate the errors but retain the functional benefits (see the discussion of revolutionary fictionalism in Richard Joyce's chapter "Fictionalism in Metaethics"). One might also advocate reforming ethical thought and talk even if you thought it involved no metaphysical error. For example, one might think that reforming it would promote important practical goals, like social justice, or that reforming it would allow us to more smoothly accomplish our epistemic goals. Influential work that explicitly aims to reform existing understandings of ethics includes Brandt 1979/1998 and Railton 1986. Reforming projects like these involve asking normative questions about which concepts we *should* use, and not just descriptive questions about the ones we do use. (Such normative questions about thought and talk are what we can call questions in *conceptual ethics*. See Burgess and Plunkett 2013a, 2013b.)

Ethical thought and talk appears to be *about* certain distinctive things, such as ethical facts, properties, and relations. Consider a paradigmatic example: some ethical sentences are about *what agents are ethically obligated to do*. Such sentences are about agents and actions, but what makes them *distinctively ethical* is the ethical feature—ethical obligation—that they are about. The sense of 'aboutness' we have in mind here is *intensional*: compare the way that the name 'Pegasus' is *about* a winged horse. As this example illustrates, ethical thought and talk might be in this sense *about* certain things without referring to anything that actually exists. Most views in contemporary metaethics take ethical thought and talk to be about something in *some* intensional sense, even if only in a minimalist or deflationary one. However, there are some views on which ethical thought and talk is not about anything, in even this thin sense. (Some views on which ethical words or concepts are too defective to generate intensions have this implication, as do some noncognitivist views; see Matthew S. Bedke's chapter "Cognitivism and Non-Cognitivism" for discussion.) This is why we say the explanatory task of metaethics partly concerns what ethical thought and talk is distinctively about, *if* that thought and talk is distinctively about anything. Our account is intended to be neutral concerning whether ethical thought and talk *is* about anything distinctive, or indeed about anything at all, since these are points of live metaethical controversy.

Just as with the other notions involved in our account of metaethics, we intend an ecumenical gloss on 'explaining', 'reality', and 'fitting in'. As with 'ethical', the interpretation of these terms is a controversial moving part in central metaethical debates. For example, explanatory ambitions are ubiquitous in philosophy, but the relevant notion of explanation can be understood variously in pragmatic terms, in terms of entailment, or in terms of a variety of asymmetric metaphysical relations. Similarly, there is a variety of importantly different philosophical conceptions of reality. These include glosses in terms of *what is* or *what is actual* (contrasted in Quine's canonical [1948]), and others which associate it with *what is fundamental* (e.g., Fine 2001). Different views on these topics will naturally lead to differing ambitions for metaethics, but our characterization of metaethics treats it as compatible with various resolutions of these debates.

We can say a bit more about the notion of 'fitting in'. As Frank Jackson says, we expect our best account of the world to be more than just a *big list* of what there is; we expect it to include some account of how different elements of reality *relate* to each other (1998, 5). For example, Jackson thinks that this account should feature *basic* and *non-basic* ingredients, together with a story about how these relate to each other. In this spirit, we can think of metaethics as attempting to spell out how ethical thought and talk—and what (if anything) such thought and talk is distinctively about—relate to each other and to the relevant other elements of reality. Note that one way that ethical reality could fit into reality could involve some elements of ethical reality being among the *basic* ingredients of reality.

Jackson's *particular* story, both about which elements are basic and about how such "fitting in" should proceed, is highly controversial: for example, his approach is based on a cognitivist understanding of the parts of thought and talk he is concerned with, and makes extensive use of a particular version of conceptual analysis. We intend the 'fitting into' locution to connect to the broad aims we can recognize in Jackson's work, while abstracting as much as possible from his controversial views about how to realize those aims.

On our account, metaethics is a theoretical activity characterized by its *aim*. Our talk of aims here should be understood in terms of *success conditions*: those conditions such that the activity—qua that activity—counts as successful. This is the sense in which an instance of chess playing is successful if it concludes in one's victory. Thus, on our view, metaethical theorizing is successful insofar as, and to the extent that, it explains how actual ethical thought and talk—and what (if anything) that thought and talk is distinctively about—fits into reality.

In what follows, for ease of presentation, we will sometimes gloss our view of meta-ethics as follows: metaethics aims to explain how *ethical thought, talk, and reality* fit into reality. This brings in the idea of *ethical reality*. As we understand it, ethical reality is that part of reality which ethical thought and talk is distinctively about. We want to empha-size that this gloss of metaethics be understood *purely* as a slightly misleading gloss on the official account we have spelled out in this section. For clarity, let us briefly mention three ways in which this gloss might be misleading. First, it elides our emphasis on *actual* (as opposed to reformed) ethical thought and talk. Second, it replaces our official talk of 'what—*if anything*—ethical thought and talk is distinctively about' with talk of 'ethical reality'. This might seem to presuppose (controversially) that there is some ethical real-ity. For example, on an 'actuality' gloss on reality, it might seem to presuppose that some ethical properties or relations are actually instantiated. Third, given our gloss on 'about' above (where we emphasized that it is an *intensional* notion of 'about' we have in mind), ethical *reality* will—on many accounts of reality and intentionality—be considerably nar-rower than what ethical thought and talk is distinctively about. We hope that, where it is important to do so, readers will read our official account back into the pithy gloss, rather than being misled by the latter.

An Illustrative Example: Simple Subjectivism

If you are reading this introductory chapter, you have likely heard of *Simple Subjectivism*. Most philosophers working in contemporary metaethics take the view to be indefensible. However, in virtue of its simplicity, it serves as a useful example to illustrate our account of metaethics, as well as some of what makes the metaethical project challenging.

The core of the view is a partial theory of ethical thought. Roughly:

Simple Subjectivism: What it is for someone to judge that x is good is for that person to believe that she approves of x.

Simple Subjectivism proposes an explanation of how a certain type of ethical thought—*goodness judgments*—fits into reality. It explains the nature of goodness judgments in terms of belief and approval. With this theory in hand, many questions about how to fit goodness judgments into reality then become natural tasks for our general accounts of the psychological states of belief and approval.

As we have emphasized above, there are many sorts of candidate explanatory relations, so the sort of constitutive account offered by Simple Subjectivism is only one possible way that one might seek to fit ethical thought into one's broader theory of mind. Indeed, one could even begin the task of fitting ethical thought into reality by stating that goodness judgment is a primitive and unanalyzable element of reality. A complete theory of fit for such a primitivist account would include things like explanations of how goodness judgments interact with non-ethical thoughts in reasoning and deliberation.

Note that a full explanation of how ethical thought *as a whole* fits into reality would need to address the many elements of ethical thought beyond goodness judgments. Simple Subjectivism is silent on these further topics. For example, this thesis says nothing about judging something right or virtuous, or about the nature of ethical deliberation. But even setting aside its focus on *good*, Simple Subjectivism is far from being a complete metaethical theory. Part of fitting ethical thought into reality involves explaining the relationship *between* ethical thought and talk.

It would be natural to extend Simple Subjectivism to address this task. For example, the subjectivist might claim that assertion of sentences of the form 'x is good' conventionally *express* the psychological state of judging that x is good. This linkage constrains but does not explain how ethical *talk* fits into reality. So it would be natural for the Simple Subjectivist to extend her view further to include a consilient *semantic* view. For example, she might claim that the semantic content of a sentence of the form 'x is good' is *that the speaker of the sentence approves of x*. The resulting partial accounts of ethical thought and talk put us into a position to ask how the developing subjectivist theory fits with our more general accounts of assertion and of the relationship between semantic and mental content. One possibility is that the resulting theory is compatible with these accounts being fully general; another is that the theory requires that we give different underlying accounts for assertion and semantics, depending on whether they have ethical content.

Our developing subjectivist theory is thus far silent concerning *ethical reality*. It would be natural to augment it with a consilient *metaphysical* view. For example, the subjectivist might argue that there is a class of properties, good-relative-to-A (good$_A$ for brevity). For something x to be good$_A$ is for A to approve of x. And for it to be a *fact* that x is good$_A$ just is for it to be a fact that A approves of x. We can further link the metaphysical account to the accounts of thought and talk by adding natural views about *truth*: for A's judgment that x is good to be *true* just is for A to approve of x (or equivalently, given our account of ethical properties, for x to be good$_A$). Similarly, for a sentence of the form 'x is good' to be true is just for the speaker of the sentence to approve of x.

It is again worth emphasizing the diversity of ways in which a metaethical theory might propose to fit ethical reality into reality overall. For example, the simple subjectivist's view is naturally glossed as a *reductive* view. It is plausible that on this account the property good$_A$ reduces to the property *being approved of by A*. Indeed, it is naturally glossed as an account of what goodness *is*, or, put another way, a real definition of goodness.

The account of truth just offered illuminates one way in which ethical thought and talk can fit (or fail to fit) with ethical reality. It also has implications for another sort of fit: *episte-*

mological connections between ethical thought and ethical reality (insofar as there is any). This ties into an aspect of metaethics that many people find pre-theoretically gripping: many people are motivated to do metaethics by puzzlement about how or whether ethical knowledge could be possible (see Matt Lutz and Jacob Ross' chapter "Moral Skepticism"). Our developing version of Simple Subjectivism does not yet include an epistemological account, but it does entail that, if someone tends to judge that x is good when she approves of x, then these judgments will be *reliable*. This potential to explain how reliability is possible in ordinary circumstances can play an important role in explaining how ethical knowledge is possible (see Joshua Schechter's chapter "Explanatory Challenges in Metaethics"). Finally, because ethical truths are, on this account, facts about one's own psychology, it may seem plausible that one can achieve justified belief or knowledge simply on the basis of intuitive reflection from the armchair (see Elizabeth Tropman's chapter "Intuitionism in Moral Epistemology").

We hope that this discussion of Simple Subjectivism and how it can be developed is helpful in at least three ways. First, it helps illustrate how broadly we are thinking of the task of fitting ethical thought, talk, and reality into reality. Second, it helps illustrate our core idea that metaethics is a unified theoretical activity. The ways that we developed the initial theory are all recognizable elements of a metaethical theory, which will be familiar to those engaged in contemporary metaethical inquiry. And far from being a random collection of theses about different topics (e.g., mental and semantic content, metaphysics, and epistemology), the collection of claims that we discussed was recognizably unified, as a candidate partial explanation of how ethical thought, talk, and reality fit into reality. The view we developed is far from complete, but we predict that if you continued to add more features to this theory, aiming to more fully achieve this explanatory aim, those features would continue to be recognizable as elements of a metaethical theory.

The version of Simple Subjectivism developed here is an elegant theory. Moreover, it has a number of features that many will take to be significant points in its favor. Here we mention two. First, consider a variant on a point that we made above: when someone sincerely judges that something is ethically good, we ordinarily expect her to be moved to pursue it. Simple Subjectivism can explain this: the judgment that sleep is good is a belief that one approves of sleep, on this account. It is not at all surprising for someone to be moved to pursue things she approves of. So, provided that one is not self-deceived about what one approves of, the account can explain why we expect people to be moved to pursue what they judge to be good. Second, the developed version of the view promises to smoothly integrate ethical thought, talk, and reality into a fully *naturalistic* account of reality overall. In light of the explanatory power and massive achievements of scientific theorizing, many philosophers take providing a naturalistic metaethical account to be an important goal (see Peter Railton's chapter "Naturalistic Realism in Metaethics").

The subjectivist account we sketched also illustrates how challenging metaethical theorizing is. For despite its virtues, this view also faces several deep problems. Consider four examples, each of which is an instance of a broad *kind* of problem that many systematic metaethical theories face.

First, simple forms of subjectivism have difficulty explaining genuine ethical disagreement. Suppose that I think that being vegan is good and you think it is not good. On Simple Subjectivism, my belief concerns my own psychology, and your belief concerns your psychology. This seems at least initially insufficient to constitute genuine disagreement. For our beliefs are about two entirely different things, and, thus, it seems there is no rational conflict between my belief and yours.

Second, the view might seem hard to fit with our experience of the deliberative significance of ethical thought. The thought that something is good appears different from the thought that I approve of it. For example, the former thought appears at least on its face more objective and less introspective than the latter (see David Enoch's chapter "Non-Naturalistic Realism in Metaethics").

Third, the view seems to yield the wrong extension for the predicate 'good'. In short: most of us think that there can be good things even if we do not currently approve of them. The Simple Subjectivist picture thus seems to conflict with our substantive views about goodness.

Fourth, the two points just made also have implications for the epistemological plausibility of the view. We often agonize over the considerations that seem to us to be on either side of an issue when trying to figure out what is good. But if the Simple Subjectivist picture we sketched were correct, this would be misguided: we should seek instead to simply introspect the truth of the matter.

In light of these and other objections, we are inclined to reject the Simple Subjectivist picture out of hand. But it is worth noting two characteristic and important methodological points here. First, it is open to the subjectivist to seek to *debunk* some of these appearances: to suggest that they are *misleading* as characterizations of actual ethical thought and talk. If successful, such a debunking explanation will entail that the appearance in question is no longer a constraint on our seeking to explain how ethical thought, talk, and reality fit into reality. Second, it is natural to ask whether the subjectivist can *modify* her view in a way that preserves the virtues of the simple view, while avoiding some or all of the objections just identified (to explore contemporary views that can be understood in this way, see Alex Silk's chapter "Metaethical Contextualism" and Isidora Stojanovic's chapter "Metaethical Relativism"). In any case, our aim here was to offer a simple instance of metaethical theorizing to exemplify our account of metaethics. We now return to that account.

CONSEQUENCES AND CLARIFICATIONS

The preceding section set out the heart of our account of metaethics, understood as a theoretical activity. This section develops the account in three ways. First, we explain our assumptions about how our proposal should be assessed. Second, we explain how we think about the relationship between metaethics as an *activity*, and the idea that certain *claims* are metaethical claims. Finally, we explain how facts about the connections between different kinds of normative standards (e.g., the standards of morality and practical rationality) matter for metaethics.

'Metaethics' as a Theoretical Term

A guiding assumption of our project is that 'metaethics' is a theoretical term, and that we should evaluate accounts of metaethics accordingly. Negatively, the meaning of theoretical terms is less beholden to prior usage than ordinary, non-theoretical terms. Consider for example the surprising discoveries that atoms are divisible and that space is not well modeled by Euclidean geometry. Positively, theoretical terms earn their keep either by referring to a theoretically interesting object of inquiry, or by being instrumentally useful to inquiry. While both of these criteria provide some reasons to favor fidelity to existing use, these reasons can be outweighed, as the examples just given suggest. This is especially true if existing use is somewhat heterogeneous (we will see in the section "Competitors, Challenges, and Complications" that this is the case with the term 'metaethics'), and there is a theoretically illuminating way of regimenting that usage. In the preceding section, we emphasized various ways that our account captures core features of existing use. However, if there are apparent intuitive counterexamples to our view, we do not take this to necessarily constitute a serious objection to our account. Depending on one's views about meaning, one may thus want to think of our proposal as providing a *reforming definition*, in the vein of Richard Brandt (1979/1998) and Peter Railton (1986). However, because 'metaethics' is a term of art, our account may not count as reforming at all: theoretical utility may be a central constraint on the "unreformed" meaning of this term.

It may be worth addressing a potential confusion here. In the previous section, we emphasized that metaethics is a *hermeneutic* project, which aims to theorize *actual* ethical thought, talk, and (maybe) reality. This may seem to be in tension with our claim that 'metaethics' is a theoretical term. An analogy shows that it is not: 'adverb of quantification' is a theoretical term from semantics, which earns its keep in virtue of its role in helping semanticists explain actual linguistic patterns. Terms that we introduce (or reform) in the process of doing metaethics—and, on our view, 'metaethics' itself—should be understood in the same basic way: namely, as earning their keep in virtue of their role in a significant theoretical project.

A second implication of our account concerns the significance of metaethics. We have occasionally encountered the assumption that the term 'metaethics' denotes inquiry that is somehow deserving of more attention, deeper, or more "properly philosophical" than issues within normative and applied ethics. Our characterization of 'metaethics' as a theoretical term rests in part upon the idea that metaethics is *an* important theoretical activity. However, it does not imply the comparative judgment just mentioned. We think the comparative judgment is too sporadically accepted to count as a conventional presupposition of the word 'metaethics'. But if it were, this would be one way that our account would reform existing usage. We think the comparative judgment is simply false: there are *many* philosophically deep and important issues within ethics itself, including the very applied ends of the field. Our account, however, is *neutral* with respect to this kind of comparative judgment: it would make little sense to build controversial judgments of comparative importance into our account of a theoretical notion.

A third implication of our account concerns fundamental vs. non-fundamental metaethics. One common pattern in metaethics is for a theorist to identify what she takes to be the most fundamental explanandum in the area—perhaps *value*, or *ought*, or *reasons*, and perhaps with a focus on concepts first, or language, or properties—and then to focus her metaethical investigations on this target. (For example, our exposition of Simple Subjectivism focused on *judging something to be good*.) If there is an explanatorily basic ethical concept (or property, or relation, etc.), then this might well be a sensible strategy. On the one hand, such an account might at least suggest illuminating answers to certain general metaethical questions. And on the other hand, an account of the basic concept (or property, or relation, etc.) might put us in an excellent position to extend our metaethical theory to non-basic explananda. On our account, however, this is at most a strategic point: even if it turns out that there *really is* some fundamental, explanatorily basic ethical concept (or property, or relation, etc.), the non-basic explananda are still part of metaethics. Non-basic ethical thought, talk, and reality are parts of ethical thought, talk, and reality, and hence part of the explanatory purview of metaethics as we understand it. Such strategic considerations aside, non-basic explananda can be at least as worthy of attention as the basic explananda.

Metaethics as an Activity, and Metaethical Claims

Our discussion of Simple Subjectivism sought to illustrate the point that metaethics can be well understood as an activity with the aim of explaining how ethical thought, talk, and reality fit into reality. This section explains how we understand the relationship between the metaethical activity and this aim, and between metaethical activity and metaethical claims.

To begin, notice that someone could seemingly make important contributions to metaethics without explicitly endorsing the aim that we identify. This is especially plausible when we consider a philosopher who is dedicated to working out the nuances of some specific problem, as opposed to building a comprehensive account of ethical thought, talk, and reality. This is possible, we suggest, because metaethics is a *collective* theoretical project: the kind of scope and unity suggested by our discussion of Simple Subjectivism need not be exemplified in the work of a single individual, but can instead be characteristic of a theoretical pattern that emerges from the work of many. The nuance-focused philosopher can count as doing metaethics in virtue of the relationship of her work to this collective project. Because of this, someone could contribute substantively to this project without thinking of herself as contributing to it, or even conceiving of the project as such.

Consider next how this collective project is organized. In expository work on metaethics, it is common to regiment metaethical views into broad clusters such as *naturalistic realism, expressivism*, etc. (we follow this common practice in Part I of this volume). We think it is useful to think of these clusters as *research programs*: families of views, each of which aims to systematically explain how ethical thought, talk, and reality fit into reality. Within each of these research programs, there are certain theses and patterns of explanation that help make it a recognizable *type* of approach to the explanatory project of metaethics. And within each of these research programs, philosophers direct a great deal of constructive and critical attention to debating the elements of specific systematic and comprehensive metaethical views. This activity can be understood as attempting to identify the theory that best realizes the overall research program.

An example here might help. Consider a classic kind of *non-naturalistic realist* view in metaethics. This sort of view characteristically accepts the metaphysical thesis that the fundamental ethical facts (or truths or properties) are *sui generis*. This might be cashed out in a variety of ways, e.g., that the *real definition* of ethical facts cannot be given in fully non-normative terms, or that the fundamental ethical facts are *ungrounded* in any other kind of fact (whether naturalistic ones, such as facts about how human brains work, or "super-naturalistic" ones, such as facts about God). This sort of metaphysical view fits smoothly with certain claims about ethical thought and talk. For example, non-naturalists typically accept some form of *cognitivism* at the level of ethical thought, according to which, roughly, ethical judgments are *beliefs* (see Matthew S. Bedke's chapter "Cognitivism and Non-Cognitivism"). Non-naturalists typically pair this with a commitment to *descriptivism* about ethical talk, according to which, roughly, the meaning of ethical terms is to be understood in terms of their contribution to the truth-conditions of the sentences in which they occur. Finally, non-naturalists typically embrace some kind of *intuitionism* in moral epistemology. Especially ambitious non-naturalists try to defend a relatively comprehensive package that includes claims about these and many other topics (e.g., Shafer-Landau 2003, Enoch 2011). However, many more philosophers contribute to the research program of non-naturalistic realism without ever developing such a package.

Our proposal gives a unified and fundamental account of what the metaethical *project* is. This leaves open the question of what makes a *claim* metaethical. We think the idea of a *metaethical claim* is less philosophically illuminating than that of the metaethical project. We favor a pluralist, context-sensitive account of talk about metaethical claims.

The basic idea of our account is that we can identify a number of different salient ways in which an individual claim or thesis can be related to the metaethical project. In different contexts, it can be philosophically helpful to focus on one or another of these relations. For example, a claim might be a key part of a certain attempted metaethical explanation. Or it might be something that, if true, would entail that this metaethical explanation is incorrect. We could also choose to focus on a claim's relation to a *specific* theory that has emerged within the metaethical project, or to all possible such theories, or to those theories that are currently considered live options, etc. We think there is a variety of sensible uses of 'metaethical claim' that align with each of these options, and that none of them is clearly more theoretically useful than the others. In different contexts, different of these relations, and different given attempts to do metaethics, will be more or less salient. We thus think that 'metaethical claim' can usefully be treated as a context-sensitive term that picks out different things in different contexts, depending on what is most salient in that context. We would offer a similar contextualist account concerning what counts as a 'metaethical question' , or a 'metaethical controversy', or a 'metaethical issue', or a 'metaethical theory', etc. For example: a 'metaethical theory' can, in some contexts, be understood as a theory that has emerged within the metaethical project. In other contexts, a 'metaethical theory' can be understood as the foundation for a given research program that aims to complete the overall explanatory project of metaethics.

One important motivation for the contextualist account just offered is that certain claims play a central role in some metaethical projects but not in others. In order to drive this point home, we will discuss an example in some detail. Consider the claim that the fundamental ethical facts are dependent on our mental states. Call this thesis *mind-dependence* (for a more detailed discussion, see Connie S. Rosati's chapter "Mind-Dependence and Moral Realism"). One clear example of mind-dependence was offered by our extended version of Simple Subjectivism. On this view, goodness facts depend on certain mental facts: for it to be a fact that x is good$_A$ just is for it to be a fact that A approves of x. It is tempting to take the question of whether ethical facts are mind-dependent to be a paradigmatic and central metaethical question. However, this becomes much less clear when we consider a paradigmatic metaethical research program: *expressivism*.

On one rough gloss, metaethical expressivism can be understood as the conjunction of three claims: (i) ethical judgments consist, at the most basic explanatory level, of some kind of *non-cognitive* attitude (e.g., desires or intentions); (ii) ethical statements consist of expression of the relevant non-cognitive attitude, rather than (e.g.) of the belief that one has that non-cognitive attitude; and (iii) the meaning of those ethical statements is to be understood or explained in terms of such expression. (For a more detailed discussion, see Elisabeth Camp's chapter "Metaethical Expressivism.") By itself, the truth of expressivism—which is a thesis about ethical thought and talk—doesn't settle whether or not mind-dependence about ethical facts (or properties, truths, etc.) is correct or not. However, within the contemporary research program, expressivism is typically coupled with significant attempts to interpret our talk of ethical reality. (This is another example of the way that metaethical research programs tend to aim to explain how ethical thought, talk, and reality fit into reality.) It is instructive to consider the implications of two such attempts.

A classic kind of *anti-realist* expressivist (e.g., Ayer 1936/1952) argues that the expressivist account of thought and talk is inconsistent with positing ethical truths, facts, or properties. Such posits would rest on false presuppositions, on this view. Compare: I say 'Hooray for bears!', thereby expressing my approval of our ursine cousins. It would betray confusion for you to say: 'Is that a fact?'. This question would rest on an obviously false presupposition. The question of mind-dependence purports to concern ethical facts. Far from being a central metaethical question, this question thus likewise rests on a false presupposition, according to the anti-realist expressivist.

Consider next one form of *quasi-realism*, which explains our entitlement to utter claims about facts, mind-independence, and the like by appealing to minimalist theories of locutions like 'fact' and 'mind-independent'. On such theories, the meaning of these expressions is exhausted by certain equivalence schemas. For example, the meaning of 'It is a mind-independent fact that it is wrong to eat bears' might be claimed to be roughly equivalent to that of 'Hooray for not eating bears, whatever anyone thinks about doing so!'. (We say 'roughly' because the meaning of the two sentences cannot be exactly equivalent; the first sentence has compositional properties the second lacks.) Importantly, on this view, the latter sentence is the more explanatorily illuminating of the two. So on this view, the question of mind-independence simply does not arise at the level on which we aim to explain how ethical thought and talk—and what (if anything) such thought and talk is distinctively about—fits into reality. Rather, on this kind of quasi-realism, 'mind-dependence' or 'mind-independence' can be understood as shorthand ways of describing the *modal* structure of certain patterns of substantive ethical commitment. In short, the issue is whether to say things like 'Hooray for ϕ-ing, whatever anyone thinks about ϕ-ing' (see Terence Cuneo's chapter "Quasi-realism" for discussion). Many quasi-realist expressivists are drawn to their view in part *because* it gives them the resources to endorse mind-independence, which they take to be an attractive substantive ethical position on independent grounds. But it might well be that this is a mistaken substantive ethical commitment on their part, and that quasi-realists should endorse mind-dependence instead. (For discussion, see Street 2011.)

These examples show that the thesis of mind-dependence is a central element of some metaethical theories (such as Simple Subjectivism), rests on a false presupposition according to others (such as anti-realist expressivism), and is better understood as a substantive ethical claim according to others (such as one prominent form of quasi-realist expressivism). In light of this, there are many contexts where it will make sense to count mind-dependence as a metaethical issue (hence our including a chapter on it in this volume), but there are other contexts where this could be unproductive or misleading.

Our general point about metaethical claims can also be illustrated by considering philosophical theses and issues that, by themselves, seemingly have little to do with ethics. For example, consider issues about the semantics of conditionals, or about real definition. On our view, tackling such issues might be crucial to certain research programs in metaethics, and irrelevant to others. Understanding the semantic properties of conditionals might be crucial to assessing the Frege-Geach problem for expressivism (see Jack Woods' chapter "The Frege-Geach Problem"). And understanding real definition might be crucial to assessing certain forms of realism (see Gideon Rosen's chapter "Metaphysical Relations in Metaethics"). It seems to us unproductive to try to settle in a context-independent way whether claims about conditionals or about real definition are 'metaethical' or not.

This point also applies to the way we introduced the theoretical activity of metaethics at the start of this chapter. We introduced this activity by connecting it to a specific group of questions which we claimed were theoretically unified—at least in many contexts. The argument of the current section explains why we said 'many' rather than 'all'. As we have been emphasizing, there are different relations that claims, questions, etc. can stand in to the theoretical activity of metaethics. In different contexts, different such relations will be relevant/salient, such that it will be sensible to categorize a different range of questions as 'metaethical'.

These points help to underscore why it is most illuminating to put the characteristic explanatory activity at the center of our understanding of metaethics. There is no principled limit to the sorts of issues that might be central to some or another metaethical research program. This includes traditionally philosophical issues, but also issues in other fields, such as anthropology, sociology, cognitive science, linguistics, and psychology. In some contexts, it might be useful to pick out certain core issues that are pressing for many different promising contemporary attempts to carry out the metaethical project, and label these 'central metaethical issues'. But there is nothing particularly deep about this: in other contexts, it will be important to expand or contract that list in order to focus on those issues that will help us make progress on the metaethical project.

The context-sensitivity we have argued for here applies naturally to questions as well as claims. This is why, in the chapter's initial discussion in the section "The Proposal," we clarified that our claim about the unity of the Group 3 questions was context-sensitive. We there argued that it makes sense to group together certain questions because of their relationship to the theoretical activity of metaethics. This grouping will indeed be sensible across many contexts, because in those contexts, addressing these questions will be relevant to engaging in that activity. However, the lesson of the current section is that there may be some contexts where it would make sense to categorize some of those questions differently.

Ethics, Morality, and Robust Normativity

Our gloss on metaethics characterizes it as an explanatory project concerning actual *ethical* thought, talk, and reality. However, self-described metaethical practice has a variety of explanatory targets, so in this section, we return to this issue in more detail. (Readers of this volume will notice that the volume as a whole varies a lot on this front, with some chapters focused more broadly on the normative and others more narrowly on the moral.) We take metaethics to concern *ethical* thought, talk, and reality. Roughly, *ethical* questions concern *how to live or act*. The purview of ethics is thus—at least at first blush—broader than that of *morality*. For example, one might engage in extended and careful deliberation in choosing between two professions that one takes to be equally morally acceptable, or one might wonder what color socks to wear to work today. These are questions about *what to do*, but not moral questions in any obvious sense. (For further discussion, see Stephen Darwall's chapter "Ethics and Morality.")

It is common to distinguish between two branches of the normative: the *evaluative* and the *deontic* (which is also sometimes called 'the narrowly normative'). For example, 'good' and 'bad' are paradigmatic evaluative terms, while 'ought' and 'should' and 'permissible' are paradigmatic deontic terms. And there are other normative categories, such as the reason relation, which do not fit neatly into either group. We take the ethical/moral distinction to cross-cut all of these distinctions. For example, it might be that in the first scenario imagined in the preceding paragraph, one has most *ethical* reason but not most *moral* reason to choose one profession over the other. Perhaps this is because considerations of prudence or self-interest favor the first profession in a way that matters for ethical reasoning about what to do, but that doesn't matter to the morality of that decision.

We think it is important to distinguish metaethics from the related metamoral project for several reasons. The first is that what is a plausible explanation of how *one* kind of thought, talk, and reality fits in with the rest of reality might well not be a good explanation of how *another*, different kind does. In short, the differences between the two kinds of thought, talk, and reality might well make it the case that one kind of explanatory account is suitable for one of them but not the other. This is reflected in the fact that many philosophers have different kinds of views in metaethics than they do in metamorality. For example, some philosophers have found error theory plausible concerning morality, but less so with respect to ethics (as well as vice versa).

Second, because authors are not always clear about their explanatory targets, pressing these distinctions can also help to produce useful interpretive clarification and to locate substantive disagreements. For example, when two philosophers each advance views about how to best explain what they each call 'moral' thought, talk, and reality, when are those rival explanations of the *same* part of thought, talk, and reality vs. when are they talking about different things, based on different meanings of the term 'moral'? And when one philosopher puts forward a view on how to explain *ethical* thought, talk, and reality, when is that in conflict with the explanation that another philosopher puts forward about *moral* thought, talk, and reality, and when is it not?

A third reason to attend to this distinction is that the relationship between the ethical and moral in ordinary thought and talk is messy; for example, 'unethical' has very similar connotations to 'immoral'. Focusing clearly on the distinction may help highlight the need for our theories to regiment ordinary use of such terms.

Another way that certain relations between the ethical and other normative categories could be important to the metaethical project is illustrated by one gloss on the thesis of *Moral Rationalism*:

Moral Rationalism: Necessarily, if someone morally ought to perform an action, she also ethically ought to perform it.

If true, Moral Rationalism would potentially entail that the correct metamoral and metaethical theories would have to be closely connected to each other, in order to yield (or at least permit) this tight relationship between ethics and morality. And this could, in turn, provide an interesting constraint on one's theorizing in these domains.

While the relation between ethics and morality is perhaps especially salient in the context of thinking about metaethics, similar connections are possible between metaethics and (e.g.,) the metaepistemic, metapolitical, metaaesthetic, and metalegal projects. As we understand them, these projects have parallel explanatory ambitions for (at least apparently) different parts of thought, talk, and reality (for the metalegal project, see Plunkett and Shapiro forthcoming). It might turn out that there are important explanatory connections between these projects, or even that a certain domain of thought, talk, and reality turns out to be a subset of another. For example, one elegant explanation of Moral Rationalism is that moral considerations are a (distinctively weighty) subset of the ethical considerations (Smith 1994, chapter 6).

Theorizing about the relations between metaethics and these parallel projects is complicated by the fact that—as with the 'ethical' and the 'moral'—there can be central controversies about how to demarcate the parts of thought and talk that are the targets of metaepistemic, metaaesthetic, and metalegal explanation. For example, it is possible to understand *epistemic* thought and talk as encompassing the *full range* of normative thought and talk about how to regulate our beliefs. However, the epistemic is often understood more narrowly, as a subset of such thought and talk that is connected in one or another specific way to *truth*.

It has also become common to talk about the *metanormative* project. Here we take it to be important to distinguish two different explanatory targets (or at least what prima facie seem to be two different targets). Consider the rules scrawled on the wall of little Alice's treehouse, or the standards of excellence qua berserker. Alice's dad may break the former rules by entering the treehouse to bring blankets and a snack at the wrong time of day, and Olaf may depart from the latter standards by trying to find a peaceful resolution with his erstwhile enemy. These actions involve violation or departure from the mentioned norms. However, the two norms just mentioned appear to lack the normative authority that we often associate with the norms in ethics and epistemology. These examples motivate distinguishing two 'metanormative' projects. One project might seek to provide a maximally *general* explanatory account, which applies to all normative thought, talk, and reality, including those relating to treehouse rules and berserker norms. Another project might seek to abstract from debates about specific contents (morality, ethics, epistemology, etc.), and to provide an account of that thought, talk, and reality that is 'genuinely' or 'authoritatively' or 'robustly' normative, or that has 'real normative force' (for discussion, see Derek Baker's chapter "The Varieties of Normativity"). We will call these two projects the *broad* and *narrow* metanormative projects, respectively. (For connected discussion, see Plunkett and Shapiro forthcoming.)

Much current work that is self-described as metaethics is best understood as engaging in the narrow metanormative project. For reasons already explored, we think it is important to distinguish these projects. However, it is widely assumed that ethics is authoritatively normative, and thus a subset of the narrow metanormative project. This suggests at least three reasons why it may be important for metaethicists to explore both the narrow metanormative project and the relationship between the ethical and the authoritatively normative.

First, the narrow project invites us to foreground a very interesting question: does the fundamental explanation of the distinctive character of authoritative normativity take place at the level of *thought and talk*, or at the *object-level* (e.g., the level of facts, properties, and relations)? Certain metanormative views invite specific answers to this question. For example, one gloss on Allan Gibbard's views in *Thinking How to Live* (2003) would suggest that authoritatively normative thought is distinctive in directly involving *planning* about what to do, think, or feel, and directly involving a distinctive set of concepts involved in such planning. A non-naturalist realist might, by contrast, suggest that authoritative normativity is first and foremost located in *sui generis* normative properties. On this view, normative thought and talk is *derivatively* authoritative, in virtue of being *about* those properties. If the ethical is authoritatively normative, adjudicating this debate will have significant implications for our metaethical theorizing.

Second, suppose that commitment to authoritative normativity is built into ethical thought and talk. In this case, arguing against the existence of authoritative normativity would be a clear way to develop a *metaethical* error theory.

Third, explicit focus on the narrow metanormative project might be important for metaethics because the narrow project might reveal that there is no single thing that is normative authority. As Philippa Foot (1972) showed, certain features like *categorical applicability*, that have sometimes been taken to be marks of authoritative normativity, are in fact much more widespread. And attempts to informatively characterize normative authority often either traffic in metaphors or descend rapidly into circularity (cf. Copp 2005, Tiffany 2007 and Baker forthcoming). The intuitive contrast with (e.g.) Alice's treehouse norms does not silence these worries. For it could be that talk of normative authority can track a multiplicity of features in different contexts, perhaps including certain connections to speaker endorsement, agent motivation, third-party emotions, religious traditions, etc.

COMPETITORS, CHALLENGES, AND COMPLICATIONS

So far, we have sought to explain our proposed characterization of metaethics and identify some of the implications of the proposal. In this section, we situate our proposal in relation to several other well-known proposals in order to highlight several virtues of our account. We then explain how our account sheds light on a range of important worries about metaethics.

Situating our Proposal

The account of metaethics that we offer here is novel and controversial. In this section, we briefly survey some salient competitors. In doing so, we aim to explain how we can accommodate what is illuminating in these accounts, and to emphasize the comparative virtues of our account. Many of the proposals that we will discuss have a common pair of features: they can function as a useful provisional orientation to the field, but it is difficult to see how they could be developed into an account that explains the unity of metaethics.

We might begin by considering an analogy: metaethics relates to normative and applied ethics as the philosophy of science relates to science, or the philosophy of math relates to math. There are attractive parallels here. For example, the task of explaining how *mathematical* thought, talk, and what (if anything) it is distinctively about, fits in with reality is at least a central part of the philosophy of math. Moreover, just as inquiry *within* ethics has different constitutive standards of success than inquiry within metaethics, so too the standards of success differ between mathematics and the philosophy of math. This analogy is thus potentially illuminating in at least these respects. However, the usefulness of the analogy is limited. This analogy is not yet a theory of metaethics. We could develop a theory by proposing that just as the philosophy of math is philosophical inquiry into mathematics, metaethics is philosophical inquiry into ethics. But while the former is a plausible gloss on the philosophy of math, the latter is not a plausible characterization of metaethics. Questions in normative and applied ethics are paradigmatic philosophical questions about ethics. And this does nothing to suggest that they are metaethical.

A second gloss is tailor-made to address this concern. According to this gloss, normative and applied ethics ask *first-order* questions about ethics, such as 'What ought I to do?' Metaethics, by contrast, asks *second-order* questions about ethics, such as 'What does it mean to ask "What ought I to do?"' (Smith 1994, 2; Miller 2013, 1). Again, this can be a useful means of getting a grip on metaethics, but it is hard to see how it explains the unity of metaethics. Consider the questions 'Are there any ethical facts?' and 'How many people are wondering "what ought I to do?" right now?'. In many contexts it will make sense to treat the first question as metaethical, despite its not obviously being second-order. And it rarely makes sense to treat the second question as metaethical, despite its manifestly being second order.

According to a third common gloss, metaethics is about the *nature* of ethics (e.g., Kagan 1998; van Roojen 2015, 1). One might interpret this as suggesting that metaethics concerns the very abstract or general or deep claims about what ethics is. While this may describe many claims that play a central role in the metaethical project, we think the account is arguably both too broad and too narrow. It is arguably too broad because many claims within normative ethics are candidates to be deep and general facts about what ethics is. For example, the thesis that everyone should always promote the good—if it were true—would be a profound and general fact about the nature of ethics. And (at least in many contexts—see the section "Metaethics as an Activity, and Metaethical Claims," above) it will make sense *not* to count this as a metaethical claim. Conversely (as we emphasized in the section "'Metaethics' as a Theoretical Term"), we think metaethical theorizing need not always be abstract or general or deep. An attempt to develop an extensionally adequate semantics for a specific ethical word like 'honorable' (e.g.) might play an important role in the metaethical project, even if it did not shed significant light on the nature of ethics in general. Another worry is that this gloss could be actively misleading: many philosophers will hear 'nature of' talk as pointing to a specific set of *metaphysical* issues, and that reading would make this gloss controversial indeed, in virtue of excluding issues about ethical thought and talk.

One might amend the gloss in light of these worries to say that metaethics concerns the nature of ethical thought, talk, and reality. This makes the account very similar to ours: it differs by substituting 'nature of' talk for our emphasis on explanation and fitting in. We think our gloss is more illuminating in virtue of this contrast. For example, our gloss can explain why the epistemology of ethics is a central part of the metaethical project: epistemological connections are one central dimension of *fit* between ethical thought and ethical reality. Our gloss is also more methodologically informative. For example, accounts of the semantics of ethical terms do not develop in a vacuum; rather, they are almost always developed against a backdrop of broader assumptions of how semantics can and does work for a range of expressions. This pattern is ubiquitous. For example, the metaphysics of ethics is deeply informed and constrained by broader metaphysical debates and assumptions. In short, an account that did not illuminate how ethical thought, talk, and reality fit into reality would, we claim, fail to address many of the central concerns that drive contemporary theorizing about the paradigm questions in Group 3, with which we introduced metaethics.

A fourth common gloss—sometimes paired with one of the ideas above—character-izes metaethics as a collection of philosophical subareas, such as the semantics, psychology, metaphysics, and epistemology of ethics. We agree that metaethical theories have often focused on parts of these familiar subareas of philosophy. However, the gloss fails to illuminate either what distinguishes metaethics from normative ethics, or what unifies metaethics itself. The first point is illustrated by the fact that according to many meta-ethical views, ordinary *ethical* claims are metaphysical claims. For example, consider the consequentialist ethical claim that actions are right in virtue of the goodness of their consequences. Many realist metaethical theories would entail that this claim should be inter-preted as a claim about the metaphysics of ethics, namely that facts about the rightness of actions are grounded in facts about the goodness of their consequences. (For connected discussion, see Berker forthcoming.) Glossing metaethics in terms of these familiar sub-areas of philosophy thus threatens to obscure the distinction between metaethics and normative ethics. The second point is a characteristic of the list-style view: this view does nothing to explain why we should group the semantics, psychology, metaphysics, and epistemology of ethics together. Why do these subareas constitute a unified area of inquiry? This issue is particularly pressing, given that different areas tend to show up on different lists of what characterizes metaethics. For example, deontic logic shows up on some (e.g., Sinnott-Armstrong 2006, 6), and moral responsibility shows up on others (e.g., Sayre-McCord 2014).

By contrast, our account does two important things. First, it makes clear why it at least often makes sense for those engaged in metaethical inquiry to work on the familiar subareas mentioned above. The reason is that work in these subareas is frequently an essential element of proposed (partial) attempts to meet the constitutive aim of metaeth-ics. (This was illustrated by the natural progression from one sort of question to another in our discussion of Simple Subjectivism, and by our discussion of metaethical research programs in the section "Metaethics as an Activity, and Metaethical Claims.") Second, because our view does not explain the unity of metaethics in terms of a specific list of types of claims, it can explain why it might be appropriate to count claims about deontic logic among metaethical claims in one context, and claims about moral responsibility among metaethical claims in another.

Finally, consider a *very* traditional gloss on metaethics. This understands metaeth-ics as the philosophical study of ethical language (e.g., Hudson 1970, 1). This proposal has the virtue of making the field of metaethics *more* unified than it is on our char-acterization: *ethical language* appears to be a recognizably unified target. This proposal, however, comes at a high cost. For example, it would entail that David Enoch's *Taking Morality Seriously* (2011)—a paradigmatic contemporary work of systematic metaethics—contains little metaethics, since Enoch's book focuses largely on metaphysical, epistemological, and psychological issues. Further, there is a ready explanation of what has gone wrong in the language-centric gloss. As Gilbert Harman (1977, viii) notes, philosophers began to conceive of metaethics as a distinctive area of philosophy inquiry within a socially/historically specific philosophical context in which linguistic analysis was widely assumed to be the uniquely legitimate philosophical methodology. The language-centric gloss is thus well understood as building those methodological assumptions into its characterization of what metaethics is trying to achieve. Our account permits us to vindicate the plausible idea that contemporary metaethicists are engaged in the *same* broad project as the canonical works of G. E. Moore (1903) and A. J. Ayer (1936, chapter 6). This is to explain how ethical thought, talk, and reality fit into reality. While contemporary metaethicists are engaged in this same broad project, their execution of that project is informed by a century of intellectual developments both within and outside of philosophy.

If we shift focus from the past to the future, we can see that this feature of our account is an advantage over any account that characterizes metaethics in terms of a specific list of types of claims or questions. Given the nature of the metaethical project as we understand it, and optimism about philosophical progress, we should expect the intellectual context that informs metaethical theorizing to continue to evolve and progress. This progress may lead philosophers aiming to explain how ethical thought, talk, and reality fit into reality to focus on claims and questions that current metaethical practice ignores. Unlike any account of metaethics that privileges a static list of claims or questions, our account allows us to understand this development as progress in the same activity—metaethics— that we are currently pursuing with less knowledge and poorer tools.

Challenges and Complications

Several prominent philosophers have worried or argued that there is something problematic about metaethics, or something problematic about the idea that there is a distinction between metaethics and normative ethics. Some worry that metaethical inquiry presupposes distinctions that cannot be sustained. Others think that metaethical theorizing renders certain important ways of theorizing about ethics invisible. And still others think that certain general philosophical theses entail that metaethics and normative ethics are not distinct. We will explain how our understanding of metaethics helps address these worries. We conclude this section by explaining two related concerns about metaethical practice that our theory does not preclude.

Begin with the suspicion about the theoretical interest of a distinction between normative ethics and metaethics. We have offered a preliminary reply to this suspicion: as we pointed out in the introduction, paradigmatic metaethical questions seem *different* from paradigmatic question in normative or applied ethics. And our account offers a vindicating explanation for this contrast, proposing that metaethical inquiry is interestingly unified by aims that are distinct from those of normative ethical inquiry.

It is a consequence of our view that metaethics is *not* constitutively about trying to make progress within normative or applied ethics. In light of this, metaethical inquiry could *conceivably* be wholly successful as such without enabling progress in ethical theorizing. However, our account of metaethics is also compatible with the opposite possibility: that the projects of metaethics and normative ethics interact in significant ways, such that the best methodology for doing metaethics involves doing normative ethics, and vice versa (for discussion, see Darwall 1998 and McPherson 2012). Briefly consider two ways of motivating this connection. First, a metaethical theory can directly entail the answer to some normative ethical questions. For example, a metaethical theory that included a reductive theory of what one ought to do might entail a maximally general account of which acts we ought to perform. More subtly, a metaethical theory might have important implications for the evidence that we should appeal to in doing normative ethics. For example, consider Richard Boyd's influential version of naturalistic moral realism (as in Boyd 1997), according to which moral kind terms refer directly to the clusters of properties that causally regulate our use of those terms. This account casts doubt on the reliability of intuitive moral judgments about unrealistic cases (McPherson 2012, 539–540). Many of the considerations that Boyd appeals to in his argument would support very similar conclusions about the metaphysics and epistemology of ethics (as opposed to morality, more narrowly construed). This is significant because appeals to such cases drive much of the most influential work in normative ethics (e.g., Parfit 1984, Thomson 1990, and Kamm 2007). We aim here only to illustrate such possible connections between metaethics and normative ethics. Our account of metaethics is itself neutral concerning the methodological significance of such connections.

Christine Korsgaard (e.g., 1996, 2003, and 2009) argues that ethical thinking and reasoning are inherently practical: they have their most fundamental home in the context of first-person deliberation about what to do, where this—at least initially—contrasts with theoretical reasoning about what to believe. It is crucial to Korsgaard that deliberation is irreducible to theoretical reasoning, and deploys its own concepts. To simplify greatly, Korsgaard argues that the metaethical project presupposes an incorrect picture of deliberation, which gives theoretical reason a misleading explanatory primacy. (For a more detailed discussion, see Melissa Barry's chapter "Constructivism.") However, our gloss on the metaethical project is compatible with giving the practical perspective a range of sorts of primacy. It is compatible, for example, with the thesis that if the norms of practical and theoretical reason deliver different verdicts concerning how to fit ethical thought, talk, and reality into reality, we are committed qua agents to accepting the verdict of practical reason. It is also compatible with the different idea that the explanatory project of fitting ethical thought, talk, and reality into reality can only be accomplished from within the deliberative perspective. We don't find such hypotheses attractive, but debating them is a matter of substantive metaethical theorizing and is hence fully compatible with the metaethical project as we understand it.

Ronald Dworkin (1996 and 2011) argues that many apparently metaethical claims have normative ethical implications. He then uses this fact to argue that it is difficult to interpret the apparently metaethical claims as anything other than normative ethical claims. Our account gives us the resources to provide a clear reply to this challenge. Dworkin appears to assume that ethics is *autonomous* in the sense that ethical claims are, in principle, not derivable from non-ethical claims, including metaethical claims. (For discussion, see Barry Maguire's chapter "The Autonomy of Ethics.") Notice that the claim that ethics is autonomous is plausibly a (negative) claim about how ethical thought, talk, or reality fit in with reality. In light of this, on our account, the claim that ethics is autonomous is itself a claim that will often be made *within* an attempt to carry out the overall metaethical project. Many candidate metaethical theories have implications inconsistent with the autonomy of ethics. If ethics is autonomous, these views are ipso facto false. But this possibility would threaten neither the status of these theories as metaethical nor the distinction between metaethics and normative ethics (cf. McPherson 2008; for a view of the relationship between metaethics and normative ethics compatible with these claims, see Mark Schroeder's chapter "Normative Ethics and Metaethics.")

Selim Berker (forthcoming) argues that the same metaphysical dependence relation is expressed by normative grounding claims (like 'Henry should give the bicycle to Claire in virtue of the fact that he promised he would') as are expressed by metaphysical grounding claims (like 'A glass is fragile in virtue of the structure of the molecules that make it up'). Berker notes that much of normative ethics involves explanatory claims like the former. He concludes from this that large parts of normative ethics concern (part of) the metaphysical structure of ethics, which is just a part of metaethics. Berker suggests that this casts doubt on the idea that there is a theoretically important cut between metaethics and normative ethics.

As we emphasized in the section "Metaethics as an Activity, and Metaethical Claims," we take the metaethical *project* to be more basic than the idea of a metaethical *claim*. This provides the basis for a reply to both Dworkin and Berker. Given our project-first account, even if many *claims* feature centrally in both the metaethical and normative ethical projects, this does nothing to undermine the distinct nature of the *projects* themselves. To illustrate, consider an explanatory form of consequentialism according to which one ought to perform an action *in virtue of* its promoting optimal consequences. Is that a normative ethical claim? Or a metaethical one? Some might think that is *obviously* a normative ethical claim, and *obviously not* a metaethical one. On our view, this form of consequentialism is clearly apt to play a role in normative ethics: it is a candidate partial explanation of what one ought to do. However, consequentialism might *also* play a crucial role in certain metaethical theories, for example as part of the explanation of how ethical reality fits in with the rest of reality. As with the issue of mind-dependence, however, this will only be true of *some* attempts to make progress within the metaethical project. For other attempts—such as those which deploy the kind of quasi-realism mentioned in the section "Metaethics as an Activity, and Metaethical Claims"—consequentialism will not be apt to play a central role in metaethical explanations. To reiterate the main point: a single claim can play an actual or a potential role in various different explanatory projects. Once we understand metaethics and normative ethics as projects, this sort of potential for overlap becomes predictable and innocuous.

So far, in this section, we have argued that our account of metaethics can help answer some prominent anxieties about the metaethical project. However, it is worth emphasizing that the points we have made are compatible with profound suspicions about the metaethical project, and how that project is currently practiced. Consider two illustrative worries.

First, one might worry that existing metaethical practice overwhelmingly uses the wrong tools or makes incorrect presuppositions. To offer just one example, much metaethical work is structured by the deployment of folk psychological categories, which in turn are examined using armchair methods. Many philosophers are suspicious of the value of such methods for providing an explanatory account of ethical thought and talk. This worry is wholly compatible with the theoretical goal we claim to characterize meta-ethical inquiry. The worry can prompt its bearer to bring her preferred tools to bear on this goal.

Second, one might worry that, on our characterization of metaethics, there are strong reasons to abandon the metaethical project. For example, one might worry that the ostensible target of metaethical inquiry—actual existing ethical thought, talk, and what (if anything) it is distinctively about—is theoretically uninteresting, ideologically suspect, or just an unsalvageable mess. As we noted above, we think that the project determining what to *replace* actual existing ethical thought and talk with—or how to reform it to make it better—is a very different project from metaethics, given how we have described the latter. Because of this, we think that this second sort of worry is well described as a worry about the metaethical project per se, and not (as with the first worry) simply about how that project is currently executed.

As we noted earlier, our characterization of 'metaethics' as a theoretical term rests in part upon the idea that metaethics is *an* important theoretical activity. However, as we also emphasized above, our aims in this introductory chapter are clarificatory, and not evaluative. While we are in fact both enthusiastic proponents of the metaethical project, we take it to be a virtue of our account that it permits us to aptly characterize and take seriously wholesale doubts about that project or its current execution, as we have just done.

CONCLUSION

In this conclusion, we do two things. First, we summarize some of the virtues of our account of metaethics. Second, we briefly explain the consequences of our conception of metaethics for a natural question: Why, if at all, does metaethics *matter*?

This introductory chapter has argued for the following conception of metaethics, and showed how this conception can be illuminating:

Metaethics: Metaethics is that theoretical activity which aims to explain how actual ethical thought and talk—and what (if anything) that thought and talk is distinctively about—fits into reality.

One virtue of this account is that it explains the theoretically interesting unity of meta-ethical inquiry. On our account, such inquiry is unified by a theoretically interesting *explanatory aim*. We used the example of Simple Subjectivism to illustrate how linguistic, psychological, metaphysical, and epistemological claims can all play a crucial and natural role in addressing this explanatory aim.

Another virtue of our account is that it is informative enough to permit a clear statement of substantive challenges to the significance of metaethical inquiry.

Our account takes metaethical inquiry to be explanatorily basic, and the meaning of 'metaethical claim' to be both explanatorily non-basic and context-sensitive. This has two important payoffs. First, our account accommodates the fact that it can make sense to discuss certain claims as 'metaethical' ones in certain contexts, but not in others. For example, consider again the claim that we earlier labeled *mind-dependence* (i.e., the claim that the fundamental ethical facts are dependent on our mental states). As we showed in the section "Metaethics as an Activity, and Metaethical Claims," it makes sense to treat the thesis of mind-dependence as a metaethical claim in many contexts involving discussion of Simple Subjectivism (given that mind-dependence is part of that metaethical theory), but as a substantive ethical claim in many contexts involving discussion of quasi-realist expressivism (given the neutrality of quasi-realist expressivism with respect to this claim, and its interpretation of what this claim amounts to). Second, our view can explain what is continuous in metaethical inquiry across a history of marked changes in prevailing conceptions of the important questions, live options, resources, and liabilities within metaethics.

Some people think that metaethics *matters* in ways that many other parts of philosophy do not. For example, Derek Parfit (2011) famously worries that many salient metaethical views have the consequence that his life doesn't matter. Parfit found this possibility distressing, and his desire to assess this possibility is central to his motivation for doing metaethics. We suspect that Parfit is wrong to be as worried as he is about the potential truth of certain metaethical views. However, it does seem that he is onto something here about the distinctive import of metaethics. Can our account contribute to vindicating that idea? Put another way: What does our account mean for why (if at all) we should *care* about the metaethical project? Our reply draws on several points that we have made in this chapter. First, ethical thought and talk is a central part of how we guide and understand our lives, including how we understand our lives as somehow *meaningful* ones. Given our gloss on metaethics as an explanatory project, it is reasonable to hope that metaethics could enable us to better understand this important and distinct dimension of our lives. Second, as we have noted, it can seem extremely difficult to understand how ethical thought, talk, and reality fit into reality. One might thus want to know (as Parfit does) whether one's central assumptions about this subject matter can be sustained upon critical reflection. Third, we have noted in the section "Challenges and Complications" that our account is compatible with the natural—though not universally held—hope that metaethical inquiry could contribute to our making progress in the projects of normative and applied ethics. If it can do this, metaethics might thereby help us better guide our lives.

While we take metaethics to matter in ways such as these, our aim in this introductory chapter is to characterize metaethics, not to defend its significance. Thus—as we emphasized earlier in these conclusions—our account is compatible with the view that we ultimately have reasons to set aside the metaethical project and focus on some alternative project instead.

ACKNOWLEDGMENTS

This introductory chapter was improved by discussions at the University of Stockholm, the University of Vermont, the Philosophy Mountain Workshop, NYU Abu Dhabi, and Dartmouth College. Thanks to everyone who participated in those discussions. Thanks also to Selim Berker, Krister Bykvist, Stephen Darwall, Shamik Dasgupta, Tyler Doggett, Jamie Dreier, Nina Emery, Stephen Finlay, Mark Greenberg, Scott Hershovitz, Kate Nolfi, Jonas Olson, Robert Pasnau, Peter Railton, Lea Schroeder, Scott Shapiro, Alex Silk, Michael Smith, Nicolas Southwood, Daniel Star, and Kenny Walden for illuminating comments and discussion.

REFERENCES

Ayer, Alfred J. 1936/1952. *Language, Truth, and Logic*. New York: Dover.

Baker, Derek. Forthcoming. Skepticism about Ought Simpliciter. In *Oxford Studies in Metaethics*, Vol. 13, edited by R. Shafer-Landau. Oxford: Oxford University Press.

Berker, Selim. Forthcoming. The Unity of Grounding. *Mind*.

Boyd, Richard. 1997. How to be a Moral Realist. In *Moral Discourse and Practice*, edited by S. Darwall, A. Gibbard, and P. Railton. New York: Oxford University Press: 105–136.

Brandt, Richard B. 1979/1998. *A Theory of the Good and the Right*. New York: Prometheus Books.

Burgess, Alexis, and David Plunkett. 2013a. Conceptual Ethics I. *Philosophy Compass* 8 (12):1091–1101.

—. 2013b. Conceptual Ethics II. *Philosophy Compass* 8 (12):1102–1110.

Copp, David. 2005. Moral Naturalism and Three Grades of Normativity. In *Normativity and Naturalism*, edited by P. Schaber. Frankfurt: Ontos-Verlag: 7–46.

Darwall, Stephen L. 1998. *Philosophical Ethics*. Boulder, CO: Westview Press.

Dworkin, Ronald. 1996. Objectivity and Truth: You'd Better Believe It. *Philosophy and Public Affairs* 25 (2):87–139.

—. 2011. *Justice for Hedgehogs*. Cambridge, MA: Harvard University Press.

Enoch, David. 2011. *Taking Morality Seriously: A Defense of Robust Realism*. Oxford: Oxford University Press.

Fine, Kit. 2001. The Question of Realism. *Philosophers' Imprint* 1 (2):1–30.

Foot, Philippa. 1972. Morality as a System of Hypothetical Imperatives. *Philosophical Review* 81 (3):305–316.

Gibbard, Allan. 2003. *Thinking How to Live*. Cambridge, MA: Harvard University Press.

Harman, Gilbert. 1977. *The Nature of Morality*. Oxford: Oxford University Press.

Hudson, W.D. 1970. *Modern Moral Philosophy*. London: Macmillan.

Jackson, Frank. 1998. *From Metaphysics to Ethics: A Defence of Conceptual Analysis*. Oxford: Clarendon Press.

Kagan, Shelly. 1998. *Normative Ethics*. Boulder, CO: Westview Press.

Kamm, F.M. 2007. *Intricate Ethics*. Oxford: Oxford University Press.

Korsgaard, Christine M. 1996. *The Sources of Normativity*. New York: Cambridge University Press.

—. 2003. Realism and Constructivism in Twentieth-Century Moral Philosophy. In *Philosophy in America at the Turn of the Century (APA Centennial Supplement Journal of Philosophical Research)*. Charlottesville, VA: Philosophy Documentation Center: 99–122.

—. 2009. *Self-Constitution: Agency, Identity, and Integrity*. Oxford: Oxford University Press.

McPherson, Tristram. 2008. Metaethics and the Autonomy of Morality. *Philosophers' Imprint* 8 (6):1–16.

—. 2012. Unifying Moral Methodology. *Pacific Philosophical Quarterly* 93 (4):523–549.

Miller, Alexander. 2013. *Contemporary Metaethics: An Introduction* (2nd Edition). Cambridge: Polity Press.

Moore, G.E. 1903/1993. *Principia Ethica*. Cambridge: Cambridge University Press.

Parfit, Derek. 1984. *Reasons and Persons*. Oxford: Clarendon Press.

—. 2011. *On What Matters*. Oxford: Oxford University Press.

Plunkett, David, and Scott Shapiro. Forthcoming. Law, Morality, and Everything Else: General Jurisprudence as a Branch of Metanormative Inquiry. *Ethics*.

Quine, W.V.O. 1948. On What There Is. *Review of Metaphysics* 2 (5):21–38.

Railton, Peter. 1986. Moral Realism. *The Philosophical Review* 95:163–207.

Sayre-McCord, Geoff. 2014. Metaethics. In *The Stanford Encyclopedia of Philosophy (Summer 2014 Edition)*, edited by E.N. Zalta. http://plato.stanford.edu/archives/sum2014/entries/metaethics/.

Shafer-Landau, Russ. 2003. *Moral Realism: A Defense*. Oxford: Oxford University Press.

Sinnott-Armstrong, Walter. 2006. *Moral Skepticisms*. Oxford: Oxford University Press.

Smith, Michael. 1994. *The Moral Problem*. Cambridge: Blackwell.

Street, Sharon. 2011. Mind-Independence Without the Mystery: Why Quasi-Realists Can't Have It Both Ways. In *Oxford Studies in Metaethics*, Vol. 6, edited by R. Shafer-Landau. Oxford: Oxford University Press: 1–32.

Thomson, Judith Jarvis. 1990. *The Realm of Rights*. Cambridge, MA: Harvard University Press.

Tiffany, Evan. 2007. Deflationary Normative Pluralism. *Canadian Journal of Philosophy* 37 (5):231–262.

van Roojen, Mark. 2015. *Metaethics: A Contemporary Introduction*. New York: Routledge.

I

Central Organizing Options in Metaethics

Non-Naturalistic Realism in Metaethics

David Enoch

Forget metaethics for a second. Think about the naïve realist about the outside world, say, or the naïve realist about abstract objects (a Platonist, perhaps). According to such naïve realists, when we talk and speak of objects in the outside world, or of abstract objects, what we *attempt* to do is to latch onto parts of reality that are out there, independent of us and our talking and thinking about them; and furthermore, in our better moments—when we succeed in thinking and talking in this way—what we think and say is straightforwardly true, as these objects and properties really are out there.

Now think of the average weight of the male, middle-aged analytic philosopher. Most of us are, I take it, naïve realists about it. We think that, for instance, the average weight of the male, middle-aged analytic philosopher is above 130 pounds. And we think that this is true independently of our thinking or talking about it. But we also think that there's nothing ontologically *exciting* about the average weight of the male, middle-aged analytic philosopher. We don't, for instance, feel a temptation to introduce this property into the so-called fabric of the universe. The reason is simple. While it's true that the average weight of the male, middle-aged analytic philosopher is over 130 pounds, this is true *entirely in virtue of* some other things being true—namely, a bunch of facts about particular male, middle-aged analytic philosophers and their weight. Facts about average weight are reducible to, or grounded in, or consist in, or are constituted by, facts about particular people's weight. Ontologically speaking, there seems to be nothing more involved in the former than the latter.

A good first pass at characterizing non-naturalist realism (sometimes called Platonism, or Robust Realism, or Moorean Realism) in metaethics is this, then: Like naïve realists elsewhere, the non-naturalist realist thinks of the relevant domain—in this case, moral thinking and talking—as entirely representational, attempting to capture a reality—now, moral reality—that is out there independently of our talking and thinking about it. Furthermore, the non-naturalist realist also thinks that in our better moments this attempt succeeds—that we do manage to think and utter straightforward truths about these normative facts and properties, as they do exist. On top of this, the non-naturalist realist thinks of moral facts, properties, and objects as ontologically exciting at least in the sense that they are unlike facts about the average weight of the male, middle-aged analytic philosopher: They are not reducible to or entirely grounded in other, non-moral facts, properties, and objects.

Now, philosophical isms are often hard to capture in a neat definition, and often enough it's futile to even try. Coming up with a clean, uncontroversial characterization of naturalism, for instance, is impossible, and the same goes for realism. So we shouldn't have higher hopes for a characterization of non-naturalist realism. Still, the above is a good start. And another good start would be to contrast, already at this early stage, non-naturalist realism with other metaethical views (rather crudely understood; many of these views are presented in much more detail elsewhere in this volume). Unlike *non-cognitivists* or *expressivists*, non-naturalist realists think that moral or normative talk is fully representational, that it is fully and straightforwardly fact-stating and truth-evaluable, that it expresses beliefs, that it attempts to describe the normative part of the universe. Unlike *response-dependence* theorists, non-naturalist realists believe that moral and normative facts are, well, independent of us and our responses. At least in this sense, non-naturalists defend morality's objectivity (see Billy Dunaway's chapter "Realism and Objectivity"). Furthermore, it's not just *our* responses that are ruled out here—even if there is a God, according to non-naturalist realists the moral and normative facts do not constitutively depend on Her responses either; thus, non-naturalists reject *Divine Command Theory* as well. Unlike *constructivists*, non-naturalist realists believe that normative facts are not made true by our decision-making procedures, or by our endorsing them, or by anything about us and our perspectives; unlike *naturalist realists*, non-naturalist realists don't think that normative and moral facts and properties are reducible to, or are entirely grounded in, or are nothing over and above, or can be given a real definition in terms of, run-of-the-mill natural facts (whatever exactly those are). Often this also means that non-naturalists think of moral facts as causally inert (for causal powers are arguably among the signs of the natural). And while *error theorists* are typically on the same page as non-naturalist realists in understanding the commitments of moral discourse and practice—they agree, for instance, that no "softer" interpretation of it, along naturalist or expressivist or constructivist lines, does it justice—still non-naturalist realists think, and error theorists reject, that, so to speak, the universe keeps its end of the deal: Non-naturalists believe that moral discourse, understood in this way, captures some non-trivial truths; error theorists differ.

In the rest of this contribution, I hope to accomplish the following: explain why there's a sense in which such realism is the view to beat, as it were, even before doing serious metaethics (Section 1); explain why, still, so many people reject this view, and some, vehemently (Section 2); revisit the characterization of the view and raise some doubts about it (Section 3); and briefly sketch arguments for the view (Section 4).

OBVIOUSLY, THE DEFAULT POSITION

There's a sense in which non-naturalist realism has to be the starting point: Other views enter the field, as it were, on the strength of some argument; non-naturalist realism is the default position, and arguments are needed to defeat it, not so much to establish it. How so?

The first thing to note is that moral (and more broadly, normative) language behaves very much like other representational language. Linguistically speaking, it is very hard to tell apart "Gender discrimination is common" and "Gender discrimination is wrong." We are pre-theoretically just as happy to assert (or deny) one as the other; to negate them; to incorporate them in propositional attitude reports and related locutions (She's not sure that gender discrimination is common; He agrees that gender discrimination is wrong; She believes both that gender discrimination is common, and that it's wrong, but she believes the latter more confidently than the former); we're happy to assign them truth values, to engage in (seemingly meaningful) disagreements about the wrongness of gender discrimination just as much as about its ubiquity; to speak of the property of wrongness (as I just did); and so on. Non-naturalist realists, then, can take language here at face value. True, they are not the only ones who can do this here—so can, perhaps, some naturalist realists, some constructivists, and also some error theorists (and perhaps others as well). Furthermore, it's not clear how much weight we should give, at the end of the day, to taking language at face value. Perhaps, somewhat metaphorically, language sometimes deceives us (see, for instance, Dennett's [1978: xix–xx] discussion of "fatigues"). Still, if we are to conclude that language does deceive us, we would need convincing. Going with face value seems to be the default. And non-naturalist realism (though not only non-naturalist realism) does that.

Another often-made point is that moral discourse seems to exhibit *objective purport*. We are (within some constraints) comfortable applying moral standards (for instance, via moral criticism) to many others, without first inquiring about their own moral inclinations, and we don't withdraw once we find out that their moral commitments differ from ours (if we think that it's wrong for an academic committee to apply stricter standards in promoting women than in promoting men, and we then find out that the committee members are actually committed to male academic supremacy, we don't withdraw our criticism—in fact, we strengthen it). We seem to endorse—pre-theoretically—counterfactuals that do not sit well with response-dependence (if eating meat is morally wrong, then presumably it would have been wrong even had no one ever acknowledged its wrongness). And we treat moral disagreement as *serious* disagreement—if you think that (given current circumstances) our appointments committee should engage in affirmative action and I think that it should not, we seem to be contradicting each other, only one of us can be right, we will proceed to offer what looks like arguments and evidence supporting the relevant position, and so on. In all these ways, moral discourse at least purports to be objective in roughly the way usual empirical discourse is (other differences remain, of course), and clearly contrasts with discourses that are (presumably) paradigmatically non-objective, such as about tastiness, coolness, or yuckiness (see Enoch 2014 for some comparative discussion). Again, this will certainly not get us all the way to non-naturalist realism. And once again, perhaps at the end of the day, we are going to have to conclude (with some error theorists, perhaps) that the claim to objectivity is illusory. But if we are to go down that road, we will need convincing. The default position is with the objective purport of moral discourse.

How, by the way, are such references to the objective purport of moral discourse compatible with the just-as-common complaints about "sophomore relativism," perhaps more an attitude to morality than a serious view, according to which, in some sense, when it comes to morality it's all a matter of convention, or perhaps even of personal preferences? I think—and I think that this is what most metaethicists think—that the commitments that come along with objective purport represent the deeper, in some sense more authentic, commitments of even the sophomore who, under the corrupting effects of some post-modern rhetoric, thinks that she doesn't accept morality's objectivity. But perhaps more should be said here.

But of course, talk of the average weight of the male, middle-aged analytic philosopher also exhibits objective purport, and yet no one (presumably) is a non-naturalist about it. Objectivity of the relevant kind, in other words, seems entirely consistent with a naturalist reduction, or grounding, or some such. So it's important to see that, even here, non-naturalist realism remains the default position. To see this, think of paradigmatically moral or normative facts and properties (if there are any, that is), and notice how different they are from paradigmatic natural ones. In the first group we have such things as the wrongness of humiliation; the value of dignity; the fact that it's wrong to take pride in one's social status; the fact that you have a reason to desire those things that are desirable; that you have a reason not to believe a contradiction; that it's virtuous to overcome fear in the face of danger (in the right circumstances, for the right reasons, to the right extent). In the second group, we have things like electrons and quarks, tables and chairs, the ubiquity of gender discrimination, the average weight of the male middle-aged analytic philosopher, the fact that the glaciers are melting, the current exchange rate between US dollars and the New Israeli Shekel, and so on. When we consider these two groups of facts, properties, and objects, it becomes clear that the two are very different. The difference seems like a difference *of kind*. True, there are borderline cases (like, perhaps, the fact that the heart's function is to pump blood, or that close relationships are healthy for humans). And perhaps, under the pressure of argument, we are going to have to accept that some of the members of the first group are really, at bottom, members of the second (or are reducible to them, or entirely grounded in them, or are constituted by them, or some such). But this is going to take the pressure of argument. Non-naturalism remains, in this way too, the view to beat.

This is sometimes obstructed by failing to distinguish between what we may call *formal* and *full-blooded* normativity (McPherson 2011; Enoch manuscript). Formal normativity is present whenever there are any relevant criteria of correctness at all. Set up a game—no one is allowed to step on the lines—and immediately some actions are correct (stepping between the lines) and some aren't (stepping on the lines). And this suffices for some normative-sounding language ("No, you shouldn't step on the lines!", "Yeah, you're okay, you didn't step on any line," and so on). This kind of normativity is very, very common— whenever people talk of any kind of rule or standard, whenever they engage in games or practices, or take part in institutions, there are some correctness conditions. And perhaps something similar is going on with certain evaluations—perhaps, for instance, the evaluative standards for motorcycles fall out of an understanding of what a motorcycle is, in a way roughly analogous to that in which the correctness conditions for moves in a game follow from the game's rules. Notice that facts that are normative or evaluative in this formal sense don't seem too far from the natural facts mentioned above—the thought that, say, the incorrectness of a certain move in a game is entirely grounded in facts about us and our practices seems quite natural, as is arguably that fact that a motorcycle's being good-as-a-motorcycle is reducible to facts about the nature of motorcycles, or perhaps their function (itself understood in naturalistically respectable terms).

So it's important to note that not all normative facts are merely formally normative, and that indeed, moral facts aren't. (Well, this, like so much else, is controversial. But we're still in the process of explaining why non-naturalist realism is the default view, so for now, this will do.) Morality is not just a game that generates criteria of correctness—it is *the right* game, a game whose correctness conditions you can't escape by refusing to play it. Moral evaluation is not just the evaluation of something-qua-something, of how good something is *as a motorcycle*, but of how good it is, period. This is why sometimes something like "This is not a bad motorcycle; it is a good motorcycle-shaped memorial" can be a good defense (against the accusation that its engine doesn't run) and requires re-evaluation, but "This is not a bad trait of character; it is a good envious-trait-of-character" is not. The normativity that morality seems to possess, and anyway the one we are most interested in, is *real* normativity, the one that connects with the genuine reasons that apply to us, or with what it makes sense to do, or with that to which we owe our allegiance. And the thought that facts and properties that are normative in this way, that are *full-bloodedly normative*, are really identical with (or grounded in, or constituted by) natural ones at the very least needs some serious positive support. The default position is to reject it.

In these ways, then, it seems like non-naturalist realism is the default view. Unless some powerful arguments can be presented against it, or (which amounts to the same thing) for some competing view, we should stick to the non-naturalist realist starting point. We can perhaps get some more support for this claim from the following socio-logical evidence: Philosophers defending alternative metaethical views often devote considerable effort to showing how they can, to an extent, cleverly accommodate the phenomena that, taken at face value, seem to support non-naturalist realism. Perhaps at the end of the day they succeed—and perhaps their views enjoy such weighty other advantages over non-naturalist realism that they should be preferred. But the fact that so much of the game for other views is to cleverly accommodate what non-naturalist realism straightforwardly accommodates at least supports the claim that it is indeed the default position.

SO WHY ISN'T EVERYONE ON BOARD?

If all is so good, why are so few metaethicists non-naturalist realists? (Though counting heads, of course, is not going to be easy; see Finlay 2010: 5; Bourget and Chalmers 2014.)

I think it is safe to say that what pushes many away from the default is the combined effect of two lines of thought. The first has already been mentioned—the phenomena mentioned in the previous section, and perhaps other important explananda for meta-ethics, can be explained, those rejecting non-naturalist realism think, even assuming the falsehood of non-naturalist realism, and replacing it with some other metaethical view. The second line of thought amounts to simply putting forward objections to non-natural-ist realism. If any objection of this sort is devastating, of course, then we should all reject non-naturalist realism. But even if such objections are not devastating all by themselves, but merely exert a price—they make non-naturalist realism less good as a metaethical theory—this may suffice to justify departure from the default, especially if everything non-naturalist realism can accommodate can also be accommodated by alternative views, views that are not as vulnerable to the relevant objections.

Let me, then, go *very* quickly through the most common objections to non-naturalist realism. Let me note, though, that this survey is offered with the usual provisos: *Everything* is controversial, including, in our context, how best to understand the relevant objections and how damaging they are to non-naturalist realism. And I try to compensate for the brevity with which I discuss these objections by referring to the other places in this volume where they are discussed in greater detail.

Many think that, as a general metaphysical view, or perhaps as a methodological one, *naturalism* is the way to go. Quite independently of making sense of moral discourse and practice, the thought goes, the only things that exist are natural things (perhaps the kind of things over which scientific theories quantify), or perhaps, as a methodological principle, we should treat the empirical sciences as the ultimate arbiters of what there is, or some such. If this is true in general, it is true when doing metaethics as well. A view that is inconsistent with such naturalism—as non-naturalist realism rather clearly is—loses plausibility for this very fact. The obvious line of response for the non-naturalist realist would be to reject metaphysical and methodological naturalism (e.g., Enoch 2011: 134). It is not clear how damaging this is, especially seeing that rejecting such naturalism need not involve rejecting *science*—merely the *exhaustiveness* of science, which may be an aspiration of many scientists but is not itself a scientific claim (for some discussion, see Peter Railton's chapter "Naturalistic Realism in Metaethics" and Daniel Nolan's chapter "Methodological Naturalism in Metaethics").

Now assume there are these moral facts. What exactly, in non-naturalist realism, is their relation to natural facts? We already know that they are supposed to be in some sense independent of them—not identical to them, not reducible to them, not entirely grounded in them. On the other hand, moral facts can't be *entirely* independent of natural facts. Certainly, not all of them can—perhaps, for instance, *fundamental* or *basic* moral facts (like that pain is pro tanto bad, or that humiliation is pro tanto wrong) are independent of natural facts, but more *derivative* moral facts (like that kicking that cat is wrong, or that spitting in your direction is wrong) clearly depend on natural facts (that kicking the cat will cause it pain, or that spitting in this context will amount to humiliation). So the non-naturalist may need something like a distinction between basic and derivative moral facts, or perhaps between different ways of *grounding* moral facts—the way in which the wrongness of kicking the cat is *normatively* grounded in its feeling pain, which the non-naturalist allows, and the way in which some naturalists seek to *metaphysically* ground moral facts in natural ones, which the non-naturalist rejects (see, for instance, Fine 2002, and Gideon Rosen's chapter "Metaphysical Relations in Metaethics"). Furthermore, and relatedly, it seems like a fairly robust intuition that if two actions are alike in all natural properties, it can't be that only one of them is wrong. Surely if, say, one action is right and another wrong, it must be that the former causes less pain than the latter, or that the latter amounts to a lie-telling and former does not, or some such; furthermore, it seems that the difference in moral status between the actions is there *virtue of* these non-moral differences between them. Moral properties, in other words, *supervene* on natural ones. But such supervenience seems to call for explanation, and it's not clear that the non-naturalist has available to her a satisfactory explanation (McPherson 2012 and forthcoming are especially helpful presentations of the challenge). Non-naturalists attempt to respond by offering such explanations (Shafer-Landau 2003: 80–97; Wedgwood 2007: 207–20, Enoch 2011: 140–50; Leary forthcoming). Interestingly, denying the explanandum—that is, denying supervenience—is not, as far as I know, a dialectical move that has been pursued in detail by non-naturalists (though see, for instance, Sturgeon 2007 and Rosen's manuscript). Another related line of response is to attempt a better understanding of the grounding relation and, in particular, the ways in which, according to non-naturalist realism, normative properties and facts are, and the ways that they are not, grounded in natural ones (for some relevant discussion, see Gideon Rosen's chapter "Metaphysical Relations in Metaethics" and Pekka Väyrynen's chapter "The Supervenience Challenge to Non-Naturalism").

Putting metaphysics to one side now, how if at all can we know anything about these purported moral facts? How can we have *epistemic access* to them? If they are abstract, outside of space-time, causally inert, utterly independent of human responses and attitudes—if, as we might say, they sit all the way out there in Plato's Heaven—how can our beliefs about them be justified, or indeed amount to knowledge? If there is no way of answering this question, the non-naturalist realist can have his metaphysics, but at the price of the most radical of metaethical skepticisms—a Pyrrhic victory if there ever was one. Non-naturalists typically respond by placing pressure on the idea of epistemic access—it is not entirely clear, after all, what exactly it means—and placing the discussion in the context of wider epistemological issues (like whether justification and knowledge require a causal relation to the things known) (Shafer-Landau 2003: chapters 10–12; Wedgwood 2007: chapter 10), and "companions-in-guilt" arguments purporting to show that in this epistemological respect morality does not do worse than mathematics, and perhaps the a priori in general) (for a general discussion of companions-in-guilt arguments, see Lillehammer 2007). Much of the recent discussion of this epistemic challenge to non-naturalist realism (and to an extent, other forms of realism as well) has taken the shape of evolutionary debunking arguments—arguments based on the purported observation that a plausible scientific account of how we came to make the moral judgments we do in fact make, together with realist assumptions, do not leave room for any plausible explanation of the reliability of those judgments, whose epistemic justification is thereby defeated (Street 2006; Joyce 2006: chapter 6; Enoch 2011: chapter 7). The discussion of this challenge is very much alive (Vavova 2015; see also Joshua Schechter's chapter "Explanatory Challenges in Metaethics").

You may think, though, that by asking about the epistemic credentials of our beliefs about moral properties, objects, and facts, already too much has been granted to the non-naturalist realist. For if the moral properties, say, float all the way out there in Plato's Heaven, it's not clear how we can even have beliefs *about them* at all. In virtue of what, in other words, does our word "good" latch onto the property *goodness* on the Platonic shelf of properties rather than onto some other property there, or nothing at all? A story seems to be called for, and the most natural stories to tell (stories we tell in other contexts, perhaps in causal terms) don't seem to be available to the non-naturalist realist. This *meta-semantic* challenge has not received as much attention from non-naturalist realists as perhaps it should. The natural way to proceed would be, again, to place it in the more general meta-semantical context, perhaps specifically that applying to other a priori domains (McPherson 2013; see also Laura Schroeter and François Schroeter's chapter "Metasemantics and Metaethics").

Putting now both metaphysical worries and worries about access (epistemic and semantic) to one side, a host of *motivational* worries face non-naturalist realism. When one pronounces a moral judgment ("Bullfighting is wrong!"), and perhaps when such a judgment is true of one (if it's true, say, that I ought to help her), one's motivations seem to be engaged, perhaps necessarily engaged, in ways in which they are not (necessarily, or even typically) engaged when one makes empirical and mathematical judgments (like that bullfighting is common in Spain, or that there is no largest prime). The precise nature of this relation to motivations is of course controversial, and distinctions will have to be drawn here (see David Faraci and Tristram McPherson's chapter "Ethical Judgment and Motivation" and Errol Lord and David Plunkett's chapter "Reasons Internalism"). And this is how the discussion has been unfolding—a strong relation between normativity and motivation is asserted (say—borrowing something from Williams (1980) and changing it a bit—it can't be the case that you are morally required to phi, unless there is a sound deliberative route leading from your current motivational set to your phi-ing); it is then asserted that non-naturalists cannot accommodate this relation, and non-naturalists respond by attempting to accommodate it or by rejecting it as offering too strong a relation between normativity and motivation (for instance, Svavarsdóttir 1999; Enoch 2011: chapter 9). Relatedly, the point is sometimes made (Korsgaard 1996; Bedke 2014) that if moral properties and facts are utterly independent of us and our concerns, it is not clear why we should care about them—why should we allow, the thought seems to be, a major role in our life to those distant, detached things on the Platonic shelf? The (non-naturalist) realist, it is thus sometimes suggested, seems especially unhelpful in responding to the age-old why-be-moral challenge. Unlike with other challenges, where the main line for non-naturalist realists is to attempt to respond to them head on, with regard to this challenge its very intelligibility is often questioned (Parfit 2011 [Vol. II]: 419–25; Enoch 2011: 242–47; Chappell's manuscript).

Lastly, many are impressed with *moral disagreement*—its scope, its persistence, its unmanageability (perhaps). Such disagreement, many think, though perhaps not incompatible with non-naturalist realism, is at least not very friendly to it. Perhaps, for instance, while alternative metaethical theories can readily explain such disagreement, non-naturalist realism cannot (or not as well, anyway) (for some discussion, see Gunnar Björnsson's chapter "The Significance of Ethical Disagreement for Theories of Ethical Thought and Talk"). Or perhaps moral disagreement does not threaten the metaphysical status of moral facts directly, but rather their epistemological status—perhaps, in other words, in the face of such disagreement, and assuming non-naturalist realism, we should all decrease our confidence in our moral views, perhaps to the point of suspension of judgment (Wedgwood 2010; Sinnott-Armstrong 2006; and Dustin Locke's chapter "The Epistemic Significance of Moral Disagreement"). Here too, then, there is a family of concerns rather than one clear challenge to non-naturalist realism, and non-naturalists can respond by distinguishing between then, offering explanations consistent with their theory of the phenomena in the vicinity of disagreement that needs explaining, and denying some other purported explananda (for instance, Enoch 2011: chapter 8, and the references therein).

Non-naturalist realists, then, have their work cut out for them. It is quite possible that, its intuitive advantages notwithstanding, under the combined pressure of these (or other) objections, the view should be rejected. On the other hand, perhaps these objections can, at least to an extent, be adequately dealt with. Even if they can, perhaps some readers will still respond to assertions of non-naturalist realism with a kind of an incredulous stare (Lewis 1986: 133): "Are you seriously suggesting," someone may ask, "that moral properties and facts inhabit the cosmos in something like the way that stars and electrons do? *Seriously*?" As Lewis himself noted, though (in a context in which an incredulous stare seems more called for), it is hard to know how to respond to an incredulous stare. Perhaps not much more can at this point be done than point out the many shortcomings of other, competing views; the success (if it is a success) of non-naturalism in dealing with more specific, manageable objections; its success in accommodating many deep, pre-theoretical intuitions; and perhaps also the fact that moral non-naturalism is not much more spooky than other, respectable views (like perhaps Platonism in the philosophy of mathematics, or indeed any other view that takes the a priori seriously).

WAIT, WHAT EXACTLY *IS* THE VIEW?

Still, in recent years, an altogether different family of worries has become just as prominent—not so much about non-naturalist realism directly, but about the debate of which it is a part. For it has become increasingly unclear what precisely the difference is between non-naturalist realism and some alternative metaethical views, and as a result also what precisely the view *is*.

A part of the problem is more general—it's no longer clear what the distinction between realism (naturalist *or* non-) and antirealism comes to. One major issue here has been the growingly popular minimalist conceptions of truth and related concepts. Such conceptions of truth contrast with attempts to find a metaphysically substantive conception of truth, such as truth as correspondence to independent facts (with "correspondence" substantively understood), or as that on which we will all converge at the end of inquiry, or some such. If there's no metaphysical substance to truth, if there's no more substance to truth than, roughly, the many instances of the truth schema ("It's true that so-and-so if and only if so-and-so"), then *of course* moral judgments are truth-apt (It's true that bullfighting is wrong if and only if bullfighting is wrong; and, as many antirealists will be happy to agree, bullfighting *is* wrong; so it's true that bullfighting is wrong). If so, the realism–anti-realism debate cannot be about truth. And if similarly minimalist lines can be pushed on such related concepts as *representation, correspondence, property, refer to, fact, proposition*, then these too can't be what the realism–anti-realism divide is about (Dreier 2004). Now, so far this is a problem for *everyone* in metaethics—we thought we knew what we were arguing about, but now things don't seem as clear anymore. But you may think (as do quasi-realists; see Terence Cuneo's chapter "Quasi-realism") that this is *especially* a problem for non-naturalist realism, because such *creeping minimalism* (again, see Dreier 2004) purportedly undermines its purported advantages (pretty much all other views can easily now accommodate those), without commitment to any extra metaphysical (or even rhetorical) baggage; or, perhaps, because such minimalism prevents the non-naturalist from even explaining what this extra baggage *is*. Non-naturalists respond as you may expect them to—by trying to emphasize, perhaps together with other realists, differences that remain between the different metaethical views, and by insisting that if the differences are now gone, what happened was a convergence on realism, not something else (Johnston 1989: 141). And of course, another option is to reject minimalism as a general view of *truth, representation, property, fact*, and the rest, perhaps even on the strength of the conviction that something big and important *is* at stake in the realism–antirealism debates.

Creeping minimalism, as I just said, is at the very least a problem for all realists, and may be a problem for all metaethicists. But there are also problems in the vicinity here that are unique to non-naturalist realism. One starts very close to home—a number of metaethicists who seem to be the non-naturalist's closest allies (in accepting that truth and response independence straightforwardly apply to moral judgments, and in rejecting something like a naturalist reduction) but who nonetheless insist on their view not being ontologically heavy in any way. Thus, Dworkin (1996) ridicules those who think that a commitment to this kind of realism entails a commitment to something like moral particles—"morons"—and Parfit (2011 [Vol. II]: 480–83), while insisting that moral facts exist, insists that they exist in "a non-ontological sense." Perhaps motivating such views is the feeling that more metaphysical concerns are—to the extent that they are even coherent—somehow irrelevant when it comes to our first-order moral concerns, and perhaps by implication, to our metaethical ones as well. Under the pressure of such so-called quietist views, it again becomes unclear what the distinctive non-naturalist realist claims exactly are. (It also becomes unclear, though ultimately perhaps not that interesting, whether such quietists should be classified as non-naturalist realists at all.) Perhaps the best way to view the discussion of quietism here is as a part of a much bigger philosophical discussion—the one now often called "metametaphysics" (Chalmers et al. 2009)—of what it is that is in dispute in seemingly ontological disputes. Most metaethical quietists don't engage in this general discussion, and it's unclear how successful they are when they do (see Scanlon 2014; Enoch and McPherson forthcoming; and Doug Kremm and Karl Schafer's chapter "Metaethical Quietism"). And to many of us, of course, it seems that the best, most intellectually honest way for the non-naturalist to proceed is to acknowledge the full, non-deflated ontological commitments of the view, and defend them (McPherson 2011; Enoch 2011: 121–33; Enoch and McPherson forthcoming).

Lastly, the initial characterization of non-naturalist realism above relied on an understanding of the *natural*. But the *natural* is anything but a philosophically transparent idea. And different understanding of what it takes, say, for a property to be natural will have different implications for the understanding of the distinction between naturalist and non-naturalist realism. Different suggestions come up in the literature. If natural properties are understood, for instance, as *causally effective*, then the non-naturalist is committed to the moral facts and properties being causally inert. And while this is a commitment some non-naturalists are happy to accept, this may not be true of all of them (see, for instance, Oddie 2005). Often (e.g., Copp 2003) the natural is characterized in epistemic terms—those things are natural that can be known in, roughly, an empirical way—but the distinction we were after was metaphysical rather than epistemic, so it's not clear that this helps. There is even a suggestion to understand the natural negatively, as, roughly, the non-normative (Ridge 2007). But it's not clear that such a characterization can help in meaningfully delineating the naturalist from the non-naturalist realists (and see Cuneo 2007b for a suggestion to understand the natural in more methodological terms). When characterizing the natural above, I spoke (following Sturgeon 2007: 64) rather loosely about the kind of properties (etc.) the empirical sciences quantify over, and perhaps this was a good start. But I don't want to pretend that we should be happy with this way of understanding the naturalist–non-naturalist divide. It's unclear what exactly the empirical sciences include (economics? sociology?), why they get the kind of metaphysical status that this way of understanding naturalism seems to give them, or, of course, how properties (and the like) are best divided into kinds. (For another suggestion of characterizing the natural–non-natural divide, see McPherson 2015.)

ARGUMENTS

Even if non-naturalist realism, somewhat naïvely understood, is the default position, then, this should not give us non-naturalists too much confidence. There are initially powerful objections to the view. And as if it's not bad enough, a naïve characterization of the view may no longer suffice, as challenges have been raised to the naïve understanding of what is at stake.

So what the non-naturalist needs, it seems, is *positive arguments*. In the dialectical situation just described, the initial plausibility of the view only goes so far. What more by way of positive argument can be offered for the view? Notice that if we had a better understanding of the arguments for the view—especially if they are *philosophically sincere*, in the sense of capturing the relevant underlying concerns that push people in non-naturalist realist directions (Enoch 2011: 9–10)—perhaps we could then revisit also worries about what the view is: The view is that view, whatever exactly its details, that best responds to those underlying concerns.

By far the most historically influential argument for something in the vicinity of non-naturalist realism is Moore's *Open Question Argument* (Moore 1903: Section 13). The argument—originally intended as an objection to some naturalist reductions, not as a positive argument for non-naturalist realism—notes how it is implausible to attribute sameness of meaning to moral and natural words or locutions. The thought that the good just is what we desire to desire, for instance, if understood as the thought that "good" and "what we desire to desire" are synonymous, is highly implausible. For if it were true, the question "Sure, I see that that's what we desire to desire, but is it good?" would sound silly, like "Sure, I see that he's a 30-year-old man who has never been married, but is he a bachelor?" But the two questions sound very different—the latter sounds *closed*, so that only someone failing to master some of the relevant concepts may genuinely ask it, but the former sounds genuinely open. Moore took this to refute this naturalist reduction—and insisted (with very little further discussion) that a similar refutation will apply to any other naturalist reduction.

Everyone knows that the Open Question Argument fails. For one thing, at most it refutes *analytic* or *a priori* naturalist reductions. Naturalists who put forward an identity relation between moral and natural properties (but not moral and natural concepts) are entirely off the hook. On such a view, the openness of Moore's question is not more surprising than the openness (perhaps several centuries ago) of the question "I see there's water in the cup, but is there H_2O there?" On this suggestion, the openness of a question is explained by the absence of an *a priori identity* statement closing it, not necessarily by the absence of *any* identity statement closing it. Even just focusing now on analytic or a priori naturalist views, Moore is wrong to assume that all true analyses are transparent in the same way that "All never-married men are bachelors" presumably is. And it's always possible that even if Moore was right that the questions relevant to many naturalist reductions are open in this way, a sufficiently clever naturalist reduction will close the question—perhaps the problem is not with naturalist reductions in general, but rather with the specific reductions we have thus far been able to come up with. Interestingly, though, despite the argument's many flaws, many metaethicists feel that Moore was nonetheless onto something here—perhaps something like the feeling that any naturalist reduction loses the very normativity it was meant to capture (see Rosati 1995), or, as I like to put it (Enoch 2011: 107–108), the intuition that normative facts and natural ones are just too different to make anything like a reduction remotely plausible.

Contemporary non-naturalist realists have not been as prolific in putting forward positive arguments for the view as they have been in responding to objections to it, and in pointing out the flaws in competing views (this seems true of Huemer 2006 and of Shafer-Landau 2003; see Korsgaard's [2006: 41] complaint against Nagel). Still, some such positive arguments can now be found in the literature. One such argument—due to Terence Cuneo 2007a—relies on promising analogies with non-naturalist realism regarding *epistemic* norms, properties, and facts. Of course, such arguments by analogy put pressure on whether non-naturalist realism is the view to accept about epistemology, and the need for positive arguments may resurface there.

In previous work (2011: chapters 2–4) I offered two arguments in support of non-naturalist realism. One argument—intended to establish something in the vicinity of the objectivity of morality, not exactly going all the way to non-naturalist realism—claims that with the help of some plausible auxiliary moral premises, different metaethical views have different *first-order, moral* implications. If so, the plausibility of the first-order implications of realism (and the implausibility of the implications of some competing views) scores some plausibility points for realism. The specific implication I was concerned with was the fact that in cases of moral disagreement and conflict the response morally called for seems very different from the kind of impartial response often morally required in cases of conflicts stemming merely from conflicting interests or preferences. This difference, I argue, is best explained by the truth of some realist metaethical view. But regardless of the details of this argument, the thought that perhaps we can gain traction on some metaethical debates by considering their first-order implications seems worth pursuing (if, that is, *there are* such implications, which is itself a controversial matter—see Enoch 2011: 41–49).

Another positive argument for non-naturalist realism (though about the normative, not necessarily about morality directly) proceeds by analogy with indispensability arguments in the philosophy of mathematics. There, that quantifying over some entities is indispensable to our best explanatory theories is often taken to be a good reason to believe that they exist. And it's not clear, of course, whether moral properties (and the like)—non-natural or otherwise—play an indispensable role in any respectable explanations (Harman 1977: chapter 1). But perhaps normative properties (and facts, and truths, and objects) do play an indispensable role in some other, non-explanatory project. I argue that they play such a role in the *deliberative* project—the project, roughly, of deciding what to do by coming up with answers to questions like what I have most reason to do—and that this kind of role is on a par with explanatory indispensability when it comes to conferring respectability on ontological commitments (for some critical discussion, see McPherson and Plunkett [2015]).

At the end of the day, then, how confident should we be in non-naturalist realism? It won't surprise you that the jury is still out. But perhaps we can get back to where we started. Non-naturalist realism is the default position. If other views are sufficiently convincing, or if the objections to non-naturalist realism are, then we should look elsewhere. But I still think—and hope—that non-naturalist realism is a major contender in metaethics.

ACKNOWLEDGMENTS

For many helpful comments on a previous version, I would like to thank Tristram McPherson, David Plunkett, and Lea Schroeder.

REFERENCES

Bedke, M. (2014) "A Menagerie of Duties? Normative Judgments Are Not Beliefs about Non-Natural Properties," *American Philosophical Quarterly* 51: 189–201.

Bourget, D. and Chalmers, D. (2014) "What Do Philosophers Believe?" *Philosophical Studies* 170: 465–500.

Chalmers, D., Manley, D. and Wasserman, R. (eds) (2009) *MetaMetaphysics*, Oxford: Oxford University Press.

Chappell, R. Y. (Manuscript) "A Non-Natural Reason by Any Other Name...."

Copp, D. (2003) "Why Naturalism?" *Ethical Theory and Moral Practice* 6: 179–200.

Cuneo, T. (2007a) *The Normative Web: An Argument for Moral Realism*, Oxford: Oxford University Press.

Cuneo, T. (2007b) "Recent Faces of Moral Nonnaturalism," *Philosophy Compass* 2(6): 850–79.

Dennett, D. (1978) *Brainstorms: Philosophical Essays on Mind and Psychology*, Montgomery, VT: Bradford Books.

Dreier, J. (2004) "Meta-Ethics and the Problem of Creeping Minimalism," *Philosophical Perspectives* 18(1): 23–44.

Dworkin, R. (1996) "Objectivity and Truth: You'd Better Believe It," *Philosophy and Public Affairs* 25: 87–139.

Enoch, D. (2011) *Taking Morality Seriously: A Defense of Robust Realism*, Oxford: Oxford University Press.

Enoch, D. (2014) "Why I'm an Objectivist about Ethics (and Why You Are Too)," in R. Shafer-Landau (ed.) *The Ethical Life*, Oxford: Oxford University Press.

Enoch, D. (Manuscript) "Is General Jurisprudence Interesting?"

Enoch, D. and McPherson, T. (Forthcoming) "What Do You Mean This Isn't the Question?" *Canadian Journal of Philosophy*.

Fine, K. (2002) "The Varieties of Necessity," in T. S. Gendler and J. Hawthorne (eds.) *Conceivability and Possibility*, Oxford: Oxford University Press; reprinted in his (2005) *Modality and Tense*, Oxford: Oxford University Press.

Finlay, S. (2010) "Normativity, Necessity, and Tense: A Recipe for Homebaked Normativity," in R. Shafer-Landau (ed.) *Oxford Studies in Metaethics*, Vol. 5, Oxford: Oxford University Press.

Harman, G. (1977) *The Nature of Morality*, Oxford: Oxford University Press.

Huemer, M. (2006) *Ethical Intuitionism*, Basingstoke: Palgrave Macmillan.

Johnston, M. (1989) "Dispositional Theories of Value," *Proceedings of the Aristotelian Society* (Supp.)63: 139–74.

Joyce, R. (2006) *The Evolution of Morality*, Cambridge, MA: MIT Press.

Korsgaard, C. (1996) *The Sources of Normativity*, Cambridge: Cambridge University Press.

Leary, S. (Forthcoming) "Non-Naturalism and Normative Necessity," in R. Shafer-Landau (ed.) *Oxford Studies in Metaethics*, Vol. 12.

Lewis, D. K. (1986) *On the Plurality of Worlds*, Oxford: Blackwell.

Lillehammer, H. (2007) *Companions in Guilt: Arguments for Ethical Objectivity*, New York: Palgrave Macmillan.

McPherson, T. (2011) "Against Quietist Normative Realism," *Philosophical Studies* 154(2): 223–40.

McPherson, T. (2012) "Ethical Non-Naturalism and the Metaphysics of Supervenience," in R. Shafer-Landau (ed.) *Oxford Studies in Metaethics*, Vol. 7, Oxford: Oxford University Press.

McPherson, T. (2013) "Semantic Challenges to Normative Realism," *Philosophy Compass* 8: 126–36.

McPherson, T. (2015) "What Is at Stake in Debates among Normative Realists?" *Noûs* 49: 123–46.

McPherson, T. (Forthcoming), "Supervenience in Ethics," in E. Zalta (ed.) *Stanford Encyclopedia of Philosophy*.

McPherson, T. and Plunkett, D. (2015) "Deliberative Indispensability and Epistemic Justification," in R. Shafer-Landau (ed.) *Oxford Studies in Metaethics*, Vol. 10, Oxford: Oxford University Press.

Moore, G. E. (1903) *Principia Ethica*, Cambridge: Cambridge University Press; rev. ed., Baldwin, T. (ed.) (1993).

Oddie, G. (2005) *Value, Reality and Desire*, Oxford: Oxford University Press.

Parfit, D. (2011) *On What Matters*, Oxford: Oxford University Press.

Ridge, M. (2007) "Anti-Reductionism and Supervenience," *Journal of Moral Philosophy* 4(3): 330–48.

Rosati, C. S. (1995) "Naturalism, Normativity, and the Open Question Argument," *Noûs* 29: 46–70.

Rosen, G. (Manuscript) "What Is Normative Necessity?"

Scanlon, T. M. (2014) *Being Realistic About Reasons*, Oxford: Oxford University Press.

Shafer-Landau, R. (2003) *Moral Realism: A Defence*, Oxford: Oxford University Press.

Sinnott-Armstrong, W. (2006) *Moral Skepticisms*, Oxford: Oxford University Press.

Street, S. (2006) "A Darwinian Dilemma for Realist Theories of Value," *Philosophical Studies* 127: 109–66.

Sturgeon, N. (2007) "Doubts about the Supervenience of the Evaluative," *Oxford Studies in Metaethics* 3: 53–90.

Svavarsdóttir, S. (1999) "Moral Cognitivism and Motivation," *Philosophical Review* 108: 161–219.

Vavova, K. (2015) "Evolutionary Debunking of Moral Realism," *Philosophy Compass* 10(2): 104–16.

Wedgwood, R. (2007) *The Nature of Normativity*, Oxford: Oxford University Press.

Wedgwood, R. (2010) "The Moral Evil Demons," in R. Feldman, and T. Warfield, (eds.) *Disagreement*, Oxford: Oxford University Press.

Williams, B. (1980) "Internal and External Reasons," reprinted in his *Moral Luck*, Cambridge: Cambridge University Press.

Naturalistic Realism in Metaethics

Peter Railton

How do ethical thought and practice relate to our experience and understanding of the world more generally? This question has many dimensions. Metaphysically, what is the place of value in a world of facts? Conceptually, how are claims about what *ought* to be the case related to claims about what *is* the case? Epistemically, how can our ethical beliefs be justified, when they often seem to be based upon "intuitions" that cannot be adjudicated by empirical experimentation or logical proof? And semantically, how can our thoughts and words successfully connect with putative ethical properties or facts? Such challenges are not limited to metaethics and can be found in some form right across the meta-normative realm, but it is with respect to ethics that attempts to meet them have been most developed, so that will be our principal focus here.

"Naturalistic realism" names a family of metaethical approaches that seek to provide a unified response to these challenges by grounding ethics in the natural world in a way that leaves no "unexplained residue"—whether metaphysical, conceptual, epistemic, or semantic—that could be considered indispensable to the well-foundedness of ethical distinctions (e.g., between intrinsically good and bad lives, morally right or wrong actions, and just or unjust practices) or to their practical significance (e.g., as objective values or rational standards to guide deliberation and action).

This would include no unexplained *super-natural* or *non-natural* residue—no need to appeal to divine commands, punishment in an afterlife, or a realm of absolute Ideas. Plato's argument in the *Euthyphro* (ca. 399–395 BCE/2002) has convinced most philosophers that, even if divine beings exist, still, ethics has an independent standing. But Plato did not think that ethics could do without the "Forms"—abstract, ideal, non-natural Ideas that stand behind our concepts. And many contemporary non-naturalists agree with Plato at least that far—the ethical realm is "just too different" from the ordinary world of experience in its principles, ways of knowing, or modes of thought and language (though whether this difference should be interpreted metaphysically is a matter of debate among non-naturalists; see Moore, 1903; Gibbard, 2003; Enoch, 2011; Parfit, 2011).

However, at least since Plato's pupil Aristotle (ca. 350 BCE/1999), naturalistic realists have countered that we can find all we need to vindicate the claims of ethics without going beyond the natural world, which of course includes humans as natural beings. What is required for vindication? At the heart of the issue are two characteristics of ethics that appear to be in some tension with one another: *factuality* and *normativity*. On the one hand, judgments about the quality of a life, the rightness of an action, or the fairness of a practice share many features with prosaic, paradigmatically factual judgments about the natural world. Ethical and prosaically factual claims are spoken of as true or false, have a shared propositional logic, and combine seamlessly in thought and language. Speakers making both kinds of judgments appear to presuppose that they are talking of a common subject matter, such that their disagreements can be genuine disputes, and such that they can be called upon to justify themselves in terms of reasons that are shareable and not wholly dependent upon their particular standpoint or opinion. Ethical and prosaically factual judgments alike characteristically go beyond immediate observation and invoke properties and relations that are general and not directly observable—such as causal connections, laws of nature, intrinsic value, and reasons for action. Further, in both domains, these properties and relations have a *modal* character and thus support expectations about the future and reasoning about hypothetical and counterfactual situations. Finally, in both domains, we strive for impartiality and objectivity, seeking to avoid personal or social bias and refusing to accept brute appeals to authority. In all these respects, judgments with ethical versus prosaically factual or naturalistic content are as alike as peas in a pod.

On the other hand, ethical judgments appear to have a *normative character* or *force* that prosaically factual judgments do not—they *prescribe* or *commend* rather than merely describe. So it seems anomalous at best, and incoherent at worst, to assert in all sincerity that an action is morally wrong or unjust while being indifferent to whether it is performed (philosophers differ considerably, however, on how to understand normative character or force, or its relation to ethical judgment; see David Faraci and Tristram McPherson's chapter "Ethical Judgment and Motivation").

A naturalistic vindication of ethics would thus need to accommodate both its factuality and its normativity. Historically, philosophers have developed several ways of accomplishing this. Aristotelian science saw nature in terms of essences and causes—including "final causes" that explain the behavior of objects and creatures in terms of a teleological striving to realize their distinguishing essential characteristics. In sentient creatures, this striving takes an *affective, intrinsically motivating* form, such that animals experience pleasure or happiness in activity that is in accord with their essence. Dogs, for example, find pleasure in the full development of their distinctive canine nature—eating, running, hunting, sociality, and nurturing their young. Humans, by contrast, find pleasure in the full development of their distinctively rational, political nature. Human virtues, including self-regulation by individual and shared deliberation, are grounded in the facts of human nature and at the same time intrinsically motivating—an inseparable part of achieving happiness (*eudaimonia*) (Aristotle, ca. 350 BCE, 1999: 1098–102). Naturalistic realism inspired by this Aristotelian linkage of essence with flourishing, and of human flourishing, in turn, with virtue and rational deliberation, can be found today in contemporary neo-Aristotelianism (Foot, 1977; McDowell, 1979).

A second tradition in naturalistic realism, and the one that will be the principal focus of this entry, got its start when Thomas Hobbes applied the Galilean Revolution to human science, banning Aristotelian "final causes" and using an empirical "resolutive-compositive" method that traces complex dynamical phenomena to the interactions of simpler constituent elements. For Hobbes, humans pursuing the fulfillment of their desires will, if rational, accept and abide by reciprocal constraints akin to morality as their best hope for peace and happiness (Hobbes, 1651/1994). David Hume improved upon Hobbes' psychology, adding both a theory of sentiments, which made humans sensitive to a wider range of values, and an inherent capacity for general sympathy, which meant that humans could adopt, and be moved by, perspectives other than their own—including the perspective of the general interest (Hume, 1738/1978). Combining these two features meant that people were disposed to approve of traits of character beneficial to others as well as the self ("natural virtues"), and to be responsive in feeling and action to mutually beneficial norms of justice and property ("artificial virtues"). And John Stuart Mill (1863/2001) gave greater theoretical and empirical content to these broad Humean ideas by introducing informed preferences as a standard for assessing personal well-being (utility), and the maximization of well-being overall as a standard for assessing social norms.

Naturalistic realism in Anglophone ethics went into decline in the early twentieth century, in part due to the influence of G.E. Moore (1903), which will be discussed below, and in part due to the rise of positivism in philosophy and the sciences, which dismissed Aristotelian essences and Millian utility alike as unverifiable and thus empirically meaningless. Those seeking a naturalistic explanation of ethics thus tended toward "emotivism" (Ayer, 1936) or "expressivism" (Gibbard, 2003) rather than realism, or, more radically, toward an "error theory" of ethics (Mackie, 1977). But the rejection of positivist strictures in the natural and social sciences in the second half of the twentieth century, along with a series of parallel developments in metaphysics and the philosophy of language, made possible the contemporary revival of naturalistic realism. Let us, then, begin with a brief discussion of realism, and then of naturalism.

REALISM

What is it to be a *realist* about a given domain of thought or practice? Like other philosophical terms of art, the meaning of "realism" is controversial and involves an interplay between common-sense language and the demands of conceptual clarity and theory construction. In contemporary philosophy, realism is often formulated in linguistic terms—realists about the external world may formulate their view by saying that our ordinary language of objects successfully refers—but it is important to see that they typically seek to defend the existence of a world of objects that is quite independent of how we speak about it.

We will speak here of realism *about a domain*, since what realism requires varies by domain. Realism about the external world is sometimes put in terms of its *mind-independent existence*, but this will hardly do for realism about mental states—or, according to most naturalists, for realism about ethics. Rather than seek a defining characteristic of realism, we will consider a branching series of *yes–no* choices, such that *yes* answers lead to successively greater degrees of realism about the domain in question.

First, realists about a domain tend to hold that (1) statements in that domain are capable of truth or falsity (or, more generically, of correctness or incorrectness) and that (2) at least some affirmative existential statements in that domain are in fact true (or correct). Early *emotivists* about ethics denied (1), and more recently ethical *error theorists* have accepted (1) but denied (2). For comparison, an atheist or error-theorist about religion might accept that (1) the statement "God exists" is capable of truth or falsity, but deny that (2) this statement is true. Of course, statements are only true or false when interpreted, and so the next branching question is whether (1) and (2) hold when (3) statements in that domain are given a *literal* interpretation. For example, a *non-literal* theist might claim that "God exists" is true, but when asked for the meaning of this statement say, "It means that I face the future with confidence." Such a position satisfies (1) and (2), but not (3). A non-literalist about ethics might claim that the statement "Torture is wrong" means "I hereby resolve to shun anyone who tortures or who tolerates torturing," or that talk of such a statement being true is "a useful fiction" for promoting social coordination. If someone accepts that affirmative ethical claims are true when literally interpreted, the next question is whether she accepts that (4) truth in this context is *opinion-independent*. For example, a theist who claims that "'God exists' is true for anyone who sincerely believes it" is denying opinion-independence, and similarly for a theist who claims that "Whether God exists is relative to a culture." Finally, there is the question whether (5) these literal, opinion-independent truths can provide a *substantive* explanation of our beliefs or practices in this domain. A stage-(5) realist about the external world might say, "The external world exists apart from whatever we believe, but nonetheless can shape our experience via sensation—thus our veridical perceptual beliefs can be said to be true *because* the world is the way it is." Call this a *tracking* account. By contrast, someone who accepts (1)–(4) but rejects (5) might give a *projectivist* account (cf. Blackburn, 1998): "Truth is not a substantive relation between our minds and the world that can be invoked to do explanatory work—to say that '*p*' is true is to say no more than *p*, and thus to explain what it is for *p* to be true is simply to explain what it is to *think* or *assert* that *p*." Tracking realists start off with an account of what it is for *p* to be true, and then seek to illuminate the perceptual or cognitive processes that permit the reality of *p* to be part of a causal explanation of why *p* is believed, while projectivist realists (who may call themselves *quasi-realists*) seek to show how an account of what it is to believe that *p* obviates the need for such an explanation and the metaphysics that would support it (see Dreier, 2004; McPherson, 2015; see also Terence Cuneo's chapter "Quasi-realism").

With this understanding of the landscape of realism, let us consider naturalism and its varieties.

NATURALISM: TWO BASIC ORIENTATIONS

Whatever their differences, philosophical naturalists tend to share a sense that the empirical, theoretical, and mathematical sciences afford our best-developed and most successful examples of inquiry aimed at obtaining a fundamental understanding of the world and ourselves. Moreover, the sciences have developed powerfully predictive explanations of many of the phenomena traditionally dealt with speculatively in philosophy, and in the process overturned long-held philosophical convictions concerning such questions as the nature of space and time, the ultimate constitution of matter, and the source of life and "design" in living organisms. Naturalists urge that we learn from this history that philosophical inquiry should be pursued in tandem with empirical science, not as a synthetic *a priori* "first science." This is not to say that philosophy can make no distinctive contributions to science—in the last half-century, e.g., Bayesian epistemology and decision theory have influenced a range of disciplines, and theories of speech acts and conversational norms have played an important role in linguistics. On the contrary, it is to say that philosophers should seek to develop theories that can be contributory parts of the larger explanatory enterprise of science.

Naturalists differ in approach. *Substantive naturalists* start off with a stand on ontological questions, according to which, strictly speaking, all bona fide fundamental entities, properties, relations, or facts are, or are reducible to or grounded in, entities, properties, relations, or facts of the kind posited in the natural sciences. (For short, we will speak of "properties and facts." For further discussion, see Gideon Rosen's chapter "Metaphysical Relations in Metaethics"). By contrast, *methodological naturalists* are committed in the first instance to a *project* rather than a metaphysics. Insofar as possible, they seek to work compatibly with the methods of the natural and social sciences as they tackle fundamental philosophical questions. Whether this will, in the end, result in the conclusion that the "natural world" is all the reality there is, is for them a question to which we have no *a priori* answer. (For additional discussion, see Daniel Nolan's chapter "Methodological Naturalism in Metaethics.")

NATURALISM AFTER MOORE: ANALYTIC AND NON-ANALYTIC APPROACHES

In the founding text of twentieth-century metaethics, *Principia Ethica*, G.E. Moore attacked what he called the "naturalistic fallacy" of attempting to define ethical concepts in naturalistic terms (Moore, 1903). (He also claimed to find a similar fallacy in attempts to define ethical concepts in super-natural or theistic terms.) His "open question" argument is meant to show why such definitions must fail. Take any alleged naturalistic definition of an ethical concept, e.g., of the moral goodness of an action in terms of whether, relative to alternatives, it maximizes net happiness overall. Moore argues that the philosopher advancing this account takes herself to be making an informative statement with which someone could disagree while displaying an adequate grasp of the concept MORALLY GOOD. (Moore framed his argument in terms of *properties* rather than concepts, but, for reasons to be discussed below, a formulation in terms of concepts seems to offer a more convincing version of the argument.) Moore concluded that we have a *sui generis* concept of "morally good," distinct from any proposed naturalistic characterization of what *makes* acts or outcomes good.

Moore was *not* saying that we cannot give definite, even naturalistic, answers to the question of what makes acts or outcomes good or right—indeed, he proposed such answers himself (1903, 1968). Rather, he claimed that any such answers must be *synthetic* rather than analytic—they involve substantive claims (what he would call "intuitions") about how we ought to live, and no one should be allowed to foist such claims upon us in the guise of "definitions." This he took to refute previous naturalisms in ethics, such as the utilitarianism of Mill (1863/2001).

Moore's argument has been enormously influential, though formulating it clearly and assessing its significance have proven difficult, and remain controversial (see Nicholas

Laskowski and Stephen Finlay's chapter "Conceptual Analysis in Metaethics"). Contemporary naturalistic replies fall into two categories: some agree that developing and defending their accounts must go beyond conceptual analysis, while others reject Moore's argument as based upon a mistake and thus propose a new form of analytic naturalism.

Non-analytic naturalists can draw upon several strategies. Some ethical concepts for which we have no naturalistic equivalent or "reduction" might be able to figure *in their own right* in legitimate scientific explanations. For example, interpersonal cooperation in a group or society can break down for various reasons—lack of resources, conflicting interests, external incursion, etc. But in many cases, the most illuminating explanation of breakdown will be that the existing arrangement was *unfair* to one or more of the parties—not "thought to be unfair," but *genuinely* unfair, even if this was not recognized at the time. UNFAIRNESS, then, might be a worthwhile organizing concept in diagnosing social dynamics, and so earn its way into the vocabulary of social-scientific explanation (for other examples, see Sturgeon, 1995). This may be especially plausible in the case of so-called *thick* normative concepts, in which descriptive and normative elements each figure essentially (see Debbie Roberts' chapter "Thick Concepts").

More generally, non-analytic naturalists can argue that even if some ethical *concepts* are not reducible to natural concepts, it may nonetheless be true that natural *properties* and *facts* suffice to explain the truth of claims involving these concepts. Consider the origin of the word "concept," which lies in two Indo-European roots, *con + kept*, "with + grasp/take." This suggests an image of concepts as "handles" with which we mentally take hold of the objects of which we wish to speak. Concepts can achieve this in a variety of ways, corresponding to different "modes of presentation" of their objects. Thus, the same individual can be "taken hold of" under the definite-descriptive concept THE TALLEST MAN IN THE BAR, the "baptized" concept JASON BEMIS, or the compound indexical concept THAT MAN TO YOUR RIGHT—three ways of conceiving this individual, none reducible to another, but the man *himself* is a single human being situated in the causal order, not a description, a name, or an indexical. If I am a bar-keep wondering how to reach a bottle on a high shelf, then the fact that this man satisfies the definite-description concept THE TALLEST MAN IN THE BAR presents him in a way that is directly relevant to my concern. But if I need to identify him to keep track of his tab, regardless of who else comes into the bar, then the individual concept JASON BEMIS is more apt. Importantly, the same individual can be also be picked out by *normative* concepts, which have special relevance to other purposes, for example, THE LEAST TRUSTWORTHY MAN IN THE ROOM or A MORAL AGENT.

Concepts are "modes of mental presentation," but *properties* are features of the world, e.g., dimensions of connection or similarity that unite a class of objects. Properties include substance types (*being iron, being made of proteins*), causal-explanatory or functional types (*being an acid*), structural types (*possessing bilateral symmetry*), dynamic types (*having angular momentum* r), genetic-historical types (*being a parent of twins, being a* Homo sapiens), and also evaluative or normative types (*being intrinsically desirable*), and so on. Unlike concepts, the man in question actually *is* (or *is not*) made of proteins, bilaterally symmetric, a parent of twins, a *Homo sapiens*, etc.

So, while concepts have roles in thought, properties have roles in the world. The ordinary-language concept ACID and the microphysical concept PROTON DONOR pick out the same underlying property with the same causal-explanatory powers, even though the concepts are not analytically equivalent. The existence of this shared, underlying property tells us that the ordinary-language concept ACID nonetheless picks out something real and explanatory, which accounts for why the ordinary-language concept ACID is so useful, and how it can be used (e.g., in "Lemon juice tarnishes metal because it is acidic") to convey genuine explanatory information.

A non-analytic naturalist about ethics can likewise seek to determine whether ordinary-language concepts like MORALLY GOOD or MORALLY RIGHT might pick out underlying real and explanatory properties, which would enable us to see why these concepts are useful and important in organizing the experience of life. Hume, for example, suggests that the property of *being morally good*, as attributed to traits of character, is constituted by *being such as to contribute reliably to the general interest* (1738/1978: 580). This property–constitution relationship could explain why grouping traits under the concept MORALLY GOOD or VIRTUOUS picks out features of a kind of fundamental importance in social groups, and thus similar concepts are likely to be found across many cultures. This "origin" of the moral distinction between good and bad traits of character cannot be discovered simply by analyzing the ordinary-language concept MORALLY GOOD or VIRTUOUS—it requires a theory of "human nature" and social dynamics, such as Hume develops in the *Treatise*. Arguably, it is this sort of explanatory theory, rather than an analytic definition, that Aristotle, Hobbes, Hume, Adam Smith (1759/1994), Jeremy Bentham (1780/2007), Mill, and other important naturalistic realists had in mind in the first place—they were trying to give an informative, vindicatory account of *what it is to be* morally good (or morally right, etc.) and *why this has an important action-guiding role* in human life, rather than an analysis of ordinary-language ethical concepts. Their accounts are "definitions" only in the sense of the "real" or "reforming" definitions typical of scientific theories, which seek to account for everyday features of the world in terms of underlying entities, structures, and processes—e.g., explaining macroscopic *heat* in terms of *molecular kinetic energy* (for realisms of this kind, see Railton, 1986a, 1986b, 1989; Boyd, 1988; Brink, 1989). Such accounts are *synthetic* rather than analytic and thus are not affected by Moore's open question argument.

Some contemporary naturalists take issue with the "open question" argument itself, arguing that it involves a question-begging assumption that analytic equivalences must be *obvious* to competent speakers of a language. "A sister is a female sibling" may seem, on a moment's reflection, obvious. But what about "A circle is a continuous set of points in a plane equidistant from a single point in that plane"? Given the complexity of ethical questions, it is likely that concepts such as MORALLY GOOD or MORALLY RIGHT will be yet more complex than CIRCLE, so we should not assume that spelling out their definitions will be obvious. Proponents of the "Canberra Plan" in metaethics (Jackson, 1998) argue that ethical terms can be defined in terms of the roles they play in mature ethical theory and practice, in much the same way that Frank Ramsey (1931) and David Lewis (1970) argued that theoretical terms in science can be defined via *their* roles in mature scientific theory and practice. By using quantification over properties, it is possible to formulate a statement of a well-developed theory that preserves the inferential relations and connections with observation or paradigm cases of the theory, but which does not contain any problematic theoretical terms ("unobservables" in science, or normative terms in ethics). MORAL GOODNESS, for example, could be defined as picking out whatever property most closely satisfies the role occupied by "moral goodness" in our best-developed ethical theory, including common-sense truisms about moral goodness (e.g., that it is impartial) and paradigm cases (e.g., that the relief of suffering is morally good, other things being equal). The resulting role-based definition can be thought of as giving the complex a "job description" to be satisfied by anything that would count as moral goodness. It might not be immediately obvious that whatever property best satisfies this job description *is* moral goodness, they argue, but if one sees this equation as giving the correct analysis of our concept of MORAL GOODNESS, then one can evade the Moorean critique of analytic naturalism—it won't be an "open question" whether a (possibly complex) natural property satisfying the job description is morally good. (For a non-analytic version of the "job description" strategy, see Railton, 1993.)

SUPERVENIENCE AND EXPLANATION

Let us return to our opening worry: Why think that it should be possible *at all* to give a naturalistic account of the ethical, given the categorical difference between *is* and *ought*? A key part of the answer lies in the profound ways in which the ethical properties are tied to the non-ethical, and to natural facts and properties in particular.

Imagine two individuals identical in all natural features, situated in two worlds also identical in their natural characteristics. Philosophers across the meta-normative spectrum largely agree that this naturalistic specification already assures that these individuals will have the same *evidence* and *practical reasons*—if one individual's beliefs are justified by his experience to date, then so are the other's; if one has good reason to take a certain action in his current situation, then so does the other. We cannot replicate natural features and then freely add or subtract normative features. This relationship between the normative and the natural is usually called *supervenience*. Very roughly, a feature or group of features S supervenes upon another feature or group of features T if, necessarily, fixing T also fixes S (see Pekka Väyrynen's chapter "The Supervenience Challenge to Non-Naturalism," for discussion of the many forms and strengths of supervenience).

A familiar example of supervenience is the *average value* of a variable in a population. For instance, once the individual ages of all the members of a given sample have been fixed, then so is the average age. The average of a variable in a population belongs to a class of higher-order statistics—including the median, the mode, the variation, etc.—which carry important information about a population in their own right, but which someone would fail to understand if he thought of them as *sui generis* or self-standing features that could be altered without changing any of the first-order features in the sample.

Indeed, these statistical relationships are actually "stronger" than mere supervenience, since they are asymmetric—the first-order distribution of ages fixes the average, median, mode, and variation in the sample, but not vice versa. (By contrast, *having a triangular shape* supervenes symmetrically on *having a trilateral shape*.) The higher-order value statistical values thus can be said to be *dependent upon* and to *hold in virtue of* the first-order values—the higher-order values are, in Moore's terminology, "consequential" from the first-order values, a notion of "consequence" that is asymmetric but need not be causal (Moore, 1968).

In these statistical examples, asymmetric dependence is mediated by the analytic definitions of the higher-order variables, but in many cases, it is not. For example, the macroscopic *heat* of a gas supervenes asymmetrically upon the kinetic behavior of the molecules composing it—a given microstate determines a unique heat value for the gas as a whole, but not the reverse. Thus we say that macroscopic heat holds in virtue of, or is "consequential" from, the gas's kinetic microstate, even though there is no purely analytic definition connecting the two.

This example illustrates two other important dimensions of asymmetric dependence: the *specificity* of the relation and the *explanatory status* of the dependent property or magnitude. For example, while the macroscopic heat of a given volume of gas is fixed by the *total microstate* of the universe, it also is fixed more specifically by the motion of *its own constituent molecules*—a key discovery of kinetic theory. This discovery does not supplant but rather vindicates the ordinary concept HEAT in many of its applications—e.g., invoking HEAT in an explanation of the ability of steam to melt ice or power a mill—since it shows that these uses of HEAT pick out a genuine underlying magnitude that accounts for these phenomena. Citing macroscopic heat is not simply redundant, however, since the ability to melt water or power a mill will be the same for two volumes of fluid or gas if they have the same *average* molecular kinetic energy, even though their molecular compositions differ. This similarity in ability is a *higher-order* characteristic, and the HEAT-invoking account captures this explanatory *generality* and *unification*, which would be missing from a mere conjunction of the two individual micro-level explanations.

Asymmetric, specific dependency in the absence of an analytic definition is a common relationship between our everyday categories of experience and underlying natural features. This holds for categories with normative dimensions as well. *Health*, for example, can be thought of as a normatively important higher-order property of organisms that depends asymmetrically and specifically upon a constellation of natural features of body and mind, ranging from cardiovascular sufficiency, to the absence of certain disease agents, to the balance of neurotransmitters in the brain, to physical mobility and resilience in the face of stress. When sufficiently many of these features are in place, the organism is healthy, and poor health can be traced to specific kinds of deficits or failures in such features. We do not need to posit health as a *sui generis* or self-subsistent property, and someone would misunderstand the concept HEALTH if he thought he could improve his pet hamster's health without changing its mental or physical condition. The concept HEALTH picks out real, complex features of individuals and populations, though the specific details will vary from individual to individual or species to species. HEALTH thus can provide general and unified explanations, and promoting health can be a unified project of inquiry and action (e.g., "Health declined when the medical system broke down, resulting in much-reduced productivity" or "Maternal health is a major determinant of infant mortality in humans and animals alike"). The concept HEALTH is what Richard Boyd (1988) termed a "homeostatic cluster concept," which collects under a single "handle" or "mode of presentation" a range of underlying physical and mental characteristics that work together in a mutually sustaining way—in this case, to underwrite organismic functionality and freedom from suffering (for criticism of this account, see Horgan & Timmons, 1992; for defense, see Merli, 2002; van Roojen, 2006; and Dowell, 2015). This connection with functionality and quality of experience helps explain why the property of being healthy is of enduring interest in human societies, and why the concept HEALTH can be used to orient shared discussion and inquiry, even among those who disagree about some of the underlying components of health—e.g., the current debate over what range of body mass indices is healthy.

Similarly, naturalistic realists characteristically think of ethical properties as "higher-order" features linked to core areas of shared human concern. Like HEALTH, ethical concepts such as GOOD, RIGHT, or FAIR collect together multiple phenomena that deeply affect our lives—e.g., well-being, cooperation, reciprocity, mutual respect, etc.—under a unifying "mode of presentation" with direct relevance for individual and shared deliberation and action-guidance. At the same time, ethical properties are not self-standing or *sui generis*—ethical facts depend asymmetrically and specifically upon constellations of natural, social, and psychological facts, and someone would show a deficient grasp of the concepts of GOODNESS or FAIRNESS, for example, if she thought she could improve a society's goodness or fairness while leaving in place all these empirical facts about people's lives. At the same time, ethical concepts can figure in informative, general explanations of various patterns of behavior and outcomes—e.g., "Rates of compliance with the tax system declined as tax policy became progressively less fair" or "After trying her hand at various things, she settled upon life-coaching because she discovered it was a good life for her" (Railton, 1986a, 1986b).

Naturalistic realists are not alone in thinking that ethical features depend asymmetrically and specifically upon natural features. "Like cases must be treated alike" is a common-sense truism in ethics. In this truism, likeness is not understood trivially in terms of "ethically alike," but substantively, in terms of likeness in features that can be understood independently of ethical judgment. In practice, these likenesses are typically quite specific—two acts of deception can differ in their location in space and time, the genotypes of the agents, the ambient temperature, and atmospheric pressure, etc., yet still be "like" enough in the intentions, expectations, and harms involved to require the same ethical evaluation or response. Even expressivists, who reject a metaphysical interpretation of supervenience, accept this sort of normative principle of treating like cases alike and thus accept that "fully opinionated" ethical judges are committed to there being some or other (possibly complex) natural features that all acts that are good, or right, share (Gibbard, 2003; for discussion, see Elisabeth Camp's chapter "Metaethical Expressivism").

Where naturalistic realism is distinctive is in the *explanation* it affords of this truism, and of the asymmetric, specific dependence of the ethical upon the natural that underwrites it. Just as the concept HEALTH is a normative "mode of presentation" of a constellation of natural features of body and mind that constitute *what it is* to be healthy, our concepts GOOD, RIGHT, and FAIR are normative "modes of presentation" of natural features of lives, acts, and practices that constitute *what is* good, right, or fair. Thus, Hume, for example, saw himself as making the substantive discovery that a combination of enduring human interests and a human capacity for general sympathy explains why we deem some traits virtues and others vices, why we should expect to find such distinctions in all societies, and how such distinctions can be motivating even in the face of self-interest. Moreover, he argues, once we understand this account, we will reflectively approve of our ethical distinctions and practices as corresponding to something real and important. "Thus upon the whole I am hopeful, that nothing is wanting to an accurate proof of this system of ethics" (1738/1978: 618).

To be sure, naturalistic realists need not seek to vindicate *all* aspects of ordinary ethics—this would be impossible given the conflicts in ethical thought found within and across societies. Often, as in the case of Bentham or Mill, naturalistic realists have sought to identify a core basis that explains a great deal of common-sense ethics but also could support the systematic reform of beliefs and practices—e.g., in the case of slavery or the subjugation of women—that traditionally represent themselves as ethical, but which are in tension with the fundamental characteristics of impartiality, treating like cases alike, and concern to avoid suffering and promote well-being. This works in much the same way that the "real" or "reforming" definitions of mature science seek to identify a core explanatory basis for many of the categories of ordinary experience, but also to eliminate conflations of categories, misleading superficial similarities, and erroneous associations, and to extend our conceptual vocabulary to accommodate novel phenomena.

Such a substantive explanation of supervenience also helps us see how epistemic and semantic access could exist for ethical facts—as we saw in connection with Boyd's "homeostatic cluster concepts." Similarly, Hume gives an account of *what it is* for a trait of character to be a "natural virtue" in terms of the trait's tendency to promote individual well-being and the "general interest" of social groups. This means that our individual and shared life experiences—as well as those of other individuals, other societies, and other times—can provide evidence that enables us to "track" whether a given trait is genuinely a natural virtue. Moreover, we can see how it is possible that more diverse experiences (Mill's "experiments in living," 1859/1978), enhanced capacity for empathic simulation, and greater understanding of human psychological and social dynamics can give us greater justification and reliability in these assessments. Social "tracking" accounts of this kind provide an explanation of how our ethical language could succeed in referring to ethical facts, providing a common ground for ethical discussion and disagreement and funding talk of truth and error in ethical judgments.

DIFFICULTIES WITH NATURALISTIC REALISM

It should be obvious from the descriptions given above that naturalistic realism of the "tracking" variety has many hostages to fortune. What follows is a brief survey of some of the difficulties faced by naturalistic realists, along with some preliminary responses.

Naturalistic realism involves a parochial attitude toward ethics. The "tracking" naturalistic realist gives an explanation of supervenience, and of the development of ethical discourse and practice, that draws essentially upon substantive ethical claims. This should not be surprising—we should hardly expect to be able to give a theory of how perception and language put us reliably in touch with features of the world without making some substantive assumptions about what those features are like. Addressing this worry requires that such assumptions be weak, and beg as few questions as possible. Thus, we have assumed that ethics strives for objectivity in the form of impartiality and opinion-independence, that prevention of harm or suffering are among the central ethical concerns, and that cases alike in their natural features must be treated alike by ethical evaluation. This list of features is compatible with all the main contemporary ethical theories, but it does contrast ethics with normative systems of a purely egocentric, ethnocentric, conventional, or divine kind, or of a kind that is entirely indifferent to suffering. Is this too parochial? Perhaps not. Would I count as having successfully taught my children the meaning of FAIR or MORALLY RIGHT if what I have instilled in them is a view according to which these terms apply always and only "because I say so," and guide action only "because otherwise you'll be in trouble"?

Interestingly, elementary school children across a range of cultures are already too skilled in making normative distinctions to be taken in by such spurious instruction (for a summary of evidence, see Smetana, 2006 and Turiel, 2006). For example, most children will follow a substitute teacher's instruction to raise both hands before speaking, but balk at his instruction to poke their seat-mates with a pencil to signal the desire to talk. Children explain their resistance in terms of avoiding harm to others, and they exhibit intrinsic motivation to accord such authority-independent norms special seriousness and priority in practice—even intervening to enforce these constraints in third-party interactions when this is at some cost to themselves. Moreover, they distinguish unprovoked harm from harm in the form of punishment for previous acts of harming others. It seems unlikely that all these children will have been given explicit instruction in making these distinctions, or in their relative importance in practice—especially since children can use these distinctions to oppose a parent's or teacher's instructions. Rather, it would appear that they have acquired—perhaps with assistance from innate predispositions (Hamlin, 2013)—an implicit, non-parochial understanding of the distinctive character and importance of the dimensions of normative assessment we have characterized as ethical.

Taking evolutionary theory seriously is incompatible with realism about ethics. Critics have argued on evolutionary grounds that a naturalistic approach to ethics will not sustain realism. While it might be clear why natural selection would have favored the emergence of perceptual systems capable of mapping the local natural environment accurately, why would it have favored the emergence of capacities to detect and be moved by putative objective moral truths? Such truths, we have claimed, would be impartial, abstract, unobservable, and modal. How could our perceptual systems, evolved to operate in the realm of the perspectival, concrete, observable, and actual, provide reliable feedback about such moral truths? And how could it contribute to one's inclusive reproductive fitness to constrain one's thought and action by an impartial concern with the well-being of all affected? (For some examples of evolutionary critiques of realism about ethics, see Joyce, 2001 and Street, 2006.)

We have seen, however, that a naturalistic realist's substantive account of ethical facts can explain how ordinary experience could permit access to the ethical features of lives, traits of character, or actions. To be sure, the moral truths thus learned are impartial, abstract, unobservable, and modal, but so are the causal truths of common sense and science—and so is the distinction between conventional versus authority-independent constraints that elementary schoolers implicitly master. Moreover, we now have very good behavioral and neuroscience evidence for the chief Humean mechanism for learning such moral truths: "general sympathy"—the ability to vicariously experience how things are from others' points of view, with attendant immediate effects on feeling and motivation (Decety & Ickes, 2009). Affective simulation of other points of view—including the points of view of one's future selves—appears to play a key role in human behavior, and individuals deficient in this ability appear to suffer both in personal decision-making and in the formation of mutually beneficial long-term social relations (Blair & Blair, 2009). Affective simulation generates expectations with respect to the course of one's own experience and the likely behavior of others, and these afford a basis for learning by feedback from experience. Infants in their early years seem to map their social as well as physical environment in non-perspectival terms, keeping track of evidence of trustworthiness and helpfulness in the behavior of third parties, and are less likely to accept information or instruction from adults whose third-party behavior has been deceptive or harmful (Doebel & Koenig, 2013; Nguyen et al., 2016; for adult social valuation, see Behrens et al., 2008). In short, humans appear to have evolved to be able to apply and be moved by impartial, abstract, aperspectival, modal, harm-based impartial assessments of behavior (for discussion of evolutionary mechanisms that would explain this, see Nesse, 2007).

Naturalistic realism does not provide a satisfactory account of the normative *character of ethical judgments.* Expressivists and "projectivist" (or quasi-) realists consider it a decisive advantage for their view that they can establish an *internal* connection between moral judgment and motivation: the state of mind expressed in ethical judgments, they argue, is a motivating one, and not a mere belief purporting to "track" a state of affairs (Gibbard, 2003). But the connection between ethical judgment and motivation is much-contested (for discussion, see Smith, 1994, 1995 and Darwall, 1997; see also David Faraci and Tristram McPherson's chapter "Ethical Judgment and Motivation"), and, in any event, it is unclear that a connection to *motivation* suffices to capture *normative* force. Consider someone who judges progressive taxation to be just because it equalizes burdens and would be agreed to as a social-insurance scheme by agents who did not know how the "natural lottery" would affect their fates, but who is not personally motivated to pay his share in such a scheme. Is he misusing the word "just"? Would it be a more accurate expression of his state of mind for him to pronounce progressive taxation "unjust"?

The evidence for a *necessary* connection between moral judgment and motivation is not decisive, but surely there should be a *general* connection of this kind, or ethics would have little role in human social existence (see David Faraci and Tristram McPherson's chapter "Ethical Judgment and Motivation"). The Humean mechanism of "general sympathy" offers a naturalistic explanation of why ethical judgment and motivation would tend to go hand-in-hand: the primary way by which we acquire, retain, refine, or revise ethical beliefs is via mentally simulating actions and outcomes in a way that is inherently sensitive to how those affected are harmed or helped, and that generates unfavorable versus favorable affective responses accordingly. Because this mechanism, when working well, "tracks" genuine good- or right-making features, it affords an explanatory advantage over "projectivist" approaches that lack a general account linking the *substantive content* of ethical judgment with psychic processes capable of yielding ethical beliefs that are *reliable* as well as motivating (Dreier, 2015; see also Joshua Schechter's chapter "Explanatory Challenges in Metaethics"). Moreover, as noted earlier, Aristotelian and Hobbesian forms of naturalistic ethical realism offer their own accounts of the connection between the content of ethical judgment and motivation.

No account of the normativity of ethical thought and language has emerged that commands wide consensus. What can be asked of naturalistic realism at present is that it exhibit resources for grappling with this difficult question that show some promise. Whether in the end one of these approaches will offer a convincing account that combines factuality with normativity remains to be seen.

REFERENCES

Aristotle (ca. 350 BCE, 1999) *Nicomachean Ethics*, trans. and ed. by T. Irwin, Indianapolis, IN: Hackett.

Ayer, A.J. (1936) *Language, Truth, and Logic*, London: Gollancz.

Behrens, T.E.J., Hunt, L.T., Woolrich, M.W., & Rushworth, M.F.S. (2008) "Associative Learning of Social Value," *Nature* 456: 245–49.

Bentham, J. (1780/2007) *An Introduction to the Principles of Morals and Legislation*, Mineola, NY: Dover Reprints.

Blackburn, S. (1998) *Ruling Passions*, Oxford: Clarendon.

Blair, R.J.R & Blair, K.S. (2009) "Empathy, Morality, and Social Convention: Evidence from the Study of Psychopathy and Other Psychiatric Disorders," in J. Decety & W. Ickes (eds.), *The Social Neuroscience of Empathy*, Cambridge, MA: MIT Press.

Boyd, R. (1988) "How to be a Moral Realist," in G. Sayre-McCord (ed.), *Essays in Moral Realism*, Ithaca, NY: Cornell University Press.

Brink, D. (1989) *Moral Realism and Its Foundations*, Cambridge: Cambridge University Press.

Darwall, S. (1997) "Reasons, Motives, and the Demands of Morality," in S. Darwall et al. (eds.), *Moral Discourse and Practice: Some Philosophical Approaches*, Oxford: Oxford University Press.

Decety, J. & Ickes, W. (eds.) (2009) *The Social Neuroscience of Empathy*, Cambridge, MA: MIT Press.

Doebel, S. & Koenig, M.A. (2013) "Children's Use of Moral Behavior in Selective Trust Discrimination versus Learning," *Developmental Psychology* 49: 462–69.

Dowell, J. (2015) "The Metaethical Insignificance of Moral Twin Earth," *Oxford Studies in Metaethics* 11: 1–27.

Dreier, J. (2004) "Meta-Ethics and the Problem of Creeping Minimalism," *Philosophical Perspectives* 18: 23–44.

Dreier, J. (2015) "Explaining the Quasi-Real," *Oxford Studies in Metaethics* 11: 273–97.

Enoch, D. (2011) *Taking Morality Seriously: A Defense of Robust Realism*, Oxford: Oxford University Press.

Foot, P. (1977) *Virtues and Vices*, Oxford: Oxford University Press.

Gibbard, A. (2003) *Thinking How to Live*, Cambridge, MA: Harvard University Press.

Hamlin, J.K. (2013) "Moral Judgement and Action in Preverbal Infants and Toddlers," *Current Directions in Psychological Science* 22: 186–193.

Hobbes, T. (1651/1994) *Leviathan*, ed. by E.M. Curley, Indianapolis, IN: Hackett.

Horgan, T. & Timmons, M. (1992) "Troubles for New Wave Moral Semantics: The Open Question Argument Revisited," *Philosophical Papers* 21: 153–75.

Hume, D. (1738/1978) *Treatise of Human Nature*, 2nd edition, ed. by L.A. Selby-Bigge & P.H. Nidditch, Oxford: Clarendon.

Jackson, F. (1998) *From Metaphysics to Ethics: A Defence of Conceptual Analysis*, Oxford: Clarendon.

Joyce, R. (2001) *The Myth of Morality*, Cambridge: Cambridge University Press.

Lewis, D. (1970) "How to Define Theoretical Terms," *Journal of Philosophy* 67: 427–46.

McDowell, J. (1979) "Virtue and Reason," *Monist* 62: 331–50.

Mackie, J.L. (1977) *Ethics: Inventing Right and Wrong*, London: Penguin.

McPherson, T. (2015) "What Is at Stake in Debates among Normative Realists?" *Noûs* 49: 123–46.

Merli, D. (2002) "Return to Moral Twin Earth," *Canadian Journal of Philosophy* 32: 207–40.

Mill, J.S. (1859/1978) *On Liberty*, ed. by E. Rapaport, Indianapolis, IN: Hackett.

Mill, J.S. (1863/2001) *Utilitarianism*, 2nd edition, ed. by G. Sher, Indianapolis, IN: Hackett.

Moore, G.E. (1903) *Principia Ethica*, Cambridge: Cambridge University Press.

Moore, G.E. (1968) "Replies to my Critics," in P.A. Schilpp, *The Philosophy of G.E. Moore*, Vol. 2, La Salle, IL: Opencourt.

Nesse, R. (2007) "Runaway Social Selection for Displays of Partner Value and Altruism," *Biological Theory* 2: 143–55.

Nguyen, S.P., Gordon, C.L., Chevalier, T., & Girgis, H. (2016) "Trust and Doubt: An Examination of Children's Decision to Believe What They Are Told about Food," *Journal of Experimental Child Psychology* 144: 66–83.

Parfit, D. (2011) *On What Matters*, Vol. 2, ed. by S. Scheffler, Oxford: Oxford University Press.

Plato (ca. 399–395 BCE, 2002) *Euthyphro*, in G.M.A. Gruber and J.S. Cooper (trans. and ed.), *Plato: Five Dialogues*. 2nd edition. Indianapolis, IN: Hackett.

Railton, Peter (1986a) "Moral Realism," *Philosophical Review* 95: 163–207.

Railton, Peter (1986b) "Facts and Values," *Philosophical Topics* 224: 5–31.

Railton, Peter (1989) "Naturalism and Prescriptivity," *Social Philosophy and Policy* 7: 154–74.

Railton, Peter (1993) "Noncognitivism about Rationality: Benefits, Costs, and an Alternative," *Philosophical Issues* 4: 36–51.

Ramsey, F. (1931) "Theories," in *The Foundations of Mathematics*, ed. by R.B. Braithewaite, London: Routledge and Kegan Paul.

Smetana, J. (2006) "Social-Cognitive Domain Theory," in J. Smetana and M. Killen (eds.), *Handbook of Moral Development*, Mahwah, NJ: Erlbaum: 119–53.

Smith, A. (1759/1994) *The Theory of Moral Sentiments*, ed. by K. Haakonssen, Cambridge: Cambridge University Press.

Smith, M. (1994) *The Moral Problem*, Oxford: Blackwell.

Smith, M. (1995) "Internalism's Wheel," *Ratio* 8 (new series): 277–302.

Street, S. (2006) "A Darwinian Dilemma for Realist Theories of Value," *Philosophical Studies* 127: 109–66.

Sturgeon, N. (1995) "Moral Explanations," in D. Copp and D. Zimmerman (eds.), *Morality, Normativity, and Society*, New York: Oxford University Press.

Turiel, E. (2006) "The Development of Morality," in N. Eisenberg (ed.), *Handbook of Child Psychology*, Vol. 3, 6th edition, New York: Wiley, 789–857.

van Roojen, M. (2006) "Knowing Enough to Disagree," *Oxford Studies in Metaethics* 1: 161–94.

Error Theory in Metaethics

Jonas Olson

INTRODUCTION: ERROR THEORY, WHAT?

Error theories have been proposed and defended in several different areas of philosophy. In addition to ethics, there are error theories about numbers, color, free will, and personal identity, just to mention a few examples. Error theory about some area of thought and discourse, D, is commonly defined as the view that D involves systematically false beliefs and that, as a consequence, all D-judgments, or some significant subset thereof, are false. That is also how we shall understand the term "error theory" in this chapter. (For a discussion of some non-standard versions of error theory, see Olson 2014: 8–11.) We shall thus take *moral* error theory to be the view that moral thought and discourse involve systematically false beliefs and that, as a consequence, all moral judgments, or some significant subset thereof, are false.

Moral error theories differ in scope. Theories at one end of the spectrum take normative judgments in general—of which moral judgments are a subclass—to be uniformly false, whereas theories at the other end of the spectrum take only a subclass of moral judgments—e.g., those concerning duty and obligation, but not those concerning virtue and vice—to be uniformly false (Anscombe 1958; Williams 1985). Positions between these two extremes are also possible.

In recent debate, there has been a consensus that prominent arguments in favor of moral error theory—such as the argument from queerness, to be discussed in the section "The Argument from Queerness and the Queerness Arguments"—generalize beyond the narrowly moral to the broadly normative domain. Consequently, critics, as well as proponents of the theory, have suggested that a plausible moral error theory must take the form of an error theory about the normative, or more particularly, about the irreducibly normative (Olson 2014; Streumer forthcoming). We shall say more about irreducible normativity in the section "What's Queer? On Irreducible Normativity." While the chapter focuses mainly on moral error theory, all the points made and concerns raised apply, *mutatis mutandis*, to error theories about the broadly normative.

A pertinent question for moral error theorists is what to do with moral thought and discourse. Error theorists who are also abolitionists argue that, since moral judgments are uniformly false, we ought to abolish moral thought and discourse (Garner 2007). An important question here that relates to the aforementioned issue about the scope of moral error theory concerns the meaning of "ought" in the claim that we ought to abolish moral thought and discourse. If moral judgments are uniformly false, it is not true that we ought morally to abolish moral thought and discourse, but it might be true that we ought to do so in some normative, yet non-moral, sense of "ought." Another possibility is that the "ought" is not to be understood as genuinely normative, but rather as a means–end recommendation about how to achieve certain ends, such as peace and mutual trust in a community. Abolitionists could thus argue that abolishing moral thought and discourse would tend to promote peace and mutual trust better than preserving moral thought and discourse would. But abolitionism is not the only option for moral error theorists. Fictionalists recommend that we take up fictional attitudes to moral thought and discourse (Joyce 2001: chapter 8). Conservationists recommend that we continue to engage in moral thought and use moral talk, although systematically error-ridden (Olson 2014: chapter 9). There are other alternatives as well, but since the moral error theorists' issue about what to do with moral thought and discourse is logically independent of the truth or falsity of moral error theory we will not consider it further here (see Richard Joyce's chapter "Fictionalism in Metaethics").

Moral error theorists typically join forces with non-naturalist realists, against naturalism and non-cognitivism. Against non-cognitivism, they hold that sincere utterances of moral sentences, like "Torture is wrong" and "Happiness is good," are assertions and not primarily expressions of non-cognitive attitudes. In the remainder of this chapter, we shall say no more in the way of critique of non-cognitivism (see, e.g., Elisabeth Camp's chapter "Metaethical Expressivism;" Jack Woods' chapter "The Frege-Geach Problem;" and Matthew S. Bedke's chapter "Cognitivism and Non-Cognitivism"). Against naturalism, they hold that, according to our ordinary concepts of moral properties and facts, moral properties and facts are irreducibly normative and therefore not reducible to, or wholly constituted by, natural properties and facts. It is initially convenient and useful to view error theory and non-naturalistic realism as jointly opposing naturalism concerning the metaphysical commitments of ordinary moral thought and discourse (Mackie 1977: 31–32). But we shall see in the section "What's Queer? On Irreducible Normativity" that the issue of naturalism need not be crucial to the debate about moral error theory after all. (On naturalism and non-naturalism, see David Enoch's chapter "Non-Naturalistic Realism in Metaethics;" Peter Railton's chapter "Naturalistic Realism in Metaethics;" and Daniel Nolan's chapter "Methodological Naturalism in Metaethics.")

In any case, moral error theorists part company with non-naturalist realists in holding that there are no moral *facts*. Whether moral error theorists hold that there are no moral *properties* is a slightly more delicate issue. Depending on their general views on the metaphysics of properties, particularly concerning the possibility of uninstantiated properties, moral error theorists may hold either that there (necessarily) are no moral properties, or that there are moral properties that are (necessarily) uninstantiated.

Many different arguments can and have been used to support moral error theory (Joyce 2011; Olson 2014: 15–17). For example, it is a common view that moral realism requires convergence in moral judgments among fully rational individuals (Smith 1994: chapter 6). If no such convergence is forthcoming, and if ordinary moral thought and talk involve commitment to moral realism, error theory looms. Another possible argument for moral error theory is that moral judgments presuppose a kind of free will that human agents cannot have, in which case moral error theory also looms large.

By far the most discussed argument for moral error theory, however, is the argument from queerness (Mackie 1977: chapter 1). In the next section, we shall look at the structure of the argument, and in the sections that follow, we shall consider in some detail one pertinent version of it. We shall also see what can be said for and against this version. But before we come to that, we shall take notice of a difficulty concerning the exact formulation of moral error theory. (The remainder of this section draws on Olson 2014: 11–15.)

According to the standard version of moral error theory, all moral judgments are false. A moral judgment, let us say, is a judgment that entails that some agent morally ought to do or not to do some action; that there are moral reasons for some agent to do or not to do some action; that some action is morally permissible; that some institution, character trait, or what have you, is morally good or bad; and the like. This raises the question of what to say about the truth-values of negated moral judgments, such as the judgment that torture is not wrong. This latter judgment appears to be a moral judgment, and since it is the negation of a judgment that moral error theory deems false, it appears that the theory should deem the negated judgment true. Yet we know that according to the standard version of moral error theory, moral judgments are uniformly false.

This leads to two worries: First, is moral error theory a coherent theory? Second, can it be maintained that moral error theory lacks moral implications? It is immediately obvious that the standard version of moral error theory has implications for moral theory since it implies that moral judgments are uniformly false. But the worry we shall now address is whether moral error theory has implications that are themselves moral.

Mackie insisted that his error theory is purely a "second-order," or metaethical, view (Mackie 1977: 15–17; on the distinction between metaethics and ethics, see Mark Schroeder's chapter "Normative Ethics and Metaethics"). But this can be doubted. If it is false that torture is wrong, it seems to follow, by the law of excluded middle, that it is true that torture is not wrong, which seems to be a first-order moral view. That torture is not morally wrong seems to imply that torture is morally permissible. More generally, then, the apparent upshot is that contrary to Mackie's contention, moral error theory does have first-order moral implications. And rather vulgar ones at that—if moral error theory is true, any action turns out to be morally permissible!

Things get in one way worse, for it seems that we can also derive an opposite conclusion. According to the standard version of moral error theory, "Torture is permissible" is false. By the law of excluded middle, it follows that torture is not morally permissible, which seems to entail that torture is morally impermissible. More generally, then, the apparent upshot is that any action is morally impermissible! This may not be a vulgar first-order moral implication, but it is surely absurd. It also transpires that moral error theory involves a straightforward logical contradiction since we have derived that it is true that, e.g., torture is morally permissible (since any action is morally permissible) and that it is false that torture is morally permissible (since any action is morally impermissible).

One possible way out of the predicament is to restrict the scope of moral error theory and hold that not all moral judgments are false, but only a significant subset thereof, namely *positive* moral judgments (Sinnott-Armstrong 2006: 34–36). A positive moral judgment is a judgment about what some agent morally ought to do or not to do, what there is moral reason for some agent to do or not to do, and so on and so forth; or what would be morally good or bad, or morally desirable or undesirable, and so on. Importantly, it says nothing about mere permissibility.

Restricting the scope of moral error theory to positive moral judgments in this way saves moral error theory from incoherence and from the absurd implication that anything is morally impermissible. But one may object that it remains a platitude that any action that is not wrong is permissible. In other words, moral error theory would still imply vulgar nihilism about wrongness, according to which anything is permissible. ("Nihilism" can mean different things in different contexts. In this chapter, it simply means the rejection of something, such as wrongness or moral facts more generally.)

A better way out is to deny that the implications from "not wrong" to "permissible" and from "not permissible" to "wrong" are conceptual, and maintain instead that they are instances of a generalized conversational implicature (Grice 1989). To illustrate, "not wrong" conversationally implicates "permissible" because normally when we claim that something is not wrong we speak from within a system of moral norms, or moral standards for short. According to most moral standards, any action that is not wrong according to that standard is permissible according to that standard. General compliance with Gricean maxims that bid us to make our statements relevant and not overly informative ensures that we do not normally state explicitly that we speak from within some moral standard when we claim that something is not wrong (Grice 1989: 26ff.). But the implicature from "not wrong" to "permissible" is cancellable. The error theorist can declare that torture is not wrong and go on to signal that she is not speaking from within a moral standard. She might say something like the following: "Torture is not wrong. But neither is it permissible. There are no moral facts and, consequently, no action has moral status." This cancels the implicature from "not wrong" to "permissible." (Analogous reasoning, of course, demonstrates why the error theorist's claim that torture is not morally permissible does not commit her to the view that torture is morally impermissible and hence morally wrong.) On this view, error theory has neither the vulgar implication that anything is permissible nor the absurd implication that anything is impermissible.

But one might object that a fatal problem remains. The law of excluded middle entails that if "Torture is wrong" is false, then "Torture is not wrong" is true. If the latter sentence expresses a moral judgment, then moral error theory after all has first-order moral implications, i.e., implications that by its own lights are false.

In response, recall that according to the definition above, moral judgments are judgments that entail that some agent morally ought to do or not to do some action; that some action is morally permissible or impermissible; that some institution, character trait, or what have you, is morally good or bad; and so on. Now, according to the view on offer, a negated judgment like the one expressed by the sentence "Torture is not wrong" does not *entail* that torture is permissible; it merely conversationally implicates that it is, since the implicature from "not wrong" to "permissible" is cancellable. Likewise, the judgment expressed by "Torture is not morally permissible" does not entail that torture is impermissible and hence wrong; it merely conversationally implicates that torture is impermissible and hence wrong. Thus negated atomic judgments involving moral terms are not strictly speaking moral judgments, but some such judgments conversationally implicate moral judgments. Since, on this view, sentences like "Torture is not wrong" express judgments that are true, we cannot derive that their negations (such as "Torture is wrong") are true. This saves moral error theory from the threat of incoherence and from implausible first-order moral implications, and it enables moral error theorists to maintain that all moral judgments, and not just a subset thereof, are false. Let us now consider arguments in favor of error theory and the alleged queerness of moral facts.

THE ARGUMENT FROM QUEERNESS AND THE QUEERNESS ARGUMENTS

The argument from queerness is profitably seen as having a bipartite structure. The first part of the argument seeks to identify ways in which moral facts would be metaphysically queer, and hence to establish a presumption against the existence of moral facts. Such arguments we can call "the queerness arguments." The second part seeks to explain why we tend to think and speak as if there are moral facts, although there are none. Such explanations typically appeal to projectivist accounts of moral judgment and belief, according to which we mistake affective attitudes (such as approval and disapproval) for perceptions of mind-independent moral properties and facts (Hume 1998: Appendix 1; Mackie 1977), and to debunking explanations, according to which moral judgment and belief originate and evolve because of their social and evolutionary advantageousness (Joyce 2006). The point is to explain how ordinary moral judgment and belief are products of processes that do not track moral truth.

The second part of the argument from queerness is needed because the queerness arguments, if successful, establish only a presumption against moral facts. There are some prima facie queer entities, whose queerness does not rule them out of existence. Some examples are dark matter, neutrinos, tardigrades, and Impressionist paintings (Platts 1980: 87). Once inquiry reveals how such entities fit into the natural order of things, we typically no longer view them as queer, or we may continue to view them as queer in the sense of appearing utterly different from most other things we encounter. But inquiry and reflection can help us realize that such entities are actually parts of the best explanations of some of our observations and beliefs, and at that point, they no longer seem *ontologically* mysterious. By contrast, moral facts do not in this way fit into the natural order of things, and they are not parts of the best explanations of our observations and beliefs. Moral facts are, according to error theory, both metaphysically queer and explanatorily redundant.

If successful, the argument from queerness shows that moral error theory is, in the end, more plausible than realism since it establishes a presumption against moral facts and explains our common-sense moral beliefs in ways that do not require or presuppose that they are or can be true.

The *locus classicus* of the argument from queerness is a dense passage from Mackie's *Ethics* (1977: 38–42). In my view, four distinct queerness arguments can be discerned in Mackie's discussion. They concern motivation, epistemology, supervenience, and irreducible normativity (Olson 2014: chapters 5–6). According to the queerness argument concerning epistemology, our ways of knowing about moral facts would have to be queer. This argument can be set aside for our purposes since it concerns the attainability of moral knowledge rather than the existence of moral facts. If successful, the argument supports moral skepticism rather than moral error theory (see Matt Lutz and Jacob Ross' chapter "Moral Skepticism"). One could argue that realism about moral facts requires a plausible epistemology of moral facts, and that failure to provide one would count against realism. But we won't pursue that line here.

The queerness argument concerning motivation has as its key premise that moral facts are such that necessarily, if one is aware of them (at least by first-hand acquaintance), one is thereby motivated to act in accordance with them. There is now a general consensus that the weakness of this argument is that its key premise is highly dubious. It seems not implausible that the connection between awareness of moral facts and motivation to act is contingent (see David Faraci and Tristram McPherson's chapter "Ethical Judgment and Motivation").

The queerness argument concerning supervenience is much more contested. Its starting point is that moral facts *depend* on natural facts; there can be no change or difference in moral facts without a change or difference in natural facts that somehow explains or determines the difference in moral facts. The challenge for realists is to account for this seemingly necessary dependence relation. Naturalist realists can respond that since moral facts are natural there is no dependence relation between metaphysically distinct kinds of facts to account for (Brink 1984). But the difficulty naturalists face is to give a naturalistic account of moral facts that accommodates their irreducible normativity. We will return to this in the next section. Non-naturalist realists face the difficulty of accounting for the dependence relation in a way that is consistent with the metaphysical distinctness of moral and natural facts (see Pekka Väyrynen's chapter "The Supervenience Challenge to Non-Naturalism"). Some error theorists who are impressed by this argument argue that there is no such plausible account to offer, and they conclude that there are no moral facts (Streumer 2013; forthcoming).

One way for non-naturalist realists to respond is to argue that some natural properties have the further property of *making* actions right, wrong, obligatory, etc. (Olson 2014: 98–99; Wielenberg 2014: 23–24, 35–36). For example, a utilitarian may argue that an action's natural property of maximizing happiness makes that action right. The property of being a right-making (wrong-making, ought-making, etc.) property is itself an irreducibly normative property and fundamental truths concerning which natural properties make actions right, wrong, obligatory, etc., may well be necessary truths that we can grasp only by a priori reflection or intuition. The notion of right-making (wrong-making, ought-making, etc.) properties, therefore, does not seem to give rise to additional metaphysical or epistemological puzzles for non-naturalistic realism.

Note that what is made right by a right-making property (such as the property of maximizing happiness) is an *action*. The relation between the fact that an action has certain natural properties and the fact that it has certain moral properties is plausibly seen as an instance of a kind of generic making-relation, which is not itself irreducibly normative but whose instances may obtain between natural and irreducibly normative relata (e.g., between the fact that an action has the natural property of maximizing happiness and the fact that it has the irreducibly normative property of being right).

Were error theorists to object to the idea of a generic making-relation, or to the idea that fundamental moral truths are *necessary* and a priori knowable, the target of their objections would be very wide and would not obviously succeed in pointing to something uniquely objectionable about moral or normative facts and properties. It seems, then, that the moral error theorist's objection will have to focus on the metaphysical queerness of irreducible normativity. In order to see whether that objection can be substantiated, we need to get a better understanding of what irreducible normativity is supposed to be.

WHAT'S QUEER? ON IRREDUCIBLE NORMATIVITY

It is not very easy to say what irreducible normativity is. Several contemporary non-naturalist realists take the notion of an irreducibly normative reason to be primitive (Parfit 2011a: 31; Scanlon 2014: 2). In order to illuminate irreducible normativity, it is therefore useful to say what it is *not* and to contrast it with adjacent but different notions. Following Derek Parfit, we can contrast normativity in the "rule-implying" sense with normativity in the "reason-implying" sense (2011b: 308–10; 326–27). Examples of normative facts of the former kind are facts about what is legal or illegal, grammatical or ungrammatical; and about what accords with rules of etiquette or chess. There is no metaphysical mystery how there can be such facts, for facts about the law and grammar, and about rules of etiquette or chess, are all facts about human conventions. It might, of course, be difficult to say exactly how and why certain conventions originate and evolve, but such difficulties invite no metaphysical mysteries (Mackie 1977: 25–27; Joyce 2001: 34–37; Olson 2014: 118–26). Moreover, for any fact that is normative in the rule-implying sense, e.g., that it is a rule of etiquette that one does not eat peas with a spoon, we can always ask whether we have *reason* to—or whether we *ought* to, or are *required* to—*comply* with that rule. Those are instances of what Christine Korsgaard and others have called "the normative question" (Korsgaard 1996; Broome 2007).

Facts that are normative in the reason-implying sense are irreducibly normative, and they are very different. Such facts do not reduce to—and are not wholly constituted by— facts about human conventions or about agents' motivational states or desires. In the words of the eighteenth-century moral rationalist Richard Price, irreducibly normative facts "have a real obligatory power antecedently to all positive laws, and independently of all will" (Price 1948: 105).

Moral facts are prime examples of irreducibly normative facts, but there may be others. This connects to the question concerning the scope of error theory, which was mentioned in the section "Introduction: Error Theory, What?". It has been argued, for example, that epistemic facts are irreducibly normative (Cuneo 2007; Bedke 2010; Olson 2014: chapter 8). But here we shall concentrate on moral facts. Many philosophers hold that according to the ordinary concept of moral facts, they are irreducibly normative, and that ordinary moral judgments are judgments about such facts. (This is of course not to say that ordinary speakers articulate the thought that moral facts are irreducibly normative.) Therefore, moral judgments do not invite the normative question. If we know or believe, e.g., that we ought morally to eat less meat, it makes no sense to ask whether we have irreducibly normative reason to eat less meat; that question will already have been answered. (We could, of course, ask different questions, such as whether eating less meat would be *comme-il-faut*, or whether there is anything that motivates us to eat less meat, or whether doing so would be conducive to fulfillment of our desires.) This explains why it would be odd, and perhaps conceptually confused, to accept that one ought morally to eat less meat and at the same time hold that one has no reason to do so because social conventions do not recommend or require that one eat less meat, or because one is not motivated to do so, or because one lacks the relevant desire.

Many non-naturalist realists and error theorists maintain that it is impossible to give a plausible naturalistic account of moral facts, precisely because they are irreducibly normative; moral naturalism therefore falls prey to the "normativity objection" (Parfit 2011b: 324–27; Olson 2014: 82–83). But moral naturalism is a broad church and it is perhaps premature to conclude that there can be no plausible naturalistic account of irreducible normativity. If there is such an account, moral naturalists too can agree that ordinary moral thought and talk involve commitment to irreducibly normative facts without thereby yielding to error theory. Note also that it is not uncontroversial that ordinary moral thought and talk do involve such commitment (Foot 1972; Finlay 2008). This indicates, as was suggested in the section "Introduction: Error Theory, What?", that the divide between naturalism and non-naturalism is not central to the debate on moral error theory after all. Instead, the crucial lines of division are between those who think that ordinary moral thought and discourse involve commitment to irreducibly normative facts (a group which includes non-naturalists, error theorists, and possibly some naturalists) and those who think not, and between those who think that there are irreducibly normative facts and those who think not.

For reasons of space, I shall not say more than I already have said above in defense of the view that ordinary moral thought and discourse involve commitment to irreducibly normative facts (see Olson 2014: 126–35). The pertinent question to consider now is the second of the two mentioned in the previous paragraph, i.e., whether there *are* any irreducibly normative facts. Here is where error theorists and other critics of irreducible normativity see a mystery: How can there be facts that have a real obligatory power, prior to human conventions and independently of agents' motivational states or desires? As was just noted, it seems no metaphysical mystery how there can be facts that require or favor certain courses of behavior, where these requiring or favoring relations reduce to facts about conventions or desires. But how can there be facts that require or favor certain courses of behavior, where the relation of requiring or favoring cannot be explained or demystified in terms of facts about human conventions and desires? Irreducibly normative facts seem in this way to involve "a peculiar combination of objectivity and prescriptivity" (Garner 2006: 101; see also Mackie 1977: 40–42; Olson 2014: 116–26). In comparison with facts that are normative in the rule-implying sense, such facts seem queer. Their queerness establishes a presumption against the view that there are irreducibly normative facts and in favor of views according to which there are none, such as the error theorist's view. To committed realists, this "sheer queerness worry" (Enoch 2011: 134–36) may appear unsophisticated. But it seems not very different from the grounds on which philosophers have worried about or objected to other theories.

Consider, for example, the reaction that Bertrand Russell reported that he once had to Leibniz's theory of monads, the monadology. It seemed to him "a kind of fantastic fairy tale, coherent perhaps, but wholly arbitrary" (Russell 1900: xiii). The error theorist's response to the realist's ontology of irreducibly normative facts is similar to Russell's reaction to the monadology. Error theorists may hold that the realist's theory of irreducibly normative facts is "fantastic" in the sense of unrealistic, odd, or incredible. They may also hold that while the theory is coherent, it is arbitrary, since moral facts are explanatorily superfluous; in particular, moral facts are not required as parts of the explanations of why we make moral judgments and form moral beliefs. We will return to this point in the next section.

RESPONSES TO THE ARGUMENT FROM QUEERNESS

According to the queerness argument—the first part of the bipartite argument from queerness—that we have explored, moral facts are irreducibly normative, and the metaphysical queerness of irreducibly normative facts establishes a presumption against them. There are various ways for moral realists to respond to the argument. As mentioned in the previous section, one line of response rejects the premise that ordinary moral thought and discourse involve commitment to irreducible normativity (Finlay 2008). As we also mentioned in the previous section, however, many realists worry that any account that denies that ordinary moral thought and discourse carry such commitment is thereby vulnerable to the normativity objection. A stubborn but natural response from realists who maintain that ordinary moral thought and discourse involve commitment to irreducible normativity is simply to deny that irreducibly normative facts are queer. Another natural but less stubborn response is to grant that irreducibly normative facts are queer, and that their queerness establishes a presumption against them, but maintain that the presumption can be conclusively rebutted.

As a simple illustration of how the less stubborn response may be developed, consider the proposition that *torturing children for fun is morally wrong*. Most people believe that this proposition is true, and many are strongly convinced that it is true. Now consider the proposition that *no action is morally wrong*, which is what moral error theory implies. These two propositions are obviously mutually inconsistent. Presumably, most people who are not already committed moral nihilists are much more confident that the first is true than that the second is true. Presumably, then, for most people, it seems at least initially much more plausible that moral error theory is false than that it is true; insofar as one is confident that, e.g., torturing children for fun is morally wrong, it is rational to reject the error theorist's claim that moral facts are queer and that no action is morally wrong (Huemer 2005: 116–17; Enoch 2011: 118–21). From this point of view, it would seem *more* queer or odd for it to be the case that torturing children for fun is *not* morally wrong than for it to be the case that there are irreducibly normative facts.

In order to respond to this attempted rebuttal, the moral error theorist needs to invoke the second part of the argument from queerness. As noted in the section "The Argument from Queerness and the Queerness Arguments", the point of the second part is to explain why we make moral judgments and hold moral beliefs, sometimes with great confidence, although they are uniformly false. As indicated, such an explanation typically involves a projectivist account of moral judgment and an account of the social and evolutionary advantageousness of moral judgment. Here, we shall only consider briefly what such accounts may look like (Olson 2014: 141–18).

According to one popular view, the psychological origins of moral norms are our emotions or affective attitudes (Nichols 2004). For example, norms against harming others originate in the intense distress most people feel when witnessing others suffer. Such feelings of distress explain, or at least partly explain, why people are typically strongly motivated to enforce and comply with norms against harming innocents, such as children and animals. It may be that we systematically mistake certain affective responses, such as the distress we typically feel when witnessing others suffer, for perceptions of mind-independent, irreducibly normative, properties, e.g., moral wrongness. In this way, we may come to experience moral wrongness as mind-independent and as independent of human conventions, and come to believe that, e.g., torturing children for fun, has the irreducibly normative property of being wrong. To use Hume's famous metaphor, the idea is that emotions and affective responses are "gilding or staining all natural objects with the colours, borrowed from internal sentiment [which] raises, in a manner, a new creation" (1998: 163).

Moral error theorists like J. L. Mackie and Richard Joyce have argued that this projective error is beneficial rather than pernicious in that it enables moral thought and talk to function well as devices for solving inter- and intrapersonal coordination problems. The thought is, in brief, that natural selection has tended to favor certain patterns of human behavior, such as reciprocating favors; sticking to agreements; punishing perpetrators; parents looking out for their kin; and so on. These selection processes have played a part in shaping our current systems of norms; they account for why we tend to believe, e.g., that there are reasons to return favors, keep promises, punish perpetrators for their misdeeds, and for parents to look after their kin. Human beings will of course sometimes be tempted to violate some of these norms. Breaking promises and omitting to return favors often make sense from a narrowly egoistic perspective, and punishing perpetrators can be costly for the punisher. Moral thought—along with its projective error and experience of moral properties and facts as irreducibly normative—and moral talk—along with its attributions of such properties and references to such facts—enter the picture as social devices that serve to enforce compliance with these norms. We judge that those who fail to return favors and keep their promises act *morally wrongly*; they are liable to *moral blame*, i.e., to attitudes of resentment and dislike.

The projective error is also what makes most people perceive a kind of authority in moral norms, which makes them feel *bound* to act in accordance with them. In this way, moral thought and talk function both intrapersonally "as a bulwark against weakness of will [and] as an interpersonal commitment device" (Joyce 2006: 208). In short, there is such a thing as moral thought and talk partly because "[w]e need [it] to regulate interpersonal relations, to control some of the ways in which people behave towards one another, often in opposition to contrary inclinations" (Mackie 1977: 43).

It is important to be clear about what projectivist debunking accounts of moral judgments and beliefs—like the one just sketched—achieve and do not achieve, if they are successful. First, they do not establish the ontological thesis that there are no moral facts. If successful, they establish at most that moral facts play no explanatory role in the formation of moral judgments and beliefs, and in moral practice more generally. Second, projectivist debunking accounts of moral judgments and beliefs do not establish the epistemological thesis that we cannot attain knowledge about necessary moral truths solely by a priori reflection or intuition. Even if it is true that ordinary moral judgments and beliefs originate in emotions and social conventions and hence are products of processes that do not track moral truth, it does not follow that we cannot attain knowledge a priori about necessary moral truths. It does not even follow that most of our current moral judgments and beliefs are erroneous. It might be that many moral judgments and beliefs that, according to realists, are true (e.g., that happiness is good; that justice should be honored; that cheaters should be punished; etc.) have been evolutionarily advantageous. If so, ordinary moral judgments and beliefs may correlate with moral truths, even though they are products of processes that do not themselves track moral truths. That could explain how it can be that many ordinary and widely held moral judgments and beliefs are true, even if projectivist debunking accounts of them are successful (Enoch 2011: 167–76; Olson 2014: 146; Wielenberg 2014: chapter 4).

It is thus a mistake to infer a nihilist view like error theory directly from the premise that projectivist debunking accounts of moral judgments and beliefs are successful. Moral realism is compatible with such accounts. This should not be surprising, since projectivist debunking accounts explain the psychological and social origins of moral judgments and beliefs, and as such, they have no direct implications for the ontology of moral properties and facts or the attainability of moral knowledge. The point that moral facts play no explanatory roles in the formation of moral judgment and beliefs is no embarrassment to those realists who take moral properties and facts to be causally inefficacious (e.g., Enoch 2011: 7, 162, 177).

What, then, is the point of projectivist debunking accounts of moral judgment and belief if realists can, after all, accept them? Their dialectical point in the error theorist's critique of realism is twofold. First, they explain why we tend to make moral judgments and hold moral beliefs even though they are uniformly false. Projectivist debunking accounts thereby offer a response to the realist's argument that moral error theory can be rationally rejected because we believe some moral propositions with comparatively very high confidence. They also defeat the evidence provided by our great confidence in some moral propositions. For if projectivist debunking accounts of moral judgments and beliefs are successful, error theorists can offer them as explanations of why we tend to believe certain moral propositions with great confidence, and these explanations do not require that the propositions are true.

A point worth making in this context is that the hypothesis that moral judgments and beliefs stem partly from affective attitudes explains why moral error theory is *emotionally* difficult to accept. When one considers the numerous atrocities committed in the past century, it may feel sickening to maintain that none of them were in fact morally wrong, even to proponents of moral error theory. Error theory about other matters, such as numbers and color, may be *intellectually* difficult to accept, but they do not face the same kind of emotional resistance. The emotional origin of moral judgments goes some way to explaining why reactions to error theory about morality are sometimes rather fierce, while reactions to error theories in other domains typically are less so (Olson 2014: 143–44).

Secondly and relatedly, projectivist debunking accounts help establish that moral error theory is a more parsimonious theory than realism about irreducible normativity. Error theory involves fewer ontologically fundamental and unexplained facts than does realism, without loss in explanatory power concerning how and why we make moral judgments and form moral beliefs (Olson 2014: 87–88, 147–48). Realists about irreducible normativity are of course likely to object that error theorists buy parsimony at the expense of plausibility, since error theory implies that many propositions that seem highly plausible are not true. But that only takes us back to the first dialectical point of the error theorist's employment of projectivist debunking accounts of moral judgments and beliefs.

However, while its greater ontological parsimony renders error theory in one respect preferable to realism, it is important to observe the limitations of ontological parsimony. Considerations of ontological parsimony do not constitute evidence of the absence of moral facts. At most, they establish the absence of such evidence. In other words, assuming again that the error theorist's proffered projectivist debunking account of moral judgments and beliefs is successful, that leaves an absence of evidence that there are moral facts; it does not provide evidence of absence of moral facts. (This point is forcefully made in Morton & Sampson 2014.)

This reinforces the importance of the bipartite structure of the argument from queerness. As I have indicated repeatedly, projectivist debunking accounts of moral judgments and beliefs do not on their own establish a presumption against moral facts. That is why the first part of the argument from queerness, what I have called a queerness argument, is needed. As before, realists can and probably will dispute the queerness of moral facts, and of irreducible normativity in particular. But this will not refute the argument from queerness, for it cannot be an adequacy condition of an argument that it suffices to convince the opponents. Consider again the criticism of Leibniz's monadology, that it seems a fantastic and wholly arbitrary theory. Imagine that the monadology enthusiast responds to this criticism in a way that parallels the realist's response to the error theorist's claim that irreducibly normative facts are queer, i.e., by simply refusing to admit that the monadology is fantastic and wholly arbitrary. Such a response notwithstanding, most philosophers presumably find the monadology fantastic and arbitrary, and the entities it concerns ontologically mysterious. And most philosophers presumably take such worries to constitute a presumption against monads and the truth of the monadology. Error theorists take the same views of realist theories that vindicate irreducibly normative facts, and of the alleged facts these theories are about.

At this point non-naturalist realists may try a somewhat different tack and argue that the claim that irreducibly normative facts are intolerably queer is implicitly or explicitly premised on a prejudicial commitment to a kind of philosophical naturalism, according to which only properties and facts that are in some relevant sense continuous with natural science exist (e.g., Scanlon 2014: 17–18). This kind of philosophical naturalism is not only philosophically contentious; it is also unclear what conclusions to draw from it, since it is notoriously unclear which kinds of properties and facts are in the relevant sense continuous with contemporary natural science, and also what it is for properties and facts to be relevantly continuous with contemporary natural science (see Daniel Nolan's chapter "Methodological Naturalism in Metaethics").

While it is true that some philosophers who find moral facts queer are or seem inclined toward some kind of philosophical naturalism (e.g., Mackie 1946: 78–80; cf. Enoch 2011: 135), queerness arguments need not be premised on any kind of philosophical naturalism. Someone who finds irreducible normativity queer need not thereby hold that Cartesian souls, abstract objects, God, or whatever other kind of entities commonly taken to conflict with philosophical naturalism—even Leibnizian monads—are queer. This confirms the suspicion that the divide between naturalism and non-naturalism need not be seen as a crucial line of conflict in the debate on moral error theory. The queerness argument against moral facts that we have explored here is not premised on a prejudicial commitment to a contentious kind of philosophical naturalism, but on the sheer queerness of irreducibly normative facts.

ACKNOWLEDGMENTS

Earlier versions of this chapter were presented at seminars at the universities of Oslo and Stirling and at a metaethics workshop at the Jean-Nicod Institute in Paris. I thank the participants for interesting discussions. I also thank Emma Beckman, Lars Bergström, Björn Eriksson, Kent Hurtig, Victor Moberger, and Frans Svensson for very useful written comments. Special thanks are due to Jens Johansson, Lea Schroeder, and the editors of this volume for their extremely helpful feedback. Work for this chapter was supported by a generous grant from Riksbankens Jubileumsfond (grant no. 1432305).

RELATED TOPICS

Chapter 1, "Non-Naturalistic Realism in Metaethics;" Chapter 2, "Naturalistic Realism in Metaethics;" Chapter 4, "Fictionalism in Metaethics;" Chapter 5, "Metaethical Expressivism;" Chapter 8, "Realism and Objectivity;" Chapter 9, "Metaphysical Relations in Metaethics;" Chapter 10, "The Supervenience Challenge to Non-Naturalism;" Chapter 14, "The Frege-Geach Problem;" Chapter 18, "Cognitivism and Non-Cognitivism;" Chapter 19, "Ethical Judgment and Motivation;" Chapter 31, "Moral Skepticism;" Chapter 36, "The Varieties of Normativity;" Chapter 41, "Metaethical Quietism;" Chapter 42, "Methodological Naturalism in Metaethics;" Chapter 43, "Normative Ethics and Metaethics."

REFERENCES

Anscombe, G. E. M. (1958) "Modern Moral Philosophy," *Philosophy* 33: 1–19.
Bedke, M. (2010) "Might All Normativity be Queer?" *Australasian Journal of Philosophy* 88: 41–58.
Brink, D. O. (1984) "Moral Realism and the Sceptical Arguments from Disagreement and Queerness," *Australasian Journal of Philosophy* 62: 112–25.
Broome, J. (2007) "Is Rationality Normative?" *Disputatio* 23: 161–78.
Cuneo, T. (2007) *The Normative Web*, Oxford: Oxford University Press.
Enoch, S. (2011) *Taking Morality Seriously: A Defense of Robust Realism*, Oxford: Oxford University Press.
Finlay, S. (2008) "The Error in the Error Theory," *Australasian Journal of Philosophy* 86: 347–69.
Foot, P. (1972) "Morality as a System of Hypothetical Imperatives," *Philosophical Review* 81: 305–16.
Garner, R. T. (2006) "On the Genuine Queerness of Moral Properties and Facts," in A. Fisher & S. Kirchin (eds.) *Arguing about Metaethics*, London: Routledge. Reprinted from *Australasian Journal of Philosophy* 68 (1990): 137–46.
Garner, R. T. (2007) "Abolishing Morality," *Ethical Theory and Moral Practice* 10: 499–513.
Grice, P. (1989) *Studies in the Way of Words*, Cambridge, MA: Harvard University Press.
Huemer, M. (2005) *Ethical Intuitionism*, New York: Palgrave Macmillan.
Hume, D. (1998) [1751] *An Enquiry Concerning the Principles of Morals*, T. Beauchamp (ed.), Oxford: Oxford University Press.
Joyce, R. (2001) *The Myth of Morality*, Cambridge: Cambridge University Press.
Joyce, R. (2006) *The Evolution of Morality*, Cambridge: MIT Press.
Joyce, R. (2011) "The Accidental Error Theorist," *Oxford Studies in Metaethics*, Vol. 6, R. Shafer-Landau (ed.), Oxford: Oxford University Press: 153–80.
Korsgaard, C. M. (1996) *The Sources of Normativity*, Cambridge: Cambridge University Press.
Mackie, J. L. (1946) "A Refutation of Morals," *Australasian Journal of Philosophy* 24: 77–90.
Mackie, J. L. (1977) *Ethics: Inventing Right and Wrong*, Harmondsworth: Penguin.
Morton, J. & Sampson, E. (2014) "Parsimony and the Argument from Queerness," *Res Philosophica* 91: 609–27.
Nichols, S. (2004) *Sentimental Rules*, New York: Oxford University Press.
Olson, J. (2014) *Moral Error Theory: History, Critique, Defense*, Oxford: Oxford University Press.
Parfit, D. (2011a) *On What Matters*, Vol. 1, Oxford: Oxford University Press.
Parfit, D. (2011b) *On What Matters*, Vol. 2, Oxford: Oxford University Press.
Platts, M. (1980) "Moral Reality and the End of Desire," in M. Platts (ed.) *Reference, Truth, and Reality: Essays on the Philosophy of Language*, London: Routledge and Kegan Paul: 69–82.
Price, R. (1948) [1758/1787] *A Review of the Principal Questions in Morals*, D. D. Raphael (ed.), Oxford: Clarendon Press.
Russell, B. (1900) *A Critical Exposition of the Philosophy of Leibniz*, London: George Allen & Unwin.
Scanlon, T. M. (2014) *Being Realistic about Reasons*, Oxford: Oxford University Press.
Sinnott-Armstrong, W. (2006) *Moral Skepticisms*, Oxford: Oxford University Press.
Smith, M. (1994) *The Moral Problem*, Oxford: Blackwell.
Streumer, B. (2013) "Why There Really Are No Irreducibly Normative Properties," in D. Bakhurst, B. Hooker, & M. O. Little (eds.), *Thinking about Reasons: Themes from the Philosophy of Jonathan Dancy*, Oxford: Oxford University Press: 310–36.

Streumer, B. (Forthcoming) *Unbelievable Errors: An Error Theory about All Normative Judgments*, Oxford: Oxford University Press.

Wielenberg, E. (2014) *Robust Ethics: The Metaphysics and Epistemology of Godless Normative Realism*, Oxford: Oxford University Press.

Williams, B. (1985) *Ethics and the Limits of Philosophy*, London: Routledge.

FURTHER READING

Daly, C. & Liggins, D. (2010) "In Defense of Error Theory," *Philosophical Studies* 149: 209–30. (An overview and defense of error theories in various philosophical areas.)

Francén Olinder, R. (2013) "Moral Relativism, Error Theory, and Ascriptions of Mistakes," *Journal of Philosophy* 110: 564–80. (Argues that moral relativism and moral error theory face similar challenges.)

Joyce, R. & Kirchin, S., eds. (2010) *A World without Values: Essays on John Mackie's Moral Error Theory*, Dordrecht: Springer. (A useful collection of essays for and against moral error theory.)

4

Fictionalism in Metaethics

Richard Joyce

INTRODUCTION

Looking back, it is clear that humans have held massively mistaken beliefs about virtually every aspect of the world: the place of the Earth in the universe, the physical nature of everyday objects, where living things come from and how they reproduce, what happens to us when we die, and so forth. We are pretty good at getting things wrong. Often these errors can be corrected while the key concepts are revised rather than rejected. We didn't decide that the Earth, stars, animals, death, etc., don't exist; rather, we rectified our false beliefs about them and carried on talking about these topics (now, hopefully, more truly). Sometimes, however, the errors are so entrenched that the concepts in question seem beyond salvaging. Regarding angels, vitalistic life force, karmic reincarnation, tapu, supernatural divination, phlogiston, astrology, and so on, we didn't simply undertake an internal correction to the concepts in question, but rather decided that the whole conceptual framework in question was faulty.

It will be widely agreed that humans have held massively mistaken beliefs about *morality*. These mistakes may pertain to the substantive content of morality (believing that women should be subservient to men, for example) or to the general nature of morality (believing that God's will determines moral properties, for example). (One might try to reduce the extent of moral error by plumping for a form of radical relativism, but then one would have to ascribe false beliefs about morality to all those absolutists.) Many philosophers maintain (or hope) that these mistakes in moral thinking are of the former variety, such that our moral concepts can be patched up and we can carry on talking (now, hopefully, more truly) about right and wrong, virtue and vice, obligations and responsibilities, and so on. But the worry lurks in the background—and is sometimes embraced—that the mistakes are actually of the latter kind, and that moral thinking is a fundamentally flawed way of conceptualizing the world and ourselves. The moral error theorist maintains that moral facts belong on the list including angels, karmic reincarnation, phlogiston, and the rest. (Moral error theorists include Mackie 1977, Joyce 2001, and Olson 2014; see Jonas Olson's chapter "Error Theory in Metaethics.")

Fictionalism can be thought of as a way of trying to rescue morality from the threat of error theory. But fictionalism comes in different stripes, forcing the need to delineate upon anyone wishing to discuss it. The first distinction has come to have the somewhat unfortunate pair of labels "revolutionary" versus "hermeneutic."

The revolutionary fictionalist thinks that the moral error theory is correct: our moral discourse really does involve systematic falsehood from which first-order moral truths cannot be salvaged. The usual view for the error theorist to take is to see actual moral discourse as ontologically committed to entities (e.g., moral properties) that do not exist. But of course not all language that involves non-denoting terms is ontologically committing. The sentences "Angels do not exist" and "Aquinas believed in angels" are ontologically innocent with regard to angels. Certain utterances surrounding fiction also do not ontologically commit the speaker. Neither talking about a story—e.g., asserting "According to *It's a Wonderful Life*, angels exist"—nor telling a story—e.g., uttering "Angels definitely exist!" without assertoric force in the course of a bedtime tale—commits the speaker to the existence of angels. The revolutionary fictionalist recommends that we carry on using moral discourse but in a manner that does not ontologically commit speakers to the problematic entities. Such a view presupposes that the non-moral values necessary to underwrite the relevant notion of *recommendation* are not infected with the problematic commitments that sink moral values. The view is *revolutionary* in that it proposes an actual change in our attitude to morality: that we should alter our mental and linguistic lives so as to become ontologically innocent with respect to the problematic entities to which ordinary participation in moral discourse currently commits us. And the view is *fictionalist* if it turns to one or more of the familiar commitment-removing devices of ordinary fiction as a model for that change.

The hermeneutic fictionalist, by contrast, is not an error theorist about our actual moral discourse, but is nevertheless likely to be someone who is alert to the threat of error theory and therefore motivated to interpret our actual moral discourse in a manner that avoids that threat. Like the error theorist (and, indeed, like the noncognitivist), the hermeneutic fictionalist thinks that moral judgments are problematic if taken at face value. One who makes the judgment "Breaking promises is morally wrong," for example, appears to assert that promise-breaking instantiates a certain property which (for a host of reasons familiar to metaethicists) proves to be metaphysically and epistemologically troublesome. So the hermeneutic fictionalist (like the noncognitivist) suggests that we therefore do not take moral judgments at face value—rather, an interpretation is offered such that discourse that appears to be problematically ontologically committed is not really thus committed. The view is *hermeneutic* in that it offers an interpretation of our actual moral discourse. And the view is *fictionalist* if it turns to one or more of the familiar commitment-removing devices of ordinary fiction as a model for that interpretation.

Note that I am restricting discussion to a fictionalist stance toward morality as a whole. One might, however, be a fictionalist about only certain parts of morality. For example, one might be a fictionalist about human rights but not about moral vices, or about evil but not about moral badness, and so on. Such possibilities of selective moral fictionalism are being put aside on this occasion.

What the revolutionary fictionalist recommends we become, the hermeneutic fictionalist declares we already are. Thus, though there is a great deal to be said about moral fictionalism that pertains to both revolutionary and hermeneutic forms, it is obvious that the two types of theory must ultimately be assessed in fundamentally different ways. Hermeneutic fictionalism purports to be *true*; we must therefore evaluate the evidence for and against it. Revolutionary fictionalism purports to be *good advice*; we must therefore evaluate its practical costs and benefits. Let us consider the prospects of the hermeneutic form first.

HERMENEUTIC MORAL FICTIONALISM

The hermeneutic fictionalist maintains that our actual moral discourse should be interpreted in a manner similar in some fashion to familiar fictional discourse. We have already seen two importantly different ways in which this "similarity" might be cashed out. On the one hand, there is what one does when one *talks about* a fiction; on the other hand, there is what one does when one *engages with* the fiction. The former view is a type of cognitivism, according to which moral discourse is genuinely assertoric; it is just that the assertions concern the content of a fiction (e.g., "According to the fiction of morality, such-and-such is wrong"). This view therefore also allows for moral beliefs, moral truths, and (potentially) moral knowledge. The latter view is best construed as a type of noncognitivism, since what we do when we engage with a fiction (most obviously when telling a story) is not assert but *make-believe* that we assert. "Once upon a time ..." is a device for showing that assertoric force is being lifted; "... and they lived happily ever after" is a device indicating its reinstatement; what comes between is generally amenable to a noncognitivist analysis. Note, though, that the noncognitivist analysis just described is one pertaining to the pragmatics of speech, not its semantics. A sentence within the story—e.g., "In this land, angels existed"—requires no translation into some special non-descriptive format; it means whatever it would mean if it were asserted; it is just that here it is uttered without that assertoric force. Some elements of story-telling, however, should be given a noncognitive analysis at the level of semantics rather than pragmatics. When one introduces an act of make-believe with the sentence "Let's pretend that ... ," the sentence is in the cohortative rather than indicative mood; it is not used to make an assertion. This raises the possibility of a hermeneutic fictionalism that interprets ordinary moral judgments as having the noncognitive logical form of "Let's pretend that ..." sentences (or some close cousin). (What I am calling "noncognitive fictionalism" might also be called "force fictionalism," and what I am calling "cognitive fictionalism" might be called "content fictionalism." See Eklund 2015.)

The chief theoretic virtue enjoyed by cognitivist and noncognitivist versions of hermeneutic moral fictionalism alike is that they permit speakers to reap the benefits of moral discourse without footing the ontological bill for problematic entities. But is this advantage sufficient to motivate either view, and do either or both of the views suffer countervailing problems?

The cognitivist version of hermeneutic fictionalism faces some special problems. A sentence employing a story operator ("According to fiction *F*, ...") makes sense only to the extent that some account of the content of the story/fiction in question is forthcoming.

(See Hussain 2004.) But even for paradigm fictions—such as the Sherlock Holmes stories, say—matters are far from straightforward. Consider the following:

1. According to the Holmes stories, Holmes lived on Baker Street.
2. According to the Holmes stories, Holmes had ten fingers.
3. According to the Holmes stories, Watson had forty-six chromosomes.
4. According to the Holmes stories, Watson had an old war wound in his shoulder.

1 is surely fine, and 2 seems safe despite the fact that the number of Holmes's fingers is never explicitly mentioned by Conan Doyle; 3, however, begins to feel problematic. And 4 is puzzling in a special way, since the position of Watson's war wound varies in different stories. However such matters should be straightened out, maintaining a degree of indeterminacy in the right places seems desirable.

But what "story" is the cognitivist hermeneutic moral fictionalist going to invoke in constructing the all-important operator? It's one thing to say, as the error theorist does, "Morality is just a fiction"; it's quite another to suppose that the fiction has sufficient determinate content to underwrite claims of the form "According to the fiction of morality …." More on this in a moment.

Another problem for the cognitivist hermeneutic moral fictionalist is accounting for how moral claims logically interact with non-moral claims, if the former but not the latter contains a tacit story operator. The following seems valid:

P1: Stealing is morally wrong.
P2: Amy stole last Tuesday.
C: Therefore Amy did something morally wrong last Tuesday.

But if premise 1 harbors a tacit "According to the fiction of morality …" prefix, then the validity evaporates. Perhaps the validity could be rescued by adding the same prefix to both P2 and C, but the problem now is that the revised P2—"According to the fiction of morality, Amy stole last Tuesday"—seems simply false. (See Vision 1994.)

This problem can potentially be solved by understanding the relevant story operator more carefully. The "fiction of morality" differs from the Sherlock Holmes stories in that it is not a well-defined set of propositions. Rather, it is an image of the world—*this* world—as containing certain properties that in fact the world does not contain. It is a *fiction* not merely because it makes reference to non-actual entities, but because the entities may not even be *possible*. (See Proudfoot 2006.) Thus the story operator might be better rendered as "In fictional world *FW*, …"—accompanied with the reminder that fictional worlds need not be possible worlds. (Exhibit A: Watson's war wound. Exhibit B: virtually any story involving time travel.) Despite the fact that we are not discussing possible worlds, it is reasonable to suppose that we can make some sense of roughly ordering fictional worlds with respect to their similarity to the actual world. The "moral *FW*" can be considered a complete world very much like the actual world but containing moral properties. (The moral fictionalist might borrow a device that Gideon Rosen employs in his discussion of modal fictionalism, according to which the *FW* contains an "encyclopedia" of non-moral truths. See Rosen 1990: 335.)

Understood in this manner, the aforementioned problem of how propositions with story operators logically interact seems more tractable. In particular, while "According to the fiction of morality, Amy stole last Tuesday" seemed false, a differently worded revision of P2—"In the moral *FW*, Amy stole last Tuesday"—stands a very good chance of turning out true. If, in the actual world, Amy did in fact steal last Tuesday, then, ceteris paribus, in the moral *FW* Amy stole last Tuesday.

Of course, what this solution requires is that all a speaker's utterances—even those that have nothing to do with morality—be interpreted as tacitly prefixed with "In the moral *FW* ..." (since at any time a speaker might consider the logical relations between her non-moral claims and her moral claims). Whatever problems there may be with this prospect, there is nothing ridiculous *in general* with the idea that a great many of our utterances should be interpreted as bearing tacit prefixes. Consider how we would usually accept that most assertions make tacit reference to how things stand in the actual world rather than some other possible world.

But the first problem remains: What is the content of the moral fictional world? We can offer some general answers like "In the moral *FW*, moral obligations exist" and "In the moral *FW*, people have moral rights," but can we hope for anything of more substance, like "In the moral *FW*, stealing is generally morally wrong"? When two people engage in moral argument—one of them claiming (we'll assume) that in the moral *FW* euthanasia is permissible and the other claiming that in the moral *FW* euthanasia is not permissible—then we face not merely an epistemological problem of how to know which party is correct, but a far more serious problem (for this kind of fictionalist) of puzzlement over what it would even take for one party to be correct and the other incorrect.

What the cognitivist hermeneutic fictionalist evidently needs is some non-arbitrary means of restricting possible moral fictional worlds, ideally reducing the infinitude of candidates down to a single privileged fiction. (For arguments that the fictionalist needs to pare fictions down merely to a *range* rather than a single fiction, see Woodward 2011.) Reflecting this desideratum, the story operator might be rendered "In the best moral *FW* ... ." But best in what way? Some sort of pragmatic appeal would be a natural thought here, starting with the very approximate idea that "the best moral *FW*" denotes whichever moral *FW* is most useful. As usual with pragmatic proposals, though, certain glaring questions jostle for attention and threaten to overturn the solution: Useful to whom? Useful in what way? And in this case, there's the special question of "Useful when how grasped?"—in other words, is the best fiction that which would be most useful *if believed*, or that which would be most useful if the object of *make-believe*?

Let us remind ourselves what the cognitivist hermeneutic fictionalist is trying to achieve. He or she wants a theory according to which moral judgments stand a chance of being true while remaining ontologically innocent with respect to problematic moral properties. Suppose that Ernie claims that Hitler was evil, while Bert (a well-known Nazi sympathizer) claims that Hitler was a moral hero. Error-theoretic worries threaten to render both speakers mistaken (along with speakers of every other first-order moral claim), a result from which most philosophers recoil. So Ernie's and Bert's moral judgments are interpreted as prefixed with a tacit story operator. If one were tolerant of relativism, then one might consider appropriately relativized moral fictions, allowing both claims to be true: In Ernie's moral fiction Hitler is indeed evil; in Bert's moral fiction Hitler is indeed a moral hero. But this too is a result from which most philosophers recoil. What most philosophers want (nice philosophers, that is, like us) is for Ernie's claim to come out as true and Bert's to come out as false. Therefore we—onlookers to their disagreement—will plump for a moral fiction that provides this result: In *our* best moral fiction, Hitler was evil and not a moral hero. We can interpret both Ernie's and Bert's claims as prefixed with the same operator concerning the same fictional world, thus providing an interpretation, sans problematic ontological commitment, according to which Ernie speaks truly and Bert speaks falsely. It would suit us very well if we could provide a non-arbitrary rationale for why our favorite moral fiction really is *the* best moral fiction, but even failing this the cognitivist fictionalist theory seems to have accomplished what was asked of it.

The noncognitivist hermeneutic fictionalist, by contrast, is not so obsessed with salvaging moral *truth*, but is nevertheless motivated to avoid attributing widespread error. Speakers whom we might be ordinarily tempted to see as making moral assertions and holding moral beliefs are interpreted as doing something else. Perhaps both Ernie's claim that Hitler was evil and Bert's claim that Hitler was a moral hero are equally false (for the kinds of reasons that impress the error theorist), but if neither of them is really *asserting* his claim (nor *believing* it), then neither can be charged with making an erroneous ontological commitment. Of course, acts of make-believe can be evaluated on other grounds. (The terms "pretense" and "make-believe" possibly do more harm than good in this context—with their implications of frivolity and superficiality—but I'll stick with them here.) Perhaps Ernie's type of make-believe is prudent or socially beneficial in some way, while Bert's is imprudent and socially injurious. So, as before, we, the onlookers to their moral disagreement, can take sides, and perhaps even have a non-arbitrary rationale for doing so. I will return to this matter later in this chapter.

BUT CAN IT REALLY BE SO EASY?

But can it really be so easy to side-step massive error simply by adding a tacit story operator or by interpreting people as "just pretending"? Should we even want to?

Ancient Romans were a superstitious bunch: divination, charms, omens, astrology, and necromancy were all widely accepted. Consider a representative claim: "An amulet can magically protect its bearer." Error looms, yet is easily avoided: We can interpret the Romans who made such claims as having asserted true sentences along the lines of "In FW so-and-so, an amulet can magically protect its bearer." Or we can interpret those speakers as having withheld assertoric force from their utterances of "An amulet can magically protect its bearer." Or we can interpret such utterances as expressing the cohortative sentence "Let's pretend that amulets can magically protect their bearers." I think it's safe to say, however, that *we feel no pressure to do any of these things*; indeed, we have no inclination at all to rescue the Romans from the falsehood and error of their superstitious ways. (Even if we were inclined to see such superstitions as serving some social good, we would classify it as a case of useful *falsehood*.)

Ancient Romans also by and large endorsed the geocentric view of the universe advocated by Plato and Aristotle and standardized by Ptolemy. This allowed them to employ an absolute notion of *motion*: things move relative to the Earth, which does not move—in other words, things move *period*. Consider a representative claim about motion: "Caesar moved his camp." If the *movement* mentioned is taken to be absolute, then, because there is no such thing, the sentence is false. In this case, however, we feel less inclination to lumber the speaker with falsehood. Rather, we charitably interpret the predicate "…

moved ... ," which the Roman speaker and audience took to be an *n*-place predicate, as an *n+1*-place predicate—as tacitly relativized to a frame of reference. (The indeterminate reference to "*n*" here is because "move" can be either a transitive or an intransitive verb.) In other words, we interpret the speaker as using the same relativistic notion of motion that we use, and we may do this even while aware that the speaker might *deny* that this is what he or she meant (after all, he or she might be a committed Platonist about geocentricity). (See Harman and Thompson 1996: 4.)

Philosophers sometimes take it as a methodological principle that we should interpret the folk charitably, but the difference between these two cases reveals complications: in one we seem entirely comfortable about ascribing pervasive false assertions. (It would be a mistake to invoke Quine's maxim of translation at this point, since this pertains to interpreting language *as a whole* and is entirely consistent with attributing massive error so long as the error is not inexplicable. See Boghossian and Velleman 1989: 97.) An obvious difference between the two cases is that in one but not the other *we* currently use a concept that is fairly obviously a close continuer to the ancients' concept. Relative motion is not so very different from absolute motion in the sense that which concept is employed makes not a jot of practical difference in 99 percent of everyday cases; nearly all the time, we and the ancients employ the same frame of reference for our motion claims (namely, the Earth)—it's just that we can recognize that this is a contingent choice while the ancients would have considered it mandatory. By contrast, we do not employ any concept that is a close continuer to the idea of the magical powers of amulets. Suppose that the closest we come is recognizing that some objects have sentimental value. But *having sentimental value* is simply not the same thing, and cannot be used for the same practical purposes, as *being magically protective*.

Charitably interpreting motion claims as involving a relativistic rather than absolute concept is one thing; charitably interpreting speakers as employing a tacit story operator, or as engaged in make-believe rather than belief, may be significantly different. For a start, either of the latter two expedients seems entirely too easy. Take any widespread apparently false belief that you like: the error of which the speakers apparently fall foul can be magicked away with a click of the fingers. Far from being a reasonable methodological principle of charity, this seems more like the manifestation of a disgraceful disregard for any epistemological standards. And it is, moreover, likely to lead to ruin, for what point is there in striving for truth when any error can be so easily ducked? When real-life natural disasters strike, rescuing *everyone* is a wonderful aspiration; but when it comes to epistemological methodology, the aim of rescuing *everyone* is itself a kind of disaster. If these devices of hermeneutic fictionalism are going to be of any use, then, there will have to be some principled way of discriminating those error-threatened discourses for which the fictionalist solution is reasonable from those many discourses that are best interpreted as simply utterly mistaken.

Possible ways of making such a discrimination can be divided into those based on external considerations and those based on internal factors. Basing the distinction on external considerations means that some discourses warrant charitable interpretation (whereas others do not) in virtue of bearing some specifiable relational property to us (which the others lack). Earlier I speculated that we are motivated to interpret the ancients' talk of motion charitably because we continue to use a concept that is for most practical purposes indistinguishable from their use of absolute *motion*. If their talk did not bear this relation to our talk, then maybe we'd be willing to pronounce all their motion talk false. Alternatively, perhaps we find that some discourse is indispensable to our belief system, making us highly motivated to interpret it as non-erroneous, but we also recognize that it is deeply problematic when taken at face value, and thus we turn to fictionalist interpretations as a kind of last resort. If this discourse were not so indispensable to us, then maybe we'd be willing to pronounce it false.

Basing the distinction on internal factors means that some discourses warrant a fictionalist interpretation (whereas others do not) in virtue of having discernible intrinsic features (which the others lack), indicating that the interpretation is actually reasonable. There are, after all, various ways in which the use of story operators or engaging in make-believe (rather than belief) can reveal themselves. To choose some simple illustrations: If a population of speakers had a tendency to consult a canonical fictional text before making any pronouncement on the topic of X, then this might encourage us to interpret their subsequent utterances about X as elliptical for "According to the fictional text … ." Or if a population of speakers showed a tendency in serious contexts to back off from the claims that they make about X in everyday contexts, then we might be inclined to interpret their everyday discourse about X as a kind of make-believe. For example, people commonly talk and think about the sun rising, but if pressed they'll admit that this is false and in fact the observer's position on the Earth is rotating toward the sun. (Of course, if they were sensibly clear-headed relativists about motion, then they could maintain that the sun really does rise relative to the chosen frame of reference [see Jackson 2007], but this is not what most educated people do say—rather, when speaking carefully they'll deny that the sun really rises.) Ordinary talk of sunrises, then, appears amenable on internal grounds to a kind of fictionalist interpretation. (See Boghossian and Velleman 1989: 101; see also Van Inwagen 1990: 102–103.)

Were the decision to interpret moral discourse in a fictionalist manner based on the observation of internal features of the discourse calling for such an interpretation, then we would no longer be motivated by charity in particular. Rather, we would be in the altogether more secure position of responding to evidence. Basing one's decision on external factors, by comparison, introduces a rather unattractive kind of relativism into the proceedings. Suppose we felt pressed to give an error-threatened discourse a fictionalist interpretation as a last resort, because we judged the discourse indispensable to our conceptual scheme and found the prospect of its failure intolerable. If aliens with a different conceptual scheme were to face the same decision regarding the same discourse, they may find it more dispensable and therefore would lack our rationale for the fictionalist interpretation; they would plump for an error-theoretic interpretation of the discourse. If the matter depended entirely on external relational factors, then there would be no saying who is correct: us or the aliens. No further scrutiny of the discourse in question would expose evidence to resolve the disagreement.

Another difficulty for the externalist hermeneutic fictionalist is that it remains questionable just how charitable the fictionalist interpretation really is if it can be foisted upon speakers who would actually object. Suppose Amy says "Stealing is morally wrong" and we philosophers, knowing that the threat of an error theory looms, decide to interpret Amy as asserting something like "In the moral *FW*, stealing is morally wrong," thereby construing her to be saying something true rather than false. But now what about Amy's belief (and, one imagines, adamant declaration) that she is *not* using anything like a story operator (nor make-believing) when she engages in moral discussion? Presumably, we'll have to interpret *these* beliefs of Amy's as false—so it's not clear what favors we'd really be doing her. (See Friend 2008: 16.) By contrast, if the fictionalist interpretation is based on *internal* factors, then at least we would have some evidence to present to Amy to attempt to persuade her that the fictionalist interpretation of her moral discourse is reasonable. What kind of evidence might this be?

Let me focus on the noncognitivist brand of hermeneutic fictionalism here. One way of posing the challenge is as a response to what Matthew Chrisman describes as "a flat-footed phenomenological worry about moral fictionalism: it just doesn't seem to me that I am operating under some pretence when I make a moral claim" (2008: 7). The fictional-ist response can begin by emphasizing that it is not being claimed that our attitude toward morality is the same as that which dominates our engagement with familiar or childish fictions. The "make-believe" of which the fictionalist speaks need only bear *some resemblance* to more ordinary pretense—but precisely what kind of or degree of resemblance is vague and unspecified. It has, for example, often been objected to hermeneutic fictional-ism that one of the hallmarks of pretense is a tendency to disengage with the fiction when the going gets tough (e.g., to abandon one's captivation with the play when someone at the back of the theater shouts "Fire!"), but no such tendency is apparent in moral dis-course (Chrisman 2008: 7; Cuneo 2014: 175). However, the kind of similarity that the hermeneutic fictionalist touts may not purport to preserve *that* feature. After all, it is doubtful that everything deserving of the name "pretense" exhibits this tendency. Lying is a kind of pretense—where the speaker pretends to believe something which he or she doesn't believe—but sometimes people will not admit their lie under any circumstances (and sometimes have very good reason to refrain from doing so). Whatever kind of simi-larity the fictionalist does focus on, the really crucial thing, recall, is that the similarity is such that the ontological non-commitment characteristic of pretense is preserved.

The second thing the fictionalist can do is highlight the many other instances where we lack first-person authority over what we are doing when we are speaking. To give a simple example: Many educated people insist that "data" is the plural of "datum" (adding that the widespread practice of using "data" as a singular term is a vulgar error). They are oblivious to the fact that *nobody* uses "data" consistently as a plural term (nobody says "One datum, two data, three data …"); rather, it operates more like a mass noun. Of course, people can be pretty easily brought to see the error of their meta-linguistic beliefs in this case. So the third and most important thing the fictionalist needs to do is provide actual evidence that reveals the error of our meta-linguistic beliefs about the cog-nitive nature of moral language. (See discussion of "attitude-hermeneutic nominalism" in Rosen and Burgess 2005.) I have here put matters in terms of language, but matching points could be put, *mutatis mutandis*, about mental states. Not many people deny that we often lack first-person authority regarding our own mental states.

Mark Kalderon (2005) sets out to do this by showing that the norms that govern moral discourse differ from those that govern assertion and belief. When one believes some-thing, Kalderon claims, then upon encountering an epistemic peer who firmly disagrees, one has a "lax obligation" to examine one's reasons for believing as one does. Kalderon calls this "noncomplacency." However, the norms surrounding morality, he argues, per-mit complacency: we feel no embarrassment in steadfastly maintaining our moral views in the face of disagreement from epistemic peers. Were this argument to succeed, then we would have grounds for doubting that moral discourse is belief-expressing, but evidently more would need to be said to establish a similarity with fiction-talk sufficient to justify the label "fictionalism." Kalderon himself offers little on this score and claims that he means "pretense" only in a thin and non-explanatory sense (2008: 36). Kalderon's argument is complex and I don't propose to critically evaluate it here (I do so at some length in Joyce 2011); I mention it only to give some idea of the kind of thing the internalist hermeneutic fictionalist might say.

Wittgenstein offers some intriguing thoughts, with the potential to develop into a fictionalist argument, when he notes that in moral discourse "we seem constantly to be using similes." He continues:

> But a simile must be the simile for something. And if I can describe a fact by means of a simile I must also be able to drop the simile and to describe the facts without it. Now in our case [i.e., ethics] as soon as we try to drop the simile and simply to state the facts which stand behind it, we find that there are no such facts. And so, what at first appeared to be simile now seems to be mere nonsense.
>
> (1965: 10)

Wittgenstein seems to be somewhat misusing the term "simile," for an explicit comparative sentence of the form "X is like Y" does not stand for anything (except in the trivial sense that applies to all sentences). (Wittgenstein's careless use of the term "simile" is noted in Erden 2012.) But moments earlier he talks of terms being used "as similes or allegorically" (1965: 9), which makes clearer that he has in mind terms that function to convey symbolic meaning, but for which the hidden meanings turn out in these cases to be absent. Since allegories are devices prevalent in fiction, where false images, sentences, and narratives are presented without ontological commitment to the manifest content of the allegory, it would not be unreasonable to classify Wittgenstein's view as a form of hermeneutic fictionalism. (It's worth mentioning that Wittgenstein's contention that the allegorical language is empty is superfluous to this classification; even if moral discourse consisted of allegories that successfully refer to specifiable truths, the fictionalist interpretation would be in order.)

After making this intriguing claim about moral language consisting of similes [sic], however, Wittgenstein pretty much leaves his audience to seek their own evidence that this might be true. I shall not attempt to add anything on that score, but simply use this as an opportunity to illustrate that the empirical nature of the internalist fictionalist enterprise is a mixed blessing. Sensitivity to empirical evidence opens the possibility of hermeneutic fictionalism's being well-grounded and confirmed; the problem is that the evidence seems thin, to say the least. Fictionalists can help themselves to whatever evidence noncognitivists have been able to muster for the hypothesis that moral discourse is not belief-expressing (this evidence is far from conclusive, but at least there's a decades-long tradition with several well-worn paths to explore); what is currently lacking is a well-developed program of seeking evidence for the positive part of the fictionalist hypothesis: that interesting similarities between moral discourse and fiction-talk exist.

Stephen Yablo (2000; 2005) has argued for something like hermeneutic fictionalism regarding numbers, partly on the basis of observations concerning both ordinary people's and mathematicians' number discourse, such as their apparent indifference to, and impatience with, questions regarding the ontology of numbers. (If one doesn't care whether numbers exist, then presumably one's mathematical discourse is not ontologically committed to them.) It is not obvious that analogous arguments would be any less plausible if pressed into the service of moral fictionalism. (See Hussain 2004 for discussion of how Yablo's ideas might apply to the moral case.)

REVOLUTIONARY MORAL FICTIONALISM

In some ways, the revolutionary fictionalist has it easier than the hermeneutic fictionalist. There is no need to locate evidence that fictionalism is *true*, for the revolutionary fictionalist doesn't claim that mark of distinction for the theory. Rather, the revolutionary fictionalist needs to sell the theory as *good advice*. (Of course, first the truth of error theory needs to be established, but, barring one exception later, we'll bracket off those arguments in this chapter.) Regarding the content of the advice, revolutionary fictionalists have the same menu of options as their hermeneutic relatives. One option is to revise one's moral utterances so they are prefixed with a (usually tacit) story operator. Another option is to alter one's attitude toward morality from belief to something akin to make-believe. As with advice in general, the recommendation must be based on some sort of cost-benefit analysis. "Morality is useful when believed," the fictionalist reasons, "so eliminating it will, ceteris paribus, be costly. Perhaps some of the benefits of morality which we stand to lose can be recouped by taking a fictionalist stance toward morality."

The first thing to notice is that the fictionalist need not claim that taking a fictional stance toward morality is *just as good* (in pragmatic terms) as believing it. Perhaps the fictional stance is, in practical terms, a sorry second best to a believed morality. But sincere belief is out of the running at this stage of the argument. The fictionalist's relevant competitor is the eliminativist, who advocates abolishing moral discourse altogether (which is not, of course, the same as declaring a moratorium on even uttering any moral terms). The second thing to notice is that the revolutionary fictionalist's reasoning (as just sketched) clumsily obscures the relativism inherent in any advice-giving. Whenever a philosopher claims that something is useful, one's immediate thought should be "To whom?" We may have knee-jerk intuitions that morality is broadly useful, but is it really useful to *everyone*? (Was it useful to the men dead in Flanders fields, brought to their sorry ends by moralistic propaganda and their sense of duty?) Perhaps taking a fictional stance toward morality will recoup costs for one person but not for another. Even the best advice is unlikely to be good for anyone in any circumstances. In light of this, the revolutionary fictionalist should be permitted a degree of modesty and a dose of vagueness: The position is reasonable if it's good advice generally for most people.

A particular aspect of this relativism is worth highlighting. One fictionalist proposal is that we give up asserting moral claims but rather use them to perform another speech act—one modeled on some aspect of fiction-talk. But speech acts occur only against a background of conventions shared by a speaker and her audience; a person cannot unilaterally decide that she isn't asserting the sentence S if she fails to signal this to her audience, all of whom take her to be asserting S. Given this, it is problematic to consider the fictionalist's advice as directed toward *individuals*, for it is not clear that it could even be coherent advice for an individual. (It would be like advising someone to become a rugby team.) Continuing to bear in mind the modesty and vagueness, then, it is best to consider the fictionalist's advice as directed toward *groups* of speakers.

There are different ways of understanding the claim that X is useful to a group, even before we get to more specific questions raised by replacing "X" with "morality." Let us suppose that we settle on one such way. If a group is motivated to adopt morality as a fiction because doing so is useful (in the manner settled upon), then when faced with the choice of *which* moral fiction to adopt (from an infinite range of possibilities), the answer is simply "The most useful one." It is important to remember that the fiction is being maintained for practical purposes; it is entirely possible that a group might adopt the wrong moral fiction.

Thus the (false) moral claims are grounded in (true) practical claims. This is often the case with fiction-centered activity. Kendall Walton (1993) distinguishes between *content-oriented* make-believe and *prop-oriented* make-believe. In the former, the players' real interest lies in the fictional world, and the props are but tools in the service of that end. (An upturned couch is a ship, a stick is a gun, and so on.) In the latter, it is the prop itself that is really of interest, and the make-believe game is a way of revealing its features. One of Walton's examples involves telling someone the location of the town of Crotone by saying "Imagine Italy is a boot; then Crotone is on the arch of the boot." (And if that's insufficient, I might even remove one of my stiletto boots and point: "Crotone is *here*.") Metaphor is a central example of a kind of pretense where the focus is not on the fiction per se, but on truths that it reveals. Someone who says "Fred is a two-faced snake" is trying to tell us something true, albeit somewhat indefinite, *about Fred*. (Versions of fictionalism that emphasize that the fiction is a means of getting at important truths include Yablo's views on mathematical discourse [2000, 2005] and Arnon Levy's views on discourse about biological information [2011].)

The fiction of morality, then, need not be just a wild and whimsical falsehood in which we indulge for practical benefit. The falsehoods of morality can be ways of drawing attention to truths about what will not be tolerated, what is most valued, what will be harmful, etc. Although pointing to the arch of a boot and saying "Crotone is here" is obviously false, saying this while pointing to *the toe* of the boot would be worse. (I am tempted to say "doubly false.") Analogously, the revolutionary fictionalist may maintain that while saying "Hitting babies is morally wrong" is false, saying "Hitting babies is morally permissible" would be worse.

One immediate question for the fictionalist is this: If one can speak truly about what will not be tolerated, what is most valued, what will be harmful, etc., then hasn't the error theory evaporated? Why not just accept that these truths *are* the moral truths (or at least the base upon which the moral truths supervene)? Clearly, however, this is not something that is generally true of metaphors. Saying that Fred is a two-faced snake does not invite the rejoinder "But if by this means you're able to make reference to traits that Fred truly has (being deceitful, sneaky, etc.), then surely it's literally true that Fred is a two-faced snake." In the case of morality, we are assuming that successful arguments for the error-theoretic position are already on the table, and these arguments will have shown that moral normativity has some special and problematic qualities that other norms (pertaining to what will be tolerated, etc.) do not have. It is not in the remit of this chapter to go into those arguments, and doing so would be time-consuming. Suffice it to say that if our discussion of revolutionary fictionalism begins "Suppose for the sake of argument that arguments for a moral error theory were successful … ,'" then we have already made the supposition (if only arguendo) that the revolutionary fictionalist has the resources to rebut this criticism.

If morality is a fiction that tracks truths that are important to us, then this explains why we might care about a fiction, and why we might care more about one moral fiction than other possible moral fictions. What it doesn't explain is why we should need or want the fiction at all. Why not just talk in terms of literal truths? Why not, in other words, embrace eliminativism?

Well, why do we use metaphors at all? Why not just talk in terms of literal truths all the time? "Metaphor," answers Dick Moran, "does appear to have a force that goes beyond agreement with what it asserts" (1989: 91).

> To call someone a tail-wagging lapdog of privilege is not simply to make an asser-
> tion of his enthusiastic submissiveness. … [T]he comprehension of the metaphor
> involves seeing this person as a lapdog, and in some detail, experiencing his dog-
> giness. This is what a successful metaphor pulls off, and this image-making quality
> is what lies behind both the force and the unparaphrasability of poetic metaphor.
>
> (1989: 90)

And here is Yablo discussing Walton:

> A certain kind of make-believe game, Walton says, can be "useful for articulating,
> remembering, and communicating facts" about aspects of the game-independent
> world. He might have added that make-believe games can make it easier to reason
> about such facts, to systematize them, to visualize them, to spot connections with
> other facts, and to evaluate potential lines of research.
>
> (1996: 279)

I will finish the discussion of revolutionary fictionalism by tying these thoughts about the power of metaphor back to the case of morality. First, though, I will need to quickly sketch an argument that might motivate the revolutionary fictionalist's error-theoretic leanings in the first place. (Bear in mind that a moral error theory might be based on a different argument entirely.)

Suppose we come to see that the only correct view of human ends is a broadly Humean picture: our ends depend on our contingent desires (though possibly those held under various kinds of idealization). Suppose also that we come to see that an essential com-ponent of moral discourse is a reference to non-Humean ends: Morality often deals in matters of what we "have to do" whether we like it or not; it is imbued with an inescap-ability that the Humean view cannot underwrite. This would be the basis of a moral error theory (see Mackie 1977; Joyce 2001). Suppose further, however, that *thinking in terms of* the Humean picture tends to reduce the probability of our actually achieving our ends. We are more likely to achieve our real Humean ends if we picture those ends in non-Humean terms: if we think of them as things that we *must* pursue whether we like it or not. Why might this be? Perhaps deliberating in terms of ends that brook no discus-sion bolsters our motivation to pursue them. By comparison, thinking of those ends in Humean terms allows them to wear their contingency on their sleeves. The thought "If I didn't desire such-and-such, then I wouldn't have the reasons that in fact I do have" can be a dangerous one; it opens the door to self-sabotaging rationalizations like "But, really, how much *do* I desire such-and-such?" We often succumb to temptations that we later regret—irrational lures that disrupt our ability to pursue our real ends. Perhaps a firmer habit of thinking in terms of *moral* norms—that is, norms that demand compliance irrespective of our desires—would help us achieve our goals. This would be an ironic twist of human psychology, to be sure, but it seems not entirely implausible that it is the bind in which we find ourselves. (See the discussion of "conversation stoppers" in Dennett 1995.)

The fictionalist response to this bind is to recommend that we exploit the foibles of our own psychology by cultivating non-Humean thinking as an expedient for tracking, and better motivating the pursuit of, our actual Humean ends. Like a metaphor's ability to draw attention to truths that might otherwise evade simple description (or regarding which, at least, the non-metaphorical description might be cumbersome), moral language, false though it is (in the error theorist's opinion), encourages speakers and their audience to see the world in a certain way that might otherwise evade simple description and without which they might be left susceptible to forms of self-subversion. If we were all fully informed, fully reflective, rational, clear-headed, and strong-willed, then perhaps we would have no need of any moral fiction. Revolutionary moral fictionalism depends on the contingent fact that we tend to fall well short of satisfying this list of admirable qualities.

REFERENCES

Boghossian, P. and Velleman, J. 1989. "Colour as a secondary quality." *Mind* 98: 81–103.

Chrisman, M. 2008. "A dilemma for moral fictionalism." *Philosophical Books* 49: 4–13.

Cuneo, T. 2014. *Speech and Morality: On the Metaethical Implications of Speaking.* Oxford: Oxford University Press.

Dennett, D. 1995. *Darwin's Dangerous Idea.* New York: Simon & Schuster.

Eklund, M. 2015. "Fictionalism." In E. Zalta (ed.), *The Stanford Encyclopedia of Philosophy.* URL = <http://plato.stanford.edu/entries/fictionalism>.

Erden, Y. 2012. "Wittgenstein on simile as the 'best thing in philosophy'." *Philosophical Investigations* 35: 127–137.

Friend, S. 2008. "Hermeneutic moral fictionalism as an anti-realist strategy." *Philosophical Books* 49: 14–22.

Harman, G. & Thomson, J.J. 1996. *Moral Relativism and Moral Objectivity.* Cambridge, MA: Blackwell.

Hussain, N. 2004. "The return of moral fictionalism." *Philosophical Perspectives* 18: 149–187.

Jackson, B. 2007. "Truth vs. pretense in discourse about motion (or, why the sun really does rise)." *Noûs* 41: 298–317.

Joyce, R. 2001. *The Myth of Morality.* Cambridge: Cambridge University Press.

Joyce, R. 2011. "Review essay: Mark Kalderon's *Moral Fictionalism.*" *Philosophy and Phenomenological Research* 85: 161–173.

Kalderon, M. 2005. *Moral Fictionalism.* Oxford: Oxford University Press.

Kalderon, M. 2008. "The trouble with terminology." *Philosophical Books* 49: 33–41.

Levy, A. 2011. "Information in biology: A fictionalist account." *Noûs* 45: 640–657.

Mackie, J.L. 1977. *Ethics: Inventing Right and Wrong.* New York: Penguin.

Moran, R. 1989. "Seeing and believing: Metaphor, image, and force." *Critical Inquiry* 16: 87–112.

Olson, J. 2014. *Moral Error Theory: History, Critique, Defence.* Oxford: Oxford University Press.

Proudfoot, D. 2006. "Possible worlds semantics and fiction." *Journal of Philosophical Logic* 35: 9–40.

Rosen, G. 1990. "Modal fictionalism." *Mind* 99: 327–354.

Rosen, G. and Burgess, J.P. 2005. "Nominalism reconsidered." In S. Shapiro (ed.), *The Oxford Handbook of Philosophy of Mathematics and Logic.* Oxford: Oxford University Press: 515–535.

Van Inwagen, P. 1990. *Material Beings*. Ithaca, NY: Cornell University Press.

Vision, G. 1994. "Fiction and fictionalist reductions." *Pacific Philosophical Quarterly* 74: 150–174.

Walton, K. 1993. "Metaphor and prop oriented make-believe." *European Journal of Philosophy* 1: 39–57.

Wittgenstein, L. 1965. "Lecture on ethics." *Philosophical Review* 74: 3–12.

Woodward, R. 2011. "Is modal fictionalism artificial?" *Pacific Philosophical Quarterly* 92: 535–550.

Yablo, S. 1996. "How in the world?" *Philosophical Topics* 24: 255–286.

Yablo, S. 2000. "A paradox of existence." In T. Hofweber and A. Everett (eds.), *Empty Names, Fiction, and the Puzzles of Non-existence*. Stanford, CA: CSLI: 275–312.

Yablo, S. 2005. "The myth of the seven." In M. Kalderon (ed.), *Fictionalism in Metaphysics*. Oxford: Clarendon Press: 88–115.

5

Metaethical Expressivism

Elisabeth Camp

Expressivism is the view that certain kinds of language have the function of expressing states of mind rather than representing facts. So according to expressivists, when I say "Murder is wrong!" I don't describe a state of affairs, but avow or display or advocate a negative attitude toward murder. More specifically, expressivism holds that words like 'ought' or 'wrong' conventionally function to express *non-cognitive* attitudes: attitudes other than straightforward belief, such as emotions or intentions. It holds that these non-cognitive attitudes *explain* those words' meanings rather than just happening to be frequently correlated with their use. And it holds that the meaning and function of these words *differ* in a fundamental way from ordinary description. Different expressivists target different kinds of language, associate them with different attitudes, and locate the contrast with description in different ways, producing a diverse family of views.

Although expressivism is a view about linguistic meaning, it is natural to assume that language and psychology operate in parallel, especially if one takes the job of language to be communicating thoughts, as many do. As a result, expressivism is naturally allied to non-cognitivism, which is a view about the basic psychology of engagement with a topic, paradigmatically ethics. For both, the core idea is that we distort the shape of ethical inquiry, commitment, and disagreement if we treat ethical thought and talk in descriptivist terms, as a matter of exchanging information about how the world is. Metaphysically, a descriptivist model threatens to commit us to 'spooky', non-natural facts: abstract properties like *being wrong* that are unanchored to time, place, or particular social practices. Epistemically, it threatens to commit us to positing information whose discovery would or should resolve disputes, where many have thought that even total information about how things *are* still leaves open the question of what is right or wrong. And practically, a descriptivist model threatens to undercut apparently intimate connections between judgment and motivation: thus, it seems that if I think murder is wrong, I will or at least should be motivated not to murder and to discourage murder, but it is unclear how bare facts could, by themselves, underwrite such motivation.

Instead, ethical non-cognitivists propose that the fundamental psychological states involved in considering what is right and wrong, or what to do, are desires, emotions, and/or intentions. Like beliefs, and unlike mere sensations or moods, these psychological attitudes are *about* more or less specific objects and situations: I desire, fear, hope for, and plan to bring about certain states of affairs. And like beliefs, they are related in at least somewhat systematic patterns of compatibility and inconsistency: if I fear that I will lose my job, there is at least *prima facie* something problematic about simultaneously planning to insult my boss to her face. But unlike beliefs, the function of such non-cognitive states is not to describe how the world *is*, but to show how the world *should* be, and to lead the agent to act accordingly. (For discussion, see Matthew S. Bedke's chapter "Cognitivism and Non-Cognitivism.")

The contrasts between belief and these other attitudes, and between factual descriptions and avowals of feeling and intention, are fairly intuitive, as is the idea that ethical commitments involve feelings, preferences, and plans in some central way. The main challenge for the ethical expressivist is to ground these contrasts in the way we actually talk about ethics, which is typically with declarative sentences that behave a lot like ordinary assertions. Thus, the fact that we regularly say things like 'John believes that murder is wrong, and I agree, but I don't think it follows that abortion is wrong' has led many contemporary expressivists to grant that ethical statements do express beliefs, and are true, in some minimal sense. At the same time, some expressivists have also targeted domains like probability, epistemic modality, and knowledge, by appealing to modified versions of many of the same basic metaphysical, epistemic, and practical motivations as ethical expressivists. However, these expressivist analyses tend to be grounded in psychological states that are more belief-like, with functions that are more tightly tied to tracking and manipulating information. Many of these modifications to and extensions of 'classic' ethical expressivism are well motivated. But they also erode the initial, intuitive contrast between expressing attitudes and describing facts. This, together with the appropriation of belief- and truth-talk by many expressivists, renders the boundary between expressivism and its competitors increasingly blurry.

An additional complication arises from the fact that although non-cognitivism and expressivism are close cousins, they are distinct views about distinct subjects. In particular, a non-cognitivist could emphasize the central importance of feelings and plans in engaging with ethics while retaining a fundamentally descriptivist analysis of the words we use to talk about it. Such a theorist might think that simple sentences like 'Murder is wrong' are false because they ascribe properties that don't exist but take those false (or perhaps, pretended) claims to aptly reflect a broader non-cognitive psychology. Or they might hold that such sentences are potentially true but that their truth is relatively unimportant because speakers use them first and foremost to communicate non-cognitive states. Thus, we should view expressivism, of whatever specific form, as one commitment which fits together with non-cognitivism and antirealism to form an especially elegant metaethical (or metaepistemological, etc.) package, with each element potentially being leveraged in other combinations to form quite different views.

In this chapter, I examine expressivism as the claim that certain classes of words, especially 'thin' normative terms like 'ought' and 'good', conventionally function to express non-cognitive psychological states. In the next section, I consider what the relation between attitudes and utterances must be like to count as expressing rather than describing. This is an issue in the general theory of meaning. In the section "How Do Words Express?", I turn to the more specific question of how language, as a conventional communicative system in which words combine to form whole sentences, might implement this relation. Throughout, we will find the expressivist striving to balance respect for the core intuition that normative language *does* something distinctive against the need to accommodate strong parallels between normative talk and straightforward description.

WHAT IS EXPRESSING?

The ethical expressivist maintains that normative utterances function to communicate non-cognitive psychological states rather than to describe worldly states of affairs. However, it is not enough for those utterances to communicate those psychological states in just any way. In particular, the expressivist denies that those utterances communicate those states by *reporting* that the speaker has them, as 'I disapprove of murder' does. Such a simple subjectivist analysis would undermine the very contrast the expressivist wants to capture. More importantly, it radically misdescribes ethical discourse. When agents make claims about, provide reasons for, and challenge each other about ethical matters, they aren't arguing about their mental states. If they were, we wouldn't find even the appearance of disagreement. Instead, ethical utterances would articulate parallel but distinct and therefore compatible states, much as 'I am hungry' in your mouth and mine do. Further, it would be appropriate to evaluate those utterances as *true*, just in case the speaker did disapprove of murder.

How, then, should the expressivist understand the contrast with reporting, whether a worldly or a psychological state? One natural place to start is with the idea of "performative" utterances. In reaction to the dominant descriptivist model of language, John Austin (1961) drew attention to utterances like 'I declare you married', which don't represent an independent state of affairs as obtaining, and so are not straightforwardly truth-apt in the way that descriptions are. Instead, Austin characterizes their success conditions in terms of 'felicity': an assessment of whether the right social and psychological background conditions—such as being of sound mind, willing, of appropriate age, and not currently married to someone else—obtain. Similarly, the expressivist might plausibly claim that normative utterances serve to *do* something in conversation, rather than saying *that* something has been done, and so that they should be assessed for appropriateness rather than truth.

While this distinction gets something right, there are at least two problems with exploiting it to identify a distinctively expressive class of utterances. The first is that, as Austin argues, the distinction is not exclusive. On the one hand, descriptive statements are themselves performative, and subject to assessment on grounds besides truth: whether the speaker has good evidence for her claim, whether it is conversationally relevant or polite, whether it employs an apt classificatory scheme. And on the other hand, many performative utterances are evaluable in terms of "a general dimension of correspondence with fact" (Austin 1961, 250); thus, a call of 'foul ball!' is apt only if the baseball landed on the far side of the line. Given that many utterances are both performative and descriptive, the expressivist can't establish that canonical normative utterances *don't* describe by showing that they *do* accomplish something else. Recently, 'hybrid' expressivists like Michael Ridge (2006, 2014) have embraced this sort of non-exclusivity, arguing that normative talk both describes and expresses (see Teemu Toppinen's chapter "Hybrid Accounts of Ethical Thought and Talk").

The second problem is that not just any connection between uttering a sentence and performing an action supports expressivism. The expressivist needs to identify, not merely a distinctive *doing* that people sometimes or often undertake in talking about ethics, but a conventional linguistic means for accomplishing it. We've already seen that subjective reports don't express in the relevant sense. But neither do utterances like 'Whenever I see a drowning baby, I rescue it', since they (at best) *implicate* the relevant non-cognitive attitude rather than communicating it directly. To establish expressivism as a claim about the function of language itself, rather than about the ways speakers exploit language in particular conversations, the expressivist needs to show that the uttered sentences' conventional role is the communication of non-cognitive attitudes. Dialectically, without evidence for a distinctive, conventional mechanism for expressing non-cognitive states, the expressivist has no argument against a standard semantic theory, with the communication of non-cognitive states being at most a pragmatic accompaniment to a conventional descriptive contribution.

The difference between direct and indirect modes of communication isn't just a matter of how meanings are produced; it also affects the role that utterances play in subsequent discourse. In particular, only content that is directly communicated and "at-issue" (Potts 2005) is available for straightforward response by other interlocutors—for instance with direct agreement or disagreement, with conditionalization through propositional anaphora (as with 'If so, then ...'), or with testimonial reports. Contents that are merely presupposed, implicated, entailed, or otherwise manifested can be targeted only by redirecting the conversational focus, by saying something like 'Hey, wait a minute! You seem to be assuming/suggesting that ... '. Thus, establishing that the central point of ethical discourse is expressive rather than descriptive, as 'pure' expressivists aim to do, requires demonstrating that the at-issue moves proffered by canonical ethical utterances are nondescriptive. By contrast, hybrid expressivists have more flexibility here, since they may locate expressive commitments as either at-issue in combination with a descriptive claim, or as outside the conversational focus.

In the section "How Do Words Express?", I look more closely at the implications of the distinction between at-issue and peripheral meaning for the analysis of individual words. In the remainder of this section, I consider what expressing itself might be: what do speakers *do* when they express, as opposed to describe?

The simplest version of expressivism, both in terms of the attitude expressed and the mode of expression, is *emotivism*, which treats sentences like 'Murder is wrong' as "ejaculations," much like grimacing or saying 'Ugh!' or 'Boo!' (Ayer 1936, 103). As Stevenson (1937, 23) says, emotive meaning is "the tendency of a word, arising through the history of its usage, to produce (result from) affective responses in people. It is the immediate aura of feeling which hovers about a word." Ayer held that ethical statements are strictly meaningless, because he countenanced only descriptive, and specifically verificationist, linguistic meaning. But emotivism is problematic even independently of these highly controversial assumptions, because it treats the connection between psychological states and utterances in ultimately *causal* terms, much like the connection between smoke and fire. As Grice (1957) and Dretske (1981) noted, one state of affairs, x, may indicate another, y, in virtue of being reliably connected to it; in such cases, we may say that x

means y, and we may use x to draw inferences about y. But this is very different from the kind of meaning that words, or even non-conventional gestures like pantomime, have. A hallmark of 'non-natural' meaning, whether linguistic or mental, is that it can come apart from how the world is. Thus, one can say, or sign, that the house is on fire even if it isn't and even if one doesn't believe (or desire) that it is; by contrast, smoke can't be wrong about, or want, fire—it just *is*. Emotivism treats ethical statements as natural signs of emotional states. But people are all too capable of misrepresenting what they take to be right or wrong. More importantly, they frequently disagree with one another, treating each other's ethical commitments as wrong. Emotivism denies all this.

Emotivism does capture a key intuitive aspect of expressing: that it involves a kind of *showing* which is more direct than describing. But it goes too far in construing the relation between attitude and utterance in purely causal terms. A more flexible construal appeals to the idea of 'avowal'. Simon Blackburn (1998) articulates the idea thus:

> So what at last is said when we say that something is good or right? ... . We can now say ... what is done when we say such things. We avow a practical state. 'Avowal' here means that we express this state, make it public, or communicate it. We intend coordination with similar avowals or potential avowals from others, and this is the point of the communication. When this coordination is achieved, an intended direction is given to our joint practical lives and choices.
>
> (1998, 68–69)

Blackburn doesn't spell out what is involved in 'making public' here. One useful model is offered by Mitchell Green's account of self-expression as "showing how things are within" (2007, 106; see also Bar-On 2004). On Green's view, expressive behaviors are indeed *grounded* in or reliably caused by a certain inner state, but they need not be involuntary. More specifically, because they have the function (whether by evolution or intention) of showing those states, they thereby serve as *signals* of them to others. When an agent produces a signal of a state that they do have, that signal shows, and thereby expresses it; while if they produce the signal in the absence of the state, they merely purport to express it. Finally, while some expressive behaviors are natural, others, like sticking out one's tongue (which functions as an expression of contempt in the United States but as an expression of humility in Thailand), are conventional; when an expressive signal is conventional, its use *commits* the agent to having the correlative inner state.

Unlike ejaculation, an 'avowal' model like Green's has the flexibility to allow that agents can express not just feelings but also desires, preferences, and intentions, some of which may be highly abstract and structured. Given the complexity of ethical discourse, this is a good thing. The problem is that on this model, agents also plausibly express *beliefs* when they make sincere factual assertions, since assertions are conventional devices which are reliably if not universally caused by beliefs, which function to signal those beliefs, and which commit speakers to having them. Of course, the expressivist need not adopt Green's view of expression. But any account flexible enough to encompass the abstractness and diversity of ethical discourse, and to account for lies and disagreement, seems likely to deliver the same result.

A common response here is to grant that *all* sincere declarative utterances express mental states. Indeed, Alan Gibbard says, this should be uncontroversial: "That words express judgments will, of course, be accepted by almost everyone" (1990, 84). On this view, what differentiates distinctively expressive utterances from descriptive ones is the *kind* of mental state they express. Schroeder (2008a) calls this the "parity thesis," and argues that it entails a substantive meta-semantic view: the Lockean doctrine of "Mentalism," on which language inherits meaning from thought, rather than the other way around (or independently or in interaction). Mentalism is at least somewhat controversial, but it is also endorsed by many theorists of meaning, especially those of a broadly Gricean orientation, who hold that particular utterances express mental states by getting their hearers to recognize those states in a certain self-reflexive way; conventional meanings are then explained derivatively, as a "standard procedure" (Grice 1989, 233) for speakers to mean or express such states.

The Parity Thesis is plausible, but it puts the expressivist in a delicate position by ruling out the most obvious place to establish a contrast between expressive discourse and straightforward assertion. It thereby shifts much of the explanatory burden onto non-cognitivism, since it seems that any differences between the particular species of expression involved in factual assertion and in more narrowly 'expressive' expression will be inherited from the distinct types of attitude that are expressed. It also highlights the need to provide positive evidence, not merely that agents often have and communicate non-cognitive attitudes about ethical topics, but that ethical language constitutes a "standard procedure" for manifesting them, as opposed to either reporting their existence or communicating them non-conventionally.

The most plausible way for a Parity-endorsing expressivist to augment the theoretical resources and range of evidence available to them is to look outward, to utterances' effects, rather than just inward, to the attitudes that produce them. As Blackburn says, an important, perhaps essential function of ethical avowals is to coordinate joint practical activities. For this reason, expressivists have typically supplemented or replaced the idea that ethical utterances express feelings with a dimension of practical engagement. (And indeed, many theorists hold that emotions themselves have an essentially motivational function.) Thus, Stevenson (1944) holds that sentences containing 'good' function both to declare the speaker's approval and to exhort others to approve. Hare (1952) goes further, analyzing moral statements as "universal prescriptions" that entail imperatives for action. More recently, Gibbard (2003) treats normative utterances as proposing plans for how to live.

The Mentalist has a straightforward, expressivist-friendly explanation of what it means for an utterance to have such exhortative, imperatival, or promissory force: in keeping with their general theory of meaning, on which utterances function to manifest attitudes, they analyze exhortations and imperatives as manifesting desires that the hearer does something, and promises as manifesting intentions to do something. While this analysis is plausible at a psychological level, it *prima facie* mischaracterizes the role that imperatives and promises play in discourse, which is to actually, directly, place the hearer or speaker under an obligation. It also doesn't yet provide the expressivist with evidence for a distinctively expressive conventional mechanism by which avowals implement the more generic relation of expression, since as far as the Mentalist story goes, the speaker could be expressing their desire or intention by simply reporting it.

Given these problems, some expressivists have complemented Mentalism with aspects of a more 'dynamic' theory of meaning, drawing on Stalnaker's (1970, 2002) notion of common ground and Lewis (1979) metaphor of the conversational score. These views are amenable to expressivism, insofar as they specify sentences' conventional meanings, not in terms of descriptive truth-conditions, but rather of conversational effects or "context change potentials." So, just as the declaration "You are now married" alters the context directly, by making it the case that the couple *is* married, rather than indirectly, by describing them as married, so too the permissive "You may now kiss your spouse" directly changes the context so that the addressee is permitted to kiss, rather than describing them as kissing-eligible. As long as these conventional conversational effects are ultimately *explained* in terms of expressed attitudes, so too that non-cognitive psychological states do the fundamental explanatory work of grounding linguistic meaning, the expressivist can supplement Mentalism with a 'dynamic', non-descriptivist specification of what those effects are.

The most direct way for an expressivist to incorporate conversational effects into their account would be to treat ethical statements as disguised imperatives, and to appropriate the standard dynamic analysis of imperatives, which treats them as updating the addressee's 'To Do List' (Portner 2004). On this analysis, imperatives directly assign an action the status of to-be-done-by-addressee, rather than indirectly obliging the addressee to act by adding information about the speaker's desires, or about what actions are obligatory, to the common ground. For reasons we'll explore in the next section, a direct implementation of the dynamic analysis is unlikely to succeed for thin ethical terms like 'is wrong'. But expressivist analyses of deontic modals like 'must' and 'might', as functioning to update the common ground of plans (Gibbard 2003) or to alter preference orderings among possibilities (Silk 2015), are similar in spirit. Meanwhile, expressivists about epistemic and probability modals like 'might' and 'probably' have argued along structurally similar lines that those terms function to 'test' the context set for coherence, or to alter accessibility relations among information states, or to advise a certain credence distribution (Blackburn 1980; Yalcin 2007, 2012).

All of these analyses capture a way that certain classes of utterances might conventionally *do* something other than contribute information to the conversation, in a way that mirrors and is explained by having a non-doxastic mental attitude. They thereby give us a better grip on how one might demonstrate that a class of utterances has a non-descriptive function. At the same time, the mere fact that these utterances do have one non-descriptive conventional function doesn't itself establish that they don't also play a descriptive role. Further, the cases of epistemic and probability modalities mark dramatic departures from the simple emotivist model, with its intimate connections to feeling and practical action. Finally, they raise the question whether ethical predicates like 'good' and 'wrong' really do have analogous 'dynamic' effects.

I turn to these challenges in the following section. Summarizing the discussion to this point: to establish their view, the expressivist needs to provide evidence that canonical utterances involving the target class of words have a conventional function of expressing an attitude other than belief. Pure expressivists, unlike hybrid expressivists, also need to show that the at-issue contribution of such utterances is *not* to express belief. For both, the best place to seek this evidence is not just upstream, to the cluster of beliefs, desires, feelings, and intentions that motivate speakers to produce those utterances, but downstream, to their conventional conversational effects.

HOW DO WORDS EXPRESS?

So far, we've focused on expressing as a relation between agents and whole utterances. We now turn to how language, as a conventional compositional communicative system, might implement this expressive relation, and in particular, how particular words might be 'semantically fitted' to perform it. Gibbard (2003, 7) advises, plausibly enough, that "to explain the meaning of a term, explain what states of mind the term can be used to express." While this seems innocuous, there is an immediate problem: most words don't express states of mind at all—at best, they express concepts, which combine to determine any of an indefinitely wide range of mental states. How do we identify a distinctively expressive role for a *word*?

The obvious strategy is to build up from simple cases. As Gideon Rosen (1998) suggests, in explaining Blackburn's 'quasi-realist' expressivism,

> The centerpiece of any quasi-realist 'account' is what I shall call a psychologistic semantics for the region: a mapping from statements in the area to the mental states they 'express' when uttered sincerely. The procedure is broadly recursive. Begin with an account of the *basic states*: the attitudes expressed by the simplest statements involving the region's characteristic vocabulary. Then assign operations on attitudes to the various constructions for generating complex statements in such a way as to determine an 'expressive role' for each of the infinitely many statements in the area.
>
> (1998, 387–88)

So, if we can specify the attitudes that are expressed when individual words like 'wrong' and 'good' are predicated of noun phrases like 'murder' and 'saving babies', we can then define functions on those basic attitudes that systematically relate them to other, more complex attitudes, in ways that mirror the relations among atomic sentences and complex phrases like 'If ... then' in language. To accomplish the first step, of assigning attitude-potentials to basic terms, we follow the same procedure of 'reverse engineering' as for any other word: first, we survey a broad range of the target word's actual uses to identify a canonical subclass where it is used literally and sincerely; second, we extrapolate a stable contribution which that specific word makes to utterances of sentences combining it with other words; and finally, we posit a constant meaning by which it makes that contribution.

We ended the last section with the idea that at least one feature distinguishing ethical thought and talk from descriptions is a kind of motivational or imperatival force. How might an expressivist capture this intuition semantically? Linguistically, imperatival force is expressed by a sentence's grammatical mood, as in 'Bring me an umbrella!' *Reductivist* analyses of mood treat imperatives as disguised declarative sentences, like 'I command you to bring an umbrella' (Lewis 1970), or 'The next sentence is imperatival in force: You will bring an umbrella' (Davidson 1979). Such views are obviously unsuitable for the expressivist—as well as empirically and theoretically inadequate in their own terms (Starr 2014)—because they eliminate force as a linguistic phenomenon, treating it either as a merely pragmatic performance or as part of a sentence's truth-conditions.

A more moderate view treats grammatical mood as an 'illocutionary force marker', denoting an operation that takes a complete proposition—for instance, *that you bring me an umbrella*—as input and delivers an illocutionary act—say, a command—as output (Frege 1893; Searle 1969). Obviously, normative words aren't themselves grammatical moods. But dynamic analyses of epistemic, probability, and deontic modals like 'must', 'might' and 'ought' adopt a model that is structurally analogous, insofar as they too take whole propositions as input and deliver 'context changes' as outputs, for instance of altering the range of what it is obligatory to do. However plausible this may be as an analysis of modal terms, extending it to predicates like 'wrong' and 'good' is not straightforward, given that such terms take noun phrases like 'murder', rather than whole sentential clauses, like 'You come to work on time', as inputs. For such predicates, a model like Portner's that analyzes imperatives as denoting properties rather than whole propositions might seem more amenable. However, it is not obvious how much this helps, because the distinctive dynamic effect of modifying the addressee's To Do list is achieved, not by the type of property denoted, but rather from the fact that its argument is syntactically restricted in such a way that only the addressee can make it true—a feature that is not shared by statements like 'Murder is wrong'.

If imperatives don't offer a suitable linguistic model for assigning expressivist values to individual predicates, perhaps we should turn to a class of terms that do, by themselves, actually express states of mind: loaded words like 'damn' and 'jerk'. Chris Potts (2005, 2007) offers the leading linguistic analysis of (what he calls) "expressives," which implements a basically emotivist model using contemporary semantic machinery. The central feature of Potts' account, both formally and substantively, is a robust segregation of expressive and descriptive meaning. Formally, he treats expressives as conveying a certain degree of positive or negative affect toward a subject. This contribution is non-descriptive, both in being simple and unarticulated, and in never altering any aspect of the context except the "expressive setting," which it updates directly, regardless of the word's location in the sentence. Expressive words and phrases that do contain descriptive content, like 'the damn dog', simply pass this content on, untouched, to the compositional machinery that determines a sentence's at-issue content and hence its truth value.

How might an expressivist apply Potts' analysis to terms like 'wrong' and 'good'? Most expressivists would want to replace Potts' pure affective feeling with a non-cognitive attitude that is more structured and/or more practically engaged. While this is possible, Potts' analysis of *what* expressives express goes hand-in-hand with *how* he takes them to express it: it makes sense to segregate pure, 'ineffable' feelings from descriptive contents syntactically because the two are so different substantively. And it is relatively plausible both that terms like 'damn' are devoid of descriptive meaning and that they don't interact significantly with the larger truth-conditional machinery. However, the deep reason why expressivists have moved away from emotivism is precisely that ethical and descriptive language are *not* segregated in these ways.

To see the problem with a segregationist analysis of ethical discourse, it will help to consider a range of alternative cases. Unlike 'pure' expressives, slurs (e.g. 'chink') clearly do make a substantive descriptive contribution as well as advocate an attitude—something like derogation of the target group. At the same time, these two contributions are still relatively distinct. Competent speakers can easily specify in (more) neutral terms which group is targeted by a slur; and typically only the predication of group membership contributes to the core at-issue content. This is especially clear with non-declarative utterances like bets and orders, which are intuitively satisfied if and only if the conditions determined by group membership are met (Camp 2013). It is also evidenced by the fact that when slurs are embedded within larger 'commitment-canceling' constructions—for instance, negations, questions, conditionals, modals, and indirect reports—typically only the descriptive content is 'bound' by the operator. The result is that on the one hand, the speaker doesn't end up committed to the actual application of that descriptive content, but instead to its negation, conditional consequences, etc., while on the other hand the expressive element typically 'scopes out' so that the speaker *is* committed to the appropriateness of derogating the targeted group.

This separability of descriptive and expressive meaning has led a range of theorists to advance 'multi-dimensional' analyses of slurs that exclude their expressive meaning from the compositional determination of at-issue content just as Potts does for 'damn', treating that meaning variously as a conventional implicature (Potts 2005, 2007; Whiting 2008; Williamson 2009), as conversationally implicated (Nunberg 2017), or as falling outside the realm of meaning altogether (Anderson and Lepore 2013). At the same time, though, slurs also differ from 'damn' in ways that challenge such a stringent segregation. Many theorists and ordinary speakers take assertions containing slurs to be false or incapable of truth, in contrast to sentences containing their neutral counterparts (Hom 2008; Richard 2008). And in an interesting range of cases, slurs' expressive element doesn't scope out of commitment-canceling constructions. Both of these features—effect on truth and binding within complex constructions—strongly suggest that with slurs, the expressive element *can* enter into the compositional determination of at-issue meaning, which is precisely what a standard multi-dimensional model like Potts' is founded on denying (Camp 2017).

Other normatively laden terms are even more of a stretch for a robustly segregationist analysis. 'Thick' terms like 'lewd', 'fair', and 'courageous' are akin to slurs in being both descriptive and expressive. But unlike slurs, they lack lexicalized neutral counterparts; and in their case, the expressive dimension does appear to contribute to determining the term's extension—indeed, it is often claimed that descriptive and evaluative aspects are so intimately intertwined that one cannot grasp their truth-conditions without trying on the evaluative perspective (McDowell 1981; Williams 1985; Gibbard 1992).[1]

Finally, what about 'thin' ethical terms like 'good' and 'wrong'? A 'pure' expressivist, who holds that those words' meanings are exclusively non-descriptive, cannot follow Potts in completely separating expressive meaning from the compositional determination of descriptive, at-issue content since this would leave sentences containing those words devoid of any at-issue contribution at all. While Ayer embraced this conclusion, few contemporary expressivists do. Hybrid expressivists have more flexibility: they can posit a more or less minimal or schematic descriptive property as the compositional contribution to at-issue content, along with an expressive attitude that 'scopes out' of complex constructions. (For instance, the descriptive property might be one of meeting certain standards, and the expressive attitude might be one of endorsing those standards.) Indeed, some hybrid expressivists explicitly analogize thin ethical terms to slurs, adopting a conventional implicature view of both (Copp 2001, 2009; Boisvert 2008; see Schroeder 2009 and Teemu Toppinen's chapter "Hybrid Accounts of Ethical Thought and Talk", for discussion). Hybridism holds important explanatory advantages over pure expressivism. But, fundamentally, both pure and hybrid expressivists face a basic problem in deploying anything like Potts' formal model: thin ethical terms markedly fail to exhibit the remarkable independence from truth-assessment and from compositional involvement in complex constructions that is displayed by 'pure' expressives and, to a lesser extent, slurs.

To see the difference, consider 'If John is an *S*, I'll beat him to a pulp' and 'If John is an *R*, then you should hire him', where *S* is replaced by a pure expressive like 'bastard' and *R* by a slur like 'kike', and contrast both with 'If lying is wrong, then John would never lie'. In none of these cases is the speaker committed to the outright applicability of the predicate in the antecedent to John. Intuitively, though, a speaker of either of the first two sentences *has* committed to the appropriateness of feeling negatively toward Ss and Rs; they've simply conditionalized on the applicability of feeling that way toward John in particular. By contrast, a speaker of the third sentence need not endorse any ethical standard at all: they might employ it in a general argument for amoralism, for instance. The same point goes for negation, questions, modals, and indirect reports: in all these cases, unlike with slurs and 'pure' expressives like 'damn', there is no incoherence in the speaker disavowing any particular set of feelings or commitments while maintaining their assertion of the complex sentence.

The lesson is a familiar one: thin ethical terms are fully and systematically entrenched within the compositional machinery of semantics. In essence, this is the Frege-Geach problem of specifying a consistent compositional contribution that an expressive word makes both to simple sentences and complex ones containing operators that block the speaker from commitments generated by a sincere utterance of the simple unembedded sentence (see Jack Woods' chapter "The Frege-Geach Problem" for discussion). This is precisely the problem that robust segregationism enables Potts to avoid. For 'pure' expressives like 'damn', and to a lesser extent for slurs, this seems appropriate. But the same does not hold for thin ethical terms.

The situation is not as hopeless as is sometimes made out. To accommodate the fact that stage actors and reporters don't actually make assertions, commands, etc., we already need to treat conventional markers of force as determining merely *potential* speech acts (Green 1997). Further, it sometimes is possible for force-contributing constructions, including imperatives, to embed, including in conditionals and disjunctions (Siegel 2006, Starr 2014). So we do need a theory of force-cancellation, including by embedding, anyway. Rather, the challenge is to specify what the relevant term *is* doing within such commitment-canceling contexts, and specifically to explain the appearance that it does much the same thing there as in simple sentences.

As with the interpretation of what it means to 'express' an attitude, one attractive strategy is to 'go global', by reinterpreting the existing logical machinery across the board in an expressivist-friendly way. The basic idea, pursued most systematically by Gibbard (2003) and Schroeder (2008b), is that attitudes like approving and intending are governed by a logic of consistency which is at least structurally analogous to the familiar truth-functional operations, and which ideally can be seen as a general schema of which truth-functions are just one instance. Making good on this project is already a significant challenge, one which Schroeder (2008b) argues is ultimately doomed to fail. But even if it succeeds, it is just one part of a larger story that must be told, given that: in addition to the logical operators, normative terms also occur smoothly in attitude and speech reports like 'X believes that P' and 'X asserts that P', in semantic claims like 'S expresses the proposition that P', and in alethic claims like 'It is true that P'. Thus, the meanings of all of these constructions, and the relations of entailment and inconsistency among them, also need to be explained in ways that don't essentially appeal to description and truth.

One way to accommodate the linguistic appearance of truth-conditionality while maintaining expressivism at a deeper level is to appeal to a deflationary or *minimalist* account of truth (Ayer 1936; Horwich 1990), on which asserting 'P is true' is equivalent to simply asserting P. The primary utility of the truth predicate, on this view, is to enable speakers to articulate generalizations about statements, as in 'Everything Janet said is true', rather than to ascribe a substantive property like correspondence to the world. Minimalism about truth is controversial; but if it works, it entitles the expressivist to adopt truth-talk without endorsing a substantively descriptivist psychology and ontology. Again, however, the problem is not limited to truth: the intimate interactions among P, asserting P, believing P, and knowing P, and among asserting 'It is true that P', 'It is a fact that P', and so on, mean that the expressivist must also embrace minimalism about assertion, belief, knowledge, and reality, in what Dreier (2004) calls "the problem of creeping minimalism" (see also Rosen 1998). The global reach of the 'mission creep' involved in accommodating the role of normative words within more complex discourse thus threatens to render 'quasi-realists' like Gibbard (2003) and Blackburn (1993) and 'cognitivist expressivists' like Horgan and Timmons (2006) nearly indistinguishable from sophisticated, naturalistically oriented cognitivists and realists like Railton (1986) and Brink (1989). The expressivist (as well as the cognitivist and the realist) must then explain what differentiates expressivism from a 'robust' analysis of all these phenomena.

The most popular response, endorsed by Gibbard (2003) and Dreier (2004) among others, is "the explanation explanation," summed up in Blackburn's dictum that "In the philosophy of these things it is not what you say, but how you get to say it that determines your 'ism'" (1998, 7). Proponents of the explanation explanation grant that a semantics for thin ethical terms can be articulated in ('minimalist') descriptive terms, and that ethical statements function to express ('minimalist') beliefs, which can be true. So far, descriptive and normative statements are on a par. But expressivists argue that in the normative case, in contrast to the factual one, the best *meta-semantic* explanation of how sentences come to have these contents makes no appeal to moral facts, but appeals instead exclusively to psychological attitudes. By contrast, although the moral realist's explanation will presumably also cite normative beliefs, they will take these beliefs to be explained in turn by relations to moral facts—just as both parties agree that the explanation of straightforward factual claims ultimately appeals to facts about the 'natural' world. Further, the expressivist holds that this difference in the ultimate explanations of normative and factual statements arises *because of* differences in the functional roles of the attitudes they each express: the job of (robust, factual) beliefs is ultimately to track how the world is independently of the agent, while the job of desires, intentions, and other non-cognitive attitudes is to produce action.

Suppose that a global response to both the Frege-Geach problem and the problem of creeping minimalism along these lines succeeds, so that expressivism turns out to be both formally coherent and at least theoretically distinct from descriptivism. Now the opposite worry arises: that in its zeal to accommodate the apparently truth-involving contours of ordinary ethical talk, the global approach has eliminated the possibility of any direct positive evidence for expressivism. If the difference between descriptivism and expressivism turns entirely on different theoretical interpretations of the ultimate grounding of 'truth', 'belief', and 'fact', what remains of the core intuition that the two sorts of language work differently in ordinary discourse?

If the expressivist could demonstrate that non-cognitive attitudes themselves interact in ways that depart from straightforward descriptive beliefs, this would support the claim that they play a distinctive role in thought, which might then be reflected in talk as well. To this end, Charlow (2015) argues that the interactions we actually observe among those attitudes, especially with respect to undecided and uncertain states of mind, are such that they will be mischaracterized by any theory which identifies agents' attitudes by specifying their *contents*—even non-truth-conditional contents, like Gibbardian hyperplans—and then defines logical operations on those contents using Boolean relations of intersection, union, and exclusion (see also Schroeder 2008b; Silk 2015). However,

Charlow also argues that the standard logical operations are inadequate to ordinary factual talk as well, and concludes that we need a global reconstruction of semantics which replaces truth and consistency with broader categories of support and coherence. Thus, even if we do have reason to embrace a more expressivist-friendly semantics in general, it is not clear that this enables us to recover a strong contrast between descriptive and expressive language.

An alternative road to resuscitating a robustly contrastive expressivism challenges the assumed connection between ethical disagreement and assessment for truth. Thus, Khoo and Knobe (2016) provide experimental results suggesting that, in contrast to factual disagreement, people do not always take moral disagreement via negation to require one speaker's claim to be incorrect. If this is right, then the global assimilationist's appeal to minimalism may have prematurely written off a crucial source of evidence against standard descriptivist accounts—although it is less clear whether this supports expressivism in particular as opposed to a contextualist or relativist form of descriptivism.

CONCLUSION

In considering how individual words might make an expressive contribution to larger sentences, we have arrived at much the same place as we did in investigating what it means to express a non-cognitive attitude. Expressivism seems like a coherent and attractive way to capture, within the analysis of language, many of the psychological and metaphysical intuitions that motivate non-cognitivists and anti-realists. The contrast with descriptive statements and beliefs is intuitive, and seems potentially explanatory. But the most plausible ways to articulate that contrast also threaten to undermine it, either by assimilating expression within the fold of description, beliefs, and truth, or by assimilating description, belief, and truth within the fold of expression and dynamic effects. Hybrid expressivists have more flexibility in explaining the intimate interactions between descriptive and expressive commitments than pure expressivists do, because they can locate non-cognitive attitudes outside the at-issue contributions of the compositional semantic machinery while retaining the claim that the target words conventionally function to express those attitudes. But their very flexibility also makes them harder to distinguish from cognitivists.

Expressivists of both stripes need positive evidence that expressive words have a conventional non-descriptive function, and a specification of how that function is implemented linguistically. Some of the most exciting recent developments within expressivism have focused on words and attitudes that are intimately connected with information and truth. Proponents of these views have brought important empirical data and formal resources from linguistics to bear; but the feasibility of marshaling these insights in support of classic expressivism about thin ethical terms is less obvious. At the same time, many of the most exciting developments within formal semantics concern aspects of language other than the at-issue presentation of descriptive content. Hybrid expressivists have begun to exploit some of these theoretical resources, but further interaction with linguistic theory is called for. From this perspective, expressivism about thin ethical terms may turn out to be the opening wedge of a more encompassing reconceptualization of semantic content, discourse structure, and communication.

NOTE

1. See Väyrynen (2014) for arguments against a semantic analysis on the basis of projective behavior, and Kyle (2013) for defense of a semantic treatment.

ACKNOWLEDGMENTS

Heartfelt thanks to David Plunkett, Tristram McPherson, and Lea Schroeder for extensive and extremely helpful comments. Thanks also to David Beaver, Dan Harris, Josh Knobe, and Eliot Michaelson for useful discussion.

REFERENCES

Anderson, Luvell and Ernie Lepore (2013): "Slurring Words," *Noûs* 47:1, 25–48.

Austin, John (1961): "Performative Utterances," in *Philosophical Papers*, ed. J. O. Urmson and G. J. Warnock (Oxford: Clarendon Press), 233–252.

Ayer, Alfred Jules (1936): *Language, Truth and Logic* (New York: Dover).

Bar-On, Dorit (2004): *Speaking My Mind: Expression and Self-Knowledge* (Oxford: Clarendon Press).

Blackburn, Simon (1980): "Truth, Realism, and the Regulation of Theory," *Midwest Studies in Philosophy* 5:1, 353–372.

Blackburn, Simon (1993): *Essays in Quasi-Realism* (New York: Oxford University Press).

Blackburn, Simon (1998): *Ruling Passions* (Oxford, Clarendon Press).

Boisvert, Daniel (2008): "Expressive-Assertivism," *Pacific Philosophical Quarterly* 892, 169–203.

Brink, David (1989): *Moral Realism and the Foundations of Ethics* (Cambridge: Cambridge University Press).

Camp, Elisabeth (2013): "Slurring Perspectives," *Analytic Philosophy* 54:3, 330–349.

Camp, Elisabeth (2017): "A Dual Act Analysis of Slurs," in *Bad Words*, ed. D. Sosa (Oxford: Oxford University Press).

Charlow, Nate (2015): "Prospects for an Expressivist Theory of Meaning," *Philosophers' Imprint* 15: 1–43.

Copp, David (2001): "Realist-Expressivism: A Neglected Option for Moral Realism," *Social Philosophy and Policy* 18: 1–43.

Copp, David (2009): "Realist-Expressivism and Conventional Implicature," *Oxford Studies in Metaethics* 4: 167–202.

Davidson, Donald (1979): "Moods and Performances," in *Meaning and Use*, ed. A. Margalit (Dordrecht: D. Reidel), 9–20.

Dreier, Jamie (2004): "Metaethics and the Problem of Creeping Minimalism," *Philosophical Perspectives* 18: 23–44.

Dretske, Fred (1981): *Knowledge and the Flow of Information* (Cambridge, MA: MIT Press).

Frege, Gottlob (1893): *Grundgesetze der Arithmetik, begriffsschriftlich abgeleitet,* Vol. 1 (Jena: H. Pohle, 1st ed.)

Gibbard, Allan (1990): *Wise Choices, Apt Feelings* (Cambridge MA: Harvard University Press).

Gibbard, Allan (1992): "Morality and Thick Concepts," *Proceedings of the Aristotelian Society* Supplementary Volume 66, 267–283.

Gibbard, Allan (2003): *Thinking How to Live* (Cambridge, MA: Harvard University Press).

Green, Mitchell (1997): "On the Autonomy of Linguistic Meaning," *Mind* 106: 217–244.

Green, Mitchell (2007): *Self-Expression* (Oxford: Oxford University Press).

Grice, H. Paul (1957): "Meaning," *Philosophical Review* 66:3, 377–388.

Grice, H. Paul (1989): *Studies in the Ways of Words* (Cambridge, MA: Harvard University Press).

Hare, Richard Mervyn (1952): *The Language of Morals* (Oxford: Oxford University Press).

Hom, Christopher (2008): "The Semantics of Racial Epithets," *Journal of Philosophy* 105:8, 416–440.

Horgan, Terry and Mark Timmons (2006): "Morality without Moral Facts," in *Contemporary Debates in Moral Theory*, ed. J. Dreier (Oxford: Blackwell), 220–238.

Horwich, Paul (1990): *Truth* (Oxford: Blackwell).

Khoo, Justin and Josh Knobe (2016): "Moral Disagreement and Moral Semantics," *Noûs*, online view; DOI:10.1111/nous.12151.

Kyle, Brent (2013): "How Are Thick Terms Evaluative?" *Philosophers' Imprint* 13:1, 1–20.

Lewis, David (1970): "General Semantics," *Synthese* 22:1/2, 18–67.

Lewis, David (1979): "Scorekeeping in a Language Game," *Journal of Philosophical Logic* 8:3, 339–359.

McDowell, John (1981): "Non-Cognitivism and Rule-Following," in *Wittgenstein: To Follow a Rule*, ed. S. Holtzman and C. Leich (London: Routledge and Kegan Paul), 141–172.

Nunberg, Geoff (2017): "The Social Life of Slurs," in *New Work on Speech Acts*, ed. D. Fogal, D. Harris, and M. Moss (Oxford: Oxford University Press).

Portner, Paul (2004): "The Semantics of Imperatives within a Theory of Clause Types," in *Proceedings of Semantics and Linguistic Theory* 14, ed. K. Watanabe and R. B. Young (Ithaca, NY: CLC Publications).

Potts, Chris (2005): *The Logic of Conventional Implicatures* (Oxford: Oxford University Press).

Potts, Chris (2007): "The Expressive Dimension," *Theoretical Linguistics* 33:2, 165–197.

Railton, Peter (1986): "Moral Realism," *Philosophical Review* 95:2, 163–207.

Richard, Mark (2008): *When Truth Gives Out* (New York: Oxford University Press).

Ridge, Michael (2006): "Ecumenical Expressivism: Finessing Frege," *Ethics* 116:2, 302–336.

Ridge, Michael (2014): *Impassioned Belief* (New York, NY: Oxford University Press).

Rosen, Gideon (1998): "Blackburn's *Essays in Quasi-Realism*," *Noûs* 32:3, 386–405.

Schroeder, Mark (2008a): "Expression for Expressivists," *Philosophy and Phenomenological Research*, 76:1, 86–116.

Schroeder, Mark (2008b): *Being For: Evaluating the Semantic Program of Expressivism* (Oxford: Oxford University Press).

Schroeder, Mark (2009): "Hybrid Expressivism: Virtues and Vices," *Ethics* 119:2, 257–309.

Searle, John (1969): *Speech Acts* (Cambridge: Cambridge University Press).

Siegel, Muffy (2006): "Biscuit Conditionals: Quantification over Potential Literal Acts," *Linguistics and Philosophy* 29: 167–203.

Silk, Alex (2015): "How to Be an Ethical Expressivist," *Philosophy and Phenomenological Research* 91:1, 47–81.

Stalnaker, Robert (1970): "Pragmatics," *Synthese* 22:1/2, 272–289.

Stalnaker, Robert (2002): "Common Ground," *Linguistics and Philosophy* 25:5/6, 701–721.

Starr, Will (2014): "Mood, Force and Truth," *Language and Value. Protosociology* 31: 160–181.

Stevenson, Charles (1937): "The Emotive Meaning of Ethical Terms," *Mind* 46: 14–31.

Stevenson, Charles (1944): *Ethics and Language* (New Haven and London: Yale University Press).

Väyrynen, Pekka (2013): *The Lewd, the Rude and the Nasty: A Study of Thick Concepts in Ethics* (New York: Oxford University Press.

Whiting, Daniel (2008): "Conservatives and Racists: Inferential Role Semantics and Pejoratives," *Philosophia* 36: 375–388.

Williams, Bernard (1985): *Ethics and the Limits of Philosophy* (London: Fontana).

Williamson, Timothy (2009): "Reference, Inference, and the Semantics of Pejoratives," in *The Philosophy of David Kaplan*, ed. J. Almog and P. Leonardi (Oxford: Oxford University Press).

Yalcin, Seth (2007): "Epistemic Modals," *Mind* 116:464, 983–1026.

Yalcin, Seth (2012): "Bayesian Expressivism," *Proceedings of the Aristotelian Society* 112:2, 123–160.

6

Metaethical Contextualism

Alex Silk

METAETHICAL CONTEXTUALISM: WHAT?

An important function of language is to create and develop interpersonal relationships in communication. In inquiry, we share and coordinate our beliefs about how the world is. But we also take a stance and socially orient ourselves toward possible acts, attitudes, and states of affairs. We evaluate possibilities as desirable, appropriate, horrible, trivial, permissible, wonderful. We make demands and grant permissions, emphasize commonality and breed antipathy. In communication, we shape our identities as thinkers and feelers in a social world; we coordinate on how to act, what to feel, and whom to be.

Language affords a variety of normative and evaluative resources for doing so. Such resources include modal verbs and adjectives, among others, as in (1)–(2).

(1) Morally speaking, Sally must give to charity.
(2) Killing is morally wrong.

Our evaluation of sentences such as (1)–(2) depends on what moral norms we accept. (1) can seem acceptable if you accept moral norms requiring Sally to give to charity, but unacceptable if you accept norms permitting her not to. Some theorists claim that this dependence of our evaluation of (1) on what moral norms we accept derives from a dependence of the interpretation of (1) on a contextually relevant body of norms. Whether (1) is true or false, on these views, can vary across contexts, even if everything else in the world—the relevant facts about Sally's circumstances, available charities, etc.—remains fixed.

Metaethical contextualism (hereafter 'contextualism'), as I will understand it, treats this context-dependence as a dependence of the semantic (conventional) *content* of (1) on features of the context of use, those features that determine a relevant body of moral norms. Contextualism claims that (1) is context-sensitive in the same way as sentences with paradigm context-sensitive expressions—'here', 'now', demonstratives ('this', 'that'), pronouns ('I', 'she'), etc. What information is conventionally conveyed in using (3) depends on which female is most salient in the context.

(3) She won a medal.

In a context where Anna is most salient, (3) conveys that Anna won a medal, but in a context where Betty is most salient, (3) conveys that Betty won a medal. Likewise, according to contextualism, using (1) conventionally conveys, roughly, that the relevant moral norms in the conversational context require Sally to give to charity. In a context where Alice's moral norms N_A are relevant, (1) conveys that N_A requires Sally to give to charity, but in a context where Bert's moral norms N_B are relevant, (1) conveys that N_B requires Sally to give to charity.

Contextualists differ on which norms are "relevant" in different contexts of use. Some theorists say that it is the norms accepted by the speaker (Dreier 1990), some that it is the norms accepted among a larger group or community (Harman 1975; Wong 1984, 2006; Copp 1995; Velleman 2013). Others opt for a more flexible approach (Finlay 2004, 2009, 2014; Silk 2016; cf. DeRose 2009). Contextualists also differ on what sort of object normative sentences are relativized to. One might treat normative sentences as sensitive to codes of practice (Copp 1995), standards (Silk 2016), ends (Finlay 2009, 2014), or motivational attitudes (Harman 1975, Dreier 1990), among other things. To fix ideas I will couch the discussion in terms of norms, but nothing substantive hangs on this. So, what unifies contextualist theories is the claim that what a sentence such as (1) conventionally conveys, and hence whether it is true or false, depends on what body of moral norms (standard, code, etc.) is relevant in the conversational context.

The target of this chapter is broadly normative uses of language. By 'normative use of language' I mean a use which expresses the speaker's endorsement of a relevant body of norms or values (cf. Gibbard 1990: 33). This includes certain aesthetic uses, moral uses, non-moral evaluative uses, legal uses, etc. Not all uses of expressions such as 'must', 'may', 'right', 'duty', 'beautiful', etc. are normative in this sense. For instance, the use of 'must' in (4) targets a relevant body of information, and the use of 'can' in (5) targets relevant biological and environmental circumstances.

(4) It must be raining outside. Look at all those people with wet umbrellas.
(5) Polar bears can survive here.

Further, some uses which concern relevant norms or values are merely descriptive. In using 'have to' in (6), the speaker is simply reporting what Dwayne's parents' rules require; (6) can be paraphrased with an explicit 'according to'-type phrase, as in (7).

(6) Dwayne has to be home by 10. Aren't his parents stupid? I'd stay out if I were him.
(7) According to Dwayne's parents' rules, Dwayne has to be home by 10.

All theories can accept that some uses of 'must', 'wrong', etc. are context-sensitive in the same way as 'she' in (3). The distinctive claim of contextualism is that the intuitively *normative* uses, in the above sense—the sorts of uses characteristic of deliberation and planning—are context-sensitive in the same kind of way as (3) and (6). (Hereafter I will use 'normative language' as short for 'normative uses of language', though the qualification in this paragraph should be kept in mind. Though I will often treat all types of normative uses on a par, it is in principle possible to accept contextualism about certain types of normative language but not others. I will use '(meta)ethics' broadly to cover not just morality but the variety of normative and evaluative domains.)

Contextualism, in this sense, sometimes goes under the heading of "Metaethical Relativism" (Harman 1975, 1996; Dreier 1990). The view has a checkered past. Serious objections have been raised, both on linguistic and on substantive (meta)normative grounds. Many respond by distinguishing the context-sensitivity of normative language from that of paradigm context-sensitive expressions, or by denying that normative language is distinctively context-sensitive at all.

There are two main classes of linguistic data that have been thought problematic for contextualism: first, discourse phenomena involving agreement and disagreement; and second, the interpretation of normative language in certain complex linguistic environments, such as in attitude ascriptions and indirect speech reports. The following section examines the discourse properties of normative language, and presents a standard version of the argument from disagreement. The section "Normative Attitudes and Attitude Ascriptions" examines the embedding behavior of normative language in ascriptions of normative attitudes. The differences between normative language and paradigm context-sensitive language in their discourse properties and embedding behavior have been largely underappreciated among contextualists. The section "Normative Language and Contextual Felicity" further presses this worry by examining the contextual underspecification characteristic of normative language in conversation. The section "Managing Context in Language Use" outlines a strategy for implementing what I regard as an improved version of contextualism (developed in Silk 2016).

Although contextualism is a linguistic thesis, contextualist theories are often motivated by broader substantive (meta)normative aims—e.g., to capture the connection between normative judgment and motivation, to avoid positing a realm of distinctively normative properties (facts, truths), and to explain the alleged faultlessness of fundamental normative disagreement. The section "Metaethics in Metaethical Contextualism" examines the relation between contextualist semantics for normative language, and broader philosophical theorizing about the nature of normativity and the distinctive features of normative discourse and thought.

Finally, the section "Further Issues" concludes by describing several limitations of the present discussion and directions for future research.

Before getting started, I would like to make two clarificatory remarks about what kind of context-sensitivity is at issue in debates about metaethical contextualism. First, contextualists sometimes motivate their views by noting that many modal verbs can have different "senses" or "readings" in different contexts, as we saw with (4)–(7). Such context-sensitivity in certain *words*, qua lexical items, is well known (Kratzer 1977). But it is insufficient for contextualism, in the relevant sense. All parties can accept that (e.g.) 'must' is context-sensitive in the sense that context determines what type of reading the modal receives. What is at issue is whether, given a specific type of normative reading—say, moral, as in (1)—some particular body of norms supplied by the context of use figures in calculating the semantic content, or compositional semantic value, of the sentence-in-context, where what norms are supplied may vary across contexts in the same world. Non-contextualist accounts deny this (more on which below). Debates about contextualism arise for words whose lexical semantics already fixes a specific reading (e.g., aesthetic for 'beautiful') and for complex expressions in which the relevant reading is linguistically specified (e.g., 'morally wrong').

Second, treating certain normative claims as relativized, in some sense, to relevant norms (standards, ends, etc.) isn't sufficient for contextualism. What is essential for contextualism is that there be a dependence of semantic *content* on norms determined as a function of the *context of use* (see above). Non-contextualist "relativizing" accounts would deny this—e.g., by positing relativization to norms determined by the circumstances of the *subject*, leading to a kind of invariantism, or to norms determined by a posited *context of assessment*, leading to a kind of relativism (in the sense of John MacFarlane's work). Informal relativizing claims—like that 'x is wrong' can be true "relative to" (as applied to, etc.) one person/group but false relative to another—fail to distinguish among the candidate semantic theories. (For this reason, it isn't always clear where many self-described "relativist" views fall on questions of contextualism, relativism, etc. in the present senses of these positions.)

NORMATIVE DISAGREEMENT IN DISCOURSE

Contextualists treat a particular body of norms determined by the context of use as figuring in the truth-conditions of a normative sentence. So, to give a proper account of the meaning of normative language, the contextualist must provide a general account of what body of norms is supplied as a function of the context of use and figures in deriving semantic content. This is no different from how an account of 'she' must provide a general specification of what individual is referred to given a context of use *c*—e.g., perhaps that 'she' refers to the maximally salient female in *c*. The putative problem is that, in the case of normative language, there doesn't seem to be any way of specifying the contextually relevant norms that explains both (a) how we're in a position to make the normative claims we seem licensed in making (call it the *justified use condition*), and (b) how we can reasonably disagree with one another's normative claims (call it the *disagreement condition*) (cf. Gibbard 1990, 2003; Kölbel 2002; Lasersohn 2005; Richard 2008; MacFarlane 2014).

Suppose Alice and Bert are considering how much, if anything, morality requires Sally to give to the poor. They agree on all the relevant non-normative facts, like how much Sally earns, how stable her job is, what the needs of the poor are like, and so on. Their question is fundamentally normative: It concerns what moral norms to accept. The following dialogue ensues:

(8) *Alice:* Morally speaking, Sally must give to charity.
    Bert: No, Sally doesn't have to give to charity. She can keep what she has for herself and her family and friends.

What body of norms should the contextualist say figures in the interpretation of Alice's and Bert's utterances?

Suppose, first, that Alice's utterance of (1) is just about her moral norms. Assuming Alice is in a position to make a claim about what moral norms she accepts, this captures how Alice is justified in producing her utterance. But it becomes unclear how Bert can reasonably disagree with her. And it becomes unclear how, in uttering (9), Bert is disagreeing with Alice, given that they are making claims about their respective moral norms.

(9) No, Sally doesn't have to give to charity.

Bert's denial in (8) is felicitous, whereas *B*'s denial in (10) is not.

(10) *A:*   In view of Alice's moral norms, Sally must give to charity.
     B: #No, in view of Bert's moral norms, Sally doesn't have to give to charity.

This puts pressure on the claim that the sentences used in (10) explicitly specify the semantic contents of the respective sentences used in (8).

Suppose instead that we treat normative claims as about a relevant group's norms. Assuming Alice's and Bert's utterances target the same group, this captures how Alice and Bert make inconsistent claims. But it becomes unclear how Alice is in a position to make a claim about whether Sally must give, which, intuitively, she is. It can be appropriate for Alice to utter (1) even if she doesn't know anything about Bert's (or whomever else's) moral views.

In sum, the objection from disagreement is that if we treat normative claims as about the speaker's norms ("speaker contextualism"), we capture the justified use condition but leave the disagreement condition unexplained. But if we treat normative claims as about the norms of a larger group ("group contextualism"), we capture the disagreement condition but leave the justified use condition unexplained. There seems to be no general way of specifying what body of norms is relevant as a function of context that captures all our intuitions.

There is much to say about the nature of disagreement, both in general and about normative matters specifically. For our purposes, we can focus on a certain discourse phenomenon: The *systematic licensing of expressions of linguistic denial* ('no', 'nu-uh', etc.) in discourses such as (8). Not all cases in which speakers intuitively disagree can be marked in this way. *B*'s "disagreement in attitude" with *A* in (11) couldn't typically be signaled with a linguistic denial.

(11) *A:*   I like Mexican food.
     B: #No, I like Thai.

A common contextualist strategy is to try to explain disagreement phenomena in the *pragmatics*, in terms of non-conventional aspects of use. Many contextualists note that denials can target various non-truth-conditional aspects of utterances (e.g., Björnsson & Finlay 2010: 19–20; Sundell 2011: 275–83; Plunkett & Sundell 2013: 11–22). *B*'s denials in (12)–(13), for instance, target a presupposition and scalar implicature, respectively.

(12) *A:*   The king of France was at the awards ceremony.
     B: No, there is no king of France.
(13) *A:*   Sally won two medals.
     B: No, she won three.

So, the speaker contextualist might say that the proposition targeted by Bert's denial in (8) isn't Alice's "autobiographical report"—the conventional content of her utterance—but rather "the proposition that he would have asserted by uttering the same sentence" (Björnsson & Finlay 2010: 20). One might say that even though, Alice's utterance semantically makes a claim about her moral norms, the primary implication Alice intends to convey is a pragmatically related proposition to which Bert *is* licensed in objecting. One plausible candidate is an implication that Bert ought to conform his moral views to Alice's. It is this implication, the reply continues, which is felicitously targeted by Bert's denial. In uttering (1)/(9), Alice and Bert "pragmatically advocate" (Plunkett & Sundell 2013) for their respective moral views.

Contextualists have been right to emphasize that incompatibility of conventionally asserted content isn't necessary for discourse disagreement. Intuitively, Alice and Bert are disagreeing, not about whether Sally's giving to charity is required by such-and-such norms, but about what norms *to accept*. They are managing their assumptions about what moral norms are operative in the context. Simply noting this, however, is insufficient. The question isn't whether such "discourse-oriented" negotiations are *possible*. The challenge is to explain why they are so *systematic* with normative language, given that a contextualist semantics is correct (Silk 2014, 2016).

The above contextualist replies posit that the implications systematically targeted by linguistic denials—and affirmations, for that matter—in normative discourse are implications other than the utterances' conventionally asserted contents. Yet surprisingly little attention has been given to what specific mechanisms are responsible for this, or how these mechanisms are linguistically constrained—i.e., how (dis)agreement phenomena can be derived from the specific semantic contents, general conversational principles, and general features of contexts of use, *and* why they can be derived so systematically with normative language but not with paradigm context-sensitive language. When speakers use paradigm context-sensitive expressions ("PCS-expressions") with different intended contents, the norm isn't disagreement, but talking past. Denials like *B*'s in (14)–(15) are typically infelicitous.

(14) *A:* I'm hungry.
　　　B: #No, I'm not hungry.
(15) *A:* That is a cute baby. [said demonstrating *b*]
　　　B: #No, that isn't a cute a baby. [said demonstrating *b′*]

Using 'I'm hungry' doesn't systematically imply that the addressee ought to be hungry. Using 'That [demonstrating *b*] is a cute baby' doesn't systematically imply that the addressee ought to be demonstrating *b*. One is left wondering why the assumed pragmatic mechanisms which license linguistic denials with normative language couldn't, and systematically don't, also apply with PCS-expressions. Why should uttering a sentence which conventionally describes given bodies of norms systematically communicate something about what norms to accept? Why would speakers systematically assert "normative propositions" they don't have a "fundamental interest" in (Finlay 2014: 147–50, 184–88, 217–22)? Why would the asserted contents of normative utterances, unlike other utterances, typically not have main point status?

In sum, a prototypical function of normative language is to manage speakers' assumptions about the very features of context on which its interpretation intuitively depends.

Normative language contrasts with paradigm context-sensitive language in this respect. The worry is that the distinctive role of normative language in discourse is unexpected, given the contextualist's semantics. The force of this worry has been underappreciated by contextualists.

NORMATIVE ATTITUDES AND ATTITUDE ASCRIPTIONS

The previous section considered various discourse properties of normative language— how context affects the interpretation of normative language, and how normative language is used to change context and manage what norms to accept. A second class of objections to contextualism concerns the interpretation of normative language in certain complex linguistic environments. I will focus on two objections in this area. (For discussion of additional objections, see Silk 2016: chapter 4 and references therein.)

Characterizing normative states of mind

The first objection is that contextualism mischaracterizes normative states of mind. Call an attitude ascription like (16) with a normative sentence as its complement clause a *normative attitude ascription*.

(16) Alice thinks Sally must give to charity.

Insofar as contextualism treats the contextually relevant norms as figuring in the content of a normative sentence, contextualism seems to treat (16) as ascribing to Alice the belief that her moral norms require Sally to give to charity. The worry is that this incorrectly treats normative attitudes as states of mind about what norms one accepts.

Consider the following example from Silk 2013 (207–208):

> Suppose you encourage Gabriel, your infant brother, to put his fingers into the electrical outlet. Gabriel, smart chap that he is, recoils; his mother has repeatedly scolded him not to do so. You say:
>
> [(17)] Gabriel knows he shouldn't put his fingers into the outlet.
>
> This seems true; you are attributing a certain normative belief to Gabriel. But it is implausible that [(17)] is true only if Gabriel has a belief about his, or anyone else's, normative views. He's just a baby.

As Silk (2013: 208) puts it, "Whether one can represent or take a certain perspective on normative standards is independent of whether one can *have* a normative standard." Likewise, (18) doesn't ascribe to Bert the sort of attitude ascribed in (19):

(18)   Bert fears that he must give to charity.
(19)   ⸮Bert fears that his/our/whoever's moral views entail that he gives to charity.

Bert's fear is about the moral status of his giving to charity, not about himself or the stringency of his moral views.

Normative attitude ascriptions don't seem to ascribe meta-attitudes about a relevant individual/group or their norms. They seem to characterize the subject's first-order normative views themselves. (16) characterizes Alice as accepting moral norms which require Sally to give to charity. The challenge is to capture this within a contextualist semantics.

Factive attitudes

A second objection is that normative language seems differently from paradigm context-sensitive (PCS) language when embedded under factive attitude verbs (Weatherson 2008, Lasersohn 2009)—roughly speaking, verbs which imply the truth of their complements, such as 'know' or 'realize'. (I will bracket whether the implication is a presupposition or entailment.)

Suppose the contextualist treats (16) as ascribing to Alice the belief that her moral norms require Sally to give to charity. Assume Alice is correct about what her moral views are, and that this belief constitutes knowledge. Nevertheless, if we take Sally's giving to charity to be supererogatory, or not required, we may be unwilling to accept (20).

(20) Alice knows that Sally must give to charity.

This is surprising, given the contextualist's semantics: If Alice's belief constitutes knowledge, why can't we report it as such? PCS-expressions don't appear to display this sort of behavior. If we accept (21a), and we accept that S's belief that we are philosophers constitutes knowledge, then we cannot coherently reject (21b).

(21) a. S thinks we are philosophers.
      b. S knows we are philosophers.

Likewise for PCS-expressions that allow being linked to the attitude subject: Suppose we accept (22a) in a context where 'local' is interpreted, roughly, as "local to Weatherson." Perhaps we think Weatherson is in Ann Arbor, and we attribute to Weatherson the belief that Al is at Ashley's, a bar in Ann Arbor. In such a context, if we accept that Weatherson's belief that Al is at Ashley's constitutes knowledge, there is no inclination to reject (22b).

(22) a. Weatherson thinks Al is at a local bar.
      b. Weatherson knows Al is at a local bar.

Intuitively, even if Alice's belief that her moral norms require Sally to give to charity constitutes knowledge, we cannot report this using (20) since doing so would seem to commit *us* to requiring Sally to give to charity. But this dual linking to the discourse context and the attitude subject seems incompatible with the contextualist's semantics, which requires a specific body of norms to determine the content of the complement clause. If we interpret 'must' in (20) with respect to Alice's norms, we fail to explain why we resist accepting (20) (still assuming we take Alice's giving to be not required). But if we interpret 'must' with respect to our moral norms, we incorrectly characterize Alice's state of mind. No single body of norms captures both what the truth of (20) commits Alice to and what its felicitous use commits the speaker to.

NORMATIVE LANGUAGE AND CONTEXTUAL FELICITY

Rather than lexically associating normative language with a specific feature of context, like the speaker, many contextualists opt for a more flexible approach which leaves a role for communicative intentions in determining what norms are supplied (see the opening section). There is an additional challenge for such views which hasn't received attention in the literature. This challenge raises interesting general questions about felicity constraints, accommodation, and interpretive strategies in cases of contextual underspecification. (See Silk 2016 for further discussion.)

Many PCS-expressions impose what Tonhauser et al. (2013) call a *strong contextual felicity* (SCF) constraint: They cannot be felicitously used if their presuppositions aren't antecedently satisfied in the context. Using 'too' in (23) is infelicitous if we haven't been talking about someone other than Sheila eating out tonight.

(23) #Sheila is eating out tonight, too.

Upon hearing (23), you won't be content to infer that (I think) some relevant person or other, besides Sheila, is eating out tonight. You will object and want to know who. Likewise with (3), as reinforced in (24):

(24)   [Context: We are standing opposite three women. You don't know any of them, and you don't think I do either. As far as you're concerned, they are relevantly indistinguishable. I say:]
        #She won a medal.

Even after my utterance, none of the three women is more salient than any other. Yet it's not as if my utterance is completely uninformative to you. You can infer that I take one of the women to be most salient, and that whichever woman I take to be most salient won a medal. But you won't rest content with accommodating these inferences. My use of 'she' is infelicitous.

By contrast, I can felicitously utter (1) even if no particular body of moral norms is antecedently salient in the discourse. Upon hearing (1), one would typically be content to infer that (I think) the relevant norms, whatever exactly they are, require that Sally gives to charity. We can make progress in moral inquiry without needing to commit to some particular body of moral norms.

The worry is this: On the type of contextualist semantics we are considering, using normative language assumes a lexically unspecified body of norms, and makes a claim about it. This is precisely analogous to the case of (e.g.) pronouns: Using 'she' assumes a certain salient female, and makes a claim about her. Why, then, in cases of contextual underspecification, is using normative language typically felicitous, but using pronouns (additives, etc.) is not? Why are interlocutors content to accommodate the presuppositions associated with normative language, but not with (e.g.) pronouns? If normative language has the same kind of semantics as (e.g.) pronouns, whence the contrast in felicity conditions?

MANAGING CONTEXT IN LANGUAGE USE

The theme of the foregoing sections is that there seem to be significant linguistic differences between normative language and paradigm context-sensitive language, as concerning their discourse properties, embedding behavior, and felicity conditions. These differences put pressure on the claim that normative language and paradigm context-sensitive language are semantically context-sensitive in the same general kind of way. Many contextualists have responded by positing linguistically unconstrained interpretive mechanisms and ad hoc pragmatic principles. What is needed, however, is a detailed explanation of the distinctive features of normative language in terms of specific features of their conventional meaning and general interpretive and pragmatic principles. Providing such an account is, in my view, the central challenge for contextualism.

Some theorists have responded by distinguishing the context-sensitivity of normative language from that of PCS-expressions, adopting relativist or expressivist semantics (Gibbard 1990, 2003; Kölbel 2002; Silk 2013; MacFarlane 2014). Others deny that normative language is distinctively context-sensitive, adopting invariantist semantics. Though non-contextualist theories may avoid the sorts of worries from the previous sections, they face non-trivial burdens of their own—for instance, for the relativist and expressivist, to provide accounts of assertion, belief, and truth; for the invariantist, to provide positive evidence that specific (meta)normative views are encoded in the conventional meaning of normative language. Some of these burdens have begun to be addressed, but accounts are often admittedly incomplete.

The remainder of this section briefly outlines what I regard as a more promising contextualist strategy of reply, developed in greater detail elsewhere in a view called *Discourse Contextualism* (Silk 2016). This should give a flavor for the kinds of explanatory resources available to the contextualist going forward.

First, contrary to initial appearances, much of the same puzzling linguistic phenomena observed with normative language can also arise with PCS-expressions (Silk 2014, 2016). Consider discourse disagreement. Suppose Amanda and Billy are playing with three children, two white and one non-white. Amanda is racist against non-whites, and Billy knows this. The two white children, Will and Wilma, are laughing, and the one non-white child, Nick, isn't. Amanda says:

(25) Look, the children (/they) are laughing!

Roughly, (25) says that everyone in the most salient group of children is laughing. Insofar as Amanda intends to say something true, it is mutually obvious that she is assuming that the most salient group of children includes only Will and Wilma. Since it is mutually accepted that there would be no non-racist grounds for treating Nick as less salient than Will and Wilma, Amanda's utterance of (25) thus implicitly suggests that Nick's being non-white is a sufficient reason not to talk about him. If Billy doesn't object to Amanda's utterance, he will accommodate her in this assumption. This can set the stage for further exclusionary behavior in the future.

To avoid such a consequence, Billy might object by explicitly calling out Amanda on her assumption; he might say something like, 'Wait a minute, why are you ignoring Nick?' But Billy needn't be so explicit; he might say:

(26) No, the children (/they) *aren't* laughing. Nick is bored out of his mind.

Insofar as Billy intends to say something true, it is mutually obvious that he intends his use of 'the children' to pick out a group that includes Nick. In uttering (26), Billy acts in a way which assumes that Nick *is* included in the group under discussion, and thus that Nick isn't to be ignored simply because of his race. This can lead to (implicit or explicit) negotiation about which children are salient and why.

Or consider factive attitude ascriptions. Suppose Billy accepts (27) in a context where 'the children' is linked to Amanda's belief state.

(27) Amanda thinks the children are laughing.

Though Billy accepts (27), and (let's suppose) he accepts that Amanda's belief that Will and Wilma are laughing constitutes knowledge, he may resist accepting (28).

(28) Amanda knows the children are laughing.

After all, Billy might say, the children *aren't* laughing; Nick is bored out of his mind.

Similar examples can be constructed with other PCS-expressions. The relevant observations: (i) The intended contents of Amanda's and Billy's utterances in (25)–(26) are compatible, and yet they disagree. (ii) Uttering (28) can express Billy's assumptions about the contextual features determining the content of 'the children' even if the content of the attitude is determined in light of Amanda's state of mind. Billy may thus resist accepting (25) or (28) on the basis of disagreeing with Amanda about those very contextual features (namely, whether the most salient group of children excludes Nick).

Examples such as these highlight that although what is typically relevant in uses of PCS-expressions is their truth-conditional content, rather than what their use assumes about the features of context which determine that content, this generalization isn't without exception. This observation illuminates a strategy for developing contextualism. Perhaps by examining what distinguishes the exceptional cases with PCS-expressions, such as (25)–(28), we can learn something about the distinctive discourse properties of normative language. Drawing on work in artificial intelligence, Silk (2016) argues that the sort of context management exhibited in certain uses of context-sensitive expressions is characteristic of collaborative action generally. The appropriateness of our actions often requires that circumstances are a certain way. *In acting*, we can exploit our mutual world knowledge and general abductive reasoning skills to communicate information and manage our assumptions about these circumstances. By acting in such a way that is appropriate only if the context is a certain way, one can implicitly propose that the context be that way. If the other party accommodates by proceeding in like manner, it can become taken for granted that the context is that way. If she doesn't, this can lead to negotiation over the state of the context. This can all happen without explicitly raising the issue of what the context is like. The linguistic case—the case of linguistic action, and interpretation—can be seen as a special instance of these phenomena. Using context-sensitive language presupposes that the concrete context determines a value for the relevant contextual parameter (body of norms, salience ordering, etc.) that renders one's utterance true and appropriate. Speakers can then integrate their mutual grammatical knowledge and general pragmatic reasoning skills to manage their assumptions about the very features of context that determine the intended contents of their uses of context-sensitive expressions.

The contextualist, of course, cannot stop here. The challenge isn't just to explain how speakers *can* communicate information about what norms context supplies in using normative language. It is also to explain the *systematicity* with which normative language, unlike paradigm context-sensitive language, is used in this way. But the above observations provide the basis for conversational explanations of certain relevant differences among context-sensitive expressions. Silk (2016) argues that many of these differences can be derived from the sentences' specific contents (truth-conditional *and* presupposed) and generate features of concrete discourses—e.g., concerning questions under discussion, speakers' (extra-)conversational goals, and speakers' substantive normative views. The account, is extended to capture the behavior of normative language in various complex linguistic environments (e.g., attitude ascriptions, conditionals), by drawing on independent principles of local interpretation. Whether the approach—labeled *Discourse Contextualism*—will ultimately succeed or prove superior to alternative non-contextualist theories remains to be seen. At minimum, examining the broader phenomena promises to shed light on general issues concerning (e.g.) the varieties of context-sensitivity in natural language, the nature and origins of presupposition, the role of context in communication and collaborative action, and the relations among truth, meaning, and assertion.

METAETHICS IN METAETHICAL CONTEXTUALISM

So far we have focused on metaethical contextualism as a *linguistic* thesis. Yet, historically speaking, what originally motivated the view—and what has kept many metaethicists attracted to it—aren't primarily linguistic issues, but substantive philosophical issues about the metaphysics of normative properties, the nature of normative knowledge, and the psychology of normative judgment. This section briefly considers several commonly cited *metaethical* payoffs of adopting a contextualist semantics. I will suggest that the relation between the semantic issues and the broader dialectic in metaethics is less straightforward than often assumed.

A first common motivation for contextualism concerns the psychology of normative judgment (Harman 1975, Dreier 1990, Finlay 2004, 2014; contrast Wong 2006: chapter 7). We typically take people to have at least some motivation to act in accordance with their sincere normative judgments. Suppose we are talking about the plight of starving children worldwide. Alice says that we must donate to Oxfam, and, just then, Oxfam calls. If Alice proceeds to express complete indifference to donating, we might question whether she was sincere in her previous judgment. Normative judgments are *practical*; they are *for action*.

Contextualism, it seems, has a straightforward explanation. If (29) implies that the speaker endorses norms which enjoin donating to Oxfam, then one won't sincerely utter (29) unless one's norms enjoin donating.

(29) I must donate to Oxfam.

Moreover a belief ascription like 'Alice thinks she must donate to Oxfam' won't be true—or, semantically descending, it won't be the case that Alice thinks she must donate to Oxfam—unless Alice endorses norms which enjoin donating (or at least unless Alice thinks she endorses such norms). So, if endorsing norms requiring one to ϕ is the sort of state of mind which motivates one to ϕ, there will be an intimate connection between thinking one must ϕ and being motivated to ϕ.

A second common motivation for contextualism concerns the metaphysics, epistemology, and metasemantics of normative thought and talk (Wong 2006; Finlay 2009, 2014). A challenge for non-contextualist descriptivist semantics is to explain what aspect of reality normative sentences describe, what its metaphysical relation is to other features of reality, and how we come to think, know, and talk about it. Contextualism seems to avoid such questions. One needn't posit a realm of distinctively normative properties or facts for normative thought and talk to be about. What normative sentences describe are just bodies of norms or states of mind. The metaphysics, epistemology, and metasemantics of normative thought and talk are no more puzzling than the metaphysics, epistemology, and metasemantics of thought and talk about bodies of norms (e.g., what is required according to utilitarianism) or psychologies (e.g., what norms Alice accepts). Further, by maintaining a descriptivist semantics, the contextualist can still integrate her treatment of normative language with standard views on (e.g.) assertion, informational and representational content, semantic explanation, logic, truth, and compositional semantics. This affords a potential advantage over theories, like expressivism or relativism, which call for revising our understanding of (at least some of) these issues. Contextualism can thus be of interest to theorists who are compelled by the idea that normative thought and talk depends, in some sense, on context, but who also have reservations about broader implications of revisionary theories.

A third motivation for contextualism concerns cases of fundamental normative disagreement (Wong 1984, 2006; Harman 1996; contrast Velleman 2013). Some theorists have claimed that at least some fundamental normative disagreements seem "faultless," or at least not rationally resolvable. Individuals may disagree, the thought goes, without any of them making any cognitive mistake. Though contextualism doesn't require accepting this idea, certain versions of contextualism may accommodate it. For example, the speaker contextualist might treat Alice and Bert's dispute as "faultless" in the sense that both speakers' assertions are true, and as constituting a "disagreement" in light of the speakers' conflicting preferences. However, it is contentious how robust intuitions of apparent faultless disagreement are in various normative domains, and whether the general notion of faultless disagreement is even coherent (Wright 2001; MacFarlane 2014: 133–36).

If contextualism is a thesis about the conventional meaning and use of a certain fragment of natural language, it may seem surprising that the view is often advanced with substantive (meta)normative considerations in mind. Prior to theorizing, one might not have expected the linguistic issues and the broader philosophical issues to be so closely intertwined. I would like to make two points about this.

First, perhaps contrary to initial appearances, accepting contextualism doesn't *itself* require taking a stand on the above metaethical issues. Take the connection with motivation. The crucial move in the above argument was this: *If* norm-acceptance is a motivating attitude, then there will be an intimate connection between (e.g.) asserting or thinking that one must ϕ and being motivated to ϕ. The antecedent of this conditional locates a place for theorizing about the nature of norm-acceptance, and hence about the nature of the connection between normative judgment and motivation. Does accepting norms which require one to ϕ essentially involve being motivated to ϕ? Does norm-acceptance at least essentially involve having certain motivational dispositions or emotional capacities? Questions such as these will plausibly receive different answers for different types of norms. The semantics is thus compatible with a range of views on the psychology of judgments characteristically expressed and ascribed using normative language (Silk 2016: sections 5.3–5.4).

Similarly, a contextualist semantics is compatible with a range of views on the nature of normativity and the metaphysics of normative properties (Silk 2016: sections 3.6, 5.4, 7.5). Compositional semantics takes as given an assignment of values to variables and other context-sensitive expressions. Compositional semantics with normative language thus, according to contextualism, takes as given a specific body of norms which figures in calculating the conventional contents of complex expressions. This leaves open the question of what makes it the case about a *concrete* context that it determines such-and-such norms for interpretation. This broadly *metasemantic* question locates a place for theorizing about the nature of, and relations among, the norms supplied across contexts. For instance, consider questions about the universality of morality. To capture 'relativist' claims, one could say that different concrete contexts can determine different moral norms. Conflicting moral judgments about a particular case could thus both be true. Those who defend the objectivity of morality would deny this. They could identify the relevant moral norms as the correct moral norms, determined independently of particular speaker attitudes. If a universal moral standard was correct, the same moral norms would be supplied in all contexts. Importantly, however, this would be a substantive (meta)normative matter rather than something built into the conventional meaning of moral language (as on certain invariantist semantics).

Of course, given that contextualism is neutral on these sorts of issues, it is *possible* to integrate it with an internalist moral psychology, parsimonious metaphysics, etc. But— and this is my second point—this needn't provide contextualism with an *advantage* over non-contextualist semantics. There are ways of doing so in non-contextualist frameworks as well (Silk 2013, 2016: sections 5.4, 6.3.3). According to relativism (in the sense of John MacFarlane's work), normative sentences are evaluated for truth/falsity with respect to the norms determined by a posited context of assessment, rather than the context of use. The above sorts of metaethical questions would be located in the *post*semantics of what makes it the case about a context of assessment that such-and-such norms are in force. Alternatively, invariantism may encode into the lexical semantics that the relevant norms are determined solely by the world of evaluation. Different bodies of norms would then correspond to different languages, i.e., fully formally precise languages (Lewis 1975). The above sorts of metaethical questions would be located in the *pre*semantics of what makes it the case about a linguistic community that such-and-such language is being spoken (e.g., that the string 'w-r-o-n-g' corresponds to the lexical item 'wrong' with such-and-such lexical entry).

The upshot is that doing semantics for normative language—theorizing about its conventional meaning and use—can, and arguably should, be neutral on certain broader philosophical issues often used to motivate metaethical contextualism. Distinguishing the latter issues from the semantics proper can free up our (meta)normative inquiries (cf. Forrester 1989: chapters 2 and 13; Silk 2013, 2016). This can motivate clearer answers and a more refined understanding of the space of overall theories. How exactly the various issues interact and mutually constrain theorizing may be more complicated than initially seemed.

FURTHER ISSUES

In closing, I would like to briefly describe several additional issues bearing on developments of metaethical contextualism.

First, I have focused on context-sensitivity concerning which body of norms is supplied for interpreting normative language. But there are other respects in which normative language can be sensitive to context. Notably, it can also be sensitive to a contextually relevant body of information (Kolodny & MacFarlane 2010; Parfit 2011). We can ask not only what one ought to do in light of all the facts, known and unknown, but also about one ought to do in light of available information. A *contextualist* about the latter talk treats the relevant information as supplied by the context of use and as figuring in deriving semantic content. Issues parallel to those considered in the foregoing sections arise for contextualism about information-sensitivity.

Second, normative language isn't limited to a single syntactic category. There are normative uses of modal verbs ('must', 'may'), adjectives ('right', 'wrong'), and nominals ('obligation', 'requirement'). Though these types of expressions may all seem apt for a contextualist treatment, if any are, they differ in important respects. It is non-trivial how precisely to implement a contextualist account in each case in the syntax and compositional semantics. Integration with general linguistic work on modals, adjectives, etc. is essential.

Third, though it is common in discussions of metaethical contextualism to focus on moral uses, there are many kinds of broadly evaluative language. A distinction is sometimes made between deontic terms ('must', 'permissible') and evaluative terms ('good', 'bad'), but there are also relevant sub-categories—expressions of aesthetics ('beautiful'), taste ('tasty'), desirability ('wonderful'), humor ('hilarious'), etc. Though these exhibit much of the same distinctive linguistic behavior discussed above, there are non-trivial differences among them—e.g., concerning performativity, multidimensionality, and embedding behavior (Silk 2016: chapter 7). Many of these differences are not yet well understood. Integration with research on linguistic expressives (Potts 2005)—epithets, slurs, honorifics, etc.—promises fruitful avenues to explore.

Fourth, there is a range of expressions exhibiting the apparently distinctive kind of context-sensitivity exhibited by normative language. Recent debates have targeted epistemic vocabulary, predicates of personal taste, and gradable adjectives, among others (Egan et al. 2005; Lasersohn 2005; Richard 2008; DeRose 2009; MacFarlane 2014; Silk 2016). Systematic investigation of the precise similarities/differences among them, as well as among context-sensitive expressions more generally, is needed (cf. Tonhauser et al. 2013; Silk 2016). Metaethical inquiry into context-sensitivity in normative language can thus be seen as part of the larger body of research on the varieties of context-sensitivity in interpretation.

ACKNOWLEDGMENTS

Thanks to Tristram McPherson, David Plunkett, and Lea Schroeder for helpful comments on a previous draft.

RELATED TOPICS

Chapter 5, "Metaethical Expressivism;" Chapter 7, "Metaethical Relativism;" Chapter 12, "Deontic Modals;" Chapter 15, "Hybrid Accounts of Ethical Thought and Talk;" Chapter 18, "Cognitivism and Non-Cognitivism;" Chapter 32, "The Epistemic Significance of Moral Disagreement;" Chapter 33, "Metasemantics and Metaethics."

REFERENCES

Björnsson, G. & Finlay, S. (2010). Metaethical contextualism defended. *Ethics*, 121, 7–36.
Copp, D. (1995). *Morality, normativity, and society*. New York: Oxford University Press.
DeRose, K. (2009). *The case for contextualism: Knowledge, skepticism, and context*, Vol. 1. Oxford: Oxford University Press.
Dreier, J. (1990). Internalism and speaker relativism. *Ethics*, 101, 6–26.
Egan, A., Hawthorne, J., & Weatherson, B. (2005). Epistemic modals in context. In G. Preyer & G. Peter (eds.) *Contextualism in philosophy: Knowledge, meaning, and truth*. Oxford: Oxford University Press.
Finlay, S. (2004). The conversational practicality of value judgment. *Journal of Ethics*, 8, 205–23.
Finlay, S. (2009). Oughts and ends. *Philosophical Studies*, 143, 315–40.
Finlay, S. (2014). *Confusion of tongues: A theory of normative language*. New York: Oxford University Press.
Forrester, J. W. (1989). *Why you should: The pragmatics of deontic speech*. Hanover: Brown University Press.
Gibbard, A. (1990). *Wise choices, apt feelings: A theory of normative judgment*. Cambridge, MA: Harvard University Press.
Gibbard, A. (2003). *Thinking how to live*. Cambridge, MA: Harvard University Press.
Harman, G. (1975). Moral relativism defended. *Philosophical Review*, 84, 3–22.
Harman, G. (1996). Moral relativism. In G. Harman & J. Thomson (eds.) *Moral relativism and moral objectivity*. Cambridge: Blackwell.
Kölbel, M. (2002). *Truth without objectivity*. London: Routledge.
Kolodny, N. & MacFarlane, J. (2010). Ifs and oughts. *Journal of Philosophy*, 107, 115–43.
Kratzer, A. (1977). What 'must' and 'can' must and can mean. *Linguistics and Philosophy*, 1, 337–55.
Lasersohn, P. (2005). Context dependence, disagreement, and predicates of personal taste. *Linguistics and Philosophy*, 28, 643–86.
Lasersohn, P. (2009). Relative truth, speaker commitment, and control of implicit arguments. *Synthese*, 166, 359–74.
Lewis, D. (1975). Languages and language. In K. Gunderson (ed.) *Minnesota studies in the philosophy of science*, Vol. 7. Minneapolis, MN: University of Minnesota Press.
MacFarlane, J. (2014). *Assessment sensitivity: Relative truth and its applications*. Oxford: Clarendon Press.
Parfit, D. (2011). *On what matters*, Vol. I. Oxford: Oxford University Press.
Plunkett, D. & Sundell, T. (2013). Disagreement and the semantics of normative and evaluative terms. *Philosophers' Imprint*, 13, 1–37.
Potts, C. (2005). *The logic of conventional implicature*. Oxford: Oxford University Press.
Richard, M. (2008). *When truth gives out*. Oxford: Oxford University Press.
Silk, A. (2013). Truth-conditions and the meanings of ethical terms. In R. Shafer-Landau (ed.) *Oxford studies in metaethics*, Vol. 8. New York: Oxford University Press.
Silk, A. (2014). Accommodation and negotiation with context-sensitive expressions. *Thought*, 3, 115–23.
Silk, A. (2016). *Discourse contextualism: A framework for contextualist semantics and pragmatics*. Oxford: Oxford University Press.
Sundell, T. (2011). Disagreements about taste. *Philosophical Studies*, 155, 267–88.

Tonhauser, J., Beaver, D., Roberts, C., & Simons, M. (2013). Towards a taxonomy of projective content. *Language*, 89, 66–109.

Velleman, D. (2013). *Foundations for moral relativism*. Cambridge: Open Book Publishers.

Weatherson, B. (2008). Attitudes and relativism. *Philosophical Perspectives*, 22, 527–44.

Wong, D. (1984). *Moral relativity*. Berkeley: University of California Press.

Wong, D. (2006). *Natural moralities: A defense of pluralistic relativism*. New York: Oxford University Press.

Wright, C. (2001). On being in a quandary: Relativism, vagueness, logical revisionism. *Mind*, 110, 45–98.

FURTHER READING

DeRose, K. (2009). *The case for contextualism: Knowledge, skepticism, and context*, Vol. 1. Oxford: Oxford University Press. (A classic development of epistemic contextualism.)

Dreier, J. (1990). Internalism and speaker relativism. *Ethics*, 101, 6–26. (Classic defenses of metaethical contextualism.)

Finlay, S. (2014). *Confusion of tongues: A theory of normative language*. New York: Oxford University Press. (An extended recent development of metaethical contextualism.)

Harman, G. (1975). Moral relativism defended. *Philosophical Review*, 84, 3–22.

Silk, A. (2016). *Discourse contextualism: A framework for contextualist semantics and pragmatics*. Oxford: Oxford University Press. (An extended defense of contextualist semantics for various types of expressions. Focuses primarily on linguistic issues but also examines connections with broader philosophical issues.)

7

Metaethical Relativism

Isidora Stojanovic

Although relativism may be said to be one of the oldest doctrines in philosophy, dating back to the teachings of Protagoras in the fifth century B.C., when it comes to contemporary philosophy, there is no consensus on what makes a view qualify as "relativist." The problem is particularly acute in metaethics, since most of the views that up to a decade ago were described as "relativist" would be more accurately described as "contextualist" or even "expressivist" in light of the distinctions currently drawn in the philosophy of language and semantics. In this chapter, we distinguish two construals of relativism, developed in the second and third section: the "metaphysical" construal, based on the idea that there is no single, absolute, universal morality, and the "semantic" construal, based on the idea that the truth value of moral claims is relative to a set of moral standards, or moral practices, or some other suitable parameter. The first section introduces the core relativist ideas in an informal way, and warns against possible misinterpretations.

GETTING A GRIP ON METAETHICAL RELATIVISM

If relativism were to be captured by a slogan, it would be the idea that what is (morally) good or bad is relative. Of course, as any slogan, it leaves many questions open. To *what* is it that moral goodness or badness is relative? Is *every* moral truth relative in this sense, or are only *some* moral truths relative? Assuming that moral truths are relative, say, to moral codes, are all of these on a par, or could it be that some moral codes are better than others? And so on. Different answers to these questions pave the way to often very different views, some of which may be less plausible than others. As a consequence, the term "relativism" as used in metaethics covers a variety of positions, making it sometimes difficult to see which positions are supported by which motivations, or which problems they face.

This chapter aims to help clarify the confusion by shifting the focus from the wide range of putative relativist views from the last century, discussed in numerous survey articles on moral and metaethical relativism, to a much narrower family of theoretical positions that have taken shape in this century, influenced by developments from formal philosophy of language, such as Kölbel (2002); Brogaard (2008, 2012); Beebe (2010); Schafer (2012); Egan (2012); or MacFarlane (2014).

I will distinguish two construals of metaethical relativism, discussed in the following two sections. On the *metaphysical* construal, relativism amounts to the idea that there is no single, absolute, universally valid morality, or set of moral values, or codes, or norms. The *semantic* construal relies on the idea that the truth value of a moral claim is relative to a special parameter, the nature of which may vary from one framework to another. Note that, on either construal, an important issue remains open, namely, *what* it is that moral questions are relative to. Possible answers include moral codes, norms, systems of values, sets of (possibly shared) beliefs and desires, and so on. In addition, *which* moral codes/norms/values/beliefs etc. are relevant to assessing the truth of a moral claim also allows for different answers. They could be those endorsed by some specific agent, or shared by a group of agents, or endorsed by a whole society, or they could be those of an "assessor" evaluating a given moral claim for its truth value.

While this important issue does ultimately require an answer (and the answer is far from obvious; see Shafer-Landau 2004), it is specific ethical theories that must provide the answer. The more general and abstract relativist frameworks discussed in metaethics need not commit to any definite answer, leaving the parameter under consideration open.

Turning back to the distinction between metaphysical vs. semantic relativism, even if the two often go hand in hand, the distinction remains important because many prominent relativist figures, including Gilbert Harman, David Wong, Carol Rovane, or David Velleman, have defended metaphysical relativism without committing themselves to any specific *semantics* for moral discourse. As regards the semantic construal, we will see that the idea that the truth of moral claims depends on some suitable parameter applies equally well to contextualist as to (genuinely) relativist views, the difference coming from how this dependence is further analyzed. Thus contextualists such as Dreier (1990) or Silk (2016) take it to be merely an instance of the more general phenomenon of context-dependence in language: a sentence containing a moral expression, such as "This action is (morally) good," can only be interpreted if one points to some specific set of moral norms, roughly in the same way in which the complex demonstrative 'this action' requires pointing to some specific action for the sentence to be interpreted. For a contextualist, then, the parameter at stake not only affects the truth value, but also the *content* that the moral sentence expresses in a given context. For a relativist, on the other hand, a given moral sentence (once its context-sensitive expressions have been resolved) always expresses the same content, regardless of the context in which it is uttered; however, it may still receive different truth values, provided that it is evaluated with respect to different sets of moral norms. Thus in a relativist semantics, the way in which the truth value of a moral claim depends on this special parameter is quite unlike the more familiar forms of context-dependence in language.

Now that the general structure of the chapter has been laid out, it will help to get some intuitive grip on the motivations that may push us toward relativism in the first place.

Consider a person—call her Saskia—who is facing a difficult moral dilemma. Saskia is in her fifth month of pregnancy, and has just found out that the fetus suffers from a serious deformation, and that if she carries the pregnancy, her child will be a severely damaged human being bound to suffer in horrible ways through their life. Saskia must choose between terminating the pregnancy or carrying on with it.

This is a fairly realistic case in which, for many people, neither horn of Saskia's dilemma will appear as the obviously right choice. At the same time, many other people will consider, without hesitation, that Saskia ought to keep the fetus (e.g., people who endorse certain Christian values and who think that abortion is not permissible under any circumstances). And conversely, many people will have no hesitation in claiming that Saskia ought to terminate the pregnancy (e.g., those who consider it to be morally wrong to give birth to an individual who is bound to suffer horribly). The aim of this example is to illustrate a situation such that from one perspective, the moral question whether Saskia ought to carry the pregnancy or not does not seem to have an objective, universally valid answer; from yet another perspective, in which a certain kind of moral value is taken for granted, the obvious answer is that she ought to keep the child; and from yet a third perspective, an equally obvious answer is that she ought to terminate the pregnancy.

We have presented the example as a case of moral *deliberation*, regarding what Saskia (morally) ought to do. But the case may also be presented as one of moral *evaluation*. Thus, someone coming from a contra-abortion perspective will judge that if Saskia terminates the pregnancy, that will be morally worse than if she doesn't, while someone else coming from a pro-abortion perspective will judge that her terminating the pregnancy is a morally better choice. The two individuals, who evaluate Saskia's action from such different moral backgrounds, are in a disagreement that does not seem to be resolvable on any objective, factual grounds. This kind of persistent and irresolvable moral disagreement suggests that there are moral issues whose answers crucially depend on the set of moral values and norms against which they are evaluated.

To be sure, those who believe in objective and absolute moral values will likely see this kind of case as merely a difficult and complex ethical case, one in which various considerations and norms pulling in different directions are at play, yet one for which at the end, there must be one and only one right answer. By contrast, a relativist has an elegant explanation of why it is so difficult to say what the right answer is: it is because, for them, there is no such thing as "the right answer" independently of some underlying set of moral values or norms. In sum, what emerges is the idea that there are moral issues that cannot be resolved unless we specify some set of moral norms or some other suitable factor that serves the same purpose, such as culture, educational background, the practices of a community, or what not. We have started with an example from everyday life, concerning an individual and the decision she faces, but the range of cases can be expanded to more general issues, such as the question whether abortion is morally permissible *tout court*, whether euthanasia, decapitation, torture, and the like, are permissible (and under which conditions), and similar ethical issues that different societies and cultures approach in different ways.

The fact that different cultures may endorse very different moral principles has often been seen as a strong motivation for relativism (Wong 1984, 2006; Prinz 2007; Velleman 2013; Rovane 2013). However, we must be cautious in what theoretical consequences we might want to draw from such cross-cultural divergences in morality, as they may easily lead to misinterpreting the view. Consider the case of female genital mutilation, a.k.a. female circumcision, a painful ritual practiced in certain countries that often brings about extremely harmful consequences to the women who undergo it. The fact that an entire society endorses a set of norms and practices that not only make genital mutilation acceptable but even required does not imply that such a set of norms constitutes indeed an admissible set of *moral* norms. In other words, the step from the claim that genital mutilation is accepted by a given society to the claim that there is a set of genuinely moral norms relative to which genital mutilation is permissible is a step that requires further argument. For instance, Kopelman (2011) takes genital mutilation as a case study to argue that certain relativist views are implausible. However, her argument targets only those relativist views that accept the abovementioned step.

We have stressed that it is unclear how precisely to define relativism and how to characterize the main tenets that the various relativist approaches have in common. But there are ideas that are often thought of as "relativist" such that it *is* clear that relativism is not committed to them. Such misconceptions are unfortunately widespread, in and outside philosophy, hence it is important to dispel them at the outset. For ease of exposition, let us provisorily take relativism to be the view that the truth of moral claims is relative to a set of moral norms, perhaps paired with the view that there isn't a single, absolute such set of moral norms. Then the view had better entail that *there are* moral claims that are true relative to one such set of norms and false relative to another. Unfortunately, moral relativism is often taken to entail something stronger, namely that for *every* moral claim, there is some set of norms relative to which the claim is true and some other set relative to which the claim is false. This view is then (and rightly so) dismissed as implausible, on the grounds that it is implausible to accept that, for example, there should be a set of moral norms with respect to which genocide is morally acceptable, or with respect to which slavery is right while altruism is wrong. Indeed, for most of us, it is even impossible to *imagine* what the world should be like for it to be the case that genocide is good, a phenomenon known as *imaginative resistance* (Gendler 2000).

However, relativism, as characterized above, only entails the weaker, not the stronger, view. This is not to say, though, there are no relativists who endorse the stronger view. Thus Brogaard notes "In a full-blown relativist framework, the sentence 'It is morally permissible to murder people' comes out true when uttered by the serial killer. To many people, this is highly unintuitive" (2012: 547), and then goes on to defend such a "full-blown" framework against the burden of intuitions. However, the important point is that moral relativism *is* compatible with the idea that there can be higher-order constraints on moralities, or on acceptable sets on moral norms, or moral codes. For instance, one such higher-order constraint may be that no set of moral norms should dictate incompatible actions: no set of norms should be such that, for some F, both "You ought to F" and "You ought not to F" are true relative to that set. Just as there may be higher-order constraints that rule out sets of norms that license incompatible deontic claims, there may be constraints that rule out sets of norms that license, for example, the claim that genocide is good, or that female circumcision is permissible. Of course, it remains an important question, perhaps ever the most pressing question for metaethical relativism, to say whether such constraints are absolute or are also relative (and if so, to what), and what it is that they ultimately rest upon.

RELATIVISM AS A PLURALITY OF MORALITIES: THE METAPHYSICAL CONSTRUAL

On the metaphysical construal, metaethical relativism is, roughly, the view that there is no single, absolute, universal morality. This contrasts with the semantic construal, on which it is the view that the truth value of a moral claim is relative to some suitable parameter: a morality, or a set of moral norms, standards, or whatever; to which parameters exactly is a debatable question, answered differently by different theories. To make the distinction more intuitive, compare it with relativism about motion. The question of whether the Eiffel Tower is moving can only be answered if we specify *relative to what*. Disregarding possible tectonic movements, the Eiffel Tower is not moving relative, say, to Palais Chaillot, and at the same time, it is moving relative to the Sun. On the metaphysical construal, relativism about motion is the (uncontroversial) thesis that there is no absolute motion, there is only motion relative to a frame of reference. On the semantic construal, it is the (equally uncontroversial) thesis that the truth value of a sentence such as "The Eiffel Tower is moving" depends on a hidden parameter, which specifies the frame of reference of the movement. Returning to the example of Saskia's dilemma, relativism, metaphysically understood, would say that there is no single, absolute, universally valid scale of comparison that makes one choice morally better than the other—and this would still hold even in the absence of a language that can express such things as "This choice is (morally) better than the other." Semantic relativism, on the other hand, would say that in order to ascribe a truth value to a statement such as "It would be morally better if Saskia terminated the pregnancy," or "She ought to terminate the pregnancy," we need to evaluate it with respect to a set of moral values (or some analogous parameter). Although the two construals are intimately linked, they are theoretically independent, as will be made clear in the next section. The remainder of this section aims to illustrate the metaphysical construal with two views: Gilbert Harman's view, considered a classic example of metaethical relativism, and a fairly different, dispositionalist view defended in Egan (2012), which builds on Lewis (1989). We see Harman as proposing a metaphysical rather than semantic version of relativism because his focus is on what morality and moral values are, rather than on how moral language works; in his own words, "Moral relativism is the theory that there is not a single true morality. It is not a theory of what people mean by their moral judgements" (2012: 13). Egan's proposal, on the other hand, lends itself equally well to a metaphysical as to a semantic interpretation. We have chosen to classify it under the metaphysical construal—even if that need not be what Egan himself would prefer—in order to demonstrate how relativism may encompass substantively different views.

***

Through a series of influential articles, united in Harman (2000), Harman became a key figure in the defense of metaethical relativism. There are two main motivations to his view. One is the observation that, in order to make a moral judgment, such as whether someone ought to act in a certain way, it is necessary to take into account the moral considerations and reasons to which this person is responsive. Harman further observes that when *we* are asked to make such moral judgments, we normally only do so if we take it for granted that the person whose moral deliberation we are judging is responsive to the same sort of reasons and considerations that we ourselves are responsive to. The second motivation relies on the idea that an agent's actions are normally motivated by their attitudes, and in particular, beliefs about what they ought to do. This motivation is tied to issues about cognitivism (see Matthew S. Bedke's chapter "Cognitivism and Non-Cognitivism") and internalism (see Darwall 1997), but for our purposes, we may simply retain the idea that the answer to the question whether an agent ought to act in a certain way or not depends on their motivating attitudes.

Harman's proposal, in a nutshell, combines the following two ideas. First, morality arises from a set of implicit, not necessarily conscious, agreements to which a group commits, and since the agreements reached by different groups may be different and evolve over time, there will be no single, absolute morality. Second, whether an agent ought to do something is relative to their considerations and, especially, their motivating attitudes, where these are shaped by the moral agreements that the agent has undertaken with respect to others. Finally, note that Harman's relativism is only a "first-order relativism," compatible with the possibility of objective higher-order constraints on moralities. He stresses: "I am not denying (nor am I asserting) that some moralities are 'objectively' better than others or that there are objective standards for assessing moralities" (1975: p. 4).

***

A very different kind of relativist proposal has recently emerged from the work of Andy Egan. His point of departure is the dispositionalist theory of value from Lewis (1989), to which he gives a relativist twist, relying once more on Lewis' ideas regarding attitude self-ascription (Lewis 1981). The general gist of dispositionalist theories may be captured by the following schema:

(Disp) x is (an instance of value) F iff
          x is disposed to elicit response R in subject(s) S in conditions C

As can be easily anticipated, there are many ways of defending dispositionalism, depending on what one does with the different variables in the schema: F, R, S, C. In particular, different ways of approaching the subject parameter S will differentiate between possible *invariantist* versions, *contextualist* versions, and *relativist* versions (one of which is Egan's). Egan's (2012) proposal concerns values in general, while Egan (2013) applies it to the case of personal taste, and a similar account (though not necessarily "relativist") is defended in Björnsson (ms.). But before we see how (Disp) may be developed into a form of relativism, let us illustrate the dispositionalist idea with an example of moral value. Let's take F to stand for "morally wrong" (hence a *negative* moral value). One way of instantiating (Disp) would be to say that Saskia's choosing to give birth to a severely damaged child who is bound to suffer horribly is morally wrong if, in normal conditions, it is likely to elicit strong moral disapproval from people. The conditions parameter C is important because it allows for different moral assessments about individuals who fully and knowingly control their actions vs. individuals who act under hypnosis, drug influence, or are forced to act as they do.

We have spoken in terms of "disapproval from people," but one might ask, *which people*? A view that says "people *in general*" would qualify as an invariantist version of dispositionalism. On the other hand, if we allow for a greater variability regarding who the relevant subjects might be, we get various forms of contextualism and relativism. One option is to say that the people at stake are *us* (which is Lewis' own take). This already leads to a form of relativity. For *we* may judge Saskia's action to be morally wrong (because it elicits strong disapproval in us) while others may judge her action *not* to be morally wrong (because it actually elicits approval in them). Whether a view along these lines is contextualist or genuinely relativist will depend on further assumptions. Anticipating a distinction introduced in the next section, let us say that a view is "contextualist" if the *content* of assertions and beliefs involving the moral value at stake depends on who S is, and "relativist" if only the *truth* of such assertions or beliefs, but not their content, depends on S. Thus on a possible contextualist interpretation of our example, when different people say "Saskia did something morally bad," they say different things: if Inma utters the sentence, she expresses the proposition that Saskia's action elicits disapproval in her kin; if Tarek utters it, he expresses the proposition that it elicits disapproval in *his* kin. On a possible relativist interpretation, Inma and Tarek say the same thing; however, what they say is not a classical proposition, since in order to deliver a truth value, it needs to be evaluated at a subject or a group of subjects. On Egan's interpretation (following Lewis), the content shared by Tarek and Inma's assertions—and beliefs—is the property of being a subject such that Saskia's action is disposed to elicit disapproval in you. Adapting the proposal from Lewis (1981), Egan suggests that to believe this kind of content is to self-ascribe the property at stake.

RELATIVISM AS A VARIABILITY IN TRUTH VALUE: THE SEMANTIC CONSTRUAL

On its semantic construal, metaethical relativism builds on the idea that the truth value of moral claims is relative to a special parameter, which, depending on the theory, may be a set of moral norms, codes, standards or considerations, proper to an agent or shared by a group, society, culture, or what not. For simplicity, let us call it the morality parameter. Because there are many ways in which truth value may depend on such a parameter, there will be many ways in which metaethical relativism may be developed into a semantic theory of moral language. One line of development leads to what is nowadays more accurately called "metaethical contextualism," a view defended, e.g., in Dreier (1990) and discussed at length in Alex Silk's chapter "Metaethical Contextualism." Other, more recent lines of development are cast within novel semantic frameworks and constitute a field of research in bloom. What exactly are the fine-grained differences between the various views, and which of them deserve to be called "relativist," are issues that are not peculiar to metaethics, but have received some interest in philosophy of language (Kölbel 2004; Stojanovic 2008; López de Sa 2011), metaphysics (Einheuser 2008), and epistemology (Kompa 2012). Although the question is to a certain extent terminological, there is a substantive aspect to it. For to pin down the respects in which relativism departs from rival views is to identify some of the important issues in metaethics, and to be able to clearly formulate those issues is to make progress in addressing them.

In discussing Egan's view in the previous section, we anticipated one way of marking the distinction between contextualism and relativism, namely, in terms of what gets contributed to the content. Another way to mark the distinction is in terms of what determines which morality is relevant to the truth value of a given moral claim. Views that insist that the context of utterance determines this would qualify as "contextualist," while those that deny it (a possible alternative being that the so-called context of assessment does it) would qualify as "relativist." In this section, we will look more closely at the two distinctions and will discuss the ways in which the truth value of a moral claim may be sensitive to various parameters. But before we do that, it may help to say a few words about the relationship between the metaphysical and the semantic characterization of relativism.

Understood as a claim that there is not a single, universally valid morality, relativism is a view that says nothing about moral language—indeed, it is a view that would make perfect sense even if we spoke a language that had no vocabulary and no other linguistic devices to describe actions as right or wrong, or to express moral imperatives such as "Thou shalt not kill." On this metaphysical construal, relativism is even compatible with views according to which moral claims are not even truth-value apt. Conversely, though less obviously, the semantic construal of relativism does not entail commitment to the metaphysical construal either. There may be reasons to develop a semantics for terms such as 'good,' 'wrong,' or 'ought' in which the truth value of any claim involving such a term is sensitive to the morality parameter, and at the same time accept the idea that for any given moral claim, there *is* one and only one correct value for this parameter, or a "single, true morality." To be sure, most of those who are inclined to defend semantic relativism will be inclined to endorse metaphysical relativism as well. However, theoretically, the two are independent. To make this clear, it may help to draw an analogy with time. It is customary to relativize truth value to times (Prior 1957; Kaplan 1977, Higginbotham 1993). For instance, "There has been life on Mars" may be seen as semantically expressing a temporal proposition that is true if evaluated at a time t_1 such that there was an earlier time t_1' at which it was true that there is life on Mars, and false when evaluated at a time t_2 such that there was no such corresponding t_2'. Yet, it is plausible to accept that, at any given time, there is one and only one time value at which it is correct to evaluate such a temporal proposition for its truth value; namely, now. Thus even if a thousand years from now it will be true that there has been life on Mars, this does not make the year 3016 an eligible time at which we could *now* evaluate the proposition that there has been life on Mars for its truth value.

***

Let us now turn to some preliminaries that will help us understand what a relativist semantics for a moral language might look like.

(i) <u>Deontic vs. Evaluative.</u> The moral vocabulary of English and most Indo-European languages typically includes, on the one hand, modal auxiliaries such as 'ought,' 'must,' and 'may,' which, among others, allow for a *deontic* reading, and, on the other hand, *evaluative* adjectives such as 'good,' 'bad,' 'evil,' and so on. This is only a rough classification, since there are adjectives, such as 'permissible,' which are taken to belong to the deontic category (Tappolet 2013). What distinguishes evaluative terms from the rest remains an open issue. Thus, for example, it can be debated whether "thick terms" such as 'courageous' belong among evaluative adjectives (see Debbie Roberts' chapter "Thick Concepts"). For the sake of simplicity, we will focus on basic evaluative terms and will leave aside the possible relativist proposals for deontic modals and for 'ought' (see Jennifer Carr's chapter "Deontic Modals"). For a relativist semantics applied to 'ought', see Kolodny and MacFarlane (2010) and MacFarlane (2014: 285–298) (although they do not explicitly distinguish the practical reading of 'ought' from a properly deontic reading).

(ii) <u>Dimensions of goodness</u>. The adjective 'good' in English (and its equivalent in other languages) is an all-purpose evaluative adjective. We speak of good weather, good cars, good meals, good books, none of which has anything to do with morality. What happens when we say that a person is good? Out of the context, it might mean almost anything: that she is a good carpenter, good company, a good mother, a good person (Geach 1956; Thomson 2008). Some of these interpretations may imply moral goodness, others not. Even when we restrict the interpretation to "a (morally) good person," there can still be implicit dimensions that, depending on the context, may be required for the attribution of goodness to hold. Thus a person may be (morally) good as regards treating others with respect, but not be so as regards helping out those who are in need. Similarly for actions. Which dimensions are required for being considered as good *tout court* is a context-sensitive matter. This form of variability in the truth value of statements involving 'good', even when narrowed down to its moral interpretation, is not yet a hallmark of truth relativity. Thus deciding which dimensions need to hold for the predicate 'good' to be correctly applied may be even seen as a metalinguistic issue, as in Plunkett and Sundell (2013).

(iii) <u>Threshold sensitivity</u>. Evaluative adjectives are typically gradable: some person may be better than some other; some actions may be very bad; others, scarcely bad. Gradability means that a property comes in degrees. When a statement contains a gradable adjective, to evaluate it for a truth value, first, we need to fix a scale, and second, a threshold on the scale (Kennedy & McNally 2005). Thus consider a case in which Lei makes a $5 donation to a charity, and suppose that we have determined the relevant scale of goodness. Then "Lei's action is good" may still have different truth values in different contexts. In a context in which hardly anyone made any donation at all, the threshold for a donation counting as a good action will be low, and the statement will be true. But in a context in which everyone made a $500 donation, and Lei is rich enough to do the same, the threshold will be higher and the statement false. Again, this variability in truth value does not yet commit to relativism.

An interesting feature about threshold sensitivity is that people may agree on how things stand with respect to each other on the scale, say, of moral goodness, but disagree on whether either of them is bad. Thus Tarek and Inma may agree that, in Saskia's case, carrying a pregnancy is a morally worse choice than terminating it. But while Tarek considers that if Saskia carried the pregnancy, she would do something morally bad, Inma, who is less stringent, may consider that Saskia's action would not yet reach the threshold for it to be considered morally bad.

(iv) As a last preliminary, let us briefly introduce some notions from the framework put forward in Kaplan (1977/1989) and widely adopted nowadays, which serves as a starting point for both ways of distinguishing relativism from contextualism that we will discuss below. The Kaplanian framework aims to handle context-dependence, in particular as it arises with indexicals—words such as 'I', 'here', 'now', and demonstratives 'this' and 'that'. A sentence such as "I live here" can be ascribed two kinds of meaning. One kind is that which does not vary from one context to another, and can be roughly paraphrased as "The speaker lives at the location where the utterance is taking place." The other kind of meaning—what Kaplan calls *content*—depends on who utters the sentence and where. Thus if Inma utters it in Paris, the content expressed by the utterance is that Inma lives in Paris, whereas if Tarek utters it in Tbilisi, the content will be that Tarek lives in Tbilisi. Furthermore, in order to determine whether the utterance is true or false, what we need is to *evaluate* this content at what Kaplan calls a circumstance of evaluation, which includes a possible world parameter and a time parameter. Thus suppose that Inma lived in Paris until 2009 and in Tbilisi from then on; however, had she got a job in Paris that year, she would still be living there. Then the content that she expresses by saying, in 2016 in Paris, "I live here," is false as evaluated with respect to that context, making her utterance false. Yet the same content, as evaluated at the actual world but, say, in the year 2008, is true; and so it will be if evaluated in the year 2016 and at the counterfactual world in which, in 2009, Inma got a job in Paris.

***

With (ii) and (iii), we have seen how the truth value of a moral claim may depend on parameters such as scales and thresholds. This kind of variability in truth value is a widespread feature of natural language, hence hardly controversial at all. More controversial is truth-value dependence on the morality parameter. The disagreement between contextualism and relativism is not about the nature of the morality parameter, but rather on the question of where it figures in semantics and how it gets to be assigned a value. What emerges from the recent literature on the contextualism-relativism debate is that there are (at least) two important lines of divide to be made, resulting in (at least) three views. Since both lines of divide were originally aimed at distinguishing "contextualism" from "relativism," the view that falls on the "relativist" side by one divide but on the "contextualist" side by the other is, somewhat confusingly, at times referred to as "moderate relativism" and at others, "nonindexical contextualism." The other two main views are "indexical contextualism" and "assessment relativism." Recall that the views under consideration all share the assumption that the truth value of a moral claim depends on the morality parameter. Here is, then, how this class of views may be partitioned:

(a) <u>Does the value assigned to the morality parameter figure in the content?</u>

> The views that answer 'yes' typically take moral terms to behave like covert indexicals, hence the label *indexical contextualism*. The views that answer 'no' hold that the morality parameter is merely needed to evaluate the content for a truth value. Let us appeal once again to the analogy with time. Consider the sentence "A man has landed on the Moon." On a contextualist approach to time-sensitivity, if uttered on the first of January 2016, the sentence expresses the content equivalent to "Prior to 01/01/2016, a man landed on the Moon." On a relativist approach, it expresses a content that does not specify the time prior to which a man is said to have landed on the Moon. Thus the content is true if evaluated at the present time, but false if evaluated, say, in the year 1926. Similarly, on a contextualist view, "Euthanasia is morally wrong" will express different contents if uttered in contexts that differ with respect to morality. On a relativist view, on the other hand, it will express the same content regardless of who utters it or in which context, but the content that it expresses comes out true when

evaluated at a morality that bans euthanasia, but false when evaluated at a morality that approves of euthanasia.

(b) Does the context of utterance supply the value for the morality parameter?

First of all, let us note that indexical contextualism answers 'yes'. As Alex Silk's chapter "Metaethical Contextualism" puts it, "the distinctive claim of contextualism is that a specific body of norms *from the context of utterance* figures in the conventional content of normative uses of language" (my italics). But it is possible to answer 'yes' to this question while answering 'no' to (a). The resulting view, "moderate relativism," corresponds to Kaplan's view regarding the time and world parameters, as applied to the morality parameter. In metaethics, possible defenders of this view are Kölbel (2002) and Brogaard (2008, 2012), but given that neither of them addresses the question explicitly, their views could be interpreted either way.

To answer 'no' to the question is, again, compatible with several views. The most popular one, "assessment relativism," comes from the work of John MacFarlane, which extends over several papers and culminates in MacFarlane (2014). Although MacFarlane himself has never laid out the view for evaluative moral terms, other authors have outlined it (Beebe 2010, Schafer 2012). MacFarlane makes a non-trivial amendment to the Kaplanian framework. He posits two context parameters: in addition to the context of utterance (CU), he introduces a context of assessment (CA). Applying MacFarlane"s framework to the moral case, we get the following picture. Just as in a Kaplanian framework, CU has two roles: first, to provide values for the interpretation of indexicals (which then figure in the content), and second, to provide values for the parameters of world and time, which do not figure in the content but for which the content is evaluated for a truth value. CA, on the other hand, provides values for various other parameters, such as standards of taste, standards of knowledge, and, crucially, moral standards.

One driving motivation for introducing a context of assessment, in addition to the context of utterance, is that one and the same sentence, as uttered in one and the same context, may still have different truth values, if assessed from morally divergent points of view. Thus even if "Euthanasia is wrong" is uttered in a society whose moral norms prohibit euthanasia, a person from a euthanasia-approving society may still assess that very utterance, and (arguably) rationally so, as being false.

Assessment relativism is not the only alternative to the idea that the context of utterance supplies the value to the morality parameter. A reason for answering 'no' to the question in (b) is that we may want to reject the assumption that this value is supplied in some unique way, fully specified by principles built into the semantic theory. Stojanovic (2012) argues that there are no good theoretical or empirical motivations for positing such rigid principles, not only regarding the morality parameter (or other novel parameters, such as standards of taste) but even regarding the traditional parameters of world and time. The resulting view is what we might call *flexible* relativism. From the point of view of compositional semantics, flexible relativism shares the features of the framework that moderate relativism and assessment relativism share.[1] The difference is that when it comes to deciding what truth value a given sentence, as uttered on a given occasion, has, the decision will depend on a variety of pragmatic and possibly other factors (2012: 631–33). Although flexible relativism may be argued to give empirically more accurate predictions, the question of how to choose between moderate relativism, assessment relativism, and flexible relativism ultimately depends on certain general assumptions about the relationship between semantics and truth-value assignment.

***

By way of conclusion, in the past four decades, relativism has gained some ground. From being a position all too easily discarded as implausible, it has developed into a family of views that deserve to be taken seriously. It is important to remember that relativism does not entail that, for *every* moral claim, there is some set of admissible moral norms that makes the claim true. It only entails the that *there are* moral claims whose truth value cannot be decided once and for all, irrespective of some set of moral norms, or codes, or some other suitable morality parameter on which the truth value depends. Moral relativism is thus compatible with the idea that there can be higher-order constraints on the values that this morality parameter may take. Not any old set of norms may constitute a genuine set of moral norms, and some moralities may be better than others. How such higher-order questions are to be dealt with, whether they allow for objective answers, or whether moralities may be ranked with respect to each other only relative to something else, remain important issues for contemporary metaethical relativism. Equally important and controversial is the issue of what precisely the nature of the morality parameter is: Is it a set of norms? A set of (possibly shared) beliefs? An agreement to which we implicitly commit? A set of dispositions? Fortunately, it is not necessary to settle that delicate issue in order to approach relativism from a more general metaethical perspective.

Parallel to its developments in metaethics, relativism has also made its way into the study of natural language, leading to more and more sophisticated semantic frameworks that are meant to model a wide range of constructions: epistemic modals, knowledge ascriptions, predicates of personal taste, and so on. Those recent developments in philosophy of language and semantics have a double impact on metaethical relativism. One is that some fine-grained distinctions regarding the different ways in which the truth value of moral claims may depend on moral norms and similar factors have led to a myriad of related but distinct positions, many of which are now preferably called "contextualist" rather than "relativist." Secondly, there is a certain pressure to look more carefully at the linguistic behavior of the expressions that form our moral vocabulary; these do not constitute a unified lexical category, but include modal auxiliaries ('may,' 'ought'), both gradable and non-gradable adjectives ('good,' 'evil'; 'wrong,' 'permissible'), but also certain adverbs, verbs, or nouns, which have hardly been studied in linguistics. There is also some pressure, when it comes to analyzing moral discourse and moral intuitions, to gather the empirical data with respect to which the predictions of a semantic theory may be tested. A growing interest in experimental research (see Chandra Sripada's chapter "Experimental Philosophy and Moral Theory") offers good prospects of providing such data. Nevertheless, despite being one of the oldest philosophical doctrines, metaethical relativism has barely begun to mark milestones on its semantic agenda.

NOTE

1. Note that the context of assessment only intervenes at a stage at which a sentence is evaluated for a truth value, which comes after the compositional derivation of its truth conditions. MacFarlane, after laying

out the formal semantics of his relativist framework, observes: "up to this point, we have not needed to mention contexts of assessment. That is because, in this semantics, contexts of assessment are not locally relevant. Contexts of assessment are needed only in the next phase, the definition of truth relative to a context of use and context of assessment in terms of truth at a context of use and index. To distinguish this phase from the definition of truth at a context of use and index, we call it the postsemantics" (2014: 151). In this respect, Schafer's claim that "[someone who endorses Moral Assessor Relativism] must be understood to be making a claim about (…) the sense of 'truth' with which one works when doing compositional semantics" (2012: 607) may be somewhat misleading.

ACKNOWLEDGMENTS

I would like to thank David Plunkett and Tristram McPherson for their encouragements, patience, and comments, and Lea Schroeder for helpful suggestions. I acknowledge institutional support from the following grants: MINECO FFI2016-80636-P, ANR-10-LABX-0087 IEC, and ANR-10-IDEX-0001-02 PSL.

RELATED TOPICS

Chapter 5, "Metaethical Expressivism;" Chapter 6, "Metaethical Contextualism;" Chapter 12, "Deontic Modals;" Chapter 13, "Thick Concepts;" Chapter 15, "Hybrid Accounts of Ethical Thought and Talk;" Chapter 17, "The Significance of Ethical Disagreement for Theories of Ethical Thought and Talk;" Chapter 18, "Cognitivism and Non-Cognitivism;" Chapter 33, "Metasemantics and Metaethics;" Chapter 39, "Experimental Philosophy and Moral Theory."

REFERENCES

Beebe, James (2010). Moral Relativism in Context. *Noûs* 44 (4): 691–724.

Björnsson, Gunnar (ms.) Disagreement in Attitude and Discourse. Paper presented at the LOGOS Colloquium, Fall 2015.

Brogaard, Berit (2008). Moral Contextualism and Moral Relativism. *Philosophical Quarterly* 58 (232): 385–409.

Brogaard, Berit (2012). Moral Relativism and Moral Expressivism. *Southern Journal of Philosophy* 50 (4): 538–556.

Darwall, Stephen (1997). Reasons, Motives, and the Demands of Morality: An Introduction. In Darwall, Stephen, Gibbard, Alan, and Railton, Peter (eds.) *Moral Discourse and Practice: Some Philosophical Approaches*. Oxford: Oxford University Press: 305–312.

Dreier, James (1990). Internalism and Speaker Relativism. *Ethics* 101 (1): 6–26.

Egan, Andy (2012). Relativist Dispositional Theories of Value. *Southern Journal of Philosophy* 50 (4): 557–582.

Egan, Andy (2013). There is Something Funny about Comedy: A Case-Study in Faultless Disagreement. *Erkenntnis* [online]. DOI 10.1007/s10670-013-9446-3.

Einheuser, Iris (2008). Three Forms of Truth-Relativism. In García-Carpintero, Manuel, and Kölbel, Max (eds.) *Relative Truth*. Oxford: Oxford University Press: 187–206.

Geach, Peter (1956). Good and Evil. *Analysis* 17 (2): 33–42.

Gendler, Tamar Szabo (2000). The Puzzle of Imaginative Resistance. *Journal of Philosophy* 97: 55–81.

Harman, Gilbert (1975). Moral Relativism Defended. *Philosophical Review* 84 (1): 3–22.

Harman, Gilbert (2000). *Explaining Value and Other Essays in Moral Philosophy*. Oxford: Oxford University Press.

Harman, Gilbert (2012). Moral Relativism Explained. *Problems of Goodness. New Essays in Metaethics* [online] June 19. Available at: http://philpapers.org/rec/HARMRE.

Higginbotham, James (2009). *Tense, Aspect, and Indexicality*. Oxford: Oxford University Press.

Kaplan, David (1977). Demonstratives. In Almog, Joseph, Perry, John, and Wettstein, Howard (eds.) *Themes from Kaplan*. Oxford: Oxford University Press (1989): 481–563.

Kennedy, Christopher and McNally, Louise (2005). Scale Structure, Degree Modification, and the Semantics of Gradable Predicates. *Language* 81, 345–381.

Kölbel, Max (2002). *Truth without Objectivity*. London: Routledge.

Kölbel, Max (2004). Indexical Relativism vs. Genuine Relativism. *International Journal of Philosophical Studies* 12: 297–313.

Kolodny, Niko and MacFarlane, John (2010). Ifs and Oughts. *Journal of Philosophy* 107 (3): 115–143.

Kompa, Nikola (2012). Nonindexical Contextualism—An Explication and Defence. In Tolksdorf, Stefan (ed.) *Conceptions of Knowledge*. Berlin: De Gruyter.

Kopelman, Loretta (2011). Female Circumcision/Genital Mutilation and Ethical Relativism. *Second Opinion* 20 (2): 55.

Lewis, David (1981). Attitudes *De Se* and *De Dicto. The Philosophical Review* 88: 513–543.

Lewis, David (1989). Dispositional Theories of Value. *Proceedings of the Aristotelian Society* 63: 113–137.

López de Sa, Dan (2011). The Many Relativisms: Index, Content and Beyond. In Hales, Stephen (ed.) *A Companion to Relativism*. Hoboken, NJ: Wiley-Blackwell: 102–117.

MacFarlane, John (2014). *Assessment-Sensitivity: Relative Truth and Its Applications*. Oxford: Oxford University Press.

Plunkett, David and Sundell, Timothy (2013). Disagreement and the Semantics of Normative and Evaluative Terms. *Philosophers' Imprint* 13: 1–37.

Prinz, Jesse (2007). *The Emotional Construction of Morals*. Oxford: Oxford University Press.

Prior, Arthur (1957). *Time and Modality*. Oxford: Clarendon.

Rovane, Carol (2013). *The Metaphysics and Ethics of Relativism*. Harvard: Harvard University Press.

Schafer, Karl (2012). Assessor Relativism and the Problem of Moral Disagreement. *Southern Journal of Philosophy* 50 (4): 602–620.

Schafer-Landau, Russ (2004). *Whatever Happened to Good and Evil*. Oxford: Oxford University Press.

Silk, Alex (2016). *Discourse Contextualism: A Framework For Contextualist Semantics and Pragmatics*. Oxford: Oxford University Press.

Stojanovic, Isidora (2008). The Scope and the Subtleties of the Contextualism–Literalism–Relativism Debate. *Language and Linguistics Compass* 2 (6): 1171–1188.

Stojanovic, Isidora (2012). On Value-Attributions: Semantics and Beyond. *Southern Journal of Philosophy* 50 (4): 621–638.

Tappolet, Christine (2013). Evaluative vs. Deontic Concepts. *The International Encyclopedia of Ethics*. Hoboken: Wiley-Blackwell.

Thomson, Judith Jarvis (2008). *Normativity*. Chicago: Open Court.

Velleman, David (2013). *Foundations for Moral Relativism*. Cambridge: Open Book Publishers.

Wong, David (1984). *Moral Relativity*. Berkeley: University of California Press.

Wong, David (2006). *Natural Moralities: A Defense of Pluralistic Relativism*. Oxford: Oxford University Press.

FURTHER READING

Boghossian, Paul (2006). What Is Relativism? In Greenough, Patrick, and Lynch, Michael (eds.) *Truth and Realism*. Oxford: Oxford University Press, 13–37.

Dreier, James (2007). Moral Relativism and Moral Nihilism. In Copp, David (ed.) *The Oxford Handbook of Ethical Theory*. Oxford: Oxford University Press, 240–264.

Fricker, Miranda (2013). Styles of Moral Relativism: A Critical Family Tree. In Crisp, Roger (ed.) *The Oxford Handbook of the History of Ethics*. Oxford: Oxford University Press.

Gowans, Chris (2015). Moral Relativism. In Zalta, Edward N. (ed.) *The Stanford Encyclopedia of Philosophy* (Fall 2015 edition).

Kölbel, Max (2015). Moral Relativism. In Crane, Tim (ed.) *Routledge Encyclopedia of Philosophy*. London: Routledge.

Moser, Paul & Carson, Thomas (eds.) (2001). *Moral Relativism: A Reader*. Oxford: Oxford University Press.

Rachels, James (1986). The Challenge of Cultural Relativism. In Rachels, James (ed.) *The Elements of Moral Philosophy*. New York: McGraw-Hill Education, 20–36.

Wong, David (2001). Moral Relativism, Revised Version. In Becker, Lawrence C., and Becker, Charlotte B. (eds.) *Encyclopedia of Ethics*. London: Routledge, 1162–1164.

II

Central Problems and Strategies
in Metaethics

8

Realism and Objectivity

Billy Dunaway

'Realism' and 'objectivity' are philosophers' terms of art with no strict synonyms in ordinary English. This has not prevented philosophers from using these terms with confidence approaching that of a native speaker. Most will not, for instance, hesitate to label a Subjectivist view of morality (on which an act is wrong for a subject just in case the subject herself disapproves of performing the act) as an irrealist view. And they will likely add that morality is not an objective matter according to the Subjectivist. Similarly, they will agree over judgments about Instrumentalism in science, and Idealism about the material world. But broad agreement over simple cases does not by itself select a single meaning for a term of art, and in fact, philosophers disagree significantly over the application of these terms to anything beyond simple cases, offering wildly divergent general accounts of the meaning of these terms.

It is probably a mistake to ask about *the* meanings these terms. One is free to use one's words as one wishes, and when terms of art are at issue, it is hard to claim that a philosopher has misused or mischaracterized a term. The aim of this entry is not therefore to legislate usage of the terms 'realism' and 'objectivity'. Rather, there are some uses of these terms on which they *seem* to mark out very interesting and worthwhile distinctions between types of philosophical views on a topic. I will outline some very simple and general structural features that would characterize these interesting uses of each term. Then, we can ask whether there actually are any very natural kinds that play these roles—that is, if there are any non-gerrymandered and theoretically interesting properties that the use of 'realism' and 'objectivity' could plausibly be *about*. It is a live possibility that some ways of using of these terms of art do not lock onto anything interesting in the world.

One clarificatory point should be noted at the outset. Some philosophers use 'realism' and 'objectivity' as if they were interchangeable synonyms: they say that a view is realist about its domain if and only if it makes its domain out to be fully objective. I will not follow this usage here. Instead, I will primarily be investigating one use of 'realism' on which it picks out a kind (if it picks out anything at all) that is typically of interest to metaphysicians. And I will work with uses of 'objectivity' that mark an epistemic notion, to be characterized in terms of paradigmatic epistemic properties like knowledge, justification, and the like. A metaphysical notion of realism and an epistemic conception of objectivity will not be equivalent.

REALISM: MOTIVATING EXAMPLES AND STRUCTURAL FEATURES

Here is a standard distinction in ethics made with the word 'realism': a Subjectivist, who holds that ethical statements are reports about an agent's psychological state, is not a realist about ethics. By way of contrast, a Non-Naturalist, who holds that wrongness is an irreducible and *sui generis* component of reality, is a realist.

'Realism' is applied to other domains to make the same kinds of distinctions. An Instrumentalist philosopher of science—who holds that talk about quarks, spin, and other "unobservables" to be shorthand for talk about how measuring instruments would respond in various circumstances—is not a realist. Meanwhile, someone who takes scientists' talk of unobservables at face value (much like we treat talk of chairs, people, and shapes) is a realist. Similarly, a Behaviorist about mental states—who takes pain and other mental states to be nothing more than complex dispositions to behave in various circumstances—is not a realist about mental states. But an Identity Theorist, who identifies pain and other mental states with particular neurophysiological states, is a realist.

These are just a few examples that pattern with a fairly common use of the word 'realism'. As a first pass, it would seem to mark a significant distinction in the alleged metaphysical status of the relevant domains: the Subjectivist has a very different view of the metaphysics of wrongness from the Non-Naturalist. Realist and Instrumentalist views of quarks disagree dramatically over the place of quarks in the world. The nature of pain is quite different in an irrealist Behaviorist understanding than it is in the Identity Theory.

From these examples, we can read off a few additional structural features that would be satisfied by any reasonably natural, non-gerrymandered referent for 'realism'.

First, it must be compatible with there being substantive truths in non-realist domains. Our irrealists do not necessarily deny that it is true that people sometimes do wrong actions, that quarks have spin, or that sharp needles can cause pain. They are irrealists in virtue of what they say the relevant truths consist of. They need not go so far as to deny that there are any truths at all in the domains in question.

Second, the realism/irrealism distinction is domain-independent: wrongness, unobservables from physical science, and mental states are all distinct kinds of things. But it is quite natural to think that, when we apply 'realism' and 'irrealism' in each area, we are using the terms with identical meanings in each case. The difference between realism and irrealism is the same, regardless of whether the issue is ethics, scientific unobservables, mental states, or something else.

Finally, realism is compatible with some reductions of the domain in question. An Identity Theorist offers a reductive view about mental states, but comes out as a realist. The Behaviorist also reduces mental states—but her reduction base is different, and this makes her view an irrealist one. This point is reinforced by focusing on the view of modality from David Lewis (1986), which reduces modal facts to facts about what occurs in maximal spatiotemporally separate regions. While many find the reduction hard to believe owing to its associated ontology, it is nonetheless natural to read Lewis as a realist about modality.

We can give these structural features labels for convenience:

Truth Compatibility: Irrealism about a domain D is compatible with the existence of substantive truths about D.

Domain Neutrality: For any domain D, 'realism' and 'irrealism' can apply nontrivially and univocally to D.

Reduction Compatibility: For some domains D, some reductive views are irrealist about D while other reductive views about D are realist.

Any property that does not have these three features will either be too gerrymandered to be an interesting property that is at issue in debates over a metaphysical conception of realism, or else will be too distant from common uses of the term 'realism' to plausibly be what philosophers are talking about. Below, I will outline three prominent and historically important metaphysical characterizations of realism. All of them fail to capture the structural features outlined here.

Realism: Existence

One way of using the word 'real' treats it as interchangeable with 'exists'. Someone might say that Santa Claus isn't real, and by this, simply mean that Santa Claus doesn't exist. Some philosophers have been impressed by this connection with existence, and have reached the conclusion that realism about a domain *just is* the view that the domain exists. Views of this kind assimilate all irrealist views to the kind of irrealism found in J. L. Mackie's "moral scepticism" or "error theory," which Mackie describes as follows:

> [W]hat I have called moral scepticism is a negative doctrine, not a positive one: it says what there isn't, not what there is. It says that there do not exist entities or relations of a certain kind, objective values or requirements, which many people have believed to exist.
>
> (1977: 17)

This suggests a characterization of realism about a domain D as equivalent to the following claim:

Existence: Discourse about D involves terms that refer to objects and properties that exist.

Thus we can read Mackie as claiming that moral discourse uses terms like 'wrong', but that wrongness doesn't exist, and hence that the central terms of moral discourse don't refer to anything. Mackie's error theory comes out as irrealist in the sense of **Existence**.

But **Existence** as a characterization of realism won't capture the **Truth Compatibility** feature. Mackie's error theory is an extreme version of irrealism; more modest versions that are compatible with **Existence** are possible. For instance, Subjectivism is compatible with it being true that telling lies is wrong. Subjectivism says that what it is for telling lies to be wrong is that telling lies is disapproved of. Since it is true that telling lies is disapproved of, it is true that telling lies is wrong. From this, it is trivial to infer that telling lies has the *property* of wrongness, and so that wrongness exists. The Subjectivist, though an irrealist, accepts **Existence**.

Realism: Mind-independence

Other philosophers start with a range of examples of irrealism which imply that the domain in question is mind-dependent. Subjectivism, which makes wrongness dependent on an agent's attitudes of disapproval, is an irrealist view. So is Instrumentalism about unobservables, where the notion of measurement which is essential to the view is plausibly to be cashed out partly in mental terms. These examples motivate a "mind-independence" condition in realism. For instance, in his chapter "What Is Realism?," Michael Devitt says that this condition for realism is satisfied by something "if it exists and has its nature whatever we believe, think, or can discover: it is independent of the cognitive activities of the mind" (Devitt 1991: 15). Realism about a domain *D*, on this characterization, is true if the following holds: .

Mind-independence: The objects and properties in *D* do not essentially depend on mental objects and properties.

In ethics, this characterization of realism can be found in Sharon Street (2006), among other places.

Mind-independence as a characterization of realism, however, is incompatible with **Domain Neutrality**. This can be seen when we apply **Mind-independence** to realism about the mind itself. Dependence is standardly taken to be an *irreflexive* relation: nothing depends on itself. But then, any view about the mental will entail that it is not dependent on mental states, and hence that it does not satisfy **Mind-independence**. Thus any view of the mental will come out as realist, and realism about the mental will be trivial, contrary to **Domain Neutrality**. Consider, by way of illustration, the intuitively irrealist Behaviorist view of pain. According to Behaviorism, that one is in pain depends on one's exhibiting pain behaviors. But behaviors are not mental entities, and so according to **Mind-independence**, Behaviorism is a realist view of pain.

Realism: Absolute fundamentality

Another approach to realism uses a notion that is central to much recent metaphysics; roughly, this is the notion of the *fundamental*. The fundamental is, roughly, that which doesn't depend on, or exist in virtue of, anything else. This is motivated by the thought that if something is metaphysically fundamental, then it is *most* real in the metaphysical sense. (For a more detailed discussion of the relationship between dependence and fundamentality, see Barnes 2012.) Kit Fine (2001) gives a seminal discussion of this approach to realism, which is adapted to a characterization in the following passage by Ralph Wedgwood:

> What exactly is realism? Following Kit Fine (2001) I shall suppose that a realist about the normative is a theorist who says that there are normative facts or truths—such as the fact that certain things ought to be the case, or that it is not

the case that certain things ought to be the case—and that at least some of these normative facts are part of reality itself.

The notion of *reality* invoked here is a notion that has its home within a certain sort of metaphysical project—namely, the project of giving a metaphysical account or explanation of everything that is the case in terms of what is real [...] [I]f certain normative facts are real, then [...] these normative facts, properties or relations may also form part of the fundamental account or explanation of certain things that are the case.

(2007: 1–2)

This suggests the claim that realism about a domain *D* is equivalent to the following:

Absolute Fundamentality *D* is absolutely fundamental.

Taking **Absolute Fundamentally** to characterize realism has some advantages. For starters, it yields a notion that is compatible with **Truth Compatibility** and **Domain Neutrality**. There can be truths about both fundamental and non-fundamental domains, and so irrealism is compatible with substantive truths. And it is coherent to adopt views on which the mental is absolutely fundamental (e.g., Cartesian Dualism) and views on which it is not. So we need not carve out special exemptions for the mental when deploying the term 'realism'.

However, **Absolute Fundamentality** is not consistent with REDUCTION COMPATIBILITY. Identity Theory is a realist view of the mental, but it is also reductivist as it identifies mental states with neurophysiological occurrences. These neuro-physiological occurrences, in turn, are not fundamental; the fundamental consists of microphysical facts about charge, mass, and so on. According to **Absolute Fundamentality**, then, it is not a realist view. The same result applies to *any* reductivist view. For instance, in ethics, so-called 'naturalist' reductions such as those found in the Railton (1986) paper "Moral Realism" claim that ethical properties depend on non-fundamental psychological properties. **Absolute Fundamentality** will again identify the resulting view as an irrealist one, and the reason is that this conception of realism is inconsistent with REDUCTION COMPATIBILITY.

Realism: Relative fundamentality

We have seen that none of the above characterizations of realism can capture all of the structural features. Perhaps there is no very natural property that does this.

But before settling for this pessimistic conclusion, there is a view in the neighborhood of **Absolute Fundamentality** that deserves to be explored. This doesn't appeal to the binary distinction between what is fundamental and what is not, but rather to the notion of *relative* fundamentality, expressed by the predicate 'is more fundamental than'. Some plausible (and relevant) claims about relative fundamentality include that the Behaviorist will need a long and complicated disjunction of behaviors to identify pain (one can be in pain either by screaming, or by clutching one's arm and grimacing, or by exhibiting another item on the long list of pain behaviors), and so pain is not very fundamental in the Behaviorist view. Meanwhile, the neurophysiological states which, according to the Identity Theory, are identical to mental states, will not be so disjunctive. Intuitively, they will constitute a psychologically natural, and somewhat fundamental, kind. It is then plausible that pain is more fundamental in the Identity Theorist's view than in the Behaviorist's view.

Analogous comparisons seem plausible for Subjectivism and Non-Naturalism about ethics, and for Instrumentalism and Realism about scientific unobservables. This suggests, as a first pass, that a view is realist about a domain D just in case it entails the following:

Relative Fundamentality: D is more fundamental than it is according to salient competing views of D.

Relative Fundamentality is also not incompatible with the structural features required of any adequate metaphysical conception of realism. It entails TRUTH COMPATIBILITY, since highly non-fundamental domains may nonetheless exist and be such that discourses about them contain true statements about the relevant non-fundamental entities. It is consistent with **Domain Neutrality** since there is no domain which is trivially highly fundamental; it is a substantive question for any domain (including the mental) how fundamental it is. And finally, it entails REDUCTION COMPATIBILITY since a domain might be reducible yet still more fundamental than other salient competing views make it out to be.

Clearly, there is much more investigation to be done into whether **Relative Fundamentality** captures a philosophically interesting metaphysical kind to serve as the referent of 'realism'. (For a fuller development of this idea, see Dunaway [ms].) Further investigation would proceed, ideally, by identifying additional structural features of the notion of realism, and would ask whether **Relative Fundamentality** or any other relatively simple metaphysical notion might have all of these features.

REALISM AND OBJECTIVITY: THE NO TRIVIALITY CONDITION

Here is one further structural feature of realism, which will also serve as a crucial structural feature in our subsequent discussion of epistemic conceptions of objectivity.

Gideon Rosen's paper "Objectivity and Modern Idealism: What Is the Question?" is a seminal discussion of various metaphysical conceptions of objectivity, which are more closely related to realism as conceived in the first half of this chapter. But it highlights what is not only an important structural feature of realism conceived metaphysically but also objectivity conceived epistemically. This is the **No Triviality** condition, which I will introduce in the context of one of Rosen's central arguments.

The structure of Rosen's argument is relatively simple but has the potential for very general application: it takes a candidate characterization of non-objectivity and alleges that it follows from the characterization that *every domain whatsoever* is objective. So, Rosen concludes that the candidate characterizations of objectivity fail to adequately capture their target.

This reveals an important structural feature of objectivity: that it must nontrivially distinguish objective from non-objective domains. Any characterization of objectivity that fails to do this will fail to capture a core feature of objectivity. We can call this the **No Triviality** condition:

No Triviality: There are at least some domains D that are objective, and at least some domains D^* (distinct from D) that are not objective.

To illustrate one application of **No Triviality**, consider (following Rosen) a "response-dependence" characterization of objectivity. A property is *response-dependent* just in case it is instantiated in virtue of how that thing affects agents like us. Rosen then takes the substantive understanding of objectivity given by **No Response-dependence** and argues that it fails to capture **No Triviality**:

No Response-dependence D does not contain properties that are response-dependent (Rosen 1994: 298).

Take *constitutionality* as an example of a response-dependent property: laws are constitutional just in case the Supreme Count is disposed, after investigation, to judge them so. (Any examples here are bound to be controversial, but the point applies to any example of a response-dependent characterization of a property in hand.) **No Response-dependence** fails to entail that constitutionality is not objective, according to ROSEN:

> So far we have been given no reason to think that the facts about what a certain group of people would think after a certain sort of investigation are anything but robustly objective. The facts about how the court would rule are facts of modal sociology … but on the face of it they possess the same status as the facts about what any other collection of animals would do if prompted with certain stimuli, or set a certain problem. The facts about what the court would do with a given case … are thus, for all we've said, features of the objective world. And if the facts [about constitutionality] just are these very facts, then [we have] no special grounds for thinking of them as less than entirely real.
>
> (1994: 300)

Since the same point applies to any response-dependent property, **No Response-dependence** will fail the **No Triviality** condition.

The central claim in Rosen's argument, the fact that constitutionality is response-dependent (i.e., that something is constitutional because the Supreme Court justices would judge it to be so), is itself a perfectly objective fact by any measure. It is just as objective as the fact that a mouse would run away if it saw a cat, or the fact that an electron would repel another nearby electron; the fact that something has any of these dispositions is an objective fact about the world, just like any other. Response-dependence is no different from these other dispositions.

The general version of this claim, which secures a failure of **No Triviality**, is that for any fact p that is response-dependent, the following holds (where O is the operator 'it is objective that' and RDp means 'p is response-dependent'):

$$O(RDp).$$

This general claim has some plausibility. Claims about Response-dependence do seem to be just as objective as any other kind of dispositional fact. But of course there are two issues here: one is the objectivity of the fact that p *is response-dependent*; this is the claim the above passage from Rosen supports. The other is the objectivity of p itself. This latter fact (if it is a fact) is the following:

$$O(p).$$

According to Rosen, it is the objectivity of the allegedly relevant feature of p—that is, the objectivity of the response-dependence of p—which implies that p itself is objective. This is the following claim, which is a substantive and non-trivial one:

$$O(RDp) \rightarrow O(p).$$

(Cf. Rosen [1994: 301]: "*Intuitively*, if the facts in the contested class can simply be read off in a mechanical way from the facts in an uncontroversially objective class, then there can be no grounds for denying the same status to facts in the contested area.")

Thus, this premise is necessary for securing the conclusion that every domain will be objective, and **No Triviality** is violated. This points toward a powerful form of argument which, if sound, would serve as a serious challenge to any substantive understanding of objectivity. I will return to the prospects for the general form of argument below.

OBJECTIVITY: EPISTEMIC SHORTCOMINGS

No Triviality not only places substantial constraints on metaphysical conceptions of realism and objectivity but also on the epistemic conceptions of objectivity which will be my focus here.

Some uses of 'objective' are explained primarily in epistemic terms. Begin with the contrast between objectivity and *relativity*. (This is, for instance, the starting point in Thomas Nagel [1989].) Roughly, relative facts are those that hold only in relation to agents: for these facts, there is no such thing as a non-objective fact holding simpliciter, but only holding in relation to some agent. In ethics, the relativity of the domain would amount to the claim that murder is wrong relative to some agents, but is not wrong relative to others. But objective domains, like physics, are not relative in this way: there is no need to specify an agent relative to which the laws of physics hold; they are true simpliciter, and hence objective.

What relativity in the intended sense amounts to is a tricky matter in need of explanation, and I will limit my attention here to some alleged defining epistemic symptoms of relativity. In picturesque terms, these approaches all aim to articulate the following idea. It is in the nature of relative (and hence non-objective) facts to be epistemically accessible to the agents they hold in relation to. That is, if the fact ϕ holds relative to agent a, then a has fairly easy epistemic access to ϕ. Objective facts, by contrast, do not by their nature bring this epistemic status. It might not be easy to know or have epistemically non-faulty beliefs about them. This epistemic aspect to objectivity is distinct from the metaphysical approach to realism in the previous section, and so represents an importantly different topic for investigation. I will introduce some substantive understandings of what the important epistemic difference between objective and non-objective domains might be in subsequent sections.

One leading epistemic approach to non-objectivity, which is developed in Crispin Wright (1992) and elsewhere, has been widely applied to articulate the intuitive absence of objectivity in matters of taste, aesthetics, humor, and ethics. (See Kölbel 2002, Dreier 2009, and Egan 2014 for more discussion of these ideas.) The central idea in Wright (1992) is that non-objective facts are those for which there is a possibility of a "shortcoming-free disagreement." When dealing with objective facts, subjects who form disagreeing opinions are such that one of them must fall prey to some kind of epistemic shortcoming in reaching their opinion. Take judgments about ordinary objects formed on the basis of perception. Two subjects might both, in the Oval Office, visually survey their surroundings and disagree about whether there is a desk in the room. It follows from the fact that there is a disagreement that one of them is epistemically non-ideal. There are various ways they might instantiate a shortcoming: this might be by virtue of having impoverished visual inputs or by having an improperly functioning perceptual apparatus, being biased, and so on. But one of these shortcomings (either in cognition or in environment) must be present in at least one of the subjects who is disagreeing about the furnishings of the Oval Office. Since the disagreement must exhibit a shortcoming, the facts about desks in the Oval Office are objective facts.

Non-objective domains differ in this respect from the Oval Office's furnishings. Take comedy as an example. According to Wright, the non-objectivity of the funniness of a particular joke shows up in our epistemic lives in the form of the possibility of a short-coming-free disagreement over the joke's funniness. You and I can arrive at distinct judgments concerning whether that joke is funny: I think it is, you think it isn't, yet it doesn't follow that one has impoverished comic inputs, or is biased, etc.

The terminology used to formulate this idea is at best suggestive. Wright recognizes this, and offers the notion of *Cognitive Command* as a sharpening of the shortcoming-free characterization of objectivity. His official definition of Cognitive Command is as follows:

> A discourse exhibits Cognitive Command if and only if it is a priori that differences of opinion arising within it can be satisfactorily explained only in terms of "divergent input," that is, the disputants' working on the basis of different information ..., or "unsuitable conditions" ..., or "malfunction."
>
> (1992: 93)

Wright goes on to give further clarification of the various shortcomings that explain disagreement of objective matters: divergent input, unsuitable conditions, or malfunction. But even without getting bogged down in these details, we can ask some initial questions about the proposal that it is a feature of objectivity in a domain D that D satisfies **Cognitive Command:**

Cognitive Command: The facts in D are such that it is a priori that disagreements in discourse about D could be explained as the product of divergent input, unsuitable conditions, or malfunction among at least one of the disputants.

Some questions can be raised about whether **Cognitive Command** satisfies the **No Triviality** feature of objectivity. One line of questioning begins with the following assumption: it is possible to know the facts in some non-objective domains. For instance, one can have comic knowledge. This assumption seems innocuous, but it is problematic for a **Cognitive Command**-based understanding of objectivity.

To see why, we can work a more precise understanding of what "divergent input" amounts to. Wright says that disputants have divergent inputs just in case two disputants are working on the basis of different information. On one very natural sharpening of this idea, the "information" one has will be one's evidence, and one's evidence will be the totality of what one knows (cf. Williamson 2000: chapter 5; see also Hawthorne and Srinivasan 2013). Hence, in any case where there is a dispute over p, if someone could know whether p, then it could be that the dispute is one for which there is divergent input. (Since *ex hypothesi* this is a dispute over p, the non-knower does not even believe the truth concerning p. She thus does not know whether p and has different evidence.)

This threatens to make the "divergent input" condition too easy to satisfy. If it is possible for someone to know whether a joke is funny, then any dispute over the funniness of the joke is one where it could be that someone knows more than the other disputants. (Since if someone knows that the joke is funny, it follows that it is true that the joke is funny. The disagreeing interlocutor doesn't even believe that the joke is funny—this is what makes for a disagreement—and so they can't know it.) Hence it will be very natural to say that a dispute about the comic can be diagnosed as one where disputants have different information, a condition of **Cognitive Command**.

This line of reasoning suggests that even paradigmatic non-objective domains will satisfy **Cognitive Command**, and the **No Triviality** feature is violated. But it is only suggestive, since one crucial assumption is that facts in non-objective domains can be known. We could, of course, reject this, and endorse **Moderate Skepticism** for non-objective domains:

Moderate Skepticism: Not all of the facts in D are such that someone could know them.

If **Moderate Skepticism** were true of the comic (and other non-objective domains), then some comic facts would be unknowable. There would then be no guarantee that disputes about them could be diagnosed as cases of divergent input. This puts **Cognitive Command** back in the running as a central feature of objectivity.

Whether it is a structural feature of objectivity that **Moderate Skepticism** is not true of non-objective domains is not a question I will try to answer here. But it is a substantial and non-trivial consequence of **Cognitive Command** that, if it can satisfy the **No Triviality** condition, non-objectivity must be accompanied by a degree of skepticism.

OBJECTIVITY: THE BELIEF-KNOWLEDGE CONNECTION

There are substantive hurdles to using **Cognitive Command** as a characterization of objectivity. But we can side-step some of these hurdles by taking a different approach to articulating the central insight behind **Cognitive Command**. Objective domains are characterized by **Cognitive Command** in terms of the features of *disagreements* about those domains. Disagreements involve two people forming incompatible beliefs, and objectivity is characterized in terms of the presence of epistemic fault on the part of one of the disagreers. However, there are closely related epistemic properties that are independent of and unrelated to what happens in disagreements. For instance, one might focus on the idea that it is in the nature of non-objective domains that beliefs about them are, or could easily be, free from epistemic defect. (This does not require the possibility that someone could, in a similarly non-defective way, form a disagreeing belief.) This alleged feature of non-objectivity is emphasized, for example, by the conclusion in Street (2006) where she introduces a kind of relativity into the ethical facts with the goal of earning epistemic advantages that a realist account cannot have. Here is a slightly more detailed gloss on this intuitive idea.

Begin with an independent characterization of *suitably ideal conditions* for forming a belief about domain D. These will include logical and probabilistic coherence, at a minimum, and perhaps will involve additional constraints that rule out other imperfect forms of reasoning. Call a belief about D that is formed in suitably ideal conditions a *competent belief*: in short, it is not infected by epistemic defects that arise from defective reasoning and the like. One motivating idea behind epistemic conceptions of non-objectivity is that if D is not objective, then a competent belief about D is guaranteed to have important epistemic credentials. Meanwhile, if D is objective, then it is possible that a belief about D is competent and yet lacks these credentials.

If we take knowledge to be the paradigm of epistemic success, then this amounts to the idea that domains D that satisfy **Belief-Knowledge Connection (BKC)** are the non-objective domains:

BKC: For any claim about D, if one forms a competent belief about D, then one thereby knows the claim about D.

Objective domains, by contrast, do not satisfy **BKC** and allow for competent belief-formation that is not knowledge. For example, one could form a competent belief about the presence of a chair in the Oval Office (an objective fact), but owing to an unfriendly epistemic environment fail to know that there is a chair in the Oval Office. Meanwhile, competently believing that a joke is funny is sufficient for knowing that the joke is funny.

BKC is just a simple instance of a family of epistemic conceptions of objectivity, and our focus here is not on whether it is right. One could refine the conditions for being a competent belief, or one could replace knowledge with other epistemic credentials like justification or warrant. However, instead of playing with these details here, we can use **BKC** as a test case to evaluate some claims about the structural features of objectivity.

OBJECTIVITY: COLLAPSE AND THE MASTER ARGUMENT

Recall that, in his argument that **No Response-dependence** fails the **No Triviality** feature, Rosen employs the following premise:

$$O(RDp) \rightarrow O(p).$$

That is, if it is objective that p is response-dependent, then p is objective.

If this premise is generally valid, then this sets up a "Master Argument" that **No Triviality** is violated by *every* conception of objectivity. We can run a Rosen-style argument by substituting any proposed characterization of non-objectivity in place of response-dependence, and show that any candidate for non-objectivity p is in fact fully objective. The general version of the premise in question is COLLAPSE, where Φ is any alleged characteristic feature of non-objectivity:

COLLAPSE $O(\Phi p) \rightarrow O(p).$

If Collapse is a structural feature of objectivity, then the following Master Argument will show that *any* substantive conception of objectivity fails the **No Triviality** condition:

The Master Argument:

$O(\Phi p)$
$O(\Phi p) \rightarrow O(p)$
Therefore, $O(p)$.

All we need to do is substitute the proposed characterization of non-objectivity for Φ, and the argument will be exactly the same in essentials as Rosen's. Triviality ensues.

COLLAPSE AND EPISTEMIC OBJECTIVITY

However, Collapse is very dubious when we are dealing with epistemic conceptions of objectivity. One way to illustrate this is by showing that, when we use **BKC** as a candidate characterization of objectivity, the resulting instance of the Collapse principle is false. This will give us a feel for how the Master Argument would apply if extended to epistemic conceptions of objectivity.

Using K to stand for 'could be known', a fact Φ that could be known can be written as $K\Phi$. We can state some features of **BKC** using this notation. First, since according to **BKC**, objective facts are not guaranteed to be known by competent believers, there are situations where the only facts that can be known by such believers are the non-objective ones. That is, the following holds for any fact Ψ in these situations:

$\neg O\Psi \leftrightarrow K\Psi$.

Next, we can look at what happens if we try to extend Collapse to any conception of non-objectivity. Assuming that satisfying **BKC** is equivalent to non-objectivity, then in situations where only non-objective facts are known, Collapse is equivalent to the claim that the following holds for any fact Φ:

$OK\Phi \rightarrow O\Phi$.

But, finally, we have seen that if we are in a setting where objective facts fail to be known by competent belief, then objectivity is equivalent to the absence of knowledge; $\neg O\Psi \leftrightarrow K\Psi$ holds. So, it being objective that Φ is known means that it is not known that Φ is known. And if Φ is objective, then this means that it is not known. Thus, Collapse is (modulo our earlier assumptions) equivalent to the following claim:

$\neg KK\Phi \leftrightarrow \neg K\Phi$.

This is just what is known as the 'KK principle' in the epistemology literature. (See especially Williamson 2000: chapter 4). Collapse implies that KK is true in settings where objective facts are unknowable. This is grounds for a *reductio*: in general, the fact that you don't know that you know something doesn't imply that you don't know that thing.

(Just as I might want a coffee right now without knowing that I want a coffee, likewise I might know that I am cold without knowing that I know I am cold.) And restricting the principle to settings where only non-objective facts are knowable by competent belief doesn't make KK any more palatable. KK implies that facts about what is knowable are guaranteed to be among the facts that are knowable, and hence (given **BKC**) are not objective. This is not an appealing result.

(Note that Rosen only applies his argument to metaphysical conceptions of objectivity, which are much more similar to the kinds of view we are labeling with the heading of 'realism' here. Since we concluded that **Relative Fundamentality** is most promising as a characterization of metaphysical realism, it is worth noting in this connection that the fundamentality-facts might be very fundamental, without every non-fundamentality-fact being very fundamental. Then, the relevant instance of COLLAPSE is false for relative fundamentality.)

CONNECTIONS: MAGNETISM

We have so far considered some various candidates for the natural kinds that might underlie talk of realism and objectivity. It should be clear that, on some of the candidate characterizations covered here, there is no strict entailment between realism and objectivity: for instance, domains can be not very fundamental and also difficult to know. But there still might be some interesting connections between the notions, and below I will give a brief discussion of some of the possibilities.

Suppose we accept a view of ethics in which it is highly fundamental: say we hold, unlike the Subjectivist, that ethical properties are fairly natural, non-gerrymandered properties studied by social science. (Cf. Boyd 1988; Sturgeon 1988.) In the **Relative Fundamentality** characterization of realism, our view of the normative is a good candidate for a realist view. Many writers, starting with David Lewis (1983), have held that highly fundamental properties have an additional feature: they are easy to refer to. Roughly, this means that a community of speakers doesn't need to use a term with a high degree of fit with a highly fundamental property in order to successfully refer to it. For instance, since gold is pretty fundamental, a community of speakers could use 'gold' with some idiosyncrasies—say they are reliably tricked into sincerely saying that iron pyrite ("fool's gold") counts as 'gold'—yet still succeed in referring to the element Au rather than the disjunction of Au and iron pyrite. The disjunction is a better fit with their use of 'gold', but is overridden by the superior fundamentality of Au.

Call the thesis that highly fundamental properties are easy to refer to *reference magnetism*. If reference magnetism is true, then realism about a domain will have some bearing on whether that domain is objective.

To illustrate, consider our realist view of obligation according to which it is highly fundamental. One can competently use 'ought', and yet use it in a way that does not fit best with obligation; rather, one's use fits better with some other obligation-like property. Let's call this other property *obligation**. (A simple example to illustrate this would take obligation to be happiness-maximization and obligation* to be a property instantiated by most happiness-maximizing actions, but not those that require violating the autonomy of a rational agent.) The phenomenon of reference magnetism will produce some false beliefs about obligation in this scenario. For even though one's use of 'ought' will track obligation*, one's beliefs will be about *obligation,* not obligation*. For instance: suppose *a* is an action that instantiates obligation* but not obligation. One's usage of 'ought' will lead one to accept sentences of the form 'one ought to do *a*'. And since reference magnetism is in operation, one will normally form the belief, when accepting such a sentence, *that one ought to do a.* This means one has a false belief about obligation—by hypothesis, *a* does not instantiate obligation, and so one's belief is false. If reference magnetism hadn't been in operation, things would have gone differently: the sentence 'one ought to do *a*' would have referred to the less fundamental property obligation*, and the resultant belief would have been true.

This gives rise to some connections between realism and objectivity. For instance, according to **Cognitive Command**, objective domains preclude shortcoming-free disagreements. Reference magnetism plus realism makes the disagreement portion easier to come by; since communities who use their terms differently for a highly fundamental domain can still refer to the same property, they stand in a position to actually disagree with each other, rather than merely talking past one another.

BKC carves out objectivity differently: it requires that, if a domain is objective, it is possible to competently believe a claim about that domain and not know it. Here again, there is an interesting and significant connection between realism and objectivity. Adding reference magnetism to realism about a domain will, as we have seen, imply that one can refer to properties in the realist domain, even if one doesn't use terms in a way that fits those properties perfectly. (In the simple illustration from above, this would involve referring to happiness-maximization, even though one treats some maximizing actions that require autonomy-violations as not obligatory.) Imperfect use of 'ought', which results from applying 'ought' to a non-obligatory action a, can still succeed in referring to obligation. And a normal process of belief-formation in these cases will result in false beliefs about obligation—one will come to falsely believe that a is obligatory. This is where is the interesting connection lies, given **BKC**: these beliefs will be competent beliefs. But since they are false beliefs, they are not knowledge. So realism entails objectivity.

MORE CONNECTIONS: SURPRISING ENTAILMENTS

We focused on some ways in which realism, as characterized by **Relative Fundamentality**, might entail objectivity in the previous subsection. In this subsection, I will focus on similar entailments that appear when we adopt alternative conceptions of realism.

Suppose, for example, that **Mind-Independence** characterizes realism about a domain, and so irrealism about a domain entails that that domain is mind-dependent. Facts about the mental are perfectly objective. So, irrealism about a domain entails that the domain in question is objective—a surprising result.

The crucial premises here are that (i) mental facts are objective, and (ii) if mental facts are objective, then whatever depends on them is also objective. Premise (ii) is a restricted version of COLLAPSE, and follows from multiple characterizations of objectivity. For instance, if **Cognitive Command** characterizes objectivity, then objective domains will be those that do not permit shortcoming-free disagreements. Facts about what mental states someone is in will not permit shortcoming-free disagreements; if (for example)

I believe that you want an ice cream, and you believe that you don't, then one of us must have made a mistake of reasoning or had inadequate evidence when arriving at our belief. If ethics is mind-dependent, then, facts about what ought to be done will depend on mental states of the same sort as the fact that you want (or don't want) an ice cream. But then the facts about what ought to be done will not permit shortcoming-free disagreements, because disagreements about ethics will either be based on a disagreement about the mental (which cannot be shortcoming-free), or else based on a mistake about how ethics depends on the mental.

Things go similarly if we work with objectivity in the sense of **BKC**. Again, suppose for illustration that ethics is mind-dependent by virtue of the facts about what ought to be done depending on mental facts—facts similar to the fact that you want an ice cream. These mental facts will be such that competent beliefs about them might not be knowledge. For instance, I might have reasoned impeccably but, owing to your deceptive testimony, come to believe that you want an ice cream when you really don't want one. So my competent belief will not be knowledge, and facts about mental states are perfectly objective according to **BKC**.

The mind-dependent ethical facts will then be objective as well. If I could competently believe and yet not know that you want an ice cream, then I could competently believe and yet not know the ethical facts that depend on it. As a very simple case, suppose it is true that, if it is a fact that you want ice cream, then it is a fact that I ought to give you ice cream. Moreover, suppose that I know this. Believing that you want ice cream, I competently infer from my knowledge of the relationship between the ethical and mental that I ought to give you ice cream. By this route, I come to believe that I ought to give you ice cream. But since I don't know that you want ice cream (since it is false that you want one, and you have misled me), then I also won't know that I ought to give you ice cream, since this belief rests on my unknown belief about your mental states. So I will competently believe, and not know, an ethical fact. It is objective, just like the mental fact it depends on.

CONCLUSION

Realism and objectivity are notions of central philosophical interest, and many classic philosophical debates have, at their heart, disputes over the reality or objectivity of a subject matter. The arguments discussed here will, hopefully, provide useful examples for philosophers who wish to make progress in understanding, in a rigorous way, what is at issue in these disputes. We can avoid disputes that rely on flimsy intuitive applications of philosophical terms of art without losing touch with the profound and exciting issues that motivate disputes over realism and objectivity in ethics and elsewhere.

RELATED TOPICS

REFERENCES

Barnes, E. (2012), "Emergence and Fundamentality," *Mind* **121**, 873–901.

Boyd, R. N. (1988), "How to be a Moral Realist," in G. Sayre-McCord, ed., *Essays on Moral Realism*, Ithaca, NY: Cornell University Press, pp. 181–228.

Devitt, M. (1991), *Realism and Truth*, Second Edition, Princeton: Princeton University Press.

Dreier, J. (2009), 'Relativism (and Expressivism) and the Problem of Disagreement," *Philosophical Perspectives* **29**, 79–110.

Dunaway, B. (ms), 'The Metaphysical Conception of Realism."

Egan, A. (2014), "There's Something Funny about Comedy: A Case Study in Faultless Disagreement," *Erkenntnis* **79**, 73–100.

Fine, K. (2001), "The Question of Realism," *Philosophers' Imprint* **1**(1), 1–30.

Hawthorne, J. and Srinivasan, A. (2013), "Disagreement without Transparency: Some Bleak Thoughts," in D. Christensen and J. Lackey, eds., *The Epistemology of Disagreement*, Oxford: Oxford University Press, pp. 9–30.

Kölbel, M. (2002), *Truth without Objectivity*, New York, NY: Routledge.

Lewis, D. (1983), "New Work for a Theory of Universals," *Australasian Journal of Philosophy* **61**(4), 343–377.

Lewis, D. (1986), *On the Plurality of Worlds*, Oxford: Basil Blackwell.

Mackie, J. (1977), *Ethics: Inventing Right and Wrong*, London: Penguin.

Nagel, T. (1989), *The View from Nowhere*, Oxford: Oxford University Press.

Railton, P. (1986), "Moral Realism," *The Philosophical Review* **95**(2), 163–207.

Rosen, G. (1994), "Objectivity and Modern Idealism: What is the Question?," in M. Michael and J. O'Leary-Hawthorne, eds., *Philosophy in Mind: The Place of Philosophy in the Study of Mind*, Dordrecht: Kluwer Academic, pp. 277–319.

Street, S. (2006), "A Darwinian Dilemma for Realist Theories of Value," *Philosophical Studies* **127**(1), 109–166.

Sturgeon, N. (1988), "Moral Explanations," in G. Sayre-McCord, ed., *Essays on Moral Realism*, Ithaca, NY: Cornell University Press, pp. 229–255.

Wedgwood, R. (2007), *The Nature of Normativity*, Oxford: Oxford University Press.

Williamson, T. (2000), *Knowledge and Its Limits*, Oxford: Oxford University Press.

Wright, C. (1992), *Truth and Objectivity*, Cambridge, MA: Harvard University Press.

9

Metaphysical Relations in Metaethics

Gideon Rosen

This chapter aims to clarify a question that can be vaguely put as follows: How are the normative facts related to the natural facts? As many philosophers have noted, the two domains appear to be distinct (Moore 1903; Enoch 2011; Parfit 2011). Comparing the fact that Sophie morally ought to feed the fish with the fact that the fish will die if she doesn't feed them, one has the palpable sense, not just that the claims are different, but that they concern categorically distinct subject matters: how things ought to be versus how things are. Of course, this appearance could be misleading. The normative facts could be natural facts in disguise. But however this may be, there is obviously some very close connection between the fact that Sophie ought to feed the fish and the various indisputably natural facts that underlie it. One central problem in metaethics is to say what that connection comes to.

Our discussion assumes that there are normative facts—facts about the normative properties of things and the normative relations in which they stand. It also assumes that some facts are clearly "natural," e.g., the fact that the fish will die if they are not fed. The challenge is to say how facts of the first sort are related to facts of the second sort. But it must be conceded at the outset that this question is not exactly clear. When we ask how the normative is "related" to the natural, what sort of information are we seeking? The best way to clarify a question that is unclear in this way is to say what would count as an answer to it, so the plan for what follows is to do just that. Recent work in general metaphysics provides a vocabulary in which hypotheses about the relation between the normative and the natural can be stated with some precision. This chapter explains that vocabulary by putting it to work for the purpose of providing a taxonomy of answers to our target question.

WHAT IS A NATURAL PROPERTY?

Ideally, we would begin with explicit definitions of the key terms, "normative" and "natural." But since the available definitions are controversial, and since it doesn't matter for our purposes exactly how the lines are drawn, we rely for the most part on the usual informal explanation, according to which the normative features are features like *right* and *wrong*, *reason* and *obligation*, and the natural features include those with which the physical sciences are concerned along with everyday "descriptive" features like *red* and *round*. A complete account will say what the paradigms in each class have in common, but at least when it comes to the normative, no such account will be attempted here.

When it comes to "natural," however, we face an ambiguity that needs resolving and which is best resolved with the tools that will be our focus. Some metaethicists use the word "natural" to mean what it often means elsewhere in philosophy, i.e., roughly: *of or pertaining to the causally efficacious features of spatiotemporal entities*, or perhaps, *similar in kind to the features posited by the natural sciences as we now have them* (Sturgeon 2007; Dowell 2013). When the word is used in this way, the main contrast is with "supernatural" and the paradigmatic alternative to Naturalism is theism. However, the word also has a broader sense, peculiar to metaethics, in which "natural" contrasts not with "supernatural" but specifically with "normative." To see the difference, consider a version of the Divine Command Theory according to which for an action to be wrong is just for it to violate God's commands, where the underlying facts about God and his commands are understood as straightforwardly descriptive, i.e., non-normative through and through. When "natural" is used in the narrow sense, this view is obviously not a form of naturalism since it posits an immaterial deity outside of nature. When the word is used in the broad sense, however, this view *is* (or easily could be) a form of Naturalism since it does not posit "non-natural" ethical features at the fundamental level.

For metaethical purposes, where our aim is to clarify the connection between the normative and *the rest*, it makes sense to adopt the broad usage in which "natural" contrasts with "normative" and means something like "descriptive." But then we face a question about how to understand this contrast. The key fact is (1):

(1) If a property is not normative, it is natural.

This what underlies our judgment that, insofar as the basic features of the deity are non-normative, they amount to "natural" (descriptive) features in the sense relevant to metaethics. But of course we don't want to affirm the converse of (1), at least not at this stage. Ethical Naturalism is the view that normative properties are *also* natural, so we need a conception of the "natural" that leaves room for this possibility. And there's the rub. Along with the illustrative examples, (1) is our main guide to what it means to call a property "natural" in the broad sense. But (1) tells us nothing about what it could possibly mean to call a *normative* property natural. If we want to use the word in this way, we must say something to close this gap.

A MODAL PROPOSAL

The simplest approach is (2):

(2) A property F is natural iff for some non-normative condition φ, necessarily, for all x, x is F iff x is φ.

A property counts as natural in this view when there exist non-normatively specifiable, necessary, and sufficient conditions for its instantiation. (These conditions need not be finite or specifiable by us. It is enough that they exist.) If we take (2) as our account, then the question of whether the ethical facts are also natural facts reduces to the familiar question whether intensional truth conditions for normative claims can be given in non-normative terms.

This view is practically forced upon us if we embrace a widely accepted theory of properties:

Intensionalism: Properties F and G are identical iff necessarily, for all x, x is F iff x is G.

This is a "coarse-grained" conception of properties on which, for example, the property of being a triangle (a polygon with three angles) and the property of being trilateral (a polygon with three sides) are identical. Intensionalism is clearly adequate for many purposes (Lewis 1986); moreover, it has the great advantage of providing a perfectly clear account of what it takes for properties to be the same or different. The case for (2), given Intensionalism, is straightforward. Suppose that F is a normative property and that F is necessarily equivalent to a non-normative condition φ. It is as clear as anything can be in this area that if a condition φ contains only non-normative ingredients, then *being φ* is a natural property. But given Intensionalism, F just *is* the property of being φ; so F must likewise count as natural. Now suppose that F is *not* equivalent to any non-normative condition φ. This means that it is possible for there to be two things that are alike in every non-normative respect, one of which is F, the other not. And surely that is enough to render F *non*-natural on any view.

The main difficulty with (2) is that it flattens the landscape in metaethics beyond recognition, conflating positions that are widely regarded as distinct and ruling out options that are widely regarded as viable. If we take (2) as our account of what it takes for a property to be natural, then

Ethical Naturalism: Every normative property is natural

is equivalent to

Supervenience: If two possible objects are alike in every non-normative respect, they are alike in every normative respect.

Ethical Naturalism entails Supervenience on any view. The trouble with (2) is that it yields the converse implication. To see this, let F be an arbitrary normative property and let a, b, … be the Fs, actual and merely possible. Each possible F has a complete non-normative profile $D_i(x)$ that encodes the whole truth about its non-normative features, intrinsic and extrinsic. Given Supervenience, the disjunction of these profiles, $D_a(x) \lor D_b(x) \lor \ldots$, is a non-normative condition equivalent to F. So given (2), Supervenience entails Ethical Naturalism. (This argument is due to Kim 1984; see also Jackson 1998. Wedgwood 2007 notes that it depends on non-trivial modal assumptions. See Schmitt and Schroeder 2011 for discussion.)

This means that if we adopt (2) as our account of what it takes for a property to count as "natural," anyone who accepts Supervenience is a naturalist and anyone who rejects naturalism must reject Supervenience. But this is unacceptable. With a small handful of exceptions, every philosopher who has considered the question has endorsed Supervenience as manifestly obvious. The idea that there cannot be two actions that are alike in every non-normative respect, one of which is right and the other wrong, is as close as we come to common ground in metaethics. Ethical Naturalism, on the other hand, is thoroughly controversial with committed partisans pro and con. Any interpretation of the vocabulary that collapses these two views is therefore to be resisted. So (2) won't do.

A DEFINITIONAL PROPOSAL

A promising alternative appeals to the ancient idea that properties and relations, like words and concepts, have definitions. For much of the history of modern philosophy, this idea was dismissed as a relic of bad metaphysics. But a commitment to **real definition** is arguably implicit in much contemporary philosophy. Consider the twenty-first-century metaphysician who wants to know what it is for an object to be green, or for one event to cause another, or for a system of rules to be a legal system. If our aim in asking these "What is F?" questions were to analyze our *concept* of an F, our answers would be constrained to employ only ingredients that anyone competent with the target concept already possesses. And yet in most philosophical contexts (and all scientific contexts), no such constraint applies. We cannot object to a proposed account of what it is for an object to be green on the grounds that it employs notions like *wavelength*, with which users of color concepts may be unfamiliar. This suggests that the object of philosophical analysis in these contexts is not our *concept* of an F, but the property for which that concept stands (Rosen 2015).

The real definition of a property is given by a statement of the form, "To be F is to be φ" or "Being F consists in/reduces to being φ," where φ is a complex condition not containing F. Every real definition entails a claim of metaphysical reduction. If being F consists in being φ, then in general, the fact that x is F reduces to the fact that x is φ. (As we will see, this does not mean that they are the *same* fact.) Of course, there is a real question about what it takes for a putative definition to be correct. We certainly require that F and φ be equivalent:

(3) If φ defines F then necessarily, for all x: x is F iff x is φ.

But this is clearly not enough. When the color theorist asks, "What is it for an object to be green?" the answer to her question is not: "For x to be green is for x to be either grue and observed or bleen and unobserved" (Goodman 1983). A correct real definition thus pairs a property F with a condition φ that is equivalent to F *and which satisfies further constraints, as yet unspecified*. We'll consider proposals for completing the account below. But for now, let us help ourselves to the notion in order to say a bit more about what it means to call a property "natural" in the broad sense.

The most important principle for this purpose is (4):

(4) If F has a definition φ whose ingredients are entirely non-normative, then F is natural.

It's common ground in metaethics that one way to vindicate Naturalism about (say) moral rightness is to provide an explicit definition of *right* in non-normative terms. (4) is the principle that underwrites this common view. (1) and (4) together provide a strong sufficient condition for a property to count as natural. But of course they tell us nothing about what it would take for an *irreducible* normative property to count as natural, and that's a lacuna.

Here it is tempting to endorse a stronger thesis:

(5) F is natural if and only if F is either non-normative or definable in non-normative terms.

(5) is a straightforward definition of *natural property*. It gives clear content to the idea that "natural" contrasts with "normative," while leaving room for the possibility that some normative properties are also natural. It would also put us in a position to see real daylight between Supervenience and Ethical Naturalism. Supervenience guarantees the existence, for each normative property F, of a non-normative condition ϕ modally equivalent to F. But there is no guarantee that ϕ *defines* F. To see why, consider an ordinary superveni- ent property like *house*. Each possible house has a complete description in the language of fundamental physics, so *house* is equivalent to the disjunction of these conditions: $H_1(x) \lor H_2(x) \lor \ldots$ but we can't define *house* by means of this disjunction. It's simply false to say that being a house consists in being in *this* fully determinate physical state, or *that* fully determinate physical state, or ... This would imply that we cannot know *what it is to be a house* without knowing about quarks and the like, and that's clearly wrong. But more importantly, the definition fails to bring out what the houses have in common in virtue of which they count as houses. For analogous reasons, even if *moral rightness* is equivalent to a long disjunction of non-normative conditions, one for each right act, as it must be given Supervenience, we cannot define *right action* by means of this disjunction. Of course, this leaves it open whether *right* is definable by some other non-normative condition that brings out what the right acts have in common, but this is as it should be. (5) thus has the advantage of blocking the quick inference from Supervenience to Ethical Naturalism.

The main reason to resist (5) is that it entails that the only intelligible form of Ethical Naturalism is:

Reductive Naturalism: For every normative property F there is a non-normative condi- tion ϕ that defines F.

And this unfortunate. It is a familiar idea from the philosophy of science that the special sciences like biology and economics pose no threat to a broadly physicalist metaphysics, despite the fact that the features in which they traffic can't be defined in the language of physics (Fodor 1974). In a similar spirit, many philosophers have supposed that it should be possible for normative features to count as "natural," even where they can't be *defined* in more basic terms (Miller 1985; Brink 1989; Sturgeon 2006). (5) may be a permissible way to sharpen the somewhat fluid notion of a "natural" feature. But it forecloses an option that many philosophers have found attractive, so let's not adopt it.

A GROUND-THEORETIC PROPOSAL

A better option invokes a notion that is closely connected to a real definition but distinguishable from it: **metaphysical grounding** (Fine 2001, 2012; Schaffer 2009; Rosen 2010; Bennett 2011; Audi 2012; Correia and Schnieder 2012; for doubts, see Wilson 2014).

For present purposes, we may think of grounding as a relation among facts. The basic form of a grounding claim is "Γ grounds p" or "p obtains *in virtue of* Γ," where p is a fact and Γ is a collection of one or more facts. The key fact about grounding is that it is meant to be a maximally intimate explanatory relation. If Γ grounds p, then p obtains *because* Γ obtains. Like any explanatory relation, grounding is asymmetric, hence irreflexive (cf. Jenkins 2011). Unlike some explanatory relations (e.g., causal explanation), grounding is a form of synchronic necessitation. If Γ grounds p then, as a matter of strictest necessity, if Γ obtains then so does p (cf. Leuenberger 2014); and if p concerns a restricted region of time or space, so do its grounds. The fact that Mary is smiling at t is presumably grounded in the spatial relations among the parts of her face at t. If so, then as a matter of metaphysical necessity, if the parts of Mary's face are so arranged, Mary smiles.

The example illustrates the sense in which grounding is meant to be an especially intimate relation. The fact that Mary is smiling is not *identical* to the class of facts about how the various parts of her face are related. For present purposes, it is best to think of facts as structured entities, built up from objects, properties, relations, and other worldly items in roughly the sense in which a sentence is built from words. So conceived, facts are individuated by their constituents and the manner of their combination. To a first approximation, the fact that Mary is smiling at t has three constituents: Mary, the property of smiling, and t. The facts that ground this fact have very different constituents: the parts of Mary's face and the spatial relations in which they stand. So we can't *identify* the fact that Mary is smiling with the complex of facts in virtue of which it obtains. (That's a good thing, since these underlying facts explain the fact they ground, and nothing explains itself.) And yet the fact that Mary is smiling is not a separate, free-floating fact. A fact and its grounds are as closely connected as distinguishable facts can be.

This is reinforced by the main principles connecting grounding with other notions. (Some of these principles may have exceptions; but if they don't hold in every case, they hold in a significant range of cases.)

Disjunctive facts are grounded in their true disjuncts. If Mary is smiling, then the fact that Mary is smiling grounds the fact that Mary is either smiling or scowling.

Conjunctive facts are grounded in their conjuncts taken together. If Al is tall and Bob is boring, then the fact that Al is tall and Bob is boring is grounded in a pair of facts: the fact that Al is tall, and the fact that Bob is boring.

Existential facts are grounded in their instances. If Mary is smiling, then this fact grounds the fact that someone is smiling.

Determinable facts are grounded in their determinates. If the rose is scarlet, it is red in virtue of being scarlet.

One especially important principle for our purposes is the

Grounding-Definition Link (GDL): If φ defines F then necessarily, for all x, if x is F, then the fact that x is F is grounded in the fact that x is φ.

Suppose that being a vixen consists in being a female fox. GDL tells us that, whenever something is vixen, it is a vixen in virtue of being female and a fox. Since grounding is irreflexive, this means that we must distinguish *the fact that Sasha is a vixen*—an atomic fact of the form *Fa*—from the fact *that Sasha is female and Sasha is a fox*, which is of the form *Ga & Ha*. The first contains Sasha and *vixen*. The second contains Sasha, *female*, and *fox* (and other bits and pieces), but not *vixen*. So the two facts are distinct.

Again, as the examples show, the relation between a fact and its grounds is almost maximally intimate. The fact that the rose is red is not identical to the fact that the rose is scarlet. The fact that Sasha is a vixen is not identical to the fact that Sasha is female and a fox. And yet there is a palpable sense in which the grounded fact is not an "addition to reality" over and above its grounds. To employ a familiar metaphor: when God makes the grounds she ipso facto makes the facts they ground. No further creative activity is required.

Although metaethicists rarely put the point in quite these terms, it seems to me that the ethical naturalist's key thought is that the normative facts stand to the non-normative facts in precisely this intimate relation. Normative properties may or may not be definable in non-normative terms. Ethical naturalists disagree about this. But they agree that the normative facts are not further facts, superadded to reality after the non-normative facts are fixed. This suggests the following account of what it takes for a property to be natural:

(6) A property F is natural iff either F is non-normative or, necessarily, every fact of the form Fα is fully grounded in the non-normative facts.

Everyone who speaks the language of grounding will agree that normative facts about particular people and particular actions are always at least *partly* grounded in the non-normative facts. Oswald's act was wrong, at least in part, because it caused the death of a human being. The debate over Ethical Naturalism, on this view, is a debate about whether it is always possible to complete such grounding explanations by adding further non-normative facts to the ground. The ethical naturalist says that every atomic ethical fact can be explained from below, citing only non-normative facts, in the same sense in which every disjunctive fact can be explained from below by citing its true disjuncts. The non-naturalist disagrees, maintaining that, in at least one case, the ethical fact either lacks a full ground or is such that every full ground for it contains a normative ingredient.

This account tells us what it takes for a property to count as "natural" in the broad metaethical sense. (The account is easily generalized to relations and items in other categories.) There are several ways to extend the taxonomy of properties to a taxonomy of facts, the most straightforward of which is as follows:

(7) A fact is normative iff it contains a normative constituent.
(8) A fact is natural iff it contains only natural constituents.

This leaves it open, as it should, whether some facts are both normative and natural, reducing this question to the question whether some normative properties (relations, etc.) are also natural.

A QUESTION ABOUT NON-REDUCTIVE NATURALISM

Given the principles of the last section, Ethical Naturalism may be formulated as follows:

Ethical Naturalism: For all normative properties F, for all x: if Fx then there exists a non-normative condition ϕ such that Fx is metaphysically grounded in $\phi(x)$.

Reductive Naturalism entails Ethical Naturalism so defined. (The reductive naturalist says that every normative F is defined by a non-normative condition ϕ; but if ϕ defines F, then Fα is always grounded in $\phi(\alpha)$, by the GDL.) On the face of it, however, the converse does not hold. Suppose, for example, that while every fact of the form Fα is grounded in some non-normative fact involving α, the grounds for Fα are heterogeneous, with Fa grounded in $\Psi_1(a)$ while Fb is grounded in some quite unrelated fact $\Psi_2(b)$, etc. (Perhaps a is wrong by virtue of being a killing while b is wrong by virtue of being a promise breaking, etc.) Then we cannot conclude without further assumptions that there is a *single* non-normative condition ϕ such that facts of the form Fα are always grounded in facts of the form $\phi(\alpha)$. But Reductive Naturalism requires a *uniform* non-normative ground for every fact of the form Fα. So on the face of it, Ethical Naturalism does not entail Reductive Naturalism.

This suggests one way in which Non-Reductive Naturalism could be true:

Type 1 Non-Reductive Naturalism (about F): Facts of the form Fα are always grounded in non-normative facts. But there is no non-normative condition ϕ such that every fact of the form Fα is grounded in $\phi(\alpha)$.

There is also, at least in principle, another version of the view. Nothing we have said so far rules out a view according to which whenever an act is right, it is right by virtue of being ϕ, but which goes on to insist that nonetheless, being right is one thing, being ϕ another. This would be an instance of:

Type 2 Non-Reductive Naturalism (about F): There is a non-normative condition ϕ such that every fact of the form Fα is grounded in $\phi(\alpha)$, but ϕ does not *define* F.

As the formulations suggest, mixed views are possible. In theory, at any rate, we can be reductive naturalists about *right*, non-reductive naturalists about *good*, etc.

We rejected (5) on the grounds that it ruled out the possibility of non-reductive naturalism by definition. The present account is clearly better in this respect since it allows for two formally coherent formulations of the view. Still, one may legitimately wonder whether these positions are really tenable. To see the problem, suppose that we are intensionalists about properties. (We noted earlier that Intensionalism flattens the landscape in metaethics by equating Naturalism with Supervenience. But for philosophers who are willing to bite this bullet, it's worth asking whether Intensionalism allows for non-reductive forms of Naturalism.) A quick argument seems to show that, for the intensionalist, the only coherent form of Naturalism is Reductive Naturalism. As we have seen, Naturalism entails Supervenience, which in turn entails that every normative F is intensionally equivalent to a normative condition Δ formed by disjoining the non-normative profiles of the possible Fs: $\Delta(x) = D_a(x) \lor D_b(x) \lor \ldots$ For the intensionalist, F just *is* the property of being Δ. But surely the property of being Δ is defined by the non-normative condition by means of which it was introduced. And from this, it follows that, on the intensional view, the only tenable form of Naturalism is Reductive Naturalism.

But this is too quick. The vulnerable premise is the assumption that the property of being D_1 or D_2 or ... is defined by the disjunctive condition that figures in its name. If this seems obvious that is because we are tempted by the

Abstraction-Definition Link (ADL): When F = the property of being ϕ, and ϕ does not contain F, then ϕ defines F.

If I introduce G as *the property of being either green or red* and then ask what it is for something to be G, the answers seem automatic: being G consists in being either green or red. The ADL is a generalization of the principle at work in this example. It says that whenever a property is given as "the property of being ϕ," the abstraction term encodes a definition of the property.

Intensionalists, however, should reject the ADL. Take *the property of being either grue and observed or bleen and unobserved*. This property is intensionally equivalent to *green*, so for the intensionalist it *is* the property of being green. The ADL would then entail that we can give a real definition of *green*—the sort of definition philosophers interested in the metaphysics of color have been seeking—in terms of grue and bleen. But if the notion of real definition makes sense at all, that's just not so. A real definition brings out what the instances of the property have in common. The bogus gruesome definition of green does not do that. So intensionalists should reject the ADL. They should say that, sometimes, the property of being ϕ is not defined by ϕ.

Of course, this does not show that the normative property F is *not* defined by the non-normative condition Δ. It simply blocks the most direct route to this conclusion. It is an obscure and open question whether there is some other way to show that on the intensionalist view, every normative property has a non-normative defini-tion given Supervenience. The answer will depend on what it means to give the real definition of a coarse-grained property, and that is a question upon which light has not yet dawned.

HYPERINTENSIONALISM

The *hyper*intensionalist, by contrast, can happily agree that from Supervenience it follows that every normative property F is equivalent to a disjunctive non-normative condition Δ, and that *the property of being Δ* is defined by Δ. (The hyperintensionalist can accept the ADL, since she can distinguish the property of being grue and observed or bleen and unobserved, which is defined in terms of *grue*, from the intensionally equivalent property of being green, which is not.) Her distinctive claim is that, be all of this as it may, we can still distinguish the normative property F from the definable non-normative property with which it is equivalent. For the hyperintensionalist, from the fact that F is necessar-ily equivalent to a property that can be defined in non-normative terms, nothing follows about whether F can be so defined.

This is certainly what many metaethicists have wished to say. Non-naturalists like Parfit (2011) and non-reductive naturalists like Brink (1989) do not deny that it may be possible to find a definable natural property that applies to all and only the right actions. Their view is that if there is such a property, it is distinct from the property of being right.

The main challenge for views of this sort is to provide a concrete alternative to Intensionalism. Hyperintensional theories of properties have been explored in the philos-ophy of science, where it is sometimes said that fine-grained properties are individuated by their causal or nomic roles (Putnam 1975; Sober 1982). But this approach is unsuited to metaethics, where on most accounts, the relevant properties are causally inert.

The apparatus of grounding and definition provides for a number of better options. To fix ideas, consider the following proposal (Rosen 2015; cf. Audi 2012):

Hyperintensionalism: F and G are the same property iff:

(a) F and G are indefinable and necessarily coextensive; or
(b) F and G are definable and for all φ, φ defines F iff φ defines G.

Clause (a) is Intensionalism for primitive properties, and while it is not forced upon us, there is no clear reason to distinguish equivalent indefinable properties in metaethics. Clause (b), by contrast, is compulsory for anyone who accepts the idiom of real definition. If the correct account of *what it is to be F* is the same as the correct account of *what it is to be G*, then obviously F and G are the same property.

Of course, the account is only as clear as the notion of real definition upon which it relies. So far we have taken this notion for granted. But many philosophers will find this unsatisfactory, so we should say more. As our formulations all assume, the definition of a property (relation, etc.) is what we have called a *condition*: a complex item with argument places (free variables) matching the argument places in the property to be defined. The challenge is to say what it takes for a condition to define a property. The Grounding-Definition Link gives us a necessary condition. It says that φ defines F *only if*, necessarily, whenever x is F, φ(x) grounds Fx. The simplest account built from these materials holds that this condition (strengthened slightly) is not only necessary but sufficient:

Real Definition (provisional): φ defines F iff necessarily, for all x, if x is F or φ, then φx grounds Fx.

This captures the intuitive idea that to define a property F is to identify a condition the satisfaction of which invariably *makes the F-things F*.

If we adopt this view, space for Type-2 Non-Reductive Naturalism disappears. The type-2 naturalist about F holds that facts of the form Fα are uniformly grounded in complex non-normative facts of the form φ(α), but that F is nonetheless irreducible. Such a theorist must therefore distinguish F from another property, G = the property of being φ. This latter property, after all, is straightforwardly reducible. By the ADL, it is defined by the condition φ. The proposed account of definition, however, forces us to identify F and G, since any fact that grounds Fα grounds Gα and vice versa. So if properties are individuated by the grounds for atomic facts involving them, it follows that F is identical to the reducible property G, and is thus reducible.

This is no great cost: Type 2 Naturalism is an odd view, and it would be no disaster if the best framework for sharpening these issues ruled it out. There are, however, independent reasons to prefer a more demanding account of definition, which turns out as an added bonus (?) to block this argument.

The improved account invokes a new metaphysical notion: a fine-grained notion of **essence** due largely, in its present form, to Kit Fine (1994a, b). The familiar modal account of essence has it that P is an essential property of S iff necessarily, S is P (if S exists). But this has odd consequences. Suppose it's a necessary truth that Socrates is not Napoleon. The modal account then entails that Socrates is essentially and *by his very nature* not Napoleon. But that sounds wrong. As Fine has emphasized, we have a notion of essence on which, whatever the essential nature of Socrates may be, we can be confident that it says nothing about Napoleon. To put the point in epistemic terms, you can know everything there is to know about Socrates' essential nature—*what it is to be Socrates*—without knowing the first thing about Napoleon. By contrast, if you know what it is to be Socrates, then you must know that Socrates is a human being. As Fine would put it:

> It lies in the nature of Socrates that Socrates is human; it does not lie in the nature of Socrates that Socrates is not Napoleon.

It would be nice to be able to say in more basic terms what it means for it to lie in the nature of x that p, but there is no known prospect for such an account. For present purposes, the notion of essence, along with the notion of metaphysical grounding, will be primitive.

The **essence of x** is the class of propositions p, such that it lies in the nature of x that p. Absolutely everything has an essence in this sense. It lies in the nature of *red* that whatever is red is colored. It lies in the nature of *disjunction* that if p is true then so is p ∨ q. But as these examples show, from the fact that a thing has an essence, it does not follow immediately that it has a definition. There can be truths about the essential features of *red* and *or* even if there is no way to say in more fundamental terms what it is for an object to be red, or for it to be the case that p or q.

If this notion of essence is admitted, then it's clear that the connection between a property F and its definition ϕ should be grounded in the nature of F itself. When we say that being a vixen consists in being a female fox, we make a claim about the essence of the property, namely that it lies in the nature of vixenhood that vixens are vixens because they are female foxes. More generally:

Real Definition: ϕ defines F iff it lies in the nature of F that for all x, if x is F or ϕ then ϕ(x) grounds Fx.

The real definition of F is a condition, the satisfaction of which always makes the F-things F *and whose status as such derives from the nature of F itself.* The clear cases of real definition fit this account, and while there may be other ways to bring out what the clear cases have in common, this approach plausibly captures one important notion in the vicinity.

VARIETIES OF NATURALISM

This account revives Type-2 Non-Reductive Naturalism as a coherent possibility. The type-2 theorist agrees with the reductionist that there exists a uniform, non-normative condition ϕ such that whenever x is F, x is F in virtue of being ϕ. But, whereas the reductionist thinks that this amounts to a definition of F, sourced in the very nature of F, the type-2 theorist regards the link between ϕ and F as a *synthetic grounding law* which associates F with a grounding condition that is, as it were, external to it. This is still Naturalism, since it holds that the atomic F-facts are always grounded without remainder in the non-normative facts. But because the view construes the relation between ϕ and F as external in this way, it allows the type-2 theorist to say that, despite their intimate connection, being F is one thing, being ϕ another.

It must be stressed, however, that while this view is coherent in principle, it is inconsistent with an attractive thought. In the clear cases of grounding, whenever p grounds q we can point to an item whose essence *mediates* the connection. A grounds A ∨ B. Why? Because it lies in the nature of *disjunction* that disjunctive facts are always grounded in their true disjuncts. X is red grounds X is colored. Why? In part because it lies in the nature of red that whatever is red is thereby colored. Such examples suggest a principle: whenever p grounds q, there must be some item internal to p or q whose essence includes a general law to the effect that every p-like fact grounds a corresponding q-like fact. If a fact and its grounds must always be internally connected in this way, then Type-2 Non-Reductive Naturalism is in trouble. The view says that $\phi(\alpha)$ always grounds $F\alpha$, but denies that it lies in the nature of F that this is so. But if the nature of F doesn't mediate the connection, it's hard to see what could. So if grounding connections must be mediated, Type-2 Non-Reductive Naturalism is once again untenable.

Type-1 Non-Reductive Naturalism faces no such problem. This view says that facts of the form $F\alpha$ have heterogeneous non-normative grounds, with $F\alpha$ grounded sometimes in $\phi_1(\alpha)$, sometimes in $\phi_2(\alpha)$, etc. If these grounding connections must all be mediated by general laws sourced in the nature of some item, the type-1 theorist must accept that for each of these grounding conditions ϕ_i:

It lies in the nature of F that for all x, if $\phi_i(x)$ then $\phi_i(x)$ grounds Fx.

Given plausible assumptions, this will entail:

It lies in the nature of F that for all x: Fx iff [$\phi_1(x)$ grounds Fx or $\phi_2(x)$ grounds Fx or ...]

But—and here is crucial point—this does not entail:

It lies in the nature of F that for all x: if Fx then [$\phi_1(x) \lor \phi_2(x) \lor$ ...] grounds Fx.

This last claim says that F is defined by the disjunctive condition [$\phi_1(x) \lor \phi_2(x) \lor$ ...]. But the non-reductive naturalist can resist this, insisting that while there are many "F-making features," each certified as such by the nature of F, the disjunction of those features is not an F-making feature. And this is not crazy. A theorist, impressed by the diversity of wrong-making features, may say: some acts are wrong because they kill people, others because they break promises, etc. But when A is wrong because it's a killing, it would be a mistake to say that A is wrong *because it's either a killing or a promise breaking or ...* . To the contrary, if A is wrong because it's a killing of a certain sort, reference to promise breaking has no place in the complete account of what makes A wrong. As a general matter, it does not follow from the fact that p grounds q and r grounds q that [p $\lor$ r] also grounds q. So it's open to the non-reductive naturalist to say that even though facts of the form α *is wrong* are always grounded in non-normative facts $\phi_i(\alpha)$, and even though each such grounding connection is mediated by a law sourced in the nature of *wrong*, there need be no single non-normative condition, not even a disjunctive one, in which facts about wrongness are always grounded.

The options for the ethical naturalist are thus as follows. The reductive naturalist says that the nature of each normative F yields a uniform non-normative ground $\phi(\alpha)$ for every fact of the form $F\alpha$. The non-reductive naturalist agrees that each particular fact $F\alpha$ is grounded in some such $\phi(\alpha)$, but insists either that this connection is non-uniform (type 1) or that it is not built into the nature of F (type 2) (Figure 9.1). Of course, we have said nothing about how one might choose among these views, but that is beyond our remit. The point of this exercise was to clarify the question we began with, namely, "What

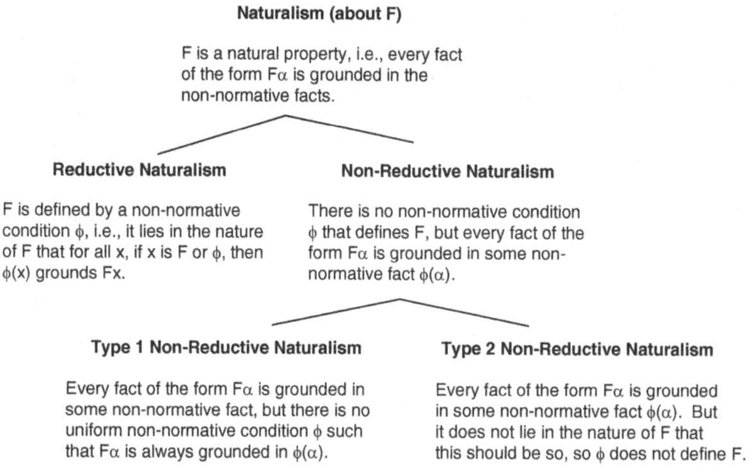

Naturalism (about F)

F is a natural property, i.e., every fact
of the form Fα is grounded in the
non-normative facts.

Reductive Naturalism

F is defined by a non-normative
condition φ, i.e., it lies in the nature
of F that for all x, if x is F or φ, then
φ(x) grounds Fx.

Non-Reductive Naturalism

There is no non-normative condition
φ that defines F, but every fact of the
form Fα is grounded in some non-
normative fact φ(α).

Type 1 Non-Reductive Naturalism

Every fact of the form Fα is grounded in
some non-normative fact, but there is no
uniform non-normative condition φ such
that Fα is always grounded in φ(α).

Type 2 Non-Reductive Naturalism

Every fact of the form Fα is grounded
in some non-normative fact φ(α). But
it does not lie in the nature of F that
this should be so, so φ does not define F.

Figure 9.1

is the relation between the normative and the natural?," and for that purpose it is enough to note that, given the apparatus we have adopted, these are the options for the naturalist.

VARIETIES OF NON-NATURALISM

If Naturalism is defined as we have defined it, then **Non-Naturalism** is the view that at least one normative fact of the form Fα is not fully grounded in the non-normative facts. The varieties of Non-Naturalism are defined by what they go on to say about how such facts *are* grounded.

One possibility is:

Brutalism: Some normative facts of the form Fα are completely ungrounded.

On this view, the normative features of actions and other particulars are like the basic physical features of fundamental particles: objects simply *have* them, but not in virtue of any of their descriptive features. Of course, this sounds preposterous to modern ears, and that's worth noting. We have said next to nothing about what distinguishes the normative features as a class. And yet somehow we know in advance that the normative features of things are always grounded at least in part in their other features. Why should this be? This is a neglected question which any complete theory of these matters should address.

Brutalism aside, non-naturalists agree that atomic normative facts of the form Fα are always somehow grounded in the natural facts, while insisting that in at least one case, this connection does not amount to a full metaphysical ground. The challenge for the non-naturalist is to give some positive account of this connection, and here the most straightforward view is:

Bridge Law Non-Naturalism (about F): Every fact of the form Fα is grounded in some non-normative fact φ(α), together with a bridge law connecting F and φ.

Views with this flavor are highly plausible in other areas. If you drive down Main Street at 80 mph, your act is *against the law*, in part because of its non-legal features and in part because, in general, it's illegal to drive down Main Street at more than 30 mph. The grounding explanation of a particular legal fact must always include a general legal fact of this sort. According to Bridge Law Non-Naturalism, the normative facts are like the legal facts in this respect. Particular facts of the form $F\alpha$ are grounded in the natural features ϕ of α, together with a general law that somehow bridges the gap between the two.

The main challenge for this view is to specify the form of the bridge laws. It is tempting to formulate them as universally quantified material conditions of the form $\forall x\,(\phi(x) \supset Fx)$. But on reflection, this can't be right. Any account of this sort will entail that when a is F,

Fa is partly grounded in $\forall x\,(\phi(x) \supset Fx)$.

(p is **partly grounded** in q when p is part of a full metaphysical ground of q.) But exotic cases aside, universal generalizations are partly grounded in their instances. So if a is F,

$\forall x\,(\phi(x) \supset Fx)$ is partly grounded in $\phi(a) \supset Fa$.

But just as a disjunctive fact is grounded in its true disjuncts, a material conditional with a true consequent is at least partly grounded in its consequent:

$\phi(a) \supset Fa$ is partly grounded in Fa.

But then it will follow, given the transitivity of partial grounding, that Fa is partly grounded in Fa. And while this may be tenable in special cases (Jenkins 2011), no metaethical view should have it as a general consequence that whenever an act is right, it is right because it is right. What this shows is that the bridge laws that figure in the grounding of particular normative facts must be proper *laws*, i.e., general principles that are not grounded in their instances and which are therefore fit to ground them.

One possibility is:

Strong Bridge Law Non-Naturalism (about F): Every fact of the form $F\alpha$ is grounded in a non-normative fact $\phi(\alpha)$ together with the fact that $\square\,\forall x\,(\phi(x) \supset Fx)$.

(Here "$\square$" means "It is metaphysically necessary that … .") On this view, when we ask what makes it the case that some particular act is wrong, a complete answer will take the form: the act is wrong because it's ϕ, and because as a matter of absolute necessity, whatever is ϕ is wrong.

This is a non-naturalist view because it locates a normative fact—the modal bridge law—in the ground of each particular normative fact. However, the contrast between this view and a corresponding naturalist view will be quite subtle. Whenever the strong bridge law non-naturalist explains a particular normative fact Fa by saying that Fa is grounded in $\phi(a)$ plus $\square\,\forall x\,(\phi(x) \supset Fx)$, his naturalist counterpart will say that Fa is grounded in $\phi(a)$ all by itself and that the modal bridge law, while true, plays no role in making it the case that a is F. This is an intelligible dispute, but an arcane one. For an analogy, we might consider a dispute between two theorists who agree that the existence of a set is always at least partly grounded in the existence of its members, one of whom thinks that the existence of {a, b} is *fully grounded* in the existence of *a* and *b*, while the other insists that we get a full ground only if we add a principle to the effect that necessarily, if two objects exist, so does the set containing them. If the grounding idiom is clear, this is a meaningful dispute, but if the answer isn't obvious, it's quite unclear what sort of argument might resolve it. The same might be said about the dispute between the strong bridge law non-naturalist and his naturalistic counterpart.

The main challenge for this view arises when we ask for an explanation of the modal bridge laws. If they cannot be explained then the view posits the sort of unexplained necessary connection between the normative and the natural that naturalists have traditionally found repugnant (Blackburn 1984; McPherson 2012; see Pekka Väyrynen's chapter "The Supervenience Challenge to Non-Naturalism"). On the other hand, if they can be explained, then the explanation will presumably advert to essences. The claim will be that $\phi(x)$ necessitates Fx because it lies in the nature of F, perhaps together with other items, that whatever is ϕ is F. But then the view will entail that the nature of the normative property F encodes non-normative necessary and sufficient conditions for being F. And while that is not quite Reductive Naturalism as we have defined it, it is very close.

The great advantage of Strong Bridge Law Non-Naturalism is that, alone among the non-naturalist views to be considered here, it vindicates Supervenience. If every normative fact of the form Fa is partly grounded in a law of the form $\Box \forall x\, \phi(x) \supset Fx$, then given standard assumptions, it follows that if two things are alike in every non-normative respect, they are alike with respect to F. We close by canvassing some non-naturalist views that are inconsistent with Supervenience.

The first is a species of Bridge Law Non-Naturalism on which the bridge laws are *normative laws* marked by a distinctive modality all their own. The pertinent analogy is with laws of nature, understood, not as patterns in nature, but as superlative facts that explain those patterns (Armstrong 1983, Maudlin 2007). Such laws may be understood as facts of the form *It is nomically necessary that p*, where nomic necessity is a *sui generis* modality with which we are antecedently familiar. When you drop a rock and it falls, this is no accident: given the circumstances, the rock *must* fall. And yet there are metaphysically possible worlds with different laws in which you drop a rock in just these circumstances and it floats away. The *must* that figures in the laws of nature is therefore weaker than the *must* of metaphysical necessity (Sidelle 2002). By analogy, some philosophers have suggested that we have a similarly *sui generis* modality in ethics (Fine 2002). When Jones kicks Smith, his act is wrong, and that's no accident. Any act of this sort, in these circumstances, *must* be wrong. But this is not the metaphysical *must*. There may be remote metaphysically possible worlds in which the normative laws are different and acts with the same non-normative features are not wrong. Still, it's no accident that Jones' act was wrong. Given its non-normative profile, it had to be. But that is to say that there exists a normative law whose content may be put as follows: it is normatively necessary that an act with just those features is wrong.

It is an open question whether normative necessity can be defined in more basic terms (Rosen forthcoming). But so long as it's in good order, we have the following possible view:

Moderate Bridge Law Non-Naturalism (about F): Every fact of the form Fa is grounded in some non-normative fact $\phi(a)$ together with a principle of the form: it is normatively necessary that $\forall x\, (\phi(x) \supset Fx)$.

Since these bridge laws need not be metaphysically necessary, this view does not vindicate Supervenience as it is usually understood, namely, as the claim that whenever two *metaphysically* possible individuals are alike in every non-normative respect, they are alike in every normative respect (cf. Scanlon 2014). However, it does license a weaker Supervenience thesis. If we say that a world is *normatively possible* relative to w iff it shares the normative laws of w, then the moderate bridge law non-naturalist may affirm:

Normative Supervenience: If two normatively possible objects are alike in every non-normative respect, they are alike in every normative respect.

It is arguable that the intuition that supports the near consensus about Supervenience in fact only supports this weaker claim. When we are invited to imagine an act that is just like A in all non-normative respects but which is (say) right when A is wrong, we balk. This suggests that *in some sense* there could not possibly be such an act. But when we are explicitly invited to consider a world in which A has the non-normative features it actually has, but in which the *moral laws are different*—e.g., a world in which Act Utilitarianism is true—we may well say, "Fine. If things had been like *that*, then A, which is in fact wrong, would have been right, despite the fact that it's non-normative features would have been no different."

Bridge law non-naturalists of every stripe hold that particular normative facts are metaphysically grounded in the natural facts together with general normative principles. An alternative and seemingly quite different view holds instead that the relation between the normative facts and the natural facts that underlie them is not a matter of *metaphysical* grounding at all, but rather involves a different relation: **normative grounding** (Fine 2012). Normative grounding resembles metaphysical grounding in some respects. Both are non-causal explanatory relations between a fact and the facts in virtue of which it obtains. Moreover, both have modal implications: if Γ grounds p in either sense, then Γ necessitates p in a corresponding sense. The difference is that while relations of metaphysical grounding yield maximally stringent metaphysically necessary connections between the underlying facts and the facts they ground, relations of normative grounding are looser: when p normatively grounds q, p entails q only as a matter of *normative* necessity.

If this notion is admitted, we have another view:

Particularist Non-Naturalism (about F): Every normative fact of the form Fα is normatively grounded in some non-normative fact of form $\phi(\alpha)$. However, Fα is not metaphysically grounded in $\phi(\alpha)$, nor in $\phi(\alpha)$ together with a general law.

The contrast between this view and Moderate Bridge Law Non-Naturalism is (once again) real but subtle. Given a normative fact Fa, both views hold there is a sense in which Fa is grounded in a normative fact $\phi(a)$ that entails Fa as a matter of normative necessity. To this, the moderate bridge law non-naturalist adds two claims: that in every such case there is a general law according to which it is normatively necessary that whatever is ϕ is F, and that $\phi(a)$ conspires with this general law to provide a complete metaphysical ground for Fa. The particularist can reject the first claim, holding that while it may be true in this particular case that $\phi(a)$ grounds Fa, there are normatively possible cases in which $\phi(b)$ fails to ground Fb. Or he can accept the first claim while insisting that the normative law connecting ϕ and F, though genuine, plays no role in grounding the normative fact Fa.

The first view is an extreme form of particularism, and it is not clear whether it is tenable. One is powerfully tempted to say that, if there are normatively possible cases in which φ(b) does not ground Fb, then φ(a) does not ground Fa *all by itself*, but rather only in conjunction with some further fact about a's identity (e.g., the fact that a is *a*). But in that case there will be a general law in the vicinity, namely, that as a matter of normative necessity, for all x, if φ(x) and x = a, then Fx. The second view amounts to a more plausible form of particularism according to which general laws, such as they are, play no role in grounding the atomic normative facts but rather emerge as consequences of the grounding relations among the atomic facts and their grounds (Dancy 1981).

Again, we have said little about how we might choose among these views. But since the aim was simply to canvas the possibilities, it suffices to say that, given the framework we have adopted, the options for the ethical non-naturalist include the following (Figure 9.2):

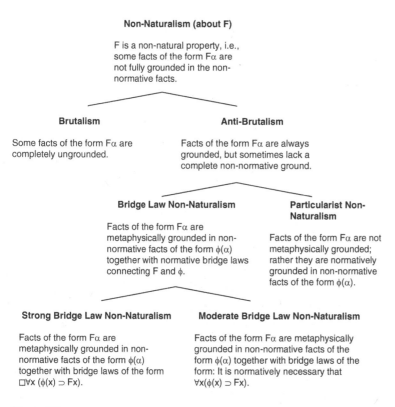

Non-Naturalism (about F)

F is a non-natural property, i.e., some facts of the form Fα are not fully grounded in the non-normative facts.

Brutalism

Some facts of the form Fα are completely ungrounded.

Anti-Brutalism

Facts of the form Fα are always grounded, but sometimes lack a complete non-normative ground.

Bridge Law Non-Naturalism

Facts of the form Fα are metaphysically grounded in non-normative facts of the form φ(α) together with normative bridge laws connecting F and φ.

Particularist Non-Naturalism

Facts of the form Fα are not metaphysically grounded; rather they are normatively grounded in non-normative facts of the form φ(α).

Strong Bridge Law Non-Naturalism

Facts of the form Fα are metaphysically grounded in non-normative facts of the form φ(α) together with bridge laws of the form □∀x (φ(x) ⊃ Fx).

Moderate Bridge Law Non-Naturalism

Facts of the form Fα are metaphysically grounded in non-normative facts of the form φ(α) together with bridge laws of the form: It is normatively necessary that ∀x(φ(x) ⊃ Fx).

Figure 9.2

CONCLUSION

We began with a vague question—What is the relation between the normative and the natural?—and the idea that the best way to clarify a question is to enumerate the possible answers to it. The rough survey we have provided appeals to a number of "fine-grained" metaphysical notions—grounding, essence, and definition. If one rejects these notions and their ilk, as many philosophers are wont to do, then our question really only has two answers: the naturalist view that the normative facts supervene on the non-normative facts and the non-naturalist view that they do not. (Naturalists may disagree about whether statements connecting the normative and the natural are to be reckoned analytic or synthetic, a priori or otherwise, but these are not metaphysical disagreements.) If one accepts the fine-grained vocabulary, an impressive landscape of possibilities opens up. Reductive Naturalism contrasts with two varieties of Non-Reductive Naturalism, all of which contrast with Non-Naturalism in its many forms. This proliferation of possibilities is neither good nor bad. It simply follows if the fine-grained idioms we have adopted are in good order.

REFERENCES

Armstrong, D. M. 1983. *What Is a Law of Nature?* Cambridge: Cambridge University Press.

Audi, P. 2012. Grounding: Toward a Theory of the *In-Virtue-Of* Relation. *Journal of Philosophy* 109: 685–711.

Bennett, K. 2011. By Our Bootstraps. *Philosophical Perspectives* 25: 27–41.

Blackburn, S. 1984. Supervenience Revisited. In I. Hacking (ed.), *Exercises in Analysis: Essays by Students of Casimir Lewy.* Cambridge: Cambridge University Press. pp. 59–94.

Brink, D. 1989. *Moral Realism and the Foundations of Ethics.* Cambridge: Cambridge University Press.

Correia, F. and B. Schnieder 2012. *Metaphysical Grounding.* Cambridge: Cambridge University Press.

Dancy, J. 1981. On Moral Properties. *Mind* 90: 367–85.

Dowell, J. 2013. Naturalism, Ethical. *International Encyclopedia of Ethics.* Malden, MA: Wiley-Blackwell.

Enoch, D. 2011. *Taking Morality Seriously: A Defense of Robust Realism.* Oxford: Oxford University Press.

Fine, K. 1994a. Essence and Modality. *Philosophical Perspectives* 8: 1–16.

Fine, K. 1994b. Senses of Essence. In W. Sinnott-Armstrong, D. Raffman, and N. Asher (eds.), *Modality, Morality and Belief. Essays in Honor of Ruth Barcan Marcus.* Cambridge: Cambridge University Press. pp. 53–73.

Fine, K. 2001. The Question of Realism. *Philosophers' Imprint* 1(2): 1–30.

Fine, K. 2002. The Varieties of Necessity. In T. Gendler and J. Hawthorne (eds.), *Conceivability and Possibility,* Oxford: Oxford University Press. pp. 253–81.

Fine, K. 2012. Guide to Ground. In F. Correia and B. Schnieder (eds.), *Metaphysical Grounding.* Cambridge: Cambridge University Press. pp. 37–80.

Fodor, J. 1974. Special Sciences (Or: The Disunity of Science as a Working Hypothesis). *Synthese* 28(2): 97–115.

Goodman, N. 1983. *Fact, Fiction and Forecast.* 4th ed. Cambridge, MA: Harvard University Press.

Jackson, F. 1998. *From Metaphysics to Ethics.* Oxford: Oxford University Press.

Jenkins, C. 2011. Is Metaphysical Dependence Irreflexive? *The Monist,* 94: 267–76.

Kim, J. 1984. Concepts of Supervenience. *Philosophy and Phenomenological Research* 45(December): 153–76.

Leuenberger, S. 2014. Grounding and Necessity. *Inquiry* 57(2):151–74.

Lewis, D. 1986. *On the Plurality of Worlds.* Oxford: Blackwell.

McPherson, T. 2012. Ethical Non-Naturalism and the Metaphysics of Supervenience. *Oxford Studies in Metaethics* 7: 205.

Maudlin, T. 2007. *The Metaphysics within Physics.* Oxford: Oxford University Press.

Miller, Richard W. 1985. Ways of Moral Learning. *Philosophical Review* 94(4): 507–56.

Moore, G. E. 1903. *Principia Ethica.* Cambridge: Cambridge University Press.

Parfit, D. 2011. *On What Matters.* Oxford: Oxford University Press.

Putnam, H. 1975. On Properties. In his *Mathematics, Matter and Method.* Cambridge: Cambridge University Press. pp. 305–22.

Rosen, G. 2010. Metaphysical Dependence: Grounding and Reduction. In B. Hale and A. Hoffman (eds.), *Modality: Metaphysics, Logic and Epistemology.* Oxford: Oxford University Press. pp. 109–35.

Rosen, G. 2015. Real Definition. *Analytic Philosophy* 56(3): 189–209.

Rosen, G. Forthcoming. Normative Necessity. In M. Dumitru (ed.), *Metaphysics, Meaning and Modality: Themes from Kit Fine.* Oxford: Oxford University Press.

Scanlon, T. 2014. *Being Realistic about Reasons.* Oxford: Oxford University Press.

Schaffer, J. 2009. On What Grounds What. In D. Chalmers, D. Manley, and R. Wasserman (eds.), *Metametaphysics: New Essays on the Foundations of Ontology*. Oxford: Oxford University Press.

Schmitt, J. and M. Schroeder. 2011. Supervenience Arguments under Relaxed Assumptions. *Philosophical Studies* 156(1): 133–60.

Sidelle, A. 2002. On the Metaphysical Contingency of the Laws of Nature. In T. Gendler and J. Hawthorne (eds.), *Conceivability and Possibility*. Oxford: Oxford University Press.

Sober, E. 1982. Why Logically Equivalent Predicates May Pick Out Different Properties. *American Philosophical Quarterly* 19(2): 183–89.

Sturgeon, N. 2006. Moral Explanations Defended. In J. Dreier (ed.), *Contemporary Debates in Moral Theory*. Oxford: Blackwell.

Sturgeon, N. 2007. Ethical Naturalism. In D. Copp (ed.), *Oxford Handbook of Ethical Theory*. Oxford: Oxford University Press.

Wedgwood, R. 2007. *The Nature of Normativity*. Oxford: Oxford University Press.

Wilson, J. 2014. No Work for a Theory of Grounding. *Inquiry* 57(5–6): 1–45.

10

The Supervenience Challenge to Non-Naturalism

Pekka Väyrynen

INTRODUCTION

It is impossible that one action is morally impermissible and another permissible unless they differ also in some other respect; perhaps one involves stealing but the other doesn't. One person cannot be morally better or more virtuous than another without there being some other difference between them, such as that one is more reliably disposed to help others or to keep her promises. It cannot be that you have a reason to run for the bus on one occasion but no reason to do so on another if the situations differ in no other qualitative respect, such as how efficient each action will be for achieving your aims or for doing something good. If two persons are qualitatively exactly alike (or "indiscernible") in all other ways, they cannot but be morally alike as well.

The above claims look immensely plausible. Each is a way of saying that some normative feature (moral permissibility, moral goodness, reasons for action) is *supervenient*. Collectively, they suggest that normative features, as a family comprising moral features and all other normative and evaluative features (such as aesthetic and prudential values and reasons) are supervenient. There are several different relations that go by the name of supervenience, but they all share this core idea: things cannot differ in one respect without differing in some other respect. (See McLaughlin and Bennett 2011 and McPherson 2015 for excellent overviews of supervenience in general and in ethics, respectively.) Because supervenience is a necessary connection, it requires explanation. Different metaethical theories may explain the connection in different ways. But if a theory cannot provide a good explanation, this makes it in one respect worse than its rivals. The supervenience challenge says this is the predicament of non-naturalist moral realism.

Non-naturalism is a form of *moral realism*—a family of views according to which there are moral truths that are objective and metaphysically robust. (If a proposition p is objectively true, in the sense realists have in mind, p is true independently of anyone's attitudes, stances, beliefs, and theories concerning whether p. Moreover, the realist notion of truth isn't merely deflationary but carries ontological commitment.) In slightly different terminology, moral predicates, such as 'good', 'wrong', and 'permissible', refer to objective moral properties in a metaphysically significant sense, and at least some such properties have instances. If the claim 'Stealing simply for one's own gain is wrong' is true, what makes it true is the fact that stealing simply for one's own gain has a metaphysically significant attitude-independent property of being wrong.

The distinctive claim of *non-naturalist* moral realism is that these moral properties, and perhaps normative properties in general, are *sui generis*—significantly different in kind from any other properties. (Contemporary non-naturalists include Hampton 1998; Shafer-Landau 2003; Cuneo 2007a; FitzPatrick 2008; Enoch 2011; Wielenberg 2014; Cuneo and Shafer-Landau 2014; and Skarsaune 2015. Some of these authors characterize non-naturalism as "robust" moral realism.) To spell this out a bit, the non-naturalist thinks that at least some normative properties aren't identical to any natural or supernatural properties, nor do they have a real definition, metaphysical reduction, or any other such tight metaphysical explanation wholly in terms of natural or supernatural properties. Normative properties are, in short, *discontinuous* with natural and supernatural properties. Supernatural properties are tricky to distinguish from the non-natural, but are meant to include non-normative properties such as being willed by God. Natural properties are (i) such that any synthetic propositions about their instantiations (including propositions stating any empirical regularities in which they could figure) are empirically defeasible or (ii) reducible to properties that satisfy (i) (Smith 2000: 95–96; Copp 2003: 185). The properties, kinds, and causal systems studied by the natural sciences, psychology, and at least some social sciences come out as natural on this criterion, but so can properties to which we have reliable non-scientific empirical access. Non-naturalists deny that normative properties are anything like that. What makes them so? Perhaps, as many non-naturalists suggest, that they are *irreducibly* normative. (That would distinguish normative properties also from mathematical properties, which might be neither natural nor supernatural.) Be that as it may, the core idea of non-naturalist moral realism is that moral (and other normative) properties are metaphysically *sui generis* and at least some of these properties have instances.

So understood, non-naturalism and the supervenience of the moral jointly entail that moral properties supervene on some properties with which they are discontinuous. The supervenience challenge says that non-naturalists cannot explain this connection without making commitments that count significantly against their view. So, unless non-naturalism has other merits worth the cost, we should reject it. In what follows, I formulate a version of this challenge more carefully, consider the most promising non-naturalist replies to it, and suggest that none of the replies are as yet fully effective.

THE SUPERVENIENCE CHALLENGE

Virtually all metaethical theories seek to accommodate in some way the idea that there can be no moral difference without some other difference. It is less clear whether any particular way of fleshing out this core idea of supervenience is similarly close to common ground in metaethics. Perhaps there is no supervenience claim that does serious argumentative work without begging any important metaethical questions (Sturgeon 2009).

But some claims might be suitably neutral for a particular philosophical purpose. I'll first identify a supervenience claim that isn't question-begging in the context of the supervenience challenge to non-naturalism, and then explain the challenge.

If things cannot differ morally without differing in some other qualitative respect, this doesn't seem to be merely a claim about how things must be in a given world. To use a classic example from R. M. Hare, if St. Francis was a good person, then *anyone* exactly like him in all other respects *couldn't but have been* good as well (Hare 1952: 145). What difference would it make whether a duplicate of St. Francis were actual or merely possible? None, it seems. Accordingly, the supervenience challenge to non-naturalism is best understood in terms of *strong* supervenience, which constrains variations among any possible entities. (The contrast is with *weak* supervenience, which only constrains entities in the same possible world; see Kim 1984.) Strong supervenience, like supervenience in general, is a *purely modal* relation. It only entails that certain patterns of variation hold between how things are in one respect and some other respect. It doesn't follow that the supervenient properties are metaphysically dependent on or explained by properties in the supervenience base. (Everything supervenes on itself, and the supervenience of one family of properties on another is compatible with the supervenience of the latter on the former.)

In what follows, it'll help to be clear about the formal structure of strong supervenience claims, in particular that they invoke necessity twice:

(SS) $\Box$ $(\forall F \text{ in } a)(\forall x)[Fx \rightarrow (\exists G \text{ in } \beta)(Gx \ \& \ \Box(\forall y)(Gy \rightarrow Fy))]$

This formula requires both explanation in ordinary language and interpretations of the schematic variables and the necessity operators (marked by '$\Box$'). Variables 'x' and 'y' pick out individuals like persons or actions. Thus, (SS) isn't a *global supervenience* claim to the effect that the *world* couldn't have been different in one type of respect without some other type of difference, but an *individual supervenience* claim. (For complications regarding strong global supervenience, see McLaughlin and Bennett 2011: §4.4.) I'll take 'a' and 'β' to pick out families of properties. We'll be interested in the case where a is the family of moral properties, so 'F' stands for some specific moral property in that family. (Of β, more below.) So interpreted, (SS) states an *ontological* connection between families of *properties*, not an *ascriptive* connection between types of *judgments* (Klagge 1988). This interpretation isn't available to metaethical expressivists, who eschew ontological commitment to moral properties and treat supervenience as a constraint on normative judgments (Hare 1952: 80–81; Hare 1981; Blackburn 1985). (Complications that arise in the context of "quasi-realist" expressivism are usefully explored in Dreier 2015.)

The interpretation of the necessity operators in (SS), taken as a moral supervenience claim, is controversial. The innermost necessity is typically taken as metaphysical: whenever something has a moral property M, it has some (possibly very complex) property that metaphysically necessitates M. (We'll revisit this assumption in the last section.) This interpretation reflects the widely held view that the basic principles of morality are metaphysically necessary. The outermost necessity is most often taken as conceptual, but sometimes as metaphysical. (For our purposes, conceptual necessity may be understood as metaphysical necessity knowable by conceptual reflection. In other contexts, this might require finessing. Taking the outermost necessity as metaphysical is compatible with but not entailed by the view that moral supervenience is a substantive *moral* truth; see Kramer 2009: chapter 10.)

Given this interpretation, (SS) says the following: as a matter of conceptual/metaphysical necessity (the outermost '$\Box$'), when something has a moral property (from class α), it has some (possibly complex) property (from class β) such that, as a matter of metaphysical necessity (the innermost '$\Box$'), anything that has the latter property has the moral property. Closer to ordinary English, we might say that absolutely any morally wrong action has some features such that anything else with those features cannot but be wrong as well, and likewise for any other moral property.

In what sort of respect must things differ in order for moral differences to be possible? Many interpretations of 'β' for moral supervenience have been proposed: the factual, the natural, the descriptive, the non-moral. These may all be different, and each interpretation comes with certain costs to metaethical neutrality (Sturgeon 2009). Fortunately, there is a way forward. Call a property *morally involving* if either it is a *sui generis* moral property or its correct analysis ineliminably mentions such properties, and say that a *base property* is any property that isn't morally involving (McPherson 2012: 213–14). This specification of the "supervenience base" generates the following strong supervenience claim:

> SUPERVENIENCE: Necessarily, when something has any moral property, it has some base property such that, as a matter of metaphysical necessity, anything that is exactly alike it with respect to the base property also has the moral property.

SUPERVENIENCE is a *general* rather than *specific* supervenience claim: it only requires *some or other* difference in base respects for a moral difference and says nothing about *which* specific base properties moral properties supervene on. Thus it is neutral between various first-order theories in normative ethics.

Nor does SUPERVENIENCE beg any important metaethical questions at stake in the supervenience challenge to non-naturalism. If moral properties are both supervenient and *sui generis*, as non-naturalists typically claim, they must supervene on a set of base properties with which they are discontinuous. So SUPERVENIENCE follows from non-naturalism. (When talking about non-naturalism, it is usually safe to assume that all base properties are non-moral properties, and I'll sometimes talk this way.) Moral realists, in general, can accept SUPERVENIENCE. Naturalist moral realism, for example, says that moral properties belong to the category of natural properties. This entails that moral properties are base properties, not morally involving properties. Thus, since everything supervenes on itself, moral properties cannot change without some base properties also changing, namely themselves. So SUPERVENIENCE follows trivially from moral naturalism. Nihilist metaethical views can also accept Supervenience. For if nothing instantiates moral properties, it follows trivially that any items that are alike with respect to all base properties are exactly alike morally. They'll be morally void.

The impossibility of moral differences without base differences is plausibly not brute, so it requires explanation. The version of the supervenience challenge to non-naturalism which I'll discuss is generated by conjoining SUPERVENIENCE with a claim concerning what non-naturalism says about SUPERVENIENCE and a plausible methodological assumption. (My formulation of the challenge will largely follow McPherson 2012: 217–19.)

The methodological assumption in question concerns necessary connections between discontinuous properties. Such connections often have explanations. Necessarily, if something is a brick, it is identical to itself. But this necessary connection between the seemingly very different kinds of properties of being a brick and being self-identical has an explanation: everything is necessarily identical to itself and any conditional with a metaphysically necessary consequence is itself metaphysically necessary (Leary 2017). Since many necessary connections between discontinuous properties have explanations, leaving such a connection brute and unexplained looks like a cost. One methodological principle that one might take this point to suggest is the following:

> MODEST HUMEAN: Commitment to brute necessary connections between discontinuous properties counts significantly against a view (McPherson 2012: 217).

MODEST HUMEAN allows that positing brute necessary connections might not rule out a view if it has merits that overall outweigh the cost (McPherson 2012: 218). Thus MODEST HUMEAN is weaker than the more familiar (and more controversial) "Hume's Dictum," which rules out any metaphysically necessary connections (brute or otherwise) between distinct entities (Lewis 1983: 366; for critical discussion, see Wilson 2010). The supervenience challenge might also get by with something weaker still than MODEST HUMEAN (Leary 2017).

Since the non-naturalist claims that moral properties are *sui generis*, she cannot explain the necessary connection in SUPERVENIENCE by the usual expedients of analysis, reduction, or identity. Such explanations would make moral properties continuous with base properties. But if moral and base properties are discontinuous, why should it be impossible for things to differ morally without differing in base respects? Whence a bar on such variations? The following claim about moral non-naturalism has at least *prima facie* plausibility:

> BRUTE CONNECTION: The non-naturalist must take the supervenience of moral properties on base properties to involve a brute necessary connection between discontinuous properties (McPherson 2012: 217).

SUPERVENIENCE, BRUTE CONNECTION, and MODEST HUMEAN jointly entail that moral non-naturalism is committed to brute necessary connections which count significantly against its plausibility.

This formulation of the supervenience challenge to moral non-naturalism differs from others that wear the same label. Perhaps the most discussed version of the challenge is due to Simon Blackburn, who takes a claim much like SUPERVENIENCE to be a *conceptual* truth and uses its alleged conceptual status to argue against moral realism in general (Blackburn 1984: 182–90; 1985). This is an overreach: supervenience doesn't raise problems for naturalist moral realism (Dreier 1992; Sturgeon 2009). The supervenience challenge above targets only moral non-naturalism. Moreover, it can be stated by treating the outermost necessity in SUPERVENIENCE as metaphysical, bracketing the question whether that necessity might also be conceptual.

I'll now turn to the most promising replies to this version of the supervenience challenge. I'll first consider the prospects of rejecting BRUTE CONNECTION and then discuss whether non-naturalists might avoid the challenge by rejecting SUPERVENIENCE. I'll largely bracket MODEST HUMEAN since it isn't special to ethics but a general methodological principle that requires broader assessment. (For a *prima facie* case that MODEST HUMEAN is self-undermining, see Wielenberg 2014: 33–34.)

REJECT BRUTE CONNECTION?

Among the three premises that generate the supervenience challenge to non-naturalism, BRUTE CONNECTION seems the most vulnerable. Even if SUPERVENIENCE isn't explicable by some continuity between moral and base properties, this doesn't entail that it has no other explanation. Non-naturalists may thus seek to reject BRUTE CONNECTION by offering a positive explanation of the kind of necessary connection between discontinuous properties which they take SUPERVENIENCE to assert.

The first response to BRUTE CONNECTION I'll discuss is the Conceptual Strategy. Many philosophers regard SUPERVENIENCE as a conceptual truth: flouting it manifests a conceptual deficiency. The Conceptual Strategy is thus to explain SUPERVENIENCE by the nature of moral concepts in general. We would be deeply puzzled by people who, for instance, regard St. Francis as a good person but at the same time think that there might have been another person with exactly the same character and behavior and placed in exactly the same circumstances, but differed from St. Francis only in not being a good person. Our puzzlement is evidence that such speakers either manifest a deficient grasp of the concept of moral goodness or are talking about something else, and thus evidence that SUPERVENIENCE is a conceptual truth. No further explanation is needed. Explaining general moral supervenience saddles non-naturalism with no additional ontological cost beyond its distinctive commitment to *sui generis* moral properties. (Stratton-Lake and Hooker 2006: 164; Enoch 2011: 149; Olson 2014: 96–99; Cuneo and Shafer-Landau 2014: 429–30.)

The Conceptual Strategy fails, for two reasons. The first is that it fails to provide a right kind of metaphysical basis for the connection which it represents as conceptually necessary. Not all analytic truths have a metaphysical basis; for example, 'I am here now' is analytic but not metaphysically necessary. (I owe this point to Jamie Dreier.) But many do. Even if (as some philosophers think) it is a conceptual necessity that magnets attract iron, it still remains to be explained why or how magnets do this. For realists about magnets and iron, it is fundamentally the world that guarantees attraction between magnets and iron, not our representations of them. The missing explanation will presumably be the same physical explanation that is accepted by people who don't assume that the necessity by which magnets attract iron is conceptual (Sturgeon 1999: 95). SUPERVENIENCE looks more like 'Magnets attract iron' than 'I am here now' in this respect, if only because it is supposed to concern a necessity irrespective of whether the necessity is conceptual. And since SUPERVENIENCE is a connection between families of properties, presumably it holds (if it does) irrespective of whether it is reflected in our concepts. (It should hold irrespective of whether a person who thinks that someone just like you in every non-moral respect could have been a much worse person is conceptually deficient or just bad at moralizing.) Thus it is hard to see how, at least given the terms and conditions of moral realism, the conceptual status of SUPERVENIENCE is supposed to explain the necessary connection it states between moral and base properties. The explanation will point to a metaphysical connection which according to this reply is *also* reflected in moral concepts. The question then arises whether that necessary metaphysical connection is brute.

The second problem with the Conceptual Strategy is that it explains the wrong necessity. (This objection is due to Dreier ms.) Recall that strong supervenience claims like SUPERVENIENCE contain two necessity operators: *necessarily,* if any two possible individuals are alike in every base respect, then they *must* be alike in every moral respect. Now, when proponents of the Conceptual Strategy say that SUPERVENIENCE is conceptually necessary, they mean that the outermost necessity is conceptual. But what about the innermost one? Reading it as conceptual would entail that the base properties (whatever they are) attach to the supervening properties with conceptual necessity. But that isn't true in the moral case. Propositions that state connections between particular non-moral and moral properties are synthetic, not analytic. That is why the innermost necessity operator in SUPERVENIENCE is typically interpreted as metaphysical. So the claim which the Conceptual Strategy represents as a conceptual truth is a truth about a metaphysical necessity. But what the supervenience challenge to non-naturalism represents as needing explanation is the metaphysical necessity by which base properties necessitate moral properties. The Conceptual Strategy thus explains the wrong necessity. The puzzle for non-naturalism remains even if SUPERVENIENCE is a conceptual truth: if moral properties are *sui generis,* how can the necessary metaphysical connection between non-moral base properties and moral properties (marked by the innermost necessity operator) be anything but brute?

A natural alternative to the Conceptual Strategy is to seek a metaphysical explanation of SUPERVENIENCE—a Metaphysical Strategy. Think of the challenge this way: how could there be properties which are *sui generis* and yet supervene in the way SUPERVENIENCE says? Any necessary connection to which non-naturalists may appeal in giving an explanation must hold between discontinuous properties, because otherwise the explanation won't be non-naturalist. And that connection must have an explanation, because explaining one necessary connection by relying on another brute necessary connection between discontinuous properties would merely relocate the problem. The Metaphysical Strategy seeks to identify a necessary metaphysical connection that avoids these problems.

One proposal here is to take moral facts to be *exhaustively constituted* by non-moral facts (Shafer-Landau 2003: 87). Suppose that the fact that Jane is generous is exhaustively constituted by non-moral facts concerning her disposition to assist those in need without a motive of self-interest, and the like (Shafer-Landau 2003: 75). If other instances of generosity can be exhaustively constituted by different non-moral facts, then generosity isn't reducible or definable by any particular non-moral constitution base. And yet, if facts to the effect that someone is generous are always exhaustively constituted by non-moral facts, then things cannot differ with respect to their generosity without differing non-morally. Thus is SUPERVENIENCE explained.

The constitution view fails to help non-naturalists, for two reasons. First, if each instance of a moral property is wholly constituted by some concatenation of non-moral properties, this threatens to make moral properties continuous with non-moral properties. The view that instances of mental properties are constituted by physical properties tends to count as a form of physicalism. And consider material constitution: a statue might have modal properties that the clay constituting it lacks without thereby being a *sui generis* type of entity. (Clay arranged statue-wise is still clay.) Second, explanations that are murkier than what they aim to explain are (all else being equal) no good. Suppose a fact is an instantiation of a property by an object (at a time). It seems that only the property component of facts can carry the structure that fact constitution would require. But the claim that one and the same *property*, F, is constituted by G, H, and I on one instantiation but by J, K, and M on another looks murky—not because it is difficult to grasp (as explanations in quantum physics might be to a lay person), but because its coherence is dubious. How can the constitution of a type entity vary across its tokens in this way? (This problem doesn't arise in the case of the material constitution of physical objects.) No murky claims about fact constitution are required if we say instead that one object can have F in virtue of having G, H, and I and another object can have F in virtue of having J, K, and M. For instance, saying that being painful and being autonomy-undermining can each make an experience bad commits us to no particular metaphysics of badness. (Ridge 2007 discusses a possible reply that goes beyond our scope: if moral properties are understood as *tropes*, or abstract particulars, then what gets constituted on different occasions is a qualitatively similar but numerically distinct entity.)

Nearby variants of the Metaphysical Strategy look to fare no better. Suppose we say instead that moral properties are *realized* by non-moral properties, on analogy with how mental states such as beliefs or pains can be realized by different physical substrata (Shafer-Landau 2003: 77). This analogy is dubious even if we can make sense of moral properties as a kind of functional properties. If a subject's beliefs are realized (at a given time) by brain states, this excludes the realization of her beliefs (at that time) also by silicon-based states or computer hardware. But one can be virtuous by manifesting various different combinations of wisdom, generosity, courage, and the like. This cannot be explained by saying that the latter are realizers of virtue. Analogies between moral non-naturalism and non-reductive physicalism in the philosophy of mind seem generally suspect (Ridge 2007; McPherson 2012: 224–27).

The Metaphysical Strategy isn't fully exhausted by these options. One might, for instance, think that it is in the nature or essence of moral properties to satisfy SUPERVENIENCE in some specific way or other (Wedgwood 2007: 151, 207). Is this necessary connection between (some or other) base properties and the nature of moral properties itself a brute connection between discontinuous properties, and would it be objectionably brute? This is difficult to assess in abstraction from concrete proposals about the nature of moral properties. Thus I'll merely note the possibility of this kind of explanation of SUPERVENIENCE. (Not all of the necessities involved with SUPERVENIENCE might be explicable this way; see Wedgwood 1999 and 2007: 207–20. Wedgwood argues that the remaining necessities involving specific supervenience facts are explicable by appeal to contingent facts. Assessing this account would require a long foray into modal logic, but see Schmitt and Schroeder 2011.)

The last response to BRUTE CONNECTION which I'll consider is the Substitute Strategy. The idea is that the non-naturalist isn't committed to necessary connections between discontinuous properties, but only to certain tolerably brute necessary normative truths. The most developed instance of the Substitute Strategy is T. M. Scanlon's explanation of normative supervenience. (Scanlon thinks that normative facts exist in an ontologically lightweight sense, so he isn't a "robust" non-naturalist realist. But the view below is compatible with non-naturalism.) Consider ordinary statements of reasons for action, such as that "the fact that the edge of a piece of metal is sharp is a reason for me, now, not to press my hand against it" (Scanlon 2014: 30). This ordinary reason relation only obtains when the piece of metal is, in fact, sharp, and it is normatively "mixed" thanks to its non-normative element. But the mixture has an essentially normative component, of the form R(p, x, c, a), where R relates a proposition p, an agent x, a circumstance c, and an action a. To get a rough intuitive grip, think of statements of the form R(p, x, c, a) as saying that "if p were true, and x were in circumstance c, then one reason for x to do a would be that p" (Schroeder 2015: 196).

These R truths are normatively "pure" in the sense that they hold irrespective of how the non-normative facts are (Scanlon 2014: 37–38). By contrast, ordinary reason claims like the one concerning my reason not to press the metal are contingent, since it is only contingent that the metal is sharp. What allows Scanlon to use the special normative relation R to explain normative supervenience is his view that R(p, x, c, a) is *always* necessary, if true in the first place (Scanlon 2014: 40–41). Provided that the agent or the circumstances are made sufficiently specific, changing the agent or circumstances in any way delivers a different tuple from <p, x, c, a>. Tuples that stand in R thus have their non-normative features necessarily. So when R holds of <p, x, c, a>, it does so necessarily, no matter how the non-normative facts had been. (We'll return to similar ideas in the last section.) But although pure normative truths of the form R(p, x, c, a) are necessary, they bear no (other) necessary connection, brute or otherwise, to non-normative facts. So they generate no commitment to BRUTE CONNECTION. It is only the mixed normative truths that cannot vary without a non-normative difference. But the supervenience of mixed normative facts on the non-normative is explained by the way they are partly constituted by a relationship to their constituent non-normative facts. So mixed normative facts generate no commitment to BRUTE CONNECTION either. In sum, SUPERVENIENCE is explained on the basis of a conception of "pure" normative facts as facts about a special relation R(p, x, c, a) such that, if they are necessary, then ordinary "mixed" normative facts supervene on the non-normative facts. (Schroeder 2014 and Skarsaune 2015 also offer to non-naturalists an explanation of supervenience based on a conception of basic normative truths on which such truths are always necessary.)

Unfortunately, the Substitute Strategy avoids brute necessary relationships between discontinuous properties only by replacing them with other sorts of brute necessary relationships in the vicinity. As Mark Schroeder notes, "to say that R ever holds of any tuple <p, x, c, a> is just to say that there are some necessary relationships that hold among wholly distinct entities" (Schroeder 2015: 197). Is the distinction between brute necessary truths and brute necessary connections really robust enough to help the Substitute Strategy avoid the kinds of theoretical costs that motivate MODEST HUMEAN?

In this vicinity lurks also a more general worry about treating normative truths as brute, which needn't appeal to MODEST HUMEAN. The Substitute Strategy aims to make it less puzzling how two discontinuous types of fact could be linked as tightly as SUPERVENIENCE says by representing the linkage between normative and non-normative facts as itself a set of normative truths, of the form R(p, x, c, a). This explains the general supervenience of normative properties on non-normative properties, whatever they are, in terms of a set of particular pure normative truths which delivers a corresponding set of truths about which specific non-normative facts are linked with which specific mixed normative facts. (The issue here isn't whether the pure normative content of the R truths can be understood in other terms by giving a reductive definition of R. The issue is what explains why R holds of some tuple when it does.) But for each pure normative truth we can ask: why does R hold of <p, x, c, a>, not of some other tuple <q, y, d, b>? The distribution of the R relationship over facts, agents, circumstances, and actions shouldn't be arbitrary. The same question extends to the necessity of these relationships: when <p, x, c, a> stands in R, why couldn't that tuple have failed to do so? When things are claimed to have some property necessarily, a demand for explanation is usually legitimate. (As the logically weaker demand, contingency is the default status for truths, at least when their modal status is open to dispute. And the view that there are no unexplained necessities is a serious contender in metaphysics.) Why should the R facts be an exception? Yet it seems to follow from Scanlon's view that the particular pure normative truths have no explanation (Scanlon 2014: 44). A theory that provides no explanation is in that respect worse than one that does, and in any case worse off insofar as the demand for explanation is legitimate. Those who find the demand for explanation legitimate are bound to regard Scanlon's explanation of SUPERVENIENCE as leaving too many significant normative truths unexplained. (Largely the same worries as above can be raised against explanations of specific supervenience relations according to which there are metaphysically necessary "normative laws" which specify that if something has certain base properties, then it has certain normative properties, but no explanation for why the normative laws are what they are; see, e.g., Enoch 2011: 142–48.)

REJECT SUPERVENIENCE?

A different way to defend moral non-naturalism against the supervenience challenge is to reject SUPERVENIENCE. This strategy might seem quixotic since SUPERVENIENCE seems to be supported by highly compelling intuitions. But if these intuitions could be captured otherwise, there would be room to reject SUPERVENIENCE. Call this the Contingency Strategy. (The label is due to Dreier ms. If SUPERVENIENCE is false when the innermost necessity is read as metaphysical, then even the most basic moral principles are metaphysically contingent.) To warrant rejecting Supervenience, the Contingency Strategy should give non-naturalism some distinctive explanatory advantage. But that is by no means clear.

The most developed form of the Contingency Strategy is due to Gideon Rosen (forthcoming). Rosen argues that SUPERVENIENCE and non-naturalism form an inconsistent triad with "essentialism" about metaphysical modality, and that out of these three claims we should reject SUPERVENIENCE. Strong supervenience entails that for each moral property M there is a condition consisting of a set of base properties, Φ, which is equivalent to M as a matter of (metaphysical) necessity. Φ may be a vast disjunction of the complete specifications of all metaphysically possible bearers of M in all of their base respects (Jackson 1998: 122–23). Rosen further supposes that Φ is a naturalistic condition specifiable in wholly non-normative terms. (Many non-naturalists agree, such as Shafer-Landau 2003.) But now assume the essentialist theory of metaphysical modality: for a proposition p to be metaphysically possible is just for p to be logically consistent with all of the essential truths, where an essential truth about a given item x (an object, property, relation, etc.) is a truth that obtains in virtue of x's nature or identity (Fine 1994). (For instance, being human is one of the things that lie in the essence of Socrates, but being a member of the singleton set {Socrates} isn't.) It follows that for each moral property M, there is a non-normatively specified naturalistic condition Φ such that for some item x, the equivalence between M and Φ is necessary in virtue of x's nature. Isn't this a form of moral naturalism? The necessary equivalence would be a synthetic truth, but Rosen takes a distinctive commitment of moral non-naturalism to be that "someone who knew the natural facts and the essences might still be in the dark about the synthetic principles that connect the normative facts to their non-normative grounds" (Rosen forthcoming: 12). In short: SUPERVENIENCE and essentialism jointly rule out non-naturalism.

Why not put essentialism in the reject pile instead of SUPERVENIENCE? Essentialism requires very substantial metaphysical commitments regarding the essences of things and casts metaphysical necessity more narrowly than many philosophers think. If, however, you are happy to work with essentialism, now ask yourself: in virtue of what item's nature might the necessary equivalence between (say) moral rightness and Φ hold? It won't be anything about Φ. For if the properties in Φ are wholly non-normative, then their natures are normatively silent. Nor will it be anything about moral rightness. For rightness won't have heard of many of the non-normative properties and relations in Φ, whatever they may be. It is hard to see what other item's nature could rule out the possibility that something is wrong but satisfies Φ. (For discussion, see Leary 2017.) Given essentialism, the metaphysically necessary equivalence between Φ and moral rightness fails if it is logically consistent with all the essential truths that something is wrong but satisfies Φ. And if the necessary equivalence fails, SUPERVENIENCE is false. The point can be brought out with putative counterexamples:

> Consider a world w that is just like the actual world in non-moral respects, but in which act utilitarianism is true. Your act of reading this paper, A, would have been wrong if w had been actual. No matter how much benefit the world derives from your reading this paper, you would have done more good licking stamps for Oxfam instead. So we have a world w in which D(A), a description that gives a complete specification of the wholly non-moral features of A, is true and A is wrong. Together with the actual world—where D(A) is true and A is not wrong— this yields a counterexample to supervenience.
>
>   (Adapted from Rosen forthcoming: 3)

The point may also be put using an epistemological heuristic. You might know all there is to know about the properties and relations in D(A) without knowing whether A is right or wrong. And you might know all there is to know about the nature of wrongness without knowing whether D(A) specifies one of the wrong acts. So it seems that nothing in the essence of things makes w impossible.

The metaphysical contingency of even the most fundamental explanatory principles of ethics—candidates for which include act utilitarianism, Kant's categorical imperative, Ross' plurality of principles of *prima facie* duty, and so on—might seem a suspect result. If St. Francis was a good person, wouldn't absolutely anyone exactly alike him in their non-moral properties have to have been good as well? Rosen offers an innovative explanation of these compelling intuitions. Although no moral truths are absolutely necessary, some are "fact-independent," where p is fact-independent if p is the case and would have been the case no matter how things had been in wholly non-normative respects (Rosen forthcoming: 16). (Cohen 2003 introduces a similar notion of the fact-independence of moral principles, but in a different context.) We might alternatively express this by saying that moral principles hold as a matter of a *sui generis* type of *normative neces-sity* which isn't reducible to metaphysical or natural necessity (Fine 2002). (Rosen offers fact-independence as an explication of Fine's notion of normative necessity. Scanlon sug-gests that the necessity of his pure normative facts is an instance of normative necessity; Scanlon 2014: 41 n. 40. See also Cuneo 2007b: 863–71.) On this view, act utilitarian-ism might still be true in some worlds even if it is false in the actual world and would have been false no matter how the non-normative facts had been. Thus it would be no objection to the moral principles governing your (hopefully permissible!) reading of this chapter to say that those principles would have been false if act utilitarianism had been true. If a moral principle is fact-independent, it would have been true no matter what we had thought or done, no matter how hard we tried to falsify it, no matter what the laws of nature had been, and so on. These claims are analogous to the view that laws of nature aren't metaphysically necessary. Those taking this view usually think that laws of nature are explained by some metaphysically contingent facts. Is anything similarly true of fact-independent moral principles? What metaphysically contingent facts would explain the important modal claims which morality supports, such as that if torture is wrong, then torture would have been wrong no matter how the non-moral facts had been?

Be that as it may, the argument offers powerful reasons to regard fact-independence as an important feature of moral principles and to think that SUPERVENIENCE, under-stood as constraining all metaphysically possible individuals, is controversial in its own right and not required to make sense of the practice of moral theory (Rosen forthcom-ing: 17–19). Perhaps nothing important is lost if we instead adopt the weaker superveni-ence thesis that moral properties supervene on base properties as a matter of normative necessity. (Non-naturalism will still be compatible with a restricted strong supervenience claim: it is metaphysically/conceptually necessary that if any items x and y *in worlds gov-erned by the same set of basic moral principles M** are alike in all base respects, then x and y must be alike in all moral respects. Note that this would make supervenience a substan-tive moral truth; cf. Kramer 2009: chapter 10. It is less clear that nothing important is lost if non-naturalists instead follow Hills 2009 and give up SUPERVENIENCE for the view that moral differences are merely constantly conjoined with base differences.) I'll close with three reservations about the Contingency Strategy.

First, the Contingency Strategy won't help non-naturalism in particular because its characterization of moral naturalism is too narrow. The distinctive commitment of moral naturalism is that moral facts and properties belong to the category of natural facts and properties. It doesn't follow that a property counts as natural only if it has a necessary equivalent specifiable in wholly non-normative terms, since moral properties might meet the criterion of naturalness directly in their own right (Sturgeon 2003: 536–40). Naturalism secures SUPERVENIENCE trivially: moral properties cannot change without a change in some natural properties, namely themselves.

Second, the Contingency Strategy might leave something morally important unex-plained. If act utilitarianism is the basic principle of morality in some possible worlds but not ours, why is that? If sexism, speciesism, or violations of other people's bod-ily integrity are moral obligations in some metaphysically possible worlds, how come ours isn't one of them? (Any particular examples will be controversial: the metaphysical contingency of moral principles doesn't imply that anything could have been morally permissible or required. But constraints on what moral principles can be like, such as consistency and universalizability, may not suffice to rule out morally problematic variation. For instance, why cannot the moral judgments of a fanatic Nazi who thinks he himself ought to have been exterminated if he had been Jewish be consistent and universalizable? For discussion, see Hare 1981.) The Contingency Strategy seems bound to say that these questions have no answer. So if it is legitimate to demand answers to them, failure to explain normative necessities would still be a strike against a theory that posits them. Should no such explanation be forthcoming, the supervenience challenge to non-naturalism might retain some of its bite even if we rejected strong supervenience claims that constrain moral differences across all metaphysically possible worlds. Moreover, even if the brute metaphysical contingency of the basic moral principles wasn't problematic in itself, its seemingly consequent brute *authority* might still be. Act utilitarianism might (as a matter of metaphysical possibility) just as well have been the basic principle of morality. So why *shouldn't* we be guided by it, in lieu of whatever moral principles are basic for our world? Those who want the basic principles of morality to close normative questions concerning their authority may, therefore, find the Contingency Strategy argument unsatisfactory. (One explication of such normative questions can be found in Korsgaard 1996.)

Third, the Contingency Strategy seems to entail too much moral luck. Given moral contingency, it is metaphysically possible that the world could have been just as it is in wholly non-moral respects but our actions had been profoundly morally wrong. For if the basic moral principles had been different, then what we regard as morally creditable might have been morally monstrous. Nor would we have known this: in any metaphysically possible world which is non-morally just like the actual world, we would have the same moral beliefs we actually have; in counter-moral worlds, these beliefs would be badly mistaken. If the basic moral principles are fact-independent but metaphysically contingent, we are extremely fortunate that the things we regard as morally innocuous aren't systematically morally monstrous. But it is incredibly hard to believe that it is *mere luck* that the concern and respect with which we try to treat others and the care and love with which we try to raise our children are morally commendable rather than grotesquely evil. Yet that is our situation, according to the Contingency Strategy. (This argument is due to Dreier ms.)

In conclusion, the Contingency Strategy is intriguing and deserves further discussion, both in its own right and as a response to the supervenience challenge to moral non-naturalism. As it stands, however, it seems to provide no distinctive explanatory advantage to non-naturalism in dealing with the supervenience challenge.

CONCLUSION

The aim of this chapter was to formulate a compelling version of the supervenience challenge to non-naturalist moral realism and assess some of the most promising responses to it. I have focused on two main strategies: rejecting the relevant supervenience thesis (SUPERVENIENCE) and rejecting the claim that non-naturalists must take moral supervenience to involve brute necessary connections between discontinuous properties (BRUTE CONNECTION). The responses I have considered raise fascinating issues. Some of these responses are nonetheless ineffective and even the most promising attempts suffer from some explanatory shortcomings. The demands for explanation on which these shortcomings are premised aren't themselves uncontroversial, however. Nor did I discuss how well some of the responses might work together if combined. The supervenience challenge to non-naturalism is thus not a closed chapter in metaethics.

ACKNOWLEDGMENTS

Thanks to John G. Bennett, Tristram McPherson, David Plunkett, Lea Schroeder, Knut Olav Skarsaune, and Mark van Roojen for comments on earlier drafts.

RELATED TOPICS

Chapter 1, "Non-Naturalistic Realism in Metaethics;" Chapter 2, "Naturalistic Realism in Metaethics;" Chapter 8, "Realism and Objectivity;" Chapter 9, "Metaphysical Relations in Metaethics;" Chapter 27, "The Autonomy of Ethics;" Chapter 40, "Quasi-realism."

REFERENCES

Blackburn, S. (1984) *Spreading the Word*, Oxford: Oxford University Press.
Blackburn, S. (1985) "Supervenience Revisited," in I. Hacking (ed.) *Exercises in Analysis*, Cambridge: Cambridge University Press: 47–67.
Cohen, G.A. (2003) "Facts and Principles," *Philosophy & Public Affairs* 31: 211–45.
Copp, D. (2003) "Why Naturalism?," *Ethical Theory and Moral Practice* 6: 179–200.
Cuneo, T. (2007a) *The Normative Web: An Argument for Moral Realism*, Oxford: Oxford University Press.
Cuneo, T. (2007b) "Recent Faces of Moral Nonnaturalism," *Philosophy Compass* 2: 850–79.
Cuneo, T. and Shafer-Landau, R. (2014) "The Moral Fixed Points: New Directions for Moral Nonnaturalism," *Philosophical Studies* 171: 399–443.
Dreier, J. (1992) "The Supervenience Argument against Moral Realism," *Southern Journal of Philosophy* 30: 13–38.
Dreier, J. (2015) "Explaining the Quasi-Real," *Oxford Studies in Metaethics* 10: 273–97.
Dreier, J. (ms) "Is There a Supervenience Problem for Robust Moral Realism?" Unpublished manuscript.
Enoch, D. (2011) *Taking Morality Seriously: A Defense of Robust Realism*, Oxford: Oxford University Press.
Fine, K. (1994) "Essence and Modality," *Philosophical Perspectives* 8: 1–16.
Fine, K. (2002) "Varieties of Necessity," in T. Gendler and J. Hawthorne (eds.) *Conceivability and Possibility*, Oxford: Oxford University Press: 253–81.
FitzPatrick, W.J. (2008) "Robust Ethical Realism, Non-Naturalism, and Normativity," *Oxford Studies in Metaethics* 3: 159–205.
Hampton, J. (1998) *The Authority of Reason*, Cambridge: Cambridge University Press.
Hare, R.M. (1952) *The Language of Morals*, Oxford: Clarendon Press.
Hare, R.M. (1981) *Moral Thinking*, Oxford: Clarendon Press.
Hills, A. (2009) "Supervenience and Moral Realism," in A. Hieke and H. Leitgeb (eds.) *Reduction—Abstraction—Analysis: Proceedings of the 31st International Ludwig Wittgenstein-Symposium*, Frankfurt: Ontos Verlag: 163–77.
Jackson, F. (1998) *From Metaphysics to Ethics*, Oxford: Oxford University Press.
Kim, J. (1984) "Concepts of Supervenience," *Philosophy and Phenomenological Research* 45: 153–76.
Klagge, J. C. (1988) "Supervenience: Ontological and Ascriptive," *Australasian Journal of Philosophy* 66: 461–70.
Korsgaard, C. (1996) *The Sources of Normativity*, Cambridge: Cambridge University Press.

Kramer, M.H. (2009) *Moral Realism as a Moral Doctrine*, Oxford: Wiley-Blackwell.

Leary, S. (2017) "Non-Naturalism and Normative Necessities," *Oxford Studies in Metaethics* 12: 76–105.

Lewis, D. (1983) "New Work for a Theory of Universals," *Australasian Journal of Philosophy* 61: 343–77.

McLaughlin, B. and Bennett, K. (2011) "Supervenience," in E.N. Zalta (ed.) *The Stanford Encyclopedia of Philosophy* (*Winter 2011 Edition*) [online]. Available at: http://plato.stanford.edu/archives/win2011/entries/supervenience/.

McPherson, T. (2012) "Ethical Non-naturalism and the Metaphysics of Supervenience," *Oxford Studies in Metaethics* 7: 205–34.

McPherson, T. (2015) "Supervenience in Ethics," in E.N. Zalta (ed.) *The Stanford Encyclopedia of Philosophy* (*Winter 2015 Edition*) [online]. Available at: http://plato.stanford.edu/archives/win2015/entries/supervenience-ethics/.

Olson, J. (2014) *Moral Error Theory: History, Critique, Defence*, Oxford: Oxford University Press.

Ridge, M. (2007) "Anti-Reductionism and Supervenience," *Journal of Moral Philosophy* 4: 330–48.

Rosen, G. (forthcoming) "Normative Necessity," in M. Dumitru (ed.) *Metaphysics, Meaning, and Modality: Themes from Kit Fine*, Oxford: Oxford University Press.

Scanlon, T.M. (2014) *Being Realistic about Reasons*, Oxford: Oxford University Press.

Schmitt, J. and Schroeder, M. (2011) "Supervenience Arguments under Relaxed Assumptions," *Philosophical Studies* 155: 133–60.

Schroeder, M. (2014) "The Price of Supervenience," in *Explaining the Reasons We Share*, Oxford: Oxford University Press, 124–44.

Schroeder, M. (2015) "*Being Realistic about Reasons* by T.M. Scanlon," *Australasian Journal of Philosophy* 93: 195–98.

Shafer-Landau, R. (2003) *Moral Realism: A Defence*, Oxford: Oxford University Press.

Skarsaune, K.O. (2015) "How to Be a Moral Platonist," *Oxford Studies in Metaethics* 10: 245–72.

Smith, M. (2000) "Does the Evaluative Supervene on the Natural?" in R. Crisp and B. Hooker (eds.) *Well-Being and Morality*, Oxford: Clarendon Press, 91–114.

Stratton-Lake, P. and Hooker, B. (2006) "Scanlon versus Moore on Goodness," in T. Horgan and M. Timmons (eds.) *Metaethics after Moore*, Oxford: Oxford University Press, 148–68.

Sturgeon, N.L. (1999) "*The Moral Problem* by Michael Smith," *Philosophical Review* 108: 94–97.

Sturgeon, N.L. (2003) "Moore on Ethical Naturalism," *Ethics* 113: 528–56.

Sturgeon, N.L. (2009) "Doubts about the Supervenience of the Evaluative," *Oxford Studies in Metaethics* 4: 53–90.

Wedgwood, R. (1999) "The Price of Non-Reductive Moral Realism," *Ethical Theory and Moral Practice* 2: 199–215.

Wedgwood, R. (2007) *The Nature of Normativity*, Oxford: Oxford University Press.

Wielenberg, E.J. (2014) *Robust Ethics: The Metaphysics and Epistemology of Godless Normative Realism*, Oxford: Oxford University Press.

Wilson, J. (2010) "What Is Hume's Dictum, and Why Believe It?" *Philosophy and Phenomenological Research* 80: 595–637.

11

Vagueness and Indeterminacy in Ethics

Tom Dougherty

EXAMPLES OF ETHICAL VAGUENESS

In an artificial incubator, a zygote gradually develops from a handful of cells to a child who is capable of surviving on its own (Manley ms). With a sufficiently powerful microscope, we would see that its continuous development is constituted by smaller processes in which cells gradually multiply and differentiate. There will come a point in these processes at which we assign the emergent human a moral status higher than that of a cat. But is there a specific millisecond, at which the entity gains this moral status? If we had to choose between terminating the human entity or terminating a cat, are there individual strands of protein that need to bind together for it to become impermissible to terminate the human entity?

This ethical question has familiar descriptive analogs. Is there a precise millisecond at which a cat stops being a kitten? A blind and mewing day-old feline is clearly a kitten. An august 15-year-old cat is clearly not. But between these clear cases, there will be a range of borderline cases—say, Cornelius, a one-year-old cat who is rapidly losing interest in playing with string. Following a common definition, let us say when a term like "kitten" has borderline cases, this term is *vague*.

In our introductory example, the zygote develops in a continuous process, and the vagueness arises because there is no definite degree in this process at which the entity acquires a new moral status. This degree-based vagueness is what gives rise to the Sorites paradox. Consider the following argument:

P1. It is permissible to terminate the single-cell zygote rather than a cat.
P2. If it is permissible to terminate X rather than a cat, and after a millisecond of development, X becomes Y, then it is permissible to terminate Y rather than a cat.
P3. In a continuous process, a zygote will develop into a three-year-old child.
C. Therefore, it is permissible to terminate a three-year-old child rather than a cat.

The conclusion is unacceptable, and yet every premise has some initial plausibility. Hence the paradox.

Ethical vagueness need not always arise from an underlying property that comes in degrees. Suppose our paradigm of a morally responsible person is someone who has a cluster of capacities, e.g., rationality, self-governance, and a capacity to act on ethical reasons. Now suppose Jones has some but not all of this cluster of capacities. We might then say that Jones is a borderline case of a morally responsible person, without explaining this vagueness of "morally responsible" in terms of degrees.

A third putative example of ethical vagueness is a little controversial. Just as some non-comparative terms are vague, so comparative terms can also be vague. For example, is Alfred, who has 1,000 hairs distributed across his head, more bald than Bert, who has 1,500 hairs clustered directly above his ears (Wasserman 2004: 396)? It seems vague which man is balder. But if there is comparative vagueness in non-ethical cases, then there seems nothing to stop it arising in ethical cases too. Just as it could be vague whether Clare is non-comparatively a good artist, it could also be vague as to who is the better artist out of Clare and Dana. If so, we should neither say that each artist is definitely better than the other, nor that both are exactly equally as good—it is not as if a smidgen more creativity in Clare's fingertips would tip the balance in her favor. In this way, we could appeal to comparative ethical vagueness to give an attractive account of how it is possible for two people to be "incommensurable" with respect to, e.g., artistic merit (Shafer-Landau 1995; Broome 1997; Constantinescu 2012; Williams 2015; Elson ms). This is an account that will prove controversial with some (Chang 2002), but it is hard to see what special reasons there would be to be dismissive of comparative ethical vagueness, once we have already taken non-comparative ethical vagueness seriously (Constantinescu 2012; Williams 2015). If value incommensurability is a form of comparative ethical vagueness, then the debate about how we should reason in the face of incommensurable values is, in effect, a debate about how to reason in the face of ethical vagueness. Since the literature on how to reason in the face of incommensurability is vast, and surveyed elsewhere (Hsieh 2007; Chang 2013), I will set it to one side here.

SEMANTIC, EPISTEMIC, AND METAPHYSICAL ACCOUNTS OF VAGUENESS

Outside of ethics, there are three standard explanations of vagueness (Williams 2008). To keep our initial exposition simple, let us first consider "pure" accounts that posit only one source of vagueness. According to a purely semantic account, vagueness is an artifact of how we represent the world in our thought and talk. For example, a semantic theorist might say that our use of the term "kitten" does not settle whether it applies to Cornelius, our two-year-old feline. If so, the statement "Cornelius is a kitten" would be ("alethically") indeterminate insofar as it lacks a determinate truth value. Since this is a view about the indeterminacy of our linguistic representations, a purely semantic theorist would hold that the world itself is perfectly precise.

A purely epistemic account agrees that the world itself is precise but denies that some statements involving vague predicates lack a determinate truth value. The epistemic theorist will say that facts about our usage of the term and facts about the rest of the world jointly determine whether the term applies or does not apply to all entities in the world.

However, the epistemic theorist will say that we are unable to know whether the term applies to certain entities, and hence these entities will be borderline cases for us. So if an epistemic account of the vagueness of "kitten" is correct, then it is either the case that Cornelius is a kitten, or it is not the case that Cornelius is not a kitten. Cornelius would only be a borderline case insofar as it is difficult, and perhaps even impossible, for us to discover whether he is a kitten or not.

Meanwhile, a purely metaphysical account will hold that the world itself is imprecise, insofar as it is metaphysically unsettled whether some entities have particular properties. These entities will be borderline cases for the terms that refer to these properties. On this account, there is genuine metaphysical indeterminacy that is not the result of our epistemic or linguistic limitations: this is vagueness written into the world, which we should continue to acknowledge even if we were omniscient and spoke a perfectly precise language (Barnes 2014). Indeed, if there is metaphysical vagueness, then a perfectly precise language would be *too* precise for accurately capturing all of reality. To capture all of reality, we would need language with imprecision that mirrors the imprecision in the world. If we accept a metaphysical account of the vagueness of "kitten," then we should conclude that the underlying reality is simply that it is metaphysically indeterminate whether Cornelius is a kitten. (This example is for illustrative purposes only; it could be that there are more plausible examples of metaphysical vagueness than that associated with the term "kitten.")

We need not hold a pure account of vagueness, though. We might think that one type of explanation is most appropriate for the vagueness of some terms, while another explanation is appropriate for other terms. For example, someone might hold a semantic account of the vagueness of a term like "kitten," while holding a metaphysical account of the vagueness of a natural kind term like "feline."

So, outside of ethics, accounts of vagueness take stances on issues in the philosophy of language, epistemology, and metaphysics. Since metaethicists aim to give accounts of ethical language, ethical knowledge, and ethical metaphysics, this means that they will need to give accounts of ethical vagueness. So what should metaethicists say about ethical vagueness?

ETHICAL VAGUENESS AND ETHICAL DISAGREEMENT

An early metaethical appeal to vagueness was made by Samuel Clarke, who held that the fittingness of certain actions is "so notoriously plain and self-evident that nothing but the extremest stupidity of mind, corruption of manners, or perverseness of spirit can possibly make any man entertain the least doubt concerning them" (Clarke 1969 [1704–1705]: 194). But if ethical knowledge is so easy, how could people who are not stupid or perverse fall into ethical error? Clarke had this to say:

> But as … two very different colours, by diluting each other very slowly and gradually, may … so run into the other, that it shall not be possible even for a skilful eye to determine exactly where the one ends, and the other begins, and yet the colours really differ as much as can be, not in degree only but entirely in kind, as … white and black: so, though it may perhaps be very difficult in some nice and perplext

cases (which yet are very far from occurring frequently), to define exactly the bounds of right and wrong, … yet right and wrong are nevertheless in themselves totally and essentially different, even altogether as much, as white and black."

(1969 [1704–1705]: 229)

Here, Clarke appears to hold an epistemic account of vagueness, and uses this to press an analogy between descriptive vagueness and ethical vagueness. Clarke's thought is that just as there are borderline cases of "white," there are also borderline cases of "wrong." And just as one may occasionally fail to discern whether a color is white, so one may fail to discern whether an action is wrong. In this way, Clarke appeals to ethical vagueness in order to explain ethical ignorance.

In the contemporary metaethics literature, some philosophers have made a similar appeal to vagueness as part of their overall explanation of ethical disagreement. Explaining ethical disagreement has become a pressing task for "ethical realists." For the purposes of this chapter, let us use the term "ethical realism" coarsely to refer to views that hold the following two commitments. First, these views hold that ethical judgments are members of a broader kind of doxastic mental state, which aims to fit the world; as such, ethical realists disagree with theorists who hold that ethical judgments are conative states that aim to change the way the world is. Second, these views hold that some ethical judgments are true by virtue of representing ethical facts; as such, ethical realists disagree with error theorists who hold that all of our ethical judgments are false because there are no ethical facts to make them true. This coarse-grained conception of ethical realism covers a host of positions that are discussed in this handbook. However, since all of these positions typically assume that we have some ethical knowledge, they face a common challenge: they need to provide a moral epistemology that explains how it is that we can have this knowledge, while simultaneously explaining how it is that we can disagree.

Typically, ethical realists' overall explanation of ethical disagreement is multi-faceted. Ethical realists will explain some ethical disagreement as resulting from non-ethical disagreement (e.g., about the deterrence effect of capital punishment). Further, they will explain other ethical disagreement as resulting from partiality or ideology. But in addition, some ethical realists have posited pockets of ethical vagueness, and argued that we should not expect people to agree when an ethical issue is vague (Brink 1984; Shafer-Landau 1994; Sosa 2001).

However, this response might seem a little quick: why would idealized ethical judges not simply agree that the issues in question are ethically vague (Shafer-Landau, 1994: 336)? After all, when we encounter one-year-old Cornelius, we presumably will not persist long in deep disagreement about whether he is really a kitten. Instead, most likely, we will soon agree that he is a borderline case.

Some ethical realists have conceded this point, but suggested that the upshot is that we have to be careful about how we characterize failures of agreement in the first place. They argue that some cases that might initially look like ethical disagreement are in fact cases in which people simply are failing to agree, insofar as they are not converging on shared judgments about which actions are determinately right and wrong (Shafer-Landau, 1994: 343; Vasile 2010). So if we both are of the opinion that it is vague whether the term "kitten" applies to Cornelius, then we might be said to be failing to agree whether Cornelius is a kitten. But we need not thereby be disagreeing in the sense that one of us judges that he is a kitten and the other judges that he is not a kitten. A similar story could be told for ethical vagueness.

REALISTS' ACCOUNTS OF ETHICAL VAGUENESS

But if an ethical realist allows that there is ethical vagueness, then what account can she give of this phenomenon? This issue rapidly becomes complex, and it is here that much of the metaethical interest in ethical vagueness lies. We quickly come to interesting and vexed questions concerning the correct metasemantics for ethical terms and the extent of our epistemic grasp of the ethical world. In order to introduce some of the key philosophical points at issue, let us abstract from much of this complexity and consider a few simplified explanations.

Suppose an ethical realist tried to replicate the following semantic explanation of the vagueness of the term "bald." According to this explanation, the extension of the term is fixed simply by how we use the term, and we never settled whether to apply it to some men. These men are the borderline cases of bald men. There are multiple ways that we could have made our term "bald" precise, and each way would generate a different extension for the precisified version of "bald." However, as things stand, we have never settled on one precisification rather than another, and so it is indeterminate which of these extensions is the referent of the term. By analogy, an ethical realist could say that we simply failed to settle whether to apply "wrong" to certain actions. This would mean that there are multiple candidate extensions of wrong actions, and it is indeterminate which our term "wrong" refers to. Consequently, none of these extensions stands out with a "special ethical glow" (Dougherty 2014; Eklund forthcoming).

Moreover, by giving a robust role to semantic conventions in determining the extension of our ethical terms, this line faces two related challenges. First, how could it be possible for us to have a substantive, non-terminological, ethical disagreement with someone from a community of people whose ethical terms are governed by different semantic conventions (Horgan & Timmons 1991; Manley ms; Eklund forthcoming.)? Given how broadly we are conceiving of ethical realism, perhaps some ethical realists will not think this scenario *is* possible. But many realists will allow that there could be a genuine ethical disagreement here, without this simply being a matter of the communities using terms differently and thereby talking past each other. Second, can practical questions be resolved by discovering more about how people use words? Suppose someone is faced with a practical dilemma about whether to perform an action that she initially judges to be borderline wrong. Should her quandary be resolved by a linguistic anthropologist informing her that, upon closer examination, her community's semantic conventions governing the word "wrong" dictate that the term determinately applies to the action (Schoenfield 2016)? Both challenges can be raised outside of the context of ethical vagueness, but they are pressing challenges for an ethical realist who offers a semantic account of vagueness in terms of linguistic conventions.

Similar problems arise for an ethical realist who gives an epistemic explanation along the lines that some people have given of the vagueness of terms like "bald" (Williamson 1994). On this epistemicist line, our linguistic usage does determine precisely whether "bald" applies to each person. However, the reference of this term is sensitive to small shifts in our community's linguistic usage (Hawthorne 2006; Schoenfield 2016). Consequently, we are sometimes unable to know whether the term applies to some people—the borderline cases. For similar reasons, we might say that we cannot know whether the term "wrong" applies to some actions. But although this is an epistemic explanation of ethical vagueness, it also gives a robust role to semantic conventions in fixing the reference of normative terms: it is because we are partially ignorant of these conventions that we do not know whether the term "wrong" applies to borderline cases. As a result, this explanation faces both the community disagreement challenge and the linguistic anthropologist challenge.

In addition, this epistemic explanation faces two further challenges. First, when we consider degree-based ethical vagueness, we will see that small descriptive changes can determine whether a normative predicate such as "permissible" applies. Consider our introductory example of an embryo's development. We supposed that there are borderline cases of embryos that it is permissible for one to terminate in order to save a cat. According to the epistemic account, among these borderline cases there will be a pair of embryos, such that one embryo is microscopically more developed than the other, and yet it is permissible to terminate the earlier embryo while impermissible to terminate the later embryo. This may cause us to revise the significance that we place on properties like permissibility (Sider 1995; Dougherty 2014; Constantinescu 2014). Antecedently, we might think that there is a huge moral difference between permissibly terminating the life of a human being and impermissibly terminating the life of a human being. But when we learn that this difference in permissibility could turn on the minutest developmental increase, we may revise this antecedent judgment. Second, the commitment to holding that there are some unknowable ethical facts will be challenged by those who argue that ethical facts need to be knowable in order to be action-guiding (Sorensen 1995; Sider 1995; Dougherty 2014; Constantinescu 2014; Schoenfield 2016). Indeed, these challenges will face anyone, realist or not, who wishes to give an epistemic account of ethical vagueness.

Alternatively, an ethical realist might deny that an ethical term's extension is simply the entities to which we actually apply the term in practice. Instead, she might say that an ethical term's extension is determined in the way that the extension of a "natural kind" term is determined (Boyd 1988). Consider the following two metasemantic stories for natural kind terms (Manley ms). The first story holds that we use natural kind terms with the intention that these terms refer to natural kinds and ethical kinds; the story continues that this intention ensures that these terms refer to natural kinds and ethical kinds, even when our patterns of using the terms fails to do so. The second story holds that the extension of a term is fixed not only by how candidate extensions *fit* our usage, but also by how "eligible" these extensions are. On this line, some extensions are more eligible than others because they are more "natural" groups (Lewis 1983, 1984). For example, the set of green things is a more natural group than the set of things that are "grue"—things that either are observed before some future time, e.g., 2025, and are green, or are blue (Goodman 1955). Consequently, the set of green things is a more eligible extension for our terms than the set of grue things. In this way, some metaphysically privileged extensions can act as "reference magnets" for our terms, even when we fail to apply these terms to these things (Lewis 1983; Sider 2011). If the ethical realist adopts either of these metasemantic stories, then she could hold that natural kind terms refer to groups that form part of the deep metaphysical structure of the world, even if in practice we do not apply the terms to all the members of these groups. Similarly, she might say that our ethical kind terms' reference is guided by the existence of ethical kinds that have a special metaphysical status. If she holds that there is a single precise set of things that forms an ethical kind associated with a particular term, then she will not be able to offer a semantic account of the vagueness of this term (since the metasemantic story would lead her to the conclusion that the term determinately refers to this precise extension). But she might say that the precise demarcations of this ethical kind are unknown and maybe even unknowable to us, and consequently offer an epistemic account of the term's vagueness. If, by contrast, she holds that there are multiple precise sets of things that each form multiple precise ethical kinds associated with a term, then she can say that it is indeterminate which of these kinds is the referent of the term. In this way, she could offer a semantic explanation of ethical vagueness (Boyd 1988).

Those are some of the ways that an ethical realist can aim to offer semantic or epistemic explanations of ethical vagueness. In addition, she might simply say that ethical vagueness is metaphysical vagueness (Schoenfield 2016). This is a claim that is compatible with accepting or rejecting the natural kind analogy. The costs of this position would seem only to be the costs that one bears for positing metaphysical vagueness in general. The nature of these costs is currently up for debate. Until relatively recently, positing metaphysical vagueness was not taken seriously as an option, and was quickly dismissed as incoherent or misguided. But the view has received sustained defense in recent years, and the debate about the viability of metaphysical vagueness continues (Williams 2008; Barnes 2010).

EXPRESSIVISTS' ACCOUNTS OF ETHICAL VAGUENESS

That brief sketch covers some—but by no means all—of the options for ethical realists. What options are there for realists' opponents? Some opponents, such as error theorists, may simply deny that there is any ethical vagueness to be accounted for in the first place. But other opponents of realism want to recover much of the surface of our ethical discourse. In the contemporary debate, the most popular position in this vicinity is expressivism, which holds that ethical judgments are conative or evaluative mental states that are different in kind from the doxastic states by which we represent the world. If ethical vagueness is included in the parts of our ethical discourse that an expressivist wishes to explain, what account should she give of ethical vagueness?

The first task for an expressivist will be to retain a robust enough account of truth that she can identify determinately, e.g., wrong actions in the first place (Sorensen 1993). But assuming for the sake of argument that an expressivist can do this, the question then is whether this account could be naturally extended to cover the borderline, e.g., wrong actions that generate ethical vagueness. For example, what is it to judge an action to be indeterminately morally wrong? Is it simply to be unsure whether the action is morally wrong? To make good on this epistemic explanation, she would need to have sufficient theoretical resources for giving an account of ethical uncertainty (Smith 2002; Baima 2014). Does giving an account of judging an action to be indeterminately wrong require finding an additional conative or evaluative mental state? Alternatively, could it be accounted for by positing ambivalence between conative or evaluative mental states besides the mental states that constitute judging actions to be determinately right or wrong? Or could it be accounted for by positing indeterminacy concerning which mental states someone is in? These are questions that would seem to interlink with the question of which conative attitudes it is appropriate to form in the face of ethical indeterminacy (Williams 2014, 2015).

DIRECTIONS FOR FUTURE RESEARCH

The topic of ethical vagueness is a relatively neglected topic in metaethics. It certainly has received nothing like the attention spent on ethical judgments about what is, e.g., determinately right or wrong, and what it would be for there to be such a determinate ethical fact. As such, it is a topic on which there is still much work to be done. Research so far has focused primarily on what ethical realists and expressivists could say about ethical vagueness. It seems unlikely that the final word has been said about either metaethical position. In particular, there remain interesting questions concerning whether accounting for ethical vagueness is easier or harder for the various positions that fly under the ethical realist banner. (Again, the term "realist" is being used coarsely here to refer to cognitivists who hold that some ethical claims are true.) In addition, could an expressivist give a semantic account of ethical vagueness—something she might feel pressured to do if she gave a semantic account of non-ethical vagueness? Moreover, ethical realism and expressivism do not exhaust the metaethical terrain. What accounts of ethical vagueness could be offered by other metaethical positions? What might an ethical fictionalist say about ethical vagueness, for example?

Carrying out this research could help us in our choice between different metaethical positions. If, as seems plausible, these positions have different explanatory options available to them when it comes to accounting for ethical vagueness, then we can evaluate these positions according to the attractiveness of these options. When doing so, we can bring to bear considerations about the viability of the standard accounts of vagueness, and we can also bring to bear specialist considerations that arise only in the ethical case. In these respects, ethical vagueness is an exciting topic, insofar as it offers us the possibility of finding new leverage with some of the most central and important debates in metaethics.

ACKNOWLEDGMENTS

Thanks to Tristram McPherson, David Plunkett, and Lea Schroeder for helpful comments.

BIBLIOGRAPHY

Baima, N. (2014) "The problem of moral vagueness for expressivism," *Ethical Theory and Moral Practice* 17: 593–605.

Barnes, E. (2010) "Ontic vagueness: A guide for the perplexed," *Noûs* 44: 601–627.

Barnes, E. (2014) "Fundamental indeterminacy," *Analytic Philosophy* 55: 339–362.

Boyd, R. (1988) "How to be a moral realist," in G. Sayre-McCord (ed.) *Essays on Ethical Realism*, Ithaca, NY: Cornell University Press, 181–228.

Brink, D. (1984) "Moral realism and the sceptical arguments from disagreement and queerness," *Australasian Journal of Philosophy* 62: 111–125.

Broome, J. (1997) "Is incommensurability vagueness?" in R. Chang (ed.) *Incommensurability, Incomparability and Practical Reason*, Cambridge, MA: Harvard University Press, 67–89.

Chang, R. (2002) "The possibility of parity," *Ethics* 112: 659–688.

Chang, R. (2013) "Incommensurablity (and incomparability)," in H. LaFollette (ed.) *The International Encyclopedia of Ethics*, Cambridge, MA: Blackwell Publishing Ltd, 2591–2604.

Clarke, S. (1969) [1704–1705] *Boyle Lectures*, in D. Raphael (ed.) *The British Moralists 1650–1800, Vols. I and II*, Oxford: Oxford University Press.

Constantinescu, C. (2012) "Value incomparability and indeterminacy," *Ethical Theory and Moral Practice* 15: 57–70.

Constantinescu, C. (2014) "Moral vagueness: A dilemma for non-naturalism," in R. Shafer-Landau (ed.) *Oxford Studies in Metaethics*, Volume 9, Oxford: Oxford University Press, 152–185.

Dougherty, T. (2014) "Vague value," *Philosophy and Phenomenological Research* 89: 352–372.

Eklund, M. (forthcoming) *Choosing Normative Concepts*, Oxford: Oxford University Press.

Elson, L. (manuscript) "Incommensurability as comparative borderlineness."

Goodman, N. (1955) *Fact, Fiction and Forecast*, Cambridge, MA: Harvard University Press.

Griffin, J. (1986) *Well-Being: Its Meaning, Measurement and Ethical Importance*, Oxford: Oxford University Press.

Hawthorne, J. (2006) "Epistemicism and semantic plasticity," in his *Metaphysical Essays*, New York: Oxford University Press, 185–210.

Horgan, T. & Timmons, M. (1991) "New wave moral realism meets moral twin earth," *Journal of Philosophical Research* 16: 447–465.

Hsieh, N.-H. (2007) "Incommensurable values," *Stanford Encyclopedia of Philosophy* (Fall 2008 Edition), Edward N. Zalta (ed.) Available at: http://plato.stanford.edu/archives/fall2008/entries/value-incommensurable/.

Lewis, D. (1983) "New work for a theory of universals," *Australasian Journal of Philosophy* 61: 343–377.

Lewis, D. (1984) "Putnam's Paradox," *Australasian Journal of Philosophy* 62: 85–93.

Manley, D. (manuscript) "Moral realism and semantic plasticity."

Raz, J. (1985–1986) "Value incommensurability: Some preliminaries," *Proceedings of the Aristotelian Society* 86: 117–134.

Schoenfield, M. (2016) "Moral vagueness is ontic vagueness," *Ethics* 126: 257–282.

Shafer-Landau, R. (1994) "Moral disagreement, moral objectivism and moral indeterminacy," *Philosophy and Phenomenological Research* 54: 331–344.

Shafer-Landau, R. (1995) "Vagueness, borderline cases and moral realism," *American Philosophical Quarterly* 32: 83–96.

Sider, T. (1995) "Sorensen on unknowable obligations," *Utilitas* 7: 273–279.

Sider, T. (2002) "Hell and vagueness," *Faith and Philosophy* 19: 58–68.

Sider, T. (2015) *Writing the Book of the World*, Oxford: Oxford University Press.

Smith, M. (2002) "Evaluation, uncertainty and motivation," *Ethical Theory and Moral Practice* 5: 305–320.

Sorensen, R. (1990) "Vagueness implies cognitivism," *American Philosophical Quarterly* 27: 1–14.

Sorensen, R. (1995) "Unknowable obligations," *Utilitas* 7: 247–271.

Sosa, E. (2001) "Objectivity without absolutes," in A. Byrne, R. Stalnaker, & R. Wedgwood (eds.) *Fact and Value: Essays on Ethics and Metaphysics for Judith Jarvis Thomson*, Cambridge, MA: MIT Press, 215–228.

Vasile, L. (2010) *Moral Disagreement and Moral Indeterminacy*, unpublished doctoral dissertation, Department of Philosophy, Central European University.

Wasserman, R. (2004) "Indeterminacy, ignorance and the possibility of parity," *Philosophical Perspectives* 18: 391–403.

Wasserman, R. (2015) "Personal identity, indeterminacy, and obligation," in G. Gasser & M. Stefan (eds.) *Personal Identity: Simple or Complex?*, Cambridge: Cambridge University Press, 63–81.

Williams, J. R. G. (2008) "Ontic vagueness and metaphysical indeterminacy," *Philosophy Compass* 3: 763–788.

Williams, J. R. G. (2014) "Non-classical minds and indeterminate survival," *Philosophical Review* 123: 379–428.

Williams, J. R. G. (2015) "Indeterminacy, angst and ethics," *Ratio Special Issue*.

Williamson, T. (2014) *Vagueness*, London: Routledge.

12

Deontic Modals

Jennifer Carr

Deontic modals are a form of normative language. They can be used to express facts about deontic modality: to talk, not about what is actually the case, but instead about what would be the case if the world accorded with some normative or evaluative standard. Various standards might be relevant, for example, moral norms, requirements for achieving one's own private goals, standards for complying with the mandates of good sportsmanship, or rules governing membership of JC's secret club.

Deontic modals are narrowly defined as a particular interpretation of modal auxiliaries: "ought," "may," "must," "can," "should," etc. But other sorts of expressions can express deontic modality:

- **verbs:** "have to," "need to," "be allowed to," "be supposed to," etc.
- **adjectives and adverbs:** "obligatory," "permissible," "impermissible," etc., as well as their adverbial forms
- **suffixes:** e.g., "desireable" to mean *worthy of desire*, rather than *possible to desire*
- **infinitival constructions:** "the thing to do," "you are to be home by 9:00," etc.

This chapter will focus strictly on deontic modals, but many of the conclusions generalize to other forms of normative and evaluative language (e.g., "good," "bad," "right," "wrong," "okay").

This chapter provides a selective survey of prominent theories on the semantics of deontic modals in logic and natural language. We focus on Kratzer's (1977; 1981; 1991) semantics and extensions to this analysis. Kratzer's semantics has been far and away the most influential theory of deontic modals, which provide a base case for the interpretation of normative language in general. Understanding the logic and truth conditions of normative language is one of the core areas of metaethics. It informs our understanding of normative arguments and normative reasoning. As this chapter will emphasize, some forms of normative language don't allow for the inferences that classical logic trains philosophers to expect. Understanding what inferences are valid for normative language should impact our understanding of how we reason, and should reason, about the normative.

We will first look at how deontic modals are understood in the context of modal logic and natural language. Then we'll survey some recent debates and discoveries in the literature on deontic modals in natural language. We close with some considerations about the relevance of natural language to metaethics.

LOGIC AND NATURAL LANGUAGE

Deontic logic

In standard intensional logic, deontic modals are treated as a form of quantifier. They quantify over possible worlds. In a deontic context, *Must α* means, roughly, that *α* is true at *all* deontically ideal worlds. *May α* means, roughly, that *α* is true at *some* deontically ideal worlds. (I omit quasi-quotation.) We can think of *Must α* as saying: *under any circumstances where things are perfect, α will be the case.* We can think of *May α* as saying: *it's compatible with things being perfect that α is the case.*

To be more precise, I'll briefly introduce a Kripke-style semantics for the deontic modals "may" and "must."

We start with a set of possible worlds *W*. Note that deontic logic is entirely neutral about the ontology of possible worlds. They could be understood as maximal sets of consistent sentences, maximally specific properties, or concrete entities, etc. Talk of possible worlds might be realist or antirealist.

Standard deontic logic is concerned with how worlds are related to each other: which worlds are deontically ideal from the perspective of some other world. For example, if, in the actual world, a murder has been committed, the actual world is not deontically ideal. A deontically ideal world, from our perspective, might be one where the murder was not committed. It might be that there's one objectively privileged set of deontically ideal worlds. Or it might be that, at different worlds, there are different norms or standards that determine different sets of worlds as deontic ideals. Logic is neutral on this question.

If a world *w* "sees" another world *w′* as deontically ideal—*w′* is ideal from the point of view of the standards at *w*—we'll say *w′* is "deontically accessible" from *w*. Call this relation of deontic accessibility *D*. If *w′* is deontically accessible from *w*, we'll say *wDw′*. For each *w*, there is a set of deontically accessible worlds. We can call this set $D(w) = \{w′ \in W : wDw′\}$.

Deontic modals are then understood as quantifiers over sets of deontically accessible worlds. We can distinguish deontic necessity modals from deontic possibility modals in terms of the type of quantification (universal or existential) they involve:

Deontic necessity modals: *must α, should α, ought α*
Notation: $\Box α$
$\Box α$ is true at a world *w* iff *α* is true at all worlds in *D(w)*.

Deontic possibility modals: *may α, can α*
Notation: $\Diamond α$
$\Diamond α$ is true at a world *w* iff *α* is true at some world in *D(w)*.

Like "all" and "some," $\Box$ is traditionally assumed to be the dual of $\Diamond$. In other words, the two are interdefinable in the following way: α can be defined as $\neg\Box\neg\alpha$, and $\Box\alpha$ can be defined as $\neg\Diamond\neg\alpha$. In English: α is permissible is true if and only if it's not the case that not-α is required, and α is required if and only if it's not the case that not-α is permissible.

The same kind of model can be used for other forms of modal logic, e.g., epistemic logic. Different logical subject matters, or modalities, can yield different constraints on the modal accessibility relation. For example, epistemic logic should be reflexive, in the sense that every world should be accessible to itself: for its accessibility relation, E, wEw for all w. This ensures that, where $\Box_s\alpha$ is read as s *knows that* α, $\Box_s\alpha$ is true only if α is true. But this is not true of deontic logic. People can sometimes fail to do what they ought to do, and so $\Box\alpha$ should not logically entail α. Deontic logic's accessibility relation should not be reflexive.

Other constraints on a deontic accessibility relation are controversial. For example, it's often suggested that deontic logic should be *serial*, such that every world has deontic access to some world: nothing is a deontic dead end. In other words, for all w there is some w' such that wDw'. This constraint ensures that, for all propositions α, either $\Diamond\alpha$ or $\Diamond\neg\alpha$ (or both). Why does this matter? The seriality constraint rules out the possibility of *dilemmas*, where no options are permissible: both α and $\neg\alpha$ are impermissible. Whether genuine dilemmas are possible is a substantive question: rather than being decided within the logic, we select a modal logic that conforms to first-order ethical considerations.

While this rudimentary deontic logic is adequate for many purposes, it remains highly idealized. It doesn't capture the ways in which uses of deontic modals in natural language are sensitive to features of context. It also doesn't capture the way in which deontic modals behave within different linguistic embeddings. (For a survey of deontic logics and discussion of their possible shortcomings, see McNamara 2014.) So we turn to natural language considerations next.

Deontic modals in natural language

Like deontic logic, natural language semantics for deontic modals is of a piece with natural language semantics for modals in general. Epistemic, circumstantial, and other "flavors" of modality can be expressed with the some of the same vocabulary as deontic modality: *Jochen could drink whiskey* can be used to express the claim that Jochen was permitted to drink whiskey (deontic); the claim that, for all the speaker knows, Jochen might be a whiskey drinker (epistemic); or the claim that Jochen was capable of drinking whiskey (circumstantial).

There are any number of different flavors of modality expressible by modals. Even among deontic modals, different sets of norms or standards can be relevant for the interpretation of modalized assertions. For example, *Jochen could drink whiskey* might be true in a context where federal laws are the salient norms (he had just turned 21), but not in a context where other norms are salient (he was in a rehab program with strict rules about drug and alcohol consumption).

If we treated the multiple readings of modals as a form of ambiguity, we would have difficulties accounting for their relative cross-linguistic stability as well as the commonalities in their embedding behavior. It makes better sense to treat the many readings of modals as a form of context-sensitivity, as Kratzer (1977) argued. This aligns with the semantics of other natural language quantifiers, the scope of which is also determined by context. If I say *All the students made it to the midterm,* context will determine whether I'm quantifying over all the students in the class, all the students in the university, or all the students in the universe. (In the section "Contextualism and relativism," we will discuss which contexts are relevant for the assessment of deontically modalized sentences.)

The context-sensitivity of deontic modals explains why, in the context of federal law, *Jochen could drink whiskey* might be true, but (at the same time, of the same person) in the context of rehab regulations, the same sentence is not true. Federal law determines a different deontic accessibility relation from the relation determined by the regulations of the rehab clinic. Both sets of norms, we can suppose, determine a set of worlds consistent with their contents. But the worlds compatible with the federal laws include at least one where Jochen drinks whiskey, while the rehab regulations don't.

The picture, so far, is that deontically modalized sentences are evaluated relative to a context, which determines a set of deontically ideal worlds given the contextually salient norms or standards. The deontic modal acts as a quantifier over deontically ideal worlds.

Problem: suppose the following sentence is uttered in a context where the salient norms are the norms of morality:

(1) You should rescue an abandoned dog (instead of buying a designer puppy).

Our current analysis of deontic modals entails that (1) is true if and only if all the morally ideal worlds are worlds in which you rescue an abandoned dog. But surely in the morally ideal worlds, there would be no abandoned dogs, since abandoning dogs is morally abhorrent. So this (highly plausible) sentence must be false! This is a simplification of Prior's (1958) Samaritan Paradox. (See also Åqvist 1967.)

One might reply: there's an easy solution. Context has made salient, here, *not* the morally ideal worlds, but the most *comparatively* morally ideal worlds that are consistent with the existence of abandoned dogs.

This explanation seems on the right track. Note that it appeals to two separate kinds of backgrounded information in a conversation: some facts about circumstances are taken for granted (in particular, the existence of abandoned dogs) and provide an absolute constraint on the domain of possible worlds that *should* quantifies over. (If there were a world with no abandoned dogs, it would be morally ideal, but in it, the addressee would not rescue a dog.) By contrast, the moral ideals do not place an absolute constraint: instead of looking to worlds that absolutely conform to moral norms, we look to those that conform as much as possible to moral norms consistent with the existence of abandoned dogs (and other circumstances taken as fixed). Moreover, this explanation suggests that the moral norms salient in the conversation are *comparative*: possible worlds can conform to the moral norms to a greater or lesser extent. This suggests that these two forms of background information (what Kratzer [1981] calls "conversational backgrounds") do not play formally equivalent roles.

These two observations lead to a semantics for deontic modals that incorporates separate parameters for conversational backgrounds: one for presupposed factual information, and one for an ordering over worlds in terms of some form of deontic ideality. This form of analysis is explored in Hansson (1969), van Fraassen (1972), and Lewis (1973). We will focus here on Kratzer's (1981; 1991) semantics for modals in natural language, which incorporates the compositional context-sensitivity in (Kratzer 1977) and is explicitly unified with the restrictor analysis of conditionals.

On Kratzer's analysis, the two conversational backgrounds that modals are sensitive to are the *modal base* and the *ordering source*. For deontic modals, the modal base is the set of circumstances that are taken as given (in our example, the existence of abandoned dogs, and probably other facts). The modal base is understood as a set of propositions. Kratzer treats propositions as sets of possible worlds. The modal base is a thus a set of sets of possible worlds. Its intersection is the set of circumstantially possible worlds.

Ordering sources are also represented as sets of propositions, but their formal role is different: they are meant to generate a (partial) ordering over possibilities in terms of their ideality. An ordering can be projected from this set as follows: call our deontic ordering source g, and let $w \leq_g w'$ be interpreted as: *w is at least as ideal as w' according to g*. Then we can project the ordering $\leq_g$ from g as follows:

$$w \leq_g w' \text{ iff } \{p \in g : w \in p\} \supseteq \{p \in g : w' \in p\}$$

In English: w is at least as ideal as w' iff the set of ordering source propositions that w satisfies includes the set of ordering source propositions that w' satisfies.

Illustrating with our dog example: suppose that the ordering is one of moral ideality. Simplifying morality a bit, our example could be represented with a comparative moral ideality relation as follows:

worlds where no one ever abandons a dog

$\wedge$

worlds where you rescue an abandoned dog

$\wedge$

worlds where there are abandoned dogs but you buy a designer puppy instead

How do we generate a domain for the modal to quantify over, given the modal base and the ordering source? First, we will assume that the domain of $\leq_d$ must always have minimal (i.e., highest ranked) elements. (This is known as the Limit Assumption; see Lewis 1973 and Stalnaker 1984 for discussion.) Then the modal's domain is, roughly, the set of highest ranked worlds compatible with the modal base. More precisely, we can define the domain of a modal as a function of a world w, modal base f, and ordering source g:

domain$(w, f, g) = \{w \in \cap f : \text{there is no } w' \text{ s.t. } w' \leq_g w \text{ and } w \leq_g w'\}$

Then:

$\Box\alpha$ is true relative to (w, f, g) iff α is true at all w' in **domain** (w, f, g)

$\Diamond\alpha$ is true relative to (w, f, g) iff α is true at some w' in **domain** (w, f, g)

(A technical note: here we treat f and g as sets of propositions immediately generating a set of worlds and an ordering over worlds. But for reasons of compositionality, each of these conversational backgrounds will actually have to be functions from worlds to sets of propositions that generate [respectively] the set of worlds and the ordering over

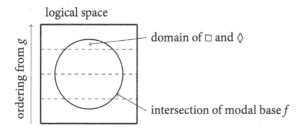

Figure 12.1

them. This allows that the same contextually salient circumstances and body of norms can generate different circumstantially possible worlds and different orderings at different worlds.)

So, in our example, the modal base eliminates worlds where no one ever abandons a dog. In context, we take it as given that abandoned dogs exist. Among the remaining worlds, worlds where you rescue an abandoned dog are better than worlds where you instead buy a designer puppy. So all the highest ranked worlds in the intersection of the modal base are worlds where you rescue an abandoned dog. And so *You should rescue an abandoned dog* is true in this context.

One of the immediate benefits of this analysis is that it provides a solution to Kratzer's (1991) version of the Samaritan Paradox. In Kratzer's version, the paradox is to give a semantics for deontic modals that accommodates the following hypothesis: that (2a) and (2b) could be true in the very same context:

(2) a. No one should abandon a dog.
    b. If there are abandoned dogs, you should rescue one of them rather than buying a designer puppy.

If deontic modals simply quantified over some immediately contextually specified domain—simply a salient set of deontically ideal worlds—then these two sentences couldn't be true relative to the same context. For (2a) requires that the ideal worlds contain no abandoned dogs, and (2b) presupposes that at least one ideal world contains an abandoned dog. But Kratzer's semantics makes sense of their consistency at a shared context. On her view, the function of the antecedent in (2b) is to restrict the modal base of the modal in the consequent to worlds where the antecedent is true. Where β is the conditional's antecedent, the conditional can be represented as shown in Figure 12.2.

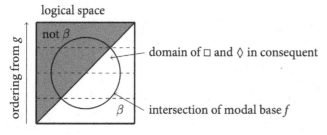

Figure 12.2

So suppose our modal base's intersection ($\cap f$) includes some worlds where there are no abandoned dogs and some worlds where there are. Then, relative to the same conversational backgrounds, both (2a) and (2b) can be true: the highest g-ranked worlds in $\cap f$ are worlds where no one abandons dogs, and when $\cap f$ is restricted by the antecedent of (2b) (*there are abandoned dogs*), the highest g-ranked are worlds where you rescue an abandoned dog rather than buying a designer puppy.

There are multiple linguistic phenomena associated with the name "The Samaritan Paradox," and Prior's original presentation is one that Kratzer's semantics doesn't immediately solve. The problem is this: with both of the quantificational semantics we've considered, the following entailment holds:

(1) You should rescue an abandoned dog (instead of buying a designer puppy).
(3) Therefore, there should be abandoned dogs.

But this entailment is obviously a bad one; it is not inconsistent to endorse (1) and reject (3).

A simple (though not uncontroversial) solution to this puzzle is to place a *diversity condition* on the interpretation of modalized sentences:

Diversity: the intersection of the modal base where $\Box\alpha$ is evaluated must include α-worlds and *not-α*-worlds.

Diversity implies that (3) must be interpreted relative to a modal background that includes worlds where there are no abandoned dogs. But, with the above assumptions about the ordering source, these worlds will be more highly ranked than worlds where the addressee rescues an abandoned dog. This means that (1) and (3) must be evaluated relative to different modal bases, and hence (1) cannot entail (3).

One potentially useful feature (or potentially problematic bug) in Kratzer's ordering sources is that they can be used to generate non-total orderings over worlds. This leaves room for incomparability between pairs of worlds: neither $w < w'$ nor $w' < w$. Consider, for example, a body of norms that included, among others, the following subset:

   {*you call your mother weekly, you refrain from speeding*}

It might be that these two norms generate incomparability: if in w you satisfy only the first norm, and in w' you satisfy only the second norm, then maybe there's no fact of the matter about how w and w' compare in terms of deontic ideality. Since neither of these worlds satisfies a superset of the norms the other world satisfies, the partial order $\leq$ projected from the ordering source g will not make a comparative ranking of the two.

Kratzer's semantics is the benchmark analysis of modals in natural language. Much of the literature on deontic modals since has focused on elaborating generalizations of Kratzer's semantics to accommodate various puzzle cases. We'll survey some such cases now.

PUZZLES IN DEONTIC SEMANTICS

Puzzles involving conditionals

The Gentle Murderer Paradox (Forrester 1984) consists of the following three premises, which are intuitively consistent:

(4) a. You shouldn't murder anyone.
  b. If you're going to murder someone, you should murder someone as painlessly as possible.
  c. You're going to murder someone.

Classically, (4b) and (4c) entail, by modus ponens:

(5) You should murder someone as painlessly as possible.

But (5) is, at least prima facie, inconsistent with (4a).

In the ethics literature, the most popular attempted solution to this problem aims to analyze the conditional (4b) in a way that makes modus ponens inapplicable in this case. On this analysis, the deontic modal *should* takes wide scope over the conditional: rather than having the logical form $\alpha \rightarrow \Box\beta$, (4b)'s logical form is $\Box(\alpha \rightarrow \beta)$. Because the main operator of the sentence is not a conditional, modus ponens doesn't apply. This wide-scoping proposal has been defended for a variety of similar problems (Broome 1999, 2002, 2004; Dancy 2000; Darwall 1983, 2001). For a host of objections to this account, see, among others, Kolodny and MacFarlane (2010) and Silk (2014b). It is worth noting that Kratzer semantics does not have to be modified to make intuitive predictions about the Gentle Murderer case. Kratzer semantics doesn't validate modus ponens, as Charlow (2013) shows. For (4c) to be true at the world of evaluation, it is not necessary that it be incorporated into the circumstantial modal base relevant for the interpretation of (5). If it is not, then all the sentences in (4) are compatible.

Another puzzle generated by a tension between classical logic and deontic modals is the Miners Puzzle, first presented by Regan (1980) and later introduced into the semantics literature by Kolodny and MacFarlane (2010). The puzzle runs as follows:

> Ten miners are trapped in one of two mineshafts, A or B, but you have no way to find out which; as far as you know, they're equally likely to be in either. Incoming floodwaters will soon flood the shafts. You can block one or the other of the mineshafts using sandbags, but you cannot block both. If you block a mineshaft, all of the floodwaters will be diverted into the other, filling it completely and drowning any miners inside. On the other hand, if you block neither shaft, then both shafts will fill halfway with water, and only the one miner who is lowest in the mineshaft will be killed.

The sentences in (6) are intuitively true in this context:

(6) a. You ought to block neither shaft.
  b. If the miners are in shaft A, you ought to block shaft A.
  c. If the miners are in shaft B, you ought to block shaft B.
  d. The miners are either in shaft A or in shaft B.

The puzzle is that (6b), (6c), and (6d) classically entail (7) (by proof by cases):

(7) Either you ought to block shaft A or you ought to block shaft B.

This example suggests that proof by cases might not be valid in natural language. Furthermore, it is impossible to accommodate within Kratzer's semantics without stipulating change of context between the sentences in (6).

Here's why: in Kratzer's semantics, the antecedent of a conditional can restrict the modal base, but it doesn't affect the ordering source. If (6a) is true, then the ordering source ranks blocking neither shaft more highly than blocking shaft A or blocking shaft B. But when the modal base is restricted to worlds where the miners are in shaft A (or in shaft B), the addressee still has the option of blocking neither shaft. And, since the antecedent doesn't affect the ordering source, it must still rank blocking neither shaft as the highest ranked option. So (6b) and (6c) are predicted to be false.

There are two strategies for addressing the Miners Puzzle. The conservative strategy explains away the Miners Puzzle as a case of shifting context; the inconsistency therefore turns on a kind of equivocation. The revisionary strategy explores how the Miners Puzzle sentences can be predicted within a single context, given a semantics that allows conditional antecedents to affect not just the modal base but also the ordering. Dowell (2012) and von Fintel (2012) provide conservative defenses of Kratzer semantics against the charge that the necessary changes in context are ad hoc. Revisionary generalizations of Kratzer semantics that accommodate the consistency of the sentences in (6) appear in Kolodny and MacFarlane (2010), Charlow (2013), Cariani et al. (2013), Silk (2014a), and Carr (forthcoming).

A final interesting puzzle for deontic modals and conditionals, which appears not to have a standard name, is what we will call the "If α, ought α, problem." The problem is that possible worlds semantics for modals, combined with various accounts of conditionals, predict that sentences of the form $if\,\alpha$, $\Box\alpha$ are logically valid, hence analytically true. Perhaps the earliest mention of this problem appears in Spohn (1975); the problem is elaborated for Kratzer semantics in Frank (1997), Zvolenszky (2002, 2006, 2007), Geurts (2004), Kratzer (2012), and Carr (2014).

The problem is relatively straightforward: in Kratzer's semantics for modals and conditionals, deontically modalized conditionals (of the form $if\,\alpha$, $\Box\beta$) are true iff the highest ranked α-worlds in the intersection of the modal base are also β-worlds. Now, suppose β and α happen to be the same proposition. It is trivial that the highest ranked α-worlds in the intersection of the modal base are also α-worlds. So $if\,\alpha$, $\Box\alpha$ must be true.

But there are sentences of that form that are contingent, and moreover, intuitively false:

(8) If you cheat at Battleship, you ought to cheat at Battleship.

Now, an easy response is available. In the section "Deontic modals in natural language," we noted that Prior's Samaritan Paradox appeared to motivate a diversity constraint on modal bases: $\Box\alpha$ can only be true if the intersection of the contextually determined modal base includes both α and $\neg\alpha$ worlds. But if the constraint applies to the modal base post-restriction when the modal is embedded in a conditional, this diversity constraint is violated in sentences like (8). And so, with this generalization of the diversity constraint, we predict the falsity of (8). But we also predict that sentences of this form are necessarily false. And as Zvolenszky (2002) notes, some sentences of the form $if\,\alpha$, $\Box\alpha$ are intuitively true. For example, suppose Rita is a gentle spirit who seldom gets angry and only does so if she's given a very good reason. Then the following sentence is intuitively true:

(9) If Rita is angry, she ought to be angry.

While *if α*, □α sentences are not trivially true, then, they are also not trivially false.

A better solution, mentioned in Zvolenszky (2002) and Kratzer (2012), and explored at length in Geurts (2004), is to explore a kind of ambiguity generated by conditionals with quantifiers in their consequents. On Kratzer's semantics, bare conditionals (with no overt quantifier in the consequent) have an unpronounced quantifier (typically an epistemic modal) that is restricted by the antecedent. When a conditional has an overt quantifier, modal or otherwise, the conditional can be ambiguously read as also containing the unpronounced epistemic modal, generating different readings. On the doubly modalized reading, where the restrictor applies only to the epistemic modal, sentences of the form *if α*, □α are neither trivially true nor trivially false, and this accommodates the falsity of (8) and the truth of (9). Zvolenszky (2002) argues that this account is inadequately predictive, however, and Carr (2014) argues this account still faces problem cases.

Puzzles involving monotonicity

The next batch of puzzles for deontic modals involves monotonicity. Kratzer's quantificational semantics is upward monotonic. An operator ∇ is upward monotonic iff, if $α$ implies $β$, then $\nabla α$ implies $\nabla β$. A variety of examples suggest that natural language deontic modals might not be upward monotonic.

Jackson and Pargetter (1986) present a case of apparent failure of upward monotonicity involving conjunction:

Professor Procrastinate.

Professor Procrastinate receives an invitation to review a book … . The best thing that can happen is that he says yes, and then writes the review when the book arrives. However, suppose it is further the case that were Procrastinate to say yes, he would not in fact get around to writing the review. Not because of incapacity or outside interference or anything like that, but because he would keep on putting the task off. (This has been known to happen.) Thus, although the best that can happen is for Procrastinate to say yes and then write, and he can do exactly this, what would in fact happen were he to say yes is that he would not write the review. Moreover, we may suppose, this latter is the worst that can happen. It would lead to the book not being reviewed at all, or at least to a review being seriously delayed.

(1986: 235)

The following two sentences are judged to be true with respect to this case:

(10) a. Professor Procrastinate should not accept the invitation.
b. Professor Procrastinate should accept the invitation and write the review in a timely way.

So Professor Procrastinate is thought to show that $\Box(\alpha \wedge \beta)$ doesn't entail $\Box\alpha$.

Ross Puzzle (Ross 1944) involves an apparent failure of upward monotonicity involving disjunction: $\Box\alpha$ doesn't entail $\Box(\alpha \wedge \beta)$ (and similarly for $\Diamond$). Examples are easy to come by:

(11) a. You should rescue an abandoned dog.
     b. So you should rescue an abandoned dog or burn down an animal shelter.

The inference from (11a) to (11b) is clearly not licensed.

One possible explanation for this phenomenon, discussed in Cariani (2013) and defended in von Fintel (2012), is that the inference is blocked because (11b) generates implications or implicatures that (11a) lacks, in particular:

(12) a. You may rescue an abandoned dog.
     b. You may burn down an animal shelter.

This is a consequence of the so-called "free choice effect" (Kamp 1973):

(13) a. $\Diamond(\alpha \vee \beta)$
     b. $\therefore \Diamond\alpha \wedge \Diamond\beta$

Combining (13) with a seriality assumption, we validate the following inference:

(14) a. $\Box(\alpha \vee \beta)$
     b. $\therefore \Diamond\alpha \wedge \Diamond\beta$

(12b) is naturally judged false. Since (11b) licenses the inference to (12b) (by free choice), it must be false as well. But (11a) does not license the inference, so it is still judged to be true.

Now, it might be that (11b) is literally true; it is merely judged unassertable because its assertion would license free choice inferences. If these inferences are a purely pragmatic phenomenon (Hare 1967; Alonso-Ovalle 2006; Wedgwood 2006) rather than semantic entailments, then Ross Puzzle generates no fundamental challenge to the compatibility of an upward monotonic logic for deontic modals. On the other hand, if free choice is semantic, then Ross Puzzle suggests that deontic modals are not upward monotonic (Cariani 2013; Lassiter 2011; Fusco 2015).

What about Professor Procrastinate? The case remains controversial. Cariani (2013) and Lassiter (2011) defend the example as a failure of upward monotonicity, while others (e.g., von Fintel 1999) argue that the case involves a surreptitious context change. (10a), the claim that he should not accept the invitation, is evaluated relative to a context where it's treated as a necessary feature of the circumstances that Procrastinate will not write the review. But this proposition is no longer treated as necessary when we evaluate claim (10b), that Procrastinate should both accept the invitation and write the review. The question, once again, is whether to accept a conservative account that requires stipulating this context change, or instead a revisionary account that predicts the data without stipulations about context.

Strong and weak necessity modals

Throughout this chapter, we've assumed that different necessity modals—*should, ought, must*—were logically interchangeable, representable with the same logical symbol (□). As various authors have argued (e.g., Sloman 1970; Horn 1972; Ninan 2005; von Fintel & Iatridou 2008; Rubinstein 2012; Silk 2014a), however, expressions like *should, ought,* and *be supposed to* are importantly different from expressions like *must, need to, have to,* and *be required to.* The former group is logically weaker than the latter: (15a) is a perfectly acceptable utterance, while (15b) is hard to interpret as consistent: the assertion is infelicitous, though not in violation of grammar (conventionally marked with the "#" symbol).

(15) a. Ian should rescue an abandoned dog, but he doesn't have to.
      b. #Ian has to rescue an abandoned dog, but it's not as if he should.

What is the difference between what's expressed with a so-called "strong necessity modal" like *must* and a so-called "weak necessity modal" like *should?*

Horn (1972) proposed a simple account: *must α* requires that α be true in all favored worlds, whereas *should α* requires only that α be true in most favored worlds. A benefit of this account is that it characterizes the relative weakness of *should*, between *may* and *must*, in the same terms that explain the logical weakness of *may* compared with *must*: in terms of their quantificational strength over a shared body of worlds. But the proposal also has shortcomings. It's not clear whether there's any sense to be made of counting possible worlds; even if there were, plausibly, the distinction between what one ought to do and what one must do is independent of the number of worlds. It might be that even among favored worlds, there could be many more ways for it to be the case that ¬α than for it to be the case that α—but why should that make *should α* false?

von Fintel and Iatridou (2008) argue that *should α* says, not that most favored worlds are α-worlds, but rather that the best-favored worlds are α-worlds. This requires some ranking within the set of favored worlds. Modals must therefore be relativized to a second ordering. So, in our example, we suppose it is permissible for Ian not to adopt an abandoned dog: there are some favored worlds in which Ian does not adopt an abandoned dog. The ordering here could, for example, be legal. But there also could be a second salient ordering—for example, in terms of maximizing overall utility—which, within the set of contextually favored worlds according to the first ordering, makes finer-grained distinctions.

Ninan (2005) describes another dimension of the strong/weak necessity modal distinction: that utterances of strong deontic necessity modals, unlike weak deontic neces-

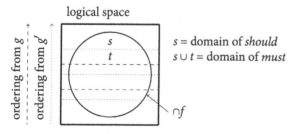

Figure 12.3

sity modals, seem incompatible with the acknowledgment that the norms they express might not be obeyed.

(16) a.   Phaedra should feed the cat, but she won't.
     b.   #Phaedra must feed the cat, but she won't.
     c.   Phaedra should feed the cat, but she might not.
     d.   #Phaedra must feed the cat, but she might not.

Ninan argues that the explanation for these data is that strong deontic necessity modals have a performative component in their conventional meaning: they are conventionally used not merely to report an obligation, but to impose one.

   Given the distinctive uses of strong and weak necessity modals, questions arise about how the puzzle cases discussed in previous sections apply when the type of necessity modal is toggled (see, e.g., Silk 2014a).

Contextualism and relativism

We now turn to the metasemantics of deontic modals. It's clear that these expressions, like other normative and evaluative vocabulary, are sensitive to features of context. But it is controversial which contexts they are sensitive to.

   Contextualism about deontic modals is the view that utterances of deontic modals are sensitive to features of the context in which they are uttered. (For canonical defenses of contextualism about related expressions, though not specifically about deontic modals, see Kratzer 1981 and DeRose 1991.)

Contextualism: whether an utterance of $\Box\alpha$ at a context c is true depends on salient background information at c.

Relativism is the view that utterances of deontic modals are also sensitive to features of the context in which the utterances are assessed, which can be different from the context in which they are uttered. There are different ways this view can be formulated:

Truth relativism: whether an utterance of $\Box\alpha$ at a context c is true as assessed from a context c' depends on salient background information at c'.

Content relativism: what proposition an utterance of $\Box\alpha$ at a context c expresses, as assessed from a context c', depends on salient background information at c'.

To see how these three views come apart, consider the following simplified example:

   Disagreement.

   Walker and Elle are considering how their friend should get to a different part of Chicago: on foot or on the L. Walker thinks the beauty of the walk makes up for the slower commute, while Elle thinks the opposite: the speed of taking the L compensates for the worse views. Walker asserts, in context c:

   (17) He should walk.

   Elle assesses (17) as false in context c'.

At which context(s) is (17) true? At which context, if any, is (17) false?

According to *contextualism*, the context of assessment can only be the context of utterance, c. At c, where the salient standards are those endorsed by Walker, (17) expresses, roughly, the proposition that according to Walker's standards, the friend should walk. This proposition is true.

According to *truth relativism*, (17) expresses the same proposition at both c and c'. But this proposition, and (17) itself, can only be assessed relative to contexts of assessment, which (at least in this case) determine a salient body of standards. The sentence and its corresponding proposition are true as assessed at c (relative to Walker's standards) but false as assessed at c' (relative to Elle's standards).

According to *content relativism*, (17) expresses different propositions as assessed at c and c'. Roughly, at c, (17) expresses the proposition that, according to Walker's standards, the friend should walk. This proposition is true; hence at c, (17) is true. At c', (17) expresses the proposition that, according to Elle's standards, the friend should walk. This proposition is false; hence at c, (17) is false.

Truth relativism (with respect to a variety of expressions, including deontic modals) is canonically defended in MacFarlane (2005, 2014) and Egan (2007). Content relativism (about epistemic rather than deontic modals) is defended in Egan et al. (2005) and Weatherson (2009) and discussed in Egan and Weatherson (2009) and MacFarlane (2014). For a more thorough discussion of arguments for and against contextualism, see Alex Silk's chapter "Metaethical Contextualism." For arguments for and against different forms of relativism, see Isidora Stojanovic's chapter "Metaethical Relativism."

DEONTIC MODALS IN ETHICS AND METAETHICS

In this chapter, we have focused on the natural language logic and semantics of deontic modals. But one might worry that, for the purposes of ethical and metaethical theorizing, investigations of natural language are moot. For in ethical and metaethical theorizing, we regiment our use of deontic modals, so that, for example, the so-called objective *ought* always expresses non-information-sensitive, all-things-considered obligations, and the so-called subjective *ought* always expresses all-things-considered obligations that are relativized to the information of the agent(s) under discussion. For these purposes, one might think, the messiness of natural language can be idealized away, and the elegantly simple deontic logic and semantics described in the first section will be adequate.

While we might allow that this regimented reading of deontic modals exists, if only within philosophy papers and philosophy classrooms, we should acknowledge that it is a philosopher's invention. We might reasonably be skeptical of the idea that we have intuitions about the truth values of claims involving a technical reading of deontic modals. Note, for example, that our reasoning and intuitions in ethics and metaethics often must be expressed using deontic modals under a variety of different embeddings. Can we really expect to have reliable intuitions about the truth conditions of the infinitely many complex sentences that our regimented deontic modals could appear in?

As a methodological point, native speaker intuitions are the primary data for facts about natural language; their correctness is the null hypothesis. Indeed, if linguistic facts are a matter of convention, then the aggregate of native speaker intuitions can't be wrong. The same methodological considerations don't apply to stipulated terms. We would need to stipulate the specific ways in which such terms are affected by embedding, rather than rely on intuition. Otherwise, our "intuitions" could (and, as a matter of sociological fact, probably do) reflect an unholy mixture of stipulation and intuition about natural language cognate terms.

Natural language is our primary mode of voicing our intuitions and expressing our reasoning in ethics and metaethics. And so we might believe we're using philosophically regimented deontic modals when we're not. This can lead to a variety of philosophical confusions: for example, misguided conclusions based on argument forms that are not valid within the logic of natural language deontic modals (like the Gentle Murderer), or illusions of paradox based on misguided assumptions about consistency and inconsistency (like the Miners Puzzle).

Note that this argument does not necessarily extend to any use of regimented terms. For example, take Lewis's regimentation of the term "natural": the term applies to properties such that the "perfectly natural" properties are those that carve nature at the joints. The phrase "perfectly natural" is not context-sensitive; embedding it in different linguistic contexts will not affect its extension. So the above argument does not motivate research on the semantics of the natural language expressions "natural" or "perfectly natural." By contrast, modals are sensitive to a number of features of context.

Moreover, modals are standardly understood as logical operators. Logical operators are understood in terms of the inferences they warrant. For this reason, understanding their embedding behavior is paramount for understanding their meaning. For cases like the Gentle Murderer or the Miners Puzzle, even if we stipulate away the context sensitivity of deontic modals in our regimentation, we still turn to intuitions about consistency and entailment. But if consistency and entailment facts are not stipulated, then we risk confusing the embedding behavior and inferential role of the context-sensitive, natural language term with that of the stipulation. Indeed, whatever intuitions we might have about regimented readings of deontic modals, we should expect them to be systematically distorted by our intuitions about ordinary language.

It may be that some regimented use of deontic modals will succeed better than natural language at cutting nature at its ethical or logical joints. But we won't know unless we know how the regimented term could differ from its natural language counterpart. So it is worth the effort to get a clear grip on the logic and semantics of natural language normative expressions.

ACKNOWLEDGMENTS

The research for this chapter has received funding from the European Research Council under the European Union's Seventh Framework Programme (FP/2007-2013)/ERC Grant Agreement no. 312938. Many thanks to all with whom I've discussed these issues, and especially to Jamie Fritz, Tristram MacPherson, David Plunkett, and Paolo Santorio.

REFERENCES

Åqvist, Lennart (1967). "Good Samaritans, Contrary-to-Duty Imperatives, and Epistemic Obligations." *Noûs*, 1(4): pp. 361–379.

Alonso-Ovalle, Luis (2006). *Disjunction in Alternative Semantics*. Ph.D. thesis, University of Massachusetts at Amherst.

Broome, John (1999). "Normative Requirements." *Ratio*, 12(4): pp. 398–419.

Broome, John (2002). "Practical Reasoning." In J. L. Bermúdez and A. Millar (eds.) *Reason and Nature: Essays in the Theory of Rationality*. Oxford: Oxford University Press, pp. 85–111.

Broome, John (2004). "Reasons." In R. J. Wallace (ed.) *Reason and Value: Themes from the Moral Philosophy of Joseph Raz*. Oxford: Oxford University Press, pp. 2004–2028.

Cariani, Fabrizio (2013). "'Ought' and Resolution Semantics." *Noûs*, 47(3): pp. 534–558.

Cariani, Fabrizio, Magdalena Kaufmann, and Stefan Kaufmann (2013). "Deliberative Modality under Epistemic Uncertainty." *Linguistics and Philosophy*, 36(3): pp. 225–259.

Carr, Jennifer (2014). "The 'If P, Ought P' Problem." *Pacific Philosophical Quarterly*, 95(4): pp. 555–583.

Carr, Jennifer (Forthcoming). "Subjective Ought." *Ergo*.

Charlow, Nate (2013). "What We Know and What to Do." *Synthese*, 190(12): pp. 2291–2323.

Dancy, Jonathan (2000). *Practical Reality*. Oxford: Oxford University Press.

Darwall, Stephen L. (1983). *Impartial Reason*. Ithaca, NY: Cornell University Press.

Darwall, Stephen L. (2001). "Because I Want It." *Social Philosophy and Policy*, 18(2): pp. 129–153.

DeRose, Keith (1991). "Epistemic Possibilities". *Philosophical Review*, 100(4): pp. 581–605.

Dowell, Janice (2012). "Contextualist Solutions to Three Puzzles about Practical Conditionals." In *Oxford Studies in Metaethics, Vol. 7*. Oxford: Oxford University Press.

Egan, Andy (2007). "Epistemic Modals, Relativism and Assertion." *Philosophical Studies*, 133(1): pp. 1–22.

Egan, Andy, and Brian Weatherson (2009). *Epistemic Modality*. Oxford: Oxford University Press.

Egan, Andy, John Hawthorne, and Brian Weatherson (2005). "Epistemic Modals in Context." In Gerhard Preyer and Georg Peter (eds.) *Contextualism in Philosophy*. Oxford: Oxford University Press.

Forrester, James William (1984). "Gentle Murder, or the Adverbial Samaritan." *Journal of Philosophy*, 81(4): pp. 193–197.

Frank, Anette (1997). Context Dependence in Modal Constructions. Ph.D. thesis, Universität Stuttgart.

Fusco, Melissa (2015). "Deontic Modality and the Semantics of Choice." *Philosophers' Imprint*, 15(28): pp. 1–27.

Geurts, Bart (2004). "On an Ambiguity in Quantified Conditionals". Manuscript.

Hansson, Bengt (1969). "An Analysis of Some Deontic Logics." *Noûs*, 3(4): pp. 373–398.

Hare, Richard M. (1967). "Some Alleged Differences between Imperatives and Indicatives." *Mind*, 76(303): pp. 309–326.

Horn, Laurence (1972). On the Semantic Properties of Logical Operators in English. Ph.D. thesis, University of California, Los Angeles.

Jackson, Frank, and Robert Pargetter (1986). "Oughts, Options, and Actualism." *Philosophical Review*, 95(2): pp. 233–255.

Kamp, Hans (1973). "Free Choice Permission". *Proceedings of the Aristotelian Society*, 74: pp. 57–74.

Kolodny, Niko, and John MacFarlane (2010). "Ifs and Oughts." *The Journal of Philosophy*, 107(3).

Kratzer, Angelika (1977). "What 'Must' and 'Can' Must and Can Mean." *Linguistics and Philosophy*, 1(3): pp. 337–355.

Kratzer, Angelika (1981). "The Notional Category of Modality." In Hans-Jürgen Eikmeyer and Hannes Rieser (eds.) *Words, Worlds, and Contexts: New Approaches in World Semantics*. Berlin: de Gruyter, pp. 38–74.

Kratzer, Angelika (1991). "Modality." In Arnim von Stechow and Dieter Wunderlich (eds.) *Semantics: An International Handbook of Contemporary Research*. Berlin: de Gruyter, 639–650.

Kratzer, Angelika (2012). *Modals and Conditionals*. Oxford: Oxford University Press.

Lassiter, Daniel (2011). *Measurement and Modality: The Scalar Basis of Modal Semantics*. Ph.D. thesis, New York University.

Lewis, David (1973). *Counterfactuals*. Oxford: Blackwell.

MacFarlane, John (2005). "Making Sense of Relative Truth." *Proceedings of the Aristotelian Society*, 105(3): pp. 321–339.

MacFarlane, John (2014). *Assessment Sensitivity: Relative Truth and Its Applications*. Oxford: Oxford University Press.

McNamara, Paul (2014). "Deontic Logic." In E. Zalta (ed.) *Stanford Encyclopedia of Philosophy* (Winter 2014 Edition). URL = http://plato.stanford.edu/archives/win2014/entries/logic-deontic/.

Ninan, Dilip (2005). "Two Puzzles About Deontic Necessity". In J. Gajewski, V. Hacquard, B. Nickel, and S. Yalcin (eds.) *New Work on Modality, MIT Working Papers in Linguistics*, 51: pp. 149–178.

Prior, Arthur N. (1958). "Escapism: The Logical Basis of Ethics". In A. I. Melden (ed.) *Journal of Symbolic Logic*. University of Washington Press, 4, pp. 610–611.

Regan, Donald (1980). *Utilitarianism and Cooperation*. New York: Oxford University Press.

Ross, Alf (1944). "Imperatives and Logic". *Philosophy of Science*, 11(1): pp. 30–46.

Rubinstein, Aynat (2012). *Roots of Modality*. Ph.D. thesis, University of Massachusetts, Amherst.

Silk, Alex (2014a). "Evidence Sensitivity in Weak Necessity Deontic Modals". *Journal of Philosophical Logic*, 43(4): pp. 691–723.

Silk, Alex (2014b). "Why 'Ought' Detaches: Or, Why You Ought to Get with My Friends (If You Want to Be My Lover)". *Philosophers' Imprint*, 14(7): pp. 1–16.

Sloman, Aaron (1970). "'Ought' and 'Better'". *Mind*, 79(315): pp. 385–394.

Spohn, Wolfgang (1975). "An Analysis of Hansson's Dyadic Deontic Logic". *Journal of Philosophical Logic*, 4(2): pp. 237–252.

Stalnaker, Robert (1984). *Inquiry*. Cambridge, MA: MIT Press.

van Fraassen, Bas (1972). "The Logic of Conditional Obligation". *Journal of Philosophical Logic*, 1(3/4): pp. 417–438.

von Fintel, Kai (1999). "NPI Licensing, Strawson Entailment, and Context Dependency". *Journal of Semantics*, 16(2): pp. 97–148.

von Fintel, Kai (2012). "The Best We Can (Expect to) Get? Challenges to the Classic Semantics for Deontic Modals". *Central Meeting of the American Philosophical Association*, February (Vol. 17).

von Fintel, Kai, and Sabine Iatridou (2008). "How to Say *Ought* in Foreign: The Composition of Weak Necessity Modals". In *Time and Modality: Studies in Natural Language and Linguistic Theory*, vol. 75, pp. 115–141.

Weatherson, Brian (2009). "Conditionals and Indexical Relativism". *Synthese*, 166(2): pp. 333–357.

Wedgwood, Ralph (2006). "The Meaning of the 'Ought'". In R. Shafer-Landau (ed.) *Oxford Studies in Metaethics: Volume 1*. Oxford: Clarendon Press, vol. 1, pp. 127–160.

Zvolenszky, Zsófia (2002). "Is a Possible-Worlds Semantics of Modality Possible? A Problem for Kratzer's Semantics". In *Proceedings of Semantics and Linguistic Theory*, 12: pp. 339–358.

Zvolenszky, Zsófia (2006). "A Semantic Constraint on the Logic of Modal Conditionals". In B. Gyuris, L. Kalman, C. Pinon, and K. Varasdi (eds.) *Proceedings of the Ninth Symposium on Logic and Language (LoLa 9)*, pp. 167–177.

Zvolenszky, Zsófia (2007). *The Lost Pillar of Deontic Modality Naming with Necessity (Part of the Dissertation Portfolio* Modality, Names and Descriptions). Ph.D. thesis, New York University.

13

Thick Concepts

Debbie Roberts

There has been a renewed flurry of interest in thick concepts in the last ten years or so. Despite this, they remain a fairly niche topic in metaethics, and in metanormative theorising more generally. In this chapter, I aim to show that thick concepts deserve more attention in general than they currently enjoy.

Metaethics, and metanormative theorising more generally, concerns giving an account of all normative thought and talk. *Prima facie*, thick terms and concepts are part of the relevant range of terms and concepts, so an account of them is part of the task of metanormative theorising. In addition, as I will argue below, thick terms and concepts are intrinsically puzzling because they seem to combine evaluation and non-evaluative description. While it would, of course, be intrinsically interesting to figure out how they do this, solving this puzzle turns out to have interesting and important implications for metanormative theory more generally.

'What Are Thick Concepts?' is a brief characterisation of what thick concepts are. I then outline the main views in the debate in the section 'The Main Views'. The section three that follows this is the meat of this chapter. There I lay out the current state of play, pointing out the main points of contention between the different views. I end that section by examining which concepts end up counting as thick according to the different positions. The final section, 'Why Are Thick Concepts Important?', considers the significance of thick concepts.

WHAT ARE THICK CONCEPTS?

What is a theory of thick concepts a theory of? There are at least two routes to answering that question. The first provides some paradigm cases. The second provides an answer in theoretical terms. Here, I take the first route.

A standard way of introducing thick concepts is to point to an intuitive contrast between concepts like GENEROUS, BRUTAL, CRUDE and TACTLESS, and concepts like GOOD,

BAD, RIGHT and WRONG (though the difference may be one of degree rather than one of kind [Scheffler 1987]). Bernard Williams (1985: 129) introduces to ethics the terminology of 'thick' and 'thin' to mark this contrast and gives the following examples of thick concepts: PROMISE, TREACHERY, BRUTALITY, COURAGE, COWARD and LIE.

As well as examples drawn from the *ethical*, and the *practical* realm more generally, like those above, paradigmatic cases in the literature are also drawn from other normative domains. In *aesthetics*, DAINTY, DUMPY, DELICATE and DASHING are among these. And specifically *political* concepts seem to belong on the list too, for example, DEMOCRACY, LEGITIMACY and DISTRIBUTIVE JUSTICE. More controversially, some have claimed that there are *legal* thick concepts, for example, NEGLIGENCE and MURDER, as well as LAW and LEGAL themselves. And others have claimed that there are *epistemic* thick concepts, for example, GULLIBLE, CONSCIENTIOUS and OPEN-MINDED (compare *Philosophical Papers* 2008 [37]).

There are other examples of terms and concepts that, like the legal and epistemic examples, don't typically feature as paradigmatic cases but seem intuitively like they might either turn out to be thick or be interestingly similar-but-different to the thick. These include *slurs and pejoratives*, like 'slut', 'kraut', 'girly' and 'poof'; *affective notions* like 'admirable', 'desirable' and 'contemptible'; certain *complex predicates* that explicitly concern ways of being good or bad, like 'good torturer' and 'bad dancer'; and, lastly, prima facie uncontroversially *nonevalutive terms* that are often used to convey evaluations pragmatically, e.g., 'painful', 'pleasurable', 'fat' and 'athletic'. Whether any of these kinds of terms end up counting as thick will depend on the details of the correct account. On the approach to answering the question that I started this section with, working out which account of thick concepts one ought to adopt will in part involve working out which generates the most plausible-looking list.

I've moved from talking about thick concepts to talking about thick terms and concepts. Roughly put, the idea that most in this literature are working with is the simple one that terms express concepts; the semantic content of a term is, or overlaps exactly with, the concept.

So how are we to characterise the intuitive contrast between thick and thin? BRUTAL and SPITEFUL are thick and BAD thin, seemingly in virtue of BRUTAL and SPITEFUL, each containing or conveying more detailed information than BAD. However, more precise accounts that nonetheless remain neutral between particular views on the nature of thick concepts are non-existent. (Compare Väyrynen 2013: 4–7; Eklund 2011.) This is because part of what is at issue in this debate is just what makes thick concepts thick.

For the moment, since we must start somewhere, let's take as a working attempt to characterise the distinction the claim that thick concepts and the terms that express them somehow combine evaluation and non-evaluative description whereas thin concepts are (or are more purely) evaluative or normative. Even this is not a neutral distinction, as should become clear below. But this seems at least an initially plausible explanation of how it is that thick terms and concepts seemingly convey or contain more detailed information than that conveyed or contained by the thin.

THE MAIN VIEWS

Broadly speaking, there are three different types of view one might have on the nature of thick terms and concepts (Roberts 2013b). The first divergence arises depending on how the evaluative aspect of thick terms and concepts is taken to be communicated. Some hold that thick terms and concepts are themselves evaluative as a matter of content ("inherently evaluative," to use Väyrynen's terminology) so the evaluation is, or is part of, the *semantic content* of the relevant terms. Others hold that the evaluations most closely associated with thick terms and concepts are communicated by some kind of *pragmatic* mechanism, and thus that thick terms and concepts are not inherently evaluative, that is, not evaluative as a matter of content.[1]

Content views can be further divided into those who think that the content of thick terms and concepts can in principle be separated into non-evaluative descriptive and thin evaluative elements of content and those who think this cannot be done. I call these *reductive* and *non-reductive* content views, respectively.

The *non-reductive content* view holds that thick terms and concepts are inherently evaluative and irreducibly thick. It is on this view that thick terms and concepts are held to have distinctive significance (e.g., as an argument against non-cognitivist views and 'the fact-value distinction'). The other kinds of views represent two different ways one might deflate the significance of the thick and avoid the problems for various theories that thick concepts are supposed to cause.

One view of the nature of thick terms and concepts, the *descriptive equivalence* view, has been widely discredited in this literature, though it is still worth mentioning here. The descriptive equivalence view claims that for every thick term (concept) there is, or could be, a purely non-evaluative descriptive term (concept) with the same extension (compare Mackie 1977: 16–17; Hare 1981: 72). Against this it is widely held that for thick terms and concepts 'evaluation drives extension', that is, in order to be able to apply the term to new cases, one has to at least imaginatively adopt the evaluative perspective within which the relevant concept has its point. If a non-evaluative descriptive term with the same extension were possible, an outsider would be able to see how to go on applying the term to new cases without ever even just imaginatively adopting the relevant evaluative perspective (see McDowell 1981: 201–202).

It seems very plausible that the descriptive equivalence view is false for at least *paradigmatic* examples of thick terms and concepts. (It is a widely held view in the slurs literature, but as I said at the start, it is controversial whether or not slurs are thick concepts.) When one starts to try to come up with extensional equivalents for 'cruel' or 'elegant', it's very difficult not to reach for other seemingly *evaluative* terms ('suffering', 'graceful') and very easy to end up using 'cruel' and 'elegant' themselves. This looks to undermine not only the claim that we have in our current vocabulary the non-evaluative term that is extensionally equivalent to cruel, but also the claim that we could in principle invent one.

One might think that the failure of the descriptive equivalence view shows that the evaluative and non-evaluative content of thick concepts cannot be separated out or 'disentangled'.[2] And, indeed, some do appear to have concluded this (see, e.g., Williams 1985: 141; Putnam 2002: 37–38). That the evaluative and non-evaluative content of thick concepts cannot be separated out, even in principle, is a crucial element of the non-reductive content view. So if we could conclude 'no separation' from the failure of descriptive equivalence, this would be good news for the non-reductivists.

However, unhappily for the non-reductive view, reductive content and pragmatic views can happily accommodate that the descriptive equivalence view is false, though they do so in very different ways. Most importantly, the reductive content view accepts the claim that evaluation drives extension for thick terms and concepts, but the pragmatic view does not.

Let's take *reductive content* views first. Prominent defenders include Gibbard (1992) and Elstein and Hurka (2009). Elstein and Hurka, for example, put forward two reduction plans for thick terms, neither of which generate descriptive equivalents, so they are both compatible with the claim that evaluation drives extension for the thick. The first is a two-component analysis where the non-evaluative descriptive component does not fully specify what something has to be like to merit the application of the thick term. 'Cruel', for example, might be handled in this way:

> 'x is cruel' means 'x is bad and there are properties P, Q & R (unspecified) of non-evaluative sort c (specified) such that x has properties P, Q & R and P, Q & R make anything that has them bad'.
>
> (2009: 522)

Elstein and Hurka's second reductive plan introduces an *embedded* evaluation, distinct from the *global* evaluation governing the whole use of the term. When it comes to thick terms and concepts, an evaluation is *global* if that evaluation applies to all the features that distinguish the things falling under that term or concept. We can contrast this with *embedded* evaluations, which are evaluations required to specify the very thing over which the global evaluation will take scope. Take 'distributively just' as an example, and assume that 'x is distributively just' means something like 'x has features X, Y and Z as a distribution and is good for having those features'. The 'good' that occurs in the analysis is a global evaluation. An embedded evaluation would be present if specifying the type of thing to which the global evaluation applies required evaluative information. In this case, if one or more of X, Y or Z were an evaluative feature (e.g., perhaps X is 'is the result of a *fair* procedure') then 'distributively just' would contain an embedded evaluation.

And now for the second reductive plan:

> 'x is courageous' means 'x is good [global evaluation], and x involves an agent accepting harm or the risk of harm for himself for the sake of *goods greater than the evil* [embedded evaluation] of that harm, where this property makes any act that has it good'.
>
> (2009: 526).

Both reductive plans are compatible with the claim that evaluation drives extension, and the falsity of the descriptive equivalence view, for in both cases, in order to determine the extension of the term, one has to make some evaluations. In the first case, evaluation is required to settle precisely which non-evaluative features of type c are the bad-making, and thus cruel, ones. In the second, evaluation is required to settle when accepting harm or the risk of harm is worthwhile and thus courageous (it's worth noting that Elsten and Hurka are assuming the 'harm' is non-evaluative).

On the *pragmatic view*, thick terms and concepts are not inherently evaluative. Prominent defenders include Hare (1952; 1963; 1981), Blackburn (1992) and Väyrynen (2013). On Väyrynen's view, the fact that the descriptive equivalence view is false, and that one can't go on to apply 'cruel' correctly in new cases without drawing on one's understanding of 'cruel', doesn't show anything more than would be shown by observing that one can't go on to apply 'red' or 'chair' correctly in new cases without drawing on one's understanding of 'red' or 'chair'. If this is correct, the 'evaluation drives extension' point that non-reductivists appear to have made so much of may really be no more than a misidentification of the unexciting point that thick terms and concepts lack a classical structure. Moreover, Väyrynen argues, thick terms should be understood as context-sensitive gradable terms (like 'tall'). And for such terms, there is really no such thing as 'the' extension (Väyrynen 2013: chapters 7 and 8).

To sum up, there are three options currently on the table: The *non-reductive* content view, the *reductive* content view and the *pragmatic* view. The main point historically taken to favour the non-reductive view, that the descriptive equivalence view is false, can be accommodated by all three. How, then, are we to decide between them? In the next section, I set out the main points of contention between these views.

THE CURRENT STATE OF PLAY

The main issues in the current debate concern objectionable thick terms and concepts, what makes a concept evaluative, the question of whether evaluation drives extension for thick terms and concepts, the distinction between global and embedded evaluation, the non-evaluative shapelessness of thick concepts and, lastly, the question of which terms and concepts get to count as thick.

Objectionable thick terms and concepts

In classifying the available positions on the nature of thick concepts, I said above that the first divergence occurs depending on whether the (global) evaluation most closely associated with a thick term is held to be a part of the semantic concept of the term or not, that is, depending on whether thick terms and concepts are held to be *inherently* evaluative. Content views claim that they are, pragmatic views that they are not. Central to the issue here is linguistic data concerning the use of *objectionable* thick terms and concepts.

This issue is best introduced by considering Väyrynen's argument for the pragmatic view. Väyrynen takes evaluation to be "information to the effect that something has a positive or negative standing—merit or demerit, worth or unworthy—relative to a certain kind of standard ... the kind that is capable of grounding claims of merit or worth" (Väyrynen 2013: 29). And a term or concept T is inherently evaluative on this view if "all literal uses of sentences of the form x is T in normal contexts entail, as a conceptual matter or by virtue of a semantic rule, that x is good or bad, depending on T in a certain way" (2013: 34). This last suggests a way to test whether T-evaluations are a part of the meaning of thick terms and concepts.

If T-evaluations were a part of the meaning of thick terms and concepts, then we would expect them to be semantic entailments, semantic presuppositions or conventional implicatures. Standard methods in linguistics give us ways to test for these things. If they turn out to be none of these things, then they are related to thick terms and concepts pragmatically.

Here is where objectionable thick terms and concepts come into the argument for the pragmatic view. A thick term or concept is objectionable if the global evaluation most closely associated with it doesn't fit the things which the term or concept is true of. For example, we might think that 'lewd' is objectionable because overt displays of sexuality are not bad for being such displays. The linchpin of the argument is a hypothesis that linguistic data concerning objectionable thick terms and concepts shows that T-evaluations *project*—they survive embedding in various contexts that cancel semantic entailments—and are *defeasible* in certain ways that semantic entailments aren't. If someone says "Miley's show is lewd", we'd be inclined to think that they thought the show was bad in a certain way. But is that it is bad in a certain way *entailed* by 'lewd'? Väyrynen argues that it is not, on the grounds that because the global evaluation projects in all of the following cases: "Is Miley's show lewd?," "Miley's show might be lewd" and "If Miley's show is lewd, the *Daily Mail* will be all over it." And one can perfectly well say things like "Miley's show is lewd, but not bad in any way."[3]

Projection and defeasibility are also key to Väyrynen's argument that T-evaluations are not conventional implicatures or semantic presuppositions. He argues that the best explanation of the behaviour of T-evaluations is that they are related to thick terms and concepts pragmatically. Specifically, his view is that global T-evaluations are implications of utterances containing thick terms which are part of background, 'not-at-issue' content in normal contexts and which arise conversationally.

Broadly speaking, there are two different strategies for replying to this argument. The first can be used by defenders of either the reductive or the non-reductive content views, and this is to directly deny that the data concerning objectionable thick terms and concepts supports the pragmatic view by challenging either the supposed data itself, or that the data shows that the relevant evaluations are not part of the semantic content of the relevant terms. Brent Kyle is an example of someone who has pursued this strategy, and he introduces further linguistic data which he argues supports what he calls the semantic view (Kyle 2013).

The second strategy for replying to Väyrynen's argument can be revealed by considering the question of whether *thin* terms and concepts can be found objectionable, that is, as embodying evaluations that ought not to be endorsed. Take 'morally good' for example. Perhaps a Marxist or a Nietzschean can think that there is such a property but offer an account in which moral goodness is something to be condemned. Any difficulty we have in imagining that moral goodness could be found objectionable could be accounted for by the imaginative difficulty in occupying evaluative perspectives very remote from our own.

We could use the case of a Nietzschean finding 'morally good' objectionable to argue that the global evaluation associated with 'morally good' projects is defeasible in the same way as the global evaluation associated with 'lewd'. Someone who found 'morally good' objectionable would be unlikely to say any of the following: "Is helpfulness morally good?," "Helpfulness might be morally good" or "If helpfulness is morally good, Bryan will help Patrick." That is, they would be unlikely to use the term in a question, embedded in a possibility modal or epistemic modal, or in the antecedent of a conditional because the positive evaluation projects. And it seems possible to deny that an action is good for being morally good.

The crucial point is that this would not necessarily show that 'morally good' is not an evaluative concept or that it fails to pick out an evaluative property. To reject a concept, as Dancy puts it, one has to see its point and reject it for that reason (Dancy 1995: 269). Given that we are talking about evaluative concepts, another way to put this would be that one has to make the evaluation and then evaluate that evaluation as objectionable. A rough-and-ready characterisation of what is going on here could be that there are two evaluations: one conceptual and one substantive. If we accept Väyrynen's account of such data, what this would show is that any substantive evaluation of 'morally good' is plausibly not itself a part of the content of 'morally good'.

Might not the same be true in the thick case? If global evaluations are no part of the semantic content of thick terms, this might be a reflection of the fact that substantive evaluations of thick properties are no part of the concept that picks out those properties. We could take as evidence for this the case familiar in the literature of the bully who is quite competent with 'cruel' but evaluates cruelty positively.

In fact, this is part of the pragmatic view as Väyrynen defends it: that the substantive evaluations that groups of people make are no part of the content of the relevant term or concept but instead ought to be viewed as communicated via pragmatic mechanisms. However, importantly for the defenders of content views, this by itself does not answer the question of whether the thick concepts or properties *themselves* are evaluative, any more than a substantive evaluation of 'morally good' being no part of its content should lead us to conclude that 'morally good' fails to be an evaluative concept or pick out an evaluative property.

What makes a concept evaluative?

The previous section brought to light an important fundamental issue raised by the thick concepts debate, that is, the question of what makes a concept evaluative in the first place. This is a tricky issue, and again one where it looks to be difficult to find an account that is appropriately metaethically neutral, and neutral between the different views in this debate. This is particularly difficult as at least some non-reductive content views hold, or at least suggest, that there is no sharp distinction to be made between evaluation and non-evaluative description (see, e.g., Putman 2002: chapter 2; Dancy 1995; Roberts 2013a).

Because, historically, much of the thick concepts debate merely assumed that thick concepts were evaluative concepts, this issue is relatively under-explored. The second reply to Väyrynen's argument in the previous section relied on the intuitive, pre-theoretical view that the concept MORALLY GOOD is an evaluative concept. But MORALLY GOOD is thicker (richer, more informative) than GOOD. Perhaps then it is open to defenders of the pragmatic view to argue that MORALLY GOOD is itself a non-evaluative descriptive concept, merely one that we tend to think is evaluative because it is so closely associated with the substantive evaluation that it is good.

For the purposes of this chapter, it is important to note that, given the nature of the debate, we cannot rely on our pre-theoretical intuitions about which concepts are evaluative, any more than we can rely solely on our intuitions concerning which concepts are thick. Part of any account of the thick, then, should be an account of what makes evaluative concepts evaluative in the first place (see Eklund 2013; Roberts 2013a; Väyrynen 2013: chapter 2).

Does evaluation drive extension?

As noted above, that thick concepts are evaluative is assumed without argument in most of the literature on the thick. Those wishing to defend this assumption, and thus some version of the content view, might look to the considerations cited in favour of the common claim in the literature that evaluation drives extension for thick terms and concepts. Borrowing Väyrynen's terminology, I consider two here: *parochiality*, or the claim that the point of these concepts is only apparent from within a particular evaluative point of view, and *underdetermination*, the way in which their non-evaluative content underdetermines their extensions.

Evidence for parochiality is taken to come from the plausible thought that an outsider would not be able to see how to 'go on' in applying the concept to new cases without at least imaginatively adopting the *evaluative* perspective within which the concept has its point. This is best illustrated by considering examples of thick concepts historically and/or culturally remote from our own, like perhaps the Quaker value of simplicity or the Southern African value of *ubuntu*.

Parochiality is closely related to the claim that the non-evaluative components of thick terms and concepts underdetermine their extensions. Here, the thought is that even the most detailed non-evaluative description which a given thick term may plausibly be thought to entail will not be sufficient to determine the extension of the term. Consider 'distributively just', an example that Elstein and Hurka discuss. If a distribution is just, that seems to entail nothing more non-evaluatively speaking than that it is a distribution. Or take 'dainty', which appears to entail nothing more than 'small', non-evaluatively speaking. One plausible explanation for this is that it is evaluation as part of the semantic content of the relevant terms that is at least partially determining extension.

Gibbard illustrates this thought nicely in his discussion of GOPA, his fictional example of a thick concept used by the (fictional) Kumi tribe for certain kinds of killings:

> I allow there might be descriptive constraints on a thick concept. Calling the eating of vegetables gopa, say, might violate a rule of language: it may just not be the sort of thing that could count as gopa. These constraints, though, will in many cases be too sparse to give the whole meaning-even when combined with an evaluative component. A good treatment of thick terms may combine clearly descriptive and clearly evaluative elements-indeed, my own analyses will. My claim has been that a statement like 'this killing was gopa' has no descriptive meaning as a whole-or not enough of one that, in some combination with its evaluative meaning, it can yield the full meaning of the statement. There is no statement 'This act was descriptively gopa' which somehow combines with an evaluative meaning to give the full meaning of 'This act was gopa'. In thick concepts, descriptive and evaluative components intermesh more tightly than that.
>
> (1992: 277–278)

Now it may seem, on the face of it, that both parochiality and underdetermination tell strongly in favour of holding that evaluation plays an extension-determining role for thick terms and concepts by being part of their content. The pragmatic view is, however, not without resources here. Väyrynen, for example, has argued that the pragmatic view, together with general features of context-sensitive gradable terms (and he argues that thick terms are plausibly context-sensitive gradable terms) can also explain these considerations. He then argues on the grounds of Grice's razor—that other things being equal, we should prefer the view that postulates fewer semantic properties—that the pragmatic explanation is to be preferred.

Defenders of reductive and non-reductive content views may reply to this in a number of ways. First, this account of parochiality and underdetermination depends on the success of the argument for the pragmatic view discussed in the section 'Objectionable thick terms and concepts' above. If the direct response to that argument (that is, denying that the data concerning objectionable thick terms and concepts supports the pragmatic view) succeeds, then this account of parochiality and underdetermination is unavailable. Second, it's worth noting that a term or concept's being evaluative is compatible with its being a context-sensitive gradable term—thin evaluative concepts fall precisely into this category. If, as I discussed in 'Objectionable thick terms and concepts,' it is substantive evaluations that are communicated pragmatically, the pragmatic view combined with general features of context-sensitive gradable terms could nonetheless be combined with the view that thick concepts and properties are evaluative.

This is perhaps just a different way of making the same point that Väyrynen makes, which is that the issue of whether thick concepts are *themselves* evaluative is really to be decided by the employment of a generalisation of Grice's razor; *other things being equal* we should prefer the pragmatic view. But are other things equal? In the rest of this section, I aim to show that there is as yet no reason to be confident that they are, so both reductive and non-reductive content views remain as live options.

Evaluation: Global and embedded?

Whether thick terms and concepts contain embedded evaluation, regardless of whether they also contain global evaluation, is an important issue. Broadly speaking, it's important for the pragmatic view that if there are any thick terms that contain embedded evaluation, that this isn't a characteristic of paradigmatic thick terms in general. And it is important for both the pragmatic and the reductive content views that this embedded evaluation is thin and that it can in principle be "unembedded," i.e., separated out from the non-evaluative content of the thick term. I explain both these points in more detail below.

The main argument for the pragmatic view, discussed above, targets only global evaluation. Väyrynen allows that paradigmatic thick terms and concepts may contain embedded evaluation but holds that thick terms and concepts won't be inherently evaluative, or have deep or distinctive significance, if their meanings only contain embedded, and not global, evaluations. This is for two reasons, he claims. First, he suggests, only some thick terms have embedded evaluation, so embedded evaluation cannot be what is in general distinctive of the thick. Second, he follows Elstein and Hurka (defenders of a reductive content view) in claiming that because embedded evaluations are independent of whether they figure in the meaning of thick terms and concepts, if embedded evaluations had deep or distinctive significance, then they'd have this independently of their relation to the thick terms and concepts that embed them.

Both these reasons can be questioned, with potentially problematic results for both pragmatic and reductive content views. First, the non-reductivist can attempt to make a case for the claim that all (or just most) paradigmatic cases of thick concepts contain embedded evaluation. Second, regardless of whether this case is successful, the claim that embedded evaluations couldn't give thick terms and concepts deep or distinctive significance because they are independent of thick terms and concepts that embed them is really only plausible if (i) all embedded evaluations are *thin*, and (ii) if they are genuinely embedded, that is, could at least in principle be unembedded. And the non-reductivist can attempt to deny these things.

Defenders of non-reductive content views might well ask why we should assume either (i) or (ii). On (i), if some embedded evaluations are *themselves* thick, why assume that there will be some chain of embeddings which bottoms out in an analysis that includes only thin evaluation and non-evaluative description?[4] Moreover, why assume that there are neat conceptual divisions such that each embedded evaluation can be regarded as independent? Our evaluative concepts may form a network with no such sharp divisions.

For example, grasping the concept 'courage' may involve grasping when it is *worthwhile* to pursue *goods* regardless of the badness of the *harm* or risk of *harm* one is accepting. Grasping 'harm' may require grasping what *welfare* and *flourishing* and the *worthwhile* are. And grasping 'welfare', 'flourishing' and 'the worthwhile' may require grasping what *courage* is.

On (ii), if so-called embedded evaluations cannot be separated from that in which they are embedded, it may not make sense to think of them as being independent or, indeed, as embedded.

At this point, it is worth noting that it may be that what is referred to as embedded evaluation, and what is dismissed as thus being unable to ground claims concerning the distinctive significance of thick concepts, may well have been what, historically, non-reductivists about the thick were concerned to focus on. That is, the issue was never really primarily whether the relevant global (thin) evaluation could be detached (be separated out by analysis on the reductive content view, or shown not to be part of the semantic content on the pragmatic view). The issue was whether the very object of the global evaluation was *itself* evaluative. In my view, the way to put this point is that the real issue in this debate is whether the object of the global evaluation is an evaluative *property*.

This gets to the heart of what at least some defenders of irreducible thickness were concerned about, that is, showing that kindness, cruelty, courage and the like are genuine evaluative features of the world and thus a problem for anti-realist views (see, e.g., McDowell 1981; Dancy 1995; Putnam 2002). The thought might be that no one, not even the metaethical anti-realist, wants to claim that kindness, generosity, cruelty, harm, suffering, brutality and courage are not genuine features of the world (using the relevant robust standard of genuineness), though they may be happy to do so in the case of thin properties. So thick terms and concepts represent the possibility of a distinctive challenge to the sharp ontological, and perhaps also semantic, fact-value distinctions made by these sorts of views, if it can be shown that the object of the global evaluation, for any thick concept, *is itself evaluative* and evaluative in such a way that cannot be reductively analyzed into some combination of thin evaluation and non-evaluative description.

Shapelessness

Another common claim, typically made by non-reductivists, is that thick terms and concepts are *non-evaluatively shapeless*. Assuming that thick concepts are themselves evaluative, this is thought by some to tell in favour of the non-reductive view.

What is non-evaluative shapelessness? The 'shape' of a concept, we can say, is what all the things falling under the concept have in common: the unifying feature or the real resemblance (Roberts 2011: 505). If evaluative concepts are non-evaluatively shapeless then that unifying feature or real resemblance is *not* non-evaluative: it is not simply that we lack a term for the non-evaluative feature of the world that we are nonetheless sensitive to in applying our evaluative concept, *it is not there.*[5]

Many have found the shapelessness thesis plausible (see, e.g., McDowell 1981; Dancy 1993, 1995; Wiggins 1993; Putnam 2002; Majors 2003, 2009; Kirchin 2010; Roberts 2011, 2013a). *If* shapelessness is the case, does this tell against either the reductive content view or the pragmatic view? The answer here is bound up with the issue of embedded evaluation discussed in the previous section. If we assume that Elstein and Hurka and Väyrynen are correct about embedded evaluation, then I think it is safe to say that both the pragmatic view and the reductive content view can accommodate shapelessness. But if they are not, then I think that shapelessness will tell in favour of the non-reductive view.

(vi) *What makes concepts thick? The list revisited*

On the pragmatic view, thick terms and concepts are not inherently evaluative. One might then ask why (paradigmatic) thick concepts have been so universally thought to be evaluative. Väyrynen's answer is that thick terms and concepts concern aspects of human life that matter: they "are widely invested with evaluative significance or systematically evoke various affective responses that are connected to evaluation" (Väyrynen 2013: 133). On this view, there is no difference in kind between 'courageous', 'cruel' and 'loyal', on the one hand, and 'fun', 'athletic' and 'chocolate', on the other, where these are non-evaluative terms commonly used to imply positive evaluation. Väyrynen holds that we can explain the appearance of a difference in kind by noting a cluster of contingent differences of degree. Chief among these are the differences in the degree to which the relevant evaluations are generalised: the greater the degree of generalisation, the easier it is for a term or concept to appear inherently evaluative.

A response open to reductive and non-reductive content views here is that it leaves it very mysterious that 'pleasure' and 'pain' aren't paradigmatic thick terms. These terms would seem to satisfy all the relevant criteria for being a paradigmatic thick term on Väyrynen's account. For one, they are typically used against a very broad and very strong background of agreement regarding their evaluative significance.

Väyrynen offers two speculations as to why 'pleasure' and 'pain' aren't regarded as thick: that the properties ascribed by thick terms are less easy to characterise in general terms, and that many of us are confident that it is no part of what it is to be pain that it be bad and no part of what it is to be pleasant that it should be good and thus see no essential need to use evaluative notions in describing pleasure and pain. The worry remains, though, for another way to put this might be that while we are confident that plain and pleasure are non-evaluative, the same cannot be said for the paradigmatically thick.

A plausible explanation here may have to do, again, with so-called embedded evaluation. Perhaps paradigmatic thick terms and concepts are those that involve this kind of evaluation. Once again, there seems to be a reason for further exploration of this issue. Moreover, appealing to embedded evaluation may be what explains the pre-theoretical intuition that complex predicates like 'bad dancer' and 'good assassin' are not thick, and these also come out as thick on Väyrynen's view.

Let us pause for a moment to take stock. The data concerning objectionable thick concepts does not conclusively favour any particular view of the nature of the thick. Moreover, all three positions are able to explain parochiality, underdetermination and shapelessness. Other things being equal, employing Grice's razor at this point means the pragmatic view comes out on top. However, there are further considerations. There is the issue of which concepts get to count as thick, as just discussed above. The pragmatic view is possibly vulnerable on this point for including too many concepts we don't ordinarily think of as evaluative or thick, and for not having a convincing rationale for excluding some that are not—i.e. pleasure and pain. At this point, plausibly, content views are out ahead. The issue of which concepts count as thick is connected to the interesting question of what makes concepts evaluative in the first place. In my view, this question is unlikely to yield non-question-begging answers.

The last remaining consideration is that of so-called "embedded evaluation". Many, if not all, of the examples of thick terms and concepts which are given as paradigmatic examples are plausibly understood as requiring evaluative information to characterise the very thing that is then subject to global evaluation. For these paradigmatic examples, it is very difficult not to reach for further thick terms when characterising that thing, as Elstein and Hurka inadvertently reveal in using the thick term 'harm' in their supposed reductive analysis of courage. Exactly what the upshot of this is, is an issue that requires more careful consideration than I have space for here. Suffice it to say that this issue concerning the nature of embedded evaluation (including whether it really makes sense to call it that) should now be centre stage in the debate about the nature of the thick.

WHY ARE THICK CONCEPTS IMPORTANT?

Precisely because these terms and concepts combine evaluation and non-evaluative description, some have held that they have significance beyond their intrinsically interesting nature. It's held to be distinctive because it is supposedly significance that isn't shared by thin concepts. Arguments for the distinctive significance of thick concepts have focussed on thick ethical terms but if there turn out to be thick concepts in other normative domains, then presumably the same kinds of significance would follow.

Typically, those who think that thick concepts have distinctive significance hold the non-reductive content view. Defenders of the pragmatic view deflate the significance of the thick by claiming that thick concepts are not inherently evaluative. And those who defend reductive content views claim that the evaluative and non-evaluative component of thick concepts can, at least in principle, be separated out by analysis. Non-reductive content views of the thick are most at home within a non-reductivist robust realist view in metaethics. Defenders of other kinds of metaethical views are likely to be drawn to one or other of the reductive content or the pragmatic view, depending on how wedded they are to the idea that thick concepts are inherently evaluative.

What then are the distinctive significances that (irreducibly) thick concepts have been claimed to have?

Fact and value

There are at least two of what may be loosely termed "fact-value" distinctions that thick terms and concepts have been held to break down. If these terms and concepts are successful in this regard, then they constitute an objection to any metaethical view that requires either or both of these distinctions.

First, we might make a *semantic* distinction between two different kinds of meaning, two different kinds of things we can do with language: we can evaluate and we can describe. One way to understand expressivism is as the view that evaluative utterances express non-cognitive attitudes, and that evaluation is thus not a species of description. On this understanding, expressivism requires a sharp distinction between evaluation and description. If thick terms and concepts are both evaluative and descriptive in such a way that they don't combine evaluative and non-evaluative descriptive elements that can in principle be separated from each other, then this is a problem for expressivism so understood. Many read Williams, McDowell, Putnam and Dancy, among others, as making this sort of thick concept argument against expressivism.

Secondly, we might make a related *ontological* distinction concerning what we admit into our ontology as genuine features of the world. The view that evaluative utterances are not truth-apt usually goes along with the view that there aren't any evaluative properties (in some appropriately robust sense) in the world. There are of course all sorts of other properties on this view, properties which, loosely speaking, are what the facts are about. Expressivism, as characterised above, thus also accepts a sharp ontological distinction between fact and value in this sense. If thick concepts were to undermine this ontological distinction, then this is a problem for expressivism. But it is a problem, too, for any anti-realist metaethical view that denies the existence of evaluative properties (compare McDowell 1981; Putnam 2002; Wiggins 1993; Dancy 1995). Error theories and fictionalist views would thus also be vulnerable to a thick concept argument.

In what way would all these anti-realisms be vulnerable? Recall from the discussion of so-called embedded evaluation above that the issue there was, for any thick concept, whether the very object of the global evaluation is *itself* evaluative. I said that the best way to put this is that the real issue in this debate is whether the object of the global evaluation is an evaluative *property*, for this gets to the heart of what at least some defenders of irreducible thickness were concerned about, that is, showing that kindness, cruelty, harm and the like are genuine evaluative features of the world. It is a significant cost to a view, one might think, if it has to claim that kindness, cruelty, harm and the like are not genuine features of the world (by the relevant robust standard of genuineness).

Interestingly, if thick concepts are a problem for anti-realist views because they're irreducibly thick and undermine an ontological distinction between fact and value, then they may also turn out to be a problem for *reductive realist* views in metaethics (Roberts 2011, 2013a). Moreover, thick concepts may even be recruited to undermine the idea that the evaluative, in general, supervenes on the non-evaluative (Dancy 1995; Roberts Forthcoming).

Of these two challenges to "fact-value distinctions," the second looks to be more fundamental and potentially more powerful, if it can be brought off, and there is still much interesting work to be done.

Evaluative practice, conceptual priority and normative ethics

If thick terms and concepts are evaluative in their own right, and they do not combine non-evaluative and evaluative elements of content in a way that can in principle be separated out, then this has been thought to have implications for evaluative thought and discourse, and normative ethical theories.

A large range of ethical theories focuses primarily, even exclusively, on thin terms and concepts. It is at least implicit in these views that all moral judgements can be expressed using thin terms and concepts, and that the thin is primary in some sense. It is also sometimes explicitly a part of these theories that thick moral concepts can be derived from the thin. If one is attracted to these kinds of views in normative ethics, one is likely to be attracted to reductive content or pragmatic views of the thick.

If thickness is irreducible, this may generate problems for the relevant theories in normative ethics. For example, we might worry, as some anti-theorists and virtue ethicists have, that ethical theories that focus only on the thin impose an oversimplified, distorting structure on ethical thought and the complexity of ethical life as we actually live it (compare Anscombe 1958; Williams 1985). In addition, we might think that the traditional approach to ethical theory is thin-centric, in that it assumes that the thin is somehow (conceptually, explanatorily) fundamental. If thick concepts are not derivable from the thin, we might question this thin-centralism and perhaps advocate either thick centralism or some kind of no-priority view in its place (compare Hurley 1989: 11).

Ethics and beyond

Lastly, whatever account of thick concepts turns out to be correct is likely to have implications for accounts of particular virtues, vices and values in ethics—and in other domains if the distinction between thick and thin turns out to hold there too. So, there are potential implications for accounts of various concepts important in ethics, applied ethics, politics, law, aesthetics and epistemology. To mention just a few potential examples, some repeated from above: CONSENT, RESPECT, DIGNITY, HARM, MORAL STANDING, LEGITIMACY, NEGLIGENCE, LEGAL, INTELLECTUAL HUMILITY and TRUSTWORTHY. Arguably, the implications for accounts of such concepts will be most profound if thickness turns out to be irreducible.

NOTES

1. Strictly speaking, the pragmatic view holds that it is the global evaluations most closely associated with thick terms and concepts that are not part of their content. See below.
2. This is a claim that is often made in this literature, and it is not always precisely clear what it means. There are at least two ways it has been interpreted: that evaluative and non-evaluative content/information cannot even in principle be separated out by conceptual/semantic analysis, or that the property picked out by the relevant term is itself an irreducibly evaluative property.
3. "Guy loves hummus" entails that Guy has very positive feelings towards hummus. Compare "Does Guy love hummus?," "Guy might love hummus" and "If Guy loves hummus, then he'll enjoy this restaurant." The entailment does not project. And nor is it plausibly defeasible: "Guy loves hummus but he doesn't have any positive feelings toward it" is infelicitous.
4. Thanks to Tristram McPherson for this point.
5. This requires adopting a certain view of the nature of properties on which massive disjunctions, for example, are not properties.

ACKNOWLEDGEMENTS

Thanks to the editors, James Fritz and Guy Fletcher for extremely helpful comments on an earlier draft.

REFERENCES

Anscombe, G. E. M. (1958) 'Modern Moral Philosophy', *Philosophy* 33 (124), 1–19.

Blackburn, S. (1992) 'Through Thick and Thin', *Proceedings of the Aristotelian Society*, Supplementary Volume 66, 285–299.

Dancy, J. (1993) *Moral Reasons* (Oxford: Blackwell).

Dancy, J. (1995) 'In Defense of Thick Concepts', in P. A. French, T. E. Uehling Jr. & H. K. Wettstein (eds.) *Midwest Studies in Philosophy XX: Moral Concepts* (Notre Dame: University of Notre Dame Press), 263–279.

Eklund, M. (2011) 'What Are Thick Concepts?', *Canadian Journal of Philosophy* 41, 25–49.

Eklund, M. (2013) 'Evaluative Language and Evaluative Reality' in S. Kirchin (ed.) *Thick Concepts* (Oxford: Oxford University Press), 162–181.

Elstein, D. & Hurka, T. (2009) 'From Thick to Thin: Two Moral Reduction Plans', *Canadian Journal of Philosophy* 39, 515–536.

Gibbard, A. (1992) 'Thick Concepts and Warrant for Feelings,' *Proceedings of the Aristotelian Society*, Supplementary Volume, 66, 267–289.

Hare, R. M. (1952) *The Language of Morals* (Oxford: Clarendon Press).

Hare, R. M. (1963) *Freedom and Reason* (Oxford: Clarendon Press).

Hare, R. M. (1981) *Moral Thinking: Its Levels, Methods and Point* (Oxford: Oxford University Press).

Hurley, S. L. (1989) *Natural Reasons: Personality and Polity* (New York: Oxford University Press).

Kirchin, S. (2010) 'The Shapelessness Hypothesis', *Philosophers' Imprint* 10 (4), 1–28.

Kyle, B. (2013) 'How Are Thick Terms Evaluative?', *Philosophers' Imprint* 13 (1), 1–20.

McDowell, J. (1981) 'Non-Cognitivism and Rule Following' in his (1998) *Mind, Value, and Reality* (Cambridge, MA: Harvard University Press), 198–218.

Mackie, J. L. (1977) *Ethics: Inventing Right and Wrong* (London: Pelican Books).

Majors, B. (2003) 'Moral Explanation and the Special Sciences,' *Philosophical Studies* 113 (2), 121–152

Majors, B. (2009) 'The Natural and the Normative' in R. Shafer-Landau (ed.) *Oxford Studies in Metaethics* (Oxford: Clarendon Press) 4, 29–52.

Putnam, H. (2002) 'The Entanglement of Fact and Value' in *The Collapse of the Fact/Value Dichotomy and Other Essays* (Cambridge, MA: Harvard University Press), 28–45.

Roberts, D. (2011) 'Shapelessness and the Thick', *Ethics* 121, 489–520.

Roberts, D. (2013a) 'It's Evaluation, Only Thicker' in S. Kirchin (ed.) *Thick Concepts* (Oxford: Oxford University Press), 79–96.

Roberts, D. (2013b) 'Thick Concepts', *Philosophy Compass* 8, 577–588.

Roberts, D. (Provisionally Forthcoming) 'Why Believe in Normative Supervenience?' in R. Shafer-Landau (ed.) *Oxford Studies in Metaethics* (Oxford: Clarendon Press), 13.

Scheffler, S. (1987) 'Morality through Thick and Thin: A Critical Notice of *Ethics and the Limits of Philosophy*', *Philosophical Review* 96, 411–434.

Väyrynen, P. (2013) *The Lewd, the Rude and the Nasty: A Study of Thick Concepts in Ethics* (Oxford: Oxford University Press).

Wiggins, D. (1993) 'A Neglected Position' in J. Haldane & C. Wright (eds.) *Reality, Representation and Projection* (Oxford: Oxford University Press), 329–336.

Williams, B. A. O. (1985) *Ethics and the Limits of Philosophy* (Cambridge MA: Harvard University Press).

14

The Frege-Geach Problem

Jack Woods

Non-cognitivist views of normative discourse, especially *emotivism*, *prescriptivism*, and their mutual successor *expressivism*, face a number of challenges in accounting for normative thought and talk. Perhaps the most prominent of these, "the Frege-Geach problem," is the challenge of explaining the content of normative thought and talk in complex constructions when the content of simple normative thought and talk are given non-cognitive treatment.[1]

The Frege-Geach problem arises for any view that takes force or analogous notions, such as *expression*, to explain content. For expressivists, the problem manifests in the fact that even if "Murder is wrong" expresses a conative state like disapproval in simple contexts, it does not do so in complex contexts like "If murder is wrong, it's not profitable." So the content of "Murder is wrong" cannot be what is expressed. Explaining how the content is related to what is expressed—solving the Frege-Geach problem—is mandatory for a satisfying expressivist theory; the inability to so explain would be a damning objection to the view.

Following Frege (1956), let us take the *content* of "The cat is on Matt" to be a certain picture of the world—one in which the relevant cat is on the relevant Matt—and the *force* to be my putting forth that the world is this way. I might utter the same *sentence* with different force, and in certain complex descriptive constructions, the force of the component is *canceled* entirely. "If the cat is on Matt, he'll get hives" does not describe the world as being such that the cat is on Matt, but rather describes a connection between one way the world could be and another. Frege used " $\vdash$ ", a combination of a vertical "judgment stroke" and horizontal "content" stroke, to indicate a forced expression. $\vdash p$ is a judgment with the content $- p$. Embedding, we obtain something like

$$\vdash \text{if} - p, \text{then} - q$$

where the indicative force, indicated by $|$, "scopes" out to the entire conditional, whose content is a connection between two ways the world could be, and which, when asserted, describes the world as obeying this connection. But the descriptive content of $-p$ is the same in the conditional just mentioned, in a simple assertion like $\vdash p$, and even in an interrogative utterance of p. So the force of an utterance separates from its content.

Frege argued, on this basis, that uttering "The cat is not on Matt" was not a case of *denial*, but an assertion in its own right, albeit an assertion of negated content. If we understand uttering this sentence as an act of *denying* that the cat is on Matt—parallel-ing the act of asserting—then we owe an account of what happens when we embed this sentence into a conditional like "If the cat is not on Matt, then he won't get hives." This conditional is asserted, not denied, and we neither assert nor deny the antecedent. For an assertion $\vdash p$, we can strip the force off when we embed it, leaving $-p$. If we try to do this with "The cat is not on Matt," understood as an act of denial, we end up with "The cat is on Matt" and this is plainly incorrect. So we cannot understand "The cat is not on Matt" in the conditional as an act of denial; when embedded, it simply does not have this force.

The problem reappears in Geach's "Ascriptivism" where he argued that R.M. Hare's *prescriptivist* account of moral discourse fails for similar reasons (Geach 1960). Hare ana-lyzed the content of moral utterances largely in terms of their *prescriptive* force—their use in prescribing or permitting actions. Contemporary expressivists similarly use the role of moral utterances in giving voice to our evaluative or conative attitudes as the locus of their content. In force-canceling contexts like the antecedents of conditionals, however, the content of moral sentences is different from what it is in simple contexts. Embedded uses of moral sentences do not prescribe or express. This problem creeps as well; things we expect content to explain, like the validity of arguments, are also affected. Consider:

(P1) Murder is wrong.
(P2) If murder is wrong, then stealing is permissible.
(C) So, stealing is permissible.

If the content of "murder is wrong" in P1 and in P2 differ, then we seemingly cannot compose P1 and P2 in order to derive C. To do so would, *prima facie*, be analogous to inferring that Barclays is the shore of a body of water from the fact that Barclays is a bank and banks are the shores of bodies of water.

Many theorists have taken the Frege-Geach problem to be the task of specifying a rela-tionship of *validity* or *inference* which applies to statements when their content is under-stood in terms of force or expression. This potentially conflates a criterion for a successful solution with a solution itself. We need to specify an adequate account of content, in terms of simple force-involving assertions or judgments, which is adequate for expressions embedded both in complex constructions like the antecedents of conditionals and alter-natively forced contexts like questions. Any reasonable account will give rise to a notion of validity which legitimates the intuitive relationships between logically complex normative sentences. The action of inference, however it is to be understood, should partially derive from the account of validity. Specifying a notion of validity directly thus seems the wrong way to approach the problem—unless logical inferentialism is correct—since it wouldn't explain *why* certain combinations of normative statements were inconsistent.

Initial reason to hope that we can solve the problem arises from the fact that *impera-tives* can be embedded (Hare 1952). Even though "If there's beer, get me one" doesn't itself express a command, the meaning of "get me a beer" is clearly exhausted—or nearly exhausted anyway—by its use in expressing a command to the relevant party to get me a beer. And whatever explains this would presumably also explain embedding normative content. But hope dwindles on inspection—constructions like "murder is wrong" cleanly embed where imperatives do not. Compare:

(1c)   If there's beer in the fridge, get me one.
(2c)   If murder is fun, it's wrong.
(1a)   #If get me a beer, there's beer.
(2a)   If murder is wrong, it's fun.

We have no problem understanding the consequent embeddings (1–2c), but the antecedent embedding (1a) is incoherent, in contrast to (2a). So the analogy to imperatives will not get us very far. We need to actually develop an account instead of presuming that we can simply poach whichever explains embeddings in imperatives.

We survey some such answers to the problem shortly, but first we will discuss criteria for a successful solution. We focus on the Frege-Geach problem for expressivism about moral or normative thought and talk, putting other contexts to the side. The majority of what we say easily transfers.

CRITERIA FOR A SOLUTION TO THE FREGE-GEACH PROBLEM

Explaining content

Explaining content in terms of what is expressed does not mean identifying content with what is expressed. Consider, as a similar example, the Gricean explanation of descriptive meaning in terms of communication of our intentions of getting our interlocutor to believe something. My intention to get you to believe that the cat is on Matt is not itself the meaning of "The cat is on Matt," even though it plays an essential role in explaining the meaning. Rather, the meaning is the actual content of the belief we intend to get our interlocutor to adopt (Grice 1957).

Similarly to the Gricean, the expressivist attempts an account of content for some fragment of our thought and talk which satisfies the constraint that expressive use is fundamental to understanding such content in any context, simple or complex. They can satisfy this constraint by explaining the meaning of "Murder is wrong" in embedded contexts by appealing to what it expresses in simple contexts without identifying the two (for useful discussion see Hare 1971, p. 93; Searle 1969; and Sinclair 2011).

Not all "content" need be expressible

An account of the content of embedded expressions, say in terms of states of mind, need not be reversible in the sense of providing an expression which corresponds to every state of mind. We need an *embedding* of normative language into states of mind, not a one-to-one mapping. This holds quite generally: consider standard possible worlds semantics where we identify *propositions*—taken as the content of interpreted sentences—with sets of worlds. Plausibly, there are least $\aleph_0$ many worlds, so there are at least $2^{\aleph_0}$ many sets of worlds and, correspondingly, at least $2^{\aleph_0}$ distinct propositions. But there are only $\aleph_0$ many sentences and, of course, $\aleph_0 < 2^{\aleph_0}$. So there can be no one-to-one mapping of sentences into propositions, so understood.

Likewise if we map normative sentences into something like commitments to possessing certain combinations of attitudes. We need not show that any particular combination of attitudes we can be committed to holding is expressible by a normative sentence of natural language. This mistake, most recently made in Skorupski (2012), conflates the project of explaining normative content in terms of expression with the dubious project of *identifying* normative content with what is expressed. These should not be conflated—expressivists and fellow travelers use reasonably well-understood social, communicative, and psychological structure to explain the content of normative language and thought. They are not attempting to identify normative language and thought with this structure.

Mixed expressions

Solving the Frege-Geach problem doesn't just mean giving an account of complex *normative* expressions—stealing is impermissible and murder is *really* impermissible—but also accommodating cases where we have composites of both normative and non-normative expressions—stealing is impermissible, but *really* fun. For example, it is not at all obvious what is expressed by assertions of disjunctions of moral and descriptive expressions: conative states, beliefs, or both?

There are obvious hurdles to the tempting route of treating normative and non-normative expressions differently. Suppose, for example, we treat moral conditionals one way and descriptive conditionals another. Consider, then, the blatantly moral conditional "If stealing is fun, it's not permitted" and its clearly descriptive contrapositive "If stealing is permitted, it's no fun". So ordinary logical transformations such as contraposition can change topic and, thereby, change what is expressed, even though we might want the two conditionals to be meaning-equivalent (this depends on taking contraposition as valid for indicative conditionals). On the other hand, treating normative and non-normative expressions alike may mean accepting non-cognitivism about descriptive expressions like "The cat is on Matt," which seems tantamount to a reductio of the approach (noted by Schroeder 2008 before he heroically attempts to provide such an account). Telling *some* story which evades these worries is mandatory for any resolution of the Frege-Geach problem.

Summary of criteria

Summing up, the Frege-Geach problem is part of the development of an adequate non-cognitivist treatment of moral thought and talk. It is the task of giving an account of the content of expressions which

- assigns a content to both embedded and unembedded occurrences of expressions, subject to the proviso that the embedded occurrences are appropriately related to the expressive or forced unembedded occurrences.
- legitimates the logical relations between the expressions so analyzed.
- accommodates intuitive data about legitimate and illegitimate embeddings (as in the case of imperatives).
- can accommodate mixed cases such as "murder is wrong and fun."

Furthermore, though it is not a no-go requirement, it is desirable if the resulting account is *compositional* in the sense that the content of complex expressions is a function of the content of the parts, *finitely specifiable* in the sense that we can lay down a set of rules for generating complex expressions on the basis of the parts, and *general* in the sense that we need not lay down special conditions to deal with complexities arising from each additional manner of composition accommodated. We will now turn to one more central framing point—whether expressivism is a view in *metasemantics* or *semantics*—before describing the most prominent extant solutions. We start with *minimalist solutions*, turn to *discordance solutions* which posit some type of conflict between expressed mental states, and then close by evaluating the resulting landscape.

THE METASEMANTIC GAMBIT

Some theorists, such as Charlow (2014), Chrisman (2015), and Ridge (2014), argue that expressivism should be understood *metasemantically* (as a theory of how normative thought and talk has the content it has). Others, such as Schroeder (2008), argue that expressivism is best interpreted as a *semantic* view (a theory of normative content). Metasemantic expressivists typically claim that we can adopt a more-or-less standard semantic theory in accounting for the meaning of complex normative utterances. This might be truth-conditional (Ridge) or more closely modeled on how we might assign meanings to imperatives (Charlow). Typically these views solve the *semantic* Frege-Geach problem by showing that there is a natural compositional account of the meaning of complex expressions, given the chosen semantic theory (Schroeder, though, argues that this undermines the use of semantic value in explaining normative judgment).

We might, however, worry that this just shifts the bump in the rug. After all, formal semantics need to be interpreted and interpreting aspects of a formal semantics can be rather difficult. See Alwood (2016), for example, for useful discussion of how Ridge's view fares on this score. Dummett once complained that Davidson's use of a compositional truth-theory as a theory of meaning did not yet, in any substantive sense, provide an adequate account of linguistic understanding (Dummett 1975). Expressivists face a similar problem in providing a metasemantic theory which simultaneously legitimates the use of a standard compositional semantic theory (solving the Frege-Geach problem) while remaining both independently plausible and true to the spirit of the expressivist program. Some metasemantic expressivists, such as Ridge (2014), have a relatively easy time with the Frege-Geach problem, but this is more due to the hybrid aspect of their views (on which, see below) than the metasemantic aspect.

Expressivists have been less than fully clear about whether their program is semantic or metasemantic and less than fully clear about what they take linguistic meaning to be. A quick look at any traditional expressivist theory reveals that expressivists are typically more interested in metasemantic issues than in giving a down-and-dirty formal semantics; accordingly, many expressivist views can be easily augmented with a deflationary theory of truth to provide a more-or-less standard truth-conditional formal semantics or are already cast halfway between a semantic and a metasemantic approach. On any expressivist view, we need to be able to provide an account of the content of complex expressions; this might mean providing a compositional theory of mental states, a way of interpreting the semantics of complex expressions, or another direct account of the meaning of complex normative expressions. As we will see below, we face some version of the Frege-Geach problem on any way of proceeding.

EXTANT SOLUTIONS TO THE FREGE-GEACH PROBLEM

Minimalist and inferentialist solutions

Hare mooted an early version of the inferentialist strategy to handle conditionals:

> To understand the "If... then" form of sentence is to understand the place that it has in logic (to understand its logical properties).
>
> (Hare 1971)

Hare's idea is that all that is needed to grasp the meaning of the conditional is to recognize the acceptability of inferring the consequent from the pair of the conditional and antecedent (or, perhaps, the disposition to do so.) Similar strategies could be used to explain most logical operations, drawing on existing work in the logical inferentialist tradition. If that's all that's needed to understand conditionals and other complex constructions embedding normative language, the Frege-Geach problem disappears. That is, it disappears as long as inferentialism is a viable program for explaining operators like the conditional.

A related strategy employs *minimalism* about truth in order to explain the content of complex constructions (Stoljar 1993). If we are willing to account for the truth of a statement ϕ in terms of the disquotational schema:

ϕ if and only if 'ϕ' is true

then we can apply ordinary compositional truth-laws in analyzing logically complex constructions like "If the cat is on Matt, murder is wrong." We analyze a conditional like the proceeding as true, just in case the consequent is true if the antecedent is, and treat "'Murder is wrong' is true" as equivalent to "Murder is wrong."

Unfortunately, these solutions face numerous difficulties. Neither inferential-role nor minimalist analyses will, by themselves, yield a plausible account of the meaning of normative language, expressivistically understood, in contexts like the antecedents of conditionals. We can bring this out by means of an example adapted from Dreier (1994). Let "Bob is hiyo" be a sentence whose primary function is to greet Bob. That is, when we see Bob and wish to greet him, we shout "Bob is hiyo." Now consider:

If Bob is hiyo, then he's in Princeton

Even if we allow that "'Bob is hiyo' is true" is meaning-equivalent to "Bob is hiyo," saying that the quoted sentence is true just in case Bob is in Princeton if he is hiyo—i.e., applying the minimalist schema to the components of the conditional—doesn't seem to explain it. Likewise, we do not have a clear sense of how and why someone would infer that Bob is in Princeton from the speech act of greeting Bob. These explanations seem incomplete—when we stipulate an expression with superficially descriptive grammar which is explicitly understood in terms of its force or expressive role, we have difficulties in understanding what it would mean to embed it in complex contexts *even given* a deflationist account of truth or a settled inferential role. So minimalism doesn't suffice to explain the content of *the components* in embedding contexts, even if we grant that it specifies a truth-condition for the complex construction, since the analysis of the truth of normative components like "Murder is wrong" outside of embedding contexts leans on what asserting that murder is wrong expresses. But in the embedded context, we have not expressed anything.

Discordance solutions

We start with a distinction, made vivid in Schroeder (2008), between A-type and B-type solutions to the Frege-Geach problem. The issue concerns the way in which a set of attitudes can be inconsistent, or, more precisely, *discordant* (Baker and Woods 2015). Since almost all expressivist solutions to the Frege-Geach rely on a property of attitudinal discordance, the question arises of whether this is a property of the *content* of the attitudes or, rather, a property of the attitudes themselves.

- **A-type discordance:** A set of attitudes is A-type discordant if and only if it is discordant by virtue of being a set of attitudes of the same type with inconsistent contents.
- **B-type discordance:** A set of attitudes is B-type discordant if and only if it is discordant but not by virtue of being a set of attitudes of the same type with inconsistent contents.

The contrast between these cases is clearest in the distinction between cases like belief and cases like approval and disapproval—a pair of beliefs is discordant by virtue of having logically inconsistent contents. But the discordance between disapproval and approval does not obviously have the same character—I can approve of two inconsistent contents or actions without discordance, whereas approving and disapproving of one and the same content or action is clearly discordant (Baker and Woods 2015, p. 409). The discordance between approving and disapproving of the same action is, at least *prima facie*, due to features of the attitudes themselves, not the action which is their content. The A-type theorist holds that all attitudinal discordance—or, anyway, all attitudinal discordance relevant for the analysis of normative thought and talk—strongly resembles belief. So if disapproving of murder and tolerating it are discordant, that's because of a subtle feature of the content. The B-type theorist denies this, holding that the appearance of B-type discordance matches the reality.

Motivating a notion of discordance, whether A- or B-type, does not by itself solve the Frege-Geach problem. We use discordance to characterize expressed mental states in such a way as to (a) license the right implicational properties between statements and (b) distinguish expressed mental states of sentences obviously different in meaning. If we can specify the action of the logical connectives in such a way that complex statements which would ordinarily be inconsistent turn out to express discordant mental states, then we have come a long way toward giving a *constructive* semantics in the sense in which the minimalist and inferentialist solutions seem to fail to. Even if one disagrees that giving a constructive semantics is necessary to solve the Frege-Geach, it is clearly the *best* type of solution.

Discordance solutions, prior to Schroeder's *Being For*, have fallen into a few determinate B-type accounts: higher-order solutions and commitment accounts (due mainly to Simon Blackburn), and norm-acceptance or planning-state solutions (due to Allen Gibbard). We will now turn to describing how these work in broad strokes before turning to A-type accounts—Schroeder's *being for* proposal and hybrid expressivism. We will close by drawing a few lessons for forward progress on the problem.

B-TYPE DISCORDANCE THEORIES: HIGHER-ORDER ATTITUDES AND COMMITMENTS

Higher-order attitude solutions were first developed in Blackburn's *Spreading the Word* (1985). They treat logical operators—and presumably cognate expressions—as indicating expression of attitudes toward holding viewpoints consisting of patterns of attitudes. Asserting "Murder is wrong" expresses *disapproval* of murder (DIS[murder]) whereas asserting a conditional like "If murder is wrong, then stealing is wrong" expresses *disapproval* of simultaneously disapproving of murder while not disapproving of stealing:

DIS[disapproving of murder while not disapproving of stealing]

In the simple case, we *express* an attitude toward murder (as indicated by capital letters), whereas in the embedded case, we *describe* this psychological state. The descriptive content of the embedded sentence is still clearly derivative from the embedded use—it *describes* possession of the attitude a sincere assertion of "Murder is wrong" would express.

Suppose we disapprove of murdering and hold that stealing is wrong if murder is. We recapture the mistake in failing to conclude stealing is wrong—failing to disapprove of stealing—by noting that we would then:

DIS[disapproving of murder while not disapproving of stealing], DIS[murder], not DIS[stealing]

But this means we would self-disapprove, resulting in a sort of fracture in our psychologies. Other cases of valid argument patterns can be treated analogously. Of course, there are problems involving refraining from approving or disapproving and the psychological fracture account requires implausibly treating mixed cases as expressing disapproval of combinations of cognitive and conative states. But put these relatively minor problems to the side for now.

Blackburn's solution is a type of B-type solution—viewpoints containing certain patterns of attitudes, such as tolerating and disapproving of murder, are "fractured," which is Blackburn's notion of discordance. But discordance, so interpreted, isn't sufficient to explain our reasons to avoid such states. Blackburn claims these reasons are derivative from our *disapproval* of fractured stances. However, this suggests a deep problem for views which explain our reasons to avoid discordance in terms of disapproving of it: we might not always so-disapprove. In fact, given work by Gil Harman and others on the benign character of much contradiction, we may not disapprove of some contradictory belief-states at all. Believing my viewpoint is inconsistent does not trigger self-loathing in me; I view it as the cost of doing epistemic business while maintaining a healthy skepticism about whether I have done it correctly. Moreover, nothing cleanly separates disapproving of stances like the above from disapproving of viewpoints involving approval of, say, anything involving chickens. But, presumably, the types of discordance involved in the two cases are significantly different.

Blackburn's solution also seems to conflate *logical* and *rational* or *practical* inconsistency (van Roojen 1996). "It's wrong to disapprove of murder and not disapprove of stealing" expresses *disapproval* of simultaneously disapproving of murder and not disapproving of stealing, just like the conditional "If murder is wrong, so is stealing." On Blackburn's account, the validity of the above argument arises from the "fractured" nature of the mental states involved in holding the premises while refraining from holding the conclusion. But this means that

P1 Murder is wrong
P2 It's wrong to disapprove of murder and not disapprove of stealing
C   Stealing is wrong

is also valid, which it is clearly not (though see Weintraub 2011 and Baker and Woods 2015 for ways to address this problem).

Blackburn, in response, started treating normative assertions as expressing *commitment states*—a type of psychological state—to accept certain patterns of attitudes (Blackburn 1988). The idea is that accepting a disjunction ordinarily *commits* you to the truth of at least one disjunct, but it does not commit you to taking either of the particular disjuncts as true. Blackburn so treats an asserted normative disjunction—murder is wrong or stealing is wrong—as expressing a *commitment*:

disapprove of murder or disapprove of stealing

but, importantly, not as expressing commitment to disapproving of either individually. In combination with, say, approval of stealing and thus inability to meet my commitment by satisfying the right disjunct, I am derivatively committed to disapproving of murder on pain of a fractured mental state. Of course, there are many ways to not disapprove of stealing—avoiding taking a stand on it, for instance—and in such cases, we have a *rational* commitment to come to disapprove of murdering absent changing our mind.

Since a trivial normal-form theorem guarantees that every sentence of propositional logic can be expressed in terms of negation and disjunction, Blackburn's account can be used to characterize a wide swath of normative and mixed claims. But this is a slightly strange strategy; giving a semantics for a language in terms of a set of logical equivalents transforms the expressivist project from one of *describing* our use of normative language to one of *replacing* or *rationally reinterpreting* normative language. The usual goal of expressivism is to *interpret* ordinary usage and, for that, providing truth-conditions merely for disjunction and negation is plainly inadequate; our language is richer than that.[2]

Blackburn's move neatly avoids Van Roojen's objection since we no longer iterate the notion of disapproval. "It's wrong to drink or drive" expresses a commitment to disapproving of drinking or driving while "It's wrong to drink or it's wrong to drive" expresses the commitment to either disapproving of drinking or disapproving of driving, and "It's wrong to approve of drinking and approve of driving" expresses a commitment to disapproving of approving of drinking while approving of driving. Notice also that it easily solves the case of mixed constructions—we need only treat a disjunction like "Murder is wrong or stealing is fun" as expressing a commitment to come to disapprove of murder if we fail to believe that stealing is fun and vice versa. Problems solved.

Or are they? Mark Schroeder and others have argued that such solutions, even though they *formally* solve the Frege-Geach problem, do so by assuming something that needs explaining. Consider the analogous theory of Horgan and Timmons (2006). They posit a pair of commitment operators (is- and ought-commitment) and claim that the negation of a commitment state φ, −φ, indicates a distinct commitment state logically inconsistent with φ. This does little to explain what these states are and *why* they are discordant with each other. Since the stipulated "logical inconsistency" that arises merely from negation isn't, by itself, obviously discordant, they assume a notion of discordance arising from certain combinations of states, mental and otherwise, which needs to be somehow reduced, explained, or made analogous to more familiar notions discordance of belief. According to Schroeder, Blackburn likewise needs to provide an explanation of why committing to approving and disapproving of the same thing is discordant. We will return to this shortly in the context of the most popular solution to the Frege-Geach, Gibbard's factual-normative semantics.

B-TYPE DISCORDANCE THEORIES: PLAN-LADEN SEMANTICS

Gibbard's factual-normative semantics (1992, 2003) uses a modification of possible-worlds semantics to account for the *semantic values* of moral language. Let a *fact-prac* world be a pair of a set of facts (the worldly component) and a plan about what to do in situations like those described by the worldly component (the practical component).[3] We can represent a claim, possibly including both practical and normative material, as a set of fact-prac worlds—the set of *fact-prac* worlds which are consistent with the plan described by the normative claim and the content of the descriptive claim.

Consider, for example, the claim that murder is wrong and stealing is fun. Its content is the intersection ({@, w}) of the set of fact-prac worlds where we plan to blame for murdering ({@, w, u}) and the set of fact-prac worlds where stealing is fun ({@, w, v}):

	S is F	S is not F
P-to-B for M	{@, w}	{u}
P-to-not-B for M	{v}	{s, t}

Accepting this claim means intersecting this set with the set of fact-prac worlds we haven't yet ruled out, typically resulting in a smaller set of worlds. Accepting its negation, analogously, means intersecting its complement ({u, v, s, t}) with the set of fact-prac worlds we haven't yet ruled out. This "semantics" models both normative and descriptive content analogously to the way ordinary (coarse-grained) linguistic semantics models descriptive content.

Of course, a formal semantics is not yet, by itself, an explanation of meaning (Burgess 2008). In order to bridge the gap between an admittedly appealing formal model of meanings and meaning itself, we need to interpret the formal semantics. Gibbard does this by taking the state of mind expressed by a set of fact-prac worlds to be a *planning state*—a state of planning to do such and so depending on the circumstances obtained. Or, in a later epicycle, by additionally taking the *complement* of a set of worlds Γ—the set of all fact-prac worlds which are not in Γ—as modeling the mental state which disagrees with the mental state indicated by Γ.

Our example of disjunction, for example, expresses that our settled-with-respect-to-every-possible-circumstance—or, in Gibbard's lingo, *hyperdecided*—state of mind is one where we plan to blame for murdering if it isn't fun. Accepting the disjunction cuts away those hyperplanes where murder isn't fun, yet we don't plan to blame for murdering—which would be the psychological state which disagrees with planning to blame for murdering if murdering isn't fun. Complexities emerge in using this framework to account for the distinction between indifference—blame for murdering or not, whatever!—and indecision—to blame for murder or not to blame for murder, that is the question! (Dreier 2006), but such complexities can be finessed. Gibbard's interpretation is rightly regarded as one of the most flexible and interesting attempts to solve the Frege-Geach problem.

It is so flexible that there have been attempts to accept something like Gibbard's *formal* framework, but to use it to model a distinct interpretation of normative thought and talk. Nate Charlow (2014), for example, uses roughly the Gibbardian framework to give a *semantics* for normative language which doesn't involve mental states at all, even though he accepts the *metasemantic claim* that expressed mental states ground the meaning of normative claims. Carballo (2014) claims that expressivists can all accept something like Gibbard's framework as a mediate *semantic* story between a standard linguistic semantics and the expressivistic metasemantic interpretation thereof. The Gibbardian framework, if it can be properly interpreted, seems to be a very promising approach to solving the Frege-Geach.

Which is not to say there aren't problems. Schroeder (2008) also charges Gibbard with taking for granted that which needs to be explained—the notion of discordance or mental fragmentation—which does the important work of rescuing the intuitive notion of inconsistency for the expressivist. To see more clearly what the objection is, note that we've interpreted the mental state expressed by "Murder is wrong" as the set of hyperplanes where we plan **to blame** *for murdering*. This two-part structure—*X*-ing for *Y*-ing—solves a problem involving negation that we will see in a minute. But Gibbard's basic normative notions are not "wrong" or "permitted," but "the thing to do" or "ought" in a generic sense, whose interpretation is simpler. "We ought to murder," in this sense, simply expresses planning to murder. And this gives rise to a problem—formulated originally in Unwin (1999)—which has been recently highlighted by Schroeder in one of the most trenchant discussions of the Frege-Geach problem to date.

THE NEGATION PROBLEM

Consider three ways of inserting a negation into normative judgment:

1a Jack thinks murdering is not the thing to do.
2a Jack thinks that not murdering is the thing to do.
3a It's not the case that Jack thinks murdering is the thing to do.

Planning states, at least in their toy implementation, only capture two of these three. Not planning to murder analyzes 3a, planning on not murdering gets us 2a, but what gets us 1a? Similar troubles arise for a Blackburn-style solution—not disapproving of murdering corresponds to not thinking that murder is wrong, disapproving of not murdering analyzes thinking that not murdering is wrong, but thinking that murdering is not wrong sits unanalyzed. Any solution to the Frege-Geach problem which fails to account for these three natural language interpretations will be extensionally inadequate. Failure to solve the negation problem thus implies failure to solve the Frege-Geach problem.

Blackburn solves this problem by treating a construction like "Thinking that murder is not wrong" as expressing something like *tolerance*—the minimal state conflicting with disapproval—of not murdering. Gibbard, by his assumption that we are dealing with *complete plans*, collapses 1a and 3a since, if my complete plan doesn't include murdering, then it must include not murdering—though one might worry about Gibbard's ability to deal with more psychologically realistic *incomplete* plans.

Schroeder grants that these types of solutions would work, but worries that they take for granted unexplained notions of discordance. Against Blackburn, he claims it is unclear why tolerance and disapproval of one and the same thing are discordant. Against Gibbard, Schroeder claims that it is unclear that there exists a mental state corresponding to sets of hyperplanes which disagree with a state like planning to murder (note, though, that this is a problem with assigning mental states to formal objects, not a direct problem with the notion of discordance itself).

Many have followed Schroeder in this (Charlow 2014, etc.), even though attitudes which are fundamentally incoherent with one another is a familiar phenomenon once we move outside of the domain of *propositional* attitudes (Baker and Woods 2015). Explaining B-type discordance likewise does not seem impossible as "... it is arguable that the root idea of inconsistency is precisely the idea of disagreeing with oneself" (Wedgwood 2010). Putting these B-oriented responses to the side, for now, Schroeder is right that expressivists need to justify that a *constructive* approach to expressivist semantics is possible. In his *Being For* (2008), he shows what an A-type constructive approach would look like.

A-TYPE DISCORDANCE THEORIES: BEING FOR

Schroeder starts by stipulating a single attitude—*being for*—that is inconsistency-transmitting. To avoid confusion, we will use *discordant* for the relevant property of attitudes and *inconsistent* for the semantic property of their contents. Then:

> An attitude A is *inconsistency-transmitting* just in case two instances of A are discordant when their contents are (semantically) inconsistent.

The idea is to see how far an expressivist theory can get if we just *assume* that there is an attitude with the right sorts of discordance properties. It is thus very important to keep in mind that *being for* is a placeholder for some existing attitude to be filled in later (if the development gets that far!). Since Schroeder has argued against B-type theories and rejects minimalist ones, he views his account as the only way for pure, not hybrid, expressivism to proceed.

Given that *being for* is, by stipulation, an inconsistency-transmitting attitude, Schroeder implements Gibbard's solution of treating a judgment of, say, wrongness in terms of the structure [X-ing for Y-ing], yielding something like [being for blaming for murdering]. We can then interpret

4a Murder is not wrong.
5a Not murdering is wrong.
6a It's not the case that murdering is wrong.

as

4b Being for not blaming for murdering.
5b Being for blaming for not murdering.
6b Not being for blaming for murdering.

Since, unlike planning attitudes, there is no reason to assume that there is a linguistic expression for attitudes like *being for drinking*, we can neatly skirt the worry about solving the negation problem for sentences expressing one-part attitudes (though see Gibbard 2014, appendix 2 for Gibbard's response).

Schroeder extends his basic interpretation to a compositional semantics for the logical operators, yielding a flexible and interesting variation on the usual sort of solution to the Frege-Geach. His view has the virtue of modeling what is expressed as almost directly analogous to the case of belief where, as Schroeder notes, we have very good reason to think that inconsistency transmission holds—even though there yet is no compelling *explanation* of *why* it does. Unfortunately, the initial solution has problems accounting for mixed expressions since if what is expressed by "Murder is wrong" is being for blaming for murdering and what is expressed by "Murder is fun" is the belief that murder is fun, then we need to find some state which is expressed by "Murder is wrong or murder is fun." It certainly isn't a belief on pain of giving up non-cognitivism.

Schroeder, in response, goes expressivist about belief as well—asserting "Grass is green" expresses being for proceeding as if grass is green—but the resulting view itself has significant problems. Schroeder puts forward a solution using what he calls *biforcated* attitude semantics—pairs of *being for* attitudes such as

> *being for* proceeding as if grass is green
> *being for* not proceeding as if grass is not green

but the overall view is clunky, requiring special pleading for each additional linguistic construction in order to accommodate iterated versions of the negation problem (violating one of our desiderata for a solution to the Frege-Geach). As Schroeder also notes, his view also has trouble with modal constructions and other complicated parts of natural language. The details are complicated and would distract here (but see chapters 8–12 of *Being For*). It should be noted that Schroeder is one of the only theorists to have even attempted to develop an expressivist semantics to this extent; most theorists stop after accounting for a logical operator or two.

On balance, if Schroeder's objections to B-type expressivism succeed and if his A-type view really is the only way to go, then expressivism and other views subject to the Frege-Geach objection are in significant trouble. But, luckily, this is plausibly not the case: none of the problems for B-type expressivism are conclusive and B-type accounts are at least superficially more descriptively adequate as an account of what normative language expresses (Baker and Woods 2015; Wedgwood 2010). Schroeder's view, on the other hand, is far more developed than many alternatives and is a flexible and useful alternative to the more usual B-type accounts. The outcome of this internecine dispute awaits an even more serious development of both. We now turn, finally, to the other extant A-type solution to the Frege-Geach problem—hybrid expressivism.

A-TYPE DISCORDANCE THEORIES: HYBRID EXPRESSIVISM

Hybrid expressivists claim that assertions of normative sentences express *both* descriptive beliefs and conative states. These views easily solve the Frege-Geach problem as long as the belief component is importantly related to the conative component. For example, consider a hybrid view where an assertion of "Murder is wrong" expresses the belief that murder is G—where G is some descriptive property of actions—and disapproval of things which are G. The belief component accounts for embedding and fixes the meaning-conditions of complex embeddings. For example, we can treat "If murder is wrong, stealing is wrong" as expressing the belief that if murder is G, then stealing is G *and* disapproval of G things. Likewise for more complex embeddings.

One might worry here that there is no property G which all linguistically competent speakers ascribe to wrong things (Schroeder 2009). But a more general solution can be developed where an assertion like "Murder is wrong" expresses a single hybrid or relational higher-order state composed of a descriptive component like murder is G and disapproval of G things—allowing that the G might be filled in by different properties (Schroeder 2013; Ridge 2014; Toppinen 2013). Perhaps when I say "Murder is wrong," I express a state consisting, descriptively, of the claim that murder is in violation of the rights of others and disapproval of things which violate the rights of others, whereas when Richard says "Murder is wrong," he expresses a functionally identical state consisting of the claim that murder is non-utility-maximizing and disapproval of things which don't maximize utility. The solution to the Frege-Geach problem on these more sophisticated accounts is analogous to the above; logical operators and other semantic operators are applied to the cognitive aspect of the higher-order state, leaving the conative portion "scoped out" over the entire complex judgment.

Since inconsistency properties are all foisted off on the expressed belief (or the belief component of a complex state), hybrid expressivism neatly solves the Frege-Geach problem. There are other worries for this sort of account; for one thing, so much is foisted off on belief that it becomes unclear in what sense it preserves the initial appeal of non-cognitivist views. It is also not obvious that the resulting views are preferable to, say, cognitivist views asserting that a normative claim *expresses* a belief and *implicates* some conative state. Views which accept the expressivist's claim about the connection between normative assertion and conative states, but claim the connection is part of the conversational *pragmatics* of normative discourse, have the advantage of fitting more closely with contemporary semantic views, after all (see Finlay 2014 for a sophisticated development of this point).

THE CONTEMPORARY LANDSCAPE

Where do things stand after our brief survey of solutions to the Frege-Geach problem? As the above demonstrates, there are a number of potential ways to solve the Frege-Geach problem. Schroeder's argument against B-type expressivism isn't conclusive—he establishes that B-type theorists face the additional burden of explaining discordance attaching to their preferred mental states *as well as* explaining discordance of belief, but not that doing so is unworkable. Dreier's problem of distinguishing between indifference and indecision seems closer to a research problem than a devastating objection. And even van Roojen's problem points toward the burden of distinguishing logical discordance from pragmatic and semantic discordance, not the inability to do so (see Baker and Woods 2015, §4).

This is fertile ground for abductive argument. Consider weighing Gibbard's view against Schroeder's *being for* approach. Each has fairly straightforward costs—Schroeder's approach requires us to go non-cognitivist about descriptive discourse, Gibbard's approach is developed for idealized agents and thereby has trouble interpreting finite and mildly irrational agents like ourselves—but each has significant advantages as well. Whether or not to adopt one or other of these approaches is a matter of weighing out the various costs and benefits of so doing so.

But at this point, it is crucial to enjoin caution. Expressivist semantics, on whichever approach, have barely left their infancy. There is simply no developed comparison of expressivist accounts to the truth or whatever-conditional accounts of the sort taken for granted in contemporary linguistic semantics. Given this situation, it is crucial to not conflate the property of not *yet* being able to solve a problem—such as interpreting modal constructions or accommodation of a sophisticated theory of subjunctive conditionals—with the property of being *unable* to solve a problem. What developments sustained development of an expressivist semantics would bring are, as yet, mostly a mystery. Even a quick glance at the theoretical maneuvers sketched above demonstrates that vastly more can be done with expressivist semantics than one might have thought at the outset.

NOTES

1. I use "content" instead of "meaning" throughout to stress there is not a shared conception of linguistic meaning neutral between the views discussed.
2. Note that the negation problem, below, could be similarly "finessed." Another equi-trivial normal-form theorem guarantees that every sentence of propositional logic is logically equivalent to a sentence either of the form ϕ or $\neg\phi$ where ϕ contains no negations. This does nothing to undermine the intuitive force of the negation problem; natural language constructions contain a rich array of negative particles.
3. Gibbard initially characterized the practical component in terms of the acceptance of norms for feeling and behavior. In his later work, he used planning states to explicate his earlier picture. The differences between these approaches aren't especially important here, so we set them aside.

ACKNOWLEDGMENTS

Thanks to the esteemed editors of this volume, and to Derek Baker, Catharine Diehl, Jamie Fritz, Barry Maguire, Teemu Toppinen, and Daniel Wodak for useful discussion.

RELATED TOPICS

Chapter 5, "Metaethical Expressivism;" Chapter 13, "Thick Concepts;" Chapter 15, "Hybrid Accounts of Ethical Thought and Talk;" Chapter 16, "Conceptual Role Accounts of Meaning in Metaethics;" Chapter 18, "Cognitivism and Non-Cognitivism;" Chapter 33, "Metasemantics and Metaethics."

REFERENCES

Alwood, A. 2016. Should Expressivism Be a Theory at the Level of Metasemantics? *Thought: A Journal of Philosophy* 5(1): 13–22.

Baker, D. and J. Woods 2015. How Expressivists Can and Should Explain Inconsistency. *Ethics* 125(2): 391–424.

Blackburn, S. 1985. *Spreading the Word*. Oxford: Oxford University Press.

Blackburn, S. 1988. Attitudes and Contents. *Ethics* 98(3): 501–517.

Burgess, J. 2008. Tarski's Tort. In *Mathematics, Models, and Modality. Selected Philosophical Essays*, 149–168. Cambridge: Cambridge University Press.

Carballo, A. P. 2014. Semantic Hermeneutics. In A. Burgess & B. Sherman eds., *Metasemantics: New Essays on the Foundations of Meaning*, 119–146. Oxford: Oxford University Press.

Charlow, N. 2014. The Problem with the Frege-Geach Problem. *Philosophical Studies* 167(3): 635–665.

Chrisman, M. 2015. *The Meaning of 'Ought': Beyond Descriptivism and Expressivism in Metaethics*. Oxford: Oxford University Press.

Dreier, J. 1996. Expressivist Embeddings and Minimalist Truth. *Philosophical Studies* 83(1): 29–51.

Dreier, J. 2006. Negation for Expressivists: A Collection of Problems with a Suggestion for Their Solution. *Oxford Studies in Metaethics* 1: 217–233.

Dummett, M. A. E. 1975. "What is a Theory of Meaning?" In S. Guttenplan ed., *Mind and Language*. Oxford University Press.

Finlay, S. 2014. *Confusion of Tongues: A Theory of Normative Language*. Oxford: Oxford University Press.

Frege, G. 1956. The Thought: A Logical Inquiry. *Mind* 65(259): 289–311.

Geach, P. T. 1960. Ascriptivism. *The Philosophical Review* 69(2): 221–225.

Gibbard, A. 1992. *Wise Choices, Apt Feelings*. Cambridge: Harvard University Press.

Gibbard, A. 2003. *Thinking How to Live*. Cambridge: Harvard University Press.

Gibbard, A. 2014. *Meaning and Normativity*. Oxford: Oxford University Press.

Grice, H. P. 1957. Meaning. *The Philosophical Review* 66(3): 377–388.

Hare, R. M. 1952. *The Language of Morals*. Oxford: Clarendon Press.

Hare, R. M. 1971. *Practical Inferences*. Cambridge: Cambridge University Press.

Horgan, T. and M. Timmons 2006. Cognitivist Expressivism. In *Metaethics after Moore*, 255–298. Oxford: Oxford University Press.

Ridge, M. 2014. *Impassioned Belief*. Oxford: Oxford University Press.

Schroeder, M. 2008. *Being For: Evaluating the Semantic Program of Expressivism*. Oxford: Oxford University Press.

Schroeder, M. 2009. Hybrid Expressivism: Virtues and Vices. *Ethics* 119(2): 257–309.

Schroeder, M. 2013. Tempered Expressivism. *Oxford Studies in Metaethics* 8: 283–314.

Searle, J. R. 1969. *Speech Acts: An Essay in the Philosophy of Language*. Cambridge: Cambridge University Press.

Sinclair, N. 2011. Moral Expressivism and Sentential Negation. *Philosophical Studies* 152(3): 385–411.

Skorupski, J. 2012. The Frege-Geach Objection to Expressivism: Still Unanswered. *Analysis* 72(1): 9–18.

Stoljar, D. 1993. Emotivism and Truth Conditions. *Philosophical Studies* 70(1): 81–101.

Toppinen, T. 2013. Believing in Expressivism. *Oxford Studies in Metaethics* 8: 252–282.

Unwin, N. 1999. Quasi-Realism, Negation and the Frege-Geach Problem. *Philosophical Quarterly* 49(196): 337–352.

van Roojen, M. 1996. Expressivism and Irrationality. *The Philosophical Review* 105(3): 311–335.

Wedgwood, R. 2010. Schroeder on Expressivism: For—or Against? *Analysis* 70(1): 117–129.

Weintraub, R. 2011. Logic for Expressivists. *Australasian Journal of Philosophy* 89(4): 601–616.

15

Hybrid Accounts of Ethical Thought and Talk

Teemu Toppinen

Some parts of language and thought plausibly mix the doxastic with the attitudinal. An effective example of this is provided by racial or ethnic slurs, such as 'roundhead', 'China Swede', or 'dumb Finn'—derisive terms used for the (allegedly) clannish, heavy-drinking, knife-fighting, radicalism-tending, trouble-breeding Finnish immigrants in Minnesota and Michigan (or thereabouts) in the early 1900s. Let us consider the following sentence:

S1 The strike was organized by roundheads.

When someone in, say, Minnesota, back then, used S1, she expressed her belief that the strike was organized by Finns, but she did more than this. She also somehow conveyed, at the same time, a derisive attitude toward Finns.

Another example of an area of discourse and thought that plausibly somehow blends the doxastic and the attitudinal is provided by ethical (or more broadly normative) talk and thought—that is, talk and thought concerning, roughly, what is good or bad, or right or wrong, or what there is reason to do. Ethical *thought* has both belief- and desire-like features. On one hand, our ethical views (about the wrongness of eating factory-farmed meat or catcalling, for example) are naturally characterized as beliefs, and occasionally also as correct or true; they figure in (sometimes valid) inferences that we draw, and so on. On the other hand, our ethical views are intimately tied to motivation and action: it is hard to make good sense of someone both as thinking that catcalling is wrong, and at the same time as engaging in catcalling. Ethical *talk* seems similarly dual-natured: on the one hand, a use of 'Eating factory-farmed meat is wrong' seems to describe eating factory-farmed meat as being a certain way; on the other hand, an utterance of this sentence also seems to express an opposing stance toward eating factory-farmed meat.

A significant part of metaethics, or metanormative theory, can be seen as the project of trying to make sense of this duality in ethical thought and talk.

Many accept a view that might be called *cognitivism*. On this view, the meaning of ethical claims, as well as the nature of moral thought, is to be explained by what they are *about*, or in terms of their *representational* content—with reference to the normative ways the world is, or with reference to the ways in which we cognitively access the normative properties and facts. For example, consider the claim that catcalling is wrong. According to a cognitivist view, the meaning of this claim will be explained, roughly, by (what determines) its truth-conditions, and the nature of a corresponding thought is explained in terms of representing catcalling as having a certain property. Whereas cognitivists seem to have an easy time explaining the 'belief-like' or 'descriptive' features of normative thought and talk, accounting for the 'desire-like' and 'expressive' features is trickier for them.

Some reject cognitivism and accept instead a view that is sometimes called *pure expressivism*. On this view, the meaning of (some) ethical claims can be satisfactorily explained with reference to the purely non-representational, 'desire-like', or sentimental states of mind that they express. Likewise, on this view, to think an ethical thought just is to be in a non-representational state of the relevant sort. Pure expressivism captures the desire-like and expressive features of ethical thought and talk neatly, but faces challenges with respect to accounting for the belief-like and descriptive phenomena.

A recently popular option (with a potentially long history—see, e.g., Ross 1939: 255; Stevenson 1944) has been to go impure. One might suggest, first, that (i) ethical claims conventionally express *both* representational beliefs and desire-like states, or states that are constituted or realized by both representational beliefs and desire-like states. Second, one might also hold that (ii) to think an ethical thought is to be in a state that is constituted by both beliefs and desire-like states. Views that incorporate one or both of (i) and (ii) are often called *hybrid views*. Some of the hybrid views appeal to analogies with the way that slurs such as 'roundhead' work. Others develop the vague, basic idea of appealing to both desire-like states and representational beliefs in accounting for normative thought and talk in different ways.

Within hybrid views, we may distinguish between *hybrid cognitivism* and *hybrid expressivism*. The former is a cognitivist view. That is, on this view, the conventional meaning of sentences such as 'Eating factory-farmed meat is wrong' is explained, at least in part, by their representational content. Also, according to this view, when someone thinks that eating factory-farmed meat is wrong (say), this is, at least in part, a matter of her having a belief (I sometimes omit the qualification 'representational' from this on), where this belief ascribes to eating factory-farmed meat the property of being wrong (or, anyway, a property such that the judgment is true, just in case eating factory-farmed meat really has it). However, according to *hybrid* cognitivism, this is not all that there is to the meaning and nature of ethical talk and thought. Rather, there is also a desire-like element to the story. Hybrid expressivism, by contrast, involves the rejection of cognitivism. That is, on this view, ethical sentences have no representational ethical content, and their meaning is to be explained, rather, in terms of the kinds of states that they conventionally express. However, according to *hybrid* forms of expressivism, representational beliefs still have a role to play in the explanation, as the states expressed by ethical sentences are partly constituted by representational beliefs. Both in the case of pure and hybrid expressivism, 'explaining' the meaning of normative sentences in terms of the states that they express can be taken to amount to giving a 'psychologistic' *semantics* for ethical language (cf. Schroeder 2010), or to giving a *metasemantic* theory, which might be compatible with, for example, a truth-conditional semantics (see Ridge 2014; Chrisman 2016).

In this chapter, I offer an overview of hybrid views, starting with the cognitivist ones.

MOTIVATIONS FOR HYBRID COGNITIVISM: INTERNALISM

I shall not be able to properly discuss all the different kinds of hybrid cognitivist views that have been proposed in the literature. I'll focus on views that seek inspiration from the way that slurs work—on views defended by David Copp (2001, 2009, 2014) and Daniel Boisvert (2008) in particular. Clearly, this does not exhaust the important work on developing hybrid cognitivist or broadly similar views (see, e.g., Barker 2000; Tresan 2006; Bar-On & Chrisman 2009).

Why would a cognitivist go hybrid? The hope would be to capture the idea that there is something more to ethical talk and thought than describing and representing. Ethical language is used to *endorse* and to *oppose*; moral thought seems to be closely connected to *motivation* as well as to our *emotional* lives. Often the hope is to be able to capture, or at least to explain the allure of, some of the following (or some relevantly similar) 'internalist' theses (see Björklund et al. 2011):

(MOTIVATIONAL INTERNALISM) Necessarily, if someone, S, thinks that she [morally] ought to φ, then, if she is rational, she is motivated to φ.

(e.g., Smith 1994: chapter 3; Ridge 2014: chapter 2)

(COMMUNAL INTERNALISM) Necessarily, if someone, S, thinks that she [morally] ought to φ, then, if she is rational, she is motivated to φ, or she is suitably related to some others, who, if rational, are motivated to act in accordance with their ought-thoughts.

(cf. Blackburn 1998)

(DISCOURSE INTERNALISM) Necessarily, if someone, S, asserts that she [morally] ought to φ, this is sufficient—though defeasible—evidence, independently of any other information concerning S's desire-like states, that S is motivated to φ.

(cf. Copp 2001: 38; Finlay 2014: 135)

These theses are quite plausible. Let us imagine planet Amorality (see Lenman 1999), on which no one is, and has never been, disposed to perform the actions to which they apply the word 'right', to refrain from performing the actions to which they apply the word 'wrong', and so on. Moreover, the inhabitants of the planet seem entirely rational (in the sense of being internally coherent). If communal internalism were false, there might be no obstacle to our taking the inhabitants of planet Amorality to be making genuine moral judgments. But it is really implausible to think that they would be doing so. Discourse internalism also seems attractive. We are reluctant to translate 'right' and 'wrong', as used on planet Amorality, as meaning right and wrong. But if discourse internalism were false, it would not be clear why. Motivational internalism is a more controversial thesis, at least if it is read as a claim about judgments concerning *moral* oughts. However, given a modestly 'rationalist' thesis, according to which a belief about what morally ought to be done is a belief about how reasons of a certain type shape up, it is quite plausible that a rational moral believer will have some motivation to act in accordance with her moral ought-thought. In any case, whatever the plausibility of these internalist claims, they provide much of the motivation for developing hybrid cognitivist views. (For non-hybrid cognitivist attempts at capturing certain forms of internalism see, e.g., Smith 1994; Wedgwood 2007; Schroeter and Schroeter 2014.)

ETHICAL TALK: SLURS, CONVENTIONAL IMPLICATURES, AND DISCOURSE INTERNALISM

Let us consider the following sentences:

S1 The strike was organized by roundheads.
S2 The strike was organized by Finns.

Plausibly, S1 says what S2 says—that the strike was organized by Finns. However, as noted above, someone who uses S1 is not just expressing this belief, but also, at the same time, somehow conveying a negative take on Finns.

Slur terms and other pejoratives have recently attracted a lot of attention from linguists and philosophers. There is much disagreement about how their workings should be understood—for instance, about the nature of the 'negative take' that they carry, and about whether they carry it as part of their content, or as a matter of pragmatics (see, e.g., Copp 2001; Hom 2008; Camp 2013; Bolinger forthcoming).

One possibility is that a use of a slur *conventionally implicates* certain attitudes. Conventional implicatures are carried by sentences in virtue of their conventional meaning, but do not contribute to their truth-conditional content (Grice 1989: 25–26; Potts 2007). (For instance, if I say that S1 is not true, I only seem to be denying that the strike was organized by Finns.) Another common example of conventional implicature is offered by the word 'but':

S3 Finns are good laborers, but troublemakers.
S4 Finns are good laborers and troublemakers.

Again, the truth-conditions of S3 plausibly are the same as those of S4. But the use of S3 also indicates that the speaker thinks that there is a contrast between being a good laborer and being a troublemaker.

Some hybrid cognitivists have proposed that ethical terms function roughly as slurs do, and that both could be understood in terms of conventional implicatures (Copp 2001, 2009, 2014; Boisvert 2008). Let us suppose that Ida accepts the following sentence:

S5 Exploiting miners is wrong.

On Copp's view, when Ida says this, she ascribes to exploiting miners the property of being wrong—that is, the property of failing to be in accord with the authoritative standards for warranted blame—and also conventionally implicates that her policy is to avoid and oppose acts that fail to be in accordance with such standards. Somewhat similarly, on Boisvert's view, when Ida uses S5, she ascribes a certain wrong-making property, F, to exploiting miners and also conventionally expresses an attitude of opposition, or disapproval, toward performing actions with this property.

Given that the expression of the relevant non-belief attitudes by moral utterances works via something like conventional implicature, the hybrid cognitivist would seem to be well positioned to capture the truth of discourse internalism. If uses of moral sentences express certain motivational states in virtue of the conventional meaning of moral sentences, an utterance of such a sentence will provide defeasible evidence of the presence of a motivational state, regardless of independent knowledge about the speakers' psychology.

ETHICAL THOUGHT: JUDGMENT-INDIVIDUATING HYBRID COGNITIVISM AND MOTIVATIONAL INTERNALISM

One might wish to capture discourse internalism without accommodating motivational internalism. On Copp's (2001, 2014) view, for instance, moral beliefs are just ordinary representational beliefs that bear no necessary or conceptual connection to motivation. If Ida *says* that exploiting miners is wrong, she thereby expresses disapproval of acting in the relevant way. But she may *believe* that exploiting miners is wrong without being in any way against doing so.

However, a hybrid cognitivist who treats the expression of desire-like states by moral utterances as a matter of the conventional meaning of moral terms could also accommodate the truth of motivational internalism. On Boisvert's view, for example, to think that exploiting miners is wrong is to (a) believe that exploiting miners has a certain wrong-making property, F, and to (b) be opposed to, or disapprove of, performing acts with this property. On this kind of view, it would make sense that if Ida thinks that exploiting miners is wrong, she will, if she is instrumentally rational, be motivated to oppose exploiting miners. Following Michael Ridge (2014: chapter 3), we may call views such as Boisvert's *judgment-individuating* forms of hybrid cognitivism. (See also Bar-On & Chrisman 2009: 154–155; Ridge 2014: chapter 3; Laskowski 2014; Schroeder 2014.)

Might a hybrid cognitivist view that rejects motivational internalism nevertheless help to explain why motivational internalism *seems* attractive—the thought being that it's easy enough to confuse the idea that ethical assertions express certain attitudes with the idea that ethical beliefs involve such attitudes (see Copp 2001: 38, 2014: 59)? This doesn't seem to work. Consider the following quartet of sentences:

S6 Ida is a roundhead.
S7 John believes that Ida is a roundhead.
S5 Exploiting miners is wrong.
S8 Ida believes that exploiting miners is wrong.

A use of S6 plausibly conventionally implicates that the speaker views Finns negatively. Still, there is no temptation to think that it would follow from S7 that *John* views Finns negatively. A use of S7 would normally seem to convey, instead, the speaker's negative attitude toward Finns (see, e.g., Schroeder 2010: 203–204). Let us assume, then, that S5 conventionally implicates that the speaker is opposed to exploiting miners. It is unclear why this should help explain the temptation to think that it follows from S8 that Ida is opposed to exploiting miners (cf. Ridge 2014: 87–89; Schroeder 2014: 283).

CHALLENGES FOR HYBRID COGNITIVISM

The idea that moral utterances conventionally express motivational attitudes along with representational beliefs faces a number of challenges, which at the very least importantly restrict the options available to a hybrid cognitivist.

Projection

First, let us consider the following sentences:

    S5 Exploiting miners is wrong.
    S6 Ida is a roundhead.
    S9 If Ida is a roundhead, she is a feminist.
    S10 If exploiting miners is wrong, the pastor will be mad.

The expression of derisive stance toward Finns, carried by the term 'roundhead', *projects* in that when an atomic sentence in which this term figures generates a commitment to this attitude, this commitment remains in place, also in complex sentences where the regular entailments are canceled (e.g., negations, conditionals). For example, an utterance of S9 conveys a derisive attitude toward Finns just as much as an utterance of S6 does. This kind of projection behavior is a feature of conventional implicatures, quite generally. By contrast, whereas S5 conveys opposition to exploiting miners, any such opposition is canceled in S10 (Strandberg 2012: 95). This generates a puzzle for the idea that moral utterances would convey attitudes via conventional implicatures.

However, according to the kinds of views considered above, utterances concerning wrongness, for instance, express opposition to any action, quite generally, insofar that it is wrong. Given that this is so, a hybrid cognitivist could say that even though S10 does not express opposition to exploiting miners, it does express opposition to actions insofar as they are wrong. Slurs and ethical terms would then work similarly in this respect (Boisvert 2008: 185–186).

Cancelation

Another concern is that the expression of non-belief attitudes via moral utterance seems (to many) to be *cancelable*, whereas conventional implicatures generally are not. Consider the following pairs of sentences:

S11 The strike was organized by roundheads. Not that I have anything against Finns.
S12 Exploiting miners is wrong. Not that I have anything against wrongdoing.

Many think that S11 is linguistically inappropriate in a sense in which S12 is not. If so, this is a strike against the conventional implicature view (Finlay 2005; Strandberg 2012;

Fletcher 2014). By contrast, Copp (2001, 2009) suggests that the expression of attitudes by moral utterances is *not* cancelable without linguistic inappropriateness, and that this is a point in favor of his view.

It seems fair to say that when it comes to cancelation behavior, moral sentences differ from those containing slurs at least in that it is much more controversial what the right data is. A hybrid cognitivist who wishes to appeal to conventional implicatures, or to the analogy with slurs, should have some explanation for this.

Detachability

A third concern is that conventional implicatures are usually *detachable*. That is, there are alternative, 'neutral', ways of making the claims involving the expressions that carry conventional implicatures. This is clearly illustrated by sentence pairs such as S1 and S2, or S3 and S4. By contrast, there seems to be no neutral way of picking out, for example, the actions that are morally wrong. In response, one could note that hybrid cognitivists need not hold that the analogy with slurs holds in every respect. Also, it may be that some other pejoratives, such as 'asshole', offer a more promising analogy in this respect (Hay 2011).

Big Hypothesis

The fourth and final concern (to be discussed here) applies to judgment-individuating forms of hybrid cognitivism, according to which, if "Exploiting miners is wrong" expresses a certain belief plus a state of opposition, then "Ida believes that exploiting miners is wrong" ascribes to Ida both this belief and this state of opposition. Schroeder (2009: 301) calls this the 'Big Hypothesis'—the name being due to the fact that, as was noted above, slurs, for instance, do not seem to obey this kind of hypothesis. Again, some other terms seem to provide a more helpful analogy:

S13 John thinks that Finns are good laborers, but troublemakers.

On Schroeder's (2010: 204) view, sentences such as S13 illustrate "that when 'but' appears inside a verb like 'thinks that', the speaker is not committed to the contrast, but rather saying that [John] thinks that there is a contrast." In many other contexts, 'but' seems to work like slurs do (e.g., projection behavior when it comes to negations and conditionals), and so it would seem like a promising model for a hybrid cognitivist.

Schroeder (2014) raises an interesting worry, though. Let us consider arguments of the following form:

S14 Everything John thinks is true.
S13 John thinks that Finns are good laborers, but troublemakers.
S3 Finns are good laborers, but troublemakers.

S15 Everything Ida believes is true.
S8 Ida believes that exploiting miners is wrong.
S5 Exploiting miners is wrong.

Someone who accepts S15 and S8 should also accept S5 (or reject one of the premises). In order to accept S5, she must, according to the judgment-individuating view, be opposed to wrongful actions. But where does the pressure to have this attitude come from? Plausibly, one may accept S15 without being opposed to wrongful actions. If so, the hybrid cognitivist should hold that accepting S8 involves being opposed to wrongful actions. Now, if this is right, then the hybrid cognitivist should think that 'wrong' works, in this respect, like 'roundhead' does. But we have also seen, in this section, that she should think that 'wrong' works like 'but' does. So, perhaps a hybrid cognitivist should hold that 'wrong' works like 'roundhead' in that S8 expresses opposition to wrongful actions, but also like 'but' in that S8 also ascribes this kind of opposition to Ida. Schroeder's worry is this: S13 ascribes a belief in contrast to John, but does *not* express the speaker's belief in the relevant contrast. But according to the current hybrid proposal, ethical terms *cannot* work in this way because we can come up with an argument of the form illustrated by the one from S15 and S8 to S5 for any relevant term. This leaves us with an explanatory challenge. Given that a belief in contrast may be expressed by a term ('but') without being expressed by belief ascriptions using the relevant term (e.g., S13), why is it that the expression of non-belief attitudes by ethical terms is bound to project also through belief ascriptions?

CONVERSATIONAL IMPLICATURES?

Let us consider the following exchange between Ida and another roundhead (it seems that I, as a Finn, can get away with using this term):

Ida: "How is Reino adjusting to his work in the mines?"
Elis: "Well, he hasn't been to prison yet."
Ida: "Just how bad is it?"
Elis: "It sure is pretty cold in Minnesota this time of the year!"

What Elis first says is that Reino has not been to prison, yet (this exhausts the truth-conditional content of her statement), but what he means by saying this is something different. Plausibly, he means to suggest that Reino has not adjusted very well. Elis does not say this, but he *implies* as much. Elis's second statement concerns the temperature in Minnesota at a certain time, but what he *conversationally implicates*, using this sentence, is that he desires to avoid further discussion of Reino and his work in the mines.

Conversational implicatures are generated when we put together the conventional meanings of our sentences with our (implicit) knowledge concerning our conversational aims and effective means of achieving them. Very roughly, our assumption is that when someone engages in speech, she is sensibly pursuing her (usually cooperative) conversational goals. This standardly requires, for instance, being sincere, and making our contributions to discussion sufficiently (but not overly) informative and relevant to the topic at hand. In the above example, Elis openly flouts the maxim of relevance, and this allows Ida (and us) to infer, given that Elis is pursuing his and Ida's conversational ends in a cooperative way, that Elis believes that Reino has not adjusted very well, and that Elis does not want to discuss the topic in question. It is only by making these assumptions that we can make sense of Elis' contributions to the conversation as being in the service of what conversational goals we assume Elis has. Thus, the conversational implicatures (Grice 1989).

Appealing to the phenomenon of conversational implicature (or some similar pragmatic mechanism), a cognitivist might suggest that there is no need for her to go hybrid, really. Rather, the idea would be, the practicality of normative language (which I have tried to encapsulate in the thesis of discourse internalism) and the temptations to accept motivational internalism can be wholly explained by the purposes for which we use purely descriptive normative language (see, e.g., Milo 1981; Finlay 2005, 2014; Strandberg 2011, 2012; Fletcher 2014; Woods 2014). Views that combine cognitivism with this kind of pragmatic account of the practicality of moral language are sometimes taken to represent a brand of hybrid accounts, but given that this strategy is available for pretty much every cognitivist, it seems better to think of it as an attempt to explain how cognitivists can capture the relevant phenomena without going hybrid.

How might this kind of story work? A conversational implicature only arises when the audience is in a position to infer, given the supposed conversational aims of the speaker, that the speaker must believe what is being implicated. Conversational implicatures are *calculable*. So, when someone asserts S5 ("Exploiting miners is wrong"), for example, how do we calculate that the speaker (believes that she) is opposed to exploiting miners? Caj Strandberg's (2011, 2012) suggestion is, *very roughly*, as follows: the (mutually accepted) purpose of moral talk is, in part, to influence behavior. Someone should not, then, use S5 in case she is not opposed to exploiting miners. And so, given that she utters S5, and that she knows what she is opposed to, we are entitled to infer that she is opposed to exploiting miners.

Strandberg proposes that moral utterances convey that the speakers have certain motivational attitudes as a matter of *generalized conversational implicature*. Generalized conversational implicatures are conversational implicatures that arise regardless of the specifics of the context of utterance, unless they are somehow defeated (Grice 1989: chapter 2). For example:

S16 She will be here on Tuesday or on Wednesday.
S17 She drank some of the beer.

Someone who uses S16 thereby implicates that the person she is talking about won't be at the relevant location both on Tuesday and on Wednesday; someone who uses S17 thereby implicates that the person she is talking about did not drink all of the beer. Plausibly, these are just conversational implicatures, which need to be calculable, in principle, but the relevant implicatures arise standardly, without any further knowledge of the specific context in which these sentences are uttered.

Some suggest that the behavior of conversational implicatures nicely fits the way that moral utterances convey our attitudes. As explained above, conventional implicatures project and are neither cancelable nor detachable, while the expression of attitudes by moral utterances works differently in these respects, or at least does not clearly match the behavior of conventional implicatures. Conversational implicatures may fit the relevant data somewhat more smoothly, as conversational implicatures are not detachable, do not standardly project, and are easier to cancel without a residual feeling of linguistic inap-propriateness (Strandberg 2012; Fletcher 2014).

However, conversational implicatures do not seem to provide a cognitivist with any very significant benefits. Appealing to conversational implicatures does not help the cognitivist to capture motivational internalism of any kind, including communal internalism. Neither does it seem to offer a debunking explanation for acceptance of motivational internalism. For instance, we are not tempted to think, on reflection, that someone who says "Ida ate some of the cookies" must believe that Ida didn't eat all the cookies (see Tresan MS).

Appealing to conversational implicatures does not, then, seem sufficient for any old cognitivist to capture the kinds of phenomena that motivate cognitivists to adopt hybrid accounts. This is not to say that appealing to conversational norms only might not be sufficient in connection with *some* cognitivist views. For example, Stephen Finlay's (2005, 2014) end-relational view, on which ethical claims concern the ways in which certain ends of ours may be satisfied, might, when combined with suitable pragmatic explanations, allow us to better capture what's plausible in internalism.

HYBRID EXPRESSIVISM

According to pure expressivists, some ethical thinking consists *solely* in having certain desire-like attitudes (Blackburn 1998, Gibbard 2003). According to hybrid expressivism, all ethical thinking consists of having desire-like attitudes *as well as* suitably related beliefs. However, even a pure expressivist may hold that judgments deploying 'thick' terms such as (perhaps) 'courageous' or 'distributively unjust' involve representational beliefs. So, we could relativize views such as pure and hybrid forms of cognitivism and expressivism, more carefully, to different types of ethical claims, and say that one can be a pure expressivist about 'ought' or 'good' (say), but a hybrid expressivist about (for example) 'courageous'. Perhaps one could also combine an expressivist view about the thin with hybrid cognitivism about the thick (cf. Ridge 2014: chapter 8). However, in the following sections, we're concerned with views that are hybrid expressivist with regard to the thin—that is, regarding judgments about oughts, goodness, wrongness, and so on.

It is helpful to introduce hybrid expressivism via *ecumenical expressivism*, a view advanced by Ridge (2006, 2007) in some of his earlier papers. On a somewhat simplified, 'plain vanilla' version of this view, S5 ("Exploiting miners is wrong"), for instance, would express, roughly, disapproval of actions insofar as they have some property, F, as well as a belief that exploiting miners has this property. Thus far, this sounds very much like the judgment-individuating hybrid cognitivist view discussed above. However, on Ridge's view, sentences such as S5 are not to be understood as being about a certain specific property across different speakers. Rather, what the relevant property, F, is, is determined by the desire-like states of the speaker, and varies from one speaker to another. For Ida, being F might be a matter of being advised against by someone with character traits, C; for Elis, being F might amount to failing to maximize happiness. (The relevant property might also be massively disjunctive.) Moreover, the idea is not that when Elis uses S5, the content of his claim is that exploiting miners fails to maximize happiness. Even though his utterance of S5 does, on Ridge's (early) view, express a belief that exploiting miners fails to maximize happiness, the content of this belief is not the representational content of his assertion, and one might sensibly think that while the belief expressed is true, the utterance isn't. (For roughly similar views, see Jackson 1999; Lenman 2003; Eriksson 2009.)

A subtly but importantly different kind of view, *relational expressivism*, rejects the idea that S5 expresses a certain desire, as well as a belief—the content of which is determined by that desire. According to relational expressivism, S5 expresses, instead, a relational state—a state of having one's desire-like states and beliefs related in certain ways (Schroeder 2013; Toppinen 2013; Ridge 2014). One version of this view would say that S5 expresses a state of having one's desire-like states and beliefs related just as Elis' disapproval of failing to maximize happiness and his belief that exploiting miners fails to maximize happiness are related. We could also put the idea as follows: S5 expresses a certain kind of *higher-order state*, that is, a state of being in a certain kind of hybrid state—a higher-order state that is massively multiply realizable by hybrid states roughly like the ones that Ridge's earlier view suggested would be expressed by ethical sentences (Toppinen 2013). If Ida is against actions that go against the advice of someone with character traits C and believes that exploiting miners goes against such advice, and Elis is against failing to maximize happiness and believes that exploiting miners fails in this respect, then Ida and Elis both are, despite the differences in the contents of their respective states of opposition and belief, in a relational higher-order state of this kind.

Ridge's (2014) more recent view (still called 'ecumenical expressivism') is the most sophisticated development of relational expressivism to date. On this view, all ethical claims concern the relation of actions, etc., to acceptable standards for practical reasoning. The state expressed by S5 (for example) would be a relational state that consists of (a) a 'normative perspective' and (b) a suitably related belief. Normative perspectives are understood roughly in terms of plans and policies that rule out certain standards. The belief-component of a state realizing the relational state expressed by S5 would then be, very roughly, a belief that exploiting miners is ruled out by the standards not ruled out by the thinker's normative perspective—a belief that exploiting miners is ruled out by the *admissible standards*, for short (to use a technical term of Ridge's). Similarly, thinking that promoting women's suffrage is good would involve having a normative perspective plus a belief that promoting women's suffrage scores high on any of the admissible standards, and so on.

SOME POTENTIAL ADVANTAGES OF HYBRID EXPRESSIVISM

Frege-Geach and wishful thinking

Why would an expressivist go hybrid? Here is a nice set of challenges for any expressivist: explain how the meanings of complex ethical sentences (e.g., S10, "If exploiting miners is wrong, the pastor will be mad") are determined by the meanings of the simpler sentences (e.g., S5) they are made up of, and do this in a way that allows us to explain why, for example, someone who accepts S5 and S10 would be inconsistent if she went on to accept S18, and why she rationally should accept S19 (or reject one of S5 and S10).

S18 The pastor won't be mad.
S19 The pastor will be mad.

This is, on one understanding, the so-called Frege-Geach problem for expressivists (Schroeder 2010: 41–54, 105–112). A related challenge is that of explaining why moving from a justified belief in S10, via simply coming to be in the desire-like state expressed by

S5, to a descriptive, representational belief in S19 does not instantiate wishful thinking (Dorr 2002).

A number of responses to these problems have been proposed on behalf of the pure expressivist, but it's controversial whether these responses succeed. Plausibly, a solution to the Frege-Geach problem should provide us with a recipe for determining what the complex sentences express as a function of what their parts express (Schroeder 2010: 48–54). The recipe offered by hybrid expressivism is quite simple. Consider, again, the following argument:

S10 If exploiting miners is wrong, the pastor will be mad.
 S5 Exploiting miners is wrong.
S19 The pastor will be mad.

According to hybrid expressivism, my acceptance of S5 is a matter of my being in a state that is realized by a desire-like state (e.g., a normative perspective à la Ridge) and a suitably related belief, let's say a belief that lying is F (e.g., such that it is ruled out by standards with some property, G). My acceptance of S10 will then involve, again, the same desire-like state, as well as a belief that if lying is F, then the pastor will be mad. Any ethical sentence will express a state realized by a certain desire-like state and a belief, the content of which we get by substituting for 'wrong', in the original sentence, the name of the corresponding wholly descriptive property (e.g., being ruled out by the admissible standards). This gives us the recipe for determining what is expressed by the complex sentences.

We can now explain why acceptance of S10 and S5 together with rejecting S19 is inconsistent (Ridge 2006, 2014: chapter 5; Toppinen 2013). This would involve having the beliefs that if lying is F, the pastor will be mad, that lying is F, and that it is not the case that the pastor will be mad—which is inconsistent. Moreover, Ridge (2014: chapter 5.5) proposes, acceptance of S10 and S5 together with rejecting S19 is *logically* inconsistent, because it involves inconsistency in belief "on any acceptable substitution of the non-logical terms of the argument." Similarly, we should now be in a position to explain why someone who accepts S10 and S5 is rationally committed to accepting S19 (or rejecting one of the premises): the beliefs involved in accepting S10 and S5 commit one to the belief involved in accepting S19. This also allows the hybrid expressivist to escape the worry of wishful thinking. According to the hybrid expressivist view, acceptance of S19 by someone, on the basis of S10 and S5, will always be based on the *beliefs* involved in accepting S10 and S5.

Many attitudes

There are a number of 'propositional attitudes' other than beliefs. For some proposition, p, we may believe that p, but we may also desire that p, hope that p, wonder whether p, and so on. This applies also to normative propositions. Just as one may believe (at least in a suitably minimalist sense) that exploiting miners is wrong, one may also desire or hope that exploiting miners is wrong. Expressivists cannot simply explain these attitudes as different attitudes that all are about exploiting miners being wrong. Even if they do have a story about what it is to believe that exploiting miners is wrong, they would also seem to owe us an account of what it is to hope that exploiting miners is wrong, and so on. Mark Schroeder (2010: 84) calls this the *Many attitudes* problem. Hybrid expressivism offers promising resources here. The idea would be that to hope that exploiting miners is wrong is to be in a state of having some suitable desire-like state in relation to a certain property as well as a state of hoping that exploiting miners has that property. The idea generalizes in obvious ways (Ridge 2014: chapter 5).

Akrasia

Expressivists also plausibly need to make sense of the possibility of akrasia—roughly, of the possibility of thinking that one ought to perform some action while having no plan or intention to act accordingly. This seems impossible if one identifies thinking that one ought to perform an action with having a plan to perform this action (Gibbard 2003). Ridge (2007) suggests that a hybrid view, according to which the desire-like element in a normative judgment is directed at actions with certain properties, quite generally, makes room for akrasia, even assuming that the relevant desire-like states are plan-like commitments. An agent might think that one ought to refrain from murder—that is, for instance, plan to maximize happiness and believe that murder fails to maximize happiness—and yet, irrationally, fail to form an intention to refrain from murdering in her particular circumstances.

Uncertainty

Expressivists also have trouble making acceptable sense of ethical uncertainty. We may think that x is really good whereas y is only moderately good (call this *importance*), but be much more certain about y being moderately good than we are about x being really good (call this *confidence*). If normative judgments are just desire-like states, it's hard to see how we can make sense of this. We might appeal to the strength of desires in accounting for importance, or perhaps in accounting for confidence, but we cannot explain both importance and confidence with reference to the strength of desires (Smith 2002). Adopting a hybrid view might be of some help here. Roughly, we could suggest that the level of confidence in some normative judgment may always be explained with reference to the belief involved in making this judgment (Lenman 2003). It is by no means clear that this will work, but hybridism offers some extra resources for an expressivist also in this context (for discussion, see Bykvist & Olson 2009; for a related challenge, see also Egan 2007; Ridge 2015b).

CHALLENGES FOR HYBRID EXPRESSIVISM

Expression

Let's suppose Elis is a hedonistic utilitarian. On the 'plain vanilla' version of Ridge's (2006, 2007) earlier view, Elis' utterance of S5 would express something like disapproval of failing to maximize happiness plus a belief that exploiting miners fails to maximize happiness. On this view, the state expressed by utterances of S5 varies from one speaker to another and is determined by what states the speaker is in. However, given that the state expressed is a function of the speaker's attitudes, it is difficult to see how Elis' utterance could express these particular states in virtue of S5's conventional meaning (Schroeder 2009).

Relational expressivism avoids this worry. According to this view, S5 may be conventionally associated with a certain relational or higher-order state (which may be differently realized in the case of different speakers). A use of this sentence may, for example, be evidence of the speaker being in such relational state, or be permissible only when the speaker is in such state—to briefly indicate two ways of understanding the expression relation (Toppinen 2013: section 4).

Disagreement

If Ida thinks that exploiting miners is wrong, and Elis thinks it's not, they disagree. Expressivists cannot explain this simply by saying that it cannot be true both that exploiting miners is wrong and that it isn't. Plausibly, their account of Ida's and Elis' disagreement should appeal to the idea that being in the states expressed by "Exploiting miners is wrong" and "Exploiting miners is not wrong" involves some relevant kind of incoherence. But now, suppose that Ida's judgment that exploiting miners is wrong is realized by her being against acting in ways that are not recommended by someone with character traits, C, and believing that exploiting miners would not be recommended by someone with character traits, C, whereas Elis' judgment that exploiting miners is not wrong is realized by Elis' being against failing to maximize happiness and believing that exploiting miners does not fail in this respect, under the relevant circumstances. It seems that being in these states does not secure incoherence of any relevant kind (Toppinen 2013: section 5; Eriksson 2015). That is, one could coherently be against actions that fail to maximize happiness as well as against actions that would not be recommended by someone with C, and one could, moreover, coherently believe both that exploiting miners would not be recommended by someone with C and that it does not fail to maximize happiness.

Relational expressivism avoids this worry, too (Toppinen 2013: section 5), for suppose that we ask whether one can coherently be in the kinds of relational states that are realized, in Ida's and Elis' case, by their respective states of opposition and belief. Being in both of these relational states would involve opposing actions that have a certain property and believing both that exploiting miners has and doesn't have this property. This would clearly be inconsistent. This does not yet amount to giving a fully satisfying account of disagreement (Toppinen 2013: section 5). However, giving a fully satisfying account of disagreement would seem to be a problem for expressivism quite generally, and not for hybrid forms of expressivism in particular (see, e.g., Dreier 2009, 2015; Ridge 2014: chapter 6, 2015a).

Ethical judgment ascriptions

The hybrid expressivist recipe for determining the states expressed by complex sentences doesn't work entirely generally. A couple of sentences:

S8 Ida believes that exploiting miners is wrong.
S21 If Kant is right, then exploiting miners is wrong.

S8 does not express a state of having some normative perspective as well as a belief that Ida believes that exploiting miners is ruled out by the standards that are admissible by the light of *that* normative perspective. Rather, S8 would seem to concern the kind of normative perspective that Ida has. Similar concerns arise in relation to sentences such as S21 (Carr 2015; Ridge 2015a). And whatever story we give of the meaning of S8 (say), it should allow us to explain how one can validly derive from S8, together with the claim that what Ida believes is true, the conclusion that exploiting miners is wrong (Schroeder 2009; Ridge 2014: chapter 7).

Details about the relational state

There is, of course, a lot more to be said about how exactly we should understand the kinds of hybrid states that, according to hybrid expressivism, realize the relational states expressed by ethical sentences. Ridge (2014: chapter 4) suggests that we should understand the desire-like component (largely) negatively, as ruling out acceptance of certain kinds of standards. This way, he suggests, we can do justice to the idea that someone engaged in ethical thought may not accept any very specific set of standards. However, normative perspectives also have certain positive elements, on Ridge's view: policies, aspirations, and propensities to act and deliberate in certain ways.

How should we, then, understand the beliefs that are relevantly related to these perspectives? One worry is that it's not plausible that these beliefs would present the relevant standards to us as *our* standards (Schafer 2015). However, a hybrid expressivist may reject the idea that the relevant beliefs concern our own standards (under that description). Rather, the idea is that these beliefs concern certain standards that are salient to us thanks to our having a certain kind of normative perspective. Ridge (2015a: 475) offers as an analogy a case of someone who hears a tune and says that he doesn't like songs 'like that one'—where this someone may not be able to say what the relevant similarity is between the tunes that he thereby groups together.

Conclusion

Even if hybrid expressivism offers resources for dealing with some of the hard problems for expressivists, it remains to be seen how it deals with the rest. Some of the worries raised above are yet to be answered. Also, expressivists of any stripe have yet to offer a fully satisfying account of, for example, disagreement and ethical uncertainty. There's also more to be said about how to capture just the sorts of internalist theses that should be captured, about how the different expressivist views generalize to normative or evaluative thought and talk outside the realm of the (broadly) ethical, and so on. But of course, all the metaethical options on the table are work in progress. Just as with cognitivism, with expressivism, too, the most plausible ways of going hybrid seem to hold considerable promise.

ACKNOWLEDGMENTS

I thank Jamie Fritz, Tristram McPherson, David Plunkett, and Pekka Väyrynen for helpful comments.

RELATED TOPICS

Chapter 5, "Metaethical Expressivism;" Chapter 13, "Thick Concepts;" Chapter 14, "The Frege-Geach Problem;" Chapter 17, "The Significance of Ethical Disagreement for Theories of Ethical Thought and Talk;" Chapter 18, "Cognitivism and Non-Cognitivism;" Chapter 19, "Ethical Judgment and Motivation;" Chapter 33, "Metasemantics and Metaethics;" Chapter 40, "Quasi-realism."

REFERENCES

Barker, S., 2000, "Is Value Content a Component of Conventional Implicature?" *Analysis* 60: 268–279.

Bar-On, D. & M. Chrisman, 2009, "Ethical Neo-Expressivism," in R. Shafer-Landau (ed.): *Oxford Studies in Metaethics, Volume 4* (Oxford: Oxford University Press).

Björklund, F., G. Björnsson, J. Eriksson, R. Francén Olinder, & C. Strandberg, 2011, "Recent Work on Motivational Internalism," *Analysis* 72: 124–137.

Blackburn, S., 1998, *Ruling Passions* (Oxford: Oxford University Press).

Boisvert, D., 2008, "Expressive-Assertivism," *Pacific Philosophical Quarterly* 89: 169–203.

Bolinger, R. J., forthcoming, "The Pragmatics of Slurs," *Noûs*.

Bykvist, K. & J. Olson, 2009, "Expressivism and Moral Certitude," *Philosophical Quarterly* 59: 202–215.

Camp, E., 2013, "Slurring Perspectives," *Analytic Philosophy* 54: 330–349.

Carr, J., 2015, "Ecumenical Expressivism Ecumenicized," *Analysis* 75: 442–450.

Chrisman, M., 2016, *The Meaning of 'Ought'* (Oxford: Oxford University Press).

Copp, D., 2001, "Realist-Expressivism: A Neglected Option for Moral Realism," in E. F. Paul, F. D. Miller, Jr., & J. Paul (eds.): *Moral Knowledge* (New York: Cambridge University Press).

Copp, D., 2009, "Realist-Expressivism and Conventional Implicature," in R. Shafer-Landau (ed.): *Oxford Studies in Metaethics, Volume 4* (Oxford: Oxford University Press).

Copp, D., 2014, "Can a Hybrid Theory Have It Both Ways? Moral Thought, Open Questions, and Moral Motivation," in G. Fletcher & M. Ridge (eds.): *Having It Both Ways* (New York: Oxford University Press).

Dorr, C., 2002, "Non-Cognitivism and Wishful Thinking," *Noûs* 36: 97–103.

Dreier, J., 2009, "Relativism (and Expressivism) and the Problem of Disagreement," *Philosophical Perspectives* 23: 79–110.

Dreier, J., 2015, "Truth and Disagreement in *Impassioned Belief*," *Analysis* 75: 450–459.

Egan, A., 2007, "Quasi-Realism and Fundamental Moral Error," *Australasian Journal of Philosophy* 85: 205–219.

Eriksson, J., 2009, "Homage to Hare: Ecumenism and the Frege-Geach Problem," *Ethics* 120: 8–35.

Eriksson, J., 2015, "Explaining Disagreement: A Problem for (Some) Hybrid Expressivists," *Pacific Philosophical Quarterly* 96: 39–53.

Finlay, S., 2005, "Value and Implicature," *Philosophers' Imprint* 5 (4): 1–20.

Finlay, S., 2014, *Confusion of Tongues: A Theory of Normative Language* (New York: Oxford University Press).

Fletcher, G., 2014, "Moral Utterances, Attitude Expression, and Implicature," in G. Fletcher & M. Ridge (eds.): *Having It Both Ways* (New York: Oxford University Press).

Gibbard, A., 2003, *Thinking How to Live* (Cambridge, MA: Harvard University Press).

Grice, P., 1989, *Studies in the Way of Words* (Cambridge, MA: Harvard University Press).

Hay, R., 2013, "Hybrid Expressivism and the Analogy between Pejoratives and Moral Language," *European Journal of Philosophy* 21: 450–474.

Hom, C., 2008, "The Semantics of Racial Epithets," *Journal of Philosophy* 105: 416–440.

Jackson, F., 1999, "Non-Cognitivism, Validity and Conditionals," in D. Jamieson (ed.): *Singer and His Critics* (Oxford: Blackwell Publishers).

Laskowski, N., 2015, "Non-Analytical Naturalism and the Nature of Normative Thought: A Reply to Parfit," *Journal of Ethics and Social Philosophy* (http://www.jesp.org/articles/download/nonanalytical-naturalism. pdf).

Lenman, J., 1999, "The Externalist and the Amoralist," *Philosophia* 27: 441–457.

Lenman, J., 2003, "Noncognitivism and the Dimensions of Evaluative Judgment," *BEARS (Brown Electronic Article Review Service)* (http://www.brown.edu/Departments/Philosophy/bears/).

Milo, R. D., 1981, "Moral Indifference," *Monist* 64: 373–393.

Potts, C., 2007, "Into the Conventional-Implicature Dimension," *Philosophy Compass* 2: 665–679.

Ridge, M., 2006, "Ecumenical Expressivism: Finessing Frege," *Ethics* 116: 302–337.

Ridge, M., 2007, "Ecumenical Expressivism: The Best of Both Worlds?" in R. Shafer-Landau (ed.): *Oxford Studies in Metaethics, Volume 2* (Oxford: Oxford University Press).

Ridge, M., 2014, *Impassioned Belief* (Oxford: Oxford University Press).

Ridge, M., 2015a, "Replies to Critics," *Analysis* 75: 471–488.

Ridge, M., 2015b, "I Might Be Fundamentally Mistaken," *Journal of Ethics and Social Philosophy* 9: 1.

Ross, W. D., 1939, *Foundations of Ethics* (Oxford: Oxford University Press).

Schafer, K., 2015, "The Unity of Normative Judgement: On Ridge's *Impassioned Belief*," *Analysis* 75: 442–450.

Schroeder, M., 2009, "Hybrid Expressivism: Virtues and Vices," *Ethics* 119: 257–309.

Schroeder, M., 2010, *Noncognitivism in Ethics* (Abingdon: Routledge).

Schroeder, M., 2013, "Tempered Expressivism," in R. Shafer-Landau (ed.): *Oxford Studies in Metaethics, Vol. 8* (Oxford: Oxford University Press).

Schroeder, M., 2014, "The Truth in Hybrid Semantics," in G. Fletcher & M. Ridge (eds.): *Having It Both Ways* (New York: Oxford University Press).

Schroeter, L. & F. Schroeter, 2014, "Why Go Hybrid? A Cognitivist Alternative to Hybrid Theories of Normative Judgment," in G. Fletcher & M. Ridge (eds.): *Having It Both Ways* (New York: Oxford University Press).

Smith, M., 1994, *The Moral Problem* (Oxford: Blackwell Publishers).

Smith, M., 2002, "Evaluation, Uncertainty and Motivation," *Ethical Theory and Moral Practice* 5: 305–320.

Strandberg, C., 2011, "The Pragmatics of Moral Motivation," *Journal of Ethics* 15: 341–369.

Strandberg, C., 2012, "A Dual Aspect Account of Moral Language," *Philosophy and Phenomenological Research* 84: 87–122.

Toppinen, T., 2013, "Believing in Expressivism," in R. Shafer-Landau (ed.): *Oxford Studies in Metaethics, Volume 8* (Oxford: Oxford University Press).

Tresan, J., 2006, "De Dicto Internalist Cognitivism," *Nôus* 40: 143–165.

Tresan, J., MS, "Communal Internalism is the Real Deal: A Defense."

Woods, J., 2014, "Expressivism and Moore's Paradox," *Philosophers' Imprint* 14 (5): 1–12.

Wedgwood, R., 2007, *The Nature of Normativity* (Oxford: Oxford University Press).

FURTHER READING

Fletcher, G. & M. Ridge (eds.), 2014, *Having It Both Ways* (New York: Oxford University Press).

Schroeder, M., 2015, *Expressing Our Attitudes: Explanation and Expression in Ethics, Vol. 2* (Oxford: Oxford University Press).

16

Conceptual Role Accounts of Meaning in Metaethics

Matthew Chrisman

INTRODUCTION

Metaethicists are interested in questions in the philosophy of language as these apply to ethical and more generally normative terms. One of the core questions in the philosophy of language is how to explain the meaning of terms and the sentences in which they figure. Hence, an important question in metaethics is how to explain the meaning of ethical terms and the sentences in which they figure. In the philosophy of language, one of the main accounts of meaning stresses the roles terms play in an interconnected web of meanings central to our linguistic practice of talking about the world and what to do in it. This general view of meaning is sometimes dubbed "conceptual role semantics." The basic idea is that the meaning of a term is not something it has, independent of conceptual connections to other words and sentences, but rather something determined by these very connections.

The label "conceptual role semantics" misleadingly suggests that the view is a competitor to standard approaches to model theoretic semantics (such as possible worlds semantics) as an attempt to model the way the meaning of whole sentences in particular languages could be a systematic function of the meaning of their parts and their logical forms. Although the issue is somewhat controversial, as I see things, the conceptual role view is best pursued instead as a *meta*semantic view (which is part of an overall theory of meaning attempting to explain the sources or foundations of meaningfulness in general). Rather than proffering explanations of how terms of a particular language compose into meaningful sentences in a way that explains the productivity and learnability of a language, the conceptual role view offers an explanation of that in virtue of which words have the semantic values that they do. If this is right, the conceptual role view is more usefully contrasted (in its appeal to "conceptual roles") with representationalist views about why terms have the meanings they do. Representationalist views stress, in contrast, the way pieces of language stand for things in the (mostly) extralinguistic environment.

As an intuitive and rough example, a representationalist and conceptual role theorist might agree that the semantic value of the predicate 'is red' is usefully thought of as something like the set of all red things. However, the representationalist will say that this predicate has that semantic value in virtue of standing for the property of redness, whereas a conceptual role theorist would say instead that this predicate has that semantic value in virtue of the conceptual connections to other predicates, such as 'is colored', 'is crimson', 'is orange, is yellow, is blue...'. Hence, in what follows, I refer to "conceptual role accounts of meaning" and "conceptual role views" rather than the more customary "conceptual role semantics."

Surprisingly, in spite of its being arguably one of the main theoretical traditions in contemporary philosophy of language, conceptual role views are somewhat difficult to locate in standard metaethical discussions of the meaning of ethical terms. Here, the debate is often conceived as one between cognitivists and noncognitivists, where (in this context) *cognitivism* is something like the thesis that ethical terms contribute representational content to the sentences in which they figure and hence function semantically primarily to determine conditions of reality that would make those sentences true; and *noncognitivism* is the view that ethical terms contribute emotive or evaluative content to the sentences in which they figure and so either don't contribute to the sentences' truth conditions or do so only in some trivial and metaphysically noncommittal way.

For example, a cognitivist might say that the predicate 'is wrong' in the sentence "Sexual assault is wrong" represents the property of being wrong, and this is why this sentence is true iff sexual assault has the property of being wrong. (Most who endorse cognitivism think that this or some other simple sentence deploying 'is wrong' is literally true, and so they embrace a form of metaethical *realism*; however, one can obviously be a cognitivist and antirealist in metaethics by developing a form of *error theory* or *fictionalism*.) A noncognitivist would typically reject this, arguing that 'is wrong' is not a term primarily for representing a property but rather a term primarily for expressing one's negative evaluation of something. Hence, noncognitivists often deny that ethical sentences such as "Sexual assault is wrong" are the sorts of sentences properly said to be true or false; or they argue that these sentences have truth conditions in a "deflationary sense" incompatible with a substantive appeal to truth in one's explanation of their meaning. In any case, they think the real action for explaining the meaning of ethical terms lies in the way they serve as vehicles for the expression of emotive or evaluative states of mind rather than the way they represent reality.

If we understand the main debate in metaethics about meaning like this, it's unclear where a view focusing on conceptual roles rather than representational purport or emotive/evaluative expressive function would fit in. With a little care, however, I think we can find versions of the conceptual role view in theories defended by some philosophers inspired by cognitivism and also by other philosophers inspired by noncognitivism. Moreover, I think there's also a third way to conceive of a conceptual role view, one which undermines the stark distinction between cognitivism and noncognitivism (at least as it's commonly understood).[1]

Because of this, in what follows, I want to explain three ways to develop a conceptual role view of meaning in metaethics. First, I'll suggest that there's a way to combine inspiration from *noncognitivism* with a particular form of the conceptual role view to form a noncognitivist view with distinctive advantages over other noncognitivist views. Second,

I'll suggest that there's also a way to combine a strong commitment to *cognitivism* with a different form of the conceptual role view to form a version of cognitivism with distinctive advantages over other cognitivist views. Finally, I argue that another way to think of the conceptual role view in metaethics is as opening up the space for a third way, beyond cognitivism and noncognitivism. But before I turn to those arguments, I begin with brief comments on some relevant distinctions about what determines conceptual roles and what kind of internal connection between ethical thought and action there may be. Then I use these distinctions to explain the three different applications of the conceptual role view.

SOME DISTINCTIONS

There isn't such a thing as *the* "conceptual role view about meaning." Rather there is a family of loosely connected views stressing the conceptual role of terms in determining their meaning (usually in contrast to the referential purport of those terms, though we'll see below that those aren't in strict tension). We can begin to understand the contours of this family of views by marking some choice points that distinguish different versions.

Here, without claims to being exhaustive, are four choices any complete conceptual role account of meaning must make (compare Whiting [2006]):

1. Functionalism vs. Normativism: What determines a "conceptual role"? Is it the connections between terms/concepts that a normal user is *disposed* to make in various circumstances or the ones a normal user *ought* to make?
2. Globalism vs. Localism about representational content: Do conceptual roles generally determine representational content or is some significant class of conceptual roles nonrepresentational?
3. Solipsistic vs. Social: Is the primary locus of a conceptual role in individuals or linguistic communities?
4. Wide vs. Narrow: Are "language-entry" (from world to mind) and "language-exit" (from mind to world) connections included in a conceptual role? Relatedly, how many conceptual connections are meaning-determining for a term—some "core" set, or all[2] of them?

In what follows, I focus on 1–2 because (somewhat surprisingly) 3–4 don't seem to matter much to distinguishing the three main ways that I think conceptual roles views might be developed in metaethics. Any complete conceptual role view, though, must settle on answers to all of these questions.

Something else that will be relevant in what follows is what kinds of "internal" connections there may be between ethical thought and action. This is because it is often seen as a benefit of conceptual role views that they can incorporate the supposedly internal connection between ethical thoughts and the actions based on them into an account of the conceptual role of ethical terms. If this works, then it might provide the best explanation of some of the distinctive features of ethical terms in their connections to actions.

As is well known, many different ideas go under the label "internalism" in metaethics, and in philosophy more generally. It would take a whole essay to develop even a highly contentious map of the different versions of internalism. In lieu of this, I propose to work with the following crude distinction between:

1. *Causal Internalism* (vague), the thesis that one's thought that one ought to φ in C *tends* in some special way to dispose one's ceteris paribus to φ whenever in C; and
2. *Normative Internalism* (vague), the thesis that one's thought that one ought to φ in C *commits one* in some special way to φ whenever in C.

With those distinctions in hand, let's turn to some possible applications of the conceptual role view in metaethics.

THE CONCEPTUAL ROLE VIEW DEVELOPED AS A FORM OF NONCOGNITIVISM

The first kind of view is inspired by noncognitivism, which I'm treating here as the view that ethical words contribute emotive or evaluative content rather than representational content to the sentences in which they figure. By drawing on the resources of conceptual role accounts of meaning, there may be room to improve on both traditional and other contemporary views in this vein.

The first step is to argue that the role of a concept is determined by the function it has in our mental economies, its application being caused by and then causing various other applications of concepts. Then, if we assume that words get their meaning from the concepts they express, we get a *Functionalist* version of the conceptual role view of meaning. (Compare Block [1986], Field [1977], and Harman [1999].)

Next, one mobilizes the metaphor of "directions of fit," whereby some mental states are conceived of as representational in that they "aim" to fit the world and other mental states are conceived of as directive in that they "aim" to get the world to fit them. Then, given a broadly Humean conception of our mental economies, which has it that the cooperation of both kinds of mental states is crucial for motivation to action as well as coordinating our preferences, one can argue that the conceptual role of ethical predicates is action-guiding and preference-coordinating rather than reality-representing. (Compare Bennett [1976].) The argument is roughly that this provides the best explanation of whatever truth there is in the Causal Internalist idea that ethical thoughts have a special causal effect with respect to motivating action and preference.

What results is a picture, according to which some predicates are reality-representing. For instance, ordinary empirical predicates will have, on this view, the conceptual (in this case, functional) role of keeping track of the properties of things in our mostly non-linguistic external environment. However, ethical predicates are different because of the way their conceptual roles are functionally connected to causing action. In terms of the second choice point above, this means the view is Localist about representational content: The conceptual role of *some* predicates determines representational content, but this is not true of all predicates, since other predicates (especially ones expressing ethical concepts) don't have representational content on this view.

I'm not sure if anyone endorses a functionalist Localist version of the conceptual role view so baldly as I have just presented it, but Blackburn (2006) speaks very favorably about it.[3] He contrasts his preferred "non-factualism" about particular areas of thought and speech with an approach to semantics that "works in terms of what words and sentences represent." And he suggests that one positive reason in favor of adopting non-factualism about ethical thought and speech concerns "functional role":

> The mental states we voice as we communicate values or moralize to each other seem to be attitudes or practical stances that orientate us towards the world rather than representing any part of it. In a familiar metaphor, they have a different 'direction of fit' with the world, behaving more like desires, whose function is to effect changes in the world rather than beliefs, whose function is to represent the world.
>
> (2006: 245)

And he describes a change in his own view about how best to respond to the Frege-Geach challenge as one moving toward a conceptual role semantics. He describes himself as having proposed, in Blackburn 1988, to modify his theory of the meaning of conditionals by "drawing on conceptual role semantics Harman 1973" and arguing that conditionals get their meaning simply by their role in forcing moves from their antecedents to their consequents, or from the negation of their consequents to the negation of their antecedents (Blackburn 2006: 247).

I take the idea here to be that, rather than suggesting, as some noncognitivists have, that the meaning of a term *is* the attitude/concept it expresses, we say that the meaning is *the conceptual role* of whatever attitude/concept is expressed by the term. Then, by allowing for directive rather than representational conceptual roles, we get the view that some terms aren't representations of reality; and by allowing for distinctive pressures on action (e.g., via desire-like directions of fit) we get the positive alternative: Ethical terms are action-guiding rather than world-representing.

In the paper discussing conceptual roles, Blackburn doesn't work through a concrete example, but a quick sketch of one might aid comprehension. I take it his idea is that a predicate such as 'is wrong' means what it does because the concept of something being wrong is connected functionally to other concepts in a complex web of interconnected concepts. It's nontrivial to map this web precisely, but it will include tendencies to make transitions like

- belief that something causes unnecessary pain and suffering → belief that it is wrong
- belief that something is right → belief that it is not wrong
- belief that something is wrong → intention not to do it
- belief that something is wrong → preference that others not do it

Is this a version of noncognitivism? Well, as long as these conceptual connections are funded by the role 'is wrong' has in evaluating things rather than what it picks out in reality, it'll be a view that denies that 'is wrong' is a term primarily for representing a property. The idea instead is to view it as a term primarily for expressing one's negative evaluation of something. (Of course, we shouldn't forget that Blackburn [1993; 1998] also pioneered the quasi-realist development of this idea, which hopes to recover talk of moral properties and moral truths via minimalist treatments of 'property' and 'truth'.) In any case, developing the idea in conceptual role terms promises to carry an advantage over other noncognitivist-inspired views in metaethics: Unlike emotivist views, Blackburn can argue that the inferential connections revealed by Frege-Geach style objections are simply special cases of the conceptual (i.e., functional) connections ethical words bear to other words. (Compare Båve [2013] and Warren [2015].) Moreover—and this is rather speculative—unlike prescriptivists like Hare and perhaps even fellow expressivists like Gibbard, Blackburn's variegated functionalism is more flexible in that the functional role of ethical concepts doesn't always have to be spelled out in terms of prescriptions or plans. So it looks like it's going to be able to handle cases where it is implausible that ethical claims are "universally prescriptive" or "plan-laden" in any plausible sense of these notions.

As I see things, to make this fly, Blackburn needs something plausible to say about how the conceptual roles (as he conceives them) of ethical terms determine their contribution to the truth conditions of the sentences in which they figure. Of course, as a quasi-realist, he'll want some kind of deflationism about truth, so that assigning truth conditions to a sentence in the way we do in compositional semantics is not viewed as ascribing it representational content. But even so, if our functionalism is too loose, allowing in all sorts of dispositional connections between various attitudes, we risk conceptual roles including extraneous stuff not plausibly thought to be determinative of the sort of *semantic* content that is supposed to determine truth conditions. So we'll want some plausible story about a term's "core" functional role, which allows us to distinguish in a non-question-begging way which functional connections are part of the meaning of ethical terms and which are extrasemantic (e.g., because of deriving from pragmatic goals or from customs of politeness, etc.). Also, a view like this one will face the sorts of challenges that have been posed by Kripke (1982) to the idea that naturalistically describable functional roles might determine semantic content. (For ideas on how to preserve noncognitivism within a broadly normative conception of meaning, which might provide a way to respond to this objection, see Price [2011] and Gibbard [2012].)

THE CONCEPTUAL ROLE VIEW DEVELOPED AS A FORM OF COGNITIVISM

A flatfooted representationalist account of meaning might say that predicates mean what they mean solely in virtue of what properties, in reality, they stand for. We know this can't be right because two different terms can stand for the same property in reality, even necessarily so, without being synonymous—'closed triangular figure' and 'closed trilateral figure' have different meanings (witness the fact that someone might understand one but not the other). As a result, many have been tempted to say that the meaning of terms is determined by something like their conventionalized role in our conceptually imbued practices. On this view, grasping a term's meaning amounts to something like cottoning onto enough of the core rules governing its use. This is one thing that might be called a term's "conceptual role."

Peacocke (1995) argued, however, that going this route is compatible with the view that concepts stand for things in reality or that the terms expressing concepts have referential purport as part of their meaning. For one might think that part of the job of terms is to express concepts, and part of the role of these concepts is to stand for something in reality (whether instantiated or not). If that's right, then although we might focus in the first instance on explaining the way one ought to use a term, this explanation could be argued to determine what in reality this term stands for. For example, a kind of conceptual role view about 'is red' might say that this means what it means because of its conceptual connection to other predicates such as 'is colored' and 'is crimson', but that this conceptual role determines what in reality the term stands for: the property of redness.

Moreover, once we had that in the picture, we could mobilize relatively standard accounts of how different terms standing for different things can, along with logical form, determine the conditions under which declarative sentences with those terms are true. Accordingly, it seems that embracing a conceptual role account of meaning is perfectly consistent with a representationalist understanding of truth-conditional semantics.

Whether that is the best understanding of truth-conditional semantics is, of course, a controversial issue. But I bring this possibility up here in order to explain how this line of thought opens up space for an account of the meaning of *ethical* terms inspired by traditional realist forms of cognitivism but also with improved resources for addressing one of the standard worries about those views.

The worry is that construing an ethical predicate such as 'is wrong' as standing for some property (such as being wrong) makes it hard to account for an apparent difference between the practical justificatory force of ethical claims and other claims. Roughly put, this difference is that ethical terms are mainly for evaluating things in a way that we take to bear pretty directly on which actions to perform, whereas other words seem to be mainly for describing things in a way that seems to bear only indirectly on which actions to perform. How could the term 'is wrong', when it's presumed to stand for being wrong, carry this extra justificatory "oomph," compared with a non-ethical term such as 'is frequent', which is presumed to stand for being frequent? For, if someone thinks an action is frequent, nothing follows about what they're justified in doing, whereas someone who thinks that an action is wrong is prima facie justified in not performing it. (As we'll see, this is clearly related to the normative internalist thesis mentioned above.)

Something like this line of thought forces some cognitivists to say that ethical properties are sui generis precisely in the sense that their attribution carries special practical justificatory force. However, a Peacocke-inspired conceptual role account of the meaning of ethical terms would have a different response: The practical justificatory force of the attribution of ethical properties could be part of their conceptual role, in the sense that it's one of the rules of use one must grasp (at least implicitly) in order to count as understanding their meaning; it doesn't have to be a sui generis feature of the things in reality that they refer to. In terms of the distinction gestured at above, this amounts to an argument that a conceptual role view of meaning might, when applied to ethical terms, offer a better explanation of whatever truth there is in Normative Internalism than competing cognitivist views.

It's possible to develop this idea in a functionalist way by arguing that ethical thoughts tend to cause other thoughts about actions being justified or thoughts about practical commitments. However, I think a Normativist development better captures the normative version of internalism, which isn't about what thoughts someone tends to have but rather what actions one is committed to in virtue of having ethical thoughts. The idea is that part of the conceptual role of ethical terms is their power to *commit* one who deploys them to act in various ways. Whether one *tends* to be motivated to so act is a separate question.

Should the view be Globalist or Localist? There's room to go either way on this choice point, though there's pressure to develop the view in *Globalist* ways: Insofar as the view is inspired by a version of cognitivism, a Normativist conceptual role account of the meaning of ethical terms will need some justification for saying that ethical predicates have (or determine) representational content. One good justification would be that *all* predicates are assumed to represent properties. This is the Globalist position. (It would be open, however, to someone developing this cognitivist view of ethical terms to argue that ethical terms are representational but some other terms are not. For example, there is more purely, narrowly linguistic evidence that epistemic modals and probability operators behave nonrepresentationally. (Compare Yalcin [2007; 2011].) So, one could be anti-representationalist about them but not about ethical terms.

Again, I don't know if anyone develops a Normativist, Globalist application of the conceptual role view to ethical terms as baldly as I just have here, but Wedgwood (2001; 2007) has developed a metaethical view in this general vein. He argues that an account of the meaning of *any* term and so ipso facto *ethical* terms should explain "what it is for someone to understand the term—that is, to be a competent user of the term" (2001: 5). Drawing on Peacocke (1987; 1995), then, he develops this idea of competence in terms of dispositions to follow the basic rules of rationality governing a term's use: "According to the version of conceptual role semantics that I wish to develop, the meaning of a term is given by the basic rules of rationality governing its use" (Wedgwood 2001: 6). What makes them "basic" for him is that "the rationality of following these rules, and the irrationality of violating them, must not be due merely to the availability of some independent justification of these rules" (Wedgwood 2001: 8), presumably ruling out nonsemantic justifications of pragmatics, politeness, etc. These comments suggest a normativist understanding of the conceptual role—indeed, one with resources for distinguishing between all of the various connections that may stand between concepts and the "core" ones determinative of meaning.

As Wedgwood notes, the conceptual role of any term will be complex in ways that are difficult to map succinctly, and even his summary treatment of 'better' and 'ought' have complexities I won't cover here. But it may aid comprehension to sketch the basic idea with these two terms. Wedgwood (2001) argues that thinking that some course of action is, all things considered, better than another commits one to having a preference for that course of action over the other. So, he thinks a core rule of rationality governing "better" is that one make transitions in thought of the form:

> belief that x is all things considered better than y for me to do → preference for doing x over doing y.

Similarly, Wedgwood (2007: chapter 4) argues that thinking that p ought to be true (in the way characteristic of all things considered deliberative normative thought for oneself) commits one to making the truth of p part of one's ideal plan about what to do. So, that means that he thinks a core rule of rationality governing 'ought' is that one make transitions in thought of the form:

> belief that p ought (all things considered, and relevantly to my practical deliberation) to be true → planning for p to be true.

So far, that sounds like something that could be incorporated into a noncognitivist version of the conceptual role view if we traded out Blackburn's functionalism for a Normativist conception of these transitions. However, Wedgwood clearly intends his view as a version of cognitivism.

In the earlier paper, he proposes to simply "…assume that every moral term has the function of standing for a property or relation," which amounts to assuming "…that cognitivism is correct, and that the meaning of moral terms is straight-forwardly truth-conditional" (2007: 6). In the book (Wedgwood 2007), he spends a chapter arguing against noncognitivist views, including sophisticated expressivist views such as Blackburn (1998) and Gibbard (2003). I don't have space here to present his argument in full, but it turns on the idea that there are preferences and plans that are *correct* in some more "external" sense than being determined by coherence with all of one's other beliefs, preferences, and plans (even when these are improved by further information and more careful reflection). Because of this, he thinks our normative thought and discourse is implicitly committed (in ways an expressivist cannot capture) to there being some property or relation that betterness- and ought-judgments are about. This will be the property or relation making the core set rules governing the use of these terms valid and complete. Insisting that the conceptual roles of predicate terms determine such properties or relations is what he takes to secure his commitment to cognitivism. Moreover, he argues that the availability of this package undermines any advantage noncognitivists might have thought they win from the internal justificatory connection between ethical concepts and action. He writes "…the idea that the meaning of moral terms is given by their role in practical reasoning is fully available to cognitivists, and so lends no support to noncognitivism" (Wedgwood 2001: 18).

Once we're working with a cognitivist conception of conceptual roles, however, there's also a more general reason to think ethical terms add representational content to the sentences in which they figure: If you thought that a term expresses a concept iff it affects the truth conditions of sentences in which it figures, and you had a representationalist conception of truth conditions, then you might think that all semantically contributing terms should be treated representationally. In other words, in order to have a semantic value, a term would have to stand for something (though what it stands for is determined by its conceptual role). This reasoning seems to be in the background of what Wedgwood says regarding the semantics of 'ought': "Within the semantic framework that I am assuming here, the semantic value of the concept '$O<A, t>$' will in effect be a certain property of propositions—presumably, a relational property that propositions have in virtue of some relation in which they stand to the agent A at the time t" (2007: 99).

Because he thinks some ethical statements are true and so successfully represent reality, Wedgwood's view faces the metaphysical challenges of other realist views: Show that the properties represented by ethical words are natural or explain why it's ok in this case (but not in most other cases) to countenance the existence of non-natural properties. Also, the conceptual role he gives for 'ought' treats it as a propositional operator, roughly akin to a necessity operator. Hence, his globalism leads him to view this as representing a property had by propositions. This commits the moral realist going this route not only to properties of goodness and wrongness but also to properties propositions have when they are correctly incorporated into plans. One might reasonably be more skeptical of such "logical" properties of propositions than of more ordinary properties of actions.

THE CONCEPTUAL ROLE VIEW AS A THIRD OPTION

The labels "cognitivism" and "noncognitivism" suggest there is no third way, but the substance of the views (at least as defined above, which I think captures one prominent way these labels are used in metaethics) doesn't rule out a view according to which ethical words contribute *neither* representational content nor emotive/evaluative content to the sentences in which they figure. To see this, notice that a common view taken about terms such as the copula ('is'), articles ('a', 'the'), logical connectives ('not', 'if'), and epistemic operators ('probably') is that they don't stand for things in reality, but neither do they carry emotive/evaluative content. Rather, they do various other jobs in our sentences, such as linking together other words with representational and/or evaluative content and qualifying, situating, or displacing some embedded piece of representational content. The third conceptual role view I discuss here takes inspiration from this model to suggest that the conceptual role of at least some ethical terms is to perform one of these other jobs.

It's not clear how to think of these "other jobs" in general, but one significant distinction is between broadly "logical" and "non-logical" terms. In this vein, with a very broad conception of the "logical," Brandom (2008) argues that we should recognize a distinction between terms directly involved in first-order conceptualization of reality and what to do in it (roughly, what we convey with simple declarative and volitive/imperative sentences) and terms whose job it is to "make explicit" the inferential commitments implicitly carried by first-order thought and discourse. (Compare also Kant [1997: 209], Frege [1879: 13], and Sellars [1958].) On Brandom's way of working out this view, terms in this latter class have a distinctively second-order conceptual role in their job of articulating inference rules. These are not descriptions of how people happen to infer but normative claims about how people ought to infer. As such, this suggests a Normativist version of the conceptual role view (with Wedgwood, against Blackburn). However (against Wedgwood, with Blackburn), it is Localist about representational content: Not all words' conceptual roles determine representational contents. Some words are treated as "meta-conceptual" devices for talking about the inferential connections between other words.

This is most plausible when applied to ethical words that are also operator-like. In Chrisman (2016), I focus on 'ought', which is plausibly construed as functioning semantically as an intensional (and more specifically, *modal*) operator. (Compare Castañeda's [1975] treatment of 'ought' as a practical necessity operator and Sellars' [1958: 282; 1968: chapter 7] suggestion that its content is partly determined by its distinguished role in practical reasoning.) According to the argument I develop, the conceptual role of this word is like other intensional operators, such as 'might' or 'probably', in that its addition to a sentence shifts something about how the sentence puts forward some embedded piece of content. For example, "Paula might be home," is not treated as representing Paula (or anyone else, such as her counterparts in some epistemically accessible possible worlds) as having some property but rather is conceived as a vehicle for putting forward a more basic piece of representational content (Paula is at home) as an epistemically open possibility, roughly something not ruled out by the beliefs held to be commonly agreed upon in an ongoing conversation.

Similarly, then, we might think that "Paula *ought* to be home" does not represent Paula (or anyone else, such as her counterparts in all normatively accessible worlds) as having some property, but rather conceive of this sentence as a vehicle for putting forward a more basic piece of content (Paula is at home) as a normative necessity, roughly something that is, so to speak, *ruled in* by the beliefs and norms/prescriptions held to be commonly agreed upon in an ongoing conversation.

In this way, we get a version of the conceptual role view that treats the conceptual role of some terms as distinctive from representational terms, not in their link to emotive/evaluative content but rather in their metaconceptual function. Because, on this view, the words with metaconceptual function do not add *representational* content to the sentences in which they figure, this view might be classed as a form of antirealism about 'ought', avoiding many ontological worries associated with realist forms of cognitivism. However, because this metaconceptual function is very specific, the hope is that the view will have an easier time than the noncognitivist-inspired conceptual role view discussed above at explaining how these words affect the truth-conditional content of the sentences in which they figure. Moreover, there should be less of a worry about how to cordon off apparently nonsemantic connections between the concepts expressed by these terms and other concepts.

In chapter 5 of Chrisman (2016), I argue that a modification of the standard truth-conditional semantics for modal operators can be developed to predict contents for many of the diverse flavors of ought-sentences we witness in natural language. This semantic account is incomplete, but insofar as it makes plausible predictions in a compositionally tractable way, I think that represents an advance over expressivist views that would assign contents to ought-sentences in some nonstandard way. In my view, developing a plausible rule for predicting truth conditions for arbitrary ought-sentences leaves open the crucial metasemantic issue of what it is in virtue of which these sentences have the truth conditions that they do. I then argue in chapter 6 that a broadly inferentialist account of meaning has resources to explain the conceptual role of 'ought' in a way that grounds its semantic content in neither a word-world representation relation nor a word-mind expression relation. This form of antirealism assimilates 'ought' more with an antirealist view of the meaning of necessity modals than with an antirealist view of the meaning of emotive/evaluative terms.

Where does a view like this stand with respect to both Causal and Normative Internalisms? Regarding the former, there is nothing to prevent someone pursuing this kind of view of the meaning of a term such as 'ought' to argue that there is a causal–functional connection between applications of this words and motivations to act. For my part, I think such a connection is plausible only in a very small percentage of the cases where we use 'ought' (roughly, whenever it's plausibly interpreted as all-things-considered and about the speaker's own future actions), so I think it's implausible to think this is a "core" element of the term's meaning, but there's nothing in the basic contours of the view that rules out developing a specific version of it with this feature. Much more plausible, I think, is some form of the normative internalist thesis. And the Normativist development of a conceptual role view of 'ought' provides ample resources to capture whatever truth there is in that thesis.

In the context of metaethics, there are two important challenges faced by views like this one. First, it is not clear that they can be extended to cover ethical (or normative) terms considered quite generally. The word 'ought' might be one of the core normative terms, but semantically it is an intensional operator, and that's what supports the idea that its conceptual role is metaconceptual. The term 'is wrong', however, is an ordinary predicate. Sure, we sometimes think that what makes such words ethical (or normative) is that they bear directly on what one ought to do, but significant work still needs to be done to show that the Brandom-inspired conceptual role view about 'ought' can be developed into a full metaethical view about the meaning of ethical words (see Chrisman [2016: chapter 7] where this is discussed in more detail). Second, it is not clear what it is in virtue of which the word 'ought' (and other so-called "metaconceptual" words) has the second-order conceptual role that I've suggested that it has. In contrast to Blackburn, a defender of this view cannot locate this in natural facts about how we happen to use these words, as this version of the conceptual role view is Normativist rather than functional-ist; and in contrast to Wedgwood, a defender of this view cannot locate this in the bits of reality that these words stand for, as its localism is designed to avoid commitment to thinking these words stand for things in reality. So, what kind of fact is it that 'ought' has a second-order or "metaconceptual" conceptual role? A full defense of this view requires a convincing answer to this difficult question. It's one that arises when we think meaning is, in some important sense, normative, but are inclined to think "the normative" is not some special realm of reality. What happens when we turn a normativist conceptual role version of antirealism about Normative terms on itself?

CONCLUSION

At the beginning of this essay, I said that it's unclear where conceptual role views about meaning apply amongst metaethical theories about the meaning of ethical terms. I think that's because the basic idea behind conceptual role views can be developed in several interesting ways. In some of Blackburn's work, we see a noncognitivist-inspired form of the view. It's a Functionalist and Localist version of the conceptual role view, explain-ing the meaning of ethical words in terms of the way the concepts they express serve to direct action and, as such, do not have representational content. By contrast, Wedgwood develops a cognitivist-inspired application of the conceptual role view to ethical terms. It appears to be a Normativist and Globalist version of the view, explaining the mean-ing of ethical words in terms of the core set of rules governing the practical reasoning of one deploying the concepts that they express, which he takes to determine the prop-erty that they denote. In my work, I've been inspired by Wedgwood's Normativism and Blackburn's Localism. By drawing on Brandom's idea to distinguish terms with a second-order metaconceptual role from terms with first-order descriptive function in our con-ceptually imbued practices, I think we might develop an explanation of the meaning of at least some core ethical terms that is not obviously cognitivist nor noncognitivist (but antirealist in a more pragmatist sort of way).

Above, I mentioned two further questions any conceptual role account of meaning must answer: Is the primary locus of conceptual role in individuals or linguistic commu-nities? And, are "language-entry" (from world to mind) and "language-exit" (from mind to world) connections included in the conceptual role? I think all of the views I have discussed here are compatible with either answer to both questions.

In the first case, this is because, for all we have said about what conceptual roles might be like, we have said very little about what grounds them or where they come from. Many in the conceptual role tradition stress the way language is a social phenomenon, which inclines those who view conceptual roles as a key to explaining linguistic meaning to favor a more social answer to the first question. However, one could also think that the psychology of individual agents and its biological development takes pride of place in the explanation of the possibility of content; and if one does, it can begin to seem like the sociality of linguistic practice depends on the prior existence of a more solipsistic kind of content. The important point here is that it is a general issue for any conceptual role view and not something that seems to bear specifically on conceptual role views in metaethics.

The second question might seem to have more bearing on metaethics, because many in the conceptual role tradition have thought that the conceptual role of ethical terms must have something to do with action, which is the paradigmatic "language-exit," where our minds, so to speak, touch the world. However, for any "wide" conceptual role view (including language-exit connections as part of conceptual roles), it seems to me that we could imagine an analogous "narrow" conceptual role view that stops the connection at the point of an intention or volition. So, again, this seems to be an issue that cuts across various developments of the conceptual role view in metaethics.

NOTES

1. Of course, one could simply define *noncognitivism* as the denial of cognitivism, in which case conceptual role views would have to fall on one side or the other. However, that way of conceiving of noncognitivism doesn't fit well with antirepresentationalist views witnessed in areas other than ethics. Some philosophers think, for example, that epistemic modals, probability operators, the truth predicate, etc. are not devices of representation. However, it's weird to refer to them as noncognitivists about these things, as they would insist that thought involving the relevant concepts is part of cognition rather than affect, and they generally think it can constitute knowledge.
2. This is related to a broader issue in the philosophy of language about holism vs. atomism about meanings. Predictably, no one in favor of a conceptual role view is an atomist, in the sense of holding that a word/concept has content all on its own, as something that then gets added atomistically to form the compound contents of phrases and sentences. However, there are differing opinions about whether it is possible to draw some non-arbitrary line between the connections language users tend or ought to track that are part of specifically semantic competence with words and those that are part of wider understanding of the world. If, following Quine, one thinks there is no sharp line between analytic and synthetic truths, then one will think it difficult to draw a sharp line between the "conceptual connections" and the "substantive" connections between various propositions. However, most conceptual role theorists will be happy to recognize that some connections are more central to a term's meaning than others.
3. See also Köhler (2014, forthcoming) for someone who endorses a view like this one. Gibbard (2003) develops a sophisticated and noncognitivism-friendly account of the contents of the mental states expressed by normative sentences. He suggests that this account, which construes all normative thought as "plan-laden," is consistent with a naturalistic account of the role normative thoughts play in our mental economies (especially in their connection to action). (See especially pp. 154 and 195.) If we take these plan-laden thoughts (and the sentences expressing them) to have those contents in virtue of playing the relevant role in guiding action, then I think we get another version of the functionalist kind of conceptual role view sketched above. It's somewhat more restrictive about the role played by normative thought than I think Blackburn wants to be, but it still would explain meaning in terms of functional role. However, Gibbard also suggests there that his view of the contents of the mental states expressed by normative sentences is consistent with the view that meaning is normative, which in his scheme would mean that the thoughts expressed by normative sentences cannot be identified in purely naturalistic terms. (This idea is

explored in much more detail in Gibbard [2012].) Going this way would constitute a departure from the functionalist kind of conceptual role view sketched above.

ACKNOWLEDGMENTS

For helpful feedback on this chapter, I'd like to thank Max Barkhausen, Samuel Dishaw, James Fritz, Sebastian Köhler, Michael Ridge, Silvan Wittwer, and the editors of this handbook.

RELATED TOPICS

Chapter 5, "Metaethical Expressivism;" Chapter 12, "Deontic Modals;" Chapter 18, "Cognitivism and Non-Cognitivism;" Chapter 33, "Metasemantics and Metaethics;" Chapter 37, "Pragmatism and Metaethics;" Chapter 40, "Quasi-realism."

REFERENCES

Båve, A. (2013) "Compositional Semantics for Expressivists," *The Philosophical Quarterly* 63 (253): 633–59.
Bennett, J. (1976) *Linguistic Behaviour*, Cambridge: Cambridge University Press.
Blackburn, S. (1993) *Essays in Quasi-Realism*, New York: Oxford University Press.
—. (1998) *Ruling Passions: A Theory of Practical Reasoning*, New York: Oxford University Press.
—. (2006) "The Semantics of Non-Factualism," in *The Blackwell Guide to the Philosophy of Language*, Devitt, M. and Hanley, R. (eds.), Oxford: Blackwell, pp. 244–52.
Block, N. (1986) "Advertisement for a Semantics for Psychology," *Midwest Studies in Philosophy* 10: 615–78.
Brandom, R. (2008) *Between Saying and Doing*, Oxford; New York: Oxford University Press.
Castañeda, H-N. (1975) *Thinking and Doing: The Philosophical Foundations of Institutions*, Berlin: Springer.
Chrisman, M. (2016) *The Meaning of 'Ought': Beyond Descriptivism and Expressivism in Metaethics*, New York: Oxford University Press.
Field, H. (1977) "Logic, Meaning and Conceptual Role," *Journal of Philosophy* 69: 379–409.
Frege, G. (1879) *Begriffsschrift, eine der arithmetischen nachgebildete Formelsprache des reinen Denkens*, Halle a/S.: L. Nebert.
Gibbard, A. (2003) *Thinking How to Live*, Cambridge, MA: Harvard University Press.
—. (2012) *Meaning and Normativity*, Oxford: Oxford University Press.
Harman, G. (1999) *Reasoning, Meaning and Mind*, Oxford: Oxford University Press.
Kant, I. (1997) *Kritik der reinen Vernunft*, Guyer, P. and Wood, A. (trans./eds.), Cambridge: Cambridge University Press.
Köhler, S. (2014) *Beyond Frege-Geach — Neglected Challenges for Expressivism*, Ph.D. Thesis, University of Edinburgh.
—. (forthcoming) "Expressivism, Belief, and All That," *Journal of Philosophy*.
Kripke, S. (1982) *Wittgenstein on Rules and Private Language: An Elementary Exposition*, Cambridge, MA: Harvard University Press.
Peacocke, C. (1987) "Understanding Logical Constants: A Realist's Account," *Proceedings of the British Academy* 73: 153–99.
—. (1995) *A Study of Concepts*, Cambridge, MA: MIT Press.
Price, H. (2011) "Expressivism for Two Voices," in *Pragmatism, Science and Naturalism*, Knowles, J., and Rydenfelt, H. (eds.), Frankfurt am Main: Peter Lang, pp. 87–113.
Sellars, W. (1958) "Counterfactuals, Dispositions, and the Causal Modalities," in *Minnesota Studies in the Philosophy of Science, Volume II*, Feigl, H., Scriven, M., and Maxwell, G. (eds.), Minneapolis: University of Minnesota Press, pp. 225–308.

—. (1968) *Science and Metaphysics: Variations on Kantian Themes*, London: Routledge and Kegan Paul.

Warren, M. (2015) "Inferentialism and the Frege Geach Problem," *Philosophical Studies* 172 (11): 2859–85.

Wedgwood, R. (2001) "Conceptual Role Semantics for Moral Terms," *Philosophical Review* 110 (1): 1–30.

—. (2007) *The Nature of Normativity*, Oxford; New York: Oxford University Press.

Whiting, D. (2006) "Conceptual Role Semantics," *Internet Encyclopedia of Philosophy*. http://www.iep. utm.edu/.

Yalcin, S. (2007) "Epistemic Modals," *Mind* 116 (464): 983–1026.

—. (2011) "Nonfactualism about Epistemic Modality," in *Epistemic Modality*, Egan, A. and Weatherson, B. (eds.), New York: Oxford University Press: 295–332.

17

The Significance of Ethical Disagreement for Theories of Ethical Thought and Talk

Gunnar Björnsson

This chapter has two sections, each focusing on a distinct way in which ethical disagreement and variations in ethical judgment matter for theories of ethical thought and talk. In the first section, we look at how the variation poses problems for both cognitivist and non-cognitivist ways of specifying the nature of ethical judgments. In the second, we look at how disagreement phenomena have been taken to undermine cognitivist accounts, but also at how the seeming variation in cognitive and non-cognitive contents between parties of deep ethical disagreement challenge both cognitivist and non-cognitivist accounts of disagreement itself.

SPECIFICATION PROBLEMS

Ethical judgments come in a wide variety. We make not only judgments about what to do or feel, but also about moral obligation, wrongness, permissibility, justice, blameworthiness, and virtue. Almost all analyses of some specific kind of ethical judgment fall into three broad categories, specifying what it is for a state to be *of that particular kind* based either on (i) its cognitive content, (ii) some non-cognitive attitude, or (iii) some combination of both (see Matthew S. Bedke's chapter "Cognitivism and Non-Cognitivism" and Elisabeth Camp's chapter "Metaethical Expressivism"). But such specifications have proven elusive, as ethical judgments of a given kind vary both with respect to features closely associated with cognitive content and with respect to accompanying non-cognitive attitudes. In this section, we look first at the specification problem for analyses in terms of judge-invariant cognitive contents, before turning to the corresponding problem for analyses appealing to non-cognitive attitudes.

The invariantist cognitivist's specification problem

A simple cognitivist analysis of ethical judgments of a given kind (e.g., judgments that an action is morally wrong) identifies them with judgments about whether something has a certain moral property (e.g., the property of moral wrongness). But ethical relativists have thought that at least in cases of deep and systematic ethical disagreement, the parties are concerned with different properties (different properties of moral wrongness, say), making judgments with different cognitive contents. If relativists are right, there is a certain sense in which ethics is *subjective* rather than *objective*: a judgment's cognitive content might vary between judges. In what follows, I will first specify the relevant idea of invariant cognitive content, before explaining how invariantist analyses are threatened by deep ethical disagreement.

Sometimes the relevant notions of invariant and variant cognitive contents are understood in terms of *truth-values*: the contents are invariant if and only if the judgment is true or false independently of who made it, otherwise variant. However, on some minimalist, expressivist, or relativist views about truth, this will fail to draw the relevant kind of distinction. On such views, to say that a judgment is true might merely reflect one's agreement with it, or the sense that it satisfies one's own fundamental standard of acceptance for such judgments. Correspondingly, the claim that the truth-values of a class of judgments are judge-independent might not reflect the assumption that people are concerned with the same aspect of reality. It might instead reflect a policy of holding these judgments to the same fundamental standards independently of whose judgments they are, a policy that might be in place in order to lead to coordination of attitudes (e.g., Blackburn 1993; 1998; Ridge 2014, chapter 7; Björnsson 2015).

To avoid this complication, the invariance of cognitive content at stake is better characterized in terms of relations between what different judges *are trying to get right* when making their judgments, and conditions under which they *succeed* in their judgmental endeavor. The key idea is that judgments about the same judge-independent matter have the same *success conditions*, independently of who is making the judgment. Suppose that Arith and Metic each tries to determine the product of 936 and 724. If they make the same judgment, it follows that if Arith's effort was successful, so was Metic's, and that if Arith's effort was a failure, so was Metic's. For contrast, consider judgments of personal taste. Suppose that both Gus and Tibus feel peckish, and that each tries to determine whether there is something tasty in the vending machine. What each is trying to get right, we can plausibly assume, is whether there is something in the machine that accords with *his* taste. Then, even if they both judge that there is something tasty in the machine, one of them might have made a successful judgment while the other has not, and if they judge differently, they might nevertheless both have been successful; they might simply have different taste preferences.

In line with this, I will understand invariantism about the cognitive content of a kind of judgment as follows:

COGNITIVE INVARIANTISM: For any two judges A and B, if both A and B judge that X is F, or both judge that X is not F, then if one is (un)successful in her judgmental endeavors, so is the other.

(Correspondingly, *variantism* says that success conditions vary between judges.) Importantly, we can see that both Gus and Tibus have judged successfully even if we do not agree with both their judgments, and thus do not want to say that both judgments are true. Attributions of judgmental success might thus come apart from agreement and attributions of truth (Björnsson 2015).

Arguably, COGNITIVE INVARIANTISM about ethical judgment—henceforth, just "invariantism"—captures views that have been assumed or defended by a variety of historical figures, including Plato, Hume, and Kant, as well as by most contemporary self-described moral realists. Invariantism can also be endorsed by some philosophers who take moral judgments to be commitments to act or feel rather than ordinary beliefs, but who think that the formation of such judgments involves commitments to satisfy strong judge-invariant constraints (see, e.g., Hare 1981; cf. Korsgaard 1996).

Notice that invariantism is only indirectly connected to the semantics of the *language* used to express ethical judgments. First, invariantism might be true even if ethical discourse employs context-dependent expressions. For example, consider the fact that terms like "ought," "should," "right," "wrong," and "good" seem to be context dependent. To say that something is wrong seems to be to say that it violates some relevant norm, but which norm varies from context to context: it might be a moral norm, a norm of etiquette, some professional procedural norm, or some grammatical rule, among others. (For recent extended defenses of metaethical contextualism, see, e.g., Wedgwood 2007; Finlay 2014; see Alex Silk's chapter "Metaethical Contextualism.") But such context dependence, or a corresponding context dependence in thought, does not rule out that when people judge that something is *morally* wrong, they always relate to the same norm (i.e., the same univocal moral norm), thereby making judgments with the same success conditions.

Second, invariantism might fail even if judgments are expressed using terms with invariant descriptive contents. Suppose, for example, that "immoral" has invariant content in English. It might still be that the corresponding terms in other languages—the terms naturally translated to "immoral" in English—have other referents. For, as many have suggested, translation need not go by referential content, as opposed to, say, role in practical deliberation (e.g., Hare 1952, chapter 9; Wong 1984: 73; Blackburn 1991: 5–9; Copp 2000; Björnsson and McPherson 2014). If so, invariantism might fail *across* linguistic communities for kinds of judgments that are naturally described as judgments about what is immoral. What judges in the other communities are trying to get right when making such judgments is whether something has the property referred to by *their* term.

If invariantism is true for a given kind of ethical judgment, we could provide an elegant (though perhaps partial) characterization of such judgments by pointing to their success conditions. But invariantism about any widely instantiated kind of ethical judgment seems to be a highly ambitious contingent claim: it says that *all* judgments of that kind have identical success conditions. As such, it is in need of substantial support.

The need for such support is especially pressing in light of deep and seemingly intractable ethical disagreement. As is generally recognized, the problem is not that intractable disagreement is incompatible with invariantism, as it might be due to the complex and difficult nature of a topic, combined with motivated reasoning (e.g., Brink 1989; Shafer-Landau 2003; Huemer 2005). What puts invariantism in question, rather, is that some ethical disagreements seem to be grounded in different fundamental conceptions of the subject matter as well as in responsiveness to systematically different features of reality (see, e.g., Westermarck 1932; Wong 1984; Gibbard 1990; Wong 2006; Prinz 2007). For example, take disagreements about our obligations to people in need, such as the poor or sick in our own community, or refugees seeking asylum from war. Some of these disagreements might be grounded in disagreements about non-moral matters, perhaps concerning positive or negative effects of help on those who give or receive it. But other disagreements are more fundamentally moral, being grounded in different conceptions of what is owed to others *given* that helping has certain effects. These disagreements might seem to involve primitive or fundamental differences concerning what ultimately grounds obligations: hypothetical contractual agreements, certain methods of moral thinking, enlightened self-interest, or certain sets of values, rights, reasons, or norms, say. Given that we often take fundamental conceptions as (defeasible) guides to what people have in mind, this variation seems to provide (defeasible) evidence that the parties are making judgments with different success conditions. Unless there is significant evidence for invariantism, variantism seems the better bet.

What sort of positive evidence might there be? The most popular argument for invariantism points to features of ethical discourse and thinking that are characteristically instantiated by paradigmatically invariant domains but, at best, partially instantiated in paradigmatically variant domains. For example, in asking ethical questions, we are typically not satisfied with answers *explicitly relativized* to different judges or ethical systems. We also typically take even judges with radically different moral views to be in *disagreement*, rather than merely seeing things from different perspectives. Non-cognitivists and relativists have proposed explanations of these phenomena. In the next section, we will look specifically at attempts at variantist-friendly explanations of disagreement, and we have already mentioned the possibility of pragmatically motivated policies of holding ethical judgments to the same judge-independent standard: such policies might explain why relativized answers to ethical questions are unsatisfactory. But many invariantists have found assumptions required for these explanations *ad hoc*. They have therefore endorsed something like the following argument (see, e.g., Brink 1989, chapter 2; Smith 1994; Shafer-Landau 2003, chapters 2–3; Streiffer 2003, chapter 1; Huemer 2005, chapters 2–3; Enoch 2011, chapter 2):

THE STRAIGHTFORWARD ARGUMENT:

(i) Ethical discourse and thinking display features characteristic of paradigmatically invariantist domains.

(ii) Invariantism can explain or make sense of these "invariantist" features in whatever way they are explained in paradigmatically invariantist domains, thus requiring no *ad hoc* assumptions.

(iii) Non-invariantist (variantist or non-cognitivist) explanations of "invariantist" features require *ad hoc* assumptions.

(iv) Invariantism thus offers the more straightforward way of explaining or making sense of these features.

Though popular, THE STRAIGHTFORWARD ARGUMENT seems to have limited force (Björnsson 2012; cf. Tersman 2006, chapter 5; Loeb 2007). Obviously, premise (iii) is undermined if there is good independent motivation for non-invariantist explanations (as many non-invariantists think). Moreover, premise (i) might be at odds with studies suggesting that people often reject the idea that at least one of the judgments constituting moral disagreement must be incorrect (Sarkissian et al. 2011; Beebe 2014; Khoo and Knobe 2016).

Less obviously, but of significant dialectical importance, premise (ii) would seem to be undermined if we lack independent positive evidence for invariantism. If displays of "invariantist" features in ethical thought and talk have not been responsive to such evidence, some special story would be needed about how invariantism explains or makes sense of these features. We cannot merely assume that it would be more straightforward than the non-invariantist alternatives. Moreover, if we could make plausible that the features have been responsive to independent positive evidence, it is unclear how much further support is added by THE STRAIGHTFORWARD ARGUMENT.

So what other sources of evidence might there be for invariantism? The striking variation in conceptions most saliently involves certain substantial natural (psychological, sociological, physical) or supernatural properties that judges take to determine whether something has a certain ethical property. This leaves open the possibility that there is agreement at some other, more fundamental, level. G. E. Moore (1903) famously thought so. On the one hand, he claimed that

OPEN QUESTION: Any description of an object in naturalistic or supernaturalistic terms leaves open and intelligible the question whether something satisfying that description has a given ethical property.

Given this, no exhaustive naturalistic or supernaturalistic conception of ethical properties is necessary for making the relevant ethical judgments. (For discussion of Moore's "open question argument," see Nicholas Laskowski and Stephen Finlay's chapter "Conceptual Analysis in Metaethics.") On the other hand, Moore thought that judges have a *non-naturalistic* or *irreducibly normative* conception of ethical properties (Moore 1903, chapter 1; cf. Shafer-Landau 2003; Huemer 2005; Parfit 2005: 330–32). Perhaps *that* conception could ground invariantism.

Before assessing that possibility, consider a different way in which invariantism might be true in spite of deep ethical disagreement. Moore took open question to show that ethical properties cannot be natural or supernatural properties because he assumed that a judge's conception of a referent reveals its nature. However, many have rejected that assumption (e.g., Putnam 1975; Burge 1979; Kripke 1980; Millikan 1984; Boyd 1988; Railton 1989; Smith 1994; Jackson 1998; Millikan 2000). Without it, open question does not rule out that parties of deep ethical disagreement have the same non-relative natural (or supernatural) property in mind when judging whether an action is obligatory.

There are various ways in which this might be true. One possibility is that judges always have some *procedural* conception of ethical properties in mind. For example, perhaps all judges are committed to correctly applying principles that would be identified in a process of reflective equilibrium, given access to the relevant non-normative facts (cf. Jackson 1998: 131–35; Brink 2001; Merli 2002; Schroeter and Schroeter 2009: 11–15). Another is that in judging whether something is, say, morally wrong, one is necessarily concerned with whether it belongs to the *same kind as paradigmatic instances of moral wrongness*, or has the same ethical property as these instances, whatever that property is. Yet another is that in judging whether something is morally wrong, one intends to be concerned with whatever others making wrongness judgments are best understood as concerned with. That intention could help ensure *de jure* that success conditions are coordinated (Schroeter and Schroeter 2009). On each of these possibilities, the conceptions guaranteeing sameness of reference—the *reference fixing* conceptions—leave open the fundamental nature of the property in question, thus leaving room for deep substantial disagreements.

Yet another possibility is that invariantism is guaranteed by factors at least partly external to judges' conceptions of the property in question (cf. the discussion of internalist and externalist metasemantic theories in Laura Schroeter and François Schroeter's chapter "Metasemantics and Metaethics"). One version of this externalist possibility is that success conditions of judgments are determined by the etiological function of the concepts involved: A judgment that X is (not) F is successful if and only if X has (lacks) the property such that prior successful tracking of that property explains why we make judgments about what is and is not F and why they play the role they play in our psychology (e.g., Millikan 1984; 2000). Even if judges themselves have no exhaustive conception of what it is for something to be F (to be water, say), the ability to make such judgments might itself have a determinate enough function to provide an account of judgmental success. Along these lines, Richard Boyd (1988; 2003) famously suggested that the term "good" (when used in moral contexts) is best seen as referring to the property of being conducive to human flourishing. Another possibility is that success conditions for moral judgments are determined by what judges commit themselves to in virtue of the practical role of these judgments. This proposal starts with the assumption that moral judgments involve various action-directed attitudes (preferences, decisions), and adds that rational agents are committed to certain constraints on such attitudes: constraints of universality, equal concern, coherence, or self-determination, say. These constraints, it is then argued, provide exhaustive success conditions for our moral judgments (see, e.g., Smith 1994; Korsgaard 1996; Wedgwood 2007; Korsgaard 2009).

All of these suggestions indicate how invariantism *might* be true in spite of deep ethical disagreement. But it is another matter to make plausible that it is, in fact, true. To do so, it is not enough to make plausible that success conditions for kinds of ethical judgment obey some universal constraints. The constraints have to be *exhaustive*. If they merely provide *some* necessary or sufficient condition for judgmental success, individual judgments might involve further necessary or sufficient conditions, and so still differ in success conditions. Because of this, evidence for invariantism often seems elusive:

Non-naturalistic conceptions: Suppose that judging whether something is morally wrong presupposes that one understands the ethical property in question as a non-natural property. Even so, it is unclear why we should assume that disagreeing parties have *the same* non-natural property in mind. When judges have very different conceptions of what natural properties make an act wrong, this assumption seems particularly problematic (see, e.g., Björnsson 2012: 386–87; cf. Eklund 2012).

Procedural conceptions: Suppose that judgments of justice aim at verdicts that are in line with the upshots of a process of reflective equilibrium. Even so, judges might understand such a process in different ways, admitting different inputs or prescribing different kinds of revision, thus yielding different views of justice. Given variations in what parties of deep moral disagreement take as evidence or as admissible forms of argument, it is unclear why we should assume that they operate with the same exhaustive procedural conceptions.

Rational practicality constraints: Suppose that kinds of ethical judgment involve specific action-directed attitudes. Even so, few have been convinced that there are rich enough judge-invariant constraints on the relevant attitudes to exhaustively account for what we are trying to get right when making moral judgments (see, e.g., Enoch 2006).

Sameness of kind: Suppose that all judgments of moral wrongness aim to determine whether the object in question is of the same kind as paradigm cases of moral wrongness. Even so, the idea that something is *of the same kind* as something else is itself unclear—things can be alike and different along many different dimensions—and judges might have different kinds of sameness in mind. An etiological account of reference like Boyd's might avoid this problem as it relies on external tracking relations rather than judges' conceptions of sameness in kind. But Boyd himself takes seriously the possibility that "good" tracks different and incompatible modes of human flourishing, thus leaving room for a certain kind of relativism (cf. Wong 1984), and other attempts to apply related accounts of reference to ethical judgments have suggested that properties tracked will vary between judges (Gibbard 1990, chapter 6).

Sameness de jure: Suppose that judges intend to be concerned with whatever others are concerned with when judging whether something has a certain property. Even so, this intention might not be best understood as fixing reference to a judge-invariant property (Björnsson 2012: 387–89). It would seem to leave open whether what others are concerned to get right is itself invariantist (as in the case of arithmetic) or variantist (as in the case of tastiness), or perhaps non-cognitivist (as when we try to jointly decide what to do).

Because of difficulties like these, the jury is still out on whether some form of invariantism is both compatible with and supported by the evidence. To my mind, we currently have little positive reason to think that central kinds of ethical judgment have some specific set of judge-invariant exhaustive success conditions. As a consequence, we also have reason to reject THE STRAIGHTFORWARD ARGUMENT: in the absence of readily available evidence for invariantism, there is no straightforward invariantist explanation of "invariantist" features of ethical talk and thought. Defenders of invariantism cannot just assume that explanations from other domains carry over to ethical judgments.

The non-cognitivist's and cognitive variantist's specification problem

Suppose that what unifies ethical judgments of a certain kind and distinguishes them from other kinds is not some invariant cognitive content. How, then, should the different kinds of judgment be specified? Here, the best-known proposals appeal to non-cognitive attitudes such as desires or preferences. On typical non-cognitivist views, ethical judgments are identified with such states: to think that it would be good that something happens is to desire or prefer that it be the case, say (see Matthew S. Bedke's chapter "Cognitivism and Non-Cognitivism"). On a typical cognitive variantist view, it is instead to think that it has a certain property, P, where P is the property the judge prefers that events have (Dreier 1990).

Though both non-cognitivist and cognitive variantist strategies avoid the invariantist's specification problem, they face a related two-pronged challenge. First, there are many kinds of ethical judgment, each requiring its own specification. Second, not any non-cognitive attitude can constitute the judgment or fix the property that a given judgment concerns: a sports fan upset with a team's tactical choice or a critic finding aesthetic fault with a performance does not thereby think that it is morally wrong.

To distinguish among kinds of ethical judgment, further specifications of the relevant non-cognitive attitudes are needed. For the case of moral wrongness judgments, some have suggested that they involve specific commitments to moral blame (indignation, guilt) (Gibbard 1990). Others have suggested that such judgments involve the idea that sanctions of some kind (punishment, public opinion, conscience) ought to be in place (Mill 1863: 71), and some have proposed that these judgments have a special etiology, being characteristically based on certain kinds of emotionally engaged processes (Kauppinen 2010). The problem is that such proposals seem to either over- or underdiscriminate. Surely one might think that there ought to be sanctions against actions of a certain kind without thinking that these actions are morally wrong, or think that an action is wrong without having engaged in the sentimentalist processes characteristic of human beings, or without being committed to having certain reactive attitudes (Miller 2003; Merli 2008; Björnsson and McPherson 2014)? More radically, motivational externalists deny that any non-cognitive attitude is required (e.g., Svavarsdóttir 1999).

Much as it is unclear what *cognitive content* might be in common between all people making judgments of moral wrongness, it is thus unclear whether they involve some common *non-cognitive attitude* capable of constituting the judgment or fixing the property it concerns. In response to this variation, one strategy has been to embrace a form of variantism about the relevant non-cognitive attitude. On this view, attributions of ethical judgments are inherently flexible because flexibility is required for normal moral judgments to serve their practical function, namely to coordinate attitudes. This purpose, the suggestion goes, is best served if we engage people who make judgments sufficiently similar to the normal cases (Blackburn 1991: 5–9; Björnsson and McPherson 2014). A potential problem for this sort of proposal, apart from capturing just the right amount of flexibility, is that it seems difficult to explain ethical disagreement between parties whose judgments involve neither a shared cognitive content nor a shared non-cognitive attitude (Sturgeon 1991: 25–27; for a response, see Björnsson and McPherson 2014). To assess that worry, we need to understand the nature of disagreement and attributions of disagreement.

DISAGREEMENT PROBLEMS

In the previous section, we saw how variations within specific kinds of ethical judgment create difficulties for both cognitivist and non-cognitivist analyses. In this section, we look at how attributions of disagreement raise problems for variantist cognitivism, before considering non-cognitivist and other non-orthodox attempts to understand ethical disagreement.

Arguments against variantist cognitivism

At least at first glance, it might seem that,

IMPLIED CONTRADICTION: If A says, "X is wrong," and B says, "X is not wrong," B has contradicted A.

Claims like IMPLIED CONTRADICTION have been taken to undermine accounts according to which the referent or satisfaction conditions of "wrong" might vary between utterances (see, e.g., Moore 1912: 100–01; cf. Hare 1952: 148–50; Smith 1994: 32–35). For example, the proposal that "wrong" just means *in violation of S*, where S is whatever standard the speaker endorses, fails to guarantee that B has contradicted A: if A and B endorse different standards, X might violate A's standard but not B's, rendering both claims correct. Given IMPLIED CONTRADICTION, our simple analysis of "wrong" thus seems mistaken. Moreover, since IMPLIED CONTRADICTION seems equally plausible when "permissible," "right," "good," and other ethical terms are substituted for "wrong," similar arguments can be raised against variantist analyses of these.

A qualification is in place. The term "wrong" can be used to convey thoughts not only about moral wrongness, but also about inappropriateness relative to various non-moral goals, aesthetic standards, and so forth. Focusing on *moral* wrongness specifically, it is furthermore common to distinguish between *prima facie* and *all things considered* moral wrongness, as well as between *subjective* wrongness (relative to the agent's evidence) and *objective* wrongness (relative to all non-moral facts). IMPLIED CONTRADICTION is implausible if A is concerned with moral wrongness and B with aesthetic wrongness, or if A and B are concerned with different kinds of moral wrongness. Though such complications are rarely discussed in relation to disagreement arguments of this sort, the arguments make best sense if we take the utterances to concern the same kind of wrongness, such as all things considered subjective moral wrongness.

Similar arguments against variantist cognitivism have been proposed in terms of *disagreement in judgment* rather than *contradiction*. The following seems as reasonable as IMPLIED CONTRADICTION (assuming the qualification just introduced):

IMPLIED DISAGREEMENT: If A judges that X is wrong and B that X is not wrong, they disagree.

However, on analyses of "wrong" given which A's and B's judgments might have compatible success conditions, IMPLIED DISAGREEMENT cannot be explained merely in terms of the cognitive content of the two judgments (see, e.g., Moore 1912: 100–101 (on "difference in opinion"); Gibbard 1990, chapter 1; Horgan and Timmons 1991; Smith 1994: 32–35).

For those operating with an orthodox cognitivist understanding of disagreement, IMPLIED DISAGREEMENT has seemed not only to undermine variantist cognitivism, but also to straightforwardly support invariantism. Consider:

ORTHODOX DISAGREEMENT: For two judges to disagree is for them to make judgments with incompatible success conditions.

To ensure orthodox disagreement between any two judges A and B, the judgment that X is wrong and the judgment that X is not wrong must have incompatible success conditions *independently of whose judgments they are*. But non-cognitivists have argued that no plausible cognitivist account of the meaning of "wrong" guarantees that success conditions for wrongness judgments are judge-independent. Given this and given IMPLIED DISAGREEMENT, it instead seems that ORTHODOX DISAGREEMENT must be false: disagreement must be explained in some other way (Stevenson 1937). (A tempting alternative formulation of the orthodox account is in terms of incompatible truth- or correctness conditions. As already noted, however, studies indicate that people confidently attribute disagreements without confidently thinking that one judgment must be incorrect. See, e.g., Sarkissian et al. 2011; Beebe 2014; Khoo 2015; Khoo and Knobe 2016.)

Recently, arguments from disagreement have most famously been invoked against causal-regulatory forms of cognitivism of the sort advocated by Richard Boyd (see, e.g., Blackburn 1991; Horgan and Timmons 1991; Smith 1994). In Horgan and Timmons' version, we are faced with two groups of judges: people on Earth and people on "Moral Twin Earth." The normative vocabularies of the two people play similar practical roles. Here on Earth, considerations about what is "wrong," "right," "good," and so forth guide action and motivation; Moral Twin Earthlings have terms playing the corresponding practical roles. However, since the terms of the two groups are relevantly causally regulated by different properties, they have different referents according to Boyd's theory. Against this background, Horgan and Timmons claim that if disagreement arises between the groups, the parties are best understood as disagreeing "in moral belief and normative moral theory, rather than ... in meaning" (1991: 460). From this they conclude that Boyd's cognitivism is mistaken.

Notably, Horgan and Timmons do not presuppose that both parties make judgments of wrongness, rightness, value, and so forth, and so do not appeal directly to claims like IMPLIED DISAGREEMENT. Instead, they take the features of the case—in particular, the fact that the terms in question play the same practical role as our terms—to make it plausible that judges in the two communities disagree in moral judgment. From that intermediate conclusion, however, the argument follows the model of arguments from IMPLIED DISAGREEMENT: since the target cognitivist account suggests that the parties make judgments with compatible success conditions, it leaves us with no explanation of why these judgments constitute disagreement. Moreover, given that intuitions of disagreement are grounded in the practical role of the terms involved, the case might seem to suggest that these terms should be understood along non-cognitivist lines.

Some critics of the Moral Twin Earth argument have objected that intuitions about such cases are unreliable guides to the nature of the judgments or claims involved because of the highly theoretical content of these intuitions and the unusual nature of the cases in question (see, especially, Dowell forthcoming). This criticism might have less force against disagreement arguments building on more familiar cases than that of Moral Twin Earth, but raises important questions about the methodology of semantic analysis.

Others have argued that disagreements of the sort figuring in Horgan and Timmons' scenario have little bearing on the content of the terms involved. Most commonly, the suggestion has been that the cognitivist can follow non-cognitivists in taking the disagreement at hand to be grounded in the practical role played by the terms, while nevertheless denying that this practical role is part of their content, strictly speaking (Sayre-McCord 1997; Copp 2000; Merli 2002; Björnsson and Finlay 2010; Plunkett and Sundell 2013; Finlay 2014, chapter 6).

Some of these replies have appealed to specific mechanisms of conversational pragmatics, arguing that disputes in ordinary language are often best understood as practically motivated attempts to impose a certain normative perspective (Björnsson and Finlay 2010) or as expressions of metalinguistic disagreement about how the terms involved should be used in certain contexts where this use has practical implications (Plunkett and Sundell 2013). If proponents are right that the pragmatic mechanisms in question play prominent roles outside of ethics, we have independent reason to resist inferring that some predicate "F" has context-invariant content from the fact that one party's assertion,

"X is not F," seem to contradict another's assertion, "X is F," or from the fact that the parties seem to disagree. More has to be said to ground that inference.

It is less clear that these pragmatic proposals are enough to explain the seeming plausibility of IMPLIED CONTRADICTION or IMPLIED DISAGREEMENT, understood as perfectly general claims. Unless whatever it is that grounds contradiction and disagreement *necessarily* accompanies the utterances or judgments involved, contradiction and disagreement are not guaranteed. But it is unclear how non-cognitive attitudes or metalinguistic views can be such necessary companions if utterances and judgments are understood purely in terms of their cognitive content.

To better understand whether and how non-invariantist accounts of moral language or moral judgments can make sense of IMPLIED CONTRADICTION and IMPLIED DISAGREEMENT, we would be helped by a more general understanding of what might ground contradiction and disagreement if orthodox cognitivist views fail to account for all cases. Such an understanding would also help us determine whether these two claims have perfectly general scope, or whether their intuitive appeal can be explained in terms of factors that only typically accompany the utterances or judgments in question.

Non-orthodox accounts of disagreement and contradiction

Suppose that invariantism is false or that, as our discussion in the first section suggested, we lack clear evidence for it. Then, unless the intuitive appeal of claims like IMPLIED DISAGREEMENT is mistaken or epistemically irresponsible, our understanding of these claims seems to operate with a non-orthodox notion of disagreement.

The best-known non-orthodox proposal understands ethical disagreement in terms of conflicts in non-cognitive attitudes:

CONFLICTING ATTITUDES: A and B disagree if A is in favor of p and B is in favor of q, where p and q cannot be simultaneously realized (see, e.g., Stevenson 1963: 2).

The account is structurally similar to ORTHODOX DISAGREEMENT, providing a tempting explanation of why both kinds of relations would be understood as *disagreement*. It also seems to straightforwardly capture central cases of ethical disagreement: characteristically, someone judging that an action morally ought to be done is in favor of doing it, and someone judging that it morally ought not to be done is in favor of not doing it. Moreover, though originating in a non-cognitivist tradition, CONFLICTING ATTITUDES might be employed by accounts that deny that non-cognitive attitudes are *semantically* implicated in moral judgments and moral claims.

Appealing as it is, however, CONFLICTING ATTITUDES is too weak, as illustrated by cases like (cf. Ridge 2013: 46–47):

Mere Clash: A wants C to sell an apartment to A and B wants C to sell that apartment to B. Though both A and B might be disappointed if C decides to sell to the other, neither would have any objection to such a decision, nor be opposed to it in any other way.

Here it is clear that A's and B's attitudes conflict, but unclear whether they disagree about anything.

The standard way of strengthening CONFLICTING ATTITUDES is to add an element of *opposition* between the parties, spelled out in terms of higher-order attitudes, as when

C. L. Stevenson requires that neither party be "content" to let the other's first-order attitude be unchanged (Stevenson 1937: 27; cf. Blackburn 1998: 14, 69). However, this proposal threatens to be either too weak or too strong. On one reading, to say that the parties are not content with the other's attitude is to say that they prefer that the other has a different attitude. But this is plausibly already part of *Mere Clash*, and still seems insufficient for disagreement. On another reading, inspired by Stevenson's illustrations of his proposal, disagreement requires active effort to change the other's mind, or perhaps willingness to engage in such efforts (see, e.g., Schafer 2012). This would make it harder to deny that there is disagreement, but this requirement seems too strong. Though willingness or effort to change the other's mind might be necessary conditions for the *activity* of disagreement, two people can disagree *in judgment* without having any active interest in changing the other's mind. (A similar problem faces Gibbard's (2003, chapter 14) suggestion that disagreement is partly a matter of choice.)

Even without amendment, CONFLICTING ATTITUDES also seems too strong to capture all cases of ethical disagreement. One problem is that of "amoralists": people whose attitudes are not aligned with their moral judgments. Motivational externalists insist that such people are possible, and many motivational internalists accept that misalignment is possible under abnormal conditions (see David Faraci and Tristram McPherson's chapter "Ethical Judgment and Motivation"). If moral judgments can be made without accompanying non-cognitive attitudes, it seems clear that there can be moral disagreement without clashes of attitudes. But CONFLICTING ATTITUDES also runs into trouble with less controversial cases:

Neutrality: A thinks that it would be better if C φ rather than not, whereas B thinks that C's φ-ing and not φ-ing are morally on a par, neither being morally better than the other. A's and B's attitudes are well aligned with their moral judgments: A prefers that C φ, whereas B is neutral or indifferent with respect to C's φ-ing.

Here, B would have nothing against C's acting in accordance with A's preferences. Nonetheless, there is a clear disagreement about whether φ-ing and not φ-ing are morally on a par. One might think that this is instead explained by a conflict in second-order attitudes, but we have already seen some difficulties for that suggestion. (For further problems with the Stevensonian account of disagreement, see Ridge 2013.)

Perhaps there are ways of amending these shortcomings. The problem is to do so without excessive *ad hoc* tinkering. Ideally, an account of *ethical* disagreement fits with a general understanding of why a variety of differences in psychological states constitute disagreement while others do not. On the one hand, we find disagreement in a variety of domains, both paradigmatically objective (arithmetic) and paradigmatically subjective (tastiness). On the other hand, two people do not disagree merely by having conflicting preferences or imagining incompatible states of affairs, nor does someone thinking that an object is *to the right* disagree with someone thinking that it is *to the left* if they judge from different spatial perspectives. As CONFLICTING ATTITUDES covers only non-cognitive disagreement, it seems ill suited to give us a unified understanding of what distinguishes cases of disagreement from cases of mere difference. Moreover, it already needs further amendments to handle *Mere Clash* and *Neutrality*, and it is unclear how it can account for disagreements in various non-normative subjective domains where clashes in attitude are non-obvious, such as disagreement about what is tasty (but see Marques and García-Carpintero 2014). Because of this, we might want to look elsewhere.

One place to look is at literature focusing on linguistic disagreement phenomena rather than on disagreement in judgment. A central observation in this literature has been that we naturally employ expressions of disagreement ("no," "I disagree"), also in response to paradigmatically "subjective" or judge-relative claims, such as claims about what might be the case, or about what is or isn't tasty:

Tasty:
A: This soup is really tasty.
B: No, it's too salty.

In *Tasty*, A makes a claim based on her personal taste reaction, but it seems that B can felicitously contradict or express disagreement with what A has said based on her own, different, taste reaction. Often, observations like these have been made in defense of the suggestion that the claims involved have *assessor-relative acceptance conditions*, and so might be competently accepted by the speaker but rejected by someone with a different palate (for gustatory taste claims), different evidence (for epistemic modals), or different norms (for moral claims) (e.g., Lasersohn 2005; Egan 2007; Stephenson 2007; Egan 2010; 2012; Schafer 2012; Willer 2013; MacFarlane 2014; Björnsson 2015; Khoo and Knobe 2016). (Assessor-relativist accounts should be distinguished from accounts taking the acceptance conditions to vary with context of utterance. See Alex Silk's chapter "Metaethical Contextualism" and Isidora Stojanovic's chapter "Metaethical Relativism.") These proposals explain the sense of contradiction in variantist discourse when combined with something like the following:

CONTRADICTION: One utterance contradicts another if and only if fully accepting the former involves rejecting the latter.

For example, even if the judgments expressed by A and B in *Tasty* have judge-relative success conditions, to fully accept A's claim is to judge, oneself, that the soup is really tasty, which is to reject B's claim.

CONTRADICTION seems to apply equally well to ethical discourse, given an intuitive understanding of what it is to accept various ethical claims. If A says "X is morally wrong" and B says, "X is not morally wrong," to fully accept A's claim would seem to involve rejecting B's: whether understood in invariantist, cognitive variantist, or non-cognitivist terms, judging that something is wrong should involve rejecting the idea that it isn't wrong. CONTRADICTION thus seems to vindicate a version of IMPLIED CONTRADICTION.

The idea that certain kinds of claims have assessor-relative acceptance conditions is relatively recent, and it is still unclear how it is best developed. One question concerns *why* certain utterances have assessor-relative acceptance conditions. Another concerns the extent to which data conform to assessor-relativist predictions, as assessors do not always accept or reject claims in the relevant domains based on their own information, palate, or norms (e.g., Stephenson 2007; von Fintel and Gillies 2008; Björnsson and Finlay 2010). For example, if a small child points towards the sauce in the pan, saying, "that's tasty," a parent who very much likes the sauce but believes that it is too spicy for the child can felicitously reply, "no dear, it's too spicy," contradicting the child's claim and expressing disagreement.

One explanation for both the existence of assessor-relative acceptance conditions and exceptions like these could be that *conversational pragmatics* determines what sort of assessment is called for. If claims of various kinds have pragmatic points—to inform about some objective fact, guide the taste expectations of others, or affect their moral attitudes, say—then for hearers to go along with that point means forming the corresponding beliefs, expectations, or attitudes. For some claims—ordinary claims about judge-independent reality—the point is to convey a belief with a certain hearer-independent representational content. For other claims, the point is to convey non-representational attitudes or hearer-relative representations. If we understand *accepting a claim* as a matter of going along with its conversational point, we would then have an explanation of why certain claims have assessor-relative acceptance conditions (e.g., Stephenson 2007; Egan 2010; 2012; Willer 2013; cf. Stalnaker 2002). This could also explain why it is sometimes natural or even mandatory to take the speaker's perspective, even in characteristically assessor-relative domains. Sometimes such assessments might simply be more in line with the point of the conversation, as when the child needs taste guidance in relation to its own palate rather than that of its parent (Björnsson and Almér 2010: 23–26, 29–32; Björnsson and Finlay 2010: 19–24, 28–34; Finlay 2014, chapter 8; Björnsson 2015).

Whether and in what form such pragmatic stories are successful, they do not directly provide an account of *disagreement in judgment* between parties that are not engaged in conversation, nor, perhaps, willing to engage. But one possibility is that disagreement in judgment consists in a certain *potential* for discursive disagreement:

DISAGREEMENT FROM CONTRADICTION: For A and B to disagree is for A and B to be in states characteristically expressed using contradictory utterances (Björnsson 2015).

This suggestion might solve problems faced by CONFLICTING ATTITUDES. First, it does not seem to overgenerate disagreement in *Mere Clash*: it is not clear what contradictory claims the parties can make merely in virtue of their conflicting attitudes. Second, it seems to handle *Neutrality*: A's and B's judgments can be characteristically expressed by "φ-ing is morally better than not φ-ing" and "φ-ing and not φ-ing are on a par," respectively. But fully accepting the first of these two claims would seem to involve rejecting the other, whether moral judgments are understood along non-cognitivist or variantist cognitivist lines. (On a non-cognitivist account, for example, accepting the first might be to morally prefer φ-ing over not φ-ing, whereas accepting the latter might be to morally prefer neither to the other [cf. Dreier 2009].) Given CONTRADICTION, DISAGREEMENT FROM CONTRADICTION thus seems to ensure that A and B disagree. It also seems to straightforwardly handle disagreement about what is tasty, relying on the treatment of *Tasty* offered by CONTRADICTION. Finally, the idea that ethical judgments are characteristically expressed with conversational points other than to convey some assessor-independent fact seems compatible with a variety of non-invariantist solutions to the specification problem discussed in the first section. (For a structurally similar account of disagreement in terms of potential to give *conflicting advice* rather than potential to make contradictory claims, see Ridge 2013.)

Though DISAGREEMENT FROM CONTRADICTION might look promising, any explanation of disagreement in judgments in terms of expressions of these judgments might seem to get the order of explanation wrong. Moreover, for DISAGREEMENT FROM CON-

TRADITION to apply to deep moral disagreement along the lines just sketched, it requires some solution to the non-invariantist's specification problem from the first section. The question about how to understand disagreement in non-invariantist discourse generally, and moral disagreement specifically, is thus still very much an open one.

Conclusion

In the first section of this chapter, we saw how deep ethical disagreements and variations in non-cognitive attitudes create difficulties for attempts to characterize specific kinds of ethical judgment. In this section, we have seen how attributions of disagreement have been taken to undermine cognitive variantist accounts. But we have also seen how the lack of clear evidence for invariantism, as well as disagreement in paradigmatically non-invariantist domains, suggests that we intuitively countenance disagreement that does not conform to the orthodox cognitivist model. Though it is still unclear what non-orthodox theory of disagreement best accounts for such disagreement phenomena, the very existence of non-orthodox disagreement undermines simple inferences from the existence of a disagreement to the cognitive content of the judgments that seem to ground that disagreement.

ACKNOWLEDGMENTS

This chapter has greatly benefited from comments from participants of the research seminar in philosophy at Umeå University, as well as from written comments by Marco Tiozzo, Jamie Fritz, and, in particular, the editors, Tristram McPherson and David Plunkett. Work on this chapter has been funded by the Swedish Research Council.

REFERENCES

Beebe, James R. 2014: 'How Different Kinds of Disagreement Impact Folk Metaethical Judgments'. *Advances in Experimental Moral Psychology*, pp. 167–87.

Björnsson, Gunnar 2012: 'Do "Objectivist" Features of Moral Discourse and Thinking Support Moral Objectivism?'. *The Journal of Ethics*, 16, pp. 367–93.

Björnsson, Gunnar 2015: 'Disagreement, Correctness, and the Evidence for Metaethical Absolutism'. In *Oxford Studies in Metaethics*. Shafer-Landau, Russ (ed) Oxford: Oxford University Press, pp. 160–87.

Björnsson, Gunnar and Almér, Alexander 2010: 'The Pragmatics of Insensitive Assessments'. In *Formal Semantics and Pragmatics. Discourse, Context and Models*. Partee, Barbara H., Glanzberg, Michael, and Skilters, Jurgis (ed) Manhattan, KS: New Prairie Press, pp. 1–45.

Björnsson, Gunnar and Finlay, Stephen 2010: 'Metaethical Contextualism Defended'. *Ethics*, 121, pp. 7–36.

Björnsson, Gunnar and McPherson, Tristram 2014: 'Moral Attitudes for Non-Cognitivists: Solving the Specification Problem'. *Mind*, 123, pp. 1–38.

Blackburn, Simon 1991: 'Just Causes'. *Philosophical Studies*, 61, pp. 3–17.

Blackburn, Simon 1993: 'How to Be an Ethical Anti-Realist'. In *Essays in Quasi-Realism*. Blackburn, Simon (ed) Oxford: Oxford University Press, pp. 166–81.

Blackburn, Simon 1998: *Ruling Passions*. Oxford: Oxford University Press.

Boyd, Richard 1988: 'How to Be a Moral Realist'. In *Essays on Moral Realism*. Sayre-McCord, Geoffrey (ed) Ithaca: Cornell University Press, pp. 181–228.

Boyd, Richard 2003: 'Finite Beings, Finite Good: The Semantics, Metaphysics and Ethics of Naturalist Consequentialism, Part 2'. *Philosophy and Phenomenological Research*, 67, pp. 24–47.

Brink, David O. 1989: *Moral Realism and the Foundations of Ethics*. Cambridge: Cambridge University Press.

Brink, David O. 2001: 'Realism, Naturalism, and Moral Semantics'. *Social Philosophy and Policy*, 18, pp. 154–76.

Burge, Tyler 1979: 'Individualism and the Mental'. *Midwest Studies in Philosophy*, 4, pp. 73–121.

Copp, David 2000: 'Milk, Honey, and the Good Life on Moral Twin Earth'. *Synthese*, 124, pp. 113–37.

Dowell, Janice L. forthcoming: 'The Metaethical Insignificance of Moral Twin Earth'. In *Oxford Studies in Metaethics*. Shafer-Landau, Russ (ed) Oxford: Oxford University Press.

Dreier, James 1990: 'Internalism and Speaker Relativism'. *Ethics*, 101:1, pp. 6–26.

Dreier, James 2009: 'Relativism (and Expressivism) and the Problem of Disagreement'. *Philosophical Perspectives*, 23, pp. 79–110.

Egan, Andy 2007: 'Epistemic Modals, Relativism and Assertion'. *Philosophical Studies*, 133, pp. 1–22.

Egan, Andy 2010: 'Disputing About Taste'. In *Disagreement*. Warfield, Ted and Feldmans, Richard (eds) Oxford: Oxford University Press.

Egan, Andy 2012: 'Relativist Dispositional Theories of Value'. *The Southern Journal of Philosophy*, 50, pp. 557–82.

Eklund, Matti 2012: 'Alternative Normative Concepts'. *Analytic Philosophy*, 53, pp. 139–57.

Enoch, David 2006: 'Agency, Shmagency: Why Normativity Won't Come from What Is Constitutive of Action'. *Philosophical Review*, 115, pp. 169–98.

Enoch, David 2011: *Taking Morality Seriously*. Oxford: Oxford University Press.

Finlay, Stephen 2014: *Confusion of Tongues: A Theory of Normative Language*. Oxford: Oxford University Press.

Gibbard, Allan 1990: *Wise Choices, Apt Feelings*. Cambridge, MA: Harvard University Press.

Gibbard, Allan 2003: *Thinking How to Live*. Cambridge, MA: Harvard University Press.

Hare, Richard M. 1952: *The Language of Morals*. Oxford: Oxford University Press.

Hare, Richard M. 1981: *Moral Thinking*. Oxford: Oxford University Press.

Horgan, Terence and Timmons, Mark 1991: 'New Wave Moral Realism Meets Moral Twin Earth'. *Journal of Philosophical Research*, 16, pp. 447–65.

Huemer, Michael 2005: *Ethical Intuitionism*. New York: Palgrave Macmillan.

Jackson, Frank 1998: *From Metaphysics to Ethics: A Defence of Conceptual Analysis*. Oxford: Oxford University Press.

Kauppinen, Antti 2010: 'What Makes a Sentiment Moral?'. In *Oxford Studies in Metaethics, Vol 5*. Shafer-Landau, Russ (ed) Oxford: Oxford University Press.

Khoo, Justin 2015: 'Modal Disagreements'. *Inquiry*, 58, pp. 511–34.

Khoo, Justin and Knobe, Joshua. 2016 'Moral Disagreement and Moral Semantics'. *Noûs*. DOI: 10.1111/nous.12151

Korsgaard, Christine M. 1996: *Creating the Kingdom of Ends*. Cambridge: Cambridge University Press.

Korsgaard, Christine M. 2009: *Self-Constitution*. Oxford: Oxford University Press.

Kripke, Saul A. 1980: *Naming and Necessity*. Cambridge, MA: Harvard University Press.

Lasersohn, Peter 2005: 'Context Dependence, Disagreement, and Predicates of Personal Taste'. *Linguistics and Philosophy*, 28, pp. 643–86.

Loeb, Don 2007: 'The Argument from Moral Experience'. *Ethical Theory and Moral Practice*, 10, pp. 469–84.

MacFarlane, John 2014: *Assessment Sensitivity: Relative Truth and Its Applications*. Oxford: Oxford University Press.

Marques, Teresa and García-Carpintero, Manuel 2014: 'Disagreement About Taste: Commonality Presuppositions and Coordination'. *Australasian Journal of Philosophy*, 92, pp. 701–23.

Merli, David 2002: 'Return to Moral Twin Earth'. *Canadian Journal of Philosophy*, 32, pp. 207–40.

Merli, David 2008: 'Expressivism and the Limits of Moral Disagreement'. *The Journal of Ethics*, 12, pp. 25–55.

Mill, John Stuart 1863: *Utilitarianism*. London: Parker, Son, and Bourn.

Miller, Alexander 2003: *Introduction to Contemporary Metaethics*. Cambridge: Polity.

Millikan, Ruth Garrett 1984: *Language, Thought, and Other Biological Categories: New Foundations for Realism*. Cambridge, MA: MIT Press.

Millikan, Ruth Garrett 2000: *On Clear and Confused Ideas: An Essay About Substance Concepts*. New York: Cambridge University Press.

Moore, George Edward 1903: *Principia Ethica*. Cambridge: Cambridge University Press.

Moore, George Edward 1912: *Ethics*. New York: Henry Holt.

Parfit, Derek 2005: 'Normativity'. In *Oxford Studies in Metaethics*. Shafer-Landau, Russ (ed) pp. 325–80.

Plunkett, David and Sundell, Timothy 2013: 'Disagreement and the Semantics of Normative and Evaluative Terms'. *Philosophers' Imprint*, 13, pp. 1–37.

Prinz, Jesse J. 2007: *The Emotional Construction of Morals*. Oxford: Oxford University Press.

Putnam, Hilary 1975: 'The Meaning of "'Meaning'". In *Mind, Language and Reality*. Cambridge: Cambridge University Press. pp. 215–71.

Railton, Peter 1989: 'Naturalism and Prescriptivity'. *Social Philosophy and Policy*, 7, pp. 151–74.

Ridge, Michael 2013: 'Disagreement'. *Philosophy and Phenomenological Research*, 86, pp. 41–63.

Ridge, Michael 2014: *Impassioned Belief*. Oxford: Oxford University Press.

Sarkissian, Hagop, Park, John, Tien, David, Wright, Jennifer and Knobe, Joshua 2011: 'Folk Moral Relativism'. *Mind and Language*, 26, pp. 482–505.

Sayre-McCord, Geoffrey 1997: '"Good" on Twin Earth'. *Philosophical Issues*, 8, pp. 267–92.

Schafer, Karl 2012: 'Assessor Relativism and the Problem of Moral Disagreement'. *The Southern Journal of Philosophy*, 50, pp. 602–20.

Schroeter, Laura and Schroeter, François 2009: 'A Third Way in Metaethics'. *Noûs*, 43, pp. 1–30.

Shafer-Landau, Russ 2003: *Moral Realism: A Defence*. Oxford: Oxford University Press.

Smith, Michael 1994: *The Moral Problem*. Oxford: Basil Blackwell.

Stalnaker, Robert 2002: 'Common Ground'. *Linguistics and Philosophy*, 25, pp. 701–21.

Stephenson, Tamina 2007: 'Judge Dependence, Epistemic Modals, and Predicates of Personal Taste'. *Linguistics and Philosophy*, 30, pp. 487–525.

Stevenson, Charles L. 1937: 'The Emotive Meaning of Ethical Terms'. *Mind*, 46, pp. 14–31.

Stevenson, Charles L. 1963: *Facts and Values: Studies in Ethical Analysis*. New Haven: Yale University Press.

Streiffer, Robert 2003: *Moral Relativism and Reasons for Action*. New York: Routledge.

Sturgeon, Nicholas L. 1991: 'Contents and Causes: A Reply to Blackburn'. *Philosophical Studies*, 61, pp. 19–37.

Svavarsdóttir, Sigrún 1999: 'Moral Cognitivism and Motivation'. *The Philosophical Review*, 108, pp. 161–219.

Tersman, Folke 2006: *Moral Disagreement*. Cambridge: Cambridge University Press.

von Fintel, Kai and Gillies, Anthony S. 2008: 'CIA Leaks'. *Philosophical Review*, 117, pp. 77–98.

Wedgwood, Ralph 2007: *The Nature of Normativity*. Oxford: Oxford University Press.

Westermarck, Edward 1932: *Ethical Relativity*. London: Kegan Paul.

Willer, Malte 2013: 'Dynamics of Epistemic Modality'. *Philosophical Review*, 122, pp. 45–92.

Wong, David 1984: *Moral Relativity*. Berkeley: University of California Press.

Wong, David 2006: *Natural Moralities*. Oxford: Oxford University Press.

18

Cognitivism and Non-Cognitivism

Matthew S. Bedke

A PROFOUND DIFFERENCE OF OPINION

Of all the ways of dividing up the metaethical terrain, arguably the greatest chasm lies between cognitivism and non-cognitivism. To see what is at issue, consider the following claims:

- Rousseau should have thanked Hume.
- Stepping on gouty toes is (morally) wrong.
- Forcing people into an agrarian lifestyle is (morally) obligatory.
- Pleasure is intrinsically good.
- That you are jealous of Sarah is not a good reason to kick her.

These claims can be thought of as sentences in English or as psychological judgments. As we shall see, 'cognitive' and 'non-cognitive' make most sense when labeling different types of psychological judgment. But the issues I wish to discuss are similar regardless of whether we consider linguistic meanings or psychological states, and I find them easier to introduce in the context of linguistic meanings.

So let us start with sentences and let us suppose someone sincerely asserts "Pleasure is intrinsically good." If you are in a particularly reflective mood, you might set aside the issue of whether pleasure is indeed intrinsically good—an issue in normative ethics—and wonder instead *what it means to say* that pleasure is intrinsically good, or for that matter, *what it means to say* that pleasure is intrinsically value-neutral, or to say that it is intrinsically bad.

Cognitivism and non-cognitivism offer two different answers to your questions. Put simply, cognitivism says that "Pleasure is intrinsically good" *purports to describe* pleasure in some way by calling it intrinsically good. This descriptive purport is meant to be a very common sort of meaning that many pedestrian sentences enjoy. If one says "Hume is frustrated," for example, the expression 'is frustrated' is fairly uncontroversially *about* a certain psychological state of mind; it *stands for* a state of mind. And you probably think "Hume is frustrated" *ascribes* that state of mind to Hume, and that is how the whole sentence then purports to *describe* how things are.

Cognitivism would say all these things about our normative sentences. For example, there is some worldly feature that 'is intrinsically good' is about, or that it stands for, and the sentence ascribes that feature to pleasure so that the whole sentence "Pleasure is intrinsically good" purports to describe how things are.[1]

We could add some wrinkles to the story. For example, we could say that the way a sentence describes things is by expressing a proposition, and it is more fundamentally the proposition that describes or represents possible states of the world. We might also wonder whether a normative sentence could describe things differently depending on the context in which it is used. Maybe when I say an action is wrong I describe it in one way (e.g., as being condemned by *my culture's* norms) whereas others who call it wrong describe it in a different way (e.g., as being condemned by *their culture's* norms). Wrinkles aside, the key thought for cognitivism is that the sentences purport to describe how things are.

Non-cognitivism takes an entirely different approach. It comes in two parts. First, it rejects cognitivism. Applied to "Pleasure is intrinsically good," the thought is that this sentence does not purport to describe pleasure in any way. The meaning of 'is intrinsically good' does not involve being about anything, or standing for anything, so the sentence is not ascribing any worldly feature to pleasure.

Second, it offers a positive story about meaning. I will elaborate later, but the rough thought is that some normative expressions have an intrinsically action-guiding meaning. Applied to "Pleasure is intrinsically good," we would say its meaning has some intimate connection with the *motivation* to bring about pleasure, or with *endorsing* pleasure, or *commanding* people to bring about, preserve, or protect pleasure, or some such. Applied to "Stepping on gouty toes is wrong," its meaning is connected to the motivation to not step on gouty toes, or to disapprove of doing so, or commanding people not to do so, or some such.

Having said all this, I hasten to add that there is no consensus as to exactly how to formulate the divide more precisely, or even if the distinction I just attempted to draw survives critical scrutiny. The bulk of this chapter is dedicated to such issues. Near the end, I briefly canvass some of the arguments for and against one camp or the other.[2]

THE HYPOTHESES: LINGUISTIC AND PSYCHOLOGICAL

Let me begin by recommending more precise formulations of cognitivist and non-cognitivist hypotheses. First, taking normative language as the object of study, here are two distinct positions concerning linguistic meaning.

linguistic cognitivism: normative expression 'N' has descriptive content as a matter of its conventional meaning, so it can help sentences in which it features describe a possible state of the world via its conventional meaning.

linguistic non-cognitivism: (negative part:) normative expression 'N' has no descriptive content as a matter of its conventional meaning, so it cannot help sentences in which it features describe a possible state of the world via its conventional meaning; (positive part:) the meaning of 'N', or a sentence in which it features, is to be understood in a more purely action-guiding way.

These hypotheses are schematic. Substitution of terms for 'N'—e.g., 'is good', 'ought to', 'is a reason to', etc.—delivers non-schematic hypotheses for particular expressions. Historically, the debates tend to focus on certain bits of moral language, though the same distinctions will crop up in other normative areas, including rationality, prudence, aesthetics, epistemology, and so on.[3] Rather than wrestle with questions of scope, I will draw examples from the sentences listed at the outset to characterize the two camps.

Turning to normative judgments and taking them as the object of study, we have the following distinct positions.

psychological cognitivism: normative judgments affirming normative status N are belief-like attitudes that represent some possible worldly feature by affirming status N.

psychological non-cognitivism: (negative part:) it is not the case that normative judgments affirming normative status N are belief-like attitudes that represent some possible worldly feature by affirming status N; (positive part:) they do, however, have a more conative, action-guiding nature.

As before, these hypotheses are schematic, allowing substitution of various statuses (being wrong, being good) that can be affirmed in thought. And the central issues are very similar to those found in the linguistic hypotheses. Instead of talking about the sentence "Stepping on gouty toes is wrong," we would talk about the psychological judgment that *stepping on gouty toes is wrong*. On one view, it is a belief that represents stepping on gouty toes as exhibiting some possible worldly feature. On another view, the judgment does not represent the action as exhibiting any worldly feature; instead, it is a conative attitude toward the action, akin to having a negative attitude toward stepping on gouty toes, planning not to step on gouty toes, or something along these lines.

Note that I put the linguistic hypotheses in terms of *description*, whereas I put the psychological hypotheses in terms of *representation*. This is not to mark any deep distinction between description and representation, but merely to help us bear in mind that the linguistic and psychological hypotheses are distinct. That is, the psychological version of one does not entail its linguistic correlate, and vice versa.

Also worth noting, the hypotheses do not make cognitivism and non-cognitivism logical contradictories. The contradictory of cognitivism would be the negative component of non-cognitivism. But to be faithful to the non-cognitivist tradition, we need to incorporate an action-guiding element into the non-cognitivist hypothesis.

POSITIVE HYPOTHESES FOR NON-COGNITIVISM

It is standard to recognize three ways of filling in the non-cognitivist's positive position on the action-guiding qualities of thought or language.

One of them is the *emotivism* of A. J. Ayer (1936). According to him, normative language 'emotes' or 'evinces' a speaker's attitudes such that the meaning of "Stepping on gouty toes is wrong" is similar to "Stepping on gouty toes" said with a special tone of horror, or followed by special exclamation marks that conventionally indicate the speaker's horror. Some philosophers have suggested that the language of booing and cheering provides an apt analogy, in which case our exemplary sentence has a meaning similar to "Boo stepping on gouty toes!"

Another option is the *prescriptivism* of R. M. Hare (1952). For him, the primary kind of meaning a bit of moral, evaluative language adds to a sentence is like the kind of mood found in imperatival sentences. A command like "Don't step on gouty toes!" nicely illustrates the imperatival mood, and on Hare's suggestion, "Stepping on gouty toes is wrong" has a meaning similar to this command. 'Is wrong' does not add any descriptive content to the sentence, but rather adds *something like* an imperatival mood.

The most popular option is the *expressivism* of Simon Blackburn (1984; 1993; 1998), Allan Gibbard (1990; 2003), Terry Horgan and Mark Timmons (2006a; 2006b), and Mark Timmons (1999). Expressivism includes two theses. First, a perfectly general thesis in the philosophy of language: the meaning of a term or sentence is understood in terms of the state of mind it is used to express.[4] Second, a thesis about the state of mind expressed by some normative expression 'N': the state of mind expressed by 'N', or expressed by the atomic, assertoric sentences in which it features, are not beliefs with representational contents but conative states.

To illustrate, under expressivism the meaning of "Stepping on gouty toes is wrong" has to do with the state of mind it is used to express in assertoric contexts. Which state of mind does it express? Well, to satisfy the action-guiding dimension of meaning it must be a conative state of mind, like some negative attitude toward stepping on gouty toes (Blackburn, and probably Horgan and Timmons), or a plan not to step on gouty toes (Gibbard), or some such.

When we turn to consider how normative judgments might be action-guiding, expressivists have a ready answer. They can say that normative judgments just are the non-cognitive state of mind expressed by the corresponding sentences. The judgment that *stepping on gouty toes is wrong* is then something like a negative attitude toward stepping on gouty toes, or a plan not to do it, or some such.

Looking at the emotivism of Ayer, or the prescriptivism or Hare, it is less obvious that they even have a psychological hypothesis to offer. This is especially true for prescriptivism. If normative language is like the language of commands, perhaps there is no such thing as a normative judgment *per se*, just as (arguably) there is no such thing as a command that is merely thought.

Given these remarks, we are in a position to appreciate an alternative taxonomy to the one I suggested above. It would characterize cognitivism as the view that the meaning of a normative sentence involves *expressing belief-like, representational psychological states,* and non-cognitivism as the view that they *express more desire-like, non-representational states.* This taxonomy would blend the linguistic and psychological issues that I have tried to keep separate. To be sure, blending them makes a lot of sense if we put attitude expression front-and-center in a theory of linguistic meaning, as expressivists do. But the broader debate between cognitivism and non-cognitivism should not be yoked to the expressivist's controversial theory of meaning. That is not to say that expressivism has a bad theory of meaning. It is merely to point out the expressivism is one version of non-cognitivism and the broader debate should not be articulated using its guiding assumptions.

So, let us stick with our more general taxonomy. Doing so brings into relief some important points. First, *if* description- and representation-relevant aspects to meaning are not tied to attitude expression, *then* arguments for linguistic non-cognitivism do not need to show that non-belief-like states are expressed, and arguments for linguistic cognitivism do not need to show that belief-like states are expressed. Second, it is possible to combine linguistic non-cognitivism with psychological cognitivism, or vice versa, though consideration of such mixing and matching is beyond the scope of this entry.

THE LAY OF THE LAND

At this point, it might help to situate the camps in the broader metaethical landscape.

The clearest example of a cognitivist metaethic, and the target of most non-cognitivist arguments, is some form of realism. Realists not only think that moral language and thought purport to describe or represent, but they think there are mind-independent moral properties and facts that we sometimes describe or represent accurately. Some realists think those properties and facts are natural (Boyd 1988; Brink 1989; Copp 1995; Finlay 2014; Jackson 1998; Railton 1986; Schroeder 2007), others think they are non-natural (or simply *sui generis*) (Cuneo 2007; Enoch 2011; Fitzpatrick 2012; Moore 1903; Shafer-Landau 2003). But realists are cognitivists, both psychologically and linguistically.[5]

So are error theorists. They think that some extant normative discourse either tries to attribute mind-independent normative properties, or presumes such properties are exhibited. They differ from realists in claiming that, in fact, *nothing* exhibits such properties, and perhaps nothing *could* exhibit such properties. As such, the discourse is shot through with error (Joyce 2001; Mackie 1977; Olson 2014).

Some positions are harder to locate on the cognitivism, non-cognitivism map. Take constructivism (Street 2010). As I understand it, its distinguishing characteristic is that some normative truths are constructed from some perspective on the world. Different constructivist positions will differ over the truths constructed (e.g., all normativity vs. just moral normativity), exactly what construction amounts to (e.g., following a procedure of deliberation from some actual perspective, generating claims from some idealized perspective), and the perspective that provides the materials of construction (e.g., practical rationality, some domain of normative judgments, the attitudes of one's culture, the attitudes of an ideal observer). If that is the nub of constructivism, it is neutral on the cognitivism, non-cognitivism divide. Constructivists are free to add that normative claims purport to describe or represent a constructed reality (thereby being cognitivist), but they need not do so.

One version of cognitivist constructivism deserves special mention here: speaker subjectivism. On that view, we take the actual attitudes of an individual as the materials of construction, and we simply say that correct normative claims for that speaker are accurate *descriptions* of her/his attitudes. If so, "Forcing people into an agrarian lifestyle is morally obligatory" is used to describe in roughly the same way as "Forcing people into an agrarian lifestyle is *approved of by me*." And both are presumably accurate descriptions (and so presumably true) when said by A, just in case A has the requisite positive conative attitudes toward forced labor.

It should be clear that non-cognitivism is not speaker subjectivism (Ayer 1936; Horgan and Timmons 2006b). For non-cognitivism says that the normative sentence is not in the business of describing anything, let alone describing the speaker's attitudes. It is doing something else that *might* have a lot to do with speakers' attitudes, but it is not describing those attitudes. As a result, non-cognitivists do not need to concede that a normative sentence, as said by A, accurately describes (and is presumably thereby true), just in case A has the requisite conative attitudes.

Another position difficult to locate on our map is *hermeneutic fictionalism*. Concerning linguistic meanings, I think there are two ways of understanding the view. One hermeneutic fictionalist position is this: in asserting normative sentences, we are *pretending* there are normative facts and properties or *making believe* that there are. An analogous situation might be that of the actor pretending that various things are true on stage, but prepared to deny them when the curtain falls. Another option is that there is an "in the fiction" operator supplied by the contexts in which we normally assert such sentences, so that, say, "Stepping on gouty toes is wrong" would normally be said in a context that gives the sentence the same content as "According to the moral fiction, stepping on gouty toes is wrong." An analogous situation might be discourse about the characters and goings-on of the Harry Potter series. In such discussions, we know we are not taking a stand on how things are with the real world, nor are we pretending to do so. The context in which we speak supplies an "in the fiction" operator.

Both views, it seems to me, are at least consistent with linguistic cognitivism. For it looks like *the language* has descriptive content. It is just that the *speakers* of the language typically use it in a special way, or use it in contexts that supply a special operator. So, I tentatively count them as linguistic cognitivists. As for psychological theses, it looks like an attitude of make-believe or pretend might count as a non-representational state, so at least that version of hermeneutic fictionalism has affinities with psychological non-cognitivism (see Kalderon 2005).

Last, I should mention so-called *hybrid views*, which try to combine aspects of the two camps. For example, they might wish to combine linguistic cognitivism with only the positive part of linguistic non-cognitivism to generate this hypothesis: some expression 'N' both has descriptive content and also has an action-guiding dimension to its meaning. For more, see Teemu Toppinen's chapter "Hybrid Accounts of Ethical Thought and Talk." As I proceed, I will set hybrid theories to one side.

TAXONOMIC TROUBLES AND CREEPING MINIMALISM

Everything I have said so far is subject to dispute. Consider again the early non-cognitivist positions of Ayer and Hare. If we take their analogies with emotings and commands seriously, we can end up with much stronger *negative* non-cognitivist theses than the ones I suggest—not the lack of descriptive or representational content, but the *lack of truth-aptitude* (Ayer 1936; Shafer-Landau 2003). For neither "Boo stepping on gouty toes!" nor "Don't step on gouty toes!" is truth-apt. And if normative sentences are not even truth-apt, then they are not true (and not false), and presumably there is no reason to posit normative facts, properties, etc.

In the salad days of non-cognitivism, non-cognitivists were happy to deny the truth-aptitude of normative sentences, and happy to deny the existence of normative properties and facts. But the vast majority of contemporary non-cognitivists think normative sentences and judgments are truth-apt, that some are true, that there are normative facts, properties, and even moral knowledge! Some of the philosophers I have put in the non-cognitivist camp have registered some discontent with the label precisely because it is associated with the old-school denial of truth-aptitude, truth, and the rest. Simon Blackburn prefers the labels 'quasi-realism' and 'projectivism', where quasi-realism is the project of earning the right to truth-, fact-, and property-talk when one is not a realist, and 'projectivism' refers to the view that moral properties and facts are projected from our sentiments (Blackburn 1996a; 1996b). Allan Gibbard has noted that the "touchstones" of cognitivism are things he embraces: normative claims can be true or false, normative questions have a right answer, and sometimes those right answers are knowable (Gibbard 2003). And Horgan and Timmons have a view they call *cognitivist expressivism* (Horgan and Timmons 2006a).

What gives? Well, most of the philosophers I label 'non-cognitivists' are engaged in a project of accommodation. They see how deeply engrained truth-, fact-, and property-talk are in moral discourse, and they think that non-cognitivists can think and talk in those terms, too.

It looks like they are right to accommodate, at least if they wish to maintain their normative views. For consider a non-cognitivist about 'wrong' who thinks that stepping on gouty toes is wrong. He says as much in English. Now suppose he goes on to say that *it isn't true that stepping on gouty toes is wrong*, or *there is no fact of the matter whether stepping on gouty toes is wrong*, or *stepping on gouty toes does not bear the property of being wrong*. By saying such things, it looks like he is taking something back—he does not think that stepping on gouty toes is wrong after all. So, in order to sustain his view that stepping on gouty toes is wrong, he has to admit that it's true, that there are moral facts and properties, etc. In fact, he might have to admit that the sentence *accurately describes* the moral facts. If he denies this, again, it looks like he is taking something back.

Herein lies a problem. If non-cognitivists and cognitivists are all on board with moral truths, properties, descriptions, etc., what is the difference between them? James Dreier calls the general problem *the problem of creeping minimalism* (Dreier 2004; see also Rosen 1998; Timmons 1999). I think it is easiest to see the problem if we start with a contrast between minimalist and correspondence theories of truth. A correspondence theory says something like this: for "S" to be true is for there to be some worldly fact F, and for "S" to correspond with F. On this view, accepting the truth of *any* sentence, whether it is about science or morals, commits you to a word-world relation of correspondence between language and fact.

By contrast, minimalism eschews any general analysis of truth in favor of something along the following lines: there is nothing more to the concept of truth aside from the following schema and its substitution instances:

"S" is true iff S.

For the minimalist, "Snow is white" is true if snow is white, and "Forced labor is wrong" is true if forced labor is wrong, but there need not be a robust word-world relation, whether it be correspondence with fact or anything else, that the truth of each sentence is committed to. That is good for a non-cognitivist who wants to maintain the truth of the normative sentence without thereby incurring any metaphysical or semantic commitments beyond what he already committed to in thinking or saying that forced labor is wrong (which, for him, might be no more than opposing forced labor and expressing this opposition in language).

And now here comes the creep. Just as the non-cognitivist wanted to talk about truth on the cheap, he might also want to talk about fact, property, and maybe accurate description on the cheap. He could give minimalist theories of these, too, using the following schemas and their substitution instances:

It is a fact that S iff S.
a has the property of being F iff *a* is F.
"*a* is F" accurately describes *a* iff *a* is F.

If such minimalist theories are right, then you can talk of normative truths, facts, properties, descriptions, and the like without incurring any metaphysical or semantic commitments than you already incur with your first-order normative opinions. Adding these extra ways of talking does not a cognitivist make (or such talk does not make one a cognitivist *as opposed to* a non-cognitivist).

Non-cognitivism can thereby complete their accommodation project. At the same time, it makes it hard to draw a distinction between the two camps. We cannot say one camp affirms normative truths, facts, properties and the other does not. Maybe we cannot even say one camp affirms descriptive content and the other does not. Maybe there is no sustainable distinction to draw.

Then again, it would be very strange if there were nothing to the cognitivist, non-cognitivist distinction. One option is just to reject minimalism about the vocabulary you would like to use to make the distinction. You might be inclined to reject minimalism about representation and description, for example.

Alternatively, James Dreier himself has suggested what he calls the "explanation" explanation as a way of maintaining a distinction in the face of fairly aggressive minimalist creep. Here is what he says: "The point, I think, is that expressivists are distinguished by their claim that there is nothing to making a normative judgment over and above being in a state that plays a certain 'non-cognitive' psychological role, a role more like desire than it is like factual belief. In particular, to explain what it is to make a moral judgment, we need not mention any normative properties" (Dreier 2004: 39).

His general idea is that there are least two sorts of things one can say when asked to *explain what it is* to make a moral judgment. The cognitivist cites properties. The non-cognitivist cites states with a certain desire-like psychological role (see also Fine 2001). Allan Gibbard (2003: 19–20, 187) also draws distinctions between the two camps in terms of the explanations they offer. When considering the interesting motivational or decision-making role that normative judgments have, for example, Gibbard says that normative judgments are *plans* for what to do, whereas (some) realists would maintain that normative judgments are special representational beliefs with the power to motivate.

Stepping back, these versions of the "explanation" explanation appear to grant all parties talk of normative truth, fact, property, description, etc., but one party (the non-cognitivist one) says these ways of talking *do not help explain* the nature of normative judgments. Presumably, the non-cognitivist would want to say that, when explaining the nature of some *non-normative* judgments, like the judgment that snow is white, truth, fact, property, description, etc. *are* explanatory. It remains unclear exactly how this fits with minimalism about all these notions. If you are a minimalist about properties, for example, how can it be explanatory in one context but not another? One would think that minimalism about properties saps it of explanatory power in every context, or at least gives it the same explanatory power in every context.

Before moving on, let me mention a slightly different approach. Mark Timmons (1999, chapter 4) distinguishes morally engaged from morally disengaged contexts. In morally engaged contexts, cognitivists and non-cognitivists can both make liberal use of truth-talk and the rest as a perfectly (semantically) appropriate way of expressing their normative views without thereby being metaphysically or semantically committal. This much sounds like minimalism. In disengaged contexts, however, non-cognitivists would want to disavow commitment to normative truths and the like, while cognitivists would like to maintain it, for in such contexts truth-talk and the like is more metaphysically and semantically committal.[6] Unfortunately, it is beyond the scope of this chapter to further discuss what looks like a contextualist theory of truth and the like.

WHAT ARE BELIEFS? WHAT ARE DESIRE-LIKE STATES?

Notice that much of the above has focused on psychological issues. One common theme has been that cognitivists explain the nature of normative judgments by saying that they are representational beliefs while non-cognitivists say they are non-representational, desire-like states. Now, we might ask, what is it to be a representational belief as opposed to a desire-like state?

In the background here is a folk psychological distinction between the different *roles* of beliefs and desires. The different roles are often characterized in terms of differing *directions of fit* (Anscombe 1957, section 32; Humberstone 1992; Searle 1984: 8; Smith 1994: 115). In brief, a representational belief is meant to fit the world, whereas a desire is meant for the world to fit it. Less briefly, the thought is that A's belief that P tends to come into existence when A is in an epistemic state indicating that P, and the belief tends to desist when A is in an epistemic state indicating that not P, whereas A's desire that P couples with true beliefs to tend to cause the agent to make it the case that P, and it tends to persist in the face of an epistemic state indicating that not P.

Plugged into our psychological hypotheses, cognitivists hypothesize that normative judgments have a certain role—the mind-fit-world role, or thetic role (terminology proliferates here)—whereas non-cognitivists hypothesize a different sort of role—a world-fit-mind role, or a telic role. This gives us some indication of what to look for if we are to discern whether psychological cognitivism or non-cognitivism is true of some judgment: look for evidence that bears on the role played by the judgment.

But there is another way of thinking about the distinction between belief-like and desire-like states. Rather than (or perhaps in addition to) thinking of beliefs as having a certain sort of role, Horgan and Timmons (2006a) have suggested that we count a judgment-type as belief if it exhibits some key generic properties associated with belief-type states. Here are some of the properties they discuss:

- Beliefs have the phenomenology of categorizing or classifying some item based on sufficient reason for so categorizing or classifying.
- Beliefs are semantically assessable for truth and falsity.
- Beliefs have contents that bear logical entailment relations with the contents of other beliefs.

Horgan and Timmons think that normative judgments tick these boxes. They conclude that normative judgments are beliefs.

There is a wrinkle. For they also want to stress that judgments that tick these boxes can *lack* what they call *overall descriptive content*, or, using our terminology, they can lack *overall representational content*. As I understand the view, a judgment like *stepping on gouty toes is wrong* can be a genuine belief, and yet to think the action wrong is not to represent it as having any worldly features. Such beliefs they call *ought-commitments*, whereas beliefs with overall representational content they call *is-commitments*. Importantly, Horgan and Timmons also think that ought-commitment beliefs have a more motivational, action-guiding role than do is-commitment beliefs.

Shall we conclude that certain normative judgments are beliefs, albeit ought-commitment beliefs rather than is-commitment beliefs? On the one hand, Horgan and Timmons have noted some interesting features that normative judgments share with states that are uncontroversially beliefs. On the other hand, it seems the hard work is not deciding whether to label these as non-belief-type states, or as ought-commitment beliefs. The hard work is explaining why a non-representational state has the key generic properties of belief that Horgan and Timmons rightly note—the phenomenology of categorization, semantic assessability for truth and falsity, and logical entailment relations. A cognitivist could argue that it is harder to explain why normative judgments have these properties with the hypothesis that they are non-representational states. This brings us to the arguments.

ARGUMENTS

With some idea of what is at stake in these debates, what reason is there to embrace one position rather than the other? Here, I briefly mention some considerations, and direct the reader to other entries in this volume where appropriate.

For cognitivism: Commonalities with other cognitivist discourse
Grammatically, normative language resembles language that is uncontroversially descriptive. Its sentences can take the declarative mood, they can be asserted, and they can embed in complex constructions. The sentences seem truth-apt, and some of them seem true. We can use the sentences to formulate valid arguments. We have genuine normative disagreements, and sometimes we think our normative views might be mistaken.

On the psychological side, normative judgments have a phenomenology much like categorization or classification. We can use normative premises in good, apparently theoretical, reasoning, exploiting logical entailment relations between the contents of our judgments. We call normative judgments beliefs in everyday speech, and we think such judgments are truth-apt and some of them true by virtue of having true contents.

The cognitivist hypotheses can deliver all these things in the same way one delivers them for non-normative, descriptive discourse. The key question is this: are non-cognitive explanations of these things *worse*? The jury is out, but all agree that non-cognitivism faces some significant challenges. For example, cognitivists think they have a relatively easier time explaining normative disagreement, for it is a familiar sort of disagreement between incompatible representations of the world, whereas non-cognitivism must posit something like disagreement in attitude (Gibbard 2003; Parfit 2011; Stevenson 1963). For more on this, see Gunnar Björnsson's chapter "The Significance of Ethical Disagreement for Theories of Ethical Thought and Talk."

Also, cognitivism might have an easier time accounting for the possibility of fundamental normative error, for that would be a failure to accurately represent or describe real features of the world, whereas non-cognitivists have tried to give an account of *the thought* that one's fundamental normative views might be in error as the thought that one's conative attitudes might be improved. This is to employ the standards of one's conative attitudes to pass judgment on some of those attitudes, and in so doing to imagine that improvement is possible by those standards (Blackburn 2009; Egan 2007).

Disagreement and error might be the deepest concerns for non-cognitivism. But lately, some more formal objections have received the most attention. Let me turn to them now.

The Frege-Geach problem(s) for non-cognitivism

Consider a constellation of issues about the compositionality of meaning, validity, and inference raised by Peter Geach and John Searle (Geach 1960; 1965; Searle 1969). Geach asks us to consider the following argument:

1. If tormenting the cat is bad, getting your little brother to do it is bad.
2. Tormenting the cat is bad.
C. Getting your little brother to torment the cat is bad.

This looks like a valid argument, poised for a theoretical inference. As we have seen, non-cognitivists have had various things to say about what (2) means. It is like emoting or commanding, or it expresses a non-cognitive attitude. But we need to ask what (2) means as embedded in the antecedent of (1). Qua antecedent, it does not appear to be emoting a negative attitude, or commanding anything, nor is it expressing a negative attitude. That is, if someone just accepts (1), he does not thereby have any negative attitude toward tormenting the cat, nor does he command anything. So we need to know: under non-cognitivism, what do all these premises mean such that the argument as a whole avoids equivocation, is valid, and can be used in inferential reasoning (c.f. Dreier 1996)?

As you can see, "the" Frege-Geach problem—or "the" problem of embeddability—is really a constellation of problems for non-cognitivism. Most basically, we want to know what logically complex sentences featuring normative expressions mean. We also want accounts of validity, inference, etc. that jibe with that theory of meaning, and some assurance that it makes sense to package all of this in the propositional, declarative surface structure that the language manifests (as opposed to, say, a more transparently imperatival structure or emotive structure).

There are some interesting non-cognitive answers to this challenge (Blackburn 1984; Gibbard 1990; 2003), but nothing is settled here (Schroeder 2010b; van Roojen 1996). For more on this, see Jack Woods' chapter "The Frege-Geach Problem." For those who develop a taste for these issues, there is a nicely focused aspect of the problem to study: *the negation problem* (Dreier 2006; Hale 2002; Schroeder 2010a).

For non-cognitivism: Motivational internalism

The single most important consideration weighing in favor of non-cognitivism—and particularly in favor of *psychological* non-cognitivism—is the motivational profile of certain normative judgments. Suppose Able judges she ought to visit her grandmother in the hospital, and Bea that she ought to donate to the charity drive on the radio. Are they motivated to do these things, at least a little? If so, is the motivation contingent? In answer, many have thought that there is some non-contingent connection between ought judgments and the motivation to act accordingly. Similar points can be made for other normative judgments.

Non-cognitivists think they have a better explanation for this motivational profile. For they can say that the motivational connection exists because a judgment that one ought to phi is a conative state, something like a desire to phi. No surprise, then, that one is non-contingently motivated to act accordingly. If, on the other hand, the judgment is a belief that represents one's phiing as having some worldly feature, it is puzzling why there would be anything more than a contingent motivation to phi. Beliefs do not normally motivate without coupling with appropriate contingent desire-type states.

There are two difficulties with this line of argument. First, it is heavily contested exactly what the motivational explanandum is. Here are some options.

- Necessarily, if A judges that she ought to phi, A is motivated to phi (insofar as she is rational).
- Necessarily, if A judges that she ought to phi, A is normally motivated to phi (insofar as she is rational) (Blackburn 1998; Dreier 1990; Korsgaard 1986; Timmons 1999).
- Necessarily, if A judges that she ought to phi, A's judgment has the purpose of helping to motivate her to phi (insofar as she is rational) (Bedke 2008).
- It is not possible to have a community of rational agents, none of which are (normally) motivated by their first-person ought judgments (Bedke 2008; Dreier 1990; Lenman 1999; Tresan 2009).
- A's judgment that she ought to phi has an entirely contingent connection to motivation.

Now, if the first option, known as strong motivational internalism, captures the motivational data, psychological non-cognitivists are in a good position to explain it. But even non-cognitivists shy away from a very strong motivational internalism in light of the so-called *amoralist* counterexample (Brink 1989). An amoralist (or a-normativist) is someone who sincerely makes the relevant first-person normative judgment but who is utterly unmoved by it. If such an agent is possible, strong motivational internalism is false. And it is widely thought that such an agent is possible.

At the other end of the spectrum, we have the entirely contingent connection to motivation. That strikes many as too weak. A person's normative judgments normally tell us something about their cares and concerns, what they are for and against, and how they are likely to behave. So you might think that some weak, but non-contingent, motivational internalism captures the data. Unfortunately, weak internalisms are a problem for both camps. To the extent the motivational data are anything other than the data we find with standard desire-like states (strong internalism) or standard belief-like states (entirely contingent), it just isn't clear whether *either* of our theories are particularly well poised to explain them.

Let us back up and suppose that the data supports some strong-ish motivational connection. You might think that this would at least *favor* psychological non-cognitivism. But even this is contested. For some maintain that certain representational beliefs are either capable of motivating without the need of any independent desires, or that such beliefs are able to spawn independent desires *ex nihilo* (Shafer-Landau 2003; Smith 1994). That is, they deny the folk theory of belief-desire psychology. You can guess which beliefs are the special ones: normative judgments with the interesting motivational profile. They are special beliefs in that they do not need to couple with contingent, independent, and *ex-ante* existent desires to generate motivation.

At this point, I leave it to the reader to ponder just what the motivational data are and how best to explain them. I also direct your attention to David Faraci and Tristram McPherson's chapter "Ethical Judgment and Motivation."

For non-cognitivism: Endorsement internalism

More directly relevant to the linguistic issues is what I like to call *endorsement internalism*. According to endorsement internalism, normative language has some tight connection to the speech acts of endorsement, or approval (or disapproval or disapprobation as the case may be) (Gibbard 1990). We get some sense of the position when we consider the oddity of saying "Stepping on gouty toes is wrong, but I have nothing against it." This is largely underexplored territory (but see Woods 2014). The menu of options we found under motivational internalism is likely to repeat here, and it is a good question what sort of linguistic hypothesis accounts for the data.

OTHER CONSIDERATIONS AND CONCLUSION

I have just scratched the surface of the considerations that need to be explained. I focus on the above issues because they seem to directly address the general question: cognitivism or non-cognitivism? Other arguments in this literature take a divide-and-conquer strategy. For example, one could mount separate arguments against different versions of cognitivism, and thereby argue in favor of some version of non-cognitivism. One might, for example, argue that non-naturalist realism is subject to epistemic and metaphysical concerns of various sorts, while naturalist realism is undermined by Moore's open question argument (Moore 1903) and, more recently, moral twin earth arguments (Horgan and Timmons 1992). I must leave all these other metaethical battles for discussion elsewhere in this volume.

What we have, though, is an important distinction that cuts deep in the metaethical landscape and reaches out to nearly every area of philosophy. A lot of work has gone into these debates. Yet many issues remain ripe for further exploration.

NOTES

1. We can set to one side what sort of worldly features are ascribed. Perhaps some normative sentences ascribe a monadic property, others relations between agents and actions, others relations between sets of possible worlds, etc.
2. Another excellent resource on these issues is the SEP entry "Moral Cognitivism vs. Non-cognitivism" (van Roojen 2015).
3. Gibbard (2012) now defends expressivism about semantic discourse.
4. Exactly what this position amounts to is disputed. Some say we are to assign mental states as semantic values in a formal treatment of the language (Rosen 1998; Schroeder 2010a). Others say we are to draw a meta-semantic distinction: sentences have whatever semantic values they have in virtue of expressing states of mind (Chrisman 2012; Ridge 2014). Another option is to locate the view in a more deeply pragmatic theory of meaning (Price et al. 2013). This is not the place to pursue these issues (but see Carballo 2014 and Elisabeth Camp's chapter "Metaethical Expressivism").
5. There are difficult cases with the so-called non-metaphysicalist or quietist positions (Parfit 2011; Scanlon 2014), which typically align themselves with cognitivism but have unclear associations with description and representation.
6. Chrisman (2008) offers another approach: distinguish the camps in terms of whether they give normative judgments pride of place in practical reasoning or theoretical reasoning. It is unclear whether this captures the debate, and whether we can sustain the distinction between practical and theoretical reasoning without recourse to description- and representation-talk.

ACKNOWLEDGMENTS

Thanks to the editors and to Lea Schroeder, Stefan Sciaraffa, Mark Timmons, and Mark van Roojen for helpful comments on previous drafts of this chapter.

RELATED TOPICS

Chapter 5, "Metaethical Expressivism;" Chapter 14, "The Frege-Geach Problem;" Chapter 15, "Hybrid Accounts of Ethical Thought and Talk;" Chapter 17, "The Significance of Ethical Disagreement for Theories of Ethical Thought and Talk;" Chapter 19, "Ethical Judgment and Motivation;" Chapter 22, "Mind-Dependence and Moral Realism;" Chapter 33, "Metasemantics and Metaethics."

REFERENCES

Anscombe, G. E. (1957). *Intention*. Cambridge, MA: Harvard University Press.
Ayer, A. J. (1936). *Language, Truth and Logic*. London: V. Gollancz, Ltd.
Bedke, M. S. (2008). Moral judgment purposivism: Saving internalism from amoralism. *Philosophical Studies*, *144*(2), 189–209.
Blackburn, S. (1984). *Spreading the Word: Groundings in the Philosophy of Language*. Oxford; New York: Clarendon Press.
Blackburn, S. (1993). *Essays in Quasi-Realism*. New York: Oxford University Press.
Blackburn, S. (1996a). Comments on Dworkin's "Objectivity and truth: You'd better believe it." Available at: http://www.brown.edu/Departments/Philosophy/bears/9611blac.html.
Blackburn, S. (1996b). Securing the nots: Moral epistemology for the quasi-realist. In W. Sinnott-Armstrong & M. Timmons (eds.), *Moral Knowledge? New Readings in Moral Epistemology*, New York: Oxford University Press, 82–100.
Blackburn, S. (1998). *Ruling Passions: A Theory of Practical Reasoning*. Oxford; New York: Oxford University Press.

Blackburn, S. (2009). Truth and a priori possibility: Egan's charge against quasi-realism. *Australasian Journal of Philosophy*, 87(2), 201–213.

Boyd, R. (1988). How to be a moral realist. In G. Sayre-McCord (ed.), *Essays on Moral Realism*, New York: Cornell University Press, 181–228.

Brink, D. O. (1989). *Moral Realism and the Foundations of Ethics*. Cambridge: Cambridge University Press.

Carballo, A. P. (2014). Semantic hermeneutics. In A. Burgess & B. Sherman (eds.), *Metasemantics: New Essays on the Foundations of Meaning*, New York: Oxford University Press, 119–146.

Chrisman, M. (2008). Expressivism, inferentialism, and saving the debate. *Philosophy and Phenomenological Research*, 77(2), 334–358.

Chrisman, M. (2012). On the meaning of "ought." *Oxford Studies in Metaethics*, 7, 304–332.

Copp, D. (1995). *Morality, Normativity, and Society*. Oxford: Oxford University Press.

Cuneo, T. (2007). *The Normative Web: An Argument for Moral Realism*. Oxford; New York: Oxford University Press.

Dreier, J. (1990). Internalism and speaker relativism. *Ethics*, 101(1), 6–26.

Dreier, J. (1996). Expressivist embeddings and minimalist truth. *Philosophical Studies*, 83(1), 29–51.

Dreier, J. (2004). Meta-ethics and the problem of creeping minimalism. *Philosophical Perspectives*, 18(1), 23–44.

Dreier, J. (2006). Disagreeing (about) what to do: Negation and completeness in Gibbard's norm-expressivism. *Philosophy and Phenomenological Research*, 72(3), 714–721.

Egan, A. (2007). Quasi-realism and fundamental moral error. *Australasian Journal of Philosophy*, 85(2), 205–219.

Enoch, D. (2011). *Taking Morality Seriously: A Defense of Robust Realism*. Oxford: Oxford University Press.

Fine, K. (2001). The question of realism. *Philosophers' Imprint*, 1(1), 1–30.

Finlay, S. (2014). *Confusion of Tongues*. New York: Oxford University Press.

Fitzpatrick, W. (2012). Ethical non-naturalism and normative properties. In M. Brady (ed.), *New Waves in Metaethics*, Chippenham and Eastbourne: Palgrave MacMillan, 7–35.

Geach, P. (1960). Ascriptivism. *The Philosophical Review*, 69(2), 221–225.

Geach, P. (1965). Assertion. *The Philosophical Review*, 74(4), 449–465.

Gibbard, A. (1990). *Wise Choices, Apt Feelings: A Theory of Normative Judgment*. Cambridge, MA: Harvard University Press.

Gibbard, A. (2003). *Thinking How to Live*. Cambridge, MA: Harvard University Press.

Gibbard, A. (2012). *Meaning and Normativity*. Oxford: Oxford University Press.

Hale, B. (2002). Can arboreal knotwork help Blackburn out of Frege's abyss? *Philosophy and Phenomenological Research*, 65(1), 144–149.

Hare, R. M. (1952). *The Language of Morals*. Oxford, UK: Clarendon Press.

Horgan, T., & Timmons, M. (1992). Troubles on moral twin earth: Moral queerness revived. *Synthese*, 92(2), 221–260.

Horgan, T., & Timmons, M. (2006a). Cognitivist expressivism. *Metaethics After Moore*, New York: Oxford University Press, 255–298.

Horgan, T., & Timmons, M. (2006b). Expressivism, yes! Relativism, no! *Oxford Studies in Metaethics*, 1, 73–98.

Humberstone, I. L. (1992). Direction of fit. *Mind*, 101(401), 59–83.

Jackson, F. (1998). *From Metaphysics to Ethics: A Defence of Conceptual Analysis*, Oxford: Oxford University Press.

Joyce, R. (2001). *The Myth of Morality*. Cambridge: Cambridge University Press.

Kalderon, M. E. (2005). *Moral Fictionalism*. Oxford: Oxford University Press.

Korsgaard, C. M. (1986). Skepticism about practical reason. *The Journal of Philosophy*, 83(1), 5–25.

Lenman, J. (1999). The externalist and the amoralist. *Philosophia*, 27(3–4), 441–457.

Mackie, J. L. (1977). *Ethics: Inventing Right and Wrong*. Harmondsworth, NY: Penguin.

Moore, G. (1903). *Principia Ethica*. Cambridge: Cambridge University Press.

Olson, J. (2014). *Moral Error Theory: History, Critique, Defence*. New York: Oxford University Press.

Parfit, D. (2011). *On What Matters: Volume Two*. New York: Oxford University Press.

Price, H., Blackburn, S., Brandom, R., Horwich, P., & Williams, M. (2013). *Expressivism, Pragmatism and Representationalism*. New York: Cambridge University Press.

Railton, P. (1986). Moral realism. *Philosophical Review*, 95: 163–207.

Ridge, M. (2014). *Impassioned Belief*. New York: Oxford University Press.

Rosen, G. (1998). Blackburn's essays in quasi-realism. *Noûs*, *32*(3), 386–405.

Scanlon, T. M. (2014). *Being Realistic About Reasons*. New York: Oxford University Press.

Schroeder, M. (2007). *Slaves of the Passions*. Oxford; New York: Oxford University Press.

Schroeder, M. (2010a). *Being For: Evaluating the Semantic Program of Expressivism*. Oxford, UK: Clarendon Press.

Schroeder, M. A. (2010b). *Noncognitivism in Ethics*. London; New York: Routledge.

Searle, J. R. (1969). *Speech Acts*. Cambridge; New York: Cambridge University Press.

Searle, J. R. (1984). *Intentionality*. Cambridge: Cambridge University Press.

Shafer-Landau, R. (2003). *Moral Realism: A Defence*. Oxford, UK: Clarendon Press.

Smith, M. (1994). *The Moral Problem*. Oxford, UK: Blackwell.

Stevenson, C. L. (1963). The nature of ethical disagreement. In *Facts and Values: Studies in Ethical Analysis*, New Haven: Yale University Press, 1–9.

Street, S. (2010). What is constructivism in ethics and metaethics? *Philosophy Compass*, *5*(5), 363–384.

Timmons, M. (1999). *Morality without Foundations: A Defense of Ethical Contextualism*. New York: Oxford University Press.

Tresan, J. (2009). The challenge of communal internalism. *The Journal of Value Inquiry*, *43*(2), 179–199.

van Roojen, M. (1996). Expressivism and irrationality. *Philosophical Review*, *105*(3), 311–335.

van Roojen, M. (2015). Moral cognitivism vs. non-cognitivism. In E. N. Zalta (ed.), *The Stanford Encyclopedia of Philosophy*. Available at: http://plato.stanford.edu/archives/fall2015/entries/moral-cognitivism/.

Woods, J. (2014). Expressivism and Moore's paradox. *Philosophers' Imprint*, *14*(5), 1–12.

19

Ethical Judgment and Motivation

David Faraci and Tristram McPherson

If you face a difficult choice, it is natural to ask yourself *what ought I to do*? And if you answer that question to your own satisfaction, we typically expect you to then perform the action that you've judged you ought to do. Related lines of thought have led many philosophers to conclude that *ethical* judgments—such as the judgment I ought to do such-and-such—have a distinctive connection to motivation and the explanation of action. And many have further taken this connection to have important implications for the nature of ethical judgment.

The literature on this topic has largely focused on the relationship between motivation and *moral* judgment, in particular. This is understandable. First, metaethicists have only recently begun distinguishing questions about ethics from questions about morality, and focusing on the former. Second, many endorse claims like:

Moral Rationalism Necessarily, if someone *morally* ought to perform an action, she also *ethically* ought to perform it.

Indeed, some claim that this is a conceptual truth (e.g., Smith 1994: 185). This might seem to suggest that ethical and moral judgments bear the same connection to motivation, so that it does not matter which we focus on. However, both Moral Rationalism and this apparent implication are controversial (for discussion, see e.g., Brink 1986; Smith 1994: §3.3; van Roojen 2010; Bromwich 2013; Markovits 2014). In light of this, we think it is fruitful to directly address the relationship between motivation and judgments about what one ethically ought to do. This is both an intrinsically interesting metaethical issue and a potentially crucial moving part in the dialectic concerning Moral Rationalism and the nature of moral judgments. This chapter thus focuses primarily on the relationship between ethical judgment and motivation, although we highlight connections to debates over moral judgment and Moral Rationalism where appropriate. It is worth noting that, in what follows, we often reference papers that focus on moral judgment when we are discussing an issue concerning ethical judgment. We only flag this difference when we think that this contrast makes a structurally important difference to the point or argument being made in that paper.

We begin by introducing the core motivations for thinking that there is some necessary connection between ethical judgment and motivation, and exploring the consequences of a strong account of the connection, which we call *Simple Internalism*. We then explore the evidence for and against this simple view. Next, we explore three influential ways of modifying the simple view. We examine the case for denying the existence of a necessary connection between ethical judgment and motivation. Finally, we briefly consider several issues about the relationship between mind and language that complicate ordinary ways of discussing this connection.

AN INTRODUCTION TO ETHICAL JUDGMENT AND MOTIVATION

This section does four things. First, it more carefully introduces the initial case for thinking that ethical judgment is linked to motivation. Second, it introduces the strongest form of this connection that has been influential in the literature. Third, it explains how this account of the connection can be used in an argument for a distinctive, *non-cognitivist* account of the nature of ethical judgment. Finally, it introduces and explains some of the central assumptions about motivation and the explanation of action that are required for this argument to work.

To begin, it will be useful to introduce some common (but controversial) assumptions about human psychology that frame our discussion. The first assumption is that much of our thought can be modeled in terms of *attitudes* and *contents*. For example, one might change from *wondering whether* <u>one should be vegetarian</u> to *judging that* <u>one should be vegetarian</u>. This is a change in the attitude (from wondering to judging) one bears towards a single content: that one should be a vegetarian. People can have many different sorts of attitudes towards a given content: *believing, hoping, fearing, desiring, supposing for the sake of argument*, etc.

Notice that some types of attitude towards an ethical content bear no apparent tie to motivation. For example, there is no reason to expect me to have any particular motivation if I merely wonder whether I ought to perform a certain action. This chapter focuses on a specific attitude-type: ethical *judgment*. Judging is an attitude that is intended to clearly and intuitively contrast with, for example, hoping, fearing, or wondering. As we'll see, the nature of such ethical judgment—whether it is a species of belief, or of desire, or of something else entirely—is one of the central controversies impacted by the debate over the relationship between ethical judgment and motivation.

The contents of attitudes also take many forms. For example, one can have attitudes towards individuals (loving <u>Achmed</u>), properties (seeking <u>happiness</u>), or propositions (worrying that <u>Alice is cruel</u>). Another important category is *self-ascribing* or *de se* content. For example, if Jane thinks <u>Jane is tired</u>, this is an ordinary propositional content that happens to be about her. In the right circumstances, Jane might have this thought without noticing that it is about her (compare Perry 1979). By contrast, if Jane has the thought <u>I am tired</u>, this *de se* thought transparently ascribes tiredness to *the thinker of the thought*.

This chapter focuses on the motivational significance of judgments with self-ascribing ethical content, of the form <u>I ought to perform action A</u>. We assume that such judgments purport to *settle what to do* in a way that contrasts with the deliverances of other normative standards, like etiquette or the rules of a game (for discussion, see Derek Baker's chapter "The Varieties of Normativity"). We can understand Moral Rationalism as the claim that the moral ought has the same authoritative purport. However, we make ethical ought judgments about cases where morality is—at least intuitively—silent. For example, imagine concluding that you will feel more confident today if you wear your favorite shirt. You might conclude that you thus ought to wear it, without thinking that morality bears on this question at all. (For discussion, see Stephen Darwall's chapter "Ethics and Morality.")

In focusing on ethical ought judgments in this chapter, we ignore the relationship between motivation and other sorts of ethical judgments. These include other *strong deontic judgments*, such as that corporal punishment is right or wrong; *evaluative judgments*, such as that pleasure is good; *aretaic judgments*, such as that courage is virtuous; *thick ethical judgments*, such as that charitable giving is generous; and *weak deontic judgements*, such as that charitable giving is supererogatory. We also set aside questions about the motivational significance of ethical judgments about *others'* behavior.

It is uncontroversial that moral judgments can take each of the above forms. Ethical judgments can take at least some of these forms, which a full account of the relationship between ethical judgment and motivation will therefore need to address. Such a full theory might significantly complicate the lessons that metaethicists have been inclined to draw based on the discussion of self-ascribing ought judgments (for one example, see Archer forthcoming). (For brevity, we call self-ascribing ought judgments 'ethical judgments', unless a contrast with other ethical judgments is important to the relevant discussion.)

With these clarifications in hand, we can ask: why think that ethical judgment is closely connected to motivation? One answer is suggested by an influential example from Michael Smith:

> Suppose we are sitting together one Sunday afternoon. World Vision is out collecting money for famine relief, so we are waiting to hear a knock on the door. I am wondering whether I should give to this particular appeal. We debate the pros and cons of contributing and, let's suppose, after some discussion, you convince me that I should contribute.
>
> (Smith 1994: 6)

Smith makes two claims about this case. The first is that if the canvasser then knocks on the door, you would expect Smith to give. The second is that only certain *special explanations* suffice to dispel this expectation. For example, one excellent explanation would be that Smith has subsequently changed his mind. Another would be that he has succumbed to weakness of will.

If correct, these claims make ethical judgments unusual. If all you knew about Smith was that he believed <u>I can contribute to World Vision's mission by giving the canvasser money</u>, it would not be puzzling if Smith then declined to give. We would be equally unsurprised if Smith were unmotivated by certain non-ethical normative judgments, such as a judgment that contributing to World Vision would meet the standards of etiquette or the rules of some game.

These contrasts seem to suggest that ethical judgment is distinctively connected to motivation. One strong thesis is that there is a *necessary* connection between ethical judgment and motivation. Because this connection is often taken to flow from the nature of ethical judgment (and hence to be 'internal' to it), we call this view *ethics/motives judgment internalism* (or, for brevity, *internalism*). By parity, we call the contrary view—that there is *no* necessary connection between ethical judgment and motivation—*externalism*. (Compare Darwall 1996: 308 for the classic characterization of judgment internalism.) The internalist claim that there is *some* necessary connection here is importantly imprecise. The next few sections address various precisifications. Begin with:

Simple Internalism Necessarily, if you judge that you ethically ought to do A, you are motivated (to some extent) to do A.

Simple Internalism is poised to help explain both of Smith's claims. First, if the truth of Simple Internalism were widely implicitly known, that would explain our strong expectation that Smith would give in his scenario. Second, because Simple Internalism merely entails that the ought-judge has *some* relevant motivation, it is compatible with explanations of failure to act that appeal to weakness of will. By contrast, consider the much stronger thesis that if you genuinely judge that you ought to do A, and you are 'of one mind' about this, you *will* make the attempt to do A (Gibbard 2003: 153). This stronger thesis can seem implausible exactly in virtue of ruling out weakness of will.

Simple Internalism has been taken to have substantial consequences for the nature of ethical judgments, in light of its relationship to the *Humean theory of motivation*. The core idea of the Humean theory is that for an agent to be motivated to do A, she must desire to do B, and believe that by doing A she will do B. That is, every intentional action is explained by the agent's belief about what she is doing, and a desire she takes that action—so understood—to fulfill.

Philosophers are often attracted to the Humean theory because they accept a *functionalist* account of the nature of belief and desire. This idea can be illustrated by a famous analogy due to Elizabeth Anscombe (1957: 56). Imagine a detective hired to follow a shopper around a grocery store and find out what he purchases. Suppose that both the detective and the shopper have lists of groceries. The shopper's list functions to *guide* his behavior: when all goes well, if 'butter' is on the list, he puts butter in his cart. The shopper's aim is to make the contents of his cart conform to the contents of his list. The detective's list, by contrast, functions to *represent* the world: when all goes well, if there is butter in the cart, the detective adds 'butter' to her list. Her aim is to make her list conform to the contents of the shopper's cart.

Psychological states can be understood in similar functional terms. A *cognitive* or *belief-like* psychological state functions like the detective's list: when all goes well, one will *believe* that there is butter in the shopper's cart only when there is. A *non-cognitive* or *desire-like* psychological state functions like the shopper's list: when all goes well, the desire to put butter in the cart will motivate one to put butter in the cart. As the Humean theory suggests, part of *all's going well* here is the presence of a relevant means-end belief: for example, <u>that picking up the butter and dropping it thusly will get it into the cart.</u> If the shopper instead believes that the way to get butter into his cart is to throw it at the wall, he will not tend to wind up with butter in his cart. Crucially, the functionalist Humean insists that the cognitive and non-cognitive functions are *distinct*: for example, while the desire that there be butter in the cart motivates you to put butter in the cart, it would be bizarre for the belief that there is butter in the cart to motivate you to put butter in the cart. (For two approaches to defending the Humean theory of motivation, see Smith 1987 and Sinhababu 2009. For challenges to the Humean theory or its typical functionalist gloss, see e.g., Little 1997; Scanlon 1998; Sobel and Copp 2001; Coleman 2008; Schueler 2009; Frost 2014.)

It is important to emphasize that the issue here is about functionally characterized states. Despite their names, it is controversial whether these functional states map neatly onto the attitudes we typically mean by 'belief' and 'desire'. (For some complications, and different ways of understanding the distinction between cognitive and non-cognitive states, see Matthew S. Bedke's chapter "Cognitivism and Non-Cognitivism.")

Combined with Simple Internalism, the Humean theory underwrites an elegant argument for *non-cognitivism* about ethical judgment: the thesis that ethical judgments are *desire-like* attitudes. If only desire-like attitudes can motivate, and ethical judgments always motivate, then wherever there is an ethical judgment, there must be a non-cognitive attitude. Arguably, the simplest explanation for this partnership is that ethical judgments *are* non-cognitive attitudes. Of course, this isn't the *only* possible explanation. For example, a cognitivist could propose to explain Simple Internalism by citing a universal desire to do what one ought to do. But why think that, *necessarily*, every ethical judge has such a desire? In light of questions like this, many philosophers have thought that non-cognitivism is the *best* explanation for theses like Simple Internalism.

THE EVIDENCE FOR AND AGAINST SIMPLE INTERNALISM

This section considers evidence for and against Simple Internalism, as well as resources that the simple internalist can use to rebut evidence against the view. It is important to emphasize in this context that Simple Internalism is in one respect an extremely *strong* view, because it claims that motivation to do A *necessarily* accompanies the judgment that one ought to do A. Because of this, showing that *in many cases* motivation accompanies such ethical judgments is not sufficient to establish the view; something more must be done to show that this connection is necessary.

A range of evidence for Simple Internalism is suggested by reflection on possible cases. Suppose, for example, that someone's avowed ethical claims fail to line up with his behavior. Which of these—the claims or the behavior—would you consider the better guide to his ethical judgments? Arguably his *behavior* is the better guide (compare Hare 1952: 1). But the idea that behavior is a good guide to ethical judgment only makes sense if ethical judgment tends to be connected to motivation. And this tendency must be quite strong, in order for the evidence of this connection to outweigh the ordinary presumption of sincere utterance. Smith's claims about the famine relief example, discussed in the previous section, provide complementary evidence: if (as Smith claims) we strongly expect motivation to accompany a *new* ethical judgment (like the one Smith makes in the example), this supports the idea that we take motivation to be connected to ethical judgment itself. (For empirical evidence that the sorts of expectations Hare and Smith suggest are widely shared, see Eggers 2015.)

One limitation of the sort of evidence offered by Hare and Smith is that it is *indirect*: if successful, it most directly identifies our widely shared tacit *beliefs* about ethical judgments rather than providing direct evidence about the nature of the judgments themselves (for a discussion that exploits this distinction, see Braddon-Mitchell 2006). One might thus attempt to complement this work by studying the nature of ethical judgments directly. Consider one discussion of *moral* judgment that provides an instructive model. Jesse Prinz (2015: §4.2.1) points to three converging lines of evidence for internalism about moral judgments: (1) that moral cognition is correlated with heightened emotion, (2) that elicited emotions can alter moral judgments, and (3) that emotional differences and deficits are correlated with differences and deficits in moral judgment. Prinz suggests that this evidence is *best explained* by a sentimentalist view on which moral judgments consist of emotional attitudes.

The form of Prinz's argument answers a central challenge to the possibility of empirical arguments for Simple Internalism: Simple Internalism is a strong modal claim, and it may be hard to see how empirical evidence alone could support such a claim. Prinz's account suggests an answer: he argues that the empirical evidence supports sentimentalism, which is a constitutive claim about the nature of moral judgments. And constitutive accounts characteristically have strong modal consequences.

What can be said *against* Simple Internalism? As we noted above, this view posits a *necessary* connection. Its modal strength thus makes it a natural target for counterexamples: establishing a single possible case of ethical judgment without motivation would suffice to refute it. One prominent style of counterexample concerns persons suffering from a quite general lack of motivation, such as deeply depressed persons. It might seem completely unsurprising that a depressed person could sincerely make an ethical judgment and yet fail wholly to be motivated by it (Stocker 1979: 744).

One line of reply to this style of objection takes advantage of a respect in which Simple Internalism is a *weak* claim. It requires only that one possess *some* motivation to do what one judges that one ought to (Finlay 2004: 209). And this makes it possible to resist putative counterexamples like Stocker's depressed person, by suggesting that the motivation exists, but is *weak*, perhaps to the extent of being unnoticeable even to the agent himself.

Another prominent style of counterexample to Simple Internalism appeals to the possibility of persons who simply do not care about ethics. Consider Plato's Thrasymachus, who believes (roughly) that justice is what is in the interests of the powerful, and is therefore not moved at all by the thought of what justice demands of him. Notice that this sort of view is easiest to make plausible with relatively 'thick' moral concepts, like justice. It is a bit harder with morally ought, although here, imagining someone who rejects Moral Rationalism—and hence believes that he *ethically* ought not to act *morally*—can make the case more plausible (compare Brink 1986).

Things get harder still with ethically ought (compare Ridge 2014: 55–56). There has not been a great deal of effort in the literature to spell out an analog for Thrasymachus with respect to ethically ought (for one exception, see Greenberg 2009: 156–158). But there are interesting resources to be explored. For example, someone might have an *alienating* conception of what she ethically ought to do: a conception on which what she ought to do simply runs roughshod over everything she most cares about. Such a person might conclude that doing what one ought to do is simply *awful*, and it might not be surprising if such a person had no motivation to do what she judged she ought to. Call such a character *anethical*.

One influential way of replying to this style of counterexample begins by noting that not all sincere claims that deploy ethical *words* thereby express the speaker's ethical *judgments*. For example, we sometimes use ethical words to talk about conventional ethical views, or some specific salient ethical view other than our own. R. M. Hare (1952: 124) noted that, in print, we can use *inverted commas* around a word to signal such a use. For example, someone might convey her distaste for local mores by writing: "Around here, 'justice' involves a *remarkable* number of public beatings." Interpreted in this way, Thrasymachus might be understood as claiming that 'justice'—i.e., *what other people call 'justice'*—amounts to the interests of the powerful. Crucially, when Thrasymachus makes these claims, he does not thereby directly express his own justice-judgments. His lack of motivation when making such claims would therefore be entirely compatible with Simple Internalism. (For arguments against the plausibility of this strategy as a reply to the relevant range of cases, see Svavarsdóttir 1999: 188–192; for a different internalist reply to this style of case, see Bromwich 2013.)

Psychopaths have received considerable attention in recent discussion of these issues as potential real-world examples of Thrasymachus-style *amoralists*. A significant part of the literature on psychopaths and internalism concerns whether psychopaths should be interpreted as making genuine moral judgments, or something more like Hare-style inverted commas judgments (e.g., Roskies 2003; Nichols 2004; Prinz 2007; Kennett and Fine 2008; Kumar 2016a).

The significance of this literature for Simple Internalism, as a view about *ethical* judgment, is less clear. The first difficulty is that psychopaths seem indifferent to morality, not to their ethical judgments per se, and there are few other candidates for real-life anethical judges. Of course, those who endorse Moral Rationalism will maintain that amoral judges are *ipso facto* anethical judges. But if psychopaths make genuine moral judgments, this might more naturally be taken to cast doubt on Moral Rationalism itself, as opposed to threatening Simple Internalism.

Ironically, a final way to challenge Simple Internalism can be developed from the fact that motivational states are functional states. Functional states are usually analyzed in terms of dispositions, and it is possible for a disposition to be present but *masked*. For example, a vase can have the dispositional property of being *fragile*, where this property is *masked* by its being packed safely in a box (Johnston 1992). One might think that a condition like depression could mask the motivational force of some of one's ethical judgments. If so, then even if ethical judgments are desire-like functional states, Simple Internalism would be false.

A substantial number of philosophers have thought that—in part in virtue of the sorts of cases explored in this section—ethical judgment is possible without motivation. However, many of these philosophers have also thought that the simple internalist is correct in thinking that there is *some* sort of necessary connection between ethical judgment and motivation. We now turn to explore such views.

DEFEASIBLE INTERNALISMS

In this section, we introduce three important ways of developing the idea that the connection between ethical judgment and motivation is necessary but not universal.

These accounts take the relationship to be mediated by *rationality*, *normalcy*, and *linguistic community*, respectively.

Rationality internalism

The first defeasible form of internalism we discuss is

Rationality Internalism Necessarily, if you judge that you ethically ought to do A, and you are structurally rational, you are motivated (to some extent) to do A.

This formulation amends Simple Internalism by adding an additional condition: structural rationality. The inclusion of 'structurally' here is important. To see why, consider the claim that in order to count as *substantively* rational you must be motivated to do what you judge that you ought to. This might be interpreted as telling us a lot about what is required to count as substantively rational, but little about the nature of ethical judgment (compare Schroeter 2005). This worry doesn't seem to apply to Rationality Internalism, because we have an independent grasp on structural rationality as a matter of the joint coherence of one's attitudes. For example, if you believe both P and not-P, then you are structurally irrational. Rationality Internalism, then, differs from Simple Internalism in proposing that ethical judgment without motivation is *possible*, but only if the agent in question is in some way incoherent.

One motivation for Rationality Internalism begins by noting that the judgment I ought to do A has its natural home in deliberation, arguably the paradigmatic mechanism for rational governance of one's own actions. This might make it seem plausible that the failure of motivation following an ought-judgment is structurally irrational, in the same way that it might seem plausible that a failure to apportion one's beliefs to what one takes to be the weight of one's evidence seems to be structurally irrational (for relevant discussion, see Pettit and Smith 1996; Burge 2000; and Schroeter 2005). Notice that this motivation is clearer than in the case of moral judgment, where the (im)plausibility of Moral Rationalism is another crucial moving part.

Rationality Internalism has resources to address some of the other alleged counterexamples to Simple Internalism, discussed in the previous section. Consider the depressed person. The lack of motivation imagined here is quite *general*: this person will also struggle to do what he judges that he would like to do, or what he judges would make him feel better. This seems like a good candidate for a rational failing: this person's motivational system fails to cohere with his own perspective on the world. Or consider the psychopath. It has been argued that psychopaths have significant deficits in practical reasoning (Nichols 2004 and, especially, Maibom 2005). This means that even if psychopaths *do* make genuine moral judgments, their existence may be compatible with both Rationality Internalism *and* Moral Rationalism, if their lack of motivation can be connected to their structural irrationality. Rationality Internalism is also poised to explain the sorts of claims that motivated Simple Internalism: the sorts of expectations that Smith and Hare pointed to can be understood as reasonable, given a background assumption that we are ordinarily (approximately) structurally rational.

What consequences does Rationality Internalism have for our theories of ethical judgment? The first thing to notice is the contrast with the non-cognitivist's explanation of Simple Internalism. According to Rationality Internalism, it is possible to have an ethical judgment without motivation. This rules out identifying ethical judgment with any necessarily motivating state. If every token non-cognitive state were necessarily motivating, this would spell trouble for the non-cognitivist. However, we should not think this (Björnsson 2002: §4). For example, Ridge (2015: 145–146) argues that *general plans* are an example of non-cognitive states that are generally but not necessarily connected to motivation. So, Rationality Internalism does not *rule out* non-cognitivism.

On the other hand, the straightforward case from Simple Internalism *against cognitivism* fails to carry over. Recall that case: on Simple Internalism, ethical judgment guarantees the presence of motivation, and according to the Humean theory of motivation, no cognitive state by itself can guarantee motivation. Given these assumptions, the best explanation of ethical motivation seemed to rule out cognitivism about ethical judgment. But Rationality Internalism rejects the guarantee of motivation, so it cannot support a parallel argument.

Instead, if Rationality Internalism has implications for this debate, they turn on the question: which kinds of states can succeed or fail to cohere with motivational states? Both cognitivists and non-cognitivists can appeal to the plausibility of so-called *enkratic* principles of structural rationality, such as: *if you judge that you ought to do A, then you intend to do A* (Broome 2013). Can one side of the cognitivism/non-cognitivism debate offer an explanation for the truth of such a principle that is unavailable to her opponent? Consider two attempts.

A simple cognitivist theory might analyze the judgment <u>I ought to do A</u> as a belief with the content: <u>were I structurally rational, I would do A</u>. This sort of analysis seems poised to explain why the enkratic principle is a principle of structural rationality, in virtue of its content. (For a sophisticated proposal along these lines, see Smith 1994: chapter 5.) *If* an analogous account is unavailable to the non-cognitivist (something we take no position on here), this would support a Rationality Internalism-based argument for cognitivism.

Conversely, it might be thought that the non-cognitivist has the advantage here since, on her view, ethical judgments are intrinsically apt to motivate, even if they do not do so in every case. But it is not obvious how this grounds rational links. For example, one might think that the ability to *mask* the motivational force of one's non-cognitive states is sometimes rational: consider someone who is able to experience anger, but control what, if anything, that anger disposes him to do.

Normality internalism

A different way to retain the core internalist idea, while granting the force of the apparent counterexamples (such as the anethical judge and the depressed person) is to focus on the idea that, in these examples, the unmotivated judges are *abnormal*. We could state the proposal this way:

Normality Internalism Necessarily, if you judge that you ethically ought to do A, and you are normal, you are motivated (to some extent) to do A.

It is crucial that the notion of normality at play here is not intended as statistical. Rather, the key idea is that we can only imagine cases of unmotivated ethical judgment as parasitic on a robust pattern of connection between ethical judgment and motivation (compare Dreier 1990). For example, the depressed person is imagined to have acquired ethical concepts, been motivated in the ordinary way, and only then fallen into a depression that deprives him of motivation. And Thrasymachus is imagined to have started out motivated to do what is just, and transitioned to his unmotivated state as a result of his investigation into the nature of justice.

One way to motivate Normality Internalism is to imagine someone who is raised without ethical concepts, then joins a society that possesses ethical concepts. He learns how to follow along in conversations, how people use 'ought', etc., but he never experiences any motivation to do what he says he judges he ought to. It may be more tempting to ascribe an inverted commas meaning—as opposed to a genuine ethical judgment—to this person's use of 'ought' than to do so with the depressed person. The normality condition can explain why: this person—unlike the depressed person—has never instantiated the normal connection between ethical judgment and motivation.

Normality Internalism can explain some of the claims that motivated Simple Internalism, but only given background empirical assumptions. For example, because normality is *not* a statistical notion, the expectations that Smith and Hare mention will only be vindicated when we believe that the relevant speakers are normal. The normality internalist might insist that this is as it should be: when we learn any of a variety of things about how an ethical judge has become abnormal, the Smith or Hare-style expectations of that judge tend to disappear. Normality Internalism also arguably has more resources to address counterexamples than Rationality Internalism. For example, the normality internalist does not need to diagnose some structural irrationality in the anethical judge, in order to defend her view.

As these points bring out, the Normality view is a recognizably more modest version of internalism. One might worry that this modesty is purchased at the price of opacity: while we have an initial gloss and motivating examples to orient us to the relevant notion of normality, it is not clear how precisely to understand that notion, or how explanatorily interesting it is (compare Svavarsdóttir 1999: 175, n. 7).

It is an interesting question what the upshot of this view is for the debate between cognitivists and non-cognitivists. As with Rationality Internalism, there is no simple argument for non-cognitivism (for relevant discussion, see Strandberg 2012 and Toppinen 2015). For example, if all abnormal conditions could be understood as conditions that mask an underlying non-cognitive disposition, this would be grist for the non-cognitivist's mill. But it is unclear why we should think that all abnormal ethical judges retain a motivational disposition. On the other hand, Normality Internalism leaves the cognitivist needing to explain what sort of cognitive state could be such that, in order to *get into it*, one must have a certain pattern of motivations, even if one can then go on to lose that pattern. One possibility is that ethical judgment is a *hybrid* state, consisting of cognitive and non-cognitive elements that are ordinarily linked by robust causal mechanisms (e.g., Kumar 2016b). Cases of abnormality might be explained as cases in which these sorts of normal mechanisms break down, or are masked by other psychological processes (for a different cognitivist explanation, see Dreier 1990).

Community-level internalism

The final way of refining internalism that we discuss sets aside the individual and focuses instead on the idea that there is a necessary connection between ethical judgment and motivation at the level of the linguistic community. Suppose you find yourself confronted with an alien linguistic community, *Anethicalia*, whose members happen, through the infinite wackiness of the cosmos, to speak a language that is identical, phonetically and grammatically, to English, and also semantically *very* similar. Their planet has tall plants they call 'trees', small, furry animals they call 'cats' and 'dogs', emotions between partners they call 'love', and so on. They often talk of what they 'ought' to do, much as we do. They often claim that they 'ought' to save the dying, avoid hurting others, give to World Vision, and care for their children. There is just one striking contrast between us and the Anethicalians: they are utterly unmotivated by these judgments.

Some philosophers have suggested that linguistic communities like this are *not* deploying ethical concepts (e.g., Lenman 1999 and Bedke 2009; for a contrary view see Gert and Mele 2005). The idea of community-level internalism, then, is that, necessarily, there is a *community-level* connection between ethical judgment and motivation, for any community of speakers that uses words to conventionally voice their ethical judgments. Stronger and weaker versions of this sort of view are possible. A stronger version would insist that, necessarily, in any linguistic community which has a term in its language that means *ethically ought*, speakers in that community are normally motivated to do A when they judge that they ethically ought to do A. By contrast, a weaker version of the view would insist that a community of normal ethical judges might retain their ethical concepts, even as they evolved into anethical judges. The internalist connection would be retained by insisting that there could not be a community that deployed ethical concepts that had *always* been overwhelmingly anethical (Bedke 2009; compare Dreier 1990).

Like the Normality view, the community-level account has the virtue of smoothly accommodating many sorts of unmotivated ethical judges, provided such judges do not constitute a whole community. However, because the community-level view posits a relatively tenuous link between ethical judgment and motivation, it may have more difficulty vindicating the stronger sorts of claims that Smith and Hare used to motivate internalism in the first place. In light of this, the view is perhaps best understood as motivated by distinct considerations, like the cases introduced in this section.

Critics can attempt to debunk the cases that are supposed to support the community-level view. Consider one such approach, which begins by noting that, on a plausible substantive account of ethical facts, such facts will be a function of something like prudence, cooperation, special relationships, satisfaction of our goals, etc. (or a subset of these things). Now consider a simple form of externalist cognitivism, on which ethical judgment consists in beliefs *about* prudence, cooperation, etc., with no necessary connection to motivation. (Focusing on this view serves only to make the point vivid; similar points hold for other views.) On this view, why would members of a community tend to make ethical judgments, or, more broadly, deploy ethical concepts at all? Presumably, because they *care* about prudence, cooperation, etc. enough to want to keep track of them. This drives home the point that the case proposed to support community-level internalism would have to be quite bizarre: *first* we would need to imagine a functioning society where the members did not typically care about prudence, cooperation, etc. This is already difficult. Then we would need to imagine that such a society nonetheless got a bit of discourse up and running to talk about these topics. This is even more puzzling. Then we are supposed to be confident that this society does not make ethical judgments. Even if we have these reactions about such bizarre cases, it is not wholly clear whether we should take them as any kind of evidence (for worries about the evidential significance of related cases, see Dowell 2015).

The relationship between community-level internalism and theories of the nature of ethical judgment is even less clear than on the Normality view. Both cognitivism and non-cognitivism, as we have spelled them out, are claims about the nature of the *individual psychological states* that constitute ethical judgment. But the community-level view suggests that we can tolerate considerable variation in the nature of such states, provided they are related appropriately to a broader communal pattern (we return to this point below).

DENYING A NECESSARY CONNECTION

Ethics/motives judgment externalists deny a necessary connection between ethical judgment and motivation. Externalists have two central tasks in arguing for their view. First, they must argue against the presence of a necessary connection. This task has already largely been explored in this chapter: many of the challenges to each form of internalism explored above can also be understood as prima facie evidence for externalism. Together, the range of such cases might be taken to constitute a powerful argument for externalism.

Whether or not there is a *necessary* connection between ethical judgment and motivation, it is uncontroversial that there is typically a *strong* correlation between these states. The externalist's second task is therefore to explain this correlation without appealing to such a necessary connection. One natural explanation is that many people—especially generally virtuous people—find appealing the idea of acting ethically; they desire <u>to do what they ought to do</u>, under that very description. Michael Smith complains that this is not the sort of motivation a good person would have (1994: §3.5). For example, a good person who judges that she ought to help you should be motivated by the fact that you need help, not simply by the desire <u>to do what she ought to</u>. (For replies to Smith on this point, see e.g., Strandberg 2007, and several of the papers cited therein.)

One straightforward externalist reply to Smith points out that we should expect ordinary good people to have a *plurality* of relevant motives that are contingently but strongly correlated with what they believe they ought to do, and so are apt to explain their acting in accordance with such ethical judgments. For example, many people are motivated by prudence or kindness or respect, or by direct concern for certain individuals in their lives. Many people also want to act justifiably, and believe that ethical action is a way of doing so.

Given this, the externalist can appeal to an *overlapping set* of these sorts of commonplace motivations to explain the robust correlation between ethical judgment and motivation. This might seem ideally suited to explain the phenomenon in question. On the one hand, by appealing to such an overlapping patchwork of motives that can be expected to vary between people, this picture can explain the wide variation in the nature, strength, and resilience of ethical motivation between people (noted by Svavarsdóttir 1999: 161). On the other, we would expect ordinary good people to possess most of the motives just mentioned: this is part of what makes them good!

This picture can also be used to explain why only certain special explanations will *ordinarily* make lack of ethical motivation intelligible. For in many ordinary cases, what someone judges that she ought to do is correlated with a wide variety of substantial emotions. But this is not always the case. Consider a fact that is familiar to every vegan philosopher. We frequently meet people who say: "I am convinced that I ought to be vegan, but I am just not motivated to do it." Yet we often take them to be sincere in these judgments. Arguably, this is because we recognize that such people are normally motivated by many of their *other* ethical judgments, but we also understand how difficult it can be to emotionally connect with distant animal suffering or to *feel* wrongness in apparently mundane activities like drinking milk. The patchwork picture of ethical motivation suggested in the previous paragraph is well-suited to vindicate these natural thoughts.

COMPLICATIONS: MIND AND LANGUAGE

Much of the discussion of ethical judgment and motivation takes as evidence claims about the relationship between what people *say*, and what they are motivated to do. But notice that facts about what people say are first and foremost facts about language, not psychology. In this section, we note three ways in which focusing on language as a crucial moving part can complicate the discussion offered thus far.

First, consider whether your favored connection between ethical judgment and motivation (if any) really demands *any* psychological explanation in terms of the nature of ethical judgment. Jon Tresan (2006) has shown that even strong internalist connections do not obviously demand this. To see this, consider the state *Tuesday belief*. 'Tuesday belief' just means any belief held on a Tuesday. There are surely Tuesday beliefs, and necessarily, if one has a Tuesday belief, one has it on a Tuesday. But it would be silly to think that we need to give a *psychological* explanation of why this mental state is necessarily instantiated on only one day of the week. The simple internalist claim that ethical judgment is necessarily accompanied by motivation (for example) might get the same treatment: it might be suggested that a certain ordinary belief only counts as an ethical judgment when accompanied by motivation. If this suggestion were right, then just as in the Tuesday belief case, there would be no special psychological puzzle about ethical judgments; they could be ordinary beliefs that cease to count as ethical judgments when their contingent connection to motivation happens to fail.

Second, consider a plausible explanation for the fact that moral and, more broadly, ethical discourse is a cultural universal: such discourse is a means of achieving coordination, shared reasoning, and influence. A functional rationale for treating someone as an ethical judge, then, is that you think of their relevant judgments as apt candidates for such discursive coordination, shared reasoning, and influence. This, in turn, requires that you take yourself to have some reasonable chance of influencing your interlocutors' behavior through ethical engagement. If correct, this picture might explain many of our judgments about who is making genuine 'ethical judgments'. But there may be no *specific* psychological states that our interlocutors would need to be in to make such engagement possible (compare Björnsson and McPherson 2014).

Third, consider a distinctive commitment of the community-level views, suggested above. These views seem committed to a sort of language-first 'anti-individualism' concerning ethical judgments (compare Burge 1979). Community-level internalists appear committed to the idea that two individuals could have qualitatively identical brain states and dispositions, and yet the first could count as making ethical judgments while the second does not, because the second individual is not located in a linguistic community with the relevant properties. This consequence is inconsistent with common assumptions about how to individuate ethical judgments. For example, we sketched the distinction between cognitivism and non-cognitivism in terms of the functional natures of elements of individual psychologies. The anti-individualist picture suggests that it may be a mistake to individuate ethical judgments in this way. If community-level evidence is compelling, it may thus warrant a shift of focus from *psychological* questions about the nature of ethical judgment to *metasemantic* questions about how best to explain the meaning of ethical words in a public language.

On the other hand, anti-individualism is a controversial feature of the community-level view, because many philosophers are tempted to think that ethical judgments are distinctively apt for psychology-level—as opposed to community-level—individuation conditions. Suppose that Sally lives in Anethicalia, discussed above. But suppose that, for whatever reason, her judgments about what she 'ought' to do play a central role in her agential life: she often plans for the future by thinking about what she 'ought' to do, she is robustly motivated by her judgments about what she 'ought' to do, etc. It may seem implausible to insist that she fails to make ethical judgments simply because the *words* she uses to express the relevant judgments are not conventionally associated with any motivational response. This might be taken as evidence that internalism really *is* a thesis about the nature of ethical judgment, rather than about how we use language.

CONCLUSIONS

It is a striking fact that our ethical judgments appear more intimately connected to motivation than many of our other judgments. Many metaethicists have taken this fact to provide the seeds of powerful arguments for distinctive accounts of the nature of ethical judgment. This chapter has aimed to introduce readers to the complexity of the issues facing these arguments, and to some of the tools that philosophers have deployed in seeking to understand that complexity. We hope this introduction is useful to readers interested in further investigating these important issues.

ACKNOWLEDGMENTS

Many thanks to Jamie Fritz and David Plunkett for helpful comments on previous drafts.

REFERENCES

Anscombe, G.E.M. 1957. *Intention*. Cambridge, MA: Harvard University Press.
Archer, A. forthcoming. "Motivational Judgement Internalism and the Problem of Supererogation." *Journal of Philosophical Research*.
Bedke, M.S. 2009. "Moral Judgment Purposivism: Saving Internalism from Amoralism." *Philosophical Studies* 144 (2): 189–209.

Björnsson, G. 2002. "How Emotivism Survives Immoralists, Irrationality, and Depression." *The Southern Journal of Philosophy* 40 (3): 327–344.

Björnsson, G., and T. McPherson. 2014. "Moral Attitudes for Non-Cognitivists: Solving the Specification Problem." *Mind* 123 (489): 1–38.

Braddon-Mitchell, D. 2006. "Believing Falsely Makes It So." *Mind* 115 (460): 833–866.

Brink, D.O. 1986. "Externalist Moral Realism." *The Southern Journal of Philosophy* 24 (S1): 23–41.

Bromwich, D. 2013. "Motivational Internalism and the Challenge of Amoralism." *European Journal of Philosophy* 24 (2): 452–471.

Broome, J. 2013. *Rationality Through Reasoning*. Hoboken, NJ: John Wiley & Sons.

Burge, T. 1979. "Individualism and the Mental." *Midwest Studies in Philosophy* 4 (1): 73–121.

—. 2000. "Reason and the First Person." In *Knowing Our Own Minds*, edited by C. Wright, B. Smith, and C. Macdonald. Oxford: Oxford University Press.

Coleman, M.C. 2008. "Directions of Fit and the Humean Theory of Motivation." *Australasian Journal of Philosophy* 86 (1): 127–139.

Darwall, S. 1996. "Reasons, Motives, and the Demands of Morality: An Introduction." In *Moral Discourse and Practice: Some Philosophical Approaches*, edited by S. Darwall, A. Gibbard, and P. Railton. New York: Oxford University Press.

Dowell, J. L. 2015. "The Metaethical Insignificance of Moral Twin Earth." In *Oxford Studies in Metaethics*, edited by R. Shafer-Landau. Vol. 11. Oxford: Oxford University Press.

Dreier, J. 1990. "Internalism and Speaker Relativism." *Ethics* 101 (1): 6–26.

Eggers, D. 2015. "Unconditional Motivational Internalism and Hume's Lesson." In *Motivational Internalism*, edited by G. Björnsson, C. Strandberg, R. Francén Olinder, J. Eriksson, and F. Björklund. New York: Oxford University Press.

Finlay, S. 2004. "The Conversational Practicality of Value Judgement." *The Journal of Ethics* 8 (3): 205–223.

Frost, K. 2014. "On the Very Idea of Direction of Fit." *Philosophical Review* 123 (4): 429–484.

Gert, J., and A. Mele. 2005. "Lenman on Externalism and Amoralism: An Interplanetary Exploration." *Philosophia* 32 (1): 275–283.

Gibbard, A. 2003. *Thinking How to Live*. Cambridge, MA: Harvard University Press.

Greenberg, M. 2009. "Moral Concepts and Motivation." *Philosophical Perspectives* 23 (1): 137–164.

Hare, R.M. 1952. *The Language of Morals*. Oxford: Clarendon.

Johnston, M. 1992. "How to Speak of the Colors." *Philosophical Studies* 68 (3): 221–263.

Kennett, J., and C. Fine. 2008. "Internalism and the Evidence from Psychopaths and 'Acquired Sociopaths'." In *The Neuroscience of Morality: Emotion, Disease, and Development*, edited by W. Sinnott-Armstrong. Vol. 3. Moral Psychology. Cambridge, MA: MIT Press.

Kumar, V. 2016a. "Psychopathy and Internalism." *Canadian Journal of Philosophy* 46 (3): 318–345.

—. 2016b. "The Empirical Identity of Moral Judgement." *The Philosophical Quarterly*, 1–22.

Lenman, J. 1999. "The Externalist and the Amoralist." *Philosophia* 27 (3): 441–457.

Little, M.O. 1997. "Virtue as Knowledge: Objections from the Philosophy of Mind." *Noûs* 31 (1): 59–79.

Maibom, H.L. 2005. "Moral Unreason: The Case of Psychopathy." *Mind & Language* 20 (2): 237–257.

Markovits, J. 2014. *Moral Reason*. Oxford: Oxford University Press.

Nichols, S. 2004. *Sentimental Rules: On the Natural Foundations of Moral Judgment*. Oxford: Oxford University Press.

Perry, J. 1979. "The Problem of the Essential Indexical." *Noûs* 13 (1): 3–21.

Pettit, P., and M. Smith. 1996. "Freedom in Belief and Desire." *The Journal of Philosophy* 93 (9): 429–449.

Prinz, J. 2007. *The Emotional Construction of Morals*. Oxford: Oxford University Press.

—. 2015. "An Empirical Case for Motivational Internalism." In *Motivational Internalism*, edited by G. Björnsson, C. Strandberg, R. Francén Olinder, J. Eriksson, and F. Björklund. New York: Oxford University Press.

Ridge, M. 2014. *Impassioned Belief*. Oxford: Oxford University Press.

—. 2015. "Internalism: Cui Bono?" In *Motivational Internalism*, edited by G. Björnsson, C. Strandberg, R. Francén Olinder, J. Eriksson, and F. Björklund. New York: Oxford University Press.

Roskies, A. 2003. "Are Ethical Judgments Intrinsically Motivational? Lessons from 'Acquired Sociopathy'." *Philosophical Psychology* 16 (1): 51–66.

Scanlon, T.M. 1998. *What We Owe to Each Other*. Cambridge, MA: Belknap Press of Harvard University Press.

Schroeter, F. 2005. "Normative Concepts and Motivation." *Philosophers' Imprint* 5 (3): 1–23.

Schueler, G.F. 2009. "The Humean Theory of Motivation Rejected." *Philosophy and Phenomenological Research* 78 (1): 103–122.

Sinhababu, N. 2009. "The Humean Theory of Motivation Reformulated and Defended." *Philosophical Review* 118 (4): 465–500.

Smith, M. 1987. "The Humean Theory of Motivation." *Mind* 96 (381): 36–61.

—. 1994. *The Moral Problem*. Malden, MA: Blackwell.

Sobel, D., and D. Copp. 2001. "Against Direction of Fit Accounts of Belief and Desire." *Analysis* 61 (269): 44–53.

Stocker, M. 1979. "Desiring the Bad: An Essay in Moral Psychology." *The Journal of Philosophy* 76 (12): 738–753.

Strandberg, C. 2007. "Externalism and the Content of Moral Motivation." *Philosophia* 35 (2): 249–260.

—. 2012. "Expressivism and Dispositional Desires." *American Philosophical Quarterly* 49 (1): 81–91.

Svavarsdóttir, S. 1999. "Moral Cognitivism and Motivation." *The Philosophical Review* 108 (2): 161–219.

Toppinen, T. 2015. "Pure Expressivism and Motivational Internalism." In *Motivational Internalism*, edited by G. Björnsson, C. Strandberg, R. Francén Olinder, J. Eriksson, and F. Björklund. New York: Oxford University Press.

Tresan, J. 2006. "De Dicto Internalist Cognitivism." *Noûs* 40 (1): 143–165.

van Roojen, M. 2010. "Moral Rationalism and Rational Amoralism." *Ethics* 120 (3): 495–525.

FURTHER READING

Björnsson, G., C. Strandberg, R. Francén Olinder, J. Eriksson, and F. Björklund (eds.). 2015. *Motivational Internalism*. New York: Oxford University Press.

Rosati, C.S. 2014. "Moral Motivation," in *The Stanford Encyclopedia of Philosophy* (Spring 2014 Edition), Edward N. Zalta (ed.), URL = <http://plato.stanford.edu/archives/spr2014/entries/moral-motivation/>.

20

Reasons Internalism

Errol Lord and David Plunkett

INTRODUCTION

The last several decades have seen *normative reasons* come to the theoretical fore all across normative philosophy, especially in ethics and epistemology. To use the orthodox introductory gloss, normative reasons are considerations that *count in favor of* various reactions; for example, acts, beliefs, intentions, desires, emotions, etc. (see Scanlon 1998). As the label "normative reasons" suggests, the basic job description of normative reasons is a *normative* one, e.g., to *justify* a given reaction. This is in contrast to a *descriptive* one, e.g., to explain *why* that reaction happened, which is the core job description of *motivating reasons*. Within ethics, philosophers have focused chiefly on normative reasons for *action* or *intention*. Such normative reasons are central to thinking about *practical* reasoning about what to do, as opposed to *theoretical* reasoning about what to believe. Hence, one might call them "practical normative reasons." Practical normative reasons are our focus. For ease of exposition, we will use "normative reasons" to refer to specifically practical normative reasons, unless we note otherwise.

One of the central issues about normative reasons concerns whether they are necessarily connected to the psychologies of the agents they are reasons for. *Internalist* views of normative reasons hold that in order for some consideration C to be a normative reason for A to φ (where φ is an action or intention), C has to bear some special relation to A's psychology. *Externalist* views deny this.

This schematic way of putting things (which draws on Finlay and Schroeder 2012) reflects an important fact about the debate over internalism. There are many different internalist views about the relation between reason-providing facts and psychology. There is also a plethora of views about which psychological feature is relevant. There are thus a wide variety of different internalist theses. Moreover, some views that posit a relatively weak connection between an agent's psychology and her normative reasons—such as the view of McDowell (1995), on which, roughly, normative reasons must be capable of motivating an ideally virtuous version of the agent—are called "externalist" in some contexts but "internalist" in others. This is partly due to the fact that, in different contexts, speakers will have different things in mind about what would count as a relevant relation to A's psychology.

These facts can make it hard to understand what exactly is at issue in the debate over internalism in general, as well as to find one's bearings within a given part of the debate. It also raises the question of whether there is a single philosophically important dividing line between internalism and externalism. However, as we will see, much of the action in the discussion over "internalism" and "externalism" in recent years does not depend on there being a single important dividing line. Rather, many of the most interesting debates are about *specific* internalist proposals, many of which can be articulated without using the labels at all. (See Finlay and Schroeder 2012 for connected discussion.)

The plan for this chapter is as follows. We will start by providing an overview of some key arguments on behalf of internalism and externalism, respectively. Following this, we will look at how the debate over internalism interacts with the debate over *moral rationalism*. Moral rationalism, as we will understand it, is the view that morality necessarily provides normative reasons. We will use the discussion of moral rationalism as a general frame to discuss some of the major versions of internalism.

INTERNALISM: CENTRAL MOTIVATIONS

In this section, we will sketch some of the central motivations for internalism.

We'll start with a straightforward motivation that Mark Schroeder puts forward at the beginning of *Slaves of the Passions* (2007). Schroeder notes that, at least prima facie, it seems obvious that at least *some* normative reasons are dependent on one's psychology. To use Schroeder's own example, suppose Ronnie loves to dance but Bradley hates it. Both of them are invited to a party where there will be dancing. Intuitively, claims Schroeder, the fact that there will be dancing at the party is a normative reason for Ronnie to go to the party, but not so for Bradley. This, claims Schroeder, seems best explained by the difference in facts about their psychologies—in particular, facts about what they each desire. Given that at least some normative reasons are explained this way, it's natural to wonder whether *all* of them are. If they are, it would yield a simple and unified theory of normative reasons. As Schroeder emphasizes, it is a tall order to carry out this task. The crucial point is just that there is a good motivation for examining whether or not this task can be carried out.

A second influential line of motivation stems from Bernard Williams, who first coined the term "internal reasons" (Williams 1979). Williams holds that the *same* consideration that *justifies* an agent's action must be something the agent could also take as her goal and actually act on, thus playing a role in the *explanation* of her action. The core idea, then, is that in order for C to be a normative reason for an agent A to φ, it must be that A is capable of actually φ-ing on the basis of C—i.e., it must be that C can be A's *motivating reason* for φ-ing. Moreover, Williams claims that if an agent were fully rational and grasps what her normative reasons are, this will motivate her to perform the action favored by those reasons. Following Julia Markovits, we can call the combination of these ideas "the motivating intuition" (Markovits 2014).

Why accept "the motivating intuition"?

First, one might argue (following Williams) that the *purpose* of normative reason ascriptions is to point out a consideration that an agent would be wrong to ignore *by her own lights*. Now consider the plausible assumption that failing by one's own lights requires some connection to potential motivating reasons. When these two ideas are combined, this gives us the motivating intuition.

A second argument starts from the plausible claim that one's normative reasons are the considerations that one would be motivated by if one were reasoning *well*. Suppose the relevant notion of "reasoning well" here is tied to the psychological capacities of the agent in question (e.g., what it is for *you* to reason well is different than for what it would be for a God-like creature to do so). If so, it's plausible that one always *can* reason well in the relevant sense. Thus, one can always be motivated by the considerations that figure in good reasoning, which by the first premise just are normative reasons. This is the motivating intuition.

Finally, and relatedly, it's plausible that we *ought* to be motivated by our normative reasons. Since ought implies can, it seems to follow that we can be motivated by our normative reasons. This is the motivating intuition. (For extensive arguments against the motivating intuition, and citations of important connected arguments both for and against it, see Markovits 2014.)

With the motivating intuition in hand, there are different paths to internalism. Here is one path, which has its roots in Williams. The motivating intuition demands that normative reasons are potential motivating reasons. The considerations that are potential motivating reasons are, plausibly, all connected to one's actual psychology in some way. (On a Williams-style view, for example, they are all connected to one's current set of motivations, at least through a chain of rational deliberation.) If all potential motivating reasons are connected to one's actual psychology and the motivating intuition is true, then it looks like some form of internalism is true. (See Van Roojen 2015, chapter 4 for helpful discussion of other, more complex paths from the motivating intuition to internalism, including ones closer to the core of Williams's work.)

A third motivation for internalism connects to the idea that the purpose of reason ascriptions is to point out a consideration that an agent would be wrong to ignore *by her own lights*. That might be wrong. But there is a more general, related idea in the background which might well support a form of reasons internalism: the idea that an agent's normative reasons should be the kinds of things that are tailored for *her*, which she should not be hopelessly alienated from. If that is right, it's natural to think that normative reasons must be connected to an agent's psychology in an appropriate way. (See Railton 1986 for connected discussion about the idea of what is *good* for a person.)

Such a non-alienation idea connects to Kate Manne's recent defense of internalism, which centers on the idea that normative reasons are tied to the activity of people reasoning together about what to do. Manne considers which attitudes are normatively appropriate in giving genuine *advice* to an agent about what to do, and, on that basis, argues for a form of internalism. Giving appropriate *advice* to an agent A, Manne argues, needs to be fundamentally tied to A's psychology, lest the "advice" simply turn into a form of brow-beating or manipulation. (See Manne 2014. See Smith 1994 for connected discussion about the normative constraints on giving genuine advice.)

A fourth important motivation for internalism concerns the epistemology of normative reasons. Consider the facts about psychology at the center of a given internalist view (e.g., facts about what an agent desires, or what would promote those desires). We are arguably capable of learning about such facts through non-mysterious methods—and, moreover, gaining knowledge about them and making reliable judgments about them. Hence, internalism seems to provide a solid foundation for the epistemology of normative reasons.

This broad idea gets developed in different ways. For example, Sharon Street argues that the psychology-dependence of ethical facts helps explain our reliability in ethical judgment, including, crucially, our judgments about normative reasons (see Street 2006). As Street (2008) makes clear, she favors a version of psychology-dependence that concerns the *agent's* psychology whose normative reasons one is making judgments about—i.e., she favors a kind of reasons internalism, as we are using the terminology here. (See Joshua Schechter's chapter "Explanatory Challenges in Metaethics" for discussion of the kind of argument at the core of Street's influential work on this topic, and see Markovits 2014 for discussion of other purported epistemological benefits of internalism. See chapter 9 of Schroeder 2007 for pushback on the idea that internalist views have the sorts of epistemic benefits that theorists such as Street appeal to. The crux of the issue is whether internalism guarantees that we have unproblematic epistemic access to the normative facts given that we have unproblematic access to the relevant psychological facts.)

A final important motivation for internalism concerns metaphysical *naturalism* about normative reality (e.g., normative facts, properties, and relations). Naturalists hold, roughly, that normative reality is metaphysically continuous with the part of reality studied by the natural and social sciences (see Peter Railton's chapter "Naturalistic Realism in Metaethics"). In contrast, non-naturalists deny this (see David Enoch's chapter "Non-Naturalistic Realism in Metaethics").

Many have thought that internalism might help secure a form of naturalism, which they take to be an attractive result for independent reasons. The basic connection rests on the idea that many facts about an agent's psychology—including facts about desires she has, and what would promote those desires—are naturalistic facts. If that is correct, and a version of internalism that invokes those psychological facts is true, then a form of naturalism about normative reasons is true. Moreover, suppose we combine these claims with an ambitious "reasons-first" view about ethical reality, according to which *all* of ethical reality (including, among other things, facts about value) can be fully explained in terms of facts about normative reasons (importantly, such reasons-first theorists will want to appeal to normative reasons for many reactions, not just to normative reasons for action or intention). This then yields a form of metaphysical naturalism about *all* of ethical reality. (For a helpful illustration of this kind of strategy, see Schroeder 2007.)

Importantly, not all internalist views support naturalism, nor do they all support the same form of it. To see this, first consider that different internalist views invoke different metaphysical relations. For example, one might hold that an agent's normative reasons are *explained* in terms of facts about her desires, but also deny that this illuminates the *real definition* or *essence* of normative reasons, and in no way support any kind of *reduction*. If one thought that naturalism required such a further claim about real definition, essence, or reduction, then this form of internalism won't yield a naturalistic account of normative reasons. (See Gideon Rosen's chapter "Metaphysical Relations in Metaethics" for discussion of the relations involved here, and how they tie into the debate over naturalism.)

Moreover, as we'll see below, different internalist views invoke different properties. A prominent kind of internalist view understands reasons in terms of *rationality*. In order for views of this kind to vindicate naturalism about *all* of normativity, they need to provide a naturalistic account of rationality. (For an important recent internalist view that appeals to rationality, but which denies that this can be done, see Markovits 2014.) Finally, and relatedly, suppose the ambitious (and controversial) form of the "reasons-first" approach we indicated above fails. Then *even if* one secures a naturalistic account of normative reasons, this by itself doesn't mean that all of ethical reality is also naturalistic, let alone all of normative reality (which includes, among other things, the normative facts discussed in such fields as epistemology, political philosophy, and aesthetics).

ARGUMENTS FOR EXTERNALISM

We have now glossed some of the main motivations for internalism. What, though, of motivations for externalism?

Return to our discussion of naturalism. In contrast to what we just saw above, some philosophers have argued *against* internalism by appeal to *non*-naturalism. Such philosophers hold that the most promising forms of internalism yield a naturalistic account of normative reasons. However, they also hold that *non*-naturalism is true about normative reasons (and, usually, also true of normative reality more generally). (For an illustrative example of this kind of argument, see Parfit 2011.)

Another motivation for externalism starts from a claim about what it is to *judge* that an agent has a normative reason to φ in circumstances C. Many have thought that such judgments involve *endorsement* of the agent φ-ing (see Gibbard 1990). This idea might be developed into a defense of *judgment internalism*, according to which there is a necessary connection between a speaker making an ethical judgment and a speaker being motivated in some way (see David Faraci and Tristram McPherson's chapter "Ethical Judgment and Motivation"). A person typically makes judgments not only about what she herself has normative reason to do, but also about what normative reasons *other* agents have. It is not clear why one would be motivated based on judgments about facts about *another* agent's psychology (which is what normative reasons judgments would be about, if reasons internalism is true). Moreover, it is not clear why, if at all, judgments about such facts would even constitute a kind of *endorsement*. Thus, the two different kinds of internalism—judgment internalism and the kind of "reasons internalism" we are focusing on in this chapter—seem to stand in at least *prima facie* tension with one another. (For further discussion of this point, see Van Roojen 2015.) If judgment internalism is correct, then this is thus the basis of an argument against reasons internalism.

Another common motivation for externalism appeals to our judgments about specific cases in ethics. In particular, externalists often appeal to cases that look to cause trouble for pretty much *any* view worth calling "internalism": cases where the fact that a certain consideration gives an agent a reason (or fails to do so) appears independent of the agent's psychology. For example, consider the idea that you have a normative reason to help another person in need, if it is easy for you to do so. Or consider the idea that you have no reason to dedicate your life to a worthless pursuit like counting blades of grass, even if you desire to do so.

Such cases are a powerful motivation for externalism—so powerful, in fact, that many take internalism to be a non-starter. It is therefore worth pausing here to emphasize that, as many internalists have pointed out, there is a lot of subtlety involved in using such judgments to support externalism. Here are four points worth emphasizing. First, we need to think there is *no* reason involved in the counting-blades-of-grass-type cases, as opposed to just a reason that doesn't have much weight. It is easy to get these things confused, especially since, in many conversational contexts, it would *not* make sense to even mention the presence of a normative reason with very little weight, since doing so would *pragmatically* communicate that the reason has relevance that it does not have. (See Schroeder 2007 for connected discussion, and for a proposed internalist-friendly way of telling apart judgments about *no* normative reason vs. judgments about reasons with very little weight.) Second, we need to be sure that our judgments really are about normative reasons, as opposed to some other kind of normative or evaluative judgment—e.g., about what would be *good* if they did, or whether they are wicked, cruel, or immoral, etc. (see Williams 1995, Street 2009, and Manne 2014 for discussion). Third, we need to be sure that we are really imagining agents that meet the conditions of the relevant internalist theories in question—that is, that we are really imagining the agents in question having the relevant psychological states (see Street 2009). Fourth, as in other areas of ethics, we can also question the degree to which case judgments should be taken as probative to this kind of foundational question in ethics (see Kagan 1998 for discussion).

Finally, and relatedly, one important kind of argument for externalism involves an appeal to *moral rationalism*. The argument is that moral rationalism is true, but that internalist views can't vindicate it. We will now turn to looking at this kind of worry in more detail. Doing so will allow us to introduce and critically assess some of the main forms of internalism that have animated recent philosophical discussion.

MORAL RATIONALISM AND INTERNALISM

Much of the critical discussion of internalism has revolved around *extensional* objections. These objections (including some which we just glossed in the last section) attempt to show that internalism predicts either that there are *too few* normative reasons or *too many* normative reasons. Some of the best work on internalism has been carried out in these extensional debates. For this reason, we will use part of this debate to introduce some specific internalist views. To focus discussion, we will focus on the relationship between internalism and a version of *moral rationalism*. Moral rationalism holds that there is some intimate connection between morality and normative reasons. (Because of this, what we are here calling "moral rationalism" is also sometimes called *morality/reasons internalism*, following Darwall 1997.)

There are three different versions of moral rationalism we will work with in what follows:

Weak Rationalism: Necessarily, if there is a moral reason for A to φ, then there is a normative reason for A to φ.

Strong Rationalism: Necessarily, if there is decisive moral reason for A to φ, then there is decisive normative reason for A to φ.

Middling Rationalism: Necessarily, if there is a moral reason for A to φ, then there is a normative reason for A to φ and, at least sometimes, normative reasons provided by moral reasons have significant weight.

There are different ways of thinking about what moral reasons are. We will proceed with the following rough idea: a moral reason to φ is a consideration that lends φ-ing a *positive* status within the system of morality, e.g., by morality *favoring* that an agent φs (as opposed to, for example, forbidding that she do so). In turn, of course, different philosophers will understand what *morality* itself is in different ways (see Stephen Darwall's chapter "Ethics and Morality"). Part of what is at issue in debates over moral rationalism is how morality compares with other systems of norms, rules, or values that we might use to guide our lives (e.g., religious codes or systems of etiquette). Moral rationalism is one way to vindicate the claim that morality is normatively *authoritative* or *important* with respect to how we should actually live, in a way that other normative systems are not.

As we will discuss, philosophers have appealed to all three forms of moral rationalism we just glossed in arguments over internalism. That said, since Middling Rationalism is perhaps closest to the pre-theoretical "common sense" view, much of the discussion has centered on something like it.

In what follows, we will focus our initial discussion on (purported) connections between the normative reasons that there are for A to φ and a particular psychological feature of A: namely, which *desires* she has. However, it should be noted that many of the issues that come up for the views we gloss in terms of *desire* will also be issues for views that appeal to other psychological states, e.g., facts about what an agent cares about, values, or intends.

Simplest internalism

Consider the following view:

Simplest Internalism: Agent A has a normative reason to φ just in case A desires to φ.

Given very plausible assumptions about the distribution of desires, Simplest Internalism cannot vindicate any of the rationalist theses. This is because there are many agents who do not desire to perform some of the actions that there is moral reason for them to do. It is plausible that we are all like this for some of the things we have moral reason to do. Most of us haven't thought through all of the particular actions we have moral reason to perform. At least before thinking of this example, neither of the authors of this article had the desire to give $4.16 to Oxfam on June 7th, 2021. Yet, it's plausible that there is *some* moral reason for both of us to do this.

Simplest Internalism makes bad predictions about other cases too. Suppose that the roasted beets at Seva are extremely tasty. Further, Daniel loves nothing more than a good beet. Plausibly, there is a normative reason for Daniel to get roasted beets from Seva. However, suppose that Daniel has never heard of Seva, and thus has never formed a desire to purchase and eat their roasted beets. It implausibly follows, from Simplest Internalism, that Daniel lacks normative reason to do so.

Simplest Internalism is not a widely held view. Insofar as it explicitly figures into philosophical discussion, it is mostly as a foil (which is how we are using it too).

Simple internalism

Simplest Internalism requires one to desire to perform a *specific* action in order for there to be a normative reason to perform that action. This is what created the above problems. Simple Internalism gets rids of this feature by insisting upon a broader requirement between normative reasons and desires:

Simple Internalism: Agent A has a normative reason to ϕ just in case one of A's desires would be promoted were A to ϕ.

Simple Internalism does not require one to have desires about specific actions. Instead, it just insists that one of A's desires be promoted by ϕ-ing. Plausibly, one way in which a desire would be promoted were one to ϕ is if a desire of A's would be satisfied were one to ϕ. Another potential way for a desire to be promoted is if its satisfaction is more likely than it otherwise would be were one to ϕ. (For helpful discussion of what the "promotion" relation involves here, see Lin 2016 and the references therein.)

Simple Internalism can handle the cases that plagued Simplest Internalism. In Daniel's case, it's clear that he has at least one desire that would be promoted by getting roasted beets from Seva. This is his desire to eat tasty beets. In our case, it is plausible that at least one desire of each of ours would be promoted were each of us to give $4.76 to Oxfam on June 7th, 2021—e.g., a desire to help other people.

That said, Simple Internalism still has a very hard time vindicating any of the rationalist theses. Start with Weak Rationalism. It is pre-theoretically plausible that there is at least *some* possible agent who has a psychology that contains *no* desires that would be promoted were that agent to perform some action she has moral reason to perform. If such an agent is possible, then there is a possible agent that does not have normative reason to do what she has moral reason to do. If Weak Rationalism is false, so is Strong and Middling Rationalism.

Further, even if Simple Internalism could vindicate Weak Rationalism, it's plausible that it won't be able to vindicate Middling or Strong Rationalism. In order to see this, we need to say something about the *weight* or *strength* of reasons.

It seems as if the internalist has a straightforward option when it comes to weight. This is what Mark Schroeder calls *Proportionalism* (Schroeder 2007). Proportionalism is the view that the weight of some normative reason to ϕ is a function of the strength of the desire that would be promoted were one to φ and the probability that the desire promoted will be satisfied if one ϕs. Proportionalism is a natural view to hold if you already think that desire is the seat of normative reasons. Further, it is a simple view that builds the scalar notion of weight out of the scalar notions of strength of desire and likelihood.

The rub is that Middling and Strong Rationalism are very unlikely to be true if Simple Internalism and Proportionalism are true, even if the Simple Internalist can somehow vindicate Weak Rationalism. In order to vindicate Middling Rationalism, the proportionalist needs to show that necessarily we all often have *strong* desires that would be promoted were we to do what there is moral reason to do. This seems very unlikely.

Many have objected to Simple Internalism on these grounds. One option for Simple Internalists is to accept this implication but argue that this implication is acceptable. (For example, see Williams 1995 and Manne 2014.) However, at least two prominent defenders of versions of Simple Internalism have provided machinery that could help show that Simple Internalism vindicates at least some of the rationalist theses.

Velleman's Common Desire Strategy

One important move that a Simple Internalist can make is to hold that there are particular desires that are *constitutive* of practical agency. This strategy maintains that there are certain desires with particular contents that one must have in order to act at all. Call this the Common Desire Strategy. David Velleman proposes this strategy in his (1996). He argues that the desire that is constitutive of action is the desire to *have conscious control.* For Velleman, this amounts to the desire to be autonomous. If one has to have this desire in order to act at all, then all agents that act will share a desire.

If this claim is correct, it vindicates the thesis that everyone shares certain normative reasons. These are the reasons whose origins lie in the desire for autonomy. In order to get from this claim to Weak Rationalism, one must also claim that the desire for autonomy is such that necessarily, for any agent A, A's desire for autonomy is promoted when A does what there is moral reason for A to do. This is a difficult claim to defend. This is because its truth would require very substantive connections between autonomy and morality. These connections might not seem implausible on their own, especially if one is attracted to Kantian views of morality. However, they start to look more suspect when you notice that the notion of autonomy at work must *also* be the notion that plays a fundamental role in the nature of action. It is not *prima facie* plausible to suppose that the notion of autonomy that explains the nature of action would be so morally loaded that the internalist could use *that same notion* to explain Weak Rationalism.

Importantly, this kind of issue does *not* just stem from Velleman's particular view about *which* desire is shared by all agents (a view that he himself adjusts in further work, where he turns to the desire for a form of self-understanding instead of the desire for autonomy). Rather, it brings out a broad *structural* worry that any proponent of the Common Desire Strategy will face.

Schroeder's Overdetermination Strategy

One of the most important internalist views in the contemporary literature is Mark Schroeder's *Hypotheticalism* (see Schroeder 2007). His particular view, which is a version of Simple Internalism, is this:

Hypotheticalism: For R to be a normative reason for A to φ is for there to be some p such that A has a desire whose object is p, and the truth of R is part of what explains why A's φ-ing promotes p.

This is a version of what is often called *The Humean Theory of Reasons*, according to which, roughly, facts about an agent's normative reasons are fully explained by facts about the contingent desires or other motivational attitudes she has. (See Schroeder 2007 for further discussion, and Street 2008 and 2012 for an alternative way of developing a Humean theory of normative reasons.)

In developing Hypotheticalism, Schroeder attempts to improve upon Velleman's story. He appeals to the *overdetermination of promotion*. The basic hypothesis is that there are some actions that are such that, no matter which particular desires you have, you will have at least one desire that is promoted by performing that action. In order to use this to vindicate Weak Rationalism, Schroeder must maintain that all actions for which there are moral reasons are like this. And so he does. If this is right, then Weak Rationalism is vindicated.

Schroeder also wants to vindicate something like Middling Rationalism. One potential route for doing so would be to accept Proportionalism and then appeal to the (purported) strength of the desires involved in performing the actions we have moral reasons to perform. Defending that second claim would be a tall order indeed. Instead, Schroeder opts to reject Proportionalism. He does this on the grounds that *weight* is a normative notion and thus demands an analysis in normative terms. Once he does this, he is in a position to hold that those who lack strong desires that would be promoted were they to perform acts there is moral reason to perform are making a *mistake*. (See Lord and Maguire 2016 for more on Schroeder's account of weight.)

In making this argument, Schroeder's main aim is to provide an existence proof of a Simple Internalist view that not only vindicates Weak Rationalism, but also something like Middling Rationalism. It seems like he does do this. But an existence proof of such a view, of course, doesn't tell us whether the view is correct.

With this in mind, Schroeder also provides some argument for the overdetermination hypothesis. He does this in two stages. In the first stage, he argues that it's plausible that normative reasons *come cheap* because the promotion relation is a very weak one. He raises significant problems for very strong views of promotion before concluding that ϕ-ing promotes a desire for p just in case the probability of p is higher conditional on A ϕ-ing than it is conditional on A doing nothing. As Schroeder points out, the weaker the promotion relation is, the more plausible the overdetermination hypothesis is. His weak promotion relation thus raises the probability of the overdetermination hypothesis, perhaps by a lot. (For important criticisms of Schroeder's weak promotion view see McPherson 2012.)

This is far from vindicating Weak Rationalism. Schroeder never attempts to do this directly. Instead—and this is the second stage of the argument—he provides a model for showing that the overdetermination hypothesis holds for some particular reaction. The model he uses provides an explanation of why, for any p, everyone has some desire that is promoted by believing p only when p is true. He considers an arbitrary agent, Mary, who wants a pair of shoes. There is no truth that Mary must believe in order to get a new pair of shoes. Indeed, as long the errors are distributed in the right way, she might be able to get a new pair of shoes even though she only has false beliefs. Nevertheless, being right about some things will promote her desire to get a new pair of shoes. This doesn't show that for every truth, believing that truth will promote getting a new pair of shoes. To fill this gap, Schroeder claims that every truth x is related to some truth y such that getting it wrong about x risks getting it wrong about y and getting it right about y promotes one's desire. He concludes from this that getting it right about x promotes one's desire. If this is right, then Mary's desire to get new shoes is promoted by believing any truth. Further, the explanation doesn't seem to turn on the content of Mary's desire. Thus, it looks like the argument will work no matter the desire. (There are worries, however, about the desire to never believe a truth.)

If all of that is right, then this looks like a model of what many have wanted: a form of Simple Internalism that vindicates Weak Rationalism. Still, it's not clear how much more confident one should become that Schroeder's Simple Internalism vindicates Weak Rationalism even if this model works. After all, this is a far cry from showing that for *every* moral reason, everyone has some desire that would be promoted if one were to perform the action that the moral reason recommends.

Idealized internalism

Simple Internalism doesn't just have problems with the rationalist theses. It also seems to deliver the wrong verdicts about individual cases. Consider the following case. Stephanie is a doctor. She has to choose whether to give a patient drug A or drug B. She believes that drug A will cure the patient and drug B will severely harm the patient. She thus desires to give the patient drug A. That desire would be promoted if Stephanie were to give her patient drug A. Thus, Simple Internalism predicts that Stephanie has a normative reason to give the patient drug A. Unbeknownst to Stephanie, though, drug B will cure the patient and drug A will harm the patient (and, if it makes a difference to you, suppose that Stephanie's mistaken view is a failure of rationality). Given this, it is not particularly plausible that there is a normative reason for Stephanie to give the patient drug A.

This sort of case motivates the most common move to make internalism more sophisticated. Rather than focusing on the desires that an agent currently has in her *actual* conditions, we focus on the desires that an agent has in conditions that are *better* or *more ideal* in some way. For example, in order to handle Stephanie's case, it's natural to add a *full information* condition. This gives us Full Information Idealized Internalism.

Full Information Idealized Internalism: There is a normative reason for A to φ just in case one of A's fully informed desires would be promoted were A to φ.

A's fully informed desires are the desires that A would have were A to have full information about the options (and have true beliefs based on that information). Full Information Idealized Internalism can handle Stephanie's case. This is because it is plausible that Stephanie would desire to give the patient drug B, and not drug A, were her desires fully informed.

Full Information Idealized Internalism also has problems with the rationalist theses. It seems possible for there to be a fully informed psychology that lacks any desires that would be promoted were one to do something there is moral reason to do. This, of course, turns on whether Velleman's common desire hypothesis or Schroeder's overdetermination hypothesis are true. Assuming that neither is true, it's not at all clear why adding a full information condition would guarantee Weak Rationalism.

That said, the full information condition—or, similarly, a full *relevant* information condition—is usually not the only idealizing condition that proponents of this strategy impose. This is because of cases like the following. Sally has full information about her dinner options. She knows that restaurant A has pizza and restaurant B has falafel. She also believes that the only consideration that matters is the quality of the food. Based on the quality, she prefers A to B. Nevertheless, she doesn't form a desire to go to A. Indeed, she has no desires that would be promoted by going to A.

Intuitively, there is a normative reason for Sally to go to A. However, it doesn't look like Full Information Idealized Internalism predicts this. Sally lacks a desire that would be promoted by going to A, even though she has full information. In response to this kind of problem, many internalists are drawn to accept Full Information Rational Idealized Internalism.

Full Information Rational Idealized Internalism: There is a normative reason for A to φ just in case were A to be fully rational and fully informed, then one of A's desires would be promoted were A to φ.

Full Information Rational Idealized Internalism seems to make the right prediction in Sally's case, given that Sally seems *irrational* in lacking a desire to go to A. After all, going to A is the best way to satisfy her preferences. And—at least so one could argue, based on common ideas about rationality—one is irrational if one doesn't desire the act that would satisfy one's preferences.

It's not immediately clear how Full Information Rational Idealized Internalism fares when it comes to the rationalist theses. In order to determine whether the view can vindicate the rationalist theses, we need to know what it takes to be *fully rational*. Since there are many different views about this, there are many different ways of filling in the view.

One important division within the resulting versions is between Humean and Kantian camps. This reflects a broader division within internalist theories of normative reasons. We will discuss each camp in turn.

The Humeans

As we saw when discussing Schroeder, one sort of Humean view about normative reasons holds that normative reasons are fully explained by contingent facts about the psychology of the agent those reasons apply to (standardly, facts about her desires). A different, but connected, kind of Humean view is a view about rationality. On this view, the requirements of rationality are relatively *thin*. For example, many Humeans claim that rationality only requires that we be coherent in certain ways. (See Street 2008 and 2012 for a Humean theory of normative reasons that is Humean in both senses.)

Humeans in both senses have long been the standard bearers for internalism. This is partly due to the influence of Bernard Williams, whose initial discussion of reasons internalism set the stage for much of the subsequent literature on this topic. In Williams (1979, 1995), he defends a Humean version of Full Information Rational Idealized Internalism. The view that Williams defends holds that "[an agent] A has a reason to [φ] only if he could reach the conclusion to [φ] by a sound deliberative route from the motivations he already has" (Williams 1995, p. 35). In Williams (1979), he famously calls the relevant motivations one's *subjective motivational set*. It is a source of controversy what is included in one's subjective motivational set. It is clear, though, that "desires, evaluations, attitudes, projects" are included (Williams 1979). He also makes it clear that motivations based on false beliefs *don't* count and that one can gain members of one's subjective motivation set through deliberation.

Williams is explicit in his rejection of the rationalist theses. He thus thinks that there are agents with fully informed rational psychologies that lack desires that would be promoted were they to perform the actions there are moral reasons to perform. He thinks there is nothing in the "subjective motivational set" of such agents that favors them performing actions that there are moral reasons to perform.

A core thought shared by many Humean internalist views is that the nature of rationality will not guarantee *weak convergence* of desires, given full information. A set of fully informed rational agents' desires weakly converges just in case all agents in the set have desires that would be promoted were they to perform acts there is moral reason to perform. Humeans hold that there are some psychologies that are such that, just by being rational, no amount of information will allow the agent in question to gain a desire that would be promoted if they were moral. If this is right, then none of the rationalist theses are true.

Many take this to be a strike against Humean versions of Full Information Rational Idealized Internalism. It should be noted that many Humeans do not see the failure of rationalism as a problem. Indeed, Williams argues *against* rationalism on the grounds that a Humean version of Full Information Rational Idealized Internalism is true. (For a more recent defense of this kind of argument, see Manne 2014.)

The Kantians

Kantian views of rationality are *thicker* than Humean views. One can spell out this idea in different ways, but one core idea that unites many Kantians is that rationality *does* guarantee weak convergence.

The two most prominent contemporary defenders of Kantian internalism are Christine Korsgaard and Michael Smith. We will outline Smith's recent view in order to illustrate some of the resources and challenges that such a view faces. (See Korsgaard 1996 and Korsgaard 2009 for two of the most important statements of Korsgaard's views on the foundations of ethics. See Schafer 2015 for a kind of Kantian internalism that differs from both Korsgaard and Smith.)

Smith argues that the best version of Full Information Rational Idealized Internalism predicts weak convergence. In fact, Smith holds not only weak convergence, but also *strong convergence*. A set of fully informed rational agents' desires strongly converge just in case all agents in the set share particular desires that would be promoted were they to do what there is moral reason for them to do. (The difference between weak and strong convergence is that strong convergence requires that the group of agents share desires with *particular* contents.)

Importantly, Smith attempts to show that strong convergence is true by appealing to a coherentist version of rationality that is very similar to the view that Williams holds. Smith argues that Williams incorrectly interprets the consequences of this sort of view. At the core of Smith's view is the idea that one's normative reasons are determined by the psychology of one's *ideal counterpart*. (See Smith 1994 for an overview of this idea.)

In recent work, Smith argues that one's ideal counterpart is the counterpart that fully and robustly exercises their capacities to realize their desires and know the world (capacities that, according to Smith, are at the heart of what it is to be an *agent* as such) (see Smith 2012). Smith argues that ideality in this sense gives rise to coherence requirements that guarantee that all ideal counterparts have certain desires.

Smith proposes that all ideal counterparts have desires to do the following things: promote the current exercise of their own rational capacities, promote the future exercise of their own rational capacities, promote the current exercise of other agents' rational capacities, not interfere with the current exercise of other agents' rational capacities, promote the future exercise of other agents' rational capacities, and not interfere with the future exercise of other agents' rational capacities (see Smith 2012). Let's call this set of desires the *capacity desires*. If every agent's ideal counterpart has the capacity desires, then it's plausible that every agent has normative reason to perform, at the very least, many of the actions they have moral reason to perform. This is because it is plausible that much of morality—at least insofar as it concerns the relations between persons—can be explained in terms of promoting and not interfering with other people's rational capacities. In other work, Smith argues that this is the case (2013). If all of that works out, it's plausible that Weak Rationalism is true.

Smith also has resources to provide an ostensible explanation of Middling Rationalism, or perhaps even Strong Rationalism. This is because, like all Full Information Rational Idealized Internalists, Smith is in a position to offer a more plausible version of proportionalism—we'll call it Full Information Rational Proportionalism. According to this version, the weight of normative reasons is determined by the strength of one's *fully informed and rational* desires. This is a powerful tool for Full Information Rational Idealized Internalists to use in order to get better extensional verdicts. It is especially powerful for Smith, who holds not only that all ideal counterparts share certain desires, but also that some of those desires have the same strength for all counterparts. This is because he holds that coherence demands that the capacity desires are *overriding*. This means that whenever there is a conflict between the capacity desires and more idiosyncratic desires, the coherent agent satisfies the capacity desires. If you combine this with Full Information Rational Proportionalism, you get the result that the normative reasons provided by the capacity desires can be very weighty.

Kantian views face a number of important challenges. One central problem for Smith's view—and this is a problem all Kantian internalists face—is that it is very hard to make the transition from the claim that coherence demands that we care about *our own* rational capacities to the claim that coherence demands that we care about *other agents'* rational capacities. Smith's own argument for this is complex and relies on unobvious claims about the metaphysics of identity. Other Kantian internalists make different moves, but all rely on highly controversial claims.

A second problem has to do with what *coherence* even is. There are some uncontroversial examples of incoherence—e.g., contradictory beliefs and intentions that are known to be jointly unrealizable. However, the sets of desires that Kantian internalists like Smith claim are incoherent are not obvious examples like this. Kantians such as Smith need a principled and plausible account of coherence that fits with the work they want the notion of "coherence" to do, and it's far from clear that there is such an account to be had.

CONCLUSION

As we have seen, there are a variety of views discussed as versions of "reasons internalism" in the literature, as well as a variety of arguments offered in favor of and against them. We have only scratched the surface of the details of the main positions and arguments that have been influential. Moreover, as we hope our schematic way of putting things makes clear, there are many different possible positions and arguments that have yet to be fully explored, or even conceived of, which might very well improve on the existing discussion in crucial ways. We hope this point is kept firmly in view and helps guide the discussion forward in the years to come.

ACKNOWLEDGMENTS

Thanks to Tristram McPherson, Lea Schroeder, and Kenny Walden for helpful feedback and discussion.

REFERENCES

Darwall, Stephen L. 1997. Reasons, Motives, and the Demands of Morality: An Introduction. In *Moral Discourse and Practice: Some Philosophical Approaches*, edited by S. L. Darwall, A. Gibbard, and P. A. Railton. New York: Oxford University Press.

Finlay, Stephen, and Mark Schroeder. 2012. Reasons for Action: Internal vs. External. *Stanford Encyclopedia of Philosophy*.

Gibbard, Allan. 1990. *Wise Choices, Apt Feelings: A Theory of Normative Judgment*. Cambridge, MA: Harvard University Press.

Kagan, Shelly. 1998. *Normative Ethics*. Boulder, CO: Westview Press.

Korsgaard, Christine M. 1996. *The Sources of Normativity*. New York: Cambridge University Press.

—. 2009. *Self-Constitution: Agency, Identity, and Integrity*. Oxford: Oxford University Press.

Lin, Eden. (2016). Simple Probabilistic Promotion. *Philosophy and Phenomenological Research*. Published online. Forthcoming.

Lord, Errol, and Barry Maguire. 2016. An Opinionated Guide to the Weight of Reasons. In *Weighing Reasons*, edited by E. Lord and B. Maguire. Oxford: Oxford University Press.

McDowell, John. 1995. Might There Be External Reasons? In *World, Mind and Ethics: Essays on the Ethical Philosophy of Bernard Williams*, edited by J. E. J. Altham and R. Harrison. Cambridge: Cambridge University Press.

McPherson, Tristram. 2012. Mark Schroeder's Hypotheticalism: Agent-Neutrality, Moral Epistemology, and Methodology. *Philosophical Studies* 157 (3):445–453.

Manne, Kate. 2014. Internalism about Reasons: Sad but True? *Philosophical Studies* 167 (1):89–117.

Markovits, Julia. 2014. *Moral Reason*. Oxford: Oxford University Press.

Parfit, Derek. 2011. *On What Matters*. Oxford: Oxford University Press.

Railton, Peter. 1986. Facts and Values. *Philosophical Topics* 14:5–31.

Scanlon, Thomas M. 1998. *What We Owe To Each Other*. Cambridge, MA: Harvard University Press.

Schafer, Karl. 2015. Realism and Constructivism in Kantian Metaethics (Parts 1 and 2). *Philosophy Compass* 10 (10):690–713.

Schroeder, Mark. 2007. *Slaves of The Passions*. Oxford: Oxford University Press.

Smith, Michael. 1994. *The Moral Problem*. Cambridge: Blackwell.

—. 2012. Agents and Patients, or: What We Learn about Reasons for Action by Reflecting on Our Choices in Process of Thought Cases. *Proceedings of the Aristotelian Society* 112 (3):309–331.

—. 2013. A Constitutivist Theory of Reasons: Its Promise and Parts. *LEAP: Law, Ethics, and Philosophy* 1:9–30.

Street, Sharon. 2006. A Darwinian Dilemma for Realist Theories of Value. *Philosophical Studies* 127 (1): 109–166.

—. 2008. Constructivism about Reasons. In *Oxford Studies in Metaethics: Volume 3*, edited by R. Shafer-Landau. Oxford: Oxford University Press.

—. 2009. In Defense of Future Tuesday Indifference: Ideally Coherent Eccentrics and the Contingency of What Matters. *Philosophical Issues* 19:273–298.

—. 2012. Coming to Terms with Contingency: Humean Constructivism about Practical Reason. In *Constructivism in Practical Philosophy*, edited by J. Lenman and Y. Shemmer. Oxford: Oxford University Press.

van Roojen, Mark. 2015. *Metaethics: A Contemporary Introduction*. New York: Routledge.

Velleman, J. David. 1996. The Possibility of Practical Reason. *Ethics* 106 (4):694–726.

Williams, Bernard. 1979. Internal and External Reasons. In *Rational Action*, edited by R. Harrison. Cambridge: Cambridge University Press.

—. 1995. Internal Reasons and the Obscurity of Blame. In *Making Sense of Humanity*. Cambridge: Cambridge University Press.

FURTHER READING

Kieran Setiya and Hille Paakkunainen's edited volume *Internal Reasons: Contemporary Readings* is an excellent collection of some of the most influential papers on the topic. It also includes a helpful introduction by Setiya. The SEP entry by Finlay and Schroeder on "Reasons for Action: Internal vs. External" is another crucial resource.

Setiya, Kieran, and Hille Paakkunainen. 2012. *Internal Reasons: Contemporary Readings*. Cambridge, Mass.: MIT Press.

21

The Wrong Kind of Reasons

Howard Nye

INTRODUCTION

An important class of metaethical views seeks to explain what it is for something to fall under an ethical or evaluative category in terms of its being something towards which we ought, or have reasons, to have certain kinds of attitudes. These *Fitting Attitude* [FA-] *Analyses* might hold, for instance, that an outcome's goodness consists in its being an outcome we should desire or have "pro-attitudes" towards (Ewing 1939); or that an action's moral blameworthiness consists in the fact that the agent who performed it ought to feel guilty, and that others are justified in feeling resentment or indignation towards her for doing it (Gibbard 1990, chapters 3 and 7).[1]

FA-analyses are attractive as a way of helping to provide a simple and unified picture of how values and reasons fit together, by explaining the distinctive normative or prescriptive features of ethical and evaluative categories as stemming from the deontic categories of oughts or reasons in terms of which they are explicated (cf. Rabinowicz and Ronnow-Rasmussen 2004: 391–392; Olson 2004: 295). The judgment that an outcome is good (or that an action is blameworthy) seems to "speak in favor" of desiring (or feeling guilt and anger towards) it, in much the same way that the judgment that a belief is warranted by one's evidence speaks in favor of the belief, or that a judgment that one should plan or intend to do something speaks in favor of intending to do it. Ethical and evaluative judgments seem to have the distinctive properties of this broader class of judgments about what attitudes we ought, or have reasons, to have—such as their being "essentially [coherently] contestable" (cf. D'Arms and Jacobson 2000b), in the sense that it seems conceptually coherent to affirm *or* deny most of them; our having to determine which of these coherent judgments are correct by means of *a priori* philosophical arguments; and their exerting a significant (if defeasible) influence on the attitudes we come to have (Gibbard 1990; Persson 2007; Raz 2009). FA-analyses can compactly explain this by holding that ethical and evaluative judgments simply *are* specific instances of judgments about what attitudes we ought, or have reasons, to have. The alternatives to FA-analyses hold either that ethical and evaluative categories are distinct from but substantively related to those of reasons for attitudes like emotions and desires (Dancy 2000; Zimmerman 2007), or that what it is to have reasons for such attitudes just is for their objects to have the relevant ethical and evaluative properties (Orisi 2013). It is much less clear on these views how ethical and evaluative categories are related to other normative categories like those of reasons for belief and intention, and how and why they share the same central normative features.

These attractions of FA-analyses are compatible with whatever one takes to be the best fundamental metaethical (or "metanormative") account of judgments or facts about what attitudes we ought, or have reasons, to have—such as robust realism, expressivism, or reductive realism (all three of which have been favored by different proponents of FA-analyses, such as Ewing 1939; Gibbard 1990; and Brandt 1946; respectively). FA-analyses thus offer a kind of "non-fundamental" metanormative account, which seeks to explain the metaphysics and/or semantics of one normative category in terms of another normative category, without committing to any particular view about the underlying metaphysics or semantics of the explaining category.

One of the main problems for FA-analyses is that—at least at the outset of inquiry—there seem to be reasons for or against having the relevant attitudes towards things that do not bear on whether those things fall under the relevant ethical or evaluative categories. For instance, suppose that an evil demon credibly threatened to harm your loved ones unless you desired to have an odd number of hairs on your head (cf. Crisp 2000). The fact that the demon will spare your loved ones just in case you desire that you have an odd number of hairs seems to be a reason—or to make it the case that you ought—to desire that you have an odd number of hairs. But it does not make your having an odd number of hairs good. Similarly, the fact that you were causally involved in a someone's death, even though you took all reasonable precautions to avoid it, seems to be a reason to feel guilt for what you did, or a factor that makes guilt on your part appropriate (Greenspan 1992). But it does not seem to make it the case that your conduct was blameworthy.

Proponents of FA-analyses (*FA-analysts*) will want to insist that, although considerations like the demon's threat or your causal involvement in the death in some sense count in favor of your having (or at least wanting or getting yourself to have) the relevant attitudes, they are not the kinds of reasons intended by FA-analyses. To mark the intended distinction, we can say that FA-analyses hold that something falls under an ethical or evaluative category just in case it is *fitting* to have the relevant attitudes towards it, and that the reasons or oughts constituted by things like the demon's threat or your causal involvement in the death do not bear on the fittingness of the relevant attitudes (hence the name "fitting attitude analyses"—cf. D'Arms and Jacobson 2000b: 746; Rabinowicz and Ronnow-Rasmussen 2004: 422–423). But herein lurks a problem for the FA-analyst— namely that, unless some further argument or account is offered, it might seem that the only thing that distinguishes considerations that bear upon an attitude's fittingness from those that do not is that the former, but not the latter, make for the instantiation of the ethical or evaluative category that the FA-analyst is trying to analyze. Why, for instance, does the fact that an outcome involves a puppy's being happy contribute to the fittingness of a desire for it, while the fact that a demon will harm one's loved ones if one does not desire some outcome *not* contribute to the fittingness of a desire for *it*? A natural explanation is that an outcome involving the puppy's happiness *contributes to its goodness*, while its being such that desiring it will spare one's loved ones does not. But if this is what the FA-analyst must say to distinguish fittingness from non-fittingness reasons, her account of the kind of reasons for attitudes she is talking about in her analyses looks viciously circular.

FA-analysts thus face a problem of explaining what distinguishes fittingness reasons to have attitudes from non-fittingness reasons with respect to those attitudes, without running into the vicious circularity of invoking the ethical concepts they are trying to analyze in the first place. This is the *Wrong Kind of Reasons* (WKR) *problem* with which I will be concerned in this chapter. I believe that this is a maximally general way of understanding the distinctive problem, described by this phrase in the literature, which is faced by all FA-analyses—regardless of whether they speak explicitly of a distinct category of fittingness (or simply different kinds of "reasons"), whether they allow that non-fittingness reasons with respect to an attitude are genuine reasons for the attitude (or insist that they are only reasons to "want to" or "make ourselves have" the attitude), and whether they offer a reductive account of the distinction between fittingness and non-fittingness reasons (or take the category of fittingness as more or less primitive). On the other hand, because solutions to this problem are constrained by the FA-analyst's need to distinguish the "right" from the "wrong" kind of reasons without invoking corresponding ethical and evaluative categories, it is (at least potentially) a more specific problem than that sometimes referred to as a "WKR problem" of distinguishing different kind of reasons for attitudes, such as epistemic from non-epistemic reasons for beliefs, and reasons to intend to do things that do as opposed to do not constitute reasons to actually do them.

I think that the main responses to the WKR problem can be divided into three general kinds of approaches. The first and, to date, most popular *material approach* seeks to explain the distinction between fittingness and non-fittingness reasons in terms of what *features of considerations* make them eligible as opposed to ineligible to serve as fittingness reasons. Perhaps the best-known version of the material approach, inspired by Parfit (2001), holds that fittingness reasons to have an attitude must be "object-given," or cite features of the attitude's object, while non-fittingness reasons with respect to the attitude are "state-given," or cite features of the state of having the attitude. A second, *constitutivist* approach seeks to distinguish fittingness from non-fittingness reasons by holding that, while fittingness reasons for an attitude pertain to the concerns or commitments constitutive of having the attitude at all, non-fittingness reasons with respect to the attitude stem from concerns external to the attitude's essence. A third, *formal approach* seeks to explain the distinction between fittingness and non-fittingness reasons in terms of *features of judgments or inferences* about these different kinds of reasons. Perhaps the most natural version of this view is that our attitudes can respond *directly* to what we take to be fittingness reasons for them, while they can only respond indirectly to what we take to be non-fittingness reasons.

In the next three sections, I will explore each of these approaches to solving the WKR problem. As I will conclude in the fifth and final section, I believe that each approach answers to distinctive motivations and faces distinctive problems. In many of the cases considered in the literature, there seems to be a common structure that separates fittingness from non-fittingness reasons, which appropriately motivates material approaches.

But proponents of material approaches seem to overlook other kinds of cases—like that of feeling guilt in response to one's causal involvement in harm from an unavoidable accident—where the reasons need not conform to this structure. Constitutivist approaches seem applicable to both the cases that animate the material approach and many of the cases it ignores. But there are concerns about whether FA-analysts can explain the idea of the relevant attitudes' constitutive aims without incurring vicious circularity. Formal approaches promise maximal generality without vicious circularity. But the features of judgments about fittingness reasons adduced by existing formal approaches do not seem sufficient to distinguish them from all judgments about non-fittingness reasons.

MATERIAL APPROACHES

Material approaches, like most existing solutions to the WKR problem, have been focused on cases that resemble (in a sense I will clarify) that of Roger Crisp's demon, who (on my telling) threatens to harm your loved ones unless you desire to have an odd number of hairs. I believe that material approaches have made genuine progress on the problem of giving a compelling, non-circular explanation of what distinguishes fittingness from non-fittingness reasons in such cases. Initially, Wlodek Rabinowicz and Toni Ronnow-Rasmussen (2004) surveyed and rejected several material approaches, including the highly influential, Parfit-inspired:

Object-Given vs. State-Given Proposal: Consideration R is a fittingness reason to have attitude A towards object O (i.e. R is the kind of reason to have A towards O, the existence of which FA-analyses should say makes it the case that O falls under some ethical or evaluative category) only if R cites properties of O. If R cites properties of the state of having A towards O, then R is not a fittingness reason to have A towards O.

Since the fact that *desiring to have an odd number of hairs will spare one's loved ones harm* cites a property of the state of desiring an odd number of hairs, this proposal seems to correctly avoid counting it as a fittingness reason to have this desire. It also seems to correctly count, for instance, the fact that *a puppy's having companions will make her happy* as a fittingness reason to desire her having companions, since the fact cites a property of the outcome of the puppy's having companions, which is the object of the desire for which it is a reason.

However, as Rabinowicz and Ronnow-Rasmussen (2004: 407–408) observed, there are cases in which non-fittingness reasons to have certain attitudes seem to cite properties of the objects of those attitudes, such as

The Admiration-Demanding Demon. This demon credibly threatens to harm your loved ones unless you admire him.

Here, the fact that *the demon will harm your loved ones unless you admire him* is surely a *non*-fittingness reason to (make yourself) admire him. But because it cites a property of the demon, the object-given vs. state-given proposal seems to incorrectly count it as a fittingness reason to admire him.

In response, Jonas Olson (2004: 299) proposed, in effect, that one must strengthen this proposal's account of fittingness reasons to

Olson's Proposal: *R* is a fittingness reason to have *A* only if *R* makes no reference to *A*.

Since the fact that *the demon will harm your loved ones unless you admire him* makes reference to admiration, Olson's proposal correctly avoids counting it as a fittingness reason. But, as Rabinowicz and Ronnow-Rasmussen (2006: 118) observed, Olson's proposal seems to go too far, since there are cases where *fittingness* reasons to have attitudes make reference to those attitudes, such as

Modesty. Allan is indifferent to whether we admire him.

The fact that *Allan is indifferent to our admiring him* seems to be a fittingness reason to admire him—such modestly genuinely contributes to his admirably. But because this fact makes reference to admiration, it appears that Olson's proposal cannot count it as such.

Generalizing a proposal by Gerald Lang (2008), in response to important criticisms of Olson (2009), Lars Samuelsson (2013) argues that we can solve the WKR problem through the appropriate interpretation of

Samuelsson's Proposal: *R* is a fittingness reason to have *A* only if *R* does not cite or depend upon the consequences of having *A*.

Samuelsson does not here wish to restrict "consequences" to causal consequences (398–392), since, like Rabinowicz and Ronnow-Rasmussen (2004: 403–404), he observes that there can be cases like those of

Mental State Axiologies. These views hold that it is intrinsically good that we have certain mental states, even if their objects lack intrinsic value (e.g. one might think deep immersion in a project is intrinsically good, even if the project lacks intrinsic value).

Such views might coherently hold, for instance, that the fact that *one's attitude towards grass counting would be one of deep immersion* is a *non*-fittingness reason to (make oneself) have that attitude—an intrinsic reason to (make ourselves) have it that does not contribute to grass counting's intrinsic value—even though the fact makes no reference to the attitude's causal consequences. But Samuelsson's proposal can allow this if we understand "the consequences of having an attitude" to include non-causal consequences, such as the bringing about of the state of affairs of one's having it. So interpreted, Samuelsson's proposal seems right that (a) the axiologies in question take us to have reasons to (make ourselves) have the relevant attitudes *in virtue of* our having reasons to value the state of affairs of our having them, and (b) this distinguishes these reasons to (make ourselves) have attitudes from fittingness reasons (e.g. the fact that *companions would make a puppy happy* as a reason to desire that she has them), which do not seem to depend upon the value of the state of affairs of our having them. With fittingness reasons, the direction of explanation may often go the other way around: we have reasons to value the state of affairs of our having certain attitudes *in virtue of* our having fittingness reasons to have them (Nye, Plunkett, and Ku 2015: 16).

I believe that the non-fittingness reasons to (make ourselves) have attitudes upon which material approaches have focused all resemble those provided by Crisp's demon, in that they depend upon our reasons to care about the consequences of those attitudes (broadly construed). There seem, however, to be non-fittingness reasons that do not fit this pattern, which material approaches appear to have ignored. These may include the example from the first section of the fact that *your conduct was causally involved in someone's death despite all reasonable precautions* as a genuine reason to (make yourself) feel guilt for your conduct, but not a fittingness reason to feel guilt that constitutes your blameworthiness. A defender of Samuelsson's proposal might insist that you have this reason because feeling such guilt partially constitutes having a good moral character, and you should desire the state of affairs of having a good moral character (cf. D'Arms and Jacobson 2014: 30). But it seems coherent—and indeed quite plausible—to think instead that, much like a fittingness reason to feel guilt (e.g. that *you deliberately harmed someone for fun*), the fact that *you were causally involved in someone's death* is a reason to (make yourself) feel guilt quite independently of the consequences of doing so, *including* the intrinsic value of the state of affairs of your feeling guilt or being morally good. One might insist that, although mere causal involvement in harm does not make guilt fitting (in the sense that entails blameworthiness), it makes guilt "morally appropriate," and that such appropriateness-making reasons cannot be explained by—but may instead help explain—which states of feeling guilt we should value.

D'Arms and Jacobson have explored many other examples of non-fittingness, "appropriateness-making" reasons to (make ourselves) have or omit having attitudes, some of which at least arguably do not depend upon the value of the states of our having them. These include factors that would make it petty to envy someone's accomplishments, even if they are genuinely good and this reflects poorly on oneself (2000a: 73–74; 2014: 24–25), factors that make genuinely funny jokes morally inappropriate (2000a: 80–81; 2014: 10–19), factors that make it admirable or noble to be unafraid of genuinely fearful odds (2000a: 85), and factors that make it morally virtuous to pity morally deserved suffering (2014: 38–40). Simply at the level of what features a reason does or does not concern (in relation to the object of an attitude or the upshot of having it), there seems to be no common feature that this wide variety of "appropriateness-making" reasons share with the broadly "pragmatic" reasons upon which material approaches have focused. This suggests that material approaches will not be successful in explaining what distinguishes all non-fittingness reasons from fittingness reasons.

It is important to understand that proponents of material approaches cannot solve this problem by arguing that, as a substantive ethical matter, there are no appropriateness-making reasons to (make ourselves) have attitudes that do not depend upon our reasons to care about the broad consequences of having those attitudes. FA-analyses are meta-ethical theories, which hold that *what is at issue* between rival substantive ethical and evaluative views is what attitudes we have fittingness reasons to have. As such, they must provide interpretations of all coherent, or at least all reasonably plausible, ethical views as views about fittingness reasons. This requires solving the WKR problem of distinguishing fittingness from non-fittingness reasons in a way that works for all coherent, or at least all reasonably plausible, ethical views—many of which are substantively false.

CONSTITUTIVIST APPROACHES

A natural way of trying to articulate what separates the fittingness reasons for attitudes that constitute something's falling under an ethical or evaluative category from both pragmatic and appropriateness-making reasons is the following. It might seem that certain evaluative concerns or questions are somehow internal to or constitutive of having the attitudes at all. For instance, envy might seem, essentially, to portray its object as having something valuable, your relative lack of which reflects badly on you (D'Arms and Jacobson 2000a: 64). Other evaluative concerns, including both whether envy would have good consequences and whether it would be morally inappropriate, petty, or ignoble, seem to be "external" to envy, in the sense that they go beyond how envy portrays its object (D'Arms and Jacobson 2000a: 73–74), or what we commit ourselves to in envying it (cf. Hieronymi 2005). If we can draw such a distinction between the concerns constitutive of as opposed to external to an attitude, we can try solving the WKR problem by appealing to some version of

The Constitutivist Proposal: Fittingness reasons for attitude A are considerations that show A to "fit" its object, by showing A's object to have the features that A is constitutively concerned with. Non-fittingness reasons to (make oneself) have A do not speak to A's constitutive concerns. (cf. D'Arms and Jacobson 2000a; 2006; Hieronymi 2005; Schroeder 2010)

In addition to offering a convincing explanation of what separates fittingness reasons from both pragmatic and appropriateness-making reasons, it seems that this approach can make sense of what is at issue between many different coherent ethical views. Suppose, for instance, that a member of an honor-loving, acetic warrior caste lives a life of immense enjoyment by killing a record number of opponents in wars of conquest. Many of us might think that the fact that

E: He enjoyed his life so much

makes his life enviable in a respect, but the fact that

K: He killed so many opponents in wars of conquest

is a reason not to (allow ourselves to) envy him, which *does not* make his life less enviable. But his fellow warriors, who think that killing opponents in wars of conquest is the highest good and despise the love of pleasure as lowly, might think instead that the fact that K makes his life enviable, while the fact that E is a reason not to (allow themselves to) envy him that, does not make his life less enviable. The constitutivist proposal can give the following compelling explanation of the difference between our thoughts. We take E to bear upon envy's constitutive concerns by showing the warrior to have something valuable that we lack, while we take K to bear upon considerations external to envy (*viz.* whether the envy is morally appropriate). His fellow warriors, on the other hand, take K to bear on envy's constitutive concerns by showing him to have something valuable that they lack, while they take E to bear upon considerations external to envy (*viz.* whether the envy would involve a cowardly desire for a pleasant life).

The main problems for constitutivist approaches concern whether they really can draw a distinction between evaluations that are constitutive of as opposed to external to attitudes, in a way that solves the WKR problem for FA-analyses. First, there are problems about what it is for an evaluation to be constitutive of an attitude. The most natural idea here is that part of what it is to have the attitude is to make the evaluation, in the form of either a judgment (Foot 1963), an entertained thought (Greenspan 1988), or a percept-like "construal" (Roberts 1988). Because D'Arms and Jacobson (2003) argue (quite convincingly) that the relevant attitudes do not actually involve any such evaluations, their talk of attitudes "presenting" things as falling under constitutive evaluations seems metaphorical. One way they suggest of cashing out the metaphor is that evaluations constitutive of attitudes must play "deep" and "wide" roles in the psychology of almost all humans, in that they fit at least many of our deeply entrenched tendencies to have them and speak to a wide variety of our other concerns (2006: 116–118). But as D'Arms and Jacobson themselves recognize, this entails a highly controversial view, on which contingent psychological facts limit the range of eligible judgments about the fittingness of different attitudes.

In defense of their attempt to tie standards of an attitude's fittingness to our actual propensities to have it, D'Arms and Jacobson suggest that because the purpose of such standards is to regulate the attitude, we should accept standards that have "significant traction" with our propensities to have it (118). But there are at least two problems with this defense. The first is that judgments about fittingness can substantially regulate our responses even when they fail to prevent us from having attitudes that we judge to be unfitting, namely by causing us to *avoid acting out of* such recalcitrant attitudes (cf. Nye 2009: 149–153). The second is that D'Arms and Jacobson's defense of their view seems to rely upon a potentially objectionable form of "rule pragmatism" about fittingness standards by portraying them as something we can or should construct to achieve certain ends. Pragmatic considerations about what will achieve various ends we care about can look just as irrelevant to the question of what fittingness standards are genuinely correct as they do to whether a token attitude is fitting.

A second set of problems concerns whether the evaluations held to be constitutive of attitudes can themselves be described in ways that will avoid making the FA-analyses that cite the attitudes viciously circular (cf. Rabinowicz and Ronnow-Rasmussen 2004: 420–422; Persson 2007: 6n4; Louise 2009: 360–362). Evaluations of undesirable differences in possession do not seem to make reference to the category of the enviable. But problems quickly arise when we consider what evaluations could be said to be constitutive of the attitudes referenced by FA-analyses of core ethical and evaluative categories, like that of *good outcomes*. What evaluation could be said to be constitutive of attitudes like desire for an outcome? There seems to be no candidate, other than "that the outcome is good." But it looks viciously circular for an FA-analysis to say that "What it is for an outcome O to be good is for desires that O to be fitting, what it is for a desire that O to be fitting is for O to meet the constitutive standards of desires that O, and what it is for O to meet the constitutive standards of desires that O is for O to be good."

More subtle vicious circularities may arise for FA-analysts' attempts to specify the constitutive concerns of other attitudes. For instance, D'Arms and Jacobson (2006: 109) suggest that shame constitutively evaluates its object as a "social disability." They recognize, however, that this is "vague and potentially misleading" and that it would be "more accurate, but rather less edifying" to say that shame constitutively evaluates its object as shameful. It seems that one can, with perfect coherence, think that intuitively non-social and non-disabling traits are shameful, and that our only grip on D'Arms and Jacobson's intended sense of "social disability" may be that of something that is, well, shameful. But if this is the case, their constitutivist account of shame's fittingness seems to make the

FA-analysis of shameful things as things it is fitting to be ashamed of viciously circular, in virtue of having to appeal to shamefulness in explaining what it is for shame to be fitting.

There may be certain attitudes, like envy, for which plausible constitutive concerns can be articulated without even tacit reference to their corresponding ethical categories. But these still seem to make at least tacit reference to other ethical or evaluative categories—e.g. *someone's having something **valuable**, your lack of which reflects **badly** on you*, makes two such references. If an FA-analyst's ambitions extend to giving FA-analyses of all ethical and evaluative categories, including those needed to explicate the allegedly constitutive concerns of attitudes like envy, then it seems that she cannot globally employ a constitutivist account of fittingness without incurring the vicious circularities described above. But perhaps constitutivism could be still be used more locally. For instance, D'Arms and Jacobson (2000b, 2006) suggest sympathetically that one might defend FA-analyses of what they call "sentimental values," which correspond to the fittingness of natural emotion kinds (constituted by robust psychological syndromes of attention, physiological response, and motivation), while eschewing FA-analyses of core ethical and evaluative categories like *good outcomes*. Such "local" deployments of constitutivist accounts of fittingness should, however, have something to say about why they are appropriate for distinguishing fittingness from non-fittingness reasons in the cases of interest, even though alterative explanations of similar differences between kinds of reasons must be given in other cases. This may include an explanation of what is attractive about being a "local" FA-analyst—distinct from the "global" motivation I presented in the first section.

FORMAL APPROACHES

Pamela Hieronymi suggests a way of understanding the concerns "constitutive of" an attitude, which has the potential to avoid at least some of the difficulties described in the previous section. According to Hieronymi (2005: 447–450), an answer to a question is "constitutive of" an attitude, just in case "settling [the] question amounts to forming the attitude." Thus, we might say that in envying a celebrity's fame, one has settled in the affirmative the question as to whether her fame is something valuable, one's relative lack of which reflects badly on oneself. As Hieronymi herself notes, this claim might sound too strong, since one can, for instance, recalcitrantly envy the celebrity's fame despite one's judgments that it is *not* valuable, or that one's relative obscurity does *not* reflect badly on oneself. But Hieronymi (2005: 454n34; 2009) wants to insist that there is a sense in which one has "settled" the relevant question simply by having the attitude, since having it makes one "vulnerable to the questions and criticisms which would be satisfied by considerations that bear positively on the question." For instance, if Hieronymi agreed that envy is constituted by commitments about relative differences in advantage that reflect badly on oneself, the idea would presumably be that, in envying the celebrity— even recalcitrantly—one can be asked "why did you envy her?", and one's answer should indicate a consideration (such as her fame and one's relative obscurity) that one "took to" make it the case that she has something valuable, one's relative lack of which reflects badly on oneself.

One might object to Hieronymi's apparent assumption that there is a literal, explanatorily powerful sense in which even recalcitrant attitudes must involve "taking" certain ethical claims to hold, despite one's judging such claims to be false (on the strength, for instance, of D'Arms and Jacobson's 2003 objections to similar "quasi-judgmentalist" views). But even if one does, Hieronymi's emphasis on the relationship between taking a consideration to be a fittingness reason for an attitude and actually having the attitude suggests an importantly different kind of approach to the WKR problem. Even if our attitudes do not always respond to what we take to be the fittingness reasons for or against having them, there seems to be a crucial attitude-guiding difference between taking a consideration to be a fittingness reason as opposed to a non-fittingness reason. This is that we *can*—and, barring special circumstances, do—have attitudes in response to what we take to be fittingness reasons for them *directly*, without our first having to do something to bring it about that we have them. Simply coming to judge that object O has a feature, which you already take to make attitude A fitting, can cause you to have A towards O. For instance, if you already accept that an outcome's having the property

PS: preventing enormous suffering at the cost of convenience and some gustatory thrills

makes it fitting to desire it, then coming to learn that everyone's becoming vegan will have property PS can directly cause you to desire everyone's becoming vegan.

Similarly, simply coming to judge that a feature, which you already take O to have, actually makes A fitting, can also cause you to have A towards O. For instance, you might initially realize that everyone's becoming vegan has the property

PAS: preventing enormous non-human animal suffering at the cost of convenience and some gustatory thrills for humans,

but start off *not* thinking that an outcome's having PAS is a fittingness reason to desire it. But, upon further consideration of whether factors like a being's intellectual ability (with reference to profoundly intellectually disabled humans) and bare biological species membership (consisting as it does of mere history of phylogenetic decent, phenotype-independent genotype, or psychology-independent morphology) should make such a difference, you might come to think that an outcome's having PAS actually *is* a fittingness reason to desire it. This too can directly cause you to desire everyone's becoming vegan.

On the other hand, it seems that we can respond to what we take to be *non*-fittingness reasons to (make ourselves) have attitudes only *indirectly*, by doing things to bring it about that we have them. Thus, those of us who take the fact that

TH: A demon will harm our loved ones if we do not admire him

to be a reason to (make ourselves) admire him, which does not contribute to his admirability, cannot admire him simply by coming to believe that TH or that TH is a reason of this kind. To respond to TH by admiring the demon, it seems that we must do something like psychologically condition ourselves to love such demons, take mind-altering drugs, or selectively attend to considerations that make him seem genuinely admirable.

This ability to respond directly to what we take to be fittingness as opposed to non-fittingness reasons corresponds to similar distinctions between judgments about reasons with respect to attitudes like intentions and beliefs (Persson 2007: 4–5, 12–13; Raz 2009: 39–40, 50–52; Skorupski 2010, chapter 10; Parfit 2011, appendix A). If we take a consideration to favor intending to φ and *actually* φ-*ing*, we can respond to it directly by intending to φ (e.g. we can intend to be vegan directly in response to taking the consideration that *being vegan avoids complicity in enormous suffering at relatively trivial personal cost to favor intending to be*—and actually being—vegan). But as Kavka (1983) observed, it does not seem that we can intend to φ simply in response to taking our intending to φ to have good consequences if they do not translate into reasons to actually φ (e.g. we cannot now intend to take a toxin tomorrow that will make us sick for a day simply because a mind reader will financially reward us for having this intention today). Similarly, we can believe that p directly in response to taking there to be epistemic or "truth-related" reasons to believe that p (e.g. we can believe there are no gods directly in response to taking the positing of them to add complexity without any additional predictive or explanatory power). But as Pascal (1670) observed, it does not seem that we can believe that P simply in response to taking the belief that P to have good consequences (e.g. you cannot believe in gods simply by taking your having this belief to have good expected consequences—as Pascal suggested, you must do things that will "naturally make you believe," like acting as if you had religious beliefs and attending religious rituals).

Several authors take these observations, together with the plausible idea that we must be able to have attitude A in response to what we take to be reasons *for A*, to be principled grounds for concluding that fittingness reasons for conative attitudes, along with epistemic reasons for beliefs and action-relevant reasons for intentions, are the only genuine reasons for these attitudes, while pragmatic reasons with respect to an attitude are merely reasons to want or get ourselves to have it (Persson 2007; Raz 2009; Parfit 2011; Rowland 2015). Whatever the merits of this (I think largely terminological) conclusion, one can use the idea of direct response to apparent reasons to try to solve the WKR problem in a highly general way, which also distinguishes judgments about epistemic reasons for beliefs and action-relevant reasons for intentions from pragmatic reasons for these attitudes.

One might try saying, for instance, that R is a fittingness reason to have A only if one can have A directly in response to R (Persson 2007; Raz 2009). Unfortunately, Jennie Louise (2009) and Andrew Reisner (2009) argue convincingly that, depending on how we interpret "can have," this either makes what genuine reasons we have too dependent upon the contingencies of our psychology or fails to distinguish fittingness from non-fittingness reasons. What the foregoing observations about responsiveness to apparent reasons seem to support, however, is a way of distinguishing *judgments about* fittingness reasons from *judgments about* non-fittingness reasons. Moreover, since FA-analyses are ultimately trying to explain what is at issue between different ethical and evaluative views in terms of their *holding different views* about fittingness reasons, FA-analyses can—and it seems should—solve the WKR problem by explaining the difference between *judgments about* fittingness and non-fittingness reasons. This, it seems, might be achieved by appealing to

The Response to Apparent Reasons Proposal: One judges that R is a fittingness reason to have A only if one can have A directly in response to one's judgment about R. If one can have A only indirectly in response to one's judgment about R, then one's judgment is that R is a non-fittingness reason to make ourselves have A.

D'Arms and Jacobson (2014: 27–30) have, however, argued that judgments about appropriateness-making reasons pose a dilemma for this proposal. On the one hand, if we understand "having A directly in response to one's judgment about R" to amount to no more than the judgment's causing one to have A without one's having to deliberately instill A in oneself, then certain judgments about appropriateness-making reasons seem to falsify the proposal. For instance, it seems that one's judgment that it would be cold or uncaring not to feel guilt for one's causal involvement in a harm can cause one to feel guilt for it, without one's having to deliberately try to instill the guilt—even if one takes oneself to be blameless. Similarly, it seems that one's judgment that a joke is morally offensive can directly cause one not to be amused by it, even if one takes such moral considerations to be irrelevant to whether the joke is genuinely funny. On the other hand, one might insist that these purported examples of attitudes *directly responding* to apparent non-fittingness reasons are merely examples of attitudes *being directly caused* by apparent non-fittingness reasons. But it would be viciously circular to say that one's attitudes cannot count as direct *responses* simply because they are being caused by judgments about non-fittingness reasons, and it is unclear how else one can distinguish between an attitude's "directly responding to" as opposed to "being directly caused by" a judgment.

Hope that the relevant kind of "response to" judgments can be non-circularly distinguished from merely "being caused by" them may be found in Persson's (2007: 5–7) suggestion that we should look to the inferences or "valid patterns of reasoning" in which judgments about fittingness as opposed to non-fittingness reasons can participate. Along these lines, Way (2012) suggests that fittingness reasons do *not*, while *non*-fittingness reasons do "transmit across facilitating attitudes," or:

Way's Proposal: R is a fittingness reason for attitude A only if one *cannot* infer from R that *attitude B facilitates attitude A* is the same kind of reason for B. If R is a reason with respect to A, and one can infer from R that B's facilitating A is a reason of the same kind for B, then R is a non-fittingness reason to bring about A.

For instance, the fact that *outcome O will make Bugsy happy* is a fittingness reason to desire O. If one irrationally hated Bugsy, and the only way one could get oneself to desire O was to first admire the people Bugsy admires, this would *not* contribute to the fittingness of admiring them. On the other hand, if one had the non-fittingness reason to (make oneself) desire an odd number of hairs constituted by the fact that a demon will harm one's loved ones unless one desires this, and the only way to instill this desire was to first desire that nothing be symmetrical, this *would* seem to give one a non-fittingness reason to (make oneself) desire that nothing be symmetrical.

Unfortunately, while Way's proposal may distinguish fittingness reasons for attitudes from *pragmatic* reasons to make oneself have them, it does not seem to distinguish fittingness reasons from *appropriateness-making* reasons. It is at least coherent, and indeed quite plausible, to think that we *cannot* infer from

(i) R contributes to the appropriateness of having A, and
(ii) B facilitates having A

that (ii) contributes to the appropriateness of having B. For instance, suppose that

(i') joke M's offensive portrayal of minorities makes it morally inappropriate to be amused by M, but (ii') the only way to suppress one's amusement at M is to be amused by joke S, which is both unfunny and portrays women in an offensive way.

It is at least coherent, and indeed quite plausible, to think that one cannot infer from (i') and (ii') that (ii') contributes in the least to the moral appropriateness of being amused by S. Similarly, suppose that

(i*) your friendship with Abigail, and envy's focus on relative positions, make it inappropriately petty to envy Abigail's accomplishments, but

(ii*) the only way to avoid envying Abigail's accomplishments is to envy your equally good friend Brittany's accomplishments.

It is at the very least coherent, and I think extremely plausible, to think that one cannot infer from (i*) and (ii*) that (ii*) makes it any less inappropriately petty to envy Brittany's accomplishments.

CONCLUSION

I have thus surveyed the primary motivations and problems for what I take to be the main approaches to solving the WKR problem. Material approaches seem to have made progress in articulating features of pragmatic reasons to make ourselves have attitudes that distinguish them from fittingness reasons to have them. But existing material approaches seem to have ignored appropriateness-making reasons, and it is unclear how they can be extended to accommodate them. Constitutivist approaches hold the promise of distinguishing fittingness from appropriateness-making reasons, but face problems explaining the alleged "constitutive evaluations" of attitudes in ways that avoid vicious circularity. Constitutivism might avoid certain (but not all) of these problems by limiting its scope to solving the WKR problem for FA-analyses of a special subset of ethical or evaluative categories, but this would be inconsistent with the ambitions and motivations of most FA-analysts, and require an alternative rationale. Formal approaches that look to the attitude-guiding or inference-licensing features of judgments about fittingness as opposed to non-fittingness reasons have the potential to explain the distinction between such judgments in a highly general way, which distinguishes similar judgments about reasons for attitudes like beliefs and intentions from judgments about pragmatic reasons for them. But existing formal approaches seem to have problems distinguishing judgments about fittingness reasons from judgments about appropriateness-making reasons.

Some might be tempted to conclude that these difficulties show the WKR problem to be insoluble, which would appear to have significant theoretical implications. Explaining the core normative features of ethical and evaluative categories by understanding them as categories of reasons for attitudes might make for a simple and unified picture of our normative categories, and justify focusing our fundamental metanormative efforts on understanding the foundational category of reasons. But if FA-analyses cannot avoid a viciously circular reference to ethical and evaluative categories in delineating the sorts of reasons that are supposed to do the explaining, this initially attractive theoretical perspective and strategy of metanormative research looks untenable.

I think, however, that FA-analysts can learn from the problems I have surveyed for existing approaches to solving the WKR problem, and that prospects for a solution remain bright. FA-analysts need to pay more attention to the theoretical motivations for FA-analyses, and the variety of coherent judgments—especially about appropriateness-making reasons—that they need to adequately interpret. Along these lines, I believe that there is, in particular, room for further fruitful developments of formal approaches that pay more attention to the functional and inferential roles of judgments about fittingness reasons beyond direct attitude causation and the non-transmission of reasons across facilitating attitudes (cf. Gibbard 1990, chapter 4; Nye 2009, chapter 6).

NOTE

1. Those who have encountered something like the idea of these analyses through Scanlon (1998, chapter 3) often refer to them as "buck-passing accounts." But as Jacobson (2011, §2.1) has observed, what Scanlon actually describes as a "buck-passing account" incorporates elements that are quite distinct from the view that we can explain something's falling under an ethical or evaluative category in terms of there being reasons to have certain kinds of attitudes towards it. These include the view that something's value does not provide reasons to value it over and above its value-makers (which opponents of explaining value in terms of reasons for attitudes can accept), and the possible view that we can explain something's value in terms of reasons to *act* towards it in certain ways. This latter idea may be problematic from the standpoint of explaining value in terms of reasons in at least two ways. First, a feature of something (e.g. someone's bravely helping others) may make for two very different kinds of value (e.g. it may make her both morally admirable and aesthetically inspiring), in a way that can be captured only by citing its status as a reason for two different kinds of attitudes (e.g. moral admiration and aesthetic appreciation), as there may be no bifurcation in the acts it is a reason to perform. Second, one may not want to build into the very idea of something's value the idea that we should act towards it in certain ways. One may want to explain the connection between values and reasons to act in terms of other principles, such as a general connection between fitting motives and reasons to act (cf. Anderson 1993; Skorupski 2010; Nye, Plunket, and Ku 2015).

    Fortunately, most of the literature on the Wrong Kind of Reasons problem that addresses itself to "buck-passing accounts" is concerned with them as FA-analyses in the sense I explain. But, because talk of "buck-passing" in this context can still threaten to obscure the core issues, I shall avoid all further use of it.

ACKNOWLEDGMENTS

I am grateful to Justin D'Arms, Daniel Jacobson, John Ku, Tristram McPherson, David Plunkett, and Lea Schroeder for extremely helpful comments on an earlier draft of this chapter.

REFERENCES

Anderson, Elizabeth. 1993. *Value in Ethics and Economics*. Cambridge: Harvard University Press.

Brandt, Richard. 1946. Moral Valuation. *Ethics* 56: 106–121.

Crisp, Rodger. 2000. Review of Value… and What Follows by Joel Kupperman. *Philosophy* 75: 458–462.

Dancy, Jonathan. 2000. Should We Pass the Buck? *Royal Institute of Philosophy Supplement* 47: 159–173.

D'Arms, Justin and Daniel Jacobson. 2000a. The Moralistic Fallacy. *Philosophy and Phenomenological Research* 61: 65–90.

—. 2000b. Sentiment and Value. *Ethics* 110: 722–748.

—. 2003. The Significance of Recalcitrant Emotion. *Philosophy: The Journal of the Royal Institute of Philosophy*, 52 (suppl.): 127–145.

—. 2006. Anthropocentric Constraints on Human Value. In R. Shafer-Landau (ed.), *Oxford Studies in Metaethics*, Vol 1, New York: Oxford University Press, 99–126.

—. 2014. Wrong Kinds of Reasons and the Opacity of Normative Force. Forthcoming in R. Shafer-Landau (ed.), *Oxford Studies in Metaethics*, Vol 9, New York: Oxford University Press.

Ewing, Alfred. 1939. A Suggested Non-Naturalistic Analysis of Good. *Mind* 48: 1–22.

Foot, Philippa. 1963. Hume on Moral Judgment. In D. Pears (ed.), *David Hume*, London: McMillan, 74–80.

Gibbard, Allan. 1990. *Wise Choices, Apt Feelings: A Theory of Normative Judgment*. Cambridge, MA: Harvard University Press.

Greenspan, Patricia. 1988. *Emotions and Reason*. London: Routledge & Kegan Paul.

—. 1992. Subjective Guilt and Responsibility. *Mind* 101: 287–303.

Hieronymi, Pamela. 2005. The Wrong Kind of Reason. *The Journal of Philosophy* 102: 437–457.

—. 2009. The Will as Reason. *Philosophical Perspectives* 23: 201–220.

Jacobson, Daniel. 2011. Fitting Attitude Theories of Value. In E. Zalta (ed.), *The Stanford Encyclopedia of Philosophy*, Spring 2011 Edition, URL = <http://plato.stanford.edu/archives/spr2011/entries/fitting-attitude-theories/>.

Kavka, Gregory. 1983. The Toxin Puzzle. *Analysis* 34: 33–36.

Lang, Gerald. 2008. The Right Kind of Solution to the Wrong Kind of Reason Problem. *Utilitas* 20: 472–489.

Louise, Jennie. 2009. Correct Responses and the Priority of the Normative. *Ethical Theory and Moral Practice* 12: 345–364.

Nye, Howard. 2009. *Ethics, Fitting Attitudes, and Practical Reasons*. Ph.D. Dissertation, University of Michigan.

Nye, Howard, David Plunkett, and John Ku. 2015. Non-Consequentialism Demystified. *Philosophers' Imprint* 15: 1–28.

Olson, Jonas. 2004. Buck-Passing and the Wrong Kind of Reasons. *Philosophical Quarterly* 54: 295–300.

—. 2009. The Wrong Kind of Solution to the Wrong Kind of Reason Problem. *Utilitas* 21: 225–232.

Orisi, Francesco. 2013. What's Wrong with Moorean Buck-Passing? *Philosophical Studies* 164: 727–746

Parfit, Derek. 2001. Rationality and Reasons. In D. Egonson, J. Josefson, B. Petterson, and T. Ronnow-Rasmussen (eds.), *Exploring Practical Philosophy*, Aldershot: Ashgate, 17–39.

—. 2011. *On What Matters: Volume One*. Oxford: Oxford University Press.

Pascal, Blaise. 1670. *Pensées*. W. F. Trotter (Trans.), London: Dent, 1910.

Persson, Ingmar. 2007. Primary and Secondary Reasons. In T. Rønnow-Rasmussen, B. Petersson, J. Josefsson, and D. Egonsson (eds.), *Homage á Wlodek*, URL = <http://www.fil.lu.se/hommageawlodek>.

Rabinowicz, Wlodek and Toni Ronnow-Rasmussen. 2004. The Strike of the Demon. *Ethics* 114: 391–423.

—. 2006. Buck-Passing and the Right Kind of Reasons. *Philosophical Quarterly* 56: 114–120.

Raz, Joseph. 2009. Reasons: Practical and Adaptive. In D. Sobel and S. Wall (eds.), *Reasons for Actions*, Cambridge: Cambridge University Press, 37–57.

Reisner, Andrew. 2009. The Possibility of Pragmatic Reasons for Belief and the Wrong Kind of Reasons Problem. *Philosophical Studies* 145: 257–272.

Roberts, Robert. 1988. What an Emotion Is: A Sketch. *The Philosophical Review* 97: 183–209.

Rowland, Richard. 2015. Dissolving the Wrong Kind of Reason Problem. *Philosophical Studies* 172: 1455–1474.

Samuelsson, Lars. 2013. The Right Version of 'The Right Kind of Solution to the Wrong Kind of Reason Problem'. *Utilitas* 25: 383–404.

Scanlon, Thomas. 1998. *What We Owe To Each Other*. Cambridge: Harvard University Press.

Schroeder, Mark. 2010. Value and the Right Kind of Reason. In R. Shafer-Landau (ed.), *Oxford Studies in Metaethics*, Vol 5, New York: Oxford University Press, 25–55.

Skorupski, John. 2010. *The Domain of Reasons*. Oxford: Oxford University Press.

Way, Jonathan. 2012. Transmission and the Wrong Kind of Reason. *Ethics* 122: 489–515.

Zimmerman, Michael. 2007. The Good and the Right. *Utilitas* 19: 326–353.

22

Mind-Dependence and Moral Realism

Connie S. Rosati

Moral realism is the view that there are objective moral truths or moral facts. But what is it for moral truths to be "objective"? A common way of characterizing moral realism has it that the objectivity of moral truths consists in their being, in some sense, mind-independent. Thus, we are variously told, moral truths are independent of our attitudes, emotions, values, responses, perspectives, or judgments; they are "stance-independent" or independent of the "practical standpoint." Derek Parfit (2011), for example, treats moral realism as response-independent, as does David Enoch (2011); and Jay Wallace (2012: 21) characterizes moral realism in terms of truths that are "prior to and independent of the will."

The chief contrast is said to be with forms of metaethical constructivism, according to which moral truths are mind- or stance-dependent: they are dependent on our attitudes, emotions, values, responses, perspectives, or judgments; they are a matter of what is entailed from the practical standpoint. But certain forms of ethical naturalism, such as Roderick Firth's (1952) Ideal Observer Theory and Richard Brandt's (1979) reforming naturalism, would also count as mind-dependent. On a mind-independence characterization of moral realism, then, only nonnaturalist views, such as the classical views of G. E. Moore (1903/1993) and W. D. Ross (1930), and perhaps some forms of nonreductive naturalism, count as forms of moral realism.

This chapter explores how best to understand these claims of dependence and independence. For ease of exposition, I will use the expressions 'mind-dependence' and 'mind-independence' to cover all of the various claimed kinds of dependence and independence, except where it is necessary to distinguish between them. I shall propose that mind-independence characterizations of moral realism are best understood as excluding from the category of moral realism metaethical views according to which all moral facts are either identical to or fully grounded in nonmoral facts of a certain type. I then argue that we ought to reject mind-independence characterizations of moral realism, for at least two reasons. First, we ought to reject any characterization of moral realism that assumes, in advance of our inquiries, a particular view about the nature of moral facts. Second, we ought to reject any characterization of moral realism that excludes as forms of realism theories that are, at least in principle, better positioned to account for the normativity of morality, as are some forms of constructivism and ethical naturalism. We therefore ought to adopt a characterization of moral realism that distinguishes realism from antirealism in ethics on grounds other than mind-independence.

UNDERSTANDING INDEPENDENCE

Not all self-described moral realists regard mind-independence as a critical feature of moral realism. For example, Terence Cuneo (2007: 45–49), a nonnaturalist, draws a distinction between what he calls "strong" and "weak" mind-independence, arguing that paradigmatic moral realism need not subscribe to either sort; and David Copp (1995), a naturalist, defends as a form of moral realism a view that treats moral facts as standpoint-dependent. As a consequence, not all metaethicists see constructivism as an alternative to moral realism (e.g., Copp 2013; Cuneo 2007: 48–49), a point to which we will return later. The more common view, however, seems to be that moral realism requires mind-independence, and in this critical respect, contrasts with constructivism (cf. Billy Dunaway's chapter "Realism and Objectivity").

Let's begin, then, by considering what motivates mind-independence characterizations of moral realism. (We will consider later what would motivate philosophers to gravitate toward mind-dependent views in metaethics.) After doing so, I will present some representative claims of mind-independence and mind-dependence. The focus thereafter will be on attempting to understand what these various claims come to.

There seem to be three basic motivations for characterizing moral realism in terms of mind-independence. The first two rest on ideas about what is necessary for a view or theory in ethics to be realist. According to the first, a view isn't realist unless it allows for the possibility that we could be quite wrong about the moral facts, much as we can be quite wrong about physical objects. But a view allows for the possibility of substantial error only if it treats moral facts as independent of our emotions, attitudes, responses, or judgments, all of which are open to normative criticism. According to the second, a view isn't realist unless it captures the "normativity" of moral facts. But the normativity of moral facts makes them seemingly just "too different from" nonmoral facts (Enoch 2011), including facts about our attitudes, emotions, values, responses, perspectives, or judgments. The third motivation rests on considerations of theoretical unity. Here, the thought is that what makes for realism in ethics ought to be the same as what makes for realism in other domains. For example, realism about physical objects or about primary qualities, like shape, seems to be a matter of their existing independently of our conceptions of or judgments about them. Similarly, realism about moral facts would seem to be a matter of their existing independently of our conceptions of or judgments about them.

Now consider some representative characterizations of moral realism and metaethical constructivism:

> [The moral realist holds that] there are moral facts (and properties) that are independent of human attitudes, conventions, and the like.
>
> (Timmons 1996: 106)

Realism is sometimes contrasted with constructivism by invoking the claim that, for realists, morality is mind-independent ... The way I would prefer to characterize the realist position is by reference to its endorsement of the stance-independence of moral reality. Realists believe that there are moral truths that obtain independently of any preferred perspective, in the sense that *the moral standards that fix the moral facts are not made true by virtue of their ratification from within any given actual or hypothetical perspective.*

(Shafer-Landau 2003: 15)

[O]ne thing that unites almost all constructivists is the idea that normative facts are somehow dependent upon the normative judgments or values of individuals or communities.

(Schafer 2012: 2)

[I]t is ... fully in keeping with philosophical tradition to understand the "realism-anti-realism" debate as concerning ... the question of mind-dependence ... On this understanding, the key point at issue between realists and antirealists is the answer to the central question of Plato's *Euthyphro* (in rough secular paraphrase), namely whether things are valuable ultimately because we value them (antirealism), or whether we value things ultimately because they possess a value independent of us (realism) ... Metaethical constructivism falls squarely on the antirealist side of this divide. As the slogan "no normative truth independent of the practical point of view" makes clear, metaethical constructivism asserts a counterfactual dependence of value on the attitudes of valuing creatures; it understands reason-giving status as conferred upon things by us. According to metaethical constructivism, there are no facts about what is valuable apart from facts about a certain point of view on the world and what is entailed from within that point of view. Normative truth, according to the constructivist, does not outrun what follows from within the evaluative standpoint, but rather consists in whatever is entailed from within it.

(Street 2010: 370–371)

We will return later to the Euthyphro question and consider whether the constructivist view that things are valuable ultimately because we value them settles where to situate it with respect to the realism-antirealism divide.

How should we understand these various independence and dependence claims? It will be helpful to have some preliminary formulation of mind-independence in front of us and to work toward a more adequate formulation. But should mind-independence be formulated as a claim about moral concepts or moral facts? As it happens, at present, mind-independence tends to be formulated in terms of moral truths, moral facts, and moral properties. As Sharon Street expresses it, "The defining claim of realism about value, as I will be understanding it, is that there are at least some *evaluative facts or truths* that hold independently of all our evaluative attitudes ..." (2006: 110–111, emphasis added). There is good reason for this. There might, after all, be a mismatch between our moral concepts and the nature of the moral properties those concepts concern. This possibility, many now think, explains why Moore's open question argument does not defeat forms of synthetic naturalism, according to which our moral concepts may not admit of naturalistic analysis, but moral properties are nevertheless natural properties. There might be an open question whether, say, GOOD is the same concept as n (where n is the concept of something natural), but for all that, *being good* might be the same property as *being N*. Our concepts MORALLY RIGHT and MORALLY WRONG might be concepts of mind-independent features of reality, but the nature of the properties of *being morally right* and *being morally wrong* might be mind-dependent. So, although mind-independence claims could be formulated as claims about our concepts, in keeping with the contemporary literature, I will continue to treat them as claims about the nature of moral truths, facts, and properties.

Let's begin our efforts to understand claims of mind-independence, then, with the following modal formulation, where A stands for an agent or group of agents:

Independence: At least some moral facts would have been the same even if A's [attitudes, emotions, values, responses, perspective, judgments] had been different.

Independence must be understood to concern all agents—actual and hypothetical. Thus understood, Independence expresses what Cuneo calls the strong form of the "mind-independence constraint": "moral facts are mind-independent inasmuch as they are existentially independent of the attitudes of actual or hypothetical human moral agents" (2007: 45).

Independence seems to capture the intuitive idea behind the various independence claims, namely, that the moral facts, ultimately, are not determined by us, any more than basic facts about the natural world are determined by us. Independence is thus consistent with the side of the Euthyphro divide that says "valuable things have their value independently of us." But it does not make clear precisely what independence and dependence come to, and in any case, it remains unclear why those moral facts that are dependent on us are any less objective or real.

Notice that many particular moral claims concern mind-dependent facts, yet moral realists would be inclined to accept these claims. As Cuneo (2007: 45–47) has stressed, it is implausible to think that particular moral truths are all (strongly) mind-independent. An example of a particular moral truth or moral fact would be that it is wrong for Smith to kill Jones, as contrasted with the general moral truth or moral fact that murder is wrong. Whether Smith murdered Jones, and so whether what he did was wrongful, depends, among other things, on whether Smith intended to kill Jones. So the moral truth that it was wrong for Smith to kill Jones is not independent of Smith's mental states. Had Smith's mental states been different, had he believed correctly, for instance, that his life was in imminent danger from Jones, then Smith's killing of Jones might not have been wrongful. Thus, had Smith's attitude been different, the moral facts might have been different. But no moral realist could plausibly think otherwise.

Likewise, some general moral claims that moral realists accept concern mind-dependent facts. After all, some general moral truths depend on facts about human psychology and its bearing on human welfare. If people's emotional capacities were such that they did not care about and so could not benefit from friendship, for example, then it would arguably be false that we ought to promote the good of friendship for their sake. People's emotions and attitudes bear on what can benefit them, and so bear on what we ought to do with respect to promoting people's welfare. But no realist could plausibly think otherwise.

The existence of some mind-dependent moral facts is thus compatible with moral realism, even when moral realism is understood as limited to nonnaturalist realism. If people's emotions or attitudes or mental states had been different, then some particular moral truths might have been otherwise. And if people's emotions or attitudes or mental states had been different, then some general moral truths might have been different.

Insofar as the mind-independence theorist's claim is only that *some* moral truths are mind-independent, the existence of some mind-dependent moral facts does not itself undercut mind-independence characterizations of moral realism. Of course, now we seem to have two sorts of moral facts, the mind-dependent ones and the mind-independent ones. Given that mind-dependent facts were supposed to be less-than-fully objective, we might wonder whether the mind-dependent moral facts are somehow less objective than those moral facts that are mind-independent. Let's allow, though, that insofar as the truth of mind-dependent moral facts ultimately depends on the truth of mind-independent moral facts, they have the sort of objectivity required for realism. The question that we need to consider, then, is whether there is a sense of objectivity on which the kinds of mind-dependent moral truths that the realist rejects are less-than-fully objective, so that moral realism ought to be characterized in terms of mind-independence. We shall consider this question along with a second question: Does it make a difference to the plausibility of mind-independence characterizations of moral realism whether claims of mind-independence concern, say, independence from emotions, desires, or responses as opposed to judgments?

Gideon Rosen (1994) has argued that extant efforts to characterize realism generally in terms of objectivity fail, whether we understand objectivity in terms of mind-independence, response-independence, or judgment-independence. "We can epitomize the realist's basic commitment by saying that for the realist as against his opponents, *the target discourse describes a domain of genuine, objective fact.* The basic foundational question is then: What is objectivity in the relevant sense, and what is the alternative?" (1994: 279). Rosen queries whether there is a "definite and debatable thesis upon whose truth the legitimacy of the rhetoric of objectivity depends"; he ultimately concludes that, "So far as I can see, it adds nothing to the claim that a certain state of affairs obtains to say that it obtains objectively" (1994: 279).

Of relevance to the present discussion is Rosen's consideration of various proposed accounts of the objectivity that is supposed to separate realism from nonrealism. He observes first that the objectivity of interest is evidently supposed to contrast with mind-dependence. "What is less-than-fully objective owes what reality it possesses to our thinking, and is to that extent something mental" (1994: 287). But the notion of mind-dependence as a mark of what is less-than-fully objective is problematic. Consider artifacts, such as chairs, soccer matches, and political and social institutions. Artifacts come into existence (and may continue in existence) partly as a result of something mental— namely, the intentions of the individuals who bring them about. Other things that exist, such as climate change, are the "unintended consequences of intentional social activity" (1994: 287). "Let us say that an item depends *causally* on the mind iff it is caused to exist or sustained in existence in part by some collection of everyday empirical mental events or states" (1994: 287). But mind-dependence in this sense clearly does not undermine the objectivity of facts about artifacts or climate change. Nor does the mind-dependence of mental states, such as pain, undermine the objectivity of facts about those states (1994: 288). So the objectivity of realism, as opposed to nonrealism, must not involve at least this sort of mind-dependence; it must be a non-causal, non-empirical sense of dependence.

An alternative way of trying to formulate the objectivity at issue, he suggests, would be in terms of the distinction between response-dependent and response-independent concepts. (Sentences employing response-dependent and response-independent concepts represent response-dependent and response-independent facts, and so we can still treat mind-independence as concerning moral facts rather than concepts.) Rosen has us consider David Lewis's (1989) response-dependent conception of value:

> x is a value iff we would be disposed to value x under conditions of fullest possible imaginative acquaintance with it.
>
> (Rosen 1994: 291)

As Rosen notes, this biconditional can be supported by a claim of conceptual identity:

> The concept of being a value = the concept of being such as to be valued by us under conditions of fullest possible imaginative acquaintance.
>
> (1994: 291)

It is worth mentioning some other response-dependent theories not discussed by Rosen, such as those offered by John McDowell (1997) and David Wiggins (1987). McDowell argues that we should understand value on the model of secondary qualities, like color, rather than primary qualities, like shape. Values, like (phenomenal) colors, are not "brutely there," independently of human sensibilities. But "this does not stop us supposing that they are there independently of any particular apparent experience of them" (1997: 208). A disanalogy, as McDowell emphasizes, is that whereas color is such as merely to *cause* our phenomenal experience of it, value is such as to *merit* certain responses (1997: 207). Though the comparison of values with secondary qualities might suggest values are less objective than primary qualities, McDowell contends that primary and secondary qualities are "on all fours" as concerns the objectivity of their objects (1997: 205).

Wiggins (1987) also likens value to secondary qualities. As he characterizes the position of the "sensible subjectivist," "x is good if and only if x is the sort of thing that calls forth and makes appropriate a certain sentiment of approbation *given the range of propensities we actually have to respond in this or that way*" (1987: 206). The sensible subjectivist's claim is that

> for each value predicate Φ … there is an attitude or response of subjects *belonging to a range of propensities that we actually have* such that an object has the property Φ stands for if and only if the object is fitted by its characteristics to bring down that extant attitude or response upon it and bring it down *precisely because* it has those characteristics.
>
> (1987: 206)

Wiggins says that although he himself would not adopt the label 'realism' for this position, we must be ready for the possibility of categories of judgment that are both subjective and objective (1987: 202).

Rosen considers the following as a proposal for understanding objectivity in terms of a contrast between response-independence and response-dependence.

When the central concepts of a discourse are response-dependent, the true sentences within that discourse represent a range of subjective or mind-dependent
facts. A fact is genuinely objective, then, when it is represented in a discourse
whose central concepts are response-independent.

(1994: 292)

Rosen argues that this proposal is problematic. Consider the mental state of annoyance,
and consider the following conceptual identity claim:

The concept of being annoying to fox terriers = the concept of being disposed to
annoy statistically normal fox terriers under ordinary conditions.

(1994: 293)

Facts about what fox terriers are disposed to find annoying seem to be quite objective,
even though they are response-dependent. To call a concept "response-dependent" is
not, Rosen thinks, to give up thinking of corresponding facts as robustly real. On the
contrary, he argues, "dispositions to bring about mental responses would seem to be on
a par, metaphysically speaking, with dispositions to produce merely physical responses
in inanimate things. ... " (1994: 293). For the same reason, facts about what is valuable,
as Lewis characterizes value, are as objective as facts about physical responses in inanimate things. Or to make the point in more qualified terms, if these facts about value are
problematic from the standpoint of realism, it is not per se because they are response-
dependent. (See Billy Dunaway's chapter "Realism and Objectivity" for further discussion of Rosen's argument and of realism and objectivity.)

   An alternative way to characterize objectivity might be in terms of judgment-
independence. Following Rosen, we can say that a concept F is judgment-dependent if
and only if

It is a priori that: x is F iff certain subjects S would judge that x is F under conditions C.

(1994: 301)

When the central concepts of a discourse are judgment-dependent, are the facts described
by such discourse any less objective than facts described by a discourse that is judg-
ment-independent? It might seem so because of the common thought that the objective
obtains, regardless of our opinions about it. But we lack adequate reason to think that
the former facts are any less objective than the latter. Consider one of Rosen's examples:

It is a priori that: x is funny iff we would judge x funny under conditions of full
information about x's relevant extra-comedic features.

(1994: 301)

An alien anthropologist who studied us might come to reliably determine which jokes
we would judge funny under the specified conditions. But, in discerning these facts
about the funny, he would seem to be discerning perfectly objective facts, even if they
"supervene on facts about our minds" (1994: 302). From the anthropologist's standpoint,
his investigation is aimed at facts that are objective and independent, even though they

are identical to or supervenient on facts about how we are disposed to use certain concepts (1994: 303). And this is so even if, from our standpoint as participants in a practice, our judgments might look to us to involve a kind of invention.

This highly condensed discussion of Rosen's arguments doesn't begin to cover the range of views that he considers under the headings of mind-, response-, and judgment-independence. But it does help us to begin to address our two questions. First, we still seem to lack a characterization of objectivity on which mind-dependent facts are less-than-fully objective. Second, it evidently makes no difference to the plausibility of mind-independence characterizations of moral realism whether claims of mind-independence concern, say, independence from emotions, desires, or responses, as opposed to judgments. There is much more to be said, but we should tentatively conclude that whether the dependence at issue concerns emotions, desires, responses, or judgments does not make a difference to how we ought to characterize the realist-antirealist divide.

Of course, it may make a difference to the comparative plausibility of mind-dependent theories in metaethics. Compare, for instance, Ideal Advisor analyses of welfare or Firth's Ideal Observer Theory to John Rawls' constructivism or Street's Humean constructivism. On Ideal Advisor theories, what is good for an individual is what she would want herself to want under ideal conditions of full information and rationality. (See, e.g., Railton 1986a and 1986b.) But what she would want herself to want would be a product, not simply of full information and ideal rationality, but also of her contingent motivational system. She does not reason her way to new desires; rather, what she would come to desire under ideal conditions depends on how she would respond to increasing information, given her motivational system. As a consequence, such views would seem to lack the normativity of welfare; we can reasonably wonder whether what those views say is good for us, really is good for us—really is something we have reason to pursue for ourselves—for our own motivational systems are normatively arbitrary (Rosati 1996a and 1996b; Michael Smith's [1994] moral rationalism may or may not be subject to similar difficulties). According to Firth's Ideal Observer theory, what is, say, morally right, is whatever would be approved of by any Ideal Observer, an observer who is omniscient, omnipercipient, disinterested, dispassionate, consistent, and "otherwise normal." But, again, what an Ideal Observer would approve of is not simply a matter of its idealized features but of its motivational system, which is not entirely specified on Firth's view and would be difficult (if not impossible) to specify fully without begging important normative questions.

Compare Rawlsian constructivism, according to which the correct principles of justice (at least for liberal democratic societies) are those that would be chosen by parties to the original position (Rawls 1971; cf. Rawls 1980). The motivational system of the parties involves some idealization—they are mutually disinterested, for example, but they choose principles of justice by considering arguments about which principles would best further their interests. Thus, the parties' motivational systems do not play the causal role that they play in Ideal Advisor and Ideal Observer theories. The same is true of Street's constructivism. According to Street, "the philosophical heart of [constructivism] is the notion of the practical point of view and what does or doesn't follow from within it" (2010: 364). What follows from within the practical point of view is what is entailed by the normative judgments a person already accepts. So, moral truths, on this view, are not, in the same way, a matter of a person's idiosyncratic motivational system, even if they are truths about what follows from what she contingently values.

Consider also whether the type of attitude on which moral facts might depend is the attitude of valuing as opposed to mere desire. Street (2012) argues, for example, that the attitude of valuing is more apt in formulating a viable version of constructivism. That attitude, she contends, is "characterized by a 'discipline' that the attitude of mere desiring lacks" (2012: 4). In contrast to mere desiring, valuing "is characterized by all the range, nuance, and depth of human emotion and feeling" (2012: 5). And it is characterized by greater "structural complexity": whereas desire tends to be directed at "a single object or state of affairs," valuing involves experiencing "very specific features of the world" as counting in favor of or demanding specific things (2012: 5).

Judgment- (or choice-) dependence may or may not produce a more defensible form of constructivism than emotion-, attitude-, or desire-dependence. The attitude of valuing may or may not be more apt than the attitude of desiring for developing a viable form of constructivism or of ethical naturalism. The important point, for now, is that we should not confuse the difference it may make to the comparative plausibility of mind-dependent theories whether the dependence at issue concerns emotions, desires, responses, or judgments for a difference it may make to how we ought to characterize the realist-antirealist divide. Of course, defenders of mind-independence characterizations of moral realism would think that these differences among mind-dependent theories are of no moment: any mind-dependent theory falls short. At least some moral truths are, in an important sense, yet to be specified, independent of our emotions, attitudes, desires, judgments, or perspectives.

What, then, might independence itself come to, given that even nonnaturalist moral realists accept as moral facts some mind-dependent facts, and given that we lack a characterization of objectivity on which mind-dependent facts are less-than-fully objective? Precisely what is being accepted (and rejected) by the mind-independence theorist? We might begin to get at what mind-independence comes to by considering how mind-independence and mind-dependence relate to supervenience, grounding, and identity, three important metaphysical relations in which the normative might stand to the nonnormative (see Gideon Rosen's chapter "Metaphysical Relations in Metaethics"; McPherson 2015).

Mind-independence theorists and mind-dependence theorists alike accept supervenience. Both accept that the normative supervenes on the nonnormative in that any two metaphysically possible worlds that are alike in their nonnormative features will be alike in their normative features. So, what mind-independence theorists must be rejecting is a more intimate relation between the normative and the nonnormative than supervenience, a more intimate relation between normative facts and nonnormative facts about our emotions, desires, and responses.

Grounding is such a relation. A grounding relation between two facts is supposed to be an explanatorily tight connection, in which one fact holds *because* or *in virtue of* some other fact(s). Though the grounded fact is distinguishable from the facts that are its grounds, the grounded fact is not a part of reality over and above the facts that ground it. Thus, the fact that I am waving my hand is grounded in facts about how the sundry parts of my arm and hand are related, but while the former fact and the latter facts are distinguishable, the former fact is not some part of reality in addition to the facts that ground it (see Gideon Rosen's chapter "Metaphysical Relations in Metaethics").

How does this relate to constructivism? Constructivism is commonly taken to be a mind-dependent, antirealist position in opposition to nonnaturalist realism, but in fact, the metaethical status of constructivism is a matter of dispute. Among those who maintain that constructivism is a metaethical view, rather than simply a normative view, some have interpreted it as a form of realism (nonnaturalist or naturalist), while others have argued that it is best understood as a version of expressivism (Lenman and Shemmer 2012; Lenman 2012). Although constructivists maintain that there are normative truths, they themselves reject both realism and expressivism. On one way of characterizing constructivism as a position distinct from either realism or expressivism, constructivism is committed to "hypothetical proceduralism" along with a distinctive strategy for defending certain procedures of construction as "constitutive standards of agency or the practical point of view" (see Melissa Barry's chapter "Constructivism"). This is said to be in contrast to Humean hypothetical proceduralist accounts, like those of Firth, Brandt, or Smith, which "typically defend the applicability of the procedures with a naturalistic reduction, according to which reason is reducible to complex natural facts about how an agent with an initial set of desires would be motivated after procedural corrections of nonnormative fact and reasoning" (see Melissa Barry's chapter "Constructivism").

Understanding constructivism in terms of how the constitutive standards of agency structure deliberation, and understanding reasons and values as a function of the commitments of rational agents, is arguably compatible with understanding constructivism as a view about the grounding of moral and value facts. For example, Street's constructivism might fairly be understood as the view that facts about what is valuable are grounded in facts about what is entailed from within the practical standpoint. And although this was not Rawls' own understanding of his view (see, e.g., Rawls 1985), Rawls' constructivism might fairly be understood as the view that the fact that a principle should govern the basic structure of society is grounded in facts about what would be agreed to by parties in the original position.

Understood in this way, constructivism treats normative truths as grounded in facts about what is constitutive of agency, how these constitutive standards structure deliberation, and what follows from the commitments of rational agents. Φ is a value for A, for example, because – or in virtue – of the fact that it follows, given the relevant hypothetical procedure, from the commitments of A. The fact that Φ is a value for A is not identical to the fact that Φ would follow from A's commitments, given the relevant hypothetical procedures, but it is not a feature of reality over and above its grounds. Understanding constructivism in terms of grounding would commit constructivism, with respect to all moral truths, to a stronger metaphysical connection between moral facts and nonmoral facts about our emotions, attitudes, or responses than would be accepted by nonnaturalist realists. So, it would be compatible with constructivism's rejection of nonnaturalist realism. It would also be compatible with constructivism's rejection of expressivism. Although it would, in these ways, have the effect of aligning constructivism with some forms of naturalist realism, reductive or nonreductive, it would preserve the constructivist idea that what is explanatorily basic is our emotions, attitudes, or responses—our valuing—as corrected by the relevant hypothetical procedure. It would thus keep constructivism on the side of the Euthyphro divide that says things are valuable because we value them. Yet, as we will, see, keeping constructivism on that side of the Euthyphro divide does not settle where it stands with respect to the realism/antirealism divide.

More would need to be considered, of course, to determine whether understanding constructivism in terms of grounding fails to capture something that is truly essential to the constructivist project. And more would need to be said to address constructivists' reasons for rejecting realism. Constructivists do, however, tend to reject moral realism, at least in part, based on an understanding of moral realism as requiring mind-independence (Street 2010: 317; see also Korsgaard 1996 and 2003). But mind-independence characterizations of moral realism are driven, in part, by the idea that mind-dependent facts are somehow not fully objective, and as we have seen, this idea does not provide a compelling reason to accept such characterizations. What's more, as I will explain shortly, we have positive reason to reject them. This leaves open the possibility of a characterization of the divide between moral realism and antirealism in terms of something other than mind-independence, and one that places at least some versions of constructivism on the realist side of the divide.

Moving beyond constructivism, as we have already seen, there are mind-dependent forms of ethical naturalism, and these can be understood as offering either grounding or identity claims. For example, moral facts and value facts on certain naturalist views are grounded in or identical to facts about our emotions, attitudes, values, or judgments under idealized conditions. If either constructivism or some form of ethical naturalism is correct, then moral facts and facts about value could not be independent of our emotions, attitudes, responses, values, or judgments, because they are either grounded in or identical to facts about our emotions, attitudes, responses, values, or judgments.

Insofar as there is a clear claim of mind-independence that distinguishes nonnaturalist realism from constructivism and ethical naturalism, that claim may be best understood as a denial of the view that all moral facts are either grounded in or identical to mind-dependent facts. We should thus replace Independence with

Independence*: At least some moral facts are independent of facts about any agent's actual or counterfactual attitudes, emotions, values, or judgments, in the sense that at least some moral facts are neither fully grounded in nor identical to facts about any agent's actual or counterfactual attitudes, emotions, values, or judgments.

Independence* makes clear, in a way that Independence does not, what sorts of mind-dependence are being rejected.

We should be unsurprised that mind-independence is best understood as a rejection of grounding and identity claims, because both rule out the idea that at least some moral facts are facts about the instantiation of sui generis moral or value properties. As we have seen, realists accept the supervenience of the normative on the nonnormative. Some realists also accept the idea that moral facts are constituted by nonmoral facts, where constitution is understood as a relation other than identity or grounding (Shafer-Landau 2003: 75–76). But nonnaturalists certainly think that moral properties are not themselves natural properties (Shafer-Landau 2003: 91). Likewise, they reject the idea that all moral facts are fully grounded in the nonnormative facts, because they maintain either that some moral facts are entirely ungrounded or that moral facts lack a complete grounding in nonnormative facts (see Gideon Rosen's chapter "Metaphysical Relations in Metaethics").

REALISM AND ANTIREALISM

If the foregoing proposal is correct, then even if claims of mind-independence sharpen our understanding of the contrast between nonnaturalist realism and certain of its metaethical competitors, appeals to mind-independence do not provide us with an acceptable way of characterizing the distinction between moral realism and antirealism.

There are at least two reasons for this. We'll turn to the second reason shortly. The first is that if there are any moral facts, it is an open question what their nature is. Moral facts, and facts about value more generally, might be facts about the instantiation of sui generis moral or value properties. Or they might be facts identical to or grounded in nonmoral facts about our emotions, desires, attitudes, or responses. Our characterization of moral realism shouldn't presuppose that moral realism is true only if moral facts have the nature nonnaturalists claim that they have. Instead, whether a metaethical view is a form of realism should turn on such matters as how well it captures what we treat as truistic or platitudinous about morality.

We might compare mind-independence characterizations of moral realism to characterizations of free will, according to which free will is contra-causal freedom. We do not know the nature of free will, so it remains an open question whether free will is or isn't compatible with determinism. To characterize the free will/non-free will distinction in terms of contra-causal freedom presupposes that soft determinism is false. But our characterization of free will should not assume in advance an answer as to the nature of free will; it shouldn't presuppose that free will exists only if the will has contra-causal freedom, which may not be genuine freedom at all.

When we consider nonnaturalist realism, ethical naturalism, and constructivism, we face the question of how best to understand the realist/antirealist divide and where to place these types of theories with respect to that divide. Because mind-independence characterizations of moral realism presuppose that moral facts must have a certain nature, we should reject such characterizations in favor of something like Geoff Sayre-McCord's or David Copp's way of drawing the realism/antirealism distinction.

According to Sayre-McCord, "realism involves embracing just two theses: (1) the claims in question, when literally construed, are literally true or false (cognitivism), and (2) some are literally true" (1988: 5). David Copp (2007) offers a fuller characterization of moral realism. According to Copp, moral realism involves the following five claims:

1. There are moral properties (and relations). There is, for example, such a thing as wrongness.
2. Some moral properties are instantiated. For example, some actions are wrong.
3. Moral predicates are used to ascribe moral properties. When we call an action "wrong," we are ascribing to it the property wrongness.
4. Moral assertions express moral beliefs. When we call an action "wrong," we are expressing the belief that the action is wrong.
5. Moral properties, in being properties, have the metaphysical status that any other property has, whatever that is (2007: 7).

Notice that this characterization of moral realism leaves entirely open the nature of moral properties. As Copp explains, what ethical naturalism adds is a sixth claim, to the effect that moral properties are natural properties (2007: 10).

These characterizations of moral realism may or may not be fully adequate. We might, for example, have reason to add universality as a feature, so that moral realism is the view that some universal moral claims are literally true. This would have the benefit of excluding, as forms of moral realism, subjectivist and relativist views. We could then say that if a view like Street's best counts as a form of antirealism, it would not be because it involves mind- or stance-dependence, as she claims, but because it apparently rejects universality. However we might ultimately best characterize moral realism, Sayre-McCord's and Copp's characterizations have the virtue of remaining appropriately neutral as to what the moral facts might turn out to be like.

MIND-DEPENDENCE AND NORMATIVITY

The dispute about how best to characterize moral realism and the realism/antirealism distinction is not merely terminological. We have, as just explained, sound methodological reasons for rejecting mind-independence characterizations of moral realism. But there is a further reason to keep our characterization appropriately neutral (Rosati 2016).

We explored earlier the motivations for mind-independence characterizations of moral realism. What motivates some to move to mind-dependence views in metaethics? The motivations of constructivists (see Melissa Barry's chapter "Constructivism") differ in some ways from those of ethical naturalists, but two motivations seem to be held in common. The first concerns the problematic metaphysical and epistemological commitments of nonnaturalist realism. As J. L. Mackie (1977) argues, nonnaturalism is committed to the existence of "queer" properties, and it is uncertain how we would have epistemic access to facts about their instantiation. The second, and most important for present purposes, concerns the apparent inability of nonnaturalism, notwithstanding its claims to the contrary, to account for the normativity of ethics (e.g., Korsgaard 1996: 38–40).

Moral facts, if there are any, are a kind of normative fact. Just what "normativity" is and what the normativity of value and morality consists of is uncertain. What we would presumably want, if normativity is to play any role in adjudicating among rival metaethical theories, is an account of the nature of normativity that is, in principle, acceptable across a broad array of objectivist metaethical theories, even if in the end it favors one over others. (The restriction to objectivist metaethical theories is meant to exclude expressivism, on the grounds that for expressivism, normativity is ultimately a feature of normative judgments, rather than a feature of normative facts.) According to one view that has found fairly broad acceptance, normativity consists (at least) in being reason-giving. "All normative phenomena are normative in as much as, and because, they provide reasons or are partly constituted by reasons. This makes the concept of a reason key to an understanding of normativity" (Raz 2010: 5). Of course, the notion of a reason is itself normative, and a complete account of the nature of normativity would have to account for the normativity of reasons as well (Copp 1995: 33; 2007). But the basic point I want to make holds even if we come to understand normativity somewhat differently.

It is an adequacy condition on a realist metaethical theory that it account for the normativity of morality (and of value more generally); the nature of morality includes its normativity. Classical nonnaturalism might seem to have an advantage in capturing the normativity of moral facts and properties (however, see Frankena 1968). At least, a common complaint against extant forms of ethical naturalism and constructivism is that they fail to do so. But nonnaturalism arguably fares worse. It is unclear why the fact that an act has the unanalyzable nonnatural property of, say, rightness gives us a reason to perform that act. What is it about the presence of such a property that would give us a reason to act? It would seem that there must be something about the nature of the property that accounts for the reason-giving force of facts about its instantiation. But the nonnaturalist maintains that it is simply a brute fact about certain properties that facts about their instantiation are reason-giving. This leaves the normativity of morality unexplained. Of course, the nonnaturalist might maintain that explanations must come to an end somewhere. But the fact that nonnaturalism leaves the normativity of morality unexplained suggests a way in which we might hope a realist metaethical theory would do better. Constructivism and mind-dependent forms of ethical naturalism provide accounts of the nature of moral facts and properties that allow us to begin to explain their reason-giving force; they are thus, at least in principle, equipped to explain the normativity of morality. For example, mind-dependent theories that are framed in terms of desires or other pro-attitudes can be paired with an instrumental conception of reasons to explain how moral and value facts are reason-giving (Railton 1986a). Constructivist views like Street's have the potential to explain the reason-giving force of normative truths insofar as they are truths about what follows from an agent's values or commitments.

Given that accounting for the normativity of morality is an adequacy condition on a realist metaethical theory, we have reason to keep our characterization of moral realism neutral as between objectivist metaethical theories and to reject mind-independence characterizations of moral realism. Suppose that some form of constructivism best explained the normativity of morality. If our characterization of moral realism limits it to mind-independent theories, we would then have the peculiar result that realist theories do not satisfy a basic adequacy condition on moral realism, while a form of mind-dependent antirealism does. The result would be particularly problematic, given that we have found no grounds to consider mind-dependent facts less objective than mind-independent facts, if that form of mind-dependent theory otherwise accounted for what we find truistic or platitudinous about morality.

CONCLUSION

According to the proposal offered herein, mind-independence characterizations of moral realism exclude, as forms of realism, views according to which all moral facts are grounded in or identical to facts about an agent's actual or counterfactual attitudes, emotions, values, or judgments. As we have seen, however, we have reasons to reject mind-independence characterizations of moral realism in favor of a characterization that allows forms of nonnaturalism, naturalism, and constructivism alike to count as forms of moral realism.

ACKNOWLEDGMENTS

I would like to thank David Plunkett, Tristram McPherson, and Jamie Fritz for extremely helpful comments on an earlier version of this essay.

REFERENCES

Bagnoli, C. (ed.) (2013) *Constructivism in Ethics*, Cambridge: Cambridge University Press.
Brandt, R. B. (1979) *A Theory of the Good and the Right*, Oxford: Clarendon Press.
Brink, D. (1987) "Rawlsian Constructivism in Moral Theory," *Canadian Journal of Philosophy* 17: 71–90.

Copp, D. (1995) *Morality, Normativity, and Society*, Oxford: Oxford University Press.

—. (2007) *Morality in a Natural World*, Cambridge: Cambridge University Press.

—. (2013) "Is Constructivism and Alternative to Moral Realism?" in Carla Bagnoli (ed.) *Constructivism in Ethics*, Cambridge: Cambridge University Press, 108–132.

Cuneo, T. (2007) *The Normative Web: An Argument for Moral Realism*, Oxford: Oxford University Press.

Enoch, D. (2011) *Taking Morality Seriously*, Oxford: Oxford University Press.

Firth, R. (1952) "Ethical Absolutism and the Ideal Observer," *Philosophy and Phenomenological Research* 12: 317–345.

Frankena, W. (1968) "Obligation and Value in the Ethics of G. E. Moore," in Paul Arthur Schilpp (ed.) *The Philosophy of G. E. Moore*, 3rd ed. La Salle, IL.: Open Court, 93–110.

Korsgaard, C. M. (1996) *The Sources of Normativity*, Cambridge: Cambridge University Press.

—. (2003) "Realism and Constructivism in Moral Philosophy," in Robert Audi (ed.) *Philosophy in America at the Turn of the Century*, 99–122.

Lenman, J. (2012) "Expressivism and Constructivism," in James Lenman and Yonatan Shemmer (eds.) *Constructivism in Practical Philosophy*, Oxford: Oxford University Press, 213–225.

Lenman, J. and Shemmer, Y. (eds.) (2012) *Constructivism in Practical Philosophy*, Oxford: Oxford University Press.

Lewis, D. (1989) "Dispositional Theories of Value," *Proceedings of the Aristotelian Society*, suppl., 63: 13–29.

McDowell, J. (1997) "Values and Secondary Qualities," in Ted Honderich (ed.), *Morality and Objectivity: A Tribute to J. L. Mackie*, London: Routledge and Kegan Paul, 1985, reprinted in Stephen Darwall, Allan Gibbard, and Peter Railton (eds.) *Moral Discourse and Practice*, Oxford: Oxford University Press, 201–213.

Mackie, J. L. (1977) *Ethics: Inventing Right and Wrong*, New York: Penguin Books.

McPherson, T. (2015) "What is at Stake in Debates among Normative Realists?" *Noûs* 49: 123–146.

Moore, G. E. (1903/1993) *Principia Ethica*, Revised Edition, Cambridge: Cambridge University Press.

Parfit, D. (2011) *On What Matters*, Volume 2, Oxford: Oxford University Press.

Railton, P. (1986a) "Facts and Values," *Philosophical Topics* 14: 5–31.

—. (1986b) "Moral Realism," *Philosophical Review* 95: 163–207.

Rawls, J. (1971) *A Theory of Justice*, Cambridge: Harvard University Press.

—. (1980) "Kantian Constructivism in Ethics," *Journal of Philosophy* 77: 515–572.

—. (1985) "Justice as Fairness: Political not Metaphysical," *Philosophy and Public Affairs* 14: 223–251.

Raz, J. (2010) "Reason, Reasons, and Normativity," *Oxford Studies in Metaethics*, Volume 5, Oxford: Oxford University Press, 5–23.

Rosati, C. S. (1995a) "Persons, Perspectives, and Full-Information Accounts of the Good," *Ethics* 105: 296–325.

—. (1995b) "Naturalism, Normativity, and the Open Question Argument," *Noûs* 29: 46–70.

—. (2016) "Agents and 'Shmagents': An Essay on Agency and Normativity," *Oxford Studies in Metaethics* 11, 182–213.

Rosen, G. (1994) "Objectivity and Modern Idealism: What is the Question?" in Michaelis Michael and John O'Leary-Hawthorne (eds.) *Philosophy in Mind*, Dordrecht: Kluwer Academic Publishers, 277–319.

Ross, W. D. (1930) *The Right and the Good*, Oxford: Clarendon Press.

Sayre-McCord, G. (1988) "Introduction: The Many Moral Realisms," in Geoffrey Sayre-McCord (ed.) *Essays on Moral Realism*, Ithaca, NY: Cornell University Press, 1–23.

Schafer, K. (2012) "Constructivism and Three Forms of Perspective-Dependence in Metaethics," *Philosophy and Phenomenological Research*, 1–34.

Shafer-Landau, R. (2003) *Moral Realism: A Defence*, Oxford: Clarendon Press.

Smith, M. (1994) *The Moral Problem*, Oxford: Basil Blackwell.

Street, S. (2008) "Constructivism About Reasons," in Russ Shafer-Landau (ed.) *Oxford Studies in Metaethics*, Volume 3, Oxford: Oxford University Press, 207–245.

—. (2010) "What is Constructivism in Ethics and Metaethics," *Philosophy Compass* 5/5: 363–384, 10.1111/j.1747-9991.2009.00280.x.

—. (2012) "Coming to Terms with Contingency: Humean Constructivism About Practical Reason," in James Lenman and Yonatan Shemmer (eds.) *Constructivism in Practical Philosophy*, Oxford: Oxford University Press, 40–59.

Timmons, M. (1996) "Moral Constructivism," in Donald M. Bouchert (ed.) *The Encyclopedia of Philosophy*, suppl. New York: Macmillan.

Wallace, R. (2012) "Constructivism About Normativity: Some Pitfalls," in James Lenman and Yonatan Shemmer (eds.) *Constructivism in Practical Philosophy*, Oxford: Oxford University Press, 18–39.

Wiggins, D. (1987) "A Sensible Subjectivism?" in *Needs, Values, Truth: Essays in the Philosophy of Value*, Oxford: Basil Blackwell, 185–214.

23

CONSTITUTIVISM

Michael Smith

There are many normative facts: we have reasons to perform certain actions, certain outcomes of actions are better than others, certain people are virtuous whereas others are vicious, and so on. What explains these very different normative facts? As I understand it, constitutivism is an answer to this question. According to constitutivists, normative facts of certain kinds are explained by facts about the constitutive features of something—that is, the features in virtue of which that thing is the kind of thing it is—where the constitutive features might be those of some person, or some action, or some state of affairs, or something else entirely. Constitutivists may disagree about this.

For those who are wary of talk of explanation, constitutivism can be restated in terms of an entailment claim and a claim about the relative fundamentality of features. Constitutivists think that we can derive claims to the effect that people, actions, or states of affairs of a certain kind have some normative feature from claims about something's constitutive features, and they further think that these constitutive features are more fundamental than the normative features that they entail. Resorting to a creationist metaphor, we can put the point in terms of what was required of God in the act of creation: all God needed to do was to create things with their constitutive features; once he had done that, the relevant normative features came for free.

Constitutivism, so understood, is a broad church. Constitutivism about *value*, for example, is the view that facts about the value of objects of a certain kind can be explained in terms of facts about the constitutive features of—of what?—perhaps the constitutive features of *objects of that kind* (Thomson 2008), or perhaps those of *valuers* (Lewis 1989), or perhaps those of something else entirely, like *God* (Zagzebski 2004). These very different views all qualify as versions of constitutivism about value, as constitutivism is being understood here, because they all take facts about something's constitutive features—whether those of objects of a certain kind, or valuers, or God—to be more fundamental than the value that those constitutive features entail.

Though we haven't yet said anything about what the constitutive features of things might be, it should be clear that, since facts about (say) a valuer's constitutive features are supposed to be more fundamental than facts about value, it is inconsistent with constitutivism to suppose that those facts themselves require facts about values for their explanation. More generally, the relevant explanatory relations hold only if facts about constitutive features can be explained without alluding to facts about the normative features they explain. This leaves it open, as it should, that the relevant constitutive features can be explained in wholly non-normative terms, but it also leaves it open that they have to be explained, *inter alia*, in terms of normative features, albeit different ones from those they explain.

Moreover, since constitutivism is just one answer to the question 'What is a normative fact?', it also leaves it open whether, in those cases in which the constitutive features of something are themselves explained by normative features, those normative features are explained by something else's constitutive features. As I understand it, constitutivism about certain normative features is thus consistent with anti-constitutivist views about others. Of course, the most ambitious form of constitutivism will explain *all* normative features in terms of objects' constitutive features. But constitutivists need not be so ambitious.

A constitutivist who thinks that we can sometimes explain facts about constitutive features in wholly non-normative terms will reject the idea that there is, in full generality, an *is-ought* gap (Pigden 2010). Moreover, such a constitutivist seems right to reject that idea, as there are kinds whose constitutive features entail normative features where the constitutive features of those kinds can be explained in wholly non-normative terms. Think of functional kinds. If the relevant function can be characterized in wholly nonnormative terms, then this will entail facts about what *properly* functioning things of that kind do, which will in turn entail facts about what *ideal* things of that kind do, what *defective* things of that kind fail to do, what things of that kind *ought* to do, and so on. There is no *is-ought* gap in such cases, so there is no *is-ought* gap in full generality.

An example will help fix ideas. Imagine you have aching limbs and cold extremities, so you go to the doctor. He examines you and then wonders aloud, 'Why isn't your heart functioning properly?' or, perhaps, 'Why isn't your heart doing what it is supposed to do?' How are we to explain his use of 'properly' and 'supposed to'? The answer lies in the fact that a heart is something whose function is to pump an adequate supply of blood around the body (an *is*-claim). This entails that a properly functioning heart pumps an adequate supply of blood around the body (an initial *ought*-claim), that a defective heart is one that fails to do so (another *ought*-claim), and that hearts are supposed to pump adequate supplies of blood around the body (yet another *ought*-claim). The doctor's uses of 'properly' and 'supposed to' are in this way explained by reference to the heart's pumping an adequate supply of blood around the body (an *is*-claim).

It should now be clear why I said that constitutivism is *an* answer to the question 'What is a normative fact?' Even those who are convinced that there are irreducibly normative features should agree that, when it comes to facts like the heart's functioning *properly*, or being *defective*, or doing what it is *supposed to do*, the constitutivist's explanation is the best available. But if these normative features can be explained in wholly non-normative terms, it cannot be absurd to suppose that all normative features are so explainable, much as the ambitious constitutivist thinks. Constitutivists needn't be so ambitious, but since we're stuck with some constitutivist explanations, parsimony tells in favor of looking for constitutivist explanations wherever we can and, when we find them, making sure that the explanations given are as ambitious as possible.

In the light of this, consider again constitutivism about value. As we saw, David Lewis tells us that for something to be of value is for that thing to be valued by ideal valuers (Lewis 1989). Lewis's explanation of value initially appears to be normatively laden— what is an *ideal* valuer?—but we can now see that it may be fully reductive for all that. According to Lewis, valuers are those with the capacity to match their valuings, which he thinks are their intrinsic second-order desirings, with those that would survive full imaginative acquaintance with their objects. Valuers thus value well to the extent that their intrinsic second-order desires are those that would survive the exercise of this capacity, and badly to the extent that they are not, and an *ideal* valuer is someone who values as well as possible. Lewis's explanation of value therefore makes no appeal to values, and it explains what an ideal valuer is in functional terms, not constitutivist terms.

We can now characterize a constitutivist view of some normative fact more precisely. What makes the earlier account of facts about defective hearts, and what hearts are supposed to do, a constitutivist account is the fact that the kind *heart*, being characterizable functionally, generates an ordering of hearts from best to worst according to how well they function. The kind *heart* is thus what Judith Jarvis Thomson calls a *goodness-fixing kind*, and the account of defective hearts and what hearts are supposed to do that we give by appealing to the functional characterization of hearts is fully reductive because that ordering, which can be understood as a specification of the functional nature of hearts, can itself be characterized in wholly non-normative terms.

Similarly, what makes Lewis's account of value a constitutivist account is the fact that the kind *valuer*, being characterizable in terms of the capacity to have second-order intrinsic desires that match those that would survive full imaginative acquaintance with their objects, also generates an ordering of valuers from best to worst—the kind *valuer* is a goodness-fixing kind—and it is fully reductive if a specification of that ordering can be given in non-normative terms. Whether this is so will depend on whether we can explain what desires are without presupposing anything normative. But if, for example, to be a desire is to be a psychological state that plays a certain functional role along with beliefs in the psychology of a *fully rational* agent, and if we could explain what an agent's being fully rational is without presupposing anything normative, perhaps by supposing that the beliefs and desires of fully rational agents bear certain structural relations to each other, and that psychologies can be ordered from best to worst depending on how similar their structural relations are to these, then the account would be fully reductive. Lewis's ambitious constitutivism about value would then follow from functionalism about psychology.

In general, an account of some normative fact is constitutivist when the account explains that normative fact in terms of some goodness-fixing kind, and the account is fully reductive when the specification of the ordering that that kind generates can be given in wholly non-normative terms. With this general characterization of constitutivism before us, it should be clear that theorists have offered very different constitutivist accounts of a diverse range of normative facts. Whether their versions are fully reductive is harder to assess, but for many, the aim doesn't seem to have been reduction, but rather a decrease the number of normative facts that require explanation. Here are some examples.

Consider Thomson's explanation of facts about what *human beings ought to do* (Thomson 2008). In her view, among other characteristics, what it is to be human is to have moral capacities like the capacity to be just and generous. The kind *human being* is therefore a goodness-fixing kind: we can order human beings from better to worse depending on how just and generous they are; we can identify defective human beings as those who lack the virtues of justice and generosity; and we can define what human beings ought to do as those things which are such that, if they knew what differences would be made by their doing those things, they would be defective human beings if they failed to do them. Thomson thinks that what human beings ought to do can in this way be explained in terms of a specification of the goodness-fixing kind *human being*, a specification which itself makes no appeal to facts about what ought to be done. But since the explanation appeals to facts about agents being just and generous, which are themselves normative facts, her account of what humans ought to do is fully reductive only if we can explain these virtues in non-normative terms.

Or consider Jurgen Habermas's explanation of what it is for *a rule of action or choice to be justified* in terms of whether all those who are affected by the rule or choice could accept it in a reasonable discourse (Habermas 1996). This turns out to be a constitutivist explanation of justified rules and choices because it is in the nature of a discourse to be a mode of communication that can more or less reasonable—the kind *discourse* is therefore a goodness-fixing kind—and because we can define what it is for a rule of action or choice to be justified in terms of what could be accepted in a reasonable discourse. Whether rules of action or choices are justified are in this way supposed to be explained by a specification of an ordering generated by the goodness-fixing kind *discourse*, a specification that itself makes no appeal to facts about which rules of action or choices are justified. But since Habermas's explanation appeals to facts about discourses, and discourses are in turn the product of our communicative intentions, his explanation is like Lewis's in being fully reductive only if we can understand psychology in wholly non-normative terms.

Or, more ambitiously, consider Sharon Street's claim that what makes claims about *what people have reason to do* true is the fact that those claims follow from the practical point of view, where the practical point of view is the point of view of someone who values various ends and the means to those ends, and a claim about what they have reason to do follows from this point of view if it is supported by the valuings that would survive if that person's values were as coherent as possible (Street 2009, 2012). This is a constitutivist explanation because the kind *practical point of view* generates an ordering of sets of valuings from best to worst depending on how coherent they are—the kind *practical point of view* is therefore a goodness-fixing kind—and a specification of that ordering makes no appeal to facts about what people have reason to do. Street's explanation looks to be more reductive, but since valuing is a kind of psychological state, her explanation is like Lewis's and Habermas's in being fully reductive only if we can understand psychology in wholly non-normative terms.

It will be helpful at this point if we focus on a specific example. Since we just considered Street's view, let's consider other versions of constitutivism about *reasons for action*, and let's note how the distinctions made so far help us understand the differences between these different versions, and how attention to these differences, so understood, helps us identify the different versions' strengths and weaknesses. To anticipate, the crucial questions will be: which goodness-fixing kind is supposed to explain facts about reasons for action; whether a specification of that goodness-fixing kind presupposes normative facts, and if so, which; and how compelling the explanation provided is. Since the answer to the last question will depend on whether the explanation gets the extension of what we have reason to do right, how compelling any particular version of constitutivism is will depend on the extent to which it survives in reflective equilibrium with our substantive views about what we have reason to do. Given theorists' disagreements about what we have reason to do, this makes the evaluation of different versions of constitutivism about reasons for action problematic.

The disagreement that will occupy center-stage in what follows is whether moral requirements entail facts about what we have reason to do, and, more specifically, given that on any plausible view of morality we are sometimes morally required to cooperate with others when doing so requires us to give up something that we care about more than cooperation, whether we sometimes have reasons to act contrary to our cares and concerns. Street's view is striking in this regard because she thinks it follows from her explanation of what we have reason to do that we never have reasons to act contrary to the cares and concerns that would survive as part of a fully coherent set. A perfectly coherent Caligula, she tells us, has no reason at all to do what's morally required (2009). Is this an objection to Street's version of constitutivism? That depends on whether you think moral requirements entail reasons for action. At this point, I invite readers to make a mental note of their answer to this question and to score Street's constitutivsm accordingly.

Street's view is striking for another reason as well. The target of her explanation is familiar facts about what we have reason to do, but she pursues her reductive ambitions by couching her explanations in unfamiliar terms. Though the details are unimportant, both the idea of a practical point of view and the more basic idea of someone's valuing something turn out to be technical terms, as Street uses them. This adds an extra dimension of difficulty to the evaluation of her view, as we first have to figure out what she takes the practical point of view and valuing to be. We then have to ask ourselves whether she is right that, for all their unfamiliarity when fully spelled out, it turns out that those of us who have reasons for action have a practical point of view and value things, and only then do we get to ask whether the explanation she provides is compelling. It is therefore worth considering some alternative explanations where the choice of goodness-fixing kind is more familiar.

In *Natural Goodness*, Philippa Foot tells us that there is the following strong similarity between living things (Foot 2001). For each species of animal and plant, there is a set of generic claims that spells out what, for that species, is the characteristic way in which its members develop, maintain themselves, and reproduce (see also Thompson 1995). These generic claims spell out what it would be for a member of that species to function properly, and hence which features would be possessed by species members that are functioning properly—these are the relevant plant and animal goods—and what it would be for them to be defective. In the case of animals where the activity necessary for development, self-maintenance, and reproduction cannot be explained in stimulus-response terms, but requires belief-desire explanations, these generic claims will include claims about actions that realize the relevant animal goods, and, in the case of social animals like human beings and wolves, they will also include claims about the cooperative activity needed to realize the relevant animal goods.

With a rich account of distinctively human goods in place, Foot thinks that we can give an account of the human virtues. Human virtues turn out to be those traits of character that a human being needs to have in order to fare well as a human being. At a minimum, this presumably requires that the desires that drive the actions of virtuous human beings have as their contents the human goods—or anyway, contents that stand in some systematic relation to human goods—and, with this account of the human virtues in place, we also have the materials out of which to construct a theory of reasons for action. Reasons for action turn out to be those features that motivate virtuous agents, so once again, these features will turn out either to be, or to stand in some systematic relation to, the human goods that virtuous agents bring into being.

In explaining reasons for action, Foot thinks we must appeal to the fact that human beings are of a kind with other living things, and that things of this kind have a characteristic function, namely, that associated with their development, self-maintenance, and reproduction, a function that can be specified in terms of an ordering from best worst. *Human being* is thus a goodness-fixing kind. Moreover, Foot thinks that once we specify this ordering we can explain all sorts of normative features: what it is to be a defective human being; what human goods are; what it is for a character trait to be a human virtue; and what the relationship is between human goods, human virtues, and reasons for action. Given that Foot makes no appeal to facts about reasons for action in her specification of this ordering, it follows that her theory meets the explanatory constraint on a constitutivist theory of reasons for action. Whether the specification could itself be explained without appealing to normative notions is an open question—note she too must appeal to beliefs and desires—but giving such a non-normative specification doesn't seem to be her main concern.

One of the great virtues of Foot's version of constitutivism, as she sees things, is that it explains why we sometimes have reasons to cooperate even when doing so requires us to act contrary to our cares and concerns. This is because whether or not some action realizes a human good isn't dependent on whether it realizes something the agent cares about, or would care about if she were coherent. Reasons to cooperate are not hostage to our cares and concerns, but are instead a consequence of the behaviors we have to engage in, as social beings, in order to develop, maintain ourselves, and reproduce. To the extent that these cooperative behaviors correspond to what's morally required, Foot's version of constitutivism thus squares with the idea that moral requirements entail reasons for action. This is a striking difference between her constitutivism and Street's, and it is a direct consequence of her choice of goodness-fixing kind.

Foot's view is not, however, without its problems. For one thing, the cooperative behaviors Foot tells us we have reasons to engage in correspond only imperfectly to what's morally required. Imagine that there are extraterrestrials who are as psychologically sophisticated as humans. Foot's view entails that, just as humans have reasons to realize human goods, such extraterrestrials have reasons to realize extraterrestrial goods. But now imagine a situation in which humans and these extraterrestrials interact, but no course of action available simultaneously realizes both human goods and extraterrestrial goods. If humans and extraterrestrials were each to do what they have reason to do then, given Foot's explanation of reasons, they would be at loggerheads with each other, each trying to realize their own species-specific good. Foot's version of constitutivism thus squares with the idea that we have reasons to do what we are morally required to do only on the assumption that morality doesn't tell us that there are fair terms on which humans and extraterrestrials could interact in such circumstances, not even fair terms that put bounds on what a competition in the pursuit of their respective species-specific good could consist in. In putting so much emphasis on *human* goods, Foot's view thus builds an implausible human chauvinism into morality.

Foot's human chauvinism has further implications. Though her explanation of reasons allows that we may sometimes have reasons to do something because we care about it, it only allows that this is so when getting what we care about doesn't come at the cost of human goods. To focus on a striking case, though many people care about having children, it is a commonplace that some don't, and we ordinarily think that the decision to have children is therefore a matter of personal preference. But now imagine that everyone had the preferences of those who don't want children. On Foot's view, independently of whether their having children would help them get other things they care about, or other human goods, everyone would still have reasons to have children. Or imagine people who care very much about the goods of dogs, and cats, and cows, and pigs, and chickens. If they cared so much about these non-human beings' goods that they sacrificed human goods for their sake, then on Foot's view they would be doing something they have no reason to do. These too are consequences of Foot's human chauvinism.

An obvious thought at this point is that Foot chose the wrong goodness-fixing kind in terms of which to explain reasons for action. She should have chosen a kind that didn't entail a species-specific ranking, and a kind that allows for the possibility that beings of the relevant kind can do well simply by doing things they care about. With this thought in mind, consider Bernard Williams's explanation of reasons for action (Williams 1980).

Williams explains what agents have a reason to do in terms of what they would be motivated to do if they deliberated correctly. Agents deliberate correctly, according to Williams, only if (i) they have all and only those intrinsic desires they would have if they exercised their imaginations concerning all of the possible objects of intrinsic desires (Williams's explanation of reasons is, in this respect, like Lewis's explanation of value); (ii) when their intrinsic desires have indeterminate content, and they could make them more determinate by bringing them into line with other things they intrinsically desire, they do so (to the extent that this sounds like a coherence requirement, Williams's explanation of reasons is in this respect like Street's); (iii) they have no false non-normative beliefs relevant to the satisfaction of their intrinsic desires; (iv) they are not ignorant of any non-normative facts relevant to the satisfaction of their intrinsic desires; and (v) they order the actions they take to satisfy their intrinsic desires over time so as to ensure the optimal satisfaction of their (current) intrinsic desires (again, to the extent that this sounds like a coherence requirement, the explanation is like Street's).

Though Williams doesn't describe his explanation of reasons for action as a version of constitutivism, it certainly seems to be a version. Williams explains reasons for action in terms of the kind *deliberator*, where deliberators have the capacity to deliberate, and where deliberators deliberate well to the extent that they exercise this capacity and their psychologies have the features he describes, and badly to the extent that they fail to exercise the capacity and their psychologies lack such features. *Deliberator* is thus a goodness-fixing kind. Williams's explanation of reasons is given in terms of a specification of those at the top of the ordering that this goodness-fixing kind generates. Given that the specification makes no appeal to facts about reasons for action, it follows that Williams's theory meets the explanatory constraint on a constitutivist theory.

In some respects, Williams's explanation is like Street's, but his explanation is unlike hers in appealing to a familiar kind whose connection with reasons for action is more or less transparent: the role of deliberation just seems to be the discovery of what there is reason to do. However, if Williams is right, this is so even though we needn't explicitly ask ourselves what there is reason to do when we deliberate: look again at (i)–(v). As with Thomson's and Foot's explanations, whether Williams's explanation is fully reductive depends on whether we can explain what it is for someone to have desires and beliefs in wholly non-normative terms. In this connection, it worth remembering the suggestion made earlier in the discussion of Lewis's view of valuing.

If desire and belief are understood functionally in terms of how they relate to each other in the psychology of a fully rational agent, then if we could we explain what an agent's being fully rational is without presupposing anything normative, perhaps by supposing that the beliefs and desires of fully rational agents bear certain structural relations to each other that generate an ordering of psychologies from best to worst, Lewis's account of valuing would be fully reductive. What is striking about Williams's (i)–(v) is that they look like an attempt to describe some of what these structural relations might be. Though Williams doesn't advertise himself as giving a fully reductive explanation of reasons for action in constitutivist terms, it does seem to be an attempt to give such an explanation.

Note that Williams's specification of deliberators is not species-specific—humans and extraterrestrials have the same deliberative capacities—but instead ranks deliberators according to how well they meet conditions (i)–(v). Moreover, note that these conditions allow that we can have reasons to act on our cares and concerns to the extent that these survive the exercise of our imagination about their objects. Williams therefore has no problem explaining why people with the relevant intrinsic desires may have no reason to reproduce, and why they may have reasons to realize non-human goods even when doing so comes at some cost to human goods. In this respect, Williams's explanation better captures what we ordinarily take to be the extension of reasons for action. But is Williams's explanation consistent with the claim that moral requirements entail reasons for action?

According to Williams, deliberators have the capacity to acquire intrinsic desires after they fully exercise their imaginations. But since the intrinsic desires they acquire are explained by facts exogenous to their being deliberators—deliberators have different embodiments, upbringings, cultures, and so on, and it is these that explain which dispositions to acquire intrinsic desires in the light of their imaginings they have—it follows that even deliberators who deliberate well could end up with very different intrinsic desires from each other. Williams's explanation is thus like Foot's in making facts about reasons for action relative, but instead of being relative to species, they are relative to the individual. The upshot is that, if Williams's explanation is correct, then whether humans have reasons to cooperate on fair terms with extraterrestrials, and indeed with each other, depends on whether, after they exercise their imaginations, they have intrinsic desires that will be satisfied by such cooperation. Williams's and Street's views are in this respect strikingly similar. Neither allows that moral requirements entail reasons for action. Once again, I invite the reader to score Williams's explanation in the light of this.

Should those who think that moral requirements entail reasons for action abandon the idea that such reasons can be explained in terms of the constitutive features of deliberators? Not necessarily. When we think of Williams as a constitutivist, his constitutivism consists of two claims: first, that we explain reasons for action in terms of the constitutive features of deliberators, and second, that the nature of deliberation is as specified in (i)–(v). A constitutivist who thinks that moral requirements entail reasons for action could think that the problem with Williams's explanation of reasons lies not in his choice of goodness-fixing kind, but rather in his specification of the nature of that kind (compare Korsgaard 1986). In particular, perhaps Williams is wrong that the only way we can correct our intrinsic desires when we deliberate is by revising our intrinsic desires in the light of exercises of our imaginations, where this is in turn explained by exogenous factors like our embodiment, upbringing, enculturation, and so on.

Unsurprisingly, Kant can be understood as a constitutivist who thinks that this is so (Kant 1786). Reasons for action are to be explained in terms of a specification of the goodness-fixing kind *deliberator*, but those who deliberate well additionally exercise the capacity to give themselves the Categorical Imperative, and so come to have motivations that conform to universal laws. What it is to deliberate well, on Kant's view so understood, just is to be so motivated—in Kant's terms, it is to have a "good will." The challenge is then to explain two things: first, what exactly it means to have motivations that conform to universal laws, and second, why the mere fact that a deliberator has such motivations entails that they have reasons to cooperate on fair terms with other deliberators. Moreover, if the explanation is to satisfy the explanatory constraint on a constitutivist theory of reasons for action, these explanations must at no point appeal to facts about what deliberators have reasons to do.

Very roughly, Kant's answer to the first question is that motivations accord with universal laws when they are motivations to act in ways that all deliberators could act at the same time as a result of their deliberating, and his answer to the second question is that it follows from this that no deliberator could end up with motivations to treat other deliberators in ways that leave them incapable of acting on the motivations that result from their own deliberations. In this way, Kant's specification of what it is to deliberate is supposed to entail that everyone has a reason to treat deliberators, whether themselves or others, never merely as a means, but also always as an end. If, as seems plausible, this entails having reasons to cooperate with other deliberators on fair terms, then the Kantian explanation of reasons for action is consistent with the claim that moral requirements entail reasons for action. Not only do human deliberators have reasons to cooperate on fair terms with each other, but they also have reasons to cooperate on fair terms with extraterrestrials, and extraterrestrials also have such reasons.

There are, of course, well-known problems with Kant's answers to each of these questions, and there are well-known Kantian attempts to address these problems (Korsgaard 1986). For present purposes, the important points are, first, that the answers to the two questions do not anywhere appeal to facts about reasons for action, so the explanation meets the constitutivist's explanatory constraint, and second, that the answers seem to be a further elaboration of the structural relations between the intrinsic desires and beliefs of those who deliberate well. Deliberators have the capacity to move from thoughts about what would be required for motivations to conform to universal laws to corresponding motivations, so a specification of what it is to deliberate well simply amounts to a description of the ways in which thoughts about universal laws and corresponding motivations in fact relate to each other in deliberators who have and fully exercise these capacities. In this respect, Kant's explanation is like Williams's. Both are well understood as a contribution to a fully reductive explanation of facts about reasons for action. At this point, the reader is invited to score Kant's explanation accordingly.

Perhaps surprisingly, Scanlon's theory of reasons for action is also well understood as a version of constitutivism that explains facts about reasons for action in terms of the goodness-fixing kind deliberator (Scanlon 1998). What is Scanlon's preferred account of what it is to deliberate well? In Scanlon's view, there is a class of judgment-sensitive attitudes, where the distinctive feature of this class is that the attitudes are acquired and lost depending on whether the person who has them takes there to be sufficient reasons for acquiring and losing them. Beliefs are judgment-sensitive attitudes *par excellence*, and intentions and intrinsic desires in the very broad sense in which we have been understanding them here are also such attitudes. To deliberate well, according to Scanlon, is therefore just to acquire and lose judgment-sensitive attitudes—that is, beliefs, intentions, and intrinsic desires—as a result of a sensitivity to the reasons for them.

The reason relation, as Scanlon understands it, is a primitive four-place relation that relates a fact, a person, a circumstance, and a judgment-sensitive attitude: the fact provides the person in that circumstances with a reason to have that judgment-sensitive attitude (Scanlon 2014). He may suppose that, in a situation of conflict, there is a certain fact—perhaps the fact that certain actions would accord with principles for the general regulation of society that no one could reasonably reject—that provides the individuals in those circumstances with a reason to intend to perform actions of that kind. If such principles captured the fair terms of cooperation, then the individuals in those circumstances would each have reasons to intend to cooperate on fair terms. They would have these reasons no matter what species of living thing they are; no matter what intrinsic desires they would happen to have after they exercised their imaginations, given their embodiment, their upbringing, and their culture; and no matter what intrinsic desires they would end up with after having thoughts about what's required for motivations to conform to universal laws.

Note that what we have here is an explanation of which judgment-sensitive attitudes agents in such circumstances have reason to have, not what they have reasons to do. This is why we do well to understand Scanlon's explanation of reasons for action in constitutivist terms, as it is constitutivism that allows us to turn reasons for judgment-sensitive attitudes into reasons for action. What agents have reason to do is explained by what they would be motivated to if they deliberated well, so if people deliberate well to the extent that they are sensitive to the independently given reasons for judgment-sensitive attitudes, and badly to the extent that lack such a sensitivity, then if there are reasons for those in circumstances of conflict to intend to cooperate on fair terms, it follows that they have reasons to cooperate on fair terms. They have such reasons because this is what they would be motivated to do if they were to deliberate well.

As I said, Scanlon seems to commit himself to constitutivism of this kind when he tells us that "'reason for action' is not to be contrasted with 'reason for intending'" (Scanlon 1998, p. 21). His idea seems to be that since what makes an event an action is the fact that it was the product of a certain judgment-sensitive attitude, namely an intention to perform the action, so what makes an action one that an agent has reason to perform is the fact there are reasons for the agent to have the intention to perform it. We get constitutivism by restating this as a counterfactual. What makes an action one that the agent has reason to perform is the fact that that the agent would intend to perform it if he were sensitive to the reasons for having intentions.

Is Scanlon's explanation of reasons for action, so understood, a reductive or a non-reductive version of constitutivism? Since it appeals to a normative feature in explaining the constitutive features of deliberators—the primitive four-place reason relation—that cannot be explained in non-normative terms, it is a non-reductive version. Deliberators are those who have the capacity to be sensitive to reasons for judgment-sensitive attitudes in the formation of such attitudes. But since this normative feature is a distinct normative feature from the normative feature that his constitutivism explains—namely, reasons for action—it follows that the requisite explanatory relations between facts about reasons for action and facts about the constitutive features of deliberators remain intact. Facts about reasons for judgment-sensitive attitudes explain facts about the constitutive features of deliberators, and facts about the constitutive features of deliberators explain facts about reasons for action. At this point, the reader is invited to score Scanlon's explanation.

Though we have considered various versions of constitutivism about reasons for action, we have not yet discussed two of the better-known versions of the view. Christine Korsgaard and David Velleman both defend versions of constitutivism, but they conceive of the view very differently from the way it has been characterized here (Korsgaard 1996, 2009; Velleman 1989, 1996). As they see things, constitutivism is the view that reasons for action are to be explained in terms of the *constitutive aim of agents.* In Korsgaard's view, this is the aim of self-constitution. In Velleman's view, it is the aim of making sense. According to some who follow Korsgaard's and Velleman's lead, the constitutive aims are something else again: Paul Katsanafas, for example, thinks that the constitutive aim of agents is some end or other plus the aim of encountering and overcoming obstacles or resistances in the pursuit of that end (Katsafanas 2013, forthcoming).

My reason for not discussing these views until now is because their way of under-standing constitutivism is so unhelpful. The claim that agents have a constitutive aim is either false or metaphorical. Suppose we understand the claim non-metaphorically, and a constitutive aim is some sort of intrinsic desire or intention that every agent is sup-posed to have simply by virtue of being an agent. The problem with this is that there are evidently agents—many non-human animals, human infants, children, and those who are cognitively impaired—who lack the conceptual sophistication required to have any of these aims. More generally, though it seems right that agents may have to have some intrinsic desires or intentions or other to count as agents, *which* desires or intentions they have seems to be an entirely contingent matter. In other words, in the non-metaphorical sense, agents do not have constitutive aims.

This leaves open the possibility that talk of agents having a constitutive aim is metaphorical, but then the question is how the metaphor is to be understood in non-metaphorical terms. The best way of understanding it, in my view, is to suppose that the kind *agent* is a goodness-fixing kind: for Korsgaard, to be an agent is to possess the capacity to constitute oneself as a unified agent; for Velleman, it is to possess the capacity to make oneself make sense; and for Katsanafas, it is to have the capacity to have ends and to encounter and overcome obstacles in the pursuit of those ends. Though each of these ways of understanding their views is more plausible than the claim that agents have the corresponding constitutive aims, the elaboration and evaluation of their views so understood would take us some distance from anything that these theorists actually say in defense of their views. It therefore seems best to leave a discussion of them for another occasion.

The main objection to constitutivism is the well-known *agency-shmagency* objection due to David Enoch (2006). Since the objection was originally stated as an objection to the constitutive aim theorists' versions of constitutivism, it will be helpful to restate it as an objection to the more plausible versions of constitutivism as the view has been understood here. These are the versions of constitutivism that explain reasons for action in terms of the constitutive features of deliberators, where deliberation is understood in Williams's or Kant's or Scanlon's way. The agency-shmagency objection is that it is opaque why reasons, understood in any of these ways, have the authority that reasons are supposed to have.

Imagine people who are motivated to act in the way that some guru instructs people to act, and imagine that what the guru instructs people to do is completely different from what they would be motivated to do if they deliberated well. According to all of these versions of constitutivism, these people act in ways they have no reasons to act. They are deliberators, so what they have reason to do is fixed by what they would be motivated to do if they deliberated well. But, the objection goes, what's so special about the goodness-fixing kind *deliberator*? We could coin the word 'shmeliberator' to pick out those who could act in the way the guru instructs people to act, and, on plausible assumptions, all and only deliberators are shmeliberators and vice-versa. *Shmeliberator*, like *deliberator*, is therefore a goodness-fixing kind—we can order people from best to worst according to how well their acts accord with the guru's instructions—and we can define 'shmeasons for action' as what people would be motivated to do if they were excellent shmeliberators. If we deliberate well, we shmeliberate badly, and if we shmeliberate well, we deliberate badly. So, what makes it the case that the considerations that would motivate us if we deliberated well have authority over us in a way that those that would motivate us if we shmeliberated well don't? The agency-shmagency objection is that constitutivism can give no good answer to this question.

There have been many replies to the agency-shmagency objection, and many replies to these replies (examples include Ferrero 2009; Tiffany 2012; and Silverstein 2015). The best reply, in my view, focuses on what it is for considerations that motivate us to be authoritative. On one view, a consideration that motivates us is authoritative if it is a consideration that motivates an excellent member of some goodness-fixing kind of which we are members. On this way of understanding authority, the considerations that motivate shmeliberators are indeed authoritative, so there is nothing for constitutivists to explain. On an alternative view, the considerations that motivate us are authoritative only if they are considerations that motivate us to do what we have reason to do. On this way of understanding authority, constitutivists do need to explain why the considerations that motivate shmeliberators are not authoritative, but this isn't a problem, as they have a good explanation of this.

Why suppose that we do not have reason to what we would be motivated to do if we shmeliberated well? The answer, according to the constitutivists we have considered, is the intrinsic plausibility of supposing that we find out what we have reason to do by deliberating, where deliberation is understood in Williams's or Kant's or Scanlon's way, and the fact that what we ordinarily take to be the extension of what we have reason to do is well captured by what we would be motivated to do if we deliberated well, where deliberation is understood in one of these ways. By contrast, it is completely implausible to suppose that we find out what we have reason to do by finding out whether what we are motivated to do corresponds to the guru's instructions, and the extension of what we would be motivated to do if we shmeliberated well is therefore a poor fit with what we ordinarily take to be the extension of what we have reason to do.

Of course, those who put forward the agency-shmagency objection might think that no one can explain what it is to have a reason for action, as such facts are explanatorily basic (see Wiland's comparison of the agency-shmagency objection to the open-question argument [2012], and McPherson's discussion of robust versus formal normativity [2011]). Though they might agree that we find out what we have reason to do by deliberating, they might think that deliberation is to be understood as the exercise of the capacity to detect instantiations of the primitive property of an act's being something there is reason to do. This primitivist view of reasons for action is indeed a competitor to constitutivism. However, to the extent that we think we can give an adequate description of deliberation without assuming this primitivist view of reasons for action, perhaps a description like Williams's or Kant's or Scanlon's, or perhaps a description in some other terms entirely, we should reject it in favor of constitutivism.

ACKNOWLEDGMENTS

Thanks to Jamie Fritz, Tristram McPherson, and David Plunkett for their very helpful comments on a draft.

REFERENCES

Enoch, David 2006: "Agency, Shmagency: Why Normativity Won't Come from What Is Constitutive of Action," *Philosophical Review* (115) pp. 169–198.

Ferrero, Luca 2009: "Constitutivism and the Inescapability of Agency" in Russ Shafer-Landau (ed.) *Oxford Studies in Metaethics: Volume 4* (Oxford: Oxford University Press) pp. 303–333.

Foot, Philippa 2001: *Natural Goodness* (Oxford: Oxford University Press).

Habermas, Jurgen 1996: *Between Facts and Norms: Contributions to a Discourse Theory of Law and Democracy*, translated by William Rehg (Cambridge, MA: MIT Press).

Kant, Immanuel 1786: *Groundwork of the Metaphysics of Morals* (London: Hutchinson and Company, 1948).

Katsafanas, Paul 2013: *Agency and the Foundations of Ethics: Nietzschean Constitutivism* (Oxford: Oxford University Press).

— forthcoming: "Constitutivism about Practical Reasons" in Daniel Star (ed.) *Oxford Handbook of Reasons and Rationality* (Oxford: Oxford University Press).

Korsgaard, Christine 1986: "Skepticism about Practical Reason," *Journal of Philosophy* (83) pp. 5–25.

— 1996: *The Sources of Normativity* (Cambridge: Cambridge University Press).

— 2009: *Self-Constitution: Agency, Identity, and Integrity* (Oxford: Oxford University Press).

Lewis, David 1989: "Dispositional Theories of Value," *Proceedings of the Aristotelian Society Supplementary Volume* (63) pp. 113–137.

McPherson, Tristram 2011: "Against Quietist Normative Realism," *Philosophical Studies* (154) pp. 223–240.

Pigden, Charles 2010: *Hume on Is and Ought* (Basingstoke: Palgrave Macmillan).

Scanlon, Thomas M. 1998: *What We Owe To Each Other* (Cambridge, MA: Harvard University Press).

— 2014: *Being Realistic About Reasons* (New York: Oxford University Press).

Silverstein, Matthew 2015: "The Shmagency Question," *Philosophical Studies* (172) pp. 1127–1142.

Street, Sharon 2009: "In Defense of Future Tuesday Indifference: Ideally Coherent Eccentrics and the Contingency of What Matters," *Philosophical Issues* (19) pp. 273–298.

— 2012: "Coming to Terms with Contingency: Humean Constructivism about Practical Reason" in James Lenman and Yonatan Shemmer (eds.) *Constructivism in Practical Philosophy* (Oxford: Oxford University Press) pp. 40–59.

Thompson, Michael 1995: "The Representation of Life" in Rosalind Hursthouse, Gavin Lawrence, and Warren Quinn (eds.) *Virtues and Reasons* (Oxford: Clarendon Press) pp. 247–296.

Thomson, Judith Jarvis 2008: *Normativity* (Chicago: Open Court Publishing Company).

Tiffany, Evan 2012: "Why Be an Agent?" *Australasian Journal of Philosophy* (90) pp. 223–233.

Velleman, J. David 1989: *Practical Reflection* (Princeton, NJ: Princeton University Press).

— 1996: "The Possibility of Practical Reason," *Ethics* (106) pp. 694–726.

Wiland, Eric 2012: *Reasons* (London: Continuum).

Williams, Bernard 1980: "Internal and External Reasons" in his *Moral Luck* (Cambridge: Cambridge University Press, 1981), pp. 101–113.

Zagzebski, Linda 2004: *Divine Motivation Theory* (New York: Cambridge University Press).

24

Constructivism

Melissa Barry

CONSTRUCTIVISM: THE BASIC IDEA

In a well-known discussion of constructivism in ethics, Darwall, Gibbard, and Railton characterize the view as a form of proceduralism:

> ... the constructivist is a hypothetical proceduralist. He endorses some hypo-
> thetical procedure as determining which principles constitute valid standards of
> morality ... A proceduralist ... maintains there are no moral facts independent
> of the finding that a certain hypothetical procedure would have such and such an
> upshot.

> (1992: 140)

Restricted or *local* constructivism confines itself to constructing normative truth in a limited domain, such as political justice or the morality of right and wrong. It aims to explain
how such truths can be arrived at, through procedural reasoning, from other normative
principles that are taken for granted for the purposes of the construction. In this sense,
it is an intranormative enterprise. Since its ambitions are thus limited, it is free to use
substantive normative judgments as inputs to construction. The role of the procedure
of construction is to articulate and extend the input ideals or principles to generate new
conclusions about the target domain. For example, John Rawls begins with a moral ideal
of free and equal persons, from which he constructs principles of justice for the basic
structure of society (1971; 1980). Likewise, Thomas Scanlon appeals to the ideal of living
on terms with others that they could not reasonably reject, along with intuitions about
substantive reasons for action, to construct principles for the morality of right and wrong
(1998). To avoid circularity and uninformativeness, the inputs to construction must be
of a clearly different sort from the outputs. Objections to restricted constructivism typically focus here, claiming, for instance, that Rawls appeals too directly to intuitions about

fairness in the inputs and the design of the procedure of construction (e.g., Daniels 1975), or that Scanlon relies on intuitions about substantive moral reasons in his constructivist reasoning to moral principles (e.g., Kamm 2002; Gibbard 2003b).

Unrestricted or global constructivism aims, more ambitiously, to construct all reasons and values, and indeed normative truth as such. It seeks to be at once non-skeptical (claiming that there are normative truths) but also non-realist (claiming that these truths are constructed). This enterprise faces an initial challenge. Since the goal is to construct all normative truth, it cannot appeal directly to normative principles in the process of construction, either in the inputs or in the specification and defense of the procedure, on pain of circularity and uninformativeness. However, appealing only to non-normative inputs and procedures threatens to reduce normative truth to something else instead of explaining it. How, then, can this enterprise proceed?

The strategy of unrestricted constructivists is to derive all normative substance from normative form, and then to derive normative form from an analysis of the activity that the norms target (e.g., practical or theoretical deliberation). For constructivism about practical reasons, the inputs to construction are typically subjective states (e.g., unreflective forms of valuing). The procedure of construction is derived from an analysis of some aspect of agency (e.g., willing). The outputs of construction are substantive normative truths, reached through procedural reasoning from the inputs. Substantive normative judgments and truths must be confined to the outputs to avoid circularity (and a return to restricted constructivism).

The ambition of this form of constructivism appears to be both metaethical and normative. Three recent defenders—Onora O'Neill (1996), Christine Korsgaard (1996; 1997; 2008; 2009), and Sharon Street (2008; 2010; 2012)—attempt to explain what normative truth as such is, in opposition to realist and skeptical metaethical accounts, but also to identify the truth conditions of judgments about reasons, which takes them into normative territory. It is a distinctive feature of constructivism that it views these levels of theorizing as closely intertwined. This aspect, more than any other, has led to disagreement over how to interpret the view. Some critics argue that, while constructivism is a metaethical position, it is not a distinctive one, and is best interpreted as a version of one or another familiar metaethical view; others claim that it is not a metaethical position at all and remains entirely at the level of normative theorizing. One explanation of this disagreement, I'll suggest, is a lack of clarity about constructivism's stance on the relationship between metaethical and normative theorizing.

In what follows, I will focus exclusively on unrestricted constructivism, with special attention to its metaethical potential. Discussion will be confined to two recent accounts: Korsgaard's Kantian constructivism and Street's Humean constructivism (for discussion of O'Neill, see Barry 2013). Of necessity, I will neglect a host of other constructivist positions in ethics (see Bagnoli 2011). For simplicity, from here on, I will use the label 'constructivism' to refer only to unrestricted forms.

MOTIVATIONS FOR CONSTRUCTIVISM

Since constructivists aim to develop a non-skeptical, non-realist account of normative truth, they typically motivate their view by arguing against skeptical and realist positions.

Against skeptical views, they offer two general forms of argument:

1. Deliberating and acting would be incoherent or impossible without normative truth; as agents we need to deliberate and act, so we should reject skepticism (Street 2010: 379, n. 60; 2011: 16 and throughout)—indeed, the fact that we *need* reasons is part of why there *are* reasons (Korsgaard 1996: 92–97, 120–123, 163–64; 2009: 23–24).
2. We take ourselves to know some normative truths, so skepticism is implausible (Street 2006: 109, 122, 125; 2011: 14).

Against realism, understood broadly as the view that normative truths and facts are mind-independent, constructivists offer several arguments, including the following:

1. Realist appeals to intuitions about substantive reasons cannot answer skeptical challenges, as an agent can always coherently ask why he *ought* to conform to such truths. An adequate answer must show the agent how a conclusion follows, as a matter of rationality or coherence, from things he is already committed to (Korsgaard 1996: 38–40; 1997: 240–242; 2008: 316–317; 2009: 5–6, 32).
2. A realist account of the principles of rationality is incoherent. If those principles were external normative truths, then an agent would need an additional norm in order to apply them since facts alone cannot obligate action; this norm could not, in turn, be just another external normative truth, on pain of regress (Korsgaard 2008: 315–316; 2009: 64–65).
3. The only non-arbitrary source of authority for a rational agent is that agent's own will or autonomous self-legislation. This means that reasons and values must be products of rational willing, not external truths (Korsgaard 1996: 90–130; 1997: 244–251; 2008: 316–317; 2009: 32, 66, 127, and throughout; Street 2008: 229–230, 237, 244).
4. Evolutionary theory implies that selective pressures pervasively shaped our normative commitments. There is no reason to think that normative truths could play any role in this evolutionary shaping, so if realism were true it would imply that we are hopeless at knowing normative truth. Since we do not regard ourselves as hopeless in this sense, and indeed could not coherently do so while deliberating, we should reject realism and conceive of normative truth as mind-dependent. (Street develops a version of this argument against both non-naturalistic and naturalistic forms of realism [2006], and also against quasi-realism [2011: 12–16].)
5. Non-naturalistic realism holds scientifically untenable metaphysical and epistemological commitments that constructivism avoids (Street 2006; 2008: 220, n. 30; Korsgaard 1996: 160–161).

Several of these arguments begin with a claim about what is necessary for coherent deliberation (or adequate justification) and conclude that realism or skepticism is untenable. This, I'll suggest in the section "The Relationship between Metaethical and Normative Theorizing," is part of a distinctive approach to metaethical theorizing.

A MORE PRECISE FORMULATION OF CONSTRUCTIVISM

The claim that reasons and values derive from the commitments of rational agents makes constructivism a response-dependent account. A further differentiating feature is a commitment to hypothetical proceduralism. Korsgaard characterizes the idea as follows:

> The procedural moral realist [the constructivist] thinks that there are answers to moral questions *because* there are correct procedures for arriving at them. But the substantive moral realist thinks that there are correct procedures for answering moral questions *because* there are moral truths or facts which exist independently of those procedures, and which those procedures track.
>
> (1996: 36–37)

While a commitment to hypothetical proceduralism is an essential element of the constructivist views under consideration here (see also Street 2008: 208, 223), it does not distinguish them clearly from familiar Humean desire-satisfaction theories, which can also be viewed as response-dependent hypothetical proceduralist accounts (in virtue of taking an agent's desires as inputs, subjecting them to procedural [theoretical and instrumental] correction, and counting the resulting desires as reasons for action [Brandt 1979; Williams 1981; Lewis 1989] or non-moral values [Railton 1986a and 1986b]). Indeed, these shared features have led some to categorize Humean desire-satisfaction accounts as forms of constructivism as well (e.g., Cullity and Gaut 1997: 4–5; Shafer-Landau 2003: 14). (See Enoch 2009: 328–330 for related discussion.)

A feature that differentiates constructivism from these other proceduralist accounts is its strategy for defending the procedure of construction. Constructivists argue that the procedure is determined by constitutive standards of agency or the practical point of view, as such, and applicable for this very reason. As Street puts the guiding ideas: (1) "the only standards of correctness that exist are those set from within the practical point of view itself" (2008: 220), and (2) normative truth consists in "what is entailed from within the practical point of view" (2010: 367). While Kantian and Humean constructivists disagree about the content of the procedure, they agree on this strategy for defending it (Street 2010: 369–370; 2012). The strategy seems intended to do both normative and metaethical work: it claims not only that the truth conditions for reasons are proceduralist in nature, but that the procedure applies in virtue of deriving from constitutive standards of agency. The defense rests ultimately on a *constitutive* argument. (See Enoch 2006 for related discussion.) In contrast, non-constructivist Humean hypothetical proceduralist accounts typically defend the content and applicability of the procedure with a naturalistic reduction, according to which a reason is reducible to a complex natural fact about how an agent would be motivated after exposure to non-normative facts and reasoning. It's worth noting that realists (either naturalistic or non-naturalistic) can appeal to constitutive arguments of a sort, but they will view their potential differently, i.e., as at most identifying conceptual truths about agential structures and related principles, not as doing foundational metaethical work. According to realists, mind-independent normative truths are needed to establish any normative significance that constitutive principles might have.

One further way the constructivist accounts under consideration here differ from other forms of hypothetical proceduralism is in characterizing the inputs to construction as phenomenologically irreducible, i.e., as normative experiences or pre-reflective normative judgments. While the content of these inputs cannot be analyzed directly in terms of the concept of a reason, on pain of circularity, the inputs are viewed as having a distinctively normative phenomenology (Street 2006: 117, 119, 128; 2008: 239–242; Korsgaard 2009: 110–132). This is in contrast to non-constructivist Humean hypothetical proceduralist accounts, which characterize the inputs as non-normative states of desire, typically with the aim of reducing the normative to the non-normative. (See Lenman and Shemmer 2012: 3, 6 for related discussion.)

Taking this last point into account, we might characterize the type of constructivism under consideration here as a *response-dependent hypothetical proceduralist constitutivist non-reductive* account of normative truth. It is the metaethical status of this view that is in dispute. I'll return to this issue in the section "The Metaethical Implications of Constructivism," after outlining the constructivist position.

THE CONSTRUCTIVIST EXPLANATION OF NORMATIVE TRUTH

As noted above, a constructivist explanation aims to derive all normative substance from normative form, and normative form from an analysis of the activity the norms target.

Here is how Korsgaard describes the strategy:

> ... the argument goes from the nature of the rational will to a principle which describes a procedure according to which such a will must operate and from there to an application of that principle which yields a conclusion about what one has reason to do ... . There are then facts, moral truths, about what we ought to do, but that is not because the actions are intrinsically normative. They inherit their normativity from principles which spring from the nature of the will—the principles of practical reasoning.
>
> (1996: 36)

Korsgaard takes the target of analysis to be *willing an end* (in contrast, Street takes it to be *making a normative judgment* [2008: 209, n. 4] or *valuing* [2010: 366–369]). The goal is to identify constitutive standards of this activity, i.e., standards one must follow to engage in it at all. Since such standards simply specify the way to do the activity, their authority is clear: rejecting them while trying to engage in the activity is incoherent (Korsgaard 1996: 235–236; 1997: 242–251; 2009: 27–34). Because the activities of willing or valuing cannot be escaped by anyone who deliberates and acts, their constitutive standards are normatively inescapable for any agent. As Korsgaard puts it, "A constitutive principle for an inescapable activity is unconditionally binding" (2009: 32). (For discussion of the difference between psychological and normative inescapability, see Fitzpatrick 2005 and 2013; Enoch 2006.)

An initial puzzle about constitutive standards is the following: if one is not an agent *at all* unless one conforms to them, how is bad or defective agency possible? Korsgaard addresses this worry by arguing that agency comes in degrees. To be an agent at all one must at least try to conform to constitutive standards of agency, and succeed to some degree; however, an agent can fail to meet these standards fully and still count as a defective agent. This is what allows constitutive standards to be normative. (2009: 31–32, 45–49, and 159–176) (Street worries that characterizing constitutive standards as normative threatens the aims of *unrestricted* constructivism. This leads her to claim that they involve *entailment* relations, not normative relations [and that "constitutive entailment is not rational entailment" (2008: 232 and 228; 2010: 367, 374)]. This seems problematic, however, since constructivism needs the procedures of construction to be normative; otherwise, why follow them, and why count the results as reasons? In any case, Street mostly treats constitutive standards as normative. [See Wallace 2012: 33–34, and n. 11; Enoch 2009: 328, n. 14; Hussain and Shah 2006: 291 for related discussion.])

The idea, then, is that the essential activities of agency have a determinate structure, represented by constitutive standards. By engaging in these activities, an agent commits himself to meeting these standards, and thereby legislates them, which makes them normative (Korsgaard 2009: 32–33; Street 2008: 229–230, 237) Failing to meet them is then irrational by his own lights (Street 2008: 228, n. 37). Korsgaard also puts her argument in terms of a problem-solution structure, claiming that constitutive standards apply to agents because they solve an inescapable problem of agency, i.e., the need for reasons and unification. As she says, "if you recognize the problem to be real, to be yours, to be one you have to solve, and the solution to be the only or the best one, then the solution is binding upon you" (2008: 322). (See also Korsgaard 1996: 92–130, 225–233; 2009.)

Kantian and Humean accounts disagree about the content of constitutive standards. Korsgaard argues that the basic activity of agency, *willing an end*, constitutively involves willing the necessary means because if one always fails to will the necessary means then one will not be willing the end at all (1997: 244–248; 2009: 69–72). More ambitiously, she argues that willing particular ends constitutively implies valuing rational agency in oneself and others. (Very roughly, willing ends requires taking them to be valuable; since they do not get their value from outside, the agent must view her rational agency as the source of their value, which requires viewing rational agency itself as valuable [1996: 120–123]. See 2009, chapter 9 for a different argument to the same conclusion.) This yields a form of Kantian constructivism, in which formal procedural reasoning supports one required substantive value (i.e., rational agency). According to Humean constructivism, in contrast, while the activity of *valuing* constitutively entails a commitment to the instrumental and logical implications of this valuing (Street 2010: 367), it does not imply any commitment to valuing rational agency, or any other particular substantive value (Street 2008: 243–245; 2010: 369–370; 2012).

We can distinguish two elements in this account: (1) the objective structure of agency, represented by constitutive standards, and (2) an agent's legislation of these standards through willing or valuing. It is not entirely clear which element is doing the work of making standards normative for an agent. Constructivists claim that it is the agent's own will—his engaging in the activity—that makes constitutive standards normative. However, as constructivists are keen to emphasize, constitutive standards have objective implications with respect to which actual agents may be mistaken. As Street notes, even in the Humean account, there are determinate answers concerning which reasons an agent has: they are the commitments implied, logically and instrumentally, by his initial pre-reflective normative commitments in combination with the non-normative facts (2008: 230). These implications are what they are even if he is not aware of them and never would be (2008: 230; 2010: 367). This, however, opens up a potential gap, for the fully (logically and instrumentally) coherent set of an agent's normative commitments may diverge sharply from his actual commitments, which in all likelihood are not systematically coherent. He may care much more about his actual commitments and their local success, even if they conflict, than about the fully coherent version of them (or indeed the standard of coherence itself). Once such a gap opens between what an agent actually wills or values and what the constitutive standards of agency indicate he *ought* to will or value given his antecedent commitments, we can ask which of these is normative for him, and why. The same question arises for a Kantian constructivist account. When what an agent wills conflicts with the value of rational agency, which principle is normative: that expressed by his actual willing, or that set by the constitutive standards of agency as such, objectively understood? (For discussion, see Gibbard 1999; Wallace 2004, 2012; Fitzpatrick 2005, 2013; Enoch 2006; Street 2012.)

A clear way to resolve this ambiguity would be to claim that if an agent isn't actually motivated to conform to constitutive standards of agency, then they don't apply to him. This would locate the ultimate authority in the individual agent's choice, not in the objective structure of agency. Some things constructivists say point in this direction. Street claims that each person faces a radical choice of whether to be an agent (2008: 238). Likewise, in discussing a Mafioso who values honor but not rational agency, Korsgaard says that as long as he has not carried out the stretch of reflection that would unseat his immoral ends, they are normative for him (1996: 256–258). These statements, however, threaten the constructivist enterprise, for if agents are subject to constitutive standards only insofar as they are actually motivated to follow them (and be agents), normative authority reduces to motivational force. Perhaps for this reason, constructivists appear to reject this line in the end. As Korsgaard goes on to say about the Mafioso, reflection has standards of its own that he ought to have followed, which would have led him to recognize the value of rational agency (1996: 257–258). The upshot seems to be that substantive reasons and values derive from an agent's *rational* willing or practical reasoning, not from his actual (bare) willing. (For related discussion, see Wallace 2004; cf. Wallace 2012: 35–38.)

With the procedures of construction in place, the next step is to construct substantive reasons and values by applying these procedures to an agent's antecedent commitments. Interpretative and critical questions arise at this stage as well. I'll mention three.

First, as noted earlier, Korsgaard and Street view the inputs to construction as having an irreducibly normative phenomenology. Both claim that humans experience things in the world as *calling for* or *making appropriate* certain responses (e.g., Street 2008: 239–242; Korsgaard 2009: 111, 122–124). What kind of mental states are involved here? Insofar as these experiences involve normative *judgments*, worries about circularity threaten: if substantive reasons and values are the targets of construction, then judgments about these cannot figure among the inputs to construction. If these experiences do not involve normative judgments, however, then the sense in which they have normative content is unclear. (For related discussion see Ridge 2012; Lenman 2012.)

Second, there are related questions about the normative status of the inputs, and the coherence of the resulting theory. According to constructivists, agents experience things in the world as calling for certain responses. While constructivists deny that this involves attributing normative properties to the world, insofar as it seems to do so constructivists must give an error theory of the experience, as Street admits (2008: 240–241, and n. 55). This, however, threatens the coherence of the constructivist account, as truths about reasons and values would be constructed from mistaken or illusory experiences (Ridge 2012).

Third, constructivism may face a bootstrapping worry. By hypothesis, subjective normative experiences are not normative in their own right; they're a matter of nature, not reason (Street 2006: 152–154; 2008: 244; Korsgaard 2009: 122). However, how can inputs with no initial normative standing become reason-giving simply through increased coherence? It seems clear that coherently willed ends can be worthless (e.g., those of the grass counter) or perverse (e.g., those of a coherent Caligula [Gibbard 1999: 145, 149; cf. Street 2009]), and so justification here may be too hostage to the initial commitments of agents.

THE METAETHICAL IMPLICATIONS OF CONSTRUCTIVISM

What are the metaethical implications of this constructivist story? For the purposes of this discussion, we can treat any claim that has direct normative implications for what we *ought* or *have reason* to do as a normative claim, and any claim that is *about* such a normative claim but does not itself have direct normative implications as metaethical. This distinction is easily blurred, however, since claims at each level can have implications for the other. Standard metaethical questions include the following: (1) Is there such a thing as normative truth? If so, is it mind-dependent, and in what sense? What are the truthmakers for normative claims? (metaphysics). (2) What do normative concepts mean, and how do they get their content? (semantics). (3) How, if at all, can we come to know normative truths? (epistemology). (4) Are normative judgments beliefs, desires, or some other kind of mental state? (moral psychology). (5) What is the connection between normative judgments, practical reasoning, and motivation? (practicality). As we'll see below, there is disagreement about how to interpret these questions, which in turn has implications for how we should view constructivism.

The question about constructivism's metaethical status comes into focus if we ask the following: at which levels does the account accept *mind-dependence*, and in what sense? Two central claims emerge from the constructivist explanation: (1) substantive reasons and values are a function of procedurally correct reasoning from an agent's commitments, and (2) the procedures of construction are principles constitutive of agency, and applicable because of this. In virtue of what are these claims true? Is their truth mind-dependent? At one level, constructivism gives an unambiguously mind-dependent account of substantive reasons and values, for it claims that these are constructed through subjecting an agent's initial commitments to procedurally correct reasoning. However, we can ask a further question here: is the truth that substantive reasons and values are constructions of procedurally correct reasoning *itself* mind-dependent? Put otherwise, what kind of fact is it (if it is a fact) that substantive reasons and values are constructions of procedurally correct reasoning? We can ask the same sort of question about the claim that the procedures of construction are constitutive standards of agency, and applicable because of this. Is the truth of this claim mind-dependent? As the discussion in the previous section revealed, this is not entirely clear.

These questions about mind-dependence are at the heart of the controversy over the metaethical status of constructivism. Some aspects of constructivism invite an interpretation along realist lines, while others fit naturally with an expressivist view. This has led critics to argue that constructivism should be viewed as a variety of realism or expressivism. Other critics, however, argue that the ambiguity in constructivism on this point means that it is not a metaethical view at all and remains at the level of normative theorizing (Hussain and Shah 2006). In addition, critics argue that constructivists leave unanswered related metaethical questions about epistemology (Hussain and Shah 2006: 284–285), semantics (Hussain and Shah 2006: 286–288; Ridge 2012; Lenman 2012; Dorsey 2012), and moral psychology (Ridge 2012; Lenman 2012). These questions are important. Since their resolution depends largely on how questions about mind-dependence are answered, however, I'll focus on the latter.

On a realist reading of constructivism, the truth that substantive reasons and values derive from an agent's commitments is a mind-*independent* truth, either natural or non-natural. That is, it is either (1) a normative fact that is identical to a complex natural fact about how initial commitments would change if subjected to procedural reasoning, or (2) a non-naturalistic normative fact that supervenes upon a complex natural fact about how initial commitments would change if subjected to procedural reasoning. Likewise, the procedures of construction (or the constitutive principles of agency) are mind-independent truths that apply to any agent as such. They are either (1) normative truths identical to complex natural facts about consistency relations among mental states of commitment (or the structure of agency), or (2) non-naturalistic normative truths that supervene on relations of consistency among mental states of commitment (or the structure of agency). For the purposes of this discussion, I'll restrict my focus to the status of the procedures of construction.

The strand of constructivism thought by critics to invite a realist interpretation is the following. We saw in the previous section that there are two elements in the constructivist account: (1) the objective structure of agency, represented by constitutive standards, and (2) an agent's legislation of these standards through willing or valuing. Constructivists often talk as if the applicability of constitutive standards is volition-dependent, contingent upon an individual agent's willing or valuing. This suggests that the agent's individual will has ultimate say over whether the standards apply to her activity. However, as we saw above, in the final analysis, constructivists seem to treat these standards as applying to *any* agent simply by virtue of the fact that she wills or values at all (i.e., that she is an agent). In this sense, the standards are not (individually) volition-dependent. Moreover, we saw that denying this would threaten the distinction between normative authority and motivational force.

Insofar as the constitutive argument needs to rely on intrinsically normative principles of agency to make good on its claims to objectivity, it can look like a form of realism about formal principles. (See Wallace 2004; Fitzpatrick 2005 and 2013 for related discussion.) The same holds if Korsgaard's problem-solution structure needs to rely on a normative conception of the problem of agency and its solution—one that agents *ought* to recognize as their own. (See Fitzpatrick 2005; Ridge 2012; Barry 2013 for related discussion.) These and related points lead critics to argue that elements of Korsgaard's account are potentially compatible with non-naturalistic realism, contrary to its goals (Fitzpatrick 2005; Enoch 2006; Hussain and Shah 2006). Likewise, some critics claim that Street's account is indistinguishable from the naturalistic realism embraced by many (non-constructivist) Humean hypothetical proceduralists (Enoch 2009: 328, n. 14; Ridge 2012).

Viewing constructivism as a form of realism provides a clear way to understand the objectivity of claims about the applicability of constitutive standards of agency. Moreover, realism restricted to *formal* principles allows for autonomy in the construction of substantive reasons and values, and it may seem less metaphysically mysterious since it posits normative facts that supervene on or reduce to structural features of agency, not independent facts about substantive reasons. The problem with this interpretation, of course, is that it conflicts with constructivists' explicit rejection of realism (including realism about formal principles) (Korsgaard 1997: 239–244; 2008: 309–310; 2009: 64–67). It also leaves constructivism subject to its own objections to realism, and threatens its global ambitions. (See Wallace 2004; Fitzpatrick 2005, 2013 for related discussion.)

How does an expressivist interpretation of constructivism go? Expressivism claims that there are no normative facts in the world. Instead of analyzing what it is to *bè* a reason, we should analyze what it is to *take* something to be a reason, which is to express a motivational state of approval or norm-acceptance toward treating that consideration as counting in favor of acting. Likewise, what it is to take a principle to be a principle of rationality is to endorse conformity with it as non-optional. Thus, an expressivist interpretation views constructivist claims about constitutive standards and the truth conditions of reason statements as normative claims that express attitudes of endorsement.

The features of constructivism thought by critics to favor an expressivist interpretation are the following. First, when speaking generally, constructivists often talk as if normative truth must be the product of volitional endorsement in order to be authoritative for rational agents. Second, they claim that normative truth exists and is detectable only *within* the first-person perspective of agency, and that from the outside, all we can see are creatures valuing things (Korsgaard 1996: 161; 2008: 325 and n. 49; Street 2008: 219–223; 2010: 364–367). Third, they claim that normative judgments are intrinsically motivating (Korsgaard 1986; 1997; Street 2008: 228, n. 37, and 230; 2010: 376) and deny that the primary function of normative judgments and concepts is to represent external normative facts (Korsgaard 1996: 44–47; 2008: 321–324; Street 2006; 2010: 376). If one holds a Humean belief-desire theory of motivation, these commitments imply that normative judgments are pro-attitudes, not beliefs. This, in turn, suggests that an expressivist semantics for normative concepts may be in order (Lehman 2012). It is considerations such as these that lead Gibbard (1999) to interpret Korsgaard's position as a form of expressivism, Hussain and Shah (2013) to argue that it is compatible with expressivism, and Lenman (2012) to read Street as a potential expressivist.

This interpretation, too, has problems. Korsgaard worries that expressivism implies that we cannot genuinely engage in *reasoning* about our attitudes (2008: 325, n. 49). This points to a general concern that expressivism may not have the resources to adequately capture the rational necessity of constitutive standards within a constructivist account. This is too large of a topic to address here, but we can at least get an initial sense of the intuitive worry.

Expressivists take the lesson of Hume's ban on deriving *ought* from *is* to be that no non-normative fact entails endorsement. About any such fact, we can acknowledge that it is a fact but still ask whether it is reason-giving. This argument applies to constitutive features of agency and formal procedures of construction as much as to any other natural facts, leaving the agent free to ask, "Yes, I can see that agency has such and such a structure, but why must I count that as giving me a reason to conclude or do anything?"

Interestingly, R.M. Hare, a well-known prescriptivist, seems to assume that some normative concepts, along with the logical principles that govern their use, are exempt from Hume's argument, for he claims that identifying the logical properties of the normative concept 'ought' reveals clear canons of reasoning for moral thinking that rationally support utilitarian conclusions (1981). It is unclear, however, why concepts and their logical properties should be exempt from the ban on deriving *ought* from *is*. About any particular normative concepts, we can ask whether they are really reason-giving, and we can presumably adopt alternatives (or use the concepts we have in an idiosyncratic fashion).

In contrast to Hare's willingness to exempt some normative concepts and logical principles from Hume's argument, quasi-realists try to "earn back" the applicability of logical standards to normative discourse by explaining why even non-representational, initially non-truth-apt motivational states of endorsement need to conform to logical structure (e.g., to rule out some commitments, combine with others, and allow for the assessment of sensibilities) (see Blackburn 1984: 171 and 181–221; 1993; 1998: 68–77; Gibbard 1990; 2003a, especially sections II and III; 2008: 167–174). The question is whether this sort of explanation can succeed in earning back logical structure, and its rationally required status, without simply helping itself to what it needs to earn. Many have doubted that it can (e.g., Hale 1986; 1993; 2002; Wright 1988; Broome 2008; Schroeder 2008, chapter 3 [cf. Gibbard 2012, appendix 2]).

To account for a principle's status as rationally required, Gibbard says that expressivists can claim, from within the attitudinal perspective, that its truth is mind-*independent* (i.e., that it would apply even if we did *not* endorse its application). As he puts it, "anyone who takes a norm to constitute a requirement of rationality takes that norm to apply independently of his own accepting it. He thinks that even if he rejected the norm, that norm would still be valid" (1990: 155). This is a familiar maneuver in quasi-realist expressivist accounts (Blackburn 1984: 217–220; 1988; 1998: 74, 307–308, 311–312; Gibbard 1990: 153–170; 1999: 142–143, n. 3; 2003a: 52–53, 183–186). It strikes many, however, as trying to have things both ways. Why is that?

According to an expressivist metaethical account, when we make normative claims we are not describing or representing mind-independent normative facts or truths (since there aren't any). What we are doing is expressing non-representational motivational attitudes of endorsement, the meaning of which derives from their expressive function. If we accept this metaethical theory, then when we claim, normatively, that some principle is mind-independently true, it seems clear that we cannot take ourselves to mean, in a descriptive sense, that the principle is mind-independently true. We must instead take ourselves to be endorsing treating the principle *as if* it were mind-independently true (in a descriptive sense). This, however, severs the link between mind-independence and objectivity, for the intuitive connection derives from the potential to refer successfully to mind-independent facts or truths—a potential which is lost with the expressive meaning. Expressivists might be tempted to invoke minimalism about truth, facts, and mind-independence here to claim that we don't mean anything very metaphysically robust even when we use these words descriptively (e.g., Blackburn 1998: 77–83; Gibbard 2003: *Preface* and chapter 9). This raises a different worry, however, for minimalism makes it difficult for expressivists to articulate an initial contrast between truth-apt representational beliefs and non-truth-apt motivational states, or between facts that do heavy explanatory lifting and those that don't, which is crucial for distinguishing quasi-realist expressivism from realism. (For early articulations of the contrast, see Blackburn 1988 and Gibbard 1990: chapter 6; for doubts that the contrast can be sustained if minimalism is embraced, see Wright 1988 and Rosen 1998 [cf. Blackburn 1998: 77–83 and Gibbard 2003, chapter 9]; see Dreier 2004 for related discussion.) While these points merit more detailed discussion, they suggest that the expressivist strategy of invoking mind-*independence* to secure the objectivity or rational necessity of principles may face serious obstacles.

The root problem with an expressivist interpretation of constructivism is the expressivist claim that endorsement can in principle attach to anything, for this means that no natural properties, not even structural features of agency or related constitutive principles, directly require endorsement. In contrast, according to constructivists, the activities of willing and deliberating have a structure that is the non-negotiable descriptive starting point for any theorizing about the normative. Normative endorsement necessarily concerns this content. To identify the constitutive standards of agency is to unpack the built-in logic of action and deliberation. These standards are not a function of our attitudes *about* the activity. They are objective features *of* the activity that require endorsement by anyone engaged in it. The quasi-realist project of "earning back" logical structure, in contrast, implies that the structure is a product of our attitudes.

A weakness of the expressivist interpretation of constructivism, then, is its potential inability to capture the content and rational necessity of principles of reasoning in the manner constructivism needs. Moreover, constructivists explicitly reject expressivism (Korsgaard 2008: 325, n. 49; Street 2010: 376–379; 2011). An expressivist interpretation would, however, provide a semantics for normative terms, allow a kind of autonomy in endorsement, and avoid naturalistic worries (although this point is trickier than it seems, as Gibbard's shifts in view illustrate [see Gibbard 2003a: 191–194, in contrast with 2012]).

This discussion suggests that while certain features of constructivism fit with realism or expressivism, constructivism is not clearly compatible with either. Where does this leave it, metaethically speaking? Is it an alternative metaethical view or should we conclude that it is not a metaethical view at all, despite what its defenders suggest in setting it up as a rival to familiar metaethical views?

THE RELATIONSHIP BETWEEN METAETHICAL AND NORMATIVE THEORIZING

Constructivists have noted in passing that they view metaethical and normative theorizing as inextricably intertwined (Korsgaard 2008: 322, n. 44; Street 2008: 217, n. 22). While they have not articulated a clear position on the interrelationship, this commitment is apparent in the way they approach the metaethical enterprise. They worry that realists and expressivists seek a metaethical basis for objectivity in an alien domain—either external facts (realists) or non-cognitive attitudes (expressivists)—with implausible results. In contrast, they suggest that we start by identifying the essential features of this distinctive subject matter—practical deliberation—in order to arrive at a view about what normative objectivity could be. Metaethical theorizing must take its start from these features. In particular, constructivists seem to take metaethical theorizing to be directly answerable to conditions of coherent deliberation and adequate justification. As we saw in the section "Motivations for Constructivism," they argue that skepticism and realism should be rejected, among other reasons, because they are incompatible with such conditions.

More generally, Korsgaard argues that an explanation of normative thinking must not only explain *why* we think normatively but enable us to view our thinking as potentially *justified* (1996: 7–18). The content of the explanation, including its metaethical content, must be coherently affirmable by an agent while she is engaged in practical deliberation. While the constructivist explanation is external to the deliberative perspective—it explains how the self-conscious structure of the mind makes normative truth possible and necessary—Korsgaard views this explanation as suited to justify endorsement because it identifies the essential role of normative principles in enabling the functioning of deliberative agency. (See 1996: lecture 3 and 251–258 for related discussion.) In contrast, neither realism nor skepticism, she claims, can be affirmed coherently by a deliberating agent.

For constructivists, conditions of coherent deliberation and adequate justification not only eliminate metaethical rivals, they also provide the only reference points for a positive foundation. In particular, the rational inescapability of a commitment within the deliberative perspective, determined by the incoherence of rejecting it, warrants accepting it as true, indeed is what *makes* it true. In the domain of agency, constructivists argue, it makes little sense to think that we need to accept certain principles to deliberate coherently and function as agents, and yet to deny that they are true. In a real sense, there are reasons and principles with a certain kind of objectivity because we need there to be in order to deliberate coherently.

This leads to a related claim: if we can identify principles of practical reasoning that require certain conclusions, and if we can come to understand the applicability of these principles as rooted in the role they play in enabling our basic functioning as deliberating agents, then all of the necessary foundational work will be done. There will be no need for further grounding from outside of practical reasoning itself. Put otherwise, if metaethics is about the foundations of normative thinking, and normative thinking rests on principles of practical reasoning that are constitutive of the functioning of deliberative agency, then foundational normative theorizing helps to reveal metaethical foundations. Constructivists deny that this amounts to quietism because they attempt to explain what normative truth is, and how it comes onto the scene, by showing its constitutive role in the basic functioning of deliberative agency.

Korsgaard's rejection of the terms of traditional metaethical debates can be understood in this light. She argues that these debates are structured by distinctions—cognitivism versus non-cognitivism, belief versus desire—that leave no space for a theory in which normative truths are conclusions of practical reasoning (2008: 309). Both distinctions have a natural home in a view like Hume's, according to which (1) reason is purely theoretical, (2) the function of concepts is to represent external facts, (3) only beliefs can be true or false (or well reasoned), and (4) motivation is the work of non-representational, non-truth-apt states of desire (Korsgaard 1986; 1997: 220–234). (See Barry 2010 for related discussion.) This way of carving up the terrain, Korsgaard argues, forces constructivists into a choice between realism and expressivism, neither of which can capture genuine rational necessity.

This discussion suggests that the ambiguity concerning constructivism's metaethical implications may stem from its distinctive approach to metaethical theorizing. It is an interesting feature of metaethical theorizing in general that philosophers of different stripes take it to be primarily answerable to different points of reference. Expressivists and reductive naturalists typically take philosophical naturalism to be their primary reference point (see especially Blackburn 1993: 166–181 and 1998; Gibbard 1990; Railton 1986a and 1986b). This leads them to reject objectively prescriptive facts and to develop an account of normative truth that either takes prescriptivity to be the essential element with objectivity earned back (expressivists), or takes facthood to be the essential element with prescriptivity earned back (reductive naturalists). Non-naturalistic realists, in contrast, take the objective-seeming form and content of normative discourse to be the primary reference point, and they reject philosophical naturalism as a result. While constructivists are concerned to offer a naturalistically acceptable account, they too seem to take features of normative thinking (in particular, conditions of coherent deliberation and adequate justification) to be their primary reference point. In this way, they share with non-naturalistic realists a tendency to take metaethical theorizing to be directly answerable to normative thinking. However, instead of taking this to justify believing in mind-independent normative truths, they take it to license embracing a conception of normative truth that is strongly answerable to conditions of coherent practical reasoning, and indeed, in the end, a function of them. With Kant, they view normative truth as existing within the structure of deliberative agency. This is a way of trying to address metaethical questions, but it views the tasks of metaethics in a distinctive manner.

There are worries, however. First, this approach strikes many as engaging in a questionable form of metaethical bootstrapping, for intuitively, at least, there is an important difference between what agents *need* to be true in order to deliberate coherently and what *is* true. (For related discussion, see Shah 2010; McPherson and Plunkett 2015.) How could truth, even truths of practical reasoning, simply be a function of conditions of coherent deliberation? Further, how, if deliberating agents need to think there are normative truths in order to deliberate coherently, could they at the same time view themselves as constructing these truths through deliberation? (See also Enoch 2009: 333–335.)

Second, there are persistent questions about what objectivity finally amounts to in this account. Objectivity is supposed to inhere in a method of reasoning. Methods of reasoning differ, however, as evidenced by the disagreement between Kantian and Humean constructivists over the content of constitutive standards. If there are no reference points external to the deliberative point of view, what makes one set of principles correct? The official answer—the structure of agency—shifts the question to this structure. What makes one particular structure, or way of exercising agency, best when there are alternatives? Is one structure, or way of functioning, intrinsically normative? In viewing the formal principles of rationality as binding on any rational agent as such, Kant seems to view their correctness as transcending human reasoning. What more this could involve, short of realism, has been a matter of interpretive controversy, with some reading Kant as a realist and others accusing him of psychologism (i.e., of reducing rational necessity to a form of psychological inescapability). Constructivists face a similar challenge: to articulate a conception of objectivity within the deliberative perspective that provides a clear alternative to these positions.

Does understanding the methodological commitments of constructivism this way endanger its goal of explaining how normative truth is *constructed*, not discovered? If an explanation of normative truth must begin with an analysis of conditions of coherent deliberation and adequate justification, does this mean that constructivists must take for granted normative presuppositions that require constructivist defense? This will depend in part on whether the intuitions appealed to are conceptual intuitions *about* the normative, as Street seems to claim, or normative intuitions proper. If the former, the worry may be avoidable, although distinguishing between these two kinds of intuitions is difficult, particularly when what are characterized as conceptual intuitions about the normative are taken to have direct normative implications, as they are within constructivism.

What are the implications if a constructivist explanation of normative truth does need to rely on high-level normative intuitions about what counts as coherent deliberation or adequate justification? Would it ruin the ambitions of constructivism? Not necessarily, but the view would need to recharacterize its aims. I started by noting that any attempt to construct normative truth from the ground up faces an initial puzzle: relying only on non-normative materials threatens to reduce the normative to the non-normative, while relying on normative materials threatens the goal of constructing normative truth from the ground up. It wouldn't be surprising if any form of constructivism had to rely on normative materials to some extent (and so remain a form of *restricted* constructivism) (see Enoch 2009; Barry 2013). The interesting question concerns the extent and nature of appeals to normative starting points. If a constructivist account restricts itself to very general and formal intuitions about conditions of coherent deliberation and adequate justification, and avoids appealing to intuitions about substantive reasons and values, then it might still constitute a distinctive and interesting account of normative truth—one in which all normative substance is derived from normative form, and normative form is derived from an analysis of deliberative agency. But it should acknowledge that the construction cannot be done entirely from the ground up without appealing to some high-level normative intuitions (or conceptual intuitions about the normative that have direct normative implications).

ACKNOWLEDGMENTS

I would like to thank the editors of this volume, Tristram McPherson and David Plunkett, for insightful comments on an earlier draft of this chapter. Thanks, too, to their research assistant Jamie Fritz for his helpful input.

RELATED TOPICS

Chapter 1, "Non-Naturalistic Realism in Metaethics;" Chapter 2, "Naturalistic Realism in Metaethics;" Chapter 3, "Error Theory in Metaethics;" Chapter 5, "Metaethical Expressivism;" Chapter 18, "Cognitivism and Non-Cognitivism;" Chapter 22, "Mind-Dependence and Moral Realism;" Chapter 23, "Constitutivism;" Chapter 30, "Intuitionism in Moral Epistemology;" Chapter 40, "Quasi-realism;" Chapter 41, "Metaethical Quietism;" Chapter 42, "Methodological Naturalism in Metaethics;" Chapter 43, "Normative Ethics and Metaethics."

REFERENCES

Bagnoli, C. (2011) "Constructivism in Metaethics," *Stanford Encyclopedia of Philosophy*.
Barry, M. (2010) "Humean Theories of Motivation," in R. Shafer-Landau (ed.) *Oxford Studies in Metaethics* 5: 195–224, Oxford: Oxford University Press.
—. (2013) "Constructivist Practical Reasoning and Objectivity," in D. Archard, M. Deveaux, N. Mason and D. Weinstock (eds.) *Reading Onora O'Neill*, New York: Routledge Press, 17–36.
Blackburn, S. (1984) *Spreading the Word*, Oxford: Clarendon Press.
—. (1988) "How to Be an Ethical Antirealist," *Midwest Studies in Philosophy* 12: 361–375.
—. (1993) *Essays in Quasi-Realism*, Oxford: Oxford University Press.
—. (1998) *Ruling Passions: A Theory of Practical Reasoning*, Oxford: Clarendon Press.
Brandt, R.B. (1979) *A Theory of the Good and the Right*, New York: Oxford University Press.
Broome, J. (2008) "Comments on Allan Gibbard's Tanner Lectures," in *Reconciling Our Aims: In Search of Bases for Ethics*, Oxford: Oxford University Press, 102–119.

Cullity, G. and B. Gaut (1997) (eds.) *Ethics and Practical Reason*, Oxford: Clarendon Press.

Daniels, N. (1975) (ed.) *Reading Rawls*, Oxford: Blackwell.

Darwall, S., A. Gibbard, and P. Railton (1992) "Towards *Fin de siècle* Ethics: Some Trends," *The Philosophical Review* 101: 115–189.

Dorsey, D. (2012) "A Puzzle for Constructivism and How to Solve It," in J. Lenman and Y. Shemmer (eds.) *Constructivism in Practical Philosophy*, Oxford: Oxford University Press, 99–118.

Dreier, J. (2004) "Meta-Ethics and the Problem of Creeping Minimalism," *Philosophical Perspectives* 18, *Ethics*: 23–44.

Enoch, D. (2006) "Agency, Schmagency: Why Normativity Won't Come from What is Constitutive of Agency," *Philosophical Review* 115: 169–198.

—. (2009) "Can There Be a Global, Interesting, Coherent Constructivism about Practical Reason?" *Philosophical Explorations* 12(3): 319–339.

Fitzpatrick, W.J. (2005) "The Practical Turn in Ethical Theory: Korsgaard's Constructivism, Realism and the Nature of Normativity," *Ethics* 115: 651–691.

—. (2013) "How Not to be an Ethical Constructivist: A Critique of Korsgaard's Neo-Kantian Constitutivism," in C. Bagnoli (ed.) *Constructivism in Ethics*, Cambridge: Cambridge University Press, 41–62.

Gibbard, A. (1990) *Wise Choices, Apt Feelings*, Cambridge, MA: Harvard University Press.

—. (1999) "Morality as Consistency in Living," *Ethics* 110: 140–164.

—. (2003a) *Thinking How to Live*, Cambridge, MA: Harvard University Press.

—. (2003b) "Reasons to Reject Allowing," *Philosophy and Phenomenological Research* LXVI(1) January 2003: 169–175.

—. (2008) *Reconciling Our Aims: In Search of Bases for Ethics*, Oxford: Oxford University Press.

—. (2012) *Meaning and Normativity*, Oxford: Oxford University Press.

Hale, B. (1986) "The Complete Projectivist," *Philosophical Quarterly* 36: 65–84.

—. (1993) "Can There Be a Logic of Attitudes?" in J. Haldane and C. Wright (eds.) *Reality, Representation, and Projection*, Oxford: Oxford University Press, 337–363.

—. (2002) "Can Arboreal Knotwork Help Blackburn out of Frege's Abyss?" *Philosophy and Phenomenological Research* 65: 144–149.

Hare, R.M. (1981) *Moral Thinking*, New York: Oxford University Press.

Hussain, N. and N. Shah (2006) "Misunderstanding Metaethics: Korsgaard's Rejection of Realism," *Oxford Studies in Metaethics* 1: 265–294.

—. (2013) "Metaethics and its Discontents: A Case Study of Korsgaard," in C. Bagnoli (ed.) *Constructivism in Ethics*, Cambridge: Cambridge University Press, 82–107.

Kamm, F. (2002) "Owing, Justifying, and Rejecting," *Mind* 111(422) April 2002: 323–354.

Korsgaard, C. (1986) "Skepticism about Practical Reason," *Journal of Philosophy* LXXXIII(1) January 1986: 5–25.

—. (1996) in O. O'Neill (ed.) *The Sources of Normativity*, Cambridge: Cambridge University Press.

—. (1997) "The Normativity of Instrumental Reason," in G. Cullity and B. Gaut (eds.) *Ethics and Practical Reason*, Oxford: Clarendon Press.

—. (2008) *The Constitution of Agency*, Oxford: Oxford University Press.

—. (2009) *Self-Constitution: Action, Identity and Integrity*, Oxford: Oxford University Press.

Lenman, J. (2012) "Expressivism and Constructivism," in J. Lenman and Y. Shemmer (eds.) *Constructivism in Practical Philosophy*, Oxford: Oxford University Press, 213–225.

Lenman, J. and Y. Shemmer (2012) (eds.) *Constructivism in Practical Philosophy*, Oxford: Oxford University Press.

Lewis, D. (1989) "Dispositional Theories of Value," *Proceedings of the Aristotelian Society*, suppl. Vol. 63: 113–137.

McPherson, T. and D. Plunkett (2015) "Deliberative Indispensability and Epistemic Justification," *Oxford Studies in Metaethics* 10: 104–133.

O'Neill, O. (1996) *Towards Justice and Virtue: A Constructivist Account of Practical Reasoning*, Cambridge: Cambridge University Press.

Railton, P. (1986a) "Facts and Values," *Philosophical Topics* 24: 5–31.

—. (1986b) "Moral Realism," *Philosophical Review* 95: 163–207.

Rawls, J. (1971) *A Theory of Justice*, Cambridge, MA: Harvard University Press.

—. (1980) "Kantian Constructivism in Moral Theory," *Journal of Philosophy* 77: 515–572.

Ridge, M. (2012) "Kantian Constructivism: Something Old, Something New," in J. Lenman and Y. Shemmer (eds.) *Constructivism in Practical Philosophy*, Oxford: Oxford University Press, 138–158.

Rosen, G. (1998) "Blackburn's *Essays in Quasi-Realism*," *Noûs* 32: 386–405.

Scanlon, T.M. (1998) *What We Owe to Each Other*, Cambridge, MA: Harvard University Press.

Schroeder, M. (2008) *Being For: Evaluating the Semantic Program of Expressivism*, Oxford: Oxford University Press.

Shah, N. (2010) "The Limits of Normative Detachment," *Proceedings of the Aristotelian Society*, Vol. CX, Part 3, 347–371.

Shafer-Landau, R. (2003) *Moral Realism*, Oxford: Clarendon Press.

Street, S. (2006) "A Darwinian Dilemma for Realist Theories of Value," *Philosophical. Studies* 127: 109–166.

—. (2008) "Constructivism about Reasons," *Oxford Studies in Metaethics* 3: 208–245.

—. (2009) "In Defense of Future Tuesday Indifference: Ideally Coherent Eccentrics and the Contingency of What Matters," *Philosophical Issues* 19, *Metaethics*: 273–298.

—. (2010) "What is Constructivism in Ethics and Metaethics?" *Philosophy Compass* 5: 363–384.

—. (2011) "Mind-Independence Without the Mystery: Why Quasi-Realists Can't Have It Both Ways," *Oxford Studies in Metaethics* 6: 1–32.

—. (2012) "Coming to Terms with Contingency: Humean Constructivism about Practical Reason," in J. Lenman and Y. Shemmer (eds.) *Constructivism in Practical Philosophy*, Oxford: Oxford University Press, 40–59.

Wallace, J. (2004) "Constructing Normativity," *Philosophical Topics* 32 (1&2): 451–476.

—. (2012) "Constructivism about Normativity: Some Pitfalls," in J. Lenman and Y. Shemmer (eds.) *Constructivism in Practical Philosophy*, Oxford: Oxford University Press, 18–39.

Williams, B. (1981) *Moral Luck*, New York: Cambridge University Press.

Wright, C. (1988) "Realism, Antirealism, Irrealism, Quasi-realism," *Midwest Studies in Philosophy* 12: 25–49.

25

Normativity and Agency

Hille Paakkunainen

Normative facts, such as the fact that you ought to do something or have good reason to do it, are often thought to bear some important general connection to facts about agency. Most non-normative facts, such as facts about the material composition of the Sun, aren't usually thought to do so. Why think that the normative bears some important general connection to agency, where the non-normative, as such, doesn't? And what forms might this connection take?

I start by explicating the phenomena of normativity and of agency at issue ("Normativity and Agency: Some Basics"). I then focus on two putative connections between normativity and agency present in the literature that are, I think, insufficiently understood, but often heavily inform one's further views: certain types of "open question" argument (OQA) ("Agency and Deliberative Open Questions"), and the claim that normative reasons for action are premises in good deliberation ("The Deliberative Constraint: Doubts, Merits, and Conceptual Choices"). I argue that while OQAs don't seem to capture any important general connection between normativity and agency, the Deliberative Constraint does; at least, it captures an important way in which *some* central normative facts depend on agency. The final section, "Further Connections and Topics," briefly connects the Constraint to further putative connections between normativity and agency present in the literature, and sketches some avenues for further exploration.

NORMATIVITY AND AGENCY: SOME BASICS

We can distinguish various normative phenomena. One broad but helpful contrast is between "formal" *versus* "robust" normativity. What it is for a standard S to be formally normative is for S to be such that one can violate it, or make a mistake by its lights (McPherson 2011: 232). For example, traffic rules and various rules of games are formally normative in this sense. Formal normativity is cheap: we can create new formally normative standards simply by inventing violable rules.

Robust normativity is a seemingly more important phenomenon that many take to be associated with *normative reasons*. Normative reasons for a response Φ are facts or true propositions, *p*, that genuinely justify, favor, or call for that response, at least *pro tanto*. The fact that a tree fell on my neighbor calls for my response of helping him. (Here, the fact, *p*, that is the reason to help is the ordinary non-normative fact that a tree fell on my neighbor. It's the further fact *that p is a reason for me to help* that is a normative fact, and *p*'s property of *being a reason for action* is the normative property. Cf. Dancy 2006: 137, Parfit 2011 Vol. 2: 330–331.) If I failed to help, I would not only be violating a formally normative standard—the "reasons standard," as we might call it (McPherson 2011: 232)—but moreover, I'd be violating a standard that has special *authority* or *normative importance* (McPherson 2011: 233). At least, I'd be violating such a standard by failing to help if my reasons to help were *decisive*, so that I *ought* to help, in a robustly normative sense. Whether we act as we have (decisive) reasons to act seems somehow more important than whether we follow or violate the rules of any old game. 'Robust normativity', 'normative authority', and 'normative importance' are labels for this intuitively familiar but difficult-to-characterize type of normativity that is more important than mere formal normativity.

It's robust normativity in particular whose connection to agency I'll discuss. I'll mostly focus on normative reasons and connected ought-facts, assuming with much of the literature that these are central robustly normative phenomena; the section "Agency and Deliberative Open Questions" also discusses the property of *being good for a person*, where this property is linked to reasons in a particular way. I'll stay neutral regarding whether some reasons and oughts have a distinctively *moral* flavor. And I'll focus on reasons for *action*, and oughts concerning actions, where actions are paradigmatic exercises of agency; leaving aside reasons for belief or emotion.

What, then, is agency in the relevant sense? It's not just being a *self-mover*, in the Aristotelian sense of a being that has its principle of movement within itself. Cockroaches are self-movers, since unlike (say) fallen leaves, they can move under their own steam, without being pushed by external forces such as wind. Our concern is with *minimally rational* agency—agency that's rational in the sense of contrasting with *non*-rational—in its various guises: practical reasoning, acting on the basis of considerations, reflecting about what one ought to do and acting on one's subsequent normative judgments. (This is a mere characterization to get an intuitive grip on the phenomenon; not a purported definition.) I'll call minimally rational agency simply 'agency'. When agents perform some agential activity such as practical reasoning *well*, they perform it in accordance with whatever its proper standards of excellence are. I'll say that these agents are being "rational" (in some respect), where the relevant sense of rationality contrasts with *irra-tionality*. "Fully rational" agents are hypothetical agents purged of all irrationalities. Different ways of connecting normativity to agency focus on slightly different agential phenomena. I'll comment on the different foci as we go.

A final orienting remark. In assuming that there are robustly normative facts, I assume the falsity of important versions of normative nihilism and error theory, on which there are no such facts even if we talk as if there are. But I *don't* assume that robustly normative facts are mind-independent or agency-independent: precisely not. They might be constructed out of, or constituted by, actual or hypothetical psychological facts, or bear some more modest connection(s) to agents' minds. This is an important terminological warning, as the term 'robust' is sometimes used for a kind of "realism" about normative facts on which they're radically mind-independent (Enoch 2011, FitzPatrick 2008). It's a substantive, disputed question what degree of mind-dependence or independence is needed for capturing 'robust' normativity in the sense of normative authority or importance. In examining forms of agency-dependence below, we examine, in part, this disputed question. (For error theory, see Jonas Olson's chapter "Error Theory in Metaethics." For realism, see David Enoch's chapter "Non-Naturalistic Realism in Metaethics," Peter Railton's chapter "Naturalistic Realism in Metaethics," and Billy Dunaway's chapter "Realism and Objectivity.")

AGENCY AND DELIBERATIVE OPEN QUESTIONS

How, then, might robust normativity be connected to agency? *Normative judgment internalism* holds that *judgments* about (putative) normative facts bear a necessary connection to agency—specifically, to motivation (see David Faraci and Tristram McPherson's chapter "Ethical Judgment and Motivation"). On a popular way of fleshing out this idea, necessarily, if one sincerely judges that one ought to Φ, then if one is fully rational, one is motivated (to some extent) to Φ. However, our concern isn't primarily with normative *judgments* and their connection to agency, but with agency and normative *facts* (and the normative *properties* ingredient in those facts). So I set aside normative judgment internalism here.

Still, normative reflection about what one ought to do or has reason to do is plausibly, itself, one kind of exercise of agency, especially if it's such as to engender motivation or action. And some have suggested that such exercises of agency bear an important general connection to normative facts, of roughly the following form:

OQA If the question whether X is F—where F is some normative predicate—remains open from the perspective of idealized normative reflection, then this impugns the claim that X is F. (The details of the idealization depend on the theorist.)

There's a trivially true version of OQA. If the relevant reflective perspective is idealized to include a grasp of the normative truths about whether X is F (and if either X is F or X isn't F), and if the question whether X is F remains open from that perspective, then it's not the case that X is F. But is there a plausible non-trivial version of OQA? This section examines two prominent proposals to the effect that there is: Christine Korsgaard's (1996) and Connie Rosati's (2003). While I cast some doubt on each, Rosati's proposal points us towards questions about agency, normativity, and normative thought that deserve much further exploration.

Korsgaard's discussion of normative reasons is framed by a familiar skeptical doubt that can afflict agents within normative reflection. If your confidence has been shaken in whether some fact, *p*—say, that morality requires you to Φ—really is a reason for you to Φ, then we cannot shore up your confidence merely by pointing to putative reasons out there, without heed to what you think (1996: 34–40). Shoring up your confidence requires engaging your own deepest commitments, including, ultimately, the commitments constitutive of reflective agency as such; and showing that *p* is a reason *as judged from the perspective of those commitments* (1996: 93ff). Otherwise, thorough and clear-eyed normative reflection will always leave it an open question for you whether *p* really is a reason. And Korsgaard thinks that such open questions impugn *p*'s status as a reason. Reasons are hostage to reflective agents' verdicts (1996: 16, 92–94 *et passim*):

OQA-K: If the question whether *p* is a reason for A to Φ remains open, as judged from the perspective of A's deepest commitments, including commitments constitutive of reflective agency, then this impugns the claim that *p* is a reason for A to Φ.

However, it remains unclear in Korsgaard's treatment why we should accept OQA-K. Korsgaard uses OQA-K to reject "substantive realist" views on which reasons exist, regardless of whether they speak to our commitments, and to argue for a Kantian constructivist view on which reasons are a function of agents' deepest commitments. (On constructivism, see Melissa Barry's chapter "Constructivism.") But why think that deliberative open questions are problematic in the way that Korsgaard thinks? We need some reason to think that a clear-eyed working out of the implications of our deepest commitments, even commitments constitutive of reflective agency, doesn't or can't itself embody or engender normative error, or leave room for failures to grasp normative facts that obtain regardless. (Cf. Enoch 2006.)

To be sure, it would be disturbing if clear-eyed normative reflection, regardless of its starting points, *necessarily* left us out of touch with an important portion of normative reality. We may have *prima facie* reason to defend a view of normativity on which this isn't the case. But we can reject OQA-K while holding that some contingent commitments lead to the right normative views *via* clear-eyed normative reflection. There may be *a* route to normative truth *via* normative reflection, even if not every agent's deepest commitments furnish such a route (cf. FitzPatrick 2008: 177–178). Of course, the easiest way to forge such a route is by building in a grasp of general normative truths or values into the relevant reflective perspective—a grasp that some agents may be lucky to have acquired, perhaps through good moral education (ibid.). Again, this front-loads normative truths into the relevant reflective perspective, without seeming to provide any interesting agency-related constraint on normativity.

In sum, we lack a good argument for OQA-K, and while it may seem partly supported by a felt need to view normative facts as not ineluctably outside of agents' reflective reach, OQA-K isn't needed to satisfy this putative need.

Rosati (2003) employs a different version of OQA, arguing that extant naturalist accounts of the property *being good for a person* fail because they leave open questions within fully autonomous, empirically well-informed normative reflection. Take the view that *being good for a person* is some natural property N—say, *being pleasurable*. Rosati's OQA is supposed to challenge such views, and also help us diagnose what goes wrong with them. Specifically, it purports to help us identify "some feature of our notion *good for person A* that the proposed account misses and that cannot [...] be abandoned without sacrificing our ability to ask and answer the questions that ordinarily concern us when we wonder what is good for us" (2003: 501). The feature of personal good that we mustn't abandon is, roughly, its "fit" with our capacity for autonomous normative reflection and subsequent action (2003: 507). As I read Rosati, the presence of open questions within autonomous reflection is supposed to indicate failure to secure the requisite "fit." In particular, if the question whether X is good for us, given that X is N, remains open within fully autonomous and empirically well-informed normative reflection, then the relevant "fit" hasn't been secured, and the account of personal good as Nness must be rejected (ibid.). Generalized for any robustly normative property F and property N:

OQA-R If the question whether X is F given that X is N remains open within fully autonomous and empirically well-informed normative reflection—so that Fness, on the account of it as Nness, doesn't "fit" with our capacity for autonomous reflection—then this impugns the claim that X really is F (even though X is N) (thereby impugning the theory that Fness is Nness).

To clarify, Rosati isn't proposing an account of personal good in terms of autonomous reflection, but a necessary condition on accounts of personal good: an adequate account must construe personal good as "fitting" with our agency so as to close the relevant reflective question (2003: 519; cf. Rosati 2016). OQA-R forces us to refine our accounts if, in their present forms, they fail to secure the requisite "fit" (2003: 524). (Notice that nothing in Rosati's challenge turns on N's being a natural property. Cf. Rosati 2003: 517.)

Why think that such a "fit" with agency *is* a necessary condition on personal good (or on some other normative property F)? Recall Rosati's claim that without the relevant "fit," we sacrifice "our ability to ask and answer the questions that ordinarily concern us when we wonder what is good for us" (2003: 501, 507). Let's unpack this idea.

As I read Rosati, our "ordinary concern" with personal good has two related facets that together require the relevant "fit" with agency. First, in wondering what's good for A, we're partly concerned with what we have reason to do, or ought to do (2003: 516–520). In ordinary thought and talk about personal good, there are "inferential links" between propositions about personal good and about reasons and obligations: for instance, if X is good for me, I have "at least a *[pro tanto]* reason to obtain X;" and "others have at least a *[pro tanto]* obligation to support" my efforts to obtain X (2003: 517). A second, related facet is that judgments of personal good, and related judgments about reasons and obligations, "function as regular guides to action and attitude" (2003: 520). And they do so not by merely causing bodily movements or attitudes, but *via* engaging those reflective, critical capacities that make us self-governing, autonomous agents (2003: 518, 520). It's through autonomous normative reflection that we can step back from a moment's impulse and ask what we really have reason to do, or ought to do, and be moved accordingly. (Judgments about wrongness plausibly enjoy similar inferential links, and a similar action-guiding role; if so, Rosati's argument should generalize to some extent. Cf. Rosati 2016.)

Rosati infers that the "content" of propositions about personal good must be "such as to engage [our] autonomy-making motives and capacities" (2003: 518–519).[1] Our account of these propositions' content must make sense of why judgments about personal good engage our autonomous agency by engendering related judgments about reasons and obligations, and by motivating action (ibid.). Rosati further infers that accounts of the *property* of *being good for a person* shouldn't "leave it mysterious why" the relevant features of ordinary thought and talk obtain (2003: 517, 522). The truth-makers for propositions about personal good should help explain why judgments about personal good exhibit the highlighted inferential and action-regulating behaviors. This, I take it, is the relevant "fit" with our agency that accounts of personal good should secure.

Suppose Rosati is right about the need for such a "fit." What does this have to do with reflective open questions? The presence of such open questions is supposed to indicate that the relevant "fit" is missing. To illustrate how, Rosati considers a toy account of personal good as blueness. While something's being good for me provides me with a reason to pursue it, and I would generally judge as much within autonomous reflection, autonomous and empirically well-informed agents can reasonably doubt whether they have any "reason to pursue [their] good as specified by an account of personal goodness as blueness" (2003: 518). The judgment that X is blue doesn't generally engender the judgment that one has reason to pursue X, nor, relatedly, does it engender motivation to pursue X, within autonomous reflection. Personal good construed as blueness palpably fails to engage our autonomous agency in the way that personal good is supposed to do. The account of personal good as blueness accordingly seems to do nothing to explain the inferential and action-regulating behaviors of judgments of personal good as made by autonomous agents. I take it that this is how the presence of open questions is supposed to indicate that a proposed account fails to secure the relevant "fit" with autonomous agency.

Moving beyond toy accounts, Rosati presses the same problem against accounts of personal good as pleasure, or as a function of informed desires (2003: 518–519). Rosati suggests that we can close the troublesome reflective questions only by construing personal good as a "relational property" that's partly defined in terms of "some connection to what makes persons self-governing actors" (2003: 521). Rosati suggests that a dispositional theory on which *being good for a person* is "roughly, the property of being such as to be approved by us when our autonomy-making motives and capacities operate effectively and other appropriate conditions obtain," might do the trick (2003: 520).

Rosati's argument deserves more discussion than I can provide here. One worry is that it's unclear how the suggested dispositional theory *does* close reflective questions. Can't a fully autonomous, empirically well-informed agent find it an open question whether X is good for A even though X is such as to be approved by her when her "autonomy-making motives and capacities operate effectively and other appropriate conditions obtain" (ibid.)? One might, after all, doubt whether one's autonomy-making motives and capacities make one approve of the right things. It's unclear why mere empirical information and autonomy would dispel the doubt. (Cf. Enoch 2006: 178, 180–185.) (Of course, much may depend on what "appropriate conditions" are.)

However, the presently most relevant worry concerns the role of open questions in Rosati's argument. What's ultimately important for Rosati seems to be just the claim that personal good should "fit" with our agency, helping to explain why judgments of personal good, as made by autonomous agents, exhibit the inferential and action-regulating behaviors they do. This demand for a "fit" may be apt, even if the presence of open questions doesn't always indicate that the "fit" is missing. Suppose that Fness is Nness, but that seeing why requires grasping a convoluted theoretical argument. And suppose that, having appreciated the argument, one can see that the account of Fness as Nness *does* help to explain the inferential and action-regulating behaviors of judgments about Fness. It's unclear why these suppositions couldn't be true and the relevant convoluted argument sound, even while fully autonomous, empirically well-informed agents can doubt whether something that is N is also F; and relatedly, can doubt whether something's being N gives one reasons to act. After all, full autonomy and empirical information presumably don't ensure grasp of the envisaged convoluted argument. Not having grasped the argument, one might fail to realize that something's being N amounts to its being F, and thus gives one reasons to act.

Of course, if full autonomy and empirical information *did* ensure grasp of the relevant argument, or belief in the account, then the question whether, given that X is N, X is F, *would* be closed within autonomous reflection. But this doesn't give us any independent grip on whether the account is true, or the envisaged argument sound. Either way, the presence or absence of open questions within autonomous reflection isn't a good adequacy test for accounts of Fness as Nness. Such open questions may function as a fallible heuristic device for directing attention to perceived shortcomings of an account. But whether the shortcomings are real or merely apparent depends on the availability of arguments that agents needn't, just in virtue of being autonomous and empirically well-informed, appreciate.

In sum, I doubt that OQA-R provides a true, non-trivial constraint on accounts of normative properties. If autonomy together with empirical information somehow ensures a grasp of an account of Fness as Nness, then the account trivially passes the test of OQA-R. But to establish the truth of the account, we still need an independent argument. On the other hand, autonomy and empirical information might not ensure a grasp of even a true account that helps to explain (in some non-obvious way) why judgments of personal good engage our agency in the ways they do. If so, reflective open questions don't tell against the account.

None of this challenges Rosati's argument that accounts of normative properties should "fit" with autonomous agency, doing something to explain why judgments about those properties engage agency in the ways they do. This argument deserves further attention. One question to consider in assessing it is whether the nature of *agency* might explain the inferential and action-regulating behaviors of normative judgments within autonomous reflection; perhaps the nature of normative properties needn't play any explanatory role (cf. Rosati 2003: 525–526). Further, our ordinary normative *concepts*, such as the concept of personal good or of a reason for action, might be inferentially articulated in a way that explains the relevant behaviors of judgments deploying those concepts, even if the properties that these concepts pick out can also be picked out by means of other concepts that lack the same inferential articulation, and even if the properties themselves don't explain the inferential and action-guiding behaviors of normative judgments. (See Matthew Chrisman's chapter "Conceptual Role Accounts of Meaning in Metaethics" for some relevant discussion.) Still, I suggest that these questions are best pursued separately from the concern with open questions.

THE DELIBERATIVE CONSTRAINT: DOUBTS, MERITS, AND CONCEPTUAL CHOICES[2]

OQA connects normativity to idealized normative reflection—idealized reflection on the explicitly normative question whether X is F. A different and common way to connect normativity to agency focuses on agents' deliberation in view of, and motivation by, the non-normative facts, *p*, whose status as reasons explicit normative questions can concern. For instance, Mark Schroeder proposes the "Deliberative Constraint" that when an agent "is reasoning well, the kinds of thing about which he should be thinking are his reasons" (2007: 26; cf. 33). Kieran Setiya sees it as a "harmlessly illuminating" starting point for further theorizing to construe reasons for A to Φ as premises for "sound reasoning to a desire or motivation to Φ whose further premises are available to A" (2014: 221). Jonathan Way says that it's "near platitudinous" that "a reason for you to Φ must be an appropriate premise for reasoning towards Φ-ing" (2015: 1). There are different ways to flesh out theses in this area. But the basic idea I'm interested in is that reasons are considerations that non-normatively well-informed good deliberation takes into account; and if the reasons are decisive, it's part of good deliberation to be moved to act on them, in the way that they support. In slightly more detail, and borrowing Schroeder's label:

> Deliberative Constraint:
> If p is a reason for A to Φ, then there's a possible course of non-normatively well-informed good deliberation such that, were A to undergo it, A would take p into account; and if p is a decisive reason to Φ, then it's part of the relevant course of good deliberation to be moved to Φ on the basis of p.

Those who explicitly articulate versions of the Constraint often see it as rather obvious. But even more often, the Constraint operates quietly in the background, unremarked-upon. Much of the literature on "existence internalism" about reasons is an example of this. (On internalism, see Errol Lord and David Plunkett's chapter "Reasons Internalism," and Paakkunainen forthcoming.) On Bernard Williams' (1981) famous internalist view, p is a reason for A to Φ only if there's a broadly instrumental "sound deliberative route" from A's "subjective motivational set" S—from A's current contingent set of desires, dispositions, and projects—to A's Φ-ing or being motivated to Φ on the basis of the consideration, p, that is the reason. Early influential critics of Williams take issue with the ideas that sound deliberation must start from merely contingent motivational elements, and that the standards of soundness in deliberation are merely instrumental, suggesting that soundness in deliberation may involve satisfying standards of Kantian universalization or ethical virtue that demand more than mere instrumental cogency (Korsgaard 1986, 1996, 2009; McDowell 1995). Neither Williams nor these critics, however, question the idea that reasons are premises in sound deliberation. Indeed, this is why they take the question of what sound deliberation involves to impact the fate of views about reasons.

Beyond debates over internalism, the background influence of the Constraint should be evident to anyone who goes looking for it in the vast literature on reasons for action. But we lack a good sense of why, if at all, the Constraint is true. Why should the normative support relations between considerations and the actions they support correspond to good deliberation, or to patterns of rational response to information? It's a fairly common view that the ultimate moral justifications of actions, as stated by general moral theories, aren't what morally good deliberation focuses on. Morally good deliberators are often moved by considerations of loyalty or love, such as "she's my wife," not by considerations such as "this act would maximize utility," or whatever the ultimate right-makers are supposed to be (Railton 1984). If normative reasons can't likewise be considerations that good, rationally excellent deliberation would ignore, it's unclear why.

Indeed, some have proposed examples that look to defeat the Constraint.

Surprise Party (paraphrased from Schroeder 2007: 33)

> The fact, *p*, that there's a surprise party waiting for Nate at home is a reason for Nate to go home, but only if Nate doesn't believe *p*. For while Nate loves successful surprise parties thrown in his honor, he hates unsuccessful ones: his believing *p* would destroy *p*'s status as a reason to go. Since taking *p* into account in deliberation requires at least believing *p*, whatever else it involves, *p* is a reason for Nate only if Nate doesn't take it into account in deliberation; and so only if Nate doesn't take it into account in good deliberation.

Deluded Belief (versions of this are in Markovits 2014: 41, Smith 2009: 523, Johnson 2003: 575)

> The fact, *p*, that I have the deluded belief that I'm Jesus is a reason for me to seek psychiatric help. But *p* is a fact, and so a reason, only if I don't believe it, and so only if I don't take it into account in deliberation. For were I to believe that I have the deluded belief that I'm Jesus—that is, were I to think of my belief that I'm Jesus *as* deluded—this would do away with my delusion.

Emergency Landing (paraphrased from Markovits 2014: 48)

> Captain Sullenberger performed a successful emergency landing of a commercial airliner on Hudson River. The fact, *p*, that so many lives were at stake was a decisive reason for Sullenberger to attempt emergency landing. But he didn't think about this reason on the way to performing the landing—and a good thing too, for he shouldn't have. Were he to have thought about it, he would likely have become very unnerved and endangered the success of the landing.

In *Surprise Party* and *Deluded Belief*, the putative reasons, *p*, are facts that A *can't* take into account in good deliberation without destroying their status as reasons, or as facts (and so as reasons).[3] In *Emergency Landing*, the putative reasons are ones that A *shouldn't* take into account; we might infer that it can't be part of good deliberation for A to take them into account and be moved by them. If the Constraint survives these examples, we must spell out why.

The rest of this section explains why these examples don't defeat the Constraint, and sketches a positive argument for the Constraint that seeks to explain its appeal.

Start with *Emergency Landing*. Plausibly the fact, *p*, about the lives at stake is a reason, indeed a *decisive* reason, for Sullenberger to attempt emergency landing. For given *p*, Sullenberger definitely *ought* to attempt it, in the robustly normative sense. Sullenberger would be failing an important authoritative demand on him if he didn't attempt landing but, say, started doing crossword puzzles instead. However, even if Sullenberger would likely get dangerously unnerved by considering the reason-giving fact, *p*, it doesn't follow that it wouldn't be good deliberation if he took *p* into account and were thereby moved to act in the way that *p* supports. It merely shows that Sullenberger is unlikely to deliberate well, given his nerves. (Compare: it's no part of Williams' internalism to deny that agents can fail, or be likely to fail, to undergo the sound deliberative routes to which their reasons correspond.)

Of course, if one is very likely to get unnerved by considering the reason-giving facts, perhaps in some sense one ought to ignore them. Still, this is a case where one ought, in some sense of 'ought', to not deliberate well; not a case of reasons for action that good deliberation would ignore. It's intuitively a case of good deliberation, a recognizably rational response to the fact about lives at stake, to attempt emergency landing on the basis of one's appreciation of that fact. The possibility of irrational or non-rational responses to the reason-giving facts shouldn't obscure this point.

Further reflection on the case supports rather than challenges the Constraint. The lives at stake are a reason for the *whole* action of attempting landing. Once this action is in progress, more relevant are facts about how specific maneuvers will affect the plane's behavior, about what one needs to communicate to whom, etc. These further facts are reasons for sub-actions, the actions by means of which one lands. It's to be expected that good deliberation while the landing is in progress focuses on these further facts, and doesn't dwell on the initial reason to attempt landing. And surely it *is* intuitively a case of good deliberation to take account of these further facts as one is landing, and to be moved by them to perform the maneuvers that they support. Certainly, this is intuitively better deliberation than choosing one's maneuvers based on, say, facts about today's crossword puzzle, or about the state of the stock market.

One might object that these claims are hard to assess without a specific account of "good deliberation" in view. Further, if good deliberation is just a matter of responding to the reason-giving facts by doing what they support, then the Constraint looks trivial and uninformative.

In response, it is indeed part of the operative notion of good deliberation that it involves taking account of the reason-giving facts, and responding to them by doing what they support. The Constraint isn't supposed to link reasons to some notion of good deliberation that's completely independent of the idea of appropriate responsiveness to one's reasons. Instead, the Constraint articulates a dependence between two putatively interconnected notions: normative reasons for action, on the one hand, and rational responsiveness to the considerations that are the reasons, on the other. In doing so, it articulates (part of) a *conception of reasons as linked to such rational responsiveness*. As we've seen, one might doubt this conception: one might doubt that reasons, as properly conceived, need correspond to anything that looks like an intuitively rational response to the reason-giving facts. Examples such as *Surprise Party* and *Deluded Belief* make this most evident. Further, the idea of rational responsiveness to the reason-giving facts isn't empty. We have some grasp of when a response to considering some facts is a rational one, and when it's an irrational or non-rational one. One can deploy this grasp in assessing my claims about the *Emergency Landing* case, above.

Of course, there's a sense in which, *if* we accept the conception of reasons that the Constraint articulates, then the Constraint will look trivial as applied to reasons thus conceived. But the question of interest is whether and why we should accept the conception; or whether there's some good reason, based perhaps on some independent, contrary intuitions concerning normative reasons, to reject the conception. Thus far I've argued, in effect, that *Emergency Landing*-style cases provide no good basis for rejecting the conception of reasons as linked to good deliberation.

None of this rules out that "good deliberation" can be further precisified. Does it involve normative ascent—thinking of the reason-giving facts under a normative guise, *as* reasons? Does it proceed in accord with an instrumental rule of deliberation, such that one is moved by those considerations that reveal courses of action as promoting the objects of one's desires? There may be good arguments for some such precisifications—perhaps partly based on what deliberation as such can involve. For example, if deliberation as such can only take an instrumental form, the same applies to good deliberation. If the Constraint holds, such further constraints on good deliberation are also constraints on reasons. Still, we can make some progress in assessing the basic idea of the Constraint without examining such further precisifications.

What, then, of cases such as *Surprise Party* and *Deluded Belief*? In these cases, there's supposed to be no such thing as responding rationally to the reason-giving facts, while the relevant reasons are in force. If so, some reasons violate the Constraint. If we find this verdict intuitive, we find in these cases some intuitive basis for rejecting the Constraint's conception of reasons.

However, we should consider different interpretations of our intuitive reactions to these cases. In *Surprise Party*, there's clearly something to be said for Nate's going home. But it's unclear why we should interpret this intuition as indicating the presence of the specific alleged normative reason for Nate to go, instead of indicating (merely) some other normative or evaluative phenomena. The relevant fact, *p*, might be an explanatory reason, one that explains why Nate's going home would be a good outcome from the perspective of Nate's preference-satisfaction. Or it might be a normative reason for Nate's friends to urge him to go; or a normative reason for Nate to be glad, should he end up home: a reason for an affective response, should a pleasant outcome occur. The fact that Nate would be glad if he went might itself be a reason for Nate to go, a reason that Nate *can* take into account and act on. (*Mutatis mutandis* for *Deluded Belief*.) These hypotheses are all compatible with the Constraint. It's not pre-theoretically clear that we should adopt an anti-Constraint interpretation of the cases instead. Our tendencies to apply the word 'reason' may, if unexamined, elide important distinctions between different normative or evaluative notions that the Constraint actually helps us mark. And even if we think, say, that agents' reasons are ultimately a function of their preference-satisfaction—even a function that allows for violations of the Constraint—this is a theoretical claim that's at least as controversial as the Constraint.

If so, the examples on their own don't defeat the Constraint. Still, is there a good positive argument for the Constraint, and so for interpreting the examples in Constraint-friendly ways?

The rest of this section sketches an argument that there are certain key jobs in theorizing and in everyday normative practice that the notion of reasons is often pressed to perform, and that these jobs are best performed by reasons as conceived by the Constraint. This leaves open that there are other important theoretical or everyday jobs that only some incompatible conception of reasons can perform. But if so, we should be explicit about what these jobs are.

Recall that part of what's important about reasons is their connection to normative authority. If A has decisive reasons to Φ, then A ought to Φ, in the robustly normative sense; decisive reasons pose authoritative demands. A qualification: some reasons, even if not overweighed by contrary reasons, might merely "entice" or recommend (Dancy 2004: 21). Still, it's an important job for the notion of reasons that some reasons can impose authoritative demands. Consider disputes about morality's authority. These disputes usually proceed on the assumption that moral requirements have authority on A if, and only if, A has some normative reason to do what morality requires. Part of the thought is that, without such reasons, A is free to take or leave morality as a guide to action. However, if even strong reasons to abide by moral requirements left it entirely normatively optional whether to do so—as they would, if they merely recommended without demanding anything—this wouldn't be much of a vindication of morality's authority. We would *still* be free to take or leave morality as a guide to action. This suggests that the operative conception of reasons in disputes about morality's authority is, at least implicitly, one on which reasons can impose not just recommendations but demands. And plausibly, this concern with "reasons to be moral" has roots in common-sense concerns about morality's authority. There are important theoretical and everyday jobs for a conception of reasons as capable of imposing authoritative demands.

The Constraint is plausibly a condition of making sense of reasons as imposing authoritative demands. This is because of a link between authoritative demands and *reasonable expectations*. If the facts in a situation demand of A that she Φ, then there must be some possible condition, X, that A might be in in the situation, such that if A encounters the situation while in that condition, then we can reasonably expect of A that she will Φ. The relevant notion of reasonable expectations is partly predictive, partly normative. The predictive part is that, if A is in condition X in a situation, it's predictable that A will end up doing precisely what the facts in the situation demand of her: condition X *well-equips* A to meet authoritative demands. Without some such possible condition X, the idea that A is under an authoritative demand to Φ seems to lapse. A might of course happen, by sheer accident, to do precisely Φ. And we might apply some positive evaluative predicate to such happy accidents. But authoritative demands to Φ require that there be some possible condition that A might be in (even if she's not in that condition, in fact) that well-equips A to meet those demands. So it seems to me.

Here is the normative aspect of the notion of reasonable expectations: if A is under an authoritative demand to Φ, then it must be reasonable to demand it *of* her that she Φs, and to criticize her if she fails to Φ—at least absent excusing conditions. (For instance, non-culpable ignorance of relevant non-normative facts plausibly excuses.) The condition X that well-equips A to meet authoritative demands must be of a type that makes sense of the appropriateness of such criticism. And roughly, it seems that A is criticizable only for what she does or fails to do under her own steam, *via* the exercise of her capacities for agency. We no more criticize A for involuntary non-rational twitches than we criticize rocks for their behavior—even though there are conditions of rocks that well-equip them for certain behaviors in certain circumstances. It seems, then, that X must be some deliberative condition of A's: a condition in which A acts on considerations, takes in information, and makes choices in its light, in a way aptly describable as an exercise of agency.

In sum, X must be (a) a possible deliberative condition of A's that (b) well-equips A to do precisely what the facts in the circumstance demand of her. Without some such X, the facts in the circumstance can't demand anything of A. What deliberative condition X best satisfies (b)? The obvious answer is the condition of deliberating well, where this involves taking account of the facts that impose the relevant demands, and being moved on their basis to do what they demand. It's certainly harder to see why deliberating *badly* (e.g., drawing bizarre conclusions from relevant reason-giving facts), or taking into account only facts that do nothing to support Φ-ing, would generally lead agents to Φ whenever the reasons so demand.

While the argument is abstract, its conclusion isn't surprising. It's *prima facie* odd to think that the facts in a situation might authoritatively demand A to Φ, even though no possible rational response to those facts would lead A to Φ on their basis. We usually think there's a point to trying to figure out facts relevant to what we should do before making important decisions, and to trying to make our decisions in light of those facts. We expect deliberating well in light of the reason-giving facts to help us to do what we should do (cf. Schroeder 2007: 132). The argument above gives some explanation of why decisive reasons and connected oughts are linked to good deliberation in these intuitive ways.

The argument is merely a sketch. A proper treatment would respond to objections, consider different types of reasons, and so on. (For instance, if there are "ultimate" and "derivative" reasons, perhaps good deliberation need only take account of one or the other; cf. Star 2015.) Recall, too, that the argument leaves room for alternative conceptions of reasons that deny the Constraint. For all I've said, there may be further important theoretical and everyday jobs that reasons can perform only on some such alternative conception. If so, we should spell out these jobs. Either way, I doubt we can resolve disputes about reasons without such explicit attention to issues of conceptual choice, and solely on the basis of attending to when we're willing to deploy the term 'normative reason' in imagined, or even real life, cases.[4]

I've argued that we have intuitive need for the Constraint's conception of reasons as linked to the agential activity of good deliberation. The next section briefly connects the Constraint to further putative connections between agency and normativity, and suggests some topics for further exploration.

FURTHER CONNECTIONS AND TOPICS

The Constraint states a necessary connection between reasons and agency, but the connection is fairly modest. It assumes nothing about the contours of good deliberation beyond its involving rational responsiveness to, and motivation in light of, the reason-giving facts. Nor does it assume that agents have a current motivational propensity to undergo the good deliberative routes to which their reasons correspond, only that there's a possible world in which they do so, while the reasons remain in force. But we might wonder whether the argument for the Constraint supports a stronger thesis. Specifically, if A isn't aptly criticizable for failures to Φ for the reason that *p*, where Φ-ing for this reason is outside of A's current motivational reach, this may suggest a stronger, "internalist" constraint on reasons. (Cf. Lord 2015 for a somewhat similar argument for an ability condition and a further epistemic condition on reasons.)

Whether the argument might be so extended depends in part on which conditions merely excuse from otherwise reasonable criticism, and which ones make the criticism, and the associated demand to Φ, lapse. Where the absence of appropriate motivational propensities merely excuses, the demand, and so the reasons that impose it, may stay in force. This would allow that thoroughly vicious people have decisive reasons to act in non-vicious ways, even if they lack the current motivational wherewithal to do so. Further, if it's reasonable to criticize mature agents for failures to acquire non-vicious motivational tendencies, lacking those tendencies might not even excuse. Whatever the case may be, I suggest that the precise contours of the link between reasons and good deliberation depend partly on such questions about excuses and reasonable criticism.

One notable consequence of the Constraint is that the Advice Model of reasons is inadequate as a model of reasons capable of imposing authoritative demands. On the Advice Model, there's (decisive) reason for A to Φ (if and) only if A+, A's fully rational and non-normatively fully informed counterpart, would, after thinking about what A is to do, *advise* A to Φ. But A+ wouldn't be moved to Φ, herself (Smith 1995). The Advice Model allows that there may be *no* version of A who is moved to Φ by rationally considering A's reasons to Φ. Since reasons in the sense associated with authoritative demands require that there be such a version of A, the Advice Model fails as a conception of reasons in this sense.

The mistake is inherited by theories of reasons that build on the Advice Model without incorporating the Constraint, such as Smith's constitutivism (2015). Smith's constitutivism seeks to ground reasons in the nature of ideal agency, where the advisor, A+, is an ideal agent. Whatever else this ideal involves, if it *doesn't* involve responsiveness to reasons by doing what those reasons demand, we should reject the account as an account of reasons as capable of imposing authoritative demands. Other constitutivists may fare better in this regard: Velleman (2009) and Korsgaard (1996, 2009) both seem to accept versions of the Constraint, at least implicitly. Whether their brands of constitutivism are otherwise adequate is of course a further question. (On constitutivism, see Michael Smith's chapter "Constitutivism.")

There is surely some need for a conception of reasons as figuring in well-informed advisors' advice. One important open question in this area is the extent to which reasons, as figuring in advice, *must* come apart from reasons as imposing authoritative demands: can we capture reasons' intuitive role in advice compatibly with the Constraint? Or will only some incompatible conception of reasons do? However we end up answering these questions, the Constraint, while modest, is an important choice point in much theorizing about reasons; and captures a central way in which some important normative phenomena depend on agency.

NOTES

1. Rosati assumes a form of cognitivism about normative judgments. On cognitivism, see Matthew S. Bedke's chapter "Cognitivism and Non-Cognitivism;" cf. Matthew Chrisman's chapter "Conceptual Role Accounts of Meaning in Metaethics."
2. This section draws on a more detailed treatment in Paakkunainen (ms).
3. We might doubt that reasons are facts or true propositions, but I'll continue to assume this with much of the literature I'm engaging.
4. Thanks to David Plunkett and Daniel Star for helpful discussion here.

ACKNOWLEDGMENTS

I'm grateful to David Sobel, Nate Sharadin, Ben Bradley, Daniel Star, Kim Frost, Tristram McPherson, and David Plunkett for extremely helpful discussion and feedback, and to the Murphy Institute's Center for Ethics and Public Affairs at Tulane for supporting part of the work on this chapter.

RELATED TOPICS

Chapter 1, "Non-Naturalistic Realism in Metaethics;" Chapter 2, "Naturalistic Realism in Metaethics;" Chapter 20, "Reasons Internalism;" Chapter 23, "Constitutivism;" Chapter 24, "Constructivism."

REFERENCES

Dancy, J. 2004. *Ethics Without Principles*. Oxford: Oxford University Press.

Dancy, J. 2006. Nonnaturalism. In Copp, D. (ed.) *Oxford Handbook of Ethical Theory*, 122–145. Oxford: Oxford University Press.

Enoch, D. 2006. Agency, Shmagency: Why Normativity Won't Come from What Is Constitutive of Action. *The Philosophical Review* 115: 169–198.

Enoch, D. 2011. *Taking Morality Seriously: A Defense of Robust Realism*. Oxford: Oxford University Press.

FitzPatrick, W. 2008. Robust Ethical Realism, Non-Naturalism and Normativity. In Shafer-Landau, R. (ed.) *Oxford Studies in Metaethics*, Vol. 3: 159–205. Oxford: Oxford University Press.

Johnson, R. 2003. Internal Reasons: Reply to Brady, Van Roojen and Gert. *The Philosophical Quarterly* 53: 573–580.

Korsgaard, C. M. 1986. Skepticism about Practical Reason. *The Journal of Philosophy* 83: 5–25.

Korsgaard, C. M. 1996. *The Sources of Normativity*. Cambridge: Cambridge University Press.

Korsgaard, C. M. 2009. *Self-Constitution: Agency, Identity, and Integrity*. Oxford: Oxford University Press.

Lord, E. 2015. Acting for the Right Reasons, Abilities, and Obligation. In Shafer-Landau, R. (ed.) *Oxford Studies in Metaethics*, Vol. 10. Oxford: Oxford University Press.

McDowell, J. 1995. Might There Be External Reasons? In Altham, J.E.J. and Harrison, R. (eds.) *World, Mind, and Ethics*. Cambridge: Cambridge University Press.

McPherson, T. 2011. Against Quietist Normative Realism. *Philosophical Studies* 154: 223–240.

Markovits, J. 2014. *Moral Reason*. Oxford: Oxford University Press.

Paakkunainen, H. Forthcoming. Internalism and Externalism about Reasons. In Star, D. (ed.) *Oxford Handbook of Reasons and Normativity*. Oxford: Oxford University Press.

Paakkunainen, H. (ms) Can There Be Government House Reasons for Action?

Parfit, D. 2011. *On What Matters*. Oxford: Oxford University Press.

Railton, P. 1984. Alienation, Consequentialism, and the Demands of Morality. *Philosophy and Public Affairs* 13: 134–171.

Rosati, C. 2003. Agency and the Open Question Argument. *Ethics* 113: 490–527.

Rosati, C. 2016. Agents and "Shmagents": An Essay on Agency and Normativity. In Shafer-Landau, R. (ed.) *Oxford Studies in Metaethics*, Vol. 11. Oxford: Oxford University Press.

Schroeder, M. 2007. *Slaves of the Passions*. Oxford: Oxford University Press.

Setiya, K. 2014. What Is a Reason to Act? *Philosophical Studies* 167: 221–235.

Smith, M. 1995. Internal Reasons. *Philosophy and Phenomenological Research* 55: 109–131.

Smith, M. 2009. Reasons With Rationalism After All. *Analysis* 69: 521–530.

Smith, M. 2015. The Magic of Constitutivism. *American Philosophical Quarterly* 52: 187–200.

Star, D. 2015. *Knowing Better: Virtue, Deliberation, and Normative Ethics*. Oxford: Oxford University Press.

Velleman, J. D. 2009. *How We Get Along*. Cambridge: Cambridge University Press.

Way, J. 2015. Reasons as Premises of Good Reasoning. *Pacific Philosophical Quarterly* 97(2): 1–20.

Williams, B. 1981. Internal and External Reasons. In Williams, *Moral Luck*. Cambridge: Cambridge University Press.

26

Mores and Morals: Metaethics and the Social World

Kenneth Walden

Anyone who has taught an introductory ethics course has found themselves having to explain that some important words can be used in different ways. There is the way social scientists talk when they refer to the *norms* of a Balinese cockfight, the *values* of early modern scientific culture, and the *morality* of Bolsheviks. And then there is the philosophers' use of the same words when they talk about the normativity of rationality, the value of persons, and the moral law.

How should we explain this duality? There are a few very simple answers. One is to say that words like "norm" and "moral" are polysemous. They have separate, unrelated meanings in the mouths of social scientists and philosophers. A second is that these uses are related, but indexed to different perspectives: one descriptive and one normative. Whereas the social scientist is describing the culture and customs of the Bolsheviks or Balinese, the philosopher is prescribing or evaluating them (Gert 2002). A third answer makes gestures about reality and appearance. The social scientists' words describe beliefs or opinions or maybe even theories about the things denoted by the philosophers. So while it is true that the Balinese take themselves to have certain reasons regarding cock-fighting, that early modern scientists valued things like intellectual self-sufficiency, and that compromise is immoral for Bolsheviks, there are further questions—philosophical questions—about whether cock-fighting considerations are *genuinely* normative, self-sufficiency is *actually* valuable, and compromise is *really* immoral. These are the questions that moral philosophers ask.

All three of these answers seem too simple. "Morality" is plainly not polysemous in the way "bank" is: its meanings are not wholly unrelated. It may be polysemous in a more subtle way, as "sanguine" is. That is, the word may carry multiple meanings connected in some interesting way. But that possibility invites the question of what that connection is, which takes us back to where we started. The suggestion that one usage is descriptive and the other normative also seems misguided, for the norms of the Balinese cockfight are certainly normative *for the cockfighter*. They are not normative for the social scientist, but that's not a feature of the norms themselves; it's a feature of the social scientist's detached perspective. (However, one could deny that they are "robustly" normative in McPherson's [2011] sense.) The last option may be most plausible, but it also seems too simple. There is more to a group adhering to a norm than their *believing* or *accepting* that they have reasons to follow it, and it seems procrustean to characterize the morality of Russian revolutionaries as tantamount to a *theory* about the true nature of morality in the way that general relativity is a theory about space-time.

These problems may lead us to a more complicated answer, and possibly to one that brooks a more substantive and intimate connection between, as it were, mores and morals. That possibility is the subject of this chapter. But before turning to that work, we should record the familiar difficulties faced by proposals in this genus—problems that make the idea that morality may be closely tied to social mores an unpopular one amongst ethicists these days. These objections all involve our considered judgments about the nature of morality. When we say that something is good or bad, wrong or right, we probably don't think that we are expressing our community's conventions; we probably think we are trying to say something that *transcends* our community. We probably think systems of mores can themselves be evaluated, as when we say that the abolition of chattel slavery was a form of moral progress. And we probably doubt that moral facts are constituted by whatever chaotic forces shape our culture. Finally, we are appropriately reluctant about aligning a subject too closely with the social practices concerning that subject: we wouldn't want to take religious practices to be the final word on the metaphysics of God. (Russ Shafer-Landau [2003] develops some of these objections in greater detail.) Any answer to our question about the relationship between mores and morals that makes them too nearly coincident is likely to clash with these judgments and end up looking like a poor characterization of morality.

On the other hand, there are considerations that favor a close connection. One motivation is naturalism. Many philosophers attribute features to morality that are hard to fit into our scientific picture of the world. For example, many think that we have reasons to be moral even when it does not advance any particular end we have adopted, but the entities we would need to countenance to vindicate this supposition seem irremediably queer, and so it is hard to square their existence with a naturalistic conception of reality (Mackie 1977). But if we turn our attention to social practices, this concern looks exaggerated. The reasons these practices give us appear to have exactly the kind of character that this argument deems queer: I have a reason to queue in line even if it's not the most direct means to satisfying some end. And yet there is good reason to suppose that we can explain social practices without leaving the aegis of naturalism, so social practices are a potential model for explaining the same features in morality. (Perhaps Mackie would also find queerness here, but his skepticism looks all the more dubious if it forces us to believe that there are no such things as social practices.)

A second reason is that the norms of morality look and function an awful lot like the norms of social convention. They claim to tell us how to treat other people, purport to be unconditional, and don't seem easily reducible to norms of rationality or prudence. Naturally, few would agree that judgments like "you really mustn't leave Cindy to be eaten by that crazed manatee" are completely on par with ones like "you really mustn't wear a hat in the clubhouse." But it is notoriously difficult to find a durable, principled, and clean way of drawing this distinction. Proposals focusing on alleged asymmetries in scope, application conditions, or the properties invoked by moral and conventional judgments face serious problems (Southwood 2011; Letsas 2014). We needn't conclude from these difficulties that there is no difference between the moral and conventional. After all, children as young as three seem to have some sense of the dichotomy (Turiel 1983). But it does suggest that our explanation of *why* a given moral principle has normative force for an individual may overlap in significant ways with our understanding of the same force in conventional norms. This would both blur the line between the reasons provided by morality and those provided by convention and promise to make studying their entanglements profitable.

A third reason is that it is part of our very idea of morality that it is a social institution. (Or, more guardedly, it must be *realized by* such institutions.) Moral principles, rules, and ideals are internalized by communities and regulate the activity of their members. This happens in overt ways, like the enforcement of laws and formal conventions and the forms of rebuke and punishment that accompany that punishment. And it happens in more subtle ways: in the normalization of certain behaviors, the sifting and structuring of the options that an agent considers in her deliberations, and the advice that one friend gives another. These are not incidental features of morality, but ones we cite when we want to say what morality is. They are part of our *concept* morality if you like. Now, not everyone would agree with this conceptual claim. It was popular in the nineteenth century: different versions of the thought motivated Hegel (1991), Marx and Engels (1998), and Nietzsche (1998). But it was less so in the twentieth century: the analyses in, e.g., Frankena (1966) and Smith (1994) don't mention these features at all. Let's bracket this disagreement. If some version of the conceptual thesis is true, then the social function of morality may produce a substantive constraint on what morality can be, not unlike the constraint that some see motivational internalism placing on our conception of morality: morality must be the kind of thing that can play a particular role in regulating the social order.

A final reason is that we find features of the social world implicated in popular candidates for the basis of moral facts. I'll mention two examples. Emotions, feelings, and allied states are affected by culture, tradition, convention, and other social phenomena in obvious ways. But some social scientists have argued that these effects are more pervasive and systematic than we might realize. In a classic study, Arlie Russell Hochschild (2012) argues that certain professions demand the cultivation of distinctive and sincere emotional responses, and, as a result, acculturation into these professions involves the internalization of certain "feeling rules" and with them an enduring reshaping of the sentimental self. This study suggests a hypothesis: that certain crucial facts about such emotions, feelings, and allied attitudes—that we are capable of certain emotional responses at all, that particular stimuli regularly produce specific responses, that our emotional attitudes are associated with certain cognitive and motivational states—can only be explained by understanding their role in enabling and regulating particular social practices. If this is right, then sentiments are social entities. This conclusion has important consequences for those who believe that the sentiments of moral arbiters are part of the ground of moral facts. For when combined with our hypothesis, this view entails that moral facts are partially constituted by whatever social conditions shape our emotions.

A similar point can be made about agency. What agency amounts to would seem to vary from one social milieu to another. When we talk about those capacities possessed by the factory worker and the pre-historical forager that enable them to efficaciously control their actions, we are probably talking about rather different things. This isn't to say that they don't share a generic kind of agency, but it also seems theoretically defensible to talk about the different *forms* that agency can take when a person internalizes the practices, rules, and schemas of a given social structure. This is the attitude of most sociologists. For them, it is not a question of *whether* agency is realized in different ways within different social contexts, but *how* social structure and agency depend on each other. For example, according to Anthony Giddens's "structuration" theory (1986), social structures and individual agency stand in a relationship of mutual interaction. Structures are enacted by the behavior of agents, while agency is enabled and constrained by the same structures. This has important consequences for constitutivism, the idea that the constitutive requirements or aims of agency correspond to norms that have authority over agents, independent of their particular aims, desires, or ends. For if such norms can be derived in the way constitutivists suggest, and agency is shaped by social structure, then it seems possible that some practices and schemas that make up that structure will turn out to have precisely this normative force.

In this introductory section, I have offered a hodgepodge of reasons for and against a "substantive" connection between mores and morals. On balance, I think we have reason to take the idea seriously. Of course, I've been pretty vague about what I mean by "substantive." In what follows, I try to get more specific by considering what a "substantive" connection might obtain and how it might figure in debates within moral philosophy and metaethics. I will consider three issues. First, I examine the possibility that the social aspects of morality might tell us something important about what morality must be, and thus inform our metaethics. Second, I will make a case for a profitable engagement between metaethics and foundational questions about the social world. Finally, I will summarize how extant metaethical views might accommodate, and indeed gain support from, the social features of morality.

DOES THE SOCIAL FUNCTION OF MORALITY CONSTRAIN WHAT MORALITY IS?

The third reason I gave for supposing a more substantive connection between mores and morals was that it is part of our very idea of morality that it plays a certain role in society. This idea has motivated an important tradition in ethical theory. It would be too much to try to survey this entire tradition, so instead I want to pick out two proposals that represent two extremes for how tightly bound morality is to particular social arrangements. The first is a sober and relatively limited account from Kurt Baier; the second is a more fervent line of thought from Alasdair MacIntyre.

Baier (1995) says that to understand what morality is we must first understand the notion of a *moral order*. This he understands on the model of Hart's "legal order": as a social order that has additional structure and institutions. Baier criticizes a "Platonistic" tradition in philosophy that aims to describe an ideal version of such an order. The attraction of these ideals is that they promise univocal, unassailable answers on all moral questions. But this promise proves unfounded when we try to actually use the ideals and find that "bridging the gap" between them and moral questions is just as difficult as the questions themselves. Baier's alternative is to characterize the minimal conditions on a social order qualifying as a moral order. The key idea here is that a moral order is distinguished from an order of "Pure Custom" by having practices, offices, and institutions devoted to the *critique* and *regulation* of the mores of the society. Whereas a social order of Pure Custom operates by simply accepting mores as *how things are done here*, the moral order includes provisions for challenging and reforming those mores. There is no independent conception of how these challenges and reforms are to go, save that they are motivated by the demands of practical reason. This, too, Baier understands as an essentially social enterprise. For him, practical reason is the dialogical practice of giving, requesting, and accepting reasons. Like any other practice it must be transmitted through training, and it may be realized according to different customs and conventions in different social orders.

So Baier offers a conception of what morality is that interacts with the social in three distinct ways. First, the raw material that morality is supposed to regulate, our mores, are features of our social order. Second, the particular mechanisms of regulation—the offices of moral critic and moral reformer—are socially constructed. Finally, the process that guides this regulation, practical reason, is itself a particular practice that can vary from one social order to another. Without these connections, Baier suggests, a system would not be a *moral* system at all.

Suppose Baier is right about the need for these interfaces. Does anything of interest for metaethics follow? One potential consequence is moral relativism. If substantial variation amongst social orders with respect to any of these points of contact is possible, then "what are sound moral guidelines in one moral order may be unsound in another" (1995: 275). I don't think a particularly full-blooded form of relativism is in the offing here, however. A comparison between Baier's view and T. M. Scanlon's contractualism may be helpful. Scanlon distinguishes between relativism, according to which there are no universal moral principles whatsoever, no matter how general, and a view he calls "parametric universalism" (1998: 329). The latter brooks universal moral principles but maintains that the application of these principles can vary quite substantially depending on context. I think Baier's view is an instance of parametric universalism that takes features of social structure as essential parameters. Indeed, the final form that Baier thinks that moral regulation tends toward—an ideal of mores that codify what members of a society, when engaged in practical reason, would want from each other—is not so far from Scanlon's own contractualism. Scanlon says that "an act is wrong if its performance under the circumstances would be disallowed by any set of principles for the general regulation of behavior that no one could reasonably reject as a basis for informed, unforced, general agreement" (1998: 153). The major difference between Baier's view and Scanlon's contractualism concerns the standard of "reasonableness." Whereas Scanlon thinks it is an objective standard, Baier sees it as determined by the rational practices of a given society. In this way, Baier's view may be *more* relativistic than Scanlon's insofar as reasonableness is determined by a community's norms rather than matters of fact, but I don't think it entails a particularly radical form of the doctrine.

A second important consequence of Baier's view is the "teachability" of morality. The moral order is distinguished by its having particular social roles like moral critic and moral reformer. The existence of both these things depends on the training up of new generations in the appropriate rules and roles. Might this requirement rule out some otherwise promising moral theories? We might think it excludes theories on which moral expertise is a significant achievement, like Plato's, Aristotle's, or the Stoics'. We cannot count on training future generations to be sages, so there is no way moral judgment could depend on sage-like insight. But maybe we are assuming an overly simplistic model of moral instruction. There may be minimal rules that members of a society must internalize for that society to be a moral order, but the way to teach these rules may not be to drill children on them. It may instead involve training them in habits and dispositions, the *perfection* of which are the virtues. So I'm not sure that even these theories are excluded by the teachability requirement.

Teachability also involves a kind of publicity: everyone must understand the moral order and its structure well enough to play their part in its enactment. But this is a very weak kind of publicity, and it is hard to see what it would exclude. A moral order in which the true strictures of morality are known only by the illuminati, in which the hoi polloi are given dummy rules that will, given their limitations, allow them to best act enact the moral order—even *this* kind of order would seem to satisfy such a weak publicity requirement, since each person knows what they need to carry out their role. There is, however, a stronger notion of publicity. According to this condition, the *reasons* justifying morality for everyone subject to morality must be accessible to everyone and this accessibility must be common knowledge (Rawls 1999: 115). (For similar constraints see Gert [2005] and Gaus [2011].) Rawls proposes this as a condition on our conception of right, and uses it as a premise in his argument for the Original Position. The trouble with this stronger publicity requirement is that even though it is commonly associated with Baieresque accounts of social morality, I don't see any way of justifying it on grounds like those produced by Baier. The justification of social conventions and mores in general, much less common knowledge of this justification, is not required for these conventions to exist and perform the function Baier specifies. Indeed, many of these conventions and mores could be expressions of false consciousness and do their job just fine. There is no reason to think that matters would be any different for the particular social roles and institutions that distinguish a moral order. (What seems to do the crucial work for Rawls is a Kantian conception of public reason not entailed by Baier's picture.)

So much for Baier's social conception of morality and what it can do to constrain moral theory. Let's look at a burlier version of the same idea. Alasdair MacIntyre (1988) has argued that different conceptions of rationality, morality, and, ultimately, justice arise out of different socially-embedded traditions of inquiry. In the lecture "Is Patriotism a Virtue?" (1984), he expounds on the significant consequences of this dependence. MacIntyre contrasts two conceptions of morality. The first is "liberal" morality, which understands the moral point of view as characterized by impartiality, impersonality, and neutrality. MacIntyre doesn't give the second conception a name, but it might as well be called communitarian morality. "On this view it is an essential characteristic of the morality which each of us acquires that it is learned from, in and through the way of life of some particular community." As a result, "the form of the rules of morality as taught and apprehended will be intimately connected with specific institutional arrangements." Morality will be "the highly specific morality of some highly specific social order."

MacIntyre gives a few reasons for adopting a communitarian conception of morality. First, morality requires us to forgo personal benefits, so to be properly motivated we need to appreciate the benefits of the form of life morality makes possible. But in this respect, we will never be motivated by generic social goods; we will rather be motivated by the *particular* social goods that we encounter in *our* community. Moreover, for many people, the integration into specific social networks is an indispensable part of moral motivation. The second reason is that MacIntyre believes that those who practice a liberal morality will not be loyal to their community in the ways required to defend the community against outside aggressors, and so liberal morality is inimical to the perpetuation of social bonds in a way that communitarian morality is not.

Unlike Baier, who argues for more or less formal conclusions about the nature of morality on the basis of its social function, MacIntyre thinks that communitarian morality entails particular values. In particular, he thinks it entails that a strong form of patriotism is a virtue.

> If first of all it is the case that I can only apprehend the rules of morality in the version in which they are incarnated in some specific community; and if secondly it is the case that the justification of morality must be in terms of particular goods enjoyed within the life of particular communities; and if thirdly it is the case that I am characteristically brought into being and maintained as a moral agent only through the particular kinds of moral sustenance afforded by my community, then it is clear that deprived of this community, I am unlikely to flourish as a moral agent. Hence my allegiance to the community and what it requires of me—even to the point of requiring me to die to sustain its life—could not meaningfully be contrasted with or counterposed to what morality required of me.

This appears to be a sort of transcendental argument: one's particular moral community is a condition on moral thought and moral motivation, therefore a commitment to the preservation of that community is entailed by the moral point of view. The argument depends on a problematic premise. MacIntyre discounts the possibility that we might abstract from particulars in our ordinary ethical thought and be motivated by such abstractions—that we can care about respect for persons as such rather than honoring our chieftain. If this *were* possible, then the purported advantages of communitarian morality over liberal morality would disappear. He assumes that moral thought could not possibly be something that transcends the concrete rules and blandishments instituted by a given community. This is a very strong assumption—much stronger than Baier's—and I can see no good reason for accepting it. After all, we are certainly capable of abstracting from particular rocks and stones and thinking about masses and forces in our theoretical endeavors, and we can be motivated towards this abstraction by values like curiosity. Why is the analogous abstraction impossible in the practical realm? Without support for this crucial premise, I don't see a good reason for accepting MacIntyre's conclusion.

In this section, I have looked at two proposals about how the "social function" of morality might constrain the nature of morality. The results have been mixed. Baier's account of "moral orders" seems plausible, but the constraints it entails on what morality must look like are relatively undemanding. On the other hand, MacIntyre's communitarianism does entail substantive conclusions—the virtue of patriotism—but to get there it relies on dubiously strong premises about the ties connecting moral thought and motivation to particular social arrangements. The lesson of these results, I think, is that if we want more interesting ethical and metaethical conclusions to follow from the place that morality occupies in the social world, then we are going to need to go further out on a limb about what precisely that place is.

CAN THE SOCIOLOGY OF MORALITY INFORM OUR PHILOSOPHICAL THEORY OF MORALITY?

To do this, it would be very nice to have an off-the-rack empirical theory about the sociology of morality. We could then rely on that instead of on armchair speculations. Unfortunately, when we look to the social sciences, we find no such thing. Instead, we find very different theories of the sociology of morality, which (I will suggest) arise from different stances on the metaphysics of social facts. Once again, instead of offering a panoramic view, I will focus on two exemplars.

On the one hand, we find Max Weber, who, as a methodological individualist, does not countenance emergent social phenomena. All social regularities must ultimately be reducible to the dispositions of individual actors. What other social theorists are apt to call social structures or institutions or practices, Weber would instead regard as clouds of probability concerning the likely behavior of individuals (1978a). This outlook leads Weber to the view that we cannot talk about morality as an objective structure like Baier's "moral order," but only as constellations of subjective judgments held by individuals. A corollary of this thesis is that there is very little that we can say to critique moral claims on the basis of their place in a social order. We can offer technical criticisms about the efficacy of actions in achieving particular ends, comment on the consistency of an agent's axioms, and calculate the costs of holding those axioms. But since there is, strictly speaking, no such thing as "social morality"—only the moral judgments of individuals and the probabilities of certain events given those judgments—we cannot expect to ground substantive and non-trivial constraints on morality from this putative feature, much less expect what Weber calls

> a "realistic" science of morality, in the sense of a demonstration of the factual influences exercised on the ethical convictions which prevail at any given time in a group of human beings by their other conditions of life and in turn by the ethical convictions on the conditions of life, [that] would produce an "ethics" which could ever say anything about what ought to be the case.
>
> (1978b: 80)

For Weber, then, we can see a relatively straight line from his methodological convictions about the nature of the social to his conclusion that there isn't much for sociology to say about morality.

The opposite extreme is occupied by Emile Durkheim, who does countenance emergent social phenomena. Sociology, Durkheim (1997: 37) says, "rests wholly on the basic principle that social facts must be studied as things, that is, as realities external to the individual." Durkheim's model for emergence is the relationship between an organism and its components. The cell contains nothing above and beyond particular chemical elements, and yet the distinctive properties of life cannot be *reduced* to these elements. These properties emerge only in the wholeness of the cell (or the organism). By the same token, even though a society contains nothing above and beyond individuals, what distinguishes a society only emerges at the level of the whole, of the society itself (2014: 10). This analogy positions Durkheim to identify social morality with a particular organismic function. Thus, he writes (1984: 331):

We must say that which is moral is everything that is a source of solidarity, everything that forces man to take account of other people, to regulate his actions by something other than the promptings of his own egoism, and the more numerous and strong these ties are, the more solid is the morality.

This functional identification gives Durkheim both a standard by which to identify morality as we find it in a given society and a standard by which to evaluate such morality. In the introduction to the same work, Durkheim explains, "because what we propose to study is above all reality, it does not follow that we should give up the idea of improving it. ... A state of moral health exists that science alone can competently determine and, as it is nowhere wholly attained, it is already an ideal to strive towards it" (1984: xxvi). A network of moral standards can be evaluated, then, by how far it succeeds in securing a state of social "health" analogous to the health of the cellular organism. Durkheim's own standard of health and pathology looked to frequency: features of healthy societies recurred in many different societies, while deviations were probably pathologies. This conception leads to a kind of moral conservatism and is contentious, to say the least. But Durkheim's basic thought of connecting morality to the health of social organism can perhaps be developed in more palatable directions (see, for example, Bosanquet [1898] and Bradley [1927]).

What we see in Weber and Durkheim is how initial assumptions about the subject matter and methodology of sociology—which amount, in part, to metaphysical views about social entities—can lead to radically different conceptions of the place of morality in society. Weber's skepticism about the very idea of social entities leads him to think that the sociality of morality places very little constraint on what morality might be. Durkheim's insistence on those same entities and his particular model for understanding their ontology gives him a muscular, if sketchy, standard by which to evaluate particular moral standards.

Obviously, these are just two examples, and, as with most subjects in philosophy, progress from metaphysical foundations to methodological upshots can be stymied at many points. Nonetheless, I think the discussion does demonstrate that there is enough place for reasonable disagreement on philosophical questions about the foundations of social science that we cannot expect the hope that I began this section with to materialize: we are not going to find a simple and uncontroversial answer to the question of *what* the putative "sociality of morality" consists in, which makes it all the harder to understand *how* that sociality might entail more substantive metaethical conclusions than we saw in the previous section.

This is not all bad news, though. What we have seen is that disagreements about the metaphysics of the social world are palpably relevant to metaethics because they are relevant to what kind of social function morality has. And that is an opportunity, for these two philosophical occupations have seldom been pursued together. If we want a metaethics that is adequate to the sociality of morality—whatever that ends up being—and an account of social actors adequate to their status as moral beings, then we must see them as connected in a way that we hitherto have not.

HOW CAN A METAETHICAL THEORY SATISFY THE DEMANDS OF SOCIALITY?

Of course, there are exceptions to the claim I just made, and in this section, I want to provide a too-brief synopsis of some of them. I have so far focused on the question of how the putative "sociality" of morality might inform us about the nature of morality, and thus offer a point of friction for metaethics. Here, I shall head in the other direction by looking at how different schools in metaethics have tried to exploit the social features of morality. I will mention four such views, corresponding roughly to four possible grounds of moral facts: nature, reason, agency, and sentiment.

Nature. Naturalists are interested in whether moral facts can earn their keep in our scientific worldview by explaining empirical phenomena. It seems unlikely, however, that moral facts will explain mundane laboratory phenomena like the conductance of copper wire, and some philosophers have argued that they are also irrelevant to the explanation of individuals' moral attitudes. Realists have countered these arguments by latching on to the possibility that moral facts may explain *social phenomena*. A simple example is Nicholas Sturgeon's (1989) suggestion that the rapid rise of anti-slavery movements in some regions is explained by the slavery practiced in those being *morally worse* in those regions. (Also see the essays in Harman [2000].) Peter Railton (2003) offers a more systematic version of the same idea. Railton begins by giving a naturalistic definition of non-moral goodness based on the "objective interests" of individuals which "are supervenient on natural and social facts." Railton goes on to propose the possibility of moral principles grounded in what he calls "social rationality"—the rationality of a perspective neutral between all members of a society. Railton proposes that, just as explanations of individuals' behavior will sometimes mention the rationality or irrationality of that individual, our explanations of a society will naturally advert to that society's distance from the ideal of social rationality. For example:

> Just as an individual who significantly discounts some of his interests will be liable to certain sorts of dissatisfaction, so will a social arrangement—for example, a form of production, a social or political hierarchy, and so forth—that departs from social rationality by significantly discounting the interests of a particular group have a potential for dissatisfaction and unrest.

One cannot help but see the specter of Durkheim in this proposal. For both Railton and Durkheim, moral facts gain explanatory significance through their connection to an assessment of the health, stability, or well-functioning of a social entity. Of course, Railton shows that we need not use dubious phrases like "the health of the social organism" in describing this entity, but it nonetheless seems that a notion of "social rationality" will be plausible precisely insofar as it tracks some salutary quality. As a result, Railton's style of naturalism will have debts similar to Durkheim's: we will need to be willing to invest the integrity or health of social entities with moral significance.

Reasoning. Motivational internalists maintain that for someone to have a reason to do something, it must be possible to motivate them to do it through a process of reasoning. But it is hard to see how any kind of reasoning could bring some knaves to moral conclusions, and so this thesis imperils the common supposition that everyone has a reason to do what is morally required. Just how imperiled this thesis is, however, depends on what kind of process reasoning is. It is often supposed that reasoning is a solitary endeavor: churning through premises or intuiting some rational reality all alone. If this is right, then the problem of the knave is acute. The products of reasoning will involve other people only if the inputs do; the act of reasoning itself has no interpersonal character.

But recently, some have argued that this is a stilted view of reasoning, and the activity is better understood as a shared activity: reasoning is a process of inviting others into our "space of reasons"—of justifying ourselves to them, making ourselves intelligible to them and they to us, planning with them, advising them (Graham 2002; Laden 2012; Manne 2013; Manne 2015). If one of these claims is correct, then motivational internalism and categorical moral reasons may live in harmony, despite the knave. Such reasons may be assured not by the inputs of reasoning but by the structure of the activity itself. For example, if practical reasoning necessarily involves certain forms of cooperative deliberation, then the norms of this deliberation may push us towards the adoption of moral systems structured by analogous formal principles (Habermas 1990, 1996). Alternatively, if reasoning necessarily involves *acting together* with another person in a substantial sense, then there is reason to think that it also encompasses what Margaret Gilbert (2014) calls "joint commitment" and thereby engenders significant obligations all by itself—maybe even a Kantian duty to respect our co-reasoner as an end in herself (Korsgaard 2009: 177ff).

Agency. I have already mentioned how constitutivism—the claim that the requirements of agency are categorical norms—may interact with the thesis that agency is socially situated. Some versions of the thesis are particularly well-positioned to capture this fact. J. David Velleman (2009) says that the constitutive aim of action is self-understanding. An action is correct just insofar as it renders the actor intelligible to himself in light of his antecedent commitments and aims. This criterion is individualistic in the sense that it concerns the ability of the actor to understand himself, but Velleman argues that it is social in practice. The best way for neighbors to secure their respective self-intelligibility, Velleman says, is to enter into patterns of interaction that render them mutually intelligible. The most effective patterns, Velleman says, are ones that push us in the direction of our "moral way of life." For example, this aim "favors developing intrapersonally coherent and interpersonally shared values." For agents who are interacting, it "requires them to join in an improvisational collaboration, which is facilitated by adherence to socially shared scenarios." Moreover, these collaborations are "generally facilitated by mutual understandings and hindered by deception" and "recognizing one another as rational agents should inspire a complex interpersonal regard." And finally, "our participation in joint improvisation fosters the development of a discrete mental process that functions in various ways ordinarily associated with conscience." These arguments suggest "a rough configuration that our dealings together would acquire from practical reasoning in the very long run: shared values and scenarios, discouraging private exceptions, minimizing occasions for deception, shaped by acknowledged common interest in comprehensibility, consequently free of unnecessary distinctions amongst persons, and supported by a psychological process recognizable as the conscience." More recently, Velleman (2013) has backed away from the suggestion that there is a substantive enough conception of agency *as such* to guarantee that this picture will see everyone nudged in the direction of the same morality. Instead, he thinks that the interpersonal demands of agency can be met in different ways by different societies, and that this possibility furnishes a foundation for moral relativism.

I have defended a similar but more radical version of the same proposal according to which intelligibility to other agents is not merely instrumentally useful to achieving the aim of action, but constitutive of agency itself (Walden 2012). The idea is that action must be subsumed by a distinctive class of natural laws—the laws of agency—but whether the principle we act on is such a law (rather than, say, a law that applies to all animals) depends on it being appropriately recognized by other actors. This makes such recognition a condition on our meeting the constitutive requirements of action. If this suggestion is correct, then we are committed to an ideal very close to what Kant calls the Realm of Ends just by dint of the nature of action.

Sentiment. I also already suggested how work on the sociology of emotion may intersect with the sentimentalist views of moral judgment. The potential for sentiments to be shaped by social processes has actually been a cornerstone of sentimentalist views since they first crawled out of the Firth of Forth in the eighteenth century. At the center of Adam Smith's (1976) view, for example, is a conception of sympathy whereby we aim to share the feelings of others as closely as possible. This concordance is not automatically assured, however, and so it leads us into an ongoing negotiation between persons "principally concerned" with a given event and those trying to sympathize with them. In the typical case, the former try to restrain the vigor of their reactions while the latter try to intensify theirs. When successful, the two meet in the middle. It is this process of mutual sentimental attunement that grounds the virtues. The "awful" virtues of self-restraint are those that allow us to rein in our sentimental reactions, and the "amiable" virtues of compassion allow us to more fully feel the joys and pains of others. For Smith, to sympathize with someone's feelings is to approve of them, and for this reason *moral* evaluation corresponds to the sympathy that would be experienced in an idealized version of this process of mutual attunement. To sympathize as we suppose a fully informed, impartial spectator would sympathize is to bestow moral approval on an individual's feelings, and moral norms are expressions of the feelings of an impartial spectator. Ultimately, then, for Smith, morality is an idealization of the process whereby our sentiments are successfully socialized.

More recent work premised on the idea that moral judgment is based on sentiment sees a more limited role for social induction. According to Jonathan Haidt's (2001) "social intuitionism" model, for example, the shaping of our sentiments in reaction to our neighbors is something that only happens in youth, and even this is restricted to the "maturation and cultural shaping of endogenous intuitions." In adulthood, "people can acquire explicit prepositional knowledge about right and wrong … but it is primarily through participation in custom complexes." At this stage, sociality is less a means of shaping moral sentiments and more an impetus for lawyerly defenses of one's rigid reactions. This restriction ends up being important. For if what moral judgment ultimately tracks are cultural articulations of endogenous intuitions and the values we soak up from our eleven-year-old peer group, then moral judgment's subject matter is hardly something that we should be happy calling *morality.* Smith's sentimentalism is different: it can be a moral theory precisely *because* it has a robust social mechanism for the negotiation of sentiments that encodes structural features of morality: concern, equity, and impartiality.

In this section, I have suggested how different metaethical schools have attempted not only to accommodate the social dimensions of morality, but to exploit them in defense of their preferred theory. What I would like to note in closing is that there is no obvious reason that all these stories about the sociality of morality—or similar ones—cannot be true at the same time. It can be the case that at least some moral norms are categorical because of their connection to socially contingent forms of agency, that these forms of agency reflect and are reflected in the particular forms that reasoning takes in a social milieu, that this reasoning is reinforced by affective systems that are similarly structured, and that this complex of agency, reason, and affect is a feature of the social "organism" that can be evaluated as well- or ill-functioning in a fashion that is explanatorily consequential. Saying all this would mean giving up on claims of explanatory priority, of course, and the details may be difficult to spell out, but our most satisfying account of the interaction between morality and the social world may very well be one that posits more than one point of contact.

RELATED TOPICS

Chapter 2, "Naturalistic Realism in Metaethics;" Chapter 19, "Ethical Judgment and Motivation;" Chapter 20, "Reasons Internalism;" Chapter 22, "Mind-Dependence and Moral Realism;" Chapter 23, "Constitutivism;" Chapter 35, "Ethics and Morality."

REFERENCES

Baier, K. (1995) *The Rational and the Moral Order: The Social Roots of Reason and Morality*, La Salle, IL: Open Court.
Bosanquet, B. (1898) "Hegel's theory of the political organism", *Mind* 7(25): 1–14.
Bradley, F. H. (1927) *Ethical Studies*, Second edn, New York: Oxford University Press.
Durkheim, E. (1984) *The Division of Labor in Society*, New York: Free Press. (Originally 1893).
—. (1997) *Suicide*, New York: Free Press. (Originally 1897).
—. (2014) *The Rules of Sociological Method*, New York: Free Press. (Originally 1895).
Frankena, W. K. (1966) "The concept of morality", *Journal of Philosophy* 63(21): 688–696.
Gaus, G. (2011) *The Order of Public Reason*, New York: Oxford University Press.
Gert, B. (2002) "The definition of morality", E. Zalta (ed), *The Stanford Encyclopedia of Philosophy*, <http:// plato.stanford.edu/entries/morality-definition/>.
—. (2005) *Morality: Its Nature and Justification*, Revised edn, New York: Oxford University Press.
Giddens, A. (1986) *The Constitution of Society*, Berkeley and Los Angeles: University of California Press.
Gilbert, M. (2014) *Joint Commitment*, New York: Oxford University Press.
Graham, K. (2002) *Practical Reasoning in a Social World*, New York: Cambridge University Press.
Habermas, J. (1990) *Moral Consciousness and Communicative Action*, C. Lenhardt and S. Nicholsen (trans), Cambridge: MIT Press.
Haidt, J. (2001) "The emotional dog and its rational tail: A social intuitionist approach to moral judgment", *Psychological Review* 108(4): 813–834.
—. (1996) *Between Facts and Norms*, W. Rehg (trans), Cambridge: MIT Press.
Harman, G. (2000) *Explaining Value and Other Essays in Moral Philosophy*, New York: Oxford University Press.
Hegel, G. W. F. (1991) *Elements of the Philosophy of Right*, A. Wood (trans), New York: Cambridge University Press. (Originally 1821).
Hochschild, A. (2012) *The Managed Heart: Commercialization of Human Feeling*, Third edn, Berkeley and Los Angeles: University of California Press.
Korsgaard, C. M. (2009) *Self-Constitution: Agency, Identity, and Integrity*, New York: Oxford University Press.
Laden, A. (2012) *Reasoning: A Social Picture*, New York: Oxford University Press.
Letsas, G. (2014) "The DNA of conventions", *Law and Philosophy* 33(5): 535–571.
MacIntyre, A. (1984) "Is patriotism a virtue?", Lawrence, KS: The Lindley Lecture at the University of Kansas.
—. (1988) *Whose Justice? Which Rationality?*, South Bend: University of Notre Dame Press.
Mackie, J. L. (1977) *Ethics: Inventing Right and Wrong*, New York: Penguin.
McPherson, T. (2011) "Against quietist normative realism", *Philosophical Studies* 154(2): 223–240.

Manne, K. (2013) "Going social in metaethics" in R. Shafer-Landau (ed), *Oxford Studies in Metaethics* vol. 8, New York: Oxford University Press.

—. (2015) "Tempered internalism and participatory stance", in G. Björnsson et al. (eds), *Motivational Internalism*, New York: Oxford University Press.

Marx, K. and Engels, F. (1998) *The German Ideology*, New York: Prometheus Books. (Originally 1846).

Nietzsche, F. (1998) *On the Genealogy of Morality*, M. Clark (trans), Indianapolis: Hackett Publishing. (Originally 1887).

Railton, P. (2003) "Moral realism", reprinted in his *Facts and Values*, New York: Cambridge University Press.

Rawls, J. (1999) *A Theory of Justice*, Revised edn, Cambridge: Harvard University Press.

Scanlon, T. M. (1998) *What We Owe to Each Other*, Cambridge: Harvard University Press.

Shafer-Landau, R. (2003) *Whatever Happened to Good and Evil?* New York: Oxford University Press.

Smith, A. (1976) *The Theory of Moral Sentiments*, D. D. Raphael and A. L. Macfie (eds), New York: Oxford University Press. (Originally 1759).

Smith, M. (1994) *The Moral Problem*, Malden, MA: Blackwell.

Southwood, N. (2011) "The moral/conventional distinction", *Mind* 120(479): 761–802.

Sturgeon, N. (1989) "Moral explanations", in G. Sayre-McCord (ed), *Essays on Moral Realism*, Ithaca: Cornell University Press.

Turiel, E. (1983) *The Development of Social Knowledge*, New York: Cambridge University Press.

Velleman, J. D. (2009) *How We Get Along*, New York: Cambridge University Press.

—. (2013) *Foundations for Moral Relativism*, Cambridge: OpenBook Publishers.

Walden, K. (2012) "Laws of nature, laws of freedom, and the social construction of normativity," in R. Shafer-Landau (ed), *Oxford Studies in Metaethics* vol. 7, New York: Oxford University Press.

Weber, M. (1978a) *Economy and Society*, Berkeley and Los Angeles: University of California Press. (Originally 1922).

—. (1978b) "Value-judgments in social science", reprinted in W. G. Runciman (ed) and E. Mathews (trans), *Weber: Selections in Translation*, New York: Cambridge University Press. (Originally 1913).

FURTHER READING

Bratman, Michael (2014) *Shared Agency*, New York: Oxford University Press.

Clark, Maudemarie (2015) "Nietzsche's immoralism and the concept of morality", reprinted in her *Nietzsche on Ethics and Politics*, New York: Oxford University Press.

Foucault, Michel (1990) *The History of Sexuality*, R. Hurley (trans), New York: Vintage.

Hitlin, Steven and Vaisey, Stephen (eds) (2010) *Handbook of the Sociology of Morality*, Dordrecht: Springer.

Parsons, Talcott (1951) *The Social System*, New York: The Free Press.

Rosen, Michael (2000) "The Marxist critique of morality and the theory of ideology", in E. Harcourt (ed), *Morality, Reflection, and Ideology*, New York: Oxford University Press.

Sewell, William (2005) *Logics of History*, Chicago: University of Chicago Press.

Simmel, G. (1950) *The Sociology of Georg Simmel*, K. H. Wolff (trans), New York: The Free Press.

Turner, Jonathan H. and Stets, Jan E. (2006) "Sociological theories of human emotions", *Annual Review of Sociology*, 32: 25–52.

Wood, Allen (1990) *Hegel's Ethical Thought*, New York: Cambridge University Press.

—. (2004) *Karl Marx*, Second edn, New York: Routledge.

27

The Autonomy of Ethics

Barry Maguire

INTRODUCTION

David Hume introduced the autonomy of ethics as follows:

> In every system of morality, which I have hitherto met with, I have always remarked, that the author proceeds for some time in the ordinary ways of reasoning, and establishes the being of a God, or makes observations concerning human affairs; when all of a sudden I am surprised to find, that instead of the usual copulations of propositions, *is*, and *is not*, I meet with no proposition that is not connected with an *ought*, or an *ought not*. This change is imperceptible; but is however, of the last consequence. For as this *ought*, or *ought not*, expresses some new relation or affirmation, 'tis necessary that it should be observed and explained; and at the same time that a reason should be given, for what seems altogether inconceivable, how this new relation can be a deduction from others, which are entirely different from it.

An autonomy thesis maintains that facts or propositions in some domain are isolated in some respect from those in some other domain, or perhaps all other domains. Some of the most interesting philosophical conjectures have been autonomy theses of one kind or another. Think of Gottlob Frege's anti-psychologism about mathematics, Donald Davidson's anomalous monism in philosophy of mind, Jerry Fodor's 'disunity of science' hypothesis or Bertrand Russell's claim that "You can never arrive at a general proposition by inference from particular propositions alone. You will always have to have at least one general proposition in your premises" (Russell 1918/19: 199). Even within the normative domain, a variety of different autonomy theses is discussed: the autonomy of morality from prudence, reasons from rationality, theoretical reason from practical reason.

In this chapter, I will stick to the general question of the autonomy of the ethical domain from the non-ethical domain. I assume that the ethical domain contains facts about good and bad states of affairs, including facts about what is good or bad for individuals. It also contains facts about how one should live, act, and feel. I use 'ethical' expansively to include prudential as well as moral considerations. I'll occasionally use substantive examples, but the arguments do not depend on any of these specific examples. Non-ethical facts (propositions, etc.) include scientific facts; other contingent facts, for instance concerning the goings-on of cats and mats; 'supernatural facts' about God's will; and psychological facts about beliefs and desires. I'll use the word 'descriptive' stipulatively to pick out the intuitively non-ethical. It is important that 'ethical' and 'descriptive' are not logical contraries. Conjunctions of ethical and descriptive propositions might turn out to be *both* ethical and descriptive.

Here is a smattering of examples of the sorts of ethical transitions that philosophers have worried about:

1. The invasion of Iraq contravened international law, therefore the invasion of Iraq was wrong (Campbell Brown 2012).
2. Individuals are motivated by personal gain, therefore the principles of justice allow inequalities so long as these improve the positions of the worst off (Cohen 2008 on Rawls).
3. Jones uttered the words "I hereby promise to pay you, Smith, five dollars," therefore Jones has an obligation to pay Smith five dollars (Searle 1964).
4. Ronnie wants to dance, therefore Ronnie has a reason to dance (Schroeder 2007).

I will discuss three types of ethical autonomy thesis, distinguished by the types of relation maintained *not* to obtain between the antecedents and consequents in arguments such as these: logical relations, metaphysical relations, and epistemic relations. (I'll talk variously in terms of facts, propositions, or sentences, as befits different types of autonomy relations.) I'll express some doubts about the serviceability of logical accounts and, in the end, some doubts about the significance of a purely metaphysical account. I'll suggest that the real motivation for metaphysical and logical autonomy arises from the importance of an epistemological thesis, namely the thesis that non-ethical propositions are irrelevant to the justification of non-derivative ethical propositions.

LOGICAL AUTONOMY

Let's start with the most familiar, and perhaps most tempting, type of proposal, one that leans (too) heavily on Hume's claim that one cannot "deduce" an ethical sentence from a descriptive sentence. Let E be some paradigmatic ethical sentence, for instance 'it is impermissible to starve the Irish' and let D be some paradigmatic descriptive sentence, for instance 'Echidnas are egg-laying mammals'. According to *logical* characterizations, the autonomy of ethics consists in the fact that certain logical relations do not obtain between sentences such as D and sentences such as E. Let's start with:

SIMPLE LOGICAL AUTONOMY: no descriptive sentence entails an ethical sentence.

There is an immediate problem with this thesis. (D & ~D) entails E, our ethical sentence. D entails ((E & (D ∨ ~D)), and D also entails (E ∨ ~E). Assuming some modest taxonomic principles, it follows that SIMPLE LOGICAL AUTONOMY is false. Now, perhaps it is not too ad hoc to respond to this problem by restricting the autonomy thesis to exclude arguments involving impossible antecedents and necessary consequents. A more interesting counterexample to simple logical autonomy is due to Arthur Prior (1960). He argued as follows:

1. D entails (D ∨ E)
2. ((D ∨ E) & ~D) entails E
3. Either (D ∨ E) is ethical or not.
4. If so, then 1 constitutes a counterexample to simple logical autonomy.
5. If not, then 2 constitutes a counterexample to simple logical autonomy.
6. Therefore simple logical autonomy is false.

Premises 1 and 2 are incontestable. We'll find occasion to doubt premise 3 later, but not on grounds shared by the simple logical autonomist, so let's grant it for now. If (D ∨ E) is ethical, premise 4 follows directly from 1. If (D ∨ E) is not ethical, then (so long as we assume that a conjunction with non-ethical conjuncts is non-ethical) premise 5 also follows. Hence it seems we should reject SIMPLE LOGICAL AUTONOMY.

One natural move in reply is to restrict the logical autonomy thesis to exclude 'vacuous' entailments. In an important series of papers, Charles Pigden defends this approach (1989, 2010). He defines a notion of vacuous entailment as follows. An expression x occurs vacuously in the conclusion of a valid inference if and only if under any interpretation of the premises and conclusion such that they both come out true, we can uniformly substitute for x any other expression of the same grammatical type without upsetting the validity. Pigden then offers the following revised thesis:

NON-VACUOUS LOGICAL AUTONOMY: no descriptive sentence non-vacuously entails an ethical sentence.

Since x might be a sentence rather than just a predicate, this definition accounts for the vacuity of arguments with necessarily false antecedents or necessarily true consequents. Here's how this principle avoids Prior's objection. Premise 1 is a vacuous entailment, since D entails the disjunction of D and anything you like. Premise 2 is also a vacuous entailment, since for any proposition P, ((D ∨ P) & ~D) entails P. Hence both fall outside the scope of NON-VACUOUS LOGICAL AUTONOMY.

The central problem with NON-VACUOUS LOGICAL AUTONOMY is that it overgeneralises. On Pigden's account, the autonomy of ethics is just an instance of the conservativity of logic. The conservativity of logic applies as much to the non-vacuous entailment of sentences about elephants as obligations.

Hence, NON-VACUOUS LOGICAL AUTONOMY is unlikely to be the distinction Hume famously drew our attention to. For instance, minimally, we want an autonomy thesis to distinguish between:

1. Ronnie has a desire to dance, therefore Ronnie has a reason to dance.
2. Ronnie has an obligation to dance, therefore Ronnie ought to dance.

Both are equally autonomous in Pigden's sense. There are no non-vacuous logical entailments from premises about desires or obligations to conclusions about reasons or ought. However, intuitively, 1 but not 2 violates the autonomy of ethics. So there is more to the autonomy of ethics than non-vacuous logical autonomy.[1]

The autonomy of ethics has been thought by many to be an exciting, controversial thesis with a wide variety of implications for ethics, for metaethics, and for general metaphysics and epistemology. T. M. Scanlon (2014) argues that a proper characterization of non-naturalism depends upon a proper understanding of autonomy. G. A. Cohen (2008) argues that the debate between liberals and socialists turns on an issue closely related to autonomy. James Dreier (2004) argues that the defence of Blackburn's quasi-realism depends on an autonomy thesis and an associated account of the metaethics/ethics distinction. Ronald Dworkin (1996, 2011) argues, from a premise about the autonomy of the ethical domain, that ethical nihilism is not merely false but incoherent. Then there are all the other great autonomy theses in other parts of philosophy. Many esteemed philosophers have taken there to be something philosophically substantive at stake. In the pursuit of an adequate characterization of an *exciting* thesis, we will need to appeal beyond Pigden's sparse logical resources.

METAPHYSICAL AUTONOMY

By 'metaphysical' accounts of autonomy, I have in mind those that make some claim about the modal status, or grounding relationships, or natures, of ethical facts or principles. Metaphysical autonomy theses deny, of at least some ethical facts, that they are identical to, or fully explained by, or modally sensitive to, or underwritten by descriptive facts or properties.

Let's start with identity. Insisting that at least one ethical fact is not identical to any descriptive fact would appear to be a necessary condition for any metaphysical characterization of ethical autonomy:

NON-IDENTITY: At least one ethical fact is not identical to any descriptive fact.

Versions of NON-IDENTITY restricted to value or morality are inconsistent with familiar brands of ethical naturalism: straightforward reductive realism (e.g. David Lewis's dispositional theory of value [1989]), analytical naturalism (e.g. in Frank Jackson [1998]) and synthetic naturalism (e.g. in Richard Boyd [1988]).

This familiar thesis – NON-IDENTITY – may not draw quite the distinction we are after. For instance, various subjectivists hope to preserve the explanatory priority of clearly non-ethical descriptive facts over all ethical facts, while also denying the 'autonomy of ethics' in some important sense. Mark Schroeder (2007) maintains that, for any A, some fact F is a reason for A to x if and only if and *in virtue of* the fact that F explains the fact that x-ing would increase the probability of the satisfaction of at least one of A's desires. The 'in virtue of relation' here is asymmetric, so this is not a straightforward identity thesis. (It may be a non-straightforward identity thesis, if one additionally defends the hypothesis that any fact fully grounded by a descriptive fact is a descriptive fact, and one identified ethical facts with these grounded descriptive facts.)

In order to characterize asymmetric descriptivist views as non-autonomous, we need a stronger, and perhaps more interesting, autonomy thesis. Some motivation for this alternative characterization is provided by G. A. Cohen (2008):

> Suppose someone affirms the principle that *we should keep our promises* (call that P) because *only when promises are kept can promises successfully pursue their projects* (call that F). Then she will surely agree that she believes that F supports P because she affirms ... that we should help people to pursue their projects.

The general version of the thought is this: if some ethical E1 seems to be explained by some non-ethical facts N1, that's only in cooperation with some underlying ethical principle E2. If E2, in turn, seems to be explained by some non-ethical N2, that's only in virtue of some deeper ethical principle E3, and so on. To borrow a metaphor from Gideon Rosen (2010), this view insists that any tree with ethical branches will have at least one ethical root. We can capture this in the following thesis (adapted from Maguire [2015]; for refinements see Jack Woods [ms]):

METAPHYSICAL AUTONOMY: If an ethical fact has grounds, these include at least one ethical fact. (Equivalently: No ethical fact is fully grounded just by descriptive facts.)

One can use METAPHYSICAL AUTONOMY as a fulcrum to argue that many enthymematic premises are ethical principles. For instance, suppose we assume that the grounds of the fact that Ronnie has a reason to dance are precisely two – some fact about his desire, and Schroeder's subjectivist thesis itself. Suppose we also assume that the fact about his desire is a non-ethical fact. Then METAPHYSICAL AUTONOMY entails that the subjectivist thesis itself is an ethical thesis. Or take Searle's example. The fact about your obligation to keep your promise is moral. That fact obtains in virtue of the preceding premises – including that Jones uttered the words "I hereby promise to pay you, Smith, five dollars" – together with some covering principles (these are spelled out by Searle). According to METAPHYSICAL AUTONOMY, at least one of these premises or principles is ethical. Or take Campbell Brown's example. The invasion of Iraq contravened international law, therefore the invasion of Iraq was wrong. If METAPHYSICAL AUTONOMY is true, some ethical principle must also be true in this case. We can look around to see whether any plausible principles underlie this transition, for instance, some principle of the form 'It is wrong to violate international law'. This, in turn, might be true for a variety of reasons: because contraventions of international law by superpowers lead to countless other wrongful infractions, or involve disrespect to international neighbours, or perhaps because it is in the nature of international law to be just.

A metaphysical principle like METAPHYSICAL AUTONOMY will avoid the troubles facing logical autonomy theses. It clearly avoids the argument from explosion, since (D & ~D) does not plausibly ground any ethical fact E, nor does any descriptive D ground (E ∨ ~E). Grounding is an explanatory relation, and there is no explanation here.

What about Prior's argument? If we swap the entailments for grounds, the premises are:

1. D grounds (D ∨ E)
2. ((D ∨ E) & ~D) grounds E

3. Either (D ∨ E) is ethical or not.

It is not plausible that 2 is true. No disjunction grounds its disjuncts; the grounding relation goes the other way around. What about 1? There are two options. If E is false, then 1 doesn't plausibly provide a counterexample to METAPHYSICAL AUTONOMY since we have no reason to think the disjunction is ethical. It has an ethical constituent, but only in a metaphysically impotent disjunct. If E is true, then since disjunctions are grounded by their disjuncts, we still don't have a counterexample. D grounds (D ∨ E), but so does E. This is a case of metaphysical overdetermination, just as when the fact that there is a large dog in the office is fully grounded both by the fact that the bloodhound is in the office, and the fact that the mastiff is in the office.

So, a principle like METAPHYSICAL AUTONOMY has several virtues. Let's now consider some related challenges, based on the thought that there are various distinct explanatory roles that putative ethical facts might play. Consider the following explanatory chain:

1. The right thing to do is to spare his life.
2. Sparing his life would maximize expected utility.
3. UTILITARIANISM: An act is right if and only if, and if so in virtue of the fact that, it maximizes expected utility.
4. METAPHYSICAL UTILITARIANISM: To be the right thing to do is to be the thing that would maximize expected utility.

Assuming utilitarianism, it is natural to think that 1 is fully grounded just in 2 and 3. Assume that 2 is a descriptive fact. Hence, by METAPHYSICAL AUTONOMY, 3 is an ethical fact. It is natural, in turn, to think that the biconditional thesis in 3 is fully grounded just in the definitional thesis in 4. The problem arises when we consider the familiar proposal that, as a metaethical thesis about essences, 4 is not itself ethical. If so, we have a counterexample to METAPHYSICAL AUTONOMY. This is the first challenge: that UTILITARIANISM, an ethical fact, is fully grounded just by METAPHYSICAL UTILITARIANISM, a non-ethical fact.

In fact, METAPHYSICAL AUTONOMY appears to be in even more trouble. For once METAPHYSICAL UTILITARIANISM is on the scene, it is less clear that 1 is grounded by 2 *and* 3. An alternative proposal has it that 1 is fully grounded just by 2. *This* fact, the fact that 2 fully grounds 1, is itself metaphysically explained by METAPHYSICAL UTILITARIANISM. On this account, we have at least one instance of a descriptive fact grounding an ethical fact, viz. the fact about the right thing to do being grounded by the fact about utility maximization. This is the second challenge: that the rightness fact in 1 is fully grounded just by the fact about expected utility in 2.

There may also be a third challenge here. Take the (putative) fact that [2 grounds 1]. If facts about the explanations of ethical facts are ethical, then the fact that [2 grounds 1] is itself an ethical fact. If we further assume that the 'underwriting' relation is the grounding relation and we continue to assume that the definitional thesis in 4 is descriptive, then the fact that 4 grounds the fact that [2 grounds 1] is another counterexample to METAPHYSICAL AUTONOMY. To repeat: this third challenge arises if one is committed to the fact that [2 grounds 1] is ethical and fully grounded just by the combination of 2, which is non-ethical, and METAPHYSICAL UTILITARIANISM, which is (thought to be) non-ethical.

There is some wiggle room here and there. One option in defence of METAPHYSICAL AUTONOMY is to concede that *if* there were enough true descriptive definitions of ethical properties to do the work of explaining every ethical fact, then METAPHYSICAL AUTONOMY would not be true. However, the defender would roll up her sleeves and deny, on first-order grounds, that there are enough such true definitions. The principle in 4, for instance, is false if UTILITARIANISM is false.

An alternative option preserves the spirit but not the letter of METAPHYSICAL AUTONOMY. One might allow that some descriptive facts fully ground ethical facts, for instance, that 2 fully grounds 1. However, one can insist that whenever some descriptive fact fully grounds some ethical fact, the fact that that descriptive fact grounds that ethical fact is itself underwritten by an ethical fact. This may be because some ethical principle is playing an explanatory role without being a *ground* (on which, see Bader [ms]). Or it may be by virtue of a definitional fact like METAPHYSICAL UTILITARIANISM itself. The ethicality of such a non-grounding ethical principle or of METAPHYSICAL UTILITARIANISM would need to be defended, not on the basis that ethicality is preserved across grounds, as such, but on the basis that the full metaphysical explanation of any ethical fact will include at least one ethical fact. This gives some leeway to allow that metaphysical explanations may have more structure than simple chains of grounds – either because grounding facts themselves have grounds, or because grounding facts are underwritten in some other way.

The metaphysical autonomist may want to avoid getting stuck in these metaphysical debates about different types of explanation or different types of reduction. There had seemed to be something in particular at stake, and it doesn't seem likely that this important thing will be fully captured by the fruits of *these* inquiries. It doesn't seem particularly plausible that the question of the autonomy of ethics is reducible to the question of whether there is only one metaphysical explanatory relation. Again, something important seems to have been left out of the analysis. I think this is evidence that the most significant thesis in the ballpark is not a metaphysical thesis. It is a thesis that has metaphysical implications, which can make these metaphysical disputes rather urgent. But the heart of the autonomy of ethics is not metaphysical. It is epistemological.

EPISTEMOLOGICAL AUTONOMY

Let's start with an analogy. Ethical facts are irrelevant to the justification of scientific theories (for discussion, see Barber [2013]). The ethical significance of some scientific result might well be relevant to the decision to *publish* the result. This would be a practical matter. But it would be irrelevant to its epistemic justification. No matter how much morally better it would be if scientific theory S1 were true than S2, just a smidgen more scientific evidence for S2 would make you epistemically unjustified in believing S1 rather than S2. Similarly, no matter how much evidence you have about the way people actually think, this would not amount to a refutation of the validity of some argument in some formal system. The domain of science sets the standards for what counts as scientific evidence; moral value is scientifically irrelevant. Different formal systems set the standards for different kinds of entailment; facts about the inference patterns of experimental subjects are irrelevant.

Just so, the thought goes, the domain of ethics (or morality, or normativity, as the case may be) sets the standards for what counts as evidence for pure ethical propositions (i.e. ethical propositions that, if true, do not partly obtain in virtue of descriptive facts). Non-ethical philosophical considerations are ruled to be justificatorily irrelevant.

The restriction to 'pure' ethical propositions is important. There are normative facts about what you should do in particular situations, and clearly some non-ethical propositions – that there is a lion in the living room – will be relevant to their justification. Epistemic autonomy applies only to ethical propositions that are not contingent on such descriptive propositions. So let's stick with non-mixed ethical principles like UTILITARI-ANISM for now, and consider, for argument's sake, the following strong principle:

SIMPLE EPISTEMIC AUTONOMY: no non-ethical evidence is relevant to the epistemic justi-fication of any pure ethical proposition.

The notion of relevance here is wide-ranging. According to this thesis, no non-ethical evidence can attenuate or defeat your justification for some non-mixed ethical proposi-tion, no non-ethical evidence can intensify your justification for some non-mixed ethical proposition and no non-ethical evidence can constitute evidence on its own for some non-mixed ethical proposition. So for instance, if we assume that Schroeder's subjectiv-ism is a metaethical thesis, and that metaethical theses are non-ethical, SIMPLE EPISTEMIC AUTONOMY entails that evidence for subjectivism is irrelevant to the epistemic justifica-tion of any pure ethical proposition. There might still be evidence for subjectivism as a substantive ethical thesis, e.g. that desires often seem to give reasons in tie-breaking cases. SIMPLE EPISTEMIC AUTONOMY dovetails nicely with METAPHYSICAL AUTONOMY.

This thesis is silent about whether, conversely, (pure or mixed) ethical propositions are ever justificatorily relevant to your descriptive propositions. Presumably, ethical proposi-tions might be relevant to your epistemic justification for *some* descriptive propositions. For instance, if there are any purely metaethical (and hence presumably descriptive) propositions – for instance, the thesis that ethical nihilism is false – one's epistemic jus-tification for these propositions will be considerably affected by one's epistemic justifica-tion for certain ethical propositions.

Hence SIMPLE EPISTEMIC AUTONOMY espouses a justificatory asymmetry between ethical and descriptive propositions. Pure ethical propositions may be justificatorily rel-evant to descriptive propositions (SIMPLE EPISTEMIC AUTONOMY is silent about this), but descriptive propositions are not justificatorily relevant to non-mixed ethical proposi-tions. On this way of thinking, metaethics is epistemically subordinated to ethics. This is not, of course, to deny that metaethics is an important enterprise.

The most natural objections to this thesis will come from 'debunking' hypotheses about the origin of our ethical beliefs or intuitions, and from issues concerning disagree-ment and moral expertise. These issues require careful consideration. I refer the reader to Sharon Street (2006) and Katia Vavova (2014), and the pertinent chapters in this volume. Something will also need to be said about perfectly general defeaters like drinking too much whisky before thinking about what to do.

Instead, we'll move on to consider a variation on the challenge from the previous sec-tion. Since METAPHYSICAL UTILITARIANISM entails UTILITARIANISM, and since it is plau-sible that evidence for P is evidence for (a non-tautologous) Q if P entails Q, it is plausible that evidence for METAPHYSICAL UTILITARIANISM is evidence for UTILITARIANISM itself. This would contradict SIMPLE EPISTEMIC AUTONOMY.

I suggest that theses like METAPHYSICAL UTILITARIANISM are best understood as complex, obtaining in virtue of an ethical thesis and an otherwise ethically neutral metaphysical thesis (which may well be non-ethical). The evidence in favour of the otherwise neutral metaphysical thesis does not provide evidence in favour of any specific ethical thesis.

Let me spell this out a bit. The idea is that METAPHYSICAL UTILITARIANISM is a hybrid of UTILITARIANISM – the thesis that, necessarily, an action is right if and only if it is utility maximizing – and some metaphysical thesis, perhaps IDENTITY, the thesis that necessarily coextensive properties are identical, or perhaps some asymmetric explanatory relationship such as in Schroeder (2007) and Rosen (2010). IDENTITY is neutral about what is right and wrong. It is neutral between UTILITARIANISM and competing ethical theories. Similarly, UTILITARIANISM is neutral concerning whether rightness is identical with whatever property is the 'rightness-maker', or whether rightness is a distinct non-descriptive property instantiated by all and only the rightness-makers. We break down the evidence for METAPHYSICAL UTILITARIANISM into distinct sets of evidence for these two distinct theses. Some evidence will be purely philosophical or metaethical, addressing ethically neutral hypotheses concerning the relationship between ethical and descriptive properties. Other evidence will be purely ethical, addressing otherwise descriptively neutral hypotheses concerning which properties are rightness-makers (or reason-givers or value-bearers or whatever). METAPHYSICAL UTILITARIANISM itself is, as it were, doubly vulnerable, since it is required to withstand both ethical scrutiny and general metaphysical scrutiny.

But suppose that the ethical theory that stood up to our most rigorous first-order ethical inquiry was *also* somehow supported by some argument from purely descriptive premises. Suppose that some specific first-order theory was vindicated by our best-going metaphysics and epistemology of ethics, and perhaps also fitted nicely with a plausible philosophy of language and an empirically respectable moral psychology. Wouldn't that constitute *some* further justification for the relevant ethical theory? Perhaps not. Such further justification would be inconsistent with SIMPLE EPISTEMIC AUTONOMY. We need to lean again on the analogy with science or mathematics. Ethical beliefs are utterly irrelevant to the justification of scientific theories, whether they would impose major revisions or minor marginal revisions. Just the same is true of scientific theories and ethical justification. (The same is true of logic – recall Frege's logic/psychology autonomy thesis.) No matter how considerable the evidence in favour of the metaethical thesis, that doesn't lend any weight to the *ethical* principle.

We are now in a position to interpret an infamous passage from Ronald Dworkin (1996, 100–101):

> There is no difference in what two people think if one thinks that the only thing that can make an act right is its maximizing power, so that it makes no sense to evaluate rightness in any other way, and the other thinks that the property of rightness and the property of maximizing power are the very same property. The second opinion uses the jargon of metaphysics, but it cannot add any genuine idea to the first, or subtract any from it. It sounds more philosophical but it is no less evaluative.

Dworkin is right in that these two remarks are ethically equivalent, but wrong in that they are metaphysically equivalent. They are ethically equivalent not just because they agree modally (as we assume) in their evaluations but because they agree in their evaluative explanations. Both maintain that it is the maximization of utility that makes some particular action right. But Dworkin is wrong to deny that there is a separate set of questions, in general metaphysics, about the relations that may or may not obtain between modally coextensive properties. Certain questions about reduction and identity and explanation – and if naturalism turns on the availability of ontological reductions or identity theses, questions about naturalism – are strictly orthogonal to questions about extensionality or normative explanation. There *is* a domain of purely metaethical questions about ethics: questions about the metaphysical status of ethical principles, the answers to which are neutral concerning questions about *which* ethical principles are true.

Let's now turn to another challenge. Let ANALYTICAL UTILITARIANISM be the thesis that the word 'right' just means 'conducive to general happiness'. Tristram McPherson (2008) writes:

> ... it is easy to find counterexamples to [SIMPLE EPISTEMIC AUTONOMY], in the form of metaethical theories with direct normative implications. ... analytical utilitarianism is an account of the semantics of a central piece of moral vocabulary, and hence a paradigmatic metaethical theory. However, it also transparently has implications for the content of the correct normative theory.

The response here must be a little different, since it is less plausible that ANALYTICAL UTILITARIANISM is a hybrid thesis.

Suppose we found ourselves with decisive sociological evidence for the hypothesis that, in the mouths of speakers in the United States in the early part of the twenty-first century, the word 'right' means 'utility maximizing'. It would remain an open question whether UTILITARIANISM is true, for it remains open whether these speakers should change what they mean by this word, or perhaps stop using it altogether. This is a familiar point. Perhaps we meant something different by 'solid' before we found that tables were mostly space, or by 'simultaneously' before we learned about general relativity. What is important is what is right, not what people happen to mean by the word 'right'.

But there is a puzzle here. When we say "what is important is what is right, not what we mean by 'right'," what do we mean by 'right' the first time it appears in that sentence? If we mean the same thing by 'right' both times, then surely finding out what we mean by 'right' *will* be a way to find out what is right?

One line of reply to this puzzle is to appeal to the notion of a 'reforming definition' (Rawls 1971; Brandt 1979) or 'critical analysis' (e.g. in Haslanger [2012, 223–225]; compare Burgess and Plunkett [2013]). Sally Haslanger says this (2000: 31–55):

> [On] an *analytical* approach to the question, "What is gender?" or "What is race?" ... the task is not to explicate our ordinary concepts; nor is it to investigate the kind that we may or may not be tracking with our everyday conceptual apparatus; instead we begin by considering more fully the pragmatics of our talk employing the terms in question. What is the point of having these concepts? What cognitive or practical task do they (or should they) enable us to accomplish? Are they effective tools to accomplish our (legitimate) purposes;

if not, what concepts would serve these purposes better? In the limit case of an analytical approach the concept in question is introduced by stipulating the meaning of a new term, and its content is determined entirely by the role it plays in the theory. ...

Suppose it turned out that we use 'right' to mean 'utility maximizing', or 'good' to mean 'good for me', or 'reason' to mean 'something that would satisfy a desire I would have under modestly idealized conditions'. We can ask whether these are the most effective conceptual tools we can use to think about the moral, the evaluative, or the normative. There are other concepts available. We might instead use 'good' to mean 'good *simpliciter*', 'reason' to mean 'promotion of states it would be good to care about' and 'right' to mean 'what I have most reason to do'. Which of these concepts is best? Which should we adopt? The obvious difficulty with answering this question is that we'll encounter the same challenge concerning these standards of 'best' and 'should', as they pertain to theory choice. What if by 'which concept is best?' you mean 'which concept favors impartial good promotion' or 'which concept defers to God's will'?

This is an important challenge. Plausibly, all we can do in response is to exercise due diligence in our ethical theorizing. The important thing is that even if some purely sociological account of the extension of some ethical word were offered, this would not *itself* settle any ethical question without admitting an *ethical* defence. The hard line here – and I continue to find it plausible – is that the sociological evidence would be justificatorily *irrelevant* to the relevant ethical thesis itself.

CONCLUSION

I distinguished accounts of the autonomy of ethics into logical, metaphysical, and epistemological proposals.

The simplest logical proposals succumb to Prior's well-known challenge. More sophisticated proposals such as Pigden's succeed in avoiding Prior's challenge but do not manage to draw the distinction we are after.

There are various metaphysical proposals available. The simplest denies that ethical facts are identical to intuitively non-ethical facts. A more sophisticated version denies that ethical facts are fully grounded just by intuitively non-ethical facts. This more sophisticated version may need to be refined if ethical principles are not grounds or partial grounds but play some other metaphysical role. These discussions become rather arcane, and it becomes less clear where the urgency lies in questions of ethical taxonomy.

That led us to the bold epistemological thesis, that intuitively non-ethical evidence is irrelevant to the justification of non-mixed ethical beliefs. This thesis has some hope of withstanding challenges from METAPHYSICAL UTILITARIANISM and ANALYTICAL UTILITARIANISM. The first is a hybrid of an ethical principle and a thesis in general metaphysics. The second is perhaps of sociological rather than ethical significance.

These discussions are complementary. Given the asymmetry of justification, we need to look for a metaphysics of ethics that is consistent with our best first-order theory of ethics, just like we need to look for a metaphysics of science that is consistent with our best scientific theory.

NOTE

1. For a critical discussion of some model theoretic characterizations of autonomy, see Maguire and Woods (forthcoming).

REFERENCES

Bader, R. (manuscript). 'Two Levels of Good-Making'.

Barber, A. 2013. 'Science's Immunity to Moral Refutation', *Australasian Journal of Philosophy*, 91 (4): 633–653.

Boyd, R. 1988. 'How to Be a Moral Realist', in G. Sayre-McCord (ed.), *Essays in Moral Realism*, Ithaca: Cornell University Press, 181–228.

Brandt, R. 1979. *A Theory of the Good and the Right*, New York: Oxford University Press.

Brown, C. 2012. 'Minding the is- ought gap', *Journal of Philosophical Logic*, 1–17.

Cohen, G.A. 2008. *Rescuing Justice, Rescuing Equality*. Cambridge: Harvard University Press.

Dreier, J. 2004. 'Metaethics and the Problem of Creeping Minimalism', *Philosophical Perspectives*, 18.

Dworkin, R. 1996. 'Objectivity and Truth: You'd Better Believe it', *Philosophy and Public Affairs*, 25 (2) (Spring, 1996): 87–139.

Dworkin, R. 2011. *Justice for Hedgehogs*, Cambridge: Harvard University Press.

Haslanger, S. 2000. 'Gender and Race: (What) Are They? (What) Do We Want Them to Be?' *Noûs* 34 (1): 31–55.

Haslanger, S. 2012. *Resisting Reality*, Oxford: Oxford University Press.

Jackson, F. 1998. *From Metaphysics to Ethics*, Oxford: Oxford University Press.

Lewis, D. 1989. 'Dispositional Theories of Value', *Proceedings of the Aristotelian Society*, supplementary volume 72.

McPherson, T. 2008. 'Metaethics and the Autonomy of Morality', *Philosophers' Imprint*, 8 (6): 1–16

Maguire, B. 2015. 'Grounding the Autonomy of Ethics', in R. Shafer-Landau (ed.), *Oxford Studies in Metaethics* 10, 188–216.

Maguire, B. & Woods, J. forthcoming. 'Model Theory, Hume's Dictum, and the Priority of Ethical Theory', *Ergo*.

Pigden, C. 1989. 'Logic and the Autonomy of Ethics', *Australasian Journal of Philosophy*, (67) (2).

Pigden, C. 2010. 'Introduction', *Hume on Is and Ought*, London: Palgrave Macmillan.

Prior, A.N. 1960. 'The Autonomy of Ethics', *Australasian Journal of Philosophy*, 38 (3): 199–206.

Rawls, J. 1971. 'Two Concepts of Rules', *The Philosophical Review*, 64 (1): 3–32.

Rosen, G. 2010. 'Metaphysical Dependence: Grounding and Reduction', in B. Hale (ed.), *Modality*. Oxford: Oxford University Press.

Russell, B. 1918. *The Philosophy of Logical Atomism*. La Salle, IL: Open Court.

Scanlon, T.M. 2014. *Being Realistic about Reasons*, Oxford: Oxford University Press.

Schroeder, M. 2007. *Slaves of the Passions*, Oxford: Oxford University Press.

Searle, J. 1964. 'How to Derive "Ought" from "Is"'. *Philosophical Review*, 73 (1): 43–58.

Street, S. 2006. 'A Darwinian Dilemma for Realist Theories of Value', *Philosophical Studies*, 107 (1): 109–166.

Vavova, K. 2014. 'Debunking Evolutionary Debunking' in R. Shafer-Landau (ed.), *Oxford Studies in Metaethics*, 9: 76–101.

Woods, J. (manuscript). 'On Vacuous Grounding: The Case Study of Ethical Autonomy'.

28

Explanatory Challenges in Metaethics

Joshua Schechter

INTRODUCTION

There are several important arguments in metaethics that rely on explanatory considerations. Gilbert Harman has presented a challenge to the existence of moral facts that depends on the claim that the best explanation of our moral beliefs does not involve moral facts. The Reliability Challenge against moral realism depends on the claim that moral realism is incompatible with there being a satisfying explanation of our reliability about moral truths. The purpose of this chapter is to examine these and related arguments. In particular, this chapter will discuss four kinds of arguments—Harman's Challenge, evolutionary debunking arguments, irrelevant influence arguments, and the Reliability Challenge—understood as arguments against moral realism. The main goals of this chapter are (i) to articulate the strongest version of these arguments, (ii) to present and assess the central epistemological principles underlying these arguments, and (iii) to determine what a realist would have to do to adequately respond to these arguments.

ROBUST MORAL REALISM

Before we get to the explanatory arguments, it will be useful to first present a strong form of non-natural moral realism. I won't defend this view here (though I am sympathetic to it). Rather, I present this view because it makes a natural target for the explanatory arguments discussed in this chapter. Versions of the arguments may have force against other metaethical views. But the issues involved are delicate, and it is easier to get a sense of the crux of the arguments when they are targeted against a strong form of realism.

The version of moral realism that will serve as the target of the explanatory arguments has seven theses. The first thesis concerns the nature of moral language and thought:

(Cognitivism) Certain sentences and mental representations purport to represent moral facts. They are both meaningful and truth-apt (that is, capable of being true or false).

This thesis should be accepted by any moral realist.

The second thesis is the denial of moral error theory:

(Non-Error Theory) Some attributions of basic moral properties and relations are true.

Moral error theory is sometimes understood to be the claim that all moral sentences are false. But this is a mistake. If a moral sentence is false then its negation is true. Instead, moral error theory is better understood as the view that sentences that attribute basic moral properties and relations are false. For example, if wrongness is a basic moral property, then according to moral error theory, any sentence that attributes wrongness to an action will be false, but its negation—and the sentence "no action is wrong"—will be true.

The third thesis is a claim about the independence of the moral:

(Independence) The fundamental moral facts do not depend on us. In particular, they do not depend on facts about our minds, language, or social practices.

On any plausible realist view, some moral facts depend on facts about our minds, language, or social practices. For example, that my friends detest the taste of strawberry ice cream is part of why it would be better to bring a tub of vanilla to their party. That certain words and gestures have the meanings that they do—which itself depends on complex facts about our social practices—is part of why uttering certain sentences or making certain gestures is morally problematic. And so on. According to Independence, what is independent of us are the fundamental moral facts—those moral facts that (in combination with non-moral facts) determine the rest.

How should "independent" be understood here? The best way to understand this notion is in terms of a kind of explanation (Fine 2012). According to Independence, facts about our minds, language, and social practices do not constitutively explain the truth of the fundamental moral facts. In other words, the fundamental moral facts do not obtain in virtue of facts about our minds, language, or social practices.

Independence captures one sense in which morality may be claimed to be objective. The fourth thesis captures a different sense in which morality may be claimed to be objective. This is the sense on which not every practice of moral assessment is on a par.

(Non-Plenitude) Of the many possible coherent practices of moral assessment, only a few are correct. Not all practices are on a par.

This thesis requires some explanation. Consider a view of the metaphysics of morality on which there are a vast number of different moral properties. For instance, there are the properties of rightness and wrongness. There are also the properties of rightness* and wrongness*, the properties of rightness** and wrongness**, and so forth. Indeed, suppose there are so many properties analogous to rightness and wrongness that every coherent practice of assessing actions as "right" or "wrong" fits one of these pairs of properties. Suppose, too, that none of the pairs of properties is metaphysically privileged over the rest. (This view is loosely analogous to plenitudinous Platonism about mathematics, according to which every consistent mathematical theory correctly describes some part of mathematical reality [Balaguer 1998].) For instance, on this view, if members of some society have a coherent practice of moral assessment that involves accepting the claim "causing gratuitous suffering is wrong, but not on Tuesdays," this claim will be true when their word "wrong" is understood to stand for a different property than what our word "wrong" stands for. Such a plenitudinous view of morality is compatible with the first four theses. But it lacks an important kind of objectivity. The Non-Plenitude thesis is intended to rule out this kind of non-objective view.

The fifth thesis is the denial of moral naturalism.

(Non-Naturalism) Moral properties and relations are not natural properties and relations.

This is a metaphysical thesis about the nature of moral properties and relations. There are two conceptions of the natural that are relevant here. According to one conception, natural properties are the kinds of properties that play a role in the natural sciences (along with any properties that are reducible to or fully grounded in such properties). According to a second (and potentially broader) conception, natural properties are descriptive properties. (See Gideon Rosen's chapter "Metaphysical Relations in Metaethics" for one way to make this precise.) The difference between these two conceptions will not be important in what follows. What will be important is the claim, plausible on either conception, that natural phenomena do not have non-natural causes. Given this claim, the fifth thesis entails that moral facts do not cause natural phenomena.

The final two theses concern the status of our moral beliefs:

(Justification) By and large, the moral claims we believe (upon reflection and discussion) are epistemically justified.

(Reliability) By and large, the moral claims we believe (upon reflection and discussion) are true. Or, at least, we do significantly better than chance would predict.

According to these two theses, we are not epistemologically hopeless about the moral. Many of our moral beliefs are justified—they are rational for us to have. Many of our moral beliefs are true. Even if our moral beliefs are imperfect, they are correct more often than they would be if they were generated at random.

These seven theses concern moral language, moral thought, moral metaphysics, and moral epistemology. Taken together, they characterize a strong form of moral realism. Borrowing a term popularized by David Enoch, in what follows I will use "robust moral realism" to stand for this package of views (Enoch 2011). Robust moral realism will serve as the main target of the explanatory challenges discussed below.

HARMAN'S CHALLENGE

The first explanatory challenge I will discuss is due to Gilbert Harman. In *The Nature of Morality*, Harman presents a challenge to our belief in the existence of moral facts (Harman 1977: 3–10). Harman begins by noting a disanalogy between moral and scientific beliefs. Consider some scientific observation. To use Harman's example, consider a physicist observing a vapor trail in a cloud chamber and immediately coming to believe that there is a proton over there. Harman points out that the best explanation of the physicist's belief involves the existence of a proton. (Roughly: The proton interacted with the vapor in the chamber, causing there to be a vapor trail. Photons bounced off the vapor trail and interacted with photoreceptors in the physicist's eye, which led to a pattern of electric impulses in the physicist's optic nerve ... which led to the physicist's belief.) By contrast, consider some "moral observation." Again to use Harman's example, consider someone who observes children lighting a cat on fire and immediately comes to believe that what the children are doing is wrong. Harman suggests that the best explanation of the observer's belief does not involve the existence of moral facts, at least not as they are conceived of by the robust moral realist. The explanation of how the observer came to have the moral belief only seems to involve facts about the psychology (and culture and social background, etc.) of the observer.

Why does this (apparent) disanalogy pose some kind of problem for robust moral realism? There are a few different arguments that one could present that make use of Harman's disanalogy. For instance, one might claim that a belief in an independent truth doesn't count as a piece of knowledge unless the best explanation of how the thinker came to have the belief involves the truth in question. (Related principles concerning the nature of knowledge have been endorsed by several epistemologists [Goldman 1988: 22; Jenkins 2006: 139].) Given this principle, one might argue that since the best explanation of our moral beliefs does not involve moral truths, either (i) the moral truths are not independent of us or (ii) our moral beliefs do not count as knowledge. (This argument is broadly analogous to Benacerraf's problem for Platonism about mathematics [Benacerraf 1973].) This argument runs into difficulty, however, since the proposed principle is false. One important kind of counterexample concerns knowledge of the future. By observing water in a pot on the stove, I can come to know that the water will boil. This is so even though the fact that the water will boil doesn't play a role in the explanation of my belief.

A second argument that could be presented goes as follows: Since moral facts don't play a role in the best explanation of our moral beliefs, it is mysterious how it could be that our moral beliefs are by and large true. This casts doubt on our reliability about morality, and provides us with reason to give up our moral beliefs. This argument is an important one, and will be discussed below. But it is not the challenge that Harman poses.

To understand Harman's Challenge, it is helpful to return to the case of protons. Why are we justified in believing that protons exist? A plausible answer is that the claim that protons exist is part of the best explanation of our observations of the world, including the observation of vapor trails in cloud chambers. Our belief that protons exist is justified because the claim that protons exist plays an important role in explaining our observations. The same does not seem to be true for our belief in moral facts—moral facts do not seem to play any role in explaining our observations. Thus, argues Harman, we have reason to worry that our belief that there are moral facts is unjustified.

This line of thought is tied to a general picture of epistemic justification. According to a popular view, many of our beliefs are justified on the basis of Inference to the Best Explanation (Lipton 2004). Given some evidence, we are justified in coming to believe a hypothesis if it (i) does a sufficiently good job of explaining the evidence and (ii) does a significantly better job of explaining the evidence than alternatives. Candidate explanations are better than alternatives when they have various explanatory virtues—e.g., they are simpler, less ad hoc, have greater predictive power, yield greater understanding, are theoretically fruitful, and so on. Harman's Challenge depends on something like a converse to Inference to the Best Explanation: If certain claims do not play a role in the best explanation of our observations, we are not justified in believing them.

Harman's Challenge thus rests on a general epistemic principle. At a first stab, we can state the principle as follows: We are justified in believing that there exist objects of a certain kind only if the existence of those objects plays a role in the best explanation of the relevant kind of observations. As stated, this principle needs several refinements. One issue is that morality doesn't obviously involve the existence of special moral objects. Rather, morality involves the attribution of moral properties and relations—the properties of rightness, wrongness, goodness, and badness, and the relations of is-morally-better-than and is-a-moral-reason-for, among others. So the epistemic principle needs to be expanded to apply to properties and relations, too.

A second refinement is that, presumably, for us to be justified in believing in the existence of objects, it is not necessary that the objects play a role in explaining our observations of those very objects. (And similarly for properties and relations.) It would suffice that they play a role in explaining something else, so long as what is explained is part of our total body of evidence. Moreover, if a claim is itself part of our total body of evidence, it doesn't need to do any explanatory work for us to be justified in believing it. That it is part of our total evidence suffices.

A third refinement is that we may be justified in having some beliefs on a basis that doesn't involve Inference to the Best Explanation—for instance, we may be justified on the basis of perception or some kind of intuition, or perhaps because the beliefs in question are included in our epistemic starting point. (Harman himself endorses the claim that the beliefs included in one's epistemic starting point have a privileged epistemic status [1995: 189–93].) The epistemic principle at issue in Harman's Challenge is better understood as a principle governing the revision of belief. A belief in some claim loses justification when we acquire good reason to believe that the claim does not play an appropriate explanatory role.

Putting this all together, we get the following epistemic principle:

> If we are justified in believing that the best explanation of our total body of evidence does not involve the existence of a certain kind of object or the exemplification of a certain property or relation (and our total body of evidence doesn't itself entail that the kind of object exists or that the property or relation is exemplified), then this defeats any initial justification we might have had to believe that the kind of object exists or the property or relation is exemplified.

This principle is a mouthful. But it captures a straightforward idea. For us to be justified in believing that there are moral facts—that is, facts that attribute basic moral properties—such facts had better "earn their keep." They had better be part of our evidence or part of the picture of the world that does the best job of explaining our evidence.

Given this principle (perhaps with additional refinements), Harman's Challenge is generated by the following line of thought: Our direct evidence about the world does not include moral facts. Moral facts are not part of the best explanation of our moral beliefs. Moral facts are not part of the best explanation of any other part of our evidence. So, by the epistemic principle, we are not justified in believing in the existence of moral facts.

As I've so far presented it, Harman's Challenge is a challenge to our justification for believing in the existence of moral facts. But it is better to view it as a challenge to robust moral realism taken as a package. This is because there are ways to avoid or answer the challenge by rejecting realist theses. It is easy to see that the challenge poses no difficulty for a moral error theorist or for someone who denies that moral beliefs are justified. What is more interesting is that some naturalists are also able to straightforwardly answer the challenge (Harman 1986). Consider a view according to which moral properties are reducible to natural properties that do explanatory work. For instance, consider a view on which the property of moral rightness just is the property of maximizing the satisfaction of preferences. Alternatively, consider a view on which the property of moral rightness just is the property of being what would be approved of by one's community if it were fully informed. On such a view, Harman's Challenge can easily be answered: The constituents of the property of moral rightness—e.g., preference, satisfaction, and the like—do important explanatory work for us. Since the property of rightness reduces to these constituents, it does not need to do any additional explanatory work to belong in our picture of the world. Such a reductive view of moral properties may raise further questions—for instance, why is it that this natural property (as opposed to some other natural property) plays such an important role in our thought and talk? And in answering these further questions, it may be helpful to show how the property of moral rightness plays a distinctive explanatory role. But to answer Harman's Challenge, no more is required.

This kind of response doesn't work for all naturalist views. Consider a naturalist view according to which moral properties are distinctive natural properties that are not reducible to other natural properties. Since moral facts are a new kind of natural fact, to directly answer Harman's Challenge one would need to show how these natural facts earn their keep. Of course, a naturalist is in a better position than a robust realist to show this. This is for two reasons. First, adding new natural facts to one's picture of the world presumably requires less justification than adding new facts of a completely novel kind. Second, since the robust realist claims that moral facts are not natural facts, such a realist will presumably claim that moral facts cannot play a role in the causal explanation of natural phenomena. So they cannot earn their place in our picture of the world by providing causal explanations.

Harman's Challenge is therefore at its strongest targeted against robust moral realism. How might a robust realist respond to this challenge? One strategy is to find an explanatory role for moral facts to fill. Indeed, much of the debate over Harman's Challenge has taken this form, though typically on behalf of the non-reductive naturalist. For instance, Nicholas Sturgeon provides examples of cases in which we are happy to treat some moral fact as explaining some natural facts (1988: 243–44). Sturgeon's examples include (i) the fact that Hitler was morally depraved helps to explain why Hitler did what he did (e.g., start a world war) and (ii) the fact that the institution of slavery was particularly bad in the eighteenth and nineteenth centuries in Europe and North America helps to explain why widespread opposition to slavery appeared then. Sturgeon argues that these examples provide an answer to Harman's Challenge.

Sturgeon is right that we are sometimes happy to treat moral facts as explaining natural facts. But his examples don't provide a good avenue of response for the robust realist. One difficulty is that, as we have seen, the robust realist claims that moral facts are not natural facts, and so will resist the claim that moral facts can play a role in the causal explanation of natural phenomena. Instead, the robust realist will presumably account for Sturgeon's examples by claiming that what does the explanatory work in each of his cases is not a moral fact but whatever natural facts the moral fact is correlated with. Strictly speaking, it is not Hitler's depravity that explains his behavior but his racism, paranoia, and megalomania. It is not the badness of the institution of slavery that explains the wide-spread opposition to it, but the fact that it caused a great deal of suffering. On this view, when someone presents an apparent moral explanation of a natural fact, this is really just an elliptical way of pointing to a natural explanation of a natural fact.

A second issue with this strategy is that it is not enough to answer Harman's Challenge to present apparent examples of moral explanations of natural facts. Rather, it needs to be shown that the moral facts are indispensable for explaining the natural facts (Sayre-McCord 1988b). If we can explain the natural facts just as well without relying on moral facts, then the moral facts are not part of the best explanation of the natural facts—expla-nations that rely only on natural facts are more parsimonious. So Sturgeon's examples do not suffice to answer Harman's Challenge.

A different strategy for the robust realist to pursue is to reject the epistemic principle at the heart of Harman's Challenge. It is plausible that we are justified in believing that there are objects of a certain kind or that certain properties are exemplified only if the objects or properties do some important work for us. But one might think that this work need not be explanatory. There are other ways that a belief in moral facts, for example, could earn its keep.

The developments of this line of thought of which I am aware are all aimed at arguing for the existence of normative—and not strictly moral—facts. Belief in the existence of normative facts is then leveraged to help support belief in the existence of moral facts.

The most well-developed proposal of this kind is due to David Enoch (2011: chapter 3). Enoch suggests that, just as we can be justified in believing in the existence of certain facts because they are indispensable to our best explanations, we can also be justified in believing in the existence of certain facts because they are indispensable to our delibera-tions. On Enoch's view, the explanatory project and the deliberative project—the project of deciding what to do—are on a par in the sense that thinkers are epistemically justified in holding those beliefs and employing those rules of inference that are indispensable for successfully carrying out either one of these projects (Enoch and Schechter 2008). Enoch further argues that belief in the existence of normative truths is indispensable to the deliberative project. Consider some difficult decision between two courses of action. For it to make sense to deliberate about which action to take, one has to assume that there is an answer to the question of what one should do. And one has to assume that this answer is independent of the deliberative process itself, and more generally, that it has the hall-marks of a robustly realist fact. This, Enoch argues, justifies us in believing that there are robustly realist normative truths.

Enoch's line of argument is appealing, but it faces a number of worries. One issue is that engaging in deliberation doesn't seem to require that one assume that there is an answer to the question of what one should do. Rather, it only seems to require that one not assume that there isn't an answer to that question. So the belief that there are nor-mative facts may not be deliberatively indispensable. A second issue is that deliberation is a non-epistemic project, so indispensability to this project may not yield genuinely epistemic justification. (To avoid this worry, Enoch could move to a different project—for instance, the explanatory project. Enoch might claim that it is indispensable to the project of explaining phenomena that we take there to be better and worse explanations, which is itself a normative fact. A version of this view has been proposed by Geoffrey

Sayre-McCord [1988b: 178–80].) A third, related, worry is that epistemic justification is closely tied to truth, but being indispensable to deliberation is not. So deliberative indispensability cannot yield epistemic justification (McPherson and Plunkett 2015).

A final strategy available to the robust moral realist is to argue that some moral facts are part of our evidence, and so do not need to play an explanatory role for us to be justified in believing in them. Harman's discussion seems to fit with a particular conception of what our evidence is—a subject's evidence consists of claims about the subject's empirical observations. But this is a contentious view of what our evidence consists of. One might argue that our evidence includes other claims, too, perhaps including simple logical, mathematical, and moral truths. If that's right, then the moral truths that are part of our evidence don't need to do any explanatory work in order for us for us to be justified in believing them. We may be justified in believing in the existence of those moral facts directly, and then gain further justification for believing in the existence of the moral facts that help to explain those moral facts, and so on. The nature of evidence is a vexed topic in epistemology (Kelly 2014), but this strikes me as a promising approach for a robust realist to take.

EVOLUTIONARY DEBUNKING ARGUMENTS

The second group of challenges I will discuss are evolutionary debunking arguments against morality. There have been many different presentations of evolutionary debunking arguments in the literature (Ruse and Wilson 1986; Joyce 2006; Street 2006). Sometimes these arguments are focused on the moral. Other times they are focused on normativity more generally. Sometimes these arguments are used to argue for error theory. Other times they are used to argue for a mind-dependent (or society-dependent) view.

My discussion will take as its starting point the evolutionary debunking argument presented by Sharon Street (2006). This is because Street's argument is among the most sophisticated in the literature, and because focusing on Street's discussion will be helpful for drawing out several lessons. Street's argument is aimed at realism about normativity in general. For simplicity, I will refocus it against realism about morality. Street also claims that her argument has force against naturalist as well as non-naturalist views. For simplicity, I'll primarily focus on non-naturalist realism.

In broad outline, Street's argument (the "Darwinian Dilemma") is as follows: Our cognitive mechanisms for making moral judgments are the products of evolution by natural selection. Indeed, "the forces of natural selection have had a tremendous influence on the content" of our moral beliefs (Street 2006: 113). According to robust moral realism, the fundamental moral truths are independent of us. However, there are good scientific reasons to think that our ancestors were not selected for believing independent moral truths (or for having the motivational tendencies that would lead to believing such truths). Rather, they were selected for having beliefs (or motivational tendencies) that would provide them with survival and reproductive advantages. There are many different possible collections of moral beliefs. It would therefore be an astonishing coincidence if our moral beliefs matched the independent moral truth. Thus, robust moral realism leads to the conclusion that it is highly likely that our moral beliefs are false. This is an unacceptable conclusion. Therefore, robust moral realism is false.

One thing to note about this argument is that it aims to show that there is an internal tension in the robust realist view. The realist claims that our moral beliefs are by and large true. If Street's line of thought is correct, there is also an argument from premises the realist should accept—a Darwinian account of the evolution of our moral capacities as well as Independence and other realist theses—to the conclusion that it is likely that our moral beliefs are false. This internal tension has epistemic force. It provides realists with reason to give up some part of their package of views. Street suggests that the best claim to give up is Independence, and that the realist should move to a mind-dependent view. But there are alternatives—one could instead give up the claim that our moral beliefs are by and large true, or the claim that moral sentences and mental representations purport to represent moral facts, or perhaps some other realist thesis.

A second thing to note is that Street's argument is not meant to be a conclusive argument against robust moral realism. The premises don't entail that robust moral realism is false. If the argument is successful, rather, it shows that there is strong reason to reject robust realism. This reason may, in principle, be outweighed by competing considerations.

How exactly should Street's argument be understood? The argument has several moving parts. It is not transparent what the crux of the argument is, or how best to characterize the epistemic principle underlying it. In what follows, I will discuss ways of trying to explicate Street's argument.

IRRELEVANT INFLUENCE ARGUMENTS

A natural suggestion is to assimilate Street's argument to an "irrelevant influence" argument (Vavova 2016). This is an argument that relies on the claim that some of our beliefs were formed in a way that reflects the impact of irrelevant causal influences. This, it is claimed, defeats our justification for those beliefs.

More carefully, the suggestion is to understand the crux of Street's argument as follows: Assuming robust moral realism, we have good reason to believe that our moral beliefs were formed in a way that reflects the significant impact of irrelevant factors—factors that are disconnected from the truth of the claims in question. (The irrelevant factors are the factors that were important in the evolution of our cognitive mechanisms for making moral judgments.) According to a general epistemic principle, if under certain background assumptions we have good reason to believe that our beliefs about a domain were formed in a way that reflects the significant impact of irrelevant factors, this puts pressure on the combination of our beliefs about the domain with the background assumptions. Thus, there is an internal tension in the robust moral realist's package of views.

The problem with this argument is that the "general epistemic principle" it relies upon has counterexamples. Many of our beliefs were formed in ways that reflect the significant impact of irrelevant factors. For example, the fact that I was bored earlier today led me to surf the Internet, which led me to read an article on the red-spotted newt, which led me to come to have several new beliefs about the red-spotted newt. But the fact that I was bored is disconnected from the truth of claims about newts. Similarly, the fact that I grew up in the United States led me to have many beliefs about what various words mean in the English language. But the fact that I grew up in the United States is disconnected from the truth of claims about the meaning of those words.

Perhaps these counterexamples can be avoided by somehow restricting the "general epistemic principle." For instance, one might note that the irrelevant influences in my examples led me to acquire evidence about red-spotted newts and about the meanings of words in English. This suggests a potential fix: Irrelevant influences are not problematic when they lead to the acquisition of evidence. According to this proposal, learning about the significant impact of an irrelevant influence only defeats the justification of a belief if one is justified in believing that the irrelevant influence did not act via leading one to acquire new evidence that supports the belief.

The proposed fix, however, doesn't work. One problem is that learning about an irrelevant influence can defeat the justification of one of my beliefs even if the influence led me to acquire new evidence—for instance, I might find out that the influence led me to acquire evidence in a biased way or to misevaluate the new evidence. A second problem is that learning about an irrelevant influence can fail to defeat the justification of one of my beliefs even if the influence did not lead to me acquire new evidence—for instance, I might find out that the influence prompted me to better evaluate the evidence that I already possessed. Finally, there are areas of thought where talk of evidence seems inappropriate. For instance, it is plausible that whatever justifies my beliefs in basic logical, mathematical, and conceptual truths is not properly described as evidence. (What is my evidence for the claim that 2 is a number or that bachelors are unmarried?) If there is a distinction between problematic and unproblematic irrelevant influences in these areas of thought, this distinction cannot be drawn by appealing to the notion of evidence.

A different proposed fix is to claim that learning of the significant impact of irrelevant influences is problematic only when one has good independent reason to think that the influences have likely led one to have false (or unjustified) beliefs. More carefully, the proposed epistemic principle is as follows: If under certain background assumptions we have good independent reason to believe that our beliefs about a domain were formed in a way that makes it likely that they are false (or unjustified), this puts pressure on the combination of our beliefs about the domain with the background assumptions. Here, "we have good independent reason" means something like "putting aside our beliefs and reasoning about the relevant domain, we have good reason." Versions of this principle have been defended by David Christensen and Adam Elga in the context of peer disagreement arguments, and by Miriam Schoenfield and Katia Vavova in the context of irrelevant influence arguments (Christensen 2007; Elga 2007; Schoenfield 2014; Vavova 2016). To make use of this principle in an argument against robust moral realism, one would also have to argue that, assuming robust realism, we have good independent reason to think that the evolutionary origin of our cognitive mechanisms for making moral judgments makes it likely that our moral beliefs are false.

This proposed fix faces difficulties, too. First, it is not clear exactly how to understand "good independent reason"—which beliefs and reasoning are we supposed to put aside, and what exactly is it to put these beliefs and reasoning aside? Second, the proposed epistemic principle has problematic consequences. Consider the case of perception. Putting aside our perceptual beliefs, we have good reason to think that perception is likely to yield false beliefs about our environment. After all, there are very many possible perceptual mechanisms that a creature could employ, and only a small proportion of them tend to yield true beliefs. (We do, of course, possess a psychophysical explanation of how perception works and an evolutionary explanation of how we ended up with a reliable perceptual mechanism that together explain how it is that our perceptual mechanism yields true beliefs about our environment. But these explanations are ultimately justified on perceptual grounds, and so presumably have to be put aside when applying the principle.) So, according to a minor generalization of the epistemic principle, there is pressure to give up our perceptual beliefs or some anodyne background assumptions. That seems wrong.

What all of this suggests is that irrelevant influence arguments against robust moral realism are problematic. It is not clear how to state a correct general principle concerning the epistemic significance of irrelevant influences. (Indeed, I suspect there isn't such a principle.) Even if there is such a principle, it is not clear that it can be used to pose a difficulty for robust moral realism. If Street's argument is to have some force, we had better understand it in a different way.

THE RELIABILITY CHALLENGE

A better idea is to understand Street's argument—or the intuitive argument underlying it—not in terms of irrelevant influences but in terms of explanation. What generates the intuitive problem for robust moral realism is that, assuming the truth of robust realism, there seems to be no satisfying explanation of how our moral beliefs are reliable (Enoch 2011: chapter 7). (This argument is analogous to the Benacerraf-Field argument against mathematical Platonism [Field 1989: 25–30]. There are also analogous arguments concerning other areas of thought, including even logic [Schechter 2010].)

Put more carefully, the argument goes as follows: According to robust moral realism, the moral claims we believe are by and large true, at least given sufficient reflection and discussion (from Reliability). This is a striking fact, one that "cries out" for explanation. In particular, explanation is needed of how it is that we have cognitive mechanisms for making moral judgments that tend to yield true beliefs. Given robust moral realism, there is no satisfying explanation of our reliability that can be provided. That is because our moral beliefs do not constitutively explain the moral facts (from Independence), the moral facts do not causally explain our moral beliefs (from Naturalism), and there is no third factor that somehow explains both our moral beliefs and the moral facts. According to a general epistemic principle, it is a cost of a theory if it treats a striking phenomenon within the scope of the theory as accidental or otherwise inexplicable. Thus, there is a tension in the robust moral realist's overall package of views.

This is a better explication of Street's argument. It correctly highlights the role that the "astonishing coincidence" that we are reliable about the moral plays in generating the problem (Bedke 2009). It also relies on a plausible epistemic principle—it is a cost of a theory if it treats a striking phenomenon within the scope of the theory as inexplicable. This general principle seems central to our practices of theory choice.

One important feature of this argument is that evolution turns out not to play a role in generating the challenge for robust moral realism. The problem for the robust realist does not stem from there being some causal story of how we came to have our cognitive mechanisms for making moral judgments. Rather, the problem stems from the fact that we seem to lack a satisfying explanation of how it is we have reliable cognitive mechanisms for making moral judgments. Or, more accurately, the problem stems from the fact that there seem to be principled reasons to think there cannot be a satisfying explanation of how we have reliable cognitive mechanisms for making moral judgments, at least assuming robust moral realism.

I think that the fact that evolution does not play a role in this argument is exactly right. Pointing to the evolution of our moral capacities is part of what makes Street's argument so arresting. But this is more of a psychological phenomenon than an epistemological one. The evolutionary story makes salient a worry the robust moral realist already should have had—namely, that there is no satisfying explanation of how it is that we are reliable about morality. One way to see this point is to note that if we did possess a satisfying explanation of our reliability about morality, the evolutionary story of how we came to have our cognitive mechanisms for making moral judgments would not seem at all worrisome. A second way to see the point is to note that the evolutionary story does not rule out any explanation of our reliability about morality compatible with robust moral realism that was not already ruled out by a broadly scientific view of the world. So the presence of the evolutionary story does not seem to put any pressure on robust moral realism that wasn't already there.

To be fair, evolution may have a role to play if the Reliability Challenge is targeted against moral naturalism. According to moral naturalism, moral facts are natural facts. So they can play a role in causing natural phenomena. At least in principle, we may be able to explain our reliability about the moral by claiming that the moral facts caused our moral beliefs. Street's evolutionary account might be seen to put pressure on this sort of approach. If Street's evolutionary account rules out (or renders less plausible) potential naturalist explanations of our reliability, it will contribute to generating the problem for moral naturalism. Of course, to see if this is really so, one would need to generate specific candidate naturalist explanations of our reliability and determine whether Street's evolutionary account rules them out (or renders them less plausible).

A second important feature of the argument is that it rests on explanatory considerations. To answer the Reliability Challenge, one does not need to provide a justification of our moral beliefs or of robust moral realism. One doesn't need to provide new evidence for these claims. Rather, what is needed is an explanation of how it is that we are reliable about the moral. In principle, this explanation could make use of our moral beliefs or robust moral realism. Since the challenge is an explanatory rather than a justificatory one—and since the challenge is generated by an internal tension within the robust realist's package of views—it is perfectly fine to make use of robust realist theses or substantive moral claims in answering the challenge.

How should we respond to the Reliability Challenge? One option is to reject robust moral realism. There are several ways in which this could be done. We could give up the claim that moral sentences and mental representations purport to represent moral facts. We could give up the claim that we are reliable about the moral. As Street recommends, we could give up the Independence thesis and instead claim that we are reliable because the moral truths are constitutively explained by our moral beliefs. Alternatively, we could move to a naturalist view and claim that we are reliable because our moral beliefs are caused by the moral truths. (Street presents arguments against such a response, most notably that if the naturalist explanation relies on our substantive views, it will be question-begging [2008: 215–17]. As we've seen, this isn't obviously correct.) Or, instead, we could move to a plenitudinous view of moral properties. If every coherent moral practice fits some set of moral properties, it is easy to explain our reliability—no matter our practice, we would be bound to get it right.

Assuming we want to retain robust moral realism, how could we respond to the Reliability Challenge? One possible response is to reject the need to answer the challenge. The most sophisticated version of this response is due to Justin Clarke-Doane (2015). He argues that information can provide a reason to give up beliefs about a domain only if it provides reason to doubt the safety or the sensitivity of those beliefs. (Beliefs about a domain count as safe just in case we could not easily have had false beliefs about the domain. Beliefs about a domain count as sensitive just in case had the truths about the domain been different, we would have had correspondingly different beliefs.) Clarke-Doane argues that arguments such as the Reliability Challenge do not provide reason to doubt the safety or sensitivity of our moral beliefs, and so have no force. Clarke-Doane further argues that we have good reason to think that our fundamental moral beliefs are both safe and sensitive. If our fundamental moral beliefs are true, they are safe, since the evolutionary origins of our moral beliefs show that we could not easily have had different fundamental moral beliefs. If our fundamental moral beliefs are true, they are necessarily true, and so are automatically sensitive.

There are several problems with Clarke-Doane's response. One issue is that we might understand the Reliability Challenge as targeting the safety and sensitivity of our moral beliefs. If there is no explanation of how it is that we are reliable, this provides reason to think that we may not be reliable, which in turn provides reason to think that our beliefs are neither safe nor sensitive. A second issue is that there is reason to think that Clarke-Doane's epistemic principle is false. The principle makes the defense of necessarily true beliefs much too easy. There can be good arguments against beliefs that thinkers take to be both necessarily true and hard to avoid. If his principle were correct, these arguments could always easily be answered.

A second potential response to the Reliability Challenge is to claim that we are reliable about morality because our powers of rational reflection helped us to arrive at the moral truth. This proposal faces two difficulties. First, a version of the Reliability Challenge applies to our beliefs about what is rational. So this response may simply move the bump under the rug. Second, rational reflection requires a starting point—it starts with some initial beliefs and (hopefully) improves them. But if our initial moral beliefs are wildly unreliable, even careful rational reflection will be unlikely to yield true moral beliefs (Street 2006: 123–24).

A third proposal is to claim that what explains our reliability involves the nature of moral concepts (Cuneo and Shafer-Landau 2014: 424–28). On this view, if one accepts claims that are far enough away from the genuine moral truths, one is no longer thinking or talking about morality but about something else entirely. So there is a limit to how unreliable thinkers can be about the moral. There are three problems with this proposal. First, even if there is a limit to how unreliable someone can be about morality, one can still be pretty unreliable about the moral. So we still need an explanation of how we are as reliable as (we think) we are. Second, if the view is not to be a plenitudinous view, practices that are sufficiently far away from the genuine moral truths must either correspond to properties that are metaphysically less privileged than genuine moral properties or they must not correspond to properties at all. So we still would need an explanation of how it is that we ended up with a practice that corresponds to metaphysically privileged properties. Third, even if this proposal were to explain our reliability about the moral, it would not explain our reliability about what one ought to do in a more general sense (i.e., the "plain vanilla" ought). It is implausible that there are significant conceptual constraints built into our most general normative concepts, so the analogous strategy would not seem to work for explaining our reliability about beliefs involving these concepts.

In my view, the most plausible direct response to the Reliability Challenge is to present a "third-factor" view, according to which there is some factor that explains both the moral truths and our moral beliefs (Wielenberg 2010; Enoch 2011: 168–74; Sarksaune 2011). For example, according to a (toy) proposal due to Enoch, our ancestors were selected to behave in ways that promoted their survival. Natural selection did this in part by encouraging our ancestors to believe that it is good to behave in those ways. Moreover, survival is (typically) a good thing, and it is (typically) good to act in ways that promote survival. This is part of what explains our reliability about what's good. On this view, facts about what promotes survival causally explain our moral beliefs and also constitutively explain the moral facts. One can challenge this specific explanation. And one might worry that this view leaves something left to explain—for instance, that what natural selection aims at has a positive normative status. But this kind of view strikes me as a plausible avenue to pursue.

There is also an indirect response to the Reliability Challenge worth mentioning: Robust moral realism has "companions in guilt." This is so in two different senses. First, other domains face analogous challenges—including logic, mathematics, modality, conceptual truth, and so on. It is implausible that we should give up realism about all of these domains. This suggests that there must be some way of responding to the challenge. Second, versions of the Reliability Challenge arise for alternatives to robust moral realism. For instance, naturalist realist views are subject to the challenge. More interestingly, mind-dependent views of morality may also be subject to the challenge. There are very many possible ways in which the moral facts could depend on facts about our minds. It is a striking fact that the way that the moral facts actually depend on facts about our minds (according to a mind-dependent view) is one where the moral truths turn out to by and large match our moral beliefs (as opposed to, for instance, their negations). This fact "cries out" for explanation, too. If this is right, then robust moral realism doesn't face a distinctive problem.

Finally, it is worth noting that, even if it is successful, the Reliability Challenge does not conclusively show that robust moral realism is false. It only generates strong reason to reject robust moral realism. This reason may, in principle, be outweighed by competing considerations.

CONCLUSION

Let's take stock. If what I've argued here is correct, there are two pressing explanatory challenges facing robust moral realism. According to Harman's Challenge, for us to be justified in believing in the existence of moral facts, such facts had better be part of the picture of the world that does the best job of explaining our evidence. Given robust moral realism, it is difficult to see how this could be so. According to the Reliability Challenge, it is a striking fact that we are reliable about morality. Given robust moral realism, it is difficult to see how there could be an explanation of our reliability. This puts pressure on robust moral realism. (And, perhaps, analogous challenges put pressure on alternative metaethical views.)

There are plausible lines of response open to the robust moral realist. In response to Harman's Challenge, the robust realist might reject the central epistemic principle generating the challenge and claim that moral facts "earn their keep" in some way that does not involve explanation. Alternatively, the robust realist might claim that certain moral claims are part of our total body of evidence. In response to the Reliability Challenge, the robust realist might claim that some "third-factor" view is correct, according to which some factor both constitutively explains the moral truths and causally explains our moral beliefs. Alternatively, the robust realist might argue that the Reliability Challenge is a challenge facing all plausible views of morality, and so does not pose a problem specific to robust realism.

It is fair to say, though, that it has not been established that these challenges can be answered, either when targeted against robust moral realism or when targeted against alternative metaethical views. These explanatory challenges are still very much alive.

ACKNOWLEDGMENTS

Thanks to Tristram McPherson and David Plunkett for their helpful comments and boundless patience. Thanks to Jamie Fritz for extremely useful comments. Thanks also to David Christensen and David Enoch for discussion of many of these issues. This chapter was written while I was a visiting fellow at the Humanities Institute at the University of Connecticut. I am grateful to the University of Connecticut for its hospitality.

RELATED TOPICS

Chapter 1, "Non-Naturalistic Realism in Metaethics;" Chapter 2, "Naturalistic Realism in Metaethics;" Chapter 8, "Realism and Objectivity;" Chapter 9, "Metaphysical Relations in Metaethics;" Chapter 31, "Moral Skepticism."

REFERENCES

Balaguer, M. (1998) *Platonism and Anti-Platonism in Mathematics*, Oxford: Oxford University Press.

Bedke, M. (2009) "Intuitive Non-Naturalism Meets Cosmic Coincidence," *Pacific Philosophical Quarterly* 90: 188–209.

Benacerraf, P. (1973) "Mathematical Truth," *The Journal of Philosophy* 70: 661–79.

Christensen, D. (2007) "Epistemology of Disagreement: The Good News," *Philosophical Review* 116: 187–217.

Clarke-Doane, J. (2015) "Justification and Explanation in Mathematics and Morality," *Oxford Studies in Metaethics* 10: 80–103.

Cuneo, T. and Shafer-Landau, R. (2014) "The Moral Fixed Points," *Philosophical Studies* 171: 399–443.

Elga, A. (2007) "Reflection and Disagreement," *Noûs* 41: 478–502.

Enoch, D. (2011) *Taking Morality Seriously*, Oxford: Oxford University Press.

Enoch, D. and Schechter, J. (2008) "How Are Basic Belief-Forming Methods Justified?" *Philosophy and Phenomenological Research* 76: 547–79.

Field, H. (1989) *Realism, Mathematics, and Modality*, Oxford: Basil Blackwell.

Fine, K. (2012) "Guide to Ground," in F. Correia and B. Schnieder (eds.), *Metaphysical Grounding*, Cambridge: Cambridge University Press, pp. 37–80.

Goldman, A. (1988) *Empirical Knowledge*, Berkeley: University of California Press.

Harman, G. (1977) *The Nature of Morality*, Oxford: Oxford University Press.

—. (1986) "Moral Explanations of Natural Facts," *The Southern Journal of Philosophy* 24 supplement: 57–68.

—. (1995) "Rationality," in E. Smith, and D. Osherson (eds.), *Thinking*, vol. 3, Cambridge, MA: MIT Press, pp. 175–211.

Jenkins, C. S. (2006) "Knowledge and Explanation," *Canadian Journal of Philosophy* 36: 137–63.

Joyce, R. (2006) *The Evolution of Morality*, Cambridge, MA: MIT Press.

Kelly, T. (2014) "Evidence," *The Stanford Encyclopedia of Philosophy* (Fall 2014 Edition). Available at: http://plato.stanford.edu/archives/fall2014/entries/evidence/.

Lipton, P. (2004) *Inference to the Best Explanation*, second edition, New York: Routledge.

McPherson, T. and Plunkett, D. (2015) "Deliberative Indispensability and Epistemic Justification," *Oxford Studies in Metaethics* 10: 104–33.

Ruse, M. and Wilson, E. O. (1986) "Moral Philosophy as Applied Science," *Philosophy* 61: 173–92.

Sarksaune, K. (2011) "Darwin and Moral Realism: Survival of the Iffiest," *Philosophical Studies* 152: 229–43.

Sayre-McCord, G. (ed.) (1988a) *Essays on Moral Realism*, Ithaca: Cornell University Press.

—. (1988b) "Moral Theory and Explanatory Impotence," in G. Sayre-McCord (1988a), pp. 256–81.

Schechter, J. (2010) "The Reliability Challenge and the Epistemology of Logic," *Philosophical Perspectives* 24: 437–64.

Schoenfield, M. (2014) "Permission to Believe: Why Permissivism Is True and What It Tells Us about Irrelevant Influences on Belief," *Noûs* 48: 193–218.

Street, S. (2006) "A Darwinian Dilemma for Realist Theories of Value," *Philosophical Studies* 127: 109–66.

—. (2008) "Reply to Copp: Naturalism, Normativity, and the Varieties of Realism Worth Worrying About," *Philosophical Issues* 18: 207–28.

Sturgeon, N. (1988) "Moral Explanations," in G. Sayre-McCord (1988a), pp. 229–55.

Vavova, K. (2016) "Irrelevant Influences," *Philosophy and Phenomenological Research*.

Wielenberg, E. (2010) "On the Evolutionary Debunking of Morality," *Ethics* 120: 441–64.

FURTHER READING

Berker, S. (2014) "Does Evolutionary Psychology Show That Normativity Is Mind-Dependent?" in J. D'Arms and D. Jacobson (eds.) *Moral Psychology and Human Agency*, Oxford: Oxford University Press, pp. 215–52. (A careful discussion of Street's evolutionary debunking argument.)

Vavova, K. (2015) "Evolutionary Debunking of Moral Realism," *Philosophy Compass* 10: 104–16. (An introduction to evolutionary debunking arguments, distinguishing them from other kinds of arguments.)

White, R. (2010) "You Just Believe That Because…," *Philosophical Perspectives* 24: 573–615. (A sensitive discussion of many different kinds of irrelevant influence arguments.)

29

Moral Expertise

Karen Jones and François Schroeter

INTRODUCTION

We recognize the existence of expertise in many domains, from plumbing to physics, meteorology to medicine. Nor do we think it problematic to defer to the opinion of those who have the expertise we lack in these and other fields. When it comes to morality, however, many have the intuition that deference is problematic. This intuition is supported by reflecting on the oddness of, for example, becoming a vegetarian on the basis of someone telling you that meat eating is wrong, without yourself fully considering the matter. This chapter is an exploration of the asymmetry thesis, or the claim that morality differs from other domains of inquiry (with the possible exception of aesthetics) insofar as deference is problematic in the moral domain in a way that it is not in other domains. The asymmetry thesis can be defended using two broad strategies: 1. Challenge the existence of moral expertise, for justified deference must be deference to expertise not mere authority, so if there is no moral expertise then there should be no moral deference. 2. Identify something distinctive about morality that precludes deference. This chapter examines a variety of attempts to pursue each of these broad strategies, and argues they fail to provide adequate support for the asymmetry thesis.

We begin by exploring what moral expertise would be like, if it exists, and how the notion of expertise relates to the notion of experts ("Varieties of Moral Expertise and the Expertise/Expert Distinction"). It turns out that there are at least three different kinds of moral expertise: expertise in judgment, in action, and in giving and assessing reasons. Next, we consider metaethical objections to the very idea of moral expertise ("Metaethics and the Possibility of Moral Expertise"). We argue that moral expertise is compatible with the majority of metaethical views: only simple versions of non-cognitivism and nihilism must be opposed to moral expertise. In the final section ("Expertise and Moral Epistemology"), we explore what follows for communities of moral inquiry, given the supposition that moral expertise exists. Would such expertise support a rich social epistemology of the kind we find in science? A rich social epistemology includes epistemic divisions of labor, different credibility rankings, relations of deference, and roles for expert testimony and advice. Defenders of the asymmetry thesis claim that nothing much follows for the structure of communities of moral inquiry from the existence of moral expertise: either we cannot or should not access such expertise and our moral epistemology should remain individualist. We raise objections to these arguments against symmetry, arguing that they are inconclusive.

VARIETIES OF MORAL EXPERTISE AND THE EXPERTISE/EXPERT DISTINCTION

There are at least three possible kinds of moral expertise: expertise in judgment, expertise in action, and expertise in giving and evaluating reasons (for a related but somewhat different taxonomy, see Driver 2013). Those with expertise in judgment tend to arrive at true or nearly true moral judgments. Those with expertise in action reliably act well, and those with expertise in giving and evaluating reasons have the ability to articulate the morally relevant features of situations. Each type of expertise can be thought of as extending across the full range of morally significant choice situations, or as being held in a more limited, domain-specific way. A fourth kind of expertise, expertise about how moral cognition and moral language work, or about the development of moral concepts and conceptions, is sometimes confused with moral expertise but is its own distinctive kind of expertise, the kind developed by the study of metaethics or history of ideas.

Crosscutting the distinctions between expertise in judgment, action, and giving and evaluating reasons are two polar opposite models of what expertise consists in, which define the conceptual space into a spectrum along which we can locate less extreme views. According to the first model, moral expertise is a matter of knowing, and knowing how to apply, correct moral principles (Caplan 1992; Singer and Wells 1984). This model privileges intellectual abilities—including reasoning ability, knowledge of moral theory, and knowledge of non-moral facts—ahead of perceptual, behavioral, or emotional dispositions and thus can be described as intellectualist. At the opposite pole is Dreyfus and Dreyfus' (1991) model of moral expertise as engaged non-reflective moral coping. Those with expertise transcend the rules that formed part of their moral education and become able to react immediately and without deliberation to diverse moral situations (see also Churchland 1995, chapters 6 and 10). A somewhat weaker position takes moral expertise to be a matter of experienced practical judgment; the moral expert is the virtuous person who possesses practical wisdom (Dancy 1993, 2004; McDowell 1979). The deliverances of practical wisdom cannot be captured in a set of rules; however, unlike the radical approach of Dreyfus and Dreyfus, this approach allows a significant role for intellectual reflection in criticizing the principles and positions governing our moral thinking (McDowell 1994, 81). Clearly, there is room for many other intermediate positions, thereby generating a spectrum of views between the poles of extreme intellectualism and extreme anti-intellectualism.

These two polar opposite models of how moral reliability is achieved have different implications for the relationship between the three types of moral expertise, expertise in judgment, action, and giving and evaluating reasons. The intellectualist's appeal to rules and principles amounts to giving priority to expertise in justification, from which expertise in judgment will follow, but expertise in action might be entirely lacking. In contrast, anti-intellectualists like Dreyfus and Dreyfus give priority to expertise in action, which can be fully decoupled from expertise in justification and does not require expertise in judgment understood as occurrent, linguistically articulated thought.

If moral expertise exists, do moral experts exist? That depends on what we think an expert is. If we hold a restrictive account of what it takes to be an expert, such that experts must have knowledge rare in kind or degree, must be credentialized, and must occupy a distinct social role that supports deference, then the existence of expertise does not imply the existence of experts. Similarly, if we think experts require comprehensive, articulable knowledge of a field, then the existence of expertise in judgment and action is compatible with the non-existence of experts, as is the existence of domain-limited expertise in giving and assessing reasons. But there is a deflationary account of what it takes to be an expert which does not have these implications, according to which simply possessing expertise is enough to qualify as an expert no matter how widely shared that expertise is, whether or not it receives social recognition, and whether or not it is comprehensive in scope. As we will see in in the "Expertise and Moral Epistemology" section, some of the objections to moral deference rest not on concerns about the very idea of moral expertise but about recognizing experts, understood as persons occupying a socially sanctioned role.

METAETHICS AND THE POSSIBILITY OF MORAL EXPERTISE

In this section, we take as our primary example expertise in moral judgment, which has attracted the most attention in metaethics. But our conclusions generalize to other normative and evaluative domains. One might think that moral expertise presupposes strong metaphysical and semantic commitments about the existence of moral facts. For example, it might be thought that only if moral facts are robustly mind-independent does talk of moral expertise make sense. Just as those with expertise in the natural sciences know more about the nature of the world than the layperson, those with expertise in moral matters know more about the nature of the world of value than the moral beginner. Thus one might think that only if we have been able to resolve a complex cluster of meta-ethical problems can we reach a verdict on the existence of moral expertise. However, what seems crucial for expertise is it being legitimate to posit moral truth and knowledge, and being able to make sense of the idea that there are better and worse epistemic positions with respect to moral truth. If a metaethical position is able to do this, then it is compatible with the existence of expertise, whatever its stance on broader metaphysical and semantic issues.

The pre-conditions for moral expertise are weaker than might be first thought, but they are not trivial. More is required for expertise than the claim that we be able to *talk* of moral positions as better or worse, for someone committed to astrology can rank practitioners' verdicts as better or worse and there might even be agreement among practitioners about such rankings. If we accept that astrology purports to offer insight into personality and into the future using methodologies that can do neither of these things, then there can be no astrological expertise. Merely being able to say that positions can be ranked as better or worse is insufficient to establish the existence of genuine expertise. In addition, some epistemic positions must be more reliable at getting at the truth than others.

Not all metaethical positions are able to meet this bar. For instance, simple non-cognitivism of the kind advocated by Ayer (1952) rejects both talk of moral truth and the idea of better and worse moral positions. Moral statements are simply expressions of pro and con attitudes, attitudes which differ between agents, but which cannot be described as more or less appropriate. However, simple non-cognitivism is now universally rejected as unable to account for the seemingly objectivist features of our moral practices. Contemporary developments of non-cognitivism want to vindicate the idea of moral truth, and once you have the idea of moral truth you open up the possibility of moral knowledge and of more or less accurate positions with respect to moral truth (see Elisabeth Camp's chapter "Metaethical Expressivism"). For this reason, Blackburn (1998) and Gibbard (2003) reject the label of non-cognitivism, finding it misleading for their views.

Whether Blackburn and Gibbard's positions are ultimately compatible with moral expertise depends on how deflationary their account of moral truth is and hence whether it is able to ground the claim that one view is correct and another false. This remains an open question. The problem comes into focus when we consider two people engaged in moral disagreement. Each can say to the other, in seemingly objectivist fashion, "I am right, you are wrong"; the problem is how to break this symmetry. It could be broken if we were able to appeal to a perspective-independent fact, which one person latches onto and the other doesn't. However, the worry is that the machinery developed by Blackburn and Gibbard only grounds *perspective-dependent ascriptions* of truth and knowledge (Schroeter and Schroeter 2005, 5–12) when moral expertise seems to require something stronger: getting things right in a way that can be intersubjectively endorsed. Perspective-dependent ascriptions of truth fall short of this. Blackburn and Gibbard may be able to vindicate the idea that different individuals can ascribe moral expertise to each other, and can *talk as if* there is moral expertise. But this is insufficient to establish the existence of genuine moral expertise.

The other metaethical position that seems in immediate tension with the existence of moral expertise is nihilism. According to the nihilist, there are no moral facts; moral discourse is truth-apt, but there are no true attributions of moral properties to actual states of affairs. Nothing is good or bad, right or wrong. Nihilists typically offer error theories to explain how we could be so very mistaken in our understanding of our own moral practices (see Jonas Olson's chapter "Error Theory in Metaethics"). If all attributions of moral properties are false then there is no moral knowledge and we cannot make sense of the idea that some people's moral judgments are better than others.

Nihilism is sometimes combined with a fictionalist approach to moral discourse (see Richard Joyce's chapter "Fictionalism in Metaethics"). While denying that moral attributions are literally true, fictionalists insist that we evaluate moral claims as true or false in roughly the same way we evaluate claims about Sherlock Holmes' professional life as true or false. Insofar as there are better and worse interpreters of standard fictional claims such as 'SH had a difficult childhood', or 'SH must have had mathematical training', there may be better or worse interpreters of moral fictions: some individuals may be better than others at getting at what's true according to the fictions. Fictionalism thus seems compatible with the existence of moral expertise.

Metaethical positions prima facie compatible with the possibility of moral expertise are constructivism and realism. We discuss each in turn. Constructivism takes a variety of forms, united by the core thought that moral facts are constituted by the deliverances of a deliberative procedure, whether of ideal reason (Kant 1991), ideal discursive practice (Apel 1990, Habermas 1990), or contractual irresistibility (Rawls 1970, Scanlon 1998) (see Melissa Barry's chapter "Constructivism"). All these theories can posit moral truth and moral knowledge because they do not reduce moral facts to the upshot of agents' actual deliberations, but rather to various forms of ideal deliberation. This idealizing move opens up the space between actual attitude and ideal attitude that is required to vindicate classifying moral views as better or worse, more or less accurate. So long as the idealizing moves are justified, constructivism in its various forms is compatible with moral expertise. The same lesson applies to ideal response theories, which take moral facts to be constituted by our idealized conative attitudes, whether idealized desire (Smith 1994) or idealized affective response (Wiggins 1987; McDowell 1998, 151–166). So long as these theorists can make good on their idealizing moves (but see Enoch 2005 for an argument that they cannot), they are compatible with moral expertise.

Moral realism is typically defined as the conjunction of the semantic claim that moral statements are truth-apt, the metaphysical claim that moral facts are independent of our attitudes and norms, and the epistemological thesis that we can know at least some moral truths (Boyd 1988, Sayre-McCord 1988; but see Billy Dunaway's chapter "Realism and Objectivity" for worries about the adequacy of this definition). Moral realists typically endorse context-invariant cognitivism, such that the truth of moral statements does not vary across the context of utterance or standards of assessment—for instance, the truth of the judgment that incest is morally wrong is not affected by the context in which the judgment is uttered or assessed. Moral realism (in its standard, context-invariant form) is so strongly associated with the idea of moral expertise that some theorists (McGrath 2011) who are skeptical of moral expertise take realism's association with expertise to count against it. Nevertheless, realism supports the existence of moral expertise only if it is able to defend its epistemological claim. Some theorists argue that realism makes moral facts so independent of our responses and attitudes that they fall outside our cognitive reach, threatening the very possibility of moral knowledge (Gibbard 2003, Joyce 2006, Street 2006). If it does, this would be a major problem for realism, both as a metaethical position and as a basis on which to support moral expertise.

One might wonder whether moral expertise is compatible with metaethical relativism. Moral relativism can be construed as:

(i) a metaphysical claim about the world: that there is no single, absolute, universal morality, or
(ii) a semantic claim about language: that the truth value of moral utterances is relative to some parameter, such as a moral code or a culture (see Isidora Stojanovic's chapter "Metaethical Relativism").

Both versions of relativism seem to be compatible with expertise. Take the metaphysical version first. What's permitted by a moral code may depend on complex facts about prevailing social norms and empirical circumstances. Those who are more reliable in discerning compatibility with the code determined by those circumstances will have moral expertise *relative to that code*. Moreover, some judges may be reliable at discerning which actions are right relative to different codes. So the relativist may hold that there can be experts in more than one moral code. Thus there is room for a kind of code-relative moral expertise on this relativist view of morality, but this will fall short of the kind of non-code-relative expertise that people might have hoped for. The semantic version will also leave room for expertise, as long as identifying the relevant parameter is not a trivial task. For instance, if the parameter for assessing truth and falsity of moral utterances is determined by mutually negotiable standards within a conversational context, then some of us may be more skilled at determining which standards are invoked and what the content of those standards is. In that case, the semantic relativist can allow for a relativized notion of moral expertise along the same lines as the metaphysical relativist.

EXPERTISE AND MORAL EPISTEMOLOGY

If there is moral expertise in judgment, whether or not that expertise extends broadly or is domain-limited, or even—at the limit case—is just the ability to do better with respect to the truth of some moral claim (Enoch 2014), what follows for moral epistemology? Should moral epistemology be fully social on the model of scientific inquiry, which permits epistemic divisions of labor, deference to expert authority, and testimonial transfer of knowledge? In the literature, these questions are taken up in the context of testimony about moral matters. Some examples support the intuition that moral and other knowledge should be treated symmetrically. For example, if you are not especially good at applying a particular moral concept, such as sexism, then it seems you might defer to someone with better experience in this area (Jones 1999); if you are unsure how to weigh up the various considerations that count for and against an action—for example how solidarity is to be weighed against consumer inconvenience in determining whether to strike—then you might defer to a more experienced friend (Hopkins 2007); or, again, if you think your moral judgment might be tainted by bias, it seems appropriate to defer to someone who is more distant from the situation (Sliwa 2012). The examples that prima facie count in favor of moral deference concern particular deficits rather than global moral impairment and subsequent global deference. The issue is whether, and if so under what circumstances, a mature and ordinarily competent moral agent should defer to another agent's expertise. No one denies the importance of deference for the moral beginner or defends global deference on the part of the morally mature to a guru figure.

If some examples seem to support moral deference, others seem to undermine it. For example, there is something decidedly odd about becoming a vegetarian on the basis of someone's telling you that eating meat is wrong (McGrath 2009, Hills 2009); nor is the situation significantly improved if they tell you that the reason meat eating is wrong is because farming methods cause unnecessary animal suffering (Hills 2009). Unless you yourself understand why causing unnecessary suffering makes an action wrong, and are therefore able to dispense with reliance on the authority of the other, there remains something odd about your deference. There is no parallel oddness in deferring to the views of your physician about what treatment to take.

Appeal to examples alone cannot resolve the asymmetry debate. Those who argue in favor of asymmetry take on the burden of demonstrating what the relevant difference is between the two cases, if that difference does not lie in general metaethical worries about the possibility of moral expertise. Arguments in favor of asymmetry divide into two kinds:

epistemic and non-epistemic (Hopkins 2007). Epistemic arguments purport to show that we cannot get moral knowledge from moral testimony; non-epistemic arguments claim that while it might be possible to get moral knowledge second-hand, there are political, moral, or other reasons for not getting our knowledge in this way.

There are two main epistemic arguments against moral testimony, even granting the existence of moral expertise: the practicality argument and the argument from the impossibility of identifying experts. According to the practicality argument, the close link between moral judgment and action makes moral knowledge a matter of knowledge how, rather than knowledge that. Testimony can transfer knowledge that, but not knowledge how; hence it is useless in the moral case (Anscombe 1981, 47–48; Hopkins 2007). This argument overstates the role of knowledge how in morality. Though it is plausible that our moral competences include some knowledge how, it is implausible to suppose that they are not in large part constituted by propositionally articulated beliefs that could be transferred by linguistic means and so could be acquired from testimony (Hopkins 2007, 618–620).

In order to gain knowledge from testimony, one must be able to pick out those who are likely to have the required expertise. If this cannot be done, then no matter whether there is expertise out there, it is unavailable to us as an epistemic resource. McGrath (2008) claims that while we can pick out experts in other domains, the existence of moral disagreement means that we cannot do so in the moral domain. In some fields we can check expertise independently; for example, we can check the expertise of weather forecasters by seeing if their predictions hold, of engineers by seeing if their bridges hold. In addition, for a wide class of experts, from plumbers to physicists, there is agreement about appropriate training. But, claims McGrath, neither of these apply in the moral case. McGrath argues that, in the moral case, there is a danger that many explanations that purport to show why one side is more likely to be in error than the other will be question-begging or circular (McGrath 2008, 99). Thus, we lack an error theory as to why one side should be right and the other wrong; hence, deferring to either would be problematic.

The problem of how to pick out those with expertise is important; however, it is not clear that it supports the asymmetry thesis, for where there is controversy about, for example, medical matters, testimony is also ruled out because even if one side or the other is correct, no one is in a position to tell which side is which (Sliwa 2012, 190). Moreover, McGrath only considers all-in judgments, and yet they form just a fraction of our moral judgments. We not only form verdicts about what is right and wrong, but also about what is just and courageous; about what kinds of moral considerations are relevant to settling an issue; about the nature and significance of different values, such as the nature and significance of respect; and so on. It is easier to understand what kinds of experience and training would put an agent in a better epistemic position with respect to the nature and significance of these specific values or virtues. Think, for example, of the moral understanding of the need and frailty of human beings that can emerge from a life, such as Mother Teresa's, spent caring for the dying destitute. Such lives might not present equivalent lessons in the value of social justice as lives spent resisting political repression (Jones 1999, 65).

When it comes to disagreement about all-in verdicts such as whether an action is right or wrong—that is, when it comes to correctly applying our thin moral concepts—it can be harder to assess the comparative epistemic qualifications of potential authorities than it is when it comes to claims using thick moral concepts such as those expressed by the virtue terms or terms for specific moral values such as respect. We currently do not have the kind of story about how such all-in expertise, especially in domain-unrestricted form, is acquired. Nevertheless, we do have theories about factors that are likely to distort all-in judgment. For example, when there is reason to think that someone is likely to be biased because they are too close to the situation and have vested interests, we have no difficulty identifying who might be better placed than them with respect to forming an all-in verdict about the right thing to do (Sliwa 2012, 179).

The second family of arguments against symmetry are non-epistemic and argue that the problem with moral testimony is not that it cannot transmit knowledge but that it should not be used as a source of such knowledge for moral or other practical reasons. The first argument of this type can be quickly dispensed with, as it rests on a slide from expertise to the socially sanctioned role of experts. On this view, experts occupy distinct and certified roles in our economy of credibility: their opinion is sometimes to be taken as definitive and always to be taken more seriously than that of a non-expert. 'Expert' is thus not only an epistemic status, it is also a social role. Some wonder whether that social role is compatible with democratic decision-making, since it privileges the views of some over others and that appears incompatible with granting equal respect for different ethical stances. Likewise, the social role of moral expert seems incompatible with joint deliberation (e.g., ethics committees), and with legal reasoning where it risks usurping deliberation by testifying to the matter at hand (Nussbaum 2002). In pluralist democratic societies committed to neutrality among conceptions of the good, it seems that there can be no space for the social role of moral expert. Perhaps it could be argued that even in such societies there can be a role for moral experts in providing specialized input into deliberation while not determining its outcome. However, in the face of moral disagreement, even this more modest proposal would face insuperable practical difficulties, for how would the experts be selected (Jones 1999)? Nevertheless, these arguments against the socially sanctioned role of moral expert do not count against recognizing the moral expertise that individuals can bring to deliberation.

The remaining two main arguments—the argument from autonomy and the argument from moral worth—are not so readily dismissed. Deference in moral matters might be thought to be incompatible with autonomy; insofar as we defer to others on moral matters, it might be thought that we are no longer self-legislators (Kant 1991), or properly in charge of our deliberative decision-making (Driver 2006, Jones 1999). The argument from autonomy is a better way of pressing the objection that might lie behind the thought that the importance of moral matters is incompatible with deference regarding them. After all, we willingly defer on important non-moral matters such as cancer treatments.

Whether the autonomy argument supports asymmetry depends on the account of autonomy you hold. If you think of autonomy as requiring independence from others, then our epistemology, whether moral or otherwise, must be individualistic. However, such accounts of autonomy have been roundly criticized, for it is hard to see why autonomy conceived as independence should be something valuable. A more plausible account of autonomy views it as involving, among other things, the capacity to reflect critically on the principles and beliefs that one adopts. Through such reflection, one exerts agency and takes responsibility for one's own views. This model of autonomy does not support the asymmetry thesis. Just as in the non-moral case, where there can be non-reflective servile deference to others, there can be non-reflective servile deference about moral matters. Just as in the non-moral case, where there can be engaged, critical deference to others, likewise there can be in the moral case. A Kantian account of autonomy, according to which the will must determine its own guiding principles free from the influence of incentive or other outside influence, would provide the necessary support for the asymmetry thesis. Such an account of autonomy, however, is highly unattractive unless combined with the additional Kantian thesis that the demands of morality are a priori knowable and equally available to all rational agents. If there is equal accessibility, then we all of us are equal in expertise, and there is no need for deference. Hence accepting this account of autonomy takes you out of the deference debate altogether.

There remains the argument from moral worth (Nickel 2001, Hills 2009). Hills offers the most systematic elaboration of this line of argument. Hills argues that agents who rely on moral testimony may get moral knowledge but they will continue to lack moral understanding. Because they lack this understanding their actions, and they themselves as agents, are morally deficient. Knowing that p is different from knowing why p, and knowing why p is different again from *understanding* why p (Hills 2009, 100–106; Hills 2016). To understand why an action is morally wrong, you must understand the reasons why it is wrong. Understanding requires more than knowing that there is a reason why it's wrong, or even knowing what that reason is; you must also grasp the support relation linking the consideration that is the reason to the action for which it is a reason. This support relation cannot be grasped in isolation from understanding the relative importance of that consideration in relation to other considerations that might bear on that action as well as how that consideration might support other actions in different contexts. Thus, this understanding cannot be easily isolated in a well-defined set of local knowledge-that claims. Hills argues that understanding why p involves the abilities to follow someone's explanation as to why p, give an explanation in your own words, draw the conclusion that p from the considerations that support it, make related inferences to somewhat different conclusions in similar but not identical cases, and give the right explanations in relevantly similar cases, even where those explanations differ somewhat (102–103). Clearly, you can know why p (that is, know what reason supports p) without having these further capacities.

Hills' account of moral understanding could be challenged as overly intellectualist, given that it requires articulacy and so demands expertise in giving and evaluating reasons. However, the articulacy requirement could be dropped in favor of a notion of implicit or tacit understanding (Hills 2016, 7). For this reason, we set aside concerns about articulacy to focus on Hills' core claim that the moral worth of action requires the agent to have abilities that extend beyond getting it right in the particular case to getting it right in related but different cases.

Moral understanding has epistemic value insofar as it equips us better to contribute to shared inquiry and insofar as it helps us get things right in a range of related cases (Hills 106–107). But, according to Hills, the central value of moral understanding is itself moral: moral understanding affects the moral worth of actions. The reasons for which an action is done make a difference to what is done: though Kant's self-interested shopkeeper does the right thing, he does not do it for the morally right reason and this deprives his action of moral worth (Kant 1991). What is distinctive about Hills' development of this thought is the requirement not only to know what the reason is, but to act with the kind of orientation towards that reason that presupposes the broader abilities required for understanding.

Hills argues that when someone does the right thing simply because they have been told that it is right by a trustworthy informant, they do not act for the right reasons and so their action lacks moral worth. While they are concerned about doing the right thing, they do not have access to the reasons that make their action right and so cannot act for them. At best their reason is "it is right, he told me," and that is no genuine right-making reason. This claim could be challenged; perhaps someone else's say-so can be a genuine right-making reason (Markovits 2010, 219), but let us grant, for the sake of argument, that there is something deficient about the actions of a person who acts from bare testimony about all-in rightness. Their actions are better than those of someone who doesn't care about the moral quality of their actions, but they are not responsive to that which makes the actions right.

Hills' point is not yet established, however, since very little moral testimony uses only thin moral concepts such as rightness. Most moral testimony concerns what reasons are and are not relevant in a particular context and even testimony about all-in rightness is typically also reason-rich: we are not told simply that φ-ing is the right thing to do, but that φ-ing is right because of reason R. The real test for Hills' view are cases where the testifier transfers their knowledge of the right-making reasons to the recipient of their testimony, as when, for example, someone says that it is right to give money to people living in poverty because justice, not just charity, requires it. In cases of this kind, the recipient of testimony is concerned about doing the right thing and has chosen a knowledgeable informant on the basis of whose testimony she now knows that an action is right, and knows the reason why it is right but still lacks the abilities required to understand why it is right. Hills claims that "more is required for morally worthy action: you need to act for the reasons that make your action right" (2009, 117). The puzzle, however, is why having been granted testimonial access to the reasons that make your action right, you are still not acting for those reasons. Hills claims you are not because you are not properly oriented towards those reasons, but that is disputable. You are not independently oriented towards those reasons—you require the assistance of someone else to turn your attention and motivation in their direction—but still it seems, with this assistance, you can come to respond to them. What is at issue here is whether an agent needs the kind of rich orientation towards reasons that requires the understanding characteristic of virtue before she counts as responding to them. Hills has not given an argument that this is necessary. We might think that those with understanding have a stronger counterfactual link to reasons than those who lack it: that is, were the situation to be somewhat changed, they would still be capable of responding appropriately to their reasons. However, reliability can be achieved second-hand, provided an agent correctly chooses their informants. Moreover, it is unclear why responding to reasons on one occasion would require the ability to reliably respond to similar reasons in different cases. In sum: acting on the basis of someone else's all-in judgment about what action is right without any explanation of what the reasons are might indeed be incompatible with the moral worth of that action; but for all that has been argued, when knowledge of the right-making reasons is also transferred, and one acts on that basis, the action has moral worth.

Any argument that purports to show that actions based on reasons, access to which is at second-hand, lack moral worth must also offer an account of how to weigh up the significance of this lost moral worth relative to the significance of the moral risk of acting wrongly because we choose to rely on our judgment rather than on the judgment of someone else who is better placed to get it right (Enoch 2014). Perhaps if we are justified in thinking that the other is more likely to be right about the matter than we are, we can be required to defer and can even be blameworthy for not doing so (Sliwa 2012, 193; Enoch 2014). There are reasons to be concerned at the very idea of weighing the value of performing a morally worthy action, understood as requiring exercise of one's own moral understanding, against the disvalue of risking a morally wrong action. An agent who is concerned with the worth of their actions, even at the risk of acting wrongly, seems overly focused on the quality of their own agency. Anyone who would weigh the value of their having the opportunity to perform a morally worthy action against the risk of performing a wrong action seems to have the vice of moral self-involvement, a vice analogous to that of the person who acts out of concern for their own virtue rather than in response to virtue-relevant features of the situation. Thus granting the highly controversial claim that moral worth requires moral understanding in fact places fewer restrictions on the scope of moral deference than it might first appear. It would prohibit deference only in cases in which you justifiably believe that your judgment is at least as good as anyone else's. But in those cases, there is no need to defer in the first place, just as there is no reason to defer regarding mathematical or scientific matters when your judgment is at least as good as anyone's to whom you might defer.

Yet the thought that there must be some asymmetry might persist: if we don't care to go in for mathematics or medicine, there is nothing wrong with our simply not developing the capacities that would be required to have an informed judgment about such matters. We are allowed to stand as consumers of, rather than contributors to, inquiry regarding non-moral matters. Life is short, and we cannot develop all our intellectual capacities; indeed, our collective ability to know as much as we know rests on epistemic divisions of labor and on our willingness to defer to those with the relevant expertise. In contrast, it seems that we cannot escape participating in moral inquiry, just by virtue of the fact that we each of us must deliberate about what to do and our individual verdicts about this, as well as the verdicts we arrive at when we deliberate together, amount to taking a stance on what ought to be done, what things matter, and how best to live. Moral decision-making is embedded in the fabric of our everyday lives and is thus inescapable. Unless we are to have someone constantly at our side making each and every decision for us, it seems that we cannot avoid developing at least those moral skills that are required to navigate that range of ethical problems we routinely encounter. Our moral outlooks might be significantly shaped by deference and we might choose to defer when it comes to novel non-everyday situations but we cannot stand as global consumers of the deliverances of other people's moral expertise in the way that we can stand as wholesale consumers of medical expertise. Even if it is an overstatement to claim that we must each of us exercise our moral understanding whenever we can, there is surely something right in the thought that we are required to develop and exercise our moral understanding in at least that range of ethical problems that form part of our daily lives. This demand does not apply in other domains of inquiry. Moreover, given the assumption that moral expertise is developed by experience, the inescapability of moral significant encounters suggests that we each have something to contribute to the necessarily shared task of working out what is worth pursuing and how to live well. If we are overly deferential, we fail to hold up our end in this communal task.

Neither of these observations establishes an obligation to cultivate all our moral capacities. Nor do they support the claim that we should use testimony only when there is no other way to secure the knowledge we need (Hills 2012), and thus that there should be no moral "specialization" equivalent to the specialization permitted in other areas of inquiry. The suggestion that we have an obligation to reduce the need for moral testimony as much as possible rests on assumptions about the nature of the world of value and about our own capacities. If the world of value is complex and if our understanding of it rests on our experience, then there is reason to think that we cannot develop all our moral capacities to an equivalent extent and we may do worse by trying than by practicing wise deference (Jones 1999, 77). Limited forms of moral specialization, with their accompanying practices of deference, will be permissible.

CONCLUSION

The question of whether there is moral expertise is connected to questions in metaethics and moral epistemology. However, the relation between these questions is not as straightforward as it might first appear. Many metaethical positions are compatible with the possibility of moral expertise, which requires not robustly mind-independent moral properties but only positing moral truth, moral knowledge, and the possibility of better and worse moral verdicts. The existence of moral expertise is compatible with denying that moral epistemology should become fully social on the model of science, for there might be epistemic, political, practical, or moral objections to accessing such expertise. Nevertheless, arguments in defense of the asymmetry thesis and hence against a genuinely social moral epistemology remain inconclusive.

REFERENCES

Anscombe, E. (1981) "Authority and Morals," in *The Collected Philosophical Papers of G.E.M. Anscombe*, Minneapolis: Minneapolis University Press.

Apel, K.-O. (1990) *Diskurs und Verantwortung*, Frankfurt am Main: Suhrkamp.

Ayer, A.J. (1952) *Language, Truth and Logic*, New York: Dover Publications.

Blackburn, S. (1998) *Ruling Passions*, Oxford: Clarendon Press.

Boyd, R. (1988) "How to Be a Moral Realist," in G. Sayre-McCord (ed.) *Essays on Moral Realism*, Ithaca, NY: Cornell University Press.

Caplan, A.L. (1992) *If I Were a Rich Man Could I Buy a Pancreas? And Other Essays on the Ethics of Health Care*, Bloomington and Indianapolis: Indiana University Press.

Churchland, P. (1995) *The Engine of Reason, the Seat of the Soul: A Philosophical Journey into the Brain*, Cambridge, MA: MIT Press.

Dancy, J. (1993) *Moral Reasons*, Oxford: Blackwell.

—. (2004) *Ethics without Principles*, Oxford: Clarendon Press.

Dreyfus, H. and S. Dreyfus (1991) "Towards a Phenomenology of Ethical Expertise," *Human Studies* 14: 229–250.

Driver, J. (2006) "Autonomy and the Asymmetry Problem for Moral Expertise," *Philosophical Studies* 128: 619–644.

—. (2013) "Moral Expertise: Judgment, Practice and Analysis," *Social Philosophy and Policy* 30: 280–296.

Enoch, D. (2005) Why Idealize? *Ethics* 115: 759–787.

—. (2014) "A Defense of Moral Deference," *Journal of Philosophy* 111: 229–258.

Gibbard, A. (2003) *Thinking How to Live*, Cambridge: Harvard University Press.

Habermas, J. (1990) *Moral Consciousness and Communicative Action*, Cambridge, MA: MIT Press.

Hills, A. (2009) "Moral Testimony and Moral Epistemology," *Ethics* 120: 94–127.

Hills, A. (2015) "Understanding Why," *Noûs* 50: 661–688.

Hopkins, R. (2007) "What Is Wrong with Moral Testimony?" *Philosophy and Phenomenological Research* 74: 611–634.

Jones, K. (1999) "Second-Hand Moral Knowledge," *Journal of Philosophy* 96: 55–78.

Joyce, R. (2006) *The Evolution of Morality*, Cambridge, MA: MIT Press.

Kant, I. (1991) *Groundwork of a Metaphysics of Morals*, trans. H.J. Paton, London: Routledge.

McDowell, J. (1979) "Virtue and Reason," *The Monist* 62: 331–350.

—. (1994) *Mind and World*, Cambridge, MA: Harvard University Press.

—. (1998) *Mind, Value, and Reality*, Cambridge, MA: Harvard University Press.

McGrath, S. (2008) "Moral Disagreement and Moral Expertise," *Oxford Studies in Metaethics* 3: 87–107.

—. (2009) "The Puzzle of Pure Moral Deference," *Philosophical Perspectives* 23: 321–344.

—. (2011) "Skepticism about Moral Expertise as a Puzzle for Moral Realism," *Journal of Philosophy* 108: 111–137.

Markovits, J. (2010) "Acting for the Right Reasons," *Philosophical Review* 119: 201–242.

Nickel, P. (2001) "Moral Testimony and Its Authority," *Ethical Theory and Moral Practice* 4: 253–266.

Nussbaum, M. (2002) "Moral Expertise? Constitutional Narratives and Philosophical Argument," *Metaphilosophy* 33: 502–520.

Rawls, J. (1970) *A Theory of Justice*, Cambridge, MA: Harvard University Press.

Sayre-McCord, G. (1988) "Introduction: The Many Moral Realisms," in *Essays on Moral Realism*, Ithaca, NY: Cornell University Press.

Scanlon, T.M. (1998) *What We Owe to Each Other*, Cambridge, MA: Harvard University Press.

Schroeter, L., and F. Schroeter (2005) "Is Gibbard a Realist?" *Journal of Ethics and Social Philosophy* 2: 1–18.

Singer, P., and D. Wells (1984) *The Reproductive Revolution*, Oxford: Oxford University Press.

Sliwa, P. (2012) "In Defense of Moral Testimony," *Philosophical Studies* 2012: 175–195.

Smith, M. (1994) *The Moral Problem*, Oxford: Wiley-Blackwell.

Street, S. (2006) "A Darwinian Dilemma for Realist Theories of Value," *Philosophical Studies* 127: 109–166.

Wiggins, D. (1987) "A Sensible Subjectivism?" in *Needs, Values, and Truth*, Oxford: Blackwell.

30

Intuitionism in Moral Epistemology

Elizabeth Tropman

Attributions of moral knowledge are common in everyday life. We say that we know that some actions are morally right or wrong, permitted or required. Yet how do we know such moral claims? Moral intuitionism is a family of theories in moral epistemology that tries to answer this question. Intuitionists are not skeptics about moral knowledge. They think that there are moral truths for us to know and, further, that knowledge of these truths is possible. What distinguishes intuitionism from other anti-skeptical moral epistemologies is the idea that we can know some moral truths directly, without inferring them from premises. According to many intuitionists, it is possible for us to know that keeping promises is morally right even if we do not hold this belief on the basis of further evidence or proof.

While intuitionism was popular in the early twentieth century, it was subsequently dismissed as implausible. Recently, there has been renewed interest in intuitionism. Philosophers have defended updated versions of the theory and argued that the view has been misunderstood. This chapter considers the merits of intuitionism in moral episte-mology. In what follows, I examine different ways of being an intuitionist and indicate the relative strengths and weaknesses of various approaches within intuitionism.

MORAL INTUITIONISM: A GENERAL CHARACTERIZATION

All moral intuitionists are united by their commitment to two claims: (1) the descriptive claim that some moral beliefs are non-inferential, and (2) the normative claim that some non-inferential moral beliefs have positive epistemic status. The first claim is about the causal history of certain moral beliefs. It asserts that the moral beliefs are not inferred from prior premises. The notion of "inference" calls for clarification. Not all reasoning occurs explicitly. Implicit inferences, while not rehearsed overtly, are accessible to the agent upon reflection, and this is why they count as inferences nonetheless. Hence beliefs held on the basis of implicit or explicit inferences are not targeted by intuitionism. The possibility of unconscious reasoning raises more difficult questions. Intuitionists are often suspicious of appeals to unconscious inferences. The alleged inferences are supposed to be completely hidden from our awareness, so it can be hard to show that we are making the arguments unconsciously. If we do reach moral beliefs on the basis of unconscious reasoning, intuitionists will have to decide if the resulting beliefs also qualify as inferential.

The descriptive side of intuitionism claims that some moral beliefs are not inferential. To defend this part of their theory, intuitionists will have to isolate a class of non-inferential moral beliefs and explain how the beliefs arise if not via inference. The normative side of intuitionism makes the further step of saying that the non-inferential moral beliefs have a positive epistemic status needed for knowledge. Intuitionists often understand this positive status in terms of being justified. According to the traditional analysis of knowledge, knowledge is justified true belief. Even if this analysis is incomplete, and something in addition to being justified and true is needed for a belief to count as knowledge, it is widely agreed that being justified is a necessary condition for knowledge. If intuitionists can establish that some non-inferential moral beliefs are justified, this would be an important step towards showing that the beliefs are candidates for moral knowledge.

Intuitionists do not always agree on how best to develop the descriptive and normative aspects of their theory. Different forms of intuitionism offer different accounts of how their targeted beliefs arise non-inferentially as well as what it is that makes them justified.

As just defined, intuitionism is essentially an epistemological doctrine according to which some non-inferential moral beliefs are justified. While intuitionism has been associated with other views, such as ethical pluralism, non-naturalism, and objectivism, the theory itself is neutral with respect to these issues. Some classic intuitionists, notably W. D. Ross (2002), were ethical pluralists and thought that there is a plurality of basic moral duties, but other intuitionists, including G. E. Moore (1993) and Henry Sidgwick (1907), rejected pluralism in favour of utilitarianism. Additionally, nothing about intuitionism per se requires that moral truths be objective or that moral properties are non-natural, though intuitionism may become more or less plausible when paired with these other commitments.

Before proceeding, a terminological point is in order. It is common to say that intuitionists hold that we can know some moral truths by intuition. Unfortunately, the term "intuition" does not have a consistent meaning in the literature. For some authors, intuitions are non-inferential beliefs. In other discussions, intuitions are not beliefs but non-doxastic seeming states, inclinations to judge, or immediate gut reactions. To avoid confusion, I shall dispense with reference to "intuition" and focus instead on the intuitionist's core idea that some moral beliefs are non-inferential and justified.

WHY BE A MORAL INTUITIONIST?

One of the key arguments in favour of moral intuitionism is that it is true to our moral experiences. We seem to arrive at moral judgements, both singular and general, immediately and without inference. Evidence from cognitive psychology suggests that automatic, non-inferential processes are responsible for many of our moral judgements (Railton, 2014).

Not all moral inquirers have a specific general moral principle in mind when they form their moral beliefs. Still, familiarity with moral theory does not seem necessary for moral knowledge. Someone could know, or justifiably believe, that lying is morally wrong without inferring this from a higher-order moral principle.

Even if one rejects the above idea and holds that singular moral beliefs must be deduced from some general moral principle to be justified, our knowledge of these moral generalities would be in need of explanation. Intuitionists have argued that the general principles of ethics, such as the Principle of Utility and the Categorical Imperative, are not empirical hypotheses, held on the basis of their ability to explain and predict what we observe, as are the theoretical principles of the empirical sciences (Shafer-Landau, 2006; Tropman, 2012). For many intuitionists, certain moral principles can be credible to us in their own rights, independent of their inferential relations to another theory or observational data.

Importantly, intuitionism can explain how sound moral thinking can get started. Moral inquiry has to begin somewhere, and according to intuitionism the initial inputs to moral thinking do not need to be inferred from something else to be justified.

OBJECTIONS TO INTUITIONISM

Despite the arguments in its favour, intuitionism has been dismissed for a host of reasons. Critics object that if intuitionism were true, we would need to posit a realm of strange, non-natural moral properties as well as an equally mysterious faculty of intuition to detect them (Mackie, 1977). It is also supposed that, for the intuitionist, the target moral beliefs would be indubitable, obviously true, and infallible, all of which flies in the face of the complexity and uncertainty of moral practice. Moreover, since the relevant moral beliefs are not held on the basis of any premises, agents would be unable to evaluate their beliefs critically. This is problematic, as it forecloses argumentation about one's moral commitments.

Additionally, there is the worry that the intuitionist's moral beliefs are not reliable and are disconnected from moral truth. This unreliability objection can be developed in multiple ways. According to one evolutionary explanation of our moral beliefs, we immediately believe that certain actions, such as cooperating with others and avoiding harm, are right not because they are right, but ultimately because having positive motivational tendencies towards these behaviours was fitness-enhancing for our ancestors (Street, 2006). If our non-inferential moral beliefs are influenced by selective forces, forces that have nothing to do with moral truth, it is hard to see how these beliefs could be accurate. Other explanations of our belief-forming practices also pose problems for intuitionism. Recent work in moral psychology suggests that many of our immediate moral judgements are due to gut reactions, emotional states, biases, framing effects, and other factors unrelated to moral reality (Sinnott-Armstrong, 2006). To the extent that our non-inferred moral beliefs are influenced by such distorting factors, we have reason to doubt the beliefs' truth and, by extension, the intuitionist's claim that the beliefs enjoy a positive epistemic status necessary for knowledge.

To evaluate the seriousness of these challenges, we need to consider specific versions of intuitionism. In what follows, I examine three kinds of intuitionism—views I call "rationalist intuitionism," "appearance intuitionism," and "response intuitionism"—and consider the extent to which they can overcome these, and other, objections.

RATIONALIST INTUITIONISM: OLD AND NEW

According to rationalist intuitionism, some moral truths are self-evident, and we can non-inferentially recognize these truths through an exercise of our rational capacities. Several philosophers in the first part of the twentieth century were rationalist intuitionists, including G. E. Moore (1993), H. A. Prichard (1912), W. D. Ross (2002), and Henry Sidgwick (1907). By the mid-1900s, the theory fell out of favour for many of the reasons outlined above. Rationalist intuitionism has recently received renewed interest in the literature. Contemporary ethicists, such as Robert Audi (2004) and Russ Shafer-Landau (2003), have reformulated the view and argue that the position warrants serious attention.

To appreciate the new developments in rationalist intuitionism, let us begin with an earlier version of the position. A classic statement of rationalist intuitionism can be found in the work of W. D. Ross (2002). Ross was both a rationalist intuitionist and an ethical pluralist. He thought that there is a plurality of irreducible prima facie moral obligations, such as the obligations of fidelity, justice, and self-improvement. Prima facie duties depend on just one aspect of a situation, whereas final or all-things-considered obligations take all morally relevant considerations into account. An action may be prima facie right insofar as it fulfils a promise, but finally wrong if some other prima facie duty, such as justice, were more important in that instance. Of our knowledge of prima facie duties, Ross wrote:

> That an act, *qua* fulfilling a promise, or *qua* effecting a just distribution of good … is *prima facie* right, is self-evident; not in the sense that it is evident from the beginning of our lives, or as soon as we attend to the proposition for the first time, but in the sense that when we have reached sufficient mental maturity and have given sufficient attention to the proposition it is evident without any need of proof, or of evidence beyond itself. It is self-evident just as a mathematical axiom, or the validity of a form of inference, is evident.
>
> (Ross, 2002: 29)

Ross (2002) thought that some moral propositions, such as the proposition that promise-keeping is prima facie right, are evident in and of themselves. The comparison to mathematics and logic underscores the rationalistic element of this moral epistemology. For Ross, non-inferential moral knowledge, like our knowledge of mathematical axioms, is a matter of adequately grasping propositions that are self-evidently true. Because mature agents can know propositions about the prima facie duties solely upon considering them sufficiently, such moral knowledge would be independent of experience in a way that qualifies it as a priori.

Moral self-evidence secures both the descriptive and normative components of Ross's intuitionism. The relevant moral beliefs are about self-evident truths, and they are held upon considering them sufficiently. The beliefs are non-inferential, as they are not held on the basis of prior premises that evidence the proposition. The beliefs are justified because they are grounded in sufficient attention to propositions that are self-evidently true.

At this point, we can see that at least some of the objections to intuitionism mentioned earlier are misplaced. Ross (2002) stated that self-evident moral propositions are not immediately evident upon encountering them. Knowledge of them requires maturity and sufficient attention. This admission should mitigate the concern that the objects of non-inferential knowledge must be obvious or intuitive. Ross would claim that a special, occult faculty of moral intuition is not needed to grasp moral truths. Nothing over and above rational reflection, of the sort employed in mathematics and logic, underwrites moral knowledge. For this reply to succeed, rationalists will have to say more about what rational reflection involves and why this reflection yields knowledge in other domains.

It should be noted that Ross said other things about self-evidence that open his view up to additional criticism. He asserted that our knowledge of self-evident truths is certain, in the sense of being free from doubt (2002: 30). Ross famously said of self-evident moral and mathematical propositions, "We are dealing with propositions that cannot be proved, but that just as certainly need no proof" (2002: 30). According to Ross, self-evident moral propositions are impossible to prove.

Contemporary rationalist intuitionists have distanced themselves from some of the claims of their predecessors. Audi (2004), a leading current rationalist intuitionist, draws inspiration from Ross's original position but moderates some of Ross's commitments. An important innovation of Audi's Rossian intuitionism is a new theory of self-evidence. On Audi's view, self-evident propositions are such that:

1. in virtue of adequately understanding them, one has justification for believing them (which does not entail that all who adequately understand them *do* believe them); and
2. believing them on the basis of adequately understanding them entails knowing them. (Audi, 2015: 65)

If a proposition is self-evident, we can justifiably believe it solely on the basis of grasping it adequately. If our beliefs in the propositions are based on this understanding, and not on some other ground, then we can be said to know them. Like Ross, Audi (2004) thinks that the Rossian principles of prima facie duty, such as the principle that promise-keeping is prima facie required, are plausibly self-evident. Were one to grasp adequately the relevant concepts that figure in the proposition and sufficiently comprehend the moral principle, this understanding is all that is needed to justifiably believe that keeping one's promises is prima facie required. By definition, any belief in a self-evident proposition held on the basis of this understanding is justified. One's understanding of the principle also does not function as some sort of premise from which one concludes that the principle is true, and this is why a belief in a self-evident truth held on the basis of understanding it is not inferred from it. Once more, self-evidence secures the descriptive and normative claims of rationalist intuitionism.

One feature of Audi's account is that self-evident propositions are not belief-entailing. Nothing in Audi's analysis requires that one believe a self-evident proposition upon considering it. One could fail to comprehend the proposition sufficiently or decide to withhold belief even in light of the adequate understanding one in fact has. Self-evident truths need not be obvious and can be subject to doubt. Notably, just because a self-evident truth is in no need of proof, since it can be known on the basis of understanding it adequately, it does not follow—as Ross (2002) thought—that these truths are unprovable. Self-evident truths may be derived from or evidenced by premises but remain self-evident all the same (Audi, 2004: 101–14). By moderating the notion of self-evidence, rationalists are able to make sense of moral argumentation and uncertainty about the objects of non-inferential moral knowledge.

Rationalists will try to ease concerns about the unreliability of intuitionistic beliefs by pointing out that the relevant beliefs result from adequate reflection upon propositions that are self-evident. Beliefs caused by gut reactions, biases, and framing effects, and not by a sufficient understanding of self-evident truths, are not targeted by their theory, so it is not a problem for rationalists if these moral beliefs are mistaken and lack justification. In response to the objection that our moral thinking has been distorted by evolutionary pressures, rationalists would likely say that the belief-forming method in question is rational reflection, which seems to yield knowledge in other areas of thought. Rationalists then must explain why reflection is a reliable or appropriate way to form beliefs, in both ethics and other domains, even if our capacity for this reflection has its roots in our evolutionary history.

A concern with the rationalist's model of moral knowledge is that it may be overly rationalistic; morality is unlike mathematics and logic, and the appeal to self-evidence seems to ignore the affective and action-guiding character of moral thought. It also remains to be seen if any moral propositions *are* self-evident. Perhaps no moral truth is such that we could know it on the basis of understanding it alone. Further, these self-evident moral propositions need to be substantive enough to matter for moral knowledge (Väyrynen, 2008). A real worry is that only analytic statements—that is, those that are true by definition—would qualify as self-evident; this could include statements such as "It is unjust to punish someone for a crime they did not commit." To reply, intuitionists need to show either that some non-analytic (synthetic) moral statements can be self-evident, or that it is not a problem if self-evidence attaches only to those that are analytic.

Even if some non-trivial moral claims are self-evident, there is the additional worry that they would only be of a very general sort, such as Ross's principles of prima facie duty or the Principle of Utility. Ross claimed that propositions about our final, as opposed to prima facie, moral duties are never self-evident (2002: 33). Weighing competing moral duties against one another in concrete situations requires more than an adequate grasp of moral propositions such as "I am morally forbidden to help Sam." We need to know a great deal about the world—for example, the kind of help Sam requires and what other moral considerations are at play. Argumentation may also be needed to reach a conclusion about what to do. A rationalist might reply that if a moral proposition were sufficiently detailed and contained a more complete non-moral description of the world, it would be self-evidently true. In other words, once fleshed out, propositions of the form "If circumstances C obtain, then I am morally forbidden to perform action A" might meet the conditions for self-evidence. Such moral conditionals could quickly become quite complex, and rationalists would need to show that sufficiently understanding them is enough to know them. Also, on this approach, our knowledge of singular moral facts would be based on our prior knowledge of the moral conditionals. Such a model of moral knowledge does not explain, as some intuitionists wish to, how we could know some singular moral facts non-inferentially.

APPEARANCE INTUITIONISM

According to other intuitionists, such as John Bengson (2015) and Michael Huemer (2005), intuitionism's target moral beliefs are not justified by an adequate understanding of self-evident propositions but by how things appear to the believer. We can call this view "appearance intuitionism."

Some moral propositions appear true prior to argument. It just seems wrong to push a large stranger over a footbridge to save five lives. Being beneficent, fair, and honest all seem like morally right things to do, and they can seem this way independent of any argument for why this is so. Appearances, or seemings, are non-doxastic mental states that represent propositions as being true. According to Bengson's (2015) quasi-perceptualist form of intuitionism, appearances are best understood as presentational states that directly present the world as being a certain way. Appearances should be distinguished from beliefs. A proposition can strike us as true, even if we do not believe it. We can believe that a stick in the water is straight, despite its seeming to be bent. Similarly, utilitarians can believe that it is morally right to exploit the poor, even though it might still seem wrong to them. That said, in most cases appearances invite belief, and when they do, the appearances do not function as premises in an argument for a proposition's truth. Appearances are not the objects of belief or pieces of evidence from which we reason to moral conclusions, and this is why beliefs based on appearances are not inferred from them (Huemer, 2005: 121–22).

Appearance intuitionists combine the above descriptive account of non-inferential moral belief formation with an epistemological view about the justificatory powers of appearances. Huemer has endorsed the Principle of Phenomenal Conservatism, which states, "If it seems to S that p, then, in the absence of defeaters, S thereby has at least some degree of justification for believing that p" (Huemer, 2007: 30). On phenomenal conservatism, appearances give us some justification for believing their contents. This justification can be defeated. Things are not always as they appear, and when we have reason to think that an appearance is misleading, this defeats the justification that the appearance would otherwise confer to the belief. Still, beliefs grounded in appearances have some, albeit defeasible, justification. Suppose that I believe that lying is wrong because it seems wrong, and not because any argument has persuaded of me of lying's wrongness. Suppose there are no defeaters to this belief, so I have no reason to distrust the appearance. Even though the belief was not a conclusion of a reasoning process, it still has some initial positive epistemic credibility on this view insofar as it was based on how things appeared to me.

Appearance intuitionists have resources to respond to many of the classic complaints about intuitionism. We do not need to suppose that there is anything strange or objectionably non-natural about morality to allow that certain moral propositions just seem true. A special faculty of moral intuition is not needed to make sense of non-inferential moral knowledge. Appearances are not specific to ethics. The claims of natural science and everyday experience lend themselves to appearances. Appearances can be deceiving, and we can deny that things really are as they seem on the basis of argument or evidence to the contrary. It might seem wrong to pay people to participate in research, but arguments can convince us otherwise. Similarly, we can construct arguments to support the belief that things *are* as they seem, and hence we can argue for or against our non-inferred beliefs. Appearance intuitionism, like its rationalist counterpart, does not preclude moral argument.

Unlike rationalist intuitionism, appearance intuitionism does not have to defend the contentious claim that some moral propositions are self-evident. A proposition does not have to be self-evident for it to appear true prior to argument. It can strike us as wrong to push the stranger off the footbridge, lie to a friend to spare her pain, or fail to obtain a subject's informed consent to undergo a routine medical procedure, even if the objects of these appearances do not meet the conditions for being self-evidently true. Indeed, a proposition need not even be true for it to seem so to us. Appearance intuitionists have a much more liberal picture of what can be justifiably believed non-inferentially, and this allows them to avoid the worry that intuitionism only accounts for how we can know trivial or highly general moral truths.

Still, appearance intuitionism faces its own set of problems. While rationalists may be too restrictive in their account of which moral beliefs are non-inferential and justified, appearance intuitionists arguably go too far in the other direction. Suppose that Smith, having given the matter no thought at all, believes that he morally ought to deceive others whenever it would further his own interests because it appears to him that he should. Any appearance, no matter how it came about—be it the result of irrationality or carelessness—is supposed to confer some justification on Smith's belief. Yet it is hard to see how such appearances would justify resulting beliefs.

This brings us back to the objection that the intuitionist's moral beliefs are tainted by factors such as bias, emotion, framing errors, cultural background, and evolutionary history. Rationalist intuitionists have a ready reply to this objection since they limit the class of non-inferential beliefs to those about self-evident truths held on the basis of adequate understanding. Appearance intuitionists do not restrict non-inferential justification in this way, so this strategy is not open to them.

In reply to these concerns, an appearance intuitionist could first point out that appearances only justify in the absence of defeaters. If someone has evidence that their moral appearance is faulty, this would defeat the appearance's justificatory powers.

This response does not account for agents who do not think that their appearances are caused by unreliable processes. Such people would lack a defeater for their beliefs, and their beliefs would once more be justified by how things appeared to them. Appearance intuitionists might claim that these cases are rare; most adults realize that certain kinds of moral appearances are influenced by bias, illusions, and emotion. In situations in which the agent is ignorant of these effects, appearance intuitionists would have to concede that the beliefs have at least some justification, but they could note that this justification may not be enough for the belief to constitute knowledge. Further, if the appearance is misleading and things are not as they appear, the belief would be false and for this reason also would not rise to the level of knowledge.

Appearance intuitionists could also put pressure on the critic's assumption that many moral appearances are in error. The framing effects, faulty heuristics, and other mistakes that psychologists see in the lab may not generalize well to everyday moral life. Responding to a contrived moral dilemma in a questionnaire is importantly unlike confronting a real moral situation. It could also be argued that being emotional and partial improves, rather than clouds, one's moral judgement (Little, 1995).

Even if some of our moral appearances are faulty, this does not mean that they all lead us astray. Huemer (2008) is willing to grant that certain kinds of moral appearances are often distorted by emotion, personal interest, cultural background, or evolutionary history. Appearances about specific cases or mid-level principles are, for Huemer, especially vulnerable to these influences, whereas other appearances are more insulated from these errors. Huemer draws our attention to abstract, formal propositions, such as "If it is permissible to do x, and it is permissible to do y given that one does x, then it is permissible to do both x and y" (Huemer, 2008: 386). Once we reflect upon what permissibility involves and what the principle says, this proposition seems true. These kinds of abstract propositions present themselves as true not because of personal bias or emotion but upon rational reflection, and this is why the appearances are highly trustworthy. Huemer thinks that some moral appearances should be given more priority in moral thinking than others.

This way of developing appearance intuitionism shares some interesting similarities with rationalist brands of intuitionism. The abstract propositions that Huemer identifies are plausibly self-evident; they could be justifiably believed solely on the basis of grasping them adequately. The difference is that appearance intuitionists maintain that it is the proposition's appearing true that justifies one's belief in it, not an adequate understanding of it. Still, like rationalist intuitionism, Huemer's appearance intuitionism faces the objection that its account of moral knowledge is too intellectual and only concerns trivial or non-substantive principles. If appearance intuitionism is to distinguish itself more clearly from its rationalist competitors, it needs to offer another picture of non-inferential moral belief formation, one that does not rely on rational reflection on abstract, general propositions. The challenge is to offer this account without falling prey to the objection that such non-inferential beliefs are unreliable and unjustified.

RESPONSE INTUITIONISM

Another class of intuitionism focuses on the role that emotion and other affective responses play in non-inferential moral knowledge. For these intuitionists, the relevant non-inferential moral beliefs are grounded in, or combine with, certain felt responses such as anger, indignation, approbation, and a sense of wrongdoing. Call this approach "response intuitionism."

The central idea here is that affective experiences can be a source of moral knowledge. Suppose that, upon witnessing a driver flee the scene of a hit-and-run accident, I am outraged and angered. In some versions of response intuitionism, this affective response can be prior to, and the basis of, my subsequent moral belief that the driver's actions were wrong (Audi, 2013). The emotional experience is not a piece of evidence from which I infer that the driver acted wrongly, and thus the grounding relation between response and moral belief is non-inferential. Other response intuitionists, such as Sabine Roeser (2011), claim that the affective response is not prior to the moral belief but instead combines with it to form a single unitary state. According to Roeser's view, which she calls "affectual intuitionism," these complex unities of moral belief and affect constitute the moral emotions such as guilt and anger. Roeser argues that these moral emotions are candidates for genuine moral knowledge. In general, response intuitionism sets itself apart by its descriptive claim that certain moral beliefs are non-inferentially grounded in, or bound up with, affective responses.

Endorsing this descriptive account of non-inferentiality is not enough to make one a moral intuitionist. One also has to show that such affective moral beliefs are epistemically justified, and this is why related views in psychology that share some affinities with response intuitionism do not count as forms of intuitionism in the sense under consideration here. Jonathan Haidt's (2001) social intuitionism, for example, holds that many moral beliefs are caused by affective responses; however, the responses are usually socially informed gut reactions or flashes of disgust, and Haidt does not defend the normative claim that the beliefs have positive epistemic status.

Unlike appearance intuitionism and rationalist intuitionism, response intuitionism is not wedded to a specific account of justification for its beliefs. Response intuitionists could adopt the appearance intuitionist's account of justification and then argue that the relevant affective responses are a species of moral appearance. Insofar as anger and outrage present their objects as morally wrong, these responses—as appearances—defeasibly justify our belief that things are as they seem (Kauppinen, 2013). Alternatively, response intuitionists could argue that the relevant felt responses reliably indicate moral truths and that the affective moral beliefs are accurate enough to count as justified (Roeser, 2011).

Response intuitionism is attractive because it does not over-intellectualize moral knowledge as other intuitionists arguably do. The focus on affective responses captures the dynamic and motivating force of moral judgements. Because these responses usually concern particular instances of moral or immoral conduct, this kind of intuitionism accounts for our non-inferential beliefs about concrete actions, as opposed to merely general, abstract moral propositions.

Response intuitionism is perhaps most vulnerable to concerns about the trustworthiness of its moral beliefs. Whatever view of epistemic justification response intuitionists endorse, they will have to overcome doubts that affective moral beliefs are justified. To do this, they will likely adopt some of the defensive strategies already discussed: showing that emotional responses help rather than hurt moral judgement; arguing that felt moral beliefs are not as unreliable as critics suppose; and even narrowing the relevant class of non-inferential moral beliefs further to exclude certain kinds of affective belief. Because response intuitionism restricts itself to felt moral beliefs, worries about the reliability of emotion and affect become more pressing.

An additional problem unique to response intuitionism is that it seems possible for an agent to believe sincerely that an action is morally wrong without experiencing any kind of emotional response like guilt or approbation. Such cases seem especially common when it comes to more general moral beliefs, such as the beliefs that one is morally required to keep one's promises and that one has a duty to take others' ends as one's own. This poses difficulties for the response intuitionist's descriptive claim that non-inferential moral beliefs are grounded in, or integrate with, affective experiences. Response intuitionists might reply that they are not interested in dispassionate moral beliefs and that if a moral belief left an agent cold in this way, it would not be targeted by their theory. The drawback with this rejoinder is that the response intuitionist's account of moral knowledge is more limited than initially supposed. Alternatively, response intuitionists could argue that in apparently dispassionate moral beliefs, a felt response is there, but it is either weak or overwhelmed by other mental states. The ultimate success of response intuitionism hinges on its ability to defend its descriptive and normative claims against these sorts of criticisms.

CONCLUSION

Moral intuitionism is frequently misunderstood. Recent work in intuitionism is trying to correct these misconceptions, and intuitionism now deserves serious consideration as a plausible option in moral epistemology. Intuitionism is currently being developed along multiple lines. Different formulations of intuitionism can be distinguished by their descriptive accounts of non-inferentiality and their normative accounts of justification. A central disagreement among intuitionists concerns which non-inferential moral beliefs should be targeted by their theory. Do the relevant moral beliefs result from rational reflection, affective experiences, or some other process? How intuitionists answer this question will affect how they respond to the most pressing challenge they face, which is to show that their moral beliefs have positive epistemic status despite not being inferred from antecedent theoretical commitments or other premises. If intuitionists can address concerns about the epistemic credentials of non-inferential moral beliefs, they hold out the hope of helping us see how sound moral thinking can get started.

ACKNOWLEDGEMENTS

I would like to thank Jamie Fritz, Tristram McPherson, David Plunkett, and Rhema Zlaten for their helpful comments on earlier versions of this chapter.

RELATED TOPICS

Chapter 1, "Non-Naturalistic Realism in Metaethics;" Chapter 28, "Explanatory Challenges in Metaethics;" Chapter 31, "Moral Skepticism;" Chapter 39, "Experimental Philosophy and Moral Theory."

REFERENCES

Audi, R. (2004) *The Good in the Right: A Theory of Intuition and Intrinsic Value*, Princeton, NJ: Princeton University Press.
Audi, R. (2013) *Moral Perception*, Princeton, NJ: Princeton University Press.
Audi, R. (2015) "Intuition and Its Place in Ethics," *Journal of the American Philosophical Association* 1(1): 57–77.
Bengson, J. (2015) "The Intellectual Given," *Mind* 124(495): 707–60.
Haidt, J. (2001) "The Emotional Dog and Its Rational Tail: A Social Intuitionist Approach to Moral Judgment," *Psychological Review* 108(4): 814–34.
Huemer, M. (2005) *Ethical Intuitionism*, New York: Palgrave Macmillan.
Huemer, M. (2007) "Compassionate Phenomenal Conservatism," *Philosophy and Phenomenological Research* 74(1): 30–55.

Huemer, M. (2008) "Revisionary Intuitionism," *Social Philosophy and Policy* 25: 368–92.

Kauppinen, A. (2013) "A Humean Theory of Moral Intuition," *Canadian Journal of Philosophy* 43(3): 361–81.

Little, M. O. (1995) "Seeing and Caring: The Role of Affect in Feminist Moral Epistemology," *Hypatia* 10: 117–37.

Mackie, J. L. (1977) *Ethics: Inventing Right and Wrong*, New York: Penguin Books.

Moore, G. E. (1993) *Principia Ethica*, rev. edn, New York: Cambridge University Press.

Prichard, H. A. (1912) "Does Moral Philosophy Rest on a Mistake?" *Mind* 21(81): 21–37.

Railton, P. (2014) "The Affective Dog and Its Rational Tale: Intuition and Attunement," *Ethics* 124(4): 813–59.

Roeser, S. (2011) *Moral Emotions and Intuitions*, New York: Palgrave Macmillan.

Ross, W. D. (2002) *The Right and the Good*, new edn, Oxford: Clarendon Press.

Shafer-Landau, R. (2003) *Moral Realism: A Defense*, Oxford: Clarendon Press.

Shafer-Landau, R. (2006) "Ethics as Philosophy: A Defense of Ethical Nonnaturalism," in T. Horgan & M. Timmons (eds.) *Metaethics after Moore*, Oxford: Oxford University Press.

Sidgwick, H. (1907) *The Methods of Ethics*, 7th edn, London: Macmillan.

Sinnott-Armstrong, W. (2006) "Moral Intuitionism Meets Empirical Psychology," in T. Horgan & M. Timmons (eds.) *Metaethics after Moore*, Oxford: Oxford University Press.

Street, S. (2006) "A Darwinian Dilemma for Realist Theories of Value," *Philosophical Studies* 127(1): 109–66.

Tropman, E. (2012) "Can Cornell Moral Realism Adequately Account for Moral Knowledge?" *Theoria* 78(1): 26–46.

Väyrynen, P. (2008) "Some Good and Bad News for Ethical Intuitionism," *Philosophical Quarterly* 58(232): 489–511.

FURTHER READING

Bedke, M. (2008) "Ethical Intuitions: What They Are, What They Are Not, and How They Justify," *American Philosophical Quarterly* 45(3): 253–69. (Critically compares appearance intuitionism and rationalist intuitionism.)

Sinnott-Armstrong, W. (ed.) (2008) *Moral Psychology, The Cognitive Science of Morality: Intuition and Diversity*, vol. 2, Cambridge, MA: MIT Press. (A collection of papers on cognitive science and moral judgement.)

Stratton-Lake, P. (ed.) (2002) *Ethical Intuitionism: Re-evaluations*, Oxford: Clarendon Press. (New work on moral intuitionism.)

31

Moral Skepticism

Matt Lutz and Jacob Ross

Most people think they know right from wrong. While there may be certain moral gray areas where there is room for reasonable disagreement, we generally think we know many moral truths—for example, that murder, torture, and rape are morally wrong, and that helping the needy is morally good. But are these claims to moral knowledge defensible?

The moral skeptic denies that we can have moral knowledge—that is, knowledge of moral truths. In this chapter, we will look at a number of influential arguments for moral skepticism. We first argue that it is helpful to understand many of these arguments as expressing the same core concern, which we will call the Connection Concern. In the section "A Refined Version of the Connection Concern Argument," we present a refined version of the Connection Concern. This argument—the Explanatory Trilemma Argument—makes a strong case for moral skepticism. And in the section "Objections and Replies: A Sketch," we examine potential avenues for objection to the argument.

We have a couple of notes to make before proceeding. First, we will assume that there are such things as moral beliefs, about which it makes sense to ask whether they are true or false, whether they are justified or unjustified, and whether they constitute or fail to constitute knowledge. Second, our focus will be on moral skepticism as a claim about moral *knowledge*. Skepticism about the possibility of moral truth will not be our focus; we will be concerned with arguments that allow, *arguendo*, that there are such truths but deny that we are in a position to know them. Other epistemic categories, such as justification, will be relevant only insofar as they are necessary conditions on knowledge. Third, we will be concerned with skepticism about *moral* knowledge and, in particular, knowledge of *right and wrong*. However, many of the arguments we consider could be extended to other kinds of ethical knowledge, such as knowledge of good and bad or virtue and vice. Fourth, our focus will be on moral skepticism, understood as the view that *we can have no moral knowledge*. We will not be asking, for example, whether there could be an omniscient being who possesses moral knowledge. Instead, we will be asking whether moral knowledge is attainable by us, in our actual circumstances. And fifth, we are concerned with arguments for the unattainability of moral knowledge in which this conclusion does not follow *a fortiori* from global skepticism. An interesting argument for moral skepticism will show why *moral* knowledge is particularly troublesome.

VARIETIES OF SKEPTICAL ARGUMENT AND THE INESCAPABILITY OF EXPLANATORY CONNECTIONS

There are many different arguments for moral skepticism. In this section, we will survey some of the most prominent such arguments and show that they can be understood to share a core concern: the Connection Concern. While there may be other skeptical arguments that cannot be so understood—for instance, Sinnott-Armstrong's regress argument (2006: chapter 4) is not a version of the Connection Concern—the Connection Concern is so central to such a large number of skeptical arguments that it will be our main focus in this chapter. In its most schematic form, the Connection Concern argument can be represented as follows:

(P1) S knows that P only if S's belief that P is connected to the fact that P in the right kind of way.
(P2) For any moral proposition P, it is not the case that our belief that P is connected to the fact that P in the right kind of way.
(C)   Therefore, for any moral proposition P, it is not the case that we know that P.

We will set aside a critical discussion of the Connection Concern argument until the section "A Refined Version of the Connection Concern Argument." For now, our interest is in the relationship between this argument and other varieties of skeptical argument.

Moral Disagreement

By far the most popular and influential argument for moral skepticism is the argument from moral disagreement. There is a substantial amount of disagreement on what counts as right or wrong between cultures and over times. On this basis, some have concluded that moral knowledge is impossible. Different people seem to have opposing moral beliefs, and who is to say which moral beliefs are correct? Yet disagreement between individuals, or between members of different cultures, over some matter of fact does not immediately preclude knowledge of that fact (see Shafer-Landau, 2004: chapter 1; see also Dustin Locke's chapter "The Epistemic Significance of Moral Disagreement"). If Alice and Brian disagree about whether human beings evolved from non-human animals, that does not imply that there can be no knowledge of human evolution, nor does it imply that neither Alice nor Brian possesses such knowledge. If Alice, who is aware of the scientific evidence supporting human evolution, believes that humans evolved from other animals on the basis of this evidence, then she may know that humans so evolved in spite of the fact that Brian, who is unaware of this evidence, believes otherwise.

Thus, if the skeptic wants to argue that moral disagreement leads to a skeptical conclusion about morality, some effort must be made to show why disagreement about morality is particularly worrisome. We must ask: when, in general, does disagreement create epistemic problems? Often, when we learn that someone disagrees with us about some proposition, it will be rational for us to become less confident that this proposition is true. In other words, disagreement can often act as a *defeater*. Defeaters are often thought of as falling into two (possibly overlapping) kinds: *rebutting* defeaters and *undercutting* defeaters (Pollock, 1987). Rebutting defeaters are defeaters that operate by providing evidence for a contrary proposition. Undercutting defeaters, on the other hand, attack the evidential connection between our old evidence and the proposition in question. They provide new evidence in light of which the old evidence no longer provides (as much) support for the belief that P. Testimony that not-P can provide a defeater for one's belief that P of either of these two kinds. Suppose, for example, that Albert believes that Betty will be at the party because Carl told him so. But then Diane comes along and tells Albert that Betty will not be at the party. Normally, Diane's testimony will provide evidence that Betty will not be at the party, and so it will be a rebutting defeater for Albert's belief that she will be at the party. But suppose that Albert knows that Diane's formed her belief on the basis of Carl's testimony to her. In this version of the case, Diane's assertion that Betty will be at the party indicates that Carl has been saying conflicting things to different people, and so it indicates that his testimony is unreliable. In this way, Diane's testimony provides an undermining defeater for Albert's initial belief.

Moral disagreement might be thought of as providing a defeater for our moral beliefs of either of these kinds. However, if we adopt the view that moral disagreement merely provides a rebutting defeater for our moral beliefs, we should not regard such disagreement as supporting moral skepticism. On this view of disagreement, someone's testimony that not-P serves as a defeater for our belief that P by providing evidence for not-P, and so moral testimony provides evidence for the moral claim asserted. But if this is right then presumably—other things being equal—the more people sincerely assert a given moral claim, the more reason we will have to believe it. Hence, if there are many more who agree with you on a question of ethics than disagree, then the defeat that comes from the few dissenters will be swamped by the support provided by the much larger number who agree with you. Consequently, while the contrary evidence provided by disagreement may jeopardize our justification for our more controversial moral beliefs (e.g. our beliefs about abortion or affirmative action), such contrary evidence won't jeopardize our justification for our relatively uncontroversial moral beliefs (e.g. our beliefs about the wrongness of torturing babies). If moral disagreement provides only a rebutting defeater, moral disagreement will not support a broad moral skepticism.

In order for moral disagreement to support general moral skepticism, disagreement concerning *controversial* topics would need to cast doubt on our moral beliefs concerning *uncontroversial* topics. Thus, for example, disagreement about affirmative action would need to cast doubt on our beliefs about torturing babies. And it may do this by providing an *undercutting* defeater. Even if I don't have a good understanding of how my moral beliefs are formed, I may have reason to suppose that my moral beliefs and the moral beliefs of others are formed on the basis of similar mechanisms. Hence, learning that others disagree with me about a range of moral issues may call into question the reliability of the mechanisms underlying my moral beliefs and hence call into question the accuracy of all the beliefs, including the uncontroversial ones, formed on the basis of these mechanisms. If our moral belief-forming mechanisms are unreliable, then it would seem that our moral beliefs are not connected, in the right sort of way, to the moral facts.

To sum up, if the Moral Disagreement Argument is to be successful in supporting a general skeptical conclusion, then moral disagreement must be thought of as providing an undercutting defeater for our moral beliefs and hence as indicating that our moral beliefs are not connected, in the right sort of way, to the moral facts. Hence, to the extent that the Moral Disagreement Argument succeeds, it does so by raising the Connection Concern.

Divergence in Moral Theory

Another common skeptical argument proceeds from the claim that there has been little or no convergence over time between competing moral theories. The differences between consequentialism and deontology, for instance, and the arguments for and against each, have long been fairly well understood. Yet there has been no convergence in expert opinion as to which of these two theories is superior, and there are no signs that such a convergence will be forthcoming any time soon. This makes moral theory notably different from scientific theory, where convergence and progress are de rigueur. (This concern is plausibly the underlying motivation for Derek Parfit's [2013] attempt to reconcile various normative theories.)

While this is a disconcerting feature of moral discourse, the lack of convergence between mature moral theories is simply an instance of protracted moral disagreement among moral theorists. We should therefore understand the Divergence in Moral Theory Argument as a special case of the Moral Disagreement Argument. As such, insofar as it is successful, it is also just a special case of the Connection Concern.

In fact, it is useful to reflect on the Divergence in Moral Theory Argument because it is a particularly good illustration of why concerns about disagreement point to the Connection Concern. Prolonged, intractable disagreement about moral matters persists, even among expert theorists. What could explain this? One possibility is that there are no moral facts to begin with, so of course the experts are spinning their wheels. If there are moral facts, on the other hand, one likely explanation of this continued disagreement between experts is the hypothesis that even experts are not forming beliefs in a manner that is conducive to finding the truth of the matter (although this is not the only explanation—see Enoch, 2011: chapter 8; Huemer, 2005: chapter 6). Such disagreement suggests that, even under the best epistemic conditions we can hope for, our beliefs aren't appropriately connected to the moral facts.

Evolutionary Debunking and Off-Track Influences

Another argument for moral skepticism that has gained substantial popularity in recent years is the Evolutionary Debunking Argument (Street, 2006; Joyce, 2006). According to the Evolutionary Debunking Argument, we know what explains our moral beliefs: evolutionary pressures. We have the moral beliefs we do because having dispositions to form such moral beliefs was conducive to the survival of our ancestors. Because our moral beliefs track evolutionary pressures so neatly, it would be a massive coincidence if those beliefs were *also* reliably correlated with a mind-independent moral truth.

The Evolutionary Debunking Argument has taken a number of different forms in recent years. Street (2006) and Joyce (2006) present the debunking concern in different ways and draw different conclusions from their arguments (Joyce thinks the argument supports moral error theory; Street deploys it in favor of constructivism). But while there are many different ways to frame the debunking argument, we see it as another instance of the Connection Concern. Whereas arguments from disagreement give us a reason to suspect that our moral beliefs don't reliably track the moral facts, the Evolutionary Debunking Argument looks at what our moral beliefs *do* track and suggests that what is being tracked has nothing to do with morality. Our moral beliefs are not connected to the moral truth, because they are connected to something else—that is, to facts about which kinds of moral dispositions happen to have promoted the survival of our Paleolithic ancestors.

In a similar vein, Sinnott-Armstrong has argued that our moral beliefs do not track the moral truth, because they track other kinds of psychological pressures (Sinnott-Armstrong, 2006: chapter 9). Drawing on contemporary psychological research, Sinnott-Armstrong shows how our moral beliefs can be affected by a huge number of morally irrelevant factors. For instance, we are somewhat more likely to judge that an action is morally wrong when we are in a dirty environment than a clean one, because dirty environments evoke emotions of disgust and those emotions affect our moral reasoning. We are also subject to *framing effects* when making our moral judgments: we are liable to describe the same action as morally wrong or morally neutral depending on whether the action is described as a loss from a high benchmark or a gain from a low benchmark.

Sinnott-Armstrong musters a battery of psychological experiments that demonstrate the many ways in which our moral beliefs can be influenced by factors that are irrelevant from the standpoint of morality. The moral permissibility of a given action may depend on many things, but it does not depend on whether there is rotting food in your vicinity when you hear about the action. This is, once again, an instance of the Connection Concern. What these experimental results suggest is that our moral beliefs are not connected to the moral facts in the right kind of way, since, in forming them, we are at the mercy of irrelevant environmental factors.

We do not claim to have shown that all of these skeptical arguments *must* be interpreted as special cases of the Connection Concern. But the Connection Concern is central to so many different arguments for moral skepticism that it is worth isolating and examining it in its own right, and attempting to present it in its strongest formulation. The success or failure of such an argument will tell us much about the prospects for moral skepticism. So, our task in the remainder of this chapter will be to identify and evaluate the strongest version of the Connection Concern.

A REFINED VERSION OF THE CONNECTION CONCERN ARGUMENT

Recall that the initial version of the Connection Concern Argument we presented ran as follows:

(P1) S knows that P only if S's belief that P is connected to the fact that P in the right kind of way.

(P2) For any moral proposition P, it is not the case that our belief that P is connected to the fact that P in the right kind of way.

(C) Therefore, for any moral proposition P, it is not the case that we know that P.

In this section, our aim will be to move from this schematic outline to a clear and defensible argument.

Defining the Relevant Connection

In order to refine this argument, we will first need to specify what we mean by *the right kind of way*. To do so, we will need to find some kind of connection between belief and the facts that is plausibly required for knowledge, and that is arguably absent in the case of moral beliefs.

To find such a connection, it may be useful to consider Gettier cases in which someone appears to have justified true beliefs that fail to constitute knowledge, and in which the reason these beliefs do not constitute knowledge is that they fail to be connected to the corresponding facts in the right kind of way. Consider the following cases:

1. **Coin Conundrum**: Your boss tells you Jones will be getting a promotion. Jones tells you that he has ten coins in his pocket. On this basis, you infer that the person who will receive the promotion has ten coins in his pocket. While you have not counted the coins in your own pocket, it happens that they are ten in number. It turns out that it is you, and not Jones, who receives the promotion. And so your belief is true (Gettier, 1963).
2. **Sheep Shenanigans**: You are standing in a field looking at a dog that has been cleverly disguised as a sheep. On this basis, you form the belief that there is a sheep in the field. As it happens, elsewhere in the field there is indeed a sheep that is hidden from your view. And so your belief is true (Chisholm, 1966).

In both these cases, it seems that while you have justified true belief, it does not amount to knowledge. One natural thought is that your belief isn't knowledge because you were *lucky* in arriving at a true belief. But this can't be quite right. If you happen to turn your head in the right direction just as a meteor appears in the sky, then you are lucky in arriving at the true belief that there is meteor in the sky, but your belief amounts to knowledge all the same. What distinguishes the meteor case from the other two cases just considered is that while, in all three cases, you are lucky to form a true belief, in the meteor case it is *no mere coincidence* that your belief is true. After all, the presence of the meteor caused your visual experience, which caused your beliefs. Hence, you believe that there is a meteor in the sky *because there is a meteor in the sky*. By contrast, in the other two cases, it is a mere coincidence that your belief is true. In the coin case, you believe that the person who will receive the promotion has ten coins in his pocket not because this person really does have ten coins in his pocket, but because someone else has ten coins in his pocket. Similarly, in the sheep case, you believe that there is a sheep in the field not because there is a sheep in the field, but because there is a dog disguised as a sheep in the field.

These cases suggest that, in order for your belief to count as knowledge, it can't be a mere coincidence that this belief is true. We should note that this is not meant to be a sufficient condition for knowledge, or even to yield a sufficient condition when added to justified true belief. However, it does appear to be plausible as a necessary condition for knowledge. Moreover, it should be widely accepted as such, since many accounts of knowledge that have been offered in the literature entail it. Many such accounts require that, in order for one's belief that P to count as knowledge, there must be some kind of counterfactually robust connection between one's belief that P and the fact that P, so that they co-vary, in some specified way, across possible worlds. (particularly prevalent here are "sensitivity" accounts [see Nozick, 1981] and "safety" accounts [see Sosa, 1999].) And since mere coincidences tend not to be counterfactually robust, these accounts will typically imply that, in order for one's belief to count as knowledge, it can't be a mere coincidence that one's belief is true.

A *mere coincidence* is a concurrence without an explanatory connection. Thus, for example, it is a mere coincidence that Thomas Jefferson and John Adams died on the same day. If, however, the death of one caused the death of the other (e.g. because the second died of grief upon hearing the news of the other's death) or if both deaths had a common cause (e.g. because they were both killed by the same explosion), then it would not be a mere coincidence that they both died on the same day. Thus, the concurrence of A and B will constitute a mere coincidence if and only if A does not explain B, B does not explain A, and no third thing explains both A and B. Consequently, in order for one's belief to count as knowledge, the concurrence between one's belief and the truth can't be a mere coincidence. This claim is equivalent to the following:

Explanatory Connection Condition: S knows that P only if either (1) the fact that P explains the fact that S believes that P, or (2) the fact that S believes that P explains the fact that P, or (3) some further fact explains both the fact that P and the fact that S believes that P.

This will be the condition on knowledge that interests us in what follows.

Pure and Impure Moral Propositions

Assuming the Explanatory Connection Condition, all we'd need in order to derive moral skepticism is the following:

(2*) For any moral proposition P, it is not the case that our belief that P is explained by the fact that P, or vice versa, and neither is it the case that the fact that P and our belief that P share a common explanation.

Unfortunately for the skeptic, however, this assumption is highly questionable. Consider, for example, our belief that Pol Pot acted wrongly. Arguably, we have this belief because Pol Pot acted wrongly. After all, if Pol Pot had minded his own business and avoided all wrongdoing, we wouldn't now believe he had acted wrongly. It seems that there is indeed an explanatory connection between the fact that Pol Pot acted wrongly and our belief that he so acted (see Sturgeon, 1988). While the existence of such explanatory connections is controversial, it would be better for the skeptic to make an argument that does not depend on denying them.

One way to solve this problem is to identify a subset of moral propositions that plausibly do not stand in such explanatory connection with our beliefs. In order to do so, it will be useful to introduce some terminology. Let us define a *complete moral theory* as a theory that specifies, for every maximally specific consistent descriptive characterization of a world, how things would stand morally in a world satisfying that description. And let us define a *pure moral proposition* as a disjunction of complete moral theories. These are the propositions that have moral content but no descriptive content. Finally, let us define an *impure moral proposition* as a proposition that has moral content but that is not a pure moral proposition.[1]

So, for example, "You acted wrongly in stealing that money" is an impure moral proposition, since it entails "You stole that money." But "Stealing money is wrong" is a pure moral proposition, because it entails no such thing (cf. Scanlon, 2014: chapter 2).

We are now in a position to see how the truth of an impure moral proposition could explain our belief that it is true. Consider, for example, the proposition that Pol Pot acted wrongly. This is clearly an impure moral proposition, since it has some descriptive content (it implies, for example, that Pol Pot did something or other). Suppose we begin with the belief that it's always wrong to order genocide. Then we encounter film footage of Pol Pot ordering genocide. Hence, we come to believe that Pol Pot ordered genocide and that doing so is wrong. And from this we infer that Pol Pot did something wrong. In this case, while it may be true that Pol Pot's doing something wrong resulted in our believing that he did something wrong, it did so through the mediation of a descriptive belief—namely, the belief that he ordered genocide. From this belief, together with our purely moral belief that genocide is always wrong, we are able to infer the impure moral proposition that Pol Pot acted wrongly.

Note, however, that we cannot acquire our belief in pure moral propositions in this manner. While a purely moral proposition that we antecedently believe together with a descriptive proposition that we come to believe may entail an *impure* moral proposition (such as the proposition that Pol Pot acted wrongly), they cannot together entail a stronger pure moral proposition. Hence, if the clearest cases in which we come to believe a moral proposition P because P is true are cases in which we infer P from some descriptive proposition, together with our background moral beliefs, then we can get around the problem we have considered by restricting our attention to pure moral propositions. Thus, we can avoid the problem by replacing the problematic premise (2*) with the following:

(2**) For any *pure* moral proposition P, it is not the case that our belief that P is explained by the fact that P, or vice versa, nor is it the case that the fact that P and our belief that P share a common explanation.

This premise, together with the Explanatory Connection Condition, entails that we can have no knowledge of *pure* moral propositions. But skeptics want more than this. They want to maintain that we can have no knowledge of any moral propositions. To get this result, we will need one further assumption.

The Bridge Principle

The further assumption we need is the following:

Bridge Principle: For any person S and moral proposition M, if S knows that M, then there is some pure moral proposition P such that S is in a position to know that P.

The motivation for this principle is fairly straightforward. Assume the antecedent of the conditional is true. That is, assume that for some arbitrary person S and moral proposition

M, S knows that M. M is either a pure moral proposition or an impure moral proposition. Suppose it's a pure moral proposition. In this case, there is clearly a pure moral proposition that S is in a position to know—namely M itself—since, obviously, if S knows that M, then S is in a position to know that M. Hence, if M is a pure moral proposition, then the consequent of the conditional is true.

Suppose, on the other hand, that M is an impure moral proposition—that is, a proposition whose content is partially moral and partially descriptive. Suppose, for concreteness, that M is the proposition that Pol Pot acted wrongly. How might S know that M is true? It seems there are three possibilities: S might know it on empirical grounds, by learning certain descriptive facts about the world; S might know it on a priori grounds; or S might know it on the basis of a combination of a priori and empirical grounds. Regardless of which of these possibilities obtains, it must be that the totality of S's descriptive information about the world, together with whatever a priori grounds S may possess, constitutes a sufficient basis for knowing that Pol Pot acted wrongly. Let C be the conjunction of all the descriptive information S possesses. Thus, C will therefore include all the information C possesses about the descriptive facts relevant to the rightness or wrongness of Pol Pot's actions, such as how many people he killed, the circumstances under which he killed them, and so on. Now if, given the relevant a priori grounds, learning that C is true in the *actual world* suffices for S to know that in the actual world Pol Pot acted wrongly, then given these same grounds, learning that C is true in any arbitrary world W should suffice for S to know that in world W Pol Pot acted wrongly. Hence, S must be in a position to know the following proposition:

(P) In any world in which C is true, Pol Pot acts wrongly.

Note, however, that P is a pure moral proposition: it is equivalent to the disjunction of all the complete moral theories that entail that Pol Pot acts wrongly in worlds in which C is true. Hence, if S knows that Pol Pot acted wrongly, then S is in a position to know a pure moral proposition.

Recall that the proposition under consideration (that Pol Pot acted wrongly) was chosen simply for illustration. The same argument could be run for any impure moral proposition—and so we may conclude that if S knows any impure moral proposition, then S is in a position to know a pure moral proposition. From this conclusion, together with what we have already established, the Bridge Principle follows.

Putting It All Together

Combining these elements, we arrive at the following argument:

Explanatory Trilemma Argument

1. (Connection Condition) For any proposition P, S knows that P only if there is some kind of explanatory connection between the fact that P and S's belief that P. In particular, if S knows that P, then either (a) the fact that P explains S's belief that P, (b) the fact that P is explained by S's belief that P, or (c) the fact that P and S's belief that P share a common explanation.
2. Therefore, for any proposition P, S is *in a position to know* that P only if S is *in a position to form a belief* that P such that either (a) this belief is explained by the fact that

P, (b) this belief explains the fact that P, or (c) this belief and the fact that P share a common explanation.

3. For any pure moral proposition P, it is not the case that we are in a position to form a belief that P such that this belief is explained by the fact that P.

4. For any pure moral proposition P, it is not the case that we are in a position to form a belief that P such that this belief explains the fact that P.

5. For any pure moral proposition P, it is not the case that we are in a position to form a belief that P such that this belief and the fact that P share a common explanation.

6. Therefore, for any pure moral proposition P, it is not the case that we are in a position to know that P.

7. (Bridge Principle) For any moral proposition M, if S knows that M, then there is some pure moral proposition P such that S is in a position to know that P.

8. Therefore, for any moral proposition M, we do not know that M.

The overall strategy of this argument is to divide and conquer. Knowledge of any fact requires explanatory connections between belief and fact (premise 1). And knowledge of *pure* moral propositions is ruled out because this requirement cannot be satisfied for pure moral propositions (premises 3–5). Then, because pure and impure moral knowledge must stand or fall together (premise 7), the unavailability of pure moral knowledge entails the unavailability of any moral knowledge.

OBJECTIONS AND REPLIES: A SKETCH

A number of objections may be raised to the argument just presented, and we will conclude by examining some of these objections and sketching the beginnings of some replies. The objections and responses listed here are not supposed to be an exhaustive categorization of the ways one can object to or defend the Explanatory Trilemma Argument, any more than the survey in the section "Varieties of Skeptical Argument and the Inescapability of Explanatory Connections" was supposed to be an exhaustive survey of all possible arguments for moral skepticism. Nor are any of these arguments intended to be conclusive. This discussion should make clear what the main points are for and against the Explanatory Trilemma Argument and thus help to frame the debate over whether the Connection Concern can be developed into a sound argument for moral skepticism.

One response to the Explanatory Trilemma Argument rejects premise 1 by drawing a distinction between *a priori* and *a posteriori* knowledge. When it comes to empirical propositions that can only be known a posteriori, our knowledge of them requires sense perception. Hence, a posteriori knowledge involves forming beliefs in a manner that is influenced by, and hence explainable in terms of, the facts. But when it comes to necessary truths that are knowable a priori, such as mathematical truths, no such explanatory connections are required (Clarke-Doane, 2014). Pure moral truths are like mathematical truths in that they are necessary and knowable a priori. Hence, pure moral knowledge likewise requires no such explanatory connections.

There is a familiar reply to this objection. While mathematical truths may not be the right sorts of things to play a *causal* role, they may nonetheless play an explanatory role (Putnam, 1972; Baker, 2005; McGrath, 2014). Thus, mathematical truths about derivatives and integrals may figure in an explanation of projectile motion. Indeed, it is not implausible to suppose that the fundamental principles of mathematics figure at least implicitly in many, if not all, scientific explanations. Moreover, it seems that all mathematical truths, or at least all the knowable ones, will be explainable in terms of the fundamental mathematical truths. Since such fundamental mathematical truths will plausibly figure both in the explanation of the *truth* of any given mathematical proposition and in the explanation of our *belief* in this proposition, it is plausible to suppose that our mathematical beliefs are explanatorily connected to the mathematical facts. Consequently, there is reason to be suspicious of the partners-in-guilt response.

But the argument just given cuts both ways. If we maintain that mathematical truths, although necessary, can play a role in the explanation of our mathematical beliefs, why can't the moral anti-skeptic say the same thing about pure moral truths? Why can't the anti-skeptic maintain that pure moral truths can figure in the explanation of our pure moral beliefs? Indeed, some philosophers have argued precisely this. One way to defend this claim is to maintain that moral truths are *analytic* or *conceptual* truths. Setiya (2012: 100 ff.) has argued that for any proposition P, if P is an analytic truth, then P might figure in the explanation of why anyone who possesses the concepts required to entertain P would be disposed to believe that P. This fact, in turn, could figure in the explanation of our belief that P.

It has been suggested that something similar may be true of purely moral propositions (Huemer, 2005: 125–27; Cuneo & Shafer-Landau, 2014). If "Torture is wrong" is an analytic or conceptual truth, then perhaps it could figure in the explanation of our belief that torture is wrong. This would allow the anti-skeptic to reject premise 3 of the Explanatory Trilemma Argument and hence resist the skeptical conclusion. This response, however, will only work if pure moral propositions are analytic or conceptual truths. And while this view has some defenders, it has far more detractors. To most philosophers, it seems that a person could have mistaken moral beliefs about the permissibility of abortion, euthanasia, or the like while fully understanding the concepts that figure in these beliefs (Moore, 1903).

Given the way we have defined the pure moral propositions, any pure moral proposition will be necessary. But it doesn't follow that it will be *analytic*. Perhaps the pure moral facts are *facts about essences*, akin to the fact that all water is composed of hydrogen and oxygen, or the fact that all human beings are mammals. Such facts appear to be necessary without being analytic—we learn them by scientific inquiry rather than by reflecting on our folk concepts. Moreover, such facts about essences appear to be facts that can figure in scientific explanations and are therefore the right kind of facts to explain our beliefs. Thus, if pure moral truths could be understood as facts about essences, then perhaps we could understand how they could be necessary, synthetic, and explanatory of our moral beliefs. This would be another way of rejecting the third premise of the Explanatory Trilemma Argument.

As an illustration of a view of this kind, one might identify the fact that, for example, "Torture is wrong" with the fact that a certain kind of attitude (say, moral disapproval) is fitting toward torture. And one might in turn identify the fact that "Moral disapproval is fitting toward torture" with the fact that "Torture possesses that natural feature that it is the functional role of moral disapproval to track" (Ross, 2015). In this way, one would identify the pure moral fact that torture is wrong with the fact that torture stands in a certain relation to the functional role of moral disapproval. And facts about the functional role of mental state types are plausibly necessary truths about the essential nature of these types. Moreover, it seems these facts could play a role in explaining our moral beliefs. Suppose it were the functional role of the attitude of moral disapproval to track a certain feature F, and that torture, by its very nature, possesses F. This could explain why we are disposed to have an attitude of moral disapproval toward torture. And this fact, in turn, could explain why we believe that torture is morally wrong. (This is not the only way such an account might go—see Copp [2008], who holds that moral facts are identical with certain natural facts that plausibly explain our moral beliefs.)

Such an approach would, however, need to tackle the problem of moral disagreement. If there really is some natural feature that it is the functional role of moral disapproval to track, then one would expect there to be a high degree of uniformity in our dispositions to morally disapprove—and so it may be difficult, on this view, to explain the seeming ubiquity of moral disagreement.

So far, we have focused on attempts to reject premise 3, which denies that we are in a position to form moral beliefs that are explained by the pure moral facts. But some philosophers have attempted to reject premises 4 and 5, which deny other kinds of explanatory connection between our beliefs and the pure moral facts. First, consider the view that the explanatory connection runs from our beliefs to the pure moral facts. On this view, we can know the moral facts not because our beliefs depend on these facts but because these facts depend on our beliefs. A view of this kind is defended by Street (2006), who proposes that "the truth of 'X is a reason for agent A to Y' is a function of whether that judgment would be among A's evaluative judgments in reflective equilibrium." On this view, whether X is a reason for me to act in some way depends on whether I would regard it as such if my evaluative judgments were in reflective equilibrium, which in turn depends on my actual evaluative judgments. Hence, facts about my reasons depend, indirectly, on my beliefs about such facts.

But there are two reasons to doubt that such an approach can provide an adequate response to the moral skeptic. First, even if it could help to ground moral knowledge, it would be limited to what we might call *egocentric moral knowledge*, or knowledge of one's own moral reasons. Even if we adopt an internalist view on which my reasons depend on my evaluative beliefs, other people's reasons still won't depend on my evaluative beliefs— it simply isn't plausible, for example, that whether Julius Caesar had reason to cross the Rubicon depends on my evaluative beliefs. Even on this view, there won't be mind-to-world explanatory connection between my beliefs and other people's reasons that would allow me to have knowledge of the latter. Moreover, since moral reasons are generally thought to be universal, a view on which I can know my own moral reasons without being in a position to know other people's moral reasons may not be coherent.

The second problem with this approach is that it doesn't seem to apply to knowledge of pure moral facts, since pure moral facts are necessary truths. (This follows from the widely accepted claim that moral supervenes on the descriptive. This claim implies that the true complete moral theory is necessarily true. From this, it follows that any true pure moral proposition (or disjunction of complete moral theories) must be necessarily true.) But since our evaluative judgments are contingent, any fact that depends on these judgments must likewise be contingent. The pure moral facts can't depend on our evaluative judgments. And while some moral anti-realists might defend an account of pure moral claims where even these conditional principles are contingent and dependent on individual attitudes, this must be counted as a substantial theoretical cost for the view.

Lastly, let us consider the rejection of premise 5, which denies that our moral beliefs and the pure moral facts can share a common explanation. A number of philosophers have proposed "third-factor accounts" according to which there is such a common explanation. This idea was first proposed in Nozick (1981) and has recently been advocated in Berker (2014), Enoch (2011), and Wielenberg (2010), *inter alia*. The basic idea is that there is some factor X that both explains why certain actions are morally required and explains why we believe they are morally required. Since many of these authors are responding to the Evolutionary Debunking Argument and accept, at least for the sake of argument, that our moral beliefs are shaped by evolutionary pressures, this third factor is typically identified with an evolutionary aim, such as "inclusive fitness" (Nozick, 1981) or "survival or reproductive success" (Enoch, 2011).

But there are several problems with this approach. One problem is that it clearly can only apply to *derivative* moral truths, or moral truths that have explanations. Many philosophers (including, we suspect, many philosophers who endorse third-factor accounts) believe that there are some fundamental moral truths that explain other moral truths but are not susceptible to further explanation. "Pain and suffering are bad" might be one example. "Survival and reproductive success are good" might be another. But if these or any other moral propositions cannot be explained, then clearly there can be no third factor that explains both them and our belief in them.

Moreover, even in the case of non-fundamental moral facts, it is dubious that the very same factor that explains our belief in them could also explain their truth. To illustrate the difficulty, suppose you believe that promise-keeping is morally required. What might explain why you believe this? Perhaps you believe this, at least in part, because dispositions to form this belief promote reproductive success. But *whose* reproductive success? From an evolutionary point of view, it's irrelevant whether these dispositions promote *your* reproductive success. Rather, what matters is that they promoted the reproductive success of your ancestors—chiefly, your Paleolithic ancestors. But it's questionable whether this could have any bearing on whether promise-keeping is now morally required.

Moreover, even if we grant, with proponents of this approach such as Enoch (2011), that the evolutionary aim that explains the formation of our beliefs is good, this would at most explain why our moral beliefs, or the dispositions that gave rise to them, are *good*—it would not explain why they are *true*. After all, false beliefs, like true beliefs, could promote good aims. This is an issue that utilitarians, beginning with Sidgwick (1907), have been acutely aware of. As Sidgwick pointed out, even if utilitarianism is true, and hence what is good is total happiness, the moral beliefs that most promote this good may be non-utilitarian and hence false beliefs. And the same may be true if what is good is survival or reproductive success. Suppose the aim I ought to promote is reproductive success, and hence that the valuable actions and moral beliefs are the ones that promote reproductive success. In this case, it might turn out that I ought to cheat when I can get away with it, since doing so is conducive to reproductive success. But it might also turn out that I am disposed to believe that I ought *not* to cheat when I can get away with it, since having this false belief may be conducive to reproductive success (this could be true, for example, because other people are able to discern to some degree what my moral beliefs are, and because they are more likely to cooperate with me if I have this false belief). Hence, even if we grant that the evolutionary aim is good, it is plausible that evolutionary pressures could result in the formation of systematically false beliefs, and hence that they could constitute an off-track influence.

Thus, while there are a number of philosophical views that seem to offer an escape from the Explanatory Trilemma Argument by allowing us to reject one of its premises, each of these views faces difficulties.

CONCLUSION

Skeptical arguments can play one of two roles: they can lead us to question *whether* we have a given kind of knowledge, or they can lead us to question *how* we can have such knowledge. This is true, in particular, of the skeptical arguments we have considered in this chapter. Some people, philosophers or non-philosophers alike, may wonder whether we have any moral knowledge, and may see some of the arguments we have considered as providing grounds for a negative answer. Others, more Moorean in their outlook, will regard it as obvious that we possess moral knowledge, and hence as obvious that these arguments must go wrong somewhere. Even for them, however, these arguments should prove illuminating, since replying to them requires giving a defensible account of how our moral beliefs are connected to the moral facts. And this, as we have seen, is no easy task.

NOTE

1. To give a more precise account of impure moral propositions, we could define a *complete descriptive theory* as a maximally specific descriptive characterization of the world, and we could define a *total theory* as a conjunction of a complete descriptive theory and a complete moral theory. Then, just as we define a *pure moral proposition* as a disjunction of complete moral theories, we may define a *pure descriptive proposition* as a disjunction of complete descriptive theories. Finally, we may define an *impure moral proposition* as a disjunction of total theories that is not equivalent either to a pure moral proposition or to a pure descriptive proposition.

RELATED TOPICS

Chapter 3, "Error Theory in Metaethics;" Chapter 28, "Explanatory Challenges in Metaethics;" Chapter 30, "Intuitionism in Moral Epistemology;" Chapter 32, "The Epistemic Significance of Moral Disagreement."

REFERENCES

Baker, A. (2005) "Are There Genuine Mathematical Explanations of Physical Phenomena?" *Mind* 114 (454): 223–38.

Berker, S. (2014) "Does Evolutionary Psychology Show That Normativity Is Mind-Dependent?" in J. D'Arms & D. Jacobson (eds.) *Moral Psychology and Human Agency: Philosophical Essays on the Science of Ethics*, New York: Oxford University Press: 215–52.

Chisholm, R. M. (1966) *Theory of Knowledge*, Englewood Cliffs, NJ: Prentice Hall.

Clarke-Doane, J. (2014) "Moral Epistemology: The Mathematics Analogy," *Noûs* 48(2): 238–55.

Copp, D. (2008) "Darwinian Skepticism about Moral Realism," *Philosophical Issues* 18(1): 186–206.

Cuneo, T. & Shafer-Landau, R. (2014) "The Moral Fixed Points: New Directions for Moral Nonnaturalism," *Philosophical Studies* 171(3): 399–443.

Enoch, D. (2011) *Taking Morality Seriously: A Defense of Robust Realism*, Oxford: Oxford University Press.

Gettier, E. (1963) "Is Justified True Belief Knowledge?" *Analysis* 23(6): 121–23.

Huemer, M. (2005) *Ethical Intuitionism*, New York: Palgrave Macmillan.

Joyce, R. (2006) *The Evolution of Morality*, Cambridge, MA: MIT Press.

McGrath, S. (2014) "Relax! Don't Do It! Why Moral Realism Won't Come Cheap," in R. Shafer-Landau (ed.) *Oxford Studies in Metaethics*, vol. 9, New York: Oxford University Press: 186–214.

Moore, G. E. (1903) *Principia Ethica*, Dover Publications.

Nozick, R. (1981) *Philosophical Explanations*, Cambridge, MA: Harvard University Press.

Parfit, D. (2013) *On What Matters: Volume One*, Oxford: Oxford University Press.

Pollock, J. (1987) "Defeasible Reasoning," *Cognitive Science* 11(4): 481–518.

Putnam, H. (1972) *Philosophy of Logic*, London: Allen and Unwin.

Ross, J. (2015) "From Moral Blame to Moral Wrongness," presented at the Arizona Workshop in Normative Ethics, 16 January 2015.

Scanlon, T. M. (2014) *Being Realistic about Reasons*, New York: Oxford University Press.

Setiya, K. (2012) *Knowing Right from Wrong*, Oxford: Oxford University Press.

Shafer-Landau, R. (2004) *Whatever Happened to Good and Evil?* New York: Oxford University Press.

Sidgwick, H. (1907) *The Methods of Ethics*, London: Macmillan.

Sinnott-Armstrong, W. (2006) *Moral Skepticisms*, New York: Oxford University Press.

Sosa, E. (1999) "How to Defeat Opposition to Moore," *Philosophical Perspectives* 13: 137–49.

Street, S. (2006) "A Darwinian Dilemma for Realist Theories of Value," *Philosophical Studies* 127(1): 109–66.

Sturgeon, N. (1988) "Moral Explanations," in G. Sayre-McCord (ed.) *Essays on Moral Realism*, Ithaca, NY: Cornell University Press: 229–55.

Wielenberg, E. J. (2010) "On the Evolutionary Debunking of Morality," *Ethics* 120(3): 441–64.

FURTHER READING

Goldman, A. (1967) "A Causal Theory of Knowing," *Journal of Philosophy* 64(12): 357–72.

Harman, G. (1977) *The Nature of Morality: An Introduction to Ethics*, New York: Oxford University Press.

32

The Epistemic Significance of Moral Disagreement

Dustin Locke

Unfortunately, we possess no analogue to an eye exam, by which we might determine whose moral vision is askew and whose is in good working order.

Sarah McGrath (2007: 99)

INTRODUCTION

Take any one of my moral beliefs. More likely than not, there is some competent person who rejects it. Is it nonetheless appropriate for me to stick to my belief? Or should I be more conciliatory, significantly reducing my confidence in the disputed belief or perhaps withdrawing my belief altogether? What, in short, is the epistemic significance of moral disagreement?

Common wisdom isn't much help here. On the one hand, we're told that people should often 'agree to disagree'. This suggests that it can be reasonable to stick to one's moral beliefs in the face of disagreement, provided that one allows others to stick to their beliefs. On the other hand, we're told that it's arrogant to think of oneself as 'knowing the truth' when other reasonable people think otherwise. This suggests that merely allowing others to think as they do is not enough: proper humility requires significantly reducing confidence in one's own belief. I think it's no surprise that common wisdom is conflicted here: our question turns out to be surprisingly complicated, hanging on some of the most nuanced and controversial claims in contemporary epistemology. The question is for that reason all the more exciting. It's also pressing: with technology making our political and cultural borders ever more permeable, the need to understand the epistemic significance of moral disagreement has never been greater.

While this chapter might have been organized around competing *views* about the epistemic significance of moral disagreement, it is instead organized around a certain 'Core Argument'—an argument roughly to the effect that known moral disagreement of a certain sort ought to lead one to suspend one's moral belief. Focusing on a particular argument will give our discussion a greater focus than it otherwise might have had. And I don't think it will be *too* focused: readers with sympathies for another argument are still likely to find most of the relevant issues touched on here.

I begin by distinguishing the kind of argument to be developed in this chapter from other kinds of argument from moral disagreement. I then consider some natural initial thoughts about the epistemic significance of moral disagreement, eventually working up to a rough statement of the Core Argument. I next give a precise statement of the Core Argument, clearly defining the kind of moral disagreement at issue. After a discussion of the applicability of the Core Argument's conclusion, I assess its various components, drawing heavily on the epistemology literature on 'peer disagreement'. Finally, I consider what the Core Argument's conclusion has to say about cases of *radical* moral disagreement.

METAPHYSICAL VERSUS EPISTEMOLOGICAL ARGUMENTS FROM DISAGREEMENT

The *locus classicus* for the kind of argument to be developed and discussed in this essay— the Core Argument—is Sarah McGrath's 'Moral Disagreement and Moral Expertise' (2007). McGrath's argument explicitly and *merely* aims to 'undermine moral knowledge by showing that … we are not in a position to have anything like the amount of moral knowledge that we ordinarily take ourselves to have' (88). This stands in contrast, McGrath notes, to 'the most familiar arguments from [moral] disagreement in the literature', which 'purport to establish conclusions about the metaphysics of morality: that there are no moral facts, or that there are no moral properties, or that the moral facts are relative rather than absolute' (87). McGrath thus draws a distinction between her 'epistemological argument'—with its purely epistemological conclusion—and familiar 'metaphysical arguments'—with their familiar metaphysical conclusions.

It's worth dwelling on this point for a bit, since it's possible to rationally reconstruct traditional metaphysical arguments in such a way that they involve epistemological arguments. Take, for example, John Mackie's (1977) famous argument from disagreement against moral realism. The central claim of Mackie's argument is that anti-realists— according to whom there are no properties such as *moral rightness* and *moral wrongness*—can offer a 'better' explanation of actual moral disagreement than moral realists can. The realist explanation of disagreement, Mackie assumes, would have to be one according to which moral judgments 'express perceptions, most of them seriously inadequate and badly distorted, of objective values' (1977: 37). Granting Mackie that this, or something near it, is the kind of explanation that the moral realist will have to offer, why is this explanation of moral disagreement supposed to be *worse* than the best explanation the anti-realist can offer? Unfortunately, Mackie doesn't say. But we can speculate.

Perhaps the thought is that once the realist appeals to whatever 'distorting influences' on our moral judgments he is prepared to appeal to—for example, self-interest—there is no reason to appeal to anything *further* in the explanation of our moral beliefs; in particular, there is no reason to appeal to objective moral properties. Thus, one might conclude that the anti-realist explanation—which merely appeals to those factors that are, according to the realist, distorting factors—is all things considered *simpler* than the realist explanation. If Mackie's argument proceeds in this way, it is open to a serious objection. From the perspective of the moral realist, who *independently believes* that there are objective moral properties, a hypothesis that appeals to objective moral properties is for that reason no worse than one that does not (Schafer-Landau, 2003: 219). The basic idea here is that when deciding which hypothesis offers the best explanation of a given phenomenon, the relevant notion of 'simplicity' is measured against what one has independent grounds for believing. Now, the anti-realist might protest that we have no independent grounds for believing in moral properties. But if that's so, then it seems that the argument from moral disagreement becomes an unnecessary fifth wheel, at best refuting a view that no one has any reason to endorse anyway.

There is, however, another way that Mackie might have argued that the realist explanation—which, we're assuming, must appeal to 'seriously inadequate and badly distorted perceptions' of objective moral properties—is worse than the anti-realist explanation. Leaving simplicity considerations aside, Mackie might have appealed to a certain *epistemological* argument from disagreement. In particular, he might have argued that what makes the realist explanation of disagreement worse than the anti-realist explanation is that one cannot endorse the realist explanation of moral disagreement without *undermining* one's endorsement of moral realism (Loeb, 1998). On this interpretation, the first step in the argument is the claim that if one endorses:

Big Trouble. Our moral judgments express seriously inadequate and badly distorted perceptions of objective moral properties.

one cannot rationally continue to endorse one's moral judgments. Consider, by analogy, someone who thinks to himself:

There's a ball of wax in front of me. But all of my empirical judgments, including the one I just made, *are based on seriously inadequate and badly distorted perceptions of my physical environment. Still, there's a ball of wax in front of me.*

This position isn't *logically inconsistent*—everything here thought might be true. But it is plausibly rationally inconsistent—it is plausibly irrational to continue to believe *p* while consciously believing that one's belief that *p* is ill-founded.

Suppose it's true, then, that one cannot rationally endorse one's moral judgments while simultaneously endorsing Big Trouble. If it's also true that the realist's belief in objective moral properties is (in part but essentially) based on her moral judgments—for example, if believing that some things are wrong forms an essential part of the basis upon which she believes that there is an objective property of moral wrongness—then it seems that she cannot rationally endorse Big Trouble without giving up her moral realism. But Big Trouble entails moral realism. So Big Trouble is not a position that one can rationally endorse. The only explanation of moral disagreement open to the realist, according to this argument, is an explanation that one cannot rationally endorse.

Much remains to be said about the strength of the argument just presented. The point here, however, is merely to illustrate that McGrath's distinction between metaphysical arguments from disagreement, on the one hand, and epistemological arguments from disagreement, on the other, is not quite as clean as we might have hoped: on the reconstruction of Mackie's argument I just gave, the argument involves an epistemological argument from disagreement. This is not to say that McGrath's distinction isn't both sound and useful. It's just to say that, in practice, we'll need to watch out for metaphysical arguments that *involve* epistemological arguments. There are, moreover, important differences between McGrath's epistemological argument and the epistemological argument at work in the reconstructed version of Mackie's metaphysical argument.

First, the epistemological argument at work in the reconstruction of Mackie's argument is a *reductio*: it aims to show that *if* one endorses a realist explanation of moral disagreement—Big Trouble—*then* one's moral judgments are unjustified, and this in turn is meant to show that a realist explanation of moral disagreement is inherently unstable. McGrath's argument, by contrast, aims to show that, given what we know about moral disagreement, one *ought* to embrace a limited moral skepticism: one ought to believe that one doesn't have as much moral knowledge as many people think they have. McGrath does not (merely) attempt to establish that this skeptical conclusion is implied by some metaphysical view—she attempts to establish this skeptical conclusion.

Second, the epistemological argument at work in the reconstruction of Mackie's argument is (crucially) ambitious: it aims to show that, from a realist perspective, actual moral disagreement reveals that there is something *deeply problematic about the basic processes* by which we form our moral beliefs, such that, from the perspective of moral realism, we ought to abandon *all* of our moral beliefs. McGrath's argument, by contrast, merely aims to show that when there is (a certain kind of) disagreement on a particular moral issue, one doesn't know the truth with respect to that particular moral issue. This is not to say that an argument like McGrath's could not be generalized so that it implies widespread or even global moral skepticism; if there is (the relevant kind of) disagreement on *all* moral issues, then an argument like McGrath's would imply global moral skepticism.

The present chapter follows McGrath's lead. Here, I develop and discuss an argument—the Core Argument—to the effect that when a certain kind of moral disagreement exists, one ought to be skeptical. In the next section, I begin with some initial thoughts along these lines, ultimately leading up to the Core Argument.

FROM INITIAL THOUGHTS TO THE CORE ARGUMENT

I believe that it's wrong to consume factory-farmed meat. Others whom I rationally believe to be my 'moral peers' disagree. By 'moral peer', I mean roughly someone who is (1) aware of all the same relevant information that I am aware of—for example, the fact that factory-farmed animals are kept in such and such conditions—and (2) just as likely as I am, given a body of information, to arrive at an appropriate moral view (Elga, 2007; cf. John, 2014). On first thought, disagreement with a moral peer seems to have profound epistemic significance. If I don't take myself to be generally better than my peer at figuring out the moral truth, and if we are aware of all of the same relevant information, shouldn't I suspend judgment on the moral permissibility of consuming factory-farmed meat, at least for now?

On second thought, moral disagreement seems to have no epistemic significance. Either I do or do not have good reasons for believing that it is wrong to consume factory-farmed meat. If I have good reasons for believing as I do, then my belief is justified. If not, then it is not. It seems, then, that moral disagreement *per se* has nothing to do with it: what matters is simply whether I have *good reasons* for believing as I do.

On third thought, my peer is pretty good at figuring stuff out, and when someone who is pretty good at figuring stuff out believes *not-p*, this very fact is itself a good reason to believe *not-p*. So we cannot just say that whether my moral belief is justified depends on whether I have good reasons for believing as I do and does not depend on whether others disagree with me: it's plausible, but not uncontroversial, that the facts about what my peers believe on moral matters are *among* the facts that count for and against believing as I do (Jones, 1999; Sliwa, 2012).

On fourth thought, the fact that someone who is pretty good at figuring stuff out believes *not-p* is not, comparatively speaking, very *much* reason to believe *not-p*. In particular, it's not very much reason when compared to my reasons for believing *p* (Kelly, 2005). I know quite a bit about how factory-farmed meat is produced, I know that the fact that there is so much suffering involved is a *pro tanto* moral reason to avoid contributing to that practice, and I know that people get a relatively small benefit from consuming factory-farmed meat. Knowing these facts gives me a strong reason to believe that it's not morally permissible to consume factory-farmed meat. The mere fact that *someone who is pretty good at figuring stuff out believes that it is not wrong to consume factory-farmed meat* seems to pale in comparison.

On fifth and final thought, my peer's dissenting opinion seems to count against my beliefs in a couple of different ways (Feldman, 2006; Matheson, 2009). One way is by *rebutting* my belief—that is, by providing me with at least some reason to believe *not-p*. This is the idea behind the third thought above. But another way that a dissenting opinion can count against my belief is by *undermining it*—that is, by turning my good reasons for believing as I do into not-so-good reasons for believing as I do.

Consider an analogy that has nothing to do with morality, and nothing to do with disagreement. Suppose that a friend's dog growls in my direction. At first, this is a good reason to believe that the dog sees me as a threat. But then my friend points out that there is a raccoon on a tree just behind me, and that his dog has been trained to growl at raccoons. This new information does not provide me with a reason to believe that the dog does *not* see me as a threat—it does not rebut my belief. But it does provide me with reason to *stop* believing that the dog *does* see me as a threat. It does this by turning what was a good reason for believing that the dog sees me as a threat—the fact that she was growling in my direction—into a not-so-good reason for thinking that she sees me as a threat. In other words, this new information *undermines* my belief that the dog sees me as a threat.

In our third thought, we noted that my peer's belief that it is not wrong to consume factory-farmed meat provides me with some reason to believe that it is not wrong. And in our fourth thought, we granted that this was so, but noted that such a reason to believe it is not wrong—the mere fact that a peer believes it is not wrong—pales in comparison to my reasons for believing that it is wrong. But the fifth thought insists that this misses the more devastating epistemic significance of my peer's dissenting opinion. According to the fifth thought, I cannot simply weigh the fact that my peer believes otherwise against my good reasons for believing as I do, *because the fact that my peer believes otherwise turns my good reasons for believing as I do into not-so-good reasons for believing as I do.* In other words, moral disagreement *undermines* justified moral belief. This is the central idea of the argument to be developed and evaluated in this chapter—the Core Argument. Let's work it out.

How might disagreement with a moral peer undermine belief? Here's a natural but ultimately unhelpful thought: if my peer and I have opposed beliefs, then at least one of us must be *wrong*. And if I rationally think that my peer's epistemic credentials are just as good as my own, then it would be inappropriate for me to believe that it is more likely that my peer has got things wrong than that I have.

While the literature contains arguments for conciliation that proceed roughly along these lines, this attempt to spell out *how* disagreement undermines justified moral belief does little more than simply assume *that* moral disagreement undermines belief. Notice that the argument simply assumes that if I rationally think that my peer's epistemic credentials are just as good as my own, then it would be inappropriate for me to believe that it is more likely that my peer has got things wrong than that I have. To assume this is to simply assume that I do not remain justified in my belief in the face of known disagreement with a peer. For if I *do* remain so justified, then I *am* justified in believing that it is more likely that my peer has got things wrong than that I have. What we want to know is *why* or *how* known disagreement with a peer undermines belief.

A better attempt to spell out how peer disagreement undermines belief starts, not with the assumption that:

(Wrong) If my peer and I have opposed beliefs, then at least one of us must be *wrong*.

But with the assumption that:

(Inappropriate) If my peer and I have opposed beliefs, then at least one of our beliefs must be *inappropriate*.

By an appropriate belief, I mean a belief that one is justified in forming, given one's body of information. Since moral peers by definition form their beliefs on the basis of the same body of information, it's plausible that if my moral peer and I have opposed moral beliefs, then one of us must have formed an inappropriate moral belief (more on this below). And if I rationally think that my peer's epistemic credentials are just as good as my own, then it is inappropriate for me to believe that it is more likely that my peer has an inappropriate moral belief than that I have an inappropriate moral belief. But this seems to imply that I am rationally required to (at least) withhold from believing that my moral view is appropriate. And this in turn seems to imply that I am rationally required to (at least) drastically reduce my confidence in my moral belief, perhaps abandoning it altogether. This, roughly, is the Core Argument.

Before proceeding to a more precise statement of the Core Argument, it's worth noting a couple of key differences between this argument and McGrath's (2007) argument. First, the Core Argument targets not (merely) moral knowledge but justified moral belief. This is no small difference: some philosophers think that when it comes to deciding how to act, it's what you *know* and not merely what you *justifiably believe* that counts. While I doubt it (see Locke, 2015), these philosophers might be right. If they are, then even if moral disagreement does not threaten justified moral belief, we might still be in trouble, since moral disagreement might threaten moral knowledge. Second, unlike the conclusion of McGrath's argument, the conclusion of the Core Argument is conditional: *if* one knows that a certain kind of moral disagreement exists, *then* one is not justified in maintaining the disputed moral belief. Aside from some general remarks below, it is beyond the scope of this chapter to consider whether the relevant kind of moral disagreement actually exists.

THE CORE ARGUMENT REFINED

To give the Core Argument a fighting chance, we'll need to formulate it a bit more carefully. Specifically, we'll need to replace the rough notion of a 'moral peer' with a more precisely defined notion.

The epistemology literature on so-called 'peer disagreement' tends to focus on cases in which someone knows that there is someone else who, despite being in a certain sense their 'epistemic equal', nonetheless disagrees with them on some particular issue. More precisely, the literature tends to focus on cases where there is a what I will call a:

Dissenting Prima Facie Peer (Definition A)
S_2 is S_1's dissenting prima facie peer (DPP) if and only if:

(1A) S_1 has a high degree of confidence that p and S_2 has a low degree of confidence that p (and thus a high degree of confidence that not-p);

(2A) S_1 rationally believes that S_1 and S_2 have formed their respective degrees of confidence that p on the basis of the same body of information E; and

(3A) Setting aside the reasons for which S_1 formed her degree of confidence that p, S_1's rational degree of confidence that she, S_1, arrived at an appropriate degree of confidence that p on the basis of E is identical to her rational degree of confidence that S_2 arrived at an appropriate degree of confidence that p on the basis of E.

A useful but imperfect heuristic for thinking about (3A) is to think about S_1 *before* she forms her degree of confidence that p. How rationally confident is S_1 that she will form the appropriate degree of confidence that p on the basis of E? How rationally confident is S_1 that S_2 will form the appropriate degree of confidence? Roughly, (3A) is satisfied if and only if these rational degrees of confidence are equal.

While Definition A provides us with a reasonably intuitive notion of a dissenting prima facie peer, there are several reasons that it won't quite do. First, one need not—nor is it the case that one often should—have a *precise* degree of confidence that some proposition is true. Is my degree of confidence that it will rain today *precisely* 0.7? No. But it is around there—as I'll say, my degree of confidence is *indeterminate* but *centered on* 0.7. I'll use the term 'doxastic attitude' to refer to both determinate and indeterminate degrees of confidence. I'll then say that two doxastic attitudes are 'opposed' when one attitude is centered on a degree of confidence below 0.5 and the other is centered on a degree of confidence above 0.5. The first change to the definition of a DPP will thus involve switching from talk of high versus low degrees of confidence to talk of 'opposed doxastic attitudes'. The other change concerns condition (2A). Note that although (2A) requires S_1 to rationally *believe* that she and S_2 have formed their respective degrees of confidence that p on the basis of the same body of information E, (2A) allows for S_1 to be rationally *more confident* that she formed her doxastic attitude on the basis of a given body of information than she is that

S_2 formed her belief on the basis of that same body of information. This allowance seems negligible, but it can have big epistemic consequences in cases of disagreement, thus leaving our discussion vulnerable to certain distractions from our main topic.

Putting these considerations together, we will replace Definition A with:

Dissenting Prima Facie Peer (Definition B)

S_2 is S_1's dissenting prima facie peer (DPP) if and only if:

(1B) S_1 and S_2 have opposed doxastic attitudes with respect to p;

(2B) S_1 is rationally certain that S_1 and S_2 have formed their respective doxastic attitudes on the basis of the same body of information E; and

(3B) Setting aside the reasons for which S_1 formed her doxastic attitude with respect to p, S_1's rational doxastic attitude towards the proposition that S_1 *has arrived at the appropriate doxastic attitude towards* p *on the basis of E* is identical to S_2's rational doxastic attitude towards the proposition that S_2 *has arrived at the appropriate doxastic attitude towards* p *on the basis of E.*

With the notion of a DPP so defined, we can now offer a step-by-step formulation of the Core Argument:

The Core Argument

Let a p-attitude be a doxastic attitude with respect to p, and let a p-DPP be a DPP with respect to p.

1. For any moral proposition p, if I know that I have a p-DPP, then I have a decisive reason to believe that at least one of us has formed an inappropriate p-attitude. (premise)

2. For any moral proposition p, if I know that I have a p-DPP, then I have no good reason to believe that it is my p-DPP, and not I, who formed an inappropriate p-attitude. (premise)

3. Thus, for any moral proposition p, if I know that I have a p-DPP, I should at least withhold from believing that my p-attitude is appropriate. (from 1, 2)

4. Thus, for any moral proposition p, if I know that I have a p-DPP, then it is inappropriate for me to continue to hold my p-attitude. (from 3)

The conclusion that it is inappropriate for me to continue to hold my p-attitude is intended to entail that, at a minimum, substantial revision to my p-attitude is epistemically rationally required. There are difficult questions about exactly *how much* revision is required (Moss, 2011) and whether we ought to be more concerned with the requirements of *practical* rationality than *epistemic* rationality (Elgin, 2010). Unfortunately, we do not have space to consider these important questions here. Another difficult question is whether the Core Argument generalizes to *all* normative disagreements, forcing us to abandon not only moral judgments but judgments of practical and epistemic rationality as well. If it does, one might think that this amounts to a *reductio* of the Core Argument (Sher, 2001). Unfortunately, we don't have space to consider this important issue either.

Most of the remainder of this essay will be concerned with a more or less direct evaluation of the component premises and inferences of the Core Argument. The inference from (1, 2) to (3) seems unassailable (but consider this a challenge to assail it!).

This leaves us with three components to consider: premise (1), premise (2), and the inference from (3) to (4). I will discuss these in turn. Before doing so, however, let us take a moment to consider the scope of the argument's conclusion.

ARE THERE DPPs? IDEALIZATION, ERROR THEORY, RELATIVISM, AND INTUITIONISM

The conclusion of the Core Argument is conditional: for any moral proposition p, if I know that I have a p-DPP, then it is inappropriate for me to continue to hold my p-attitude. But I almost certainly have no actual DPPs. For someone to be my DPP, I must be rationally certain that they formed their doxastic attitude on the basis of the *exact* same body of information on which I formed mine. Surely there are no such people. One might be tempted to conclude from this that we're wasting our time on DPPs and thus wasting our time on the Core Argument. Shouldn't we be considering more realistic cases of disagreement?

It is a mistake, I think, to focus directly and exclusively on realistic cases. Realistic cases are incredibly complicated, making it almost impossible to separate the epistemic significance of disagreement from the epistemic significance of other features. Consider an analogy. There are no frictionless pucks or perfect vacuums, but theorizing about such idealizations is central to the practice of physics. Doing so enables physicists to isolate features of more realistic cases that, considered directly, are simply too complicated to allow for fruitful theorizing. I think it is useful to take a similar approach in philosophy (Kamm, 2011; Locke, 2014), although this approach has been rejected by others (Wilkes, 1994).

That said, one might reasonably insist that we spend time on the Core Argument only if there are actual cases that relevantly resemble DPP disagreement. Such cases will involve at a minimum (1) moral disagreement, and, more controversially, (2) parties who formed their respective doxastic attitudes on the basis of bodies of information that are *not so dissimilar* as to make appropriate radically different doxastic attitudes.

Let's start with (1). Are any ostensible cases of moral disagreement *genuine* cases of moral disagreement? This is partially an empirical question—a question about what sorts of doxastic attitudes people do as a matter of fact have—and partially a philosophical question—about what exactly it is for there to be a *disagreement* between people, and what exactly it is for a disagreement to be a *moral* disagreement (Wong, 1984). With respect to the latter, a plausible place to begin is with the thought that there is moral disagreement only if there is some moral proposition p with respect to which two people have opposed doxastic attitudes.

On some metaethical theories, combined with certain theories of propositions, there are no such propositions. Consider, for example, Mackie's error theory (1977). On Mackie's view, there are no moral properties—no such thing as moral *rightness*, *wrongness*, and so on. Now, consider a version of the so-called 'structured propositions' view, according to which propositions are structures composed of objects, events, properties, and so on. On some versions of this view, the proposition that *it is wrong to consume factory-farmed meat* is a structure composed of the action-type *consuming factory-farmed meat* and the property *moral wrongness*. Given Mackie's error theory, there is no such property as *moral wrongness*, thus no such structure, thus—on the view of propositions under consideration—no such proposition, and thus no such proposition over which people might disagree. Some might see this argument as a *reductio* on the combination of views that generates its conclusion.

A view that might have similar implications is moral subjectivism. On a simple subjectivist view, what I believe when I believe that consuming factory-farmed meat is wrong is: *I* [thought in reference to Dustin] *disapprove of consuming factory-farmed meat*. When Bridget believes that it is not wrong to consume factory-farmed meat, what she believes, on a simple subjectivist view is: *I* [thought in reference to Bridget] *do not disapprove of consuming factory-farmed meat*. On such a view, is there one moral proposition about which we disagree? It doesn't seem so. My belief is *about me*, while Bridget's belief is *about her*. This simple argument is by no means uncontroversial (see Marques, 2014; Garcia-Carpintero & Torre, forthcoming).

Let us turn to issue (2). Is it plausible that all actual cases of moral disagreement—supposing there are any—involve people who form their respective moral judgments on the basis of bodies of information that are so dissimilar as to make appropriate radically different doxastic attitudes? To address this question, we should be careful to separate non-moral information—information about, for example, the hedonic consequences of taking a certain course of action—from moral information—information about, for example, what kinds of outcomes are morally good or bad or what kinds of acts are morally right or wrong. It is controversial whether there exists such a thing as 'moral information' and, if there is, whether two people could have the same non-moral information while having different moral information. But there are views that make this possible. Consider, for example, a view according to which we have 'intuitive' access to a realm of non-natural moral truths. A proponent of such a view might insist that it is at least logically possible that some of us have better access to this realm than others (Audi, 2004: 60). If this is what is happening in cases of actual moral disagreement—that is, if actual moral disagreement is the result of people having different degrees of access to the relevant *moral* information—then the lessons we learn from consideration of DPP disagreement might not straightforwardly carry over to cases of actual moral disagreement (cf. Ernest Sosa's [2010: 287] discussion of 'the rational given' and its relation to the epistemic significance of disagreement).

ON REJECTING PREMISE (1): EPISTEMIC PERMISSIVISM AND EPISTEMIC EGOCENTRISM

Recall:

1. For any moral proposition *p*, if I know that I have a *p*-DPP, then I have a decisive reason to believe that at least one of us has formed an inappropriate *p*-attitude. (premise)

Epistemic permissivists maintain that for some bodies of information, there is no *unique* appropriate doxastic attitude to form on the basis of that body of information; it is, rather, appropriate to form any one of a set of permissible attitudes. If this is right, then it would seem that the mere fact that my DPP and I have formed distinct attitudes gives me no reason to believe that at least one of us has formed an inappropriate attitude.

Sophisticated versions of epistemic permissivism have been defended against common objections to less sophisticated versions (Schoenfield, 2013). But why would one be tempted to endorse such a view in the first place? To deny permissivism is to insist that there is always a unique doxastic attitude supported by a given body of evidence. This might seem to entail that there is always a unique *and precise* degree of confidence supported by a given body of evidence, which strikes many as implausible (Christensen, 2007: fn. 8; cf. Feldman, 2000: 681). But this particular argument for permissivism ignores a rather well-known alternative: indeterminate degrees of confidence (Christensen, 2007: fn. 8). Whereas the permissivist will insist, say, that both credence 0.45 is appropriate and credence 0.55 is appropriate, the proponent of indeterminate credence will insist that the unique appropriate doxastic is one of indeterminate credence, in which this indeterminacy ranges (at least) over both 0.45 and 0.55.

Another way to try to resist premise (1) of the Core Argument is by appeal to epistemic egocentrism. On this view, the doxastic attitude that it is appropriate for me to have need not be the same as the doxastic attitude it is appropriate for someone else to have, despite the fact that we form our respective doxastic attitude on the basis of the same body of information. Suppose that I believe that p and Bridget believes that *not-p*. Suppose also that I know that I have formed my belief that p partially on the basis of the fact that *it seems to me* that p and Bridget has formed her belief that *not-p* partially on the basis of the fact that *it seems to her* that *not-p*. If Bridget is my DPP, then I must be rationally certain that we have formed our respective beliefs on the basis of the *same* body of information. This means that I know that *it seems to Bridget* that *not-p*, and I formed my belief that p partially on the basis of this fact. *Mutatis mutandis* for Bridget and the fact that *it seems to me* that p. Now, despite the fact that I know that Bridget has formed her belief partially on the basis of the fact that it seems to me that p, I also know (and so does Bridget) that I have a certain 'personal relationship' to that fact that she does not have. I know that I am the subject of that fact; I know (and so does Bridget) that it is *me*, and not her, to whom it seems that p. Michael Huemer (2011) argues that such distinct relationships to the same information can create an asymmetry in virtue of which Bridget and I are justified in believing different things (Ralph Wedgwood [2010] makes a similar argument). Specifically, Huemer defends a principle I will call:

Treat Yourself! When it seems to A that p, this fact provides S with prima facie justification for believing p. But for any B ≠ A, the fact that it seems to B that p provides A with no prima facie justification for believing p, even when A knows (with absolute certainty) that it seems to B that p.

Given how I've described the case so far, Treat Yourself! implies that the mere fact that it seems to me that p provides me with prima facie justification for believing p. But Treat Yourself! also implies that, despite the fact that Bridget knows that it seems to me that p, the mere fact that it seems to me that p does not provide her with any prima facie justification for believing that p. Hence, according to Treat Yourself!, Bridget and I might be justified in having different doxastic attitudes on the basis of the same body of information. Hence, if Treat Yourself! is true, and I know it's true, the mere fact that I have a DPP with respect to p provides me with no reason to think that one of us have formed an inappropriate doxastic attitude, contrary to (1) of the Core Argument.

ON REJECTING PREMISE (2): DEMOTING ONE'S PEER

Recall:

2. For any moral proposition p, if I know that I have a p-DPP, then I have no good reason to believe that it is my p-DPP, and not I, who formed an inappropriate p-attitude.

Premises along the lines of (2) are at the center of most of the literature on peer disagreement. For better or worse, there is now a mild consensus that the controversy over (2) hangs on the following question: can the very fact that *my DPP has the p-attitude she does* count as a reason for believing that it is her and not me who has formed an inappropriate p-attitude? That is, can I legitimately 'demote' someone from peer status on the mere basis of her opinion about the issue now under dispute? Some philosophers maintain that to do so would be to dismiss my DPP in a 'blatantly question-begging' kind of way (Christensen, 2011: 2); others disagree (Kelly, 2005).

Consider the following kind of reasoning:

Well, on the basis of our common body of information E, my DPP came to believe not-p. *But she ought not to have come to believe* not-p—*on the basis of E, one ought to believe* p. *So she formed an inappropriate* p-attitude.

Call this 'the prima facie question-begging reasoning'. Some philosophers maintain that, despite appearances, the prima facie question-begging reasoning is perfectly legitimate (Kelly, 2005). As noted above, proponents of the Core Argument will be happy to grant that in many cases in which the known existence of a DPP leaves one's belief unjustified, one was, prior to learning of the existence of a DPP, justified in believing as one did. Let's call this:

The Prior-Justification Assumption. Prior to finding out that I have a DPP, I am justified in believing p on the basis of E.

Consider a case in which this assumption holds, and upon finding out about the existence of a DPP I engage in the prima facie question-begging reasoning. While such reasoning will not be *dialectically* effective—that is, it won't persuade someone who doesn't already think that I am justified in believing p—it's hard to say what, from the perspective of rationality, is wrong with reasoning in this way. Given the Prior-Justification Assumption, I was justified in believing p on the basis of E prior to finding out about my DPP. And it is surely rational for me to reason on the basis of my justified beliefs. Thus, to simply assume that it is not rational for me to engage in the prima facie question-begging reasoning is to simply assume that learning of the existence of a DPP has undermined my previously justified belief that p. But to simply assume *that* is to assume what the Core Argument is meant to show—namely, that the known existence of a DPP undermines previously justified belief. Hence, the argument now under consideration concludes, to reject the prima facie question-begging reasoning is to beg the question in favor of the conclusion of the Core Argument.

This is a powerful line of argument. Nevertheless, it faces a serious challenge. The trouble begins to emerge when we notice that the prima facie question-begging reasoning doesn't actually rest on the assumption that p—rather, it rests on the assumption that *on the basis of E, one ought to believe* p. The distinction is subtle but crucial. Given

The Prior-Justification Assumption, prior to learning about my DPP, I am justified in believing p. But it doesn't follow from this that, prior to learning about my DPP, I am justified in believing that *on the basis of E, one ought to believe* p. Thus, a proponent of the Core Argument can reject the prima facie question-begging reasoning without simply assuming that the known existence of a DPP undermines my justified belief that p—she merely needs to assume that, after learning of the existence of my DPP, I am no longer justified in believing that *on the basis of E, one ought to believe* p. It's plausible that a proponent of the Core Argument could make this assumption without begging the question in favor of the conclusion of the Core Argument and without denying the Prior-Justification Assumption.

ON REJECTING THE INFERENCE FROM (3) TO (4): LEVEL-SPLITTING

Recall:

3. Thus, for any moral proposition p, if I know that I have a p-DPP, I should at least withhold from believing that my p-attitude is appropriate. (from 1, 2)
4. Thus, for any moral proposition p, if I know that I have a p-DPP, then it is inappropriate for me to continue to hold my p-attitude. (from 3)

The inference from (3) to (4) rests on what David Christensen (2013) calls a 'level-connecting' principle. Roughly, a level-connecting principle connects beliefs to beliefs about beliefs. A bit more precisely, a level-connecting principle connects facts about what it is *rational* to believe with facts about what it is *rational* to believe about what it is rational to believe; we might say that it connects rational beliefs to rational beliefs about rational beliefs. For example, the claim that *it is rational to believe that p only if it is rational to believe that it is rational to believe that* p is a level-connecting principle. More precisely still, a level-connecting principle connects rational doxastic attitudes to rational doxastic attitudes about rational doxastic attitudes. The specific level-connecting principle at work in the inference from (3) to (4) is:

3.5. For any proposition p, if I should at least withhold from believing that my p-attitude is appropriate, then it is inappropriate for me to continue to hold my p-attitude.

To deny (3.5) is to maintain that it is sometimes appropriate to maintain one's doxastic attitude even when one ought to withhold from believing that one's doxastic attitude is appropriate. Since (3.5) is a level-connecting principle, we'll say that to deny (3.5) is to endorse *level-splitting*. To see what level-splitting amounts to, let's distinguish it from a couple of nearby theses, one stronger and one weaker.

Sophie Horowitz (2014) criticizes a thesis I'll call 'strong level-splitting', according to which it is sometimes appropriate to maintain one's doxastic attitude even when one ought to *believe* that one's doxastic attitude is *not* appropriate (cf. Lasonen-Aarnio, 2014). To deny (3.5), however, is merely to claim that it is sometimes appropriate to maintain one's doxastic attitude even though one ought to be *agnostic* about the appropriateness of that attitude. It is also important not to confuse level-splitting with the weaker thesis famously advocated by William Alston (1980). According to Alston, it is sometimes appropriate to maintain one's doxastic attitude even when one ought to withhold from any particular belief about what *makes* one's doxastic attitude appropriate. Level-splitting thus goes beyond Alston's thesis to say that even if you ought to go as far as withholding from believing *that your doxastic attitude is appropriate*, your doxastic attitude might still be appropriate.

Where does this leave us? With work to do. While some authors have more or less explicitly rejected level-splitting, carefully distinguishing level-splitting from nearby theses (Feldman, 2006; Matheson, 2009), I know of none who has offered much by way of an *argument* either for or against level-splitting. The authors who have addressed the thesis have, rather, simply noted that level-splitting is fairly counterintuitive. This is not to say that these authors have failed us. But it is to say that this is an area of research that remains to be explored.

RADICAL MORAL DISAGREEMENT: DEEP, WIDESPREAD, EXTREME

Before closing, I want to briefly touch on what the conclusion of the Core Argument has to say about various types of 'radical' moral disagreement. There are at least three interestingly different types of radical moral disagreement to be considered, not all of which are always carefully distinguished in the literature on peer disagreement.

First, there is what I will call 'deep moral disagreement'. Here, there is a moral disagreement between two parties over some particular moral issue—say, the permissibility of consuming factory-farmed meat—that is due to a deeper moral disagreement between them—say, over the moral standing of non-human animals. Second, there is what I will call 'widespread moral disagreement'. Here, there is moral disagreement on *many* moral issues. Widespread moral disagreement may or may not be due to deep moral disagreement; you and your interlocutor might agree on all the more 'fundamental moral issues'—say, the moral standing of non-human animals—but just so happen to disagree on lots of particular moral issues.

Two comments about widespread moral disagreement are in order. First, when widespread moral disagreement is *shallow*—that is, not deep—this doesn't mean that the disagreement must be purely based on some non-moral disagreement. Despite agreement on both the fundamental moral principles and the relevant non-moral facts, you and your interlocutor might simply disagree on how those moral principles *apply* to those non-moral facts. Second, widespread moral disagreement might exist either between you and another person—as when the two of you disagree on a lot of issues—or between you and a *group* of people—as when for most of your individual moral beliefs, there is someone in the group who rejects that moral belief. In the latter case, there may or may not be widespread disagreement between you and any one member of the group.

If the conclusion of the Core Argument applies to these kinds of disagreements, then these kinds of disagreements, should they exist, threaten us with radical moral skepticism—the thesis that few of our moral beliefs are justified—or even complete moral skepticism—the thesis that none of our moral beliefs are justified. But it is no simple matter to determine whether the conclusion of the Core Argument could apply to these kinds of moral disagreements. The crucial question is whether someone, or the members of some group, with whom you have such radical moral disagreement could possibly count as your 'peers' in the relevant sense (Elga, 2007; McGrath, 2007; Vavova, 2014). In the context of the Core Argument, the main point of contention will be over whether such people could possibly satisfy condition (3B) of the definition of a DPP. This matter is delicate and complicated, and I won't pursue it further here. Instead, I'll use the remaining space to discuss a different type of radical moral disagreement—a type that has received relatively little attention in the literature on the epistemic significance of moral disagreement.

Suppose that I believe that consuming factory-farmed meat is wrong, and I come to find out that my friend, who I antecedently and justifiably believed was as likely as I was to have the correct moral view of the matter, believes not only that it is not wrong to consume factory-farmed meat but that, of the meats available for consumption, one is morally required to consume whatever meat was produced in the way that involved the *most suffering for animals*. As it happens, our moral disagreement is neither deep nor widespread: we agree on fundamental moral principles, and we agree about the vast majority of particular moral issues. On this one issue, however, our disagreement is *extreme*.

Is it possible that my friend is my DPP with respect to the proposition that it is wrong to consume factory-farmed meat? Recall condition (3B) of the definition of a DPP:

(3B) Setting aside the reasons upon which S_1 form her doxastic attitude with respect to p, S_1's rational doxastic attitude towards the proposition that S_1 *has arrived at the appropriate doxastic attitude towards* p *on the basis of E* is identical to S_2's rational doxastic attitude towards the proposition that S_2 *has arrived at the appropriate doxastic attitude towards* p *on the basis of E*.

There's a good case to be made that my friend and I could not satisfy condition (3B).

To see why, consider an analogy involving non-moral disagreement. Suppose that you are virtually certain that you are sober and that you are pretty good at mental math—when dividing triple-digit numbers by two, you get the right answer 99 percent of the time, a wrong but *nearby* answer 0.99 percent of the time, and a *way off* answer only 0.01 percent of the time. Your friend, however, is a real mathlete. When she's sober, she gets the right answer 100 percent of the time. But when she's drunk, she gets the right answer only 50 percent of the time, a wrong but *nearby* answer 40 percent of the time, and a *way off* answer 10 percent of the time. Moreover, you are only 98 percent certain that your friend is sober. Notice that your friend's prowess at math, on the one hand, and the small chance that she is drunk, on the other, are in a certain sense offsetting, so that you are just as confident (i.e. 99%) that she will get the right answer when dividing a triple-digit number by two as you are that you will get the right answer. Hence, (3B) of the definition is, for now, met.

Now, suppose that you and your friend are asked to divide 324 by two. You get 162, but your friend disagrees: she insists that the answer is 405. Here, you are rationally certain (let's suppose) that you and your friend formed your judgments on the basis of the same body of information—condition (2B)—and yet you have opposed doxastic attitudes towards the proposition that 324 divided by two is 162—condition (1B). However, upon learning of your friend's view, you don't learn *just* that she has an opposing doxastic attitude with respect to the proposition that 324 divided by two is 162; you also learn that she *endorses* the answer 405. Thus, you learn that you and your friend have come up with wildly different answers. From this you conclude that at least one of you has come up with an answer that is *way off*. As Jennifer Lackey (2008) and Christensen (2011) have pointed out, you can, without 'begging the question' against your friend's answer, use this information to conclude that your friend has probably come up with the wrong answer. Given the facts of the case—that you are virtually certain that you are sober; that when you are sober, you get an answer that is way off only 0.01 percent of the time; that you are only 98 percent certain that your friend is sober; and that when your friend is drunk, she gets an answer that is way off 10 percent of the time—you can rationally conclude that if one of you has come up with an answer that is way off, it is most likely your friend and not you. And you do this, moreover, while setting aside the reasons for which you believe that 324 divided by two is 162. What you rely on, instead, is (1) your antecedent information about you and your friend, and (2) the mere fact that you and your friend have come up with *wildly different answers*. Hence, after you learn of your friend's view of the matter, she no longer satisfies condition (3B).

The case of my extreme disagreement with my friend over the moral permissibility of consuming factory-farmed meat might be analogous. While I have learned that my friend has an opposing doxastic attitude towards the proposition that it is wrong to consume factory-farmed meat, this is not all that I have learned: I have also learned that he believes that, of the meats available for consumption, one is morally required to consume what-ever meat was produced in the way that involved the most suffering for animals. Going into this dispute, it may have been reasonable for me to have an attitude towards my friend analogous to the attitude that it was reasonable for you to have towards your friend in the math case: roughly, it may have been reasonable for me to believe that when my friend is cognitively well-functioning, he comes up with the right moral view more often than I do, but because of certain personal information I have with respect to myself but lack with respect to my friend, I am rationally less certain that he is functioning well than I am that I am functioning well. Since these two factors might be offsetting, I might thus rationally have the same attitude towards the proposition that he will come up with the right answer that I have towards the proposition that I will come up with the right answer. And yet, since I rationally believe that if we come up with *extremely different* answers, it is more likely that my interlocutor is not functioning well than that I am not functioning well, I might rationally retain my moral belief in the face of extreme disagreement.

Some cases of extreme moral disagreement are thus cases in which less would have been more—that is, in some cases of extreme moral disagreement, the disagreement has little or no undermining effect, because one can legitimately downgrade one's interlocu-tor partially on the basis of the very fact that the disagreement is extreme. Notice, moreo-ver, that the degree to which one can downgrade one's interlocutor will depend, in part, on just how extreme one's moral disagreement is: the more extreme, the more likely it is that one of you is not cognitively functioning well, and thus, given that certain conditions are met, the more likely it is that your friend is not functioning well. In short, this sug-gests the somewhat paradoxical conclusion that, at least under certain conditions, there is an inverse relationship between how extreme a piece of moral disagreement is, on the one hand, and how epistemically significant it is, on the other. Katia Vavova (2014) argues for a similar point with respect to widespread and deep moral disagreement. However, Vavova's argument and the argument presented here proceed via different routes, and thus it's possible to endorse one while rejecting the other.

ACKNOWLEDGMENTS

This chapter would not exist without the help of other philosophers, especially the members of the "Board Certified Epistemologists" Facebook group created by Clayton Littlejohn. Some of the literature covered in this essay was unknown to me before members of that Facebook group brought it to my attention, and their helpful comments played a crucial role in the creation of this chapter. I also owe thanks to the participants of the 2015 Prindle Institute of Ethic's Summer Research Retreat on Moral Epistemology at DePauw University, organized by Andy Cullison. Specific individuals to whom I owe a special debt include Mathew Benton, Michael Bergmann, Pat Bondy, Matthew Braddock, David Christensen, Cory Davia, Travis Dumsday, Andy Egan, Kenny Easwaran, Neil Feit, Daniel Greco, Sophie Horowitz, Matthew Jernberg, Dan Korman, Clayton Littlejohn, Theresa Lopez, Heather Lowe, Jon Matheson, Josh May, Tristram McPherson, Andrew Moon, Ángel Pinillos, John Pittard, David Plunkett, Alex Rajczi, Jake Ross, Neil Sinhababu, Jack Spencer, Josh Thurow, Katia Vavova, Brad Weslake, and Robin Zheng.

REFERENCES

Alston, W. (1980) "Level Confusions in Epistemology," *Midwest Studies in Philosophy* 5: 135–50.

Audi, R. (2004) *The Right in the Good*, Princeton: Princeton University Press.

Christensen, D. (2007) "The Epistemology of Disagreement: The Good News," *Philosophical Review* 116: 187–217.

Christensen, D. (2011) "Disagreement, Question-Begging, and Epistemic Self-Criticism," *Philosophers' Imprint* 11 (6): 1–22.

Christensen, D. (2013) "Epistemic Modesty Defended," in D. Christensen and J. Lackey (eds.) *The Epistemology of Disagreement: New Essays*, Oxford: Oxford University Press.

Elga, A. (2007) "Reflection and Disagreement," *Noûs* 41: 478–502.

Elgin, C. (2010) "Persistent Disagreement," in R. Feldman and T. A. Warfield (eds.) *Disagreement*, Oxford: Oxford University Press: 53–68.

Feldman, R. (2000) "The Ethics of Belief," *Philosophy and Phenomenological Research* 60(3): 667–95.

Feldman, R. (2006) "Epistemological Puzzles about Disagreement," in S. Hetherington (ed.) *Epistemology Futures*, Oxford: Oxford University Press: 216–36.

Garcia-Carpintero, M. & Torre, S. (eds.) (forthcoming) *About Oneself: De Se Thought and Communication*, Oxford: Oxford University Press.

Horowitz, S. (2014) "Epistemic Akrasia," *Noûs* 48(4): 718–44.

Huemer, H. (2011) "Epistemological Egoism and Agent-Centered Norms," in T. Dougherty (ed.) *Evidentialism and its Discontents*, Oxford: Oxford University Press: 17–33.

John, E. (2014) "XI—Literature and Disagreement," *Proceedings of the Aristotelian Society* 114: 239–60.

Jones, K. (1999) "Second-Hand Moral Knowledge," *Journal of Philosophy* 96(2): 55–78.

Kamm, F. (2011) *Ethics for Enemies: Terror, Torture, and War*, Oxford: Oxford University Press.

Kelly, T. (2005) "The Epistemic Significance of Disagreement," in J. Hawthorne & T. Gendler (eds.) *Oxford Studies in Epistemology*, vol. 1, Oxford: Oxford University Press: 167–96.

Lackey, J. (2008) "A Justificationist View of Disagreement's Epistemic Significance," in A. Millar, A. Haddock and D. Pritchard (eds.) *Proceedings of the XXII World Congress of Philosophy*, Oxford: Oxford University Press: 145–54.

Lasonen-Aarnio, M. (2014) "Higher-Order Evidence and the Limits of Defeat," *Philosophy and Phenomenological Research* 88: 314–45.

Locke, D. (2014) "Darwinian Normative Skepticism," in M. Bergmann and P. Kain (eds.) *Challenges to Moral and Religious Belief: Disagreement and Evolution*, Oxford: Oxford University Press: 220–36.

Locke, D. (2015) "Practical Certainty," *Philosophy and Phenomenological Research* 90: 72–95.

Loeb, D. (1998) "Moral Realism and the Argument from Disagreement," *Philosophical Studies* 90: 281–303.

McGrath, S. (2007) "Moral Disagreement and Moral Expertise," in R. Shafer-Landau (ed.) *Oxford Studies in Metaethics*, vol. 3, Oxford: Oxford University Press: 87–108.

Mackie, J. L. (1977) *Ethics: Inventing Right and Wrong*, Harmondsworth: Penguin.

Marques, T. (2014) "Doxastic Disagreement," *Erkenntnis* 79(1): 121–42.

Matheson, J. (2009) "Conciliatory Views of Disagreement and Higher-Order Evidence," *Episteme: A Journal of Social Epistemology* 6(3): 269–79.

Moss, S. (2011) "Scoring Rules and Epistemic Compromise," *Mind* 120(480): 1053–69.

Schoenfield, M. (2013) "Permission to Believe: Why Permissivism Is True and What It Tells Us About Irrelevant Influences on Belief," *Noûs* 47(1): 193–218.

Shafer-Landau, R. (2003) *Moral Realism: A Defense*, Oxford: Oxford University Press.

Sher, G. (2001) "But I Could Be Wrong," *Social Philosophy and Policy* 18(2): 64–78.

Sliwa, P. (2012) "In Defense of Moral Testimony," *Philosophical Studies* 158(2): 175–95.

Sosa, E. (2010) "The Epistemology of Disagreement," in A. Haddock, A. Millar and D. Pritchard (eds.) *Social Epistemology*, Oxford: Oxford University Press.

Vavova, K. (2014) "Moral Disagreement and Moral Skepticism," *Philosophical Perspectives* 28(1): 302–33.

Wedgwood, R. (2010) "The Moral Evil Demons," in R. Feldman and T. Warfield (eds.) *Disagreement*, Oxford: Oxford University Press: 216–46.

Wilkes, K. (1994) *Real People: Personal Identity without Thought Experiment*, Oxford: Oxford University Press.

Wong, D. (1984) *Moral Relativity*, Berkeley: University of California Press.

The Status and Methodology
of Metaethics

33

Metasemantics and Metaethics

Laura Schroeter and François Schroeter

Metaethicists disagree about the semantic content of normative and evaluative terms. According to traditional metaethical realists, the semantic role of normative terms is similar to that of natural kind terms: adjectives like 'morally right' pick out a property as their reference, and all competent users of the expression co-refer. Error theorists and fictionalists agree that the semantic role of normative terms is to pick out a property, but they doubt that any such property is instantiated. Contextualists hold that the reference of normative terms varies according to the context of utterance; relativists hold that the truth of normative claims should be evaluated with respect to the standards of an interpreter; and expressivists maintain that the semantic role of normative terms is to express the motivational states of the speaker. Similar positions have been developed for evaluative terms like 'morally good' and 'brave'. For ease of exposition, we'll focus primarily on normative terms in this chapter, but the issues discussed generalize to evaluative terms.

To adjudicate such disagreements, we need to ask how the semantic content of linguistic expressions in general gets determined. What makes it the case that certain words (and the thoughts they express) have the semantic content they do? A metasemantic theory seeks to answer this question. Ultimately, metasemantics should explain the relationship between a *psychological state* (competence with the meaning of a normative term) and a *semantic content* (the contribution made by that word to the correct interpretation of the utterance in which it occurs). For instance, if proper names refer to individuals, then what makes it the case that competence with the meaning of a name like 'Aristotle' guarantees that one refers to a specific individual on every occasion of use? To answer such questions, a metasemantic theory must explain which facts about the subject's use of a name are relevant to fixing the reference (e.g. facts about her internal cognitive organization, her inferential or recognitional dispositions, her history of worldly interactions, her social interactions with others, etc.) and how those facts suffice to single out a specific individual as the reference regardless of variation in background beliefs and empirical facts about the context of use. More generally, a metasemantics must explain how the states that constitute semantic competence ground the assignment of specific semantic content.

There are a wide range of views in the literature about which specific factors may be relevant to determining the semantic content of expressions. These include, for example, facts about the subject's cognitive and motivational dispositions; sociological facts about her linguistic community; facts about her physical environment; anthropological facts about human nature; historical facts about natural selection; and irreducible normative facts about morality or rationality (assuming there are any). But an account that reduces meaning facts to, say, sociological facts still needs to go on to explain how those facts are linked to *this particular utterance* if it's to ground an interpretation of that utterance. The same goes for dispositional, anthropological, historical, and other factors that might figure in a full account of how content is determined—the relevant factors must all be linked to token utterances to explain how the semantic content of the utterance is fixed. So metasemantic theories can all be thought of as providing competing accounts of the relation in virtue of which particular psychological states—like a competent use of a term or a thought deploying a particular concept—have their semantic content.

In the case of normative terms, we can formulate the metasemantic challenge as follows:

How does the state that constitutes competence with the meaning of a normative term guarantee that any competent use of that term has semantic content X?

All metaethical positions assume that normative terms have specific semantic content, so they all assume that a correct metasemantics would vindicate their preferred account of semantic content.

Answering this metasemantic question has been seen as a particularly difficult challenge for traditional normative realists. Because they hold that all competent speakers pick out the very same property with their use of normative terms, traditional realists must explain how such co-reference is possible given persistent disagreement about the applicability conditions of normative terms. On the face of it, there seems to be much wider scope for disagreement about the applicability conditions for 'right' than for such terms as 'chair' or 'water'. Radical and persistent disagreement about which things are chairs would normally lead us to conclude that we were not using words to pick out the same property. The worry is that we should draw a similar conclusion in the normative case. If there is no plausible way to explain co-reference in the face of normative disagreement (Björnsson, 2012), this would be a good reason to favour other metaethical positions that can explain how sameness of semantic content is guaranteed by speakers' competence. More generally, the challenge for all metaethicists is to show how semantic contents can be settled despite non-convergence among competent speakers' understanding and use of normative terms.

In this chapter, we survey different metasemantic approaches to explaining how the content of normative terms is determined. We divide the accounts into two broad groups—internalist approaches and externalist approaches—that diverge over what's required for semantic competence and how facts about competence determine semantic content. Since the non-convergence problem for context-invariant realism has received the most critical attention in the literature, we will use that position as our primary example for illustrating different metasemantic approaches. But along the way, we'll highlight how the issues we discuss generalize to other metaethical positions. In the final section, we focus on recent developments in metaethics that bring a more nuanced understanding of the role of compositional semantic theorizing in linguistics into the metaethical debate. Metaethicists have traditionally assumed a straightforward relationship between the content of normative and evaluative terms and the content of the thoughts those terms are used to express. But a theory of the compositional semantics for language is not equivalent to a theory of thought content, and recently some theorists have argued that this insight can help to counter one of the main challenges to expressivism, the Frege-Geach problem.

THE METASEMANTIC TASK

A metasemantic theory should explain both (1) what constitutes competence with the meaning of a particular expression, and (2) how meeting those competence conditions ensures that the use of that expression has a particular semantic content (see Peacocke [1992] for this two-part division of labour).

We'll assume that there are genuine semantic facts of both these types. In doing so, we set aside both skepticism about the determinacy of semantic content (e.g. Kripke, 1982) and skepticism about individuating fine-grained meanings (e.g. Quine, 1951; Stalnaker, 2008). This semantic realism is the default assumption within mainstream metaethics.

It's worth saying a few words about how *meaning, semantic competence*, and *semantic content* are related. A semantic content is the contribution made by a word to the correct interpretation of an utterance in which it occurs. For instance, a name like 'Hesperus' may contribute a reference, Venus, to the truth-conditions of utterances in which it occurs, or it may contribute a contextually restricted variable, or a descriptive condition. We'd like to stress that semantic contents in this sense need not be referential—they can be context-dependent functions or markers of expressive significance.

On our usage, meaning is a finer-grained notion than semantic content. For instance, 'Hesperus' and 'Phosphorus' may share the same semantic content yet differ in meaning. This fine-grained notion of meaning is grounded in (broadly psychological) *ways* of grasping an expression's semantic content. We call these ways of grasping a given semantic content 'competence conditions'. Thus, token uses of 'Hesperus' and 'Phosphorus' differ in meaning just in case they are governed by distinct competence conditions. Conversely, when token uses of an expression are governed by the same competence conditions (as in 'Hesperus = Hesperus'), those uses are guaranteed to have the same semantic content—since particular ways of grasping a content must determine which content is grasped.

Now let's consider our dual metasemantic task. Suppose that 'x is nuba' is a normative predicate in a foreign language. The first metasemantic question is:

Semantic competence: In virtue of what does someone count as competent with the meaning of this term?

To fully answer this question, we must specify *competence conditions*: particular psychological facts about the use of an expression (perhaps together with non-psychological background facts) that are necessary and sufficient for competence with the standard meaning of 'nuba'. Notice that these conditions must be *specific enough* to distinguish competence with the meaning of 'nuba' from competence with any other possible meaning. In effect, a theory of semantic competence individuates distinct ways of grasping particular semantic contents. An account of competence with specific expressions like 'nuba', moreover, should fit within a general theory of semantic competence with arbitrary expressions in a language.

'Nuba', we are supposing, has certain semantic properties: it is either representational or expressive, context-sensitive or context-neutral, and so on. Within these general categories, moreover, we can distinguish the specific content expressed by 'nuba' from that of other terms with similar representational, expressive, or context-sensitive contents. So the second metasemantic question is:

Semantic determination: In virtue of what do competent uses of 'nuba' have these semantic properties?

To fully answer this question, we need a *determination theory*, which explains how specific psychological or non-psychological facts about the use of an expression are relevant to determining its semantic content. Once again, the determination theory for a particular expression like 'nuba' must fit within a general determination theory for language and thought content. The task of the determination theory is complicated by the fact that there are indefinitely many different natural, functional, and gerrymandered properties, and indefinitely many of them will have significantly overlapping instantiation conditions. Similarly, there are potentially infinitely many distinct psychological state types that could be expressed, and infinitely many functions from contexts to extensions. Explaining why just one of these semantic contents is the one expressed by 'x is nuba' is a highly non-trivial task.

We take it as common ground in metaethics that competence with the same meaning guarantees sameness of semantic content: anyone who satisfies the competence conditions for 'x is nuba' expresses the same content, regardless of how their background beliefs, motivations, or social and physical circumstances may vary. Even relativists and contextualists hold that a particular normative term like 'nuba' will always contribute the very same function from contexts of use and standards of assessment to extensions.

This requirement that semantic competence secure sameness of semantic content places an important constraint on the relationship between a theory of competence and a determination theory:

Linking constraint: The determination theory must appeal *only* to facts about a subject's understanding or circumstances that figure in the competence conditions for particular meanings.

Suppose a specific belief or disposition is not part of the necessary and sufficient conditions for competence with the meaning of 'nuba'. Obviously, the determination theory for 'nuba' cannot appeal to this belief or disposition to explain how all competent subjects—including those who lack the belief or disposition in question—share the same semantic content. This means that competence conditions must be rich enough to single out a determinate content. At the same time, however, competence conditions must not build in too many substantive constraints on understanding if we are to allow for shared meanings over time and between subjects.

Metaethicists have traditionally assumed there is a straightforward relationship between the contents of normative terms and the contents of the thoughts those terms express. One natural picture is that the meaning of the adjective 'morally right' is partly constituted by its connection to a corresponding concept, [morally right], which is what determines the distinctive semantic content expressed by that adjective (e.g. the property of *moral rightness* or the attitude of *moral approval*). There are different ways of conceiving the relation between the lexical entry for an expression and the corresponding concept it expresses. On one approach, lexical entries involve formal semantic "packaging" that determines how an expression will contribute to compositional semantics in a language and "pointers" to specific concepts that lie outside of the language faculty (Glanzberg, 2014; Pietroski, 2010). For instance, the lexical entry for 'is tall' might point to the concept of *height* packaged with a place-holder for a *scale* and a *cut-off point*, which can be supplied by context. This approach ties lexical semantics to the thought contents literally expressed, while allowing for the possibility of linguistic context dependence. See Väyrynen (2013) for an application to thick concepts. For a purely formal conception of linguistic meaning that leaves out any tie to the thought contents expressed by uses of sentences, see Yalcin (2014). As we'll see, this distinction between formal compositional semantics and the substantive thought contents expressed is important to contemporary debates about expressivism.

INTERNALIST THEORIES

The traditional approach to the dual metasemantic task is an internalist one:

Internalism: Semantic competence and semantic contents are determined exclusively by physical factors inside the individual or psychological resources available to the individual.

The intuitive idea is that subjects implicitly know (or have a priori access to) the semantic contents of their own words and thoughts. On standard internalist accounts, to count as competent with a given meaning, one must rely on *rules* or *criteria* for the correct use of an expression. The semantic content of the expression is then settled by those criteria, independently of facts about the individual's external circumstances such as facts about (a) her own past states, (b) her linguistic community, (c) the metaphysical nature of features of her environment, or (d) causal relations linking the speaker to (a)–(c).

From Simple Descriptivism to Neo-Descriptivism

Simple descriptivism is a paradigm internalist metasemantics. According to simple descriptivism, competence with the meaning of a name or predicate consists in an (implicit) understanding of its applicability conditions in any possible circumstance. To count as competent with the name 'Aristotle', for instance, you must be disposed to rely on a specific criterion that serves as your ultimate standard for identifying what the name applies to. The name's semantic content is simply read off of this internal criterion of application. So the content of 'Aristotle' will be a descriptive condition specifiable by a definite description like 'the last great philosopher of antiquity'. Since competence with the same meaning requires reliance on the same criterion, and the criterion fully determines semantic content, it's clear why anyone who meets the competence conditions is guaranteed to pick out the same content. And the linking constraint will be satisfied: semantic assignments depend exclusively on the internal states that constitute semantic competence.

Simple descriptivism, however, came under sustained attack by semantic externalists in the 1970s and 1980s. One central objection was that construing proper names and natural kind terms as semantically equivalent to definite descriptions conflicts with our semantic intuitions about *de re* modal claims like 'Aristotle could have died as a child' or 'Lemons might be blue' (Kripke, 1980; Putnam, 1970). A further objection was that simple descriptivism underestimates the scope for ignorance and error on the part of competent speakers: one can be competent with the meaning of 'gold' without grasping a failsafe criterion for the correct application of that expression (Kripke, 1980; Putnam, 1970; Burge, 1979). This fallibility, moreover, is crucial to the stability of meaning through open-ended inquiry and debate (Putnam, 1973) and to our ability to represent genuinely objective features of our environment (Putnam, 1975; Millikan, 1984; Stalnaker, 2008). If such objections are sound, then simple descriptivism is extensionally inadequate: its semantic competence conditions are too demanding, and its determination theory generates implausible contents.

In response, internalists developed neo-descriptivist metasemantic theories. Neo-descriptivists seek to vindicate the commonsense view that the semantic function of expressions like 'Gödel', 'water' and 'arthritis' is to stably represent particular objects, kinds, or properties, even though we may be ignorant or mistaken about the instantiation conditions of these features. Their proposal is to loosen the connection between competence conditions and semantic content. On this approach, semantic competence may consist in criteria that determine the reference only relative to empirical facts about one's actual environment. Competence with 'water', for instance, may consist in having a conditional criterion for identifying the essential nature of the reference on the basis of information about the chemical nature of the liquids in one's actual historical environment: *if* your environment is like Twin Earth *then* water = XYZ, *if* your environment is like Earth *then* water = H_2O, and so on. But you cannot know what water is without empirical information about your actual environment. So neo-descriptivists can agree that a competent speaker may be ignorant or mistaken about the essential nature of water. Even so, neo-descriptivism holds that competence with the same meaning provides a *conditional guarantee* of sameness of reference: *if* the relevant environmental facts are the same, *then* two competent uses of 'water' are guaranteed to pick out the same reference (Peacocke, 1992; Jackson, 1998a, 1998b). Thus, neo-descriptivism vindicates the core internalist idea that both competence conditions and semantic content are determined (in part or wholly) by a speaker's internal criteria for using an expression.

In metaethics, neo-descriptivism has been used to explain competent speakers' ignorance and error about the instantiation conditions of normative properties. According to Frank Jackson and Philip Pettit's 'moral functionalism', for instance, competence with the meaning of the moral term 'fair' is constituted by a specific pattern of inferential, recognitional, epistemic, predictive, and motivational dispositions, which together constitute the subject's implicit 'folk theory' of morality (Jackson & Pettit, 1995: 22–3). The semantic content of 'x is fair' is the property determined by the upshot of ideal reflective equilibrium, starting from this folk theory and taking into account any empirical facts that are relevant from the point of view of that theory. In a similar spirit, Christopher

Peacocke holds that competence with moral terms consists in the subject's dispositions to reason in accord with a set of core moral principles. The applicability conditions of moral terms—and hence the properties they pick out—must be justifiable on the basis of these a priori moral principles together with empirical facts about circumstances of evaluation (Peacocke, 2004). These neo-descriptivist accounts share a common internalist structure: the competence conditions allow one to identify the precise instantiation conditions for normative properties through empirical inquiry and ideal reflection. So, on this account, ordinary speakers can be ignorant or mistaken about the instantiation conditions of moral rightness, even though the upshot of ideal empirically informed reflection is guaranteed to be correct.

An important advantage of neo-descriptivism is its capacity to vindicate intuitive judgements about the semantic contents of our words and thoughts. Although externalists emphasize our fallibility about *de re* necessities, their arguments typically rely on our reflective, empirically informed judgements about which properties are picked out. Because neo-descriptivism takes reference to be determined by ideal, empirically informed reflection, the approach is immune to intuitive counterexamples. Neo-descriptivism also affords a clear explanation of why all competent speakers are guaranteed to co-refer: any two individuals who rely on the same criteria must co-refer if they share the same empirical context. Moreover, the neo-descriptivist metasemantics is perfectly general; neo-descriptivism about normative terms is part of a well-motivated uniform metasemantics of *all* terms, including names, natural kind terms, commonsense functional kind terms, and logical operators (Peacocke, 1992).

Meaning Stability and Convergence

One central difficulty for neo-descriptivism is vindicating the stability of meaning over time and between speakers. By commonsense standards, novices and experts share the same meanings when they use terms like 'water' or 'is morally right', and there is no change in meaning when rational inquiry leads novices to become more expert. But prior to further empirical inquiry, the novice's ultimate reference-fixing criterion might hinge on deference to experts' criterion, whereas the expert's criterion will not. In such cases, neo-descriptivists must deny there are stable shared meanings; novices and experts rely on different criteria, which will generate divergent verdicts about reference relative to variations in the social environment.

The problem of vindicating stability of meaning is particularly acute for normative terms, since competence with terms like 'x is right' seems consistent with disagreement about any particular application of the term or any general criterion of application. Explaining meaning stability is thus the crux of the familiar disagreement problem in metaethics: how can different speakers be competent with the same meaning if they diverge in their criteria for using a term?

The disagreement problem is endemic to internalist metasemantics. It is generated by internalists' commitment to explaining competence with the same meaning in terms of matching internal criteria of use and then using these criteria to explain the determination of semantic content. Because traditional realists claim that normative terms always pick out the very same property, the disagreement problem for realism will arise from divergence in speakers' applicability criteria. By commonsense standards, two speakers can diverge in virtually any aspect of their understanding of which actions are right without compromising their competence with the same meaning. If their criteria of application diverge substantially, how can their internal states guarantee that they single out the very same property as the reference? A similar problem arises for expressivists who identify competence with normative terms with internal criteria for using those terms to express motivational states. An internalist determination theory might then assign an expressive semantic content on the basis of these criteria of use. Intuitively, however, competent speakers can diverge in the precise motivational dispositions they associate with normative judgements like 'x is fair' or 'x is right': one can become disaffected or cynical without *eo ipso* losing competence with the meaning of moral terms (Merli, 2008). But on an internalist metasemantics, a shift in core motivational criteria suffices for a difference in expressivist meaning. A similar problem will face internalists who favour contextualist or relativist semantic contents. In order to share precisely the same meanings, different individuals must rely on implicit criteria for using a term that relativize normative and evaluative claims to the same parameters in the same ways. But given the scope of normative disagreement, it's not obvious that there is any such convergence among competent speakers (Silk, 2013).

A natural reply on behalf of internalists of all stripes is to appeal to ideal convergence in order to explain sameness of meaning. At the ideal limit of reflection, competent speakers would independently converge on precisely the same criteria for using an expression. But skeptics can argue that there is no good empirical reason to believe in ideal convergence. And appealing to ideal convergence would make sameness of meaning epistemically opaque to ordinary subjects placed in non-ideal circumstances: it may be far from obvious, for instance, whether two tokens of 'Hesperus' express the same meaning.

One might wonder why an internalist should be worried by the failure to explain meaning identity over time and between subjects. Mere similarity of meaning might suffice to explain how information is normally preserved in communication and memory.

However, meaning identity is crucial to explaining logical relations. In order for two claims to stand in a relation of direct logical contradiction (e.g. 'Hesperus is bright' vs. 'Hesperus is not bright'), the contents of the non-logical expressions must be strictly identical. Moreover, mere sameness of semantic content does not suffice for logical relations: the sameness must be guaranteed by competence with the same meaning. Consider the contrast between 'Hesperus = Hesperus' and 'Hesperus = Phosphorus'. The first claim is logically guaranteed to be true in virtue of the meaning of '=' and the fact that both tokens of 'Hesperus' express the same meaning (and therefore must represent the very same thing if they represent anything at all). If you're competent with the meaning of the sentence, its truth will seem obvious and rationally incontrovertible. Not so for 'Hesperus = Phosphorus'; one may firmly believe this claim, but its truth seems to depend on contingent empirical facts, and hence it won't be rationally incontrovertible. Insofar as internalists wish to explain logical relations like direct contradiction, entailment, and trivial identity of content over time and between subjects, they must offer an account of meaning identity, not just similarity of meaning. One possible response on behalf of the internalist is to deny such logical relations hold over time and between speakers using normative terms. For an internalist-friendly explanation of the surface phenomena of disagreement between subjects that does not posit such logical relations, see Plunkett and Sundell (2013).

EXTERNALISM

Metasemantic externalism is simply the negation of internalism:

Externalism: It's not the case that both semantic competence and semantic contents are determined exclusively by physical factors inside the individual or psychological resources available to the individual.

We'll focus first on externalist accounts of content determination, which have played a prominent role in defending traditional realism in both the philosophy of science and metaethics. We'll then consider externalist approaches to competence conditions.

Causal Theories of Reference

A central theoretical advantage of externalism is its ability to explain the stability of reference despite variation in understanding over time and between subjects. In the case of names and natural kind terms, many externalists have suggested that content is partly determined by causal-historical or nomic relations linking subjects' representational states to particular objects, kinds, or properties in their environment. It's important to distinguish such causal externalist theories from neo-descriptivist theories that include a subject's conception of causal roles as part of her core criteria for applying certain terms—a position known as 'causal descriptivism' (Kroon, 1987). Whereas causal descriptivists take the ultimate arbiter of reference determination to be the subjects' *conception* of the relevant causal role, causal externalists take the ultimate arbiter of reference determination to be a *causal-explanatory theory* of the subject's linguistic or conceptual practices. For instance, Michael Devitt defends his causal-historical account of reference determination as meeting general desiderata on empirical theorizing in linguistics (Devitt, 1981, 1991), and Ruth Millikan defends her teleosemantic account as fitting within the explanatory paradigm for theorizing about biological systems honed by natural selection (Millikan, 1984). On such causal externalist accounts, an individual's current criteria for applying a term play no decisive role in settling its reference.

In metaethics, Richard Boyd's "causal regulation" theory is the most fully developed and influential version of the causal externalist approach (Boyd, 1988; see also Brink, 1989; Railton, 1986; Sturgeon, 1985). The reference of both scientific and moral predicates, Boyd argues, depends on a causal feedback relation of "accommodation" between a system of representations and a system of homeostatic property clusters in the world. This account allows for variability in speakers' criteria for applying a term without risk of changing the reference: an external causal relation can still causally "lock" subjects' use of a word onto the same property despite differences in their internal criteria.

In the philosophy of mind and language, causal externalism has been criticized as: (1) too vague to single out a determinate reference, and (2) singling out the intuitively wrong reference in many cases (for overviews, see Loewer, 1999; Neander, 2006). In metaethics, these general problems for causal externalism seem especially damaging in the case of normative terms, which are less tolerant of indeterminacy and less beholden to causal-explanatory considerations than scientific terms (Schroeter & Schroeter, 2013).

Terry Horgan and Mark Timmons press a different objection to causal externalism: they contend that Putnam's Twin Earth argument in favour of externalism for natural kind terms like 'water' does not generalize to normative terms like 'good' (Horgan & Timmons, 1992). Horgan and Timmons argue that, while we have reason to accept that causal factors affect the reference of natural kind terms like 'water', we have no such reason to accept that causal factors affect the reference of moral terms. However, the Moral Twin Earth argument is controversial. Janice Dowell argues that the MTE argument does not parallel Putnam's original Twin Earth argument, and that the sort of intuitions elicited by MTE are not relevant to the explanatory project of causal externalist metasemantics. She concludes that MTE has no probative force against causal externalism (Dowell, 2015).

Reference Magnets

A second type of externalist account of reference-fixing appeals to metaphysical facts about the referential candidates themselves, rather than causal relations linking representational states to referential candidates. Many metaphysicians hold that some objects, kinds, and properties are objectively more *natural* or *fundamental* than others. David Lewis suggested objective metaphysical naturalness makes a feature a better referential candidate: a property's naturalness makes it a "reference magnet" (Lewis, 1983).

Lewis originally proposed this metaphysical constraint on reference determination as a way of avoiding "Putnam's paradox." Hilary Putnam argued that Lewis's global neo-descriptivism together with his metaphysical realism about referential candidates leads to radical indeterminacy of reference. In response, Lewis added a further, mind-independent metaphysical constraint on reference determination (Lewis, 1984). On Lewis's account, the correct semantic interpretation of an individual's words and thoughts is determined by the total assignment of semantic contents that provides the best balance between two factors:

1. *Fit*: The assignment construes the subject's overall pattern of practical and cognitive dispositions as *approximately satisfying norms of ideal practical and theoretical rationality*.
2. *Naturalness*: The assignment construes the subject's words and thoughts as picking out a set of objects, kinds, and properties that, considered as a group, are *overall more natural* than competing sets of referential candidates.

The problem with Lewis's earlier account was that fit alone could not single out a determinate reference.

We'd like to emphasize four points about the role of reference magnetism in a determination theory. First, the metaphysical facts about naturalness must be *entirely independent* of the subject's understanding if they're to solve Putnam's paradox. The naturalness constraint comes into play only after we take into account the subject's ideally reflective and empirically informed dispositions to make judgements about the instantiation conditions of the properties picked out. So the relative naturalness of a property is not constrained by the subject's intuitions about plausible referential candidates for a given domain. Second, the naturalness constraint is part of a *holistic* approach to reference determination. Causal theories like Boyd's link individual representations (or clusters of representations) to referential candidates on a case-by-case basis. In contrast, Lewis's global descriptivism provides a holistic constraint on the semantic interpretation of the representational system considered as a whole, which allows for interpretive trade-offs that generate semantic indeterminacy. The naturalness constraint is designed to counteract the effects of this holism. Third, any plausible interpretation must include both natural and unnatural properties in the total semantic assignment. On Lewis's account, one's use of words like 'grue' or 'groovy' can pick out highly unnatural properties, provided that this interpretation is part of a total semantic assignment that maximizes naturalness overall. Fourth, it follows that there must be two sorts of ordinal rankings of naturalness on Lewis's account: (1) ranking naturalness of individual referential candidates (such as objects, properties, and kinds) and (2) ranking the relative naturalness of sets of such referential candidates (which include both highly natural and highly unnatural referential candidates). Lewis himself only provides a toy example of such rankings, so objective ranking remains an outstanding issue for the approach. For a discussion of the structure and commitments of Lewis's account, see Williams (2015).

Recently, some metaethicists have suggested that reference magnetism can be used to defend traditional context-invariant normative realism (van Roojen, 2006; Dunaway & McPherson, 2016). If moral properties are highly metaphysically natural (or fundamental), then they would be good referential candidates on a Lewisian approach. So a Lewisian metasemantics might be able to vindicate co-reference despite disagreement at the ideal limit of reflection, which would neutralize the disagreement objection.

However, the metasemantic story behind this approach has yet to be fully elaborated. There are general worries about whether a reference magnet approach can secure determinate and plausible referential assignments for ordinary descriptive vocabulary (e.g. Williams, 2007; Sundell, 2012). In the case of metaethics, moreover, the problem is exacerbated by the fact that normative terms do not seem to be easily ranked on a single uniform scale of naturalness with causal-explanatory properties. For instance, it's not obvious that there's a principled way of ordinally ranking properties and sets of properties for "naturalness" that would privilege a justificatory property over a sociological property as the reference of "morally right" (Schroeter & Schroeter, 2013).

Externalist Competence Conditions

Let's turn to externalist approaches to competence conditions. According to internalism, two speakers cannot share the same meaning unless they share precisely matching internal criteria of use. Externalists deny this claim. Indeed, most externalists hold that a precise match in criteria is *neither necessary nor sufficient* for sameness of meaning or concept. Tyler Burge's anti-individualism is a version of this position:

Anti-individualism: Semantic competence doesn't depend exclusively on physical factors in the individual or psychological resources cognitively available to the individual at a time (see Burge, 2007: 153).

A theory of competence, of course, must go beyond this purely negative thesis: it must explain how external factors combine with internal factors to ground competence with particular meanings.

A promising approach to competence externalism is to treat *inter-cognitive relations* as necessary for competence with the same meaning:

Relational competence: Two token cognitive states express the same meaning only if those tokens are linked by a specific causal-historical relation R.

Relational theories of competence disagree about the nature of R. On a Kripkean "causal chain" account of names, for instance, relation R consists in being actually linked by co-referential intentions: two speakers are competent with the same linguistic meaning only if they are connected via a continuous chain of linked co-referential intentions (Kripke, 1980; Devitt, 1981). In contrast, Ruth Millikan's teleosemantic theory takes two uses of a term to express the same meaning only if they are connected by a certain naturally selected for "copying" relation (Millikan, 1984). Tyler Burge holds that sameness of conceptual content requires anaphora-like semantic memory relations linking token elements of thought within an individual and similar "content-preserving" causal links between individuals (Burge, 2007). Philosophical proponents of "mental files" like John Perry and Sam Cumming have posited causal coordinating relations linking individuals' mental files to those of others in their linguistic community (Perry, 2001; Cumming, 2013). In the philosophy of language, some theorists have argued for relationally individuated syntactic units of interpretation (Kaplan, 1990; Fiengo & May, 2006), and others have posited relational semantic rules linking token expressions (Fine, 2007; Pinillos, 2011).

One important advantage of a relational constraint on competence is that it allows for more variation in competent subjects' substantive understanding than is possible on internalist accounts. Causal-historical relations between token representational states are supposed to carry some of the burden of securing semantic competence and sameness of semantic content. As a consequence, a relational account may be better placed to vindicate commonsense epistemic commitments about open-ended inquiry and debate: no particular criterion is required for logical relations among token uses of a term.

However, such variability in understanding raises a challenge: if internal criteria associated with R-linked token states are highly variable, what ensures that all R-linked tokens have precisely the same semantic content? One natural response on behalf of a relational theorist is to take the *default unit for semantic interpretation* to be the R-linked states considered as a group rather than a token state considered in isolation (Schroeter, 2012). The default assumption would be that all R-linked uses of 'Aristotle' should be assigned the same semantic content—whether it's the shipping magnate, or the philosopher, or a descriptive content, or nothing at all. *Mutatis mutandis* for 'x is right': the default presumption is that all R-linked tokens should be assigned the same semantic content. For an application of this relational approach to competence with normative concepts, see Schroeter & Schroeter (2014). Blackburn (1991: 4–11, 1998: 59–68) also assumes social units for semantic interpretation.

One counterintuitive consequence of relational models of competence is that subjects who are not connected by R will not share the same meaning. So a perfect qualitative duplicate of you living on a perfect duplicate planet on the other side of the galaxy (Duplicate Earth) would not be competent with the same meanings that you associate with 'water' or 'right'. In response, relational theorists have explained the theoretical advantages of relationally individuated competence conditions that in their view outweigh this counterintuitive consequence (cf. Millikan, 1984; Burge, 2007). And the relational theorist can point out that non-relational internalist accounts also have highly counterintuitive consequences if they make meaning unstable within rational inquiry and debate (Schroeter & Schroeter, 2016).

A second challenge to relational theories is to explain how a shift in meaning is possible. If being R-related is sufficient for competence with a given meaning, then it must also be sufficient for sameness of content. But that seems implausible. For instance, our current use of 'Madagascar' may be R-related to early Malay and Arabic uses of the name that refer to a part of the African mainland, but clearly there has been a shift in reference between then and now (Evans, 1973). To allow for shifts in content, a relational theorist has a number of options. One is to offer an account of R that explains how new meanings get initiated—for example, by new implicit "baptisms" (Donnellan, 1974). A second option is to accept that contents are always preserved by R-relations but hold that new contents get layered on top of old ones—so token states within an R-linked tradition become multiply ambiguous (Devitt, 1981; Millikan, 2000). A third option is to appeal to further constraints on sameness of meaning that can defeat the default presumption that R individuates the unit for semantic interpretation (Schroeter & Schroeter, 2014). A fourth option is to deny that R can define a genuine meaning identity relation (i.e. reflexive, symmetric, and transitive): it can only define ad hoc local relations of guaranteed sameness of content (Fine, 2007; Pinillos, 2011).

THE METASEMANTIC CONSTRUAL OF EXPRESSIVISM

One important new development in metaethics is the metasemantic construal of expressivism. Expressivism has traditionally been characterized as a theory at the level of semantics: the semantic function of normative predicates in sentences like 'x is wrong' is not to attribute a property to x but to conventionally express the speaker's conative attitude towards x. This position generates the Frege-Geach problem: how can these expressive contents contribute to the content of complex sentences like 'Jane believes that surfing isn't wrong'? In effect, the Frege-Geach problem is to explain the role played by the expressive contents of subsentential expressions in a compositional semantic theory for a language. Given that standard compositional semantics is truth-conditional, it seems that expressivists must rebuild compositional semantics from the ground up to explain how expressive contents contribute to the contents of complex sentences. (For influential recent versions of the Frege-Geach challenge, see Zangwill, 1992; van Roojen, 1996; Unwin, 1999; Schroeder, 2008. For expressivist responses that reinterpret the function of logical operators, see Blackburn, 1988; Gibbard, 2003.)

In recent years, some theorists have argued that expressivists can accept a standard compositional semantics that uses a "possible worlds" framework to specify the truth-conditions of normative sentences. To understand this proposal, it's important to bear in mind that for the purposes of compositional semantics, possible worlds are just set-theoretic constructs whose structure is suited to modelling the contribution of subsentential expressions to the content of whole sentences. What the elements of these structures represent, if anything, is irrelevant to their role in compositional semantics. On this approach, compositional semantics functions as an autonomous domain of linguistic theorizing, with its own proprietary theoretical and empirical constraints (cf. Yalcin, 2014; Glanzberg, 2014). Roughly, compositional semantics tells us how the language faculty delivers formal constraints on which thought contents can be literally expressed by uses of natural language expressions. Expressivists then have an easy answer to the Frege-Geach embedding problem: they can accept whichever compositional semantics is supported by empirical linguistics.

If we reserve the term 'semantics' for formal compositional semantics and use the term 'semantic value' for the abstract objects posited by such a theory, then different metaethical positions might be thought of as disagreeing at the level of metasemantics. Expressivists and representationalists can accept that the basic compositional structure of language is perspicuously modelled by a particular compositional theory. Their disagreement is over *what makes it the case* that normative expressions have certain semantic values within that compositional semantic theory (Chrisman, 2015; Ridge, 2014; Silk, 2015; Pérez Carballo, 2015). For closely related suggestions, see Stojanovic (2012) and Yalcin (2014).

However, the philosophical difficulties for expressivism haven't disappeared; they've just been relocated. The central questions in metaethics are not about formal semantics but about the nature of normative thought and the use of normative language to communicate those thoughts. The fact that normative language conforms to standard compositional semantics means that the thoughts expressed by normative language must conform to the entailment, consistency, and inconsistency relations posited by the correct compositional theory. This metasemantic requirement is a non-trivial *hermeneutical* constraint on acceptable theories of which attitudes are literally expressed by normative language (Pérez Carballo, 2014). The challenge for expressivists is to identify non-cognitive attitudes expressed by normative terms (in simple predications, in complex embedded contexts, in non-indicative sentences, in non-assertoric speech acts, etc.), which reflect the entailment and consistency relations posited by the compositional semantics for those sentences. In other words, expressivists must show how the semantic relations posited by the compositional theory are reflected in relations among the psychological states that they take to be expressed. This metasemantic challenge seems less daunting if one can invoke entailment and consistency relations among the *representational contents* of thought rather than abstracting them from relations among the *attitudinal aspect* of thought. See Ridge (2014) and Silk (2015) for two recent proposals for how to meet this metasemantic challenge to attitude expressivism, and see Chrisman (2015) for an inferential role expressivism in the spirit of Robert Brandom's (1994) inferential role semantics.

Expressivists also face a challenge in explaining logical relations among normative sentences. What makes your claim 'lying is wrong' logically inconsistent with my claim 'lying is not wrong' if the contents expressed are simply divergent conative states towards lying? This problem is often assimilated to the Frege-Geach problem. But the semantic entailment captured by compositional semantics isn't the same as strict logical entailment: 'x is a bachelor' semantically entails 'x is unmarried', but there is no logical relation among the claims expressed. Strict logical relations are needed to explain the nature of deductive arguments across all domains. In response, Baker and Woods (2015) argue that expressivists and representationalists alike should appeal to the syntactic structure of sentences to explain logical relations. On standard accounts of philosophical logic, after all, logical relations are purely formal: 'x is an unmarried man' logically entails 'x is a man' because it holds true regardless of how one interprets the non-logical expressions. If logical relations are determined by formal syntactic relations, then any acceptable metasemantic theory must assign the same content to the same syntactic unit. Thus, the expressivist need not locate logical relations in the clashes among attitudes expressed. The availability of this formal account of logic, of course, does not guarantee that there is a plausible expressivist interpretation of the thought contents literally communicated by normative sentences. Moreover, as we noted previously, such an account will need to say something about apparent shifts in the content of syntactically individuated words.

The general lesson of this recent work is that metaethicists of all stripes can help themselves to independently justified theories of the syntactic structure and combinatorial semantics of normative language. This move dissolves some traditional worries for metaethical expressivism, but structurally similar concerns may arise once again at the level of the thought contents expressed.

ACKNOWLEDGEMENTS

Thanks to the editors and James Fritz for very helpful advice and feedback.

REFERENCES

Baker, D. & Woods, J. (2015) "How Expressivists Can and Should Explain Inconsistency," *Ethics* 125: 391–424.

Björnsson, G. (2012) "Do 'Objectivist' Features of Moral Discourse and Thinking Support Moral Objectivism?" *Journal of Ethics* 16: 367–93.

Blackburn, S. (1991) "Just Causes," *Philosophical Studies* 61: 3–17.

Blackburn, S. (1998) *Ruling Passions*, Oxford: Oxford University Press.

Boyd, R. N. (1988) "How to be a Moral Realist," in G. Sayre-McCord (ed.) *Essays on Moral Realism*, Ithaca, NY: Cornell University Press, 181–228.

Brandom, R. (1994) *Making It Explicit: Reasoning, Representing and Discursive Commitment*, Cambridge, MA: Harvard University Press.

Brink, D. O. (1989) *Moral Realism and the Foundations of Ethics*, New York: Cambridge University Press.

Burge, T. (1979) "Individualism and the Mental," *Midwest Studies in Philosophy* 4: 73–121.

Burge, T. (2007) *Foundations of Mind*, Oxford: Oxford University Press.

Chrisman, M. (2015) *The Meaning of "Ought": Beyond Descriptivism and Expressivism in Metaethics*, Oxford: Oxford University Press.

Cumming, S. (2013) "From Coordination to Content," *Philosophers' Imprint* 13(4): 1–17.

Devitt, M. (1981) *Designation*, New York: Columbia University Press.

Devitt, M. (1991) *Realism and Truth*, 2nd edn, Princeton, NJ: Princeton University Press.

Donnellan, K. S. (1974) "Speaking of Nothing," *Philosophical Review* 83: 1–31.

Dowell, J. L. (2015) "The Metaethical Insignificance of Moral Twin Earth," in R. Shafer-Landau (ed.) *Oxford Studies in Metaethics*, vol. 11, Oxford: Oxford University Press, 1–27.

Dunaway, B. & McPherson, T. (2016) "Reference Magnetism as a Solution to the Moral Twin Earth Problem," *Ergo* 3 (25): 1–42.

Evans, G. (1973) "The Causal Theory of Names," *Proceedings of the Aristotelian Society* supp. 47: 187–208.

Fiengo, R. & May, R. (2006) *De Lingua Belief*, Cambridge, MA: MIT Press.

Fine, K. (2007) *Semantic Relationalism*, Oxford: Blackwell.

Gibbard, A. (2003) *Thinking How to Live*, Cambridge, MA: Harvard University Press.

Glanzberg, M. (2014) "Explanation and Partiality in Semantic Theory," in A. Burgess & B. Sherman (eds.) *Metasemantics: New Essays on the Foundations of Meaning*, Oxford: Oxford University Press, 259–92.

Horgan, T. & Timmons. M. (1992) "Troubles for New Wave Moral Semantics: The 'Open Question Argument' Revived," *Philosophical Papers* 21: 153–75.

Jackson, F. (1998a) *From Metaphysics to Ethics: A Defence of Conceptual Analysis*, Oxford: Oxford University Press.

Jackson, F. (1998b) "Reference and Description Revisited," *Philosophical Perspective* 12: 201–18.

Jackson, F. & Pettit, P. (1995) "Moral Functionalism and Moral Motivation," *Philosophical Quarterly* 45: 20–40.

Kaplan, D. (1990) "Words," *Proceedings of the Aristotelian Society* supp. 64: 93–119.

Kripke, S. (1980) *Naming and Necessity*, Cambridge, MA: Harvard University Press.

Kripke, S. (1982) *Wittgenstein on Rules and Private Language*, Cambridge, MA: Harvard University Press.

Kroon, F. (1987) "Causal Descriptivism," *Australasian Journal of Philosophy* 65: 1–17.

Lewis, D. (1983) "New Work for a Theory of Universals," *Australasian Journal of Philosophy* 61: 343–77.

Lewis, D. (1984) "Putnam's Paradox," *Australasian Journal of Philosophy* 62: 221–36.

Loewer, B. (1999) "A Guide to Naturalizing Semantics," in B. Hale & C. Wright (eds.) *A Companion to the Philosophy of Language*, Oxford: Blackwell, 108–26.

Merli, D. (2008) "Expressivism and the Limits of Moral Disagreement," *Journal of Ethics* 12: 25–55.

Millikan, R. G. (1984) *Language, Thought, and Other Biological Categories*, Cambridge, MA: MIT Press.

Millikan, R. G. (2000) *On Clear and Confused Ideas*, Cambridge: Cambridge University Press.

Neander, K. (2006) "Naturalistic Theories of Reference," in M. Devitt & R. Hanley (eds.) *The Blackwell Guide to the Philosophy of Language*, Oxford: Blackwell, 374–91.

Peacocke, C. (1992) *A Study of Concepts*, Cambridge, MA: MIT Press.

Peacocke, C. (2004) "Moral Rationalism," *Journal of Philosophy* 101: 499–526.

Pérez Carballo, A. (2014) "Semantic Hermeneutics," in A. Burgess & B. Sherman (eds.) *Metasemantics: New Essays on the Foundations of Meaning*, Oxford: Oxford University Press.

Perry, J. (2001) *Reference and Reflexivity*, Palo Alto, CA: CSLI Publications.

Pietroski, P. (2010) "Concepts, Meanings, and Truth: First Nature, Second Nature, and Hard Work," *Mind and Language* 25: 247–78.

Pinillos, N. Á. (2011) "Coreference and Meaning," *Philosophical Studies* 154: 301–24.

Plunkett, D. & Sundell, T. (2013) "Disagreement and the Semantics of Normative and Evaluative Terms," *Philosophers' Imprint* 13(23): 1–37.

Putnam, H. (1970) "Is Semantics Possible?" in H. E. Kiefer & M. K. Munitz (eds.) *Language, Belief and Metaphysics*, New York: SUNY Press, 50–63.

Putnam, H. (1973) "Explanation and Reference," in G. Pearce & P. Maynard (eds.) *Conceptual Change*, Dordrecht: Reidel Publishing: Kluwer, 199–221.

Putnam, H. (1975) "The Meaning of 'Meaning'," *Minnesota Studies in the Philosophy of Science* 7: 131–93.

Quine, W. V. O. (1951) "Two Dogmas of Empiricism," in *From a Logical Point of View*, Cambridge, MA: Harvard University Press, 20–46.

Railton, P. (1986) "Moral Realism," *Philosophical Review* 95: 163–207.

Ridge, M. (2014) *Impassioned Belief*, Oxford: Oxford University Press.

Schroeder, M. (2008) *Being For: Evaluating the Semantic Program of Expressivism*, Oxford: Oxford University Press.

Schroeter, L. (2012) "Bootstrapping Our Way to Samesaying," *Synthese* 189: 177–97.

Schroeter, L. & Schroeter, F. (2013) "Normative Realism: Co-reference without Convergence?" *Philosophers' Imprint* 13(13): 1–24.

Schroeter, L. & Schroeter, F. (2014) "Normative Concepts: A Connectedness Model," *Philosophers' Imprint* 14(25): 1–26.

Schroeter, L. & Schroeter, F. (2016) "Semantic Deference vs Semantic Coordination," *American Philosophical Quarterly* 53: 193–210.

Silk, A. (2013) "Truth Conditions and the Meanings of Ethical Terms," in R. Shafer-Landau (ed.) *Oxford Studies in Metaethics*, vol. 8, Oxford: Oxford University Press: 195–222.

Silk, A. (2015) "How to Be an Ethical Expressivist," *Philosophy and Phenomenological Research* 91: 47–81.

Stalnaker, R. (2008) *Our Knowledge of the Internal World*, Oxford: Clarendon Press.

Stojanovic, I. (2012) "On Value-Attributions: Semantics and Beyond," *Southern Journal of Philosophy* 50: 621–38.

Sturgeon, N. (1985) "Moral Explanation," in D. Copp & D. Zimmerman (eds.) *Morality, Reason, and Truth: New Essays on the Foundations of Ethics*, Totowa, NJ: Rowman & Allanheld, 46–78.

Sundell, T. (2012) "Disagreement, Error, and an Alternative to Reference Magnetism," *Australasian Journal of Philosophy* 90: 743–59.

Unwin, N. (1999) "Quasi-Realism, Negation, and the Frege-Geach Problem," *Philosophical Quarterly* 49: 337–52.

Van Roojen, M. (1996) "Expressivism and Irrationality," *Philosophical Review* 105: 311–35.

Van Roojen, M. (2006) "Knowing Enough to Disagree: A New Response to the Moral Twin Earth Argument," in R. Shafer-Landau (ed.) *Oxford Studies in Metaethics*, vol. 1, Oxford: Oxford University Press: 164–94.

Väyrynen, P. (2013) *The Lewd, the Rude, and the Nasty*, Oxford: Oxford University Press.

Williams, J. R. G. (2007) "Eligibility and Inscrutability," *Philosophical Review* 116: 361–99.

Williams, J. R. G. (2015) "Lewis on Reference and Eligibility," in B. Loewer & J. Shaffer (eds.) *A Companion to David Lewis*, Oxford: Wiley Blackwell, 367–81.

Yalcin, S. (2014) "Semantics and Metasemantics in the Context of Generative Grammar," in A. Burgess & B. Sherman (eds.) *Metasemantics: New Essays on the Foundations of Meaning*, Oxford: Oxford University Press, 17–54.

Zangwill, N. (1992) "Moral Modus Ponens," *Ratio* 2: 177–93.

34

Conceptual Analysis in Metaethics

Nicholas Laskowski and Stephen Finlay

INTRODUCTION

Despite being considered the traditional and prototypical philosophical method, conceptual analysis is an approach to philosophical inquiry with a checkered past and a tarnished reputation. This is particularly true in metaethics, which we understand here as concerned not only with ethics or morality proper but also with the normative more generally. In recent decades, metaethicists have often consigned conceptual analysis to the trash pile of philosophical mistakes, yet it has always had adherents and today enjoys a renaissance. In this selective and opinionated chapter, we explore various dimensions of the debate, framed around two foundational questions: (1) what is it to *use* and *possess* a normative concept? and (2) what is it to *analyze* a normative concept? We attempt to avoid broader questions about the nature and analysis of concepts in general (for orientation, see Margolis & Laurence, 1999, 2015).

Analysis we understand, most broadly, as investigation into or explication of something's nature. All we assume at the outset about the nature of *concepts* is (1) that they are psychological resources employed in and enabling us to have *thoughts*, and (2) that they are psychological *types* of some kind rather than tokens—whether of mental representations, contents, abilities, processes, or similar—and therefore that different people can share the same concept. We make no assumptions about what makes a concept *normative*, except that normative concepts are those whose involvement in a thought make that thought normative—as it is the involvement of the concept WRONG that makes the thought that killing is wrong normative, rather than the concept KILLING. The extension of the class of normative concepts is controversial—contested cases include CRUEL, TRUE, and MEANING—but our treatment focuses on less controversially normative concepts such as WRONG, GOOD, OUGHT, and REASON.

The conceptual domain is helpfully juxtaposed against the linguistic and metaphysical domains, which it is commonly viewed as mediating. First, consider the relationship between the conceptual and the linguistic. A common assumption is that many (so-called *lexical*) concepts can be identified as the conventional meanings of words, a connection we'll call the *word-concept nexus*. Conceptual analysis is therefore often equated with, and pursued by means of, semantic analysis or study of linguistic meaning. This article focuses on such lexical concepts, following the convention of denoting them with corresponding words in small caps; for example, 'WRONG' refers to the conceptual meaning of the English word 'wrong'. For convenience, we will typically speak as if words and concepts stand in a one-to-one relationship, although readers should be wary of this assumption. On one hand, WRONG is potentially also the meaning of the German word 'unrecht' and the Swahili word 'vibaya', for example; on the other hand, some normative words may be ambiguous or context-sensitive in meaning, so it may be necessary to distinguish between WRONG$_1$, WRONG$_2$, and so on.

Second, consider the relationship between the conceptual and metaphysical domains. The latter potentially includes normative *entities* such as reasons and obligations, normative *properties* such as wrongness and goodness, normative *relations* such as counting-in-favor-of, and normative *states of affairs* such as that lying is sometimes wrong. Philosophical discussion often takes for granted that the basic function of concepts is to "pick out" entities or properties in the world, enabling us to talk and think *about* them; we'll call this connection the *concept-world nexus*. On this basis, conceptual analysis is traditionally thought to provide a path to understanding not only normative concepts and thoughts but also the nature of normative properties and facts. This hoped-for metaphysical payoff is a central motivation of conceptual analysis in metaethics, but, as we will show, normative concepts can also be of interest for their own sake.

THE CLASSICAL THEORY, PRIMITIVISM, AND THE OPEN QUESTION ARGUMENT

Philosophical tradition presents the Classical Theory of the nature of concepts and conceptual analysis, which traces its (Western) roots back at least to a foundational metaethical text, Plato's *Euthyphro*. Our discussion is organized around this view (following the model of Margolis & Laurence, 1999): after sketching its central tenets, in subsequent sections we introduce more recent, alternative views on normative concepts in terms of their departures from the Classical Theory.

The Classical Theory involves at least the following core tenets:

1. *Cognitivism*: Concepts have an essentially referential or representational function (or "role") of picking out items at the metaphysical level. For example, the concept WRONG enables us to ascribe and think about the property of wrongness, and the concept OBLIGATION enables us to ascribe and think about obligations, as normative entities.
2. *Definitionism*: Concepts fulfill this referential function by providing necessary and sufficient conditions for something's falling within the concept's extension—a set of conditions that may be articulated in the form of a descriptive definition. For example, Socrates' stalking horse in the *Euthyphro* is the proposed definition of PIOUS as *what is approved by the Gods*.
3. *Compositionality*: Concepts can be either complex (structured) or simple (primitive, atomic). Complex concepts are composed out of simpler conceptual parts. For

example, on Euthyphro's view, the concept PIOUS is composed at least of the simpler concepts APPROVED and GODS.

4. *Reductivism*: To analyze a concept is to decompose it, revealing its constituent parts and how they are interrelated—particularly, by providing its descriptive definition.
5. *Analyticity*: Some thoughts and sentences (termed "analytic") are guaranteed true simply because of the concepts or meanings of the terms involved. On Euthyphro's view, for example, it is analytic that if the gods approve of prosecuting one's father for murder then it is pious to prosecute one's father for murder.
6. *Essentialism*: The internal structure of a concept mirrors the internal metaphysical structure of the normative property (entity, etc.) that it picks out. A corollary: by reductive analysis of a concept, we can also derive a reductive metaphysical analysis of the corresponding property.

Additionally, the Classical Theory accepts the following tenets about the epistemology of concepts:

7. *Competency as Grasping a Definition*: Possession of a concept consists in (some kind of) psychological grasp of its descriptive definition; competence with a word consists in associating it with its definition.
8. *Transparency*: Being mental entities, concepts are transparent to reflection. They therefore can be analyzed, and any analytic truths identified, from the armchair in exercises of purely a priori or nonempirical inquiry (i.e. by "intuition").

The application of this classical package to normative concepts is exemplified in the early twentieth century in the work of G.E. Moore (1903). However, Moore also sent an early shot across the bow of the ambitions of conceptual analysis in metaethics, independent of any of the objections later raised against the Classical Theory, with a challenge that largely set the stage for subsequent debate.

By the classical tenet of compositionality, all concepts are ultimately made up out of simple or primitive conceptual elements. This raises the possibility that some *normative* concepts are among these simple elements. By the tenet of reductivism, such simple normative concepts would be unanalyzable, since they do not admit of further decomposition or definition. By the tenet of essentialism, this possibility further implies that some normative properties or entities are similarly simple and unanalyzable. This combination of views, which we'll call *primitivism*, is embraced by Moore and many contemporary metaethicists. (It is often labeled "nonnaturalism," but we'll stay neutral about the correct use of this terminology.) Primitivists disagree over which normative concept or concepts to identify as basic. We'll follow Moore in privileging GOOD, although today REASON or COUNTS-IN-FAVOR-OF are more commonly preferred (e.g. Scanlon, 1998).

Primitivism might seem a relatively minor challenge to the ambitions of conceptual analysis. On Moore's view, for example, every other normative concept is complex and thus analyzable, including RIGHT as PRODUCES MOST GOOD. Even as the Classical Theory has fallen into general disrepute, few metaethicists have denied that there are at least some illuminating analyses of normative concepts along classical lines, such as the popular reductive analysis of MURDER as (at least partly) WRONGFUL KILLING. But a guiding aim of metaethical inquiry has been to explicate the puzzling nature of normativity *per se*, and hence of normative concepts as a *class*. Therefore, metaethicists have typically been interested primarily in the possibility of (conceptual and metaphysical) analysis of the normative at the *global* level rather than of any individual normative concept or property. Most metaethical discussion of conceptual analysis is therefore directed at the prospects for analyzing all or any normative concepts into complexes of entirely nonnormative elements, a Holy Grail widely equated with "analytic reduction" of the normative as such.

Why believe any normative concepts are simple and unanalyzable? The primary motivation is Moore's famous and still influential *Open Question Argument* (OQA), which relies heavily on the tenets of the Classical Theory. For our purposes, this argument can be presented as follows:

OQ1. For any description D and concept M, if D is a correct definition or analysis of M, then it must be a *closed question* (roughly, one with a self-evidently positive answer) for competent users of M that whatever is D is also M, and vice versa.

OQ2. There exists no description D such that it is a closed question for competent users of the concept GOOD that whatever is D is also good, or vice versa.

OQ3. Therefore, there exists no description D that is a correct definition or analysis of the concept GOOD.

OQ4. (*Conceptual Conclusion*) Therefore, GOOD is a simple and unanalyzable concept.

OQ5. (*Metaphysical Conclusion*) Therefore, goodness is a simple and unanalyzable property.

Many metaethicists view Moore's ultimate, metaphysical conclusion as unacceptable and therefore reject one or another of the argument's steps or assumptions—which usually involves the rejection of one or more classical tenets. Subsequent sections investigate the major responses in roughly reverse order of how radically they depart from the Classical Theory. We will suggest that more extreme rejections of the Classical Theory may be overreactions and that a subtler departure may be a better course. However, we first conclude this section by observing some problems for the primitivist's (typically classical) treatment of normative concepts. (We largely ignore primitivist treatments of normative properties, as they fall outside our scope.)

One thorny issue for primitivism derives from a puzzle for the Classical Theory about simple concepts, its basic building blocks. Notice that the tenet of definitionism (Classical Theory's official story of how concepts refer to properties in the world) as well as the tenet of competency as grasping a definition (the official story of what it is to possess a concept) cannot extend to simple concepts, which as such lack descriptive definitions. Primitivism therefore owes some other account of how simple normative concepts pick out normative properties and of what possession of them consists in. This challenge might not seem especially difficult, since it is a well-established view in general philosophy of mind that some—perhaps even all—concepts are primitive (e.g. Jerry Fodor's conceptual atomism; for discussion, see Margolis & Laurence, 1999: 59–71). However, metaethical primitivists face a special problem because conceptual atomists generally explain the concept-world nexus by appeal to causal connections between the properties in the world and the concepts in our minds. This answer is not available to most metaethical primitivists, who hold that basic normative properties are not causally efficacious.

A related difficulty concerns how simple normative concepts are acquired if normative properties never causally interact with us or our senses in any way. Here, primitivists might seem obliged to embrace nativism, the Platonic idea that normative concepts are innate. This in turn raises difficult questions about how we could ever be justified in believing that our normative concepts successfully pick out anything that actually exists or that our normative thoughts ever correspond to reality. Metaethicists who have flirted with nativism have indeed tended to be error theorists, denying that normative concepts and thoughts ever correspond to anything actually existing in the world (e.g. Joyce, 2006). In our opinion, primitivists owe these problems of concept reference, possession, and acquisition greater attention than they have received.

Primitivists generally maintain that basic normative truths are a priori and knowable from the armchair by intuition alone—as is widely accepted. This forces an awkward choice. The a priori status and intuitionistic methodology of ethics seem easily explained (by the classical tenet of transparency) if these propositions are *analytic* and therefore knowable through conceptual analysis—but this explanation seems (prima facie) unavailable to primitivism and would apparently falsify OQ2, which denies the existence of any closed questions linking GOOD with a description D in nonnormative terms. The second option is to maintain that the propositions are nonanalytic—or *synthetic*—in which case their a priori status is widely perceived to be mysterious.

Traditionally, primitivists take this second path, embracing (e.g. Enoch, 2011) or denying (e.g. Scanlon, 2014) the mystery. As is seldom noticed, this choice also stands in a potentially embarrassing tension with the OQA. This is because the notion of a "closed question" is perilously close to that of an a priori truth (see further discussion below). Premise OQ2 may therefore prove incompatible with the intuitionist claim that first-order normative propositions are knowable a priori (Soames, 2011). Recently, some primitivists have reached for the first option above, conceding that a priori normative propositions are indeed conceptual truths. They maintain their rejection of analytic reductions of normative concepts by allowing only conditionals and never biconditionals: for example, an action is wrong *if* it is an intentional infliction of suffering on the innocent for fun, but not *only if* (Audi, 2004; Huemer, 2005; Cuneo & Shafer-Landau, 2014). We worry that this strategy may succeed only in moving the bump in the rug. To avoid the result that normative concepts can be reductively analyzed after all, as massive disjunctions of such conditionals, it seems committed to some further (basic) normative element in a concept like WRONG or GOOD, and the possibility of knowing (nonanalytic) truths involving this further element remains unaccounted for.

NATURALISM, SYNTHETIC DEFINITIONS, AND SEMANTIC EXTERNALISM

These problems seem easily avoided if we reject primitivism in favor of a metaethical naturalism that identifies or reduces normative properties to causally efficacious, "natural" properties. This option is supposed to be ruled out by the OQA's final inference, from its conceptual to its metaphysical conclusion. However, the inference is fallacious: basic normative *properties* could be complex and analyzable, contra primitivism, even if normative *concepts* aren't. This amounts to rejecting at least the classical tenet of essentialism, which looks vulnerable: plausibly, not every concept picks out its object by that object's essence or basic composition. On most theories, the same objects or properties can be picked out by different concepts; famously, the planet Venus can be picked out by either the concept MORNING STAR or the concept EVENING STAR. So the correct reductive or essential definitions of normative properties like goodness could be *synthetic* rather than analytic, like the definition of water as H_2O (e.g. Railton, 1986; Copp, 2007). In that case, their discovery wouldn't be possible through a priori conceptual analysis alone and might require empirical investigation. Rejection of essentialism and appeal to synthetic definitions doesn't dispose of all the puzzles about normative concepts, however. For example, it doesn't by itself explain why it would be so difficult to find *any* analytic truths connecting normative and nonnormative terms. Helen and Richard Yetter-Chappell (2013) argue that synthetic naturalists might take inspiration from strategies deployed in the philosophy of mind to explain away "explanatory gaps" left by physicalist definitions of consciousness.

A particularly radical departure from the Classical Theory is found in "Cornell Realism" (e.g. Brink, 1984; Boyd, 1988), which seeks at once to evade the OQA's challenge and put metaphysical analysis of normative properties on a respectably naturalistic footing by freeing it from conceptual analysis altogether. This combines synthetic naturalism with the doctrine of *semantic externalism*, which rejects the classical tenet of competency as grasping a definition (or "description theory"). The 1970s saw the introduction and embrace of the view that making reference to something in speech or thought requires only acquisition of a term linked to the referent by an appropriate causal chain—even if one lacks any individuating description. This can be seen as denying a necessary role for concepts in language and thought altogether (in Hilary Putnam's slogan, "Meaning ain't in the head") and replacing the word-concept nexus and concept-world nexus with a direct *word-world* nexus. The strongest version of such naturalism repudiates not only the highest ambitions but also the very possibility of armchair conceptual analysis, and its dominance over philosophical thought in the 1980s contributed greatly to the disrepute of this methodology.

Over recent years, however, the popularity of this kind of naturalism in metaethics seems to have faded. Observing that normative thought and language could conceivably function this way is one thing; demonstrating they actually function this way is quite another, and the case for synthetic definitions of and causal reference to normative properties seems weak. Not every class of words is as amenable to this treatment as the paradigmatic examples of names ('Aristotle') and natural kind terms ('water', 'tiger')—consider mathematical vocabulary, for example—and it seems a particularly poor fit for normative vocabulary (see Pigden, 2012). A primary problem is the already mentioned intuitionist or a priori epistemology of a robust range of normative truths, which is a primary motivation for primitivists' denials that normative properties could be "naturalistic." Commonly cited examples include both basic first-order normative propositions such as that intentionally inflicting suffering on the innocent for fun is wrong, and propositions about the nature of normative properties such as that they supervene on the nonnormative state of the world. This suggests that basic competence with normative thought involves substantial acquaintance with the essences of normative properties. While many philosophers have followed Immanuel Kant in embracing the possibility of synthetic a priori knowledge, particularly in ethics, this doesn't seem a genuine option for Cornell Realists, since it is implausible that causally efficacious or natural facts and properties are the kinds of things into which we could have a priori insight.

NONCOGNITIVISM, ATTITUDES, AND INFERENCES

An entirely different and perennially popular way of reacting to the OQA involves rejecting the inference from OQ3 (there is no description that is a correct definition of a basic normative concept) to the conceptual conclusion OQ4 (basic normative concepts are simple and unanalyzable) by way of rejecting the core classical tenet of *cognitivism*, that normative concepts have the essentially referential or representational role in thought of picking out normative properties. This *noncognitivist* approach has the virtue of easily avoiding all the problems observed above for primitivism and synthetic naturalism, as explained below. *Hybrid* approaches postulating a combination of cognitive and noncognitive functions are also popular today, although more often formulated at the linguistic than the conceptual level; these have their own strengths and weaknesses (see Teemu Toppinen's chapter "Hybrid Accounts of Ethical Thought and Talk").

General philosophical discussions of concepts often assume that the essential role of concepts is to pick out or refer to things in the metaphysical domain, such as individual entities (Aristotle), kinds (bachelor, horse), and properties (yellow). However, if taking our cues to the range in the conceptual domain from the variety in the linguistic domain, we should notice that cognitivism seems an unpromising approach to the meaning of many classes of words other than ordinary nouns, adjectives, verbs, and adverbs. Consider logical connectives ('and', 'or', 'if', 'not'), modal and sentential operators ('must', 'might', 'perhaps'), interjections ('hurray!', 'ouch!') and performatives ('hello', 'please'); what *in the world* could they be picking out? Rather than denying that these words express any concepts at all, we might expand our understanding of concepts to include other kinds of contribution to thought. So perhaps the essential role of normative concepts also is something other than—or on a hybrid approach, isn't exhausted by—such (so-called) cognitive functions, as many philosophers have proposed since the 1930s. (However, some early noncognitivist accounts, like A. J. Ayer's emotivist theory that 'wrong' is a device for conveying disapproval and/or influencing others, seem best characterized as claiming there are no normative thoughts or concepts, only normative language.)

Noncognitivism is a radical repudiation of the Classical Theory, because it entails rejection also of most of the other tenets we observed, which presuppose cognitivism. Against the tenet of definitionism, it denies the possibility of capturing the meaning of normative terms by a synonymous or intersubstitutable description providing a set of necessary and sufficient conditions. Simply put, the (cognitive) conceptual role of a description is fundamentally different than the (noncognitive) conceptual role of a normative term. This would explain the truth of OQ3, the lack of correct descriptive definitions of normative concepts, in a way that doesn't license Moore's conceptual conclusion (OQ4) that normative concepts are simple and unanalyzable. This is because noncognitivists also reject the tenets of compositionality and reductivism, endorsing a broader, nonclassical account of what it is to analyze a normative concept. On this account, we analyze a normative concept indirectly (from "sideways on") by describing what someone is doing or like when they possess or use it. Noncognitivism is also well placed to explain how substantive and nonanalytic normative thoughts can have an apparently a priori character, and the intuitionistic epistemology of ethics. Whatever they might be, normative thoughts are not about the obtaining of some (metaphysically objective, mind-independent) state of affairs.

What might conceptual analysis of this kind reveal the noncognitive roles of normative concepts to be? Here, there are many options, but existing views largely fall into two classes. *Expressivist* theories analyze normative thought in terms of "noncognitive," motivational attitudes like desires, intentions, and emotions, as opposed to the "cognitive" attitude of (ordinary) belief (e.g. Blackburn, 1998; Gibbard, 2003; see Elisabeth Camp's chapter "Metaethical Expressivism"). *Inferentialist* theories analyze normative thought in terms of inferences to and from other attitudes that it either psychologically or rationally requires (e.g. Wedgwood, 2007; Chrisman, 2015; see Matthew Chrisman's chapter "Conceptual Role Accounts of Meaning in Metaethics"). For example, an inferentialist analysis of OUGHT might claim that to use the concept is to rationally commit oneself to certain patterns of intention. (Note that such a theory may reject the possibility of broadly reductive analysis in nonnormative terms, since RATIONAL seems itself a normative concept.)

Noncognitivist views are a popular choice from the smorgasbord of metaethical theories, partly because they emphasize practical aspects of normative thought (e.g. in eliciting action, intention, or emotion) that cognitivist views have struggled to accommodate. However, noncognitivists face some difficult challenges. This includes (1) a prima facie problem accounting for recalcitrant characters like *amoralists*, who allegedly have moral thoughts without manifesting the motivational attitudes or inferential dispositions that noncognitivists claim to be constitutive of such thoughts, and (2) the avowals of many people that their normative thoughts are cognitivist, representing metaphysically robust normative states of affairs ("moral facts"). These claims are potentially embarrassing for noncognitivists given the classical tenet of transparency—one element of the Classical Theory they generally don't reject, since it undergirds their appropriation of (the first step of) the OQA. However, we wish to focus on a different issue.

Notoriously, noncognitivist views are faced with an "embedding" (or "Frege-Geach") problem about compositionality (see Jack Woods' chapter "The Frege-Geach Problem"). For illustration, consider the simple and naive form of expressivism that analyzes WRONG directly in terms of *disapproving* of something. This may yield a plausible analysis of thinking that lying is wrong as disapproving of lying, but it seems unable to account for the more complex thought that lying is *not* wrong, which apparently doesn't involve disapproving of anything. Similarly, the complex thoughts that *if* lying is wrong *then* deceiving is wrong, and that *S believes that* lying is wrong, are presumably uses of the concept WRONG, but they also apparently don't involve disapproving of anything. While debate often focuses exclusively on these kinds of logically complex thoughts (or sentences), at its most general the embedding problem concerns noncognitivism's ability to provide an analysis of a concept or word's meaning that accounts for the full range of different ways the concept or word can be used or deployed. This includes, for example, explaining what it is to *wonder* whether lying is wrong or to *suppose* or *hope* that lying is wrong, none of which apparently involve disapproving of anything. More sophisticated (and recent) noncognitivist theories are designed with the aim of solving the embedding problem, at least with respect to logically complex thoughts—but despite decades of debate there is little consensus over whether it can be solved or even what a solution must accomplish, and noncognitivists have barely attempted to address it for wondering and other non-belief-like thoughts. Here we focus on two aspects of the problem that have largely been overlooked but that emerge from thinking particularly about normative concepts rather than sentences or thoughts.

First, despite apparently disowning simple views of what it is to *deploy* a normative concept, noncognitivists still sometimes endorse a correspondingly simple view of the normative concept *possession*: that to possess a concept like WRONG is just to be capable of having the associated attitude, like disapproval or blame (e.g. Schroeder, 2008). Given the range of permissible uses of WRONG, this view makes concept possession come apart from concept deployment in an awkward way. It isn't obviously incoherent to imagine a person thinking that lying is not wrong, despite her being psychologically incapable of disapproval or blame. According to the suggested view, however, she would apparently be using a concept that she doesn't possess! Noncognitivists must either challenge the possibility as characterized or provide a different account of concept possession.

Second, while noncognitivists have focused on solving the embedding problem at the *sentential* level, or the level of embeddable normative thoughts such as that lying is wrong, even if these efforts succeed it can be questioned whether noncognitivism offers a viable *alternative* to the Classical Theory at the level of individual normative concepts like WRONG. To illustrate this, consider an expressivist theory designed expressly to address the embedding problem, *biforcated attitude semantics* or BAS (Schroeder, 2008). This attempts to solve the problem by splitting the attitudinal component of normative thought into two parts, identifying the attitude of belief as a generic pro-attitude of "being for" taken towards other mental states. BAS analyzes the belief that lying is wrong as the state of mind of *being for blaming for lying*. By splitting the attitudinal component, BAS creates space for logical operators like *not* and *if* in the thought's content. For example, the belief that lying is not wrong is analyzed as *being for* not *blaming for lying*. Unlike simple expressivist theories, then, BAS can apparently identify a common contribution 'wrong' makes to the states of mind expressed by the sentences 'Lying is wrong' and 'Lying is not wrong': in each case, it contributes the concept BLAMING FOR.

Notice, however, that the attitude-type of blaming for is not *itself* involved in thinking that lying is not wrong (nor, indeed, in thinking that lying is wrong!). Rather, the thought is analyzed as an attitude *towards/about* the state of mind, *not blaming for lying*. BAS thus assigns the concept WRONG a traditionally "cognitive" role (of picking out a particular type of psychological attitude), the same *kind* of role as (on a classically cognitivist theory) the concept LYING. The noncognitive character of the thought expressed by asserting 'Lying is wrong' is contributed by the noncognitivist treatment of belief itself. (BAS recovers a distinction between cognitive and noncognitive thoughts by offering a radically nonclassical analysis of the former.) Schroeder (2008) claims, controversially, that the embedding problem can only be solved by a noncognitivist theory with this split-attitude structure. If this is correct, noncognitivism may fail to provide a viable distinctive approach to normative concepts like WRONG, which must make a classically cognitive contribution to normative thoughts to support the full range of ways we use them. To be clear, this is not an objection to noncognitivism at the level of whole normative thoughts, but we suggest it is an unappreciated obstacle to conceiving of noncognitivism as a distinct option at the lexical level of individual normative concepts, as it is being considered here.

DEFINITIONS, PROTOTYPES, AND NETWORKS

This section presents two different approaches to normative concepts and their analysis—Prototype Theory and Network Theory—that depart from the Classical Theory in a less radical way, accepting the central tenet of cognitivism but rejecting the tenet of definitionism, at least as classically understood.

Prototype Theory is a broad family of views tracing their lineage back at least to Ludwig Wittgenstein's discussion of family resemblance. Concepts are understood in terms of a prototype or exemplar that a subject has in mind, which applies to things depending on the degree to which they approximate the prototype as *sufficiently like THAT*. For a (classic) example, one's mental prototype for GAME might be soccer, in which case a central application could be to rugby (conventional rules, a team sport, involves a ball, competitive, involves scoring points, played on a field) and less centrally to chess (conventional rules, competitive, but doesn't involve teams, balls, a field, or scoring points). This rejects definitionism's reliance on necessary and sufficient conditions as the criteria of concept-application. Perhaps no single feature is *necessary* for something to fall under a concept like GAME: games needn't have conventional rules, for instance, or be competitive. Other classical tenets that presuppose definitionism are collateral damage. Contra compositionality, concepts are not constructed out of simpler parts, and so, contra reductivism, they are not analyzed by decomposition. Conceptual analysis instead takes the form of identifying the prototype or listing and weighting the features relevant to falling under the concept. There might be no analytic truths involving the concept (other than, perhaps, applications to the prototype itself), since the concept can in principle apply in the absence of any paradigmatic feature provided enough others are present. This supplies a potential explanation for OQ2, the lack of closed questions connecting basic normative properties with nonnormative features (Goldman, 1993). Competency isn't grasping a descriptive definition but the ability to represent and compare the prototype.

Although Prototype Theory is an important and influential competitor to the Classical Theory in the general theory of concepts, in metaethics it lies outside the mainstream. (Proponents include Stich, 1993; Wong, 2006; Park, 2013.) To hazard an explanation, while it seems easy to imagine exemplars for a central normative concept like WRONG, philosophers remain unable to agree on the relevant features of even paradigmatically wrong actions, like inflicting suffering for fun. Prototype Theory seems more plausible and popular for so-called *thick* normative concepts like CRUEL—but the thicker the concept, the more controversial its classification as "normative" becomes. (For discussion of the strengths and weaknesses of Prototype Theory in general, see Margolis & Laurence, 1999: 27–43.)

By contrast, Network Theory, as championed particularly by Frank Jackson (1998; see also Jackson & Pettit, 1995), has made significant noise in metaethics. This approach is often characterized as a return to traditional conceptual analysis, and indeed Jackson is occasionally represented, erroneously, as virtually a lone voice defending conceptual analysis in the metaethical wilderness. However, Network Theory seems well classified as an application of what is known in the general theory of concepts as the Theory Theory (for an overview, see Margolis & Laurence, 1999: 43–51) and thereby is better understood as a modest departure from the Classical Theory.

Network Theory treats normative concepts or terms on the model of the theoretical terms of a scientific theory, with meanings or definitions determined not individually but rather holistically by their role or position in the overall theory, or *network*. It can be roughly but usefully understood as the result of applying Classical Theory directly to the total network rather than to individual normative concepts. In Jackson's hands, the relevant network is that of *fully matured folk moral theory* and consists in three kinds of connections, which have the status of constitutive but revisable "platitudes": (1) internal connections between different normative concepts (e.g. that WRONG applies to an action just in case CONCLUSIVE REASON AGAINST applies to it), (2) "input" platitudes connecting observable states of affairs with normative concepts (e.g. if an action involves inflicting suffering for fun, then it falls under WRONG), and (3) "output" platitudes connecting normative concepts with various responsive behaviors (e.g. aversion in response to applications of WRONG) (1998).

The departures from the Classical Theory are significant. Network Theory may not even recognize the existence of concepts at the lexical or individual level, the conceptual unit instead being the network. Although Jackson seems to invoke individual concepts, like WRONG, he explains that this is just a way of speaking about words (1998: 33). The conceptual and referential role of words like 'wrong' is determined by their relations to other parts of the theory, as revealed by the various platitudes. Contra (classical) definitionism, it is the theory that provides necessary and sufficient conditions—for the application of the entire network. Against the tenets of compositionality and reductivism, conceptual analysis proceeds not by decomposing complex individual concepts into simpler parts but by assembling the relevant platitudes (by pumping intuitions from the armchair) into a map of the network, taking the form of an extremely complex description. While Jackson understands conceptual analysis as an exercise in global reduction, translating a description of reality in one (e.g. normative) vocabulary into a discontinuous (e.g. scientific) vocabulary, the actual reductive work is assigned to a separate, empirical inquiry into which overall constellation of entities, properties, and relations at the metaphysical level contingently manifests (close enough to) the same relations. So contra the tenet of essentialism, the essential or reductive definitions of normative properties are synthetic rather than analytic. This provides one part of Jackson's strategy for accommodating OQ2, the lack of analytic connections between normative and nonnormative terms; additionally, the platitudes themselves are not fully analytic or guaranteed true, since each individually is potentially defeasible under the pressure towards the mature or ideal folk theory.

A general difficulty confronting Network Theory is a *Permutation Problem*: there is no clear guarantee that the complex description of the network will correspond uniquely to one complex of properties, in which case the theory underdetermines references for normative terms (Smith, 1994). We suggest additionally that these departures from the Classical Theory intuitively put the cart before the horse. Whereas Network Theory suggests that we are able to recognize wrongness only derivatively, through our knowledge of platitudes such as that inflicting suffering for fun is wrong, it seems more natural to suppose instead that we know the truth of such "platitudes" because we are able immediately to recognize wrongness (when we see it) much of the time.

CHALLENGING THE PREMISES OF OQA: NONTRANSPARENCY AND EMPIRICAL LINGUISTICS

We have examined a number of ways in which ambitious conceptual analysis has been defended against the OQA by rejecting one or another core tenet of the Classical Theory as applied to normative concepts. In this section, we consider whether these responses might be overreactions, because we should instead reject the initial premises of Moore's argument. Consider first OQ2: is it really impossible to provide reductive definitions of basic normative words or concepts that yield "closed questions"? A very few philosophers have been bold enough to reject the premise as demonstrably false: for example, Paul Ziff (1960) proposes a reductive analysis of 'good' as meaning *answers to the interests in question*. No such proposal has won widespread acknowledgment, but the premise can be resisted without being refuted. How such a bold premise can be justifiably *accepted* is unclear when it is impossible to consider every possible definition of 'good'. Perhaps the correct analysis has simply yet to be considered; then what we need is redoubled effort at classical conceptual analysis rather than its abandonment.

A modest approach seeks to support OQ2 by induction: we've tried enough potential conceptual analyses of 'good' without yielding closed questions that we can safely infer that anything we could try will similarly fail. This seems an exceptionally weak induction, however, moving from a small sample to a conclusion about all possible definitions. Another approach proposes an abductive justification: unanalyzability is the *best explanation* for why efforts at conceptual analysis of 'good' have been unsuccessful so far (e.g. Ridge, 2014). But this has yet to be demonstrated; perhaps GOOD is just very complex, for example.

The most ambitious defense of OQ2 involves a particularly strong interpretation of the classical tenet of transparency. Perhaps our normative concepts are so transparent that we can immediately recognize not only that a proposed definition is correct when it is but also what the correct definition or composition of a concept is. Therefore, we can directly perceive, in a "flash of light" (Wittgenstein, 1997) or a "just-too-different intuition" (Enoch, 2011), that our normative concepts are unanalyzable in nonnormative terms. However, even among primitivists, there is widespread disagreement over which normative concepts are basic and over the correct (nonreductive or normative) definitions of others. This stance therefore requires a difficult balancing act, finding sufficient transparency to license the just-too-different intuitions but not so much as to predict that definitional connections between normative concepts would be obvious.

These interpretative issues about the tenet of transparency also point towards an important challenge to premise OQ1, that correct analyses always produce closed questions (having self-evident positive answers). Ambitiously reductive conceptual analysis can be defended against the OQA by either abandoning or weakening the classical tenets of transparency and competency as grasping a definition. This is a minimal departure from the Classical Theory, because it is compatible with retaining all the core (non-epistemological) tenets concerning the nature of normative concepts and conceptual analysis: cognitivism, definitionism, compositionality, reductivism, analyticity, and essentialism.

Just how transparent must our own concepts be to us? At one extreme is a view we'll call *strong transparency* (or strong aprioricity): that nobody could fail to know the analysis of their own concept upon reflection. This may follow if "grasping" a concept is simply mentally tokening its descriptive definition. However, the psychological link between concept and definition may be interpreted in subtler ways. At the other extreme is the view that our own concepts are entirely opaque to us. Perhaps our minds are so compartmentalized that the resources employed in first-order thought about the world are impenetrable to conscious introspection. In this case, a normative proposition could be analytically true without being a priori in even the most attenuated sense. Between these extremes lie many possibilities we can collectively call *weak transparency* (or weak aprioricity). Perhaps possessing a concept merely entails a disposition to recognize the correct definition when presented with it? Or perhaps, more weakly still, possessing a concept merely entails that it is *possible* (although perhaps extremely difficult, requiring advanced philosophical skills and extensive focus) to identify correct definitions and analytic truths.

For the widely accepted first step of the OQA to be both sound and compelling, a fairly strong form of transparency is required. But strong forms of transparency lead to the so-called Paradox of Analysis, as follows: if a conceptual analysis is correct then it must be uninformative because already known, and if it is informative because not already known then it must be incorrect. Since some conceptual analyses are plausibly both informative and correct, there seem to be some *unobvious analyticities* (see King, 1998). David Lewis (1989) exploits this point to defend a variant of the very analysis Moore originally attacked, that GOOD is the concept WHAT WE DESIRE TO DESIRE.

If we reject the tenet of transparency altogether, by what method can conceptual analysis be conducted? Or if we accept only a weak version of transparency, how can we adjudicate between competing analyses or claims to conceptual expertise? One answer is provided by the approach of contemporary linguistic semantics, in the tradition of Ordinary Language philosophy. Although not typically characterized as analysis of "concepts," this employs methods that, although neutral with regard to the theories we've surveyed, are at least compatible with a minimal departure from the Classical Theory. Assuming the word-concept nexus, *lexical* concepts are ripe for investigation by abductive and scientific methods. Different hypotheses about the conceptual meanings of normative words yield differing, testable predictions about competent speakers' dispositions to use them and assent to their use. The primary data here include speakers' intuitions about the acceptability of individual sentences incorporating these words, but this can be supplemented with usage, etymological, and cross-linguistic data. Speakers' intuitions can be gathered by fieldwork (such as the surveys favored by experimental philosophy), but the most common methodology is for the researcher to mine her own linguistic intuitions as a competent speaker herself.

The appeal here to intuitions might be thought at odds with our characterization of this method as empirical rather than a priori. But although practiced from the armchair, it is a process of abductive reasoning from observed phenomena (our introspected "gut reactions" to individual uses of a word) to underlying and hidden causes (our implicit concepts). This approach to normative language has made great progress in linguistics since the 1970s—especially in the work of Angelika Kratzer (1981) on the meaning of modal verbs like 'ought' and 'must', which was largely overlooked by metaethicists until very recently. However, similarly abductive linguistic methods have also been effectively practiced in metaethics for decades, as in the analysis of GOOD as a predicate modifier on the basis of identifying 'good' as an *attributive adjective* (e.g. Geach, 1956; Foot, 2001; Thomson, 2008).

One distinctive break from more traditional conceptions of conceptual analysis is that because this method is self-consciously linguistic, it seeks to identify the full range of different sentential and conversational contexts in which a particular word like 'ought' or 'good' is used rather than looking narrowly at the distinctly moral or (slightly less narrowly) normative uses of particular metaethical interest. For example, a sentence like 'Ben ought to be at work' allows two very different kinds of readings, one normative and the other epistemic or predictive. Ignoring the latter might seem appropriate given the metaethicist's interest in *normative* concepts, but if the same lexical concept OUGHT occurs in each reading then this is to ignore potentially important clues to its meaning. One might think that since the two readings involve different thoughts, the word 'ought' must be ambiguous between at least two concepts, $OUGHT_{NORMATIVE}$ and $OUGHT_{EPISTEMIC}$. But not every element of our thoughts is explicitly represented in the grammar of the sentences that express them. Linguists and philosophers have successfully developed unifying *contextualist* theories of meaning for words like 'ought' by identifying other, usually implicit elements that vary between different uses of the same sentence (see Alex Silk's chapter "Metaethical Contextualism"). The differences between the concepts $OUGHT_{NORMATIVE}$ and $OUGHT_{EPISTEMIC}$ are then located not in the (unified) *lexical* concept OUGHT but in contextually supplied parameters that aren't explicit in the sentence. This contextualist approach also offers a further response to the OQA (e.g. Prior, 1964; Foot, 2001; Thomson, 2008). Perhaps the reason why any proposed reductive definition of a normative term fails to generate closed questions is that for every definition that correctly analyzes *one* way of supplementing the lexical concept, there are indefinitely many other ways of supplementing that concept to reach a complete thought or predicate; for example, even if 'good' isn't lexically ambiguous, 'Is it good?' may be a radically ambiguous question.

This neo-classical approach to conceptual analysis faces important challenges, but its proponents are not without replies. One challenge is that because words can be lexically ambiguous—like 'bank', which expresses at least the concepts $BANK_{RIVER}$ and $BANK_{FINANCIAL}$—a linguistic methodology faces the risk of wild goose chases after nonexistent unifying concepts. However, we believe that the track record of this approach warrants considerable optimism (for a sustained case, see Finlay, 2014). Another challenge is the possibility that different people use the same words with different concepts—a threat to take seriously given divergences in people's moral intuitions. However, moral disputes seem pretheoretically like substantive disagreements rather than cases of talking past one another, suggesting common concepts with disputed application. (For discussion of the problem of normative concept identity and a novel solution, see Schroeter & Schroeter, 2014.) A related complaint is that it is objectionably parochial to focus on English words like 'good' and 'ought' or to assume that speakers of other languages employ the same concepts in their normative thought. However, plausibly at least "thin" normative concepts like those expressed by 'good', 'wrong', and 'ought' are practically universal in human thought, since interpreters seldom hesitate to offer these words as translations of central words in other languages. Additionally, if a society were to conduct its normative thought with different concepts it is unclear what bearing this would have on our metaethical questions, which presumably are couched in our own concepts. Rather, such a discovery would just bring to light new questions we hadn't previously entertained.

Finally, it is complained that the normative concepts most relevant for philosophy aren't necessarily those that happen to be lexicalized in natural language. A rival model of philosophical inquiry enjoins abandoning conceptual analysis in favor of "reforming definition" (Brandt, 1979), addressed to the question of what concepts we ought to use our words to express. But determining which concepts we ought to use plausibly requires an understanding of the concepts we're already using (Plunkett, 2016), which is what neo-classical conceptual analysis seeks to provide. Since metaethicists' interests are plausibly continuous with those of the "folk," and metaethical questions plausibly arise out of reflection on ordinary normative thought and speech, it is also far from clear that the concepts of metaethical significance aren't just those expressed by our everyday normative vocabulary.

In conclusion, although conceptual analysis remains a controversial approach to meta-ethics, we suggest there are many more conceptions or varieties of it than is commonly recognized, each of which supports an active research program with devoted champions.

ACKNOWLEDGMENTS

We thank James Fritz, Tristram McPherson, David Plunkett, and Mark Schroeder for helpful comments.

REFERENCES

Audi, R. (2004) *The Good in the Right*, Princeton, NJ: Princeton University Press.

Blackburn, S. (1998) *Ruling Passions*, Oxford: Oxford University Press.

Boyd, R. (1988) "How to Be a Moral Realist," in G. Sayre-McCord (ed.) *Essays on Moral Realism*, Ithaca, NY: Cornell University Press: 181–228.

Brandt, R. (1979) *A Theory of the Good and the Right*, Oxford: Oxford University Press.

Brink, D. (1984) "Moral Realism and the Skeptical Arguments from Disagreement and Queerness," *Australasian Journal of Philosophy* 62: 111–25.

Chrisman, M. (2015) *The Meaning of "Ought,"* Oxford: Oxford University Press.

Copp, D. (2007) *Morality in a Natural World*, Cambridge: Cambridge University Press.

Cuneo, T. and Shafer-Landau, R. (2014) "The Moral Fixed Points: New Direction for Moral Nonnaturalism," *Philosophical Studies* 17(3): 399–443.

Enoch, D. (2011) *Taking Morality Seriously*, Oxford: Oxford University Press.

Finlay, S. (2014) *Confusion of Tongues*, Oxford: Oxford University Press.

Foot, P. (2001) *Natural Goodness*, Oxford: Oxford University Press.

Geach, P. (1956) "Good and Evil," *Analysis* 17(2): 33–42.

Gibbard, A. (2003) *Thinking How to Live*, Cambridge, MA: Harvard University Press.

Goldman, A. (1993) "Ethics and Cognitive Science," *Ethics* 103: 337–60.

Huemer, M. (2005) *Ethical Intuitionism*, Houndmills: Palgrave MacMillan.

Jackson, F. (1998) *From Metaphysics to Ethics*, Oxford: Oxford University Press.

Jackson, F. & Pettit, P. (1995) "Moral Functionalism and Moral Motivation," *Philosophical Quarterly* 45(178): 20–40.

Joyce, R. (2006) *The Evolution of Morality*, Cambridge, MA: MIT Press.

King, J. (1998) "What Is a Philosophical Analysis?" *Philosophical Studies* 90(2): 155–79.

Kratzer, A. (1981) "The Notional Category of Modality," in H. J. Eikmeyer & H. Rieser (eds.) *Words, Worlds, and Contexts*, Berlin: De Gruyter: 38–74.

Lewis, D. (1989) "Dispositional Theories of Value," *Proceedings of the Aristotelian Society* 63: 113–37.

Margolis, E. & Laurence, S. (eds.) (1999) *Concepts: Core Readings*, Cambridge, MA: MIT Press.

Margolis, E. & Laurence, S. (eds.) (2015) *The Conceptual Mind*, Cambridge, MA: MIT Press.

Moore, G. E. (1903) *Principia Ethica*, Cambridge: Cambridge University Press.

Park, J. J. (2013) "Prototypes, Exemplars, and Theoretical & Applied Ethics," *Neuroethics*, DOI:10.1007/s12152-011-9106-8.

Pigden, C. (2012) "Identifying Goodness," *Australasian Journal of Philosophy* 90(1): 93–109.

Plunkett, D. (2016) "Conceptual History, Conceptual Ethics, and the Aims of Inquiry," *Ergo* 3(2): 27–64.

Prior, A. N. (1964) *Logic and the Basis of Ethics*, Oxford: Clarendon Press.

Railton, P. (1986) "Moral Realism," *Philosophical Review* 95(2): 163–207.

Ridge, M. (2014) "Moral Nonnaturalism," *Stanford Encyclopedia of Philosophy*. Available at: https://plato.stanford.edu/entries/moral-non-naturalism/ [Accessed 16 February 2017].

Scanlon, T. M. (1998) *What We Owe to Each Other*, Cambridge, MA: Belknap Press.

Scanlon, T. M. (2014) *Being Realistic About Reasons*, Oxford: Oxford University Press.

Schroeder, M. (2008) *Being For*, Oxford: Oxford University Press.

Schroeter, L. & Schroeter, F. (2014) "Normative Concepts: A Connectedness Model," *Philosophers' Imprint* 14(25): 1–26.

Smith, M. (1994) *The Moral Problem*, London: Blackwell.

Soames, S. (2011) *Philosophical Analysis in the Twentieth Century, Volume 1*, Princeton, NJ: Princeton University Press.

Stich, S. (1993) "Moral Philosophy and Mental Representation," in M. Hechter, L. Nadel, & R. Michod (eds.) *The Origin of Value*, Berlin: De Gruyter: 215–28.

Thomson, J. J. (2008) *Normativity*, Chicago, IL: Open Court.

Wedgwood, R. (2007) *The Nature of Normativity*, Oxford: Oxford University Press.

Wittgenstein, L. (1997) "Lecture on Ethics," in S. Darwall, A. Gibbard, & P. Railton (eds.) *Moral Discourse and Practice*, Oxford: Oxford University Press.

Wong, D. (2006) *Natural Moralities*, Oxford: Oxford University Press.

Yetter-Chappell, H. & Yetter-Chappell, R. (2013) "Mind-Body Meets Metaethics: A Moral Concept Strategy," *Philosophical Studies* 165(3): 865–78.

Ziff, P. (1960) *Semantic Analysis*, Ithaca, NY: Cornell University Press.

35

Ethics and Morality

Stephen Darwall

Bernard Williams begins *Ethics and the Limits of Philosophy* with "Socrates's Question": how should one live? (Williams, 1985: 1). Ever since Socrates, Williams says, philosophers have taken this to be the fundamental question of *ethics*. Williams observes, however, that his contemporaries are usually concerned with "distinctive issues of morality," such as "What is our duty?" (Williams, 1985: 4). But although the narrower ethical conception of *morality* "has a special significance in modern Western culture," it is "something we should treat with a special skepticism" (Williams, 1985: 6). What is distinctive and, Williams goes on to argue, dubious about morality among ethical conceptions is its "peculiar" notion of moral *obligation*: the idea that all persons, just by virtue of having certain general capacities of agency, stand under universal, categorical, and inescapable moral requirements of right and wrong (Williams, 1985: 174–96; for a critique, see Darwall, 1987).

Not all philosophers follow Williams's usage of 'ethics' and 'morality'. But most accept the distinction he marks with it: between the broadest normative questions of how to live (also construed broadly to include motivations and feelings), on the one hand, and deontic moral questions of right and wrong, on the other. Ethics is the genus of which morality is a species. Thus Ronald Dworkin writes that "ethics includes convictions about which kinds of lives are good or bad for a person to lead, and morality includes principles about how a person should treat other people" (Dworkin, 2000: fn. 485; see also Appiah, 2005: xiii). And Allan Gibbard and T. M. Scanlon distinguish similarly between narrower and wider senses of 'moral' and 'morality', although Scanlon's narrow morality, comprising obligations "we owe to each other," may be even narrower than (deontic) morality, since the latter may include moral obligations owed to no one in particular (Gibbard, 1990: 40–1; Scanlon, 1998: 172).

It does not really matter what we call these two different ideas, so long as we recognize the conceptual distinction between them, and Williams's terms 'ethics' and 'morality' are as good as any. Without real loss, we might simply regard Williams's as a *stipulative definition*, or as a *reforming definition* that aims to replace undisciplined ordinary usage. What matters is whether, so used, these terms carve out an important conceptual distinction.

And they do. We cannot even understand Williams's simultaneous embrace of ethics and suspicion of morality—nor that of other morality critics like Friedrich Nietzsche and G. E. M. Anscombe—unless we mark this difference (Nietzsche, 1994; Anscombe, 1958; see also Slote, 1992). Nietzsche famously rejects morality, but he does so partly on the ethical grounds that morality undermines much that makes life worth living, at least for those capable of higher forms of human excellence.

In addition, some philosophers, like Philippa Foot and Richard Joyce, argue that morality raises special metaethical questions that do not arise in all ethical domains. Thus Foot famously argues that morality's pretension to provide "categorical imperatives" that give every agent (overriding) reasons for complying with them, irrespective of the agent's desires or interests, cannot be sustained (Foot, 1972). And Richard Joyce argues similarly that first-order moral claims are therefore "fictions" (Joyce, 2007a, 2007b).

For their part, morality's philosophical defenders—"moral philosophers," as we can call them—also insist on the distinctiveness of morality as an ethical conception. They think that the "modern" conception of morality is a significant historical achievement that, like the complementary modern doctrine of universal human rights, is well worth defending.

'Morality' refers alternately, then, to this narrower ethical conception and/or to what this conception is *of*, as we have so far identified it: universally binding norms of right and wrong. But this is probably too narrow a characterization. We will consider other proposals philosophers have made for demarcating the moral below. On all these views, morality comprises a proper subset of what is relevant to how human beings should live their lives in the broadest sense. Following Williams, we will use 'ethics' to refer to this broad normative subject.

Wilfrid Sellars famously defined philosophy as "the study of how things in the broadest possible sense of the term hang together in the broadest possible sense of the term" (Sellars, 2007: 369). Paraphrasing liberally, we might say that ethics is the subject of how we should (in the broadest possible sense of the term) live (in the broadest possible sense of the term). In effect, this identifies ethics with the normative in general, since all actions and attitudes (things for which we can have normative reasons) are parts of our lives in the broadest sense. Traditionally, however, certain normative subjects—epistemology, for example—have been distinguished from ethics, though even here, epistemologists sometimes talk about the "ethics of belief" (Chignell, 2010).

On this use of 'ethics', *metaethics*—the inquiry into philosophical questions about ethics—shares much with what philosophers increasingly call *metanormative* inquiry. Indeed, the very origins of metaethics, whether in G. E. Moore's *Principia Ethica* or earlier in Henry Sidgwick's path-breaking chapter on "Ethical Judgments" in *The Methods of Ethics*, are mostly driven by general issues about normativity (Moore, 1993; Sidgwick, 1967: 23–38). Moore's well-known "open question" argument, which Moore uses to argue that the ethical property of (intrinsic) goodness cannot be identified with any natural property, arguably implicitly relies on the fact that goodness is a normative concept—one that entails normative reasons, or "oughts" (Frankena, 1976: 14; see also Darwall, 1997: 690–2).

This point is only implicit and unacknowledged in Moore, but it is explicit in Sidgwick's earlier argument, from which Moore drew, that ethical judgments "cannot legitimately be interpreted as judgments respecting … any facts of the sensible world" (Sidgwick, 1967: 25). The reason that ethical judgements are not reducible to empirical judgments, Sidgwick says, is that they all contain the "fundamental notion expressed by the word 'ought'" (Sidgwick, 1967: 32). Even "instrumental" oughts like 'If you want not to burn the cake, you ought to take it out of the oven' cannot be so reduced, Sidgwick showed, since unlike 'If you do not take the cake out of the oven, it will burn', the former contains a "dictate of reason" (Sidgwick, 1967: 34).

By and large, then, use of the term 'metaethics' is consonant with the broad sense of 'ethics' as concerned with normative questions of how we should live (in the broadest sense). Metaethical questions are a subpart of metanormative questions in general.

Of course, if morality, by contrast, is a specific ethical conception, it is nonetheless *an* ethical conception. So metanormative questions about morality are also metaethical questions. Some of these—for example, those concerning the nature, conditions, and possibility of moral obligation—differ from those concerning normativity in general. They concern, among other things, morality's distinctive normativity.

We do not really have a term that stands to 'morality' as 'metaethics' stands to 'ethics'. Perhaps we should call this *metamorality* or, more felicitously, *metamorals*. Just as metaethics deals with philosophical questions about ethics, which are mostly about normativity in general, so also is metamorals concerned with philosophical issues about morality. Metamorals will thus be concerned with philosophical issues that arise with respect to this distinctive normative conception and its putative object—moral right and wrong.

SOME HISTORY

As Williams's invocation of Socrates suggests, ethics is at least as old as the ancient Greeks. And Williams is not alone in suggesting that morality is a distinctively modern ethical conception. In her famous "Modern Moral Philosophy," Anscombe criticized the preoccupation ethical philosophers have had since the seventeenth century with morality and its deontic, "juridical," or "law conception of ethics" (Anscombe, 1958). Modern moral philosophers posit a moral law, but Anscombe argued that just like legislated law, a moral law could not exist without a lawgiver.

Societies are, of course, structured by social obligations or *mores*, so they might be thought to legislate these obligations for their members. But *morality* is held to transcend any such locally posited norms. We can always ask of any contingent social or legal obligation whether we are morally obligated to follow it or not. The latter question cannot be settled simply by looking to social mores or to a society's laws; it turns on *morality's* norms. Although we sometimes use 'morality' to refer to "a *society's* morality" or even "an *individual's* morality," these are positive social facts. 'Morality', as modern moral philosophers use the term, refers to an essentially normative order that stands in potential criticism of all positive *moralities*. *Moral agents*, those subject to morality, are defined not by their membership in any particular society but by certain capacities of rational moral agency that make them capable of guiding themselves by the moral law, which binds them simply as one moral agent among others.

Anscombe thought there could be such a moral law only if it has a legislator that transcends any earthly jurisdiction. However, with notable exceptions, most modern moral philosophers have not been prepared to ground morality in theology. Most argue, indeed, that morality is not the sort of thing that could derive from any being's will, even God's. Anscombe thought this left modern moral philosophy with deontic concepts lacking any "discernible content except a certain compelling force," which could only be "psychological" (Anscombe, 1958: 18). She has not been alone in holding the metamoral position that what Hare called "prescriptivity" is a mark of moral judgment (Hare, 1963).

To appreciate the distinctiveness of morality as an ethical conception, compare it to the view of ethics one finds in Plato and Aristotle. It is notable that 'morality' does not even appear in standard English translations of Plato's *Republic* or Aristotle's *Nicomachean Ethics*. Aristotle does contrast "moral virtues" with "intellectual virtues," but by this he just means virtues that have to do with passions, actions, and character rather than with the intellect. For Plato and Aristotle, the central ethical concepts are all species of the good: virtue; intrinsically choiceworthy, noble (*kalon*) action; and the good or benefit of human beings. Much of what modern ethical philosophers consider under the heading of morality, Plato and Aristotle discuss under the virtue of justice or intrinsically choiceworthy just action.

When Socrates is asked by Glaucon and Adeimantus at the beginning of Plato's *Republic* to say why we should be just, his reply is not that justice is morally obligatory or that others' rights provide, in themselves, reasons to respect them. Rather Plato has Socrates argue that justice is both instrumentally and intrinsically good for the just person. For a modern like H. A. Prichard, however, who takes justice to be a central part of obligating morality, Socrates's argument seems to "rest moral philosophy on a mistake" (Prichard, 2002: 7–20). That complying with the moral law can benefit us, even intrinsically, is an important fact, but it cannot explain why morality obligates or establish any reason for being moral that might flow directly from that. For these tasks, Socrates's argument seems to provide a reason of the wrong kind.

Sidgwick makes a similar point when he writes that according to ancient Greek ethics, "right action is commonly regarded as only a species of the good" (Sidgwick, 1967: 106). To fully understand their ideas, we have to "throw the quasi-jural notions of modern ethics aside" (Sidgwick, 1967: 106). He thus agrees with Anscombe that modern moral philosophy differs from ancient ethical thought in holding that the "quasi-jural" or deontic notions of morality are not simply a different "species of the good."

Sidgwick draws a further, related contrast between ancient and modern ethics that concerns normativity or normative force. Whereas Greek ethical philosophy recognizes "but one regulative and governing faculty" or form of practical reason, in the modern view "there are found to be two—Universal Reason and Egoistic Reason, or Conscience and Self-Love" (Sidgwick, 1964: 198). Plato, Aristotle, and other ancients tend to be *eudaimonists*, holding that all normative reasons for action must derive from the agent's own good or happiness (eudaimonia). In Socrates's exchange with Glaucon and Adeimantus, it is simply assumed by all parties that if Socrates cannot establish that it is intrinsically or extrinsically beneficial to the just person to be just, he will not have shown any reason to act justly.

According to Sidgwick, however, the modern ethical view allows for the position that Prichard clearly assumes: namely, that the fact that an action would unjustly wrong someone and therefore be morally wrong is or entails itself sufficient reason not to do it. "Conscience," the mental power through which we make moral judgments, is itself a "regulative and governing faculty," an aspect of practical reason (Sidgwick, 1964: 198).

According to Sidgwick's moderns, morality can be an independent source of normative reasons for acting that are additional to any provided by any species of the good.

Notably, Sidgwick makes *two* contrasts between ancient and modern ethical conceptions (Sidgwick, 1964: 198). The moderns recognize both "Universal Reason" and "Egoistic Reason," whereas the ancients recognize only the latter. And the moderns accept the demands of "Conscience" no less than the recommendations of "Self-Love." These are potentially different contrasts that track two different ways of juxtaposing the moral and the prudential that had currency in the early modern period and continue to today. "Conscience," whose contrast with "Self-Love" Sidgwick draws from Joseph Butler, has a conceptual link to the deontic notions of right, wrong, culpability, and so on that both Williams and Anscombe take to define morality. It is a mental faculty through which we hold ourselves accountable for complying with the moral law (Butler, 1983; Sorabji, 2014; Darwall, 2015b).

By "Universal Reason," however, Sidgwick means nothing deontic but rather considerations either of overall benefit or well-being or of impersonal good (as he puts it, what is good "from the point of view of the Universe") (Sidgwick, 1967: 382; Parfit, 2011). The idea that an impartial or impersonal perspective marks out a standpoint of moral, as opposed to personal, assessment—a "moral point of view"—runs through a proto-utilitarian (later utilitarian) tradition of Francis Hutcheson, David Hume, and John Stuart Mill and then through more contemporary figures like Kurt Baier and Peter Railton (Hutcheson, 2004; Hume, 1978; Mill, 2002; Baier, 1958; Railton, 1986: 189).

In the 1960s, there was a debate concerning whether the "concept of morality" could be captured in formal terms of universality, prescriptivity, and categorical bindingness, or whether it had a necessary "material" content such as human flourishing, interpersonal relations, or the general good (e.g. Baier, 1958; Foot, 2003a, 2000b; Frankena, 1965, 1966; Hare, 1963; Falk, 1965). More recently, "moral functionalist" views, like that of Frank Jackson, tie morality to "mature folk morality" (Jackson, 2000; see also Smith, 1994). This contrast between formal and material conceptions of morality answers to Sidgwick's two different markers of modern conceptions that we noted two paragraphs above.

If (philosophical) ethics is as old as the ancient Greeks, moral philosophy—the philosophical exploration of morality—is arguably a more recent development. All origin narratives involve some arbitrariness and artificiality, but the figure who most stands to modern moral philosophy as René Descartes stands to modern theoretical philosophy might be Hugo Grotius, whose *On the Law of War and Peace* was published in 1625 (Grotius, 2005; for discussion see Darwall, 2012). There, Grotius argues that all moral agents are subject to a common natural (moral) law that obligates them independently of their interests or whether God commands it, and that this law enshrines basic human rights. He thereby sets for the modern period the fundamental metamoral problem of how the distinctive normativity of moral obligations is to be grounded, since he raises the question and denies that it can be answered either by the agent's interest or divine command. (Grotius's own answer is what he calls "sociability" [Darwall, 2012].)

ETHICAL AND MORAL CONCEPTS

A simple way of expressing Sidgwick's contrast is to say that while ancient Greek ethics recognized only one fundamental normative ethical concept, the good, the moderns came to recognize two, the good and the right. But this simple formula masks a good deal of complexity that is implicit in Sidgwick's proposal. Even for Sidgwick (1967: 106), Greek ethics recognized different "species of the good," including, he says, "right action." But the notion of "right action" we find in Plato and Aristotle is nothing deontic; it is simply that of an intrinsically choiceworthy (fine or noble) act, something that is worth doing simply because it is the kind of action it is. Similarly, Greek ethics clearly has the idea of *virtue*, as we see in Aristotle's claim that the best life for human beings is a life of virtuous activity. This already gives us three different species of the good: virtue; intrinsically good (choiceworthy) action; and eudaimonia, meaning the agent's good or well-being. These three concepts are knit together in what we might think of as the fundamental thesis of Aristotelian virtue ethics: the *best* life is one of *virtuous* activity—that is, of activities that express virtuous dispositions to choose intrinsically *good* acts.

Now, 'best life' is actually ambiguous. It can mean life that most realizes the agent's good. Or it can mean life that there is most normative reason for the agent to realize (perhaps because it most realizes the agent's good, or perhaps not)—that is, the life that answers Socrates's question. Ancient ethical writers tend to be eudaimonists. Even when, like Aristotle, they see the agent's good as consisting in virtue, they nonetheless hold that the agent should aim at such a life because it will realize her eudaimonia. Moreover, eudaimonism is such an unquestioned assumption of their ethical framework that the distinction we make between the claim that a life will most realize the agent's good, on the one hand, and the claim that because such a life will most realize the agent's good, it is how the agent should live (how she has most normative reason to live), on the other, is not a distinction that they tend to mark explicitly. Eudaimonism is not so much an explicit, contestable ethical doctrine in ancient Greek ethics as a basic framework principle that governs implicitly and unquestionably. This does, however, give us a fourth ethical (normative) notion—that of a normative reason—that is at least implicit in ancient Greek ethics, even if it is not explicit.

So far, we have four ethical concepts: *a person's good* or well-being; *virtue*; *intrinsically choiceworthy action*; and a *normative reason* for acting. In the sense of 'good' that contrasts with 'right', only three of these refer to species of the good. The concept of normative reasons, or 'oughts', is both more general than and arguably contained within *both* concepts of the good and concepts of the right. (How this might be, we will consider presently.) Modern moral philosophers (in our sense of philosophical defenders of morality) hold that morality is a source of normative reasons that are not reducible to the good.

Normative reasons are also more general than reasons *for acting*. There are many different attitudes (intentions, beliefs, desires, and emotions) that we can have for reasons. Indeed, what we call attitudes arguably just *are* mental states of which it is intelligible to ask: *for* what reason do we hold the attitude? (Anscombe, 1957; Hieronymi, 2005). And when we have an attitude—say, a belief or a desire—for some reason, the reason for which we have it will be a consideration we take to be a *normative reason to* have it—that is, a consideration we take to count in favor of having it (Darwall, 1983; Scanlon, 1998).

Take desire, for example. When we desire something—say, a refreshing drink—there will generally be aspects of the object of our desire that we take to be reasons *to* desire it: for example, that drinking it will be refreshing and pleasant-tasting. There being reasons to desire it makes the drink good in the sense of being *desirable*, and this is similar for any attitude for which there can be normative reasons. The choiceworthy is what there is reason to choose; the estimable, what there is reason to esteem; the credible, what there is reason to believe; and so on. For every attitude, it seems, we can frame a normative concept that is necessarily instantiated just in case there are reasons (of "the right kind") for having that attitude (Hieronymi, 2005; Darwall, 2006: 16–17). This gives us a host of further ethical concepts in addition to those of someone's good or well-being, virtue, and the intrinsically choiceworthy (Anderson, 1993; Scanlon, 1998).

What do *moral* concepts add to these other ethical concepts? Again, we mean concepts, unlike Aristotle's concept of moral virtue, that are essentially related to *morality*. Most obviously, there are the deontic moral concepts. These include the concept of *moral obligation* and its equivalents, moral demand, requirement, or duty; the contrary concept of *moral wrong*, or the morally prohibited; and the concept of the *morally permitted*. Though it may sound odd to say, what is morally *right* is what morality permits. When we speak of what is morally obligatory as *the* right action, that is because it is the only act morality then permits.

To deontic concepts we must add the concepts of *moral virtue, worth, or goodness* that enter into the moral appraisal of agents, motives, and (motivated) actions. How these concepts are related to deontic moral concepts is an important question. Immanuel Kant held, for example, that actions have moral worth and show (moral) good will only if they are done for the motive of duty (Kant, 1996: 4: 398). For virtue theorists, like Rosalind Hursthouse, who advance their virtue ethics as a moral theory, however, the concept of right is based on that of virtue rather than vice versa. What is right, Hursthouse holds, is what a virtuous person would characteristically do (Hursthouse, 2002: 17; see also Swanton, 2003). A virtue theorist might, however, like Hutcheson, attempt to avoid deontic moral concepts while grounding claims about what is morally best to do (most *morally choiceworthy*) in claims about what the morally best motives would prompt the agent to do (Hutcheson, 2004: 125).

A very different kind of moral goodness is the concept that takes the lead in utilitarian or consequentialist theories and related conceptions of morality and the moral point of view. This is the concept of what might best be called *moral desirability*, or what is desirable from the moral point of view. In "Moral Realism," Railton equates "moral rightness with rationality from a social point of view," by which he means the moral point of view of equal concern for the interests of all (Railton, 1986: 190). (In a subsequent work, however, Railton [1988] suggests a more indirect kind of utilitarian view that links the concept of right, as does Mill, to blameworthiness. We will consider this conceptual point below.)

Scanlon defines "philosophical utilitarianism" as the view that "the only fundamental moral facts are facts about individual well-being" (Scanlon, 1982: 107). But consequentialist utilitarians are also committed to the claim that it is morally desirable that people do well, and this means that they need the concept of moral desirability in addition to that of well-being. That individuals' goods are realized is, they hold, a (morally) desirable thing itself.

Moral desirability in this sense is roughly equivalent to Derek Parfit's "impersonally good," or "good in the impartial-reasons-implying sense" (Parfit, 2011: vol. 1, 47). Impersonal goodness is not, we should note, essentially moral. Consequentialists, for whom promoting impersonal goodness provides the "point" or "goal" of morality, hold that impersonally good states of affairs would be good regardless of whether there were such a thing as morality or not. Even so, it is crucial to philosophical utilitarianism and consequentialism as *moral* theories that these states are desirable from the moral point of view. This gives us two different senses of 'morally good': the morally estimable (or virtuous) and the morally desirable.

Whether these are the only kinds of moral value is an issue for normative moral theory. For consequentialists, the morally desirable and morally estimable senses of moral goodness exhaust the kinds of moral value, whereas Kantians and other non-consequentialists tend to hold that there is a fundamentally different kind of moral value—what Kant calls *dignity*—to which the appropriate response is neither esteem (as an appraisal of moral character and conduct) nor desire (as a response to possible of states that may be promoted) but rather a form of recognition or *respect* that shows itself in how we govern our conduct in relation to it (Kant, 1996: 4:434). (For a consequentialist attempt to accommodate the distinction between (desirable or promotable) goods and values to which the appropriate response is respect see Pettit 1989. Kant's idea that persons have an inviolable dignity as ends in themselves is not that they or their existence are good, but that that they are entitled to respect (Darwall 1977).)

ETHICS, MORALITY, AND NORMATIVITY

We began with Williams's identification of ethics with the broadest normative question of how to live. We can put this question in various different ways. How is it good or best to live? How should we live? How do we have most normative reason to live? And we can ask these questions of different components of our lives: actions, habits, emotions, motives, traits of character, and perhaps even modes of perception, attention, and outlook. There is also the question of what ways of living are best *for us*: which best promote our good or well-being? And there is the question of how the answer to this question relates to Socrates's Question. Socrates didn't distinguish between these two questions, but we can. That these are different issues is shown by the fact that it is obviously an intelligible position to hold that it is better to lead one's life in a way that leads to greater well-being overall (that is, impartially considered) even if such a life benefits oneself less.

We contrasted these and other broad ethical questions with more specific questions of morality. How is it morally right and wrong to act? What ways of living are morally best? And what is the relation between living rightly and living well?

Now, as we just noted, it is possible to make the normativity of other ethical concepts explicit by spelling out their conceptual connections to normative reasons. Thus, necessarily, something is good in the sense of being desirable only in the case that there are reasons (of the right kind) to desire it; estimable only if there are reasons to esteem it; and so on. A number of philosophers have argued that taking normative reasons—what Gibbard calls the "flavorless" ought—as fundamental provides the best explanation of normativity (Scanlon, 2014; Gibbard, 1990: 49; Skorupski, 2013). But what about moral concepts? In what does their distinctive normativity consist?

A familiar thought is that moral obligations purport to provide those to whom they apply with normative reasons for acting that are categorical, in the sense of not depending on the agent's ends or interests, and that also override other reasons for acting. There are, however, significant problems with holding that this is what *defines* moral obligations. First, it makes unintelligible any question about whether moral obligations actually do override other reasons in all cases, since it makes it true that they do by definition. Anyone who asks such a question thereby shows a misunderstanding of the concept of moral obligation by asking it. Second, if providing overriding reasons is part of the nature of moral obligations rather than something that flows from it, then we cannot say that these reasons exist *because* the moral obligation does. The claim that moral obligations override is not simply that there can be categorical reasons (independent of the agent's interests and desires); that these can override any reasons for acting that are grounded in them; and that we use "morally obligatory" to refer to these reasons. There might, for example, be such reasons flowing from some intrinsic impersonal values—of precious artworks, say, or parts of nature—that have nothing to do with morality. 'Moral obligation' is not simply a term that we use to refer to such reasons, if there are any. The traditional idea that moral obligations override is that it is the independent fact of being morally obligatory that guarantees conclusive reasons.

Perhaps, however, we call reasons for acting "moral" when they have certain contents—being concerned with others' welfare, for example—and we say that these amount to a moral obligation when the reasons are overriding. But again, we thereby lose the capacity to *explain* the overridingness of the reasons by the existence of a moral obligation. The overridingness of moral obligations becomes a "concealed tautology," in Parfit's phrase (Parfit, 2011).

We should note, by the way, that nothing in the idea that moral obligations provide universal, categorical, overriding reasons entails that moral considerations or reasons always override. Nothing prevents the thought that though there are reasons that recommend an action as a morally good thing to do, they are not sufficient to make failure to do it morally wrong, hence they do not necessarily override reasons to do it as they would if the action were wrong. If there can be such so-called "supererogatory acts," (and my only point here is that nothing seems to rule them out conceptually), then the moral reasons that favor the action might not override other reasons for not doing it without any threat to the thesis that moral *obligations* are always overriding.

So the problem remains: if the existence of overriding normative reasons for action is not simply definitive of the concept of moral obligation in the way that the existence of reasons for desire is definitive of the desirable—and as the existence of normative reasons for other attitudes is, in general, definitive of the normative ethical concepts connected to those attitudes—how then are we to understand the distinctive normativity of morality and moral obligation? And how, given that understanding, might we attempt to account for the thesis that moral obligations do indeed provide overriding reasons? A promising approach to this question takes its cue from a passage from Mill:

> We do not call anything wrong, unless we mean to imply that a person ought to be punished in some way or other for doing it ... by the reproaches of his own conscience. This seems the real turning point of the distinction between morality and simple expediency.
>
> (Mill, 2002: chapter 5, para. 14)

Like Mill, a number of philosophers have argued recently that the defining normativity of deontic moral concepts of obligation, right, and wrong is tied to distinctive attitudes through which we hold ourselves and one another *accountable*, attitudes that Strawson famously dubbed "reactive attitudes," like resentment, guilt, and moral blame (Strawson,

1968; see also Brandt, 1979: 163–76; Gibbard, 1990: 42; Skorupski, 1999: 142; Darwall, 2006: 94–118). Moral blameworthiness can be understood in terms of normative reasons (or Gibbard's "flavorless" 'ought') as what there is normative reason (of the right kind) to blame. The Millian point, then, is that it is a conceptual truth that:

An action is wrong if, and only if, it is an action of a kind that it would be blameworthy to perform were one to do so without excuse.

Similarly, an action is necessarily morally obligatory if, and only if, it is of a kind that it would be blameworthy to fail to perform were one to fail to perform it without excuse.

This proposal ties the moral normativity of deontic moral notions to that of blameworthiness. The thought is not that moral wrongness—being a violation of a moral obligation—and blameworthiness are the same idea. They are not. An action may be wrong without being blameworthy, since there may be reasons to excuse it. The claim is that the above conceptual links exist between wrongness, blameworthiness, and excuse—and, through wrongness's entailments with other deontic moral notions, between these latter and blameworthiness.

Another way of putting this point is that we are accountable for complying with moral obligations in a way we are not for acting in accordance with normative reasons for acting generally—even, indeed, with moral reasons. Blame and related reactive attitudes like resentment and guilt implicitly hold their objects answerable for their conduct; they implicitly address a demand to their objects and bid for their objects to hold themselves answerable through a reciprocating attitude like moral guilt, which Mill calls "the reproaches of ... conscience" (Strawson, 1968: 85; Darwall, 2006: 94–118; Mill, 2002: chapter 5, para. 14). Nothing like this follows from doing what fails to accord with other normative standards.

But if the normativity that is distinctive of deontic morality is justification for reactive, holding-accountable attitudes, what then is the relation between moral obligations and reasons *for acting*? What can vindicate morality's implicit claim that there is never sufficient reason to do moral wrong? We will return to this at the end of the next and final section, in which we discuss how the difference we have noted throughout between ethics in general and morality in particular is reflected in the difference between metaethics, or metanormative theory, on the one hand, and metamorality, or metamorals, on the other.

METAMORALS

The distinctiveness of morality and moral concepts within ethics more generally bears careful attention at the level of metaethics and metamorals. Consider, for example, the debate between different varieties of internalism and externalism. *Judgment internalists* about some part of the ethical domain hold that actual or counterfactual motivation is essential to a genuinely ethical (or normative) judgment in that domain. And *existence* or *motivational internalists* hold that actual or counterfactual motivation (of the agent) is a necessary condition of the truth of some relevant ethical judgment about what the agent should do. Focusing on the latter, note the difference between two different kinds of internalist arguments that Williams gives. Most famously, Williams argues in "Internal and External Reasons" that any normative reason for acting must be something on which the agent could act in the sense that she would do so were she to deliberate correctly from her "motivational set" (Williams, 1981). Williams's famous claim that there are no "external reasons," and that all practical reasons must be "internal" in this sense, is a claim about ethical (normative) reasons for acting in general. In "Internal Reasons and the Obscurity of Blame," however, Williams makes a very different kind of argument about the role of internal reasons in *morality* (Williams, 1995). He argues, I think correctly, that it is a presupposition of *blame* as a reactive attitude that the person one is blaming could not have had sufficient reason to do what she is being blamed for doing. It is a kind of pragmatic contradiction to blame someone and simultaneously acknowledge that she had good reason to do what one is blaming her for doing. This means that moral blame for some action can be justified only if there was conclusive reason not to have so acted.

Williams's object in making this point is to put pressure on the idea of morality from a different direction than he pursued in *Ethics and the Limits of Philosophy* (1985). There, he held that morality tends to overreach and constrain agents in ways that undermine their integrity. But in "Internal Reasons and the Obscurity of Blame" (1995), Williams argues that deontic morality's signature reactive attitudes, like moral blame, cannot always be justified if his general "internal reasons" thesis is correct. Presently, I will argue that his observation can actually be turned into a defense of morality and its claim to provide conclusively overriding reasons for acting. My point here, however, is simply that we need to take care in metaethical debates, whether they concern ethics in general or morality in particular.

Another example occurs in debates over what Jonathan Dancy calls "moral particularism" (Dancy, 1993, 2006, 2009). Dancy argues that "moral thought and judgment" do not require general "moral principles" and that moral truth can be irreducibly particularistic (Dancy, 2006: 76). However, Dancy's arguments for this position seem insufficiently attentive to morality's distinctiveness as an ethical conception. His case for moral particularism largely depends upon a general holism about normative practical reasons—that, for example, the valence of a practical reason is not intrinsic to it but can be affected by other "defeaters" or "enablers" in a way that is familiar from epistemology—so that there are unlikely to be true general principles about normative reasons. This may seem plausible enough about normative reasons in general, but that is nonetheless consistent with the existence of features of morality that make general principles requisite there.

If, for example, deontic moral truths about moral obligation, right, and wrong are tied conceptually to accountability—if, that is, it is a conceptual truth that an action can be morally wrong if, and only if, it is an action of a kind that would be blameworthy to do without excuse—then deontic moral truth is likewise tied to conditions for intelligible accountability. That this may provide a necessary role for moral principle can be shown by deontic morality's similarity to law. An essential feature of the contrast between rule by decree and the rule of law is that the latter involves publicly accessible rules whose interpretation is backed by judicial principle. Of course, morality differs from law in various ways—for example, in not being promulgated. But if morality is like law in respect of accountability for violations, and if accountability in general requires a sharable public standard, since a person cannot intelligibly be held accountable for complying with standards that are inaccessible to her, then there may well be a rationale for general principles in morality that does not hold in general in other normative or ethical domains (Darwall, 2013).

Similarly, Rawls held that it is essential to a conception of justice that it be publicizable, and this "publicity condition" figures centrally in his argument from the original position for justice as fairness and against forms of utilitarianism (Rawls, 1971: 130). Critics sometimes pointed out against Rawls that this is an implausible condition, since whether everyone should accept some doctrine and whether it is true seem to be different matters (see Parfit, 1986: 41; Scheffler, 1982). However, although this is often true, and there is no simple entailment in general from the fact that a claim should be (even) universally disbelieved to the claim's being false, this entailment may nonetheless be valid for deontic moral claims. This is owing to deontic morality's connection to accountability. While there is certainly no conceptual bar to essentially esoteric normative truth in various domains—for example, in aesthetics, or even concerning well-being or ethical vice and virtue broadly conceived—there does seem to be a conceptual bar to esoteric *morality* as a standard of moral accountability. Here, insensitivity to differences between morality and other normative or ethical conceptions can lead to error.

Again similarly, issues in metamorals about the possibility of moral expertise, about the general accessibility of moral knowledge, and about moral testimony depend upon features of morality that do not hold true across the ethical domain. There seems to be nothing problematic in the idea of esoteric aesthetic knowledge, or even of great swaths of normative truth that are inaccessible to many. But if, again, moral obligations are what we are accountable for doing, it is hard to see how these could be similarly inaccessible. We can hardly be accountable for not doing wrong if we are not also accountable for knowing what is wrong. Arguably, however, we cannot intelligibly be held accountable for that unless it is possible for us to know what is wrong. But this line of thought, plausible as it is in *metamorals*, hardly holds in metaethics across the board.

Finally, let us return to the issue of how moral philosophers might defend the claim, seemingly essential to morality, that moral obligations entail overriding reasons for compliance. As we saw before, it is little help to simply define moral obligations in terms of overriding reasons, since that makes the claim that moral obligations override a concealed tautology. Foot argues that there is an uncontroversial sense in which moral obligations are "categorical" and "inescapably" require us to act contrary to our interests and aims, but that this is similarly true of any putative normative requirement—for example, etiquette. Both sets of requirements hold categorically *from their respective "points of view"* (Foot, 1972: 308–11). However, this does not entail that either hold *sans phrase*, much less that moral obligations and oughts override other reasons.

A promising way of trying to meet Foot's challenge is to recall Williams's point about blame presupposing that moral obligations provide genuine (not just perspective-relative) reasons that override other reasons. Putting this point together with a Strawsonian analysis of moral blame—as a reactive attitude that has various presuppositions and therefore justification conditions—may form the basis of a promising line of response.

Notice, first, that skeptical questions (like those of Williams, Anscombe, and Nietzsche) about morality's normativity and about whether moral obligations provide overriding reasons differ from skepticism about normativity and normative reasons in general. This is itself an aspect of the distinction between ethics and morality that we have been exploring throughout this essay. Even if normative reasons for attitudes and actions exist in general, moral skeptics argue, there is reason to be suspicious of *morality's* claim that moral obligations provide overriding reasons for acting. Their skepticism about morality is not supposed to depend on a general skepticism about normativity and normative reasons.

The next point is that moral blame is an attitude that can be had *for reasons*, and so is justifiable or not dependent upon whether there are normative reasons to blame. In this way, blame and its kindred reactive attitudes are like belief, desire, intention, and other attitudes. Assuming there can be normative reasons for attitudes in general, we should suppose that there can be normative reasons for blame, unless we have some special reason for skepticism in this particular case.

Assume, then, that Williams (1995) is right in thinking that blame presupposes sufficient reason not to have done what the person is being blamed for doing. Blame is a form of holding someone answerable. But if the person blamed can show that she had sufficient reason for acting as she did, then she will have successfully answered the blame and shown it to be unwarranted—that is, shown that there was not in fact sufficient reason to blame her for her action.

But if it is a conceptual truth that an action is a violation of a moral obligation only if it is of a kind that *would* be blameworthy were it to be done without excuse, it necessarily follows that if the action is morally required (and no excuse exists), then sufficient reason to blame the person would exist. And since this reason would not exist if there were not sufficient reason for the person not to have done what she is blameworthy for doing, it follows further that if there was a moral obligation for her not to have done it, then there was sufficient reason for her not to have done it (Darwall, 2015a).

This is much too brief a presentation to show that an argument along these lines can actually work. I present it in conclusion here to reinforce the difference between general skeptical issues about normative reasons and normativity—which is a staple of *metaethics* and metanormative theory in general—and skeptical worries about the normativity of morality more specifically in *metamorals* in particular. The strategy of the argument is to claim that the normativity of morality stands or falls with normative reasons for (deontic) reactive attitudes like moral blame. So long as the general problem of normativity can be solved and there can be normative reasons for attitudes, it would seem that reactive attitudes like moral blame can be justified also. And if they are, they bring normative reasons for acting in their train.

ACKNOWLEDGMENTS

I am grateful to the editors and to Leah Schroeder for very helpful advice and comments.

REFERENCES

Anderson, E. (1993) *Value in Ethics and Economics*, Cambridge, MA: Harvard University Press.
Anscombe, G. E. M. (1957) *Intention*, Oxford: Basil Blackwell.
Anscombe, G. E. M. (1958) "Modern Moral Philosophy," *Philosophy* 33: 1–19.
Appiah, K. A. (2005) *The Ethics of Identity*, Princeton, NJ: Princeton University Press.
Baier, K. (1958) *The Moral Point of View*, Ithaca, NY: Cornell University Press.
Brandt, R. B. (1979) *A Theory of Good and Right*, Oxford: Oxford University Press.
Butler, J. (1983) *Sermons*, ed. by S. Darwall, Indianapolis, IN: Hackett.

Chignell, A. (2010) "The Ethics of Belief," *Stanford Encyclopedia of Philosophy*, http://plato.stanford.edu/entries/ethics-belief.

Dancy, J. (1993) *Moral Reasons*, Oxford: Basil Blackwell.

Dancy, J. (2006) *Ethics without Principles*, Oxford: Oxford University Press.

Dancy, J. (2009) "Moral Particularism," *Stanford Encyclopedia of Philosophy*, http://plato.stanford.edu/entries/moral-particularism.

Darwall, S. (1977) "Two Kinds of Respect," *Ethics* 88: 36–49.

Darwall, S. (1983) *Imperial Reason*, Ithaca, NY: Cornell University Press.

Darwall, S. (1987) "Abolishing Morality," *Synthese* 72: 71–89.

Darwall, S. (1997) "Learning from Frankena: A Memorial Essay," *Ethics* 107: 685–705.

Darwall, S. (2006) *The Second-Person Standpoint: Morality, Authority, and Accountability*, Cambridge, MA: Harvard University Press.

Darwall, S. (2012) "Grotius at the Creation of Modern Moral Philosophy," *Archiv für Geschichte der Philosophie* 94: 296–325.

Darwall, S. (2013) "Morality and Principle," in D. Bakhurst, M. O. Little & B. Hooker (eds.) *Thinking about Reasons: Themes from the Philosophy of Jonathan Dancy*, Oxford: Oxford University Press: 168–91.

Darwall, S. (2015a) "Making the Hard Problem of Moral Normativity Easier," in E. Lord & B. Maguire (eds.) *Weighing Reasons*, Oxford: Oxford University Press.

Darwall, S. (2015b) "*Moral Conscience through the Ages: Fifth Century BCE to the Present*," book review, *Notre Dame Philosophical Reviews*, https://ndpr.nd.edu/news/56313-moral-conscience-through-the-ages-fifth-century-bce-to-the-present.

Dworkin, R. (2000) *Sovereign Virtue: The Theory and Practice of Equality*, Cambridge, MA: Harvard University Press.

Falk, W. D. (1965) "Morality, Self, and Others," in H. Neri-Castañeda & G. Nakhnikian (eds.) *Morality and the Language of Conduct*, Detroit, MI: Wayne State University Press, 25–67.

Foot, P. (1972) "Morality as a System of Hypothetical Imperatives," *Philosophical Review* 81: 305–16.

Foot, P. (2003a) *Natural Goodness*, Oxford: Clarendon Press.

Foot, P. (2003b) *Virtues and Vices: And Other Essays in Moral Philosophy*, Oxford: Clarendon Press.

Frankena, W. (1965) "Recent Conceptions of Morality," in H. Neri-Castañeda & G. Nakhnikian (eds.) *Morality and the Language of Conduct*, Detroit, MI: Wayne State University Press, 1–24.

Frankena, W. (1966) "The Concept of Morality," *Journal of Philosophy* 63: 688–96.

Frankena, W. (1976) *Perspectives on Morality: Essays of William K. Frankena*, ed. by K. Goodpaster, Notre Dame, IN: University of Notre Dame Press.

Gibbard, A. (1990) *Wise Choices, Apt Feelings.* Cambridge, MA: Harvard University Press.

Grotius, H. (2005) *The Rights of War and Peace*, 3 vols., ed. by R. Tuck, from the 1738 English trans. by J. Morrice from J. Barbeyrac's French trans. and original notes, Indianapolis, IN: Liberty Classics. [Originally published in 1625].

Hare, R. M. (1963) *Freedom and Reason*, Oxford: Clarendon Press.

Hieronymi, P. (2005) "The Wrong Kind of Reason," *Journal of Philosophy* 102: 437–57.

Hume, D. (1978) *A Treatise of Human Nature*, 2nd edn, ed. by L. A. Selby-Bigge, rev. by P. H. Nidditch, Oxford: Oxford University Press.

Hursthouse, R. (2002) *On Virtue Ethics*, Oxford: Oxford University Press.

Hutcheson, F. (2004) *An Inquiry into the Original of Our Ideas of Beauty and Virtue in Two Treatises*, ed. by W. Leidhold, Indianapolis, IN: Liberty Fund.

Jackson, F. (2000) *From Metaphysics to Ethics: A Defence of Conceptual Analysis*, Oxford: Clarendon Press.

Joyce, R. (2007a) *The Evolution of Morality*, Cambridge, MA: MIT Press.

Joyce, R. (2007b) *The Myth of Morality*, Cambridge: Cambridge University Press.

Kant, I. (1996) *Groundwork of the Metaphysics of Morals*, in *Practical Philosophy*, trans. and ed. by M. J. Gregor, Cambridge: Cambridge University Press. [References are to volume and page numbers of the Preussische Akademie edition.]

Mill, J. S. (2002) *Utilitarianism*, ed. by G. Sher, Indianapolis, IN: Hackett.

Moore, G. E. (1993) *Principia Ethica*, rev. edn, Cambridge: Cambridge University Press.

Nietzsche, F. (1994) *On the Genealogy of Morals*, ed. by K. Ansell-Pearson & C. Diethe, Cambridge: Cambridge University Press.

Parfit, D. (1986) *Reasons and Persons*, Oxford: Oxford University Press.

Parfit, D. (2011) *On What Matters*, 2 vols, Oxford: Oxford University Press.

Pettit, P. (1989) "Consequentialism and Respect for Persons," *Ethics* 100: 116–26.

Prichard, H. A. (2002) "Does Moral Philosophy Rest on a Mistake?" in J. McAdams (ed.) *Moral Writings*, Oxford: Oxford University Press.

Railton, P. (1986) "Moral Realism," *Philosophical Review* 95: 163–207.

Railton, P. (1988) "How Thinking About Character Might Lead to Rethinking the Character of Utilitarianism," *Midwest Studies in Philosophy* 13: 398–416.

Rawls, J. (1971) *A Theory of Justice*, Cambridge, MA: Harvard University Press.

Scanlon, T. M. (1982) "Contractualism and Utilitarianism," in A. Sen & B. Williams (eds.) *Utilitarianism and Beyond*, Cambridge: Cambridge University Press, 103–28.

Scanlon, T. M. (1998) *What We Owe to Each Other*, Cambridge, MA: Harvard University Press.

Scanlon, T. M. (2014) *Being Realistic about Reasons*, Oxford: Oxford University Press.

Scheffler, S. (1982) *The Rejection of Consequentialism*, Oxford: Oxford University Press.

Sellars, W. (2007) *In the Space of Reasons: Selected Essays of Wilfrid Sellars*, ed. by K. Sharp & R. Brandom, Cambridge, MA: Harvard University Press.

Sidgwick, H. (1964) *Outlines of the History of Ethics for English Readers*, 6th edn, Boston, MA: Beacon Press.

Sidgwick, H. (1967) *The Methods of Ethics*, 7th edn, London: Macmillan.

Skorupski, J. (1999) *Ethical Explorations*, Oxford: Oxford University Press.

Skorupski, J. (2013) *The Domain of Reasons*, Oxford: Oxford University Press.

Slote, M. (1992) *From Morality to Virtue*, New York: Oxford University Press.

Smith, M. (1994) *The Moral Problem*, Oxford: Blackwell.

Sorabji, R. (2015) *Moral Conscience through the Ages*, Chicago, IL: University of Chicago Press.

Strawson, P. F. (1968) "Freedom and Resentment," in *Studies in the Philosophy of Thought and Action*, London: Oxford University Press.

Swanton, C. (2003) *Virtue Ethics: A Pluralistic View*, Oxford: Oxford University Press.

Williams, B. (1981) "Internal and External Reasons," in *Moral Luck*, Cambridge: Cambridge University Press, 101–13.

Williams, B. (1985) *Ethics and the Limits of Philosophy*, Cambridge, MA: Harvard University Press.

Williams, B. (1995) "Internal Reasons and the Obscurity of Blame," in *Making Sense of Humanity*, Cambridge: Cambridge University Press, 35–45.

36

The Varieties of Normativity

Derek Baker

INTRODUCTION

There are things we *should* do, and other things we *should* not. Some choices are *permitted*, others are *required*, and others are *impermissible*. Some behavior is *appropriate*, some feelings *unwarranted*. Happiness is *good*. Nazis are *bad*. Italian fascists are also *bad*, but Nazis are *worse*. Some think eating meat is *immoral*; others, that mentioning such beliefs in the presence of the Thanksgiving turkey is *impolite*. Double-parking is *illegal*; so is murder, even murder of a Nazi.

We use these terms, in some sense, to tell people what to do, what to think, and how to feel—that is, we use them to prescribe, forbid, and advise. We also use them to praise, censure, and evaluate. Finally, we use them to justify. If I did what I was supposed to, any criticism others might register is off base.

In short, these terms (or their objects) display *normativity*, which more than any other notion organizes the subject matter of metaethics, to the point that some theorists prefer to replace talk of metaethics with talk of the meta-*normative* (Enoch, 2007, 2011). It is not enough that we account for the metaphysics, epistemology, and psychology of morality and our moral judgments. We should aim at offering an account of the metaphysics, epistemology, and psychology of normative phenomena and normative judgments in general.

There are a variety of phenomena that appear to be normative in one way or another, and not always in the same way. The first part of this chapter will start by presenting what I take to be the most fundamental division within the normative: that between merely *formal normativity* and full-blooded *authoritative normativity*. It will then canvass a series of further distinctions within the normative and argue that all of these crosscut the formal-authoritative distinction, which is *sui generis*. The second part of this chapter will present reasons for skepticism about authoritative normativity. This, like most forms of philosophical skepticism, is advocated not so much because the author is convinced;

rather, it is part of the venerable tradition of trying to get philosophers to stop being so easy on themselves.

THE TAXONOMY OF NORMATIVITY

I will assume that normative properties fall into different *normative systems*. There is the system of morality, the system of etiquette, and the laws of the state of California; there is practical reason, epistemic (or theoretical) reason, prudence (or self-interest), and so on. Some of these systems apply to actions (the rules of chess). Some apply to attitudes (epistemic norms apply to beliefs). Some seem to apply to both—morality, for example, prescribes conduct but perhaps also certain emotional responses.

What are these systems? Unfortunately, they may not be the same in every case. Etiquette and the law do seem to be genuine systems of tacit or explicit rules; and normative terms such as "impolite" or "illegal" assert a *relation* between the object of evaluation and the system. But not all systems are obviously so. It could well be that what makes the values, virtues, and prescriptions we call "moral" into a single system, distinct from those values, virtues, and prescriptions we call "aesthetic," is shared subject matter. But it could also be shared reduction-base or family resemblance. I will assume that we have some intuitive grip of what these normative systems are, and that we are more confident of what kind of normative properties belong to one system or another than of why they belong (for more elaboration, see Foot, 1972; Hubin, 2001; Tiffany, 2007; Broome, 2007; for skepticism about such normative systems, see Thomson, 2008: chapter 10).

As noted, these systems tell you what to do, but they also tell you what to believe and what to feel. I will sum this up by saying that normative systems prescribe, recommend, or evaluate *options*—where these are understood to be broad enough to include possible conclusions, beliefs, or other attitudes, and not just choices.

Formal and Authoritative Normativity

The most important division among normative systems is between those that are inherently significant and those that are not. Following McPherson (2011), I will call this the distinction between *authoritative* and *formal* normativity (similar distinctions are found in Copp, 2004; Broome, 2007; Tiffany, 2007; Southwood, 2008). Formal normativity is the normativity displayed by any standard one can meet or fall short of. The rules of chess are formally normative, as are club rules, ancient honor codes, the law, and the standards of beauty employed by the Miss America pageant.

A person can ignore or even wilfully violate the above standards, however, without any implication that she is guilty of some sort of mistake or that her behavior is in any interesting sense defective. In contrast, consider the requirements of morality, prudence, authenticity, and especially theoretical and practical reason. To ignore or wilfully violate these standards does arguably involve a mistake and behavior (or reasoning) that is defective—though theorists may differ on which of these systems deserve to be excluded.

We could also put the distinction like this: normative facts and properties, in some sense, tell you what to do (or think, or feel). But authoritatively normative facts *really* tell you what to do. The distinction is also sometimes put in terms of normative properties with *normative force* and those without (e.g. Parfit, 2011: 34–5).

It should be obvious that these statements of the distinction are meant to evoke an intuitive contrast, not as definitions of either class. Some characterizations explain the difference in further normative terms ("mistake," "defect," "significant," "important," "must heed"). Others characterize the difference simply through emphatic uses of language ("really tell you what to do"), or through metaphor ("normative force").

This distinction is not helpfully identified with the familiar distinction between categorical and hypothetical imperatives; it certainly cannot be explained by that distinction. In contrast to hypothetical imperatives, categorical imperatives can be identified as those ought-claims that remain valid even when the person to whom we apply them does not care about the ends that complying with the imperative would realize. But on this definition, the rules of chess and etiquette are categorical, though obviously not authoritative (cf. Foot, 1972). Alternately, we could define categorical requirements as those that entail the existence of reasons. On this definition, categorical requirements may well be co-intentional with authoritative ones, but then that is presumably because facts about reasons are unlike most other normative facts—they don't just tell you what to do, they really tell you what to do! This doesn't explain but rather presupposes the distinction between formal and authoritative normativity.

In the following subsections, I will consider other natural distinctions in the forms that normative facts and properties can take, none of which are easily identifiable with the formal-authoritative distinction.

The Structure of Normative Systems

Normative claims seem to describe facts or properties that fall into one of four basic structural categories.

Deontic Relations

Within a normative system, certain options are ruled out and others ruled in. For example, certain moves in a game of chess may be better or worse moves, but some are *illegal*. Chess rules them out. To say that one has a moral duty of keeping a promise isn't simply to say that violating the promise is shabby; it is to say that morality instructs us not to treat this option like a genuine alternative at all. More generally, actions are *right* or *wrong, permitted* or *forbidden, legal* or *illegal, against the rules* or *in accordance* with them; feelings are *appropriate* or *inappropriate, correct* or *incorrect*. Beliefs are *justified* or *unjustified*. These types of relations are often described using modal verbs: "ought," "should," "must," and "may."

Sets of these terms seem to be interdefinable—quite obviously in the case of those terms that are cognates (e.g. "legal" and "illegal")—but *forbidden* can be defined as that which is *not permitted*, and *required* or *obligatory* can be defined as that which is *uniquely permitted*. This seems to follow from the ruling-out/ruling-in role played by deontic properties.

It should be noted that nothing about these deontic *structures* depends on voluntary control. It may be that talk of *obligations* or *duties* presupposes voluntary control. But this is presumably a feature of moral deontic norms. There is no reason to assume it is a feature of deontic norms in general. The basic structure of ruling out some responses and ruling others in applies to responses that are not voluntary: our emotions, for example, can be *appropriate* or *inappropriate*, *fitting* or *unfitting*. A standard reason for rejecting deontic understandings of epistemic justification is that beliefs are not subject to voluntary control (e.g. Alston, 2005); but this objection seems to depend on building more into the idea of a deontic structure than is necessary (cf. Feldman, 2000).

Considerations

Not all normative properties or relations imply a binary structure in which some options are ruled out and others ruled in. A standard normative relation is a *consideration in favor of*—the classic case being a *reason*. Rather than establishing that a particular option is correct or incorrect, considerations have a contributory role: they count towards an option being correct or incorrect but are not necessarily decisive. There can be one consideration in favor of continuing to work (*that one would get more work done*, for example) and another consideration in favor of taking a nap (*that napping is pleasant*). In such a case, the considerations are weighed against one another, with one or the other counting for more in determining what the normative system prescribes. In case of many reasons on either side, reasoning about which option is prescribed will require intelligently "adding up" various conflicting and congruous considerations (for more discussion, see the papers collected in Lord & Maguire, 2016).

Having a consideration-structure is not unique to authoritative normative systems. It is true that philosophers use "reason" to label those considerations that are authoritative. But we can talk about reasons of etiquette and reasons of chess without linguistic strain, and it is a live question in metaethics whether moral reasons are reasons *full stop* or reasons possessing and lacking *normative force*. Some obviously formally normative systems have a consideration-structure: the Miss America pageant may work with an offensively narrow definition of female beauty, but it is not so narrow that the judges cannot add up multiple, potentially competing considerations to get a final, overall ranking.

Teleological Structures

Within some normative systems, certain outcomes are identified as *ends*, *goals*, or *aims* to be realized. For example, the rules of chess provide players with the dual goals of checkmating one's opponent while preventing one's own checkmate. According to utilitarians, there is a single moral aim: happiness. This end can be described as an *intrinsic good* within the normative system. If utilitarians are right, happiness is the only intrinsic moral good. Admittedly, it sounds strained to call checkmate or victory a good in chess. Yet it would be correct to say that, in chess, checkmating one's opponent is *better than* a stalemate, but achieving a stalemate is better than losing.

These ends determine which options, traits, resources, and so on are instrumentally valuable in a straightforward way: they are those things that promote the realization of the end. A chess move that increases the likelihood that the player will win is a good move; those traits of his that make him more likely to win against a variety of skilled opponents are good traits in a chess player. If utilitarians are right, keeping a promise is morally good because it contributes to human happiness.

Unlike deontic structures, the evaluations corresponding to teleological structures are not binary but graded (for discussion, see Railton, 1988). Options and outcomes are better or worse. This presumably follows from three features of how teleological normative systems apply to real situations. First, various alternatives can promote an end *more* or *less* efficiently. Thus, instrumental values must be gradable. Second, any system that proposes multiple, potentially competing ends will need some ranking of those ends as better or worse if it is to provide definitive advice in complex situations. Third, the realization of some ends is itself gradable. Whether I checkmate my opponent or not is binary, but happiness can be realized to a greater or lesser extent.

Virtues

Philosophers have proposed understanding both morality and epistemology in terms of *virtues*—stable character traits that produce or prevent certain characteristic effects. The trait of *kindness*, for example, characteristically leads its possessor to act helpfully. *Bravery* characteristically prevents an agent from giving up on important goals out of fear.

Virtues seem conceptually linked to some end that they typically (perhaps necessarily) promote (e.g. Foot, 1994; Thomson, 2008). This seems to follow from the fact that they are defined as dispositions or capacities to produce certain characteristic effects. It is unclear how we could regard these dispositions to produce certain outcomes as *virtues* if we did not regard the outcomes produced as normatively salient as well. Nonetheless, virtues deserve to be treated as distinct structural features of a normative system, because, despite the link to teleological structures, they are not necessarily derivative of such structures. In some cases, they are explanatory of them. Patience is a virtue in chess, because it makes its possessor more likely to achieve the end of chess. But within some normative systems, a certain state may be an end or intrinsic good of that system because it is the characteristic product of a certain virtue. A work of art may be aesthetically superior, for example, in virtue of being the product of the artist's creativity or expressing her skill and talent.

Two points are worth making. First, we have already noted that ends and virtues are conceptually linked. The linkages go further than this, however. Considerations, for example, will be entailed by both ends and requirements. Roughly, if some outcome is an end within a normative system, then any facts in virtue of which response R promotes that end will be considerations in favor of R. Similarly, if there is a requirement, facts in virtue of which some response satisfies that requirement will be considerations in favor of that response. By the same token, to know that a consideration within some system favors response R is to know that, within the system, R is good in some way. We can construct teleological or consideration structures out of deontic structures. It may not follow, however, that a required option is always *better* within the relevant system. The system of requirements may be inconsistent, requiring and forbidding the same act. In that case, the option will simply be worthy of promotion, though also worthy of avoidance. It will be an open question whether, in that system, the good of the option outweighs the bad.

Facts about requirements thus imply facts about considerations, ends, and virtues. Does the entailment go the other way? Do facts about considerations, ends, or virtues imply facts about what a normative system requires? There is reason to think that they do not. It may seem that once you know which option there is most reason to take, or which option is best within the normative system, you know which option is required. But if morally supererogatory actions exist, then there are actions—such as throwing oneself on a live hand grenade to save others—that are morally best and have the most moral considerations in their favor but are not morally required. Chess arguably works this way as well. The rules of chess define what it is to win or lose, and moves can be evaluated in light of that. The rules of chess do not forbid losing, however, and suboptimal moves are not illegal.

These facts about entailments among normative structural kinds still leave open questions about which kinds are more explanatorily basic. Presumably, this will vary with the normative system in question. The law is fundamentally a system of requirements. The norms of chess show an interesting hybrid structure (as do the rules of most games): ends are to be promoted, but within the constraints set by the rules. What is fundamental in morality, epistemology, and practical reason is the subject of systematic normative theorizing in those areas.

The second point to note is that none of these normative structures is *sufficient* for making a normative system authoritative. This is unsurprising if one kind of structural property entails the existence of others (if requirements entail the existence of ends or considerations). But even possessing some structure *fundamentally* is not enough to entail the authority of the normative system. As noted above, etiquette and the standards of judging in beauty pageants are plausibly made up of lots of prima facie considerations that people are supposed to put together into a holistic assessment of what would be polite or of who is most conventionally beautiful. That we can talk about a good knife or a good thief indicates that neither teleological- nor virtue-structures are unique to authoritative systems (cf. Thomson, 2008: chapter 3, 9–10; chapter 5). The rules of games have requirement structures, and these are paradigmatically formally normative systems.

As to whether any of these structural properties—or, more precisely, the normative fundamentality of any of these structural properties—is *necessary* to authoritativeness, this is a substantive philosophical problem. In the debates on the nature of practical and theoretical reason, philosophers have endorsed reasons-fundamentalism (Scanlon, 1998; Parfit, 2011), treating various aims—such as truth, desire-satisfaction, and realizing the good—as fundamental (Velleman, 2000; Alston, 2005; Tenenbaum, 2007; Finlay, 2009) and treating virtues as fundamental (Setiya, 2007). And for Kant, at least, practical reason was a matter of acting according to maxims.

It may be that no fundamental structure is necessary to a normative system's authoritativeness. This would be the case for two or more authoritative normative systems that are structurally unalike. Kieran Setiya (2007) has argued that practical reason cannot be modeled off theoretical reason. Action or intention have no substantive aim, and so practical reason will be, at the normatively fundamental level, a matter of virtues (or "good dispositions of practical thought"); theoretical reason, on the other hand, has a substantive aim of discovering truth.

Some philosophers seem to assume that epistemology must have a deontic structure if it is to succeed in telling us what beliefs to have (see Goldman [1999] for this reading of a number of prominent epistemologists). But, especially in light of the above, it is not clear why this would be so. If epistemology only offered virtues, aims of belief, or considerations, some conclusions would still be epistemically superior to others—or some beliefs would be better or worse justified—even if none were unjustified *full stop*. The thought may be that instances of theoretical reasoning—attempts to appreciate evidence and arguments—could not be correct or incorrect unless some conclusions were required and others forbidden. That is in some sense, however, the position of the theorist who denies epistemology has a deontic structure: instances of reasoning are *more* or *less* correct rather than simply right or wrong (cf. Alston, 2005; also, see Railton, 1988, for an analogous position on morality). There may also be a worry that if epistemic normativity only provides evaluations of conclusions but does not forbid some and mandate others, nothing compels us to reach the better-supported conclusions. But nothing compels us to reason well anyway: normative *obligations* can be flouted—and often are—and epistemic normativity, deontic or not, does not generate its own police force.

Procedural and Substantive Norms

Another distinction in normative systems has to do with those that provide substantive prescriptions or evaluations versus those that are purely procedural. The difference can be understood as between those normative systems that tell us to take a certain stance towards the world and its objects, as opposed to those that tell each agent to reach a certain kind of agreement with herself. For example, morality prescribes certain actions, goals, and attitudes. It tells you to keep your promises and refrain from murder. It also tells you not to desire to murder, but it goes on to tell you that even if you do desire to murder, you should refrain anyway. Instrumental rationality, on the other hand, does not mandate any actions or aims at all. It instead tells you how your aims should fit together: for example, you should desire those states that you believe are more likely to promote the satisfaction of other states you desire. But as long as your desires meet *that* structure, the actual objects of your desire are a matter of indifference as far as instrumental rationality is concerned. And insofar as instrumental rationality prescribes actions, these will be those actions that best fit with your desires. Refraining from murder when murder's what you most desire is instrumentally irrational.

The procedural versus substantive distinction is at the heart of debates about the nature of reason, both theoretical and practical. Within epistemology, a central dividing line is between coherentists and foundationalists. Coherentists hold that beliefs are justified by how well they fit in or agree with the rest of one's beliefs. Foundationalists hold that certain foundational beliefs—which are responsible for justifying all others—are justified in virtue of how they relate to the world, either being based on certain forms of evidence, or having certain epistemically privileged content. Within debates about practical reason, the *internalist-externalist* debate about reasons is effectively a debate about whether reasons for action follow from one's practical attitudes—wants, desires, and other motives—plus certain procedural or coherence-based standards that tell us how to derive prescriptions from a given set of such attitudes; or whether certain facts about the world give reason for action (or reason for intention or desire) independently of what agents do or would intend or desire.

It is worth noting a puzzle that arises when one holds that an agent's reasons for action, belief, and so on are substantive and not explained by what would make the agent more coherent or by what follows procedurally given certain prior attitudes. The normative status of rational coherence itself becomes contentious. On the one hand, it is normal to characterize rational coherence in terms of requirements. It seems like a requirement of rationality, for example, to not believe both p and $\sim p$ simultaneously. It seems like a requirement of rationality that one take the most effective means to one's most highly ranked end. We call people irrational, it seems, because they violate these requirements; and "irrational" seems like a criticism.

But problems immediately arise. First, if rational coherence is normative, then horrible people have very strong reasons to do horrible things. As noted above, it may be instrumentally irrational for some agents to refrain from murder; but the idea that their powerful desires to kill make it true that they *should* murder is bizarre (Broome, 1999). Second, it is unclear why rational coherence would be *that* important. Some of my beliefs are inevitably inconsistent. Who cares? (Kolodny, 2005).

The debate is vast, and most of it is outside the scope of this chapter (for an excellent overview, see Way, 2010). Two potential solutions to the problem are, however, of importance in this discussion. First, it may seem like an obvious solution to propose that rational coherence is normative but only formally so—and a solution along these lines can be found elsewhere (Broome, 2007). Jonathan Way (2010) objects, however, that all the formally normative systems with which we are familiar are contingent normative systems. But the requirements of rationality seem to be necessary, and those necessary norms with which we are familiar seem to all be authoritative. (This objection will be assessed below in a discussion of the distinction between contingent and necessary norms.)

Nicholas Southwood (2008), on the other hand, has argued that rational coherence possesses a distinctive, *sui generis* form of authoritative normativity that neither reduces to nor explains substantive reasons for action or belief. One might wonder how rational coherence could be authoritative without being based on reasons, but it should be kept in mind that the authoritativeness of reasons themselves has never been explained (except in the trivial sense that philosophers use "reasons" to mean those considerations, whatever they are, that happen to be authoritative). It is unclear, then, why special explanation would be called for before conjecturing that other normative systems possess independent authority. To put it another way, "authority" may pick out a disjunction of properties, a point Southwood (2008: fn. 53) alludes to when he mentions the possibility of normative incommensurability between what rational coherence requires of a subject and what substantive reasons for action and belief prescribe.

That said, Southwood's (2008) proposal is inconsistent with a powerful motivation for proceduralist or coherentist theories of reasons—namely, that of giving a reductive account of authority, one that explains authority in terms of our *experience* of certain normative demands as authoritative.[1] Agents who are instrumentally irrational fail to do what they can to make the world as they want it to be. But this means that those who fail to follow the instrumental principle will experience their choices as defective or inferior in a very visceral sense. Possibly this can be generalized. If norms of rational coherence are norms I must follow to be in agreement with myself, then plausibly any violation of them will strike me as a genuine mistake: it is mistaken by my own lights. There are admittedly difficulties here. If I am in disagreement with myself and thus committed to thinking my choice was a mistake, I must also then think it was correct—otherwise, no disagreement. Presumably some attitudes are outliers, and so the overall weight of my perspective will be towards regarding the choice as one or the other. The question is whether this idea can be spelled out in theoretically satisfying detail or left at the level of metaphor.

Neither being substantive nor procedural is *sufficient* to make a normative system authoritative, and whether either half is *necessary* is a matter of philosophical debate—as the debates between coherentists and foundationalists, or reasons-internalists and externalists, demonstrate. It may seem, however, that either one or the other must be a necessary condition on being authoritative, even if we do not yet know which one. But readers should notice that Southwood's (2008) proposal puts even that into question.

Constitutive versus Non-Constitutive Norms

Some norms constitute the very activities, actions, or states that they govern; others do not. The classic example of the former is the rules of chess. For two people to play a game of chess, their moves must conform, at least generally, to the rules of chess. If both players simply flouted or ignored the rules, whatever they were doing could not be regarded as a game of chess.

On the other hand, criminal law is generally not constitutive of the actions it proscribes. One man can kill another in the absence of laws regarding homicide. Law may be constitutive of other actions, however: incorporating a business or voting in an official election, for example.

The distinction is straightforward, but constitutive norms present a mystery. If a system of norms is constitutive of the governed activity, how can it be normative? If we do not follow the rules of chess, we are not playing chess. But if we are not playing chess, the rules do not tell us what to do. On the other hand, if we are playing chess, we are following the rules of chess, so the prescriptive nature of the rules seems otiose.

The solution is to recognize this as an overly strong reading of the idea of a constitutive norm. The claim that the rules of chess are constitutive should not be understood as denying the conceptual possibility of cheating. Rather, moves in a game of chess must *generally* and *for the most part* accord with the rules of chess if they are to count as moves in a game of chess. Cheating must be episodic to be possible. This is also true of sports games, such as football, in which illegal conduct by players cannot be taken back and does not always result in forfeiture of the match; rather, violations of rules are met with penalties. What's more, the referees will not catch every violation. Obviously, in this case, it is possible to have a game in which some actions violate the rules. Nonetheless, if the rules were completely ignored, the resulting activity would no longer count as a football match.

In light of this, we can see how it is not simply deontic normative structures that can be constitutive of their governed object but also teleological structures (Velleman, 2000; Korsgaard, 2008). The function of a heart is to pump blood; the aims of chess are to checkmate one's opponent and avoid being checkmated. But this does not mean that with a heart attack the muscle tissue in one's chest ceases to be a heart, nor that with an inept queen sacrifice one has ceased to play chess. It means that making a series of "moves" that are legal but otherwise chosen at random, without any discernible aim of advancing victory or forestalling defeat, does not count as playing chess. Likewise, a heart has many structural components working together, and some may remain conducive to pumping blood while others are defective in some way. It is only if many aspects of the organ are defective that it ceases to be a heart and is instead a pulpy mass or tumor where a heart should be. (Admittedly, there will be vagueness about where the cut-off point between heart and tumor belongs.)

One may object here that the constitutive relation so described is a very weak relation. But this is not an objection if such a weak relation exists, though it may be grounds for objecting to attempts to use the constitutive relation to *explain* authoritative normativity.

It may seem that being constitutive is not sufficient for being authoritative, since the rules of chess are both paradigmatically constitutive and formal. But this overlooks a possibility: the rules of chess are authoritative *for chess*. There is no authoritative requirement that I play chess, but if I am playing chess, then questioning the authority of its rules makes no sense: I am committed to these rules in virtue of my activity. Now, I can escape this authority by avoiding the game in the first place. But if there are activities that I cannot avoid—if, by analogy, there are constitutive norms of action or belief—these will be authoritative and inescapably so (Korsgaard, 2008).

There are reasons why we should be sympathetic to this constitutivist strategy for explaining normative authority—most notably, it would be an *explanation*. However, the weakness of the constitutive relation makes it doubtful it could bear the requisite explanatory weight. Returning to the chess example, the intention of playing a game of chess does not commit me to following the rules of chess *simpliciter*. Rather, it commits me to following the rules *enough* (Dreier, 1997).[2] So the authoritative prescriptions we can derive from the constitutive nature of the rules of chess seem only to prohibit *excessive* cheating.

Following the analogy, insofar as I act or form beliefs, I am committed to responding to reasons for action or reasons for belief to a degree sufficient that I count as an agent. But this is consistent with ignoring such reasons, so long as I don't cease to be an agent—which is no danger for all but the extremely mentally ill (cf. Kolodny, 2005: 545).

What is more, this all seems to assume that I *should* aim to be an agent. But that "should" must be authoritative if it is to explain the authority of meeting those requirements instrumental to being an agent. But then we have assumed, rather than explained, authoritative normativity (cf. Enoch, 2006). Finally, the constitutivist strategy seems to conflate normative with psychological inescapability (e.g. Enoch, 2006).

Necessary versus Contingent Norms

Normative facts can either be necessary or contingent. For example, most philosophers have held that moral truths are necessary (but see Harman, 1975). It may be that whether a particular act of lying is wrong is contingent—but this is because of the contingent circumstances in which the act is performed. Specific moral prescriptions derive, however, from more general moral principles that hold necessarily. If lying in these circumstances is wrong, it could not be that lying in these circumstance could have been right. On the other hand, the laws of the state of California are contingent. They may forbid smoking in bars, but they could have allowed it and even did at one point.

Notice that some normative systems can be grounded in social convention and yet still apply necessarily to the activities within their "jurisdictions." Obviously, the state of California can survive changes to its legal code. But would a game in which the knight could move diagonally still be chess? Not if the rules of chess are constitutive of the game. So if there are constitutive norms, they apply necessarily to the activities they govern. Constitutive normative systems are trivially necessary.

Consequently, that a normative system is necessary does not imply that it is authoritative. Way (2010) claims that all familiar cases of formal normativity involve contingent normativity. But this is a mistake. As the case of chess shows, constitutive rules necessarily apply to instances of the constituted activity, and constitutive rules can possess only formal normativity. This is not a narrow point. As noted earlier, Way uses the claim that necessary normative systems are authoritative to argue against Broome's (2007) suggestion that rational coherence might be merely formally normative. But rational coherence is plausibly constitutive of agency (Davidson, 1985), and thus we would have an explanation of its necessary character that made no appeal to authoritativeness.

Can contingent norms, on the other hand, be authoritative? Possibly. Perhaps I can form personal, existential commitments to certain otherwise formally normative rules or ends, making them authoritative for me (see Frankfurt, 1999; for positions in the neighborhood, see Chang, 2009). There is natural pressure, of course, to explain the authority of such commitments in terms of some necessary normative system. Practical reason, for example, might prescribe sticking by prior commitments, all else being equal. Thus, it is not really a case of a contingent yet authoritative norm but of the application of a necessary normative system to contingent circumstances.

But perhaps this misrepresents the phenomenon. Harry Frankfurt (1999) argues that we do not experience the normative authority of personal commitments as deriving from the impersonal authority of reason but as something potentially in conflict with reason. Again, as with Southwood's (2008) proposal about rationality, this seems to imply that *authority* itself names a disjunction of properties: there are in fact distinctive kinds of authority. Given that 'authority' is a placeholder for a set of connected but admittedly obscure phenomena, we should not rule this possibility out, though it risks making our theories less parsimonious.

SKEPTICISM ABOUT NORMATIVE AUTHORITY[3]

There are reasons for skepticism about the existence of normative authority. It is not simply that it is unclear what would explain authoritativeness. This is not any different than any other area of philosophy (claims about what explains intentionality or even the existence of everyday composite objects are hardly uncontroversial)—and in any case, authority could turn out to be a non-natural property. In fact, the non-naturalist intuition that the normative is "just too different" from the natural to be a special instance of it (Enoch, 2011; see also Parfit, 2011) is plausibly intended as a claim about those normative facts with the obscure property of *really* telling people what to do (cf. Tiffany, 2007: 259–60).

The problem rather derives from the obscurity of what is meant by "authority." We had to indicate what we were after by using "really," not in the sense of genuineness but in that special sense that is only conveyed through italics, scare quotes, or table-thumping; or else we had to resort to metaphor ("grip," "normative force"), which remains unpacked. Of course, we should be careful here—the demand that we unpack our metaphors or table-thumps can sound like the demand for a definition of "authority" *in advance of our theory of it*, and this would make all theorizing impossible. The metaphor and italics were not a definition; they were to help us catch on. "Authority" is a term of art, but it is drawing a distinction we were already implicitly aware of in practice—or so the non-skeptic can claim.

There are more specific reasons for the skepticism, however. First, it is easy to offer a debunking account of our intuitions of authority. This argument follows Mill's (1863/1998) argument explaining our sense that certain moral requirements are in some sense *necessary*. Growing up, we face punishment and social sanction for ignoring certain kinds of norms but not others. We internalize this compulsion and come to associate it with the relevant normative standards. These standards do not have any authority themselves (because there could not be such a property), but we naturally come to project our own subjective feelings of being compelled onto the objects that excite such feelings. It is worth noting that our ways of indicating the phenomena of authoritativeness used metaphors of compulsion like "getting a grip on us" and "normative force" (also see Foot, 1972: 308 ff.).

Second, it is not at all clear that what's being called "authority" is really the same property in every normative system. Morality is intuitively authoritative, as is epistemology. But consider the "force" of morality. It seems tied to a number of very hot emotions, such as anger, guilt, disgust, shame, pride, and compassion. In the case of epistemic norms, on the other hand, the "force" feels quite different. It is simply psychologically very difficult for us to bring ourselves to believe what we acknowledge to be badly supported by evidence. Aesthetic norms are plausibly authoritative, but in a still different way: one is missing out, and is perhaps a little annoying, if one is insensitive to them. Prudence is authoritative, but that seems to be in the sense that one ignores it at one's own peril. We already saw as well the suggestion that norms of psychological coherence and personal commitment possess distinctive forms of authority, different from that possessed by substantive reason. We could finally add that while it is generally treated as merely formally normative, someone facing a life sentence could be forgiven for thinking the law authoritative. The plethora of plausibly authoritative norms, the dissimilarities in their phenomenology, and the presence of borderline cases all give reason to doubt that there is any single phenomenon of authoritativeness at work here; rather, we face a host of formally normative systems, each with its own different form of psychological or sociological *relevance*. Evan Tiffany (2007) calls this position *deflationary normative pluralism*.

Notice that both arguments explain our sense that certain norms are authoritative in terms of psychological reactions. Some inchoate sense of this possibility is probably a motivation for various forms of subjectivism, response-dependence, and expressivism about authoritative normativity. This would be an instance of the standard strategy of answering skepticism with some form of idealism or deflationary (quasi-)realism about the subject matter—that is, answering skepticism about a target phenomenon by making it ontologically dependent on our responses to it or, in the case of quasi-realist forms of expressivism, denying that any standpoint from which we could question the reality of phenomenon is possible (on semantic grounds).

The idealist maneuver may be supported in this particular case by more than just epistemic worries. Critics have complained that, besides the standard worries—epistemic and metaphysical—that accompany any form of non-naturalism, in the normative case positing non-natural properties is objectionable because it is beside the point—a kind of non sequitur (Jackson, 1998; Korsgaard, 2003). Non-naturalism, it seems, contributes nothing to understanding the authoritativeness of certain forms of normativity. On a stone tablet it is written, *thou shalt not kill*. It tells me what to do, but so what? Well, let's add that the tablet is not in fact stone but is actually made of immaterial Platonic ether existing eternally outside space and time. But again, so what? Stone tablets are arguably *more* imposing: immaterial ether never smashed anyone's head. Simply positing non-naturalness does nothing to explain how these norms succeed in *really* telling us what to do. The idealist maneuver looks more attractive in the light of this worry, because it can seem that there is no "force" a normative system could possess save the impact it has on agents' psychologies.

There is a third reason for skepticism about normative authority, for which idealism looks less relevant as a reply. It is very hard to communicate what the term "authority" is supposed to refer to without falling into inadvertent and seemingly vicious circularity. Let's say morality is authoritative and etiquette is not. Let's say further that in this case they conflict: the first telling me to confront my host's racist bile, and the second to change the subject. It is natural to think that the authoritative prescription *overrides* or *trumps* the merely formal prescription. But what does this mean? Given our stipulation, it does not mean that the action is not impolite.

It is very natural to say that this talk of overriding or trumping means the demands of morality are *more important* than those of etiquette, or that one ought to listen to morality rather than etiquette, or that it is much *worse* to be immoral than rude. But these are all normative characterizations—and from what system do these evaluations come? If the only way of characterizing normative authority is in further normative terms, then we are not characterizing anything at all. Merely formal systems will endorse themselves (or at least some will) or will be endorsed by some other merely formal system. Etiquette presumably requires that I heed the prescriptions of etiquette. But then it follows that the fact that one ought to obey the ought of system A rather than the ought of system B does not imply that system A has any special feature at all—certainly nothing that could be unique to authoritative systems (cf. Copp, 1997: 101 ff.).

All of this is to say that we need some other way of saying what it is for one normative system to trump another; or we need some other way of indicating the phenomenon we have in mind. Otherwise talk of *normative authority* is among that class of confusions which Lionel Trilling, in a different context, named "irritable mental gestures which seek to resemble ideas (Trilling, 1950)."

There is admittedly an assumption in the above that all prescriptions are system-relative, but it isn't clear that this is avoidable.[4] Consider the idea of an *all-things-considered ought*. At first glance, this ought is issued from a particular normative system, albeit one that takes the verdicts of certain other normative systems as inputs. But it is unclear how this latter fact would help us characterize what the authority of the all-things-considered ought consists in. Perhaps there is a better way of characterizing the all-things-considered ought, but what?[5]

This skepticism is different, because it doesn't challenge our justification for believing in authority. It challenges whether we are justified in believing we possess a coherent concept corresponding to this term—that is, whether we ever really were implicitly aware in practice of any distinction that the term is supposed to make explicit.

I want to conclude with two brief points about another possible response to skepticism about authority—namely, error-theory about normative authority. Is this something we could live with?

We could still admit a wide range of normative facts. There are the rules of chess, the reasons of epistemology, the demands of morality, and so on. We can still tell people that murder is wrong. We can still debate whether acting wrongly could ever be reasonable and whether the reasonable reduces to the rational. We can worry about the reduction-base of various normative systems. Some normative systems could turn out to be constitutive of agency. Some may be written on tablets of Platonic ether. These would be philosophically interesting properties. What none of them should be identified with, however, is any sort of normative superiority (Tiffany, 2007). *Superiority*, after all, is a normative notion, and so it must be system-relative. If reason and morality conflict, then the virtuous man will be a fool and the wise man will be a sinner. But which is worse? Well, morally it is worse to be a sinner, but from the point of view of reason it is worse to be a fool (Hubin, 1999).

This all seems fine until I am trying to deliberate about what to do. Should I be wise? Should I be good? Perhaps that question can only be settled arbitrarily. But does that mean I *should* settle the question arbitrarily? Well, the answer is obviously *yes*. What worries me is that it's just as obviously *no*.

NOTES

1. This is inspired by the accounts of practical reasons found in Hubin (1999) and Street (2008, especially pp. 239–42).
2. Note that Dreier does not take this objection to be decisive. His answer, however, is outside the scope of this chapter.
3. Beyond specific points or arguments, the general concerns of this section I owe in large part to Copp (1997, 2004), Hubin (1999, 2001), and Tiffany (2007).
4. Thanks to Matti Eklund for pushing me to address this point.
5. Or see Thomson (2008: chapter 10) for a rejection of system-relative prescriptions, precisely because their existence would seem to open up problems such as this one.

ACKNOWLEDGMENTS

Research appearing in this chapter was partially funded by a grant from the Research Grants Council of Hong Kong Special Administrative Region, China (LU342612). Thanks to Matti Eklund, Tristram McPherson, David Plunkett, Lea Schroeder, and Jack Woods for comments and criticism.

REFERENCES

Alston, W. (2005) *Beyond "Justification": Dimensions of Epistemic Evaluation*, Ithaca, NY: Cornell University Press.

Broome, J. (1999) "Normative Requirements," *Ratio* 12(4): 398–419.

Broome, J. (2007) "Requirements," in T. Rønnow-Rasmussen, B. Petersson, J. Josefsson, & D. Egonsson (eds.) *Hommage à Wlodek: Philosophical Papers Dedicated to Wlodek Rabinowicz*, www.fil.lu.se/hommageawlodek.

Chang, R. (2009) "Voluntarist Reasons and the Sources of Normativity," in D. Sobel & S. Wall (eds.) *Reasons for Action*, Cambridge: Cambridge University Press.

Copp, D. (1997) "The Ring of Gyges: Overridingness and the Unity of Reason," *Social Philosophy and Policy* 14(1): 86–101.

Copp, D. (2004) "Moral Naturalism and Three Grades of Normativity," in P. Schaber (ed.) *Normativity and Naturalism*, Frankfurt: Ontos-Verlag.

Davidson, D. (1985) "Incoherence and Irrationality," *Dialectica* 39: 345–54.

Dreier, J. (1997) "Humean Doubts about the Practical Justification of Morality," in G. Cullity & B. Gaut (eds.) *Ethics and Practical Reason*, Oxford: Oxford University Press.

Enoch, D. (2006) "Agency, Shmagency: Why Normativity Won't Come of What Is Constitutive of Action," *Philosophical Review* 115(2): 169–98.

Enoch, D. (2007) "An Outline of an Argument for Robust Metanormative Realism," In R. Shafer-Landau (ed.) *Oxford Studies in Metaethics* 2: 21–50. Oxford: Oxford University Press.

Enoch, D. (2011) *Taking Morality Seriously: A Defense of Robust Realism*, Oxford: Oxford University Press.

Feldman, R. (2000) "The Ethics of Belief," *Philosophy and Phenomenological Research* 60(3): 667–95.

Finlay, S. (2009) "Oughts and Ends," *Philosophical Studies* 143(3): 315–40.

Foot, P. (1972) "Morality as a System of Hypothetical Imperatives," *Philosophical Review* 81(3): 305–16.

Foot, P. (1994) "Rationality and Virtue," *Vienna Circle Institute Yearbook* 2: 205–16.

Frankfurt, H. (1999) "Autonomy, Necessity, and Love," in *Necessity, Volition, and Love*, Cambridge: Cambridge University Press.

Goldman, A. (1999) "Internalism Exposed," *Journal of Philosophy* 96(6): 271–93.

Harman, G. (1975) "Moral Relativism Defended," *Philosophical Review* 84(1): 3–22.

Hubin, D. (1999) "What's Special about Humeanism?" *Noûs* 33(1): 30–45.

Hubin, D. (2001) "The Groundless Normativity of Instrumental Reason," *Journal of Philosophy* 98: 445–68.

Jackson, F. (1998) *From Metaphysics to Ethics: A Defence of Conceptual Analysis*, Oxford: Oxford University Press.

Kolodny, N. (2005) "Why Be Rational?" *Mind* 114: 509–63.

Korsgaard, C. (2003) "Realism and Constructivism in Twentieth-Century Moral Philosophy," *Journal of Philosophical Research* 28: 99–122.

Korsgaard, C. (2008) *The Constitution of Agency: Essays on Practical Reason and Moral Psychology*, Oxford: Oxford University Press.

Lord, E. & Maguire, B. (eds.) (2016) *Weighing Reasons*, Oxford: Oxford University Press.

McPherson, T. (2011) "Against Quietist Normative Realism," *Philosophical Studies* 154(2): 223–40.

Mill, J. S. (1863/1998) "Utilitarianism," in R. Crisp (ed.) *Oxford Philosophical Texts*, Oxford: Oxford University Press.

Parfit, D. (2011) *On What Matters, Volume 1*, Oxford: Oxford University Press.

Railton, P. (1988) "How Thinking about the Character of Utilitarianism Might Lead to Rethinking the Character of Utilitarianism," *Midwest Studies in Philosophy* 13: 398–417.

Scanlon, T. (1998) *What We Owe to Each Other*, Cambridge, MA: Belknap Press of Harvard University Press.

Setiya, K. (2007) *Reasons without Rationalism*, Princeton, NJ: Princeton University Press.

Southwood, N. (2008) "Vindicating the Normativity of Rationality," *Ethics* 119(1): 9–30.

Street, S. (2008) "Constructivism about Reasons," in R. Shafer-Landau (ed.) *Oxford Studies in Metaethics*, vol. 3, Oxford: Oxford University Press, 207–45.

Tenenbaum, S. (2007) *Appearances of the Good: An Essay on Practical Reason*, Oxford: Oxford University Press.

Thomson, J. J. (2008) *Normativity*, Peru, IL: Open Court.

Tiffany, E. (2007) "Deflationary Normative Pluralism," *Canadian Journal of Philosophy* 37(5): 231–62.

Trilling, L. (1950) *The Liberal Imagination*, New York: Viking Press.

Velleman, J. D. (2000) "On the Aim of Belief," in *The Possibility of Practical Reason*, Oxford: Oxford University Press.

Way, J. (2010) "The Normativity of Rationality," *Philosophy Compass* 5(12): 1057–68.

37

Pragmatism and Metaethics

Andrew Sepielli

Among analytic philosophers, pragmatism tends to elicit two reactions that might seem to stand in tension with one other. The first reaction is confusion about what pragmatism *is*, exactly. The second is steadfast rejection of it.

It's easier to reconcile these disparate responses when we consider that pragmatism tends to show up under two different guises. The first is as a woolly gestalt, expressed through support for experiment, democracy, fallibilism, and solidarity, and condemnation of authoritarianism, representationalism, Cartesianism, and dogmatic metaphysics. The second is as the simple doctrine that truth is what's good *in any way whatsoever* to believe. In its first guise, pragmatism tends to provoke confusion; in its second, rejection. As a result, pragmatism occupies at best a precarious position within the mainstream of analytic philosophy. Its influence on contemporary metaethics has been especially weak.

My target reader for this chapter, then, is someone who is familiar with the basic problem-spaces in contemporary metaethics and the moves commonly made within those spaces but who is not already sympathetic to pragmatism. I want to help such a reader to make sense of pragmatism in some of its many guises, to appreciate both its subtlety and its power as a philosophical stance, and to understand its bearing on some of the main debates within metaethics.

WHAT IS PRAGMATISM?

Let me begin by offering a characterization of pragmatism that will cover as many of those commonly called "pragmatists" as possible without being so capacious as to be useless. First, let us say that to be a pragmatist, one must focus in one's inquiry on normative and evaluative questions concerning thought and its expression. Now, this alone doesn't make one a pragmatist; if it did, then anyone who worked on, say, norms of assertion would count as one. So, let us add a second condition: to be a pragmatist, one must take one's theorizing about the norms of thought and expression to obviate the need to vindicate our practices by appeal to at least some of the first-order metaphysical claims that other philosophers think such vindication rests on. Pragmatism, then, is both (1) focused on norms and values, and (2) anti-metaphysical. Furthermore, its anti-metaphysical stance is *due to* its focus on norms and values; a philosopher whose anti-metaphysical stance is not driven by explicitly normative or evaluative considerations—for example, a certain sort of logical positivist—is for that reason not a pragmatist.

Now, different pragmatists will couple this focus with different stances towards things like truth, knowledge, rationality, and so on. Some may want to give a positive account of truth in terms of the practical significance of a belief or set of beliefs. Of these, some will go the extra step of saying that claims do not become true until their practical significance is actually manifested (James, 1907; Dewey, 1911). Others will offer not so much a theory of truth as something rather weaker—an elucidation of what happens when you believe something true or something false (see Misak's [2013] discussion of Pierce [1878]). Still others will adopt the stance that we can't say anything illuminating in general about truth, and so partly for that reason we should focus instead on practical utility *as an alternative* (Rorty, 1982: introduction). Others might say that we ought to focus on practical consequences *in lieu* of things like truth even if we *can* offer an illuminating account of the latter, since the former are just more worthy of our focus.

A characterization of pragmatism in terms of "focus" may strike you as unsatisfying if you're looking instead for some philosophical *thesis* that pragmatists, qua "-ists," all believe in. But as a matter of the sociology of ideas, pragmatists are united more by the aforementioned focus, plus their views about its anti-metaphysical significance, than by any philosophical thesis. I would also say that an insistence on theses as opposed to focuses is just the kind of thing that many pragmatists will reject. From my point of view, at least, the difference between a pragmatist who purports to ground truth in practical significance and one who wishes to scrap talk of truth for talk of practical significance is of little, well, practical significance and as such does not merit our focus.

Because I've defined pragmatism as a stance according to which the need for first-order metaphysics is obviated, I want to try to introduce the different pragmatisms by considering them as departures, to various extents, from a sort of metaphysically-inflected position that is very common in Anglo-American metaethics. I call this view "archetypal realism" and characterize it in terms of four more specific commitments, which I label "Correctness," "Domain-External/General," "Subject-Object," and "Structure." Then I will start "cutting" commitments and see, with each cut, what views we end up with in philosophy generally and in metaethics specifically. Additionally, I will try to show how the various sorts of pragmatism provide rationales for dropping the various commitments.

PRAGMATISM AS A DEPARTURE FROM ARCHETYPAL REALISM

Let's start with the archetypical realist's *focus*. Like everyone, she will see that thought and talk can be good or useful in lots of different ways. A belief can be good in the sense that holding it makes me happy. A spoken sentence can be bad in the sense that it is offensive.

But in her role as a philosopher, the archetypical realist's focus on the value of an item will be mainly on whether it is good qua the kind of item it is—for example, whether a belief is good in the way that beliefs, specifically, can be good. There are different ways of explicating the notion of a belief being good in this way. We might talk about its function or "aim," or about its being supported by (conclusive) object-given, as opposed to state-given, reasons (see Parfit, 2001). But it's easiest to understand the archetypical realist's focus as follows: it is on whether a belief is *correct*, such that a belief's being true is the paradigmatic way of its being correct, and its making its holder happy is not a way of being correct. Call the commitment to this focus *Correctness*.

The archetypical realist will *also* think there's some domain-external or at least domain-general explanation you can give of a belief's correctness conditions. By "domain-external," I mean that the explanation does not merely advert to facts internal to the domain that the belief is *about*. So, for example, an explanation of the correctness of the belief that causing pain is wrong that simply went "Causing pain *is* wrong," would not be domain-external, nor would an explanation that went "Causing pain is regarded as wrong by virtuous people." Now, of course, if the belief in question is *about* the correctness of beliefs or about the things that make them correct, it's going to be difficult for anyone to give a domain-external explanation of their correctness. Any explanation of this sort will be within the domain of the belief. But we can nonetheless, perhaps, give a domain-*general* explanation of such beliefs—"general" in that it explains not only *their* correctness but also that of beliefs about giraffes, bosons, numbers, seasons, and swag. Call this commitment *Domain-External/General*.

The archetypical realist will also have a particular view about the *content* of these domain-general or domain-external explanations—namely, a view on which the correctness of a belief or a claim is a matter of the relation between things like thought and talk, on the one hand, and *the world* more generally, on the other. This relation is the sort that may obtain between things on the "subject" side of the subject/object divide and things on the "object" side, like reference or truth-making. This may be contrasted with a view on which what explains the correctness of a belief or claim is a matter of relations that can obtain only *between* thoughts, utterances, and other broadly "subjecty" things—for example, the relation of rational commitment. Call this archetypal realist commitment *Subject-Object*.

Finally, the archetypical realist has a view about the *kind* of Subject-Object connection that explains a belief's correctness and, correspondingly, about what the *relata* on the "object" side are. Specifically, the view is that a belief is correct on the grounds that the world is structured in a way that corresponds to the syntactic structure of the belief's content (or to the paradigmatic expression of that content). Consider the belief that Barry is tall. Our archetypical realist would explain the correctness of this belief by adverting to an individual, Barry, corresponding to the subject-term "Barry," and Barry's having the property of being tall, corresponding to the predicate "is tall" (see MacBride, 2013). (She might further explain Barry's having this property by appealing to his having the property of being 6'7" in height, but this latter property is not what explains, in the relevant way, the truth of the belief.) Call this last commitment *Structure*.

If the archetypal realist applies this set of commitments to ethical thought, she arrives at either moral realism (if she believes the world does contain moral properties of the right sort) or error theory (if she believes it does not).

CUTTING STRUCTURE

Let us see what a view would look like that kept Correctness, Domain-External/General, and Subject-Object, but cut Structure. Such a view would focus on the correctness of the thought that, say, water is wet and offer a domain-external or domain-general explanation of that correctness in terms of the value or usefulness of that thought—but, importantly, without invoking the property of wetness.

The most obvious way of doing that is to offer what, following William James (1907: 512), I'll call an "instrumental" account of truth—one that explains the correctness of a belief in terms of the values of the thoughts and practices that the belief enables. (Views of broadly this sort appear in James, 1907; Dewey, 1911; Ramsey, 1927; van Fraassen, 1980; Whyte, 1990; Blackburn, 2005.) Now, it seems to me that some such accounts allow us to avoid metaphysics only in part. I have in mind those views that purport to explain the correctness of a belief by appealing to the truth of *other*, in some sense more "basic," beliefs or to the veridicality of experiences, which are in turn explained in the archetypical realist manner—by finding properties to match predicates, and so on. I'm also thinking of views that appeal, ultimately, to the satisfaction of desires, where this is a matter of the truth of their propositional contents, which is explained, again, by finding properties to match predicates, and so on. The first strategy might ground the truth of a belief that there's a hole in the bucket by appealing to the truth of beliefs formed on the basis of it: for example, that water placed in the bucket will escape. The second strategy might ground the same by appealing to the fulfillment of desires by actions done on the basis of the belief: for example, I might choose to put my water in another bucket instead, which will fulfill my desire of not having water escape. In each case, I am purchasing the right to avoid the metaphysics of holes by indulging in the metaphysics of water and escaping (see Thomasson, 2015). (So far, then, pragmatism hasn't delivered on what many take to be its aim—to give us a metaphysical "free lunch.")

Other views, however, may allow us to avoid the metaphysics of properties through accounts of predictive accuracy and desire-satisfaction that avoid truth and therefore truth-*makers* entirely. Jerry Fodor (2007) has argued that we can make sense of the idea of a *non-conceptual* representation being accurate without settling questions of ontology. Because such representations lack logical forms, they can't express predication and quantification, and a representation's ontological commitments are determined by its predicative and quantificational structure (Fodor, 2007: 109; cf. Balog, 2009). Consider the difference between pictorial and discursive representation. Suppose first that a book describes Caligula as doing "an evil deed." One can imagine a moral error theorist saying that this description is, strictly speaking, false, since nothing is good or evil. One can also imagine an austere metaphysician who believes there are no such things as actions objecting to the positing of a "deed." That these different theorists disagree shows that discursive representations like a book carry ontological commitments. But now imagine that a painting depicts what I, qua skeptic about neither morals nor actions, would call "an evil deed." It seems that all three of the theorists just described could agree that the painting accurately represents reality.

This points the way towards an "instrumental" theory of true belief that avoids properties on the "object" side altogether. We might explain a belief's truth in terms of the non-conceptual representational accuracy of predictions formed on the basis of it;

and we might explain the same in terms of the satisfaction of desires, understood in non-conceptual terms as well (see Sepielli, 2016). (The latter view allows us to avoid the strange result that the degree to which my desires are satisfied depends upon whether there *really are* tables, or just particles arranged tablewise, say; or on whether a "vodka martini" *really is* a martini.)

What does this all have to do with metaethics? Well, we might imagine that, in certain contexts, ethical thoughts could be useful to prediction in just the way that non-ethical ones can be. Recall Nicholas Sturgeon's (1985) famous case involving Selim Woodworth—the midshipman whose bad character, Sturgeon argued, can help us to explain his lack of success as leader of the Donner Party rescue mission. But what can be a basis for explanation can, in principle, serve as a basis for prediction and control as well. Had those in charge of putting together the rescue team known in 1846 that Woodworth was, in one historian's words, "no damned good," they could have predicted his failure and would have been in a position to avoid it.

You may be skeptical that this really demonstrates the truth of a belief that Woodworth is a bad guy. This belief may be useful in a context in which you don't already have beliefs about Woodworth's tendencies, described non-ethically—but if we already have enough of this other information in mind, the additional belief that he's a bad guy seems to afford no more predictive or practical value than the belief that he's a *good* guy. This might make us think that the belief's content is not so much true as it is a fiction that's convenient in some contexts of inquiry and action.

It seems to me that there are two ways for the pragmatist to address this skepticism. One is to tell some story other than the "instrumental truth" one according to which the "good guy" belief, rather than the "bad guy" one, is correct even in this context of inquiry. We'll look at two very different sorts of stories along these lines in the next two sections. The other option is to show how ethical thought and talk can add either predictive or practical power even when the thinker's mind is replete with relevant non-ethical beliefs.

This might be possible if there are representational attitudes to which ethical thoughts bear a special relationship. And indeed, it seems that there may be. For while ethical thoughts and non-ethical ones alike can play a role in prediction, or in guiding action in accordance with our desires, ethical ones seem uniquely positioned to mediate our *emotions*, and it is at least arguable that emotions themselves are representational. However, most of those who've argued for the representational theory of emotion have held that emotions are representations with conceptual content and that the concepts contained are ethical (Solomon, 1993; Nussbaum, 2001). This doesn't seem like a promising *domain-external* way of vindicating ethics. But lately some have defended the view that emotions are *non-conceptual* representations (Gunther 2003; Tappolet 2003). If that is right, then it allows us, perhaps, to say that moral beliefs are true insofar as they form the basis for emotions that accurately represent the world non-conceptually. In doing so, not only would we not have to posit ethical properties—we wouldn't have to posit *any* properties.

To summarize, then, it seems that we might sidestep the metaphysics of *morality*, specifically, by conceiving of the correctness of an ethical judgment "instrumentally"—as the basis for a further, correct representation or else for a successful action. Additionally, we may be able to avoid the metaphysics of truth-making *generally* by accounting for the correctness of representations or the satisfaction of desires in terms of a match between their *non-conceptual* content and the world.

CUTTING SUBJECT-OBJECT

Now, let's cut the next of the traditional realist's commitments—Subject-Object. One might think that this can't really be done if we want to maintain Correctness, for how else can we explain the correctness of a belief, ethical or otherwise, except by saying something about how it hooks up with the world? Two ways suggest themselves.

One is adopted by constitutivist writers like Kant and Habermas. Kant (1785: book 3) famously argues that we are rationally committed to accepting the categorical imperative by features that are constitutive of something very basic—our agency. Habermas (1990) tells us that we are committed to accepting a set of criteria for the correctness of moral norms by virtue of something that is almost as basic, and perhaps more generative of substantive commitments—our participation in moral discourse. It is no part of their arguments that the agent be hooked up correctly with the world.

Habermas, at least, is explicit in labeling his view as "pragmatist," and he cites as inspiration for it C. S. Pierce's (1878) gloss on truth as what is settled upon at the end of idealized, social inquiry. But Habermas is equally explicit in denying that that his project of "communicative ethics" offers us a theory of ethical truth (1990: 52–57). Especially in his later work, he characterizes truth as requiring some Subject-Object connection (Habermas, 2003; see also Levine, 2011). He argues, however, that claims about rightness can nonetheless be "valid" just in virtue of being the ones we'd agree upon in accordance with discourse-constitutive criteria. The ultimate tribunal for a "rightness" claim is not the world, generally, that we should understand such a claim as describing; rather, the tribunals are ourselves, albeit ourselves as rational participants in discourse. Habermas writes:

> Moral beliefs do not falter against the resistance of an objective world that all participants suppose to be one and the same. Rather, they falter against the irresolvability of normative dissensus about opposing parties in a shared social world.
>
> (2003: 248)

Another way to drop Subject-Object while maintaining Correctness and Domain-External/General is to embrace something like Robert Brandom's inferentialist program. On Brandom's view, we explain when the application of a concept is correct by appealing to the propriety of social, discursive behavior involving that concept—moves in the "game of giving and asking for reasons" for our commitments. Brandom is not concerned to metaphysically reduce these norms to anything non-normative or to state the content of the norms in non-normative vocabulary. He is comfortable, then, with there being "norms all the way down," such that the "sanctions" for fallacies and poorly supported claims are nothing other than diminutions in deontic status—"internal" sanctions, as he calls them, rather than "external" ones. Brandom is concerned to account for semantic phenomena through a rich explanatory picture, but not to dispel any perceived air of "mystery" involving the normative as such (Brandom, 1994a).

So far there's been no sign of the extra-linguistic world on Brandom's picture, and no mention of any constitutive features (of agency, say, or of discourse) that might rationally commit us to certain beliefs. We might wonder, then, how any norm of the aforementioned sort could be correct or incorrect. Brandom brings in the world in two ways. First, he recognizes that what might *cause* us to make, support, accept, or reject an assertion is something about the external world. He is not imagining us as floating in an isolation chamber, tossing around assertions. It is just that what *makes* an assertion correct or incorrect is the network of norms governing discursive behavior, rather than the existence of truth-makers for that assertion. Second, Brandom ingeniously tries to get a subject-object connection "out the back end," as it were: among the many, many things we talk about are representational phenomena like truth, objectivity, representation, and so on. Insofar as he provides an account of what makes assertions correct generally, this applies to assertions about these Subject-Object notions from which we can read off facts about when, in fact, a claim is true, or represents the world accurately, and so on (Brandom, 1994a; cf. Price, 2011).

Brandom's work has made its way into metaethics through writers like Matthew Chrisman. As Chrisman (2008) conceives of it, inferentialism is an alternative to both realism and expressivism in explaining the meanings of ethical expressions. The realist will want to say that what makes an expression an ethical one is the sort of property it represents objects as having—namely, an ethical property. The expressivist will want to say that what makes an expression ethical is the kind of mental state it expresses—namely, a pro-attitude or a plan or whatever the story is. The inferentialist rejects the realist's representationalism and the expressivist's "psychologism," holding instead that the meanings of expressions are explanatorily prior to the contents of mental states they express, and that the former are explainable in the manner described above—by their standing vis-à-vis a network of norms of public discursive behavior.

Now, Brandom labels his work "pragmatist"—but on what grounds? The idea seems to be this: Brandom's focus is on concept use as a kind of activity and on the norms governing this activity, and he believes that in so focusing he can skirt metaphysical questions of the sort that seem to confront the moral realist. It is important to be clear on what *kind* of pragmatism this is, though: first, the inferentialists are focused on only a particular *kind* of action—discursive action; and second, they are focused only on a particular kind of *value* that this action may have—the kind of value that is proprietary to linguistic action, the kind that inheres in correct or well-supported assertions.

This focus makes sense given the inferentialists' (semantic-theoretic) aims—and indeed, Brandom (1994b) has criticized the aforementioned project of trying to ground correctness of use in the instrumental value of the actions, generally speaking, that a thought produces. But it is open to other pragmatists to have theoretical projects other than semantic ones, and thus to focus on actions more generally and value more generally.

CUTTING "DOMAIN-EXTERNAL/GENERAL"

The view that I call "quietism" differs from traditional realism in that not only does it fail to offer an explanation of how moral thoughts represent the world in terms of moral properties; and not only does it fail to offer an explanation in terms of a relationship between the mind and the world; but it fails to offer *any* general explanation in terms of representation, or rationality, of why some ethical views are correct and others aren't. In other words, quietism is what we get when we drop not only Structure and Subject-Object but also Domain-External/General.

The "neo-pragmatist" Richard Rorty gives voice to metaethical quietism in his rejection of attempts to provide "foundations" for human rights and moral theories generally, on which he offers the following gloss:

> Foundationalist philosophers, such as Plato, Aquinas, and Kant, have hoped to provide independent support for [moral theories]. They would like to infer these … from further premises, premises capable of being known to be true independently of the truth of the moral intuition which have been summarized [by the theories]. … To claim such knowledge is to claim to know something which, though not itself a moral intuition, can *correct* moral intuitions.
>
> (Rorty, 1998: 171)

Notably, Rorty doesn't reject the idea that some moral views are better than others; he is not a nihilist. Nor does he accept categorization as a subjectivist or relativist. What he rejects is the project of trying to ground the idea that some moral views are better in terms that are not themselves moral. Rorty does so at least partly on the jarringly pragmatic grounds that providing foundations for things like human rights isn't actually a very effective way to make opponents of a human rights regime into supporters. We, the supporters of human rights broadly construed, ought to abandon this project in favor of sentimental education or, just generally, whatever *works*. Rorty says that we cling to the foundational project for the very same reason he once yearned for the ability to prove to the schoolyard bullies that they should not torment him—out of a desire for power, to bring about change through domination (in this case in argument) rather than playing on the sentiments of the powerful (Rorty, 1998: 182; see also Nietzsche, 1901: book 1).

There is something very appealing, to me at least, about this stance—of considering the development of domain-external vindications of ethics as just another thing one could do with one's time, and judging it, *on practical grounds*, not a very good or helpful thing to do. Still, one might worry that unless someone *could* do this, it can't be the case that some moral claims are correct, or better than others, or anything like that. After all, it seems on the face of it that we *can* provide these sorts of domain-external vindications of claims within other domains—specifically, I'm thinking, by adverting to the link between such claims and a believer's ability to predict or control the world, but also, perhaps, by providing some other non-trivial account of which cognitive defects those on the wrong side of an ethical debate have exhibited (see Wright, 1992). Even if the interest in providing domain-external foundations in ethics can be attributed to power-lust, it nonetheless may be that the existence of such foundations is required for there to be any correct claims in ethics.

There are different ways to answer this question, perhaps the most prominent of which come from metaethicists working in the Wittgensteinian tradition (e.g. McDowell, 1979; Crary, 2009). But let me offer a sketch of an answer along more traditionally pragmatist lines.

Recall the earlier worry about my initial deployment of the Woodworth case: the belief that Woodworth is "no damned good" is predictively and practically useful only in contexts in which the thinker is presumed to believe (or at least, occurrently believe) little about, say, Woodworth's mental makeup and past deeds. But some moral inquiry— and, we might fairly say, particularly *fundamental* moral inquiry—takes place against the background of a great many beliefs about the non-moral facts; we are asking about the normative significance of those very facts. In those contexts, we observed, it's not clear that any moral conclusion helps us to predict the world and bring about the general fulfillment of our desires more than any other.

What, then, would be a sensible thing to say about moral conclusions reached in these contexts? It seems to me that these instances of moral inquiry are akin to certain non-moral debates that many would label "merely verbal" or "nonsubstantive." James (1907) provides the classic example of the latter: two people agree that a man is chasing a squirrel around a tree and are at odds about whether he is truly going "around the squirrel." In this case, as in the moral one, it does not seem that either answer will help or hurt our overall ability to predict and control the world.

Both in cases of fundamental ethical inquiry and in cases of "nonsubstantive" non-evaluative inquiry, I am inclined to think that there can be no domain-general or domain-external vindication of any answer as worthy of acceptance. This is because, as a pragmatist, I think that such a vindication would have to account for the links between such answers and predictive/control value, but in the contexts in which these debates occur, there are no such links (see Stich [1990] on similar themes). No such value is afforded by any answer. In cases like James's squirrel debate, though, I am also inclined to say that there will generally be *no grounds whatsoever* for designating either answer as meriting acceptance. I and others will want to say, further, that "It doesn't matter" and "You could go either way."

This is not, however, what I'd want to say about fundamental ethical debates. I would not say of the debate between the sadist and his opponent, "You could go either way." Rather it seems like the resolution of the debate matters; it matters in a way that is specifically moral. These disputes, we might say, are *important* without being *substantive*; they're ones in which value is afforded by the outcome, but not predictive/control value—just plain old moral value. In these debates, then, I'm inclined to say that anti-sadism is preferable in that accepting it affords more value than does acceptance of sadism. But its preferability cannot be explained from "outside" of ethics, for such an explanation would, in my view, have to also explain how a belief in anti-sadism, formed in the relevant context of inquiry, contributes to its holder's ability to predict and control the world. And we've seen that it doesn't (see Sepielli, 2017).

So the pragmatist-quietist will say, expressing her ethical judgment, that sadism is wrong. Pressed as to *why*, she may express more ethical judgments—about the badness of pain, about our obligations to others, and so on. But if she is asked what makes these judgments the right ones, and is debarred from further expression of ethical judgments, she will say nothing other than what makes the judgment that the man truly is going "around the squirrel" the right one—that is to say, nothing.

CUTTING CORRECTNESS

The most radical view emerges as we drop the last of the archetypal realist's commitments: Correctness. On this view, our focus in asking about anything—a belief, a desire, an emotion, a speech act—should be on its value, generally, or the all-things-considered reasons in its favor. This approach views all things instrumentally: a belief is thought of as just one more tool, alongside and in competition with anything else, that might help us to pursue the good and avoid the bad. This view does not say that we should not ultimately care about a belief's or assertion's correctness at all, although some who hold it might say that. It says only that we ought not to focus on correctness exclusively, or mostly, or necessarily.

There are two ways we might work ourselves into such a focus, it seems to me—one more theoretical, the second more practical. The more theoretical one goes like this:

> Some philosophers write as though all action is mediated by these *re*-presentations of the world in our heads. But whether we look at the phenomenology or the physiology, it doesn't seem like it really works that way (unless we twist the notion of representation beyond recognition). Most of the time, we just sort of, well, *cope* with the world, engaging in little trials and errors, enacting little feedback-and-response cycles that are not mediated by any representation. So philosophy's traditional focus on accurate representations—for example, on true belief—is out of proportion given representation's really quite limited role in human action. And not only is representation less ubiquitous than is commonly thought, it is also less fundamental. The capacity to represent the world can only be fully explained by invoking other, more "primitive" capacities. Our theorizing should focus on what's explanatorily more fundamental.

This stance has roots going back at least to Aristotle, and its defenders include John Dewey (1925, 1929); Martin Heidegger (1927) and his followers (e.g. Dreyfus, 1990; Haugeland, 2013; Dreyfus & Taylor, 2015); and the various proponents of anti-representationalist cognitive science and artificial intelligence (Beer, 1990; Brooks, 1991; van Gelder, 1995; Thelen & Smith, 1994; Chemero, 2011; an excellent philosophical look at work like the foregoing is Clark, 1997).

The more practical path towards a focus on value generally can be put simply:

> There is simply no ground for discounting, as theorists, the non-veritistic value that a belief has or helps bring about. After all, it's *value*, right? Additionally, it is arguable that other sorts of value are more important than the veritistic sort, and even that there is no such thing as veritistic value independent of these other sorts of value—specifically, practical and predictive value. So a near-exclusive focus on whether a belief is correct reflects an assignment of values—deliberate or not—that is mistaken.

But how, exactly, does dropping Correctness make a difference to *ethical* theorizing? One might think that when we're dealing with beliefs about what's valuable, surely the most valuable of these beliefs for a person to have will generally be the one that's *true*.

We are familiar, though, with the distinction between the correctness of a moral theory and the usefulness of that theory as a guide to action. For example, some writers reject utilitarianism as a moral theory on the grounds that it is an inadequate guide to action. Utilitarians typically respond either by arguing that (some sort of) utilitarianism can serve as a good guide to action, or by denying that a theory's usefulness in directly guiding action is really all that pertinent to its correctness.

One thing that both sides tend to agree on, if only tacitly, is that the question of a view's correctness is primary—that what ethics is really, fundamentally about is which theory is right. Usefulness bears on acceptability just insofar as it bears on correctness.

A certain sort of pragmatism is concerned to reject this picture of ethical theorizing. No philosopher has understood and articulated the consequences of this rejection better than Dewey. The following passage from *The Quest for Certainty* gives compelling expression to his radical reimagining of ethical inquiry:

> Instead of being rigidly fixed, [moral rules] would be treated as intellectual instruments to be tested and confirmed—and altered—through consequences effected by acting upon them. They would lose all pretence of finality.
>
> ...
>
> The transformation does not imply merely that men are responsible for acting upon what they profess to believe; that is an old doctrine. It goes much further. Any belief … is not just to be acted upon, but is to be *framed* with reference to its office as a guide to action. … When it is apprehended as a tool and only as a tool, an instrumentality of direction, the same scrupulous attention will go to its formulation as now goes into the making of instruments of precision in technical fields.
>
> (Dewey, 1929: 277–8)

The question that others see as secondary—"Which cognitive tools would be most effective to solve *this* problem, *here, now* (although it may be a temporally extended problem)?"—is what Dewey regards as paramount.

It seems, nonetheless, that we do often take a stand on which ethical theories are correct. We do this explicitly, as the culmination of ethical inquiry as understood by much of the philosophical tradition—and indeed, it is plausible to think that we must do this implicitly, even in Deweyian inquiry, as part of our assessment of the candidate theories and tools. For even if we manage to get ourselves in the mindset where we stop thinking about a theory's correctness and start thinking about its value as a tool, don't we judge its value as a tool by the lights of some background theory or disjunction of theories? And don't we thereby implicitly treat these theories as correct?

The Deweyian will regard the explicit inquiry into correctness as mistaken, except on the off-chance that this practice really does furnish *us*, what with our various limitations, with the best tools for solving practical problems as they arise. Dewey was also concerned, in his later work, to provide debunking genealogies of our concern to settle on a final, correct theory in ethics and in other domains (see Dewey, 1929: chapter 1; see also Koopman, 2011).

As to the background ethical views to which we appeal in Deweyian inquiry, it is open to question why we should think of agents as implicitly treating these theories as correct. One would need to hear why we should not, instead, think of agents as implicitly treating *these theories, too*, as useful tools—tools for assessing tools, or "meta-tools," you might say. But suppose we do say that even the Deweyian inquirer must, at some level, represent theories as correct. It matters, I think, how we theorize about this alleged necessity. We all recognize some patterns of thinking as *heuristics* with respect to the truth—implementable procedures that tend, over the long term, to maximize the probability of arriving at the truth for beings like ourselves. Similarly, we might think of Dewey as regarding represen-tational activity as a heuristic with respect to value. I think of the Deweyian ideal agent as a kind of super-*phronimos*, who we might imagine as turning to the good without the intermediate, usually costly, step of representing some view of the good as correct in just the way a sunflower turns to the sun without representing the sun as being here or there. We mere humans, without a sunflower-like ability to immediately track the good, track it mediately at best. But the Deweyian would say that it is distortive to think of mediating representations as objects of fundamental philosophical concern, rather than simply as a kind of crutch upon which limited beings may occasionally rely.

ACKNOWLEDGMENTS

Thanks to Tristram McPherson, David Plunkett, and James Fritz for their helpful comments on this chapter.

RELATED TOPICS

Chapter 8, "Realism and Objectivity;" Chapter 27, "The Autonomy of Ethics;" Chapter 41, "Metaethical Quietism."

REFERENCES

Balog, K. (2009) "Jerry Fodor on Non-Conceptual Content," *Synthese* 167(3): 311–20.
Beer, R. (1990) *Intelligence as Adaptive Behaviour*, San Diego, CA: Academic Press.
Blackburn, S. (2005) "Success Semantics," in H. Lillehammer & D. H. Mellor (eds.) *Ramsey's Legacy*, Oxford, UK: Oxford University Press, 22–36.
Brandom, R. (1994a) *Making It Explicit*, Cambridge, MA: Harvard University Press.
Brandom, R. (1994b) "Unsuccessful Semantics," *Analysis* 54(3): 175–8.
Brooks, R. (1991) "Intelligence without Representation," *Artificial Intelligence* 47: 139–59.
Chemero, A. (2011) *Radical Embodied Cognitive Science*, Cambridge, MA: Bradford Books.
Chrisman, M. (2008) "Expressivism, Inferentialism, and Saving the Debate," *Philosophy and Phenomenological Research* 77(2): 334–58.
Clark, A. (1997) *Being There: Putting Brain, Body, and World Together Again*, Cambridge, MA: MIT Press.
Crary, A. (2009) *Beyond Moral Judgment*, Cambridge, MA: Harvard University Press.
Dewey, J. (1911) "The Problem of Truth," in L. Hickman & T. Alexander (eds.) *The Essential Dewey, Volume 2: Ethics, Logic, Psychology*, Indianapolis: Indiana University Press, 101–30.
Dewey, J. (1958) [1925] *Experience and Nature*, London: Dover Publications.
Dewey, J. (1960) [1929] *The Quest for Certainty*, New York: Putnam Publishing Group.
Dreyfus, H. (1990) *Being-in-the-World: A Commentary on Heidegger's Being in Time, Division I*, Cambridge, MA: Bradford Books.
Dreyfus, H. & Taylor, C. (2015) *Retrieving Realism*, Cambridge, MA: Harvard University Press.
Fodor, J. (2007) "The Revenge of the Given," in B. McLaughlin & J. Cohen (eds.) *Contemporary Debates in the Philosophy of Mind*, Malden, MA: Blackwell, 105–16.
Gunther, Y. (2003) "Emotion and Force," in Y. Gunther (ed.) *Essays on Nonconceptual Content*, Cambridge, MA: MIT Press, 279–88.
Habermas, J. (1990) "Discourse Ethics: Notes on a Program of Philosophical Justification," in *Moral Consciousness and Communicative Action*, trans. by C. Lenhardt & S. W. Nicholsen, Cambridge, MA: MIT Press, 43–115.
Habermas, J. (2003) *Truth and Justification*, Cambridge, MA: MIT Press.
Haugeland, J. (2013) *Dasein Disclosed: John Haugeland's Heidegger*, Cambridge, MA: Harvard University Press.
Heidegger, M. (1962) [1927] *Being and Time*, trans. by J. MacQuarrie, New York: Harper & Row.

James, W. (1995) [1907] *Pragmatism*, London: Dover Publications.

Kant, I. (1785) [2009] *Groundwork of the Metaphysics of Morals*, trans. by H. J. Paton, New York: Harper Perennial.

Koopman, C. (2011) "Genealogical Pragmatism: How History Matters for Foucault and Dewey," *Journal of the History of Philosophy* 5(3): 533–61.

Levine, S. (2011) "Truth and Moral Validity: On Habermas' Domesticated Pragmatism," *Constellations* 18(2): 244–59.

MacBride, F. (2013) "Truthmakers," *Stanford Encyclopedia of Philosophy*, available at: https://plato.stanford.edu/entries/truthmakers/.

McDowell, J. (1979) "Virtue and Reason," *Monist* 62(3): 331–50.

Misak, C. (2013) *The American Pragmatists*, Oxford: Oxford University Press.

Nietzsche, F. (1968) [1901] *The Will to Power*, trans. by W. Kaufman & R. J. Hollingdale, New York: Vintage.

Nussbaum, M. (2001) *Upheavals of Thought: The Intelligence of Emotions*, Cambridge, MA: Cambridge University Press.

Parfit, D. (2001) "Rationality and Reasons," in D. Egonsson, J. Josefsson, B. Petersson, & T. Rönnow-Rasmussen (eds.) *Exploring Practical Philosophy*, Burlington, VT: Ashgate, 17–40.

Pierce, C. S. (1878) "How to Make Our Ideas Clear," *Popular Science Monthly* 12: 286–302.

Price, H. (2011) *Naturalism without Mirrors*, Oxford: Oxford University Press.

Ramsey, F. P. (2010) [1927] "Truth and Probability," in R. B. Braithwaite, (ed.) *The Foundations of Mathematics and Other Logical Essays*. London: Routledge and Kegan Paul, 156–98.

Rorty, R. (1982) *Consequences of Pragmatism*, Cambridge, MA: Cambridge University Press, 167–85.

Rorty, R. (1998) "Human Rights, Rationality, and Sentimentality," in *Truth and Progress: Philosophical Papers*, Cambridge, MA: Cambridge University Press.

Sepielli, A. (2016) "Moral Realism without Moral Metaphysics," in R. Shafer-Landau (ed.) *Oxford Studies in Metaethics*, vol. 11, Oxford: Oxford University Press, 265–92.

Sepielli, A. (2017) *Significance without Substance: A Defence of Pragmatist Quietism in Meta-Ethics*. On file with Andrew Sepielli, Toronto, ON.

Solomon, R. (1993) *The Passions: Emotions and the Meaning of Life*, 2nd rev. edn, Indianapolis: Hackett Publishing.

Stich, S. (1990) *The Fragmentation of Reason: Preface to a Pragmatic Theory of Cognitive Evaluation*, Cambridge, MA: MIT Press.

Sturgeon, N. (1988) [1985] "Moral Explanations," in G. Sayre-McCord (ed.) *Essays on Moral Realism*, Ithaca, NY: Cornell University Press, 229–55.

Tappolet, C. (2003) "Emotions and the Intelligibility of Akratic Action," in S. Stroud & C. Tappolet (eds.) *Weakness of Will and Practical Irrationality*, Oxford: Oxford University Press, 97–120.

Thelen, E. & L. Smith (1994) *A Dynamic Systems Approach to the Development of Cognition and Action*, Cambridge, MA: MIT Press.

Thomasson, A. (2015) *Ontology Made Easy*, Oxford: Oxford University Press.

Van Fraassen, B. (1980) *The Scientific Image*, Oxford: Oxford University Press.

Van Gelder, T. (1995) "What Might Cognition Be If Not Computation?" *Journal of Philosophy* 92(7): 345–81.

Whyte, J. T. (1990) "Success Semantics," *Analysis* 50(3): 149–57.

Wright, C. (1992) *Truth and Objectivity*, Cambridge, MA: Harvard University Press.

FURTHER READING

For critical introductions to pragmatism generally, see Misak (2013, cited above); R. Bernstein (2010), *The Pragmatic Turn*, New York: Polity Press; H. S. Thayer (1973), *Meaning and Action: A Critical History of Pragmatism*, Indianapolis, IN: Bobbs-Merrill. For more on pragmatist metaethics, see D. Heney (2016), *Toward A Pragmatist Metaethics*, London: Routledge; S. Pihlstrom (2005), *Pragmatic Moral Realism: A Defence*, Amsterdam: Rodopi; C. Misak (2000), *Truth, Politics, and Morality*, London: Routledge. For reading on pragmatism and ethics more broadly, see S. Fesmire (2003), *John Dewey and Moral Imagination: Pragmatism in Ethics*, Bloomington, IN: Indiana University Press; T. Lekan (2003), *Making Morality: Pragmatist Reconstruction in Ethical Theory*, Nashville, TN: Vanderbilt University Press; J. Welchman (1997), *Dewey's Ethical Thought*, Ithaca, NY: Cornell University Press. Finally, I recommend to anyone with an interest in moral psychology G. H. Mead, *Mind, Self, and Society*, ed. by C. Morris, Chicago, IL: University of Chicago Press.

38

Feminism and Metaethics

Amia Srinivasan

INTRODUCTION

Feminism is first and foremost a political project: a project aimed at the liberation of women and the destruction of patriarchy. This project does not have a particular meta-ethics; there is no feminist consensus, for example, on the epistemology of moral belief or the metaphysics of moral truth. But the work of feminist philosophers—that is, philosophers who identify with the political project of feminism, and moreover see that political project as informing their philosophical work—raises significant metaethical questions: about the need to rehabilitate traditional moral philosophy, about the extent to which political and moral considerations can play a role in philosophical theorizing, and about the importance of rival metaethical conceptions for first-order political practice. I discuss some of the contributions that feminist philosophy makes to each of these questions in turn. I hope to call attention to the way in which feminist thought bears on traditional topics in metaethics (particularly moral epistemology and ethical methodology) but also to how feminist thought might inform metaethical practice itself.

I should say from the outset that this is by no means a complete taxonomy of all the metaethical issues raised by feminist philosophy or feminism. Given the richness of not only feminist philosophy but the entire feminist tradition, such a task is beyond the scope of this chapter. But I do hope to offer some sense of the significant metaethical questions thrown up by feminism and feminist philosophers.

REHABILITATING TRADITIONAL MORAL PHILOSOPHY

Extant moral philosophy (like all philosophy) is largely the product of men, and men operating under patriarchal assumptions: the inherent superiority of men to women; the inherent superiority of the symbolically masculine over the symbolically feminine (reason over emotion, individual over community, mind over body); and the centering of male experience as normative or ideal, with female experience (if attended to at all) treated as marginal, aberrant, or non-ideal.

Recognizing this, how should the feminist moral philosopher (or indeed any moral philosopher suspicious of patriarchy) proceed? One radical proposal is to repudiate extant moral philosophy as a hopelessly masculinist project, necessarily bound up with the subordination of women. We can distinguish two different forms of this radical stance. On the first view—call it the 'radical political critique'—the very project of *theorizing* morality, as opposed to embracing it as a form of lived practice, is antithetical to the project of women's emancipation. The theoretical stance, with its idealization and cool remove, is one that (powerful) men take up in order to entrench their privilege; women (and other subordinated groups), meanwhile, must jettison theory and embrace practice in order to secure their political emancipation. Unsurprisingly, this isn't a view that feminist philosophers, qua philosophers, typically endorse, though it is certainly a view endorsed by some feminists. (There are of course many moral philosophers, feminist and not, who think that moral theorizing, done properly, should not resemble 'theory' in the scientistic sense of the term [e.g. Murdoch, 1970; Williams, 1985; Rorty, 1999]. But I take it that insofar as these philosophers write systematic and dense texts, they do not eschew theory entirely, just 'theory' in the pejorative, scientistic sense.) I will later return to the relationship between philosophical theory and feminist political practice.

On a second view—call it the 'radical epistemic critique'—extant moral philosophy is *epistemically* contaminated and condemned by its bad origins in patriarchy: because extant moral philosophy is (at least in part) the product of a distorted worldview (viz. patriarchy), it must be false. This sort of view runs the risk of committing the genetic fallacy, making a bad inference from a feature of the context of theory-construction to a claim about the truth of the theory. Suspect contexts can produce true theories, and vice versa. That said, reflecting on the 'bad' origins of a philosophical theory can give us strong reason to think that our belief in it is unjustified. If it turns out that we believe a theory merely because it is conducive to patriarchy, then we might be required to abandon the belief—just as learning that we formed a belief on a hallucinogenic drug might very well require us to abandon that belief. But such debunking claims must be vindicated in a piecemeal fashion, by showing in each case how the forces of patriarchy have distorted our ethical or metaethical theorizing in a way that renders a particular received theory epistemically suspect. Thus, the radical epistemic critique gives way to a moderate epistemic critique, according to which moral philosophy need not be entirely jettisoned but instead *rehabilitated*.

Much of the work done by feminist ethicists can be characterized as taking this moderate or rehabilitative approach. Below, I detail some aspects of this proposed rehabilitation.

New Topics, Themes, and Questions

As a political practice, feminism is deeply concerned with women's experience: what it is like, what concepts we need to capture it, and how we can transform it. In feminist ethics, this concern with women's experience most obviously means a shift in the topics seen as appropriate for ethical theorizing towards topics of particular concern to women, including rape, pornography, objectification, the family, pregnancy, and motherhood. Where these topics have already been discussed in mainstream ethical theory, feminist ethicists often draw attention to new aspects of them, aspects neglected because of the male bias of those doing the theorizing. For example, in the case of pornography, which had already been the subject of philosophical debate before the rise of feminist ethics, ethicists typically focused on whether it was morally permissible to *consume* pornography, and thus implicitly took up a male perspective. Feminist philosophers have shifted the debate by attending to how pornography affects women, both as participants in the production of pornography and as foci of sexualized objectification (MacKinnon, 1989, 1993; Hornsby, 1983; Langton, 2009; Bauer, 2015). Thus, feminist ethicists remind us that even when mainstream ethicists attend to 'women's topics', the very questions they find interesting are motivated by particular, often privileged perspectives.

The development of feminist ethics has been much influenced by Carol Gilligan's (1982) argument that ways of moral reasoning are gendered, with men typically concerned with issues of rules, justice, individualism, and autonomy, and aspiring to abstraction and universalism; and women typically concerned with issues of care, interpersonal relationships, and the emotions, and more focused on the particular and the contextual. While Gilligan's claim has been subject to much feminist criticism for involving suspect empirical generalizations that re-enforce patriarchal gender stereotypes (Card, 1995; Houston, 1987; Bartky, 1990; Moody-Adams, 1991), it nonetheless catalyzed a turn in feminist ethics towards dimensions of ethical reality that are culturally associated with the feminine—including the moral psychology of emotions, especially the 'negative' emotions (e.g. Narayan, 1988; Jaggar, 1989; Tessman, 2005; Bell, 2009; cf. Lorde, 1984), and the ethics of interpersonal relationships (e.g. Noddings, 1984; Benhabib, 1992; Friedman, 1993; Baier, 1995; Held, 1995; Hekman, 1995). This work in turn threatens the related distinctions between the personal and the political, and between ethics and politics.

Power, and its particular role in the subordination of women—but also, crucially for many feminists, its role in the subordination of other oppressed groups—has been another central focus for feminist ethicists, particularly radical, Marxist, multicultural, postcolonial, global, lesbian, phenomenological, psychoanalytical, postmodern, and third-wave feminists. Some of the many questions about power that feminists raise are: what is the value of choice in women's liberation? What is the relationship between my subordination qua woman and other axes of subordination (e.g. class, race, disability status)? In what ways do some women subordinate others? What is the relationship between patriarchy and state-sponsored violence? What conditions (the psychodynamics of the family, society's need for reproduction) give rise to and sustain the ideology of patriarchy? How does liberation differ for different women? What relationship ought women have to culturally enforced gender expectations? What does it feel like to be constructed as a woman? What are the possibilities for moral agency under patriarchy? Does it even make sense to talk of 'women' as a group, or is this merely to participate in a renewed subordination of those who do not neatly fit our proposed category? For discussion of some of these questions, and many others, see Irigaray (1985a, 1985b), hooks (1981), Lugones and Spelman (1983), Moraga and Anzaldúa (1983), Spivak (1988), Fraser (1989), MacKinnon (1989), Young (1990), Butler (1990), Frye (1991), Mouffe (1992, 1993), Kristeva (1995), Ackerly and Okin (1999), Mitchell and Mishra (2000),

Narayan and Harding (2000), Benhabib (2002, 2008), Gould (2004), Mahmood (2005), Zerelli (2005), and Krause (2008).

It is important to note just how very diverse the topics, questions, and themes addressed by feminist ethicists are, and how inaccurate the common identification of feminist ethics with 'care ethics' is.

New Starting Points: Experience and the Non-ideal

The centrality of women's experience to feminism has not only meant a proposed shift in topics for ethics; it has also meant a proposed shift in how we theorize those topics. In particular, many feminist ethicists have argued that ethics must start from actual, lived experience. We can distinguish in this demand at least two claims: one about the proper *objects* of ethical theorizing, and a second about the kind of *evidence* or *methods* appropriate to ethical theorizing.

Idealization is central to ethics in at least three senses. First, in being a branch of *normative* theory—that is, the branch of philosophy concerned with how things ought to be—ethics invokes various normative ideals, such as justice, fairness, caring, and emancipation. Second, like all philosophical (as well as social/natural scientific) theorizing, ethics involves a certain amount of abstraction; in order to theorize a given phenomenon, ethicists imagine a paradigm case of whatever they wish to discuss—abortion, disability, charitable donation—stripping away incidental details to leave only (what they take to be) the phenomenon's essential properties. Third, ethics often involves idealization, in the sense that it offers theories about how things ought to be without saying much about how they actually are (Mills, 2004).

Both the second and third kinds of idealization have been criticized by feminist philosophers. For example, Nancy Bauer has recently argued that feminist debate about pornography is hampered by its refusal to consider the phenomenology of pornography: what it is to watch and moreover be aroused by it, for both men and women (Bauer, 2015). In so doing, Bauer accuses feminist philosophers of having changed the subject, from pornography as it really is to a hypothetical pornography that has few if any real instantiations. Similarly, we might worry that mainstream philosophical debates that think about abortion as the mere wilfull destruction of a human fetus—rather than as an act that takes place within a social context of deep gender inequality—again idealize to the point of subject-changing (Jaggar, 1997). In both cases, the worry is not with abstraction as such—after all, to make any general claim about a real phenomenon, we must represent it and thus ignore some of its properties—but with the kind of abstraction that deforms the real thing into a purely philosophical construct. Philosophizing about philosophical representations that differ greatly from the objects represented can lead to substantive mistakes about what we ought to do in our actual circumstances.

The third kind of idealization—describing how things ought to be while not paying attention to how far short actuality falls from that hypothetical ideal—has come under attack, most notably by Onora O'Neill (1987), Charles Mills (2004) and Catharine MacKinnon (2012). According to Mills, the problem with ideal theory (in the third sense of 'ideal') is that in neglecting to discuss the histories of subordination, oppression, inequality, and violence that shape our highly non-ideal realities, ideal theory does not guide us towards any achievement of the (putative) ideal. Indeed, Mills suggests that ideal theory serves to re-enforce the non-ideal status quo, constituting an ideology that serves the interests of socioeconomically privileged white men—that is, the interests of most philosophers. MacKinnon suggests something similar when she writes:

> One cannot help wondering why some schools of philosophy have become a place where what something actually does is not considered pertinent to the exploration of what it could or might do. Life is not a game of logic, an argument's plausibility is not unaffected by the social reality to which it refers, and power's denial of abuse is not a function of not having read a philosophical proof that such abuse is possible.
>
> (MacKinnon, 2012: xv)

In his critique of ideal theory, Mills takes it as self-evident that ethics aims not only to describe the moral ideal but to provide some practical guidance on how to enact it. He writes: "Nor could it seriously be claimed that moral theory is concerned only with mapping beautiful ideals, not their actual implementation. If any ethicist actually said this, it would be an astonishing abdication of the classic goal of ethics" (Mills, 2004: 171). Certainly, feminist philosophers, qua feminists, would join Mills in thinking that philosophy ought not merely describe the world. But one might think that Mills misunderstands his colleagues in assuming, as he seems to, that all ethicists would join him in this. Looking at much of contemporary ethics—with its unabashedly recherché thought experiments and its seeming drive to formalization for its own sake—it's hard not to suspect that merely 'mapping ideals' *is* the ultimate goal for at least some ethicists. If so, then the critique of ideal theory advanced by Mills, O'Neill, and MacKinnon contains a demand for a fundamental reorientation in how we conceive of the aim of moral philosophy. Ethical theories should not only be judged for their truth or plausibility but also for their practical significance.

The second version of the feminist claim that ethics must start from actual experience is about the *evidence* that should be used in ethical theorizing. According to feminist standpoint theory—a descendant of Marxist standpoint theory—women, because of their social and material subordination to men, have privileged epistemic access to certain truths (Hartsock, 1987). Most feminists (and, presumably, many non-feminists as well) would agree that women are epistemically privileged vis-à-vis their own experience: they are in a better position to know what being a woman *is like* than those who aren't women. (Indeed, perhaps *only* women are in a position to know what it's like to be women; cf. Nagel, 1974.) But standpoint epistemologists are generally committed to the stronger claim that women are also in a better position to know truths about the social world that lie beyond their own experience—specifically, the truth about how gender subordination operates at both a material and an ideological level. This is because men, as beneficiaries of the subordination of women, are motivated (however unconsciously) to accept a belief system that distorts their grasp on reality; men's ability to understand patriarchy is thus undermined by their own material interests in perpetuating it. Women, meanwhile, need to both understand the ideology of their male oppressors in order to survive (e.g. to avoid being raped or killed) and have a material interest in uncovering the truth of patriarchy.

Feminist standpoint theory, like Marxist standpoint theories—which make analogous claims of epistemic privilege for the proletariat vis-à-vis bourgeois ideology—is not a variety of relativism. It does not merely claim that men and women have different understandings of the world. Rather, it claims that, *ceteris paribus*, women are in a position to have a *superior* understanding of certain dimensions of the social world. (This *ceteris paribus* caveat is vital if standpoint epistemology is going to accommodate the phenomenon of women who, in the Marxist terms, suffer from 'false consciousness'—that is, an internalization of patriarchal ideology. Whether the phenomenon of false consciousness undermines the force and interest of feminist standpoint epistemology remains an open question within feminism.)

Thus, feminist standpoint epistemology is a substantive and provocative claim in moral epistemology. Its popularity amongst feminists has, however, diminished in recent decades, mostly because of the important turn towards *intersectionality* within feminism (hooks, 1981; Crenshaw, 1989; Collins, 2000). According to an intersectional analysis, to understand a person's particular oppression, we must think about intersecting axes of oppression: not just one's gender but also one's position within capitalist work relations; one's race, ethnicity, or caste; one's disability status; one's sexuality; and so on. Importantly, these axes of oppression are not merely additive: if one is a black woman, one is subordinated *as a black woman*, and not just as a woman and as a black person. Many feminists have thought that an intersectional orientation requires one to jettison feminist standpoint epistemology (e.g. Narayan, 1992), since the latter might seem to presuppose a single standpoint that all women share, and thus does not duly take note of the many differences in oppression between women. But there is arguably still a place for a moderate standpoint epistemology within an intersectional feminism. Different, intersecting forms of oppression might give one particular forms of epistemic advantage: qua woman, one might be especially well placed to recognize misogyny, but qua white person, one might be badly placed to recognize racism. A commitment to intersectionality might then simply require us to think more carefully about the multiple ways that our epistemic situation is shaped by our social position (cf. Bubeck, 2000). While considerations of intersectionality have led some feminist ethicists to insist that they are theorizing only about *their* particular, individual situations—that they speak only for themselves (e.g. Trebilcot, 1991)—another option is for thinkers to theorize in a way that is explicitly defeasible by critique from women who experience forms of oppression that they do not.

Whether or not they endorse standpoint epistemology, most feminists agree that lived experience is vital for the acquisition of moral knowledge. But just what sort of role does experience play in such acquisition? In *The Sovereignty of Good*, Iris Murdoch (1970) argues that what is needed is a particular quality of *attention* to reality—the kind of careful, egoless attention we give to those we truly love. Only through such attention to our everyday worlds—and not through mere meditation on abstract moral principles or ethical puzzle-solving—can we come to see, and act in accordance with, the good. Many feminist ethicists join Murdoch in this broad outlook, insisting that there are certain forms of moral knowledge that can only be had by attending carefully to the real details of actual human experience, including Eva Kittay (1998), Nancy Bauer (2001), Martha Nussbaum (1990), and Alice Crary (forthcoming). Here, for example, is Kittay discussing what she learned through having a disabled daughter:

The worst anticipation was that her handicap involved her intellectual faculties. …
I was committed to a life of the mind. … How was I to raise a daughter that would
have no part of this? If my life took its meaning from thought, what kind of meaning would her life have? … We already knew that we had learned something. That
which we believed we valued, what we—I—thought was at the center of humanity—the capacity for thought or reason, was not it, not it at all.

(Kittay, 1998: 150)

Like Kittay, many feminist ethicists are often particularly concerned with the capacity of
literary narrative and first-personal testimony to transform our moral understanding,
and they urge that such narrative should have a more central role in our ethical theorizing. If they are right, then it will turn out that much of mainstream ethics is misguided in
the cursory way it treats experience only as fodder for cases—examples for the elicitation
and testing of intuitions—rather than as a deep source of moral knowledge. Rather than
assume we know which are and are not the essential features of a case, or that our immediate responses to highly abstracted cases are epistemically reliable, we should patiently
engage with actual phenomena in all its detail, in the hope of coming to a deeper insight
than that afforded by standard methods.

THE PLACE OF POLITICS IN PHILOSOPHICAL THEORIZING

The term 'feminist philosophy' raises a fundamental metaphilosophical question: how
can philosophy, qua indifferent pursuit of the truth, have a specific political or moral
orientation? Isn't 'feminist philosophy' a contradiction in terms, suggesting a form of
inquiry that is at once (qua philosophy) oriented towards the truth and (qua feminist)
oriented towards a particular political goal (cf. Bauer, 2001: chapter 1; Haack, 1993)? This
is a common but mistaken view, presupposing a naive conception of 'standard' philosophical method. (At least, it's a mistaken view that feminist philosophy can be at best
sham-philosophy; I touch on the question of whether feminist philosophy can be genuinely *feminist* below.) That is, on any plausible way of filling out the worry, either it doesn't
really apply to feminist philosophy as practiced, or it applies equally to philosophy in
general. I'll discuss the most plausible ways of unpacking the charge that feminist philosophy is a contradiction in terms—at best sham-philosophy—and show, in turn, why
they miss the mark. In so doing, I will try to speak to the ways that political and moral
considerations can legitimately enter our philosophical theorizing.

The Genetic Fallacy

First, one might worry that feminist philosophy—by rejecting views that are produced
by and conducive to patriarchy—commits the genetic fallacy, wrongly inferring from
the badness of a theory's origin to the conclusion that the theory must be false. But, as
mentioned earlier, feminist philosophy need not be engaged in any such fallacious reasoning. Of course, the moral badness of the context of the development of a view does not
entail the falsity of that view. (The view that women should have access to birth control
might have emerged from a eugenicist context, but that doesn't mean it's false.) But the

fact that a view was created by biased inquirers, and moreover that the view is useful in securing those inquirers' privileged status, does give us at least a prima facie reason to doubt the truth of the view. When feminist ethicists comb through historical and contemporary moral philosophy on the lookout for possible masculinist distortions that they aim to fix, they are engaged in good reasoning, not bad.

The Unrevisability of Feminist Belief

Second, one might worry that feminist philosophy is not really philosophy because feminist philosophers are not sufficiently open to revising their core feminist commitments—for example, about the reality and badness of patriarchy. It is of course true that one of the hallmarks of good inquirers is that they demonstrate a certain openness to challenge and revision. But it is a mistake to think that philosophers are in the habit of leaving *every* one of their commitments open to revision, or that they are capable of defending all of their fundamental commitments to the satisfaction of the skeptic. After all, I cannot defend my conviction that I have hands to the satisfaction of the external world skeptic, and the proponent of classical logic cannot defend his views to the satisfaction of the dialethist (and vice versa). As Willard Van Orman Quine (1951) said, our webs of belief encounter the tribunal of experience (and, we might add, argument) as a whole, and each of us is distinguished by which beliefs are located centrally in our webs (that is, relatively immune from revision) and which lie at the periphery (that is, susceptible to revision). This is no less true of non-feminist philosophers than of feminist philosophers. Utilitarians, for example, are notable for their ardent commitment to the rule of utility-maximization even in the face of what others take to be decisive counterexamples. Epistemicists about vagueness would rather accept (what many think of as) the metaphysically odd view that *bald* or *tall* has a sharp cut-off than sacrifice the law of the excluded middle. And so on. Philosophy in general is characterized by a great diversity in how revisable different claims are taken to be—which claims are thought of as unrevisable, fixed points, and which are thought of as expendable moving parts. Indeed, this diversity partly explains how, in philosophy, intelligent people can disagree so vehemently about so many things.

Still the skeptic of feminist philosophy might insist that feminist philosophers are wrong to hold *ethical* and *political* beliefs so near the center of their webs. But why? It is often taken for granted in philosophy that claims from philosophy's 'core' (metaphysics, epistemology, language) enjoy some sort of methodological priority over ethical or political claims. According to this view, our ethics can be guided by results in core areas, but not vice versa; we cannot, for example, dismiss a metaphysical view because it implies that rape isn't bad or that the patriarchy doesn't exist. But feminism should lead us to query this orthodoxy and, in particular, the view of metaethics—as an exercise in discovering the nature of moral truth and belief independent of any substantive moral claims—that goes along with it. (Indeed, it's not just feminist philosophers who prompt such questions. Some non-feminist philosophers explicitly reject certain metaphysical, epistemological, and even scientific views on the grounds that they clash with their deeply held moral beliefs [e.g. Dworkin, 1996; Nagel, 2012].) For example, if a certain view in epistemology implies that there is no such thing as ideology, why shouldn't that be taken to count against the view? No doubt those who are skeptical of ideology will not think this a persuasive reason to reject the epistemological view in question. But for those who take the existence of ideology to be a fairly obvious fact about the social world, wouldn't there be reason to reject an epistemology that couldn't accommodate it? If so, then it isn't at all clear that claims from philosophy's 'core' should take methodological priority over 'political' claims.

Conflating Practical Reasons with Epistemic Reasons

Third, one might charge feminist philosophy with conflating practical and epistemic reasons—specifically, believing certain views not because they are supported by the evidence but because they are politically useful or convenient to believe. In other words, feminist philosophers stand accused of engaging in a certain kind of vulgar pragmatism. In response to this, we can begin by noting that pragmatist philosophy, though scorned by many mainstream philosophers, is not usually considered a contradiction in terms. Second, one could query whether it is even conceptually possible to engage in such 'vulgar' pragmatism: a reason to believe p is a reason to believe that p is true, and so although it might very well be possible to take the usefulness of believing p as reason to *try to make oneself* believe p, it's not at all clear that it is possible—given the conceptual links between belief and truth—to take the usefulness of believing p as a reason simply to believe p. If so, it is not possible for feminist philosophers to commit the sin they are accused of committing.

Perhaps, then, the charge should be revised: feminist philosophers don't believe their views because they are politically useful, but they do *promote* and perhaps *present themselves as believing* their views because it would be politically useful if others adopted those views. Here, one might ask: what is wrong with this? Do non-feminist philosophers only promote their views because they believe they are true? Do they not sometimes, for example, promote views to which they are not entirely committed because it would be in their professional interests to have their views adopted? One might of course think there is something dishonest about exhorting others to believe a view of which one is not oneself convinced. But one's reasons for doing so might matter to the ethical question. Perhaps it is one thing to advance a view of which one is not entirely convinced in a bid to win fame, and another to advance a view of which one is not entirely convinced because it would serve justice if others were to adopt it.

Relevant to this is a program that Sally Haslanger (2000, 2005, 2012) calls *ameliorative metaphysics*, and that Alexis Burgess and David Plunkett have elaborated under the heading *conceptual ethics* (Burgess & Plunkett, 2013; Plunkett & Burgess 2013). According to this program, it is a legitimate philosophical question to ask, in the face of competing concepts (e.g. of *terrorism* or *woman*) or conceptual schema (e.g. justice vs. care), which of these concepts or schema best serve our practical purposes. That is, we can ask not only descriptive questions about how we do in fact represent the world, but also *normative* questions about how we should *choose* to represent the world. And in some cases, Haslanger argues, we can legitimately exhort others to adopt certain concepts or schema on the grounds that they are most ethically apt. This program is promising in large part because it makes explicit something that we as philosophers already do—consider the standard metaphysician's answer as to why we should speak in terms of green/blue rather than grue/bleen (because the former predicates 'carve nature at its joints')—and points to a way in which practical considerations can (and already do) play a role in our seemingly non-ethical theorizing.

Conceptual ethics thus nods towards a certain pragmatist spirit while retaining a fairly orthodox understanding of what success in ethical theorizing looks like. That's because the conceptual ethicist takes success in ethical inquiry to be a *true* answer to a question—namely, which concepts or schema best serve our practical purposes?—and takes the philosopher to be particularly good at getting at this truth. A good question, one raised by some feminist ethicists, is whether a more radical reconceptualization of success in ethics is possible, one that shifts away from the orthodox focus on truth. One potentially radical proposal is to understand success in ethics to involve the acquisition not of truth but of *justification*, where justification is taken to be an immanent property that exists within the social world rather than an epistemic property that attaches to a particular individual's belief.

Various traditions in moral philosophy—most obviously, universalizability theories (Kant, 1788; Hare, 1963, 1981) and contractarian theories (Rawls, 1971)—insist that the justification of some putative ethical norm depends on people's hypothetical acceptance of that norm. This conception of moral justification as dependent on groups of people rather than on individuals is welcomed by many feminist philosophers. Nonetheless, universalizability and contractarian theories have come under frequent attack by feminist philosophers for ignoring the differences between people and thus overestimating our ability to reliably predict agreement (Arnault, 1989; Jaggar, 1993). Even Habermasian discourse ethics—which insists that moral justification is borne out of actual 'domination-free' discussions between people—has been criticized for idealizing away the machinations of power in conversation (Fraser, 1986; Young, 1997; cf. Benhabib, 1992). According to such feminist critics, a real process of moral justification must be thoroughly non-idealized; it must not presuppose a basic similarity of all people or prize some styles of thinking over others, and it must be accessible to all people regardless of formal training and educational background. In other words, the discursive processes that give rise to moral justification must be genuinely and radically inclusive (Jaggar & Tobin, 2013). On such a view, ethics becomes not a method for arriving at moral truth but a practical, partly empirical, inquiry into how we might create the conditions for moral justification (Tobin & Jaggar, 2013). In other words, on such a view, ethics gives out onto politics.

THE IMPORTANCE OF PHILOSOPHY FOR FEMINISM

In the introduction to the last section, I suggested that while feminist philosophy cannot reasonably be thought of as insufficiently *philosophical*, it might nonetheless be thought of as insufficiently *feminist*. Many feminists have felt that philosophy—at least mainstream analytic philosophy—is antithetical to the feminist political project because of its insistence on the traditional ideals of reason, objectivity, and truth. For such feminists, genuine liberation requires liberation from such strictures as well. Consider these quotations from Bauer and MacKinnon, respectively:

From the point of view of sceptical feminists, philosophy—with its emphasis on passionless thinking, reason, objectivity, universality, essences, and so forth—

apotheosizes a way of encountering the world that is inherently and hopelessly tailored to serve the interests of men and thwart those of women.

(Bauer, 2001: 19)

Objectivity is the epistemological stance of which objectification is the social process, of which male dominance is the politics, the acted out social practice. That is, to look at the world objectively is to objectify it.

(MacKinnon, 1987: 50)

Against such worries, analytic feminist philosophers have been at pains to defend the importance of such notions as reason and objectivity for feminism:

The insistence on the localness of all norms of judgement renders postmodernism incapable of sustaining ordinary judgements, such as the judgement that some forms of social organization are plain unjust, or that some beliefs are plain false. ... Suppose someone protests 'Equal pay for equal work!', or 'Slavery is wrong!'. And suppose the protest is met with a shrug of cynical insouciance from the powers that be. Postmodernism is unfit to characterize that response as unreasonable, or unjustified, or even inappropriate.

(Fricker, 2000: 151)

In order to make any complaint whatever about the way things are, a feminist must at least implicitly appeal to standards that determine when one state of affairs or kind of conduct is better or worse than another. ... She must be appealing to moral standards of good and bad or right and wrong.

(Radcliffe Richards, 1995: 369)

These debates are thorny, and they raise familiar metaethical questions about the sources and nature of moral authority and truth. But these debates also raise a less familiar metaethical question: to what extent does political or moral action require certain metaethical commitments, and in what sense 'require'?

For many philosophers, it might seem obvious that one cannot pursue a political goal without believing in its objective value or without taking oneself to have reason and truth on one's side. But this claim sits in tension with the empirical evidence of many feminist (and anti-colonial, LGBTQ and other) activists who have repudiated reason, truth, and objectivity while pursuing real, material change. Philosophers might respond that those feminists who claim to jettison objectivity, reason and truth are mistaken about their own psychology. But philosophers might do well here not to assume that everyone has the drive to coherence that is so characteristic of philosophers. Politics and people are messy things, replete with surprises not predicted by our best theory. Perhaps the only meaningful sense in which feminism 'requires' philosophy is the sense in which those who already identify with philosophy (myself included) are driven to reconcile our theory with our practice. But as a political practice, feminism is fundamentally about transforming the world, not theorizing it. Whether philosophy has an important role to play in that transformation is ultimately itself a practical, not theoretical, question.

ACKNOWLEDGMENTS

I'd like to thank the editors, David Plunkett and Tristram McPherson, as well as Lea Schroeder, for their helpful comments on earlier drafts.

RELATED TOPICS

Chapter 8, "Realism and Objectivity;" Chapter 26, "Mores and Morals: Metaethics and the Social World;" Chapter 27, "The Autonomy of Ethics;" Chapter 30, "Intuitionism in Moral Epistemology;" Chapter 34, "Conceptual Analysis in Metaethics."

REFERENCES

Ackerly, B. & Okin, S. (1999) "Feminist Social Criticism and the International Movement for Women's Rights as Human Rights," in I. Shapiro & C. Hacker-Cordon (eds.) *Democracy's Edges*, Cambridge: Cambridge University Press: 134–62.

Arnault, L. (1989) "The Radical Future of a Classic Moral Theory," in A. M. Jaggar & S. R. Bordo (eds.) *Gender/Body/Knowledge: Feminist Reconstructions of Being and Knowing*, New Brunswick: Rutgers University Press: 188–206.

Baier, A. (1995) *Moral Prejudices*, Cambridge, MA: Harvard University Press.

Bartky, S. L. (ed.) (1990) *Femininity and Domination*, New York, NY: Routledge.

Bauer, N. (2001) *Simone de Beauvoir, Philosophy, and Feminism*, New York, NY: Columbia University Press.

Bauer, N. (2015) *How to Do Things with Pornography*, Cambridge, MA: Harvard University Press.

Bell, M. (2009) "Anger, Virtue and Oppression," in L. Tessman (ed.) *Feminist Ethics and Social and Political Philosophy: Theorizing the Non-Ideal*, London: Springer: 165–83.

Benhabib, S. (1992) *Situating the Self: Gender, Community and Postmodernism in Contemporary Ethics*, New York, NY: Routledge.

Benhabib, S. (2002) *The Claims of Culture: Equality and Diversity in the Global Era*, Princeton, NJ: Princeton University Press.

Benhabib, S. (2008) *Another Cosmopolitanism*, Oxford: Oxford University Press.

Bubeck, D. (2000) "Feminism in Political Philosophy: Women's Difference," in M. Fricker & J. Hornsby (eds.) *The Cambridge Companion to Feminism in Philosophy*, Cambridge: Cambridge University Press: 185–204.

Burgess, A. & Plunkett, D. (2013) "Conceptual Ethics I," *Philosophy Compass* 8(12): 1091–101.

Butler, J. (1990) *Gender Trouble: Feminism and the Subversion of Identity*, New York, NY: Routledge.

Card, C. (1995) "Gender and Moral Luck," in V. Held (ed.) *Justice and Care*, Boulder, CO: Westview Press: 79–98.

Collins, P. H. (2000) "Gender, Black Feminism, and Black Political Economy," *Annals of the American Academy of Political and Social Science* 568(1): 41–53.

Crary, A. (forthcoming) *Inside Ethics: On the Demands of Moral Thought*, Cambridge, MA: Harvard University Press.

Crenshaw, K. (1989) "Demarginalizing the Intersection of Race and Sex: A Black Feminist Critique of Antidiscrimination Doctrine, Feminist Theory and Antiracist Politics," *Chicago Legal Forum: Feminism in the Law: Theory, Practice and Criticism* 140: 139–67.

Dworkin, R. (1996) "Objectivity and Truth: You'd Better Believe It," *Philosophy and Public Affairs* 25(2): 87–139.

Fraser, N. (1986) "Toward a Discourse Ethic of Solidarity," *Praxis International* 5(4): 425–9.

Fraser, N. (1989) *Unruly Practices: Power, Discourse, and Gender in Contemporary Social Theory*, Minneapolis, MN: University of Minnesota Press.

Fricker, M. (2000) "Feminism in Epistemology: Pluralism without Postmodernism," in M. Fricker & J. Hornsby (eds.) *The Cambridge Companion to Feminism in Philosophy*, Cambridge: Cambridge University Press: 146–65.

Friedman, M. (1993) *What Are Friends For? Feminist Perspectives on Personal Relationships and Moral Theory*, Ithaca, NY: Cornell University Press.

Frye, M. (1991) "A Response to *Lesbian Ethics*: Why Ethics?" in C. Card (ed.) *Feminist Ethics*, Lawrence, KS: University Press of Kansas: 52–59.

Gilligan, C. (1982) *In a Different Voice: Psychological Theory and Women's Development*, Cambridge, MA: Harvard University Press.

Gould, C. (2004) *Globalizing Democracy and Human Rights*, Cambridge: Cambridge University Press.

Haack, S. (1993) "Epistemological Reflections of an Old Feminist," *Reason Papers* 18: 31–42.

Hare, R. M. (1963) *Freedom and Reason*, Oxford: Clarendon Press.

Hare, R. M. (1981) *Moral Thinking: Its Levels, Method and Point*, Oxford: Clarendon Press.

Hartsock, N. (1987) "The Feminist Standpoint: Developing the Ground for a Specifically Feminist Historical Materialism," in S. Harding (ed.) *Feminism and Methodology*, Bloomington: Indiana University Press: 157–80.

Haslanger, S. (2000) "Gender and Race: (What) Are They? (What) Do We Want Them to Be?" *Noûs* 34(1): 31–55.

Haslanger, S. (2005) "What Are We Talking About? The Semantics and Politics of Social Kinds," *Hypatia* 20(4): 10–26.

Haslanger, S. (2012) *Resisting Reality: Social Construction and Social Critique*, Oxford: Oxford University Press.

Hekman, S. (1995) *Moral Voices, Moral Selves: Carol Gilligan and Feminist Moral Theory*, University Park, PA: Pennsylvania State University Press.

Held, V. (ed.) (1995) *Justice and Care: Essential Readings in Feminist Ethics*, Boulder, CO: Westview Press.

hooks, b. (1981) *Ain't I a Woman: Black Women and Feminism*, Boston: South End Press.

Hornsby, J. (1993) "Speech Acts and Pornography," *Women's Philosophy Review* 10: 38–45.

Houston, B. (1987) "Rescuing Womanly Virtues: Some Dangers of Moral Reclamation," in M. Hanen & K. Nielsen (eds.) *Canadian Journal of Philosophy: Science, Morality and Feminist Theory*, supp. 13: 237–62.

Irigaray, L. (1985a) *Speculum of the Other Woman*, trans. by G. C. Gill, Ithaca, NY: Cornell University Press.

Irigaray, L. (1985b) *This Sex Which Is Not One*, trans. by C. Porter & C. Burks, Ithaca, NY: Cornell University Press.

Jaggar, A. (1989) "Love and Knowledge: Emotion in Feminist Epistemology," *Inquiry* 32(2): 151–76.

Jaggar, A. (1993) "Taking Consent Seriously: Feminist Practical Ethics and Actual Moral Dialogue," in E. R. Winkler & J. R. Coombs (eds.) *Applied Ethics: A Reader*, Oxford: Blackwell: 67–86.

Jaggar, A. (1997) "Regendering the U.S. Abortion Debate," *Journal of Social Philosophy* 28(1): 127–40.

Jaggar, T. and Tobin, T. (2013) "Situating Moral Justification: Rethinking the Mission of Moral Epistemology," *Metaphilosophy* 44(4): 383–408.

Kant, I. (1788) *Critique of Practical Reason*, Riga: Friedrich Hartknoch.

Kittay, E. (1998) *Love's Labor: Essays on Women, Equality, and Dependency*, New York, NY: Routledge.

Krause, S. (2008) *Civil Passions: Moral Sentiment and Democratic Deliberation*, Princeton, NJ: Princeton University Press.

Kristeva, J. (1995) *New Maladies of the Soul*, New York, NY: Columbia University Press.

Langton, R. (2009) *Sexual Solipsism: Philosophical Essays on Pornography and Objectification*, Oxford: Oxford University Press.

Lorde, A. (1984) "The Uses of Anger: Women Responding to Racism," in *Sister Outsider*, Trumansburg, NY: Crossing Press.

Lugones, M. & Spelman, M. (1983) "Have We Got a Theory for You! Feminist Theory, Cultural Imperialism, and the Demand for 'the Woman's Voice'," *Women's Studies International Forum* 6(6): 573–81.

MacKinnon, C. (1987) *Feminism Unmodified*, Cambridge, MA: Harvard University Press.

MacKinnon, C. (1989) *Toward a Feminist Theory of the State*, Cambridge, MA: Harvard University Press.

MacKinnon, C. (1993) *Only Words*, Cambridge, MA: Harvard University Press.

MacKinnon, C. (2012) "Foreword," in I. Maitra & M. McGowan (eds.) *Speech and Harm: Controversies over Free Speech*, Oxford: Oxford University Press: vi–xviii.

Mahmood, S. (2005) *Politics of Piety: The Islamic Revival and the Feminist Subject*, Princeton, NJ: Princeton University Press.

Mills, C. (2004) "'Ideal Theory' as Ideology," in P. DesAutels & M. U. Walker (eds.) *Moral Psychology: Feminist Ethics and Social Theory*, Lanham, MD: Rowman & Littlefield: 163–81.

Mitchell, J. & Mishra, S. K. (2000) *Psychoanalysis and Feminism: A Radical Reassessment of Freudian Psychoanalysis*, New York: Basic Books.

Moody-Adams, M. (1991) "Gender and the Complexity of Moral Voices," in C. Card (ed.) *Feminist Ethics*, Lawrence, KS: University Press of Kansas: 195–212.

Moraga, C. & Anzaldúa, G. (eds.) (1983) *This Bridge Called My Back: Writings by Radical Women of Color*, New York, NY: Kitchen Table: Women of Color Press.

Mouffe, C. (1992) *Dimensions of Radical Democracy: Pluralism, Citizenship, Community*, London: Verso.

Mouffe, C. (1993) *The Return of the Political*, London: Verso.

Murdoch, I. (1970) *The Sovereignty of Good*, Oxford: Blackwell.

Nagel, T. (1974) "What Is It Like to Be a Bat?" *Philosophical Review* 83(4): 435–50.

Nagel, T. (2012) *Mind and Cosmos*, Oxford: Oxford University Press.

Narayan, U. (1988) "Working Together across Differences: Some Considerations on Emotions and Political Practice," *Hypatia* 3(2): 31–47.

Narayan, U. (1992) "The Project of Feminist Epistemology: Perspectives from a Nonwestern Feminist," in A. M. Jaggar & S. R. Bordo (eds.) *Gender/Body/Knowledge*, New Brunswick, NJ: Rutgers University Press: 256–72.

Narayan, U. & Harding, S. (eds.) (2000) *Decentering the Center: Philosophy for a Multicultural, Postcolonial, and Feminist World*, Bloomington, IN: Indiana University Press.

Noddings, N. (1984) *Caring: A Feminine Approach to Ethics and Moral Education*, Berkeley, CA: University of California Press.

O'Neill, O. (1987) "Abstraction, Idealization and Ideology in Ethics," in J. D. G. Evans (ed.) *Moral Philosophy and Contemporary Problems*, Cambridge: Cambridge University Press.

Plunkett, D. & Burgess, A. (2013) "Conceptual Ethics II," *Philosophy Compass* 8(12): 1102–10.

Quine, W. V. O. (1951) "Two Dogmas of Experience," *Philosophical Review* 60(1): 20–43.

Radcliffe Richards, J. (1995) "Why Feminist Epistemology Isn't (and the Implications for Feminist Jurisprudence)," *Legal Theory* 1(4): 365–400.

Rawls, J. (1971) *A Theory of Justice*, Cambridge, MA: Harvard University Press.

Rorty, R. (1999) "Ethics without Principles," in *Philosophy and Social Hope*, London: Penguin: chapter 2.

Spivak, G. (1988) "Can the Subaltern Speak?" in C. Nelson & L. Grossberg (eds.) *Marxism and the Interpretation of Culture*, Champaign, IL: University of Illinois Press: 271–313.

Tessman, L. (2005) *Burdened Virtues: Virtue Ethics for Liberatory Struggles*, New York: Oxford University Press.

Tobin, T. and Jagger, A. (2013) "Naturalizing Moral Justification: Rethinking the Method of Moral Epistemology," *Metaphilosophy* 44 (4): 409–39.

Trebilcot, J. (1991) *Dyke Ideas: Process, Politics, Daily Life*, Albany, NY: State University of New York Press.

Williams, B. (1985) *Ethics and the Limits of Philosophy*, London: Fontana.

Young, I. M. (1990) *Justice and the Politics of Difference*, Princeton, NJ: Princeton University Press.

Young, I. M. (1997) *Intersecting Voices: Dilemmas of Gender, Political Philosophy and Policy*, Princeton, NJ: Princeton University Press.

Zerilli, L. (2005) *Feminism and the Abyss of Freedom*, Chicago, IL: University of Chicago Press.

FURTHER READING

For overviews of feminist ethics, see S. Brennan (1999) "Recent Work in Feminist Ethics," *Ethics* 109: 858–93; M. Friedman (2000) "Feminism in Ethics: Conceptions of Autonomy," in M. Fricker & J. Hornsby (eds.) *The Cambridge Companion to Feminism in Philosophy*, Cambridge: Cambridge University Press: 205–24; A. Jaggar (2000) "Ethics Naturalized: Feminism's Contribution to Moral Epistemology," *Metaphilosophy* 31: 452–68. For general reading about feminist theory, see R. Tong (2014) *Feminist Thought: A More Comprehensive Introduction*, Boulder, CO: Westview Press; L. Finlayson (2016) *An Introduction to Feminism*, Cambridge: Cambridge University Press. For further discussion of whether feminist political practice requires a certain philosophical orientation, see S. Lovibond (1989) "Feminism and Postmodernism," *New Left Review* 178: 5–28; S. Lovibond (1994) "Feminism and the 'Crisis of Rationality'," *New Left Review* 207: 72–86; L. Alcoff (1996) "Is the Feminist Critique of Reason Rational?" in *Philosophic Exchange* 26(1): 59–79.

39

Experimental Philosophy and Moral Theory

Chandra Sripada

In the course of philosophical debates, philosophers routinely appeal to intuitions about cases as a way of supporting their positions and challenging those of their opponents. Experimental philosophy is a relatively new field that uses the methods of psychology (and other sciences of mind, brain, and behavior) to study and scrutinize these intuitive judgments, with the ultimate goal of making progress in these philosophical debates. In this chapter, I distinguish between two important experimental philosophy projects, the sociological project and the psychological project, that are particularly relevant for moral theory. These two projects aren't exhaustive, as there are a number of other research programs that are part of experimental philosophy. Nonetheless, examining these two projects will give us a good sense of how experimental philosophy can potentially help us make progress in long-standing debates in moral philosophy.

THE SOCIOLOGICAL PROJECT

At critical junctures of philosophical arguments, one routinely encounters a family of assertions made by theorists as a way of supporting certain key claims. Where p is the claim at issue, theorists say such things as: "we intuitively judge that" p or that p is "common sense," "a platitude of the folk," "pre-reflectively endorsed," "part of our ordinary understanding," and other similar statements. One might raise doubts about whether the fact that we intuitively assent to a claim or regard it as part of common sense *ought* to count in its favor. Let us, however, put this serious issue aside. The main aim of the sociological project is to use experimental methods, especially survey methods, to test the preceding assertions by philosophers, in particular the contention that *we* intuitively endorse certain claims or that these claims form part of a *widely shared* folk common-sense understanding (see Knobe and Nichols 2008, where what I am calling the sociological project is closely related to what they call the "diversity" project).

One reason there is a need to undertake systematic testing, it is argued, is because philosophers constitute a self-selected and highly unrepresentative group. As Stephen Stich and Jonathan Weinberg put the point, why think "that the intuitions of high socio-economic status males … who have advanced degrees in philosophy, and whose cultural background is Western European can serve as a basis for generalizations about the intuitions of 'the folk'" (2001: 642)? There is thus a need to check philosophers' assertions about what is part of the folk understanding with careful studies of what is in fact part of the folk understanding.

In moral philosophy, debates about moral objectivity and motivational internalism have been a fruitful area for investigation by experimental philosophers pursuing the sociological project; let us examine some of the work on these topics.

Moral Objectivity

Many philosophers say the folk are committed to the objectivity of morality or that it is implicit or "presupposed" in ordinary moral discourse and practice. Here are two examples:

> [W]e seem to think moral questions have correct answers; that the correct answers are made correct by the objective moral facts; that moral facts are wholly determined by circumstances; and that, by engaging in moral conversation and argument, we can determine what these objective moral facts determined by the circumstances are.
>
> (Smith 1994: 6)

> …[W]e often see ourselves as engaged in a search for the truth about who is in the right, or where our obligations lie. We can well explain the point and persistence of moral disagreement by attributing to agents the presupposition that there is a right answer awaiting discovery.
>
> (Shafer-Landau 2003: 23)

In the psychological literature, most studies have examined the *content* of people's morals, the first-order principles they endorse, and the justifications they offer for their moral views. The metaethical question of moral objectivity has, in contrast, been widely neglected.

One exception is perhaps the large body of work on the so-called moral/conventional distinction that finds that children reliably distinguish moral wrongs and social/conventional wrongs (Turiel 1983; Smetana 1981; Nucci 1981). This work offers some suggestive evidence that the folk have objectivist leanings, but drawing conclusions from this work is challenging for a number of reasons. Most importantly, the theorists who did these studies weren't directly interested in the issue of moral objectivity, and so did not ask about it specifically. Additionally, this work remains highly controversial, with a number of theorists, including philosophers, offering systematic critiques of its theoretical assumptions, methods, and findings (see for example Kelly et al. 2007).

Geoffrey Goodwin and John Darley, two psychologists, performed an interesting early study that directly investigated folk views on the objectivity of morality (in this case, the relevant folk were undergraduates at Princeton University) (Goodwin and Darley 2008). They constructed a list of 26 statements that they classified into four types: factual, ethical, convention, and taste. In the first part of the experiment, participants indicated whether each statement is true, false, or a matter of opinion. In the second part, the experimenters told the participants that others who had previously rated the statements had disagreed with them on a number of specific items. They were then presented with questions intended to assess whether one party is mistaken or whether it is possible that neither is mistaken. A statement was assessed as having greater objectivity if participants viewed it as true or false (rather than being a matter of opinion) and endorsed that in cases of disagreement, one of the parties is mistaken. According to this measure, Goodwin and Darley found that participants rated ethical statements as being nearly as objective as factual statements and clearly more objective than convention and taste statements.

Goodwin and Darley's results extended previous work that also suggested the folk have objectivist leanings. For example, in a pioneering early study, Shaun Nichols found most participants (78 percent) rejected statements designed to capture a non-objectivist metaethical perspective (e.g., "There is no objective fact, independent of what different people think, about whether it was wrong for Frank to hit Bill or Lisa to shove Nancy. These actions were 'wrong for Ted' and maybe 'wrong for me', but they aren't *objectively wrong* independent of what people think about them.") (Nichols 2004). Similarly, Wainryb and colleagues (2004) found initial evidence that in cases of moral disagreement, children tended to say only one party is right, rather than that both are right, potentially suggesting that these children reject certain non-objectivist views that allow both parties to be correct.

In more recent investigations, Sarkissian and colleagues (2011) challenged the objectivist implications of the preceding body of work. They observed that prior work tended to present participants with moral disagreements in which it could be assumed the disagreeing parties come from the same sociocultural group. For example, in the Goodwin and Darley study previously discussed, participants were told the individuals disagreeing with them were other participants studied by the experimenters, and thus it could be readily inferred that these individuals were Princeton undergraduates. This is important because certain kinds of relativist views say the truth of a moral judgment depends on the culture of the person making the judgment. These relativist views would thus say that—just like objectivist views—if two individuals drawn from the same cultural group disagree about a moral matter, then one must be making a mistake.

Based on these observations, Sarkissian and colleagues performed studies designed to better distinguish the hypothesis that the folk are genuinely non-relativist realists versus the hypothesis that they are relativists who think the moral status of an action depends on the cultural standards of the person making the judgment.

In part of the study, all participants were given a statement:

Horace finds his youngest child extremely unattractive and therefore kills him.

Participants were next told about a disagreement about the statement between one of their classmates, who thinks the act is not permissible, and another party who thinks the act is permissible. Participants were assigned to one of three conditions. In the Same-Culture condition, they were told the other party is Sam, "a fairly ordinary student at their own college who enjoyed watching college football and hanging out with friends."

In the Other-Culture condition, the other party is a member of the Mamilon tribe, a tribe which "lives in the Amazon rainforests and has preserved a traditional warrior culture, with quite different values from those of the people in the surrounding society." In the Extraterrestrial condition, the other party is a member of a race of extraterrestrial beings called the Pentars. Participants were told that "Pentars have a very different sort of psychology from human beings, that they are not at all interested in friendship or love and that their main goal is simply to increase the total number of equilateral pentagons in the universe." Participants in all three conditions were then asked to rate their agreement on a 7-point scale (1=strongly disagree and 7=strongly agree) with the claim: "Since your classmate and (Sam, the Mamilon, the Pentar) have different judgments about this case, at least one of them must be wrong."

Results for this question for the three conditions are shown below:

Same Culture: 5.4
Other Culture: 4.4
Extraterrestrial: 3.2

These results show participants tend to provide an "objectivist" response when the two parties in the disagreement are drawn from the same culture. But as cultural distance increases, participants are less likely to agree that at least one of the parties in the disagreement is making a mistake. This pattern is exactly what is predicted if the folk are cultural relativists about morality.

Sarkissian and colleagues report the results of several other studies that also support the idea that the folk have moral relativist leanings. For example, they replicated the results of the study reported above in an independent Singaporean sample, as well as a separate American sample, where participants were allowed to rate all three scenarios (i.e., Same Culture, Other Culture, Extraterrestrial). Finally, they showed that the tendency to give answers consistent with relativism is specific to the moral domain and does not extend to straightforward matters of fact, e.g., whether Napoleon used horses or helicopters in battle.

A potential weakness of moral relativism is that it can be hard to see why we should call a "faultless" disagreement—one in which neither party is making a mistake—a disagreement at all. In a follow-up to the Sarkissian et al. study, Justin Khoo and Joshua Knobe address this worry. Drawing on experimental findings that propose contextualist "non-exclusionary" semantics for moral statements, they show how parties who aren't disagreeing about the facts can nonetheless be disagreeing (Khoo and Knobe 2016).

Sarkissian and colleagues' findings have at least two notable implications. The first is for experimentalists. Their study highlights the need to use experimental designs that better pull apart the predictions of realist versus relativist views, something that hadn't always been accomplished in previous studies. The second implication is for philosophers. Sarkissian and colleagues' findings call into doubt the claims of philosophers cited earlier that the folk are moral objectivists, and this point is discussed further below.

Motivational Internalism

Another area in metaethics where philosophers have frequently made appeals to common sense concerns the issue of motivational internalism. There are many internalist theses in metaethics (see David Faraci and Tristram McPherson's chapter "Ethical Judgment and Motivation" and Errol Lord and David Plunkett's chapter "Reasons Internalism" for discussion). Motivational internalism (hereafter "internalism") posits a necessary connection between moral judgments and motivation. According to this thesis, if a person makes a moral judgment that she should A, then necessarily the person has at least some degree of motivation in favor of A-ing. Most theorists think this bare statement of the view needs to be qualified in various ways, though there is no consensus on how. The two most common qualifications proposed are that the person must be *rational* and *psychologically healthy*, but a number of others have been put forward (see Björklund et al. 2012 for a review).

Some philosophers have claimed that internalism is part of the ordinary, shared understanding of moral judgment.

> It seems to be a conceptual truth that to regard something as good is to feel a pull towards promoting or choosing it, or towards wanting other people to feel the pull towards promoting or choosing it.
>
> (Blackburn 1984: 188)

Other philosophers have denied that common sense supports internalism (e.g. Brink 1986) and some have even suggested that externalism, i.e., the denial of internalism, is supported by common sense (see, for example, Svavarsdottir 1999).

Against the background of this dispute, a body of experimental work has developed over the last decade or so assessing whether folk opinion supports internalism. In an early and influential study, Nichols (2002) presented participants with the following vignette.

> John is a psychopathic criminal. He is an adult of normal intelligence, but he has no emotional reaction to hurting other people. John has hurt and indeed killed other people when he has wanted to steal their money. He says that he knows that hurting others is wrong, but that he just doesn't care if he does things that are wrong.

Participants were then asked whether "John really understands that hurting others is morally wrong?" Results showed that 85 percent of the subjects answered "Yes" and 15 percent answered "No." Nichols took these results to provide some initial support for externalism.

What about the additional qualifications that internalists often insist on? Nichols' study seems best positioned to address the rationality qualification as John is described as an adult with normal intelligence. In describing John as a psychopath, however, it is possible that participants infer he has a serious mental disorder. This would violate the qualification that some internalists insist on that the relevant agent be psychologically healthy.

Strandberg and Björkland (2013) performed a study that probed in more detail whether the folk endorse internalism, directly comparing a scenario in which the agent is psychologically healthy from scenarios in which she is psychologically impaired. In their study, all participants were assigned to one of five groups. The Simple group read the following story.

> Anna is watching a TV program about a famine in Sudan. In the TV program, it is shown how the starving are suffering and desperately looking for food. At the

same time, Anna is not motivated at all, not to any extent, to give any money to those who are starving.

Participants in the Normal Functioning group next read the following additional information.

Anna is mentally healthy and functions normally. For example, she is not depressed, apathetic, emotionally disturbed, psychopathic, or the like.

Participants in the other three groups read information describing a person with severe apathy, depression, and psychopathy, respectively. Finally, all participants received the following question: Could it be the case that Anna thinks she is morally required to give some of her money to the starving even if she is not motivated at all to do so?

Results showed the following percentages of people who answered affirmatively to this question:

Simple: 75.6 percent
Normal Functioning: 79.0 percent
Apathy: 60.0 percent
Depression: 79.4 percent
Psychopathy: 42.3 percent

The results for the first four conditions suggest the folk have externalist leanings. Moreover, the fact that participants gave a similar percentage of affirmative responses to the Simple condition compared to the Depression condition provides evidence against versions of internalism that require the agent to be psychologically healthy.

Why did participants tend to answer "No" more frequently in the Psychopathy condition? Strandberg and Björkland propose that their participants tended to think of psychopaths as persons who do not hold moral judgments at all. That is, they propose that participants think it is not possible that a psychopath ever thinks she is morally required to perform an action. If this is right, the fact that participants tended to answer "No" in this condition does not provide any support for the internalist.

One potential problem with the studies by Nichol and by Strandberg and Björkland is that they asked whether the character in the vignette *really understands* moral claims (Nichols) or whether the character could *think* something is morally required and remain unmotivated (Strandberg and Björkland). Björnsson and colleagues (2015) note that internalism is a thesis that concerns the necessary upshots of moral *judgment*, understood as a species of *belief*, rather than the upshots of understanding and thinking.

Based on this observation, Björnsson and colleagues constructed scenarios that manipulated the character's attitude to the relevant proposition, i.e., whether the character understands, thinks, or believes that something is morally wrong. Their vignettes are far more detailed than typical experimental philosophy studies and the results of their careful study resist easy summary, and so I will focus on one aspect. They presented participants with a detailed vignette about a character who makes correct classifications of actions as being morally right and morally wrong, but she remains entirely unmotivated to act accordingly. Participants were then randomly assigned to three conditions. In each condition, they were asked, respectively, whether the character "understands," "herself thinks," or "believes" that the relevant action is morally wrong. Results for these three conditions are shown below:

Understands: 76 percent
Herself thinks: 49 percent
Believes: 46 percent

Similar to Nichols' study discussed earlier, they found the majority of participants (76 percent) in the Understands condition responded affirmatively. Notice, however, that results differed substantially in the other two conditions. In the Believes condition in particular, which Björnsson and colleagues contend (plausibly) is most relevant for the philosophical thesis of internalism, participants were essentially evenly split. These results suggest the folk are quite divided about internalism and don't appear to provide much support for either internalism or externalism.

Implications of the Sociological Project for Philosophical Debates

Let us suppose that years in the future, substantial experimental philosophy research on the preceding topics has been completed and scholarly consensuses on key positions emerge. What impact might these findings have on philosophical debates such as the debates about moral objectivity and internalism?

Recall earlier it was pointed out that philosophers frequently assert that certain claims are intuitive or are commonsense as a way of supporting their theories. Experimental philosophy findings, specifically those coming from the sociological project, provide empirical tests of such assertions. Where the empirical findings disagree with such assertions, a (purported) source of support for the relevant theories is thereby challenged. Where the empirical findings agree with such assertions, a (purported) source of support for the relevant theories is thereby corroborated.

Critics of experimental philosophy sometimes say it tries to settle philosophical matters by surveying the masses; it trades polls for substantive philosophical arguments. This critique misses the mark, however, at least when the project is pursued carefully, in the way being advocated for here. Theorists pursuing the sociological project in experimental philosophy should not argue (and as far as I know, they mostly haven't) that their work provides evidence *directly* for or against philosophical views. Rather, their aim should be to scrutinize one kind of (purported) evidence put forward for those views, i.e., appeals to intuitions and commonsense judgments that are claimed to be shared by the folk.

THE PSYCHOLOGICAL PROJECT

The sociological project looks at the distribution of intuitions and commonsense judgments within and across societies. The psychological project in experimental philosophy, in contrast, investigates psychological structure. In particular, it studies the mentally represented information structures that give rise to intuitive judgments.

To get started in understanding this project, consider the following case proposed by Edmund Gettier that is widely viewed as a counterexample to the "justified true belief" analysis of knowledge:

> Suppose that Smith and Jones have applied for a certain job. And suppose that Smith has strong evidence for the following conjunctive proposition:
>
> (d) Jones is the man who will get the job, and Jones has ten coins in his pocket.
>
> Smith's evidence for (d) might be that the president of the company assured him that Jones would in the end be selected, and that he, Smith, had counted the coins in Jones's pocket ten minutes ago. Proposition (d) entails:
>
> (e) The man who will get the job has ten coins in his pocket.
>
> Let us suppose that Smith sees the entailment from (d) to (e), and accepts (e) on the grounds of (d), for which he has strong evidence. In this case, Smith is clearly justified in believing that (e) is true.
>
> But imagine, further, that unknown to Smith, he himself, not Jones, will get the job. And, also, unknown to Smith, he himself has ten coins in his pocket.
>
> (Gettier 1963: 122)

Though Smith has a justified true belief in (e), most people intuitively judge that he does not know (e). (Note: While early studies suggested some cross-cultural variation in intuitive judgments about Gettier cases [Weinberg et al. 2001], more recent studies performed by some of the same authors, among others, found these judgments were similar across cultural groups [Machery et al. 2015].) Notice further that it is notoriously hard to say why we make this judgment, that is, on what basis it was made. If asked, we would typically say it just seems to us that Smith does not know (e) or that it strikes us that way, but we can't provide more information about how we ourselves came to form this judgment. Call this feature—the lack of conscious awareness of the basis of the intuitive judgment—*source opacity*.

There are interesting parallels between these observations about intuitions in the Gettier case and intuitions about the grammaticality of sentences, as can be seen from the following example (based on Anderson and Lightfoot 2000). Everyone knows that for the following sentence:

(1a) Kim is happy

you can reduce the "is" by changing the sentence to:

(1b) Kim's happy

But in the following sentence, the "is" that follows Tim cannot be reduced:

(2a) Kim is happier than Tim is

Reducing this second "is" results in the following ungrammatical sentence:

(2b) *Kim's happier than Tim's

When people are asked what underlying principles they are applying in accepting (1b) but rejecting (2b), they are typically flummoxed. They are clearly applying systematic principles, but they cannot state their contents.

The actual principles being applied, which we know from linguistic and psycholinguistic investigations, turn out to be surprisingly complex. One of the principles says, very roughly: An "is" can be reduced except when it is on the left side of an extracted phrase (a phrase is "extracted" when it remains in the underlying syntactic description of the sentence but is absent in the surface representation). In (2a), the second "is" sits to the left of an extracted phrase, as prior to extraction, the sentence would have read: "Kim is happier than Tim is *happy*." In (1a), the "is" does *not* sit to the left of an extracted phrase, and thus the change to (1b) is allowed.

This principle is a good example of what cognitive scientists call *tacit information*. The principle is applied in producing a judgment, but the content of the principle itself is not something that we can readily introspect or articulate. It is likely that judgments across various domains (grammar, physics, biological kinds, social cognition, etc.) are associated with distinct, sizable bodies of tacit information. I will use the term *tacit information structure* to refer to the collection of mentally represented packets of information that play an inferential role in underwriting a certain well-defined class of judgments. Importantly, this usage allows the units of information within a structure (which I will refer to as "principles") to be encoded in a variety of different formats, for example, sentential representations, map-like representations, distributed representations, etc.

In the case of the Gettier intuition as well as other philosophically relevant intuitions, there have to be information structures that are utilized in generating the relevant intuitions. The alternative, it would seem, would be to say that the intuitive judgment arises by magic. Furthermore, it is plausible that the relevant information structures are, like in the case of grammar, tacit. When presented with hypothetical cases, we find ourselves making intuitive judgments, but we cannot readily articulate the contents of the information structures that are the basis for these judgments.

A primary aim of the psychological project in experimental philosophy is to uncover the tacit information structures that are utilized in generating certain philosophically relevant intuitions. It is claimed that by scrutinizing the contents of these structures, we can better assess the evidential value of the relevant intuitions. (Note: There is vigorous ongoing debate about whether philosophers actually do rely on intuitions as a source of evidence for their views. See Cappelen 2012 and Williamson 2007 for the anti-intuition position and Nagel 2012, and Sripada in preparation for responses.)

To provide a concrete illustration of the psychological project and how it can yield findings that can potentially advance philosophical debates, let us examine in some detail recent psychological investigations into "trolley problems." These cases originated with Philippa Foot (1967) and Judith Jarvis Thomson (1985), and they have been extensively discussed by other philosophers. Joshua Greene was an early leader in empirical investigation of these problems, and though other scientists have subsequently joined in, Greene's work is the focus in what follows.

Consider the following two cases:

Bystander

A runaway trolley is headed for five people who will be killed if it proceeds on its present course. The only way to save the five people is to hit a switch that will turn the trolley onto an alternate set of tracks where it will kill one person instead of five. Should you turn the trolley in order to save five people at the expense of one?

Footbridge

A runaway trolley is headed for five people who will be killed if it proceeds on its present course. You are standing next to a large stranger on a footbridge that spans the tracks. The only way to save the five people is to push this stranger off the bridge, onto the tracks below. He will die if you do this, but his body will stop the trolley from reaching the others. Should you save the others by pushing this stranger to his death?

Most people intuitively judge that it is permissible to turn the switch in Bystander, but it is not permissible to push the stranger to his death in Footbridge. But what are the underlying (tacit) information structures that give rise to these differing intuitive judgments? Greene's research program uses a variety of empirical methods to answer this question and in turn uses the answers generated to inform philosophically relevant conclusions.

Let me start by sketching the form of one of Greene's main arguments and then the individual premises will be scrutinized. Greene himself helpfully offers a three-step argument along the following lines (based on Greene 2014a; Greene in preparation):

1. Intuitions in response to Footbridge are strongly influenced by the presence of personal force (i.e., being the initiator of the causal force that harms another person).
2. The presence of personal force is morally irrelevant to the moral acceptability of what one should do in this case.
3. Conclusion. Since intuitions in response to Footbridge are strongly influenced by at least one morally irrelevant factor, personal force, they are therefore at least somewhat unreliable.

Before going forward, it is worth underscoring that the preceding is *one of* the main arguments that Greene has defended (he calls it the "Direct Route" argument, see Greene 2014a). There is in addition a substantially more ambitious argument that Greene has advanced that he calls the "Indirect Route" argument. This argument seeks to distinguish cases that elicit "characteristically deontological" intuitions from cases that elicit "characteristically consequentialist" intuitions. Greene understands these two categories of intuitive judgment as something like natural kinds, with distinctive psychological and neural etiologies and distinctive features of cases that they track. The goal of the Indirect Route argument is not simply to challenge the reliability of intuitions associated with individual cases (e.g., the Footbridge case) but rather to challenge deontological theories writ large (Greene's argument for this conclusion is complex and cannot be sketched here). Going forward, the more ambitious (and substantially more controversial) Indirect Route argument is put aside. The Direct Route argument provides a better illustration of the pattern of reasoning that occurs as part of the psychological program in experimental philosophy, so this argument will be our focus.

Returning now to the three-step argument presented above, Greene and his colleagues have conducted a number of studies in support of premise 1. In one set of studies (Greene et al. 2009), they presented participants with a series of systematically varied vignettes in order to identify the factors that might be driving the different judgments in Footbridge and Bystander. One factor that might influence people's intuitive judgments in Footbridge is physical contact, having to lay one's hands on another person and push him to his death. Another factor is what Greene calls "personal force," being the initiator of the causal force that harms another person. Still another potential factor is spatial proximity, being spatially near to the site where a horrible harm occurs.

Participants were presented with a series of scenarios in which these factors were selectively present or absent. In one scenario, the agent on the footbridge can only use a pole to knock the stranger off the bridge, and like in the original Footbridge case, the stranger's body stops the runaway trolley. In this scenario, the agent doesn't put his hands directly on the stranger (physical contact is absent), but he is the initiator of the causal force that harms the stranger (personal force is present). In another pair of scenarios, the agent has access to a switch that opens a trapdoor on the footbridge. If the switch is flipped, the stranger falls through and, like in the original Footbridge case, his body stops the runaway trolley. In one version of this "switch" scenario, the switch is right next to the stranger and in another version, the switch is far away from the footbridge; this pair of cases tests for the influence of spatial proximity. After tabulating results from across all the various scenarios, Greene and his colleagues found evidence that people's moral intuitions in these trolley problems are selectively sensitive to the personal force factor and not the physical contact and spatial proximity factors.

Why might we have moral intuitions that are highly sensitive to harms generated by personal force? Greene offers an evolutionary explanation in which there is a suite of relatively simple, "alarm-bell"-like emotions that serve to selectively detect such harms:

> Given that personal violence is evolutionarily ancient, predating our recently evolved human capacities for complex abstract reasoning, it should come as no surprise if we have innate responses to personal violence that are powerful but rather primitive... In contrast, when a harm is impersonal, it should fail to trigger this alarm like emotional response.... As Josef Stalin once said, "A single death is a tragedy; a million deaths is a statistic." His remarks suggest that when harmful actions are sufficiently impersonal, they fail to push our emotional buttons, despite their seriousness.
>
> (Greene 2008: 43)

Greene supports this evolutionary speculation with a review (see Greene 2008) of a large psychological literature that finds a highly similar "personal" versus "impersonal" distinction made across a number of domains: people's decisions to help victims in distress; people's decisions to invest in collective action games; people's decisions to punish violators of moral rules; and people's attitudes towards so-called "harmless" norm violations. In all these domains, psychologists have posited that simple emotional responses lead people to treat harms that happen to identifiable, concrete victims substantially differently than seemingly identical harms that happen to abstract, unnamed, unidentifiable victims.

Another line of evidence for Greene's hypothesis comes from a heavily discussed fMRI study that Greene and his colleagues conducted (Greene et al. 2001). They found brain regions linked to emotional responses were implicated in hypothetical cases that involve personal harm, while brain regions linked to "cool" deliberative reasoning were involved in hypothetical cases that—like Bystander—involve impersonal harms.

To sum up, Greene attempts to support premise 1 of his argument by combining psychological, evolutionary, and neuroscientific arguments. Other theorists have pushed back, offering alternative hypotheses. One of the most influential perspectives is advanced by the philosopher and legal theorist John Mikhail, who explains differing judgments in Footbridge versus Bystander in terms of the application of the doctrine of double effect. This principle draws a distinction between (1) bringing about a good outcome while foreseeing that an unintended harm will occur as a side effect (which is permissible); and (2) causing that same harm in order to bring about a good outcome (which is not permissible). In a number of studies, some of which were done in collaboration with psychologists and neuroscientists, Mikhail assembles a sophisticated and convergent theoretical and empirical case for his position (Mikhail 2007; Mikhail 2011). Greene, in turn, has offered trenchant replies (Greene 2014b), and the debate is ongoing.

For the purpose of continuing to explicate Greene's argument, let us assume that he is right about premise 1. Premise 2 of Greene's argument is a normative premise that Greene unabashedly grants is got from the armchair. According to Greene, it is obvious, simply by reflecting on the issue, that personal force ought not to be a morally relevant consideration. That is, we should not judge that an action that sacrifices one to save five is impermissible *only* because it involves personal force-type harm (while an otherwise similar action that does not involve personal force is judged to be permissible).

Finally, the conclusion of Greene's argument regarding the reliability of intuitions in Footbridge follows fairly directly from the premises. If the conclusion of Greene's argument is correct, this has implications for certain debates in normative ethics. Trolley cases along the lines of Footbridge are often used in arguments against utilitarianism. Utilitarianism would seem to predict that we should sacrifice the one to save five in Footbridge just as we should in Bystander. The fact that utilitarianism can't capture our intuitions about the case, it is argued, counts against the view. If the conclusion of Greene's argument is correct and intuitions in Footbridge are shown to be at least somewhat unreliable, then this helps to undercut one important source of evidence against utilitarian theories. Theorists relying on this source of evidence should, other things being equal, correspondingly increase their credence in utilitarian theories.

One sometimes hears criticisms of Greene that say he is attempting to extract a normative conclusion from empirical premises. This critique of Greene is misguided because premise 2 of his argument is straightforwardly a normative premise, not an empirical one. (It is in fact a normative premise that Greene says he gets from the armchair.) So there is no obvious way in which Greene is deducing an *ought* exclusively from an *is*.

Another objection is that Greene's argument is somehow circular or question begging. The objection begins by noting that Greene is employing a normative claim as premise 2 of his argument (and thus it is conceded he is not deducing an *ought* from an *is*). It is then argued that since Greene already presupposes a normative claim as a premise, any normative conclusions that follow from the argument beg the question.

The problem with this argument is that it fails to notice that premise 2 of Greene's argument relies on a normative claim that is quite a bit less controversial than the normative conclusions that follow from the argument. The normative claim in premise 2 is that personal force is not a morally relevant factor. This is a claim that has support given a wide range of plausible normative theories, including utilitarian and deontological theories. The conclusions of Greene's argument involve normative claims that are quite a bit more controversial. For example, earlier it was shown that if Greene's argument is correct, then at least some theorists (those who rely on intuitions in Footbridge as evidence against utilitarianism) should increase their credence in utilitarianism. In short, Greene's argument is not question begging because the normative premises are different from, and in an important sense "less weighty" than, the normative conclusions that the argument supports.

Perhaps the best-known critique of Greene's research was put forward by Selim Berker in his article "The Normative Insignificance of Neuroscience" (Berker 2009). It turns out, however, that Berker's argument has relatively little relevance to the aspects of Greene's research discussed here for two reasons. First, Berker's critique targets Greene's more ambitious (and more controversial) Indirect Route argument. We, however, have focused exclusively on Greene's more modest Direct Route argument, since the pattern of reasoning in this argument is more representative of the psychological project in experimental philosophy. Second, Berker is concerned specifically with Greene's *neuroscience* results. As we have seen, however, these results play at best a small (and largely inessential) role in the Direct Route argument, while Greene's psychological results play a much larger role. Readers interested in a detailed response to Berker's critique should consult Greene (in preparation).

From Greene's three-step argument, we can extract a more general three-step template for how the psychological program in experimental philosophy works. Start with the following background: Some philosophical debate is unfolding and theorists on one side appeal to an intuitive judgment *I* in order to advance their position. *I* exhibits a high degree of source opacity; there are mentally represented principles that are applied in producing *I* but the theorists can't articulate their contents. The first step in the psychological program is to use experimental methods from psychology, neuroscience, or other fields in the behavioral sciences, in order to identify these mentally represented principles that are the basis for *I*. The next step is to subject the contents so identified to reflective scrutiny. For example, are the contents reasonable in light of other principles, commitments, considered judgments about cases, etc.? The third step consists of adjustment of the evidential weight of the relevant intuitions upwards or downwards. For example, if the contents identified in the second step are found to be unjustifiable, then the intuitions that are rooted in these contents should commensurately lose some of their evidential status. This adjustment can in turn change theorists' credences in philosophical theories.

Thus far, we have been focusing on the information structures that are the inferential basis of intuitive judgments. There are, however, a variety of *other* factors that also influence one's intuitive judgments that are not naturally understood to be elements of the information structures associated with the judgment process. For example, one's judgments about whether to push the man in the Footbridge case might be influenced by one's mood (happy or depressed), state of inebriation, attitudes to the race of the person being pushed, and so on. An additional goal of the psychological program in experimental philosophy is to characterize the effects of factors such as these on intuitive judgment. Just like factors that are part of an intuition's information basis, uncovering the influence of these "extraneous" factors on an intuition can, through the three steps outlined in the preceding paragraph, lead to adjustment of the intuition's evidential worth. Information structures, nonetheless, continue to be emphasized going forward for ease of exposition, with the understanding that what is said applies equally well to influences exerted by these "extraneous" factors.

A critic of the psychological program in experimental philosophy might argue that empirical research is unnecessary; it is possible to uncover the contents of the underlying information structures that are the basis for intuitive judgments from the armchair alone. There are two versions of this argument. The first version says we can discover these contents from the armchair simply by "looking inside" our own minds. The information structures are represented in the head, so we can just introspect and see what their contents are. The problem with this argument is that, as the discussion of the Gettier case underscores, the kinds of mentally represented information structures at issue are *tacit*. They are not readily introspectable or available for verbal report.

The second version of this argument says theorists can pursue a quasi-experimental approach from the armchair. Consider how linguists make progress. They frequently test their own (armchair) intuitions systematically across a large number of cases, operating with the assumption that their own intuitive reactions are widely shared by the folk (or at least that they are good at predicting folk intuitive reactions; see Dunaway, Edmonds, and Manley 2013). They then use this armchair data to propose hypotheses about the mentally represented information structures that underlie grammaticality judgments. Why can't philosophers do the same?

This second argument is on much sounder footing; philosophers often do make progress in uncovering tacit principles, commitments, and other informational elements from the armchair by using the quasi-empirical method. The problem with using this observation as part of an argument against the psychological project in experimental philosophy is that the argument assumes there is some kind of all-or-none competition: we must pursue the goal of uncovering the mentally represented information structures underlying intuitive judgments *either* from the armchair or from the lab. But there is no restriction that we pursue one or the other; we can pursue both.

Armchair methods have certain advantages. For example, the "subjects" in the experiments, i.e., philosophers themselves, tend to be reflective, have extensive background knowledge, and are motivated to engage deeply with cases.

Experimental methods have their own advantages. One of the most important is that they provide quantitative precision in measuring key variables, such as the strength of an intuitive response. Look at Greene's study earlier using a series of cases to distinguish the role of physical contact, personal force, and spatial proximity in trolley problem judgments. Differences in intuitive responses to the cases are subtle, and it would be easy for a single philosopher in the armchair (especially one in the grip of a theory) to miss these subtleties. But by assembling hundreds of participants, Greene was able to identify clear quantitative differences in how people respond to these cases, which in turn points to a pivotal role for the personal force factor influencing their judgments. Experimental methods also have other advantages. For example, theorists can use a variety of methods (causal modeling, neuroimaging, reaction time measures) to understand how different psychological processes interact to produce the eventual judgment (Sinnott-Armstrong et al. 2008; Sripada and Konrath 2011; Sripada 2012). This is something that cannot be easily achieved by from the armchair, for example by introspection.

Overall, since armchair methods and experimental methods each have advantages for pursuing the goals of the psychological project (i.e., uncovering tacit information structures that are the basis for intuitive judgments), and since we are under no pressure to pursue one or the other, then it seems reasonable that we should pursue them both.

Before concluding, it is worth raising an issue that is likely to be on the minds of many readers. Philosophers have been drawing on empirical observations for centuries, and in the last few decades, many moral philosophers have explicitly strived to propose theories that are richly informed by theories and findings from the natural sciences. For example, in "Wise Choices, Apt Feelings" (1992), Allan Gibbard proposes a theory of normative judgment that draws on evolutionary theory and psychological research on decision-making. In "Lack of Character" (2002), John Doris critiques virtue ethics based on a large body of findings from social psychology that seem to put the existence of morally relevant character traits in question.

On the conception of experimental philosophy put forward in this chapter, the preceding are examples of *empirically informed philosophy*, not experimental philosophy. The distinctive feature of experimental philosophy is that it seeks to better understand philosophically relevant intuitions specifically, especially their sociological distribution and psychological roots. This conception of experimental philosophy lines up with what at least some of its leading practitioners say (Alexander 2010; Nadelhoffer and Nahmias 2007), though others offer more expansive conceptions of the field (e.g., Knobe and Nichols 2008). Perhaps more importantly, it also seems to capture what most self-identified experimental philosophers actually *do*.

CONCLUSION

The core idea of experimental philosophy is that systematic investigation of intuitive judgment, using the methods of cognitive science, can be useful in making progress in philosophical debates. In this chapter, two major programs in experimental philosophy research, the sociological and psychological projects, were distinguished and their contributions to debates in moral theory were explored. The sociological project was illustrated with summaries of research on moral objectivity and motivational internalism. The psychological project was illustrated with research into the psychological basis of judgments in trolley problems conducted by Joshua Greene and his colleagues. Research by experimental philosophers into these topics, as well as other important issues in moral theory, is active and ongoing. Experimental philosophy is a relatively new field, but there is great promise that it can complement and enrich traditional armchair methods.

ACKNOWLEDGMENTS

Many thanks to Jamie Fritz, Tristram McPherson, and David Plunkett, whose extensive comments improved virtually every aspect of this chapter.

REFERENCES

Alexander, J. (2010) Is Experimental Philosophy Philosophically Significant? *Philosophical Psychology*, 23(3): 377–389.

Anderson, S.R. and Lightfoot, D.W. (2000) The Human Language Faculty as an Organ. *Annual Review of Physiology*, 62(1): 697–722.

Berker, S. (2009) The Normative Insignificance of Neuroscience. *Philosophy & Public Affairs*, 37(4): 293–329.

Björklund, F. et al. (2012) Recent Work on Motivational Internalism. *Analysis*, 72(1): 124–137.

Björnsson, G. et al. (2015) Motivational Internalism and Folk Intuitions. *Philosophical Psychology*, 28(5): 715–734.

Blackburn, S. (1984) *Spreading the Word*, Oxford: Clarendon Press.

Brink, D.O. (1986) Externalist Moral Realism. *The Southern Journal of Philosophy*, 24(S1): 23–41.

Cappelen, H. (2012) *Philosophy without Intuitions*, Reprint edition, Oxford: Oxford University Press.

Doris, J.M. (2002) *Lack of Character: Personality and Moral Behavior*, Cambridge: Cambridge University Press.

Dunaway, B., Edmonds, A. and Manley, D. (2013) The Folk Probably Do Think What You Think They Think. *Australasian Journal of Philosophy*, 91(3): 421–441.

Foot, P. (1967) The Problem of Abortion and the Doctrine of the Double Effect. *Oxford Review*, 5.

Gettier, E.L. (1963) Is Justified True Belief Knowledge? *Analysis*, 23: 121–123.

Gibbard, A. (1992)*Wise Choices, Apt Feelings: A Theory of Normative Judgment*, Cambridge, MA: Harvard University Press.

Goodwin, G.P. and Darley, J.M. (2008) The Psychology of Meta-Ethics: Exploring Objectivism. *Cognition*, 106(3): 1339–1366.

Greene, J.D., in preparation. Notes on "The Normative Insignificance of Neuroscience" by Selim Berker. Available at: https://joshgreene.squarespace.com/s/notes-on-berker.pdf.

Greene, J.D. (2014a) Beyond Point-and-Shoot Morality: Why Cognitive (Neuro)Science Matters for Ethics. *Ethics*, 124(4): 695–726.

Greene, J.D. (2014b) *Moral Tribes: Emotion, Reason, and the Gap Between Us and Them*, Reprint edition, New York: Penguin Books.

Greene, J.D. (2008) The Secret Joke of Kant's Soul. In W. Sinnott-Armstrong, ed. *Moral Psychology, Vol 3: The Neuroscience of Morality: Emotion, Brain Disorders, and Development*. Cambridge, MA: MIT Press: 35–80.

Greene, J.D. et al. (2009) Pushing Moral Buttons: The Interaction between Personal Force and Intention in Moral Judgment. *Cognition*, 111(3): 364–371.

Greene, J.D. et al. (2001) An fMRI Investigation of Emotional Engagement in Moral Judgment. *Science*, 293: 2105–2108.

Kelly, D. et al. (2007) Harm, Affect, and the Moral/Conventional Distinction. *Mind & Language*, 22(2): 117–131.

Khoo, J. and Knobe, J. (2016) Moral Disagreement and Moral Semantics. *Noûs* (advance online publication).

Knobe, J. and Nichols, S. (2008) *Experimental Philosophy*, Oxford: Oxford University Press.

Machery, E. et al. (2015) Gettier Across Cultures. *Noûs* (advance online publication).

Mikhail, J. (2011) *Elements of Moral Cognition: Rawls' Linguistic Analogy and the Cognitive Science of Moral and Legal Judgment* 1st ed., Cambridge: Cambridge University Press.

Mikhail, J. (2007) Universal Moral Grammar: Theory, Evidence and the Future. *Trends in Cognitive Sciences*, 11(4): 143–152.

Nadelhoffer, T. and Nahmias, E. (2007) The Past and Future of Experimental Philosophy. *Philosophical Explorations*, 10(2): 123–149.

Nagel, J. (2012) Intuitions and Experiments: A Defense of the Case Method in Epistemology. *Philosophy and Phenomenological Research*, 85(3): 495–527.

Nichols, S. (2004) After Objectivity: An Empirical Study of Moral Judgment. *Philosophical Psychology*, 17(1): 3–26.

Nichols, S. (2002) How Psychopaths Threaten Moral Rationalism: Is It Irrational to Be Amoral? *The Monist*, 85(2): 285–303.

Nucci, L. (1981) Conceptions of Personal Issues: A Domain Distinct from Moral or Societal Concepts. *Child Development*, 52(1): 114–121.

Sarkissian, H. et al. (2011) Folk Moral Relativism. *Mind & Language*, 26(4): 482–505.

Shafer-Landau, R. (2003) *Moral Realism: A Defence*, Oxford: Oxford University Press.

Sinnott-Armstrong, W. et al. (2008) Intention, Temporal Order, and Moral Judgments. *Mind & Language*, 23(1): 90–106.

Smetana, J.G. (1981) Preschool Children's Conceptions of Moral and Social Rules. *Child Development*, 52(4): 1333–1336.

Smith, M. (1994) *The Moral Problem*, Oxford: Blackwell Publishing.

Sripada, C., in preparation. Intuitions, Tacit Theories, and Experimental Philosophy.

Sripada, C. (2012) What Makes a Manipulated Agent Unfree? *Philosophy and Phenomenological Research*, 85(3): 563–593.

Sripada, C.S. and Konrath, S. (2011) Telling More than We Know about Intentional Action. *Mind & Language*, 26: 353–380.

Stich, S. and Weinberg, J.M. (2001) Jackson's Empirical Assumptions. *Philosophy and Phenomenological Research*, 62(3): 637–643.

Strandberg, C. and Björklund, F. (2013) Is Moral Internalism Supported by Folk Intuitions? *Philosophical Psychology*, 26(3): 319–335.

Svavarsdottir, S. (1999) Moral Cognitivism and Motivation. *The Philosophical Review*, 108(2): 161–219.

Thomson, J.J. (1985) The Trolley Problem. *The Yale Law Journal*, 94(6): 1395–1415.

Turiel, E. (1983) *The Development of Social Knowledge: Morality and Convention*, Cambridge: Cambridge University Press.

Wainryb, C. et al. (2004) Children's Thinking About Diversity of Belief in the Early School Years: Judgments of Relativism, Tolerance, and Disagreeing Persons. *Child Development*, 75(3): 687–703.

Weinberg, J.M., Nichols, S. and Stich, S. (2001) Normativity and Epistemic Intuitions. *Philosophical Topics*, 29: 429–460.

Williamson, T. (2007)*The Philosophy of Philosophy*, Oxford: Blackwell Publishing.

40

Quasi-realism

Terence Cuneo

Over forty years ago, Simon Blackburn introduced the philosophical world to a figure he called the "quasi-realist." According to Blackburn, the quasi-realist is someone who "starting from an antirealist position finds himself progressively able to mimic the thoughts and practices supposedly definitive of realism" (Blackburn 1993: 4; see Blackburn 1994, 1998). In the intervening years, other philosophers – most notably, Allan Gibbard – have joined Blackburn in developing the quasi-realist research program in metaethics, defending it from objections and arguing that it exhibits considerable promise (Gibbard 2003, 2012). These efforts at developing and defending quasi-realism have garnered considerable attention from sympathizers and critics alike. Still, the view has remained elusive: it proves extraordinarily difficult to formulate an accurate and informative statement of what quasi-realism is.

It is no accident that quasi-realism defies ready characterization. A close look at what its proponents say when characterizing the view reveals two ambiguities that explain not just why the position is so difficult to characterize but also to assess. I dedicate the first part of this chapter to identifying these ambiguities and their import. Having located these ambiguities, I close by articulating a challenge that the view must address, which is that it offers no satisfactory account of how we can make moral mistakes.

PRELIMINARIES

Let us begin with some preliminary matters. In the passage quoted above from Blackburn, we're told that the quasi-realist starts from an antirealist position and then progressively mimics the thoughts and practices (supposedly) definitive of realism. When Blackburn says that the quasi-realist starts metaethical theorizing from an antirealist position, he has a particular type of moral antirealist position in mind. The position is a close relative of A. J. Ayer's expressivist view according to which there are no moral facts or truths, and all moral thought and discourse are, or express, states of approbation or disapprobation toward non-moral reality (Blackburn 1993: 187). Similarly, when Blackburn says that the quasi-realist progressively mimics the "thoughts and practices supposedly definitive of realism," he also has a particular version of moral realism in mind. The version of realism in question is something close to G. E. Moore's nonnaturalism according to which moral thought and discourse represent moral reality, which is itself not part of the natural order investigated by the sciences (Blackburn 1998: chapter 3; Gibbard 2003). In short, the quasi-realist begins metaethical theorizing from an expressivist starting point but ends up affirming claims that sound a lot like nonnaturalist moral realism.

To make sense of this strategy, we need to understand what distinguishes expressivist positions such as Ayer's from realist ones such as Moore's. I propose to do so as follows. Suppose we were to reflect on everyday moral thought and practice in our capacity as ethical theorists. Such reflection reveals that:

(i) Moral judgments have the marks of a descriptive belief: they are classificatory, truth-evaluable, apt candidates for knowledge, and apt for inference.
(ii) Not any response to a moral question will do; we can make moral mistakes. Moreover, some answers to moral questions are better than others.
(iii) Moral judgments have the marks of a practical attitude: they are often directive and motivationally efficacious.

Let us call these the *core metaethical data* (or the "core data," for short). Much of what transpires in metaethical theorizing consists in different theories attempting to accommodate and explain these (and other) data – or to explain why they do not require accommodation.

Realism typically attempts to accommodate and explain the full range of data stated above. It does so by appeal to the following two theses:

Moral Representation: moral thought and discourse represent moral facts. That is, they have moral representational content.

And:

Moral Facts: there are moral facts.

According to realism, its first thesis fully accommodates and explains data such as (i) and partially accommodates and explains data such as (iii). It is because moral thought and discourse represent moral reality that moral judgments have the marks of descriptive beliefs and can guide our behavior. Realism adds that it's the combination of its two theses that accommodates and explains data such as (ii). In at least some cases, we make moral mistakes when we inaccurately represent the moral facts. The point to underscore for our purposes is that realism does not simply embrace Moral Representation and Moral Facts. It also commits itself to:

Explanation: when attempting to accommodate and explain the core moral data, appeal to Moral Representation and Moral Facts.

For ease of reference, call these the *realist theses*.

Expressivists have devoted most of their energies attempting to accommodate and explain (i). Their attempted accommodation and explanation is distinctive in two respects. First, unlike realism, it does not appeal to Moral Representation. Instead, it appeals to:

Attitude: moral thought and discourse are, or express, attitudinal states. These are states of commendation and condemnation that lack moral representational content.

Second, in its most sophisticated quasi-realist guises, expressivism has often *embraced* the first two realist theses stated above. Nonetheless, it has steadfastly maintained that it is not a version of realism, since it rejects Explanation in favor of:

No Explanation: when attempting to accommodate and explain the core moral data, do not appeal to Moral Representation or Moral Facts. Rather, appeal to claims such as Attitude.

Blackburn is explicit about the negative component of this commitment when he writes that expressivism is "visibly antirealist, for the explanations offered make no irreducible or essential appeal to the existence of moral 'properties' or 'facts.'" (Blackburn 1993: 175; cf. Gibbard 2003: 183; Dreier 2004).

I have said that expressivism has devoted most of its energies to accommodating and explaining (i). No Explanation, however, implies that expressivism endeavors to accommodate and explain not just (i) but the full range of core moral data. The textual evidence appears to favor attributing this claim to expressivism. For example, when Gibbard writes that "[a]lmost all of what descriptivists insist on can be embraced and explained by an expressivist" and that what "quasi-realism mimics is not tempered realism as a whole but tempered realism in all but one respect," he indicates that expressivism has wide ambitions (Gibbard 2003: 20; 2011: 45). The position attempts to "mimic" what realism attempts to accommodate and explain while also embracing No Explanation. Moreover, a look at how expressivists have responded to the charge that it fails to accommodate and explain items that are plausibly viewed as belonging to the core data reveals a distinctive pattern. For example, when Nicholas Sturgeon charges that expressivism cannot capture the explanatory role of moral reality, Blackburn replies that it can (Sturgeon 1991; Blackburn 1993: chapter 11). When Andy Egan contends that expressivism cannot explain certain kinds of moral mistakes, Blackburn maintains that the charge is untrue (Egan 2007; Blackburn 2009). And when Sharon Street charges that expressivism cannot vindicate the trustworthiness of moral judgments, Gibbard replies that this is not so (Street 2011; Gibbard 2011). In this respect, expressivism is unlike positions such as subjectivism and error theory, which do not attempt to accommodate and explain the full range of core moral data, and like realism, which does attempt to accommodate and explain the full range of core data. At any rate, in what follows I'll refer to the two theses stated above as the *expressivist theses*.

WHAT IS QUASI-REALISM?

Having addressed these preliminary matters, we're now ready to address the question of how best to understand the quasi-realist project. To help us address this question, let's have before us a series of passages in which quasi-realists articulate their view. Earlier we heard Blackburn note that he:

invented the figure of the quasi-realist, or someone who "starting from an anti-realist position finds himself progressively able to mimic the thoughts and practices supposedly definitive of realism."

After describing quasi-realism as an approach that "mimics Moore's and Ewing's non-naturalistic moral realism," Gibbard qualifies what he says, writing that quasi-realism endeavors to thoroughly mimic the "tempered" nonnaturalism of Derek Parfit, T. M. Scanlon, and others:

> What quasi-realism mimics is not tempered realism as a whole but tempered realism in all but one respect ... . We [quasi-realists] can't mimic the claim that understanding normative properties and relations as objective matters of fact is basic to explaining how moral judgments of wrongness work.
>
> (Gibbard 2011: 44)

In the terminology that I've used, Gibbard maintains in this passage that quasi-realism mimics tempered realism but not in every respect, since quasi-realism rejects Explanation, which implies that moral reality explains elements of the core moral data.

There are some important differences between these passages from Blackburn and Gibbard that I'll discuss in a moment. For now, I want to focus on what they have in common: each passage states that quasi-realism ends up saying things that sound very much like realism because the quasi-realist engages in mimicry (Blackburn 1993: 4, 15; Gibbard 2011: 45, 47; 2003: 9, 43, 81, 112, 180–81, 220). What is it for a metaethical approach to engage in mimicry? And what would it be for such mimicry to be successful? Quasi-realists say less about these matters than one might anticipate, given how prominent the activity of mimicry seems to be to their project. And some of what they say is perplexing (compare Blackburn 2005b: 323 and 1993: 16, 52). But even without offering an informative answer to these questions, we can say some informative things about *how* quasi-realists endeavor to mimic what Blackburn calls "the apparently 'realist' appearance of ordinary moral thought" (Blackburn 1993: 151). In the first place, mimicking the realist appearances consists in formulating and defending an elaborate "logic of attitudes," which endeavors to establish that attitudinal states can behave more or less exactly like ordinary beliefs (Hale 1993; Schroeder 2008). If this project were successful, it would help quasi-realists to accommodate and explain data such as:

(i) Moral judgments have the marks of a descriptive belief: they are classificatory, truth-evaluable, apt candidates for knowledge, and apt for inference.

Second, in order to mimic the realist appearances, quasi-realism embraces deflationist or "minimalist" views regarding representation, truth, and facthood. This approach is manifest in passages such as the following in which Gibbard writes:

> In one sense there clearly are "facts" of what a person ought to do, and in a sense of the word "true" there is a truth of the matter. That's a minimalist sense, in which "It's *true* that pain is to be avoided" just amounts to saying that pain is to be avoided – and likewise for "It's a fact that."
>
> (Gibbard 2003: x; cf. Gibbard 2012: 49; cf. Blackburn 1998: 79)

For reasons that will emerge in the final section, it is a delicate matter to state exactly what the theoretical benefits of propounding deflationary views regarding representation, truth, and facthood are supposed to be. The passages just quoted seem to suggest that "going deflationary" allows quasi-realists to rather closely mimic the sorts of things that nonnaturalist realists say when stating their views. And that, in turn, may help quasi-realists to affirm the legitimacy of certain areas of ordinary moral thought and discourse in which agents claim not only that torture is wrong but also that it is *true* (or that it is a fact) that it is wrong.

So far, we've canvassed two strategies that quasi-realism employs to mimic "realist-sounding" moral thought and discourse: developing a logic of attitudes and embracing deflationism with regard to representation, truth, and facthood. This helps us to understand the means by which quasi-realism engages in mimicry. But we don't yet have a clear understanding of what the central aim of the quasi-realist project is, and what the view would affirm were it to achieve its central aim. As indicated earlier, answering these questions is more challenging than it might seem because each question reveals an ambiguity that must be addressed if we're to have a firm grip on the aims and claims of the quasi-realist project.

Let's begin with the first ambiguity. A close look at the passages I've quoted from Blackburn and Gibbard reveals that these philosophers formulate their views in importantly different and not clearly compatible ways. Moreover, not only are these formulations different, some incorporate puzzling assumptions about how theories relate to what they are supposed to explain.

Begin with the passage from Blackburn that I've already quoted twice. In this passage, Blackburn writes that the quasi-realist finds himself progressively able to mimic "the thoughts and practices supposedly definitive of realism" – where is it clear that by this last phrase Blackburn means the "central elements of our ethical thought and practice" (Blackburn 1993: 4). Elsewhere, Blackburn characterizes quasi-realism differently, writing that the view endeavors to mimic "the realist-sounding discourse within which we promote and debate (our) views," and to show "how much of the apparently 'realist' appearance of ordinary moral thought is explicable and justifiable on an anti-realist picture" (Blackburn 1994: 315; 1993: 151; cf. Blackburn 1993: 77; 1994: 180). Let's call these formulations, which state that quasi-realism aims to mimic the "realist-sounding" or "realist-seeming" dimensions of ordinary moral thought and practice, the *practice-mimicking* formulations of quasi-realism.

Gibbard's formulations of quasi-realism are different. When Gibbard characterizes quasi-realism, he typically states that its aim is to mimic, not realist-sounding ordinary moral thought and discourse, but the particular metaethical theses to which realism commits itself (see Gibbard 2011). These theses include claims about how moral concepts work (they represent moral reality) and the existence and character of moral facts (they are among those things that moral concepts represent). Let's call these formulations, which state that quasi-realism aims to mimic the elements of realism itself, the *theory-mimicking* formulations of quasi-realism.

The practice-mimicking and theory-mimicking formulations of quasi-realism might seem like minor variations on a common theme. But they are not. They are formulations that can diverge in important respects.

Consider the practice-mimicking formulations to start with. Note that quasi-realists could coherently accept these formulations but reject the theory-mimicking formulations of their view. They might do this, moreover, because they hold that much of what realism says – such as that there is a "world of norms and Forms" – is false (Blackburn 2005a: 59). Since (in their view) what realism says is by-and-large false, there would be no point in mimicking realism's claims and commitments. This is, in fact, what some of those sympathetic with the view say (PEA Soup 2015).

Now turn to the theory-mimicking formulations. Note that quasi-realists could coherently accept these formulations but reject the practice-mimicking formulations. They might do this for two reasons. First, quasi-realists might deny that ordinary moral thought and practice is "realist-sounding," holding, for example, that such thought and discourse is largely metaethically neutral (Carter and Chrisman 2012). And, second, quasi-realists might affirm – contrary to what some advocates of the practice-mimicking formulations say – that there is excellent reason for quasi-realism to mimic what realism says. After all, realism commits itself to claims such as:

It is a fact that torture is wrong.

And:

We know that torture is wrong,

which appear to be true. In addition, realism rejects other claims such as:

Torture is wrong simply because we presently disapprove of it.

And:

Were we to approve of torture, then (in those circumstances) we would know that torturing is right,

which we have excellent reason to take to be false. If realism is correct to affirm the first pair of claims and to reject the second pair, then there would be a clear and principled rationale for developing a theory that endeavors to mimic what realism says.

The practice-mimicking and the theory-mimicking formulations of quasi-realism, then, are importantly different. Not only are they importantly different, the reasons for accepting formulations of one sort can be incompatible with the reasons for accepting formulations of the other sort. The fact that these formulations can have divergent and even incompatible implications and justifications raises interpretive questions for those who want to understand the quasi-realist project. And the interpretive questions do not end here. In some cases, they become more acute the more carefully one examines the formulations themselves.

This is especially true of the practice-mimicking formulations of quasi-realism. Recall that these formulations tell us that quasi-realism endeavors to mimic the thoughts and practices that are allegedly definitive of realism or are "realist-sounding." With our earlier distinction between the core metaethical data and the theses to which metaethical theories appeal when attempting to accommodate and explain these data, consider the practice-mimicking formulations of quasi-realism once again. (I assume that the core metaethical data include, but are not limited to, what Blackburn calls "central elements of our ethical thought and practice.")

Take the claim that the core metaethical data are "supposedly definitive of realism." A moment's reflection reveals that there are no such data. For what is definitive of realism are not the core metaethical data, but the realist theses. Or consider the formulations of quasi-realism which say that there are "realist-seeming" or "realist-sounding" data. Again, we have excellent reason to hold that there are no such data for the simple reason that the core metaethical data do not seem or sound like the metaethical theses that realism affirms (or, for that matter, the theses that any major metaethical theory affirms). For example, there is no interesting sense in which the datum:

(ii) Not any response to a moral question will do; we can make moral mistakes. Moreover, some answers to moral questions are better than others,

seems or sounds like any of the realist theses. To say it again, realism endeavors to *explain* this datum (and others like it) by appeal to the realist theses. In general, however, there is little reason to suppose that what explains some range of data sounds or seems like the data themselves (or that what is doing the explaining is somehow "built into" the data).

These observations raise the concern that the practice-mimicking formulations of quasi-realism do not admit of a cogent characterization. Think of the concern like this: suppose that advocates of the practice-mimicking formulations were to concede that there is nothing "realist-like" about the core metaethical data, since these data do not seem or sound like the realist theses. Still, proponents of the practice-mimicking formulations of quasi-realism might insist that there are "realist-friendly" data that realism smoothly accommodates and explains, which quasi-realism aims to mimic. But, in fact, quasi-realists do not attempt to mimic data such as (i), which tells us that moral judgments have the marks of descriptive belief. Rather, they attempt to accommodate and explain them from an antirealist and expressivist basis. To accommodate and explain, however, is not *ipso facto* to mimic. Were realism to accommodate and explain (i) in one way and quasi-realism to do so in another way, it would not follow that realism had thereby mimicked these data (or quasi-realism, for that matter).

Suppose, then, we characterize practice-mimicking formulations of quasi-realism as follows: they describe a position that endeavors to accommodate and explain realist-friendly data from a starkly antirealist and expressivist basis. The problem with this formulation is that there appears to be nothing particularly quasi-realist about the view it describes. After all, the view it describes attempts to neither mimic the realist-seeming data (because there are none) nor the realist theses (since it rejects theory-mimicking formulations of quasi-realism). Moreover, the mere fact that this view endeavors to accommodate and explain realist-friendly data from an antirealist starting point does not appear to render it distinctively quasi-realist. After all, rival metaethical views, such as versions of constructivism and error theory, do the same (see Blackburn 1998: chapter 4; 2005a: chapter 5; Olson 2014).

We have been discussing how best to characterize the central aim of the quasi-realist project. When looking at passages in which quasi-realists state their view, we noticed that they characterize it differently. Some endorse practice-mimicking formulations, while others accept theory-mimicking formulations. We've also seen that these formulations diverge in important ways. Practice-mimicking formulations, moreover, appear to incorporate some puzzling assumptions about the relations in which theories and the data that they try to accommodate and explain stand. In fact, I've claimed that when we try to free these formulations from these assumptions, it is unclear that what remains is quasi-realist in any interesting sense.

Admittedly, all metaethical theories incorporate ambiguities. Some matter and some do not. In drawing attention to the difference between practice-mimicking and theory-mimicking formulations of quasi-realism, I have tried to identify an ambiguity that matters. It matters because metaethical theories are often accompanied by two sorts of adequacy conditions. One sort of adequacy condition is internal: it specifies the conditions that a theory must satisfy by its own lights. For example, theory-mimicking formulations of quasi-realism state that quasi-realism must thoroughly mimic the realist theses. Another type of adequacy conditions is external: it specifies the conditions that any metaethical theory must satisfy to be worthy of acceptance. Satisfying these conditions, for example, might consist in a theory accommodating and explaining the core metaethical data. We can determine whether quasi-realism satisfies the first sort of adequacy condition, however, only if we know what the aim of quasi-realism is – what it endeavors to accomplish. And this, we've seen, is not apparent.

Let us now turn to the second ambiguity, which concerns not quasi-realism's central aim, but what the view would commit itself to, were it to satisfy its central aim. The concern that quasi-realists ought to be wary of whether their view satisfies its central aim has long animated critics. The concern can be expressed in a dilemma: either quasi-realism successfully mimics realism or it does not. If the project is successful, then quasi-realism ceases to be a distinctive position: it collapses into a version of realism (see Dreier 2004). If the project is not successful, then it fails to satisfy its own aims. Either option is unacceptable. The first is unacceptable because quasi-realism is supposed to be an alternative to realism that is immune to the problems that afflict realism. The second option is also unacceptable because then the view fails to satisfy adequacy conditions of its own devising (see Wright 1988; Dworkin 1996).

While this dilemma deserves consideration, I am concerned not to press it but to explore a question to which it directs our attention, which is this: Suppose quasi-realists were to execute their project successfully. What claims would it thereby commit both itself and ordinary moral agents to? I am going to suggest that, on this issue, the textual evidence pulls us in two different directions. Some texts suggest that quasi-realists commit themselves to a position I call *Thin expressivism*, while other texts suggest that quasi-realists commit themselves to a different and incompatible position that I call *Thick expressivism*.

To appreciate the differences between these views, consider a moral sentence such as:

(E) "It is a fact that torture is wrong."

According to Thin expressivism, to sincerely utter (E) is:

(1) to express an attitudinal state (say, that of condemning torture).

And:

(2) not to state that there is (or otherwise commit oneself to the existence of) a moral fact, namely, *that torture is wrong*.

Thin expressivism holds that an agent would make no mistake by not committing herself to the existence of moral facts when uttering (E), for it embraces:

(3) either there are no moral facts or it is not possible to state that there are such facts using standard moral (or metaethical) discourse.

In contrast, according to *Thick expressivism*, to sincerely utter (E) is:

(4) to express an attitudinal state.

And also:

(5) to state or otherwise commit oneself to the existence of moral facts.

Thick expressivism maintains that an agent would make no mistake by committing herself to the existence of moral facts when uttering (E) because it holds:

(6) there are moral facts (although they do not explain the core metaethical data).

In what follows, I want to look at some passages in which quasi-realists appear to endorse Thin expressivism. I'll then turn to passages in which they appear to endorse Thick expressivism.

In *Ruling Passions*, Blackburn writes:

> The theory I want to defend is one that gives a story about the way in which ethical thought functions. Valuing something, it says, is not to be understood as *describing* it in certain terms, any more than hoping for or desiring something are describing it in particular terms.
>
> (Blackburn 1998: 49)

On the assumption that to value something is to express one's thoughts "in terms of what is good, bad, obligatory, right, justifiable," this passage appears to commit quasi-realism to claims (1) and (2) stated above.

But if there were moral facts, wouldn't this position commit ordinary agents to a mistake of sorts – a mistake that consists not in misrepresenting ethical reality, but in failing to represent it and be guided by it? In various places, Blackburn explains why such agents would commit no mistake:

> Protected by quasi-realism, my projectivist says the things that sound so realist to begin with – that there are real obligations and values, and that many of them are independent of us, for example … . He *affirms all that could ever properly be meant by saying that there are real obligations* … . It is just that the explanation of why there are obligations … is not quite that of untutored common sense. It deserves to be called anti-realist because it avoids the view that when we moralize we respond to, and describe, an independent aspect of [moral] reality.
>
> (Blackburn 1993: 157)

Elsewhere, Blackburn states more forthrightly why an agent who sincerely uttered (E) but did not commit herself to there being moral facts would make no mistake. Discussing the issue of whether his view commits itself to the thesis that actions are wrong because we disapprove of them, Blackburn writes:

> According to me, there is only one proper way to take the question "On what does the wrongness of wanton cruelty depend?": as a moral question, with an answer in which no mention of our actual responses properly figures. There *would* be an external (i.e., metaethical) reading if realism were true. For in that case there would be a fact, a state of affairs (the wrongness of cruelty) whose rise and fall and dependency on others could be charted. But antirealism acknowledges no such state of affairs and no such issue of dependency.
>
> (Blackburn 1993: 173)

In these two passages, Blackburn appears to affirm (3), stating either that there are no moral facts (as in the second passage quoted) or that talk of such facts must be "heard in an ethical tone of voice" in which we are merely "trying to express and systemize our actual values" (as in the first passage quoted) (Blackburn 1998: 50). In fact, in various places, Blackburn suggests that there is no such thing as distinctively metaethical discourse regarding a range of putatively central metaethical questions and that, in fact, moral realism is not really a philosophical position at all (Blackburn 2010). For any attempt to formulate or defend realism, Blackburn says, is simply a matter of expressing attitudinal states: "this is why any 'cognitivism' or 'realism' that supposes itself to be protecting (moral objectivity) actually marks no philosophical position. It amounts, at best to an ethical commitment: something like an injunction to get involved" (Blackburn 1998: 297; Blackburn 2010).

Thin expressivism is not, however, the only interpretation of quasi-realism that receives textual support. Consider, for example, what Blackburn says in this passage:

> Now, if the projectivist adopts quasi-realism, he ends up friendly to moral predicates and moral truth. He can say with everyone else that various social arrangements are unjust, and that it is true that this is so. Once this is said, no further theoretical risks are taken by saying that injustice is a *feature* of such arrangements, or a quality that they possess and that others do not. The first step, in other words, is to allow propositional forms of discourse, and once that is done we have the moral predicate, and features are simply abstractions from predicates.
>
> (Blackburn 1993: 206; cf. 8, 181)

Elsewhere, Blackburn expands upon this idea:

> Yes, I am an anti-realist; no, this does not mean that there are no facts of an ethical or normative kind.
>
> Quasi-realism … refuses to give ethical facts a typical explanatory role. This is already heralded when we turn our back on ethical representation. A representation of something as F is typically explained by the fact that it is F. A

representation *answers* to what is representational. I hold that ethical facts do not play this explanatory role.

(Blackburn 1999: 216)

Far from denying that moral facts exist, these passages find Blackburn affirming that they exist. As such, these passages appear to commit quasi-realism to (5) and (6). In the first passage, Blackburn seems to commit quasi-realism to the claim that uttering a sentence such as (E) commits an agent to things having moral properties (but not necessarily to the claim that the agent thereby describes these properties when engaging in moral thought and discourse). In the second passage, Blackburn affirms that there are moral facts but denies that they play the explanatory roles attributed to them by realists.

In some places, Gibbard appears to go even further than this, writing that, according to quasi-realists, "normative terms like 'ought' … signify natural properties." Using Sidgwick's position as an example, Gibbard suggests that "ought" might refer to the property "being *unihedonic*." Of course this observation is consistent with Thin expressivism; advocates of this view needn't deny that moral predicates refer to natural properties. However, Gibbard goes on to claim that quasi-realism can affirm that "the property being what one ought to do just *is* the property of being unihedonic" (Gibbard 2002: 56). That is, Gibbard appears to affirm that there is a property *being what one ought to do*, which actions have, and it is identical with a natural property. In saying this, Gibbard appears to commit quasi-realism to a claim that is stronger than (6). The difference between his view and Blackburn's is that Gibbard does not claim that moral properties are "abstractions" from or "shadows" of moral predicates. Rather, Gibbard affirms that they are simply natural properties that are part of the causal order and, hence, explanatorily robust. (I'll return to this position at the end of this discussion.)

The question that we are exploring is what quasi-realism would commit itself to were it to successfully journey from its stark antirealist starting point to its more realist-friendly end point. Thin expressivism provides one answer; Thick expressivism provides another. These answers are not compatible. Therefore, any attempt to assess quasi-realism must address the questions of whether one of these positions is the best interpretation of quasi-realism or whether there is no unified quasi-realist program but only versions of quasi-realism – some staying close to the program's antirealist roots, others venturing very close to (if not collapsing into) a version of realism. Like the first ambiguity we considered, this ambiguity is also important. Not only would it be illegitimate for quasi-realists to slide back and forth between these two versions of their view when responding to objections (as might be feared), any assessment of quasi-realism must also pay close attention to which version of quasi-realism is under consideration. Which version of quasi-realism is under consideration can, moreover, have important ramifications regarding how highly one rates the view's prospects.

ASSESSING QUASI-REALISM

A natural conclusion to draw from the preceding section is that we are in no position to assess the viability of the quasi-realist program because it is unclear how to understand the program's aims and commitments. Indeed, one might conclude that there is no unified view or research program designated by the term "quasi-realism." There are only a variety of incompatible views flying under the banner of quasi-realism that must be distinguished and considered on an individual basis.

Rather than conclude that we should forestall any assessment of quasi-realism until we settle this interpretational situation, let me try to push the discussion forward by voicing a challenge to the view (or family of views). In voicing this challenge, we need to keep in mind that it may apply only to some versions of quasi-realism.

Quasi-realism's advocates often present the view as representing a metaethical via media, an approach that strikes a path between equally unattractive metaethical options. On the one hand, quasi-realism is supposed to represent an alternative to the realist's way of theorizing in which realism simply helps itself "to normative facts at the outset" (Gibbard 2003: 183). On the other hand, quasi-realism is designed to be a viable antirealist alternative to error theory and subjectivism (Blackburn 1993: chapters 8, 9). Critics have charged, however, that the contrast between quasi-realism and these rival antirealist views is much less pronounced than it might seem: *all* these views are subject to the objection that they fail to accommodate and explain some deeply entrenched features of the moral life (see FitzPatrick 2010; Parfit 2011: chapter 28).

Perhaps the best way to articulate the challenge in question is to return to the core metaethical data and, in particular, the datum that:

(ii) Not any response to a moral question will do; we can make moral mistakes. Moreover, some answers to moral questions are better than others.

Let us dub this the *Mistake datum*. One point of deep dissatisfaction with both error theoretic and subjectivist positions is that they do not accommodate this datum. True, the error theory, which holds that all of our moral judgments are untrue, can accommodate the fact that we make moral mistakes. This is because the view implies that *all* our moral judgments are mistaken. But the view also implies that no moral response is better than any other: all are equally erroneous. Subjectivism, which holds that what makes an act right (for an agent) is that she approves of it and that what makes an act wrong (for an agent) is that she disapproves of it, is (in this regard) the mirror image of error theory. For, given the plausible assumption that we tend to know what we approve of and disapprove of, subjectivism implies that (nearly) all our moral judgments (which concern what we approve of and disapprove of) are correct. It also implies that it is very difficult to make moral mistakes. Most importantly, subjectivism implies that it is impossible for one response to a moral question to be better than another: they are all equally good.

Quasi-realism rejects both error theory and subjectivism. So, critics cannot plausibly charge that it fails to accommodate the Mistake datum for the same reasons that these views fail to. Even so, it may be that quasi-realism fails to accommodate the Mistake datum for different reasons.

Let us pursue this possibility by considering Thin expressivism once again. Thin expressivism offers an account of what it is to say or think that performing an action is wrong: to think or say that an action is wrong is to be in, or to express, an attitudinal state. Thin expressivism also tells us what it is to say or think things such as:

It is a fact that torture is wrong.

And:

It is true that torture is wrong.

Given their deflationary or minimalist commitments, Thin expressivists typically tell us that to say or think these things is simply to say or think:

Torture is wrong,

which is itself an attitudinal state or the expression thereof.

But it is one thing for a position to affirm that we can say or think that it is true (or correct) that torture is wrong, and to explain what it is to say or think such things. It is another thing for a view to imply that it *is* true (or correct) that torture is wrong, and to explain *what it is* for it to be true (or correct) that torture is wrong. Admittedly, Gibbard seems to run the two issues together when he writes:

> In one sense there clearly are "facts" of what a person ought to do, and in a sense of the word "true" there is a truth of the matter. That's a minimalist sense, in which "It's *true* that pain is to be avoided" just amounts to saying that pain is to be avoided – and likewise for "It's a fact that."
>
> (Gibbard 2003: x)

But the issues are different, and we can draw no conclusions about whether there are moral facts or truths by appealing to minimalist or deflationist accounts of what it is to think or say something factual or true, as this passage appears to.

We are now positioned to formulate what I'll call the *No Mistake challenge*:

(A) If Thin expressivism fails to accommodate and explain the Mistake datum, then there is an important respect in which it is identical with other antirealist positions such as error theory and subjectivism.

(B) Thin expressivism fails to accommodate and explain this datum.

(C) So, there is an important respect in which Thin expressivism is identical with other antirealist positions such as error theory and subjectivism: it fails to accommodate and explain the Mistake datum.

Now suppose we assume:

(7) If a metaethical position fails to accommodate and explain the Mistake datum, then that is prima facie reason to reject it.

It follows that we have prima facie reason to reject error theory, subjectivism, and Thin expressivism because none of them accommodates and explains the Mistake datum.

Let's consider four replies that quasi-realists might offer in response to the No Mistake challenge. These responses range from those that are not at all concessive to those that are quite concessive to realism.

The first reply: The No Mistake challenge assumes that a metaethical position could attempt to accommodate and explain the Mistake datum by appealing to moral facts. Thin expressivism rejects this assumption, at least when it is understood along non-expressivist lines. Instead, Thin expressivism holds that all talk of moral facts and moral mistakes must be understood simply to be the expression of attitudinal states. The impression that there is a cogent non-expressivist account of such talk is illusory.

Here is an argument for this claim, which might be implicit in some of the passages quoted earlier from Blackburn (see Blackburn 1993: 174). Suppose Thin expressivism were true, offering an accurate account of the character of moral/metaethical thought and discourse across the board. If it were, then moral/metaethical sentences would not even purport to represent moral reality or standards that could render some moral judgments mistaken; they would express attitudinal states. But when non-expressivists, such as realists and constructivists, engage in moral/metaethical discourse, they use moral/metaethical sentences. So, they cannot be stating moral propositions (i.e., moral representational contents) when using these sentences. Instead, they must be using these sentences to express attitudinal states. If this is right, then the claim that all moral/metaethical discourse must express attitudinal states is simply an implication of Thin expressivism.

The argument is problematic. It is problematic not just because it implies that realists and other "factualists" do not know what they are saying when they say that there are moral facts or that we make moral mistakes, which looks deeply uncharitable (see Cuneo n.d.). The argument is also problematic because its premises do not imply its conclusion. To see why, distinguish *standard* from *non-standard* moral/metaethical discourse. Such discourse is standard, let's assume, just in case it conforms to the ordinary use of moral/ metaethical sentences. Otherwise, it is non-standard. Now suppose, for argument's sake, that Thin expressivism offers us an account of standard moral/metaethical discourse and that its advocates engage in such discourse when developing their position.

Note that these assumptions are compatible with the following two claims. First, realism offers us an account of non-standard moral/metaethical discourse and its proponents engage in such discourse when developing their position. Second, they have good reason to, because standard moral/metaethical discourse is deeply problematic, lacking expressive power. Among other things, such discourse lacks the resources that would enable its users to talk about moral reality (however that is understood) and moral mistakes. It is probably worth adding that if the scenario I am presenting were to describe the actual character of contemporary metaethical debate, it follows that there would be no genuine moral or metaethical disagreement between Thin expressivism and realism (and nearly all other metaethical positions). At best, there would be a meta-semantic disagreement about how to engage in moral/metaethical discourse (see Plunkett and Sundell 2013).

The second reply: The No Mistake challenge overlooks an important sense in which expressivism is different from other antirealist positions. The primary difference is that expressivists employ "the core expressivist maneuver" (Carter and Chrisman 2012). Think of the maneuver as having three steps. The first step is to switch the subject: rather than concern itself with the question of what it is for something to be a moral fact or truth, expressivism concerns itself with what it is to express a normative judgment. The second step is to remind us that expressivism offers a distinctive account of what moral thought and discourse are, which rejects the claim that moral judgments have moral representational content. The third step consists in expressivists concluding that they (in their role as theorists) can "just stop talking" about moral facts or the accuracy of moral judgments and, instead, issue first-order moral judgments "inside the domain of ethics" (Carter and Chrisman 2012: 334; cf. Blackburn 1998: 50; Gibbard 2003: x). By ceasing to talk about the topic of moral facts or truths, advocates of the core expressivist maneuver needn't claim that these facts or truths do not exist. They can simply note that they are not of ethical interest, and that the view can remain agnostic about whether they exist (Carter and Chrisman 2012).

This reply fails to engage the No Mistake challenge. Remaining agnostic about the existence of moral facts or truths does not accommodate or explain the Mistake datum. It goes no distance toward explaining how agents could make moral mistakes if quasi-realism were true (as opposed to explaining how we can think and say that there are such mistakes). Since it fails to do this, when taken on its own, the core expressivist maneuver does not explain why quasi-realism fares better with regard to the No Mistake challenge than error theory or subjectivism.

The third reply: The No Mistake challenge is directed at Thin expressivism. Quasi-realists should reject this view, opting instead for Thick expressivism. The benefit of doing so is that critics cannot charge quasi-realism with failing to account for the possibility of moral mistakes because quasi-realism denies that moral facts exist. Thick expressivism does not reject but affirms their existence.

This reply also fails to engage the No Mistake challenge. The No Mistake challenge charges Thin expressivism with being unable to explain how we could make moral mistakes. This charge also applies to Thick expressivism. This is because Thick expressivism endorses No Explanation, which tells us that moral facts fail to play explanatory roles, which enables a theory to accommodate and explain the core metaethical data, such as the Mistake datum.

The fourth reply: Quasi-realists should opt for a version of Thick expressivism according to which moral facts *can* explain various elements of the core metaethical data. Since these facts are simply natural facts, this admission does not compromise the integrity of the quasi-realist project.

We have seen that there are passages in which quasi-realists seem to endorse this view (Gibbard 2002; cf. Ridge 2014). I'll make only two observations about it in closing.

The first is that this position is not clearly quasi-realist. It does not "start from an anti-realist position." Rather, it helps itself to the natural world and all its denizens, including among its denizens the moral facts. It is true that this version of Thick expressivism does not invoke these facts in order to do exactly the same explanatory work that they do in a realist scheme. But these facts do explanatory work nonetheless: they explain how we can make moral mistakes. Indeed, if appeal to such "mistake conditions" is necessary to explain how attitudinal states could behave like ordinary beliefs – as Schroeder (2008: chapter 10) argues – then this view would appeal to these facts *at the outset of theorizing* to explain the workings of moral thought and discourse. This, however, is exactly what quasi-realists maintain that their view does not do. To which I'll add, that once moral facts are added to the quasi-realist picture, many of the moves quasi-realists make, in response to certain kinds of objections, would be puzzling at best.

Take, for example, the accusation that quasi-realism cannot account for the fact that kicking dogs for fun would be wrong even if we approved of it. In reply to this accusation, quasi-realists have appealed to metalinguistic/semantic theses about what we are saying when we say that kicking dogs would be wrong even if we approved of it (Blackburn 1994: 218; Dreier 2012). This type of reply would be unnecessary – and puzzling! – if Thick expressivism were true. It is enough for Thick expressivists to point out that the relevant moral facts are attitude-independent, and they settle the issue of whether kicking dogs would be wrong in those circumstances that we approved of it.

The second observation is that quasi-realists have assiduously avoided delving into such issues as the ontology of moral facts, focusing nearly exclusively on what it is to think or express moral thoughts. In fact, a persistent selling point of quasi-realism is that it can avoid wading into the waters of moral ontology (Blackburn 1993: 171; cf. Schroeder 2010: 8). But if quasi-realists are just reductive naturalists about moral reality, then they will have to address these issues and respond to the many objections raised against reductive naturalism. In a way, embracing this last Thick expressivist reply to the No Mistake challenge commits quasi-realism to a two-flank battle: a battle against those who reject an expressivist account of moral thought and discourse, and those who reject a reductive naturalist metaphysic of moral reality. Given the hard work that remains to be done on both these issues, it may be that the attempt to vindicate quasi-realism – assuming that there is a unified approach that answers to the label – has just begun.

ACKNOWLEDGMENT

Thanks to the editors and Jamie Fritz for their comments on an earlier draft of this chapter.

REFERENCES

Blackburn, S. (1993) *Essays in Quasi-Realism*, Oxford: Oxford University Press.

Blackburn, S. (1994) "Quasi-realism," *The Oxford Dictionary of Philosophy*, Oxford: Oxford University Press: 315.

Blackburn, S. (1998) *Ruling Passions*, Oxford: Oxford University Press.

Blackburn, S. (1999) "Is Objective Moral Justification Possible on Quasi-Realist Foundations?" *Inquiry* 42: 213–28.

Blackburn, S. (2005a) *Truth: A Guide for the Perplexed*, Oxford: Oxford University Press.

Blackburn, S. (2005b) "Quasi-realism Is No Fictionalism," in M. Kalderon (ed.) *Fictionalism in Metaphysics*, Oxford: Oxford University Press.

Blackburn, S. (2009) "Truth and A Priori Possibility: Egan's Charge against Quasi-Realism," *Australasian Journal of Philosophy* 87(2): 201–213.

Blackburn, S. (2010) "Truth, Beauty, and Goodness," in R. Shafer-Landau (ed.) *Oxford Studies in Metaethics*, Vol. V, Oxford: Oxford University Press: 295–314.

Carter, J. A. and Chrisman, M. (2012) "Is Expressivism Incompatible with Inquiry?" *Philosophical Studies* 159: 323–39.

Cuneo, T. (n.d.) "The Expressivist Gap."

Dreier, J. (2004) "Meta-ethics and the Problem of Creeping Minimalism," in J. Hawthorne (ed.) *Philosophical Perspectives* 18, *Ethics*, Oxford: Blackwell: 23–44.

Dreier, J. (2012) "Quasi-Realism and the Problem of Unexplained Coincidence," *Analytic Philosophy* 53: 269–87.

Dworkin, R. (1996) "Objectivity and Truth: You'd Better Believe It," *Philosophy and Public Affairs* 25: 87–139.

Egan, A. (2007) "Quasi-Realism and Fundamental Moral Error," *Australasian Journal of Philosophy* 85: 205–219.

FitzPatrick, W. (2010) "Ethical Non-naturalism and Normative Properties," in M. Brady (ed.) *New Waves in Metaethics*, London: Palgrave: 7–35.

Gibbard, A. (2002) "Reasons of a Living Being," *Proceedings and Addresses of the Aristotelian Society* 76: 45–60.

Gibbard, A. (2003) *Thinking How To Live*, Cambridge, MA: Harvard University Press.

Gibbard, A. (2011) "How Much Realism?" in R. Shafer-Landau (ed.) *Oxford Studies in Metaethics*, Vol. V, Oxford: Oxford University Press.

Gibbard, A. (2012) *Meaning and Normativity*, Oxford: Oxford University Press.

Hale, B. (1993) "Can There Be A Logic of Attitudes?" in J. Haldane and C. Wright (eds.) *Reality, Representation, and Projection*, Oxford: Oxford University Press: 337–63.

Olson, J. (2014) *Moral Error Theory: History, Critique, Defense*, Oxford: Oxford University Press.

Parfit, D. (2011) *On What Matters, Vol. II*, Oxford: Oxford University Press.

PEA Soup (2015) "Does Expressivism Have a Knowledge Problem?" March 16. Available at http://peasoup. typepad.com/peasoup/2015/03/does-expressivism-have-a-knowledge-problem-by-featured-philosopher-terence-cuneo.html.

Plunkett, D. and Sundell, T. (2013) "Disagreement and the Semantics of Normative and Evaluative Terms," *Philosophers' Imprint* 13. http://hdl.handle.net/2027/spo.3521354.0013.023.

Ridge, M. (2014) *Impassioned Belief*, Oxford: Oxford University Press.

Schroeder, M. (2008) *Being For*, Oxford: Oxford University Press.

Schroeder, M. (2010) *Noncognitivism*, London: Routledge.

Street, S. (2011) "Mind-Independence without the Mystery: Why Quasi-Realists Can't Have It Both Ways." in R. Shafer-Landau (ed.) *Oxford Studies in Metaethics*, Vol. 6, Oxford: Oxford University Press: 1–32.

Sturgeon, N.L. (1991) "Contents and Causes: A Reply to Blackburn," *Philosophical Studies*, 61: 19–37.

Wright, C. (1988) "Realism, Antirealism, Irrrealism, Quasirealism," in P. French, T. Uehling, and H. Wettstein (eds.) *Midwest Studies in Philosophy* 12: 12–49.

41

Metaethical Quietism

Doug Kremm and Karl Schafer

Much like fanatics and hipsters, quietists are seldom quick to describe themselves as such. So it's unsurprising that contemporary metaethicists tend to avoid describing themselves in such terms. Indeed, many of the authors discussed below would actively oppose any such label. And yet analytic metaethics has often been haunted by the specter of various forms of metaethical quietism. For it is distinctive of quietism that it calls into question, if not the very intelligibility of much of metaethics, then at least its point.

In this essay, we begin by discussing how to understand metaethical quietism. In doing so, we distinguish several attitudes towards canonical metaethical questions that might be regarded as quietist. Then we discuss some prominent motivations for quietism—before turning to some recent objections to these views. We conclude by saying a bit about the relationship between these issues and more general questions of philosophical methodology. In discussing these issues, we will attempt to be as charitable as possible to the quietist—not because we are necessarily quietists ourselves—but because we want these views to have as fair a hearing as possible.

CHARACTERIZING QUIETISM

As we understand it, quietism in its various forms can be characterized in terms of the rejection of some range of questions as unworthy of philosophical debate. As a first pass, then, a metaethical quietist can be understood as someone who rejects at least a significant subset of metaethical questions in this way.

So understood, as a question-directed attitude (Friedman 2013), quietism can be made precise in at least two ways: First, with respect to the precise sort of "rejection" it involves, and, second, with respect to the set of questions it rejects.

On the first issue, we can distinguish the following grounds on which someone might reject a set of questions, Q:

Unintelligible: The questions within Q lack meaning or sense.
Indeterminate: The answers to the questions within Q lack determinate truth-conditions.
Presupposition Failure: The questions within Q involve a false presupposition.
Irresolvable: The questions within Q are in principle rationally irresolvable.
Inaccessible: The answers to the questions within Q are epistemically inaccessible.
Irrelevant: The questions within Q are irrelevant to the underlying concerns that are sup-
            posed to make these questions interesting or significant.

As we will see, quietists are often less than fully clear about exactly which sort of rejection they mean to endorse. But it will be useful to keep these possibilities in mind in what follows.

Similar difficulties of interpretation also arise with the second issue. Here it is important to stress two things. First, as will become clear, most forms of quietism are motivated by views that might reasonably be regarded as metaethical—such as views about the nature of normative concepts or inquiry. Thus, most "metaethical quietists" are not really quietists about *all* aspects of metaethics. Rather, they are quietists about *certain sorts* of metaethical questions, and their quietism about these questions is grounded in their views about other areas of metaethics. Most often, their quietism relates to the metaphysical aspects of contemporary metaethics, but it often extends to epistemological and semantic questions within metaethics—especially if these are understood in a manner that involves implicit metaphysical commitments. But all the same, this local quietism is usually motivated by further commitments about the nature of normative talk and thought. As such—while there is tendency for localized quietism to "creep" out to other areas—truly universal metaethical quietism is a creature seldom seen in the wild.

In addition, most metaethical quietists do not adopt a quietist stance towards substantive questions *within* ethical or normative discourse. This is significant here because quietists often hold that many apparently "metaethical" questions can be interpreted as *merely* raising first-order normative questions. Thus, many quietists draw a distinction between questions that are "internal" to first-order normative debate and those that are, at least in part, "external" to it—with their quietism only applying to (some of) the latter.

As is familiar from similar debates in metametaphysics, drawing such a distinction is no easy task (Eklund 2009; Chalmers 2009). Thus, by making use of it, the quietist is taking on a significant philosophical burden. That said, the rough idea here is familiar enough: The quietist takes a question to be "internal" to ethical or normative discourse if it can be settled *solely* through an appeal to the standards of good ethical or normative reasoning. Thus, the idea here is that whatever you're doing when you engage in good normative reasoning, that's all you need to do in order to answer apparently "metaethical" questions that are interpreted "internally."

Given this, it is best to characterize metaethical quietism, not simply in terms of the rejection of certain metaethical questions, but rather in terms of the rejection of these questions *when they are interpreted in an "external" fashion*:

Metaethical Quietism: A view is *metaethically quietist* insofar as it rejects certain metaethical questions as unworthy of philosophical debate, when these questions are interpreted in an "external" fashion.

On this definition, quietism is a matter of degree. The result is a very broad definition of quietism, which catches in its net (at least to some degree) many views that fail to count as "quietist" on other characterizations. For example, compare McPherson's definition of "quietist realism" (see also Enoch 2011):

> Quietist realism is characterized by two claims. On the one hand, it is a form of realism, accepting that there are normative facts and properties. On the other, it suggests that accepting the existence of such facts and properties does not lead to the sort of explanatory burdens (that require metaphysical answers as opposed to substantive normative theorizing).
>
> (2011: 224)

McPherson's "quietist realism" counts as a form of metaethical quietism in our sense since it rejects certain explanatory questions when these are understood in an external or metaphysical sense. But it is only one instance of quietism in this sense. For example, as we will explore below, many forms of quasi-realism also count as *somewhat* quietist by our standard. This will, we know, seem a mistake to some. After all, while quasi-realists do claim that many apparently metaethical questions are only meaningful insofar as they are given an "internal" or normative reading, they also attempt to *explain* this fact in terms of a systematic account of normative thought and talk.

These further explanatory ambitions might be thought to place the quasi-realist outside of the quietist camp. But this seems to us too quick. After all, even McPherson's quietist realists—such as Dworkin, Parfit, and Scanlon—generally offer *some* explanation of their rejection of many "external" metaethical questions. And these explanations, like those of the quasi-realists, generally rely on claims about the nature of normative thought and inquiry. So while there is no doubt that the explanatory ambitions of (say) Blackburn and Gibbard go beyond those of Parfit and Scanlon, this difference is more a matter of degree than it might seem (compare Dreier forthcoming-1). In short, if *any* attempt to explain one's rejection of certain metaethical questions in terms of further metaethical claims is sufficient to disqualify one from the quietist camp, it will be hard to find *any* instances of metaethical quietism. Thus, it seems to us better to think of metaethical quietism as a loose family of views, whose "quietism" is a matter of degree. This helps to illuminate the important commonalities between expressivist, pragmatist, and realist motivations for local quietism. And it has the additional advantage of fitting well with the tendency of some quietists to describe quietism, not as a particular philosophical view, but rather as a general orientation towards, or suspicion of, certain traditional philosophical questions.

MOTIVATIONS FOR QUIETISM

In this section, we'll discuss a number of possible motivations for metaethical quietism. But there are other motivations in the literature. And one very general motivation is worth stressing at the start. Quietists often argue that their view improves on non-quietist alternatives by allowing us to avoid many of the perennial sources of meta-ethical controversy via giving a "minimal" or "purely internal" reading of the questions that haunt metaethicists (Dworkin 1996). Thus, a very general motivation for quietism is simply the hope of explaining away a sense that the absence of a distinctively meta-ethical answer to such questions is a philosophical failing. (For this theme in a general philosophical context, see the development of Wittgensteinian themes in McDowell 1996, 1998a, 1998b.)

Quietism and Meaningfulness

Let us begin with what would perhaps be the simplest and most straightforward moti-vation for quietism about metaethics. One might simply dismiss metaethical questions because one thinks that such questions lack meaning or sense. This was the motiva-tion behind the logical positivists' dismissal of many normative questions, as well as many metaphysical questions more generally (Carnap 1935; Ayer 1936). And, as we will see, some forms of contemporary metaethical quietism may be seen as develop-ing this general line of thought. But there is a prima facie challenge to such views that explains the rejection of Carnap's or Ayer's criteria for meaningfulness. One criterion of success for a theory of meaning is that it counts as intelligible questions which tend to be treated as such by a wide range of competent speakers. In particular, if a wide range of competent speakers are able to engage in what seems like coherent and systematic discussion of metaethical questions, it seems fair to assume—absent of any argument to the contrary—that those questions are intelligible. And a theory of meaning which renders such questions unintelligible thus seems to be, to that extent, defective—unless some further account can be given of why the appearance of meaning in such cases is an illusion.

One way of doing this might be to insist that metaethical questions are posed in terms that are, for reasons that can be explained, systematically misleading. One might say, for example, that questions posed in terms of 'truths' and 'facts' are of this sort. Call such terms *the culprit terms*. If the quietist could provide an account of the meaning of these terms which shows why certain questions posed in terms of them are unintelligible, and if she could provide a corresponding explanation of why such questions would naturally seem intelligible to a wide range of competent speakers, then the problem just mentioned would not arise. Given such an account, the debate between quietists and their opponents would turn on whether the latter could provide an alternative and independently plau-sible account of the culprit terms—one that vindicates the intelligibility of the relevant metaethical questions.

Minimalism and Quietism

A sophisticated version of this line of thought involves distinguishing two uses of the terms in question—the first of which is perfectly meaningful but plays into the quietist's hands, while the second can only be made meaningful at the cost of losing its metaethi-cal significance. As an example of this strategy, we can consider the case of *generalized minimalism*. According to minimalism about terms like 'true', 'property', and 'fact', the ordinary meaning of these terms or concepts is exhausted by certain simple patterns of inference. So, for example, on a simple version of these views, the meaning of 'true' is exhausted by the inference rule that allows us to move freely between 'P' and 'It is true that P', and the meaning of 'fact' is exhausted by the inference rule that licenses moving between 'P' and 'It is a fact that P'. If an account along these lines is correct, then the ordinary meaning of these terms will be quite minimal, and in general it will add little to the meaning of 'P' to say that 'It is true that P' or 'It is a fact that P'. In the normative case, the upshot of this will be that the ordinary meaning of seemingly metaethical claims like 'It is a fact that murder is wrong' will be more-or-less equivalent to the meaning of first-order normative claims like 'Murder is wrong'.

Thus, for the minimalist, the ordinary notions of 'true', 'fact', 'belief' and the like do not provide us with a mechanism for raising metaethical questions that are distinct from first-order normative questions. Instead, these terms only provide us with a mechanism for raising first-order normative questions in a form that would otherwise be impossible. Thus, if these are the only meanings that can be attached to terms like 'true' and 'fact', we cannot use these terms to raise questions of a *distinctively* metaethical sort. (See Dreier 2004.) For a recent proposal along these lines, see Blackburn (2013) (also Gibbard 2003; Price 2009). Similarly, it often seems charitable to read the references of quietists like Parfit (2011) to a "non-ontological sense" of 'existence' or 'fact' as referring to a broadly minimalist use of these terms.

Of course, such claims rest on a controversial view of the meaning of terms like 'true' and 'fact'. And even if one accepts that minimalism is the correct theory of our ordinary use of these terms, one could go on to argue that there are *also* more philosophical uses of them that allow us to build more substance into their meaning. If so, while minimalism would show that our ordinary notions of 'true' and the like are ill-suited to give meaning to distinctively metaethical questions, this would not show that such questions are meaningless—only that we must look beyond the ordinary notions of 'true' and the like to give them meaning. In this way, debates about quietism often develop into debates about *which* concepts to use in doing philosophy (Burgess and Plunkett 2013; Plunkett 2015).

There is, however, a risk in making this move. For if the opponent of quietism gives up on the idea that metaethical questions are concerned with moral truths or facts in the ordinary sense, and insists that such questions are instead invoking a "more philosophical" sense of 'true' or 'fact', then she needs to explain why those questions are interesting or significant in the ways that metaethical questions are generally assumed to be. (Obviously it would not do, for example, to simply define a notion of truth as *whatever would have been endorsed by Ayer*, and then to pronounce that there are no moral truths.) What the anti-quietist needs here, then, is a notion of 'true' or 'fact' which is substantial enough to give meaning to distinctively metaethical questions while also preserving their significance. In this way, debates about whether metaethical questions are *intelligible* often lead into debates about whether they are *relevant*.

Expressivist/Pragmatist Motivations

Closely related ideas can be found in expressivist or pragmatist motivations for quietism. One central commitment of expressivist or pragmatist views about moral practice is the idea that the best theoretical understanding of moral judgments construes them as something other than representational beliefs—as emotions, practical commitments, or the like. (Note that this is different from saying that such judgments aren't beliefs. The central claim of these views is that we can best *explain* such judgments without appealing to a non-deflationary notion of belief or representation; this is compatible with maintaining that such judgments are beliefs, although as theorists we need to earn the right to say this.) Philosophers who endorse such views sometimes then go on to insist that, given an expressivist or pragmatist understanding of moral practice, any attempt to pose certain sorts of wholly "external" questions about moral reality or truth will amount to a kind of *category mistake*.

The reasoning here goes roughly like this. Suppose that normative judgments are best explained as a kind of practical commitment, so that in the most basic case, judging that you ought now to φ is (roughly) deciding to φ (Gibbard 2003). Notice, then, that it makes no sense—on this level of description—to ask whether such a judgment is true in the sense of accurately representing the facts. Such judgments are, after all, a kind of decision, and it seems strange to ask whether decisions accurately represent the facts (Dreier 2012). Suppose, next, that we explain other normative judgments in terms of these basic elements (e.g., to judge that you ought to have φed in circumstances C is (roughly) to adopt a practical commitment to φing in C), and that we tell a consistent story about how such judgments come to be embedded in complex logical contexts (Blackburn 1998: chapter 3; Gibbard 2003: chapter 4). Finally, suppose that we then tell a story about how various "culprit terms" such as 'true' and 'fact' come to have a role in all of this (e.g., in thinking about whether to accept Jane's views on torture, one might ask whether Jane's views are true, whether they get the facts right, etc.). Then, questions about moral truths, facts, etc. will make sense if they are understood "internally"—e.g., as questions about which practical commitments to adopt—but if such questions are understood "externally" they will involve a kind of category mistake, akin to the mistake involved in asking whether some decision accurately represents the facts.

This line of thought supports a kind of *conditional local quietism*: the idea is that, *if* one is an expressivist or a pragmatist, *then* the only way to pose the kinds of metaphysical questions that have formed much of the subject matter of metaethics is as first-order normative questions. The case for this kind of quietism thus depends, ultimately, on the case for an expressivist or pragmatist treatment of moral practice. Moreover, since expressivist and pragmatist treatments of moral practice often appeal to a broadly minimalist understanding of the culprit terms (at least insofar as those terms figure in *moral* practice), the work required to sort out these debates will end up overlapping to some extent with the work required to sort out the debates over minimalism that we encountered and left open above. (It is worth noting that a similar line of thought—but one that starts from a constructivist view of normative concepts—seems to lie behind some of Korsgaard's remarks about metaethics. See, for example, Korsgaard 2008: 322n.44; 1997: 66–7. Compare James 2012, 2013.)

Moral or Normative Motivations

Before discussing normative motivations for quietism, we should note at the outset that quietism itself may need to be understood as a kind of normative view, if it is going to be capable of drawing support from normative considerations. Rorty is admirably clear on this point in his introduction to *Consequences of Pragmatism*:

> [P]ragmatists see the Platonic tradition as having outlived its usefulness. ... [T]hey do not think we should ask [Platonic] questions anymore. When they suggest that we not ask questions about the nature of Truth or Goodness, they do not invoke a theory ... which says that "there is no such thing" as Truth or Goodness. They would simply like to change the subject.
>
> (1982: xiv)

There are two important points here. The first is that Rorty uses explicitly normative language to state his view: the idea is that we *should* stop asking certain kinds of questions. The second point is that Rorty does not intend to support this view by appealing to a general theory about the subject matter of those questions (e.g. Truth or Goodness). For Rorty, the essential point is not that these questions make no sense, but that they're "bad questions," in the sense that they are at best *utterly unhelpful* and at worst *positively harmful*. As Rorty says in a number of places, there is nothing wrong with talking about facts or "inner representations," so long as these are not taken to do any explanatory or justificatory work (Rorty 1979: chapter 4). Such talk becomes problematic only when it is understood in a certain way—viz., as issuing the sorts of claims that could be established by engaging in a domain-neutral inquiry, and that could adjudicate debates within or across domains by providing some kind of *grounding* for them. Thus, so long as such talk does no real explanatory or justificatory work, we can regard it as innocuous, but as soon as we try to make it do such work, it becomes not just unhelpful, but misleading and dangerous.

For Rorty this follows in part from the (very controversial) view that, even if we can form a coherent idea of *reality as it exists independently of any representation of it*, or of *the truths that "outstrip" any way of knowing about them*, we lack any way of settling questions about such matters that does not question-beggingly presuppose an answer to them. Thus, Rorty believes that it is useless to ask questions about that world or about those truths, and then to try assessing the "status" of various domains in terms of how well they succeed in representing that world or capturing those truths. The conclusion Rorty draws from this is that there is simply *no point* in preserving the relevant notions of reality and truth in terms of which such questions are posed (1982: xxiv); his claim is that we ought to abandon those notions altogether, and to "extirpate" the philosophical intuitions and puzzles to which they give rise (ibid.: xxxi). An interesting upshot here is that, since Rorty's position is a normative one—since it is a view about which concepts we ought to use, which questions we ought to try answering, which problems are worth taking seriously, and so on—his opponent needs to defend an opposing normative view. As Rorty puts it, he needs to defend the idea that "the raising of the good old metaphysical problems ... served some good purpose, brought something to light, was important" (ibid.: xxix; cf. 1979: 281). (For an important criticism of Rorty's view, see Boghossian 2006. For an argument that the world *does* have a metaphysically privileged description, see Sider 2011.)

Another broadly normative motivation for quietism is suggested in Blackburn's remark that to insist that morality must have an "external" metaphysical grounding is to express a "defective sensibility" (1993: 156–7). To see how this line of thought might be developed, start with Blackburn's idea of a sensibility as a kind of "fact-in/attitude-out grinder" (1993: 92). An agent's sensibility takes in bits of information and churns out various kinds of emotional and practical responses. Particularly important here are those emotions and practical attitudes that an agent needs to have in order to count as *taking morality seriously.* An agent who takes morality seriously presumably feels a certain way about her own moral attitudes and those of other agents; she's inclined to let these attitudes influence her deliberation; to encourage, admire, and praise the cultivation of such attitudes in herself and others; to resist, oppose, and criticize conflicting attitudes and behavior; and so on.

Now, the way that an agent is disposed to revise these attitudes is also relevant for the moral assessment of her sensibility. Someone who's inclined to give up taking morality seriously in these ways, upon learning that doing so would bring her fame and fortune, would seem to have a defective sensibility, for example.

So consider someone who's inclined to give up taking morality seriously upon learning that there are no moral facts in an "external" sense of 'fact'. The "defective-sensibility" quietist believes that "external" metaethical claims, insofar as they're genuinely external, should be irrelevant to whether we take morality seriously. He might support this by pointing out what such questions would have to be like, simply in virtue of being "external." They would have to be the sorts of questions that one could not answer by means of normatively engaged, moral reflection. Given this, the quietist might then say, it would amount to a kind of defect—a defect in one's moral sensibility—to take the answers to such questions to bear directly on moral matters. In short, the thought goes, such a sensibility would hold moral reflection hostage to the results of non-moral reflection in a morally objectionable manner.

This argument rests on a substantive moral evaluation of the decision to change the way that one relates to one's moral attitudes on the basis of wholly "external" claims. How could someone find it appropriate to give up, say, the seriousness with which she regards others' suffering, solely in response to wholly "external" claims? According to Blackburn, she could only do this if "a defective sensibility leads [her] to respect the wrong things"—e.g. if it leads her to respect only those attitudes that have "external" support (ibid.: 156). On the other hand, if someone *doesn't* think that it would be at all appropriate to stop taking morality seriously upon learning that it has no external grounding, it will be hard to make sense of her as genuinely believing that morality *needs* such a grounding in order to be taken seriously. (See Kremm [ms] for further development of this line of argument.)

Appeals to the "Fragmentation of Inquiry"

Finally, there are motivations for quietism that appeal to the idea that inquiry is "fragmented" into distinct and more-or-less autonomous domains of thought. This idea has been suggested by Nagel (1986, 1997), Dworkin (1996, 2011), and Scanlon (2003, 2014), among others. According to these philosophers, normative thought is different in kind from, say, thought about the physical world, or thought about mathematical objects, and because of this fundamental normative judgments are *autonomous,* in the sense that they "do not need and could not have" the support of judgments outside of the normative domain. This means, of course, that if judgments about the existence of normative truths or facts are not understood as being normative judgments (of a suitably abstract kind), they will be incapable of supporting (or undermining) fundamental normative judgments. And if that's right, we would have a strong case for thinking that "external" questions about normative truths or facts are irrelevant to the underlying concerns that were supposed to make them interesting or significant to begin with.

Why do these philosophers think that inquiry is "fragmented" in this way? Unfortunately, they do not address this question directly, so it is somewhat difficult to say. Scanlon says that this is the view that "makes most sense" (2014: 19), and Dworkin says that the alternative "radically misunderstands what value judgments are" (2011: 25). Nonetheless, the basic idea seems to be roughly as follows. Think about the claim that *the butler did it*, and contrast this with the claim that *there is a largest prime number*. These are two different kinds of claim, and they call for different kinds of inquiry. You can't figure out whether the butler did it by going through mathematical proofs, and you can't figure out whether there's a largest prime number by interrogating witnesses from a crime scene. Similarly, the thought goes, for normative claims, such as the claim that we all have reason to want to avoid agony. You can't figure out whether we have such reasons by engaging in anything other than normative inquiry, just as you can't figure out whether there's a largest prime by engaging in anything other than mathematical reasoning. But all of these claims can be cast in "ontological" form, using the existential quantifier (e.g., there exist reasons to want to avoid future agony; there exists a largest prime number; there exists a property of *having done it*, which the butler instantiates). The "fragmentation theorist" will thus insist that these questions, at least on the most fundamental level, need to be settled by domain-specific reasoning; if we can't figure out whether we have reason to avoid future agony by engaging in anything other than normative reasoning, then we can't figure out whether there *exist* such reasons by engaging in metaethical inquiry if this is understood as something distinct from normative inquiry.

For example, Scanlon advocates a kind of *domain-autonomism*, which he illustrates by considering the autonomy of mathematics, taking set theory as his primary example. Scanlon's view takes for granted a plurality of "domains," understood not (in the first instance) in terms of *objects*, but rather in terms of certain kinds of *claims* and associated *concepts* (e.g., mathematics, natural science, practical reasoning). Insofar as these domains license claims that can be expressed using the existential quantifier, they can be said to embody certain ontological commitments. But this notion of an ontological commitment is *domain-specific*. According to Scanlon, all ontological questions are "domain-specific," in the sense that they are to be settled by standards that are internal to the respective domains in which they arise; the standards for existence thus depend on the kind of claim in question. For example, questions such as whether there is an empty set, or whether there are such things as imaginary numbers, are settled by reasoning that is "internal" to the mathematical domain, whereas questions about whether there are magnetic fields are settled by reasoning that's internal to the domain of natural science. Crucially, these standards are not *merely* epistemic in character—they determine, not just when we are justified in making some claim, but also whether this claim is true or false. Thus, there is a sense in which the "universe" over which we quantify is fundamentally disjunctive for Scanlon. (Compare McDaniels 2009.) In short, for Scanlon, *what there is* is only as unified as our discourse or inquiry into what there is.

Importantly, Scanlon allows that we could conduct a kind of domain-neutral inquiry into "everything we are committed to quantifying over in a range of particular domains," but he thinks that this sort of inquiry would not have much of a point, since the general idea of existence *as such* is not capable of providing any "bases for standards of existence beyond those of ... particular domains" (24). Against this, one might emphasize the importance of giving a unified explanation of all of these varied domains. But, to some degree at least, Scanlon takes the project of unifying these various domains to be *pointless* because he believes that there are no determinate standards for its success or failure. (There are many reasonable questions one might raise about this approach—for some discussion of the issues here, see Enoch and McPherson [forthcoming] and Dreier [forthcoming-1].)

Dworkin, on the other hand, emphasizes the autonomy of *interpretive* domains, such as Constitutional law and literary criticism (Dworkin 2011: part 2). For reasons of space, we'll leave the complexities of Dworkin's views to the side. What we do want to stress about both Scanlon and Dworkin is that their motivations end up coinciding to a perhaps surprising degree with those of expressivists and pragmatists. As we have seen, according to Scanlon, all ontological questions are to be understood as "domain-specific," in the sense that they are to be settled by standards that are internal to the respective domains in which they arise; the standards for existence thus depend on the kind of claim in question. Similarly, according to Dworkin, truth is simply "what counts as the uniquely successful solution to a challenge of inquiry," and different kinds of inquiry pose different kinds of challenges (e.g., scientific inquiry poses a different kind of challenge from interpretive inquiry, of which moral inquiry is a species) (2011: 177).

These claims—that there is a plurality of autonomous "domains of inquiry," and that truth is the name of a "uniquely successful solution" to a "challenge" in one of those domains—can be read in a variety of ways. Following Wright (1996), one could see them as an endorsement of a form of anti-realism or constructivism about normative truths, on which the standards of normative reasoning are prior to and explain the correct answers to normative questions (Korsgaard 2008; Schafer 2015). But in making such claims of explanatory priority, this view would be "less quietist" than what Scanlon or Dworkin intend. So it seems more apt to understand these claims as similar in spirit to those made by the pragmatist above. Indeed, as Dworkin himself points out, these claims depend on accepting "what Wittgenstein pointed out: that concepts are tools and that we have different kinds of tools in our conceptual toolbox" (ibid. 160). (Cf. Scanlon's claim that not all domains "aim at the same kinds of understanding" [2014: 27].) This yields an explanation of quietism somewhat similar to that given by pragmatists: if truth is the successful solution to a challenge of inquiry, we have to engage in that kind of inquiry in order to figure out whether there's any such thing. Whether there is such a thing as moral truth is thus, for Dworkin, a question of whether we can successfully solve the challenges of moral interpretation. And whether there exist such things as reasons is, for Scanlon, a normative question about whether there are any possible features of an agent's circumstances which might count in favor of her adopting some attitude.

Importantly, both of these moves depend on a particular understanding of moral or normative judgment, as well as a particular understanding of truth and ontological commitment. Thus, Dworkin's and Scanlon's forms of quietism should only be attractive insofar as we find this understanding of truth in ethics preferable to the more explanatorily ambitious forms of realism, constructivism, and expressivism on the metaethical market. Indeed, as one presses Dworkin and Scanlon to explain their view, there is a temptation to think that their views occupy a fundamentally instable position in the metaethical landscape. For example, in his related discussion of truth in ethics, Nagel writes:

> The connection between objectivity and truth is … closer in ethics than it is in science. I do not believe that the truth about how we should live *could* extend radically beyond any capacity we might have to discover it … .
>
> (1986: 139)

At first glance, this seems an odd use of 'objectivity' on Nagel's part. After all, one might have thought that one of the central marks of an objective truth is precisely that it *is* independent from our capacities of discovery in the way that Nagel here seems to be denying for ethical truth. But if there is such a difference between truths about ethics and, say, scientific truths, it is natural to expect some explanation of this difference (Svavarsdóttir 2001; James 2012; Schafer 2015; Enoch and McPherson forthcoming). And much the same might be said of the special connection between judgments about ethics and motivation (Dreier forthcoming-1 and -2). The problem here is that such an explanation seems to require the endorsement of a form of realism or constructivism or expressivism that goes beyond the quietism we find in Dworkin or Scanlon. Thus, whether or not we find their quietism compelling will depend a good deal on how much we expect our metaethical theories to explain.

OBJECTIONS TO QUIETISM

There are a number of important objections to philosophical quietism in the literature. For example, Zangwill (1992) has argued that local quietism requires global quietism, which (in turn) is untenable. And a number of authors have suggested that philosophical quietism of this general sort is somehow self-defeating (Cassam 1986). But for reasons of space, we will focus here on objections that target *metaethical* quietism in particular. The most important of these are what we might call *symmetry arguments*, which attempt to show that, if we accept the quietist view, we will be unable to distinguish the normative domain from other "normative-ish" domains that seem defective or problematic in some way (McPherson 2011; Enoch 2011).

Enoch gives the example of a linguistic community engaged in what he calls "counter-reasons discourse" (compare McPherson's "schmeasoners"). These people judge, for instance, that the fact "that an action will cause the agent pain is counter-reason *for* performing it," and they "treat counter-reasons much as we treat reasons," e.g., they tend to do what they think there's counter-reason to do, to criticize those who don't do what they have counter-reason to do, and so on (124–5). Enoch then points out that, in just the same way that the "internal standards" of the normative domain license claims about the existence of reasons, normative truths, facts, and so on, the "internal standards" of the counter-normative domain also license claims about the existence of counter-reasons, counter-normative truths, facts, and so on. So by the quietist's lights it would seem that, just as we are entitled to believe that there are such things as reasons (etc.), so too the counter-reasoners are entitled to believe that there are such things as counter-reasons (etc.). But intuitively, it seems the counter-reasoners are making some kind of mistake when they go in for this practice; counter-normative discourse seems to be defective in a way that normative discourse isn't. The problem for the quietist is to explain this.

The natural response to this for the quietist is to give a normative explanation of the sense in which the counter-reasons practice is defective. What's wrong with the counter-reasoners is (roughly speaking) that they aren't responsive to *reasons* in the right ways. After all, they treat the fact that an action would cause someone pain as a reason for performing it; of course, they don't *say* that it's a reason—they call it a "counter-reason"— but they still treat it as a reason, in the sense of giving it a certain weight in their decisions about what to do, and this is the sense in which their practice is defective. We shouldn't weigh the fact that an action would cause someone pain in favor of performing that action, and we shouldn't criticize people for failing to perform actions that would cause them pain. More generally, the problem with the counter-reasons practice is that engaging in that practice requires people to do all sorts of things that they shouldn't be doing. That's the rough idea behind the quietist's *normative* response to the symmetry arguments. (An alternative response here would be to insist that the counter-reasoners aren't really conceivable after all. For a version of this line of thought, see Stroud 1965.)

Not surprisingly, for Enoch and McPherson, this reply is inadequate. As Enoch points out, while we can offer a normative criticism of the counter-reasoners, the counter-reasoners can make a parallel claim about us:

> Of course, [counter-reasons] are not as *normatively* respectable as reasons are. And so those acting on them are to be criticized for not acting on the reasons that apply to them. But then again, reasons aren't as *counter*-normatively respectable as counter-reasons are, and we may be counter-criticizable for failing to act on the counter-reasons that apply to us.
>
> (2011: 125)

So, while there is a *normative* asymmetry between reasons and counter-reasons, this asymmetry is matched by a corresponding *counter-normative* asymmetry in the opposite direction. In short, then, the normative asymmetry between reasons and counter-reasons is part of a larger, higher-order symmetry between reasons and counter-reasons.

Once again, our sense is that many quietists (rightly or wrongly) will be unconcerned by this—for they will feel that a *normative* asymmetry between reasons and counter-reasons is all we should have wanted in the first place, and that these further forms of symmetry do not take away from the normative significance of this asymmetry. Quite simply, for the quietist realist, this normative difference between reasons and counter-reasons gives us everything we should want.[1]

All that having been said, it will seem to many non-quietists that we can better capture the intuitive asymmetry between these two domains by turning to a more metaphysically committal form of normative realism. This is just what Enoch and McPherson (forthcoming) suggest. There they argue that only such a form of realism "can say that only the ‑asoners—and not the schmeasoners [or counter-reasoners]—track the normative struc- ‑ of reality." That is to say, the metaphysically committed realist can appeal to the truth ‑external, ontological claim—viz., that reasons exist and counter-reasons don't—in order to explain the sense in which reasons discourse is "better" than counter-reasons discourse. Since this isn't an internal normative claim—but rather an "external" metaphysical or semantic claim—it can't be mirrored by a parallel counter-normative claim in the way that caused problems for the quietist.

Here the quietist is likely to respond by asking whether anything is really gained by this explanation. Is it true that we need to be able to give an external, ontological or semantic explanation of the difference between reasons and counter-reasons? In fact, is such an explanation even possible? The denial of its possibility would be natural if, following Scanlon, we believed that the standards of truth and falsity for normative questions are internal to the domain of normative inquiry. If something like this were true, then questions about the aptness of some system of concepts for describing reality would only acquire determinate answers when viewed within the context of (say) normative inquiry—a sort of inquiry that, for Scanlon, is already structured around certain substantive norms. Thus, Scanlon might insist that the activity of trying to answer such questions only makes sense insofar as they are seen as "internal" to the normative domain.

Indeed, following Blackburn's discussion, we might wonder here whether the search for such an explanation is even appropriate in this case. After all, we will only think that facts about metaphysics or ontology will settle these issues if we think that normative questions should ultimately be sensitive to metaphysics in the manner Enoch and McPherson suggest. And it was this sort of claim that Blackburn objected to above as indicative of a "distorted normative sensibility." So at this stage the quietist may feel—not just that Enoch and McPherson's explanation is no improvement on quietism—but indeed that that explanation is objectionable on normative grounds (Kremm [ms]; compare Erdur 2015).

In short, then, what seems to Enoch and McPherson to be a fatal problem with the quietist view may well seem to the quietist to be one of its main advantages. In this way, the debate here is not merely about *how* a particular problem in metaethics is best solved, but also about *whether* some aspect of the quietist's view is really a problem at all. Once again, this points to the meta-metaethical character of these debates. For what is at issue here is not just the truth about metaethical questions, but also what the terms of success in metaethics, and so the preferred metaethical methodology, should look like in the first place.

QUIETISM AND PHILOSOPHICAL METHODOLOGY

Quietist views are often rejected simply because they seem to be "first and foremost expressions of impatience" (Enoch 2011: 132; cf. Zangwill 1996). This charge is surely fair against some forms of quietism. But many arguments for quietism are less "impatient" or "lazy" than they might at first seem. Rather, they rely on positive theorizing about the nature of normative thought and talk that is quite substantial and controversial in its own right. Of course, this opens these arguments to a variety of objections—including the objection that they are "less quietist" about these issues than they claim to be—but it also makes it harder to dismiss quietism as the expression of a simple distaste for (say) metaphysical theorizing.

Thus, even if quietists need to "earn the right" to their quietism, either through argument or through the sort of "Wittgensteinian therapy" associated with Rorty and

McDowell, it remains an open question whether such attempts might succeed, at least with respect to some of the forms of quietism noted above (Mulhall 2002). And more fundamentally, there is the question of whether quietism might sometimes be the appropriate default attitude to take to certain philosophical questions. At this point, there is often a fundamental methodological gap between quietists and their opponents about the place of explanation within a proper conception of philosophy.

This is just one instance of a more general feature of debates about quietism—namely, the manner in which they bring to the fore deep assumptions that structure the methodology of different schools within contemporary metaethics. This often makes it difficult to discuss these issues without begging the question against one side of the debate. To borrow a quote from Rorty, this may well be "one of those issues which puts everything up for grabs at once" (1982: xliii). Of course, the degree to which this is true will depend in part on how global a philosopher's quietism is. But even local quietists tend to challenge the basic methodological assumptions behind the way the contemporary "metaethics game" is played. Thus, while engagement with quietism can be frustrating, it can also promote reflection on the assumptions which structure our philosophical theorizing—a sort of reflection that is often difficult to achieve from within more local metaethical debates.

NOTE

1. As such, it would be a mistake to confuse this view with the sort of "deflationary normative pluralism" that rejects the claim that there is any "free unsubscripted" sense of 'ought' or 'reason' that has special significance in a normative context (Tiffany 2007). In short, to say that reasons and counter-reasons are structurally on a par is not, for the quietist, to treat them as having the same sort of *normative* significance.

ACKNOWLEDGMENTS

In writing this chapter we were greatly helped by comments from the editors of this collection. Thanks also to Aaron James, Kathryn Lindeman, and Barry Maguire for very useful comments on drafts of it.

RELATED TOPICS

Chapter 5, "Metaethical Expressivism;" Chapter 16, "Conceptual Role Accounts of Meaning in Metaethics;" Chapter 27, The Autonomy of Ethics;" Chapter 37, "Pragmatism and Metaethics;" Chapter 43, "Normative Ethics and Metaethics."

REFERENCES

ver, A. J. (1936) *Language, Truth and Logic*, London: V. Gollancz, Ltd.
kburn, S. (1993) *Essays in Quasi-Realism*, Oxford: Oxford University Press.
urn, S. (1996) "Blackburn Reviews Dworkin," *Brown Electronic Article Review Service*, ed. J. Dreier and stlund, available at http://www.brown.edu/Departments/Philosophy/bears/homepage.html, posted ry 12, 1996.

—. (1998) *Ruling Passions*, Oxford: Oxford University Press.

—. (2013) "Pragmatism: All or Some?" in H. Price (ed.) *Expressivism, Pragmatism, and Representationalism*, pp. 67–84. Cambridge: Cambridge University Press.

Boghossian, P. (2006) *Fear of Knowledge: Against Relativism and Constructivism*, Oxford: Oxford University Press.

Burgess, A. and Plunkett, D. (2013) "Conceptual Ethics" (I and II), *Philosophy Compass* 8: 1091–10.

Carnap, R. (1935) *Philosophy and Logical Syntax*, New York: AMS Press.

Cassam, Q. (1986) "Necessity and Externality," *Mind* 95 (380): 446–64.

Chalmers, D. (2009) "Ontological Anti-Realism," in D. Chalmers, D. Manley, and R. Wasserman (eds.) *Metametaphysics*, Oxford: Oxford University Press.

Dreier, J. (2004) "Metaethics and the Problem of Creeping Minimalism," *Philosophical Perspectives* 18 (1): 23–44.

—. (2012) "Quasi-Realism and the Problem of Unexplained Coincidence," *Analytic Philosophy* 53 (3): 269–87.

—. (forthcoming-1) "Another World: The Metaethics and Metametaethics of Reasons Fundamentalism."

—. (forthcoming-2) "Can Reasons Fundamentalism Answer the Normative Question?"

Dworkin, R. (1996) "Objectivity and Truth: You'd Better Believe It," *Philosophy and Public Affairs* 25 (2): 87–139.

—. (2011) *Justice For Hedgehogs*, Cambridge: Harvard University Press.

Eklund, M. (2009) "Carnap and Ontological Pluralism," in D. Chalmers, D. Manley, and R. Wasserman (eds.) *Metametaphysics*, Oxford: Oxford University Press.

Enoch, D. (2011) *Taking Morality Seriously*, Oxford: Oxford University Press.

Enoch, D. and McPherson, T. (forthcoming) "What Do You Mean 'This Isn't the Question'?" *Canadian Journal of Philosophy*.

Erdur, M. (2015) "A Moral Argument Against Moral Realism," *Ethical Theory and Moral Practice* 1–12.

Friedman, J. (2013) "Question-Directed Attitudes," *Philosophical Perspectives* 27: 145–74.

Gibbard, A. (2003) *Thinking How to Live*, Cambridge: Harvard University Press.

James, A. (2012) "Constructing Protagorean Objectivity," in J. Lenman and Y. Shemmer (eds.) *Constructivism in Practical Philosophy*, Oxford: Oxford University Press.

—. (2013) "Moral Constructivism," in H. LaFollette (ed.) *The International Encyclopedia of Ethics*, Oxford: Blackwell.

Korsgaard, Christine. (1996) *Creating the Kingdom of Ends*, Cambridge: Cambridge University Press.

Korsgaard, C. (2008) "Realism and Constructivism in Twentieth-Century Moral Philosophy," *The Constitution of Agency: Essays on Practical Reason and Moral Psychology*, Oxford: Oxford University Press: 302–326.

Kremm, D. (ms) "A Normative Defense of Meta-Normative Quietism."

McDaniels, K. (2009) "Ways of Being," in D. Chalmers, D. Manley, and R. Wasserman (eds.) *Metametaphysics*, Oxford: Oxford University Press

McDowell, J. (1996) *Mind and World*, Cambridge: Harvard University Press.

—. (1998a) *Meaning, Knowledge, and Reality*, Cambridge: Harvard University Press.

—. (1998b) *Mind, Value, and Reality*, Cambridge: Harvard University Press.

McPherson, T. (2011) "Against Quietist Normative Realism," *Philosophical Studies* 154 (2): 223–40.

Mulhall, S. (2002) "Ethics in the Light of Wittgenstein," *Philosophical Papers* 31 (3): 293–321.

Nagel, T. (1986) *The View from Nowhere*, Oxford: Oxford University Press.

—. (1997) *The Last Word*, New York: Oxford University Press.

Plunkett, D. (2015) "Which Concepts Should We Use?: Metalinguistic Negotiations and the Methodology of Philosophy," *Inquiry* 58 (7–8): 828–74.

Price, H. (2009) "The Semantic Foundations of Metaphysics." Reprinted in Price (2011): 253–79.

—. (2011) *Naturalism Without Mirrors*, Oxford: Oxford University Press.

Rawls, J. (1993) *Political Liberalism*, New York: Columbia University Press.

Rorty, R. (1979) *Philosophy and the Mirror of Nature*, Princeton, NJ: Princeton University Press.

—. (1982) *Consequences of Pragmatism*, Minneapolis: University of Minnesota Press.

Scanlon, T. M. (2003) "Metaphysics and Morals," *Proceedings and Addresses of the American Philosophical Association* 77 (2): 7–22.

—. (2014) *Being Realistic About Reasons*, Oxford: Oxford University Press.

Schafer, K. (2015) "Realism and Constructivism in Kantian Metaethics (1 and 2)," *Philosophy Compass* 10 (10): 690–713.

Sider, T. (2011) *Writing the Book of the World*, Oxford: Oxford University Press.

Stroud, B. (1965) "Wittgenstein and Logical Necessity," *Philosophical Review* 74: 504–18.

Svavarsdottir, S. (2001) "Objective Values: Does Metaethics Rest on a Mistake?" in B. Leiter (ed.) *Objectivity in Law and Morals*, Cambridge: Cambridge University Press.

Tiffany, E. (2007) "Deflationary Normative Pluralism," *Canadian Journal of Philosophy Supp.* Vol 37 (5): 231–62.

Wright, C. (1996) "Truth in Ethics," in B. Hooker (ed.) *Truth in Ethics*, Oxford: Blackwell: 1–18.

Zangwill, N. (1992) "Quietism," *Midwest Studies in Philosophy*, XVII: 160–76.

—. (1996) "Zangwill Reviews Dworkin," *Brown Electronic Article Review Service*, ed. J. Dreier and D. Estlund, available at http://www.brown.edu/Departments/Philosophy/bears/homepage.html, posted February 12, 1996.

FURTHER READING

Ayer, A. J. (1949) "On the Analysis of Moral Judgements." *Horizon*: 171–83. (An early article anticipating some quietist concerns about relevance.)

Pettit, P. (2004) "Existentialism, Quietism, and the Role of Philosophy," in B. Leiter (ed.) *The Future for Philosophy*. Oxford: Clarendon, 304–28. (A more general discussion of the role of quietism in contemporary analytic philosophy.)

Sumner, L. W. (1967) "Normative Ethics and Metaethics." *Ethics* 77 (2): 95–106. (An early article anticipating a number of points made by recent quietists and expressing doubt about the coherence of certain metaethical projects.)

Wick, W. (1953) "Moral Problems, Moral Philosophy, and Metaethics: Some Further Dogmas of Empiricism." *The Philosophical Review* 62 (1): 3–22. (An early article expressing doubts about the idea of a morally neutral investigation of fundamental normative issues.)

42

Methodological Naturalism in Metaethics

Daniel Nolan

INTRODUCTION

The philosophical movement of *naturalism* is normally divided into two strands. One is a methodological one: roughly, that philosophy (or some area of philosophy) should proceed using the methods of the sciences, particularly the natural sciences. The other is a metaphysical one: roughly, that the theory of the world that results from our philosophical inquiries should match, or at least not conflict with, what the sciences tell us there is. This chapter focuses on the first strand of naturalism. What does investigation of metaethics and ethics look like if we take a naturalist approach?

The focus of this chapter will be on methodological naturalism as an approach to metaethics. Part of metaethics, however, involves questions about the epistemology and method of ethics. These include questions about how we know what is morally right or wrong, good or bad, virtuous or vicious, etc., and what method we should use for determining answers to tricky questions about what we should do, how we should be, and what sort of world to aim for (morally speaking). Methodological naturalism about metaethical questions would typically go with methodological naturalism in the epistemology and method of ethics itself, though as we will see below one important strand of contemporary metaethical thinking treats *metaethics* as a naturalistic enquiry but does not treat *ethics* in this way.

A wide range of methodological approaches are claimed to be naturalistic by their proponents. Perhaps this is not surprising—there are many ways an inquiry can be like scientific inquiry, and when there is a lot of disagreement in metaethics, there is likely to be a lot of disagreement even among self-styled naturalists. Rather than trying to determine who are the *real* naturalists, it is more useful to look at the different ways different metaethical theorists take the guiding idea of naturalism in different directions.

Naturalism, of one sort or another, about the epistemology and method of ethical theorising is these days very widespread, but I think this state of affairs would have come as a great surprise to early analytic ethicists. In the first few decades of the twentieth century, one of the great divides in metaethics was between G.E. Moore and other non-naturalists, on the one hand, and the non-cognitivists such as Wittgenstein, Ayer, and Stevenson. Despite their deep disagreements, each camp was convinced that ethics was *not* like science, either in its methods or results.

Moore and other non-naturalists in his camp saw moral intuition as the core of ethical method though metaethics involved conceptual analysis as well: for example, Moore thought it was analytic that right action was a matter of maximising the good (Moore 1993:196).While it is somewhat controversial exactly how Moore saw moral intuition, it was clearly a very different process from scientific inquiry: intuitions were more like verdicts or seemings directly produced by reflection on scenarios, whether actual or imagined, than the results of theorising or observation.

While use of our supposed faculty of intuition was in the first instance a method for determining ethical questions rather than metaethical ones, it is natural to see it as indirectly providing some of the materials for metaethical conclusions as well. For example, why should Moore think that subjectivism about ethics is false? In part because he intuits that the amount of moral goodness of an act of feeding the hungry does not depend very much, or perhaps at all, on who approves of it. Likewise, for intuitions about a range of other scenarios where the difference between cases is only who judges which things are good or bad, or who approves or disapproves of them. (Moore would have likely found this pattern even in scenarios where Moore himself has different attitudes. To adapt a case of Russell's, Moore would have likely intuited that the suffering in bull-fighting is bad even where, counterfactually, Moore himself approves of it.) A good explanation of this pattern (given intuitionist assumptions) is that the goodness of an outcome does not depend very much on who takes it to be good, or who approves of it, and so appears to count against subjectivism.

Non-cognitivists, on the other hand, were equally convinced that ethics was not like science, but for quite different reasons. They rejected a non-naturalistic faculty of moral intuition, along with the idea that there were a special range of moral facts to be discovered. Instead, moral attitudes and moral disagreements involved something other than competing opinions about the facts: clashes of attitudes, perhaps, or conflicting imperatives. One illustration of the methodological anti-naturalism of non-cognitivists is found in an influential paper by Charles Stevenson. Stevenson endorsed a strong form of naturalism about every factual question, but because, in his view, moral disagreements involved clashes in desires as well as beliefs, "scientific methods cannot be guaranteed the definite role in the so-called normative sciences that they may have in the natural sciences" (Stevenson 1963:8).The suggestion that ethics is not concerned with matters of fact, particularly the sort discoverable by the sciences, is an even stronger motif in Wittgenstein's *Lecture on Ethics*: a complete scientific book of the world would "simply be facts, facts, and facts but no Ethics" (Wittgenstein 1965:7).

As the twentieth century went on, the idea that good ethical and metaethical inquiry little in common with the sciences was more widespread even than those who up to either Moorean non-naturalism or the non-cognitivism of Ayer, Stevenson, tein, etc. Traditional methods of ethical inquiry, both in metaethics and in first-s, included at least three important components. The first was the use of philo-moral *intuitions*, direct seemings that perhaps required some experience to prepare an intuiter, but did not seem to require any scientific investigation to produce or evaluate. The second was the use of *conceptual analysis*, which seemed to involve nothing more than *a priori* reflection either on the meaning of what we say or the concepts we employ in ethical thought. Later in the twentieth century, a third method, the method of *reflective equilibrium*, became popular: this was seen largely as a matter of harmonising the moral principles we accept with the mass of individual moral judgements we accept, together with various other philosophical commitments we may have. (Reflective equilibrium was most famously presented by Rawls [1971].) This coherentist method, especially if the inputs were delivered by intuition or proposed conceptual analyses, again seemed very different from the methods of e.g. chemistry or demography.

These methods were not just central to how first-order ethics was practised, but in metaethical discussions as well. It is easy to find entire metaethical works with very little discussion of scientific questions, but plenty of arguments that look like appeals to conceptual analysis, ethical and metaethical intuitions, and attempts to harmonise clashing parts of our ethical and metaethical starting points. One influential example of this sort of work in metaethics is Michael Smith's *The Moral Problem* (1994), which on the face of it at least proceeds in a very different way from typical scientific investigations.

There are some clear reasons naturalism about metaethical method is attractive, despite it having been far from orthodoxy at times in the past century. The sciences, particularly natural sciences like physics and biology, have discovered all sorts of facts that were not even dreamed of a hundred years ago. Furthermore, science is good at producing rational agreement: while there will always be scientific disputes, few seriously doubt e.g. that there is oxygen in the air or that antibiotics can cure bacterial infections. If we could turn these very successful methods to metaethical and ethical questions, we might hope for some of the same progress in discovery and in resolution of disagreements. Another reason to hope that naturalistic methods will be useful in metaethics is possessed by people who are *holists* about inquiry. Answers we give in one area of inquiry often seem to have consequences in other areas of inquiry, and any particular piece of evidence we get can be handled by modifying different parts of our overall theory. If our picture of the world faces the tribunal of experience as a whole, as for example Quine would have it (Quine 1951:38), then it seems reasonable to think that our methods for going from our experience to our theories should have important similarities across subject matters. This suggests that our methods in metaethics should not be too different from our methods in science. This line of thought will be particularly pressing for those who are naturalists about other parts of philosophical inquiry. So much of metaethics tackles questions about ethical language, or epistemology of ethics, or the metaphysics of ethics, or questions about moral judgements and moral reasoning that if we are naturalists about philosophy of language, epistemology, metaphysics, and philosophy of mind, naturalism about metaethics is virtually forced on us.

A third reason may stem from metaphysical naturalism. If we became convinced e.g. that all phenomena in the world were ultimately physical, or that our nature was exhausted by biological and social features of us, we might come to expect that any ethical truths about our situation would also ultimately have a physical or biological or social basis. And if they do, that might suggest they are best investigated by inquiries like those we use for physical or biological or social facts. Of course, establishing this as a reason for methodological naturalism in ethics would require an argument that facts about us are ultimately physical, or biological, or social (or a combination): but arguments for physicalism and other forms of methodological naturalism are familiar from other areas of philosophy, including metaphysics, philosophy of science, and the philosophy of mind.

Pursuing metaethics and ethics in a naturalistic spirit may be appealing: but how, exactly, ought we bring to bear the methods of the natural and social sciences? One way is through critique. Standard methods of ethics can be assessed for how naturalistic they are, and to the extent they are not, a methodological naturalist may wish to modify, supplement, or even reject them. Another way is through developing positive naturalistic metaethical research projects employing scientific methods. Before discussing critiques and naturalistic projects, however, it will be worth doing some ground-clearing, to see where methodological naturalism may go beyond uses of science that virtually everyone agrees are relevant to ethics, and distinguishing naturalism approaches to metaethics from naturalism about some other topics.

THE ROLE OF SCIENCE IN ETHICS: PRELIMINARIES

Everyone (or almost everyone) thinks that scientific methods are *somewhat* relevant to resolving ethical decisions. When deciding whether to administer a treatment to a patient, a doctor needs to take into account scientific evidence about what the likely outcomes of that treatment will be. When a government is contemplating a change in social welfare payments, one thing they should consider is the economic implications: what will this change do to inflation, employment, food availability to those affected, etc. Sometimes estimating these impacts will require specialised economic knowledge. When deciding what countries or individuals should do about climate change, the science of the impact of carbon dioxide on world weather patterns is relevant. And so on. What is at issue between the naturalists and others is whether, as well as these "descriptive" matters, there are "pure" moral principles concerning what we should do, and how we are to determine what *those* principles are.

One might be suspicious that moral questions and "descriptive" questions can be divided up into entirely descriptive and purely moral claims. One way to separate out descriptive and moral questions is to use conditionals. For a given case, let the uncontroversially descriptive facts be represented by D, and some moral verdict be represented by M. Then the question of whether "if D, then M" is correct can be a matter of disagreement even for two people who both accept D (or both reject D, for that matter). We can disagree about the conditional "if John took the car (and such-and-such else was descriptively the case), then he was wrong to take it," even if we agree on whether or not he took the car, for example. (Or for that matter two people could agree with the conditional even if we disagreed about whether John took any cars.) The conditional seems to capture a moral commitment that goes beyond descriptive commitments (or at least the specific commitment of D, at any rate).

Specifying "purely" moral issues in this way avoids two tricky issues. One is whether moral claims can be captured by entirely general moral principles with no apparent moral commitments: one might doubt this can be done because of a general about moral principles of that generality. The other issue avoided is finding a d for all drawing a line between moral and non-moral vocabulary. Many think that so-called "thick" moral terms bring with them both moral and descriptive commitments: to describe a policy as cruel says something descriptive about the motives and potential for producing suffering of the policy, but also something moral about those who engage in it, for example (see Debbie Roberts' chapter "Thick Concepts"). Some think these "thick" terms cannot be disentangled into those two components, at least in any language we have. If we wish to isolate "pure" moral claims using the conditional strategy, we can often leave any allegedly thick moral expressions in the consequent, thus allowing us to state moral disagreements, including ones stated in thick terms, between people who agree on all of their descriptive commitments.

Note that in dividing up claims into descriptive ones and moral ones, I do not mean to imply that the truth of moral claims is not fixed by the truth of the descriptive ones. Moral facts might even *just be* descriptive facts, for all that has been said here. (One simple example of a theory like this: one could be a hedonistic utilitarian that *identifies* the property of being the morally best outcome with the property of being the outcome having the greatest balance of pleasure over pain.) Nevertheless, even those who wish to identify facts specified with moral language and facts specified by non-moral language face controversy about whether, in settling a question posed in non-moral vocabulary, science goes very far towards settling questions posed in moral vocabulary, since the science of pleasure and pain is unlikely to itself tell us that hedonism is the correct moral theory.

The next things to be careful about, when working out the role of science in ethics, is to keep in mind two distinctions. Let us first distinguish morality and *mores*: the difference between what is morally right or wrong, and what *the conventions of a given society treat as* morally right or wrong. Many people believe that what is right, on the one hand, and what a society currently treats as right, on the other, come apart. Some societies have had (and have) the death penalty for consensual sodomy: that by itself does not establish that consensual sodomy is sometimes in itself gravely wrong. Some societies have had (and do have) permissive attitudes towards slavery: that by itself does not show that slavery was morally permissible. Scientific discoveries about what a group's mores are are only controversially of relevance to the question of what really is right or wrong. Even for those few who do identify morality and social mores, the question of what justifies that identification, at least, is presumably not settled by discovering what the mores in fact are.

The second distinction worth keeping in mind is the distinction between morality and *altruism*. The exact definition of altruism is contested, but at a first pass altruistic behaviour is behaviour that benefits others at a cost to oneself. Sometimes in the popular media discoveries about the "science of morality" only concern the science of *altruism*: how it developed, why evolutionary pressure does not eliminate altruistic dispositions and why they are sometimes maintained by evolutionary mechanisms, and so on. We should not assume too quickly, however, that discoveries about altruistic behaviour will be discoveries about morality. For one thing, some altruistic behaviour seems immoral: nepotism and corruption are often engaged in to help relatives or friends, and the fanatic who slaughters innocents for The Cause might well be behaving altruistically even if what he does is horrendously evil. Even when altruistic acts are morally good, understanding and explaining their altruistic nature may not give us much insight into why they are morally good.

So achievements in the anthropology or sociology of conventional standards, or the psychology or biology of altruism, do not seem to answer moral questions in any *obvious* way. It is tempting to think that we can gain some better answers to moral questions once we are sensitive to these discoveries, but getting those answers requires some further philosophical work. One valuable contribution naturalistic metaethics can make is to explain how and why we can draw conclusions about ethical and metaethical questions from evidence about the workings of mores and altruism. But we should not think that ethical and metaethical work is done *just* by investigating mores and altruism.

METAETHICAL NATURALISM: TWO EXAMPLES

There are many naturalistic projects, small and large, that are being carried out in metaethics. To get a sense of the range, let us look at two general approaches that stress methodological naturalism but which come to very different conclusions. The first is realist and cognitivist about ethical claims, the second anti-realist and expressivist.

One influential approach to metaethics in the late twentieth century was pursued by a group of philosophers known as the Cornell realists, due to connections they had to the philosophy department at Cornell University. Major figures in this tradition included Richard Boyd (1988), David Brink (1989), and Nicholas Sturgeon (1988), while other philosophers like Peter Railton (1986) have metaethical views that resemble the Cornell realists in important ways. What unified the Cornell realists was the view that we could learn about moral language and moral metaphysics by looking at what scientific realist philosophers of science had to say about scientific language and metaphysics. Part of this involved the thought that we can judge theories using so-called "inference to the best explanation." Something similar can be used in metaethics to choose between theories: and just as we can use scientific method to tell us about all sorts of physical and social phenomena, we can use similar methods to tell us about moral phenomena.

The best theory that enables us to predict and explain the spread of diseases, for example, is one that employs talk of bacteria and viruses in its predictions and explanations. When we test our theories of disease and they pass those tests, and our theory yields satisfying explanations of initially puzzling disease phenomena, that provides us with good reason to *believe* our theories of bacteria and viruses, or to believe those theories are approximately correct. Or at least that is a picture of inquiry, known as "inference to the best explanation" (IBE), which many scientific realists would accept. Cornell realists hold that we can apply something like this approach to investigating morality. Some packages of ethical and metaethical views do better in explaining the truth of our secure moral judgements, the behaviour of agents, and various other things. And we can test these explanations through further investigation, comparison with rival explanations, and in other ways. When we come upon a package that passes our tests and offers satisfying explanations of previously puzzling phenomena, we can use roughly the same method as we use in the sciences to infer, using inference to the best explanation that we are onto truth in our moral and metaethical theorising. (Or we are at least close to the truth.) Furthermore, just as the facts about viruses and bacteria are objective, and do not depend on what we happen to believe or desire about viruses, so too are the facts about morality not depending on the theorist's standpoint or preferences.

The "moral observations," that go into our ethical and metaethical theorizing some willingness to categorise the world we encounter in moral terms:

presumably an alien observer could detect all the same movements, masses, and even colours and sounds without necessarily recognising any actions as just or unjust, right or wrong. But this is not a barrier to treating moral observations as being like scientific observations, according to Cornell realists, since scientific observations presuppose theoretical commitments as well. An observer with no concepts of distances or planets can look through a telescope and see nothing but spots and regions of coloured lights, but this should not make us think that using telescopes in astronomy is somehow unscientific. Indeed, for any experimental or observational science, we must make assumptions about the world to gather information from observation: we can test those assumptions piecemeal, but we cannot do without them altogether. Since this is the situation when it comes to any scientific observation, it is no worry, in principle, that it also obtains in the case of moral observations.

Likewise, with moral explanations someone who does not recognise that anything is right or wrong, good or bad, will not feel the need to explain anything they encounter in moral terms. But likewise, a hypothetical alien observer who can only detect living cells and chemical interactions might never feel the need to offer psychological or economic explanations for phenomena that they observe, and this should not make us sceptical that there are minds or economies, or make us think that psychology or economics cannot be sciences. Cornell realists tend to go even further, and argue that there are explanations in moral terms of phenomena described in non-moral terms (Sturgeon 1988): the failure of a certain rescue mission, for example, can be explained on the basis that its leader is "no damned good" (Sturgeon 1988: 243). If our best explanations, by scientific standards, of some phenomena described in non-moral terms turn out to be moral explanations, all the better for the Cornell realist story about confirming moral theories, and the metaethical package that goes along with those theories.

The second form of naturalism we will look at in some detail takes a radically different approach to the subject matter of ethics, but also in a way that permits us to see metaethical investigation as fundamentally like a scientific enterprise in many respects. This approach is the quasi-realist approach of figures like Simon Blackburn and Allan Gibbard. While Gibbard is more explicit about tying his approach to metaethics to an understanding of ourselves enriched by the social sciences (especially in Gibbard 1990 and Gibbard 2003), other quasi-realists such as Blackburn (Blackburn 1993) do not present their work as having a particularly scientific methodology.

In very rough outline, Blackburn and Gibbard see the central role for moral language as expressing certain attitudes other than belief: patterns of approval and disapproval for Blackburn, and plans for Gibbard (Gibbard 2003). However, despite this primarily expressive function of moral language, it behaves as if it states facts and makes claims to objective truth. After telling a story about how to express an attitude (or pattern of attitudes), a further story can be told about how to express a pattern of attitudes through calling various moral claims true or false, moral arguments valid or invalid, expressing claims about the connections between moral matters and non-moral matters (e.g. organised dogfights are wrong in part because of the unnecessary suffering of the dogs involved), and so on. Despite its core function as expressing attitudes other than belief, moral thought and language can come to have many of the features moral realists have claimed for it. (Arguably, Gibbard 2003 ends up slipping back into a kind of moral realism, though he would not describe the view that way.)

What should expressivists say about moral method: how should we work out what to think about moral questions, and argue with others about them? Blackburn and Gibbard say a limited amount about this topic, but plausibly, this will be a matter of engaging with our own non-cognitive states, together with an evaluation of whether they would be different were we more ideal. Are any the product of false or dubious factual beliefs? Are any produced by distorting processes that would be absent in more idealised versions of ourselves? Are their conflicts between our patterns of approvals or patterns of planning, and if so what is our attitude to how they should best be resolved? And so on. This internally focused project of self-improvement, together with related interpersonal exchanges aimed at this sort of thing and perhaps at exercising more-or-less respectful pressure on each other, seem like a radically different sort of 'inquiry' from scientific investigation of fully factual questions. (This seems to fit Gibbard's discussion of moral method [Gibbard 1990:253–337] and his explicit rejection of moral inquiry using just the methods of social science [Gibbard 2003:161].) So when it comes to making moral judgements, the method that seems to mesh best with quasi-realism is more like that proposed by traditional non-cognitivists such as Stevenson rather than those who want to assimilate moral inquiry to scientific inquiry.

Despite this, when it comes to methods for resolving *metaethical* questions, quasi-realists are methodological naturalists. While *moral* questions are distinctively different from scientific ones, questions about *what it is to make a moral judgement*, or *the function of moral language*, or in general the psychologies of moral agents and the language used by moral communities are naturalistic questions. Indeed, one motivation for expressivism is a naturalistic conception of ourselves and our responses, and a desire to avoid postulating non-naturalistic moral facts, or non-natural facts about the nature of rationality. That motivation in the first instance comes from metaphysical naturalism rather than methodological naturalism, but it goes hand in hand with thinking that scientific means are the way to improve our theories of human agents and their interactions. Quasi-realists should think, and do think, that psychology and linguistics will reveal what mental states we have and how we express them in language. Philosophers of language and mind and those who work on metaethics and moral psychology have contributions to make here too, but as part of an integrated project of understanding ourselves as natural creatures in natural environments, rather than seeking a special philosophical realm of objective facts about morality or rationality. Ethics does not look much like science from a quasi-realist perspective, but metaethics does. In treating metaethics naturalistically despite not taking a naturalistic approach to ethical questions, quasi-realists resemble some earlier non-cognitivists such as Stevenson (1963), though I would hesitate to classify some other traditional non-cognitivists, such as Wittgenstein, as metaethical naturalists.

NATURALISM AND TRADITIONAL METHODS OF METAETHICAL INQUIRY

Naturalism in ethics can seem like a radical doctrine, especially against the background of insistence by people like Moore and Wittgenstein that ethics cannot be science. So you might have thought, and some naturalists do think, that methodological naturalism precludes relying on the methods traditionally used by analytic philosophers to answer metaethical and ethical questions. However, some self-identified naturalists have tried to vindicate the use of moral intuitions, reflective equilibrium, and even conceptual analysis as important parts of ethical inquiry. This section will look at some attempts to reconcile these methods with naturalism.

Debates in moral philosophy frequently feature appeals to "intuition," and some theories of the source of moral intuitions make using intuitions radically different from engaging in scientific method. G.E. Moore's theory of moral intuition, for example, maintained that moral intuition was a distinct psychological faculty that gave us access to a special kind of property, even when contemplating non-actual scenarios. Some theories of this sort of intuition take it to be a special rational faculty that delivers us information about the world: see Bealer (1998) for a defence of this view of philosophical intuitions in general. Metaethical positions are also often justified by appeal to "intuition": it is supposed to be our intuitions about the subject matter that support the doctrine that moral facts are objective, for example. Understandably, naturalists have often wanted to reject the psychological picture on which we have this sort of special faculty, or other distinctive moral detectors such as a "moral sense."

However, there are other theories of intuitions and appeals to intuitions that make them seem less anti-naturalistic. Perhaps intuitions are just our judgements about cases: David Lewis claims about philosophical intuitions that "[o]ur intuitions are simply opinions" (Lewis 1983:x). Or perhaps they are a special class of judgements, such as the relatively unreflective ones or the ones not arrived at by explicit inference from other judgements. Or perhaps they are *inclinations* to make such judgements. Seen in these ways, starting from our moral intuitions may be no more mysterious than starting from our ordinary opinions in any other inquiry. Historically, this seems to have been where many successful scientific inquiries came from: even physics and chemistry have their origins in plausible speculations about motion and the interactions of matter. Even today, many mature scientific inquiries still employ elements of good sense, hunches, and other moves that look like they are supported by something like educated "intuition." It would make no sense for a methodological naturalist to demand that ethical and metaethical theorizing have no place for intuition if intuitions can be found playing a helpful role even in paradigm scientific enterprises.

The method of reflective equilibrium, very roughly, is the method of beginning by articulating particular moral judgements and pre-theoretic moral generalisations, perhaps supplementing both of these with moral intuitions, and then bringing the resulting theory into "equilibrium" by working out the strengths of the various judgements and in cases of clashes, modifying those held less strongly so as to cohere with the more certain ones. As mentioned above, this procedure can seem suspicious to naturalists: it does not seem to be constrained by what the world is like, as opposed to what we are inclined to believe about the world. It suggests that ethics is constructed, rather than discovered, which seems in stark contrast with scientific inquiry. Indeed, Rawls himself seems to have favoured a constructivist approach to ethical truth. Finally, the starting point of reflective equilibrium involves giving a central role to intuitions, so suspicion of intuitions naturally carry over to suspicion of reflective equilibrium.

However, it is far from obvious that there is anything naturalistically objectionable about using reflective equilibrium. Historically, Rawls's conception of reflective equilibrium derives from Goodman's (1955) account of how we should establish the correct theory of inductive inference. Goodman's project was, in part, giving a theory of good scientific method: and so trying to do the same thing for ethics looks like a methodologically *naturalist* move, not an anti-naturalist one. Those sympathetic to Goodman, at least, are likely to see scientific inquiry itself as engaging in something like reflective equilibrium, trading off views about the soundness of particular judgements about the world and principles of unifying and revising those particular judgements. So it is not clear that employing reflective equilibrium is somehow unscientific.

When evaluating how naturalistic reflective equilibrium is, it can matter whether we conceive of reflective equilibrium in a *narrow* or a *wide* way (for the distinction see Daniels 1979). Narrow reflective equilibrium looks only at one's own particular and general moral judgements, and trades them off to reach a stable equilibrium. *Wide* reflective equilibrium takes into account many more considerations when trying to reach a stable resting place, including what judgements others are likely to make, different conjectures that could explain the judgements of oneself and others, and beliefs other than moral beliefs, e.g. beliefs about how it is reasonable to criticise initial judgements, beliefs about human psychology and sociology, and so on. At its widest, reflective equilibrium could be performed on all our beliefs at once. A wide enough reflective equilibrium can take into account anything a naturalist might want to bring to bear on moral inquiry, so whether a particular project of reflective equilibrium is objectionable on naturalist grounds is likely to have more to do with how narrow it is than that it involves reflective equilibrium per se.

Using conceptual analysis to reach metaethical conclusions is widespread, and seems to often be what is going on when philosophers offer an "analysis" of justice, or supererogation, or moral goodness in terms of reasons, etc. Conceptual analysis is often thought to be anti-naturalist, both because the results of conceptual analysis are meant to be a priori (and many methodological naturalists are suspicious of the a priori), and because resolving a question through conceptual analysis seems to be a method that insulates that inquiry from what science has to tell us, and from scientific testing of that answer. These suspicions of conceptual analysis are not particularly to do with conceptual analysis as used in ethics: many naturalists are suspicious of conceptual analysis across the board. (See for example Devitt 1996 or Kornblith 2002.)

However, a number of theorists have wanted to defend conceptual analysis as naturalistically respectable. Just two examples are the accounts of conceptual analysis offered by Rey (1998) and Jenkins (2008, 2013). While these accounts have many psychological and epistemological differences, a shared idea is that what concepts we have and what those concepts represent about the world is a matter of past engagement with the world itself. Once we think of concepts as mental representations bearing reliable information about the external world, a connection produced by ordinary causal interactions, it does not sound particularly anti-naturalistic to think that conceptual analysis is in part a process of making that information available for belief. If conceptual analysis is widely used, at least implicitly, in the sciences, that would make it even more naturalistically acceptable. For example, if Jenkins (2008) is right that conceptual analysis, as she conceives of it, is the source of our basic arithmetical knowledge, the results of conceptual analysis sit at the core of most contemporary natural and social sciences: neither would get very far without numbers.

One strand of recent metaethical theorising that would describe itself as naturalist, despite relying heavily on conceptual analysis, is the *moral functionalism* defended by Frank Jackson and Philip Pettit (see Jackson and Pettit 1995, Jackson 1998). The core of metaethical inquiry, according to this view, consists of two steps. The first is to assemble "commonplaces" about ethics, particularly generalisations about ethical matters that we could reasonably think are shared among those who use ethical concepts and are at least implicit, if not explicit, in their use of moral expressions. Once we have our commonplaces assembled, we can treat them as implicitly defining the subject matter of our inquiry. This network can be treated as implicitly defining many pieces of moral vocabulary together. For example, if we define just actions partly in terms of which distributions of resources are morally good, for example, then information we have about what paradigm examples of just actions are might help constrain what counts, in our "folk" theory of morality, as being a morally good outcome.

Armed with our networked implicit definition of moral vocabulary, the second step is to examine the world to determine what properties and objects best satisfy that network definition of our moral terms. Jackson and Pettit (1995), for example, suggest that the right actions are the ones we would approve of under various (descriptively specified) improvements to our situation. Jackson (1998), on the other hand, suggests that the property of goodness, as implicitly defined, might end up being maximising desire satisfaction. The question of what sequence of properties fits the networked implicit definition supplied by moral commonplaces, however, is in principle a matter for scientific inquiry, particularly social and psychological scientific inquiry.

The theory that results from the moral functionalist procedure is intended to be *metaphysically* naturalistic, or "descriptivist," since the aim of the moral functionalist is to determine what it is in the world, specified in non-moral vocabulary, which plays the functional roles specified for moral properties like goodness and obligatory action and justice. But it is natural to see it is as *methodologically* naturalistic as well—or at least intended to be by its proponents. The first step of the project is one they think is needed in a wide variety of areas to fix the subject matter of an inquiry: indeed, they model their strategy on that of the *analytic functionalists* in the philosophy of mind, who think that this kind of approach will provide the foundations for cognitive psychology, by offering us a way of understanding what for example, beliefs and desires are. And the second step, locating the things that best play those roles in the world that science tells us about, looks like a fairly standard scientific inquiry. Despite the heavy reliance on conceptual analysis in the first step of establishing the networked interdefinition of moral vocabulary, the moral functionalist approach is intended to be part of a methodologically naturalistic approach to metaethics.

This section has attempted to establish, not that naturalists must be sympathetic to methods such as reliance on intuitions, use of reflective equilibrium, and use of conceptual analysis, but rather that being a naturalist about moral methodology does not per se mean that a theorist must reject any of these three tools for moral inquiry. Methodological naturalism *need* not be a revolutionary doctrine when it comes to the question of how to do moral inquiry.

However, those who retain any of these methods but who wish to be methodological naturalists may want to treat them in particular ways. It would be natural to not *just* rely on intuitions in metaethics, especially if intuitions are something like trained hunches or what seems plausible before detailed inquiry. Methodological naturalists are likely to think that conceptual analysis cannot be the full story about the metaphysics and epistemology of morality or the key to moral psychology: all of these areas seem to have substantive questions in them to be resolved by theoretical inquiry and not just reflection on concepts. Finally, insofar as reflective equilibrium plays a role, it is more plausible that information about ourselves and the world other than just the particular judgements and principles we begin with should be the inputs into our theoretical trade-offs.

Methodological naturalism in metaethics offers more than a new take on traditional methods, however. Bringing scientific methods to bear on metaethical questions gives us more options than just pursuing metaethical business-as-usual. Let us turn to examine some of these new options.

NEW USES FOR SCIENCE IN METAETHICS

Perhaps naturalists can keep some or all of the traditional methods of ethics, and approaches to metaethics, employed in analytic philosophy. But naturalism can make a distinctive contribution if there are new, promising, methods available through applying scientific techniques to address ethical and metaethical questions.

We have already seen one suggested above in the discussion of Cornell realism. It is that we can use inference to the best explanation (IBE) to reach ethical conclusions. Cornell realists talk less about the justification for their approach to metaethics, but it is natural to see this as a matter of applying IBE as well. Note that the general kind of project pursued by the Cornell realists could be pursued by naturalists who disagree with particular views the Cornell realists may have had about science, language, or ethics: just as rival scientific theories can appeal to the same canons of scientific method, rival meta-ethical approaches can share a view about what it would take to vindicate one approach over the other.

A second use of the methods of the sciences, particularly the social sciences, can be found in the contemporary "experimental philosophy" or "x-phi" movement. Narrowly construed, this movement seeks to discover what non-philosopher's judgements are about topics of philosophical interest, for example to test whether "intuitions" philoso-phers rely upon are widespread in the general public, and to do so through empirical surveys. Why would the results be valuable for metaethics? If intuitions or the results of conceptual analysis were legitimate inputs to metaethical theorising, then drawing intui-tions from a broader range of informants and observing how they deploy concepts that they are presumptively competent with could provide better data for those inputs. On the other hand, if there is no particular reason to trust intuitive judgements or information apparently drawn from concepts, it is less clear why the judgements of the person on the street are relevant. Experimental philosophy might still be able to serve a debunking function if it turned out that philosophers' intuitions were not widely shared beyond the ivory tower, for example. But its role in positive theorising about the nature of ethical facts, the epistemology of moral judgement, their objectivity, etc. would likely be limited.

Despite its name, "experimental philosophy," in the most common use of that term, covers a comparatively narrow range of experimental work being drawn on by contem-porary philosophers. Another major source of evidence is coming from psychological investigations into how we make moral judgements. Some of that work takes the form of asking informants for their moral judgements and theorising about what best explains those patterns (i.e. x-phi in the more narrow sense). But psychologists can take advantage of more sources of evidence than that. To give one example, one debate with metaethical relevance is the debate about how much moral behaviour is influenced by relatively transitory features of an environment that an agent finds herself in. This debate, about *situationism*, seems to have implications for whether there are moral virtues, or at least whether moral virtues can play the kind of central role that virtue ethicists have traditionally thought: if it is an illusion that there are kind people and cruel people, as opposed to people acting kindly or cruelly because of local situational factors, then a virtue ethics that builds an account of moral behaviour around virtues such as kindness and vices such as cruelty, would be refuted.

The experimental evidence assembled about situationism is typically drawn from putting experimental subjects in a variety of conditions and seeing what they do. A famous early experiment in this area is the notorious experiment carried out by Stanley Milgram, where experimental subjects would administer what they thought were severe, and potentially fatal, electric shocks to other people as punishment for mistakes in a test, merely because the experimenter told them sternly to do so. These punishments continued despite the screams and pleas of those apparently affected by those shocks (Milgram 1974). More recent experiments have demonstrated significant differences in moral behaviour based on relatively small differences in circumstances: for example, the likelihood someone will stop to help an apparently injured man who has dropped some books is radically decreased if there is loud ambient noise, such as a mower running nearby (Mathews and Canon 1975). The cumulative effect of these sorts of experiments leads Doris (2004) to argue that the psychological presuppositions of traditional virtue ethics must be rejected.

Of course, experimental evidence on its own does not settle the issue of whether traditional virtue ethics has been refuted, and Doris is sensitive to the need to do serious theoretical work to show that these experiments bear on the viability of virtue ethics (Doris 1998). There are still debates to be had about the connection between evidence about people's behaviour in morally charged situations and what conclusions we can draw about whether there is moral character, and if so what it is like. Doris and Stitch (2014) have a good introductory discussion of the back-and-forth about situationism and virtue ethics, as well as a discussion of many other places where psychological results (including more narrowly x-phi ones) play into metaethical debates. Whatever conclusions should be drawn in the end about situationism and virtue theory, it is clear that psychological experiments other than surveys have a role to play in metaethical debates, as well as x-phi narrowly conceived.

There is no reason why psychological research is the only place where metaethicists should find useful scientific resources, either. Investigation of the evolution of human behaviour, and how it is influenced by genetics and transmitted culture are others. Both economics and political science have, in their own ways, always been close cousins of ethical inquiry, and the project of working out what sort of thing moral agents are and how they best interact is naturally one that disciplines such as anthropology and sociology can also contribute to. There is often careful theoretical work to be done to show how scientific results bear on traditional metaethical questions. But in this respect metaethics need be no different from science either: the links between results of experiments and general theoretical questions often require careful work to make out, despite the mythology of entire theories being immediately swept away by single "crucial experiments."

CONCLUSION

This introduction could not hope to be comprehensive: many ethicists see themselves as naturalists to a greater or lesser extent, and the temptation to conduct metaethical and ethical inquiry along scientific lines is perennial. Given the disputes between card-carrying naturalists, it is unlikely that a commitment to methodological naturalism all by itself can determine very much about how to carry out moral inquiry. My own view is that it is very unlikely that naturalism could provide a shortcut that is some kind of alternative to the careful inquiry and deliberation that making progress on moral issues requires. However, construing moral method in naturalistic terms does shift the focus of some methodological debates, and it can direct attention to avenues of inquiry too often neglected by traditional moral philosophy. Whatever turns out to be the truth of the matter about the methodological similarities between moral inquiry and scientific inquiry, or between metaethical inquiry and scientific inquiry, the debate between naturalists and non-naturalists, and among different naturalists, promises to both improve our understanding of moral inquiry and improve our methods for that inquiry.

ACKNOWLEDGEMENTS

Thanks to Frank Jackson, Carrie Jenkins, and Alex King for discussion and to Tristram McPherson, David Plunkett, and Lea Schroeder for comments. Work on this chapter was supported by the National Humanities Center.

REFERENCES

Bealer, G. (1998) "Intuition and the Autonomy of Philosophy" in DePaul, M. and Ramsey, W. (eds) *Rethinking Intuition: The Psychology of Intuition and Is Role in Philosophical Inquiry*, Lanham, MD: Rowman and Littlefield: 201–240.

Blackburn, S. (1993) *Essays in Quasi Realism*, Oxford: Oxford University Press.

Boyd, R. (1988) "How to Be a Moral Realist" in Sayre-McCord, G. (ed.) *Essays on Moral Realism*, Ithaca, NY: Cornell University Press: 181–228.

Brink, D. (1989) *Moral Realism and the Foundations of Ethics*, New York: Cambridge University Press.

Daniels, N. (1979) "Wide Reflective Equilibrium and Theory Acceptance in Ethics," *Journal of Philosophy* 76.5: 256–282.

Devitt, M. (1996) *Coming to Our Senses*, Cambridge: Cambridge University Press.

Doris, J. (1998) "Persons, Situations and Virtue Ethics," *Noûs* 32.4: 504–530.

Doris, J. (2004) *Lack of Character: Personality and Moral Behavior*, Cambridge: Cambridge University Press.

Doris, J. and Stich, S. (2014) "Moral Psychology: Empirical Approaches." *Stanford Encyclopedia of Philosophy*, accessed 22 October 2015. Available at "http://plato.stanford.edu/archives/fall2014/entries/moral-psych-emp/>.

Gibbard, A. (1990) *Wise Choices, Apt Feelings*, Cambridge, MA: Harvard University Press.

Gibbard, A. (2003) *Thinking How to Live*, Cambridge, MA: Harvard University Press.

Goodman, N. (1955) *Fact, Fiction and Forecast*, Cambridge, MA: Harvard University Press.

Jackson, F.C. (1998) *From Metaphysics to Ethics: A Defence of Conceptual Analysis*, Oxford: Oxford University Press.

Jackson, F.C. and Pettit, P. (1995) "Moral Functionalism and Moral Motivation," *Philosophical Quarterly* 45.178: 20–40.

Jenkins, C.S. (2008) *Grounding Concepts: An Empirical Basis of Arithmetic*, Oxford: Oxford University Press.

Jenkins, C.S.I. (2013) "Naturalistic Challenges to the A Priori" in Casullo, A. and Thurow, J.C. (eds) *The A Priori in Philosophy*. Oxford: Oxford University Press: 274–290.

Kornblith, H. (2002) *Knowledge and its Place in Nature*, Oxford: Oxford University Press.

Lewis, D. (1983) *Philosophical Papers Volume 1*, Oxford: Oxford University Press.

Mathews, K.E. and Canon, L.K. (1975) "Environmental Noise Level as a Determinant of Helping Behavior," *Journal of Personality and Social Psychology* 32.4: 571–577.

Milgram, S. (1974) *Obedience to Authority: An Experimental View*, New York: Harper and Row.

Moore, G.E. (1993) *Principia Ethica*, Cambridge: Cambridge University Press.

Quine, W.V. (1951) "Two Dogmas of Empiricism," *Philosophical Review* 60.1: 20–43.

Railton, P. (1986) "Moral Realism," *The Philosophical Review* 95.2: 163–207.

Rawls, J. (1971) *A Theory of Justice*, Cambridge, MA: Belknap Press.

Rey, G. (1998) "A Naturalistic A Priori," *Philosophical Studies* 92: 25–43.

Smith, M. (1994) *The Moral Problem*, Oxford: Wiley-Blackwell.

Stevenson, C. (1963) *Facts and Values: Studies in Ethical Analysis*, New Haven, CT: Yale University Press.

Sturgeon, N. (1988) "Moral Explanations" in Sayre-McCord, G. (ed.) *Essays on Moral Realism*, Ithaca, NY: Cornell University Press: 229–255.

Wittgenstein, L. (1965) "A Lecture on Ethics," *Philosophical Review* 74.1: 3–12.

43

Normative Ethics and Metaethics

Mark Schroeder

By its very name, the field of metaethics is contrasted with another field of inquiry, that of normative ethics. Metaethics concerns questions *about* normative inquiry, rather than questions *within* normative inquiry. Whereas normative ethics concerns questions like what is good or bad, what we must or ought to do, and why, metaethics is said to be concerned with questions like what it means to say that something is 'good' or 'bad', whether such claims correspond to facts about the world, and how we know or manage to talk or think about such facts, if there are any. Metaethics may also be contrasted with normative ethics as philosophy of science is contrasted with science. Metaethicists, it is sometimes said, no more make claims within normative ethics than philosophers of science make claims within science, or pundits are engaged in playing football:

> What is metaethics anyway? One useful way of answering this question is by contrasting metaethics with applied ethics and normative ethics. Consider an analogy that will illustrate the contrast: imagine ethics as football. We can equate different things associated with football with the different disciplines of ethics... there is the referee, who helps interpret the rules that the players are following. The referee can be thought of as the normative ethicist... Finally, there is the football analyst or pundit, who does not kick a ball or interpret the rules for the players but tries to understand and comment on what is going on in the game itself. This is like the metaethicist, who asks questions about the very practice of ethics, some of which we shall consider below.
>
> (Fisher 2011:1–2)

On this conception of the distinction between normative ethics and metaethics, the divide between normative ethics and metaethics runs two ways. By its very nature, metaethics is concerned with questions that cross-cut the concerns of normative ethics, and so no answer to any metaethical question commits you in any way to any answer to a normative ethical question. Similarly, no answer to any normative ethical question commits you to any answer to a metaethical question. As we'll see in what follows, this conception of the relationship between normative ethics and metaethics is mistaken. *Some* answers to *some* metaethical questions *do* carry commitments within normative ethics, and likewise, some answers to some normative ethical questions do carry commitments within metaethics. Indeed, as we'll see, there is a very interesting set of views on which metaethics and normative ethics greatly overlap. Yet it is also a mistake to think that there is no real distinction between normative ethics and metaethics. As we will see, there are, in fact, *some* answers to some very important and central metaethical questions that indeed do not carry any commitments for the answers to any normative ethical questions. Moreover, among the most prominent of such answers, are the ones espoused by the philosophers who defended the sharp distinction between metaethics and normative ethics. So it is not hard to understand where the traditional conception of the distinction between normative ethics and metaethics could have come from.

I will *not* attempt, here, to provide a set of necessary and sufficient conditions on what counts as metaethics and what counts as normative ethics. Indeed, it is a consequence of my arguments that there may be no completely satisfactory way of drawing such a distinction, and I don't think that it is important to be able to draw one. Instead, I will rely in all of what follows on the classification of easy paradigms. Views which make claims about the nature of moral language, thought, epistemology, or reality, including noncognitivism, moral error theory, contextualism, relativism, and reductive realism, are all paradigmatically metaethical. Normative ethical theory, I will assume, paradigmatically includes both particular and highly general claims about what is good, best, right, wrong, or apt, as well as attempts to explain why. I will be arguing that many, but not all, paradigmatic metaethical views carry straightforward commitments for paradigmatic normative ethical questions, and that at least one kind of paradigmatically normative ethical view carries straightforward commitments for metaethics.

TRADITIONAL NONCOGNITIVISM

One important and central question in metaethics concerns the nature of the meaning of moral words like 'good', 'ought', and 'wrong'. One important and central answer to this question is that we can get the most illuminating gloss on what gives these words their meanings, without either using these terms or applying predicates to them like 'true' or 'satisfies', which license inferences to sentences that use these terms. Instead, we understand what they mean by saying what they can be used to *do*—to praise or condemn, or to express attitudes of praise or condemnation. Answers which take roughly this form belong to the noncognitivist tradition in metaethics, and can be and have been developed in many different ways.

Noncognitivist accounts of the meaning of moral words are typically held by their proponents to be independent of commitments in normative ethics. To say what a moral word is used to do is not to use that word to do anything in particular, and so it is compatible not only with using the word 'wrong' to apply to, for example, stealing, and also with using the words 'not wrong' to apply to stealing, but with using the word 'wrong' in neither of these ways. Moreover, there are no valid inferences from sentences like 'the word wrong is used to condemn' to sentences that use the word 'wrong'. And this contrasts with more familiar, cognitivist or descriptivist, approaches to meaning, on which we say what the word 'wrong' means using sentences like 'the word 'wrong' is satisfied by all and only actions that fail to maximize happiness'. Semantic descent licenses us, from this premise, to infer, 'an action is wrong just in case it fails to maximize happiness'. Because noncognitivist theories do not rely on words like 'true', 'false', or 'satisfies' that license such inferences, they carry no similar commitments.

It is important to qualify this point, however. Some views which can for some purposes be classified as 'noncognitivist' *are* committed to answers to questions within normative ethics. Some noncognitivist views—sometimes called *hybrid* views, such as those developed in or discussed by Copp (2001), Boisvert (2008), Schroeder (2009), and Hay (2011)—model moral claims by analogy to epithets or slurs. According to these views, we cannot understand the meaning of moral words without understanding that they are used to endorse or to condemn, and that is what makes them count as 'noncognitivist'. But according to these hybrid forms of noncognitivism, it is not enough to understand the meaning of moral words, to know that they are used to endorse or to condemn; we must also understand what they are *about*, and hence what they are endorsing or condemning.

The relationship between normative ethics and metaethics is more complex for hybrid theorists. Just as you do not know the meaning of the word 'kraut' until you know that it is a slur for Germans, the hybrid theorist has not told us the meaning of the word 'wrong' until she has told us what it is used to condemn. A theorist can tell us that 'kraut' is a slur for Germans without taking a stand on whether anyone is a kraut; for if 'kraut' is not one of her words, because she does not have contempt for Germans, she may refuse to use it. So it is not possible to say what the word 'kraut' means without taking a stand on who is a kraut. But unless the word 'wrong' is not one of her words in the very same sense, the hybrid noncognitivist cannot refuse to take a stand on which actions are wrong. Once she has told us what the word 'wrong' is used to condemn, she must accept that actions with those features are wrong, on pain of not being able to use the word 'wrong' at all. So her view carries commitments for normative ethics.[1]

ERROR THEORY

Another traditional and central question of metaethics concerns whether there are any moral truths at all. An important skeptical answer to this question is that there are not. Views that maintain as such are known as versions of the moral *error theory*.

Error theoretic views can take different forms. Some claim not only that there are no moral truths (as in Finlay [2014:10–11]), but that moral claims are *false* (Mackie [1977:35], Loeb [2007:471], Olson [2014:8]). This claim requires refinement. Compare the properties of being permissible and of being required. On a standard conception, these properties are *duals*—an action is permissible just in case its negation is not required. So if it is false that A is permissible, then A is not permissible, and hence ~A is required—so it is true that ~A is required. Conversely, if it is false that ~A is required, then ~A is not required, and so A is permissible—so it is true that A is permissible. If *permissible* and *required* are duals, therefore, then some very simple reasoning—which appeals only to very minimal assumptions about truth and falsity—leads to the conclusion that it is incoherent to say that *all* moral claims are false.

The simplest answer to this puzzle, leading to one intelligible form of error theory, is to take sides.[2] The natural side to take is to say that nothing is *required*. In fact, some of the standard motivations for the moral error theory are particularly naturally construed as arguments for precisely this thesis. For example, it is sometimes argued that nothing can be wrong unless there is a categorical reason not to do it, but that since there are no categorical reasons, nothing can be wrong. This is an argument that nothing is required (since an action is required just in case its negation is not wrong), but not an argument that nothing is permissible. On the contrary, given the duality of *permissible* and *required*, it is an argument that *everything* is permissible.

It should be clear that an error theory which takes this form is deeply committed to claims within normative ethics, and not only because 'nothing is required' sounds like a 'first-order' normative claim. Most ambitious explanatory normative ethical theories aspire to endorse biconditionals of the form, 'for all *x*, *x* is wrong just in case *x* is F', where F is a non-trivial condition. The naïve error theory that I have just described is inconsistent with every such view, and so it carries commitments within normative ethics in a very deep sense.

However, there are other ways of developing the moral error theory. A different response to the problem of the duality of *permissible* and *required* is to hold that both 'permissible' and 'required' share a mistaken presupposition. On this view, 'stealing is permissible' says something like 'stealing is permitted by code C', but carries some problematic presupposition about code C, for example that C is the code of conduct preferred by God. If no code of conduct is preferred by God, therefore, claims of the form 'stealing is permissible' will all carry a false presupposition. It is an important property of presuppositions that they *project*. This means that if 'stealing is permissible' and 'not stealing is permissible' both carry the presupposition that C is the code of conduct preferred by God, then so do 'stealing is not permissible' and 'not stealing is not permissible'. But by the duality of 'permissible' and 'required', these are just the claims that not stealing is required and that stealing is required. So if claims about permissibility carry a presupposition, claims about requirement carry the very same presupposition.[3]

The error theorist who holds that 'permissible' and 'required' carry a problematic presupposition will go one of two ways, depending on what she thinks it is most apt to say about claims that carry false presuppositions. She may say that both 'stealing is permissible' and 'stealing is not permissible' are *false*, because they carry the false presupposition that (in our example), C is the code of conduct preferred by God. Or she may say that neither is true nor false, because of their false presupposition. If she takes the latter course, then she will say that no moral claim is true, but she will not say that all moral claims are false. Instead, she will say that no moral claim is false, either. If she takes the former course, then she will say that all moral claims—at least, all claims about permissibility and requirement—are false. But this will not lead her into trouble with the problem of duality, because that problem started, at its first step, with the inference from, 'it is false that stealing is permissible' to 'stealing is not permissible'. But if we classify claims with false presuppositions as false, then this is not a valid inference—and indeed, it breaks down precisely when 'P' carries a false presupposition, and according to this form of the error theory, this is precisely such a case. So this form of the error theory evades the problem of duality, as well.

The forms of error theory that I have surveyed here are not the only ways of responding to the problem of duality. Another response to the problem of duality is to reject the premise that 'permissible' and 'required' are duals.[4] This can be motivated by the observation that 'permissible' has semantic structure—it is composed out of the parts 'permit' and 'ible'. And like other predicates of this structure, including 'laughable', 'laudable', and 'loveable', this makes 'permissible' plausibly analyzed as meaning something like 'aptly permitted' or 'appropriately permitted'. If we understand 'required' analogously, as 'aptly required', then there will be an alternative to stealing being either aptly permitted or aptly required—it may be that it is neither aptly permitted nor aptly required, perhaps because nothing is apt. On this view, 'impermissible' means 'aptly impermitted', rather than 'not aptly permitted'.

Error theories which reject the duality of 'permissible' and 'required' in this way, like the naïve error theory we considered earlier, carry commitments in normative ethics. Their reason for claiming that moral claims like 'stealing is permissible' and 'stealing is impermissible' are both false, is that a third alternative is true—that it is neither apt to permit stealing nor to require not stealing. But this is a substantive claim about what is apt. Given that 'permissible' really does mean 'aptly permitted', as this view claims, it follows that every interesting substantive theory in normative ethics is committed to a non-trivial condition on whether something is apt. But this form of the error theory is inconsistent with every such condition on aptness. So it is incompatible with every substantive interesting theory in normative ethics.

In contrast, the forms of error theory which appeal to a problematic shared presupposition of moral words do not necessarily carry commitments for normative ethics. Of course, if the false shared presupposition is itself a moral claim—such as that code C is the one that it is best for everyone to follow—then this view has not avoided commitments in normative ethics, because it is committed to the view that the presupposition is false. So such error theories, at best, would avoid commitments about what is *wrong*, but would not avoid commitments about what is *best*. But if the presupposition is *not* itself a moral claim—for example, if it is the claim that code C is the code of conduct preferred by God—then the error theorist can claim that this presupposition is false without making any substantive moral claims. The advocate of presupposition who claims that all moral claims are truth-valueless does not make any claims from which any normative ethical claim can be deduced, because on her view 'it is not true that P' does not entail 'it is false that P', and hence does not entail '~P'. Similarly, the advocate of presupposition who claims that all moral claims are false does not make any claims from which any normative ethical claim can be deduced, because on her view 'it is false that P' does not entail '~P'.

Moreover, the failures of these entailments, on each view, are not ad hoc additions to each view, but follow immediately from the core claims that they make about the nature of moral language. Once we accept that moral claims carry any presupposition at all, we will get the failure of one of these entailments, and which one fails will be determined by our view about whether claims with false presuppositions are false, or merely lack truth values (see Strawson (1950)).

There is a sense, of course, in which even presupposition-based error theories preclude certain commitments within normative ethical theory. Endorsing such a theory, after all, is like responding to the question, 'when did you stop beating your wife?' by pointing out that you have never beat your wife. It would not make a lot of sense to point this out and then to go on to suggest that you stopped last week. Nor would it make a lot of sense for the presupposition-based error theorist to go on to make claims about what is permissible or impermissible. That is why error theories constitute a threat to normative ethics. But in contrast to the naïve error theory and the duality-denying error theory, presupposition-based error theories *may*—depending on the presupposition which they attribute and deny—pose such a threat without carrying any commitments for the answers to any normative ethical questions whatsoever. Such views have consequences *for* normative ethical theory, but they do not have normative ethical consequences.

CONTEXTUALISM/RELATIVISM

As we've seen, traditional, non-hybrid, noncognitivist views appear to make claims that are orthogonal to normative ethics. In contrast, whether the moral error theory is committed or not to claims within normative ethics depends very much on how the error theory is developed, but there are *some* intelligible versions of the error theory which clearly carry no commitments to claims within normative ethics. Contrasting sharply with such views, are forms of *contextualism* and *relativism*.

According to contextualist metaethical theories, moral words may be used to make different claims in different contexts of utterance. Actually, even views that are not interestingly contextualist can accept this much. On a plausible and well-supported view about modal terms like 'must', 'may', and 'ought', for example, they are not ambiguous between distinct moral and non-moral senses, just because they can be used to make moral claims in some contexts, as in 'Jack must not steal—it's wrong', and also used to make clearly non-moral claims in other contexts, as in 'Jack must have stolen the cookie—no one else could reach the shelf'. Rather, such terms are context-dependent, and allow for both moral and non-moral claims to be made, given a single, contextually flexible, meaning. All interesting metaethical views can take this insight about modal words on board, but *interestingly* contextualist metaethical views such as that developed by Finlay (2014) maintain that even once we have fixed the context so that a moral reading of 'must' is required, different speakers or different conversations may fix on interestingly different claims as expressed by the very same sentence.

The bare claim that one and the same sentence—for example, 'stealing is wrong'—may express different propositions in the mouths of different speakers or in different conversational settings does not, in and of itself, carry any commitments for normative ethics. But no contextualist view is complete without telling us *how* context affects what claim can be made using such a sentence. The general form that such theories take, is to tell us, for an arbitrary context C, under what conditions the proposition expressed by 'stealing is wrong' in C is true.

Views of this structure do not avoid commitments in normative ethics. On the contrary, once we know which proposition is expressed by 'stealing is wrong' relative to an arbitrary context C, and know which context C we occupy, we can determine the conditions under which 'stealing is wrong' expresses a truth in our own context. In knowing which context we are in, we know a claim of the form, 'C is our context'. And in knowing the consequences of our theory, we know a claim of the form, "'stealing is wrong' expresses a truth in C just in case S', where 'S' is some sentence specifying the truth-conditions of 'stealing is wrong' in context C. And from these two claims, we can infer, "stealing is wrong' expresses a truth in our context just in case S'. But no matter what context we occupy, claims of the form "P' expresses a truth in my context just in case P' express a truth in that context. So we are also committed to accepting the claim, "stealing is wrong' expresses a truth in our context just in case stealing is wrong'. But now putting these two claims together, we can infer, 'stealing is wrong just in case S'. But this is a normative ethical claim—indeed, it is a highly general one, asserting a condition of the highest possible generality for when stealing is wrong. In general, all that it takes to be committed to such claims, once we endorse a complete contextualist theory, is to know what context we are in.

Relativist metaethical theories are usefully contrasted with contextualist theories for most purposes, but are committed to normative ethical consequences in a very similar way. In general, whereas contextualists say that one and the same moral sentence may make different claims in different contexts of utterance, even once we have narrowed our attention to a particular moral use of the words in question, relativism such as that developed by MacFarlane (2014) and discussed in Brogaard (2008), as applied to metaethics, says that moral sentences make the *same* claim across such contexts, but that such claims are not absolutely true or false, but only relative to some perspective.

As with contextualism, the bare form of relativism does not carry any substantive commitments within normative ethics, but as soon as we start to spell out a particular relativist view, we get such commitments. The general form that a relativist view takes, is to tell us, for each context C and perspective P, whether some sentence S expresses a claim in C that is true with respect to P. But as soon as we have such a theory in hand, all that it takes to generate normative commitments is to know what context we are in and what our perspective is. If you know 'my context is C' you can get from "stealing is wrong' expresses a claim in C that is true with respect to P just in case S' to "stealing is wrong' expresses a claim in my context that is true with respect to P just in case S'. But in general, as before, claims of the form "R' expresses a claim in my context that is true with respect to P just in case it is true that R with respect to P' express a truth in every context, and so we are committed to the claim, "stealing is wrong' expresses a claim in my context that is true with respect to P just in case it is true that stealing is wrong with respect to P'. So we can infer, 'it is true that stealing is wrong with respect to P just in case S'. But 'it is true that stealing is wrong with respect to P just in case stealing is wrong' expresses a truth with respect to perspective P. So if we know that our perspective is P, we must accept this claim, and hence we may infer, 'stealing is wrong just in case S'. So again, we get a commitment to highly general normative consequences, merely by knowing our theory, knowing our context, and knowing our own perspective.

The reason why contextualist and relativist theories, once they amount to concrete theories and not just the bare assertion of contextualism or relativism, are committed to normative consequences, though traditional noncognitivist theories are not, is simple. Each class of theory purports to tell us something about the meaning of moral words. To do so, each theory mentions moral words or sentences involving moral words, and says things about those sentences. But the contextualist and relativist say things about moral sentences from which some moral sentences themselves follow, given appropriate, and available, background assumptions. That is because the things they tell us about moral sentences include things like ''stealing is wrong' is true if P'. But for speakers who speak the language in which S is formulated, from this follows 'stealing is wrong if P'. Noncognitivists do not use semantic vocabulary that is disquotational in this way. From ''stealing is wrong' is used to condemn stealing' no sentence that *uses* 'wrong' follows. This is because 'is used to' does not have any disquotational properties.

REDUCTIVE NATURALISM

Like contextualism and relativism, (noncontextualist) reductive naturalism is an important class of views in metaethics that cannot avoid substantive, deep, commitments within normative ethical theory. According to reductive naturalism, moral properties like *wrong* reduce to or are analyzable in terms of ordinary, non-moral, naturalistically respectable properties like desire, promotion, and explanation (Schroeder 2007).

Of course, as with contextualism and relativism, it is possible to endorse the bare thesis of reductive naturalism without making any substantive normative ethical claims. It is even possible to give arguments that reductive naturalism must be true (as in Jackson 1998) or to defend reductive naturalism from at least some important objections without taking on any such commitments. But as with contextualism and relativism, any complete statement of a reductive naturalist theory must tell us *how* moral properties reduce in naturalistic terms.

In fact, it is particularly pressing for the reductive naturalist to defend a particular reductive naturalist view, or at least a view about the neighborhood in which such a view will lie, and not simply to argue for reductive naturalism in the abstract. This is because reductive naturalism is often discussed by imagining particular reductive views that are clearly false. Everyone, even advocates of reductive naturalism, should agree that at most one particular reduction of moral properties in naturalistic terms is true (compare Finlay [2014] on the Open Question Argument). So if a reductive naturalist refuses to take on the task of defending a *particular* reductive view, she leaves discussion of reductive naturalism in the hands of her critic, who may choose to illustrate it with the example of views that everyone can agree are not true.

Michael Huemer, for example, argues against reductive naturalism like this:

On the face of it, *wrongness* seems to be a completely different *kind* of property from, say, *weighing 5 pounds*. In brief:

1. Value properties are radically different from natural properties.
2. If two things are radically different, then one is not reducible to the other.
3. So value properties are not reducible to natural properties.

[...] To illustrate, suppose a philosopher proposes that the planet Neptune is Beethoven's Ninth Symphony. I think we can see that that is false, simply by virtue of our concept of Neptune and our concept of symphonies. Neptune is an entirely different kind of thing from Beethoven's Ninth Symphony. No further argument is needed.

(Huemer 2005:94)

Huemer argues against reductive naturalism by observing that an obviously false view is false, and then generalizing. But arguments do not need to be as bad as Huemer's in order to illustrate this point; indeed, the *best* objection to reductive naturalism is that no one has offered a proposed reduction that seems like it could possibly be true. High-level arguments that some reductive view *must* be true simply do not address the source of skepticism that no such view *could* be. The only antidote to this—the only dialectically fruitful way forward—is to defend better views, and to show that they are not obviously false.[5]

In fact, other objections to reductive naturalism actually turn on skepticism about whether there is any plausible naturalistic reductive analysis. The most famous of these is Terry Horgan and Mark Timmons' (1991) Moral Twin Earth argument. The Moral Twin Earth argument is based on a thought experiment that is designed to test and provide intuitive counterexamples to theories of reference-determination for moral words. But in its full generality, it claims to provide reason to think that *no matter what* reductive analysis we give to moral properties, and *no matter what* theory we have about in virtue of what moral words pick out those properties, there will be intuitive counterexamples to that combination of theories.

It is very puzzling, however, what could lead anyone to think that there will be intuitive counterexamples to *every* possible theory of reference-determination for moral words, without surveying every possible such theory. After all, in order for the counterexamples to be intuitive, there must be some features of the case that pump the intuition in question. But then a different theory of reference-determination could make those features relevant. In general, once we know what features of cases pump the intuition that speakers mean *wrong* by 'wrong', we can design our theory of reference-determination so that it assigns *wrong* as the meaning of 'wrong' under precisely those conditions. This makes it very puzzling indeed how anything general could follow from the structure of Horgan and Timmons' argument.

But although they claim that their argument is an argument against any reductive theory, Horgan and Timmons help themselves to a helpful stipulation, in order to pump intuitions. They assume, for purposes of their argument, that the correct analysis of what we mean by 'wrong' makes it pick out what they call a 'consequentialist property'. So they are stipulating for convenience that the reductive naturalist view under consideration claims something like that to be wrong is to fail to maximize happiness. Similarly, they stipulate that speakers on 'moral twin earth' use the word 'wrong' to pick out a 'deontological property'. Since we know that consequentialists disagree with deontologists, this serves to pump the intuition that we disagree with speakers on 'moral twin earth', and hence that they also mean *wrong* by 'wrong'. An alternative diagnosis, however, is that either the consequentialist analysis is wrong—perhaps because it is insufficiently charitable to the deontologists among us—or that 'moral twin earth' would have to be much more different from ours than Horgan and Timmons go to pains to make us think, in order for speakers there to mean something else by 'wrong'—so different that it would not be intuitive, after all, that we disagree with them, once the differences are made vivid.

So I infer that one of the most pressing tasks facing the reductive naturalist is to defend actual reductive, naturalistic analyses of moral properties like *wrong*. Such an analysis will tell us *what it is* to be wrong. But once we know what it is to be wrong, we will know a condition that is necessary and sufficient for something to be wrong—indeed, we will know the most fundamental and explanatory such condition, in virtue of which all other generalizations about what is wrong are true. So we will have not just *some* commitment or other within normative theory, we will have attained the holy grail of the most ambitious and general kind of explanatory normative ethical theory. So the commitments of reductive naturalism for normative ethics run deep.

AMBITION IN NORMATIVE THEORY

Indeed, I think the relationship between reductive naturalism and ambitiously general theorizing within normative ethics runs in both directions. This because general, explanatory normative ethical theories can take one of two forms, and of these two forms, the one with the better claim to generality and explanatory power is committed to a reductive thesis.

To see the distinction between the two forms of general, explanatory, normative ethical theory, compare two possible interpretations of consequentialism. According to the first interpretation, endorsed by Sidgwick (1907), there is only one act-type that is universally obligatory, and that is maximizing the good. No matter what your situation, you are morally obligated to maximize the good. And insofar as you are obligated to do anything else, that is because given your situation that is what you must do in order to fulfill your obligation to maximize good. So on this view, facts about what will maximize the good explain what you are obligated to do because they are the features of your circumstances that affect what you need to do in order to fulfill your basic obligation. On this interpretation, consequentialism differs from deontological theories that consist in basic lists of obligations only by having fewer obligations on its list.

In contrast, Moore (1903) endorsed a strikingly different interpretation of his consequentialism. According to Moore's form of consequentialism, the reason why facts about what will maximize the good explain what you are obligated to do is that *what it is* for an action to be obligatory is for it to maximize the good. On this view, there is no basic obligation to maximize the good at all—only a fact about what *obligation* (Moore himself framed the view in terms of *rightness*) consists in.

Setting aside the act of maximizing the good, these two interpretations of consequentialism agree about what explains why obligatory actions are obligatory, though they disagree about how this explanation works. Each agrees that for every action that is obligatory for any agent in any circumstances except for maximizing the good, this action is obligatory for that agent in those circumstances because given those circumstances, unless the agent performs that action, she will not maximize the good. So over the scope of most of normative ethical theory, these two interpretations of consequentialism agree about a lot. But with respect to the act of maximizing the good, they disagree. Sidgwick's form of consequentialism offers no explanation at all of why the act-type of maximizing the good is obligatory. On the contrary, that it is obligatory is an unexplained posit of the Sidgwickian theory. So the Sidgwickian theory, though it offers a *highly* general explanatory theory, is not *perfectly* general. In contrast, Moore's form of consequentialism *is* perfectly general. According to the Moorean form of consequentialism, *if* it is obligatory to maximize the good, that is because compared to all of its alternatives, the act of maximizing the good will result in better consequences than the alternatives.[6]

So of these two forms of consequentialism, the Moorean form offers an explanation that is strictly more general. That means that it is motivated purely from an ambition for generality in our normative ethical theorizing. But the way that the Moorean view works is by making a *constitutive* claim, about *what it is* for an action to be obligatory. And such claims are intuitively the province of metaethics—they tell us about the nature or analysis of some moral property.

Of course, Moore's analysis does not make him a reductive naturalist. On the contrary, Moore's analysis treats *right* (and derivatively, obligatory) in terms of *good*, itself a further normative property. But now the very same questions arise in ambitiously general explanatory normative theory of the good, as arose in such theory about the right. We can ask for general theories about what is good and why, just as we can ask for general theories about what is right and why. As it happens, whereas Moore advocated a powerful and general explanatory theory about right action, he was content in the case of the good, to settle for a list. With respect to the good, Moore takes the same sort of view as Clarke, Price, and Prichard take about the right.

There is nothing inconsistent about Moore's position. But if we were attracted to his view about right action because of its ambitious explanatory power, then we will be attracted to theories of the good with similar scope and generality. And as with consequentialism, these will come in two forms: those that advert to a list of one or more basic intrinsic goods, such that everything else that is good is good because it results in one of the things on this list, and those that tell us *what it is* for something to be good.

For example, consider the view that things are good because there are reasons to prefer them. On one interpretation, this view claims that what is intrinsically good is there being something that there are reasons to prefer. What makes happiness good, on this interpretation, is that given our circumstances, we have reasons to prefer it, and hence by getting happiness, we are getting something that is of genuine intrinsic value—namely, having something that we have reasons to prefer. On a different interpretation, however, this view claims that *what it is* for something to have intrinsic value is that there are reasons to prefer it (Korsgaard 1983). Like Moore's form of consequentialism, this view does not claim that there being something that there are reasons to prefer is itself good (this is a substantive question), and it does not use this claim to explain why other things are good. Like Moore's form of consequentialism, it is strictly *more general* in its explanatory power. And like Moore's form of consequentialism, it adverts to a constitutive or reductive claim about *what it is* for something to be intrinsically good.

Again, this view (as it happens) is not reductively naturalistic. But if we continue down this path, then at some point we will run out of further moral or normative concepts to appeal to, in making our constitutive claims. At that point, in order to follow Moore's path over Sidgwick's, the constitutive account that we appeal to *will* have to be reductively naturalistic. But the Moorean path can be motivated over the Sidgwickian path purely on grounds of greater explanatory generality. And greater explanatory generality is an ambition that makes perfect sense even purely within normative ethical theory. Hence, pressure toward accepting a reductive naturalistic view can be motivated purely within normative ethical theory.

Shelly Kagan puts a similar thought this way:

> [A]s we go deeper in our attempt to articulate the fundamental moral principles, relatively specific first-order claims about the content of morality give way gradually to more general overall characterizations of morality's content; and as these

in turn become more general still, we find ourselves making what increasingly come to seem like second-order claims about the very nature of morality. This is especially so when we attempt to provide a foundation for the substantive moral claims of normative ethics. Such foundational theories will inevitably grow out of and appeal to larger metaethical conceptions of morality's purpose and point. That is, in the course of defending a given theory about the foundations of normative ethics, when we try to explain why it is that the various features of that theory should seem attractive and plausible, inevitably the claims we make will themselves simply be metaethical claims about the nature of morality. At a deep enough level, normative ethics does not merely draw upon metaethics—it simply becomes metaethics.

(Kagan 1997:5–6)

SUMMARY

Though distinct in their primary questions and concerns, metaethics and normative ethics are not fully independent. Indeed, it follows from what I have argued that they are deeply intertwined enterprises, to such an extent that it is not surprising that it is sometimes hard to say of some philosophical issue, such as particularism, whether it belongs to normative ethics or to metaethics. Still, some interesting and central metaethical views can be stated in full without adopting any commitments in normative ethics. These theories were the ones being advocated most often in the middle of the twentieth century, by those who insisted most sharply on the distinction between metaethics and normative ethics, so it is no surprise where we came by the idea that these closely related domains of inquiry can be so easily separated.[7]

NOTES

1. These remarks do not apply to a close relative of hybrid expressivism, *relational* expressivism. See Schroeder (2013) and Toppinen (2013) for discussion. Relational expressivism is also endorsed by Ridge (2014).
2. Loeb (2007:471), for example, restricts his characterization of error theory to the falsity of 'positive' claims. Olson (2014:14–15) says that all moral claims are false, but he defines 'moral claims' so that 'stealing is not wrong' does not count.
3. Caleb Perl (ms) argues that all deontic claims carry presuppositions without arguing for the error theory. His idea is that this thesis solves multiple problems about the semantics of deontic vocabulary and in moral epistemology.
4. Olson (2014:14) takes this route, but not the following explanation. In his terminology, he denies that 'stealing is not wrong' entails 'stealing is permissible'. According to Olson, 'permissible' is a generalized conversational implicature of 'wrong', which is what leads us to assume that there is an entailment.
5. Nick Laskowski (ms) argues, quite strikingly, that if reductive realism is true, then the correct reduction is not knowable. He contends that reductivists should restrict their ambition to claiming to know that *some* reductive thesis is true, without being able to know which one, and that this perspective solves independent problems for reductive realism, including addressing the objection that if reductive realism is true, then moral concepts are dispensable (for which, see Parfit 2011). However, my points in this section can survive Laskowski's idea, provided that we can at least make progress in narrowing down the right *kind* of reductive theory.

6. If this sounds trivial to you, compare the same claim about the Divine Command Theory, according to which an act is obligatory, just in case and because, it was commanded by God. The Sidgwickian Divine Command Theory appeals to a basic obligation to obey God, while the Moorean version claims that the fact that God has commanded something is what it is for it to be obligatory (compare Schroeder 2005). The Moorean may or may not think that it is obligatory to obey God; whether this is so will depend, on her view, on whether God has commanded us to obey Him. Similarly, even for consequentialism, whether the Moorean consequentialist thinks that it is obligatory to maximize the good will depend on details about what it means to maximize consequences.

7. Special thanks to Tristram McPherson, David Plunkett, Caleb Perl, Jonas Olson, Lea Schroeder, and especially to Nick Laskowski.

REFERENCES

Boisvert, D. (2008) 'Expressive-Assertivism'. *Pacific Philosophical Quarterly* 89(2): 169–203.

Brogaard, B. (2008) 'Moral Contextualism and Moral Relativism'. *Philosophical Quarterly* 58(4): 385–409.

Copp, D. (2001) 'Realist Expressivism: A Neglected Option for Moral Realism'. *Social Philosophy and Policy* 18: 1–43.

Finlay, S. (2014) *A Confusion of Tongues*. New York: Oxford University Press.

Fisher, A. (2014) *Metaethics: An Introduction*. New York: Routledge.

Hay, R. (2011) 'Hybrid Expressivism and the Analogy Between Pejoratives and Moral Language'. *European Journal of Philosophy* 21(3): 450–474.

Horgan, T. and Timmons, M. (1991) 'New Wave Moral Realism Meets Moral Twin Earth'. *Journal of Philosophical Research* 16: 447–465.

Huemer, M. (2005) *Ethical Intuitionism*. New York: Palgrave MacMillan.

Jackson, F. (1998) *From Metaphysics to Ethics*. Oxford: Oxford University Press.

Kagan, S. (1997) *Normative Ethics*. New York: Westview Press.

Korsgaard, C. (1983) 'Two Distinctions in Goodness'. *The Philosophical Review* 92(2): 169–195.

Laskowski, N. (ms) *On Moral Thought*. Doctoral Dissertation, University of Southern California.

Loeb, D. (2007) 'The Argument from Moral Experience'. *Ethical Theory and Practice* 10(5): 469–484.

MacFarlane, J. (2014) *Assessment-Sensitivity: Relative Truth and Its Applications*. Oxford: Oxford University Press.

Mackie, J.L. (1977) *Ethics: Inventing Right and Wrong*. New York: Penguin.

Moore, G.E. (1903) *Principia Ethica*. Cambridge: Cambridge University Press.

Olson, J. (2014) *Moral Error Theory: History, Critique, Defense*. Oxford: Oxford University Press.

Parfit, D. (2011) *On What Matters*, volumes 1 and 2. Oxford: Oxford University Press.

Perl, C. (ms) *Deontic Positivism*. Doctoral Dissertation, University of Southern California.

Ridge, M. (2014) *Impassioned Belief*. Oxford: Oxford University Press.

Schroeder, M. (2005) 'Cudworth and Normative Explanations'. *Journal of Ethics and Social Philosophy*. www.jesp.org.

—. (2007) *Slaves of the Passions*. Oxford: Oxford University Press.

—. (2009) 'Hybrid Expressivism: Virtues and Vices'. *Ethics* 119(2): 257–309.

—. (2013) 'Tempered Expressivism'. *Oxford Studies in Metaethics* 8: 283–314.

Sidgwick, H. (1907) *The Methods of Ethics*, 7th edition. Indianapolis, IN: Hackett.

Strawson, P.F. (1950) 'On Referring'. *Mind* 59: 320–344.

Toppinen, T. (2013) 'Belief in Expressivism'. *Oxford Studies in Metaethics* 8: 252–282.

Index